The Politics of Labour in the British Caribbean:

The Social Origins of Authoritarianism and Democracy in the Labour Movement

The Politics of Labour in the British Caribbean:

The Social Origins of Authoritarianism and Democracy in the Labour Movement

O. Nigel Bolland

Ian Randle Publishers
Kingston

James Currey
Oxford

Markus Wiener Publishers
Princeton

© O. Nigel Bolland 2001

First published in Jamaica, 2001 by
Ian Randle Publishers Ltd
11 Cunningham Avenue
Kingston 6

ISBN 976-8123-94-X paperback
ISBN 976-8123-95-8 hardcover

A catalogue record for this book is available from the National Library of Jamaica

First published in the United Kingdom, 2001 by
James Currey Ltd
73 Botley Rd
Oxford
OX2 OBS

British Library Cataloguing in Publication Data

Bolland, Nigel O.
    The politics of labour in the British Caribbean: the
    social origins of authoritarianism and democracy in the
    labour movement, 1934 - 54
    1. Labour movement - Caribbean, English-speaking - History -
    20th century
    I. Title
    331.8'09729

    ISBN   0-85255-830-9 paperback

First published in the United States of America, 2001 by
Markus Wiener Publishers
231 Nassau Street
Princeton, NJ 08542

ISBN 1-55876-277-9 hardcover
ISBN 1-55876-278-7 paperback

Library of Congress Cataloging-in-Publication Data
available upon request

Cover art 'Faces through the Ages' by Soeki Irodikromo.
Cover and book design by Errol Stennett
Printed and bound in the USA

This one is for Ellie, with all my love

Contents

Part I The Origins of Organised Labour

Part II The Institutionalisation of Labour Politics

Foreword

It is indeed extremely difficult to exaggerate the pervasive importance of the growth of organised labour to the political and social development of the Caribbean. The adoption of the system of slavery (along with other forms of coerced servitude) in the seventeenth century as the principal mode of labour organisation and the subsequent implementation of various forms of indentured labour systems after the nineteenth century represented a sort of organisation directed and controlled from above. But it was an organisational structure in which the workers had little or no input. Nor was it designed to respond to their aspirations. Concomitant with the transformation of labour systems across the Caribbean occurred a dramatic reconstitution of basic society, culture and ecology that has been implicitly reflected in such encompassing terms as 'slave societies' 'sugar revolutions' and 'plantation societies.' The constitution of the multi-ethnic and multi-racial plantation society along with the development of the slave society left indelible characteristics on Caribbean history. The early history of the slave society has attracted far more attention than the later history of wage-earning workers trying to carve out their place and space in the social, economic and political structure of the free Caribbean societies of the later nineteenth and throughout the twentieth century. Nevertheless the struggle of organised free labourers is no less important in the history of the Caribbean. That history of the labour movement in the British Caribbean, as Professor Nigel Bolland so immaculately illustrates, was tantamount to a desire to build democratic societies across the Caribbean. The history of organised labour that played itself out throughout most of the twentieth century also constitutes one of the truly distinguished achievements in the modern history of the peoples of the Caribbean. For it is the workers, more than any other group that shaped the political cultures of the modern Caribbean.

More than most other societies in the colonial world after the age of Christopher Columbus, Caribbean societies were singular in their original-ity and their genesis. This, perhaps, requires some explanation. Unlike the forms of colonisation that took place under the Greeks, or the Romans, or the medieval Europeans, colonisation in the Americas was fundamentally different. In the islands of the eastern Atlantic (the Azores, Madeira, the

Canary Islands and the Cape Verde Islands) along the African coast – at least until the African tropics – the Iberians either moved members of their domestic populations or transported mainland populations to construct what became essentially trading post empires. Trading post empires did not require much administrative structure. They were scattered points where commerce brought together divers types in uneasy relationships. That was the model that Columbus had in mind in his westward quest in 1492. Things did not work out the way he planned, however. After ten frustrating years the dream of establishing a rich new trade route to China slowly died in the Spanish court. As Columbus himself admitted when talking about the people of the Bahamas, the Caribbean was an area 'very short of everything.' But if the newly discovered lands could not provide trade then they would provide a new domain for the export of restless, sometimes undesirable metropolitan types, and the always important garnering of souls in the service of a revitalised Spanish Catholicism. The Caribbean in particular and the Americas in general represented long distance settlement efforts that, at least in the formative phase, did not involve the idea of constructing maritime trade networks. Early Spanish colonisation already indicated signs of that significant transformation. For Nicolas Ovando, Isabel of Castile and Ferdinand of Aragon the first Spanish colony 'planted' in Hispaniola in 1502 represented a transatlantic continuation of the southern Catholic Reconquista that finally reclaimed Iberia for their Catholic kingdoms. The frightful demographic disaster of the original Caribbean populations along with the unexpected discovery of vast deposits of gold and silver on the mainland after 1519 radically altered the imperial concept of 1502. The discovery of gold and silver forever changed the vision of small, loyal colonies of Iberians living overseas and communing as best they could with non-Iberians. Thereafter the Americas were no longer remote areas marginal to the divided and often contradictory interests of the Crown and citizens of the Spanish metropolis. The Americas became the place where any Spaniard, in the words of Bernal Díaz del Castillo, could go 'to serve God and His Majesty, to bring light to them that dwell in darkness, and to get rich as all men desire.' But the Caribbean did not provide many opportunities to get rich before the middle of the seventeenth century. Soldiers and sailors served the Castillian monarchs from fortified cities like Havana, San Juan, Cartagena and Barranquilla built across the Caribbean after 1580. Provisioning the troops was good business for a connected few, but did not constitute an attractive environment for financial specula-tion. Despite the occasional discovery of small amounts of gold on some islands, the Caribbean was no place for the ordinary fortune seeking Spanish emigrant. Better prospects existed by far on the mainland, in New Spain or

New Granada, or Upper Peru. The fortified city of Havana, however, quickly established a primary position among urban concentrations throughout the hemisphere, and remained the third largest city in the Americas until the beginning of the nineteenth century. Elsewhere in the Caribbean cities were not much more than large villages, and true urban life arrived only in the middle of the twentieth century.

The magnetic attraction of the mainland after 1519 confined the Caribbean islands to an extended period of relative neglect that altered their recently acquired importance within the newly expanded imagination of Europe. Outside the main enclaves of administration and fortifications, a sort of frontier peasant society slowly developed for the first hundred years. Then two dramatic changes took place. The first was the methodical rupturing of Spanish colonial monopoly in the Caribbean as the other Europeans, especially from France, the Netherlands and England, eventually established small settlements of their own. These settlements were in many respects, microcosms of the culture and society of their respective motherlands. The second was the extensive cultivation of tropical staples, some of which were imported to the region just like the population. These tropical staples destined for a European market necessitated vast amounts of labour, and eventually made labour provision an important component of both commerce and colonialism in the Caribbean. But it was not just any kind of labour for any kind of tropical produce. The Caribbean colonists wanted slave labour to produce tobacco, sugar, coffee, cotton, cochineal and dyewoods. The expanding demand for slaves created a major trading link between Africa and the Caribbean and gave birth to the Caribbean exploitation society with its scant regard for the conditions of the workers who generated the wealth that put the 'great' in Great Britain.

Staple production made trade - rather than bullion production or piracy - a new agent of wealth creation. It also gave the Caribbean a new importance to Europeans. The silver fleets sailing from Havana to Cadiz gave way to a complex system of commerce with tentacles that connected numerous ports along the American Atlantic coast as well as throughout western Europe and the western coast of tropical Africa. For nearly three centuries - from roughly 1640 to 1940 - the Caribbean became identified with sugar and plantation agriculture. For much of that time plantation labour was equated with slavery, and the worst working conditions anywhere in those particular types of societies. Caribbean slave societies were distinct in that nowhere else in the world did slaves consistently comprise the majority of the population. Slavery was in every respect a wretched form of labour organisation. The abolition of slavery did not ameliorate working conditions substantially either on or off the plantations. Caribbean workers, therefore, had to struggle in ways that would be quite unfamiliar to other workers in Europe and North America - or more precisely, the non-plantation zones of North America. Caribbean workers were struggling for more than merely an economic place in their society. They were struggling to build a new society congruent to their peculiar historical experience. This is what Professor Bolland captures so magnificently in this superb study of the role of organised labour in the British Caribbean. This is a consummate study of the extremely complex process of democratising both society and political culture.

It is obvious that Professor Bolland provides an outstanding intellectual contribution to the history of the labour movement in the Caribbean, and to many other fields of history. The Politics of Labour in the British Caribbean is definitive, delightfully written, and regionally comprehensive for the English-speaking Caribbean. Its signal importance may be gauged in both its intrinsic contribution to our understanding of labour history and in its stimulating methodology. At one level this study meticulously documents the valiant struggle of Caribbean workers in the English-speaking territories over the span of almost a century. Professor Bolland provides richly detailed information about workers and their leaders in the various territories from Belize to Guyana and Suriname, and all the English-speaking islands in between. He also draws a subtly nuanced picture of the changing context against which all Caribbean peoples struggled. His trenchant observations continually place Caribbean events in the larger hemisphere of the Americas and the wider Atlantic world. As he notes early in chapter seven, 'the global context encouraged Caribbean people to continue to aspire towards democracy and national liberation.' Ordinary people from the Caribbean participated regularly in the various international congresses that tried to shape the world of the twentieth centuries. Henry Sylvester Williams, a black Trinidadian founded the Pan-African Association in London at the end of the nineteenth century. Richard B. Moore of Barbados and W. A Domingo of Jamaica attended the San Francisco meeting in April 1945 that established the United Nations. Fully one-third of the delegates at the Sixth Pan-African Congress that met in Manchester, England in October 1945 came from the British West Indies. By the middle of the twentieth century Caribbean labour leaders such as A. A. Thorne, H.J.M. Hubbard and Hubert Critchlow of then British Guiana, or Albert Gomes and A A. Cipriani of Trinidad, Grantley Adams of Barbados, Albert Marryshow of Grenada, Richard Hart and Ken Hill of Jamaica were individuals with a sophisticated awareness of the Caribbean as well as the wider world. Above all they were keenly knowledgeable of the Caribbean region and tried to construct a society that reflected their vision of the region in the divided and divisive wider world. Professor Bolland's pan-Caribbean approach makes it easier to expand the comparison with worker activity in the non-English speaking Caribbean at the same time. For it is often overlooked how parallel were the manifestations of Caribbean worker agitation across the regional divides of politics, language, and custom. All workers throughout the region shared similar goals. They all wanted better wages and better working conditions but they also wanted respect and a meaningful share of political power. Caribbean labour leaders never doubted that their multiple aims were integrally connected, and many ended up being the political leaders implementing the goals they loudly advocated. With the expansion of radio communication and air transportation services across the Caribbean especially after 1945, common ideas began to flow more easily between the scattered territories. This gave impetus to the growth of a common awareness, and within the English-speaking area, the sense of a community. Yet, this history shows that these commonalties should not be confused with unanimity on how the society was to be structured or the labourers led.

The Politics of Labour in the British Caribbean provides a veritable encyclopaedia of the labour movements across the region and represents an exemplary attempt to provide even-handed attention to the various units. This landmark study defies easy disciplinary compartmentalisation. Indeed, it is a brilliant example of the benefits of genuine interdisciplinary studies. The exhaustive research and seamless way in which this outstanding book astutely ties politics and economics with social and cultural issues allow a rare understanding of what truly constitutes Caribbean distinctiveness. The issues themselves are neither original nor unique. The politics of colonialism and issues of race, ethnicity, economic injustice, inequality, or charismatic leadership can be found anywhere in the world. But the uneasy way that these issues resolved themselves democratically in the British Caribbean seem to reflect profoundly the singular experience of the Caribbean historical past. Nevertheless, Professor Bolland repeatedly warns that the resolution of the various issues was neither easy nor direct. The democratic result was not an inevitable conclusion, and the tendency toward authoritarianism was never far from the surface. Throughout the book the author raises a number of intriguing questions, not only about the British Caribbean but also about democratic politics in general. The intellectually challenging way that Professor Bolland consistently handles these questions throughout this brilliant study makes this essential reading for anyone interested in the politics of inequality, diversity and ethnicity not just in the British Caribbean but anywhere in the contemporary world. This is a truly magnificent contribution to scholarship.

Franklin W. Knight
The Johns Hopkins University

Preface and Acknowledgements

Ever since I became interested in history, as a schoolboy reading J.H. Parry, Alfred Cobban, G.M. Trevelyan and C.V. Wedgwood, I have sought to know how the many aspects of past life - social, cultural, economic, and political - hang together, and why. Following Eric Hobsbawm (1987), I want to see and express history as a coherent whole, rather than as a shopping bag full of separate topics. My subsequent education in sociology and anthropology, which some historians may consider a handicap, led me to a more deliberately comparative view of history.

The risk entailed in writing about topics in which other people are specialists is, of course, that this will reveal my limitations. My hope, however, is that these admitted limitations will be compensated by a broader view that will achieve some coherence and more understanding of the whole. The historical sociology that is my guide and method seeks to explore the intersections of history, biography, and social structure (Mills 1958: 6) in such a way that we understand the activities of individuals and the constraints of social structure within the process of history. An eminent historian wrote, 'Merely to recount the course of events, even on a world-wide scale, it is unlikely to result in a better understanding of the forces at play in the world today unless we are aware at the same time of the underlying structural changes. What we require first of all is a new framework and new terms of reference.' (Barraclough 1964: 1)

He has stated my goals. Not satisfied with a mere recounting of events, I seek explanations of the great changes and continuities of culture and social structure that we can see only if we take a long view.

Much of the world came together in the Caribbean in the period I am considering. Indeed, since 1492 the Caribbean has been an extraordinary crucible in which the peoples and cultures of the world have intersected. It is the fact that Columbus' voyages to the Caribbean initiated a restructuring of the world and its inhabitants, however inadvertently, that 'remains the essential importance of 1492 and the Columbus episode' (Knight 1992: 32). The modern Caribbean is as intimately tied to the wider world as it is to its own past (Richardson 1992a), and this book aims to contribute to our understanding of these connections.

The purpose of this book is to examine and interpret aspects of the political culture and organisations of the working people of the British Caribbean by integrating their struggle into the relevant national, regional and global contexts. My chief focus is on the politics of labour in the period between 1934, when a series of labour rebellions began, and about 1954, by which time universal suffrage had been achieved and most of the colonies were moving towards 'constitutional decolonization' (Munroe 1972). The labour rebellions gave rise to many trade unions, and new political parties, many of them based on organised labour, took advantage of democratic reforms and the evolution of self-government in this period. In order to understand developments in the political economy and their relation to emerging racial and class consciousness, however, it is necessary to begin with a review of the chief changes and continuities following Emancipation in 1838. While the former slave-owners sought to continue to recruit and coerce labour for their enterprises, the former slaves and the indentured workers struggled to achieve land, better wages and working conditions, respect and civil rights.

My primary argument is that the economic crisis in the 1930s intensified the social changes that had been developing since Emancipation and provoked a political crisis when the series of labour rebellions brought an increasingly conscious working class on to the stage. The rapid development of trade unions provided for the first time an organised basis for negotiating wages and working conditions and also a power base for ambitious members of the middle classes who were creating political parties. The UK came to accept, though it still insisted on controlling, a gradual process of decolonisation towards self-government and eventual independence. However, the circumstances in which democracy was achieved in these colonies, including the context of the Second World War, the Cold War, and the increasing hegemony of the United States in the region precluded the development of a really socialist labour movement, despite the early leaders' rhetoric. On the contrary, the middle-class politicians, having come to power on the basis of the labour movement, used the state to control this movement, and even the unions that they led, in order to be accepted by the UK and to attract the investment on which their economic development strategies depended. The consequences of this pattern of labour politics were that the new institutions - trade unions and political parties - that were ostensibly democratic in purpose, structure and procedures, often exhibited authoritarian tendencies. These tendencies, therefore, are both deeply rooted in the political culture inherited from colonialism and slavery and also are the product of the wider context within which these newly independent democratic authoritarian states emerged.

A brief word on my approach, method and sources: my approach reflects my view that we need a long historical perspective in order to understand broad continuities as well as changes in cultures and societies. This is not a comprehensive or exhaustive history, but an interpretation, with relevant examples chosen from across the region, including Antigua, the Bahamas, Barbados, Belize, Grenada, Guyana, Jamaica, St Kitts, St Lucia, St Vincent, and Trinidad and Tobago. My approach is multi-disciplinary and uses the comparative method, drawing on the work of historians, economists, geographers, sociologists, anthropologists and political scientists, but I rely on primary sources wherever possible.

In the course of this enterprise, over many years, I have worked in archives in several countries and have pillaged the work of many writers whom I consider to be my colleagues in scholarly labour. I cannot adequately acknowledge all my debts to them, but the notes show who they are, and I hope I have not done too much damage to their ideas. Even when I have disagreed with them I have tried to treat them fairly, so I must apologise if I have got them wrong.

I should like to thank many scholars and friends who have given comments, encouragement, or inspiration during the course of this project, including David Abdulah, Sara Abraham, Anton Allahar, Sir Roy Augier, Fitzroy Baptiste, Hilary Beckles, Jean Besson, Lynn Bolles, Bridget Brereton, Roy Bryce-Laporte, Richard Burton, Mary Butler, Carl Campbell, Horace Campbell, Mary Chamberlain, Ashton Chase, Barry Chevannes, Colin Clarke, Donna Coombs-Montrose, Edward Cox, Michael Craton, Michaeline Crichlow, Seymour Drescher, Peter Fraser, David Barry Gaspar, Cedric Grant, William Green, Jerome Handler, Kusha Haraksingh, Richard Hart, Maurits Hassankhan, Alistair Hennessy, Paget Henry, Gad Heuman, Barry Higman, Robert Hill, Percy Hintzen, Christine Ho, Rosemarijn Hoefte, Winston James, Howard Johnson, Grant Jones, Roberta Kilkenny, Franklin Knight, John La Rose, Keith Laurence, Linden Lewis, Rupert Lewis, Richard Lobdell, Walton Look Lai, Anne Macpherson, Jay Mandle, Tota Charran Mangar, Woodville Marshall, Luis Martinez-Fernandez, Teresita Martinez-Vergne, Irma McClaurin, Roderick McDonald, James Millette, Sidney Mintz, Mark Moberg, Pat Mohammed, Janet Momsen, Brian Moore, Robert Morris, Nancy Naro, David Nicholls, Pedro Noguera, Gert Oostindie, Ivar Oxaal, Erik Perez, Ken Post, Ralph Premdas, Richard Price, Kenneth Ramchand, Rhoda Reddock, Glenn Richards, Bonham Richardson, Selwyn Ryan, Brinsley Samaroo, Veront Satchell, Gail Saunders, Gabby Scott, Rebecca Scott, Verene Shepherd, Assad Shoman, Kelvin Singh, Arnold Sio, Jean Stubbs, Clive Thomas, David Trotman, Mary Turner, James Walvin, Hilbourne Watson, Brackette Williams, Swithin Wilmot and Kevin Yelvington. A special place belongs to those scholars and colleagues I knew in Jamaica who are now deceased, to whose work I refer in this book: George Beckford, Lloyd Braithwaite, George Cumper, Douglas Hall, George Roberts, Walter Rodney, Archie Singham and Ann Spackman.

I am grateful to the staff of the following archives and libraries, who provided a professional and friendly service: the Barbados Department of Archives, the Barbados Workers' Union in Bridgetown, the National Archives of Belize in Belmopan, the Colgate University libraries, the Institute of Commonwealth Studies of the University of London, the Public Records Office at Kew, the Rhodes House Library in Oxford, the Oilfield Workers' Trade Union in San Fernando, and the University of the West Indies libraries in Mona and St Augustine. They have earned my thanks because without their assistance I could not have completed this study.

I thank the National Endowment of the Humanities, for providing funds to visit some of these libraries and for a generous fellowship in 1994, and the Colgate University Research Council for several grants.

I wish to thank the University of Pittsburgh Press for permission to use material previously published in 'The Politics of Freedom in the British Caribbean,' in The Meaning of Freedom: Economics, Politics, and Culture after Slavery, Frank McGlynn and Seymour Drescher, editors, 1992. I thank Macmillan Publishers for permission to use material from my article, 'The Labour Movement and the Genesis of Modern Politics in Belize', in Labour in the Caribbean: From Emancipation to Independence, edited by Malcolm Cross and Gad Heuman, 1988. And I thank Vasant Kaiwar, editor of Comparative Studies of South Asia, Africa, and the Middle East, for permission to use material from 'Democracy and Authoritarianism in the Struggle for National Liberation: The Caribbean Labour Congress and the Cold War, 1945-52', that appeared in Vol. XVII, No. 1, 1997. An earlier version of chapter 5 appeared as On the March: Labour Rebellions in the British Caribbean, 1934-39 (Kingston, Ian Randle, and London, James Currey, 1995).

I owe a special debt of thanks to my colleagues at Colgate University who have helped me keep going, to Howard Johnson and Linden Lewis who valiantly read and commented on the whole manuscript, to Penny Butler for editing it so professionally and to Franklin Knight for contributing the Foreword. Ian Randle has shown great faith in this project and patience while I completed it and for this he has my heartfelt thanks.

Above all, I thank my family, and especially my wife, Ellen Bolland, for the sustained support that made this book possible.

Abbreviations

The following abbreviations are used in the notes.

BA refers to the Belize Archives, Belmopan, Belize

BWUMB refers to the Barbados Workers' Union Minute Books, Solidarity House, Bridgetown, Barbados

CO refers to the Colonial Office Records, Public Record Office, Kew

HP refers to the Hart Papers, Institute of Commonwealth Studies, University of London

OWTUL refers to the Oilfield Workers' Trade Union Library, San Fernando, Trinidad

RHL refers to the Rhodes House Library, Oxford

Notes

In quotations the emphases are the original authors' unless I have stated that I added them. If several successive quotations are from the same source in one or two adjacent paragraphs, the source is not given every time.

Currencies varied from one colony to another, in the same colony at different times, and some colonies even used and referred to different currencies at the same time. I have made no attempt to convert them to a hypothetical standard and generally refer to the currency that was mentioned in my source.

List of tables

Abbreviations

Abbreviations of organisations (Spanish names have been translated into English)

AACC	Anglo-American Caribbean Commission
ABWU	Amalgamated Building and Woodworkers union
AEA	Agricultural Employers' Association
AFL	American Federation of Labour
AIFLD	American Institute for Free Labour Development
ALP	Antigua Labour Party
ATLU	Antigua Trades and Labour Union
ATSEFWTU	All Trinidad Sugar Estates and Factory Workers' Trade Union
AWA	Antigua Workingmen's Association
BAWTU	Builders and Allied Workers Trade Union
BCN	Black Cross Nurses
BDL	Barbados Democratic League
BEA	Barbados Electors' Association
BEC	Belize Estate and Produce Company Ltd
BESC	Barbados Electric Supply Corporation
BEWCHRP	British Empire Workers and Citizens Home Rule Party
BGLU	British Guiana Labour Union
BGMU	British Guiana Mineworkers' Union
BGTUC	British Guiana Trades Union Council
BGWILC	British Guiana and West Indies Labour Congress
BGWL	British Guiana Workers' League
BHUA	British Honduras Unemployed Association
BHWTU	British Honduras Workers and Tradesmen Union
BITU	Bustamante Industrial Trade Union
BLP	Barbados Labour Party
BPL	Barbados Progressive League
BSL	Black Star Line
BWA	Barbados Workingmen's Association
BWILP	British West Indies Labour Party
BWIR	British West Indies Regiment
BWU	Barbados Worker's Union
CADORIT	Caribbean Area Division of the Inter-American Regional Organisation of Workers
CDU	Christian Democratic Union
CEC	Citizens Emergency Council
CIA	Central Intelligence Agency

CIO	Committee of Industrial Organisation
CIO	Congress of Industrial Organisations (US)
CIT	Inter-American Confederation of Workers
CLC	Caribbean Labour Congress
CSA	Civil Service Association
CSAG	Christian Social Action Group
CSP	Caribbean Socialist Party
CTAL	Confederation of Latin American Workers
DLP	Democratic Labour Party
DTU	Dominican Trades Union
EIA	East Indian Association
FCA	Federation of Citizens' Associations
FTU	Federation of Trade Unions
FWTU	Federated Workers' Trade Union
GAU	Grenada Agriculturists' Union
GAWU	Guyana Agricultural Workers' Union
GIWU	Guiana Industrial Workers Union
GLP	Grenada Labour Party
GMMWU	Grenada Manual and Mental Workers' Union
GREU	Government Railway Employees Union
GTUC	Grenada Trades Union Council
GULP	Grenada United Labour Party
GWA	Grenada Workingmen's Association
GWIFTULP	Guianese and West Indian Federation of Trade Unions and Labour Parties
GWU	General Workers' Union
ICFTU	International Confederation of Free Trade Unions
ILO	International Labour Organisation
JBPA	Jamaica Banana Producers' Association
JDP	Jamaica Democratic Party
JESU	Jamaican Ex-Servicemen's Union
JFL	Jamaican Federation of Labour
JLP	Jamaica Labour Party
JPL	Jamaica Progressive League
JTLU	Jamaica Trades and Labour Union
JTUC	Jamaica Trade Union Council/Congress
JUL	Jamaica Unemployed League
JUT	Jamaica Union of Teachers
JUWU	Jamaica United Workers Union
JWTU	Jamaica Workers and Tradesmen Union
LCP	League of Coloured Peoples
LUA	Labourers and Unemployed Association
MCU	Mercantile Clerk Union
MPCA	Manpower Citizen's Association
NDP	National Democratic Party
NIP	National Independence Party
NLP	National Labour Party

NMU	National Maritime Union
NP	National Party
NRA	National Reform Association
NUM	National Unemployed Movement
NWCSA	Negro Welfare Cultural and Social Association
NWEL	Negro Workers' Education League
NWU	National Workers Union
OEAT	Oilfileld Employers' Association of Trinidad
ORIT	Inter-American Regional Organisation of Workers
OWTU	Oilfield Workers' Trade Union
PAC	Political Affairs Committee
PAWU	Printers and Allied Workers Union
PC	People's Committee
PDP	People's Democratic Party (Trinidad and Tobago)
PDP	Progressive Democratic Party (Trinidad and Tobago)
PITU	Printers' Industrial Trade Union
PLM	Progressive Labour Movement
PMILSA	Poor Man's Improvement Land Settlement
PNC	People's National Congress
PNM	People's National Movement
PNP	People's National Party (Guyana)
PNP	People's National Party (Jamaica)
PPG	Political Progress Party
PPP	People's Political Party (Jamaica)
PPP	People's Progressive Party (Guyana)
PRI	Institutional Revolutionary Party
PTWU	Postal and Telegraph Workers' Union
PUP	People's United Party
PWEU	Public Works Employees Union
PWPSWU	Public Works and Public Service Workers' Union
PWU	Public Works Union
RPA	Ratepayers' Association
RWTU	Railway Workers' Trade Union
SCAC	Standing Closer Association Committee
SCSAU	Shop Clerks and Shop Assistants Union
SILU	Sugar Industry Labour Union
SKNTLU	St Kitts-Nevis Trades and Labour Union
SKNUBA	St Kitts-Nevis Universal Benevolent Association
SLWU	St Lucia Workers' Union
SMA	Sugar Manufacturers' Association
SPA	Sugar Producers Association
SPTT	Socialist Party of Trinidad and Tobago
SVLP	St Vincent Labour Party
SVWCA	St Vincent Workingmen's Cooperative Association
SWU	Sugar Workers' Union
SWWTU	Seamen and Waterfront Workers' Trade Union
TCL	Trinidad Citizens League

TITU	Tobago Industrial Trade Union
TIU	Tailor's Industrial Union
TLP	Trinidad Labour Party
TTGWU	Tramway, Transport and General Workers' Union
TITUC	Trinidad and Tobago Trades Union Congress
TTUSAC	Trinidad Union of Shop Assistants and Clerks
TUC	Trades Union Congress (UK)
TWA	Trinidad Workingmen's Association
TWU	Trinidad Workers' Union
UDP	United Democratic Party
UF	United Force (Guyana)
UF	United Front (Trinidad)
UFC	United Fruit Company
UFWP	United Farmers and Workers Party
UGP	United Guianese Party
UNIA	Universal Negro Improvement Association
UWTA	United Workers Trading Association
WFM	Workers' Freedom Movement
WFTU	World Federation of Trade Unions
WIIP	West Indian Independence Party
WINCP	West Indian National Congress Party

Part 1

The Origins of Organised Labour

Chapter 1

The social and cultural legacies of colonialism and slavery

Caribbean peoples have been as active in shaping their history in the twentieth century as in the nineteenth, yet still they do not shape it in circumstances of their choice. The burdens of history weigh heavily on Caribbean peoples, as the social and cultural legacies of colonialism and slavery continue to shape their societies and the ways they think about them. Their struggle for democracy and independence in the mid-twentieth century has been part of a longer and continuing struggle for freedom and justice, and the forms that this struggle have taken are shaped by the past. The history of labour has been central to the history of the Caribbean: first, in the institution of slavery; second, in the relation of the control over labour and land to political control in the aftermath of Emancipation[1] (Bolland 1981); and third, with the rise of organised labour in the twentieth century. And, in order to understand the dynamics of this history we must focus on the centrality of social conflict, on the political dimension, in Caribbean history (Bolland 1984: 125; Higman 1985-6: 20-1).

One of the most characteristic features of the history of Caribbean societies is the prolonged and pervasive nature of colonialism and labour coercion. Associated with the extreme social inequalities and injustices inherent in this situation is an extraordinary degree of authoritarianism, in personal as well as in labour and political relations. However, the political culture is shaped also by the resistance to inequality, injustice and authoritarianism, not only in the riots and rebellions that punctuate the region's history but also in the countless acts of self-assertion, both individual and collective, that have enabled the peoples of the Caribbean to survive such prolonged oppression. Indeed, it is through such acts, in myriad ways, that these people have changed the oppressive institutions in which they have been confined, and thus have shaped their cultures and societies. Certainly, we must recognise 'the importance of culture in shaping the form and content of labour movements' (Cross and Heuman 1988: 9), for example in the kinds of leadership and the repertoire of resistance, but we must also recognise how crucial labour movements have been in shaping the political culture of the Caribbean.

The plantations of the Caribbean, which were the destination of millions of workers whose job it was to produce sugar and other agricultural goods for European, and later North American, markets and consumers, provided a chapter in 'the evolving saga of the world division of labor' (Mintz 1993a: xxiii). These workers included enslaved Amerindians and indentured Europeans, but they were largely enslaved Africans and indentured Asians. The evolution of this plantation system, which was an important part of the evolution of the world capitalist system from the sixteenth century, reached a peak in the British and French colonies in the eighteenth century and in Cuba in the nineteenth century. New societies emerged, based on the two horrors of colonialism and slavery, which were not unique to the Caribbean, but were more pervasive and persistent there than elsewhere. They were shaped by coercion and conflicts that were centred on, but by no means limited to, the labour process.

Resistance to these pervasive structures of coercion was endemic in the system and took many forms, individual and collective, overt and covert, violent and non-violent. Most dramatically, Saint Domingue, the richest colony of the eighteenth century, was destroyed by a revolution that began in 1791 and ended with the independence of Haiti in 1804. This successful slave revolution was the beginning of the end of legal slavery in the Americas, which finally terminated in Brazil in 1888. However, Emancipation from slavery in the law did not bring real human emancipation, and everywhere the struggle for freedom and justice has continued. The abolition of slavery as the chief form of plantation labour in the nineteenth century gave rise to a variety of other forms of labour exaction, including sharecropping, debt peonage, wage labour and the revival of a system of indenture. This last form of labour coercion depended on new waves of mass immigration between the 1840s and 1930s which resulted, particularly in such colonies as Trinidad, British Guiana and Suriname, in ethnically heterogeneous societies in which workers who differed from each other physically and culturally were often competing for jobs and land.[2]

Twentieth-century struggles for freedom and justice in the Caribbean are rooted in the structures of domination that emerged in the nineteenth century. The legacies of colonialism and slavery, and of indenture and cultural pluralism, have shaped the forms of resistance to these structures of domination in several crucial ways. The central thesis of this book is that the democratic procedures and institutions that developed in the course of this struggle, while constituting the prevailing forms of resistance to domination in the mid-twentieth century, nevertheless contain within them quite contrary authoritarian tendencies that are, in part, the social legacy of colonialism and slavery. In other words, authoritarian traditions in the political culture permeated the struggle to create democratic institutions and societies. Of course, to say that colonialism and slavery, together with the plantation, which was the predominant institutional form of labour exploitation, had important long-term legacies is merely to state a truism. It would be a mistake, however, to attribute all the contemporary problems of the Caribbean to these legacies, as many contemporary problems have contemporary sources. With the demise of slavery in the nineteenth century and the decline of European colonialism in the twentieth century, other factors need to be given their due. If post-Columbian Caribbean history may be conceived in 'three crudely defined epochs' (Mintz 1993b: 7), beginning with Spanish hegemony, followed by the 'North European plantation era', and 'the epoch of North American power', this study is set in the transition from the second to the third epochs, as the United States' presence becomes increasingly pervasive after 1898 until today it is almost inescapable. While US economic and political influences, not to mention military interventions, were more apparent in the Hispanic Caribbean than the British, French and Dutch colonies, the 'imperial succession' was a world phenomenon, so no place in the Caribbean entirely escaped its consequences (Bolland 1997c).

This study begins with an evaluation of the social and cultural legacies of colonialism and slavery, because in the British Caribbean in the 1930s and 1940s, a century after legal Emancipation from slavery, these factors were still important, and they were understood to be by the working people of the Caribbean who initiated a great labour movement that transformed the politics of the region. This study of the labour movement in the British Caribbean, a movement that exploded in a series of labour rebellions between 1934 and 1939, examines the contradictory authoritarian and democratic tendencies within the trade unions and political parties which, by the early 1950s, formed the basis of the struggle for independence. The institutions created out of the struggle in the 1930s and 1940s, therefore, have their own powerful legacy, as the trade unions and political parties that took shape during those years have had a profound and lasting influence on the political culture of all these former colonies.

It has been said that 'the history of the Caribbean can be defined as the history of labour' (Cross and Heuman 1988: 1), and in the aftermath of Emancipation in the British Caribbean the interrelated struggles for the control of labour and land constituted the central political issue of these societies (Bolland 1981, 1992a). With the rise of organised labour and political parties between 1934 and 1954 this struggle took a new form. Although other studies have drawn attention to this period as a watershed in 'the growth of the modern West Indies' (see G.Lewis' book with this title, 1968), and have studied the labour movement in individual colonies in considerable detail (Chase n.d., Post 1978, Ramdin 1982), this is the first study to draw attention to the regional aspects of the movement and to make comparisons that show both similarities and differences between the features of the movement in the various colonies from British Guiana to British Honduras. Moreover, in taking a long as well as a comparative view, this study seeks to illuminate the considerable continuities as well as changes that existed in the politics of labour in the century after Emancipation. Such continuities are evident, as Woodville Marshall points out, in people's protests as well as the forms of coercion and control of labour. Marshall refers to 'the basic continuity in culture, between the institutions and values of our past and those of our present', and emphasises that 'protest itself helped to establish the continuity' (1993: 20). In this study I intend to show that the contradictory tendencies of authoritarianism and democracy, which were apparent within the politics of labour in general, were also present in the culture of protest. As Marshall asserts, 'emancipation was unfinished business' (1993: 20), and this essential business will remain unfinished so long as these contradictory tendencies in the political culture persist.

The analysis of the political economies and social structures of these colonial societies as systems of domination is a sine qua non, but it is equally essential to study the variety of responses of the peoples who were subordinated to these systems. As Peter Worsley says, 'Despite the political power of the conqueror, each colony was the product of a dialectic, a synthesis, not just a simple imposition, in which the social institutions and cultural values of the conquered was one of the terms of the dialectic' (Worsley 1984: 4). Thus a dialectical analysis of the interrelations of oppression and resistance will reveal and explain the dynamics of Caribbean social history. The purpose of this introductory chapter is to identify the nature of colonialism in the Caribbean, the characteristic systems of labour coercion and authoritarianism and some broad patterns of resistance, and, finally, to outline an approach to the historical sociology of the Caribbean in terms of dialectical theory.[3]

Colonialism

A distinctive feature of the history of the Caribbean is the peculiarly prolonged and pervasive nature of its colonial experience. People had been living in the Caribbean for almost 6,000 years before Columbus. Evidence of human settlement dating from around 3500 - 4000 BC has been found in Cuba, Haiti and the Dominican Republic (Wilson 1997: 4). In 1492, 'the Caribbean contained many different ethnic groups, spread out through the Lesser Antilles, Greater Antilles, and Bahamas' (Wilson 1997: 7). After 1492, when the Lucayan Taino people discovered Columbus on a Bahamian beach, several European powers competed to control trade and territory in the Caribbean. France, Great Britain and the Netherlands, in particular, challenged the early Spanish monopoly and in the late nineteenth century the United States became a major player in this competition of imperial succession. The intense imperial rivalries resulted in frequent wars and the extension of colonial conquest to every island, with many colonies changing hands over the years. The rivalry was so intense and persistent because these small colonies were immensely valuable and the region was strategically located in relation to trade with and control of empires on the mainland. However, at about the time Great Britain finally succeeded in achieving predominance over its Spanish, French and Dutch rivals in the early nineteenth century, its Caribbean colonies ceased to be so important in the greater imperial scheme. Great Britain's loss of its most valuable North American colonies, followed by its expansion in South Asia, Africa and Australasia, reduced the relative importance of such old Caribbean colonies as Barbados and Jamaica, and even of newer ones such as Trinidad and British Guiana, in the nineteenth century.

In 1898 the United States invaded the remaining Spanish colonies of Cuba and Puerto Rico and in the early twentieth century, as the European powers continued to decline, the United States purchased the Virgin Islands from Denmark and occupied the independent countries of Haiti and the Dominican Republic. 'On no less than twenty separate occasions between 1898 and 1920, United States Marines or soldiers entered the territory of states in the Caribbean area' (Wood 1961: 5), although the colonies of European powers remained immune from such interventions. When the British empire, the last of the great European empires, disintegrated after the Second World War, the United States was left supreme in a region it had long considered its zone of influence, but 'U.S. plans, goals, and ideology were incoherent, inconsistent, and unintelligently pursued' because the United States 'never attempted to understand the complex world of the Caribbean' (Knight 1990: 224). From a Caribbean perspective the decades of the Cold War are best understood less as a regional example of a new political phenomenon but more as another version of the old pattern of imperial rivalries, with anti-communist rhetoric providing a rationale for US interventions. The United States, after all, was busy invading the Caribbean long before the Soviet Union existed, and will undoubtedly continue to dominate the region long after its rival's demise.

The Caribbean colonies are distinctive not simply because of their great age but also because the colonisers created these societies almost as if they were dealing with empty lands. The first phase of colonisation was marked by plunder, including the plunder of the indigenous peoples, mistakenly called Indians. Spanish settlers in the Greater Antilles introduced diseases such as smallpox and pulmonary plague from which the Amerindians had no immunities. The resultant epidemics, combined with losses due to warfare, forced labour and social disruption, devastated the island populations. This wholesale destruction was so rapid that by 1524 the Taino people 'had ceased to exist as a separate population group' (Rouse 1992: 169) and few Amerindian habitation sites of the sixteenth century can be identified. The Spanish colonisers sought to replace what they thought of as their labour through slaving raids, undertaken in ever-widening circles as they hunted people from the Bahamas, the Bay Islands and the Central American coast, and transported them to the Greater Antilles. During the sixteenth century hundreds of thousands of people were caught in this slave trade and at least as many died of disease or in war, from overwork, ill treatment, starvation and the disruption of their communities (Bolland 1994). This was genocide, leading to the virtual depopulation of the region. Undoubtedly, 'the indigenous people of the Caribbean have played a crucial part in the historical processes that produced the modern Caribbean … in economic patterns, language, myth, and even in the genetic makeup of modern Caribbean people' (Wilson 1997: 206-7), and there are some survivors and even a few surviving communities on some islands. Above all, the indigenous people are present today 'as a link between people and the land, as a symbol of shared identity, and as a symbol of resistance to external domination' (Wilson 1997: 211), but it is nonetheless true that the largest surviving indigenous community in the islands consists of fewer than 3,000 people in Dominica. After this rapid and massive depopulation, the Caribbean colonies were repopulated according to the demands and dictates of the colonisers. Voluntary, indentured and penal labour from Europe did not sufficiently meet the demand, so the colonisers turned increasingly to enslaving and transporting the peoples of Africa, a continent that they viewed chiefly as an inexhaustible reservoir of labour.

From early in the sixteenth century the patterns of migration and settlement, and the subsequent mixture of peoples and cultures in the Caribbean, were determined to an extraordinary degree by the expansionist character of emerging European capitalism. The Europeans did not simply impose themselves on pristine economies and societies, rather, they destroyed them and started over again, creating new economies and societies tailored to their needs. These Caribbean colonies, created in a dual policy of genocide and slavery, became the most valuable possessions of the expanding European powers with the development of sugar plantations in the seventeenth century. By the middle of the seventeenth century the Caribbean was 'irrevocably harnessed to the European economy' (Richardson 1992a: 4) and so the region played an important part in the world's transition from mercantilism to modern industrial capitalism. It is important to understand that for several hundred years the Caribbean, far from being a backward or a traditional region, has been intimately involved in and shaped by the modern forces of global capitalism. The patterns of trade and investment, the predominant systems of land tenure, economic enterprise and social organisation, are all integral to this world capitalist system.

Sidney Mintz makes some interesting observations about the distinctive, and sometimes rather deceptive, features of colonialism in the Caribbean:

> The Caribbean colonies were not European imperial possessions erected upon massive indigenous bases in areas of declining great literate civilizations ... they were not mere ports of trade ... they were not "tribal" mosaics ... nor were they areas of intense European settlement ....They were, in fact, the oldest "industrial" colonies of the West outside Europe, manned almost entirely with introduced populations, and fitted to European needs with peculiar intensity and pervasiveness. It is extremely important to note that in the Caribbean region, the plantation system was a capitalistic form of development, a fact partly concealed by its dependence on slavery; that its organization was highly industrial, though this is difficult to discern because of its basis in agriculture. (Mintz 1971: 36-7)

The status and condition of the labourers, as well as the social and economic structure of the colonies, was thus in a peculiarly absolute way the consequence of colonial forces, and this remained true to a very large degree after slavery.

The interrelated patterns of dependency, powerlessness and poverty at the level of the colonial society had a parallel at the levels of community and individual experience. The imperial rivalries that resulted in the region's fragmentation were often duplicated in the competition and disunity within each colony, which perpetuated the dependency, powerlessness and poverty of the majority of people. Colonialism spread a similar set of institutions across the Caribbean, but not a common culture or common identity. 'European imperialism could not create a common sense of identity in the Caribbean. Instead, the environment, the nature of the colonial economies, the nature of the relationships to the metropolises, and even accidental circumstances combined to accentuate the schismatic tendencies of Caribbean societies by the 1790s. The political changes, then, were in some ways reflections of the separate consciousnesses that developed during the eighteenth century.' (Knight 1990: 190-1)

The Caribbean societies, constituting a colonial zone of the capitalist system, were based on the extensive exploitation of both land and labour. They enriched the slave-traders and slave-owners, the merchants and capitalists, many of whom resided in Europe. 'As artificial creations tied to the metropolis by the Acts of Trade, the export economies in the West Indies came to play a significant role in the economic development of Great Britain' (Sheridan 1994: 15). In this Atlantic system, therefore, most of the wealth produced by slaves was exported, thus contributing to the simultaneous development of Europe and underdevelopment of the Caribbean. The 'colonial slave mode of production', in the words of Clive Thomas, the Guyanese economist, 'oriented these economies towards serving the capital expansion requirements of Europe and thus prevented the development of an internal momentum strong enough to ensure that surpluses were ploughed back into the region' (Thomas 1988: 27). While the roots of present-day dependency and poverty clearly lie in the period of the colonial slave mode of production, the forms of colonial domination have changed, as have the forms of labour coercion.

Labour coercion

The genocide of the indigenous inhabitants of the Caribbean resulted in dependency on imported labour and, for so long as land was accessible in this depopulated region, free labourers could not be induced to work on the expanding plantations. The mass labour required for these plantations had to be coerced, so the owners of the plantations obtained the authority to tie their workers to the enterprise and to discipline them more or less without restraint. This combination of immigrant and coerced labour became a distinctive feature of the Caribbean plantation economy.

From early in the sixteenth century enslaved Africans were transported to work in the Caribbean colonies, alongside the coerced labour of Amerindians and Europeans. Sugar plantations, initiated by Spanish colonists in Hispaniola, were more fully developed by Dutch, French and British colonisers in the eastern Caribbean in the 1630s and 1640s. The sugar revolution spread in response to the great profits from the trade and in the eighteenth century Saint Domingue and Jamaica became the most valuable colonies of France and Great Britain, respectively. In the nineteenth century sugar production was revived in the Hispanic Caribbean and Cuba became the primary producer in the region. Although cotton, coffee and other products were also based on slave labour, sugar and slavery were especially interdependent in Caribbean history. In all these cases, the chief form of labour exaction was slavery and the majority of the enslaved were Africans. About 10 million Africans were transported to the Americas in the slave trade over a period of three and a half centuries, and almost half of these (4,602,200) came to the Caribbean: 1,665,000 to the British Caribbean; 1,600,200 to the French Caribbean; 809,000 to the Hispanic Caribbean; 500,000 to the Dutch Caribbean; and 28,000 to the Danish Caribbean (Curtin 1969: 46, 268). The Caribbean colonies became essentially bipolar societies of slaves and slave-owners, in which the social cleavages of property and prestige, race and culture were defined by law and enforced by terror.

Whether or not these colonies sought precedents in Roman laws or medieval social customs, slavery was not an ancient or traditional institution in the Caribbean. On the contrary, it was part of the early capitalist system that developed in western Europe in the seventeenth and eighteenth centuries and shaped the modern world. When the history of labour coercion in the Caribbean is seen as part of the evolving saga of the world division of labour, we can understand the relationship between the different forms of labour exaction, both more and less coerced, that coexisted within the same worldwide system of capitalism. This system depended from early times on a combination of more or less legally free workers in the metropolitan countries and largely coerced labour in the colonies, but there were also varied mixes within each region. Mintz (1977: 254) argues: 'the integration of varied forms of labour-exaction within any component region addresses the way that region, as a totality, fits within the so-called world-system. There was give-and-take between the demands and initiatives originating with the metropolitan centers of the world-system, and the ensemble of labor forms typical of the local zones with which they were enmeshed.'

The specific ways that the Caribbean was integrated into the world - economy, and the specific local responses to labour coercion, such as the slave revolutions in Saint Domingue and Jamaica, affected the manner and timing of the transition from slavery to other forms of labour in the different parts of that regional economy. There was not a sudden shift from slave to free labour, conceived dualistically, but a lengthy 'succession of different mixes of forms of labor exaction' (Mintz 1978: 87). This prolonged transition from slave markets, in which the labourers were commodities, to labour markets, in which the labour power of legally free labourers is the commodity, lasted over a century in the Caribbean, and it was everywhere a contested transition.

The predominant agricultural enterprise of the Caribbean was the plantation, whether it used slave, indentured, or wage labour, or combinations of these. Both in terms of its dependence on the world economy and its internal structure and dynamics, the plantation is simply a particular institutional expression of the capitalist system, not a distinct mode of production or type of economy in itself (Bolland 1992b: 54-5). The capitalist process of commodification was extended in the colonies with the expansion of wage labour after slavery, but the slave-based plantations were always part of the capitalist system. The extreme social inequalities and pervasive authoritarianism that characterised the plantation, and led to it being seen as a total institution, are thus simply a particular form of capitalist relations of production in which the distinctions between owner and worker are peculiarly acute, with the former monopolising authority, even to the extent of claiming chattel property rights in the latter. This perspective helps us understand the ways the former slave-owners continued to coerce their workers after slavery became illegal in order to maintain their plantations and profits. The decline of the colonial slave economy, which occurred throughout the Caribbean during the nineteenth century and ended formally with the Emancipation of the last slaves in Cuba in 1886, did not result in the rapid formation of free labour markets. On the contrary, new forms of labour coercion, and some old forms that were revived, persisted into the twentieth century in order to sustain the plantations and the profitability of the colonies.

After legal Emancipation the plantation-owners sought to keep the former slaves dependent, to keep their wages low, and to maintain tight discipline over them, by a variety of means, depending on circumstances. Often the planters' monopolisation of land reduced the former slaves' options, while their use of rents, wage advances and truck shops induced indebtedness and kept many workers in a state resembling debt peonage (Bolland 1981; Johnson 1986). A legal system, codified in the masters and servants laws in the British Caribbean, was intended to control and discipline the legally free but dependent workers by threatening them with imprisonment, often with hard labour, for minor infringements of their labour contracts. In some colonies the planters succeeded in obtaining the sponsored immigration of indentured labourers, particularly from Asia, to form the controllable core of their labour force and to reduce the bargaining power of the former slaves. The immigration of almost 500,000 indentured workers from India to the British Caribbean - including 238,909 to British Guiana, 143,939 to Trinidad, and 36,412 to Jamaica - between 1838 and 1918 extended the systems of labour coercion and the profits of the plantations (Look Lai 1993).

The transition from old to new forms of labour coercion cannot be understood adequately in terms of a simple antinomy of slavery and freedom (Finley 1964: 236). Rather, we must distinguish carefully between a variety of forms of coerced labour - including slavery, debt peonage, indentured labour and coerced wage labour - not only in terms of the legal concepts defined by the ruling class but also in terms of the meanings of the labour system as understood by the workers themselves. Above all, we must recognise that domination persists even when the forms and relations of domination may change. 'By rejecting the simple antinomy of slavery and freedom, we can view the nineteenth century as a period of transition from one system of domination to another, each involving different forms of labor control' (Bolland 1981: 617). This focus on the actual social relations, rather than the legal forms, of domination and exploitation emphasises the continuities rather than the breaks between slavery and freedom.

The status of legally free people, even in the twentieth century, has often been diminished to various kinds of dependency and unfreedom, and the study of the workers' resistance, in wage as well as slave labour societies, clarifies the nature of the coercive system. The total and explicit political control over labour under slavery, when the worker is defined as chattel property, ceased to be a prerequisite for its exploitation. At the level of the colonies themselves, direct political and administrative control became less and less necessary for their continued economic exploitation. Instead, economic mechanisms for appropriating surplus, defined as market forces, increasingly predominated. The working of our contemporary version of the world capitalist system is still predicated on processes and structures of inequality and authoritarianism, albeit less explicit than those of the colonial slave mode of production. When challenged, however, the system still relies on the threat or use of force.

Authoritarianism

The movement in the metropoles from mercantilist policies to a preference for free trade and free labour was linked in complex ways to the decline of slavery, but the freed labourers in the colonies continued to struggle in a system that was profoundly authoritarian. The pervasiveness of authoritarianism was the result of many interrelated factors, including the origin of the colonies in conquest, genocide and slavery, the creation of specific institutions of social control and the persistence of profound social cleavages, inequalities and hierarchies. Colonialism is essentially an authoritarian phenomenon, created and maintained through violence. 'The colonial world is a world cut in two', wrote Frantz Fanon, the Martiniquan psychiatrist, in 1961. 'The dividing line, the frontiers are shown by barracks and police stations' (1968: 38). And authoritarianism is closely linked with racism because the 'sharp and rigid class distinctions were integrated into an equally severe system of racial differentiation, in which the various ethnic groups were physically separated' (Thomas 1988: 25), in fact, their 'ethnicity' was largely defined in terms of the imposed hierarchy of 'race'. Authoritarianism was perceived to be essential by, and became the habit of, those who were in control, and so, whether in legal, or racist or paternalist guise, it became the central and traditional feature of the dominant political culture.

The early decades of these colonial societies, in which the colonists faced challenges from indigenous people, slaves, Maroons, buccaneers and rival colonisers, were marked by lawlessness and unregulated conflict. Even after the great powers agreed to suppress piracy at the Treaty of Madrid in 1670, the internal threats from slave rebellions and Maroon wars persisted. The colonial officials and settler elites imposed a variety of controls, such as slave codes, and created institutions, such as municipal councils and courts, to impose their power over the majority, while they continued to rely in a crisis on the military might of the metropole. Though conflicts frequently arose between the local planters and merchants, on the one hand, and the imperial power and its colonial officials, on the other, they generally acted together to deny the majority of the population any civil rights, much less any say in government. In most of the British Caribbean in the early nineteenth century the whites were less than 10 per cent and the slaves were over 80 per cent of the population (Higman

1984: 77), a situation that was guaranteed to produce a siege mentality among the minority who had power over the majority. The old legislative assemblies, though claiming to be democratic, were actually self-perpetuating oligarchies whose primary purpose was the protection of the elite's wealth and privileges. Limited rights and privileges were sometimes extended to the free people of colour, though on a discriminatory basis, to try to shore up the system.

The old political system was surrendered in the British Caribbean (except in Barbados and the Bahamas) in favour of the Crown colony system when the local elite gave up its political privileges in return for obtaining greater support from the imperial government. The elite accepted an autocratic regime rather than permit the growth of a more democratic system that could have challenged it. Crown colony government, even when some unofficial advisers were appointed from among the elite to the legislative councils, extended the power of the imperial government, excluded the masses completely, and thus reinforced the authoritarian tradition. 'Final power, always, lay in the hands of the executive and, within the executive, in the hands of the Governor and, through the Governor, of course, in the hands of the distant Colonial Office' (Lewis 1968: 98). The old ruling class of planters and slave-owners, merchant monopolists and colonial officials, when challenged by rising groups of the free coloured, peasant farmers and native politicians, intensified their defences of racial and class oppression, even as they gave up their particular political privileges. The ruling class ensured that Emancipation did not herald a fundamental reconstruction of the society. 'The class-colour alignments shifted; but they did not disappear . . . 1834 removed the gross features of the slave system without basically upsetting the underlying class-colour differentiations of the society. The three hierarchically ordered sections - white, coloured, and black - remained as solidly entrenched as ever . . . . The slave regime was dead. But it was replaced by a regime almost equally oppressive, imbued still with the slavery spirit.' (Lewis 1968: 73-4, 78)

This 'slavery spirit' was manifest in many ways and in many relationships and institutions. This is not to say that such a spirit does not exist in situations where slavery was unknown, because it surely does, but certainly it is more likely to be widespread and persistent wherever slavery has been such a pervasive institution as it was in the Caribbean, and particularly when it was associated with the disciplined plantation regimen and prolonged colonialism. Among the ways it was manifest were the arrogant attitude and overbearing actions of overseers and managers towards workers, and the high-handed and aggressive treatment of clients and citizens by police and government officials. We should also consider the degree to which it affected the paternalistic relations of religious leaders with their followers, teachers with their students and even parents with their children. The prevalence of authoritarian attitudes and behaviour, including widespread corporal punishment, is striking in these societies to this day. It exists in the spirit of 'spare the rod and spoil the child'. Merle Hodge, the Trinidadian novelist and educator, has commented perceptively on this legacy of violence, the 'shadow of the whip', as she calls it, in Caribbean societies. 'But the violence of our history has not evaporated. It is still there. It is there in the relations between adult and child, between black and white, between man and woman. It has been internalized, it has seeped down into our personal lives. Drastic brutality - physical and verbal - upon children is an accepted part of child rearing in the Caribbean'. (Hodge 1974: 111)

The slavery spirit, at the same time that it strengthened authoritarianism, contributed to the weakening of self-respect and self-discipline, and to undermining self-confidence and individual initiative, as well as inhibiting the growth of community spirit and more egalitarian and democratic relations. The pervasiveness of racial prejudice and ethnic stereotyping, as well as class snobbery and gender stereotyping and oppression, also strengthened mutual distrust at the expense of a spirit of community and participatory democracy. People who are completely denied authority in their society will often be driven to extremes in expressing their legitimate desire for a share of authority, the frustration of which produces insecurity, resentment and anger. When the risks entailed by the powerless in challenging the powerful are too great, as is often the case, an angry and frustrated person may displace the target and victimise someone who is vulnerable. Fanon referred to this common colonial phenomenon, when the threatened 'native' defends his own personality by turning on those who are like himself, as 'autodestruction'. 'The settler keeps alive in the native an anger which he deprives of outlet; the native is trapped in the tight links of the chains of colonialism. But we have seen that inwardly the settler can only achieve a pseudo petrification. The native's muscular tension finds outlet regularly in bloodthirsty explosions - in tribal warfare, in feuds between septs, and in quarrels between individuals'. (Fanon 1968: 54)

In these situations, the most vulnerable, and hence often the most victimised people, are women and children. The physical and verbal abuse of women and children, which is not only widespread but is also widely accepted as being part and parcel of normal relations between men and women, and between adults and children, is therefore an important aspect of the deeply rooted authoritarian political culture of the Caribbean.

Cultural colonialism is central to the process of control through an authoritarian political culture. The role of churches and their mission schools was to 'civilise' the former slaves and the Asian 'heathens' in terms drawn from the European religious tradition, and more specifically its patriarchal Victorian Christian variant. The missionaries who took up the white man's burden sought to produce 'an individuated and economically rational Christian black ensconced within a European family form' (Austin-Broos 1992: 226), most specifically a patriarchal family that emphasised female submissiveness and filial obedience. The links of obedience and duty, beginning in patriarchal homes and continuing through the employer and governor to the monarchy, were intended to create binding chains on these ostensibly free people. The education system, also, was designed to promote a white and European bias, so it is not surprising that some of the most educated West Indians were Anglicized gentlemen, complete with the mother country's racial prejudices and class snobberies, who had learned to despise their own people and countries. They were no accident, but were the products of a deliberate cultural colonialism and they themselves contributed towards redefining a moral and cultural order after slavery that tended to perpetuate extant patterns of domination. In the political sphere many of these West Indian gentlemen - those who were promoted and won scholarships in the system were chiefly men, and men alone could participate in formal politics - sought to extend their own limited rights and privileges. While eschewing contact with popular social bases, as they had been taught, the only way these people could promote themselves was by petitioning the colonial establishment and, in so doing, promote the further acceptance of its values, procedures and institutions.[4]

Some of these educated West Indians believed in British democratic values and institutions, but the mother country did not apply them to the Caribbean colonies until the 1940s. The planter class resisted any move towards democratisation and maintained its hegemony to a large degree through its influence with the colonial officials, both locally and in London. The Crown colony system, while eliminating the elite's legislative assemblies, assured it of continuing influence through the nominated unofficial members of legislative councils. The planters used their influence with governors and colonial officials to protect their monopolistic control over land and labour, to ensure tax systems that would benefit them, and even to sponsor mass immigration schemes to provide new supplies of coerced labour. Regressive taxation schemes generally meant that the poor peasantry and estate workers contributed disproportionately to the sponsorship of the immigrants who would compete with them for jobs and land, thereby driving down the price of the former and driving up the price of the latter, all to the advantage of the planters. Expanded systems of police and courts, much of whose activity consisted of enforcing the labour laws and disciplining the workers, were also paid for by the regressive taxation, and they, too, benefited the rich and powerful.

The colonial state after slavery, whether or not it was in the form of a Crown colony, took on new roles in relation to the slowly changing Caribbean economies and societies, but always it was in the service of the capitalist class. Thus, the state sought to protect markets for plantation products, to facilitate and regulate banking and trade, to develop infrastructure in the form of roads, irrigation and port facilities that favoured the planters, to sponsor immigration where planters needed it, and even, to a limited extent, to take responsibility for education and health services. In these ways, therefore, the internal planter hegemony and the external imperial administration were intertwined in a system of domination that continued to exploit the people of the colonies in order to accumulate more capital in the metropole.

When the elective principle was reintroduced in the colonies in the twentieth century it was on the basis of an extremely narrow franchise until the 1940s and, in some colonies, the 1950s. The slow constitutional reforms maintained the influence of the small ruling class and the powerlessness of the vast majority of Caribbean people. As Thomas, George Beckford and others have pointed out, this powerlessness is interrelated with the 'persistent poverty'of Caribbean people (Beckford 1972; Thomas 1988), but it was also dialectically related to their traditions of resistance. The assault on authoritarianism was undertaken, during slavery and after, by those who were most oppressed. Hence, we must seek an explanation for the relations of authoritarianism and the rise of democracy in the internal struggle in these colonies as well as the position they occupied in the world capitalist system.

Resistance

C.L.R. James argued that 'in the history of the West Indies there is one dominant fact and that is the desire, sometimes expressed, sometimes unexpressed, but always there, the desire for liberty' (James 1980: 177). The tradition of resistance in the Caribbean is as old as the existence of oppression. Conquest, colonialism and coerced labour, in their various manifestations, have all been resisted in numerous ways, by the Amerindians, the enslaved Africans and their exploited successors. Amerindians resisted the European invasion and their subsequent enslavement, but they were massacred or transported when they rebelled. Resistance against slavery was endemic in the Caribbean. For example, there were 75 known plots and rebellions by slaves in the British Caribbean between 1638 and 1837, 22 of them in Jamaica alone (Craton 1982: 335-9).

James, in his classic study of the revolution in Saint Domingue, The Black Jacobins, first published in 1938, showed how the slaves liberated themselves in the late eighteenth century and created the first free and independent nation state in the Americas. Elsewhere, slave resistance contributed to the modification and eventual abolition of slavery. Acts of sabotage and marronage, revenge and rebellion, increased the costs of slavery for the slave-owners, and innumerable but less overt and risky forms of everyday resistance were part of the way slaves negotiated for more humane conditions and treatment. Cultural resistance, too, was widespread, as attested by the persistence of aspects of African cultures - particularly in religion, language, music and folklore (Alleyne 1988) - despite the efforts of the dominant Europeans to suppress them. When slave-owners sought to destroy the self-respect and cultural heritage of their slaves in order to degrade and control them, every effort by slaves to maintain their dignity and heritage was an act of resistance. The rejection of racist notions of white superiority, also, was an expression of the desire for liberty and resistance against the system of oppression.

The most outstanding victory over colonialism and slavery, and over British as well as French armies, was the revolution that began in 1791 and culminated in the independence of Haiti in 1804. The Haitian revolution, unlike the earlier rebellion of white settlers in Great Britain's North American colonies, achieved not only political autonomy from the metropole but also the liberation of the slaves through a social revolution. Haiti's example inspired independence movements in the Spanish American colonies and slave revolts in Barbados, Cuba, the United States and elsewhere. Although one major consequence of the destruction of the Saint Domingue sugar and coffee plantations was the intensification of production elsewhere - in Cuba, Jamaica, Brazil and Puerto Rico - the slaves of Saint Domingue had served notice that the system could be destroyed. Slave-owners and whites in the slave societies of the Americas could never feel so secure again, for fear of 'the horrors of St. Domingo'.[5] The major rebellions among slaves in British Guiana in 1823 and Jamaica in 1831-2 were to a degree provoked by the parliamentary debates about slavery in London and the feeling that emancipation was in the offing. The great Jamaican rebellion, involving 60,000 slaves (at least 200 of whom were killed in the fighting and over 300 killed by judicial murder) hastened these debates (Craton 1982: 291-323). A week after the slave leader, Sam Sharpe, was hanged on 23 May 1832, a parliamentary committee was appointed to consider how to effect Emancipation 'at the earliest period compatible with the safety of all Classes in the Colonies'.[6] The lawmakers in London preferred Emancipation to come from above rather than, as in Haiti, from below. The first Emancipation Act was passed on 31 July 1833, and its terms - including £20 million compensation to the slave-owners for their loss of property and a period of apprenticeship to ensure that they retained control of their labour - were designed to minimize social change.[7]

Immediately after this legal Emancipation in the British colonies the movement of former slaves from the plantations led to the rapid growth of free villages and a peasantry wherever land was available. Though many plantations survived the end of slavery, the rise of a peasantry constituted a 'mode of resistance' to the plantation system and its 'imposed style of life' (Mintz 1974: 132-3). As a counterpoint to the plantation system, Maroon communities had preceded peasants in those places, like Jamaica and Dutch Guiana, where the terrain made them possible. The peasantries constituted not merely an economic alternative but also a more autonomous and egalitarian way of life, based on the community, though they still had people in authority and many of the communities remained dependent in various ways on the wider economy. Access to land was not only a source of material benefit but was also of symbolic value in defining the free communities that emerged in resistance to the domination of slavery and the plantation system (Besson 1992). A piece of land could provide some means of subsistence, but it also provided a base from which the former slaves and their descendants could bargain for better terms of employment on the estates. The struggle between their dependence and independence was real and symbolic, material and social, and is related to competing visions of what constitutes a free and fair society (Bolland 1992a). The labour rebellions that erupted throughout the British Caribbean a century after legal Emancipation were an important part of this lengthy struggle for freedom and justice, and they were so understood by many of the protagonists. These rebellions, in turn, transformed the forms of the struggle itself, but many of the same items remained on the agenda, including the demand for fair wages, land and respect.

If the role of resistance is not given its due weight in Caribbean social history we would be in danger of seeing Caribbean people merely as victims, or 'as faceless automatons energized only by metropolitan stimuli, rather than the adaptive and creative peoples that they truly are' (Richardson 1992a: 12). Of course, we need to give due weight to the extraordinary forces of oppression and exploitation in Caribbean history, but a one-sided focus on the impact of slavery, poverty, powerlessness and cultural colonialism results in seeing only social disorganisation, demoralisation and even dehumanization. Lewis, for example, concludes, 'By 1900, then, the West Indies, altogether, were a bizarre mixture of racial discord, crass commercialism, and cultural imitativeness' (Lewis 1968: 80). Although we do not deny the existence of these features, we cannot agree that this emphasis adequately describes West Indian culture and society, because even where these bizarre features were present they competed always with their opposites.[8] For example, the terrible pattern of abuse of women and children, to which reference has been made, coexists with a quite contrary pattern of love and self-sacrifice, by men as well as women, that has enabled children in the Caribbean to survive through generations.

The struggles of the various oppressed peoples of the Caribbean - Amerindian, African and Asian - to preserve and sustain a sense of their identity and solidarity is a crucial part of the entire struggle for freedom and justice. There has been an understandable tendency in recent decades to identify and honour selected national heroes in this struggle, people like Nanny, Sam Sharpe and Paul Bogle in Jamaica, and Cuffee or Kofi in Berbice, Guyana. Although those who were leaders in the more overt confrontations played an important role, the less easily identifiable people who resisted oppression also contributed in myriad ways to the political culture of resistance in the Caribbean. Michel de Certeau's work on the 'practice of everyday life' shows how the subordinate people in a society contribute to shaping their own culture and making their own history.[9] De Certeau rejects a 'social atomism' that posits the individual as the elementary unit of society, and shows instead, in his analysis of everyday practices, 'that a relation (always social) determines its terms, and not the reverse, and that each individual is a locus in which an incoherent (and often contradictory) plurality of such relational determinations interacts' (De Certeau 1984: xi). People whose social status is that of 'dominee' are neither passive nor docile but, on the contrary, frequently subvert in their actions the goals and structures of the dominators. For example, de Certeau refers to the apparent success of Spanish colonisers who impose their culture on indigenous Indians:

> Submissive, and even consenting to their subjection, the Indians nevertheless often made of the rituals, representations, and laws imposed on them something quite different from what their conquerors had in mind; they subverted them not by rejecting or altering them, but by using them with respect to ends and references foreign to the system they had no choice but to accept. They were other within the very colonization that outwardly assimilated them; their use of the dominant social order deflected its power, which they lacked the means to challenge. (De Certeau 1984: xiii)

This formulation is appropriate to the study of the politics of cultural resistance developed in the period of colonialism, slavery and indenture in the Caribbean, when there were many direct challenges to the dominant social order but also innumerable less visible 'murmurings' in everyday practices, like drops of water that could eventually wear down a stone.

Cultural resistance in social contexts of extreme domination is often not externally manifest. For obvious reasons, the modes of resistance of people whose status is subordinate, who are threatened with violence for the slightest offence, often conceal their contributions to the formation of culture, but they are no less real and perhaps just as important as the more defiant examples. It is surely significant that Anansi, the spider trickster of West African tales who 'play fool fe catch wise', is the popular folk hero of slaves and their descendants throughout the Caribbean, people who often had to choose strategies involving guile and stealth rather than open defiance. Traditions of resistance are related to the symbols and styles of authority of those who become the people's leaders. It has been suggested, for example, that Alexander Bustamante, the Jamaican labour leader, epitomized the 'trickster' who could 'manipulate the system on behalf of his followers and deceive the rich and powerful into granting concessions' (Post 1978: 185). When people grant leaders like Bustamante authority, however, they may be sowing the seed of a new kind of authoritarianism, distinct from but rooted still in the old forms. A trickster who demands obedience, as did Bustamante, may eventually fool his own followers.

The strengths and achievements of Caribbean people emerged in the crucible of their struggle with the systems of extreme domination under which they were forced to live. The shortcomings and continuing contradictions in the institutions and culture that they created are also shaped in this struggle. Understanding this central struggle is therefore the key to interpreting the history of Caribbean cultures and societies.

Dialectics

The Caribbean is an area that has been dominated by the expanding political economy of Europe, and more recently the United States, for five centuries, during which the people have resisted oppression in various ways. The history of these societies should place this relationship of oppression and resistance at the centre of the study of social change. James, one of the great Caribbean intellectuals of the twentieth century,[10] identified dialectics as the appropriate 'theory of knowledge' for understanding the contradictory nature of human society (James 1980: 80), and in The Black Jacobins he used a dialectical approach to analyse a specific example of Caribbean history in order to show the self-emancipatory potential of revolutionary politics.

In the most general sense the dialectic is a branch of logic, a mode of reasoning, and a method of scientific investigation, but in its more specific Hegelian and Marxist sense it is a theory of knowledge that identifies conflicts or contradictions as the source of change. Marx accepted the logical form of Hegel's dialectic but sought the process of development in the contradictions of society instead of in forms of thought or the 'Idea', so the primary sources of social change are in the relations of people in society. Dialectical theory conceives of social life as essentially practical activity and of people as essentially social beings. On the one hand, society consists of the social relations in which people engage, and is not reducible to individuals. On the other hand, people make their institutions and history, but under conditions and constraints that exist already in their society. Marx acknowledged the role of culture, in the form of traditions, ideas, customs, languages and institutions, in shaping social action, while these actions, in turn, modify the social structure and culture within which the people act: 'Men make their own history, but they do not make it just as they please; they do not make it under circumstances chosen by themselves, but under circumstances directly found, given and transmitted from the past'.[11]

The central dialectic of Marx's theory of history is 'the dynamic tension between the subjective and the objective . . . in its simplest and most extreme terms, between ideas and the social arrangements within which we lead our lives' (Worsley 1982: 113). What greater tension could there be than that between 'the desire for liberty', which James identified as the dominant fact of Caribbean history, and the oppressive social arrangements of colonialism and slavery, that were so extraordinarily pervasive and persistent in the region? This dialectic between the aspiration for freedom, as an ideal, and the brutal reality of colonialism and slavery, which was the experience of everyday life, constitutes the central dynamic of Caribbean history and political culture.

Dialectics, as a theory of knowledge, helps us to understand the complex relations between social structure and human agency by recognizing that while history and society are made by the more or less purposeful social action of individuals, in the same process social action and individuals are shaped by history and society. This dialectical approach to historical sociology recognizes the mutually constitutive nature of social structure and human agency, and comprehends the paradox that though 'we make our own world - the world confronts us as an implacable order of social facts set over against us' (Abrams 1980: 8). The 'dialectics of structuring' (Abrams 1980: 13) consists of dynamic tension and conflict because most important social relationships are defined and differentiated in terms of power, between the dominant and the subordinate. As the forms of oppression and the distribution of power vary from time to time and from one society to another, so does the location, kind and intensity of social conflict and change. Marx himself understood the distinction and the relationship between different forms of oppression in the development of the Atlantic capitalist world. 'Liverpool waxed fat on the slave-trade. This was its method of primitive accumulation . . . . Whilst the cotton industry introduced child-slavery in England, it gave in the United States a stimulus to the transformation of the earlier, more or less patriarchal slavery, into a system of commercial exploitation. In fact, the veiled slavery of wage-workers in Europe needed, for its pedestal, slavery pure and simple in the new world'.[12]

Various forms of oppression are based on status inequalities, defined in terms of race, ethnicity, gender, age and legal status, or a combination of these, as well as class. Such status-based inequalities may or may not coincide with the class relationship, or with each other, and they will vary in the nature of their connections with class, but all societies that exhibit relations of domination/subordination, of oppressor and oppressed, on whatever basis, cannot be free of social conflicts and these conflicts are the chief source of social change.

The absence of the explicit use of force is not evidence of genuine stability and consensus, for so long as relations of oppression persist so will the potential for conflict and change. Antonio Gramsci's work on cultural hegemony shows how the persistence of a regime of exploitation often depends on the capacity of the rulers to persuade the oppressed of the inevitability, or even justice, of the system. Whatever can be defined as 'natural', such as racial or gender oppression, for example, is thereby removed from the social agenda. Regimes of oppression are sustained by the manipulation of consent as well as by force - indeed, the ability to manipulate consent is an important attribute of power, as the more successful the rulers are in that regard the less they will need to rely upon force. Hence, too, the importance of understanding the political nature of processes of cultural resistance which may redefine the social agenda. The strength of dialectical theory as an explanation of both social change and persistence, therefore, is that it focuses 'on material interest, on the economics, power and status rewards enjoyed by those who control society, and the exploitation suffered by the great majority who do the producing, and upon the mechanisms which justify these basic inequalities and which cope with resistance to them' (Worsley 1982: 67).

James was one of the first Caribbean intellectuals to grasp and use dialectical theory as a means of analysing and understanding the history of Caribbean societies. For James, the task and promise of dialectics was to make manifest the historical tendencies of Caribbean society through analysing and understanding the dialectics of history itself (Cambridge 1992: 166). Central to this process of analysis and understanding is the actual struggle for freedom and justice because, for James, 'dialectics encapsulates the very idea of freedom itself', the comprehension that capitalist society 'creates the pre-conditions for a free and rational human existence yet precludes the realization of freedom and happiness' (Cambridge 1992: 167). Dialectics, James understood, is at once a theory of knowledge, in the sense of a way of comprehending the world, and a political methodology, in the sense of providing a means of changing the world. In short, it is revolutionary praxis, the relationship of theory and practice in Marxian socialism.

For James, then, a correct political diagnosis depends on understanding the prevailing objective conditions and historical tendencies. This means not only that we must comprehend the limitations and constraints of capitalist society but also how socialist society emerges from capitalist society, and hence is already present in it in a subordinate but imminent form. To comprehend phenomena dialectically is to comprehend them as a whole, as a totality, because everything unfolds through struggle into something implied by, but other than, what it was. But this process needs to be comprehended concretely and historically, as distinct from abstractly, or merely philosophically. In The Black Jacobins, therefore, James explored the broad implications for continuing human liberation of the revolution in Saint Domingue between 1791 and 1804. He was particularly interested in the meaning of this revolution for the struggle for freedom that was taking place in the Caribbean in the 1930s, while he was writing his study. James's intention was to show, a century after legal emancipation in the British Caribbean, that the people were ready 'to embark on the uncharted seas of independence and nationhood', but the imperial government 'poisoned and corrupted that sense of self-confidence and political dynamic' which had been demonstrated historically in Saint Domingue (James 1980: 189).

In a lecture, 'The Making of the Caribbean People', given in Montreal in 1966, James reflected on the lasting meaning of The Black Jacobins and commented on 'the savage ferocity of some of the West Indian rulers today to the populations who have put them in power' (James 1980: 184).[13] He characterized the 'new masters', who were miseducated by the former colonial power, as 'house-slaves' who were rewarded for keeping the rest of the people in order. James's intention was to show the continuing dialectic in Caribbean societies: not only is freedom imminent within the structures of domination, but also domination reappears 'at the very moment when freedom was won' (James 1980: 184). From the viewpoint of dialectics, colonialism is constitutive of Caribbean society, not just external to it, so the formal and largely symbolic constitutional decolonization does not eradicate the deeply rooted colonial political culture of authoritarianism.

The dialectics of colonialism and resistance reveal the cleavage within Caribbean society itself. The fact that the metropole is geographically overseas should not obscure the reality that colonialism has been constitutive of Caribbean society for about 500 years. Colonialism is, by its very nature, neither internal nor external, in the usual sense of those words, because it refers to the nature of the relationship between the parts of a single social system, not to discrete units that are geographically defined. From the dialectical viewpoint, metropole and colony, colonizer and colonized, like master and slave, are the differentiated parts of a whole, constituting a unity of opposites, that have no independent existence apart from each other. Each is simply a part of the system, defined in terms of its relation with the other part (Bolland 1992b: 71). Dialectical theory draws attention unequivocally to the elements of resistance that are inherent in the domination-subordination relationship between the metropole and the colony, and hence within the colony also. Resistance and conflict are therefore constituent aspects of the political cultures and the social and economic structures that are the legacies of these colonial societies.

The struggle of former slaves in the British Caribbean to make their legal freedom a reality, the resistance of indentured workers to their exploitation, the labour rebellions and movements for political rights and independence from the 1930s to the 1950s, and the continuing struggle of Caribbean people for 'bread, justice and freedom' (see Kambon's book with this title, 1988), are specific but connected phases of the entire historic struggle for human liberation.

Notes

[1] In order to distinguish between the event and the process, Emancipation will refer to the former and emancipation to the latter throughout the book.

[2] Between 1873 and 1917, 34,304 labourers were brought from India into Suriname, and between 1890 and 1940, 32,956 Javanese came to Suriname, most of them as contract labourers (Hoefte 1987: 2-3).

[3] An earlier version was outlined in Bolland 1988b: 2-8; see also Bolland 1981 and 1992b.

[4] There were some notable exceptions to this pattern, of course. Outstanding among the critics of colonialism and racism was the Jamaican, Marcus Garvey (1887-1940), but his importance lies precisely in the fact that he was so exceptional in this regard.

[5] On 18 August 1800, a Public Meeting of the self-styled Principal Inhabitants of the British settlement at Belize, in the Bay of Honduras, discussed their 'apprehension of internal convulsion and the horrors of St. Domingo' (Burdon 1935: vol.1, 282).

[6] Quoted in Craton 1988.

[7] Higman argues that the changing demographic pattern after 1807 that resulted from the abolition of the slave trade led to greater stress among the slaves and a decline in output which, in turn, contributed to the 1831 rebellion and the slave-owners' willingness to cooperate with Emancipation in return for compensation (1976: 231-2).

[8] For example, Austin-Broos points out that Rastafarianism is a kind of revolt against 'the respectable image of the Christian black' that the missionaries seemed to have so successfully promoted in Jamaica (Austin-Broos 1992: 239).

[9] I want to thank my colleague Gary Urton for drawing this work to my attention.

[10] James, born near Port of Spain, Trinidad in 1901, died in London in 1989. He influenced many students of Caribbean history and society, as diverse in their views and activities as Eric Williams, Walter Rodney and Orlando Patterson.

[11] 'The Eighteenth Brumaire of Louis Bonaparte', in Tucker 1972: 437.

[12] Capital, in Tucker 1972: 314-15.

[13] In 1965 James was placed under house arrest when he returned to Trinidad, as a cricket correspondent to report on a Test series, for the first time since his country became independent in 1962.

Chapter 2

Systems of domination
and the politics of freedom

The theme of this chapter[1] is informed by three closely connected propositions. First, Caribbean societies and cultures are shaped by basic and long-term continuities, from the years of slavery through Emancipation to independence and the present. Rather than emphasising a periodisation of Caribbean history by focusing on key dates that imply sharp breaks and ruptures with the past, we should seek to identify and understand these crucial continuities.

Second, the issue of labour, and specifically of its control and exploitation, is central in Caribbean social history. There are basic and long-term continuities in the contradictions of the relations of production, despite changes in the legal forms of these contradictions. The resultant struggles associated with the labour process reflect and shape the political culture and social structure of Caribbean societies.

Third, the prolonged and pervasive nature of colonialism in the Caribbean has led to a particularly close interrelationship between the internal and external aspects of the political dimensions of this struggle. Though we may analytically distinguish between the internal and external aspects, it is important to remember that they are really not separate. The dependent nature of the largely plantation economies and the crucial role of the state, both during and after the period of direct control through colonial administration, are organically and dynamically interrelated with the extreme inequalities of power, wealth and privilege within these societies. So we must think of continuities in the systems of domination and consider the politics of freedom in terms of the long traditions of resistance to such systems.

Beckles and Shepherd comment on the ubiquitous nature of the class struggle in the history of Caribbean societies:

[T]he role of labour as a factor of production within the economics of emancipation, and the rights and expectations of labourers as 'citizens' within the politics of freedom, proved contradictory. As a result, political conflict (occasionally characterized by armed struggle) between traditional owners of the means of production on the one hand, and the continuing disenfranchized majority on the other, constituted the principal dialectical force that shaped the nature of the post-slavery period.

Since emancipation as an event did not produce any immediate success in the area of redressing major imbalances, such as extreme inequality in wealth distribution, and minority ethnic domination of political institutions, conflict over the use of state power, ownership and possession of land, and terms and conditions on the labour market, also remained endemic. That the emancipated should pursue the political franchise and ownership of land, in themselves directly related, with as much tenacity as their determination to receive a reasonable wage and honourable working conditions, should be interpreted as constituting proof of the broad-based nature of their expectations of freedom. (Beckles and Shepherd 1993: ix-x)

Coercion and resistance in the labour process

The meaning of freedom for former slaves involved not only the struggle to gain control over their own labour power but also a search for ways to take control of their own lives. As George Cumper said, 'the legal change did not of itself destroy the whole social nexus of slavery . . . . The social subordination established under slavery cannot yet be said to be extinct' (1954:46). Freedom of movement was vital, for its symbolic value and also because former slaves sought to be reunited with family members and friends from whom they had been forcibly separated, and to create communities in which they could freely participate in their churches and mutual-aid societies. Their search for space and mobility was itself a manifestation of freedom and was also a way to find opportunities for a more independent livelihood or better terms of employment. Former slaves sometimes left the estates to escape the personal domination of their former owner or simply to turn their backs on a place associated with bad memories. Emancipation made it legally possible for former slaves to move but did not 'of itself make away with all, or even perhaps the greater part, of the forces holding the former slave to his geographical location on the estate' (Cumper 1954: 46).

As Douglas Hall argues, the movement of former slaves from the estates was not just 'a flight from the horrors of slavery. It was a protest against the inequities of early freedom' (Hall 1978: 23). Many former slave-owners sought to continue to coerce their former slaves in order to control the supply of labour that was essential to the survival of their plantations. But they also sought continued control because they continued to define themselves as 'masters', even though they could no longer legally own slaves.

> Many of the practices which aroused the ill-will of the labourers in the post-emancipation period - the charging of high and capricious rents for estate housing, the offsetting of rent against wages - can be seen as attempts by the planters to reduce their cash expenditure on labour and to draw some kind of cash return from their existing assets. This was seen by the labourers, essentially correctly, as an attempt to restore the type of status relationship which had existed before emancipation between planter and slave. By making of the Negro village and of the provision ground a symbol of insecurity it deprived the former slave of his strongest point of attachment to the physical confines of the estate and was particularly important in stimulating the exodus of labour from the estates which began soon after emancipation. (Cumper 1954: 48)

In many respects, then, the struggle over the labour process, which was central to the entire emancipation process, continued the struggle that had taken place during the period of slavery. The planters' efforts to maintain control over people whom they still considered to be their social subordinates provoked many former slaves to leave the estates. The former slaves used their new legal freedom, including the freedom of movement, to begin to shape new social relations that were unlike those that had been forced on them during slavery. In this struggle, as we will see, the former slaves upheld a meaning of freedom and a vision of a free society that was quite different from that held by their former owners.

The promise of freedom made Emancipation a great moment for the freed people themselves, a moment that should still be celebrated. Nevertheless, to the extent that this promise was largely unfulfilled, that real freedom was denied the former slaves, the whole process of emancipation needs to be re-evaluated. Emancipation should be analysed more as a prolonged process than an overnight event, and a central issue in this process is the continuing power struggle over the control of labour. From a narrowly legalistic viewpoint, slavery is a special case in which human beings are defined as chattel property, but from the broader vantage point of historical sociology, slavery is seen more as a variant, in extreme form, of relations of domination and subordination. From the former perspective, it follows that the change in legal status brought about by Emancipation is, however compromised, 'by definition a liberation', whereas from the latter perspective the legal change is 'almost epiphenomenal, for the essential facts of coercion and hardship remain' (R. Scott 1985: 282). The key issue is the actual distribution of power, rather than the particular legal expression of that power, so the political dimension - which includes questions of armed force, personal intimidation, cultural hegemony, and legal and administrative institutions – is crucial to understanding the limits as well as the promise of the process of emancipation.

The ability of the former slaves to exercise their initiatives and fulfil their aspirations was decisively affected by the economic forces as well as the political constraints against which they struggled in this emancipation process. Their struggle for 'personal mobility, autonomy, and dignity' and against 'labor in tasks not freely chosen' (R. Scott 1985: 282) existed after as well as during slavery. Of course, the change in their legal and social status in 1838 affected the ways, and perhaps the degree to which, the former slaves could achieve their goals, but to the extent that the vast majority of them remained virtually powerless the odds always weighed heavily against them. 'Emancipation involved different degrees of escape from different aspects of bondage' (R. Scott 1985: 282), and the social relations involved in the labour process, because they are central in the social system as a whole, influenced other aspects of the emancipation process. This is why, in the United States, for example, 'the fulfillment of blacks' "noneconomic" aspirations, from family autonomy to the creation of schools and churches, all depended in considerable measure on success in winning control of their working lives and gaining access to the economic resources of the South' (Foner 1988: 110). In the British Caribbean after 1838 – like the United States after the civil war and Cuba and Brazil after 1886 and 1888, respectively – those who had been slaves found themselves struggling against extant power structures and market forces while they tried to forge a new and more fully free society. The former slave-owners in the British Caribbean, unlike those in the United States, were not a defeated class, and in essential respects they retained the support of their imperial government.

Economic relations and the class structure do not determine all other social relations, nor do the people who control the economy thereby have total power over all other people. This was not so even in slave societies, where the relations of domination and subordination were most extreme. However, it is surely true that the struggle over the means of existence in societies emerging from slavery, in which control over resources had been monopolised for so long by so few, was a central struggle in the process of adjustment to Emancipation. More than a century after the end of legal slavery, this remains true throughout the Americas, wherever the enslavement of Africans was predominant.

Throughout the Caribbean, as in other parts of the Americas, the nineteenth century was 'a period of transition from one system of domination to another, each involving distinct forms of labour control and patterns of labour resistance' (Bolland 1986b: 175). Surplus labour is extracted under capitalism increasingly by economic rather than by political means, but this should not be allowed to obscure the fact that coercion continues to be a feature of labour exaction. Even after the legal abolition of slavery, then, a central conflict of interest, and hence locus of struggle, persisted between those who hired and those who must offer labour power in a more or less free society.

The key distinction between the polar types of slave labour and free wage labour is not in the question of compulsion, which exists in both types, but in the distinction between the labourer as a commodity and the labourer's labour power as a commodity. The existence of legally free wage labour 'implies the conceptual abstraction of a man's labor power from the man himself' (Finley 1980: 68), and this form of hired labour becomes increasingly the defining, though not the only characteristic of capitalist relations of production. Forms of hired labour, including even slaves who were paid wages (Bolland 1995a), coexisted with slave labour in the early capitalist economies. Even after slavery was made illegal, varieties of economic compulsion and exploitation persisted, and the state continued to play a crucial role in the institutionalised system of organising labour and exacting surplus value.

Of the two extremes, slavery may be seen as involving the loss of legal control by the labourer not only over his or her labour power but also over his or her own person, and even his or her children. To conceive of a person as having the status of a marketable commodity, of chattel property, is to conceive of 'one of the most extreme forms of the relation of domination, approaching the limits of total power from the viewpoint of the master, and of total powerlessness from the viewpoint of the slave' (Patterson 1982: 1). In this relation, the slave's deracination is important, as is his natal alienation, that is, 'the loss of ties of birth in both ascending and descending generations . . . . It was this alienation of the slave from all formal, legally enforceable ties of "blood," and from any attachment to groups or localities other than those chosen for him by the master, that gave the relation of slavery its peculiar value to the master. The slave was the ultimate human tool.' (Patterson 1982: 7)

The extreme authority of the slave–owner was matched to the absence of any legal claims by others on the slave, either as rights or responsibilities. Of course, such extreme authority was what the owner sought and the law defined, but slaves resisted this definition by various means and were not always 'as imprintable and as disposable as the master wished' (Patterson 1982: 7). As Harriet Jacobs, a slave in North Carolina, expressed her struggle, 'My master had power and law on his side; I had a determined will. There is might in each' (Jacobs 1987: 85).

Free wage labour, the other polar extreme in a continuum of labour relations, cannot be adequately understood simply as the absence of some of the features of compulsion associated with slavery. Rather, wage labour needs to be understood in terms of the existence of a variety of mechanisms of coercion, including but not limited to such economic mechanisms as rents, taxes, and debts, by means of which labourers are compelled to sell their labour power to others. Moreover, the market in which labour power is traded is rarely a free market, in the sense of there being equality between buyer and seller. Hence, we must examine the many legal, political, cultural and economic influences upon the relations of those who offer and those who hire labour power.

The transition from slave to free status, seen in this light, occurred 'only in ideal terms. In practice it involved a series of ongoing adjustments intended to sustain the economic and political power of those who needed labor over those who provided it' (Mintz 1985a: 275). What changed in this transition, then, was not the fact of domination and subordination, which persists, but the dimension of the ties between them (Finley 1980: 36), as the dialectic of power in the master-slave relationship was transformed into the dialectic of capitalist and wage worker.

The multiplicity of ways by which authority is formulated, implemented and resisted, must be at the centre of our analysis of post-Emancipation societies. The central issue of this political dimension is the ubiquitous struggle between those who attempt to depress legally free people into various conditions of dependency and compulsion in order to exploit their labour power and those who resist such measures. The former slaves recognised, as did their former owners, that the struggle for political power was a collective struggle, intimately related to control over the labour process and to cultural autonomy, because their security and freedom depended very largely on the outcome of this struggle (Scott 1988: 423).

The architects of Emancipation in the British Caribbean, responding to the great slave rebellion in Jamaica in 1831-2, sought to abolish slavery in order to prevent the far-reaching social changes that had occurred in Haiti. The British government and the West Indian planters disagreed about the necessity of slavery but they agreed that the plantation economies, which were based chiefly on the production and export of cane sugar, should continue because they constituted the colonies' primary value to the planters and to Great Britain. From the viewpoint of the planters, the problem created by the abolition of slavery was one of ensuring the continued existence of an adequate labour force to maintain the plantations and hence their profits. 'Planters, assuming blacks were either inherently indolent or simply determined to escape plantation labor, insisted that only coercion of some kind could maintain sugar production after abolition.' (Foner 1983: 15) Racist notions about the former slaves and their descendants, reinforced by the emergence of social Darwinism, constituted an important element of the political culture, an element that continued to shape labour relations and systems of authority long after Emancipation. The British government, with a few exceptions, agreed with these views and generally supported the planters.

The parliamentary committee that was created after the Jamaican slave rebellion to examine the slavery question concluded in 1832 that the danger of further rebellion was so great that freedom should be withheld no longer. Viscount Howick, the under-secretary for the colonies, and Henry Taylor, senior clerk in the West India Department, concluded that peace could be preserved only by prompt abolition. The reform of Parliament in 1832 removed many West Indian members and increased the support for abolition, and in December the Colonial Office informed the Cabinet: 'the policy of amelioration had run its course and that the constant peril of insurrection rendered full emancipation necessary .... The fear that emancipation might provoke bloodshed was only exceeded by the conviction that a withholding of freedom would probably produce even greater bloodshed.' (Green 1976: 115) Howick warned bluntly that if government did not arrange abolition with the West Indian planters, it would be achieved directly by a vote in the reformed Parliament or by a slave insurrection.[2]

The Abolition Act, passed in the British Parliament in June 1833, contained two important elements calculated to appease the proprietors of slaves, namely the apprenticeship system and compensation. Under the system called apprenticeship, all slaves over the age of six years were compelled to become apprenticed labourers for the same 'masters' who had been their owners, and were paid wages only for work done in excess of 45 hours per week. This scheme was designed to ensure that the former slave-owners retained tight control over their labour and the wages paid for overtime were a means of keeping the apprentices' work up to the mark. The apprenticeship system was intended to last for six years, as full freedom was to be received by non-field workers in 1838 and by field workers in 1840. Antigua and Bermuda rejected this system and conferred immediate freedom on the slaves in 1834.

The other element, compensation, was given to the former slave-owners for their loss of property, but no compensation was offered the former slaves for their years of unrequited toil.[3] An earlier version of the abolition bill, introduced by Edward Stanley, the secretary of state for the colonies, had proposed a 12-year apprenticeship period and £15 million of compensation. The final version, drafted by James Stephen, was a concession on the first element to the Anti-Slavery Society, which wanted immediate abolition, and on the second element to the planters who, if they could not be assured of continuing control over their labourers, demanded more compensation (Green 1976: 118-19). The treasury was empowered to raise £20 million to be paid to the slave-owners, a prodigious sum that was intended not only to shore up the planters' enterprises during this critical period but also to reassure the property-owning class that the principle of private property was not itself under attack. The compensation was to be paid based on the average value of each slave in the eight years before 1830. The average paid overall was about £21 per slave, or about 49 per cent of their estimated average value (Fogel and Engerman 1974: 395-6), but the amount varied between colonies. In Barbados and Jamaica slave-owners received an average of about £20 per slave, whereas in Belize, Guyana and Trinidad they received an average of over £50 per slave. Of the compensation fund 30 per cent was awarded to Jamaica, but a great deal of the money actually went to British merchant firms rather than to the slave-owners themselves (Butler 1988).

The terms of Emancipation, then, were intended to avoid, not to produce a social revolution. These elements of the Abolition Act, generous and sympathetic as they were to the slave-owners, were intended to limit social change in the colonies, and specifically 'to avoid any significant alterations in the plantation system of agriculture or the hierarchical character of society' (Green 1976: 126). Meanwhile, the abolitionists, paternalist as they were, felt the freed slaves were obliged to work diligently on the West Indian plantations in order to prove the superiority of free labour and to undersell the sugar planters of Cuba and Brazil, 'so as to drive all slave-grown sugar out of the markets of the world.'[4]

The British government left the framing of many of the rules and regulations concerning the conduct of apprentices and planters to the local colonial legislatures, which were dominated by the planters, but the Colonial Office reviewed these colonial emancipation acts. James Stephen, who as legal adviser had drafted the final abolition measure, was from 1836 to 1847 the permanent under-secretary at the Colonial Office. Stephen, a son and brother of leading abolitionists, was influenced by the Anti-Slavery Society and saw himself as a watchdog for the former slaves. He 'doubted both the willingness and capacity of the planters to initiate meaningful social reform' (Green 1976: 85) and was often critical of the colonial legislatures' acts. He played a key role in the government's refusal to consent to several West Indian bills that included draconian restrictions on the freedom of the former slaves. In the Jamaican act, for example, he found 'an inequality between the liability of apprentices and the liability of masters' and thought that as soon as the latter had received their compensation they would interpret the act's vague terms 'in a manner decidedly hostile to the interests of the apprentices' (Green 1976: 123). E.G.S. Stanley, the secretary of state for the colonies from April 1833 to June 1834, thought that a conciliatory policy toward the planters was preferable to a forcible one that might alienate them further. A hundred stipendiary magistrates were appointed to supervise the equitable functioning of apprenticeship and to adjudicate disputes between masters and apprentices, but many magistrates were patronised by the planters and there were never enough to provide adequate legal protection for the apprentices. Not surprisingly, given these problems, the apprenticeship system failed.

From its inception, apprenticeship had provoked resistance from the ex-slaves, many of whom considered it a conspiracy on the part of the local elites to keep freedom from them. There were disorders and disturbances in several colonies, including St Kitts, Montserrat, Guyana and Trinidad. In St Kitts martial law was declared and militiamen had to force many apprentices who refused to submit to further coercion back to the estates (Green 1976: 131). In Trinidad, a crowd of apprentices demonstrated in Port of Spain near Government House, shouting 'Point de six ans!' ('Not six years more!') Several were arrested and publicly flogged for protesting against the prolongation of coercion and the delay of full freedom (Brereton 1981: 63). Moreover, though they knew that apprenticeship was a temporary condition, many apprentices in the British Caribbean purchased their freedom, perhaps to achieve the dignity of freedman status on the basis of their own efforts, and perhaps also because they had concluded that 'freedom could be a temporary state unless vigorously defended, and they should trust no other agency but themselves to maintain its existence' (Marshall 1993: 15). As 1 August 1838 approached, it became clear that there would be widespread trouble if the praedial apprentices were still required to work under the same conditions for a further two years after the others had been freed, so the entire system was ended on that date throughout the colonies.

The planters, knowing that the apprenticeship system was to last for only a few years, sought a variety of means of coercion to ensure a continuing supply of manageable labourers. The concept of apprenticeship implied that the former slaves were to learn their obligations as wage-earning estate workers during this period, that they 'would continue to work on the plantations, but would gain legal equality while at the same time developing the economic wants, the familiarity with the marketplace, which would ensure their continued, voluntary labor once emancipation was complete' (Foner 1983: 16). The planter-dominated legislatures in the colonies enacted a series of oppressive laws concerning such offences as vagrancy, insubordination and neglecting work, in an attempt to maintain their tight regulation and control of labour.

Trinidad's Legislative Council, for example, passed the law 'to consolidate and amend the laws relative to Vagrants, Rogues and Vagabonds', Ordinance No.12 of 1838, one month after Emancipation. The law shows that the planters sought to stop, or at least to inconvenience, all forms of non-plantation or independent work. The law defined vagrants broadly and vaguely and put the burden of proof on the accused in such a way that almost anyone who did not work on a plantation had to prove they were not idle and disorderly. The Colonial Office disallowed this ordinance which was superseded by the order-in-council for the prevention and punishment of vagrancy, issued on 7 September 1838 (Trotman 1986: 208-9).

Whereas Trinidad was a Crown colony, Jamaica retained the planter-dominated Assembly and the governors between 1839 and 1846, Sir Charles Metcalfe and the Earl of Elgin, followed a conciliatory policy towards the island's oligarchs. Stephen considered the proposed Jamaica Vagrancy Act more severe than the 1838 order-in-council, particularly a provision giving local magistrates, who were often planters, summary jurisdiction over allegedly vagrant labourers, who included their former slaves. When the Colonial Office assented to the act on the provision that the governor weeded out the bad magistrates, Metcalfe declared that he trusted them all and that the Colonial Office should rely on him to work out the laws with the island's legislative and judicial institutions – a fine example of putting the foxes in charge of the chicken coop. Despite many serious reservations by Stephen, only five of the 65 Jamaican acts passed in the 1839-40 sessions were disallowed (Holt 1992: 187). The planters were able to maintain their power after Emancipation because wherever there were local legislatures they continued to control them, and they generally had the support of the colonial governors and the imperial government. Even in a Crown colony like Trinidad they remained powerful.

The parliamentary select committee on the West Indian Colonies in 1842 accepted the planters' view of the post-Emancipation crisis, attributing the planters' inability to secure sufficient labour at low wages to 'the easy terms upon which the use of land has been obtained by Negroes', and recommended that 'planters should exercise greater control over the alienation of estate lands'. The committee also urged the immigration of 'a fresh labouring population, to such an extent as to create competition for employment, thereby containing or possibly even reducing wage rates', recommended the revision of labour laws, and particularly urged that 'steps should be taken to control vagrancy and eliminate squatting by freedmen on abandoned estates or crown lands' (Lobdell 1988: 196).

As the economic crisis deepened in the 1840s, the imperial government increasingly adopted the planters' perspective. Earl Grey, the secretary of state for the colonies from 1846 to 1852, agreed with the planting interest that a productive export economy was essential for the prosperity and stability of the West Indian colonies. He stated in 1847 that 'the highest interests of the Negroes require that the cultivation of sugar should not be abandoned, and that the proprietors of European race should be enabled to maintain their present place in the society ... which can only be done by giving them a greater command of labour' (quoted in Lobdell 1988: 198). The Bentinck committee of 1848 expressed similar views, stating that the most pressing problem was the insufficiency of estate labour and recommending indentured immigration and laws against vagrancy and squatting to deter the emergence of a native peasantry. In general, from the late 1840s until the 1880s, when some officials favoured the West Indian peasantry, the prevailing official view was that 'West Indian prosperity might be rejuvenated if planters were afforded more effective control over wage labour' (Lobdell 1988: 198).

The masters, as they continued to think of themselves, tried a variety of techniques of labour control after 1838 in the British Caribbean colonies. These included the enactment of laws to restrict emigration and vagrancy and to deter independent forms of livelihood, various forms of taxation to pressure people into wage labour, the use of wage–rent and advance–truck systems to make workers dependent, and the development of systems of police, courts and prisons to punish those who broke the labour laws and to intimidate the others. They also sponsored mass immigration, particularly of indentured Asian workers, and monopolised land ownership in order to increase competition and reduce the options for the former slaves. In short, these elements, in whatever combinations they appeared in the different colonies, created new systems of domination that perpetuated the old social hierarchies throughout the British Caribbean, keeping the planters in control and the former slaves poor and dependent (Bolland 1981).

Several of these techniques of labour control had been tried already in Antigua, where planters were confident they could keep their former slaves dependent on estate work, and planters in other British colonies sought to benefit from the Antiguan experience. One such technique was the use of contracts to ensure regular and obedient supplies of labour. According to an act passed in the Antiguan legislature on 29 December 1834, labour contracts were not required to be written but needed only to be made orally in the presence of two witnesses. If a labourer under contract absented himself from work, even with a reasonable excuse, he forfeited his wages for the lost time, and if absent without such an excuse for half a day or less (a term sufficiently elastic to be used to enforce promptness), he forfeited the whole day's wages. If absent for two successive days, or for two whole days within any two-week period, the labourer would be liable to a week's imprisonment with hard labour. Other offences, such as drunkenness or the careless use of fire or the abuse of cattle, could be punished with up to three months' imprisonment with hard labour. In contrast, the maximum punishment for an employer, for any violation of a contract, was a fine of £5.

The imperial government, still sensitive to the criticisms of the anti-slavery party, disallowed this Antiguan act, but it was replaced the following year by another only slightly less severe. The new act provided that verbal or implied contracts should be for a year, terminable only at a month's notice, and that the occupation of a tenement should be prima facie evidence of the existence of such a contract between the tenant and his landlord. Antiguan labourers, under this act, worked nine hours a day, with one day free in a week or sometimes only one in every two weeks, for wages of 9 pence a day. Not surprisingly, it was concluded that 'the purely material condition of the Antiguan labourers showed little real advance over that of the days of slavery' (Hall 1971: 28).

Similar contract systems were widespread and persistent in the British Caribbean. In Trinidad the masters and servants ordinance of 1846 provided punishments of fines and/or imprisonment for workers who broke their labour contracts, or were convicted of misconduct on the job (Trotman 1986: 196). In Belize, a worker who failed to perform according to the labour contract could be apprehended by his employer, without warrant, and forcibly removed from his place of work. A century after Emancipation, workers who infringed their contracts were treated as criminals and were subject to imprisonment with hard labour for up to three months (Bolland 1986b: 180). Sometimes, however, the workers' antipathy to such contracts resulted in consequences contrary to those the planters intended. In Barbados, for example, many labourers refused to accept yearly hiring contracts in the first weeks after Emancipation because they felt that in so doing they would forfeit their freedom and suffer an extension of apprenticeship (Marshall 1993: 15). The attempt to control workers through labour contracts, far from resolving the problems of labour relations after Emancipation, contributed to social tension and class antagonism. For obvious reasons, the planters sought tight and long-term contracted employment and the former slaves preferred looser arrangements which would give them greater freedom.

The planters achieved the tightest control over indentured immigrant workers, both by law and through intimidation. Throughout the period of indentureship, which evolved particularly in Trinidad and Guyana and lasted until 1920, 'the assumptions and premises of slavery continued to inform management attitudes' (Haraksingh 1981: 7). Indentured workers could not move off the estate without the employer's permission. Even though legally entitled to lodge complaints against his employer to the protector of immigrants, the worker had to obtain his employer's permission to leave the estate in order to travel to the protector's office. As most magistrates shared the planters' attitudes, and were often hosted by them in rural areas, it is not surprising that 'the regulations notwithstanding, the plantocracy hardly hesitated to impose upon the workers an array of punitive devices – floggings and beatings on some estates, arbitrary fines and court-sanctioned imprisonment, which had the effect of lengthening the time under indenture, for periods spent in jail were not discounted' (Haraksingh 1981: 7). As in slavery, some indentured workers were made gang leaders in order to help control the others.

Some indentured workers decided not to risk resistance in order not to forfeit a return trip to India, and others undoubtedly became dejected and demoralised by the rigours of plantation life and labour, subjected as they were to similar conditions of work, housing, malnutrition and diseases as had prevailed during slavery. Many became indebted to their employers who deliberately sold them rations at inflated prices in order to keep the workers poor and dependent. Planters also sought to induce workers coming to the end of their contracts to re-indenture themselves by offering cash bounties. They also rented portions of their land to contract-expired workers in order to keep a pool of labour nearby, so-called free workers over whose heads hung the threat of eviction. In Trinidad, by the 1890s, this mixture of indentured and time-expired but dependent workers so favoured the planters that even free workers who were not resident on the estates were reduced to accepting work at indentured rates. In these circumstances,

> the presence of a group of workers who were legally bound to work under-mined the bargaining power of free workers and reduced the pressure which a strike could exert on the planters. When the free workers contemplated withholding their services, they had to consider that the critical work might continue to be done by the indentureds. Thus . . . the planters, in holding a part of the labour force "captive", could use it to capture another part. They were well aware of the value of their contract workers in this regard, so that even though by 1900 there was a surfeit of labour, they continued to press for the retention of indentured immigration. (Haraksingh 1981: 13)

Though some indentured workers resigned themselves to working off their contracts, intending then to return to India or to start a more independent life in the West Indies, others did resist this system of coercion, often by means similar to those the slaves had used – malingering and slow-downs, sabotage by burning canes, damaging machinery or mistreating draught animals and occasionally even violence, though this was more often directed against the drivers than the planters. Many fled the estates and 'were often found wandering on the rural roads or in the city – ill-clad, hungry, and destitute,' or were found dead (Trotman 1986: 186).

The law bound the indentured worker to the estate, and if found elsewhere he had to have in his possession a ticket of leave, specifying his name, period of leave, plantation to which he was attached and locality he was permitted to visit. In Trinidad, Ordinance No.24 of 1854 codified the existing regulations pertaining to indentured immigrants, other ordinances were passed and a new consolidated act in 1899 remained in force until 1917. The enforcement of these laws constituted a major mechanism for the control of workers. Between 1871 and 1874, for example, 12,198 infractions of the 1854 ordinance resulted in 5,214 convictions and 3,856 committals to prison, and even in the early twentieth century 'prison continued to be the most favored method of disciplining recalcitrant labor' (Trotman 1986: 188-9). In 1900, 64 workers left Harmony Hall in Naparima to go to San Fernando to complain about discrepancies in their wages. They were arrested for leaving the estate without permission and were sentenced to 21 days of hard labour (Trotman 1986: 192).

Another mechanism of labour control, the wage–rent system, was adopted in Antigua and, with variations, by planters elsewhere. This system also heightened the tension between employers and workers. The wage–rent system combined the roles of employer and landlord, on the one hand, and those of employee and tenant, on the other, so that the employer could use his position as landlord to control and reduce the cost of his labour force. The former slaves found that they had to pay rent for access to the provision grounds and family homes, often made by themselves, that they had occupied as slaves. These provision grounds and houses were among the few fruits of the slaves' hard labour from which they and their families actually benefited. Throughout slavery, many slaves had 'to a large degree fed themselves, had built and maintained houses, nurtured families, established kin networks in particular locations' (Marshall 1993: 13), based on their access to provision grounds. Work on these grounds and houses created an attachment to place, and offered an opportunity for slaves to exercise a degree of autonomy and self-reliance that was antithetical to the spirit of slavery.

Not surprisingly, then, many former slaves desired to continue to occupy the grounds and houses to which they felt they had customary rights of usage, supplementing a peasant livelihood with occasional cash earnings from casual estate labour. The planters, however, wanted labour on their terms and at their convenience, especially during crop time, and so used their property rights over the houses and grounds to coerce such labour from their former slaves. As employer-landlords, the planters could threaten their employee-tenants with eviction if they did not work satisfactorily on the estates. Moreover, by paying wages with one hand and receiving rents with the other, the employer-landlords were also able to reduce their labour costs. The conflicting interests of these classes was clear in the wage–rent system: the planters continued to seek plentiful and regular supplies of cheap labour, which they were accustomed to controlling in a coercive manner, while their former slaves sought to avoid estate work under these persistently oppressive conditions.

The application of the wage-rent system varied considerably from one colony to another. In Barbados, a house was often occupied rent-free on the condition that the tenant work on his landlord's estate five days a week. Those who worked less were fined, and the fine effectively constituted a rent. In order to prevent their tenants from paying rent with money earned by marketing provisions or working elsewhere, the planters deducted the rents from estate wages, thereby obliging their tenants to work for wages on the home estates, on pain of eviction. Until the mid-1840s, rents and wages were generally associated in Barbados, with resident labourers being paid 10 pence daily and non-residents 1 shilling or 1 shilling and a halfpenny, making the rent effectively 2 pence or 2 pence daily. If such tenants did not work satisfactorily they could be evicted, and if they refused to leave when evicted they were subject to arrest (Levy 1980: 79).

There were wide variations in the rents charged. In Jamaica, where wages were generally about 1 shilling per day, the average rent for a house was 2 shillings per week, but it was sometimes as high as 6 shillings and 8 pence per household. In some cases in Jamaica, rent was charged 'per capita against husband, wife, and each of the children, as a penal exaction, to compel labor' (Gurney [1840] 1969: 79). Rent was a burning issue in St George's parish, in northeast Jamaica: 'On some properties rent was levied on each occupant of a cottage while on others no rent was collected at all so that the labourers could be ejected as no tenancy would exist. Workers' requests for annual tenancy were turned down. Generally rent was manipulated in such a fashion that it was a penalty rather than a charge for the use of estate property.' (Wilmot 1993: 51)

Anger and resentment over rent issues adversely affected labour relations in many other Jamaican parishes. In Trinidad and Guyana, however, many of the former slaves who worked on the estates continued to enjoy their houses and grounds rent-free, and also had allowances of rum and salt fish and relatively high wages in the years immediately after Emancipation. In Trinidad it was so hard to stop the former slaves from squatting that some planters offered rent-free houses and grounds as an inducement to keep labour near their estates.

There was variation among the colonies in rents as a percentage of wages. In Tobago and Barbados, rents were about 20 per cent of wages, in St Vincent they were 33 per cent, in Grenada 35 per cent and in Jamaica as high as 48 per cent (Riviere 1972: 7-8). There was also variation in the planters' ability to collect rents. On Worthy Park estate in Jamaica, £342, more than 10 per cent of the total wages, was deducted directly from the labourers' pay in 1839, but in the following year, when the total rent on houses and provision grounds was assessed at £2,827, attempts to collect it proved futile. 'Those from whom rents were collected proved even less willing to work, and those who did not work had no money to pay' (Craton and Walvin 1970: 217). In 1842, less than £50 was collected for all rents at Worthy Park, 'and within a few more years it was nothing at all. In effect Worthy Park was then offering rent-free cottages and land to its regular workers. But even this did not effectively tie cottagers to the estate . . . until it was backed up by a fairly ruthless policy of evictions.' (Craton 1978: 288)

The ability of the wage-rent system to promote continuous supplies of reliable labour for the planters varied considerably. In some colonies, the planters maintained control over labour supplies, but in others the system became self-defeating. Although the threat of eviction might coerce some tenants to work on the estate, implementation of the threat would alienate the workers still further from the landlord and would-be employer who had evicted them and thereby thrown them on the general market. Often, as in Jamaica, the coercive nature of the tenure arrangements was sufficient to cause the newly freed slaves to reject the system and flee the estates. Whether the workers fled or were evicted, the planters lost their labour force through trying to coerce it. By the mid-1840s, Jamaican planters had recognised the failure of the system and grudgingly abandoned it.

The reasons why the wage-rent system worked in some instances and not in others are complex. Variations in the success of the system in securing labour supplies for the estates depended to a large extent on the availability of alternatives to the former slaves. Though some former slaves became artisans and small traders, the chief option was peasant farming on a small scale, producing a variety of crops and keeping some livestock for family consumption and for sale. Mintz has called these people a 'reconstituted peasantry', in order to draw attention to their origins in the 'proto-peasantry' who originated a peasant style of life while they were still enslaved (Mintz 1974: 151). Clearly, an important factor in determining whether peasant agriculture could become an alternative to estate labour was the availability of land.

The relation between the availability of land and population density, or the man-land ratio as it is sometimes called, has been debated at some length (Bolland 1981, 1984a; Green 1984; Richardson 1984; Marshall 1991). The density of population is only one aspect of the availability of land and does not determine it as is frequently implied. The availability of land for a peasantry is chiefly determined by the degree of concentration or monopolisation of land, and that is itself primarily determined by the power structure in the society and not simply by population density. To the extent that the planters, through their control of local legislatures and with the support of the imperial government, could control access to land in the interests of their plantation economy they were able to keep a supply of workers dependent on the estates. The plantation monopoly of land, represented classically in the latifundia type of economy, is one of the chief means by which land-owners coerce labour. To say that land is unavailable and hence that labour is dependent because of population density per se is to suggest that a mere man:land ratio rather than human agency determines social relations, but it is actually the power factor, through influencing policies, that is crucial in determining the availability of land.

It is typical of a latifundia or plantation economy that much of the land monopolised by the large estates is not actually used for agriculture. In Trinidad in 1838, for example, only 43,265 acres, or about one-fifth, of the 208,379 acres in private ownership were in cultivation (Wood 1968: 49). It was not uncultivated simply because there was not sufficient labour available, but the land-owners, by making all that land unavailable to those who would cultivate it on their own account, kept them dependent. In other words, 'one primary purpose of the ownership of large amounts of land, both on the individual and on the social level, is not to use it but to prevent its use by others. These others, denied access to the primary resource, necessarily fall under the domination of the few who do control it. And then they are exploited in all conceivable ways.' (Frank 1971: 288) Far from population density being 'the principal factor determining postemancipation labor relations' (Green 1984: 112), it was the ability of the planters, a mostly white and often absentee minority, to continue to monopolize land resources that augmented their ability to control labour supplies. They could also use their power to influence immigration policy in order to increase the availability of coerced workers, thus directly influencing the population density. It is thus the dialectical interrelationship between the control of land and the control of labour that determined the availability of land, consequently affecting post-Emancipation labour relations.

Beckford argues:

> throughout the first-established New World plantation areas the basic pattern of adjustment to the abolition of slavery was the same: plantation monopoly of the land to prevent the ex-slaves from being independent of plantation work; legislation by planter-controlled governments to force the ex-slaves to continue working on the plantations; other measures to keep the ex-slaves "attached" to the plantations; and immigration of new laborers where all else failed. The question of land was intimately bound to the problem of securing plantation labor supplies and the degree of its availability materially influenced the fate of the former slaves. Where land was available, peasant production was established; and where it was not, laborers were largely forced to continue with plantation work until during the post-World War II period. (Beckford 1972: 96-7)

The fact is that land monopoly and labour dependency can coexist with very low population density. Even if we discount the example of Guyana, where some 90 per cent of the population was concentrated in 5 per cent of the land along the coastal plain, the case of Belize, where there was a very low population density, shows that an extreme monopolisation of land-ownership, resembling a latifundia economy, inhibited the emergence of a peasantry in the nineteenth century (Bolland and Shoman 1977). My study of Belize led me to re-evaluate the relationships between land and labour control, and to conclude that labour power and land resources continued to be subject to the persisting power structures after Emancipation. In Jamaica where, unlike Barbados and Belize, a substantial peasantry developed after Emancipation, there is evidence that workers in the Western parishes of Westmoreland, St Elizabeth, St James and Trelawny were prepared to fight to gain land. One worker, Edward Campbell, said that the 1831 slave rebellion was their model: 'the black people were going to fight in August [1839], if the white and brown people did not deliver up the land to them .... That there must be a fight to get their lands; that if the last fight [in 1831] did not happen, they would not get their freedom so soon; and that everybody did not join in the last war, but now all were free, and must help in the fight that was coming.'[5]

When the plantation economy suffered a crisis there was a substantial growth of the peasantry, but the later revival of the plantation economy, which led to 'a renewed tendency towards the concentration of land in the hands of a few owners' (Satchell 1990: 151), resulted in continuing land scarcity for small farmers. The former slaves and indentured workers and their descendants were everywhere subjected to coercion, particularly where the land resources were monopolised, in what was but a new form of the old hierarchy of domination.

Other mechanisms of labour control, such as systems of credit, and wage advances and truck shops, existed in several places, including St Lucia, Belize and the Bahamas, and often persisted well into the twentieth century. By entrapping working people in debt, these mechanisms tied them to wage labour and even to particular employers, often in conditions amounting to debt servitude.

Belizeans who worked in the forest industry were given advances on their wages when they signed contracts at the beginning of the season, around Christmastime. Ostensibly, the advances were intended to enable the worker to purchase supplies prior to going to the forests for the season, but the money was generally spent in 'keeping Christmas' with his family and friends in Belize Town. The result was that labourers had to purchase their supplies on credit and at exorbitant prices from the employers' truck shops at the isolated camps in the forest. Often, the balance of the wages a worker received was insufficient to meet his expenses, and he ended his season in debt to his employer. To work off his debt, the worker would sign another contract with that employer the next season, with the result that the advance and truck system effectively bound the workers to their employers in a form of debt servitude. Fifty years after Emancipation, the colony's handbook admitted that, by this system, the labourers 'become virtually enslaved for life' (Bristowe and Wright 1888: 199). Though the custom of advances declined as the supply of workers came to exceed the demand, the truck system, and even the partial payment of workers in rations and commissary tickets, was still widespread in the mahogany camps of Belize in the 1930s (Bolland 1986b: 180).

On the abolition of slavery in St Lucia, according to H. Breen, writing in 1844, 'almost every planter was induced to establish a shop upon his estate, with the two-fold object of attaching the labourers to the property, and of drawing back in exorbitant profits a portion of the exorbitant wages he was compelled to give them' (quoted in Fraser 1981: 329). The chief purpose of credit and truck systems appears not to have been to make a profit directly, though the exploitation of captive consumers certainly contributed to that result, but rather to limit the opportunities of the former slaves and thus to make them dependent upon the employers.

In the Bahamas, a system of credit and truck indebted and coerced working people to such an extent that the governor referred to their status in 1884 as 'practical slavery'. Howard Johnson describes: 'the control mechanisms which enabled a white mercantile minority to consolidate its position as a ruling elite in the postemancipation period. Rather than a monopoly of land, the important elements in this elite's economic and social control were a monopoly of the credit available to the majority of the population and the operation of a system of payment in truck.' (Johnson 1986: 729) Such systems were also known in Belize and the sugar colonies of Trinidad, Tobago, Guyana and Jamaica. Johnson (1986: 752) concludes: 'these systems of labour control appeared in those British West Indian colonies where the roles of employer, landlord, or entrepreneur and of supplier of subsistence and production loans were combined in a single individual and where there were few alternative opportunites for employment'.

The growth of peasantries

Wherever dependency and control could not be maintained and alternatives to estate labour were available, there was a substantial flight from the estates. Often, in fact, this flight resulted largely from the planters' efforts to retain control over their former slaves. As the former slaves sought to realize their freedom, they did not simply calculate their material advantage in terms of political economy. Although wage rates were important, without a doubt, the former slaves were also interested in access to land on which they could grow crops for their subsistence or for sale, and they preferred some flexibility in the allocation of their own labour time between estate or wage work and their own self-employment. Some planters, facing the loss of labour, learned to limit their efforts to restrict their workers, and even to offer them more attractive terms of employment. Undoubtedly there were variations between places, and at different times, in the relative influences of what have been called the pull and push factors that led so many of the former slaves to leave the plantations (Marshall 1991), but after 1846, when the British Parliament passed the Sugar Duties Act, the sugar industry in most of the British Caribbean suffered a sustained decline that made it harder for the planters to offer decent wages even if they wanted to. Michael Craton observes that there was no great change in the population of Worthy Park estate in Jamaica until tumbling sugar prices made a resident population impractical for the planters and wages became too low for the former slaves. As the preferential tariff for colonial muscovado was eliminated, 'the transition began to the modern system of employing the minimum number of workers, and only when needed, for minimal wages. This naturally increased the ex-slaves' preference for peasant cultivation, making them more than ever determined to work for wages only when they had to'. (Craton 1978: 293)

The planters' policy of conditional tenancy, or labour for rent, revealed the underlying relationship between the control of land and control of labour as the planters' coercive propensities collided with the former slaves' aspirations. 'Ex-slaves wanted continued access to provision grounds and accomodation which were technically the property of their employers, and were prepared in turn to sell a portion of their labour to the estates on which they were located at a price they hoped to influence. The employers insisted that they wanted daily labour at stipulated wages, and labour immobilized by conditional tenancy or labour-rent'. (Marshall 1991: 11)

Moreover, the planters wanted labour only when they needed it, which was chiefly during crop time, and not necessarily when the workers most needed wages. Not surprisingly, then, as wage labour on declining sugar estates became more exploitative, irregular, insecure and degrading, the former slaves increasingly sought access to land on which they could control their own labour, on their own account, as small farmers.

The plantation and peasant spheres of activity, though in a limited sense coexistent, really competed for access to land and control of labour. Mintz shows that the cultivation of provision grounds came to be seen by slaves as a customary right and that the experience of this 'proto-peasantry' (Mintz 1961) in producing and marketing crops and livestock was an important aspect of their transition to emancipation. Both during slavery and after, the rise of such peasantries constituted 'some kind of resistant response' to the dominant plantation system (Mintz 1974: 132), and for many reasons the former slaves valued peasant farming as a basis for their independence. The cultivation of provision grounds, even during slavery, was largely free of supervision, unlike the gang labour on the plantations, and during the apprenticeship period 'apprentices guarded closely the labour time in their control' (Marshall 1985: 211). The problem for them all - whether slaves, apprentices, or ex-slaves, indentured or former indentured workers - was how to secure their access to land and how to allocate their labour, without oppressive supervision, more on their own account and under their own control. They understood from experience that achieving greater autonomy in their economic activity was significant and perhaps key to greater autonomy in their lives as a whole.

When the employer-landlords asserted their property rights over the houses and grounds of their former slaves, demanding rent and labour from their tenants, some of the former slaves contested the claim. In Grenada, for example, former slaves residing on the estates told the magistrates and constables who tried to evict them at the end of apprenticeship that 'they would not surrender their houses and grounds because these had been "given them by the Queen"' (Marshall 1985: 219). When the workers were told they had no right to the provision grounds if they left the plantation residence, the conflict sharpened. Former slaves may have stayed on the plantations so long as they felt their wages were adequate, or that they had adequate access to land and control over their own labour time, but may have left if they felt the balance was changing and better opportunities for more independent or remunerative economic activity were available elsewhere, even if that was abroad (Marshall 1991: 12). Emancipation had at least made such choices legally possible.

The extent to which the former slaves achieved greater control of their labour time within the confines of the plantations or left the estates and formed a more independent peasant class, varied a great deal in the British Caribbean. In Antigua, St Kitts and Barbados, for example, there was little change in the patterns of land tenure after 1838: the plantations continued more or less intact and sugar production actually increased after Emancipation. In Jamaica, Trinidad and Guyana, however, peasant communities arose rapidly and the plantation system entered a crisis. Many former slaves in these three colonies purchased land, and many more were renting or squatting on land without acquiring a legal title.

In Jamaica, the number of large estates fell from 646 in 1834 to 330 in 1854, while the number of freeholds of less than 10 acres increased from 883 in 1840 to 20,724 in 1845 (Hall 1959: 162), and by 1860 there were about 50,000 holdings under 50 acres in extent (Eisner 1961: 220). An American correspondent reported in 1861: 'there are possibly forty thousand laborers in all who give transient work to the estates, but at one and the same time the number actually at work, or the number that can be commanded, does not average more than twenty thousand. These twenty thousand laborers, taking them en masse, do not work for estates more than one hundred and seventy days in the year, sometimes three and sometimes four days in the week'. (Sewell 1861: 265)

By 1861, there were more peasant proprietors in Jamaica than there were people employed in casual estate labour. The planters sought to make their workers dependent by tying them to a bit of land, but the former slaves sought independence by obtaining a piece of land on their own account, thereby freeing them from the planters' threats of eviction and strengthening their bargaining position when they negotiated their terms of work on the estates. The crucial point determining the nature of the relationship, then, is not simply a question of whether the former slaves had access to any land. The point is, rather, what the terms were under which they had access to land, because this affected whether it further bound or freed them.

Guyana, meanwhile, 'witnessed one of the greatest expressions of land hunger among the ex-slaves of the region' (Moore 1987: 35) and a prolonged struggle between peasants and planters. The number of estates fell dramatically from 308 in 1838 to 196 in 1849. Plantation production declined between 1838 and 1844: sugar and molasses production fell by 25 per cent and rum by 36.5 per cent (Moore 1987: 33). By 1848, some 32,717 people resided on freehold lands and the total value of property (including buildings and other improvements as well as land) in the hands of former slaves was estimated to amount to almost $2.5 million. Remarkably, some of these former slaves bought not only small plots of land but also whole plantations, which they worked cooperatively. However, as most of their capital was exhausted by purchasing the land, nothing was left to maintain the irrigation and drainage or to invest in technical renovation, so the communal villages collapsed in the 1840s. In 1851, Buxton, one of the communal villages, was converted into a proprietary village of individual plots and the others followed suit (Adamson 1972: 36). Moreover, communalism became prohibited by law: Ordinance No.1 of 1852 prohibited the joint purchase of land by more than 20 persons (Adamson 1972: 57). By that time there were 11,152 small holdings in Guyana and 46,368 people lived in villages that had been formed since Emancipation.

Nevertheless, about 38,000 former slaves, or about 43 per cent of the labour force at Emancipation, still worked on the estates in the mid-1840s (Moore 1987: 37). A reduction in their wages made it harder for them to buy land, as did government policy which actively sought to inhibit the growth of the peasantry. In 1861 an ordinance raised the price of Crown land from $5 to $10 per acre and required the minimum parcel to be 100 acres, thereby putting such land beyond the peasant proprietors. Some 20 years after their formation, the proprietary villages had 'failed to develop a viable economy' (Adamson 1972: 60), which was exactly what the planters wanted. Though the village population more than doubled between 1851 and 1891, growing slightly faster than the colony as a whole, much of this growth was due to the movement of recent immigrants into villages after 1872. The creole villages stagnated and the majority of peasants, who held an acre or less, became chronically poor. Some moved to Georgetown but many who could not survive through subsistence cultivation on small plots returned to work on the plantations, compelled to compete with indentured immigrants and to suffer reduced wages.

One expedient adopted by sugar planters in Nevis and the Windward Islands (to a limited extent in Grenada and St Vincent, and more extensively in Tobago and St Lucia) during the depression of the 1840s was a share system called metayage or metairie.[6] This system, in which the workers shared the risks of production with the land-owners in return for a share (usually between one-third and one-half) of the profits, gave the planters the advantages of retaining ownership of their estates and mills, and not having to pay wages when they were short of cash. For the workers, the advantages were that they had access to land which was, in effect, rented to them by the land-owners, and they were less supervised and more free to tend their provision grounds, almost as if they were small cane farmers. In 1857, it was commented that this semi-independent peasantry in Nevis enjoyed a more 'advanced' condition than the estate workers on neighbouring islands (Richardson 1983: 99). However, the planters saw metayage only as a temporary expedient that enabled them to retain access to labour and so keep supplying their mills and refineries. There were many complaints about the system. Planters gave priority to using cane reaped from the fields where they still used wage labour, so the metayers some-times found that their canes were not reaped and they gained nothing for all their work. Metayers also complained that planters did not account honestly for the division of costs and profits, and so felt that they did not get their fair returns. However, litigation was too expensive for poor labourers and some of them thought that they risked their freedom if they became involved with the courts. Even though the metayers hoped that this system would amount to emancipation in action, a stepping-stone towards a more independent peasant status, the planters did not want to lose their control entirely and 'were utterly opposed to any innovation which might loosen or shake their dominance of the socio-economic structure' (Marshall 1993: 76). Consequently, when the price of sugar improved temporarily in the late 1850s many planters changed to the wage labour system, but the return of hard times in the 1880s led to the resumption of metayage, especially in Tobago (Green 1976: 255).

When the former slaves of the British Caribbean could not acquire land legally, by purchase, lease, or some kind of sharecropping arrangement, many of them invaded land. As the sugar crisis deepened and more estates fell into disuse or were abandoned, the occupation by squatters of such derelict land, as well as Crown lands, increased. The price of Crown land was deliberately raised after Emancipation in order to prevent most former slaves from buying it, so if they could not afford or find such private lands as were for sale, squatting was an alternative. In Dominica and Trinidad squatting was extensive, in the former chiefly on Crown lands and in the latter often on the estates' backlands (Marshall 1991: 13). In Jamaica some former slaves, unobtrusively occupying remote parts of sugar estates without challenge, 'concluded erroneously that the backlands were the Queen's gift to them at emancipation' (Satchell 1990: 64) and they resisted encroachment on what they considered to be their land. The major general of police, reporting on the use of police in ejecting squatters, expressed the opinion that 'the payment of taxes by the occupier of the land resulted in the peasants seeing the law as giving them unquestionable title deeds and an unalienable right to the possession of such land' (Satchell 1990: 67). Squatting was certainly an islandwide phenomenon, but between 1869 and 1879 some 1,196 squatters were ejected by the government from about 28,800 acres of land, the vast majority of these being small peasant farmers, and it may be supposed that even more were ejected by private proprietors. Many of the people ejected from their farms as squatters may have had legal or equitable interest in the land but did not have secure deeds or undisputed tenure. Whatever the legal status of their tenure, many peasants resisted eviction, as in Bushy Park, St Catherine in 1867, when 70-80 people were arrested for riotous assembly and forcible trespass as they sought to enforce their claims against the 'legal owner' (Satchell 1990: 74-8).

In Trinidad, the number of proprietors, mostly smallholders, increased from about 2,000 in 1832 to over 7,000 in 1849, and only 3,116 labourers were said to work regularly on the plantations in 1851. Squatting, which 'rankled with those who wanted to see disciplined labourers working regularly on the estates', was widespread (Wood 1968: 50). Land-owners viewed squatting as 'an evil of much detriment' and the squatter as: 'a man who violates the right of property, and to a certain extent, frees himself from the obligations which are imposed on the other members of the community .... [Squatting] evidently tends to create in individuals a disposition to insubordination.' (De Verteuil 1858, quoted in Trotman 1986: 196-7) The squatter-peasantry, who used the land chiefly to grow provisions, some of which they sold in local markets, did not constitute a dangerous class, as planters claimed, except in so far as they demonstrated the very freedom that the law had ostensibly awarded them and that the planters sought to curb. The squatters were not really opposing private property, as was claimed, but were responding outside the law simply because the forces of the market had been manipulated so as to exclude them from legally owning land.

The high cost of land and the regulation that Crown land could be sold only in large lots - the minimum size was raised from 340 acres to 640 acres in 1841 - as well as the inconvenience of requiring all sales to be finalized in Port of Spain, unintentionally encouraged squatting. In 1868, after French creoles pressed for opening up Crown lands for cocoa production, the cost of land was reduced, procedures for its purchase were simplified and those people who did not have legal title were given time to purchase and register titles at the Crown Lands Office. In 1869, in the Montserrat district of central Trinidad some 200 squatters paid for their lands, but those who did not were ejected and several were fined or imprisoned. One squatter who was ejected insisted on returning to his grounds, was arrested for trespass, convicted and imprisoned for two months (Trotman 1986: 198). However, the authorities' attempts to evict squatters, who could be imprisoned for up to six months if they did not remove themselves, was largely ineffective because there were not enough police, and, ironically, 'planters themselves were unwilling to lay information before the Magistrates about those squatters who were a source of labour for their own estates' (Wood 1968: 51). Here, the ability of the former slaves to gain access to land, even without legal title, enabled them to wring some concessions in their struggle with the planters.

The struggle over wages

Other important issues in labour relations after Emancipation concerned the terms of work, particularly the struggle over wages. In Jamaica[7] the newly freed workers bargained for their wages in August 1838. Generally they asked for the same daily rate they had obtained on their free days during apprentice-ship, namely 1 shilling and 6 pence, but some demanded more. Most planters, however, offered only 7 pence per day with two days' labour in lieu of rent for occupation of houses and provision grounds on the estates. On 8 August, Governor Sir Lionel Smith, concerned that both sides were unwilling to nego-tiate, urged the workers to accept 1 shilling per day and to pay 2 shillings per week as rent for their houses and grounds. The workers politely replied that they would not work for less than 1 shilling and 6 pence. Smith toured several parishes and convinced many workers to accept 1 shilling per day along with free occupation of their houses and grounds for three months. By the middle of September work resumed on plantations when the planters raised their offer to 1 shilling per day and showed they could deal with their workers as free people.

Swithin Wilmot concludes that the workers 'were eager to resume labour on the estates .... All that was required was fair treatment and conciliatory action on the part of their employers' (Wilmot 1993: 49). When the workers felt they were not being treated fairly and with respect, however, there was conflict. In the Plantain Garden River District of St Thomas planters offered only 7 pence per day and gave the workers three months' notice to quit estate houses and provision grounds. The workers, led by Richard Edwards, a former slave on Golden Grove estate, went on strike until September when the planters agreed to offer task work, from which it was possible to earn up to 1 shilling and 9 pence per day, and withdrew the notices to quit. However, women refused to resume field work, thereby increasing the men's bargaining power, while the planters revived their rent claims in order to force their tenants to work on the estate. The workers, still led by Edwards, refused to pay rent until January 1839, when a stipendiary magistrate convinced them they would have to. The workers, with good reason, did not trust the planters to deal fairly with them. 'The workers, though eager to make arrangements to secure their tenancies, steadfastly refused to enter into any contract with their employers unless the stipendiary magistrates were present .... Whenever the employers again arbitrarily altered the agreed terms of rent or wages, the workers promptly struck until the status quo was restored. All the workers asked for was even-handed treatment.' (Wilmot 1993: 50)

These conflicts over wages and rents, during the first months after Emancipation, show that the former slaves had a strong sense of their rights and, as free workers, they were prepared to defend them. Indeed, they suggest that the workers, as former slaves, probably expected to have to fight the planters over the terms of their labour and for the respect that they deserved as free people. With a clear memory of recent abuse and injustice, these women and men defended their new legal status, asserting, as a group of apprentices addressed Governor MacGregor in Barbados, that 'it will be our constant duty to Guard against future Tyranny and Oppression' (Marshall 1993: 14). When they felt it necessary, when they were harassed and exploited by their employer-landlords, they downed tools, took to the hills and occasionally even fought back with violence. On Spring Hill coffee plantation in St George, Jamaica, there was serious conflict in July 1839. Workers, especially the women, confronted parish constables who were sent to take their property for outstanding rent and they drove them off with violent language and missiles. The governor dispatched military forces which arrested one woman who had wounded a constable and they supported the civil authorities in making the levy.

Violent confrontations were rare, however, as the workers more often exercised their option of moving, either to try to make a better deal on another estate, or to find a small piece of land, or settle in one of the new free villages.

When Jamaican planters tried to reduce wages in 1841 from 1 shilling and 6 pence to 1 shilling per day, the workers struck. William Allen, a worker on Virgin Valley, spoke forcefully to over 2,000 workers at Salters Hill Baptist Church, urging them to stick out for good pay:

> De Busha dem all hab five to six harse; dem lib well nyam belly full; lib na good house; we lib no hut .... We pay half a dollar rent; den dem want to gib we shilling a day. Tell me now, how much lef fa you when week out? No half a dollar lef fe you? Den what fe buy fish? Den wha fe gib paason? ... De Busha get ten shilling a day; dem want to rob we .... Unoo will take one shilling a day; (Cries of no, no, no, no, from the audience) ... Well den, tick out fe good pay and see if dem no blige and bound fee gee whà we ax a day. (quoted in Wilmot 1993: 52)

When the planters restored the original level of wages these strikes were called off. 'Gradually, between 1839 and 1842 labour relations [in Jamaica] improved as the employers abandoned their coercive tactics in the face of determined opposition from the workers' (Wilmot 1993: 51). This was the period when the number of small farms was increasing substantially, so more people were finding alternatives to estate labour and this applied pressure on the planters.

In Trinidad planters had to pay high wages in order to attract labour after 1838. By 1840, some field workers were receiving 50 cents a task, and sometimes as much as 65 cents, compared with 20 cents per day in Barbados. When planters tried to combine in order to reduce wages in 1841 and 1842 they were unsuccessful, but they did stop granting the customary allowances. Some planters paid more in order to secure workers at the expense of the anti-labour combines. A decline in sugar prices in 1844 stimulated another effort by the planters and, after some strikes, including one in Carapichaima that lasted as long as six weeks, the workers accepted reduced wages. Wages remained at about 30 cents a task for the rest of the 1840s, but the planters' managers still complained that workers were irregular and unpredictable, turning up to work only three or four days a week, so they were never sure how many workers they would have (Wood 1968: 53-4). Absenteeism is a sure sign of worker dissatisfaction, and it may also have been a way, by withdrawing their labour when they felt like it, for them to show they were not giving up the struggle over their terms of work.

In Guyana Emancipation and the subsequent rapid growth of an independent peasantry resulted in a scarcity of labour on the sugar plantations and a rise in wages, especially for the heavier tasks like digging canals. On the already overburdened estates, the wages bills rose to constitute at least half of total currency outlay (Adamson 1972: 162). As sugar prices declined in 1841 the Guyanese planters, like those in Trinidad, tried to reduce wages, to turn out workers who did not work regularly and to eliminate such customary allowances as free medical attention, housing and provision grounds. The former slaves felt they were being ill-treated and went on strike. In January 1842 they complained to a stipendiary magistrate:

> Sir! We free labourers of Plantation Walton Hall are already to work our liberty hours in putting hands and heart providing in we getting what is right. As to say for taking one guilder[8] per day, we can not take it at all. Sir, you will be pleased to understand us to what we say (those few years since we got free), and so soon brought on a reducing price, which is now offered to we labourers. We certainly thinks it to be very hard. If you take it in consideration, when calling on us. We shall be proud to know from, if such laws came from the Queen, or any of Her Majesties Justice of Peace. During our slavery we was clothed, ration, and seported in all manner of respects. Now we are free men (free indeed), we are to work for nothing. Then we might actually say, we becomes slaves again. We will be glad to know from the proprietors of the estates, if they are to take from us our rights altogether. You will be please to understand very well. Satisfied we labourers with the former price we was getting. For we were also allowed a doctor in case of sickness. But now it is said we must pay house rent, and we is also made to understand that our negroe ground to be taken from us. Therefore we cannot work for a smaller price. You will be please to take the law in consideration in settling this matter. (Quoted in Hall 1978: 12)

Nothing in this petition suggests that these former slaves were rushing from the estates simply because of their association with slavery, even though their memories of servitude were certainly miserable. Rather, they express the understandable resentment that they were being forced to pay for continuing to use what had previously been available free. They struck because it was obvious that 'emancipation should only mean a bettering of their condition . . . . These masters' policies seemed to the ex-slaves to be a betrayal of the principles of emancipation'. (Hall 1978: 17)

In 1842 the sugar workers of Guyana 'won a quick and easy victory' (Adamson 1972: 166) and their wages remained at the previous level. Five years later, however, when the planters combined again to depress wages, Governor Light instructed the stipendiary magistrates to persuade the workers to accept a 25 per cent cut in their wages. The workers went on strike and completely shut down some estates, but on others indentured immigrants, recently introduced in the colony, continued to work. Contrary to some reports of terror and violence, the strike was remarkably peaceful, but by the end of April 1848 the workers were defeated and were working for the reduced rate. The problem of solidarity during strikes became worse as some 15,000 immigrants came to Guyana between 1848 and 1851, so, as the planters recovered control over the large body of continuous labour that they wanted, wages declined. The production of sugar recovered, increasing from 32,871 hogsheads in 1841 to 47,890 in 1851, but the total wages paid declined from £474,600 to £421,466, so the average wage cost per hogshead fell dramatically in this period from £70 to £42.66. Production revived, therefore, at the expense of the former slaves, thousands of whom, facing reduced wages and intensified work, withdrew from the estates (Adamson 1972: 167).

In 1842 there were 15,906 people living in villages in Guyana that had been formed since Emancipation, which had increased to 18,511 by 1844. Another surge occurred after the 1847-8 strike, and by the end of 1848 there were 44,443 people living in these villages. Then the village population declined for a few years as many former slaves settled up the rivers and creeks of the interior, moving away from both the plantations and the villages near the coast, perhaps to find a context 'free of the demands of the plantation economy' (Adamson 1972: 37). With a continuing flow of indentured immigrants in the 1850s, the Guyanese planters regained control of the labour market and many creole villagers, who could not maintain their families on small subsistence plots, were compelled to return to estate work in the 1860s. The withdrawal of former slaves from estate labour in the 1840s was reversed and the number of non-resident workers at hire rose from 17,252 in 1852, to 18,469 in 1861 and about 22,000 in 1868. This increased pool of labour for hire, along with the flow of indentured immigrants, had a further depressing effect on wages. Not surprisingly, therefore, a commission of inquiry in 1870 concluded simply that Creole estate workers had not shared in the 'growing material prosperity of the Colony' (quoted in Adamson 1972: 72) to which they had contributed.

The former slaves were generally in an even weaker bargaining position on the plantations in those colonies, such as Barbados, where the concentration of land ownership limited their options away from the estates. In the 1830s, sugar production rose more in Barbados than elsewhere in the British West Indies. Barbados exported 13,325 tons of sugar in 1832, 17,234 tons in 1835 and 23,679 tons in 1838, and planters were quite confident they could continue to control their workers even after apprenticeship. The first contract law passed by the planter-dominated Assembly in 1838 was disallowed for being too close to the spirit of slavery. However, the contract law of 1840, which was only mildly modified, was accepted, though 'it allowed for planters to coerce blacks on a labour market that already favoured the plantation' (Beckles 1990: 110-11). Estate worker-tenants had to pay their employer-landlords rent amounting to one-sixth of their wages, while wage levels for resident fieldhands, fluctuating between 9 pence and 11 pence per day in 1840 and declining to around 6 pence per day in 1846-50, were the lowest in any major sugar colony in the West Indies. Tenants were required to provide labour exclusively on the estates where they resided, in return for reduced rent on their houses and provision grounds, and irregular labour could lead to eviction. The planters' more or less complete monopoly of agricultural land (441 of the 508 estates controlled 81 percent of the 106,000 acres of land in the colony in 1842 - Beckles 1990: 114), and the absence of Crown lands severely restricted the development of a peasantry on freehold land or as independent squatters. Although a tenantry system allowed some former slaves access to land, it was under insecure tenure and generally consisted of only enough land for them to grow a little food around their houses to supplement their meagre wages. The tenantry system, therefore, supported cheap labour for the estates rather than making the labourers at all independent of wage work. Because of this situation, thousands of Barbadians migrated in the hope of improvement - at least 16,000 had emigrated to other colonies by 1870 (Beckles 1990: 113) - and this may have helped somewhat those who remained in the labour market.

With their options so limited, about 30,000 people still provided regular labour to the estates in Barbados in the mid-1840s, at very low wages, and sugar production and exports reached new record levels. Sugar production rose from 33,111 hogsheads in 1847 to 35,302 hogsheads in 1850 and 50,778 hogsheads in 1858, and the total value of all exports rose from £659,073 in 1848 to £1,468,449 in 1858. In the 1880s the price of sugar dropped, but output increased until almost 75,000 tons of sugar were exported in 1890. Few estates were sold up until 1887 and the average price remained above £50 per acre. Small farmers could not afford to buy land at such prices, so very few of the former slaves could qualify to vote as freeholders. There were less than 5,000 freeholders in 1878 and, as some of these were whites, or coloured or black artisans who had not been slaves, it seems that not enough ex-slaves were able to accumulate savings and buy land in order to challenge the domination of the planter and merchant elite (Beckles 1990: 116-32). The persistence of the existing structure of domination in Barbados, albeit on a new legal basis, was not a function of simple population density but was the result of the interrelationship of the control of land and labour by the planter class.

For all the variations between these colonies, the pattern that emerges reveals fundamental continuities in the struggles between labour and capital in a labour process that was still based on coercion. Mary Turner has shown in the case of Jamaica that 'the methods of struggle customarily identified with contract and wage workers were first developed by slave workers cognisant of the crucial value of labour power' (Turner 1988: 26). Their methods included making informal deals and understandings, as well as the collective presentation of grievances and the withdrawal of labour. Such actions were taken by slaves against abusive treatment and also to command more of their own labour and produce. Marshall, too, shows the continuities in the expectations of plantation workers, whether they were slaves, apprentices, or legally free wage labourers, and how these expectations clashed with what the planters offered. He draws attention specifically to the continuities with slavery and apprenticeship in the labour problems in the Windward Islands after 1838:

> Planters held fast to coercion as the means of extracting a sufficient quantity of labour from what appeared to be a reluctant labour force, and they were not deflected either by evidence of apprentices' alienation or by the creation of a wage labour force. For their part, ex-slaves, deeply influenced by participation in the provision ground/marketing complex, apparently drew the conclusion from their experience during the Apprenticeship that they could secure some insulation from coercion as well as greater rewards for their labour power by emphasizing proto-peasant activity. (Marshall 1985: 221)

Marshall suggests, in particular, that the slaves' participation in these proto-peasant activities fostered the growth of attitudes to plantation labour that continued to affect labour relations during and after the apprenticeship period.

> From the slaves' perspective, their own-account activities were as important as coerced labour in defining their status, their humanity and their notions of freedom. Perhaps it is not too fanciful to suggest that humanity and freedom may have been equated by them with own-account activities. Further, they may have concluded that their forced involvement in plantation labour was the factor which constrained their exploitation of the potential in proto-peasant activities, and was therefore the critical limiting factor on their acquisition of freedom and full expression of humanity . . . . Both apprentices and ex-slaves utilized the greater control of the labour time, which slavery abolition conferred, to de-emphasize regular plantation labour and to emphasize own-account activities. (Marshall 1988: 38-9)

Of course, the former slaves could opt out of estate labour, or bargain over the terms of such labour only when some option was available; hence the planters' desire to limit their options as much as possible.

In short, the planters found new means of coercion after Emancipation in order to obtain a regular and disciplined supply of labour, while the former slaves showed great determination, especially in Jamaica and Guyana, in their struggle for decent wages, better working conditions and greater autonomy. Many former slaves left the estates when the terms were unsatisfactory and in Barbados, where there were fewer options off the estates, thousands left the island. However, throughout the British Caribbean the odds were heavily weighted against the former slaves because Emancipation was managed in such a way as to maintain the existing economy and social hierarchy. The ability of the plantocracy to recover control of the labour market, which was not really free, and to intimidate and discipline their workers depended to a large extent on their continuing influence in the state.

The role of the state

The continuing political influence of the planters in the imperial power structure, both in the colonies and in Great Britain, was crucial to their power in the bitter struggle over the control of land and labour after 1838. The planter class by influencing legislation directly affected the outcome of this struggle, and indirectly they were effective through shaping taxation and imperial policies and controlling colonial judiciaries. Indeed, it is to a large extent through this political struggle that the planters increasingly became a self-conscious class, the plantocracy. Though the planters did not always have their own way when there were disagreements with the British government, the Colonial Office sided with the planters on most major issues because the maintenance of the plantation economy was considered to be essential to the health and vitality of the colonies. It was not until the late nineteenth century, when a prolonged economic depression prompted re-evaluation, that some colonial officials favoured the West Indian peasantry over the sugar plantations, and even then it was more in word than deed.

Planter hegemony in the social order was maintained by direct threat and coercion, which was exercised more by the state after 1838 than by individual planters, but also by cultural hegemony, as supremacist and authoritarian patterns of attitudes and behaviour were fostered by the courts, churches and schools, in particular, and by the awesome symbolism of empire in general. Against these formidable odds, the poor and powerless former slaves, for all their courage and determination in resistance, had little chance to really shape the free society according to their hopes and values. There were exceptions, however, particularly in the Afro-Caribbean churches and free villages, and the former slaves managed to keep their hopes and values alive during this struggle for real emancipation.

It was made clear, in the first months after Emancipation, that on the issues of wage rates and rights of occupancy to houses and grounds, the former slaves and apprentices faced not only their employer-landlords but also the power of the colonial state. In Grenada, Tobago, St Vincent and Jamaica, strikes occurred, but 'Troops were sent to the aid of the civil authorities and to overawe labourers in districts of Grenada and St Lucia' (Marshall 1985: 220). The civil authorities (governors, police magistrates and stipendiary magistrates) toured the districts to explain to the former slaves that they would be breaking the law if they tried to retain possession of their houses and grounds, properties that the former slaves knew to be the products of their own labours but which the law insisted belonged to the planters. In the Windward Islands, for example, the 'Labourers' protest effected no real change on the crucial questions of wage rates and secure rights of occupancy because their tactics of withholding labour while maintaining themselves on the provision grounds were robbed of their effectiveness when they were forced to accept the legality of planters' ownership of house and ground' (Marshall 1985: 220). The point is that the question of occupancy and ownership was not taken for granted but was contested. The former slaves could not win this particular struggle because the power of the state was against them, though some retreated to squat on land that was beyond the reach of the state's agents.

The planters could rely on the machinery of state to enforce their property claims against those of the former slaves, but the Colonial Office sometimes baulked at their efforts to force freed slaves to work on the plantations. The Colonial Office, when represented by Lord Glenelg and James Stephen, initially defended the freedmen's liberty against the attempts of the colonial legislatures to keep them working on the estates through draconian vagrancy and contract laws. Some of these smacked too much of the spirit of slavery and were disallowed. But whenever the plantation was threatened by crisis, as the planters frequently claimed, the imperial government rallied to support the planters. After Lord Stanley returned to the Colonial Office in 1841, numerous concessions were made to the planter–dominated colonial legislatures. Even William Green, who claims that 'the Colonial Office constituted a third force in Caribbean affairs, standing between the colonial oligarchy and the emancipated population' (Green 1986: 160), concedes that in this crucial period of struggle the imperial government sided with the planters. 'On every issue the British Government retreated from positions it had taken during the initial year of freedom, conceding points of principle and positions of power to the planter elites ... In every category of legislation the imperial Government modified its initial formula for the free society in order to accomodate the needs of an increasingly distressed planter class'. (Green 1976: 176, 187)

For example, legislation passed in the colonies to raise the property qualifications for the franchise so as to exclude most black voters, to strengthen the organization of police, militias and courts, to allow contracted labour migration from West Africa and India and to increase the duration of the indentures, and to strengthen measures against vagrancy and squatting and for the collection of rents, was all approved by the British government. Moreover, 'concessions were made to the planters perpetuating their control over the political, judicial, and law-enforcement machinery of the colonies' (Green 1976: 188), at the expense of the former slaves and their descendants, and the immigrant workers who augmented the planters' labour supply.

A series of masters and servants acts was passed in the British Caribbean, the chief purpose of which was to control and discipline the estate workers. Labourers who broke their contracts, or who were convicted of wilful misconduct, ill-behaviour or disobedience while at work, could be fined or imprisoned. The role of the courts in the continuing struggle between employers and workers in the mid-nineteenth century is indicated by the fact that between 1849 and 1854 a total of 967 people in Trinidad were committed for breach of contract under the masters and servants ordinance of 1846, compared with 830 committals for offences against the person in the same period (Trotman 1986: 278). A similar ordinance, passed in Guyana in 1846, empowered magistrates to fine workers $24 for wilful misconduct or ill-behaviour while at work and to stop all or part of a convicted worker's wages and hand it to the employer. Moreover, the employer was empowered 'to forfeit a day's rent from the wages of a worker for each day absent from work', thereby reinforcing 'the iniquitous system of tying wages to rents' as a means of labour discipline (Moore 1987: 41).

Much of the time and effort of the magistrates and courts was taken up with enforcing the labour laws in ways that favoured the employers and served to intimidate, control and discipline the workers. In Belize, for example, the district magistrate in Corozal reported that in 1869 all of the 286 cases he decided under the colony's masters and servants laws were against employees: 245 were punished for 'absenting themselves from work without leave', 30 for 'insolence and disobedience', six for 'assaults on bookkeepers', and five for 'entering into second contracts before the expiry of the period of former ones'.[9] These infringements of the labour laws were criminal offences and were commonly punished with three months' imprisonment with hard labour. In 1868 and 1869, only one of the 147 workers brought to court by their employers in Belize Town was freed without punishment, whereas only one of the ten employers brought to the court in the same period was convicted and he was given a $2 fine.[10] The workers must have concluded that it was pointless to try to bring an employer to court, whereas if they were brought to court by their employers they knew they would be convicted and punished. This policing system appears to have been a practical means of enforcing labour discipline, long after the workers were declared legally free, but the court records of absenteeism, neglect of work, disobedience and even assaults of supervisors, show that unrest among workers was widespread and persistent.

Expenditure on police, prisons and courts rose shortly after Emancipation. While under slavery much of the responsibility for social control and punishment was in the private hands of the slave-owners, unless there was a question of public safety, after Emancipation the state's police forces and penal systems took over these functions. The cost of the expanded law enforcement system, meanwhile, shifted from the slave-owners to the former slaves, upon whom the burden of taxation fell most heavily.

In Barbados, between 1835 and 1840, prison costs doubled and the expenses of the judiciary trebled, and in Guyana the amount spent on police and jails rose from £812 in 1833 to £27,796 in 1840. Total public expenditure in Guyana increased in those years from £53,996 to £125,209 (Green 1976: 184), and the chief burden of taxation fell on the former slaves. In 1833, direct taxes in the form of property and income taxes produced 76.5 per cent of Guyana's government revenue, but by 1845 customs duties and excise taxes, which fell disproportionately on the poorer consumers, brought in 74.3 per cent of the vastly enlarged revenue (Moohr 1972: 605). In Jamaica, similarly, two-thirds of the colonial government's revenue in the mid-1840s was derived from import duties (Green 1976: 185). By increasing import duties, especially on the basic necessities, the colonial authorities not only raised more revenue and shifted the cost of various responsibilities formerly borne by the owners of slaves to the former slaves, but in so doing they sought also 'to stimulate the freedmen to perform wage work on the estates' (Green 1976: 184). Earl Grey, who was secretary of state for the colonies from 1846 to 1852, 'advocated heavy capitation taxes which would force freedmen to perform steady wage work in order to satisfy the tax collector. Those who could not pay, he argued [in 1848], should be forced to labour on the roads or be hired out in gangs to the planters'. (Green 1976: 186)

In Guyana, the increases of taxes on consumer goods and imported commodities that were in general demand, such as wheat flour, tobacco, tea, cornmeal, dried codfish, pickled beef and pork, soap and salt, caused considerable distress among former slaves. In addition to import duties, licences were required for porters, hucksters and shopkeepers, in order to deter former slaves from these independent means of livelihood, and a poll tax of $2 per year for males (equivalent to two months' wages) and $1 per year for females was imposed in 1856. Brian Moore concludes, 'High indirect taxation thus remained a major instrument in suppressing the Creole population and in perpetuating their dependence on the plantation system' (Moore 1987: 117). The instrument was not always entirely successful, however, as the colonial administration generally lacked the means to collect some of the unpopular taxes. The former slaves sometimes resisted tax increases, as in Jamaica where attempts to collect a tax on hereditaments 'led to serious altercations in which a collector and police constable were beaten' (Green 1976: 188).

Immigration and indenture

The most dramatic attempt by the British West Indian planters to solve their labour problem after Emancipation was to replace slave labour on the plantations with newly imported and indentured labour. The massive import of impoverished and mainly indentured workers would, the planters hoped, create a new pool of dependable labour and at the same time make the former slaves more tractable by reducing their bargaining power.

Immigration was seen not only as a way of expanding a sparse population in an underdeveloped frontier environment (which Trinidad and British Guiana essentially were in relation to the older sugar islands), but also as a weapon in the class struggle against the newly freed Blacks. It was the ultimate way that they could be disciplined and controlled to suit the needs of the plantation system.

Even the 1842 Stanley Committee in its recommendations had made the objectives of immigration policy quite explicit: to introduce a fresh laboring population whose purpose would be to act as a competitive element against the Black labor force and thereby to depress wages to what the plantocracy would consider manageable and reasonable levels. (Look Lai 1993:12)

The indenture system varied in importance in the British Caribbean: it was central to plantation production in Trinidad and Guyana, less important in Jamaica, Grenada, St Lucia and St Vincent, and never introduced in Barbados and the Leeward Islands where the legally free labour system proved adequate for the planters' demands.

Even before 1838, the West Indian planters sought to encourage white immigration, both to augment the white population for security reasons and to create a middle class that would help keep the former slaves entrapped in dependency. Between 1834 and 1838, Guyana received over 1,000, and Jamaica over 2,000 European immigrants, but their mortality rate was high, and they were unwilling to stay on the estates. Jamaica received 4,087 out of a total of 4,582 European immigrants into the British Caribbean between 1834 and 1845, but they made little impact on the society (Look Lai 1993: 17). Governor Sir Henry Blake of Jamaica advocated white immigration until 1895, when he admitted that the German settlement at Seaford Town was not a success (Bryan 1991: 47). In 1841, Guyana supported the cost of passage for immigrants from Madeira, and up until 1850 some 17,000 Portuguese migrated there, mainly on two-, three- or five-year indentures. Mortality rates were high and most left the estates after their term of indenture to enter petty trade or small farming, sometimes in close-knit ethnic communities. In all, between 1835 and 1881, some 40,971 Portuguese Madeirans entered the British Caribbean, 32,216 (about 79 per cent) of them to Guyana, 2,527 to Antigua, and a little over 2,000 each to St Vincent and St Kitts–Nevis (Look Lai 1993: 276), but European immigration did not meet the planters' labour requirements after Emancipation.

In the circumstances, it was to be expected that the planters, as former slave-owners, would seek immigrants of African origin and descent, from other Caribbean colonies, West Africa and even the United States. Some Africans who had been liberated from slave ships and the slave centres at Rio and Havana, along with others recruited in West Africa (chiefly Liberia and Sierra Leone), were brought to the British Caribbean. Between 1834 and 1867 a total of 39,332 Africans were landed in the British Caribbean, of whom 14,060 arrived in Guyana, 11,391 in Jamaica and 8,854 in Trinidad. These Africans made a more important contribution to the plantation economy than the African Americans, most of whom were free blacks from urban areas of the northern states. Most of the 1,333 African Americans who arrived in Trinidad before 1848 rejected agricultural labour on the estates and returned to the United States (Look Lai: 1993: 15).

There was a substantial migration from the smaller Caribbean islands, where wages were lowest, to the labour-hungry colonies of Trinidad and Guyana. Between 1839 and 1849 alone, 10,278 West Indians migrated to Trinidad and 7,582 to Guyana (Wood 1968: 66). The 1851 censuses of these colonies recorded 10,800 British West Indian immigrants in Trinidad, or 15.5 per cent of the island's population, and 9,278 West Indians in Guyana, where they were 7 per cent of the population. Barbados was the chief exporter, contributing about 40,650 immigrants to Guyana between 1835 and 1893, while the 1891 Trinidad census recorded that 13,890 of the 30,689 West Indian immigrants were from Barbados (Look Lai 1993: 14). This was considered to be a problem by Barbadian planters, who saw the larger colonies as enticing away their labour force. Barbados, the Windward and Leeward Islands and the Bahamas made it illegal for immigration agents to act on those territories, and on several islands 'laborers who did register for emigration were presented with accounts for false debts to prevent their going' (Adamson 1972: 44). However, as these West Indians were using their new right to mobility to seek improvement, it is doubtful that many would have chosen to stay working on the plantations of Trinidad and Guyana. Like the former slaves of those colonies, many of these immigrants sought their own land or moved to town. The Trinidad police force was composed almost entirely of immigrants: in 1895, of the 529 police whose countries of origin were listed, only 47 were from Trinidad; 453 were from other British Caribbean colonies, 301 of them from Barbados alone; and the 13 English and 14 Irish were senior officers and non-commissioned officers, respectively (Trotman 1986: 284). As Trotman comments, this police force must have seemed to Trinidadians like 'an alien army of occupation' (Trotman 1986: 97).

From the 1840s to the 1860s, when the labour-hungry colonies were experimenting with Asian immigration, some 17,904 Chinese workers entered the British Caribbean, 13,533 or about 76 per cent of them to Guyana, 2,645 to Trinidad, 1,152 to Jamaica and 474 to Belize. These remained a small and marginal group in British Caribbean societies, however. India became the chief source of immigrants, mainly as indentured labourers for the plantation economies of the British Caribbean. Between 1834 and 1918 a total of 429,623 people came from India, constituting 80 per cent of the 536,310 immigrants who entered the British Caribbean in that period. Of these Indians, 98 per cent landed in three colonies: 238,909 in Guyana, 143,939 in Trinidad and 36,412 in Jamaica. Of the rest, 4,354 arrived in St Lucia, 3,200 in Grenada and 2,472 in St Vincent (Look Lai 1993: 276). Fewer than one in four indentured immigrants, or about 111,300, had returned to India by 1916 (Roberts and Byrne 1966: 132). This massive immigration of Asian, mainly Indian, indentured labourers revived the West Indian plantation system, particularly in Trinidad and Guyana where the cultural and social effects of this influx were permanent and profound.

In 1838, a group of 396 Indians were brought under five-year contracts into Guyana, but due to reports of their ill-treatment and high mortality rates, publicised by the Anti-Slavery Society, further emigration was suspended by the Council of India (Moore 1987: 45). By the mid-1840s, West Indian planters had persuaded the British government to support Indian immigration on a large scale (a loan of £5,000,000 helped finance the scheme) and by 1851 it was well under way. Most of these Indian immigrants came from Bengal, Bihar, the North-West Provinces, Oudh and Central India. During the peak years of immigration, between 1866 and 1880, 127,905 Indians arrived in the British Caribbean, 74,165 of them in Guyana. In 1841 there were only 343 Indians in Guyana, and in 1851 the 7,682 Indians constituted 5.6 per cent of the total population. The black and coloured Creoles of largely African descent constituted 93 per cent of the population of Guyana in 1841 but were only 49 per cent by 1911. In 1911, the 126,517 Indians were 43 per cent of the population of Guyana. In Trinidad, meanwhile, the proportion of Indians in the population rose from 6 per cent in 1851 to 33 per cent in 1911 (Look Lai 1993: 302).

This massive influx of indentured immigrants through the second half of the nineteenth century enabled the planters in Trinidad and Guyana to displace most of the former slaves who were willing to work on the plantations and to reduce their labour costs by replacing them with mainly Indian workers. By the mid-1870s, Indians constituted about 90 per cent of the labour force on Trinidad's sugar estates. They comprised three categories of workers: those indentured workers who were still working under contract, and those whose contracts had expired and who lived either in the estate barracks or in villages near the estates. The presence of a proportion of indentured workers made it easier for the planters to control the others. Indentured workers were legally obliged to work, of course, but many of those whose contracts had expired were indebted to the planters and were consequently under compulsion to work, with little scope to negotiate their terms.

The introduction of these indentured workers was intended to solve two problems for the planters: the short-term problem of providing enough coerced and dependable workers to maintain plantation production after Emancipation, and the long-term problem of increasing the potential plantation labour supply. The first problem was solved by the terms of the contracts that bound the workers for a period of years, normally five. The second problem 'was expected to be solved by having the time-expired workers remain as settlers' (Engerman 1985: 234), thereby expanding the pool of available labourers and, not coincidentally, reducing their bargaining power and hence their wage rates.[11] The competition induced in this situation between indentured workers, time-expired indentured workers, and the former slaves and their descendants conspired against them all by setting them against each other, thereby favouring the planters. As one planter in Guyana succinctly explained, 'So long as an estate has a large Coolie gang, Creoles must give way in prices asked.' (quoted in Foner 1983: 22) The former slaves even contributed through their taxes to the local immigration funds that were supported from the general revenue. Ironically, 'Indian immigration was thus financed to a considerable extent by those with whom it was intended that the Indian immigrants should compete' (Williams 1970: 358).

Although the planters persistently complained that their labour supply was inadequate, these mainly Asian indentured and, subsequently, time-expired immigrants enabled them to revive the plantations. The critical competition provided by the indentured workers actually meant that the legally free workers, both former slaves and time-expired workers, were not selling their labour power in a free market but in a situation that was biased in favour of those who hired their labour. What the planters really meant when they said that their labour force was inadequate was that 'they were not able to command as much labour as they chose for whatever wage they chose' (Laurence 1985: 270), and this is the reason that the indenture system lasted so long. Regardless of the actual supply of labour, the planters continued to complain because, short of slavery, they would never have been satisfied.

Most of the plantations that failed in the second half of the nineteenth century were smaller, inefficient and encumbered with debt, and many were absorbed by larger metropolitan companies in a continuing process of capitalist concentration. In Guyana the number of plantations declined from 173 in 1851 to 95 in 1890, but the acreage under sugar cane increased from 48,087 acres in 1855 to 79,243 acres in 1890, and sugar production increased from 29,584 tons in 1841 to 105,484 tons in 1890 (Moore 1987: 46). In Trinidad, likewise, the surviving planters invested capital, expanded cultivation and increased production from 12,228 tons of sugar in 1840 to 53,436 tons in 1880. The Trinidad sugar industry became dominated by British capital at the expense of local, and particularly French creole, planters. The Colonial Company, a giant conglomerate incorporated in 1866, built the largest and most modern sugar factory in the British empire, the Usine Ste Madeleine, in 1872. By 1895, of the 59 estates in Trinidad, 34 were owned by British corporations and these were the largest and most productive. In 1897, most of Trinidad's sugar was produced by just 11 of these consolidated units, and 'an overstocked labour market...depressed agricultural wages' (Brereton 1981: 86).

In short, as Eric Foner (1983: 23) writes: 'The use of government-sponsored immigration to transform the labor market and labor relations is a striking example of how the power of the state helped to determine the ultimate fate of planters and freedmen in the postemancipation Caribbean .... Emancipation in the British Caribbean did not challenge the local political hegemony of the planter class.'

The political hegemony of the planter class

Political hegemony was maintained in a variety of ways, including cultural hegemony and the rule of law, but not least by the severely restricted franchise that deliberately excluded the vast majority of the former slaves from the electorate in those colonies where there was an elected legislative assembly. Trinidad was a Crown colony, but in most Caribbean colonies, such as Antigua, Barbados and Jamaica, the planters continued to dominate the oligarchic legislative assemblies after Emancipation. The fact that the majority of people in Great Britain were also excluded from the vote at this time means that a broader franchise was not seriously considered in Britain's tropical colonies. The ruling classes in nineteenth-century liberal bourgeois society still viewed democracy as a threat to their system of domination and had not yet come to accept that it was compatible with, and might even help stabilise, capitalist regimes.

Trinidad did not have an elected assembly. The British government was disillusioned with the colonial assemblies in the early nineteenth century, particularly in Grenada and Quebec where the majority of electors were French-speaking and in those Caribbean colonies where there were many free people of colour. By 1810, the British government had decided to keep greater control over Trinidad, which had many French-speaking and free coloured subjects, by keeping it a Crown colony. In 1831 a purely nominated Legislative Council was established, consisting of official members, who constituted a majority until 1862, and unofficials who were nominated by the governor 'from the principal proprietors of the Colony' (Brereton 1981: 136). Between 1862 and 1898 the council had an unofficial majority, but the Colonial Office allowed this on the understanding that if they voted together to defeat the colonial officials the official majority would be restored. In any case, the governor was generally careful to nominate only those men who would support his policies, so there was no effective independent opposition to the colonial government. The unofficials were independent only in theory because their nomination was dependent on the governor's good will. The Colonial Office claimed that this Crown colony form of government 'was the best guardian of the interests of the masses as against the propertied few' (Brereton 1981: 139), but really it worked with the propertied few to keep the masses out of politics. In the view of the Colonial Office, this autocratic form of government worked well, so as opportunities arose, it was imposed throughout most of the British Caribbean.

Barbados, however, retained its wholly elected House of Assembly, with a very restricted franchise, and never became a Crown colony. In 1840 there were just 1,153 voters. Samuel Prescod, who was a free coloured leader of anti-slavery opinion in the 1830s, and was the first man of African ancestry elected to the Assembly, agitated for an extension of the franchise. Lord Stanley 'approved a complicated and restrictive law which had the effect of preserving a uniformly white Barbados Assembly throughout the mid-century' (Green 1976: 176). In 1849, there were 1,322 voters, less than 5 per cent of the population (Beckles 1990: 120), and in 1857 there were still only 1,350 registered voters in a population exceeding 135,000. A franchise act passed in 1884 reduced property qualifications from almost £13 to £5 and enfranchised all men whose annual income was £50 or more. However, the number of voters was only slightly increased and few blacks could exercise the franchise. In 1900 there were still fewer than 2,000 registered voters in Barbados (Beckles 1990: 126).

In 1854 Grenada, with a population of 32,600, had 191 electors; St Vincent, with a population of 30,125, had 273 electors; and Tobago, with 14,500 persons, had 135 electors (Green 1976: 177). In Dominica, where some of the coloured elite occupied middle-level positions within the state apparatus and had significant private sources of income, a few launched political careers, but 'they generally backed authoritarian measures ... in an effort to maintain the ex-slaves on the estates' (Trouillot 1992: 166). One of their leaders, Charles Gordon Falconer, an immigrant from Barbados, was appointed printer of the legislature in 1842, elected to the Assembly in 1845 and named colonial registrar in 1868, but 'Dominican politics were for a long time a game played primarily between white and light-skinned individuals' (Trouillot 1992: 170), a game from which the black majority was excluded.

In Jamaica, where eight of the 43 members of the Assembly elected in 1837 were free coloured men, chiefly from the city of Kingston, the planters sought to restrict the franchise further in order to maintain their political power after Emancipation. 'The Franchise Act of 1859 imposed a ten-shilling poll tax on all voters, which had the effect of slashing the voter rolls and drastically curtailing black and brown representation in the Assembly' (Holt 1992: 256). In the 1863 election for the Jamaican Assembly, only 1,457 votes were cast out of a population exceeding 440,000 (Green 1976: 177). After the peasant rebellion at Morant

Bay in 1865, this Assembly was abolished in favour of the Crown colony form of government, thereby ensuring the exclusion of any African-Jamaicans in politics.

There had been agitation and disturbances in Nevis, Tobago and St Vincent in the early 1860s and the planters sought more direct imperial intervention and control. 'Metropolitan capitalists made it clear that constitutional reforms designed to enhance executive authority would afford them greater security of capital, and their opinion carried authority in a community of debtors desperately in need of credit.' (Green 1976: 378-9) The Morant Bay rebellion provided the occasion for Jamaica to become a Crown colony and other British colonies in the Caribbean soon followed suit. This was a constitutional change from an oligarchic form of government to an autocratic one, and whether or not the legislative councils that replaced the old assemblies (except in Barbados and the Bahamas) had elected as well as nominated members, the planter class maintained its powerful infuence. Indeed, such influence was so strong that, even though the constitution asserted autocracy in theory, the 'practice of politics assumed an oligarchy' (Augier 1966: 33). It was through fear of more radical, democratic change that the planters and their allies in Great Britain 'warmly endorsed the change to Crown colony government believing that it provided greater security for their investments' (Green 1976: 398).

In 1865 the Dominica House, over the protests of Falconer's supporters, was transformed from 19 elected and nine appointed members to a council of seven elected and seven nominated members. 'Engineered by the Lt.-Governor, with full support from the Colonial Office, the measure was clearly a victory for the planting interest and their allies' (Green 1976: 378). By 1868 the legislative councils of Antigua, Nevis and St Kitts likewise consisted of half elected and half ex-officio and nominated members, with the Crown's representative exercising a casting vote. In Montserrat there was no elected member after 1866. The common feature of these legislative councils, whether or not they included elected members, was the reinforced power of the Crown, exercised through the governor. As in Jamaica and Dominica, 'the dominant whites surrendered to the British government rather than to the infiltration of coloured and other non-planter interests into the elected legislatures' (Hall 1971: 176).

In Guyana, where the unique constitutional framework was influenced by the Dutch heritage, there was a Court of Policy, an electoral college called the College of Kiezers and a College of Financial Representatives, as well as the governor, who was appointed by the imperial government. Though technically a Crown colony, there was a representative tradition that enabled the planters to have a strong voice in formulating legislation and the budget. The numbers of whites actually increased from 2,776 in 1841 to 4,551 in 1891, but their proportion in the total population decreased from 2.8 per cent to 1.6 per cent. Whether they were local whites or British-born, 'it was the wealthy resident planters and attorneys representing metropolitan principals who dominated the colonial society and formed a kind of aristocracy with a quasi-monopoly of political and social power' (Moore 1987: 52). Monetary qualifications, amounting to the payment of taxes on an annual income of 2,001 guilders (about £143) or the payment of 70 guilders (£5) in direct taxes, restricted the franchise after Emancipation to a minority of this minority (Moore 1987: 54).

The franchise was extended in 1849 to include freeholders with property valued at $96 (£20) per year in the country or $500 (£104) in the towns, rural leaseholders with land valued at $192 (£40) per year and urban leaseholders paying an annual rent of $120 (£25), and persons paying taxes on an income of $600 (£125) per year, or $20 (£4) per year in direct taxes. As a result, the number of voters increased from 561 in 1847 to 962 in 1851, but the electorate remained less than 1 per cent of the total population, 'a small privileged category' (Moore 1987: 55). When there appeared to be a chance that some of the former slaves, urban as well as rural, could meet the property qualifications, many were excluded by a literacy qualification. Moreover, the maintenance of an electoral college with high property qualifications for its members preserved planter and white dominance: 'in the absence of overt racial disqualifications of the black and coloured majority high property qualifications and the literacy test were designed to be an effective debarment of the non-white population' (Moore 1987: 57). These measures were so effective that no non-white entered the legislature in Guyana until after the 1891 constitutional reforms. The number of registered voters increased from 1,973 in 1890, to 2,046 in 1891 and 2,479 in 1896, but they were still less than 1 per cent of the population (Moore 1987: 73-4). These limited reforms did little to change the structure of colonial politics and the persistent dominance of the planters was unaffected - indeed, one must conclude that this was intended.

In Belize, it was not the fear of the former slaves that prompted the change to Crown colony government but a resurgence of Maya resistance to colonial rule. Until the 1830s the leading colonial settlers, who called themselves Baymen or the Principal Inhabitants in the Bay of Honduras, controlled the land, labour, commerce and the instruments of government in the settlement. As Belize was not formally a colony, the superintendents who were appointed by the Crown were in a weak and anomalous position when opposed by the settler elite of merchants and mahogany cutters who controlled the public meeting and magistracy. James Stephen stated in 1838, 'The Crown is represented by a Superintendent who is not much more than a Looker-on, and who supplies the want of authority by dexterity and address in acquiring and using influence over the general meeting and the Magistracy.'[12] The public meeting struggled to maintain its exclusive character after Emancipation in order to perpetuate the old settler oligarchy's political dominance, but a transformation of the economic structure coincided with the British government's desire to regularise the settlement's colonial status in the 1850s.

The authority of the superintendent increased as that of the public meeting and magistracy decreased in the 1840s, while economic control shifted decisively from the old settler families to metropolitan companies. These companies and their investors wanted greater security for their investments in land. In 1854, Great Britain approved the settlement's first recognised constitution, clearly defined the Crown's authority as vested in the superintendent, and created a Legislative Assembly of 18 elected members and three members appointed by the superintendent. Elected members were British men over the age of 21 years, in possession of property worth £400, and the franchise was restricted to men with real property yielding an income of £7 per year or a salary of £100 per year (Bolland 1977: 190). The vast majority of people in the settlement - Maya, Mestizo, Garifuna, Creoles and former slaves - were excluded from political participation. The Assembly petitioned for colonial status, and in 1862 Great Britain declared British Honduras a colony and made its superintendent a lieutenant-governor, under the authority of the governor of Jamaica.

In 1871, after a life of only 17 years, the Legislative Assembly abolished itself and Belize became a Crown colony. The expenses of administering the colony had increased in the late 1860s, largely as a result of costly military expeditions against the Maya, undertaken at a time when the economy was severely depressed. The Legislative Assembly, which controlled the colony's revenues and expenditure, was dominated by the great land-owners and merchants, and their conflicting interests produced a stalemate. On the one hand, the merchants of Belize Town felt relatively secure from Maya attacks and were unwilling to pay increased import duties toward the military expenditure necessary to resist them. On the other, the land-owners were unwilling to bear the expense themselves and argued that it was unjust to require them to pay taxes on lands that were inadequately protected. The Assembly failed to authorise the raising of sufficient revenue and the public debt, being 'chiefly for military expenditure' (Gibbs 1883: 155), rose to about $150,000 by 1870 (Bolland 1977: 191). The Assembly, agreeing to surrender its privilege of self-government in return for greater security against the persistent Maya threat, 'committed political suicide' (Gibbs 1883: 152).

Under the new constitution, inaugurated in 1871, the colony was governed by the governor-in-council, with the Council consisting of five official and four nominated members. Three of the first four members nominated to the new Council represented the landed interests and the fourth represented the merchants. The Council promptly raised import duties from 4 per cent to 10 per cent – 'another victory for the landowners' (Clegern 1967: 53). As the system of government moved from oligarchy to autocracy, the real losers were the vast majority of the population, which remained completely unrepresented. The local elite pressed in the 1890s for a restoration of the elective principle but the British government was concerned that there were too few whites in the colony and so only increased the number of unofficial members. They became a majority of the Council in 1892, but they were still nominated by and dependent upon the governor. The vested interests of the colony, and particularly the largest land-owner, the Belize Estate and Produce Company, remained dominant in its political as well as economic affairs.

Crown colony regimes were formally autocratic, even when the planters exercised great political influence. 'Final power, always, lay in the hands of the executive and, within the executive, in the hands of the Governor and, through the Governor, of course, in the hands of the distant Colonial Office' (Lewis 1968: 98). The governors were, at best, benevolent despots, shaped by paternalistic attitudes of the imperial government and by what they considered to be re- sponsible public opinion in their colonies. The unofficial, nominated members of the legislative councils were frequently chastised for being irresponsible if they dared to engage in opposition, but they had no constitutional responsi- bility. Gordon Lewis argues (1968: 99) that, in fact, 'the executive was equally irresponsible' and the Crown colony system, even when modified with some elected members, 'bred an arrogance of attitude on the part of the official side towards the nominated unofficials and the elected politicians'. This is hardly surprising, as the chief purpose of the colonies was to benefit the metropole by enabling the propertied classes to exploit the colonies' human and natural resources. The Crown colony system was intended to be a system of domination and it was not until after reforms were initiated in the 1920s and the labour rebellions erupted in the 1930s that the floodgates of change were opened. The Colonial Office created the rules and its governors and administrators were the local rulers, whether or not they were good men.

Barbados, where the old House of Assembly was fully elective and Crown colony rule was never established, was 'notorious for its entrenched system of racialist prejudice' (Lewis 1968: 226). This is explicable when we understand that Barbados, to an extraordinary degree even by Caribbean standards, remained economically dominated by the sugar planters. In an economy characterised by monopolised and expensive land, over-abundant labour and low wages, the black majority remained economically and socially subservient after Emancipation to an extreme degree. George Lamming's quasi-autobiographical novel, In the Castle of My Skin, depicts the domination of a white landlord and his overseers over a village of poor blacks in the 1930s. The social dynamics Lamming describes had lasted a century in this Caribbean version of Victorian 'little England'.

When examined in terms of constitutional forms, Barbados is at one extreme and Trinidad at the other, with Jamaica and the other colonies moving from elected assemblies to Crown colony regimes. But when seen as systems of domination, rather than in formal terms, these colonial states have more in common than otherwise because they all sought to contain the latent political threat of the former slaves. 'What imperial authorities feared in 1833 and deplored thereafter was the loss of control by Europeans over a large portion of the emancipated population' (Green 1976: 404). Barbados, Trinidad and Jamaica all managed to constrain the political aspirations of the former slaves and their descendents, though in different ways. In Trinidad there was no elective principle, and in Jamaica the oligarchy gave up its old political privileges in order to protect its property. In Barbados this was not necessary because the former slaves remained so well-regulated that the planters did not generally feel so threatened. In all cases, however, the propertied class maintained its political influence, generally supporting, because it was supported by, the representatives of the Colonial Office.

Policing and educating the workers

Local judicial authority remained totally in the hands of the planters. 'With emancipation ... the judiciary became a major means of disciplining the black labor force. Heavy fines for vagrancy, theft, and trespass were routinely imposed on the freedmen.' (Foner 1983: 24)

In Jamaica the cruellest emblem of the new forms of labour discipline after Emancipation was the treadmill, which was considered to be 'a rational and humane way to impose discipline' in two senses: 'punishment and routinized labor' (Holt 1992: 106). In fact, the treadmill was an instrument of torture, used in workhouses and jails to terrorise former slaves into submission to the new regime of state rather than personal power. 'The treadmill became emblematic of the abuses of the Jamaican prison system, which in turn symbolized that colony's general failure to make the transition from a slave to a free society' (Holt 1992: 107). The whip, emblem of slavery itself, continued to be widely used. In Trinidad, for example, flogging was 'used liberally for those convicted of practising Obeah and praedial larceny or for the unemployed convicted of being incorrigible rogues or vagabonds .... The harshest punishment for the lower classes came for those who dared to interfere with property or for those who, by their attitude, showed a disinclination to work, but not for those who did bodily harm to their fellow sufferers.' (Trotman 1986: 137-8)

In a society that originated in and continued to depend upon violence, 'The whip was as commonly used as a mechanism for labor persuasion as it had been in the worst days of slavery. In a number of cases, a severe whipping resulted in death' (Trotman 1986: 139), but the courts, which saw such matters from the planters' viewpoint, rarely found the perpetrators guilty. In Jamaica, also, whipping was a common punishment used by the state. In 1865 whipping was extended to punishment for praedial larceny and 'administered with increased severity' (Holt 1992: 287). The Colonial Office objected only to the limit of 50 lashes and asked that it be reduced to 39.

With Emancipation, the problem of policing labour was largely transferred from the individual planters, as slave-owners, to the apparatus of the state. David Trotman describes the 'concentrated attack on labor' in Trinidad, including prosecutions resulting in fines and imprisonment for squatting, vagrancy and begging, 'which had as its intention the coercion of those segments of the labor force that were not indentured and refused to bend to the demands of the plantation' (Trotman 1986: 211). This attack reached its culmination with the passage of the habitual idlers ordinance in 1918, in which the definition of a habitual idler was left to the discretion of the magistrate. With the demise of indentured immigration in 1917, this law was to provide a means 'to continue control of the labor force already on the island' and many of those convicted as vagrants were time-expired Indian workers (Trotman 1986: 211).

Members of the judiciary were generally planters or their agents, and they could rarely act independently of the planter class, even if they wanted to. Joseph Beaumont, a former chief justice of Guyana, wrote in 1871 that, 'when acts of the Executive Government or the interests or privileges of the planters come into question, no judge or magistrate can decide adversely to them, without being exposed to the risk of punishment' (quoted in Moore 1987: 61). A magistrate in San Fernando, Trinidad, upset the planters because of his rulings on immigration cases, so they had him removed and transferred to Barbados (Trotman 1986: 82).

Many magistrates had no legal training, but even when they were competent they suffered from prejudices that biased their judgements. A network of social ties and sentiments linked the judiciary to the planters, while the vast majority of defendants were working people of African and Indian origin. 'Many of the planters themselves were justices of the peace. The planters and the judiciary – in fact, the entire legal profession – were connected by blood relationships, by marriage ties, by the old school tie, by membership in the same social clubs, and of course by their common allegiance to the race and color stratification that was an integral part of the ideology that dominated the plantation society. Few of them made any effort to hide these connections.'

(Trotman 1986: 85)

The storm that broke over the Morant Bay courthouse in 1865 stemmed from many causes, not least of which was frustration about the issue of unequal justice in the local courts. On matters pertaining to access to land, rents, wages and taxes, the magistrates of St Thomas parish, epitomised by the local custos, Baron von Ketelhodt, weighted the law in favour of the planter class (Holt 1992: 300).

The planters' domination of local government was not only through the magistrates and justices of the peace, but also through their control of the vestries, statutory boards and village administrations. When these legal and administrative mechanisms were insufficient to intimidate and discipline the former slaves and indentured workers, the planters used the local armed forces in the form of the police, militia and volunteer forces. In Guyana, in the wake of disturbances in 1856, when the predominantly white militia had proved inadequate, the estates' armed force was created. Composed mainly of white employees of the planters, this armed force strengthened 'the security and coercive power of the planters on individual estates' (Moore 1987: 204). The militia and estates' armed force virtually disappeared in the 1870s, but the volunteer force established in 1878 was sufficiently strong to help suppress the Georgetown riots in 1889. Moore concludes, 'Above all, white authorities placed great emphasis on coercion - the show and actual use of armed force - to promote social stability by instilling fear and awe of white power in the minds of the subordinate population. They never equivocated about the absolute need for military force to keep these subordinates in submission to the lawful authority of the ruling white minority.' (Moore 1987: 203)

Throughout the British Caribbean the regular police forces themselves often showed characteristics of paramilitary organisations, with the emphasis on force rather than public service. Officers were generally white and of military background, and the ranks were frequently from other colonies and were stationed in barracks, like troops in a colonial army, to keep them from fraternising with the general public. When the question of reorganising the Bahamian police force was raised in 1888, Lord Knutsford, the secretary of state for the colonies, urged that the police should be recruited from other West Indian colonies, 'to prevent any feeling of local sympathy between [the] Police and the inhabitants of the Bahamas.'[13] The governor expressed concern that police recruited locally 'would be found in the time of trial on the wrong side'.[14] United by their fear of the black majority, Bahamian whites wanted a police force that could be relied on to control the black population.

The Bahamas, like Belize, Trinidad and other parts of the British Caribbean, recruited its police force largely in Barbados. Led by an officer from the Royal

Artillery, the Bahamian constabulary was organised as a paramilitary force and quartered in barracks at Nassau. Not surprisingly, many of the local people were hostile to this constabulary, as became apparent during disturbances that occurred in the black neighbourhood of Grant's Town in 1893 (Johnson 1986). In the colonies where there was no permanent detachment of troops, these paramilitary police forces were the chief defence of the propertied classes. They must have seemed to the 'natives' like an imperial garrison.

Coercion, whether by troops, police or armed volunteers, was emphasised by the white minorities in the British Caribbean and was the bottom line of social control, both during and after slavery. Cultural hegemony also played a key part in social control, but it is harder to assess its role precisely. The planters and colonial administrators recognised that organised religion and the schools that were run by missionaries could contribute to creating a consensus, though they had often been concerned about the uncontrollable effects of religious conversion and education on their slaves. At the time of Emancipation, the moral and religious education of the former slaves seemed to offer the best chance of gaining 'power over their minds'. In 1835 the Reverend John Sterling, a special commissioner appointed by the British government to advise on an education system for the West Indies, argued that the religious schools could play a key role:

> For although the Negroes are now under a system of limited control [apprentice-ship] which secures to a certain extent their orderly and industrious conduct, in the short space of five years from the 1st of next August, their performance of the functions of a labouring class in a civilized community will depend entirely on the power over their minds of the same prudential and moral motives which govern more or less the mass of the people here. If they are not so disposed as to fulfil these functions, property will perish in the colonies for lack of human impulsion .... There has been since the 1st of August a great increase of the desire for knowledge ... its certain result where the minds of the people are at all in movement will be a consciousness of their own independent value as rational beings without reference to the purposes for which they may be profitable to others. (quoted in Gordon 1968: 59-60, emphasis added)

The British government agreed with Sterling, and from 1835 to 1845 the negro education grant subsidised the religious bodies and missionary societies to pay teachers and build schools, but the provision for the education of the former slaves and their children was quite limited. Over that decade, a total of £235,000 was granted to educate the former slaves, a sum that was less than 1.2 per cent of the amount paid to the slave-owners in compensation for their loss of property (Bacchus 1990: 245). When the foundations of an elementary school system had been established, the British government decided that West

Indians should henceforth pay for their own education.

The emphasis in the curriculum was on moral improvement and this was to be achieved by Christianizing the population. Consistent with the dominant vision of the society, the teaching methods emphasised the authority of the teachers and, beyond the teachers, the inspectors who represented imperial standards and culture. Students were taught above all to be obedient, to follow orders, however absurd or inexplicable, promptly and without question. Rather than encouraging an independent spirit of enquiry or 'a consciousness of their own independent value', such methods, reinforced by the continual threat and use of corporal punishment, were intended to perpetuate the subservient roles most people were expected to occupy in the society. These goals conflicted with the hopes of parents who thought that education could provide opportunities for the occupational and social mobility of their children, but the system was not designed for that. On the contrary, 'education was to impress on the ex-slaves the need to accept the new social order and their own place within it – which was still to be on the lowest rungs of the social and economic ladder' (Bacchus 1990: 269).

The director of education in Jamaica recommended in 1886 that a simple manual to teach the 'leading principles of Christian Morality' should be used in the schools because 'in the present course of instruction there is perhaps not sufficient direct provision for training children in habits of discipline and subordination' (quoted in Bryan 1991: 116-17). The Anglican and Methodist clergy, in particular, intended to foster among the former slaves and their children a deference to authority, an acceptance of their subordinate social position and industrious, disciplined work habits. Hence religious education, in the form of catechisation with a lot of rote learning and hymn singing, and a little reading and writing, predominated at the expense of instruction in practical subjects or the development of learning skills. Even the more independent missionaries, who insisted on the rights of the former slaves and were often involved in campaigns for political reforms and the establishment of free villages, also emphasised European cultural superiority in their teaching. Convinced as they were that theirs was the only true religion, they could hardly have done otherwise. Their paternalism and ethnocentricity, however benevolent it may have been in its intentions, was oriented towards fostering lasting dependency among the former slaves. The teaching methods, backed up by widespread corporal punishment, further promoted passivity and self-deprecation rather than a critical intellect and a sense of self-worth and autonomy. Children were ferociously flogged not only for misconduct but also when they made mistakes in their work. The classroom 'was not intended to encourage love of learning as much as fear of punishment, under the guise of discipline' (Bryan

1991: 120). Above all, for Archbishop Enos Nuttall and other prominent clerics in the West Indies, 'education remained an important tool to maintain social stability' (Bryan 1991: 118).

The elementary school system was oriented towards keeping the working people in their place, and the few secondary schools were meant largely for the children of the whites and upper classes. Meanwhile, hundreds of school-teachers joined the ranks of the lower middle classes. Though most poor rural children attended school irregularly and left early, elementary schoolteaching was almost the only way any of them could escape the status of their parents. The limited but highly visible evidence of social mobility provided by the teachers reinforced the idea that social conformity was the avenue to success. Nevertheless, it was from among these people that many of the new coloured and black reformers - and even some independent-minded intellectuals and radicals - eventually emerged. Education in the British Caribbean colonies, though not intended to be an instrument of social change, 'helped to raise the levels of aspiration of those who attended schools and resulted in some of them increasingly putting pressure on the ruling elites to open more avenues for their economic and social betterment' (Bacchus 1990: 367).

The religious educational system instituted after Emancipation did not systematically indoctrinate the former slaves and their children, however hard it tried, simply because it lacked sufficient resources. The missionaries tried to make model 'Christian Blacks' of the freed slaves (Russell 1983) and contrib-uted to their continued subjugation to the plantation system by buttressing the colonial authority structure, inculcating an allegiance to the empire and even an admiration of 'whiteness', and helping to maintain the so-called good behaviour of the working people. Their moral order was contested, however, and, in Guyana amongst other places, 'the results of schooling and religious proselytization in instilling the superiority of white culture, religion and values among the Creole population were at best ambiguous' (Moore 1987: 198). In Jamaica the missionaries were first delighted by the great revival of evangelical religion in 1860-1, but when the new fervour turned African they despaired. Spirit possession and forms of dance, masquerade and worship that reflected the Myal and Native Baptist traditions soon animated the Great Revival (Cur-tin 1970: 170; Austin-Broos 1992: 234). 'The Myal tradition formed the core of a strong, self-confident counter-culture' which 'led to periodic confrontations with island authorities' (Schuler 1980: 44). Many Jamaicans who participated in the more orthodox church services on Sundays engaged in revival ceremonies and curing activities at other times. The various Zionist, Pentacostal and Ras-tafarian churches that have flourished in the twentieth century are evidence of the continuing resistance of many Jamaicans to the European model of

Christianity and Christian behaviour.

The widespread persistence of Afro-Caribbean beliefs and customs, as well as the continuing resentment of and resistance to the authority systems of the colonial plantation society, are eloquent testimony to the ultimate failure of the indoctrination process. Many people more or less escaped the colonial influence through the schools because enrolment and attendance rates were generally low, often for economic reasons. And often the schools were so dilapidated and overcrowded that conditions were too chaotic for teachers to successfully inculcate work discipline and an allegiance to the empire, however much they lashed the children in their care. One could conclude that those who were the most educated were, with some exceptions, often the most indoctrinated, for whom the world view of their colonial rulers became their own commonsense view of the world, while those people who were less exposed to the colonial education system were more likely to preserve their traditional culture of resistance. However, some people, like C.L.R. James, who had been educated in 'the general intellectual ideas of the British and the European intellectual', found that some of these ideas, such as democracy, 'were not being applied in the island in which we lived' (Hall 1996: 19-20). The contradiction between these ideas and the reality shocked some educated West Indians into a radical critique and political activity.

In Trinidad and Guyana, the school system also educated and Christianised Indians. In Trinidad, the Canadian Presbyterian mission, founded in 1868, was successful in converting and educating thousands of Indians, some of whom became schoolteachers and ministers themselves. Though educated mainly in separate institutions, these Indians obtained skills and qualifications that enabled them to compete and also to become more integrated in the wider society, sometimes even attaining middle-class status (Campbell 1992: 18). In Guyana, however, such integration occurred more slowly and, in the late nineteenth century, 'there was no common social will or value system shared by all segments of the society. Even though at emancipation the Creoles were arguably already in the process of assimilating white culture through the powerful religious and cultural influence of the white missionaries, there was no shared system of values which integrated the new immigrant groups into the colonial society.' (Moore 1987: 215)

This brings us to consider the pervasive but elusive role of 'race'[15] and racism in these colonial societies. The fear of revolt that was endemic among the white and upper classes in the slave societies of the Caribbean did not end with Emancipation. The siege mentality of a minority that exploited and oppressed a majority from whom they were divided by 'race', culture and class, led to frequent overreactions to minor incidents, which then sometimes became major disturbances. Persistent unrest among the former slaves, and major disturbances in Guyana in 1856, Jamaica in 1865 and Barbados in 1876, reinforced the paranoia of the colonial elite and administrators. The elite's fear of the masses was compounded in these former slave societies by deeply rooted racism.

At the same time that the British were attempting to assimilate the ex-slaves into the post-Emancipation society by emphasising the supposed superiority of English culture, they excluded them from equal participation in that society on racial grounds. The obvious, but crucial, point is that an important element of the English culture was (and is) its racism. Raymond Smith emphasises the conflicts and contradictions that existed in the process of creolisation after emancipation:

> The basic facts about creole society are that it was rooted in the political and economic dominance of the metropolitan power, it was colour stratified and was integrated around the conception of the moral and cultural superiority of things English .... It was an integral part of the process of 'creolization' to stress the differences between groups identified as 'racial' groups, despite tendencies toward cultural assimilation. This resulted from the fact that the value standards pertaining to the whole society were 'English' or 'white' people's and thus total conformity to them was impossible for non-whites no matter how well they commanded the culture of the mother country (Smith 1967: 234-5).

The Europeans believed that however much they tried to 'civilise the natives' they could not succeed, because non-Europeans were congenitally incapable of the kind of virtues and self-discipline that defined European civilisation. Consequently, the British used the coercive forces of the state to control and suppress popular culture by defining much of it as subversive and criminal behaviour. Popular entertainment, including gambling and drumming, were often banned and so was a great deal of religious activity, including, for example, the practice of obeah throughout the Caribbean and the Spiritual Baptists in Trinidad. When popular festivals in Trinidad were banned or curbed, people resisted, as in the carnival riots of 1881, 1883 and 1884, and the Hosein massacre of 1884. Trotman (1986: 270) concludes that 'The struggle for cultural hegemony in the nineteenth century therefore depended less on the socializing agencies of church and school to win consent and more on the coercive arms of the state to enforce compliance, and in the process, large segments of the population were forced into criminal activity'.

The racial factor affected not only the status of the former slaves and indentured labourers and their descendants within the colonies after Emancipation, but also the status of the British Caribbean colonies vis-a-vis the imperial government. The legacy of slavery left a mark in the social consciousness of race, and specifically in the social status of the former slave which was based after Emancipation on his racial identity (Sio 1979: 271). The exclusion of the vast majority of the people of the British Caribbean colonies from the political process, ostensibly on the basis of property and literacy qualifications, was intended to maintain some form of 'white' rule. British ideas of representative democracy in the nineteenth century were highly exclusive, tainted by racism, sexism and classism. Within Great Britain, and among 'whites' in the colonies who identified closely with their mother country, racism provided a rationale for the conquest of remote territories and rule over 'dusky races'. The coronation ceremony of 1902, among many other rituals of empire, was designed to express 'the recognition, by a free democracy, of a hereditary crown, as a symbol of the world-wide dominion of their race' (quoted in Hobsbawm 1987: 70). The Earl of Newcastle, in a speech in the House of Lords in 1858, said that the principle of self-government was 'only applicable to colonists of the English race' (Williams 1970: 399). Hence, just two years before Canada, which was considered a largely 'white' colony, achieved dominion status on its road to democracy, the Jamaican Assembly was abolished and Jamaica was governed as a Crown colony.

The Canadian model, which assumed a preponderance of the 'British race', was deemed unworkable in the British Caribbean where the white 'kith and kin' were such a tiny minority. The imperial government thought that Canada, despite the French faction, would become increasingly British and hence capable of democracy, while the British Caribbean would inevitably become blacker and more alien (Holt 1992: 243), and therefore had to be protected from democracy. Moore (1987: 78-9) concludes that the factors of race and imperialism determined the predominant form of colonial polity in the British Caribbean after Emancipation: 'The issue of race was used to deny the black and coloured majority the right of political participation, while their consequent non-representation was in turn used to justify the need to maintain the supremacy of the authority and power of the imperial Crown in the colonial polity. Thus race and imperialism went hand-in-hand with the preservation of white political domination in the colonial society.'

The British government accepted the dominant political influence of the planters within a colonial state structure in which the imperial Crown, as represented by the governor, remained the supreme authority. The periodic local struggles between the planters and colonial administrators were resolved (except in Barbados where the planters felt most secure) in the form of Crown colony rule. This occurred most dramatically in Jamaica after the Morant Bay rebellion when the planters settled for a strong government that would maintain white rule in their interests. The British, rather than extending political participation to the former slaves and their descendants, whom they deemed unfit for representative government, curtailed the elective principle by replacing the old assemblies with autocratic regimes in which the planter class continued to have political influence through its membership of the councils. Though the elective principle was reintroduced subsequently in some West

Indian colonies, the franchise remained extremely narrow, as it had remained in Barbados, until the great outbreak of labour rebellions in the 1930s ushered in the modern political era of democratic reforms and independence. Crown colony status, therefore, was a way to keep political power out of the hands of the freed slaves, indentured labourers and their descendants, 'the better to guarantee the survival of the plantation system' (Foner 1983: 29), and it worked for over a century after slavery was abolished.

Social structures and the culture of resistance

Rather than trying to define the former slaves as if they were undifferentiated, we should recognise the wide variety of their attitudes, aspirations and activities. They varied a great deal, by age and gender, whether they were Creole or African-born, by their skills and work experience, religious affiliation and status in the community, and in all the different Caribbean colonies. Hence, no single response was characteristic of the newly freed slaves and their descendants, or the various indentured workers and their descendants. In part, the variety of their responses resulted from the wide variety of peoples and cultures that constituted the British Caribbean after Emancipation, but it was also because of variations in the social structures of the colonies and of communities within each of the colonies. The complex interrelation of class, race and status, along with gender and cultural pluralism, in various mixtures, has made diversity itself a common characteristic of Caribbean societies.

In one of the most influential models of Caribbean societies, M.G. Smith has emphasised that culture, race and class define the British West Indies as plural societies (Smith 1965, 1984, 1991). He classified the Creole societies of the non–Hispanic Caribbean in three groups: first, the miniscule units such as Carriacou and the Cayman Islands, where the people are either entirely of African descent or mixtures of blacks and whites, are socially more or less homogeneous and are less hierarchically stratified than in societies in the second category; second, the larger societies, such as Barbados and Jamaica, which are 'modally biracial', and make cultural and hierarchic distinctions of race and colour between their black, white and mixed peoples; and third, the multiracial and segmental societies, including Belize, Guyana and Trinidad, where there are other major ethnic groups in addition to the hierarchic Creole segments that resemble the societies of the second type. 'Besides their differences of plural structure and social composition, Creole Caribbean societies differ also in area, population size, density and structure, in their metropolitan affiliations, location, climate, terrain, language and dominant religion, and in their histories of slavery, colonial rule and plantation agriculture" (Smith 1991: 12). These differences are related to differences in the politics of these societies, even between those that Smith assigned to the same type in his threefold classification. Thus, for example, the differences in the politicisation of ethnicity between Belize and Guyana are greater than Smith's plural society model leads us to expect (Bolland 1997a: 259-313). Ironically, while Smith, an anthropologist from Jamaica where class distinctions are prominent, emphasised cultural pluralism, it was Lloyd Braithwaite, a sociologist from the more pluralistic society of Trinidad, who emphasised class stratification in Caribbean societies (Braithwaite 1975). Braithwaite argued that Smith's plural society thesis overemphasised sectional cultural differences and that, despite differences of class and racial identity, there are some common social values that integrate these societies, at least to a greater degree than Smith acknowledged.

Raymond Smith, in a detailed study of kinship in Jamaica and Guyana, points to the importance of the urban–rural distinction in addition to the dimensions of race and class (Smith 1988: 11). Within societies that vary according to the characteristics and relations between class and race, and the degree of urbanisation, there are differences between kinds of community. Consequently, culture and behaviour vary significantly not only between, say, Jamaica and Guyana, but also between rural Guyanese communities that are either of predominantly African or Indian descent, between Jamaican communities that, though predominantly African, are rural or urban, between the working–class and middle–class members, all black, of a Jamaican urban community, and between rural Jamaican communities that are composed primarily of land-owning peasants or of plantation wage workers. The analysis of culture consequently varies according to the kind of community an ethnographer studies. For example, Diane Austin emphasises class differences in two contrasting Jamaican urban communities, in which culture is relatively uniform within each community but very different between them (Austin 1984), and Virginia Heyer Young argues that in rural Vincentian communities, 'The gamut of European and African values characteristic of West Indian culture is itself a bridge between different economic statuses' (Young 1993: 91).

The existence of such varieties of social structure and culture make generalisations about political culture and behaviour hazardous. Nevertheless, we must remember that none of these examples constitutes a separate unit, as if it were a closed system. On the contrary, they all exist in relation to each other and the much wider whole of which they are parts, so some overarching generalisations are not merely possible, but are essential in order to comprehend the political dynamics of the British Caribbean during emancipation.

In order to understand the varied responses of the former slaves, indentured workers and their descendants in the period of emancipation, we must examine the politics of everyday practice as well as the major disturbances and rebellions, not only because they are related but also because they show different aspects of a range of responses that together constitutes their culture of resistance. This culture of resistance, created during and after slavery and indentureship, provided a basis for the great labour rebellions that broke out in the 1930s. Hard though it is to define this culture of resistance, it should be understood that it is one of the most important and defining long continuities between the Caribbean past and present.

The working people of the British Caribbean, as peasants, indentured workers and wage-earning proletarians, resisted their oppression in dozens of strikes and disturbances after 1838. Strikes began in Jamaica in 1838 and became violent in 1839, and by 1848 the crisis exploded and led the executive 'to intervene to forestall a class war' (Wilmot 1993: 53). Some former slaves were concerned that 1 August, the tenth anniversary of their full freedom, was 'the day the whites would choose to re-enslave the blacks' (Heuman 1994: 39). Others were angered by high taxes, low wages and their treatment by overseers on the plantations. When planters, faced by the loss of protection for sugar produced in the British colonies, tried to depress wages, many former slaves thought this was 'a first step toward the reintroduction of slavery' (Heuman 1994: 39). Some planters were, in fact, denouncing the British government and were raising the possibility of annexation by the United States, which would bring the benefit – from their point of view – of reimposing slavery in Jamaica. The governor, Charles Grey, thought it necessary not only to send a warship and members of the West India Regiment to the areas where unrest threatened, but also to issue a proclamation declaring there was no intention of revoking Emancipation. 'While there was no general outbreak, there were localised protests in various parts of the island' (Heuman 1994: 40), in Black River, St Elizabeth, in Clarendon, in Brown's Town, St Ann, where two people were killed, in St Thomas in the Vale, and there was a major outbreak on Goshen estate in St Mary in August. The chief issue in the Goshen disturbances was high tax assessments. The tax-collecting constable was attacked and wounded by a crowd of at least 200 people, and when the police returned a week later to arrest people involved in that event they were confronted by 500 armed men and women. Some police were seriously wounded and all fled, other police 'met the same fate the following week, and it took the 2nd West India Regiment to restore order' (Heuman 1994: 41).

These disturbances not only show that the former slaves were concerned and angry about several problems, but also that their protests were determined and often persistent. Gad Heuman concludes that 'The 1831 rebellion as well as the Haitian revolution continued to serve as models of protest' (1994: 40), and that these post-Emancipation protests were part of a long tradition of resistance that led to the Morant Bay rebellion. This tradition of resistance was manifest in many ways, but the clearest evidence is in the dramatic unrest among former slaves and indentured workers in the form of riots and rebellions, four of which will be briefly examined: the Angel Gabriel riots in Guyana in 1856, the Morant Bay rebellion in Jamaica in 1865, the Federation riots in Barbados in 1876 and the Hosein massacre in Trinidad in 1884.[16]

Guyana

In Guyana the former slaves became increasingly frustrated by the efforts made to deny them land, to undermine their free villages and to reduce their wages. The plantation workers won their strike in 1842 but lost in 1847-8 when they again tried to stop the planters reducing their wages. Indentured immigrants continued to be brought into Guyana, including 23,301 Portuguese from Madeira and 22,355 Indians between 1841 and 1855 (Moore 1987: 273); wages declined and many former slaves found they could not sustain their families on small subsistence plots. In February 1856, John Sayers Orr, a coloured preacher from Georgetown who became known as the Angel Gabriel, aroused the former slaves. According to Governor Philip Wodehouse, Orr's preaching skilfully blended together 'political and religious subjects in a manner calculated to arouse the passions of the Black and Coloured Population against the Portuguese Immigrants'.[17] Rioting began on 16 February, then spread rapidly from Georgetown through Demerara and parts of Essequibo and Berbice after 18 February, when Orr was jailed for unlawful assembly. Within a few days virtually every Portuguese shop had been looted and the police who tried to intervene were attacked with bottles and stones. Men, women and children participated, but Wodehouse said the women in particular took 'a most active part in the Riots' throughout the colony. The governor presumed the existence of a conspiracy, rapidly deployed troops of the 2nd West India Regiment (who, like the rioters, were black) and called for help from Barbados and the neighbouring Dutch and French Guianas. The old militia regulations, in abeyance since 1839, were revived, and hundreds of white and 'reliable' coloured special constables were sworn in to help restore order. Hundreds of people were jailed, tried and convicted. Over 100 people, defined as ringleaders, were sentenced to jail terms of between one and three years with hard labour, often with fines and flogging. Orr received three years with hard labour. Another 600 prisoners were pardoned, conditional on their concluding six months' work for each month's sentence on designated estates, to the planters' satisfaction.

Though the rioters mostly plundered food from the shops, indicating that they were hungry and unable to afford the prices charged, the colonial administration did nothing to ease their plight. On the contrary, ordinances were passed to strengthen the police force and local courts, to define vagrants to mean virtually anyone who did not work on the estates, and to 'put all the onus of observing labour contracts on the labourers' (Craton 1997: 330). This, like the court sentences, clearly reveals the planter bias in Guyana. When a local tribunal agreed to the payment of £53,000 compensation to the Portuguese, more than the colony's annual budget, a petition signed by 18,000 people objected to the fact this would be paid for by a poll tax which would press most heavily on the poorest people. The riots solved nothing because prices remained high,

> both on account of high taxation and the excessive profiteering of the Portuguese traders. When in 1862 this was combined with a general economic recession occasioned by low sugar prices, resulting, in turn, in reduced plantation wages and increased unemployment, the economic plight of the Creoles became virtually insufferable. As before (and not without good reason), the Portuguese were held accountable and the Creoles petitioned for their repatriation to Madeira, and threatened to attack their shops again. (Moore 1987: 151)

The Creoles or Afro-Guyanese despised the Portuguese, whom they saw as profiteering and dominating the retail trade at their expense. Racial feelings combined with the poor economic conditions, which were fostered by low wages and high taxation as well as high prices, and resulted in violence. Despite the intensity of the racial factor, however, it was primarily Portuguese property that the rioters attacked. In similar circumstances, other riots against Portuguese traders occurred in 1889 and 1891 (Moore 1987: 152), further heightening tension between people of Portuguese and African origin in Guyana.

Jamaica

In Jamaica the economic collapse of the late 1840s was followed by a succession of floods and droughts, and about 30,000 people died in a cholera epidemic in 1850-1. Major riots occurred in Falmouth and Savanna-la-Mar in 1859. The civil war in the United States worsened Jamaica's depression and raised the prices of imports, so social tensions in the island continued to mount in the early 1860s. There were conflicts over many issues, including access to land, which was scarce for peasant farmers because of tightened policies about squatting and formal land titles, while the price of Crown land was high and many bankrupt estates were bought up to be converted into cattle pens by middle-class Jamaicans. The Great Revival of 1860-1 heightened tensions between the white and anglicised Jamaicans, on the one hand, and those whose culture remained profoundly infuenced by African beliefs and practices, on the other. The old alliance between the missionaries and former slaves, which used to cut across this division, was weakened after the revival turned African and the former were increasingly seen as part of white Jamaica (Curtin 1970: 172). Religion was 'highly politicized' in Jamaica in the 1860s, and the Native Baptists, in particular, 'provided a structure around which resistance could develop' (Heuman 1994: 87). People were also angry about 'the one-sided administration of justice' (Heuman 1994: 183-4) because planters dominated the magistracy and the courts imposed exorbitant fees.

In addition to these economic, social and cultural issues, many Jamaicans were simply hungry. In the summer of 1864, Governor Edward Eyre toured the eastern parishes and was told by some 300 peasants that they did not have enough 'continuous and remunerating labour', that the costs of food and clothing were 'intolerable', that it was very difficult 'to obtain land to cultivate extensively', that cattle overran their provision grounds because their owners did not maintain fences, and that the roads serving their properties were in 'the most deplorable condition' (Holt 1992: 272-3). These impressively specific petitions and protests reached an English Baptist minister, Dr Edward B. Underhill, who wrote a strong letter to the Colonial Office in which he linked the grim conditions on the island to the government's misguided and failed policies. Underhill's letter was widely debated in the press and a series of public meetings throughout Jamaica. The reply, written by Henry Taylor, but sent over the colonial secretary's signature and known as the 'Queen's Advice', was read from pulpits and 50,000 copies were distributed throughout the island. This callous response was not only evidence of the bankruptcy of government policy but it also, unintentionally, further provoked the petitioners. The 'Advice' urged poor Jamaicans to work hard and be thrifty, saying,

> that the prosperity of the Labouring Classes, as well as that of other Classes, depends in Jamaica, and in other Countries, upon their working for Wages, not uncertainly and capriciously, but steadily and continuously, at the times when their labour is wanted, and for so long as it is wanted; and that if they would use this industry, and thereby render the Plantations productive, they would enable the Planters to pay them higher Wages for the same hours of work than are received by the best Field Labourers in this Country; and as the cost of the necessaries of life is much less in Jamaica than it is here, they would be enabled, by adding prudence to industry, to lay by an ample provision for seasons of drought and dearth; and ... that it is from their own industry and prudence, in availing themselves of the means of prospering that are before them, and not from any such schemes as have been suggested to them, that they must look for an improvement in their condition; and that Her Majesty will regard with interest and satisfaction their advancement through their own merits and efforts.[18]

This Advice was not only in error - the cost of living was actually between 30-50 per cent higher in Jamaica than in Great Britain (Curtin 1954) - but it also completely missed the chief point of the petitioners: that sufficient wage labour was not regularly available and that they could not save for seasons of drought because they were too poor. The Advice, typically, blamed the victims for not working steadily and continuously when their labour was wanted, but the petitioners' point was precisely that their labour was not wanted steadily and continuously. And to ask starving people to save was to rub salt in their wounds.

What lay behind this insulting Advice was a set of capitalist convictions and racist prejudices. In place of a constructive policy, the Advice urged people who were presumed to be congenitally lazy to work hard for the planters, at their convenience, and to save against a wageless and rainless day. The Colonial Office failed to face the fact that the sugar estates, which were the chief employers of labour, could not provide sufficient regular work at decent wages, and that the alternative was to make land available to the people who wanted to work it. This was what the petitioners had demanded. One of the men who participated in the protest meetings held in September and October 1865 compared the level of wages with slavery: 'Why cause me to hold this meeting; myself was born free, but my mother and father was slave; but now I am still a slave by working from days to days. I cannot get money to feed my family, and I working at Coley estate for 35 chains for 1s., and after five days' working I get 2s. 6d. for my family. Is that able to sustain a house full of family?' (Quoted in Heuman 1994: 184)

In Jamaica in 1865 the central issue was not a simple matter of either wages or of land. Rather, 'the central issue was access to land as a means of resisting the necessity to work on the estates' (Bakan 1990: 88) on the planters' terms. Four months after the Queen's Advice, a major rebellion erupted in St Thomas-in-the-East.

Paul Bogle, a peasant farmer and Native Baptist deacon of the village of Stony Gut in St Thomas, was organising resistance before 1865. In a district where there were many sugar estates and thousands of land-hungry former slaves, wages and land were important, but another of the chief issues was the local judiciary which enforced the entrenched rule of the planter class. In 1864, only two of the 256 cases handled by the magistrates were against planters, while the defendants in 250 of the cases were black workers or peasants. In fact, 24 of the 28 magistrates in St Thomas were members of the planter class and the one neutral magistrate in the parish was removed in September 1865 (Heuman 1994: 68). Not surprisingly, the poor workers and peasants 'no longer had faith in the justice of magisterial courts' (Curtin 1970: 194). Bogle organised and directed an alternative court in 1863 in the area of Serge Island, in the centre of St Thomas. Bogle's court, which was probably linked with his church community, 'issued summonses, tried cases, and levied fines. It involved a completely parallel judicial and police system' (Holt 1992: 289), as did the Maroon communities of Moore Town and Scotts Hall in the nearby Blue Mountains. The chapel at Stony Gut was opened in 1864 and in March 1865 Bogle was ordained deacon by George William Gordon, a coloured planter who had been born a slave but was freed by his father. Gordon became a successful merchant and land-owner, and was elected to the Assembly in 1844. He became converted to the Baptist faith in 1861, participated in the Great Revival, and had his own Native Baptist chapel in Kingston. As representative of St Thomas, where Bogle was his political agent, Gordon was a prominent champion of the poor and, consequently, a political enemy of Governor Eyre (Heuman 1981, 1994).

Stony Gut, like most other Jamaican peasant villages, was near to and interactive with the estates, but the activities of Bogle's court and chapel suggest that the villagers wanted greater autonomy to run their own lives. The Native Baptist churches, though not overtly political, clearly provided a focus for the community and 'a vehicle for cultural resistance, giving moral authority to an alternative world-view' (Holt 1992: 291). This culture of resistance traced its roots back through the great slave rebellion of 1831 to eighteenth-century Myalism and African religious traditions (Schuler 1980: 32-3). The relationship of Bogle and Gordon, and their struggle for social justice for the people of Stony Gut and St Thomas, was shaped by the millennial world-view of their religion.

On 7 October 1865, a market day, a large crowd gathered at Morant Bay courthouse. People were agitated about the rents they had to pay and some felt that 'the land was given to them free, some years ago' (quoted in Heuman 1994: 5); they had come to hear a case in which a small settler, accused of trespass on land near Stony Gut, had been fined 20 shillings. Though it is clear that Bogle and his fellow villagers had prepared for trouble, what transpired may have been largely spontaneous and unplanned. A black spectator in the court urged a boy, who had been found guilty of assault and fined 4 shillings, not to pay the costs, amounting to 12 shillings and 6 pence. When the police attempted to seize him for disrupting the trial, the crowd protected him and beat the police, thereby demonstrating their 'growing impatience with and disdain for the system of law and justice in the parish' (Holt 1992: 295). Three days after this minor incident, police sent to Stony Gut to arrest Bogle and others for disrupting the court were overpowered and threatened by several hundred men armed with cutlasses and sticks. Bogle complained to the governor that they had been forced to resist an outrageous assault committed against them by the police, but the local custos, Baron von Ketelhodt, called out the volunteers and asked the governor to send troops. On 11 October, several hundred crudely armed women and men marched to the sound of drums, cow horns and conch shells from Stony Gut to Morant Bay where the hated vestry was meeting in the courthouse. They sacked the police station, looking for arms, and then converged on the courthouse. Thirty-two militiamen fired on the crowd, killing seven people in the first volley, but the people rushed them. Some were beaten and others retreated into the courthouse. The troops continued to fire on the rebels, who, after about two hours, set fire to the courthouse and burned it down. In all, the rebels killed about 18 militiamen and civilians, including the baron and several unpopular magistrates, planters and estate managers. The rebels released 51 prisoners from the jail and, over the following three days, spread the rebellion to many towns and estates to the north and east of Morant Bay. The affair started as a local protest against the police and magistracy, but the social conditions prevalent in Jamaica were leading it to develop rapidly into a more widespread peasant rebellion, though 'there was no proof of an island-wide conspiracy' (Heuman 1994: 185).

The Morant Bay rebellion did not develop into an islandwide peasant war, however, because the retribution was swift, merciless and overwhelming. The disturbances had not spread so far, but all the same martial law was declared in the entire eastern third of the island and the militia, joined by British troops and naval forces and the Maroons of Moore Town, fell on the rebels - and also on many people who surely had not been involved. By the final tallies, almost 500 women and men were killed, about 600 were publicly flogged (some with whips made of twisted and knotted wires) and over 1,000 houses were burned. Among those summarily tried and hanged were Bogle and Gordon, the latter having been captured in Kingston, where he had been throughout the rebellion, and transported to Morant Bay so he could be tried by court martial. The purpose of these officially condoned atrocities was to strike terror into poor Jamaicans and to exact vengeance for those prominent citizens who had been killed on 11 October. The extent and ferocity of the suppression shows, in Gad Heuman's words, 'that the government was intent on establishing its authority and on stifling black political expression of any kind' (1994: 143).

Although there was a debate in Great Britain about Eyre's excesses, and a commission of enquiry was duly instituted, the rebellion was generally taken as evidence of the need for greater British control over Jamaica. The roots of the rebellion lay in social and economic conditions concerning prices, taxes, access to land, work and wages, and the local judiciary system, but the outcome was merely a constitutional change that did not address these issues. The Crown colony government that commenced in 1866 put government entirely beyond the reach of the black majority.[19] An extremely limited franchise was gradually reinstated after 1884, but 'land policy, laws and magistracy were not substantially changed in the nineteenth century' (Craton 1997: 336), so the planter hegemony remained essentially intact into the twentieth century.

Barbados

Barbados, unlike Guyana and Jamaica, was generally quite peaceful in the period between the slave revolt of 1816 and the Federation riots, or confederation rebellion, of 1876. This was not because of an absence of suffering and injustice, however. As we have seen, the planters retained even tighter economic and political control in Barbados than in Guyana and Jamaica, severely limiting alternatives to wage labour on the estates for the former slaves. The economy remained heavily dependent on sugar production, with land monopolised by the planters, so when sugar prices continued to fall after 1856 as the beet industry contributed an increasing share of the world's sugar supply, Barbadians suffered great hardships. Wages were extremely low and the cost of food was rising, yet workers could not secure more land on which to grow provisions. Field workers received only 8 pence per day in wages, and generally only in the six months of the crop season, but rice cost 3 pence per pound, bread 3 pence per pound, beef 10 pence per pound, sugar 7 pence per pound, cheese 1 shilling and 6 pence per pound, and milk 1 shilling and 4 pence per gallon (Belle 1984: 3). Thousands of Barbadians migrated overseas, some temporarily but many permanently, in what became a persistent search for better opportunities, as small farmers or traders, policemen or domestic servants. Between 1873 and 1876 over 5,000 Barbadians emigrated, 71 per cent of them men (Belle 1984: 4).

In the 1860s and 1870s sporadic rioting and looting occurred and the governors and planters feared a more general rebellion. The Assembly voted considerable sums of money to religious and moral education programmes to dissuade the poor people from violence. 'Where such moral training failed, the Colonial Office recommended the substitution of penal sentences' (Levy 1980: 137). By the 1870s, although many planters and merchants were threatened with bankruptcy, they still clung to their social and political dominance. The white planters and their merchant bankers presented a united front to deny a share of power even to those few people of colour who had some land and capital. The population increased from 101,000 in 1838 to 162,000 in 1874, despite cholera epidemics and emigration, and many of the blacks, who were two-thirds of this population, remained in persistent poverty. 'At the best times wages were close to subsistence, and in times of depression or drought destitution was common and starvation not unknown' (Craton 1997: 339). Not surprisingly, canefield arson increased, from 68 fires in 1873, to 116 in 1874 and 141 in 1875, and in the month before the 1876 riots, 152 persons were charged with stealing food, compared with 75 charged for all other offences (Craton 1997: 339, 500). By 1876, then, conditions were desperate for many Barbadians and they were not as passive as the planters would have liked.

The immediate provocation of the riots concerned heated debates about the colony's constitutional status. The Colonial Office was trying to create a union between the Windward Islands and Barbados, with a Crown colony government. The administration of the Leeward Islands had already been centralized in 1871, and in 1875 John Pope Hennessey was appointed governor of Barbados with the duty of implementing the imperial government's policy. The Barbados Assembly, jealous of its powers and privileges, resisted the proposed change. The anti-confederate defenders of the status quo organised the Barbados Defence Association (BDA) and mounted an islandwide campaign against Hennessey and the imperial policy he represented. Hennessey, who not only argued for federation but also spoke out against the low level of wages, the high taxes on ordinary people, the lack of social services and the Bridgetown jail that was like a dungeon, was seen by many poor black Barbadians as on their side. Many blacks 'saw no practical advantage in a federation' but felt that if the white oligarchy was against it and the governor was for it, then it was probably good (Craton 1997: 340). As some rallied behind the Governor, others were urged by members of the black and coloured middle classes to support the BDA. For the first time, then, 'blacks found themselves at the centre of ruling-class conflict' (Beckles 1990: 123).

Violence broke out on 28 March 1876, when white members of the BDA, holding a meeting at Mount Prospect in St Peter's, were stoned by the audience. A black worker, Moses Boyce, was shot and several other people injured in the fracas. The secretary of state for the colonies, fearing a rebellion, instructed Hennessey to make it clear that a federation would not be forced on Barbados and that he was to prevent further excitement among the blacks (Levy 1980: 153). As the debate about federation continued, however, the situation provided an opportunity for poor people to mobilise and express their anger over their conditions. Between 17 and 26 April bands of black workers marched behind flags and conch shells, destroyed plantation property and looted food from ships, stores and estate provision grounds. Rioters designated at least two of their leaders as general and colonel, which suggests that they were organising themselves and not merely being used by the confederationists. George Belle, who calls the event an 'abortive revolution', avers, 'the disturbances were not spontaneous; organization, planning and coordination are quite apparent in the way in which the rebels went about their business' (Belle 1984: 13). Most probably, as in the Morant Bay rebellion, there was a mixture of organisation and spontaneous response, but the people's courage cannot be doubted. Police and armed whites were defied by people armed only with sticks, stones and agricultural tools, but the rebels killed nobody. Governor Hennessey mobilised troops on 21 April and authorised the swearing-in of hundreds of special constables to restore order. The most intense fighting occurred on April 21 and 22, and the rebellion was suppressed within a week, leaving seven or eight black people dead, eight police and at least 25 other people wounded, and 450 people taken prisoner. This was 'the nearest post-slavery Barbados has ever come to revolution' (Belle 1984: 13). Compared with Jamaica in 1865, the rebels were treated with leniency, but the outcome was that the Barbadian oligarchy used the riots as a pretext to retain their political as well as socioeconomic dominance.

Though a franchise act in 1884 reduced the property qualification somewhat, it remained beyond the reach of the vast black majority, and in 1900 there were still fewer than 2,000 registered voters (Beckles 1990: 126). Crown colony government was never imposed and the Barbados Assembly remained a vehicle of the white oligarchy's power until the mid-twentieth century.

Trinidad

The nature of the disturbance in Trinidad, like those in Guyana, Jamaica and Barbados, was shaped by the social and cultural composition of that colony. Alhough the event in 1884 is generally referred to as the Hosein riots, the people's resistance to oppression was actually orderly, and the violence that occurred was really in the nature of a massacre (K. Singh 1988). The elite's paranoia about the 'aliens' often took the form of fear of their popular entertainment, particularly mass public displays that involved drumming, dancing and great excitement. Shango and Rada religious gatherings and carnival bands suffered persecution at the hands of the authorities. Carnival was a popular Creole street festival that developed out of a synthesis of elements of African and French masked pageants. It became an important cultural expression when poor black people in Port of Spain in the 1860s and 1870s organised into bands based on their barrack yards. When police tried to suppress them they rioted, in 1881, 1883 and 1884 (Trotman 1986: 270). The Creole working people of Trinidad resented the police, who were predominantly Barbadian, interfering with their cultural traditions.

The elite also considered the Indians' Hosein festival to be potentially dangerous. Originally the Shi'ite Muslim celebration of Muharram commemorating the deaths of Mohammed's grandsons, Hassan and Hussein, the Hosein or Hosay festival, as it came to be known in Trinidad, had lost some of its particular religious meaning and most of the celebrants were Hindu. Hosein became a general Indian holiday, in which all Indians joined to remember their 'old country', but there was also some rivalry and competition between workers from different estates and communities. By the 1870s, some working–class Creoles were joining in. Social tensions increased in the early 1880s because of police action against carnival and because wages were being reduced and tasks increased on the estates. The number of strikes increased from seven in 1882 and six in 1883 to 12 in 1884 (Look Lai 1993: 146).

When regulations were introduced in 1884 to prevent Indians from processing along any public highway and excluding the celebration of Hosein from Port of Spain and San Fernando, the discontent mounted. Street processions in which the celebrants carried model mausoleums called tazias, or tadjahs in Trinidad, were the culmination of the ten-day festival, accompanied by chanting, drumming and mock combat, which occasionally turned serious, as each group carrying a tazia vied for precedence. The climax came when over 100 tazias were thrown into the sea from a jetty in San Fernando. Apart from two fatalities, one in Chaguanas in 1865 and one in San Fernando in 1881, the Hosein festivals passed without any serious disorder, but by 1884 the elite was paranoid about the increasing social unrest (K. Singh 1988: 6-8).

In 1882 the San Fernando Gazette implied there was a link between unrest on the plantations and the Hosein festival, and called for a strong police presence to enforce discipline (K. Singh 1988: 11). In January 1884 the Port of Spain Gazette carried an even more alarmist editorial, suggesting that non-Indians – that is, Creoles of African descent – might join the Indians in attacking the police. The chief cause of unrest was the crisis in the sugar industry, yet this paper, in August 1884, supported a reduction in the wages paid to plantation workers. On 13 September the Port of Spain Gazette, responding to the deteriorating situation on the estates, urged restrictions of the Hosein festival (K. Singh 1988: 13-14). Moreover, once restrictions had been placed on carnival, the authorities feared that Creole Trinidadians would be angry if the Hosein festivals were left unrestricted.

When the government passed an ordinance to regulate the processions a group of 32 Indians protested. The government responded by saying that the strictly religious aspects were not being interfered with and, in any case, as it was a Muslim festival, the Hindus should have no part in it (K. Singh 1988: 17). This crude attempt to divide the participants from each other on a religious basis defied the fact that Hosein had become a unifying social event. Both sides made their preparations: the Indians meant to enter the towns in defiance of the ban, while the police, backed by marines and a volunteer force, planned to keep them out. Some Indians may have thought they could be fined or imprisoned if they persisted, and others may have prepared to resist if they were stopped, but few could have expected what happened, which was a brutal display of police force.

On 30 October, at two separate entrances to San Fernando, the police fired on peaceful processions at close range. Over 100 people were wounded and at least 16 people died of their injuries. The San Fernando Gazette commented that this massacre was 'brought on by the unjustifiable defiance of the Government by the coolies . . . . Their miscarriage was that they did not expect to be fired at' (quoted in K. Singh 1988: 23). The Port of Spain Gazette, equally callously, expressed the hope that 'this lesson may have a salutary effect not only on coolies but also on the heterogeneous collections of loafers, prostitutes, roughs, rogues and vagabonds which infest our two towns' (quoted in K. Singh 1988: 24).

Although unrest and strikes had increased on the estates before the festival, and the Indians' persistence in defying the government's ban was a clear act of resistance, there was no evidence of any violence, or expectation of a riot, during the procession until the police fired. At an official enquiry, two Presbyterian missionaries referred to the processions as riots and agreed that the government had to be firm in putting them down, but this simply exposed their prejudice. The sole commissioner of the official enquiry, Sir Henry Norman, governor of Jamaica, contended that 'the Indian immigrants looked upon the processions as a sort of means of demonstrating their power', which may have been true in a symbolic sense but which cannot justify the massacre (K. Singh 1988: 145). Nevertheless, Norman vindicated the action of the colonial authorities and advised that at least one company of British infantry should be kept in Trinidad to back the police.

The government continued in subsequent years to enforce rigidly its regulations against processions and thereby succeeded in preventing the urban Creoles from further participation in the Hosein festival (Brereton 1979: 184). The festival survived in St James, a largely Indian suburb of Port of Spain (K. Singh 1988: 30-1), but remained outlawed in San Fernando and Port of Spain itself. The potential for the Hosein festival to become an event linking not only Muslim and Hindu, but also Indian and Creole, rural and urban Trinidadians, was destroyed in the massacre of 1884 and the subsequent repression. The massacre exposed the lengths to which the colonial authorities were prepared to go to maintain hegemony and, as was intended, it helped to sustain the lines of demarcation between race, culture, class and place of residence that divided the working people and thereby facilitated colonial rule.

Struggles for freedom

Each of these disturbances reveals a different aspect of social tension and unrest, particular to the circumstances of each society, but they overlap in crucial respects. In Guyana the riots were directed largely against Portuguese shopkeepers who had come to be seen as exploiters; in Jamaica the rebellion was by small farmers and rural workers who wanted land and resented the injustices of the local magistracy; in Barbados the poor plantation workers drew attention to their basic needs as the ruling regime debated constitutional issues; and in Trinidad Indian people who defied an official ban on their popular street processions were shot down by the police. On the one hand, each event shows the frustration and determination of the working people in these, the four major colonies of the British Caribbean, as they struggled against the hegemony of the planter class and the colonial authorities. On the other hand, the colonial elite and the authorities showed their willingness to kill people, not just rioters but also non-violent demonstrators and even uninvolved bystanders, in order to demonstrate the omnipotence of imperial power and to intimidate the rest of the people.

In all these events, the 'governors invariably aligned themselves with plantocracies in the cause of law and order, and the imperial authories automatically endorsed the activities of local regimes in suppressing disorder' (Craton 1997: 346). The suppression of the Morant Bay rebellion, in particular, was as massive and brutal as if Jamaica had still been a slave society. These events show that the politics of freedom continued for decades after 1838, involving new immigrants and generations in the emancipation process, and that economic, social and cultural issues were generally closely interrelated with politics. The evidence of these events supports the view that 'The struggle for cultural hegemony in the nineteenth century therefore depended less on the socializing agencies of church and school to win consent and more on the coercive arms of the state to enforce compliance' (Trotman 1986: 270). It was precisely the failure to achieve consensus in these colonial societies that required the state to use such force. On the one hand, the chief concern of the government was to avoid further disturbances, yet the government's brutality and authoritarianism promoted unrest. On the other, despite the popular unrest, and in some cases even prompted by it, the colonial governments remained authoritarian. Trinidad and Guyana retained autocratic Crown colony governments, and Jamaica, Belize and the Leeward and Windward Islands abandoned their local representative assemblies in favour of the Crown colony system. The Bahamas and Barbados retained the old oligarchic regimes, as did Guyana until it became a Crown colony in 1928, largely because they felt the most secure.

Whatever the constitutional form, however, the planters and merchants, the most prominent of whom were still mostly whites, were everywhere influential and often completely dominant in the colonies' institutional political life. The possibility that politics would become more democratised after 1838 was remote, of course, given the continuity of the plantocracy's economic power and the racism of the imperial government, and by the 1860s and 1870s it had receded beyond the century's horizon. One consequence was that 'protest has been an enduring feature of the Caribbean peoples as they struggled to free themselves from oppressive regimes' (Beckles and Shepherd 1993: 169), and because they were excluded from the institutionalised political system their struggle most often was in terms of everyday practice.

The everyday struggle took place chiefly within the labour process, and Walter Rodney reminds us not to oversimplify distinctions between people's responses:

> Each day in the life of a member of the working population was a day on which there was both struggle and accomodation. Struggle was implicit in the application of labor power to earn wages or to grow crops, while accommoda-

tion was a necessary aspect of survival within a system in which power was so comprehensively monopolized by the planter class. Some persons resisted more tenaciously and consistently than others; but there was no simple distinction between those who resisted and those who accomodated. (Rodney 1981: 151)

In studying this dialectic of domination and resistance in the period of emancipation, it is appropriate to focus attention again on the politics of the labour process, and on the related issues of the control of land and the state, which was the central issue of that dialectic.

In the transition from slavery to wage labour, the degree to which the former slaves were able to acquire and retain access to land was important, not only in affecting whether they would offer their labour power to the plantations, but also in affecting the prevailing wage rates. For many plantation workers, who experienced only seasonal employment, their access to the means of subsistence was often crucial to survival. In their search for employment and the means of subsistence, former slaves and indentured workers and their descendants moved in ever expanding circles, first temporarily and then permanently, to neighbouring estates and provision grounds, to more remote villages and lands in the hills or the interior, to other colonies or countries in the Caribbean and Central America, until, in the twentieth century, the perimeters of migration had extended to the metropolitan centres of Europe and North America - what Louise Bennett calls 'colonizin' in reverse' (Bennett 1966: 179–80).

The ability of former slaves to undertake this search for the means of subsistence was, of course, one of the chief consequences of their legal Emancipation, but their desire to undertake the search was frequently fostered by the continuing attempts of their former masters to coerce them into plantation labour. Moreover, as seen from their viewpoint, 'their own-account activities were as important as coerced labour in defining their status, their humanity and their notions of freedom' (Marshall 1988: 38). So, while we should evaluate the economic options of the former slaves, including their ability to choose employment, to move in search of work, to rise in the occupational scale, to bargain for better wages and working conditions and to have more autonomy at the workplace, we must not neglect the non-economic aspects of their freedom. In other words, when we ask the question how free the ex-slave was, we must not, like former masters, think of him or her only as a labourer. The issues of working conditions and autonomy at the workplace are not economic issues, narrowly defined, because they are inseparable from questions about respect and dignity. For many of the former slaves the labour process was to be, unavoidably, the focal point of their everyday struggles for freedom, but there is abundant evidence that freedom meant more for them than simply the freedom to sell or to withhold their own labour power in the marketplace. Moreover, as Rodney reminds us, individuals may have accommodated at some times in order to resist at others, or accommodated over some issues in order to be able to resist over others. When we examine the wide range of responses, and the complexity of the emancipation people were trying to achieve, we should avoid making simplistic judgements that divide people into categories such as accommodators or resisters.

Rodney suggests that 'Over the course of the nineteenth century Creole labourers had developed a conception of themselves that was incompatible with an increasing number of estate jobs and, ultimately, with field labor as a whole ... given the terms on which estate labor was organized' (Rodney 1981: 162, emphasis in original). If we take as given the place of the plantation within the world economy, and the racist and authoritarian ideologies and institutions of the colonial polities, then these terms on which estate labour was organised in the nineteenth-century Caribbean were pretty much inevitable. The features of a plantation system (which include monocrop production for export, strong monopolistic tendencies, a rigid system of social stratification which includes a high correlation between racial and class hierarchies and a weak community structure) conspire to ensure that estate labour will be casual and seasonal, poorly paid, closely supervised, socially degraded and hard to organise.

As several features of the plantation system are common to both the period of slavery and those of emancipation and indenture, we should not be surprised that so many people caught in this system of domination continued to resist it. Though it took a considerable amount of time, the experience of resistance to estate labour gave rise, throughout the Caribbean, to increasing class consciousness and the creation of a range of working-class institutions, including trade unions. However, these features of the proletarianisation of West Indian workers (which will be examined in the following chapters), though key to understanding their social and political history, do not exhaust what Rodney calls their 'concept of themselves'.

Former slaves, like former slave-owners, brought a whole complex of attitudes, values, self-images, and notions of rights and entitlements out of the period of slavery. The meaning of freedom, for both the enslaved and the enslavers, was historically and dialectically interconnected with the system and experience of slavery, but in different ways, so we should not expect that the former slaves shared the dominant conception of freedom that was held by their former owners. The concept of personal freedom or autonomy, and the antithetical concept of dependence, is culturally and historically variable. The liberal concept of freedom, which has predominated in western societies at least since the nineteenth century, stresses not only the absence of human restraint on the individual but also the supposedly inherent need or desire of the individual for autonomy. This non-prescriptive meaning of freedom contrasts with prescriptive freedom, which accepts limits on personal behaviour as a consequence of acknowledging that freedom is bestowed as a gift by a superior power. In the context of this distinction, Orlando Patterson (1985: 26) draws attention to the socio-historical connection between slavery and freedom in modern western consciousness: 'Personal freedom in the liberal sense, even more than its illiberal prescriptive counterpart, requires the menace of an endangering power to be meaningful. Slavery and the dread of social death was once again that menace, both symbolically and realistically. In political terms we find a growing tendency to identify the state with slavery during the late eighteenth and nineteenth centuries'.

The identification of the state with slavery in former slave societies, in particular, is associated with the fact that, with the transition from slave to free status, the locus of authority and social control passes from an individual master to the impersonal state, and personal relations of domination are transformed into a more formally defined bureaucratic structure of domination. With this transformation in the system of domination, the former slave-owners conceived of market relations as compatible with, and even as the guarantors of, their own personal freedoms, including especially their freedom to hold and dispose of private property and to hire and fire labour power without interference. But it would be naive to assume that former slaves, given their radically different experience and place in society, shared this liberal-bourgeois concept of freedom. On the contrary, in these bipolar societies characterised by an ubiquitous class struggle, we should expect that the former slaves would seek to develop a quite different moral economy from that imposed by their former owners.

We know that many former slaves had goals and priorities that were associated with a concept of personal autonomy and, as we have seen, many of these were dialectically connected to their experiences of oppression and exploitation at the workplace. We know also that former slaves had important goals connected with their family life, with conceptions of the home and of domestic authority, with religious and cultural life and with education, and these goals were affected by, but certainly were not determined by or limited to their work situation. Rebecca Scott reminds us, even while it is appropriate to 'place particular emphasis on the search for land and for control over one's own pace of work', we should bear in mind that 'it is not simply the autonomy of the individual that is at stake, but the degree of achievement of several goals by an entire family' (Scott 1987: 576). She also points out that 'former slaves often placed goals of family and community above the assertion of simple individual autonomy .... Moreover, family welfare and individual well-being were frequently intertwined, making the concept of individual autonomy misleading.' (Scott 1988: 423)

The need to look beyond the liberal notion of freedom and its association with the political economy of the bourgeois marketplace, is apparent when we focus on the former slaves' attitude towards land. We must consider not only the economic and material importance of land to the former slaves, both as a means of subsistence and as a base from which to bargain with the former slave-owners, but also its symbolic significance. Jean Besson's historical anthropology of family land in Jamaica provides an important insight:

> Freehold land was not only of obvious economic importance to those ex-slaves who managed to obtain it, giving some independence from the plantations and a bargaining position for higher wages when working on them, but it also had considerable symbolic significance to a people who had not only once been landless, but property themselves. For such land symbolized their freedom, and provided property rights, prestige, and personhood. Family land was also the basis for the creation of family lines and the maximization of kinship ties, in contrast to the kinlessness of the enslaved. (Besson 1987: 18)

In so far as slavery involved the natal alienation of the slave and his social death through the loss of kinship ties, the transcendence of slavery must recover or re-establish such ties. Family land, then, is not valued simply as a bit of material security, however important that was, but it becomes, more significantly, a means of creating and maintaining just such a network of ties and mutual obligations as slavery had denied. For many, this network extended from past to future generations in a vast web, reinforced through 'a religious respect for the earth, for a piece of ground where the living could settle, the unborn enter, the dead could be buried, the deities could descend, and the ancestors could be venerated locally' (Stewart 1992: 197). All this implies something about the kind of moral economy the former slaves sought to create in their free society.

An ideal slave society as conceived by the masters is one in which the only meaningful relationship allowed the slave is that with his owner, a relation of total domination and subordination. This is really the very negation of sociality, in so far as slaves would be merely dehumanised tools who are socially isolated from each other and hence denied their human, social existence. The negation of this society, then, is not a liberal society of autonomous citizens, a mere aggregate of self-interested individuals pursuing their personal happiness, but rather a genuine community of people linked by kinship, friendship and other strong social ties. Family land emerged as one 'resistant response' (Mintz 1974: 132-3) to the slavery-plantation system, and as a symbol and potential core of a different kind of free society, in which the relation between personal autonomy and dependence seems to be conceived in ways that differ from those predominating in the liberal-bourgeois society.

The moral economy of many communities of African origin in the Americas suggests that for women as well as men a wide network of social relations and supports provides an important basis for independence and autonomy. In contrast to the western concept of individual autonomy and equality, which implies a shedding of social attachments, the Afro-Caribbean and black American concept of autonomy is linked to a strong sense of interpersonal connectedness - an involvement in the lives of others. (Sutton and Makiesky-Barrow 1977: 322)

Personal autonomy, rather than being defined over and against the rights of others, as in liberal-bourgeois ideology, becomes achievable only in connection with others, some of whom are living but the majority of whom are dead or as yet unborn. In this vision of a free society as a vast network of people linked by mutual ties, the principles of mutuality, cooperation and interdependence, in contrast to social hierarchy, competition and the dependency of subordinates, are deemed to be the very fabric of society itself. For the former slaves, then, the process of emancipation involved a struggle to recover or re-establish a lost birthright, usually established through kinship, that included notions of association, property and personhood that differed radically from those held by their former owners who still dominated the society, because they were linked to an alternative set of values of society.

Though slavery attempted to deny all meaningful ties between slaves and to promote individuation, there is ample evidence that cooperative and collective values and activities persisted among the slaves and were often revived in freedom, for example, in cooperative work groups, community churches and religious rituals, mutual aid societies and credit institutions, as well as family land. There is ample evidence of strong family ties, but the growth of peasantries frequently involved a tension between individualistic goals and more communitarian aspirations. For obvious reasons, however, these aspirations were rarely articulated and recorded, so 'we must infer what slaves wanted from freedom from what they did with it' (Mintz 1992: 255). We can see, for example, that the former slaves struggled for the right of women and children to withdraw from estate labour, though planters often complained bitterly about this. Bridget Brereton has argued convincingly that the withdrawal of women from such work does not mean that they sought to become bourgeois Victorian ladies in patriarchal families.

Caribbean freedwomen did not withdraw from estate labour because they, or their men, had become aspirants to European bourgeois gender norms. They did so in order to exchange hard, dangerous and degrading gang labour for work in the household, on the family farm, in marketing and in child care. One reason for the withdrawal was certainly to escape the risks of sexual and other abuses which were still inseparable from gang labour on the sugar estates, even after slavery had ended; another was to allow mothers to devote more attention to rearing their children. But ex-slave men and women were not blindly obeying hegemonic gender ideologies nor seeking to transform freedwomen into dependent housewives confined to the home. They were pursuing rational family strategies aimed at securing the survival and welfare of their kin groups, in the face of appalling odds. (Brereton 1999: 107)[20]

In short, these women were engaged in reconstructing the society in terms of their own values, including the idea that women had rights to economic independence, whether or not they were wives and mothers. Caribbean women today reject male authoritarianism and emphasise the importance of their own freedom and independence (Senior 1991: 93-7), so it is reasonable to suppose that this was part of their interpretation of the meaning of freedom after 1838.

Mintz (1992: 254) is correct in saying: 'We are unable to specify the extent to which ideas of individual productive independence on the land may have been tied to larger political and philosophical conceptions of the good, the just, or the ideal society', but we may engage in informed speculation. The abstract distinction between individualistic and communitarian ideals, so dear to western political philosophy, was perhaps irrelevant to the former slaves, who may have seen their version of individual fulfilment and happiness as perfectly compatible with, and perhaps only attainable within, close family and community life. Among our reasons to think so is the rapid emergence of the free villages in the emancipation period.

Jamaica provides the most prolific evidence of free villages after 1838, even though planter policies sought to restrict them. Actually, these oppressive policies, which were aimed at keeping the former slaves on the estates, often spurred the move to establish free villages. Under the sponsorship of the Baptists, the villages of Trelawny and St Ann's parishes, including Alps, Sligoville, Refuge, Kettering, Granville, Sturge Town and Martha Brae, 'became the vanguard of the British West Indian postemancipation village movement' (Besson 1992: 192). Other examples were established in Guyana and Trinidad, and in the mountainous islands of Dominica, Grenada and St Vincent. Besson argues (1992: 200) that family relationships, often rooted in family land, 'reflecting its continuity and identity', were a common central theme of freedom and community in resistance to the coercion of the plantation system. The interrelationship between family and land, freedom and community, led to women playing a central, but too often overlooked, role in the political culture of resistance. Women in their daily lives were engaged in a struggle for survival, centred on their houses, yards and churches, their families, networks and communities, that provided a nucleus of resistance to the dominant culture (Besson 1993).

The continuing struggle over the control of land and labour, and later of the state, was always crucial in the process of emancipation to the degree that it offered to the former slaves opportunities to gain greater control over their own lives and communities. It is in this much broader sense, and not in the narrow calculations of political economy, that we should seek the myriad ways that the former slaves gave meaning to their freedom. For the British abolitionists, the meaning of freedom appeared in the context of the rise of the liberal state and the capitalist economy. Hence, for them as for the former slave-owners and the colonial officials, 'Slavery meant subordination to the physical coercion and personal dominion of an arbitrary master; freedom meant submission only to the impersonal forces of the marketplace and to the rational and uniform constraints of law' (Holt 1982: 286). But these market forces and colonial laws in the British Caribbean in the nineteenth century helped to perpetuate the poverty and powerlessness of the ex-slaves and their descendants, and the indentured workers and their descendants, who were denied the civil rights of liberal society for over a century. This limited kind of freedom - where the former slaves and other workers were conceived primarily as free labour to be hired in free markets - was really a new form of domination, albeit one more impersonal and disguised than the naked domination of slavery. Those who had formerly been slaves, it seems, aspired to a kind of freedom that their legal emancipation appeared to promise, but that could not be achieved in the societies where they lived. Hence a central aspect of the struggle between the former slaves and slave-owners was concerned with their respective visions of a free society.

The culture of resistance developed in the Caribbean with its roots in opposition to conquest, colonialism and slavery. In the British Caribbean after 1838, the majority of the population, formerly slaves, were denied access to power in the economic and political systems which remained dominated by the planter class and the colonial authorities. Through the persistent concentration of land ownership and white control of other key economic institutions, most people were kept dependent and poor, and the exclusion of the vast majority of people from participation in the legal and political system was confirmed wherever Crown colony government was established. Caribbean people, women and men, of African and of Indian origin, resisted this system of domination and sought in their everyday practice, as well as in major disturbances and rebellions, to achieve their vision of what a truly free society should be. The odds were heavily against them but as changes took place in the dominant political economy new opportunities eventually emerged for the politics of freedom.

Notes

[1] This chapter is a substantial expansion of my paper, 'The Politics of Freedom in the British Caribbean' (1992), which was first given at a conference on 'The Meaning of Freedom' at the University of Pittsburgh in 1988.

[2] Viscount Howick to Lord John Russell, 8 Dec. 1832, CO 318/116.

[3] Henry George Grey, son of the prime minister, commented that the slaves deserved compensation as much as the slave-owners, but this was really his way of saying that the planters did not deserve too much (see Holt 1992: 29).

[4] Proceedings of the General Anti-Slavery Convention (London 1841), quoted in Green 1976: 127).

[5] PP, 1840 (212) XXXV, 43, quoted in Heuman 1994: 39.

[6] This paragraph relies heavily on Marshall 1993 (originally 1965) and Richardson 1983: 99-100.

[7] This information is from Wilmot 1993.

[8] One guilder was about 1 shilling and 5 pence.

[9] Edwin Adolphus to Gov. James R. Longden, 15 Jan. 1870, BA 92.

[10] Police Magistrate Cockburn to Longden, 24 Feb. 1870, BA 106.

[11] K.O. Laurence has noted, however, that 'the concept of permanent settlement by Indian contract labour hardly emerged before 1870. In my view it never really gained much currency as a deliberate method of solving the problem of estate labour. If it had, efforts to promote settlement would have been less trivial, for trivial is what they were . … Contract labour was sought because it was unfree, rather than because a new labour force was needed' (1985: 270).

[12] James Stephen to Lord Glenelg, 4 Oct. 1838, CO 123/54.

[13] Lord Knutsford to Gov. Sir Ambrose Shea, 19 Jan. 1888, CO 23/230.

[14] Shea to Knutsford, 22 Nov. 1888, CO 23/230.

[15] It is important to note that the term "race", contrary to popular belief, is an ideological concept, lacking biological basis or scientific validity, and is a social construction created by some people to explain themselves and their relations with others. Racism, as an ideology, has a history, of course, that is intimately linked with the process of European conquest and colonisation around the world.

[16] My summary of the first three disturbances relies heavily on Craton 1997 and Heuman 1994.

[17] Gov. Philip Wodehouse to Col. Sec., 24 Feb. 1856, CO 111/309.

[18] Edward Cardwell to Gov. Sir Edward Eyre, 14 Jun. 1865, CO 137/391, quoted in Curtin 1970: 119.

[19] In 1866, Frederick Douglass had faith, however misplaced, in the ability of the US constitution and federal government to bring justice and equality to Americans of African descent, though the Freedmen's Bureau Act had already been emasculated (McFeely 1991: 246). The former slaves in the British Caribbean had no reason for such faith at that time, however, though slavery had been abolished there a generation earlier, because they would have no vote.

20 Jacqueline Jones makes a similar point about freed women in the United States during Reconstruction (1995: 57-8, 68). My thanks to Howard Johnson for reminding me of this.

Chapter 3

The political economy of
dependency and depression

Sugar remained king[1] throughout most of the British Caribbean until the mid-twentieth century, but the old king had been sick and declining for over a hundred years in some of the older colonies. Many of the problems in the sugar economy of Jamaica, for example, were apparent before the 1846 Sugar Duties Act exposed the British West Indian planters to the competition of free trade, and even before the end of slavery. However, these acts of the British Parliament, which reflected the declining influence of the West Indian planters in the metropole, certainly sharpened the problems. At the same time, British capital moved into expanding opportunities in Latin American railways, wheat farms and mining, rather than the old plantation economies of the West Indies. In the second half of the nineteenth century the expansion of sugar production in the Spanish Caribbean colonies, aided by United States investments and markets, and in Brazil, along with the growing competition from European beet sugar, produced a staggering crisis in the dependent and declining British West Indian plantation economies. This economic crisis had serious social and political repercussions in the closing years of the nineteenth and the early twentieth centuries, leading to widespread emigration and urbanisation, to demands for political reforms and new social policies, to sporadic social unrest, and to the emergence of increasing race and class consciousness. These decades, from the 1880s to the 1920s, foreshadowed and established the conditions for the responses to the Great Depression in the 1930s, when labour rebellions erupted throughout the British Caribbean.

The structure and history of the plantation economy

The poverty and powerlessness of Caribbean people derives from the subordinate position they have occupied for so long within the political economy of the capitalist world. In the British Caribbean this has been defined since the seventeenth century largely by the economic, political and social organisation of the plantation system. By plantation system we mean 'the totality of institutional arrangements surrounding the production and marketing of plantation crops' (Beckford 1972: 8), along with the colonial relations between the plantation societies and the metropolitan powers which exploit them and perpetuate their dependency. The plantation system was fundamental in shaping the lives and cultures of Caribbean people for over 300 years.

However, the insular nature of the Caribbean environment and the dominance of the plantation as the basic socioeconomic unit of production has misled some people into a reductionist perspective in which the plantation, or a particular island plantation economy, is seen as a microcosm of the whole system. 'The Caribbean plantation is a global, not a regional, enterprise, and it has always been so' (Richardson 1992a: 38); consequently, the nature of the plantation as an institution or the plantation economy of a specific colony cannot be understood, in terms of its economy, social relations and cultural attributes, except in relation to the global context in which it has been embedded from its inception.

What may be called the plantation-society thesis, which was one of the most influential models of Caribbean society developed in the 1960s, identifies the plantation, and along with it the experience and legacy of slavery, as the central determinant of Caribbean social and political life. The distinctive features of the plantation - which include monocrop production for export, strong monopolistic tendencies, a rigid system of social stratification that includes a high correlation between racial and class hierarchies, a weak community structure and the marginality of peasants who engage in subsistence production as well as periodic wage work on the plantations - make it the nexus of cultural and political as well as economic activities. The psychological consequences of extreme relations of domination and subordination have led to the plantation being compared with a 'total institution',[2] in which a new identity is imposed on the inmates (Smith 1967: 229-32).

The zone extending from the southern United States, through the entire Caribbean to Brazil, has been defined as 'Plantation America: A Culture Sphere' (Wagley 1957), in which people who are the descendants of enslaved Africans, for the most part, predominate. The connections with slavery, which was the chief method of labour control throughout the development of Plantation America, have led to a conflation of the characteristics of slavery and those of the plantation, particularly in those societies of the Caribbean where enslaved Africans became the overwhelming majority of the population. Patterson (1967: 70), for example, emphasises the importance of the plantation as the basic unit of social organisation during slavery: 'Jamaican slave society was loosely integrated; so much so, that one hesitates to call it a society since all that it amounted to was an ill-organized system of exploitation .... Jamaica is best seen more as a collection of autonomous plantations, each a self-contained community with its internal mechanisms of power, than as a total social system.'

However, although the slaves' movements were constricted and planters acted as if they were a law to themselves, this overstates the case. Although each individual plantation may have seemed to its inmates to be a total, self-contained institution, it was not really an isolated social unit but was always interrelated with the political economy of the metropolis, and hence with the imperial system and the world capitalist system as a whole. Indeed, the slaves themselves quickly discovered the importance of imperial military resources which were regularly used to suppress their rebellions.

Beckford, who emphasised the persistence of the characteristics of the slave and plantation society in the present day, drew attention to the interrelationship between the 'plantation as a social system in the territory in which it is located (the internal dimension) and ... the plantation as an economic system both in the territory of its location and in the wider world community (the external dimension)' (Beckford 1972: 10). Beckford's distinction, however, arbitrarily separates the social from the economic dimensions of the system and confines the former to the local level rather than acknowledging the essentially social nature of the entire system of which the individual plantation or plantation society is only a part, and a part that is dependent on its relations with the whole for the maintenance of its power structure as well as its economic arrangements.

The plantation-society thesis appropriately emphasises the socioeconomic structure of the plantation, which is seen as a central institution with an all-pervasive and essentially coercive and exploitative character, in the dependent society, but it tends to identify the institutional arrangement of production with the entire society in such a way as 'to leave the analysis at an institutional level' (Thomas 1984: 9). The social organisation of plantation production undoubtedly has distinctive and widely influential institutional features, but it should not be simply conflated with the entire social system which includes features other than those identified with the plantation as such.

Although the legacies of slavery and the plantation have continued to dominate much of Caribbean social life long after they have ceased to be central (or have even ceased to exist), we must not underestimate the ability of the system's victims to influence the system itself, as we saw in chapter 2.

'The appealing attempt to derive social structure [and culture, I would add] from the plantation experience is too simple and too reductionist' (Craig 1982: 150). Consequently, even while we conceive of Caribbean societies in relation to the fundamental impact of the plantation economy, seen as a system of domination as well as production, we must take account of other social and cultural dimensions, including the competing conceptions of rights and duties, beliefs and ideas, values and visions, of the various protagonists within the society. Although the predominant system defined the majority of the people as slaves and attempted to deracinate them, the fact is that these people were enslaved Africans whose cultures of origin contributed in crucial ways to the traditions of opposition to enslavement in the Americas. The colonial system, even during the heyday of slavery, was never able to guarantee the organisation of the plantation without recourse to the use of force because it failed to achieve cultural hegemony over the workers. This remained true, whether the workers were defined in the law as slaves, apprentices, indentured labourers or free workers. A narrowly economistic account of the plantation society too easily underestimates the centrality of this prolonged struggle. As was shown in chapter 2, these social and cultural aspects, which include the political culture of resistance, are generally influenced by, but are surely not limited to, the plantation as such.

With this in mind, emphasising that however dominant the plantation economy was it always had its limits, I will now identify some of the key features of the structure and history of that economy in the British Caribbean in the late nineteenth and early twentieth centuries.

There were changes within the structure of the plantation economy before the Great Depression of the 1930s, but that structure itself changed very little in the 300 years following its origins in the 1640s, when English planters in Barbados shifted from tobacco to sugar production. Other crops, including cotton, coffee, cacao and tobacco, as well as the extraction of timber and cattle raising, contributed to the Caribbean economy to various degrees in different places, but the cultivation and processing of sugar cane (Saccharum officinarum) soon became overwhelmingly important. The result, as is well known, was a revolutionary transformation of the economic and social structures of the colonies as the demands of sugar production resulted in a concentration of land ownership, wealth and power, along with the importation of enslaved Africans who soon constituted the majority of people in these societies. Moreover, the orientation of the economy to the more or less exclusive production of sugar, which was established in the mercantilist era, intensified the dependency of the colonial economies on the metropole, as the colonies remained passively respondent to metropolitan demand while relying on metropolitan investment and imports. The locus of key economic decisions, as well as the dominant market forces, was likewise metropolitan. The socioeconomic structure of plantation agriculture (which was similar in Belize, though the economy was there based on timber extraction) was dominant and resistant to change, even when it experienced economic crisis and decline.

The original mercantilist framework, which defined exclusive arrangements in legal terms, served to secure the transfer of surpluses from colonial economies to the metropole. In the Caribbean these economies were restructured to an extraordinary degree to serve the needs of the metropole by exporting staple products, with processing limited as much as possible to the metropole. In the case of sugar, the sugar cane had to be partially processed at the location where it was grown because the sucrose content begins to fall within hours of the cane being cut. Consequently, as the stalks of cane are chopped and ground to extract the juice, and the juice is heated to evaporate liquid and produce raw sugar, the plantation necessarily involves the coordination of agricultural and manufacturing activities. Nevertheless, the subsequent refining of the raw sugar, when most value was added, was undertaken in the metropole. The metropole controlled all transport of goods and associated services, and dominated the banking system and access to credit. The mercantilist framework also established a system of imperial trade preferences, allowing colonial exports to enter the metropole at lower tariffs than the competition in return for providing preferential entry for metropolitan capital, equipment and consumer goods into the colonies. This overall framework was expressed in laws enacted in the metropole, and enforced by the military and naval power of the metropole.

The plantations, initially established by settlers from the metropole, came increasingly under the influence, and eventually the control if not outright ownership, of the metropolitan merchants who bought the staple and were the source of supplies and credit. The economic ties between the plantations and the metropole, which were always close, became increasingly the ties that bind, as plantations became mere subsidiaries of metropolitan firms that had branches in more than one colony. The purpose of the plantation being to produce a staple for the metropole, any diversion of land or labour was resisted, even when it could have improved the nutrition of the population of the colony. When demand and prices for the staple were high, production was a priority in order to maximise profits, and when demand and prices fell, production had to be increased in order to minimise losses. Consequently, the production of sugar increased through the eighteenth century when profits were rising, and in the nineteenth century, when there was a secular decline in the price of raw sugar in London after 1815 (Deerr 1949: Vol. 2, 531; Ward 1985: 9), diversification was resisted. With either trend there was thus a tendency to intensify monoculture, which was associated with soil exhaustion, the increased exploitation of labour, dependence on foreign supplies of food, and worsening nutrition for the working people and their families. Moreover, the exclusive focus of monoculture hindered the development of backward linkages or spread effects in the colonial economy, and left the advantages of forward linkages to the processing facilities located in the metropole. Domestic demand in the colonial economy was met largely through imports from the metropole, with plantation workers as captive consumers, thus establishing long-term consumer preferences that further limited the possibility of local diversification and development even when the export of the staple declined.

Another consequence of the structure of the plantation economy may be called leapfrogging. The soil exhaustion produced by intensive monoculture often coincided with the decline or obsolescence of the mill facilities, with the result that metropolitan investors might choose to invest in a new plantation rather than reinvest in the old one. As the frontier of Caribbean colonisation expanded from the seventeenth century, so did the sugar revolution, in a leapfrogging process. Thus, Barbados, which was the richest British Caribbean colony in the seventeeth century, was overtaken by Jamaica around 1720. By the early nineteenth century, however, Jamaica was less attractive to new investors than the recently acquired and relatively undeveloped British colonies of Guyana and Trinidad, which offered vast new acreage for plantation development. However, these options were not limited to the British Caribbean, nor even to the British empire. West Indian producers of unrefined muscovado sugar enjoyed the lowest rate of duty until 1825 when Mauritius was given the same rate; in 1835 the East Indies was also given the same rate. Although still protected from foreign competition, this broke the virtual monopoly the British West Indies had enjoyed in the British sugar market and metropolitan investors were tempted to look elsewhere.

As this process of leapfrogging illustrates, the structural characteristics of the plantation system are inseparable from its history, and that history is inextricable from the world capitalist system in which it is embedded. It has been suggested that there is a staple cycle of distinct phases in the typical plantation economy, from the times of slavery to the present: 'The cycle can be divided into a foundation period, a golden age, and a period of maturity and decline. Maturity and decline tends to be a chronic condition, terminated by the total collapse of the system or the arrival of a new staple.' (Levitt and Best 1993: 411)

The entire British Caribbean has experienced this cycle in some fashion, though the component colonies experienced it at different times and in various ways, so it would be unsatisfactory to generalise about the region from just one or two examples. Rather, we must explore the economic history of the British Caribbean with reference to these important variations, and seek to generalise about overall factors and trends. We will see that the period of maturity and decline is initiated or postponed in the various colonies at different times in the late nineteenth and early twentieth centuries, reflecting the particular varieties of circumstance in these locations, but that it did occur everywhere.

West Indian planters vociferously attributed their problems to imperial policy and to the cost and unreliability of labour since Emancipation. However, neither the abolition of slavery nor the removal of tariff preferences were, by themselves, the cause of West Indian decline. The end of slavery certainly challenged the planters to reorganise labour on a legally free basis and, as we have seen, some recovered control of the still unfree labour market more successfully than others. The planters' access to capital and credit was also an issue, particularly with regard to the need to invest in technological innovation. New equipment and techniques in sugar processing, including vacuum and centrifugal processes in refining, and the use of steam power and railways for transporting cane to central factories, all required considerable investment and here, again, some planters were more innovative and successful than others. Finally, as we have seen, the removal of protection and the shift to free trade took place in stages beginning in 1825, when sugar from Mauritius began to be imported into the UK at the same rate of duty as West Indian sugar. The Sugar Duties Act of 1846 reduced the advantage of colonial muscovado over foreign sugar until, in 1854, there was a single rate on all muscovado, regardless of its source, and in 1874 all sugar began to enter the UK free of duty. The Sugar Duties Act caused 'a short-run difficulty' (Curtin 1954: 164) but was not, by itself, the major cause of the long-term decline of West Indian sugar economies. The tariffs before 1846 had not protected West Indian sugar from competition from other parts of the Empire, or of weaker West Indian planters from the more successful ones, but only from foreign competition.

Four conclusions may be drawn regarding the evidence of economic decline in the West Indies in the second half of the nineteenth century. First, the lowering of duties on sugar from all areas resulted in a huge increase in the size of the British market, so while the share of West Indian sugar in this market declined from 57.9 per cent of imports to 37.4 per cent, the amount imported from the West Indies actually increased slightly. Second, there was a sharp fall in the price of sugar in London in the 1840s and the price continued to decline until the First World War. Consequently, though annual averages of sugar production increased by 45 per cent between 1839 and 1846 and 1857 and 1866, from 131,177 to 190,690 tons, the real value received declined by 6 per cent, from £59.2 million to £55.8 million, so the planters 'had to run in order to stay in the same place' (Curtin 1954: 161). Initially, then, and even before the 1846 Act, many West Indian planters were losing relative to sugar imported into the UK from other parts of the empire, and subsequently also to foreign competition. Third, there was great variation among the West Indian colonies. Jamaica, which had been the largest and most valuable of the sugar colonies since about 1720, was in rapid decline between the 1840s and 1860s, as was Grenada, and Antigua and St Vincent barely held their own. Meanwhile, however, Guyana, Trinidad, St Kitts and especially Barbados greatly increased sugar production. When people write of the West Indies they are often thinking of Jamaica, but Jamaica's experience is atypical and, at this period, its decline was by far the most marked. Fourth, the greatest competition was yet to come, not from other sugar cane producers but from beet sugar, the annual average production of which increased between 1839 and 1846 and 1857 and 1866 by almost 800 per cent. 'In the last three decades of the century, all West Indian planters, and, indeed, all sugar cane producers, suffered increasing competition from beet sugar,' so, Curtin concludes (1954: 164), one should not place the blame for the economic problems of the 1880s and 1890s on the policy-makers of the 1840s.

West Indian planters' problems with free trade between 1846 and 1883 resulted largely from declining prices in the British market, not from production difficulties. Increasingly, West Indian sugar was being exported to the American market, where prices were unstable but were still more advantageous than in the UK. Exports to the UK declined in the early 1880s, and nearly half of all West Indian sugar went to the United States. This softened the shock of the crisis for those colonies - chiefly Barbados, Guyana and Trinidad - that invested in new equipment and kept labour cheap. This was also a period when estates were consolidated. In Jamaica many encumbered estates were taken out of sugar production and some concentrated on producing rum. In Trinidad and Guyana many smaller estates were amalgamated into a few huge ones, often with central factories, owned by non-resident companies. This consolidation of sugar estates after 1846 'tended to concentrate plantation ownership in the hand of British merchant houses specializing in sugar. The non-resident nature of these companies, which possessed considerable non-estate assets, gave them a creditworthiness which the smaller estates could not hope to rival. The extensive use of such credit and the more thorough organization of existing assets enabled these new enterprises to dominate the industry by 1883.' (Lobdell 1972: 44-5)

There was considerable variety in the ways that sugar colonies responded to the problems caused by free trade and declining prices. By the 1890s some colonies had curtailed sugar production, but others increased it. In Grenada, sugar was still the dominant crop in the 1860s, but by 1884 the value of sugar exported was only one-tenth the value of exported cocoa, and by 1896-7 the production of sugar had virtually ceased (Richardson 1997: 45-7). In several colonies, however, sugar exports remained a high proportion of total exports (see Table 3.1), so these economies were the most vulnerable to the sugar depression.

TABLE 3.1 SUGAR PRODUCTS AS PERCENTAGE OF TOTAL EXPORTS, 1896

Barbados	97.00
St Kitts-Nevis	96.5
Antigua	94.5
St Lucia	74.00
British Guiana	70.5
Montserrat	62.00
Trinidad	57.00
St Vincent	42.00
Tobago	35.00
Jamaica	18.00
Dominica	15.00
Grenada	0.00

Source: Data from Royal Commission Report, 1897, p.3, in Richardson 1997: 35.

The process of consolidation of estates was not limited to the sugar colonies. It was just one manifestation of a global process of economic concentration and the rationalisation of the old form of personal private enterprise into ever larger and more impersonal corporations, often in the form of joint-stock companies. An example of this was in Belize, which was not a sugar colony but which exhibited the characteristics of a plantation economy. In 1859 the British Honduras Company (BHCo) registered in the UK under the Joint Stock Companies Act. This company had its roots in one of the oldest settler families in Belize, that of James Hyde, one of the self-styled Principal Inhabitants of the settlement in the late eighteenth century. Hyde, who was born in Scotland in 1763, went to Belize in his early 20s and lived with his uncle, James Bartlett. Along with Hyde's free coloured son, George Hyde, and his white son, James Bartlett Hyde, they were among the chief slave-owners and land-owners who allocated land to themselves under the old location laws before 1817. The Hyde family subsequently bought and foreclosed on large areas of land from other settlers, and the participation of a London merchant, John Hodge, who became the agent for the settlement in 1848, enabled them to become the biggest land-owner of all. James Hyde died in the UK in 1858, but in 1862 Hodge, who had become the firm's Belize-based partner, was elected to the Legislative Assembly and he served until his death in 1868 (Judd 1992: 233). The lands of the BHCo were transferred to it from 'John Hodge, of London, merchant, presently residing in Belize, on behalf of himself and James Bartlett Hyde, the surviving copartners of the late firm of James Hyde & Co., who lately carried on business in this Settlement as Merchants and Mahogany cutters'.[3] The BHCo was the only company in Belize to take advantage of the Joint Stock Companies Act, passed in 1856, and while other firms of the 1850s ceased to exist, the BHCo grew stronger and larger. In 1875 the company's name was changed to the Belize Estate and Produce Company Ltd (BEC), and in 1881 it bought nine mahogany works from its chief rival, Young Toledo & Co, which had gone bankrupt. BEC consolidated its wealth, owned well over 500,000 acres, or about half of all the freehold land in the colony, and was the most powerful organisation in Belize for the following century (Bolland and Shoman 1977: 77-83). Moreover, this extreme monopolisation of land inhibited the development of a peasantry and resulted in the severe underutilisation of resources, the classic characteristics of a plantation economy.

In some other colonies, unlike Belize, a substantial peasantry developed. In Grenada, for example, where the sugar economy declined in the second half of the nineteenth century, there were 7,715 landholdings of 10 acres or less in 1898, and 94 per cent of these were small holdings of 5 acres or less (Richardson 1997: 186). Small-scale cocoa farming provided the basis for some prosperity in Grenada, which was in contrast to the poverty of sugar workers in, for example, the plantation economy of Barbados. In Jamaica, however, where a large peasantry had developed after 1838, the small farmers struggled to maintain a share of the land through the 1880s. Veront Satchell (1990: 115) shows how the bulk of the 2.5 million acres that changed ownership in Jamaica between 1866 and 1900 was bought and sold in large lots by planters and other big land-owners, but that the majority of acquisitions were by small farmers, generally of lots of under 10 acres. 'Holdings over 50 acres accounted for 33.1 per cent of the total [private] transfers but covered 97.4 per cent of the total area transferred. The indication is that the holdings under 50 acres that were transferred were small in size, and this suggests that there was a strong tendency towards the concentration of large tracts of land.' Holdings of over 1,000 acres accounted for only 9 per cent of transactions but covered 62 per cent of the area transferred. The large holdings were increasing in size, but the small holdings were either remaining static or, as with those of under 5 acres, were becoming smaller as prices increased. 'This had serious implications for the expansion of the peasant class ... [as] fewer acres were being made available for distribution among a rising population of would-be small settlers.' (Satchell 1990: 118, 150) The pattern of small farms fragmenting while large estates became increasingly concentrated in a few hands - and the larger estates generally had the better land - severely circumscribed the development of the peasantry in Jamaica while the plantation economy revived to some extent. Indeed, the plantations' concentration of land at the expense of small farmers was one of the chief ways the planters maintained their power and kept a large labour force dependent upon them.

These examples suggest that, although the peasantry was more successful in its struggle for land in some places than in others, the structure of the plantation economy was resilient even in depression conditions and over a long period of time. The consolidation of estates, the concentration of capital, and the shift of ownership and control towards metropolitan companies, were not changes in the structure of the typical plantation economy, but rather an intensification of the character of that economy - which was essentially monopolistic, monocultural, exploitative, dependent and metropolitan-dominated - as a result of the general logic of capitalist development. In Guyana, for example, there was in the second half of the nineteenth century a 'remorseless weeding out of undercapitalized proprietors' as mortgages fell under the control of absentee firms. By 1884, the seven largest concerns, all absentee-controlled, were responsible for nearly half the sugar production of the colony (Adamson 1972: 204).

The beet sugar crisis after 1884, when massive quantities of European beet sugar were dumped on the British market, further strengthened this process of consolidation and concentration in the plantation economies of the British Caribbean. The price of sugar in the UK, which was around 20 shillings per hundredweight in the 1870s, fell precipitously to 13 shillings and 3 pence per hundredweight in 1884 and to below 10 shillings by 1897. Sugar prices did not recover to 1883 levels until the First World War. The planters sought to reduce their costs of production with improved varieties of cane and factory operations and by reducing wage rates, with the latter reaching a pitiful level by the 1890s. Those firms, which were generally the larger ones, that had the capital and credit to invest in technical improvements were able to reduce their production costs by increasing efficiency. Between £1.4 million and £2.2 million were invested in sugar machinery in Guyana between 1879 and 1897, and by 1897 about £2.5 million had been invested in Trinidad's sugar industry, some 75 per cent of it in modern machinery. By 1896, about 53 per cent of the sugar exported from Trinidad was produced by vacuum pans. Meanwhile, however, the technologically backward sugar producers in Grenada, Dominica, Montserrat and St Vincent had mostly gone out of business by the 1890s, and Jamaican sugar estates, where methods of production were backward, concentrated on producing rum. The amalgamation of sugar estates, which continued in Guyana and Trinidad, and especially the establishment of central factories, such as the Usine Ste Madeleine which was completed for the giant Colonial Company in Trinidad, reduced production costs by about half between 1884 and 1894 (Lobdell 1972: 47-9). In a few cases, the government provided aid for the sugar industry. In St Lucia, the colonial government granted £40,000 for the construction of a central sugar factory, and the Barbados government passed the Agricultural Aids Act in 1887 to allow planters to borrow money on the security of their crops. By 1896, some 138 estates in Barbados, comprising about one-third of the total plantation acreage, had borrowed over £100,000 under this scheme (Lobdell 1972: 51). In general, however, it was the British merchant companies' investments in Trinidad and Guyana that most benefited the sugar industry during the beet sugar crisis, and these large, vertically integrated firms came to dominate the West Indian sugar industry.

> Dispassionately shifting production and investment from estate to estate and colony to colony, these new enterprises were no longer bound by the tradition, nostalgia, and status considerations which had proved so important to earlier planters. With consummate skill and almost ruthless efficiency, these firms combined their ability to command massive outside credit with their talent for vertical integration. The ultimate result was the transformation of family based plantations into modern, impersonal, industrial enterprises. (Lobdell 1972: 53)

The impact of this transformation within the plantation economy on the sugar workers, which has been vividly described for Puerto Rico in Mintz's account of Don Taso (Mintz 1960), was profound, as it deepened their poverty and alienation in a process of proletarianisation.

In Guyana, where the sugar industry continued to be quite successful, the number of estates declined, from 173 in 1835, to 105 in 1885, to 84 in 1890 and only 46 in 1904, when just four estates accounted for 58 per cent of the industry's output (Thomas 1984: 24). Only the largest corporations, organised as limited-liability companies, could survive the long-term decline in sugar prices, and they dominated land ownership. The persistent dominance of estate land ownership within the plantation economy is evident from the distribution of landholdings by size and their share of agricultural land in the region during the 1960s. Table 3.2 shows that everywhere, except Trinidad and Tobago, farms of less than 5 acres were three-quarters or more of all farms, but they generally occupied less than one-quarter of the farm land, and often less than 15 per cent. In Barbados, 98.3 per cent of all farms controlled a mere 13.4 per cent of the farm land, and in St Kitts 94.5 per cent of farms controlled 15 per cent of the farm land. In contrast, the estates of over 500 acres were everywhere less than 1 per cent of all farms, but they controlled, typically, between about one-third and over one-half of all agricultural land. In St Kitts, 0.4 per cent of the farms controlled 56.6 per cent of the farm land, and in Jamaica 0.2 per cent of the farms controlled 44.9 per cent of the farm land.
Source: Beckford 1975: 87.

In Belize, where most land was not used for agriculture but was for forest products or just held for speculation, 3 per cent of the land-owners in 1971 held 95 per cent of the freehold land, and 91 per cent of the land-owners held a mere 1 per cent (Bolland and Shoman 1977: 104-5). Moreover, as is typical of these

3.2 DISTRIBUTION OF FARM SIZE AND SHARE OF FARMLAND
IN THE BRITISH CARIBBEAN ISLANDS, 1961

	Percentage of farms		Percentage of farmland	
	Less than 5 acres	More than 500 acres	Less than 5 acres	More than 500 acres
Antigua	91.5	0.3	26.7	42.2
Barbados	98.3	0.2	13.4	31.3
Dominica	75.2	0.3	13.2	32.2
Grenada	89.7	0.1	23.9	15.0
Jamaica	78.6	0.2	14.9	44.9
Montserrat	92.7	0.7	-	-
St Kitts	94.5	0.4	15.0	56.6
St Lucia	82.5	0.2	18.0	33.8
St Vincent	89.0	0.1	27.0	24.2
Trinidad and Tobago	46.5	0.3	6.9	31.1

plantation economies, many of the largest estates, which generally monopolised the best and most accessible land, were owned by metropolitan companies.

As was shown in chapter 2, these giant estates held huge amounts of land, much of which was underutilised in order to deny its use by others, thereby increasing the pool of dependent labour in order to keep wage rates low and to maintain their profits. Established throughout most of the British Caribbean by the late nineteenth century, they represented the latest stage in the development of the plantation economy and were among the first modern transnational corporations. As a result of their economic power in the colonies these corporations exerted a tremendous political influence, not only in the colonies but also in the UK. Moreover, it is important to recognise that the emergence of these modern corporations in the British Caribbean colonies overlapped with the existence of legally sanctioned forms of labour coercion for the exaction of surplus value. Indeed, it was in Guyana and Trinidad, the two colonies where indentured labour was retained until 1921, that these corporations were the most advanced and successful in the British Caribbean. This shows that capitalism, far from being incompatible with systems of coerced labour, actually flourishes by exploiting such systems and so seeks to prolong them as long as politically possible. In 1917 the government of India suspended emigration, and in July 1917 the British government declared that indentured immigration would not be revived after the war. This was a blow to the planters, but the colonial authorities collaborated in the prolongation of legally sanctioned servitude until 1921, when indenture could no longer be sustained.[4]

The system of sugar production was reformed between 1838 and 1921, but still remained within the persistent structures of the plantation economy. For example, as Clive Thomas says (1984: 25-6) in relation to Guyana: 'A labor market, consolidation of land and capital, diversification, the greater use of scientific cultivation practices, and factory processes all heralded new departures in plantation organization. But among the newer forms, the old bases of exploitative social relations continued. There was therefore both continuity and profound change underlying the history of the [sugar] industry from the 1830s to World War II.'

The dominance of the plantation economy, which involved a particular form of exploitation by and dependence on the metropole, was responsible for the distorted economic development of the British Caribbean. In Jamaica, which was one of the most developed of the colonies in the 1830s, labour productivity in agriculture declined until in 1890 it was 22 per cent below what it had been in 1832, when slavery prevailed. Although productivity increased between 1890 and 1930, 'output per worker in agriculture in 1930 was only 18 percent higher than it had been at the end of the slave era. In the rest of the economy the level achieved in 1930 had not yet reached that of 1832.' (Mandle 1989: 232, referring to Eisner 1961)

Some of the planters adapted to pressures in the nineteenth century successfully, though generally, as we have seen, the sugar industry became dominated by corporations rather than by planters as such. But the plantation economy, in order to survive, stifled other developments, particularly the development of an independent peasantry, wherever and whenever it could. The plantations needed to keep the costs of production low, including labour costs, in order to remain competitive, and so they had to ensure that any alternatives to plantation labour, especially small farming, would yield only the most meagre incomes. As Jay Mandle argues (1989: 233-4), 'if the peasantry had been allowed to become more productive, the small farmers might have reached the stage where they no longer would have supplied their labor to the estates. If that had occurred the continued existence of the plantation sector would have been placed at risk.'

The fact that a peasantry did emerge in several parts of the British Caribbean, including Jamaica, despite the power of the planters and official discouragement, is testimony to the determination and persistence of the peasants themselves. They not only survived, but also showed considerable vitality and a pioneering creativity in the face of plantation dominance.

Two examples will illustrate the contributions made by the innovative peasantry of the British Caribbean to the diversification and growth of the economies, despite the strength of the plantation sector: the banana industry in Jamaica and rice production in Guyana. In both cases, the small farmers' economy was highly successful, but it remained vulnerable vis-à-vis the plantation.

Jamaica

The banana plant (Musa), which was introduced to the Caribbean in the early sixteenth century, flourishes in the damp climate and good soils of Jamaica's eastern parishes. Long a staple in the peasants' diet, the early production of bananas in Jamaica was by enterprising small farmers. In the 1870s the export of bananas was just one part of a growing fruit trade that included the export of oranges, limes, coconuts and pineapples to the United States. Two related changes were occurring simultaneously. First, the traditional exports of sugar, rum and coffee, the old plantation products which had accounted for over two-thirds of Jamaica's export earnings in 1865, were overtaken by fruit, which constituted 41.4 per cent of the value of all exports in 1899 and 56 per cent by 1903. Second, the British share of Jamaican trade declined as that of the United States increased. By the end of the nineteenth century, the United States was Jamaica's most important trading partner, both in exports (59.1 per cent) and imports (45.1 per cent) (Holt 1992: 348).

As bananas became Jamaica's chief export crop, however, 'the peasants who originated this crop soon lost their economic independence' (Holt 1992: 350) for a US company developed a virtual monopoly in the trade. Lorenzo D. Baker, the owner of a New England fishing fleet, visited Jamaica in 1872 and realised that the fruit trade could be very profitable. He moved permanently to Jamaica in 1881 and started the Boston Fruit Company in 1884. By 1886 he was shipping 42 per cent of Jamaica's bananas. His son became the US consular agent in Port Morant in 1885 and 'gave the family important advantages over their competitors in arranging shipments' (Holt 1992: 350). Baker bought several sugar estates in northeastern Jamaica and converted them to banana plantations in order to directly control production and to be able to dictate prices to the peasant farmers, many of whom were subsequently driven out of business by a manipulation of prices. By the 1890s, Baker controlled not only the Jamaica-United States fruit trade (Holt 1992: 354), but also the emerging tourist trade, which began as an 'economic adjunct to the banana business' (Taylor 1993: 44). The Boston Fruit Company merged with Minor Keith's[5] extensive Central American banana holdings to become the United Fruit Company (UFC) in 1899. By 1911 the UFC also controlled much of the growing tourist industry in Jamaica, including the Titchfield and Myrtle Bank hotels (Taylor 1993: 87-9). A British fruit and shipping company, Elders & Fyffes, was taken over by the UFC which, by 1914, effectively monopolised fruit supplies and shipment to the UK as well as the United States.

The formerly independent peasant producers, who had pioneered the banana industry, could no longer bargain effectively over prices and 'were more like wage workers paid at a piece rate than independent contractors' (Holt 1992: 355). Keith expanded the UFC's Central American holdings from Costa Rica into Honduras, where it owned 14,000 acres in 1918 and 88,000 acres by 1924.[6] In 1929 the UFC bought up Samuel Zemurray's banana empire and became the dominant company in Nicaragua and Guatemala as well as Costa Rica and Honduras. The proletarianisation of Jamaica's banana farmers thus became a sideshow of the emergence of the US economic empire in Central America, which was frequently maintained by political and military intervention (LaFeber 1993).

The impact of these developments became very important in Jamaica in the 1920s and particularly affected the social and political events of the 1930s. In 1925 the Jamaican government agreed to help organise and finance the Jamaica Banana Producers' Association (JBPA), a cooperative of mostly small farmers with less than 5 acres. In its first year, 1929, the JBPA's 7,694 members delivered over 4 million stems of bananas, and by 1932 its 11,628 contractors produced about 24 million stems, or one-third of the bananas shipped from Jamaica (Holt 1992: 356-8). However, devastating hurricanes in 1934 and 1935, together with the collapse of the US fruit market in the depression, created a crisis for small producers. The UFC used its immense corporate resources and power to offer higher prices to small banana growers in order to seduce them into defecting from the JBPA at a time when they were finding it hard to repay their loans to the cooperative. With its much larger properties and cheaper bananas in Central America, the UFC could compete successfully with the JBPA. Moreover, as first Panama disease and then leaf spot affected banana cultivation, the UFC began to reduce its acreage by selling land back to Jamaican capitalists. Reducing its role and therefore its risks as a producer, the UFC still remained the chief buyer of bananas.

In December 1935, when the JBPA appealed to the government for assistance, the UFC proposed that it would permit the cooperative to survive if it stopped marketing fruit in the UK and sold its ships to Elders & Fyffes, the UFC subsidiary. The small farmers had no political leverage and the elected members of the Legislative Council favoured the UFC. The Colonial Office accepted the idea that a small cooperative could not compete with a giant transnational corporation, so it should cooperate with it. The UFC was adamant that the JBPA should cease to be a growers' cooperative and become a limited company, like any other capitalist business. The JBPA was represented in the negotiations with the UFC by Norman Washington Manley, Jamaica's leading lawyer. In 1936 the JBPA was reorganised as the Jamaica Banana Producers' Association Ltd, and its farmer members became, nominally, shareholders in the company. The UFC, having got what it wanted, gave in return 1US cent on every count (nine bunches) of bananas that it exported, to serve as a development fund. This became the basis of Manley's Jamaica Welfare Ltd, formed in 1937, 'to try to repair some of the economic and social distress' (Post 1978: 89) which was then so apparent in the island. The JBPA had been unable to stem the tide of United States' corporate capital, which was proletarianising the small banana producers, and Manley's Jamaica Welfare was left to try to cope with some of the negative social consequences.

Guyana

In Guyana, unlike Jamaica, sugar remained the dominant export product, though the period of rapid expansion of sugar production that had begun in the 1840s and 1850s came to an end in the 1880s. Sugar exports from Guyana rose from an annual average between 1841 and 1845 of 25,870 tons per year to an average of 115,184 tons per year between 1886 and 1890. Sugar exports then declined in the last years of the nineteenth century to 96,817 tons per year, increased to a peak of 118,999 tons per year at the beginning of the twentieth century, and then fell again to an average of 95,292 tons per year between 1916 and 1920 (Mandle 1973: 20). As a result of the problems in the sugar industry, there was a decline in the demand for labour on the estates and the estate population fell from 89,807 in 1891 to 77,699 in 1921, that is, from 33 per cent to 27 per cent of the total population (Mandle 1973: 19). Immigration declined from its peak of almost 70,000 in the 1870s to 40,171 in the 1890s, the smallest number since the indenture scheme began in the 1840s. The addition of 74,734 immigrants between 1891 and 1920, however, at a time of declining sugar production, 'tended to oversupply the domestic labor requirements' (Mandle 1973: 34).

Many redundant workers returned to India. A total of 36,913 were repatriated between 1891 and 1920, and many others moved off the estates and settled in villages. The proportion of Guyana's population living in villages increased from 40 per cent in 1861 to 55 per cent in 1911. Many of these people sought estate employment during the crop season, but wages were low because of the abundance of labour, and there was widespread hardship. In 1890 the government sought to encourage the permanent settlement of Indians in Guyana by reducing the price of Crown land from $10 to $1 per acre, and in 1898 it was further reduced to 15 cents per acre, with land being made available in 25–acre lots, instead of a minimum of 100 acres as had been the case since 1839 when the development of a peasantry was officially discouraged. During the 1890s Indian small farmers developed rice cultivation, initially for local consumption but, by the early twentieth century, for export also. Between 1898 and 1902, some 3,824 tons of rice were produced on 6,778 acres. By 1913-17 this had increased to 36,336 tons on 49,695 acres, and over 10,000 tons were exported; rice imports were more or less eliminated. Sugar estates, too, shifted to the new crop in order to use valuable irrigated land and to help maintain their indentured labourers while sugar prices were low. The percentage of total acreage under paddy that was estate land declined, however, from 44 per cent between 1903 and 1907 to less than 18 per cent between 1912 and 1914. As village rice production increased, sugar estate owners were concerned that it was reducing their labour supply. By the First World War, the first period of the rapid expansion of rice production was over: between 1918 and 1922 production fell to 28,508 tons, of which less than 7,000 tons were exported (Mandle 1973: 34–42).

The period between 1850 and 1890 was the 'heyday of the plantation society in Guyana', and the emergence of rice production in the 1890s reflected the decline of sugar production and the rise of small farmers. However, this was an 'adjustment made by the plantation society to changed circumstances, but not a fundamental change in that society' (Mandle 1973: 67–8). When, in 1927, H.C. Sampson (1927: 7) noted that 'cane lands were allotted to East Indian labourers, working on the cane estates, to grow rice as an inducement for them to work on the plantation', he was drawing attention to the fact that many of the rice cultivators and other villagers had not broken free of their dependence on the estates. Even after the end of indentured immigration in 1917 the plantations had an abundant supply of labour because there were few other employment opportunities.

During the depression years of the 1930s, ownership of the plantations of Guyana became even more concentrated, and the plantation economy 'became more domineering and rigid' (Mandle 1973: 70). By the Second World War, one British firm, Bookers Brothers, McConnell & Co, totally dominated the Guyanese economy. Josias Booker came to Guyana in 1815 and prospered in the cotton industry before expanding into retailing and shipping. John McConnell, who came to Guyana in 1846, represented the sugar-producing interest. Booker Brothers and John McConnell and Company merged in 1900 and became a London-based company. The most rapid period of its growth was between 1920 and 1940, by which date Bookers, as it became known, owned 18 of the 28 estates in Guyana. By taking advantage of its control of shipping and of access to British capital, Bookers was able to survive the depression years and to buy up other estates whose owners lacked its advantages. While Bookers dominated Guyana's most important industry, sugar production increased in the face of low prices, from 100,447 tons in 1921-5, to 114,737 tons in 1926-30, to 145,403 tons in 1931-5, and to a peak of 187,242 tons in 1936-40. At the same time as this dramatic increase in sugar production occurred, the average weekly field labour force grew from 18,029 to 24,254, so the average production per field labourer increased over these 20 years from 5.57 tons to 7.72 tons. Technical improvements in cultivation and production, made possible by the concentration of ownership in Bookers, enabled the sugar industry - and with it, the plantation economy – to survive the Great Depression in Guyana.

The rice industry, meanwhile, was in a disastrous state, with total production falling from 43,695 tons to 38,812 tons and exports falling from 21,211 tons to 15,087 tons, from the period 1931-5 to the period 1936-40. Yields per acre remained at low levels, and milling facilities were poor. There was a potentially large market for rice in the Caribbean islands, but the poverty of most of the population meant that the market did not grow as fast as the need for food. Moreover, Guyana's rice industry was not competitive, often because it was grown on poorly drained and irrigated land and credit was inadequate and expensive. Though the Rice Marketing Board was established in 1932, public policy generally neglected rice, which was a 'demoralized industry' (Mandle 1973: 78). Thus although the sugar industry had become more efficient and competitive, the reverse occurred in the rice industry. Consequently, Guyana's plantation economy, though modified, remained intact, with a rejuvenated and even more concentrated sugar industry that was dominated by a single metropolitan corporation. The rice industry, far from seriously challenging sugar's predominance, had existed only at the edges of the estates and had enabled the plantation economy to get through the crisis at the turn of the century. The changes that had taken place, in the form of further consolidation and modernisation of the sugar industry, actually enhanced the domination and apparent stability of the plantation economy of Guyana.

These examples of the Jamaican banana industry and the Guyanese rice industry show, in their different ways, that despite vigorous and creative efforts by small farmers of African and Indian origin, respectively, the large-scale, labour-intensive plantation system remained predominant. The peasant farmers in Jamaica were so successful in pioneering bananas that their enterprise became engulfed by a giant transnational corporation, and those in Guyana were not sufficiently successful to challenge the rise of the giant transnational in that colony. The plantation economies of Jamaica and Guyana did not remain the same, but the old struggle between peasant and plantation sectors became even harder for the former, and the latter became increasingly concentrated into such powerful organisations as the UFC and Bookers, both of which were backed by the colonial administrations.[7] Against such giant transnational corporations, which were backed when necessary with the military might of the imperial powers, the poor peasants of Jamaica and Guyana had little chance of success. Although they had pioneered the cultivation of new crops in the nineteenth century and contributed significantly to the economies of these colonies in the twentieth century, they remained highly dependent and unable to break free of the power of the plantation system. The survival of the plantation system meant the persistence of the monoculture economy, of dependency and foreign control, and consequently of the absence of sustained diversification and development. As the plantation system was victorious, the working people remained condemned to poverty and powerlessness.

United States expansion, new economic sectors, and old problems

While the British Caribbean, along with the French and Dutch, suffered generally from economic stagnation from the 1870s to the First World War, US business interests were increasingly penetrating the Caribbean, even before the invasion of Cuba and Puerto Rico in 1898. The expansion of the United States to the west coast of the continent in the first half of the nineteenth century was followed in the 1860s by growing interest overseas. Across the Pacific and in the Caribbean, 'the growth of economic interests led to political entanglements and to increased military responsibilities' (LaFeber 1963: 408), culminating in 1898 in the annexation of Hawaii and the war with Spain. US expansionism was the latest phase of imperialism in the Caribbean, and its impact was greatest in Cuba and Puerto Rico. Whether nominally independent, as was Cuba after 1902, or made a colony, as in the case of Puerto Rico, these islands' economies, like those of the rest of the Caribbean, were shattered by the international crisis in the capitalist system in the 1930s. US investments and markets had created a boom for the sugar economies of Cuba and Puerto Rico, but also made their economies more monocultural, dependent and vulnerable. British West Indian sugar production, with a restoration of tariff protection in the metropolitan market in 1919, enjoyed a modest revival, while other non–plantation developments, such as tourism in the Bahamas, bauxite in Guyana and oil in Trinidad, were economically promising in so far as they offered alternatives to King Sugar. However, these developments were highly dependent on external capital and demand and eventually led the economies of those colonies into an ever closer relationship with the United States.

The economy of the Bahamas, first settled by the English in 1648, was never based on sugar. Many Loyalists who settled in the Bahamas in the 1780s brought their slaves from plantations in the southern colonies and expanded cotton production. Privateering and wrecking supplemented the economy. By Emancipation, cotton was a minor crop and some estates were exporting pineapples to the United States. No major export staple replaced cotton, however, and former slaves engaged in salt production, fishing, raising small livestock and cultivating varied crops for food, often on a share system. The pineapple industry grew in the late nineteenth century, with landlords extending credit, pineapple slips, manure and fertiliser to their share-tenants (Johnson 1991: 62). The expansion of pineapple production led to a concentration of land ownership in a few hands and to a demand for a stable labour force which was recruited and retained 'by the operation of a credit system whose effect was to bind labourers to regular employment by the creation of a debt relationship' (Johnson 1991: 64). The share system remained predominant in the pineapple industry and also in the sponging industry, which expanded in the 1860s, where crew members needed credit to buy their supplies before each 6-12 week voyage.

Though the Bahamas did not have the sugar plantation economy that predominated in most of the British Caribbean, there was a similar social structure. The largely white elite, whose economic power was based on land ownership and its control of credit and retailing as well as the import-export trade, dominated the pineapple and sponge industries. After Emancipation, the credit and truck systems were a form of labour exploitation that reinforced the economic and political dominance of this merchant elite. 'Wage labour became the norm only after the 1930s with the decline of the sponging and pineapple industries and the development of the colony as a service economy based on tourism' (Johnson 1991: 80), though the tourist industry had a shaky start. The winter tourist trade in the Bahamas collapsed in the First World War and the Colonial Hotel, Nassau's largest, was destroyed in a fire in 1922. The construction of the new hotel employed as many as 1,800 people, many of them skilled workers from outside the Bahamas. The government modernised the electricity, water and sewerage systems and expanded the harbour and wharves for more tourist ships. Another big hotel was built in 1926, by private investors but with the government's assistance (Johnson 1991: 149-51). This construction boom, much of it tourism-oriented, coincided with the bootlegging years between 1919 and 1933.

The Eighteenth Amendment to the United States Constitution, which prohibited the manufacture, import and sale of all intoxicating drinks, provided a windfall for the Bahamas, which, close to the American coast, is a natural base for smuggling. Wages rose, as did government revenues from customs receipts, but the biggest beneficiaries were members of the merchant elite. So long as there was Prohibition in the United States the worst effects of the slump after 1929 were masked in the Bahamas, but the repeal of Prohibition in 1933 resulted in a brutal depression which was made even worse by the collapse of the sponging industry early in 1939 (Craton 1986: 255). The political economy of the Bahamas, though not a pure plantation economy, was equally dominated by a tiny elite and, vulnerable to the economic fluctuations of external markets, it suffered from the typical boom-and-bust cycles of dependency.

Trinidad's economy was essentially agricultural, and plantations still dominated well into the twentieth century. The sugar industry remained quite prosperous until about 1884 and after a liberalisation of the policy regarding the sale of Crown lands in 1869, cocoa production expanded in the 1870s. 'Cocoa was a cash crop ideally suited to the peasant proprietor for it required little capital or labor (outside of the family unit) to operate a cocoa farm' (Johnson

1987: 27), and the cocoa industry developed, like the production of rice and coconuts, without government aid. During the sugar crisis in the 1880s and 1890s, the local government made little effort to diversify the economy, while the cocoa peasantry lost their properties by foreclosure to the merchants who monopolised credit and increasingly dominated cocoa production. The growth of cocoa exports in the 1880s was linked to a rise in land prices, so many small-holders became indebted to merchant-creditors. A decline in cocoa prices in the late 1890s led to the widespread dispossession and proletarianisation of this insecure cocoa peasantry. In a process that was quite similar to the history of the banana industry in Jamaica, therefore, the initial success of a black peasantry that pioneered a new crop was followed by a concentration of what had been their lands in the hands of capitalist planters and 'the consequent expansion of a rural and urban proletariat' (Johnson 1987: 35). Between about 1900 and 1920, when the sugar industry and cocoa production revived, the plantation economy had a new lease of life. Although most Trinidadians continued to be employed in agriculture, the value of exported oil overtook all agricultural products in the 1930s.

The first oil wells were drilled in Trinidad in the 1850s and 1860s, but produc-tion stopped in 1868 and did not begin again until 1902, when the oil age really started. The British government became interested after 1904 because of plans to convert the navy to oil-powered ships, and British capital was invested increasingly after 1909. By 1913 two companies, United British Oilfields of Trinidad (UBOT), a subsidiary of Shell, and Trinidad Leaseholds Ltd (TLL), based in Point Fortin and Forest Reserve/Point-a-Pierre, respectively, began to dominate the industry. In 1920 they were joined by Apex Trinidad Oilfields (ATO), based in Fyzabad. Between 1914 and 1924, the oil industry boomed and this region of southwest-ern Trinidad, which was previously forested and inaccessible, developed roads, railways, pipelines and boom-towns (Brereton 1981: 199-203).

Around 1930, when oil prices slumped, drilling was suspended in some fields and workers were laid off. New technology was applied, however, and new, high-yielding fields were opened up. Crude oil production increased during the 1930s, from 5.4 million barrels in 1927 to 20 million barrels in 1939, and the two major companies declared dividends of 35 per cent and 25 per cent in 1935-6. Oil, which accounted for only 10 per cent of exports in 1919, was worth 50 per cent by 1932, and by 1938, on the eve of the Second World War, Trinidad's oil supplied 44.2 per cent of the British empire's production. In that year, the world's first iso-octane fuel plant was built at Point-a-Pierre to produce aviation fuel for the Royal Air Force. Though Trinidad had become vital to the UK's preparations for war, and the oil industry was technologically advanced in comparison with the agricultural sector, the social relations of the oil industry remained backward and exploitative. The administrative and technical staff were chiefly British and the drillers American; the semi-skilled and unskilled workers were Trinidadian or immigrants from other West Indian islands. The social life and residential patterns, as well as the occupational hierarchy, was racially segregated and many of those few blacks who became technicians left for Venezuela rather than suffer discrimination at home. 'Low wages and a number of objectionable labour policies by the major oil companies led directly to the strikes of 1937', (Brereton 1981: 204), as the oil industry, rather than overcoming the social contradictions of the plantation economy, appears to have intensified them.

In Guyana, as we have seen, the sugar industry became increasingly concentrated in a caricature of the plantation economy and the expansion of rice production was stifled. Beginning in 1914, however, a non-plantation sector emerged with the bauxite mining industry. From its inception, this industry was dominated by North American capital. The Demerara Bauxite Company, established at Mackenzie (later Linden), about 70 miles up the Demerara River from Georgetown, was controlled by Aluminium of Canada (Alcan). Guyana's high-grade bauxite and large reserves made it a source of profitable unrefined ore, but as the smelting and further processing occurred entirely in North America most of the profits did not accrue to Guyanese people. When prices for sugar, rice and bauxite fell in the Great Depression of the 1930s, high unemployment and widespread poverty followed because, despite the great latent wealth of bauxite, Guyana's was still a dependent plantation economy.

Historically, King Sugar, for so long associated with slavery, had been the centre of the Caribbean's plantation economy, but even in those cases where sugar was not central, like Belize and the Bahamas, or when other products and industries had become important, like Jamaica, Guyana and Trinidad, the essential shape and structures of plantation economy persisted. None of these colonial economies showed any sign in the 1930s of becoming less dependent and more self-sufficient, and in spite of the considerable wealth and even great fortunes that were being generated in some places, the vast majority of working people remained desperately poor, in many cases as poor as their forebears had been a century earlier when just emerging from the slavery period. The most significant change, perhaps, was not to be found in the structure of these economies so much as in their orientation, as several of these still British colonies - among them Jamaica, Belize, the Bahamas and Guyana - became more tied to the North American economy for imports, markets and capital. Traditional ties of ownership, trade and colonial control were giving way to the changing realities of the global capitalist system and the logic of geography, as the rising United States became the chief power - economically, politically and militarily - in the Caribbean after 1898. This became increasingly true, too, in the British Caribbean, from Belize to Guyana.

The integration of the capitalist world economy, which the Caribbean had experienced since the sixteenth century as a central part of the developing Atlantic World, accelerated between 1875 and 1914, when much of the rest of the world was formally partitioned among empires dominated by a handful of states. In Africa, Liberia remained nominally free and Ethiopia defeated Italy at the battle of Aduwa in 1896, but the rest of the continent was divided between European powers. This new imperialism, which was made possible by technological developments in communications, transport and warfare, was related to the demands of the metropolitan markets for supplies of food staples and minerals, and for markets for the manufactured goods of the metropoles. Although the organisation of the new imperialism was different from the old, with capital more concentrated in modern corporations, the Caribbean was all too familiar with the disadvantages of being a peripheral region subject to the political rivalries and economic cycles of the metropolitan powers.

The Great Depression of the late nineteenth century had a massive impact on the dependent plantation economies of the Caribbean, but the most important long-term change in the political economy of the region at this time was the see-saw shift in the relative global status of Great Britain and the United States. Whereas Great Britain was undoubtedly the workshop of the world and the greatest imperial power in the 1860s, by the end of the nineteenth century its position had declined in relation to both Germany and the United States. It was inevitable, given this shift in the global balance of economic and political power, that the United States would become the greatest power in the Caribbean. Ever since its unilateral declaration of the Monroe Doctrine in 1823, the United States had opposed political intervention by European powers in the Americas, but by the end of the nineteenth century this doctrine was reinterpreted to mean that the United States was the only power with a right to intervene in the hemisphere. This transparent rationale for imperial expansion was made with Cuba in mind. By 1877, already, more than 82 per cent of Cuba's exports went to the United States, compared to only 6 per cent to Spain, and by the 1890s the United States had invested $50 million in Cuba.

In 1898, the United States ended the second Cuban war of independence by invading the island, and at the Treaty of Paris in 1899 Spain ceded Cuba and Puerto Rico, along with the Philippines, to the United States. When the United States became the political as well as effective economic metropolis of these remnants of the formerly great Spanish American empire it marked the beginning of the United States' growing hegemony in the region. By the 1920s, with the exception of those territories that were still colonies of European powers, 'the United States had established military intervention as a standard political procedure in its neighboring states' (Knight 1978: 182). Puerto Rico was made a US territory in 1900, Cuba was reoccupied between 1906 and 1909, and the

United States occupied Haiti from 1915 to 1934 and the Dominican Republic from 1916 to 1924. Meanwhile, in 1917, Puerto Ricans were made US citizens, though without equal political rights, Denmark sold its Virgin Islands to the United States, and US troops returned to Cuba, where they stayed until 1922. This series of military interventions prefaced the intensification of US investments in plantations. 'The period between 1897 and 1930 saw the enormous concentration of latifundia in the Caribbean under the stimulus of American capital investment' (Williams 1970: 429), and the migration of large numbers of people to those places stimulated by such investment.

Although the British Caribbean was immune from military interventions,[8] it was not immune from the increasing integration of the world capitalist economy under the United States hegemony. Consequently, the impact of the worldwide depression of the 1930s on these dependent economies, some of which were by 1929 more integrated with the United States than with the UK, was quite as catastrophic in the British Caribbean as in, say, Cuba and Puerto Rico. Throughout the Caribbean, in colonies and in nominally independent countries that were under US influence, there was an explosion of class and race consciousness and nationalism. This explosion redefined the politics of the entire region in the following decades.

The political agitation was everywhere rooted in social discontent and economic deprivation. The dismal economic situation that resulted from the Great Depression produced more unemployment, rising prices and lower wages, at the same time reducing opportunities for migration. The plantation sector, which remained dominant in most of these colonial economies, continued to control the best agricultural land even while the estates reduced their labour forces. Consequently, in the 1930s as in the 1830s, the plantation economy was a major obstacle to the diversification of agriculture, while it took advantage of labour that was cheap because it was so abundant. Similarly, the widespread unemployment and poverty reduced the potential domestic market for locally produced goods, either agricultural or manufactured, and so inhibited local development still further. The effect of the Great Depression in the British Caribbean was 'the last straw which broke the camel's back. Where the crash of 1929 might have been seen as heralding a remarkable and unprecedented crisis in American capitalism, this could not be said for the British Caribbean which had been experiencing the impact of crisis and depression from the mid-nineteenth century, with isolated periods of prosperity.' (Morris 1988: 39-40)

The economic breakdown of the plantation sector is evident above all in the collapse of the price of sugar because the sugar industry remained dominant in many colonies, such as Barbados, Antigua, St Kitts and Guyana, and even where it was less dominant it was generally one of the largest employers, as in Trinidad, Jamaica and St Lucia. In 1928 sugar and its by-products constituted 97 per cent of the value of all exports from Antigua, 95 per cent of those from Barbados, 86 per cent of those from St Kitts-Nevis, 60 per cent of Guyana's exports and 45 per cent of St Lucia's (Williams 1970: 440). In Barbados, the price of sugar per ton fell from $73.20 in 1927 to $41.52 in 1931, and it remained low until the Second World War (Morris 1988: 42). In Jamaica, the sugar price fell from £16 15 shillings in 1927 to £11 5 shillings in 1931, and to a low of £9 10 shillings and 9 pence in 1936 (Post 1978: 88). In Guyana, the price received for sugar exports averaged £26 per ton between 1920 and 1924, fell to £12 per ton between 1925 and 1929, and then to £6 per ton between 1930 and 1939 (Mandle 1973: 39).

In short, the average annual production of sugar in the British Caribbean increased from 312,000 tons in the 1920s to 485,000 tons in the 1930s (Ward 1985: 27), but the price received fell catastrophically after 1929 to less than £5 per ton in 1934, the lowest figure in its history (Parry and Sherlock 1971: 285-6). Those men and women who still managed to obtain work on the sugar estates found their jobs were insecure and their wages pitiful, at 28-60 cents per day for unskilled sugar workers (Williams 1970: 444). The survival of the plantation economy during the century after Emancipation was at the expense of those who worked in it, and the effect of the Great Depression was to sharpen the contradictions and lead to more militant and organised demands for reforms.

Social policies and political reforms

When the British empire was in its heyday before the First World War, the British government was unlikely to consider serious political reforms or undertake major revisions of its social policies in the colonies. Though a royal commission visited the Caribbean colonies in 1897 to investigate social and economic conditions, major changes were not undertaken until after the recommendations made by the royal commission chaired by Lord Moyne which toured the British Caribbean in 1938-9 in the wake of the labour rebellions. In the meantime, the Colonial Office merely tinkered with the system in order to limit agitation while continuing to support the plantation economy and protect British investments and interests. In spite of several recommendations, discussions of policy and minor reforms, therefore, it was not until the great labour rebellion in Jamaica in 1938, a century after Emancipation, that the British government began to change its approach to its colonies in the Caribbean.

The 1897 commission, chaired by Sir Henry Norman, who had been the governor of Jamaica from 1884 to 1889, was appointed in the wake of a virtual collapse of world sugar prices and in response to a series of disturbances in the Caribbean colonies. Whereas a previous commission, in 1884, had commented on 'the natural indolence of the negro' and regarded the question of 'a reliable supply of labour' to the planters as the key problem (Lobdell 1988: 199), the Norman Commission drew attention to the importance of peasant farming. This commission acknowledged the obvious fact that the sugar industry remained predominant while it was declining in value, yet its three members 'fell short of making a single unanimous practical decision about the underlying macro-economic cause of the depression' (Richardson 1997: 212). They could not agree, for example, on whether to propose countervailing tariffs to protect sugar from the British Caribbean from the bounty-supported European sugar. However, they did agree that there was no alternative to sugar in Barbados, so there the issue was about what changes could be made within the industry. In Grenada they saw the benefits that could accrue to small farmers. For other colonies, like St Vincent and St Lucia, they noted, with a revealing double negative, 'that it is not impossible for the two systems, of large estates and peasant holdings, to exist side by side with mutual advantage'.[9] For the first time, then, in the face of the prolonged sugar crisis, British officials were asked to consider substitutions for the sugar economy, at least in some places. No reform, recommended the commissioners, 'affords so good a prospect for the permanent welfare in future of the West Indies as the settlement of the labouring population on the land as small peasant proprietors' (quoted in Lobdell 1988: 200). Not only Crown lands should be made available but also, where circumstances were sufficiently dire, private estates should be expropriated and sold to small farmers. Remarkably, the commissioners asserted, in a break with the assumptions and priorities of the plantation economy, 'A monopoly of the most accessible and fertile lands by a few persons who are unable any longer to make a beneficial use of them cannot, in the general interest of the island, be tolerated, and is a source of public danger' (quoted in Lobdell 1988: 200). They acknowledged, as Bonham Richardson has pointed out, that the differences in 'local topographies, vegetation, soil types and climatic conditions' (1997: 213) meant there should be different plans and responses for different places. Moreover, the commissioners recommended the development of roads, bridges and shipping to facilitate the farmers' access to local markets and intercolonial trade, and the creation of a college of agriculture in Trinidad to improve knowledge and techniques of cultivation of a variety of crops. Their recognition that economies that remained dependent on sugar could not be secure, and that the British government had a moral responsibility to the working people of the Caribbean and not just the planters, however paternalistic, was quite radical in terms of nineteenth-century doctrines.

The secretary of the Norman Commission was Sydney Olivier, a Colonial Office staff member who was active in the Fabian Society from 1885. From 1890 to 1891 he was the colonial secretary in Belize, where he witnessed an extreme example of the monopolisation of land by the BEC. He then spent several years working in the South African Department before being transferred in

1895 to the West India Department. In a memorandum on the Norman Commission's report, Olivier commented that in many British Caribbean colonies the sugar plantations were sustained 'by a strict land monopoly and an entire subjection of the negro which is equivalent to the system of slavery' (quoted in Rich 1988: 217).

Olivier, who believed in benevolent colonial administration and a West Indian development scheme that would include a role for the peasants, was colonial secretary of Jamaica from 1900 to 1904 and was appointed governor of Jamaica in 1907. This provided him with an opportunity to apply some of his reformist ideas in the period immediately after a massive earthquake had shattered Kingston. However, Olivier showed 'no particularly strong faith in the existing black peasantry on the island' (Rich 1988: 225) and advocated, quite to the contrary, the continued importation of Indian indentured labourers. After visiting Panama and Costa Rica in 1911, he decided that Jamaican emigration would promise long-term benefits through settlement in Central America while dealing with some of the 'surplus population' of Jamaica. The poverty of the peasantry had spawned a major migration from rural Jamaica to the towns and overseas even while Olivier was governor. He ended his governorship in 1913, 'having failed to shift British colonial policy in any substantial manner, though imprinting some of his ideas on later colonial thinking' (Rich 1988: 226). He remained an advocate for the peasantry, wrote of 'The Scandal of West Indian Labour Conditions' in 1938, and urged the Moyne Commission to support peasant settlement schemes combined with 'liberal education' (Rich 1988: 228). At the turn of the century, the Norman Commission and Olivier were ahead of their times in recommending that the working people of the Caribbean should have access to land as small farmers rather than as wage labourers, and the idea still sounded quite radical in 1938.

Land policy was slow to change, but changes made in the medical and educational systems in the late nineteenth and early twentieth centuries had a long-term impact on the societies of the British Caribbean. The frequent incidence of sickness and death among recent indentured Portuguese and Indian immigrants in Guyana in the 1840s prompted the local government in 1847 to require their employers to maintain hospitals on each estate and to pay doctors to visit every 48 hours. By January 1848, some 98 of the 220 estates had hospitals and 24 more were being built, but it was acknowledged that the doctors' visits were insufficient. The hospitals ordinance of 1848 forbade the allocation of new immigrants to estates lacking hospitals and, although the planters grumbled, most seemed to comply if only to keep their newest workers healthier. Their legal obligation did not extend to former slaves who, even if they worked regularly on the estates, would not necessarily be allowed to use the medical services. Some planters let all their estate workers use the hospitals, but villagers who worked elsewhere had no access to medicine other than the overcrowded public hospital in Georgetown and what they could provide for themselves. A revised hospitals ordinance in 1859 required each hospital to have a nurse and certain minimum equipment, and to keep a register, and 'by 1864 the system, within its limitations, was working tolerably well' (Laurence 1964: 62).

Trinidad lagged behind Guyana in these provisions. Until 1866, when a hospitals ordinance required estates employing indentured immigrants to erect hospitals, with medical visits twice a week, the government had merely appealed to the planters to honour their obligations. By 1867, some 92 of the 155 estates in Trinidad had hospitals and 50 more were under construction, but they were not all adequately equipped. In 1870, under the immigration ordinance, government doctors were appointed to care for sick immigrants, with Trinidad divided into 15 districts, each with a district medical officer. This made possible 'a more efficient and more easily controlled service' (Laurence 1964: 65).

A more comprehensive system was introduced in Guyana in 1873, with a government medical service organised by districts for the whole population, not just the immigrants on the estates. What began as a limited service to the newly arrived immigrants in the 1840s had developed into an acceptance of responsibility by the colonial government to maintain a rudimentary medical service for everyone. In the 1860s the mortality rate among recent immigrants in Guyana, which had been higher than in any other West Indian colony, fell sharply as a result of the improved and more accessible medical care (Laurence 1964: 64). The development of these medical services was also a development in social policy, as the principle that the colonial government had responsibility for people it had encouraged to migrate became extended into a service from which everyone could benefit.

In Jamaica, where the problem regarding the health of new immigrants was not so salient as in Guyana and Trinidad, the colonial government was slower to become involved in medical services. Such primitive medical services as there were in Jamaica may actually have declined after Emancipation (Sheridan 1985: 342), and in 1861, when there were only 50 qualified doctors in the island, most people continued to rely on informal or folk medicine. Government annual expenditure on health rose from £2,300 in 1852 to £11,325 in 1870-1, and in the last two decades of the nineteenth century was £30,000 - £35,000 annually. The colonial government recruited doctors in the UK and in 1872 the governor established the Medical Council to frame the rules, assess the qualifications and serve in a disciplinary function with regard to the practice of medicine in Jamaica. The number of doctors doubled between 1861 and 1900, but the number of hospital beds increased only marginally, from 945 to 1,171, between 1880 and 1900. The problem of transportation facilities, combined with the continuing shortage of qualified medical personnel and the expense of medical services, made modern medicine inaccessible to most poor, and especially rural, people. In 1890, the 23 doctors in Kingston constituted one for every 2,109 people, but elsewhere in the island there was one doctor for every 8,803 people (Bryan 1991: 166).

The chief health problems for most Jamaicans resulted less from the shortage of doctors or hospital beds, however, than from their poor diet, inadequate housing and unhygienic water supplies and sanitation. In other words, the poverty and exploitation from which most Jamaicans suffered were the cause of malnutrition and overcrowding, which in turn contributed to many health problems, including diseases such as dysentery, tuberculosis, yaws, cholera and bronchitis. Mortality rates continued to be high, averaging about 23.5 per thousand, and climbed steeply to about 28 per thousand in epidemic years such as 1879-80 and 1889-90. Infant mortality rates were extremely high, and even increased from 158 per thousand live births in 1881-5 to 192 per thousand in 1906-10 (Roberts 1957: 187). Patrick Bryan concludes (1991: 186) that in late nineteenth-century Jamaica 'there were problems of health whose solution dictated social policy initiatives towards the improvement of housing, improvement of sanitation, water supplies, and diet. Medical facilities could not solve problems which were deeply rooted in a policy of social exploitation'. Measures to improve sanitation, including regulations for slaughterhouse facilities and for the burial of the dead, and for cleaning and providing a sewerage system for Kingston, helped reduce the possibility of epidemics, but the social environment of poverty remained responsible for most people's health problems.

Yet Jamaica was actually one of the healthiest colonies in the British Caribbean, with lower mortality rates than Barbados, Guyana and Trinidad between 1879 and 1913 (Roberts 1957: 185). Beginning after the First World War, when greater control was gained over a widening range of diseases, the mortality rate in Jamaica began a steady decline, from a peak of 26.89 per thousand in 1916-20 to 12.94 in 1946-50, and infant mortality rates also declined in this period from 174.2 per thousand live births to 85.5 (Roberts 1957: 187). In Barbados, where mortality rates were generally higher, malnutrition caused by the economic crisis of the 1890s raised them even higher. The death rate rose from 23.9 per thousand in 1882, before the crisis, to 40.7 per thousand in 1898. In the latter year, infant mortality was also exceptionally high: there were 712 still births and 2,610 infant deaths compared with 7,107 live births (Richardson 1997: 237). By the 1920s the death rate in Barbados had declined to about 23 per thousand (Beckles 1990: 164).

In general, conspicuous declines in the mortality rate have occurred in all populations of the British Caribbean since about 1920. In Guyana, which was generally the unhealthiest colony, the natural growth rate was negative until about the 1870s. Even there, however, the death rate declined from 35.1 per thousand in 1871-80 to 29.5 per thousand in 1911-20, and then more rapidly to 14.9 per thousand in 1946-50, largely due to the decline in deaths resulting from malaria and undefined fevers, pneumonia and bronchitis, diarrhoea and enteritis, tuberculosis and kidney disease (Mandle 1973: 52, 81, 87). Infant mortality rates in Guyana averaged 190 per thousand live births in 1911-20, with a peak of 223.21 in 1918, but a steady downward trend from the early 1920s reduced the rate to 121.83 per thousand live births in 1935 (Mandle 1973: 88). Many of Guyana's health problems were attributable to the poor housing and sanitary conditions associated with poverty, and to the swampy conditions of the coastal plain in which most people lived and worked. As the income levels stagnated between 1911 and 1940, the improvements in health in this period are attributed chiefly to the efforts of the public health department which was organised in 1912. By the 1930s, improvements had been made in sanitation problems, the drainage of swampy areas and water supplies, and by 1920 most milk was subject to government control. Tuberculosis and malaria, two of the greatest causes of death, were objects of special public health programmes, particularly on the sugar estates (Mandle 1973: 91-5). Mandle concludes (1973: 109) that 'the effect, if not the cause, of the investment in public health facilities, which occurred before 1940 was, to some extent, to offset the loss in estate population and labor force, caused by the termination of indentured immigration'.

In education, as health services, the colonial governments began to take more responsibility in the twentieth century, though the great influence of the various religious denominations that had long dominated the educational systems in many colonies continued to inhibit change.[10] Although much of the parlous state of education in the early twentieth century could be attributed to lack of finances, the system was severely flawed from its conception after Emancipation. In general, the formal education system, which was developed in the nineteenth century in association with the Christian churches, 'was mainly geared toward attempting to build up among the young moral support for, and acceptance of, the emerging social order of plantation society and their own place on the lowest rungs of the social hierarchy' (Bacchus 1990: 358). Even those people who wanted to reform the system were more concerned with questions of economy and efficiency than with criticising its goals and philosophy. The Lumb Commission, for example, when it attacked the inadequacies of education in Jamaica in 1898, recommended the amalgamation of voluntary, that is denominational, schools and achieving compulsory attendance in order to obtain better value for the outlay of public funds. The Lumb report also recommended a more limited curriculum, though still including the singing of approved songs and hymns, and fewer textbooks, while seeking to overcome the 'general distaste for manual and agricultural labour' (Gordon 1968: 116-28).

Some of the critics of the existing system were far from being radical innovators. After the First World War, many of the new colonial education officers were former officers in the British armed forces who continued to use their military titles and were used to authoritarian command structures. 'They were impatient of inefficiency, scandalised by the inadequacies they found, and ruthless in their administration for reform' (Gordon 1968: 6-7). Major Bain Gray, who was the director of education in Guyana, was typical, conducting his administrative career in the spirit of a military campaign. In 1925, three months after starting his job, he wrote a trenchant report which, among other matters, criticised the limitation of his own powers. Within a few years the board of education had been disbanded, and was then reconstituted only as an advisory body. Bain Gray criticised the system as being unchanged for at least 30 years: the buildings, furniture, books, and curriculum suggesting 'the general atmosphere of late Victorianism' (Report, 1925, in Gordon 1968: 150).

In the 1930s British professionals like F.C. Marriott and Arthur Mayhew, who wrote a report on Trinidad, Barbados, and the Leeward and Windward Islands in 1933, were urging reform of the colonial educational system. Marriott and Mayhew thought the systems in Barbados and Trinidad were better than those in the small islands, but they found many school buildings and the facilities for training teachers were inadequate. In most islands where an examination closed the primary school course, less than 1 per cent of the children attending obtained a certificate, and in many cases as much as one-third of the children was not attending school. They urged 'a gradual advance towards universal compulsion' between the ages of 6 and 12 years. They found that only 16 per cent of the teachers overall had any kind of training, though Trinidad was better with 27 per cent (Report, 1933, in Gordon 1968: 168). With regard to the curriculum, they found 'The time-table of the average school is littered with subjects or fragments of subjects that bear no relation to the lives of the pupils or the qualifications and ability of the teachers' (Report, 1933, in Gordon 1968: 172), and they urged simplification of the curriculum, including concentration on 'correctly spoken English'. They also noted that it was one of the chief functions of the primary school teachers to set an example of a 'willingness to work', as many people, including the employers of labour, felt that the school system 'fails to check, if it is not actually responsible for creating, an unreadiness for hard work, which is said to be on the increase' (Report, 1933, in Gordon 1968: 175). By the 1930s, however, such recommendations were too late, as 'West Indians were no longer willing to accept their solutions from colonial officials whom they regarded as responsible for the shortcomings' (Gordon 1968: 8). When Marriott, as Trinidad's director of education, urged the setting of local examinations at the secondary level, some parents suspected him of 'trying to sabotage the opportunities of non-whites to take and pass the Cambridge examinations' (Campbell 1992: 31).

The most revealing and moving testimony to the personal cost of the colonial educational system to its victims is provided in several novels of childhood, among them George Lamming's In the Castle of My Skin (1953), Merle Hodge's Crick Crack, Monkey (1970), Zee Edgell's Beka Lamb (1982) and Cecil Foster's No Man in the House (1991). Many poor parents continued to view education as providing opportunities for their children, and made sacrifices in order that their children could have the opportunities that had been denied them, but the harsh reality often failed to meet their expectations. Not only were school buildings and equipment poor and the teachers inadequately trained, but economic pressures often kept the children from school. In Barbados, which had one of the best records, 88 per cent of the children aged between six and 14 years were enrolled in school, but the average daily attendance of those enrolled was only 74 per cent. Meanwhile, in Grenada and St Vincent, enrolment was as low as 51.5 per cent and 46.5 per cent, respectively, and in St Lucia an average of only 57 per cent of those who were enrolled actually attended (Brereton 1989: 107–8). Only a tiny handful of these students continued into the secondary schools, which remained largely the preserve of the mostly fair-skinned elite and middle classes. This highly exclusive and elitist system of colonial education, rather than permitting social mobility, ensured that the secondary schools served to perpetuate deep class and racial distinctions by maintaining privileges across generations, at the same time that it propagated colonial values and a sense of imperial hegemony. Far from providing a vehicle for social change, therefore, the education system in the 1930s was essentially, as it was intended from its inception in the 1830s, a means of social reproduction.

Although the government's assumption of greater responsibility for social policies on health and education services in part reflected the changes occurring within the UK in the nineteenth century, it also reflected its concern with the social stability and economic viability of the colonies. Some black people, and a few Indians in Guyana and Trinidad, managed to take advantage of such limited educational opportunities as were available to become socially mobile, entering professions hitherto monopolised by the whites and fair-skinned, as lawyers, doctors and particularly as teachers. These last often reinforced the authoritarian and imperialistic orientation of the colonies, but some were dedicated to reform and to the advancement of their people by the expansion of education as well as their own economic and professional interests. The Association of Schoolmasters, formed in Jamaica in 1884, was followed in 1894 by the Jamaican Union of Teachers (JUT). J.H. Reid, an educated black Jamaican who contributed frequently to Dr Robert Love's Jamaica Advocate, viewed the JUT and the dockworkers' strike in 1895 as signs of a growing unity, across classes, of 'the Negro race'. Calling Crown colony government 'a hired government [that] could not promote national sentiment', Reid supported Love and others who adopted populist positions.[11]

In 1901 the People's Convention discussed several reform issues, including women's rights, the registration of voters, the abuse of Jamaican migrant workers and the use of flogging as a punishment for praedial larceny, as well as the general social and economic conditions of the island. The delegates consciously chose to focus their activities around Emancipation Day, to make it 'an occasion of intellectual, and patriotic improvement .... It is a day on which to recall the history of our Fathers, and to contemplate the destinies of our children. It should be utilized to the end that the Negro subjects of the British Crown will eventually rise to the full dignity of their national privileges, and enjoy without any distinction the full political manhood embraced in British citizenship'.[12] Black leaders like Love and Reid, and members of the JUT and People's Convention, far from advocating a revolutionary break with colonialism, advocated increasing Jamaican's rights within the British empire. Nevertheless, their intense identification with Jamaica and increasingly Pan-African sentiment represented an emerging nationalism and racial consciousness that developed anti-colonial ideas.

The Pan-African Association was founded in London in 1897 by a black Trinidadian lawyer, H. Sylvester Williams. By 1901 it had branches in Trinidad, supported by educated members of the middle class whose emerging sense of racial pride and solidarity was a response to the pervasive racism in these societies (Brereton 1981: 130). Their goal of the educational, cultural and economic development of the black population could not be realised within the existing colonial system that denied political representation to the majority. Opposition to Crown colony government and demands for political reforms grew in many parts of the British Caribbean in the 1890s and the early twentieth century. As working people were still denied the vote, reformist organisations expressed primarily middle-class aspirations to broaden the franchise and increase their representation in local government. The Ratepayers Association (RPA) of Trinidad, founded in 1901, and the Reform Association in Guyana, formed in 1889, exemplify these middle-class organisations and their political limitations.

The Crown colony system of government in Guyana, with the governor as the autocratic linchpin, was modified by the peculiar incorporation of the old Dutch institutions of the Court of Policy and the Combined Court (Lewis 1968: 259). A College of Electors (Kiezers), whose members served for life, nominated the unofficial members of the Court of Policy. Until 1891, an extremely narrow franchise, and even more restrictive qualifications for membership of the Court of Policy, ensured the planters' domination of local politics. The Combined Court used its powers of taxation to impose heavy indirect taxes, which hurt the poor people the hardest, and deployed expenditures to advance the planters' interests (Rodney 1981: 125). In the depression of the 1880s, many of the smaller planters were squeezed out and an urban Creole middle class arose, producing 'a situation that offered prospects of political change' (Rodney 1981: 127). A cross-section of these middle classes sought elective representation in the legislature in which big planters were the majority, but this could be achieved only through constitutional reform.

At a public meeting in Georgetown in 1886, demands were made to abolish the College of Electors, reform the Court of Policy into a House of Assembly with ten elected members, lower the franchise from $600 per year to $300 per year for urban voters, and for regular biennial elections (Rodney 1981: 136). A Political Reform Club was formed in 1887 and, though its leadership was middle-class, it aimed at mass mobilisation to achieve reform. D. M. Hutson, a coloured Creole attorney, was president and David Straughn, a journalist whose father was a cabinet maker from Barbados, was the articulate secretary. Other leaders were lawyers, journalists and schoolteachers, but when they decided to reorganise as a constitutional Reform Association in 1889 they invited a white planter, R.P. Drysdale, to become their first chairman. Drysdale, who had come to Guyana from Scotland as a plantation employee, had become a planter himself and then concentrated on a commercial business in Georgetown. He was a member of the Combined Court and was often the mayor of Georgetown. The middle-class Creoles chose him because they believed that he, as their social superior in this colonial society, could more effectively attack the power of his peers in the planter oligarchy. Though Straughn was on the new association's executive, the young black and coloured professionals became 'partly superseded' by Creole whites and Portuguese businessmen (Rodney 1981: 142). The petitions of the Reform Club and Reform Association drew attention to the need for remodelling the constitution because of the growth of what they called intermediary classes in the society, the number of registered electors having almost doubled from 1,001 in 1881 to 1,973 in 1890 (Rodney 1981: 145, 239).

Some working people who supported this reform movement could not hope to obtain the vote as their income was less than the $300 per year that was being demanded. Presumably, these people supported the movement because they hoped that even a slightly broader political system and new representatives might encourage other social and economic developments in the colony, such as the opening up of Crown lands, an end to state-aided immigration, the advancement of Creoles in the civil service, and improved health and educational services. There is also evidence that people saw the proposed reforms as related to a struggle for justice and against discrimination (Rodney 1981: 148-9). In 1891, the College of Electors was abolished, the Court of Policy became a purely legislative body, and property qualifications for election to the Court of Policy were lowered. A new Executive Council took on the executive and administrative functions of government, but the Combined

Court retained its fiscal powers. The 1891 constitutional reforms, though very modest, nevertheless encouraged a new political consciousness and energy in the struggle against planter domination and authoritarian colonial rule. Creole professionals and businessmen were the leaders of this political group that persisted into the twentieth century. Men like A.A. Thorne, Ayube Edun and Hubert Critchlow, who 'fought, generally, the abuses of colonialism rather than the idea of colonialism' (Lewis 1968: 269), sought a share in government.

After the 1891 reforms the number of registered electors in Guyana increased from 2,046 in 1891 to 2,928 in 1898, declined to 2,427 in 1900 and then increased again to reach 3,185 in 1905 (Rodney 1981: 239). After a further extension of the franchise in 1909, the coloured and black Creoles became the majority. However, the people of British and Portuguese origin were still over-represented, and those of Indian origin remained severely under-represented. In 1915, for example, when the electorate consisted of 4,312 people, 46.1 per cent of the British adult males were registered as voters, compared with 17.7 per cent of the Portuguese, 12.3 per cent of Chinese, 6.8 per cent of Africans, and only 0.6 per cent of Indians. Although 51.8 per cent of the adult male population was Indian they constituted only 6.4 per cent of the electorate, compared to men of African origin who were 42.3 per cent of the adult male population and 62.7 per cent of the electorate, and of British origin who were 1.7 per cent and 17 per cent, respectively (Despres 1967: 40).

By 1927, the colony of Guyana had accumulated a debt of £4.3 million and the Colonial Office appointed a commission to investigate economic conditions. The commission reported that the colony's constitution separated responsibility from power by enabling the elected members to oppose the government. In 1928, the Court of Policy and Combined Court were abolished, and Guyana became a Crown colony with a Legislative Council in which official and nominated members (comprising the governor, colonial secretary, attorney-general, eight nominated officials and five nominated unofficial members) outnumbered the 14 elected members. The governor had power to veto legislation enacted by the Legislative Council in the unlikely event that some of the men he had nominated voted with the elected members against official policy. This constitution did not change the property qualifications for the franchise; however, women were included in the electorate for the first time. These constitutional changes were not intended to liberalise the political system, but to ensure that the colonial government would have the power to enforce its financial policies, even against the wishes of the elected members. The basic structure of the colonial system was not altered, as the governor's powers were reinforced, the sugar industry, particularly Booker Brothers, McConnell & Co, continued to exert a dominant influence and the working people remained entirely unrepresented.

In Trinidad, where there was an autocratic Crown colony system throughout the nineteenth century, the sugar interests continued to exert their traditional influence in the political–constitutional structure long after the sugar industry was relegated to a less important rank, economically, than cocoa agriculture and, later, the oil industry. Though some urban Creole nationalists pressed for reforms between 1895 and 1914 (Magid 1988), it was not until after the First World War, when Captain Arthur A. Cipriani led the Trinidad Workingmen's Association (TWA), that an effective reform movement developed. The beginnings of this more populist and radical politics of the twentieth century lay in the growing opposition to Crown colony government in the decade after 1895. The chief issues of this agitation concerned the question of the unofficial majority in the Legislative Council and the borough council of Port of Spain, neither of which were well suited to win the support of working people who were disenfranchised.

Trinidad not only failed to acquire a semi–elective council, such as some other colonies were granted, but it even lost the majority of unofficials that it had had in the Legislative Council since 1862. The secretary of state for the colonies, Joseph Chamberlain, had been a reforming mayor of Birmingham, but he was a racist in imperial affairs. In 1896 he wrote: 'local government (falsely so–called) is the curse of the West Indies. In many islands it means only the rule of a local oligarchy of whites and half-breeds – always incapable and frequently corrupt. In other cases it is the rule of the negroes, totally unfit for representative institutions and the dupes of unscrupulous adventurers.' (quoted in Brereton 1981: 146-7) In 1898, on the basis of an unsubstantiated report by the colonial secretary, who was acting as governor in Trinidad, that unofficial members were organising in opposition to the government, Chamberlain appointed the commander of the local military forces an official member and thereby restored the official majority in the Council.

Chamberlain was equally high-handed with regard to the Port of Spain borough council, which had been an elected body since its establishment in 1853. Though the property qualifications were still high, this council was 'an important forum for local politicians, especially black and coloured radicals' (Brereton 1981: 147), who were opponents of Crown colony government. Borough council members argued that their powers to manage municipal affairs should be enlarged and that, as it was in financial straits, the government should provide relief by granting it exemption from some charges and providing some new revenues. When Chamberlain announced that financial relief would be offered only on condition that the council submitted its budget annually for government approval, the councillors rejected these conditions on the grounds that the borough council would then no longer be an independent body. On Chamberlain's instructions, an ordinance was rushed through the Legislative

Council in 1898 abolishing the borough council. In January 1899, the borough councillors made a formal protest: 'This Council, at its last meeting and on the eve of its abolition, wishes to place on record its strongest protests against the injustices and unfair treatment they have received from the Government of this Island' (quoted in Brereton 1981: 148). In place of the elected council the city's administration henceforth rested in a board of commissioners nominated by the governor, constituting a further extension of autocratic power within the Crown colony system.

Although the TWA, founded in 1897, and local branches of the Pan-African Association (PAA), founded in 1901, kept dissent alive, it was the Ratepayers Association (RPA), founded by Port of Spain businessmen in September 1901, that became the centre of a furore. In 1902 the RPA had only 84 members, chiefly white and coloured lawyers and merchants, and voting on matters of finance and governance in the organisation was limited to members who were rate-payers (Magid 1988: 111). After Emmanuel Lazare, a radical black solicitor who was the leader of the Port of Spain branch of the PAA, joined the RPA in 1902 it became more active and broadly based. Lazare had been impressed by the TWA's earlier call for an alliance between black workers and coloured professionals (Magid 1988: 112). By 1903 the RPA had 185 members and a wider influence.

The issue that exploded in Port of Spain was the control of water, itself a persistent problem, that became a question of rights. The director of public works tried to control wastage by inspecting private homes on unannounced visits, and cutting off the water supply if leaking taps were found, and the government prepared legislation to instal meters in city homes. Though this was not an issue that directly affected most residents, whose water came from communal stand-pipes, the RPA made this a question of governmental interference and the authoritarian character of Crown colony rule (Brereton 1981: 149). The meeting of the Legislative Council on 16 March 1903 was postponed because of disorders in and outside the Red House, the chief government building, and government announced that only people issued with special tickets could attend the next meeting on 23 March. The RPA claimed this was illegal and at a public meeting in Brunswick (now Woodford) Square on 21 March people were told to meet in order to prevent the second reading of the water bill. Lazare used the issue of the water rates to attack the principle of taxation without popular representation. Governor Sir Alfred Moloney prepared to meet any demonstration by a show of force, with some 200 heavily armed policemen (Magid 1988: 125).

At about 11.20 in the morning of 23 March, several hundred people, led by members of the RPA, tried to enter the Red House without tickets. As the crowd grew to more than 1,000, Lazare urged them to follow him across the street to Brunswick Square for a meeting. When the legislative session began at noon, Henry Alcazar, a coloured lawyer, moved an adjournment, but this was defeated by 14 to 6, the majority consisting of four unofficials and all the official members. Alcazar stated, before he walked out in protest, 'this public movement . . . is the inauguration of a more serious movement which I hope will end in the people having their own representatives at this table' (quoted in Brereton 1981: 151). This statement, and the fact that most protesters outside the building were not middle-class ratepayers, shows that the water issue had provided the occasion for the expression of resentment about the wider issues of the rights of representation and the conduct of government.

At about 1.30 pm, when some protesters forced their way into the Red House, the Governor and other officials fled. Mounted police and sailors from HMS Pallas were summoned. The crowd, now estimated at 5,000, threw stones at the police and by about 2.30 the Red House was on fire. The Riot Act was read and several volleys were fired on the crowd before it dispersed. Some 200 shots were fired, killing 16 people, and 44 were treated for their wounds at the city hospital. The Red House was destroyed (Magid 1988: 125–30).

After the tragedy of the water riots, the government of Trinidad and Tobago (the sister island was made a ward of the united colony in 1898) sought to conciliate the unofficial members, while opponents of Crown colony government focused on the restoration of the borough council. C.P. David, a lawyer and prominent member of the RPA who was the first black Island Scholar in 1885, was the first black unofficial member of the Legislative Council, nominated in 1904. Stephen Laurence, a coloured doctor who had studied at Edinburgh University on an Island Scholarship, qualifying in 1888, and who was also a prominent spokesman for reform, was appointed in 1911 (Brereton 1981: 151). Meanwhile, a committee was formed to study what kind of municipal authority should manage Port of Spain. Its members included several reformers, such as David, Lazare and Alcazar, who were active agitators since before the water riots. These 'radicals' sought an entirely elected council, but the majority of the committee recommended one composed of electives and nominees. In 1906, however, a wholly nominated town board was established. The TWA, which consisted largely of skilled artisans and white-collar workers in Port of Spain, consistently supported an elected council with low property qualifications for voting. By 1913 there were five unofficial members of the Legislative Council who favoured an elected borough council, including Laurence, Alcazar and George Fitzpatrick, the first Trinidadian Indian member. A 1914 ordinance reconstituted an elected borough council, to be restored in stages between 1914 and 1917, but with a narrow electorate and even higher qualifications for membership. Women could vote if they qualified, but they could not be members. The restoration of the Port of Spain council 'was regarded as a victory for the opposition to Crown Colony government, and it meant that the major objective of politically minded Trinidadians, after 1914, was elected representation in the central government, the legislative council' (Brereton 1981: 152).

Most political activity ceased during the war, but in the 1920s the issue of constitutional reform dominated politics in Trinidad and Tobago. A revitalised TWA, with Howard Bishop as secretary, joined the renewed campaign for constitutional reform. Bishop edited a paper, the Labour Leader, from 1922, in which demands for an eight-hour day, the recognition of trade unions, and overtime pay and workmen's compensation appeared alongside the constitutional issues. Cipriani, who had been an outspoken opponent of racism and discrimination in the British West Indies Regiment during the war, joined the TWA in 1919 and was elected its president in 1923, further linking the middle-class liberal reformers with a nascent working class.

These examples from Guyana and Trinidad and Tobago show that, while there was increasing dissatisfaction with the authoritarianism of Crown colony rule from the late nineteenth century, the middle classes alone, however articulate, determined and organised they were from time to time, lacked the political leverage to achieve major constitutional reforms so long as the British government remained intransigent. By 1921, however, the British government was prepared to make some concessions in the direction of reform and sent a senior official, E.F.L. Wood[13] to the Caribbean to study the issue of constitutional reform and to make a report. In the 1920s, there were differences among the various constitutions of the British Caribbean colonies, ranging from the more pure Crown colony type of Trinidad and Tobago, through those, like Jamaica, in which part of the legislature was elected, to Barbados, where the old House of Assembly remained fully elective.

In Barbados, where the merchants of Bridgetown had joined the traditional plantocracy during the depression of the late nineteenth century, the elite continued to dominate the elective House of Assembly in the twentieth century. This merchant-planter elite exercised a symbolic and cultural domination, correlative with its economic and political power, through social clubs such as the white Wanderers Cricket Club, formed in 1877 (Beckles 1990: 149). By the early 1920s, however, a new critical spirit had emerged, comparable with what was happening in Trinidad. The narrow franchise defined by the Representation of the People Act (1901), which required voters to have an income of at least £50 per year or freehold property worth £5 rent or more annually, enabled a growing, but still small, number of middle-class people to vote. Clennell W. Wickham, a veteran of the First World War who became editor of the Barbados Herald, criticised the elite's domination of society, but it was Dr Charles Duncan O'Neale, who returned to Barbados in 1924 after many years qualifying in and practising medicine in the UK and Trinidad, who initiated the organisational expression of political reform.

O'Neale, inspired by the British Labour Party, which he had represented on the Sunderland Council, launched the Democratic League (BDL), Barbados' first political party, in October 1924. Marcus Garvey's UNIA had established a branch in Barbados in 1920 and hundreds of Garveyites supported the league, though the restricted franchise meant that most could not actually vote for its candidates. In December 1924, just two months after the league's formation, C.A. (Chrissie) Brathwaite was elected to the House on the league's ticket in a by-election in St Michael, and O'Neale himself was elected in Bridgetown in 1932, retaining the seat until his death in 1936 (Beckles 1990: 156-9). The BDL heralded a new political era in Barbados, though the old constitution, which the governing class defended so proudly, remained intact and the Legislative Council remained dominated by the conservative merchant-planter elite.

In Jamaica the Crown colony system was reformed in 1884 and 1895, when elected members were included on the Legislative Council: nine in 1884 and 14 in 1895. After 1895, when the council had 29 members, the majority was still composed of the officials and those who were appointed by the governor, and council members could vote only yes or no to legislative proposals that originated with the governor. The power of the governor could not really be challenged and the council was little more than a debating society of the elite. Consequently, these 'modifications were more in the nature of concessions to oligarchy rather than . . . mileposts on the return-journey to democracy' (Munroe 1972: 14). Though the number of coloured and black members increased, the restrictive qualifications for membership (an annual income of £300, or £150 from landed property), and the narrow franchise ensured that they would remain a minority of the elected members. In 1884, all nine elected members were white, five of them planters, two were businessmen, one a planter-businessman and one a lawyer. The first black man to be elected was Alexander Dixon, a schoolteacher, in 1900, followed by the Bahamian-born Dr Robert Love in 1906. In 1910, of the 14 elected members, five were coloured and one black. Moreover, many of the seats were uncontested in elections, for example, in 1906, 1911, and 1920, six, five, and nine, respectively, of the 14 seats were uncontested. Jamaican politics in this period was a game limited to the elite, and 'in the prolonged constitutional negotiations of the twenties the local legislators wanted greater power for their class rather than a broadening of the base of the political order' (Munroe 1972: 15-16). In 1935, only 68,636 people were registered to vote in a population of over 1 million (Hurwitz and Hurwitz 1971: 189). The chief significance of the shift from the first period of Crown colony rule, between 1866 and 1884, to the second, between 1884 and 1944, is that after 1884 the elected members of the council, who were chosen for five-year terms, served in effect as consultants to the governor, whose powers remained intact.

In Belize, the elective principle was not reintroduced until 1936, though the colony's elite had pressed for a limited change in the 1890s and the 1920s. In the late nineteenth century a European minority of large land-owners and mahogany cutters, joined by a clique of Scottish and German merchants, exercised great influence in the colony's politics because the governor selected his nominees for the Legislative Council from among them, including the manager of the huge BEC. When members of an emerging Belizean Creole elite sought elections in the 1890s, they were denied, but after 1892 the governor appointed some token Creole members to the council. Despite continuing agitation in the 1920s, the restoration of elections was postponed so long as the governor lacked reserve powers to push through any measures he considered essential without the council's consent. The unofficial members, who were unwilling to trade financial control for the elective principle, 'were protecting their political monopoly which they feared was being threatened by the growing political awareness' (Grant 1976: 59).

By 1927, Creole and Mestizo merchants and professionals had largely replaced the whites on the council, but this made little difference to the actual governance of the colony.

> European-oriented Creoles and Mestizos ... were accepted and were acceptable ... principally because they maintained the class values and pretensions of the establishment .... When European land-owning countenances gave way, in the late twenties, to those of Creole and Mestizo merchants and the seat of power shifted from the land to the counting houses, the priorities of the new elite were indistinguishable from those of their predecessor. Labour had still to be kept submissive, direct taxation had still to be resisted and the constitution, which equated wealth with political influence, had still to be maintained. (Ashdown 1979b, quoted in Shoman 1987: 18)

In the aftermath of a terrible hurricane that destroyed Belize Town in 1931, the British government made a reconstruction loan contingent upon the governor being granted reserve powers and ultimate control over the colony's finances. The six unofficial members of the council were divided on the proposal: the three local businessmen were unwilling to approve the deal, in part because the loan included $100,000 for their chief competitor, the BEC, but the three English members supported the officials and this enabled the legislation to amend the constitution to be passed in March 1932 (Grant 1976: 79). White Creoles and expatriates and the business element of the elite remained predominant in the council in this period. In 1933, five of the unofficial members, who were still all nominated, were owners or representatives of big business interests (mahogany or chicle firms, merchants and land-owners), and the other two were professionals, namely a lawyer and a minister of religion. Even while so little changed in the formal world of constitutionally defined politics, however, the political culture of Belize was changing and new forces erupted on to the colonial scene in 1934.

The Crown colony system, which was established in the British Caribbean in the nineteenth century to confirm imperial control over the local oligarchies while excluding the masses from politics, had become by the early twentieth century the bastion of those oligarchies' defences against the masses. These oligarchies sought to defend their political privileges by resisting constitutional reforms, but the British government by the 1920s had shifted towards the idea that limited concessions to the elective principle could help stabilise the colonies. The Wood Commission's report, issued in 1922, repeatedly referred to 'responsible opinion' and the 'substantial elements' in the colonies as justification for a policy of limited reforms, while ensuring that real imperial power remained intact (Lewis 1968: 122). The strategy was to make some political concessions to the educated and largely light-skinned members of the colonies, like T.A. Marryshow of Grenada, in order to assure their loyalty to the empire.[14] E. F. L. Wood urged the Colonial Office to avoid the mistake of 'witholding a concession ultimately inevitable until it has been robbed by delay of most of its usefulness and all of its grace' (Wood 1922, quoted in Lewis 1968: 123-4), but this mistake continued to characterise official policy.

The Colonial Office tended 'to grant miniscule reforms at the last moment ... seeking every way to delay the inevitable' (Lewis 1968: 108), with the result that constitutional reforms were generally both too little and too late. Tiny increases in the elective component of legislative councils may have won over a few of the middle-class reformers in the various representative government associations, but they could not stop the growing radical demand for mass suffrage elections and a real change of power. With the great economic crash of 1929 and the social distress of the 1930s, the source of the impetus for change shifted dramatically from the small and largely brown middle classes to the large and overwhelmingly black working class of the Caribbean colonies. When Garvey launched his People's Political Party in Jamaica in 1929, the constitution denied him any chance of success at the polls, but this development 'emphasized the bankruptcy of the rule of the elective independents in the Crown Colony system' (Lewis 1968: 177). Real reforms of the Crown colony system came only with the democratisation of politics that began after the labour rebellions, the Moyne Commission and the Second World War, and led eventually to self-government and independence.

The question of labour

In addition to constitutional reforms, another area in which there were glacial changes in colonial policy in the 1920s concerned labour issues. The International Labour Organization (ILO), established in 1919, put pressure upon the British government because, by article 35 of the ILO constitution, all members were bound to apply ratified conventions in their colonies, protectorates and possessions. Between August 1921 and the end of 1923, the Colonial Office sent several circulars to the colonies requesting information on labour legislation and the application of the ILO conventions concerning such issues as night work, child labour, rights of association and combination, and workmen's compensation. The British Labour Party and Trades Union Congress, meanwhile, added pressure on the government to implement labour reforms in the colonies. As a result of this pressure, some improvements were made in the interwar years in aspects of labour policy, such as the employment of women and young persons in night work, workmen's compensation, forced labour, the recruitment and employment of indigenous workers, minimum wages and penal sanctions.

The Labour Commonwealth Conference in 1925, in which Hubert Critchlow of the British Guiana Labour Union (BGLU) participated, helped develop the colonial policies of the British Labour Party. At Critchlow's invitation, F.O. Roberts, a British Labour Party MP and trade unionist, visited Trinidad and Guyana in 1926 in support of a united British Caribbean labour movement. Roberts spent two weeks in Trinidad in January 1926 as a guest of the TWA, during which he gave several talks on trade unionism, and then attended the annual conference of the BGLU and the first regional West Indian labour conference in Georgetown with Cipriani and Howard Bishop from Trinidad and two delegates from Suriname. Roberts emphasised the goal of settling industrial disputes peacefully, 'by calm and deliberate consideration round a table', and avoiding 'the bitterness of an industrial struggle' (quoted in Basdeo 1983: 64), but he did not seem to take into account that the Caribbean colonies, where trade unions were still illegal everywhere except Guyana and Jamaica, were not like the UK. Roberts supported Cipriani's efforts to introduce labour legislation to reduce working hours and to establish a standard 48-hour week, and to set up a scheme of workmen's compensation.

In Georgetown Roberts spoke optimistically and broadly about the future role of a British Caribbean labour movement, but again without recognising that such a movement would come about only through industrial struggle: 'I feel ... that from this somewhat simple beginning or representation of the working class organizations of this part of the world there is bound to grow a movement, which would spread its influence and power until it begins to take that bigger share in the Government of the people by the people, and eventually perhaps ... take a fair share in the destiny of the government of your own people and of your own land.' (quoted in Basdeo 1983: 67) Resolutions were adopted at the conference dealing with social and labour legislation, including the eight-hour day, workmen's compensation, a minimum wage, child labour, non-contributory old age pensions, national health insurance, the repeal of all penal sanctions in the masters and servants ordinances, and the need for a system of compulsory education throughout the West Indies. Connections between the British and the British Caribbean labour movements were reinforced. Roberts' reports to the British Labour Party and TUC were 'a glaring indictment of labour conditions' in the British Caribbean, including workers' wages and welfare, and the lack of labour legislation and of protection for working women and children (Basdeo 1983: 69). Henceforth, the British labour movement took a paternalistic interest in the Caribbean labour movement, and many leaders of the latter looked with high expectations to the former for guidance and assistance.

In parts of the British Caribbean, local governments, under the urging of the ILO, the Colonial Office and local organisations, introduced reforming labour legislation. In Trinidad and Tobago, for example, the TWA had urged the abolition of child labour since the First World War and the Colonial Office, pressed by the ILO, had pushed for it since 1921. After Roberts' visit to central Trinidad, where he saw a serious problem of child workers among the Indians, Cipriani and Sarran Teelucksingh, the president and vice-president of the TWA who, in 1925, were among the first people elected to the Legislative Council, petitioned for legislation on the matter. Cipriani argued that the abolition of child labour should be followed immediately by legislation for compulsory education. Though the planters and government were willing to support the former, which was passed in 1927, they opposed the latter until the Colonial Office forced it on them in 1935 (Basdeo 1983: 72-3).

When the British Labour Party held its second British Labour Commonwealth Conference in London in 1928, Cipriani participated. He was convinced that the promises made by top Labour Party spokesmen would be implemented when they came to office. Cipriani's optimism regarding the imperial policies of the British Labour Party, and his faith in the efficacy of legislation to solve working people's problems, affected his entire future strategy and the political orientation of the TWA. The British Labour Party, in turn, pledged itself to encourage the growth of trade unions in the colonies along sound, constitutional lines, adopted resolutions supporting colonial labour and social legislation, and promised to institute the reforms to which it was committed as soon as it formed the government (Basdeo 1983: 78-9).

However, the Labour government, which was in power from 1929 to 1931, failed to change colonial policies along the lines it had promised. Of course, it was preoccupied with the problems of the Great Depression and its commitment to a policy of free trade did not help the staggering sugar industry of the Caribbean colonies. The new secretary of state for the colonies was Lord Passfield, formerly Sidney Webb, the Fabian socialist and associate of Lord Olivier. The royal commission on the West Indian sugar industry, which Olivier chaired in 1930, recognised that without subsidies or a protected market the industry would not survive. Cipriani, knowing this would be disastrous for the West Indian working people, petitioned the British government to reconsider its free-trade policy, as did a group of West Indian bishops and the Trinidad Chamber of Commerce, but Passfield refused to act.

> Cipriani was bitterly disappointed and felt betrayed. He told the Legislative Council: 'Those who have the best interests of the working class at heart are bitterly disappointed at the attitude of the Labour Government towards the working classes in these colonies, and it is only another illustration ... of the continuous neglect of the West Indies ... by the British Government; and whether it be Conservative, Liberal or Labour, the situation is exactly the same. We are too small and have not got sufficient influence to make our position or representation really felt.' (quoted in Basdeo 1983: 83-4) Despite his disillusionment and frustration, however, Cipriani would not lead his organisation towards the politics of confrontation. In 1934, on the advice of the British TUC, he chose not to register the TWA as a trade union because the ordinance of 1932 did not legalise peaceful picketing or protect unions from legal actions for damages arising out of strike action. Instead, he made the TWA into the Trinidad Labour Party (TLP) and continued to rely on political efforts in the Legislative Council. Increasing dissatisfaction with his authoritarian leadership and the lack of results in the crisis of the depression led to serious challenges and divisions in the TLP over the next few years, when a series of demonstrations and strikes led up to the rebellion of 1937.

Although Lord Passfield refused to protect the sugar industry, he did press to revise the anachronistic and repressive masters and servants laws and urged that legislation enabling trade unions to be formed should be passed. He was influenced by Dr Drummond Shiels, the Labour MP for Edinburgh East who was his parliamentary under-secretary and who became an advocate of labour reform in the Caribbean colonies. At the end of a Colonial Office conference in June–July 1930, Shiels brought up, in an informal way, 'the absence of adequate labour and social legislation' and 'the obsolete character' of some of the existing legislation in the Caribbean colonies.

> Certain of the "Master and Servant" ordinances, for instance, which obtain in many Colonies are much out of date. One thing I have noticed especially is the penalties, sometimes severe penalties, for a breach of contract, which in this country and in most other countries is only a civil and not a criminal offense. That, perhaps, is not quite so bad where you have a definite and clear written contract. But in many of these "Master and Servant" ordinances, there is a penalty for a breach of a verbal contract, where there is nothing in writing

at all. That, it seems to me, is open to serious abuse if and when it comes to be a question of the relative truth or accuracy of the statements of a master, and of, perhaps, a humble and illiterate servant. I think that is one of the things that should be done away with.[15]

Shiels went on to speak of the need for workmen's compensation and insurance, and for factory legislation to ensure fair and healthy working conditions. With regard to wages, he said he was 'not very happy about conditions in the West Indies' which 'have always suffered from a low wage policy.' He referred to the Blue Book[16] of Jamaica which gave agricultural wages as 18 shillings for a 50-hour week and manufacturing workers' wages as 26 shillings per 54-hour week. In Barbados, the equivalent was between 1 shilling and 3 pence and 2 shillings per day for six 9-hour days, and between 3 shillings and 5 shillings per day for the same length of week, respectively.

> Some reference was made the other day, I think by the Governor of Jamaica, to the fact that the people in the West Indies sometimes only work four and a half days a week, and he said that they were not very fond of hard work. I do believe that a part explanation of that is the low wages .... There is no doubt that a large part of the successful Cuban sugar industry was built up by Jamaican labour. In Panama, in 1923, there was an enormous number of people from the West Indies working there, and there are regular emigrations to plantations in San Domingo, Costa Rica, and various other places. They go to these places for higher wages .... Anybody who has travelled in Canada or the United States will agree that a great many of the hotel and railway attendants are West Indians. They think a great deal of them in Canada and regard them as hard working and efficient.[17]

To this mild and even diffident complaint about the wages of Caribbean workers, the governor of Jamaica, Sir Edward Stubbs, replied in a manner redolent of a nineteenth-century Tory planter:

> The fact of the matter is that the Jamaican works when he wants to get money to pay taxes or to pay a fine for being drunk, and on any other occasion he refrains from working except to cultivate his own ground, which he does very well. The attitude of the Jamaican towards wages is such that there is no use raising wages if you want the man to do any more work, because if you raise the wage from 2s. to 4s. a day it means he will work for one day instead of two. The average Jamaican does not think that work is a thing to be proud of; he avoids it if possible.[18]

This exchange suggests that on the rare occasions when there were reformers in the Colonial Office, the old racial and class prejudices that pervaded the colonial service resisted any change from the authoritarian relations of the nineteenth century.

Two of the other topics raised by Shiels, namely native taxation and the conditions of women and children were addressed to African rather than Caribbean colonies. He also urged that governors should 'not be too afraid of organisations of workers' such as trade unions, that could 'act as safety valves', and said that it would be much better for colonial governments 'to deal with organised bodies rather than with odd individuals who are irresponsible and who yet can make a lot of trouble'. However, Shiels ended weakly on the topic of trade unions, saying only that when speaking with representatives from the colonies at the Colonial Labour Conference he 'would like to be able to say that these matters were being considered sympathetically, and that there was no fear among Governors of Trade Unions or other bodies, so long as these organisations were conducted on a proper basis, but, rather, that they would welcome their establishment'.[19] This sounded more like a plea than a definite instruction to a group of colonial governors who were not only anti-union but probably also anti-labour.

Shiels was quite outspoken on the issue of the franchise, but again he ended with a weak plea rather than a firm instruction or any real change in policy.

> Some of the West Indian Colonies badly need a new franchise .... A member of a Legislature concerns himself mainly with those who are his electors; and to those who have no votes, who cannot influence his political fortunes in any way, he is often, though he should not be comparatively indifferent. One of the best ways therefore in which those can help who are anxious to see a better state of things, is to see that the basis of the franchise is broadened and that the humblest worker has a political weapon which he may use for his own economic salvation .... There will be undoubtedly increasing restless-ness and pressure in these places where there are elected Councils and where the franchise is on the narrow basis that it is to-day. I commend, therefore, a broad franchise as one of the best methods of improving the condition of the common people. Of course, I know that the extension of the franchise itself is a difficulty. Legislative Councillors may not be keen on it, but I would like it to be kept in mind and pushed whenever and wherever possible.[20]

One aspect of colonial labour reform that the Labour government addressed within its first year of office was the anachronistic masters and servants laws. The secretary of state for the colonies in the previous administration, L.S. Amery, had requested the colonial governments to revise these laws, especially 'the abolition of imprisonment as a punishment for breach of contract, except in default of the payment of a fine'.[21] Amery pointed out that Lord Milner, when secretary of state for the colonies in 1919, had outlined suggestions for reforms of these laws, but apparently no revision had been undertaken in Jamaica, while in Guyana, under Ordinance No. 26 of 1909, a labourer could still be imprisoned for six months with hard labour for breach of contract. Amery considered offences such as 'wilful misconduct or ill-behaviour' to be ill-defined. In Jamaica, under a law passed in 1842, workers convicted of 'misconduct, miscarriage, misdemeanor, ill-behaviour in service' could still be imprisoned for up to 30 days with hard labour. In Guyana, under the Apprenticeship of Children Act No. 1 of 1854, 'misdemeanor, miscarriage, ill-behaviour' were offences punishable by solitary confinement. Avery expressed the view that these surviving nineteenth century laws were 'obsolete and out of keeping with modern opinion as to the relations of employers and servants'. An official in the Colonial Office minuted, 'It may be well not to push reforming zeal too far, but there are certainly serious drawbacks about leaving on the Statute Books legislation reaking with the taint of slavery, and providing for insolence, misdemeanor, miscarriage, ill-behaviour and other obsolete and undefinable offences.' Jamaica, he commented, had been 'decidedly obstructive' regarding the amendment of this labour legislation.[22]

Following the half-hearted efforts of his predecessors, Lord Passfield sent separate despatches to the governors of Guyana, Bermuda, the Bahamas, the Windward and Leeward Islands, Trinidad and Tobago, Jamaica and Barbados, on 14 May 1930, regarding 'the proposed revision of the Masters and Servants legislation in force in the West Indian Colonies' and asked for reports on the working of those laws at present in force.[23] To the governor of Trinidad and Tobago, for example, he wrote advising the repeal of the colony's masters and servants law, originally passed in 1846 and revised in 1921, which contained many clauses 'that were obsolete and repugnant to current opinion'.[24] In the Bahamas, workers could be imprisoned for up to 30 days with hard labour for breach of contract under section 17 of the Contracts, Servants, Act, 1861. In Barbados, domestic servants could still be imprisoned without the option of a fine in cases of wilful negligence or improper conduct causing injury to property. In Jamaica, by Law No. 3 of 1925, the courts were given discretion to impose fines in any case in place of imprisonment, or to revoke a sentence of imprisonment in proportion to the amount of fine paid when default was made after part payment.[25]

During 1930, information about the working of the labour laws came into the Colonial Office, often in the form of reports forwarded from district magistrates. From these reports it appears that most of the workers convicted under the masters and servants laws in the 1920s were fined, often for minor offences, but some were imprisoned with hard labour if they could not pay the fine, and some were whipped. However, employers often got away with not paying all the wages due their workers. In Antigua, for example, a magistrate wrote that the law 'compels the labourer to labour but not the employer to employ ... a labourer can be bound to a master for a given time and yet, because he is paid by daily job work, he is only able to draw wages for a proportion of that time'. He commented that most workers understood their rights but were nervous of exercising them, and so only two or three, all of them women, had applied to him to prosecute an employer for wrongfully withholding wages.[26] Another Antiguan magistrate reported that all contracts entered into under Ordinance No. 3 of 1922 were verbal, that very few workers were able to read and write, that they hardly earned a living wage, and that many were indebted to their employers. 'A few cases have been brought before the Court by labourers for refusal by the Masters to pay wages due, and the defence raised has always been that the labourer had not completed his contract of service'. Children were compelled, through economic necessity, to seek employment at an early age, and many planters, because of the sugar industry crisis, were giving notice to their workers or compelling them to pay rent as tenants for the houses on estates where they had previously been residential labourers. He wrote that workers convicted in his court generally paid fines, but when in default they were given seven days in prison with hard labour, and offenders under the age of 16 years were whipped. Of a total 1,358 persons charged for offences against the master and servant act between 1 January 1925 and 31 October 1929, 557 were discharged for want of prosecution and 23 discharged on the merits of the case. Of the 778 who were convicted, 547 were fined, 226 were bound over and five were whipped.[27]

A magistrate in Montserrat reported that labour contracts were verbal, but that it was generally implied that anyone having a house on an estate or working land on a share system 'agrees to work for the Estate whenever required to do so'. The employer could not 'say beforehand what daily work each of his labourers would be required to perform, or the number of hours that he would require a given labourer to work', because of changes in the weather, so 'he could not be expected to pay for work which was not required'. But the worker was expected to be available and was compelled to work, even to work overtime, at his employer's convenience, or face prosecution, fines and eviction from his home.[28]

The governor of Barbados reported that of 312 cases dealt with under the masters and servants laws, 266 were against agricultural workers and the other 46 against domestic servants. Of these 312 cases, 35 were dismissed, 372 resulted in fines, and two were bound over to keep the peace. Fifteen were imprisoned in default of the payment of a fine. Domestic servants who neglected their duties according to unwritten contracts could be peremptorily imprisoned, but none had been in the previous 5 years. Instead, they were fined 1-20 shillings, on average about 8 shillings.[29]

From Grenada it was reported that some workers were fined on average 28 shillings and 6 pence, and some were whipped as many as ten strokes. In St Lucia most offences were of 'a trifling nature' yet they resulted in fines or imprisonment for periods of between 7 and 14 days, and in one case for over a month.[30] The governor of the Bahamas agreed that the existing masters and servants act was 'obsolete and virtually inoperative' and that its amendment was 'entirely desirable'.[31] The governor of Jamaica, the same Sir Edward Stubbs who had revealed his attitude towards Jamaican workers at the conference in 1930, reported that most cases prosecuted under the labour laws between 1925 and 1929 were for leaving service without notice, while others included misconduct as servants. Penalties ranged from fines of 1 shilling plus costs to 30 days of imprisonment with hard labour.[32]

This sample of reports regarding the working of the colonial labour laws shows how much they continued to exhibit the spirit of coercion associated with the nineteenth century. The courts were still primarily a means of disciplining labour, of keeping the workers up to the mark with threats of fines and even the use of whipping and imprisonment with hard labour for mere non-attendance at work or for such poorly defined offences as ill-behaviour and wilful misconduct. Moreover, as contracts were still generally verbal, dispute would come down to a matter of the worker's word against his employer, who was often also his landlord, and it is safe to assume that the class and race bias of the magistrates would generally favour the latter at the expense of the former. Most workers, even if they could overcome their nervousness about challenging their employers for wages due or breach of contract in a court that they knew was biased against them, would probably assume that it would be a waste of time, or might even affect them adversely if they were victimised. These laws were not simply obsolete, as several people observed at the time, they were also quite clearly class laws, which were manifestly biased, unjust and calculated to intimidate the workers, as the workers surely realised.

Several West Indian reformers who attended the third British Commonwealth Labour Conference in London, held between 21 and 25 July 1930, must have been hopeful that the Labour government would quickly make good on its promises regarding social and labour reform in the colonies. The conference was attended by Cipriani and Timothy Roodal, the Indian vice-president of the TWA, Critchlow and A.F.R. Webber of the Guyana labour movement and Marryshow from Grenada. Marryshow was the treasurer of the Representative Government Association, established in 1918, had participated in the second Pan-African Congress in London in 1921, and been elected unopposed as representative for St George's under the new Grenadian constitution of 1925. Marryshow, like Cipriani, trusted the British labour movement and looked to it for guidance and help in Caribbean affairs. After attending the conference in London in 1930, Marryshow referred to the 'dominant, conquering influences in Great Britain ready to help the West Indies as soon as the working classes line up in orderly fashion to help themselves'.[33] In 1931 he founded and became president of the Grenada Workingmen's Association (GWA). The faith that such men as Cipriani and Marryshow placed in the British labour movement's influence and capacity was premature, however, if not altogether misplaced.

Lord Passfield issued a directive supporting trade unionism in the colonies in 1930. His memorandum, which was surely the work of Shiels, instructed colonial governments to enact legislation declaring that trade unions were not criminal and providing for their compulsory registration. The goal of the Colonial Office was to provide a paternalistic guiding hand to ensure that colonial trade unions developed in a controlled manner:

> I recognise that there is a danger that, without sympathetic supervision and guidance, organizations of labourers without experience of combination for any social or economic purposes may fall under the domination of disaffected persons, by whom their activities may be diverted to improper and mischievous ends. I accordingly feel that it is the duty of Colonial Governments to take such steps as may be possible to smooth the passage of such organizations, as they emerge, into constitutional channels.[34]

Seven months later, Lord Passfield reprimanded several colonial governments for failing to comply with the Colonial Office policy regarding labour legislation.[35] The conservative colonial governments generally delayed reform measures and the Labour government fell in 1931.

Though the Colonial Office under the Labour government encouraged groups like the TWA to press for the legalisation of trade unions, there continued to be 'little or no positive response from the colonial government' (Basdeo 1983: 96), on the grounds that the economic depression made it an inopportune time because such legislation 'would increase the number and activities of agitators who may become a source of danger in difficult times'.[36] The Trade Union Ordinance that was passed in Trinidad and Tobago in 1932 made trade unions legal and gave the government power over registration, but it did not legalise peaceful picketing or protect the unions from legal actions for damages arising out of strikes. 'Far from helping the growth of trade unionism in Trinidad, this Ordinance frustrated the development of organized labour until after the 1937 riots' (Brereton 1981: 170).

Throughout the British Caribbean, it was not the 'dominant, conquering influences in Great Britain' that instigated the most important changes in the colonies, nor did the 'working classes line up in orderly fashion', as Marryshow wanted them to. On the contrary, it was only after the working classes erupted in widespread rebellion – a great series of demonstrations, strikes and riots throughout the colonies between 1934 and 1939 – that the British government was forced to reconsider its colonial policies and speed up the process of reform.

Notes

1. The metaphor of King Sugar is said to have originated in 1928 with Lowell Joseph Ragatz who, following the popular model of King Cotton in the United States, asserted that 'Sugar was king' in the Caribbean in the middle of the eighteenth century (Higman 1999: 171-8).

2. Erving Goffman, an American sociologist, studied the culture of enclosed or total institutions, in which people are cut off from normal everyday life. See his Asylums (Harmondsworth, Penguin, 1961).

3. Claims Book, 1859-62, General Registry, Belize.

4. In the Dutch colony of Suriname indentured labour was employed even until the Second World War. Over 34,000 indentured workers were imported from India between 1873 and 1917, and almost 33,000 from Java between 1890 and 1940 (Hoefte 1987: 2-3).

5. Minor Cooper Keith, an American, received large tracts of land from his uncle, Henry Meiggs, who built a railway for the Costa Rican government. Keith's business began by transporting bananas by rail to Limón and selling them in New Orleans. As one of the architects of the UFC, he played a major role in Costa Rica and Guatemala, in particular.

6. The UFC obtained a transport monopoly in British Honduras by 1902 and extracted substantial concessions from the government to establish banana plantations there. However, losses from a hurricane in 1915 and from the Panama disease caused the UFC to abandon production by 1920 and it withdrew from the colony (Moberg 1996).

7. Referring to the great and overweening power of these corporations, the UFC became known as the octopus because its tentacles reached everywhere, and British Guiana was called Bookers Guiana because of the company's dominant influence in the colony.

8. The invasion of Grenada in 1983 was the first time the United States directly intervened in a former British colony in the Caribbean.

9. Report of the West India Royal Commission (1897), p. 18.

10. For the influences of religious denominations on education in Belize, for example, see Bolland 1998.

11. J.R. Reid, 'The Negro Slave', Jamaica Advocate, 25 May 1895, quoted in Bryan 1991: 18.

12. Jamaica Advocate, 27 Jul. 1901, quoted in Bryan 1991: 261.

13. Wood, later Lord Halifax, was then parliamentary under-secretary for the colonies.

14. My thanks to Howard Johnson for this point.

15. Colonial Office Conference, Jun.-Jul. 1930, notes of meetings, p. 182, CO 854/173.

16. Blue Books are government publications that include, for example, statistical information on expenditures and revenues, exports and imports, production and population, wages and food costs.

17. Colonial Office Conference, Jun.-Jul. 1930, notes of meetings, p. 183, CO 854/173.

18. Ibid., p. 186.

19. Ibid., p. 184.

20. Ibid., pp. 183-4.

21. L.S. Amery to governors of British Guiana and Jamaica, 23 Jul. 1928, CO 318/393/10.

22. Minute by C.R. Darnley, 27 Jun. 1929, CO 318/393/10.

23. Passfield to governors of West Indian colonies, 14 May 1930, CO 318/396/12.

24. Lord Passfield to governor of Trinidad and Tobago, 14 May 1930, CO 318/396/12.

25. Statement summarising the position regarding the masters and servants ordinances at present in force in the West Indian Colonies, 19 Mar. 1930, CO 318/396/12.

26. Raymond Browne, magistrate of district A, Antigua, 17 Aug. 1930, encl. in Gov. Johnston to Passfield, 12 Nov. 1930, CO 318/401/3.

27. S.L. Athill, magistrate of district B, Antigua, 12 Aug. 1930, encl. in Johnston to Passfield, 12 Nov. 1930, CO 318/401/3.

28. S.A. McKinstry, magistrate of Montserrat, 8 Sept. 1930, CO 318/401/3.

29. Gov. Robertson to Passfield, 17 Oct. 1930, CO 318/401/3.

30. Act. Gov. Charles W. Doorly to Passfield, 18 Sept. 1930, CO 318/401/3.

31. Gov. Charles Dundas to Passfield, 21 Jun. 1930, CO 318/401/3.

[32] Gov. Sir R.E. Stubbs to Passfield, 11 Feb. 1931, CO 318/403/4.
[33] The West Indian, 29 Oct. 1930, quoted in Sheppard 1987: 30.
[34] Confidential circular from Passfield, 17 Sept. 1930, CO 295/599.
[35] Circular from Passfield to governors, 8 Apr. 1931, CO 854/80.
[36] Gov. Hollis to Passfield, 24 Feb. 1931, CO 295/573.

Chapter 4

Racial consciousness and class formation

The working class of the British Caribbean emerged as a political force through waves of activity from the 1880s to the 1930s (Hart 1988). It was largely through these activities that the working people became increasingly conscious of themselves as a class in relation to the other classes. Though attempts were made to organise the working class in this period, trade unions were still illegal throughout the British Caribbean until 1919 and did not become legal everywhere until after the great labour rebellions of the 1930s. It was during the half century before these labour rebellions erupted in 1934 that emerging class and racial consciousness prepared the way for the development of organised labour.

The process of class formation in the Caribbean, as elsewhere, is related to demographic changes and shifting demands for labour, with patterns of migration and urbanisation, and with connections between the emerging middle classes and the proletarianisation of working people. In addition, in the British Caribbean the process of class formation is intimately linked to the development of racial consciousness, and particularly to the Garvey movement,[1] and to the series of protests and strikes that occurred in several colonies between the 1880s and 1920s. During this period many organisations were formed among working people, including mutual aid societies, branches of the Garvey movement and 'proto-unions', which developed experience for the subsequent growth of trade unionism in the 1930s and 1940s.

In the process of class formation there are many interrelated aspects. Thus, for example, when demobilised soldiers protested after returning to Belize in 1919, they were responding to frustrations over local economic and political conditions, which reflected the colony's dependent status, as well as their recent experience of racial discrimination and politicisation during the First World War. And these riots in Belize Town, in turn, played a part in the developing consciousness of race, class and nation that gave rise to a more organised social movement in Belize after 1934, a movement which marked the start of the great labour rebellions throughout the region.

Demographic changes, migration and urbanisation

Improvements in health services, sanitation and hygiene that reduced mortality rates in the early twentieth century gave rise to higher population growth after 1921 in the whole British Caribbean, although between 1911 and 1921, Guyana, Barbados and the Leeward Islands experienced a population

TABLE 4.1 ANNUAL INTERCENSAL RATES OF GROWTH FOR BRITISH CARIBBEAN POPULATIONS, 1891-1946, PERCENT INTERCENSAL INTERVAL

	1891-1911	1911-21	1921-31	1931-46
Barbados	-0.29	-0.95	0.84	
Belize	1.26	1.13	1.26	0.96
Guyana	0.33	-0.02	0.48	1.15
Jamaica	1.32	0.32	1.67*	
Leewards	-0.39	-0.91	0.98	
Trinidad	2.14	0.92	1.21	2.03
Windwards	0.79	0.42	0.94	

decline (see Table 4.1).

*1921-43
Source: Roberts 1957: 50.

The total population of 13 colonies of the British Caribbean, that is, Barbados, Belize, Guyana, Jamaica, the Leeward Islands (Antigua, Montserrat, St Kitts-Nevis, the Virgin Islands), Trinidad and Tobago, and the Windward Islands (Dominica, Grenada, St Lucia, St Vincent), increased slowly until 1921 and then more dramatically, from 1,607,218 in 1891 to 1,999,159 in 1921 and to 2,851,032 in 1946. Jamaica, the largest colony, exhibited a comparatively stable rate of population growth, from 639,491 in 1891 to 1,321,054 in 1946 (and increased from 40 per cent to 46 per cent of the total British Caribbean population), while Trinidad, Belize and Guyana experienced periods of higher rates of growth when immigration was substantial, and Barbados, Antigua and St Kitts-Nevis experienced periods of decline due to heavy emigration. In St Kitts-Nevis the population in 1946 was actually less than it had been

Table 4.2 Populations of British Caribbean colonies according to the censuses, 1891-1946

	1891	1911	1921	1946
Barbados	182,867	172,337	156,774	192,800
Belize	31,471	40,458	45,317	59,220
Guyana*	270,865	289,140	288,541	359,379
Jamaica	639,491	831,383	858,118	1,321,054+
Leeward Islands				
Antigua	36,819	32,269	29,767	41,757
Montserrat	11,762	12,196	12,120	14,333
St Kitts-Nevis	47,662	43,303	38,214	46,243
Virgin Islands	4,639	5,562	5,082	6,505
Trinidad-Tobago	218,381	333,552	365,913	557,970
Windward Islands				
Dominica	26,841	33,863	37,059	47,624
Grenada	53,209	66,750	66,302	72,387
St Lucia	42,220	48,637	51,505	70,113
St Vincent	41,054	41,877	44,447	61,647
Total	1,607,218	1,951,327	1,999,159	2,851,032

in 1891 (see Table 4.2).

* Excludes Amerindians who were not accurately enumerated.

+ Estimate based on 1943 census total of 1,237,063, and Registrar-General's end-of-year estimates for 1945 and 1946.

Source: Roberts 1957: 330-1.

Rapid population growth in the 1920s and 1930s created increased pressure on resources, particularly in rural areas where an increase in the density of the population often resulted in the further fragmentation of small landholdings that were already inadequate. Apart from the mainland territories of Belize and Guyana, where the existence of huge underpopulated areas reduced the overall density of population figures quite deceptively, the islands were mostly heavily populated. In 1950, the overall density of population, in people per square km, was 110 in the Leeward Islands, 123 in Trinidad and Tobago, 125 in Jamaica, 128 in the Windward Islands and in the extreme case of Barbados 491 (Cross 1979: 64). Access to farm land was limited by social as well as by environmental factors because of the persistence of the plantation economy, so increasing numbers of people sought a better livelihood by migrating from rural areas to the towns or overseas, particularly when the economy stagnated and then collapsed in the interwar period.

Migration between the British Caribbean colonies was quite substantial after 1834, particularly from the old plantation societies of Barbados and the

Leeward Islands to the labour-hungry plantations of Guyana and Trinidad. Migration continued, in ever widening circles, in the late nineteenth and early twentieth centuries, often in response to the rapid economic development of regions that received infusions of US capital. Thousands of people left the eroded landscapes and rigid social hierarchies of the old plantation societies, such as Antigua, Barbados and St Kitts, to seek new opportunities in Panama, Costa Rica, Cuba, the Dominican Republic and the United States.

The construction of the Panama Canal between 1904 and 1914 led tens of thousands of West Indians to seek work there, but they had been preceded by as many as 50,000 West Indians, mostly Jamaicans, who worked on the isthmian railway in the 1850s and the French attempt to construct a canal in the 1880s. In the disease-ridden environment, thousands of workers succumbed to malaria, yellow fever and the bubonic plague, but thousands sent home Panama money, which encouraged others to follow them. Between 1905 and 1913, US labour recruiters in Barbados shipped 20,000 Barbadian male contract workers and hundreds of others from neighbouring islands for construction work in the Canal Zone (Richardson 1989: 210). Perhaps 40,000 other Barbadians and between 80,000 and 90,000 male and female Jamaicans travelled informally to work on the canal (Newton 1984). It is estimated that over 15,000 British West Indian workers, or about 10 per cent of the total, died from diseases, exhaustion and accidents in this enterprise (Richardson 1989: 210).

Thousands of workers stayed in Panama, and others moved northwest to Costa Rica and Honduras where the expanding banana plantations and a railway project out of Puerto Limón sought more labour. By 1927 there were 19,136 West Indians in Costa Rica, of whom 18,003 were concentrated in Limón province (Purcell 1993: 27). Panama money and remittances from work elsewhere in Central America often made life a little easier for families back home in islands where the economy was depressed by the crisis in the sugar industry. Some people used their savings to purchase houses, small plots of land, or retail shops, in order to gain a degree of independence from local plantocracies, and the example they set encouraged others to migrate in search of work (Richardson 1989: 211).

While Cuba's sugar industry was booming in Camaguey and Oriente, there was a huge demand there for migrant workers until 1920. Between 1912 and 1924, 230,000 contract workers were imported into Cuba from Haiti and Jamaica. In 1919 alone, about 24,000 Jamaicans and 10,000 Haitians arrived in Cuba, but sugar prices crashed in 1920. 'Workers who recently had been actively recruited from abroad suddenly became unwanted surplus labor, and pressures to rid the island of the West Indians began to intensify' (Petras 1988: 238). Altogether, between 1912 and the crash in 1929, over 113,000 Jamaicans entered Cuba legally, and the 1931 census recorded 40,471 Jamaicans as legally residing in Cuba (Petras 1988: 232). In the Dominican Republic, also, where US capital was modernising and expanding sugar production, thousands of West Indians sought wage work, some of them veterans from Panama, others from Jamaica or from the Leeward Islands, along with thousands of Haitians. Native Dominicans derided these culturally distinct and darker-skinned aliens as cocolos, despising and resenting them for being poor, black cane-cutters (Richardson 1989: 211). Many of these workers were seasonal migrants, a mobile, chiefly male, international labour force, but some settled, legally or otherwise.

The pattern of labour migration followed the 'application and withdrawal of US capital at various locations throughout the circum-Caribbean region' (Richardson 1989: 212), as thousands of working people pursued these generally ephemeral opportunities. Some of them sought work within the metropole itself: 'from 1901, when 520 "Negro Immigrant Aliens" were admitted from the West Indies, until 1924 when 10,630 arrived, 102,000 black West Indians entered the United States' (Richardson 1989: 212). Many of them were disappointed to find themselves, as educated or skilled workers, reduced to accepting menial jobs, and many experienced racial discrimination, as a minority in their new surroundings. Perhaps a third of them returned home, but many of those who stayed sent remittances home. Others, like Marcus Garvey, Claude McKay, Eric Walrond, Richard B. Moore and W.A. Domingo, contributed to the cultural and political life of the United States and its African-American community in particular (James 1998). On 1 July 1924 the United States abruptly closed its doors to Caribbean immigrants, when its national origins immigrant quota law went into effect. In the first six months of 1924 over 10,000 West Indians had entered the United States, but in the following year this was reduced to only 308 (Richardson 1989: 214). It was not until the Second World War, when labour migrants from the Caribbean went to the United States to contribute to the war effort, that this migration destination was reopened, and then on very different and extremely limited terms.

Thus the numbers of West Indian migrants going to Cuba and the Dominican Republic were reduced in the 1920s when sugar prices, which were inflated during the First World War, plummeted, and migration to the United States was reduced to a trickle after 1924. Meanwhile, the construction of oil refineries drew many workers from the British Caribbean to Aruba, Curaçao and northern Venezeula in the 1920s. However, the economic depression of the 1930s affected all industries everywhere. Not only were migrants laid off because of the lack of jobs but also, on returning home, they often augmented the ranks of the unemployed and the loss of their remittances added to the poverty at home. The depression heightened social tensions in places where immigrant workers were perceived as taking jobs from or reducing the wages of local workers. In Cuba, the Nationalization of Labour Decree was passed in 1933, requiring that 50 percent of employees in all industrial, commercial and agricultural enterprises must be native Cubans, that at least one-half of all payrolls should be reserved for Cubans and all vacant and new positions were to be filled by Cubans; discharged personnel should be from among the foreigners. Jamaicans, as well as Haitians and Spaniards, were affected by this 'Fifty Percent Law', were the 'targets of hostilities' (Petras 1988: 241) and were in danger of being deported if they engaged in political or labour action in defence of their rights and wages. The worst example of violence resulting from such tensions occurred in the Dominican Republic in 1937, when between 15,000 and 20,000 Haitians were massacred.

The migration, both seasonal and permanent, of workers from the British Caribbean to the zones of expanding US investment reflects the fact that these people constituted a floating labour force, or pool of reserve labour, for the global capitalist system. Whether and where they were recruited, shipped and employed, or discharged, deported and victimised, depended on the expansions and contractions of labour markets that were determined by the evolution of the global capitalist political economy. Everywhere, these workers were seen as the most expendable pawns in the game, because they were poor, black and foreign, and consequently powerless. The opportunities provided by the construction of the Panama Canal and of railways in Central America, and by the expansion of sugar and banana plantations in Central America, Cuba and the Dominican Republic, largely on the basis of US investments, declined rapidly in the 1920s and disappeared in the 1930s, and most of the dependent economies of the British Caribbean remained stagnant or in decline throughout this period. The migrant workers contributed to developments outside their home territories, but although they may have been able to send back remittances or eventually take home some savings, they were not contributing directly to the development of their own countries and they did not constitute a stable component of the emerging working class in their countries of origin.

The movement of these workers both reflected and contributed to the underdevelopment of the British Caribbean. It has been estimated that in Jamaica, for example, there was a net emigration from the island of 69,000 people between 1881 and 1911, and of 77,100, 63 per cent of whom were male, between 1911 and 1921. During those 40 years, some 46,000 Jamaican emigrants went to the United States, 45,000 to Panama, at least 22,000 to Cuba, and thousands more to Costa Rica and other Latin American countries. Between 1921 and 1943, however, there was a net immigration into Jamaica of some 25,800 people, almost 59 per cent of whom were male, most of them returning emigrants (Roberts 1957: 139–41). While the migrating workers obtained short-term gains of jobs in zones that paid relatively higher wages than at home, they were contributing to the long-term capital accumulation of investors and corporations outside the region, and increasingly in the United States. This clear relationship between 'white capital and black labor', therefore, was part of 'the ongoing evolution of capitalist production and capital accumulation' (Petras 1988: 265) in the global economy within which the Caribbean was so tightly integrated.

The causes and patterns of external migration were related to the process of urbanisation in the colonies of the British Caribbean. Often there was a two-stage process, with rural migrants moving first to the city and then moving overseas in the hope of finding better opportunities (Cross 1979: 71). Undoubtedly, internal migration was the chief cause of urbanisation, meaning an increasing proportion of the total population in urban areas, within the Caribbean as a whole (Cross 1979: 73), and in particular of the predominance of the first or primate cities. In the British Caribbean, only two colonies had what could be called second cities, namely Spanish Town and Montego Bay in Jamaica and San Fernando in Trinidad. In all the other colonies there was a marked difference between the primate city and the small towns and villages. This pattern is not only the result of the process of urbanisation within the colonies, but also reflects the relationship between each colony and the metropole, in which one town has emerged as dominant because it is the key link in this relationship. In most cases, the first city constitutes one-fifth or more of the total population of the country, and the concentration of resources, in terms of services and wealth, is generally even more striking than the concentration of the population. The first city is usually the seat of government and the commercial and communications centre, and the place where health, educational and financial services are concentrated. For poor rural people, the perception of better educational opportunities for their children, as well as the hope of jobs providing higher income for themselves, is a major attraction of the town, and the education system is biased in favour of urban lifestyles. The movement towards the city and orientation towards urban life tend to be mutually reinforcing, therefore, and the process of urbanisation is consequently linear.

The attraction to the city coincided for a long time with push factors, as population pressure on the land and labour-saving changes in the sugar industry reduced opportunities in the rural areas. Although external migration to some extent relieved the pressure on the land before 1921, the decline in opportunities overseas and the return of many migrant workers added to the mounting problems, with the result that the drift to urban areas increased in the 1920s and 1930s. In Jamaica, for example, from 1911 to 1921, emigrants were primarily of rural origin: 88 per cent of the 49,000 men and 21 per cent of the 28,000 women were from the 12 rural parishes, thereby curtailing population growth in the rural areas. In this period, the rural population lost 6,500 people through external migration and only 1,400 to internal migration. Between 1921 and 1943, however, when the rate of natural increase was higher than in the preceding period, there was actually a small net immigration of 300 people and 3,100 were lost to rural areas by internal migration. So, 'despite the relief afforded by out-migration to the urban centre [of Kingston-St Andrew], the annual increments to the rural population in 1921-43 (11,800) was about five times that prevailing during the period 1911-21 when emigration was at its height' (Roberts 1957: 160).

By 1943 there were 201,911 people living in the urban centre of Kingston-St Andrew, and 23,554 people living in the next largest towns, Spanish Town and Montego Bay. Another 11,520 people lived in the two towns with populations between 5,000 and 10,000 (May Pen and Port Antonio), and 39,947 in the 15 towns of more than 1,000 and less than 5,000 people. The total urban population in Jamaica in 1943, in the 20 towns of over 1,000 people, was 276,932, or 22.4 per cent of the population of the island (Roberts 1957: 161). A striking feature of the urbanisation of Jamaica, as elsewhere in the Caribbean, is that it was increasingly the growth of a single urban area. Kingston, which became the capital of Jamaica in 1872, increased in population from 37,300 in 1871 to 48,500 in 1891. Migration then became increasingly important as Kingston grew to 59,674 in 1911, 63,711 in 1921 and 110,083 in 1943. Kingston lost some of its population to the surrounding largely suburban parish of St Andrew, which increased from 54,598 in 1921 to 128,146 in 1943, overtaking the urban centre of Kingston (Roberts 1957: 51).

Similar developments were taking place in the less populated colonies. In Belize, for example, Belize Town grew from 5,767 in 1881 to 16,687 in 1931 and 21,886 in 1946, and the six next largest towns (Dangriga, Orange Walk, Corozal, San Ignacio, Punta Gorda and Benque Viejo del Carmen) grew from a total of 4,930 in 1881 to 11,186 in 1946. The urban population as a proportion of the total Belizean population grew from 39 per cent in 1881 to 51.4 per cent in 1931 and 55.8 per cent in 1946 (Bolland 1977: 6).

The urbanisation of the British Caribbean, and particularly the concentration of this phenomenon in the primate cities, had several important consequences. In addition to the challenge to the public policy-makers to provide an adequate expansion of housing and services for this population, there was the basic fact that the majority of the migrants were poor young adults, who in their search for economic opportunities were flooding the labour market. These job seekers, mostly unskilled or having only redundant farming skills, increased the rates of urban unemployment and drove down wage rates because work opportunities did not keep pace with urban population growth. Not only were urban services - schools, hospitals and transport - unable to keep pace with people's needs, but also the expansion of overcrowded and poor housing resulted from this rapid urban growth. Not surprisingly, these aspects - high unemployment and poverty, poor housing and inadequate services - were directly correlated with increasing crime rates and substance abuse, malnutrition and ill health.

A more positive consequence was that the concentration of people, often including returned emigrants who had diverse experiences elsewhere, facilitated their participation in voluntary associations of various kinds, which developed their political aspirations and organisational skills. Many of the returned emigrants, in particular, had acquired experience of political, trade union or Garveyite organisations[2] overseas. Some of them, having retained ties with their families and rural areas of origin, were able to provide important links between rural and urban people within the colonies, and sometimes even between them and the other places where they had worked. Among the long-term social and economic consequences of this pattern of migration and rapid urbanisation, therefore, was the increasing ability of people with broadening horizons and ambitions to develop the contacts that would enable them to participate in movements for social change. Thus religious groups, reading clubs,[3] friendly societies and lodges, as well as networks based on kinship and community of origin, generated a greater capacity to organise and to participate in the wider society. Many people were undoubtedly dispirited by the social disruption and poverty they experienced in the interwar years, but others were challenged and provoked into more political action. Hopelessness was one response to the horrors of the growing squatter shacks of the urban Caribbean, but another was rebelliousness.

Class and race in the social structure

The urbanisation of the British Caribbean in the early twentieth century was accompanied by the development of a typical urban class system. The modern relations between class, race and gender are integral to the patterns of development of these Caribbean colonial societies, so the 'particular form that Caribbean classes take is a direct result of ties of economic dependence and the legal and political systems and traditions which these have created' (Cross 1979: 117). New occupations, economic sectors and educational opportunities gave rise to emerging middle classes, but these were not determined entirely by criteria of achievement. Everywhere they were affected by the ascriptive criteria of race and gender. Colour, for example, might not have determined class membership, boundaries and relations, but it certainly affected them and racial status was closely correlated with class. 'The development of capitalist class relations in dependent economies alters the caste-like proscriptions of the early colonial period, but nowhere does it destroy them' (Cross 1979: 118). As this remains true in the late twentieth century, it was certainly even more apparent in the 1920s and 1930s, when small and largely powerless Caribbean middle classes strove for status and large and completely powerless working classes strove to survive. In the course of their struggles, class consciousness emerged along with an increasing consciousness of race and nationalism, so the process of class formation in these Caribbean colonies was always extremely complex in its relation to other aspects of the changing political culture.

From the early colonial period to the present, there has been a close association in these societies, based as they were on plantation economies, between the hierarchies of class and of racial groups. These British Caribbean colonies were controlled until the mid-twentieth century by an elite of planters, merchants and colonial administrators, some of whom were temporary residents if not absentee proprietors. Most of this elite considered themselves to be white. The lower class of working people, composed largely of the descendants of slaves and indentured labourers, was chiefly engaged in manual agricultural work, as plantation workers or peasants, and sometimes both small farming and estate labour, or were small craftsmen (such as carpenters, masons, tailors and seamstresses), casual unskilled labourers and domestic workers. This class of people was overwhelmingly black, except in colonies like Belize, Guyana and Trinidad where there were also substantial and growing numbers of Mestizo and Maya people, in the case of Belize, and of East Indians in the other colonies. In these more racially varied populations the racial groups were economically and residentially segmented to a large extent, with the people of African descent quite concentrated in the towns and the others more dispersed in the rural areas.

Within this bipolar social structure there emerged in the late nineteenth century a small middle class of educated and chiefly professional people (doctors, lawyers, clergymen, journalists, teachers and junior civil servants), whose core was the old free coloured group in the slave society. Many were the descendants of white men and black or coloured women, but the group had become self-perpetuating and was augmented by small increments of upwardly mobile blacks. 'This class was the peculiar creation of colonial society itself... vital to the maintenance of the colonial regime and enjoyed high status on that account. But this class also embodied the contradictions of the colonial regime. Highly "civilized" in its possession of English culture but excluded on account of race, it became the spearhead of a growing demand for national self-determination and its members now constitute the ruling elite — or contend among themselves for the right to lead.' (Smith 1988: 13)

This middle class absorbed, in various proportions and to differing degrees in the different societies, other groups during the last century, including Portuguese, Chinese, Arabs, Jews, upwardly mobile Indians and, in Belize, some Mestizos and Garifuna. For lower-class children, careers in the police, nursing and teaching provided some opportunities for mobility into this middle class, but very few moved as far as the elite, and educational opportunities beyond primary school remained very limited and exclusive until well after the Second World War.

Important social distinctions persisted between those members of this middle stratum who had been born into families of middle-class status and those who had themselves achieved mobility into it (Smith 1988: 15), and between the more educated professional members of this class and those who were chiefly in trade and business. This very status-conscious middle stratum made distinctions not only on the basis of social origin, occupation, education and income, but also in terms of ethnicity and race. Among this mixed middle stratum such status distinctions were very important, and fine nuances of colour, or the possession of English cultural attributes, loomed large in people's consciousness. Teachers, clergymen and minor civil servants, who suffered from small salaries that made it hard for them to sustain the class position to which they felt entitled, struggled above all to maintain their social status on the basis of a respectability that kept them socially distinguishable and apart from those whom they considered to be below them. Social standing could, of course, be enhanced by education and income, but experience reinforced the harsh fact that 'social prestige as measured by cultural attainments was no barrier to discrimination on the grounds of race' (Bryan 1991: 226). The experience of racial discrimination often shocked respectable middle-class blacks into a rising racial consciousness and incipient nationalism. The pervasiveness of race as a basis for social distinctions is such that, long after constitutional decolonisation, it remains an ascriptive criterion for occupational placement as well as political and personal relations in these former British colonies.

In the slave societies of the Americas, 'race was built into the very fabric of the social formation' (Smith 1992: 273), so that even when Emancipation changed the legal basis on which the social hierarchy was constructed, the class system was sustained by persistent racial discrimination. Indeed, in the absence of the former legal distinctions, racial discrimination became more important as a way to sustain the social hierarchy. In the British Caribbean after 1838, racism was such a pervasive force of social control and discrimination that the struggle for justice and equality was more often expressed in racial than in class terms, and even expressed as a struggle against slavery a century and more after legal Emancipation. However, the post-Emancipation problems of former slaves and their descendants were 'not caused by slavery but by the forces that reproduce the social systems established after slavery' (Smith 1992: 257), so we must understand the nature of the racial and class basis of politics that emerged after 1838. In the post-Emancipation struggle for justice, 'a working class did not spring into being overnight; it had to be made and to make itself in resistance to state and class coercion .... [I]t was forced to develop within the boundaries set by the racial ideologies of the dominant class, boundaries that engendered a deep, abiding, and wholly rational sense of injustice' (Smith 1992: 273). As we have seen, the planters in the British Caribbean colonies, often joining with merchant interests and in conjunction with the colonial administrators, excluded the vast majority of the black former slaves from ownership of good land and from participation in electing the legislatures. Then they used their power in the legislatures to pass laws and raise taxes that kept the former slaves and their descendants in a poor and dependent position. The class and race aspects of the social relations of domination and subordination, though analytically distinguishable, were intimately related in reality. This was true also in those colonies, like Guyana, Belize and Trinidad, where the social structure became increasingly complex in the nineteenth century.

The race–class system has been represented by pyramidal diagrams (Braith-waite 1975: 42-8), in which the three-tier Creole matrix of white, brown and black is intersected by the new racial and ethnic groups, but the complex dynamics of the system cannot be conveyed so simply. Such simple diagrams cannot convey the crucial shifts in consciousness and alliances that occured within and between these social groups, the very constitution of which was situationally negotiated and defined in the course of political struggle after 1838. In Guyana in the 1840s, for example, where many former slaves became peasant farmers and part-time plantation wage workers, they formed a class alliance with some of the import merchants who, like them, were 'resentful of planter-dominated legislatures that used import taxes to finance the impor-tation of cheap Indian labor. This process struck at the prosperity of African laborers, whose wages were depressed, and of the merchant class, whose prime customers were thereby impoverished. By the end of the nineteenth century many, if not most, of those merchants were Portuguese, Chinese, or Coloured.' (Smith 1992: 283) However, in the Angel Gabriel riots of 1856, and again in 1889 when Creoles attacked Portuguese shops, the racial factor was intertwined with class and broke up the former alliance.

In Caribbean consciousness and social idiom the intimate relationship between race and class frequently results in the latter, which is strictly speaking an economic phenomenon, being attributed a genetic component, so 'The overall discourse is one of hereditable identity in which race and class both play as separable but thoroughly intertwined conceptions' (Austin-Broos 1988: 8). The ways that people think of themselves is an aspect of the ways they perceive their relations with others, relations that are rooted in the past but are also reproduced and redefined by their actions in the present. Although the state and the dominant ideology play a major role in defining the categories and boundaries of the groups to which people are assigned, people are themselves continually negotiating and redefining these groups. In the struggles that took place in the race–class system in the British Caribbean in the late nineteenth and early twentieth centuries, growing racial consciousness was not a substitute for or a diversion from class consciousness but an intrinsic and necessary aspect of the nature of class formation in these societies.

There is a complex and dialectical relationship between ethnic solidarity, in which strong racial and cultural ties may divide people of the same class, and class consciousness, in which solidarity is promoted between people of different racial and ethnic identity at the middle-class and working-class levels, thus dividing the wider society in different ways. Racial categories, which had played such an important part in the system of social differentiation and domination from the formation of these colonial societies, continued to be a central component of their ideology and social economy after Emancipation. Indeed, in the nineteenth century, racist consciousness was increasingly provided with a pseudo-scientific basis as social relations became 'biologized' (Smith 1992: 264). Not only were the racist values and institutions pervasive and difficult to root out, but they also continued to play a vital role in maintaining the myth of white and European superiority and, by dividing those people who were not white from each other, in enabling the small numbers of colonisers to maintain their rule over the majority. The social construction of race and the ideology of racism helped to maintain, to the extent that it seemed to explain, a social system of inequality between races.

The economic and political power of the colonial elite was based, therefore, not only on the economic exploitation but also the racial segmentation of the labour force, whose members were more or less systematically devalued and discriminated against. Norman Girvan, the Jamaican economist, comments: 'Racist ideologies ... became an integral and structurally "necessary" component of these societies, given the racial characteristics of the labour regimes which formed their base. Hence, ideologies of racial nationalism and race pride became equally necessary for the oppressed groups to defend and reclaim their sense of humanity, as well as to resist the most extreme and obvious forms of labour exploitation.' (Girvan 1988: 11) The most prominent and influential example of this racial nationalism that originated in the British Caribbean was that associated with Garvey and his Pan-African social movement in the 1920s and 1930s.

Marcus Garvey and black nationalism

The 'development of a black ethnicity' (Robotham 1988) may have been further advanced in Jamaica than elsewhere in the British Caribbean in the nineteenth century. The political experience of black Jamaicans, both before and after Emancipation, and particularly the series of revolts and the extreme repression they provoked, stimulated its emergence (Robotham 1988: 32). The tripartite division of Jamaica into whites "backra", browns "malatta" and blacks "nayga" was based on class as well as racial criteria. With the revolts of 1831 and 1865, 'a distinct new black ethnic group had evolved but within a system of racial and national oppression and on the basis of a definite system of property relations' (Robotham 1988: 38). Though only two black men, Edward Vickars and Charles Price, were elected to the Jamaican House of Assembly before its dissolution, their efforts to get elected and the support they galvanized laid 'the tradition of black political activity ... in this formative period of free Jamaica' (Wilmot 1988: 39). The growing political influence of black small farmers and artisans in the 1840s provoked concern in the Colonial Office and near hysteria among many absentee planters and Jamaican white and brown politicians. A variety of measures was adopted to reduce the influence of black voters, including more stringent registration procedures and a poll tax on voters of 20 shillings. Vickars and Price lost the election in 1863. In August 1865, at a time of growing hardship, unemployment and agitation, one of the speakers at a meeting in St Ann's Bay was Garvey's father, a mason. Garvey became the most prominent Jamaican in the development of black politics and the Pan-African movement, building on 'the traditions laid in the post-Emancipation period.' (Wilmot 1988: 44)

It is necessary to acknowledge, as Judith Stein emphasizes, that concepts such as race and nation have specifically historical and therefore changing meanings. 'The different appellations and meanings undermine the common belief that racial identity or consciousness is fixed. The ways people define themselves are determined by their history, politics, and class. They change. The same words have conveyed vastly different meanings and encouraged diverse actions.' (Stein 1988: 200)

This is true, but while the concepts and consciousness are changing they also express continuities in the political culture that are deeply rooted. Garveyism, as a black nationalist and Pan-Africanist ideology, is rooted in the nineteenth century and became a crucial aspect of Caribbean political culture of the twentieth century.

Garvey shared certain opinions, goals and ideas with his Jamaican forerunners, Dr Robert Love and Alexander Bedward, as well as with Pan-Africanists elsewhere, such as H. Sylvester Williams and W.E.B. DuBois. Yet, at the same time, Garvey was more successful and influential than most other Africanist leaders of his period. Men like Love and Bedward were influential only among particular sections of Jamaican society, but most of the Pan-Africanists who gathered in London in 1900 'were modern men, cut loose from traditional communities in Africa, the West Indies, and the United States . . . . They were an elite and their racial consciousness was shaped by their class experiences' (Stein 1988: 202). Garvey was extraordinarily successful in creating a broadly based social movement because he combined an appeal to the internationalist racial consciousness of the Pan-Africanist elite with an appeal to the growing nationalist consciousness of less educated people whose dissatisfaction was more focused on local social and political issues, wherever they lived. Hence, Garveyism thrived at the crossroads where two dialectical processes intersected: the dialectic of social class and ethnicity, on the one hand, and the dialectic of black nationalism and Pan-Africanism, on the other.

Garvey, in his own life history, experienced the contradictory forces that formed this complex dialectic at the turn of the century. Born in 1887 in St Ann's Bay in northern Jamaica, Marcus Mosiah Garvey retained a love and sense of pride in the place and people among whom he grew up. His father found it hard to maintain the family's status in the depression of the 1890s in this declining rural area. The boy left school after completing 6th standard and became a printer's apprentice. In 1904 he moved to Port Maria and two years later to Kingston, where he was employed in the printing department of P.A. Benjamin Manufacturing Co. To his rural upbringing and experience of economic depression was added the perspective of a skilled worker and migration to the capital. Within a few years, Garvey also gained experience of trade unionism and international migration.

In 1907 Garvey was elected vice-president of the compositors' branch of a printers' union, affiliated with the American Federation of Labor, which went on strike the next year with disastrous consequences. This small union of skilled workers disintegrated in 1909. In April 1910 Garvey was elected assistant secretary of the National Club of Jamaica, an early anti-colonial organisation that called for self-government within the British empire. S.A.G. Cox, the club's founder and leader until 1911, was a barrister who published a fortnightly journal, Our Own, that attacked racism in the colonial bureaucracy, called for the legalisation of trade unions and for Crown lands to be made available to the peasantry, and opposed the policy of subsidising Indian immigration (Lewis 1987: 42-3). In the final issue of Our Own, Cox wrote, 'The coloured and black people in Jamaica can only hope to better their condition by uniting with the coloured and black people of the United States of America and with those of other West Indian islands, and indeed with all Negroes in all parts of the world'.[4] This became Garvey's life mission. Other National Club members included S.M. DeLeon and Domingo, who became important figures in the movements of the 1930s.[5]

In late 1910 and 1911 Garvey travelled in Central America. In Costa Rica he was a time-keeper on a plantation and in Panama he became involved with the newspaper La Prense. During these travels he protested 'the racist treatment and savage exploitation meted out to his people' (Lewis 1987: 44). He returned to Jamaica in 1911 and around 1912 or 1913 went to the UK. He attended some lectures at Birkbeck College in London, met people from other parts of the empire, worked as a journalist and added further to his personal perspectives and political development. In particular, he was influenced by an Egyptian journalist, Duse Mohammed Ali, and the international black community around his journal, The African Times and Orient Review, which appeared between 1912 and 1919. When Garvey returned to Jamaica in 1914 he founded the Universal Negro Improvement Association (UNIA) and African Communities League (ACL), and wrote a pamphlet, A Talk with Afro-West Indians: The Negro Race and its Problems.

Though Garvey's political philosophy continued to develop, it is clear that the essential core of his values and vision was formed by this time, even before he went to the United States in 1916 and developed the UNIA into a major international organisation. The Jamaican branch grew after Garvey's departure, a New York branch was formed in 1918 and other branches were opened during his tour of the Caribbean and Central America in 1921. Garvey was imprisoned in the United States in 1923 and again in 1925. Deported back to Jamaica in 1927, he spoke to an overflowing crowd at the Ward Theatre in Kingston. After travelling in Europe in 1928, he returned to Jamaica and formed the People's Political Party (PPP). Garvey started a daily newspaper, Blackman, in 1929, but the next year it became a weekly and publication ceased in 1931. Meanwhile, the UNIA split between the branches based in New York and Jamaica. Garvey succeeded in getting elected to the Kingston and St Andrew corporation in 1929 and 1931, but was defeated in his attempt to win a seat on the Legislative Council in 1930. He founded the Jamaica Labourers and Workers Association in 1930, organised the Edelweiss Amusement Co to sponsor shows and concerts in 1931, and started publishing a monthly magazine, Black Man, in 1933. His political efforts in Jamaica were frustrated by the legal constraints on trade unionism and the limited franchise.

Garvey relocated to London in 1935, where he denounced the Italian invasion of Ethiopia, but then began criticising Haile Selassie and his policies in 1936. On 8 August 1937, soon after the great labour rebellions in Barbados and Trinidad, Garvey was heckled in Hyde Park by the Trinidadians C.L.R. James and George Padmore, 'who called upon him to declare his stand on the working class struggle' (Lewis 1987: 269). Garvey visited Trinidad in October 1937, where he was welcomed by Cipriani and an enthusiastic crowd. He also visited Grenada and Guyana on that trip. By this time, however, new and more radical leadership was supplanting men like Garvey and Cipriani. Long before he died in 1940, Garvey's political star had waned.[6]

Garvey was overtaken by the labour crisis and the new leaders of the 1930s, but the social movement he created had an important and lasting impact in many parts of the Caribbean. His political legacy included, in particular, the experience that members of the UNIA gained in speaking and organising in its many branches in the Caribbean, Central America and the United States, and the influence on ideological developments in the political culture of the British Caribbean, especially Jamaica. For a few years after the First World War, Garvey had succeeded in bridging the gaps between nationalists and internationalists, black workers, businessmen and professionals, and in articulating a powerful appeal to racial pride and self-sufficiency. This was epitomised by the publication of the Negro World, the development of a network of community centres called Liberty Halls and the Black Cross Nurses organisation, and by the creation of the Black Star Line (BSL) in 1919.

Stein argues that it was 'the Black Star Line that elevated Garvey from his position as a local leader into a world leader' (Stein 1988: 204) by providing a rallying point and concrete evidence for the abstract doctrines of black nationalism. As shipping lines were the early twentieth-century symbols of national power, much like airlines today, the BSL became the embodiment of the national aspirations of black people. Initially the property of a small group of UNIA members in New York, the BSL linked the aspirations of black businessmen in the United States, black merchants in the Caribbean and Africa, and many of the under- and unemployed black workers who were suffering in the postwar economy. 'Garvey brought this project to the masses' (Stein 1988: 205) and at the same time created a symbol of black achievement that linked the nationalist aspirations of local communities with a Pan-Africanist vision. However radical and inspirational the BSL was in terms of black nationalist consciousness, however, it was conservative in terms of class. The assumption was that black entrepreneurs and businesses would uplift the black masses, and even when Garvey criticised the black elite for failing to support his enterprise financially, he shared and reinforced their essentially capitalist view of racial progress. The US government nevertheless defined Garvey's efforts to bring together so many diverse black people as a grand conspiracy. Garvey was placed under surveillance, arrested on charges of mail fraud, then jailed for three months in 1923, and again between February 1925 and November 1927, before being deported. The demise of the BSL in 1922, Garvey's harassment and imprisonment, and a serious split that occurred within the UNIA in 1932, marked the decline of his movement.

Garvey's movement was weakened by repression, but also by its own contradictions. Garvey was the leader of a popular mass movement who advocated black pride and self-sufficiency but who left his followers in a largely passive role. He was an anti-colonial leader who liked to dress like a colonial governor and who, after about 1922, demanded loyalty from his followers. 'Garveyites paraded and petitioned; they did not demonstrate. The organization was hierarchical, not democratic. Its bonding was loose because Garvey did not require programmatic action, only loyalty and support of UNIA projects.' (Stein 1988: 209) Garvey's ideas and organisation helped stimulate working people in the Caribbean, providing them inspiration and experience that often proved to be invaluable in the subsequent development of trade unions and political parties, but when these people, many of them Garveyites, rose in rebellion in the 1930s, Garvey himself declared that they were misled by agitators (Lewis 1987: 270).

Many former Garveyites became active, often as leaders, in the labour and independence movements of the 1930s and 1940s in the British Caribbean, but they did so in new organisations, in the trade unions and political parties that were more effective than the UNIA in channelling people's activities toward the achievement of concrete benefits. Because Garvey's movement was based on an essentially elite model of racial progress it was transcended by the more activist, mass-based and democratic labour movement of the 1930s.

> Just as Garvey's early politics were grounded in the models of British social imperialism and then those of American nationalism, so black strategies of the 1930s and 1940s were influenced by a new labour movement, radical politics, and a transformed state compelled to intervene in the affairs of civil society on the side of its working classes because of the militancy of organized workers.... Racial leaders no longer appealed to the masses, as Garvey once did, to support elite institutions by buying stock and deferring immediate popular needs. Quite the contrary. (Stein 1988: 210-11)

While it is true that Jamaicans, and others in the British Caribbean, 'chose nation over race' and many 'chose community and class over race' (Stein 1988: 208), the ways they defined their nation, community and class were shaped by the racial consciousness to which Garvey and his UNIA had contributed. Garvey, in building on Love and Cox's message of racial pride and unity, developed an ideology that was relevant and had a broad appeal throughout the British Caribbean. Although his own attempts to create a political party and workers' association in Jamaica were unsuccessful, there is no doubt that many of the labour and political leaders of the 1930s and 1940s were, or had once been, Garveyites, in Barbados, Belize and Trinidad, as well as Jamaica. However, the nature of Garveyism's racial consciousness, which was a particular asset in colonies such as Jamaica and Barbados where the people were largely of African descent, was problematic in the more racially heterogeneous societies of Belize, Guyana and Trinidad. More than half a century after Garvey's death, this continues to be true.

The emergence of new relationships in the colonial societies, including growing class distinctions within the black community, and the massive impact of the Great Depression on the working people in particular, led to a rapid rise in the class component of the national consciousness in the 1930s. Garvey's legacy, nevertheless, should not be underestimated, as it would be if we were to focus solely on class analysis at the expense of race. 'Garvey's legacy is essentially one of a fight against racism and colonialism' (Lewis 1987: 274) and this influence has been felt not only in the Caribbean but also in the United States and Africa. Indeed, it was precisely Garvey's ability to connect the struggle to liberate Africa with the struggles of Africans in the diaspora that constitutes his chief contribution to anti-racism and anti-colonialism. These have continued to be central components of the struggle for liberation since Garvey's death, and even long after the constitutional end of colonialism in most of the Caribbean and Africa. A century after Garvey's birth, a leader of the Marxist left in Jamaica recommended 'a re-examination of Garvey's own treatment of the inter-relationship between race and class in Jamaican society' (Munroe 1988: 297), as the question of race was still inadequately incorporated in the struggle for liberation.[7]

Class struggle, class formation and early labour organisations

A rise in class consciousness, appearing in conjunction with increasing racial consciousness, was manifest in parts of the British Caribbean from the late nineteenth century. Some forms of class struggle, including strikes and collective verbal protests, had occurred since Emancipation and even before (Turner 1988), but the first major wave of working-class activity was between the 1890s and the beginning of the First World War (Hart 1988: 43-50). Several labour protests and strikes, together with the emergence of the early unions and other working-class organisations, accelerated the process of proletarianisation at the same time that middle classes were developing in these colonies.

Though there were generally racial and ethnic as well as educational and occupational divisions within the middle stratum, these people shared the goal of a secure income and material standard of living that would support their claims for a respectable status in a system of prestige that was still largely dictated by the mother country. Even those members of the intelligentsia who sought more rights and privileges for themselves generally did so in terms of the values of a civilisation that was defined by the British. A diffuse group of occupations - including some wealthy peasants and farmers, professionals such as teachers, civil servants, clergymen, lawyers, doctors and nurses, as well as some merchants and the upper echelons of artisans, and some members of the police and armed forces - lay between the European-dominated elite and the mostly black masses. Though members of this middle stratum made some fine distinctions between each other in terms of education, colour and consumption patterns, their shared goal of respectability distinguished them, in their own minds at least, from the poorer peasants and workers whom they believed were less civilized.

The chief problems for this emerging middle class were the threat that the depression of the late nineteenth century posed to their material circumstances and the fact that, however educated and culturally assimilated they became, they were still subject to racial discrimination from those who were whiter than themselves (Bryan 1991: 226). Anxiety and resentment about these issues fed their growing class and race consciousness and their incipient sense of nationalism. One source of their nationalism was their resentment that many government jobs were reserved for British men, some of whom were less qualified than local people.[8] The first labour organisations of workers and the growing propensity of poor people to demonstrate and even to strike, while more respectable people only petitioned to maintain or extend their social and political privileges, augmented the feeling in this middle stratum that they constituted a distinct class. Class is a social relationship, after all, so the class consciousness of this middle stratum and of the working people evolved in relation to each other as well as to the persistence of the largely white and increasingly absentee or expatriate colonial elite.

The depression and the reorganisation of the sugar industry in the late nineteenth century increased unemployment, lowered wages and heightened suffering throughout the British Caribbean. Angry protests broke out in many colonies in the 1890s and the first years of the twentieth century. While each disturbance responded to local problems, their increasing frequency shows that they were caused by 'overarching issues of economic inequality buttressed by colonial control' (Richardson 1992a: 179). At least 17 serious disturbances occurred between 1884 and 1905, most of them in Jamaica (in 1884, 1894, 1895, 1901, 1902) and Guyana (1889, 1896, 1903, 1905). Others occurred in Grenada (1885), St Vincent (1891), Dominica (1893, 1898), Belize (1894), St Kitts-Nevis (1896), Montserrat (1898) and Trinidad (1903). Further disturbances occurred in 1908 in St Lucia and in 1912 in Kingston, Jamaica.

For most black Jamaicans, who were extremely poor, 'the struggle was not against racism defined as such but against class oppression, heavy taxation, and injustice' (Bryan 1991: 266). Strikes on estates in St Thomas, Portland, St Elizabeth, St James and Hanover in 1867, 1868 and 1878 were directed against low wages, or the planters' irregularity or failure to pay wages due. In February 1884, sugar workers and stevedores sought higher wages in St Ann and, during this bad year in the sugar industry, several strikes broke out. The inspector of police reported that an agent recruiting labourers for work in Panama had agitated people by promising them higher wages. Workers crowded into the town of St Ann's Bay, some of them waiting to embark to Colón and others planning their struggle for better wages at home. Planters and their managers conceded increased wages in order to end the strikes and slow the loss of labour to Panama. In September 1884, when recently imported Chinese workers rioted at the Gray's Town Estate in St Mary, one of them was killed and five wounded (Bryan 1991: 266-7, 276). These events show the complexity of the relationship between labour supply and wages, immigration and emigration, and the crisis in the sugar industry. The planters responded to the fall in sugar prices, from 25 shillings and 6 pence per hundredweight in 1873 to 19 shillings in 1883 and 13 shillings and 3 pence in 1884, by lowering wages and importing indentured labourers. The Jamaican workers sought higher wages, if not at home then abroad.

Trade unions were illegal and the colonial administration saw labour conflict as a matter for the police. The colonial state strengthened its police forces in order to coerce workers and suppress disorders. Riots at Cumberland Penn in 1894, provoked by the attempt of the police to arrest a poor young man for gambling illegally at the races, convinced the governor that the constabulary would not have been able to contain a more serious disturbance. Playing on the elite's fears of a race war, he sought to strengthen the police by importing white sergeants and sergeant-majors from the Royal Irish Constabulary. Conflicts between soldiers of the West India Regiment and members of the Jamaica Constabulary, which was created after the Morant Bay rebellion, sometimes resulted in riots. On 8 June 1894, for example, soldiers, joined by women and men of the town, attacked two police stations and roughed up the police at Fletcher's Land and Sutton Street. A similar pitched battle occurred in 1900 and in 1901 police intervened in riots in Portland and St Mary, which were sparked, respectively, by disputes over the sale of bananas and wage rates (Bryan 1991: 270-1). As in the period of slavery, coercion was the standard method of social control and any protest or demonstration by the working people of Jamaica was defined by the authorities as a riot.

Jamaican workers, however, sought to develop strike action 'as a legitimate method of protest against conditions' (Bryan 1991: 268) and they were supported by some middle-class Jamaicans. Love, the editor of the Jamaica

Advocate, described the strike by wharf workers in Kingston in May 1895 as a 'new chapter' in Jamaica's social history. For four days 800-1,000 dock workers 'continued to maintain, with more or less obstinacy, their hostile attitude .. .. Strikes are in reality the mode of warfare adopted by the labourers against the capitalist. It is the former's method of bringing the latter to terms'.[9] The dock workers sought wages of 5-6 shillings per day. When employers sought to break the strike by employing sailors at 6 shillings per day, the sailors would not cooperate, 'partly as a gesture of solidarity, but mainly out of fear of reprisals from angry workers' (Bryan 1991: 269). Love encouraged workers to form associations all over the island, to 'organise themselves everywhere into Labour Clubs, or Labour Unions (or whatever else they may choose to call it)',[10] in order to make their collective voice heard in the Legislative Council, where they were unrepresented. Despite the growing class conflict and class consciousness, however, this did not happen until the late 1930s.

Other sources of class conflict in Jamaica were over land and taxes. In 1901 and 1902 several attempts were made by poor people to seize land from large land-owners. In 1901 in St Mary, a major banana-producing parish, small settlers tried to possess land owned by the Hon. Dr John Pringle. The police report stated this was one of several attempts, 'The persons so acting in all cases try to put forward some bogus title, and incite the more ignorant portion of the peasantry by telling them that the lands in St Mary were belonging to the black people' (quoted in Bryan 1991: 271). Additional taxes were imposed on land in 1901 and by 1902 taxation was a burning issue. Many poor taxpayers in Montego Bay were taken 'before the resident magistrate for the non-payment of taxes, and given the alternative of either paying their obligations in full within a certain period - or going to prison' (quoted in Bryan 1991: 271). As these people borrowed money from friends and relations to avoid going to prison, there was widespread indignation and anger in the area.

Montego Bay was a rapidly growing town, whose population increased from 4,803 people in 1891 to 6,616 in 1911, but unemployment was a major problem because of the depression in the sugar industry. On 5 April 1902, a market day when the town's population was swollen with people from its environs, a constable tried to arrest a drunken sailor. People disliked this policeman in particular and a crowd of about 2,000 gathered around the court house. They pelted the building with stones and other missiles, breaking the windows, and then attacked the policeman's home. The sailor whose arrest had sparked the protest was released, but people continued to attack the police in the town after dark. The police had to retreat and released others they had arrested. Special constables were sworn in and 60 armed men and other police officers arrived the next day to reinforce the local police. Rioting was renewed the next night, the police barracks was attacked and police were forced to seek shelter in houses. An inspector then ordered the crowd to be attacked with fixed bayonets and bullets. After two and a half hours of skirmishing, one man, who was not a rioter, had been shot dead and another died subsequently of his wounds, before the people dispersed. Some of the fighting was at close quarters, as one person was wounded by a bayonet and one of the injured police was knocked senseless by a bottle. HMS Tribune came from Port Royal and its 300 sailors increased the security forces to 750 armed men, who effectively crushed the protest (Bryan 1991: 272-4).

The Jamaica Advocate blamed the Montego Bay disturbances on the 'chronic irritation and discontent which have for some time existed among the poorer classes as the consequence of the grinding, crushing, weight of the taxes which they are unable to pay, and of the prosecutions which have been recently instituted against them for not being able to pay'.[11] The harsh efforts of the police and magistrates to enforce this oppressive taxation made them prime targets of the protest. Though the police were 'simply the uniformed symbol of a system of justice which was unduly oppressive on the poor' (Bryan 1991: 275), they were also the front line of the system. As at Morant Bay in 1865, the police barracks and court house, which were not merely the symbols but the actual vehicles of domination, were attacked. The white officers and colonial officials, no doubt haunted by the example of Morant Bay, were anxious about the loyalties of their black constables. One of the inspectors who helped suppress the Montego Bay disturbances, obsessed with fears about a race war, was reassured that his men were willing to 'use their weapons against their kith and kin. I am proud to have had the honour of thus "blooding" the Jamaica Constabulary, especially in such trying circumstances . . . . They proved their loyalty to the hilt on the night of 6 April, 1902; and they have done so repeatedly since then'.[12]

The use of black police by the colonial state to repress poor black people divided the majority racial group, but also exposed how the force of the law was used to maintain class dominance in the colony. Such prominent events as the Montego Bay disturbances of 1902, therefore, may have strengthened the emerging sense of class consciousness at the expense of racial solidarity, though it was clear that race remained a central component in the maintenance of this extremely unjust society.

In Grenada, St Vincent, Dominica, Belize, St Kitts and Trinidad, also, the disturbances in this period concerned wages, prices, taxes and frustration with the local colonial authorities. The riot in St George's, Grenada, on 5 November 1885, was provoked by the authorities' banning fireworks at the annual Guy Fawkes commemoration. Several hundred men and women attacked the police with rocks, sticks and bottles, and some were imprisoned for up to three months. Handbills printed before the riot 'expressed resentment against the curtailment of customary rights, indicated an intention to "lash and go" against the police, and demonstrated an obvious capacity to organize' (Richardson 1997: 60-1). However, the riot was 'not a potentially infectious rebellion among an impoverished sugar proletariat' (Richardson 1997: 61) but a protest against the urban merchants and the colonial authorities. There was a more serious threat in St Vincent where the belief that a poll tax was going to be imposed and emigration banned led to a near-riot in Kingstown in November 1891. Threats of disturbances led the governor of the Windwards to summon HMS Buzzard, but when marines were landed they were greeted by the waiting crowd with a shower of stones. When some 2,000 people from the countryside, armed with sticks and marching to a drum, joined the crowd in Kingstown the marines set up a machine-gun and limited further disturbances. Nevertheless, these near-riots were 'an obvious result of how depression and despair had created an explosive social atmosphere, whose ignition was prevented only by an extraordinary show of force' (Richardson 1997: 62). St Vincent was still regarded as a potential trouble spot when the royal commission was told in 1897 of a 'strong and growing spirit of discontent and disaffection throughout the island, in many quarters openly expressed. The labourer, ordinarily fatalistic, is assuming a sullen, discontented, insolent attitude, which may culminate in open revolt and lawlessness for which we are little prepared' (quoted in Richardson 1997: 62).

In Dominica, where a substantial peasantry developed after 1838, access to land and taxation were key issues. The governor sought to extend taxes throughout the colony in 1886 and set a land tax which led to a confrontation with the authorities in April 1893. Pierre Collard, who lived in La Plaine, in a very poor region of Dominica from which the peasants took arrowroot and farine to sell to the merchants in Roseau, could not pay his taxes. His house lot was ordered to be sold, but when the bailiff and police inspector arrived to take possession an angry crowd forced them to flee. The governor arrived with additional police and 25 armed soldiers, and when Collard refused to vacate his property he ordered him to be ejected. The police and soldiers were stoned by the villagers. They opened fire, killing four men and wounding others (Baker 1994: 121-2). The crowd dispersed because, as unarmed peasants, they lacked the means to resist the armed force of the state successfully.

In Belize, the small elite that controlled the land, commerce and administration of the colony consisted of expatriates and an emerging Creole elite, some of whom were the descendents of old settler families. Some of the local elite pressed for constitutional change, including a return to the elective principle, but they succeeded only in obtaining a majority of unofficial members, all nominated by the governor, on the Legislative Council in 1892. The governor appointed some Creole members to the council but whites remained the majority. Two years later, the linking of the colony's currency to the gold standard effectively devalued it. This increased the price of imported goods, on which people were highly dependent, and hence reduced their real income. Mercantile clerks in Belize Town received salary raises of about 25 per cent, but government workers and forest workers did not. A strike by government workers was unsuccessful. A group of workers petitioned Governor Moloney, saying, 'That there has been a great fall for sometime past in the price paid for labour in this Colony . . . . Your petitioners are the real inhabitants of this Colony, the men by the sweat of whose brow in the forests, all its prosperity has been achieved. Yet they are without a voice in the Legislative Council of this Colony, without anyone to protect their interests while both Councils are filled with merchants and other employers of labourers'.[13]

The merchants denounced the petitioners as loafers and called their leader, John Alexander Tom, a 'public house politician', and the governor advised the workers to wait for a revival of trade to restore their wages to the pre-1894 levels. Some would not wait. Frustrated by the responses to their peaceful petition, and angered by the attitude of the merchants who continued to profit while they were forced into increasing poverty, about 100 forest workers attacked the chief stores in Belize Town on 11 December 1894. Some stores were looted. After the governor called in an armed detachment from HMS Partridge and the workers were offered a 50 percent wage increase, the disorders quickly subsided (Ashdown 1979b: 79-86). This episode, though sparked by a currency issue, was really about wages and prices. It suggests that the working people were developing a sense of themselves as a distinct class, whose particular interests were not represented in the Legislative Council, and showed that when their petition was rudely dismissed they could react more aggressively to obtain results.

In St Kitts and Nevis in the 1890s, working people were said to be starving and forced to resort to begging for food. Wages were severely depressed, the rate for cutting cane having been reduced from 8 pence per ton to 7 pence in 1895 and then to 6 pence in 1896, and emigration did not sufficiently relieve the persistent distress. Demands for higher wages erupted into disorders during the sugar crop in 1896.[14] Unrest broke out on 28 January at the adjoining estates of Ponds and Needsmust, east of Basseterre, when canefields were set alight and onlookers impeded attempts to extinguish them. These estates were owned by Joaquin Farara, a Portuguese planter who was widely disliked for having reduced wages below the prevailing rate. When the crop was due to begin on 10 February, the factory workers at Needsmust refused to work until their original wages were restored. They were joined in their strike by the field workers and by the workers at Ponds estate, and they mounted pickets.

Farara was forced to concede wage increases and news of the concessions stimulated similar action on other estates.

Bands of strikers and demonstrators patrolled the roads, accompanied by the sounds of fifes, drums and conch shells, and armed with sticks. By 17 February over 400 acres of cane had been burned. When the manager of Walter R. Boon's estate at Stone Fort tried to put out a fire on 16 February he was stoned by onlookers. He fired his revolver at the crowd, wounding two women, and he required police protection. Three weeks of this rural unrest climaxed on 17 February when waterfront workers in Basseterre went on strike. A warship, HMS Cordelia, had anchored in the harbour that morning, but the demonstrators were not intimidated. A large crowd of strikers, joined by unemployed men and women and workers from the estates, took over the streets of the town for the day, armed with sticks and machetes, and playing fifes, drums and conch shells. The police inspector felt he could not challenge them because he would incite further disorder and risk defeat. In Old Road village, police who tried to arrest a worker who was accused of breaking an overseer's arm were overpowered by the villagers and forced to retreat to their barracks. Other unrest, involving stone-throwing, was reported from Challengers Village and from the northeastern districts.

At the administrator's urgent request, 60 armed marines were landed from the warship to assist the police, but when he drove into town at 7.30 pm his carriage was stoned and bottles smashed on it by an angry crowd. Several properties belonging to the 'better classes' were attacked, including stores owned by Farara, and street lights were smashed, so another 26 marines were landed. When the marines charged the crowd with their bayonets fixed they were met with a barrage of stones and bottles, and when the fire brigade tried to put out fires their hoses were cut. An eye-witness reported that the struggle was so fierce that a 'whole body of rioters charged the marines and there was a hand to hand fight for a minute or two'. After the marines fired two volleys the people dispersed, but then they formed smaller groups and continued to throw stones and bottles from behind house fences. Some marines were said to have been fired on with revolvers. The unrest did not subside until after 3 am on 18 February, by which time two young men had been shot dead and several other people received gun shot wounds. Many marines were struck by missiles and two were badly injured. Some 11 stores, most of them owned by Portuguese, were burned during the night.

Even when Basseterre had been quieted, labour protests continued in the countryside, with large crowds of estate workers and villagers patrolling the roads, shouting in chorus, 'Higher wages! Higher wages!' and entering estates in an attempt to enforce a general strike. Parties of marines were despatched to restore order in the countryside, where estate managers and Portuguese shopkeepers felt vulnerable. At a meeting of planters and merchants on 18 February, a resolution was passed calling for the retention of a warship and the establishment of a 'permanent protective force'. Meanwhile, 43 special constables and 83 rural constables were sworn in, most of them store-owners or estate managers, and 216 people were arrested. A British warship remained in harbour while the cases were being tried. Several of the 99 people who were convicted received harsh sentences of as long as 7 years in prison with hard labour. A detachment of marines was sent to Nevis in response to rumours of similar protests there (Richardson 1983: 106). The ruling elite and the colonial administration responded to this strike as if it was primarily a civil disorder, and thereby provoked what they were ostensibly trying to prevent. Not everyone was intimidated, however, as reports of lawlessness and disorder, including further outbreaks of canefires, persisted throughout the year.

In St Kitts, the severe depression in the sugar trade had provoked labour protests, resulting in violence and death, but no long-term gains were achieved by the working people. Planters, merchants and colonial officials in other parts of the Caribbean were disturbed by these events. A few months after the St Kitts disturbances, a Colonial Office spokesman hypothesised what could happen in Barbados if many estates went out of cultivation: 'When that happens in Barbados, the too large working population, which in the best of times does not get continuous employment even at a very low wage, is reduced to starvation - incendiary fires become numerous, and there is a rising which the troops can with difficulty put down'.[15]

Some of the largest and most persistent disturbances occurred in Guyana between 1889 and 1905. The expansion of plantation production and the massive importation of indentured workers after Emancipation resulted in persistent poverty and widespread hardship among the majority of people in Guyana. The social structure made the process of class formation very complex because the working people were divided between peasants, rural and urban wage-earners, and those who were both 'peasant' and 'proletarian' (Frucht 1967; Rodney 1981: 218), as well as by race and ethnicity. Nevertheless, as Rodney and others have shown in detail, the Guyanese working class began to constitute itself through its own activities immediately after the period of slavery: 'it was through political struggle that the working people (and the middle class) clarified their identity and tested their relationship with other classes and strata' (Rodney 1981: 220). While members of the middle stratum periodically sought an alliance with working people in the late nineteenth century to support such goals as constitutional reform, the interests of the working class were distinct and frequently diverged from those of the middle classes. This can be seen in the series of protests and disturbances that culminated in the Ruimveldt riots of 1905.

Disturbances and strikes occurred in nineteenth-century Guyana among the largely Indian indentured immigrants as well as the ex-slaves, though the former could not legally cease work. Immigrant discontent rose in the 1860s and at least seven large-scale strikes and demonstrations broke out on the estates between August 1869, when immigrants rioted at Plantation Leonora, and January 1870. Even when not on strike, 'immigrants massed in delegations of one hundred or more became a common sight in Georgetown' (Adamson 1972: 130), and strikes on five plantations in November 1870 were repressed by armed police. In 1872 and 1873 there were other strikes at several estates. In September 1872 five Indian workers were shot dead by the police at Plantation Devonshire Castle, and in just six weeks in July and August 1873, there were at least 14 strikes, some of which involved assaults on overseers and managers, arson in the canefields, and open rioting (Moore 1987: 173).

With this history and experience of labour disturbances, it is not surprising that labour relations in Guyana were tense and strikes frequent during the sugar depression in the late nineteenth century. A hundred strikes on sugar estates were recorded between 1886 and 1889, 49 between 1895 and 1897, and another 60 between 1899 and 1903 (Adamson 1972: 155). Every stoppage or demonstration by indentured workers was regarded by their employers and the state as a riot and 'as such was usually brought to an abrupt end through the use of armed police' (Adamson 1972: 154). The police had been armed and reinforced after the disturbances at Leonora in 1869, and in 1881 the force was reorganised along military lines. The presence of this paramilitary force and its proven readiness to fire on crowds may have deterred some workers, but it is evident that many remained highly active and militant throughout this period despite these threats.

African Guyanese, also, were active in the late nineteenth and early twentieth centuries. In March 1889 they became angry when a Portuguese merchant brutally beat a black boy in a dispute over a pennyworth of bread in the Stabroek market. 'Over the preceding months, Creoles had taken note of the tendency to treat very lightly the taking of a black man's life' (Rodney 1981: 163). Their frustration with racial discrimination in the judicial system, which favoured whites at their expense, erupted in an attack on Portuguese shops and other properties in Georgetown, resulting in considerable damage. This event, which was spontaneous and unorganised, 'was analogous to the enraged attacks by sugar workers on overseers and drivers on the estates' (Rodney 1981: 164). Demonstrations, which were sometimes violent, were one of the few resources of poor African and Indian Guyanese who could find no justice in the courts and had no representation in the government. Moreover, 'given the heavy-handed, authoritarian responses of those in power' (Rodney 1981: 158), strikers and demonstrators who might have started their protests peacefully were often incited to fight back in self-defence. The pattern became a vicious circle, as the police saw any protest as a riot that must be suppressed with armed force, and demonstrators became violent when they anticipated that the police would open fire.

The dialectic between the authoritarian colonial system and the workers' resistance is clearly demonstrated in the events that took place at Plantation Non Pareil on the east coast of Demerara in October 1896. Indentured immigrants' wages had been lowered beyond the statutory rate, yet the workers were willing to negotiate with the plantation manager and immigration officials. They would tolerate lower wages if they received cheap rations and access to provision grounds in compensation. The manager, however, asked for five of the workers who had been identified as promoting grievance claims to be transferred, a standard practice for people who had been defined as troublemakers, in order 'to avoid breaches of the peace'.[16] Four of them were arrested on 13 October when they were returning from participating in a deputation to the Immigration Office. The chief spokesman of the Non Pareil workers was Gooljar, an Indian who had arrived in Guyana in 1871, served his indenture, sold clothing and worked in the police force, returned to Calcutta in 1890, and then reindentured and returned to Guyana in 1894 (Adamson 1972: 156). The planters and colonial officials anticipated that such an experienced man would give them trouble. Workers who were defined as rioters were dealt with peremptorily, though the colonial administration made a pretence of following legal formalities. The governor claimed to have issued instructions that arrests should be made only with proper warrants issued by a stipendiary magistrate and in the normal course of the law, that immigrants who came to state their grievances before the officials in town should not be interfered with, and that armed force was not to be used for the removal of any immigrant. However, Captain de Rinzy, who was in charge of the armed police party, broke all these instructions. When fellow estate workers sought to stop the arrest of the men, the police opened fire without even the formality of reading the Riot Act. Two workers died on the spot. Three others died later of the injuries they received, one of them a well-known militant named Jungali, and 59 others were wounded. De Rinzy, as Rodney stated, 'was acting within the planter milieu and according to certain accepted norms' (Rodney 1981: 159), though the governor tried to disassociate himself. De Rinzy, who became notorious as a trigger-happy officer, had obtained a warrant from a local justice of the peace who was a planter, and he was later vindicated for ordering his men to fire on the grounds of self-defence before a riotous mob.

Perhaps each act of violent repression intimidated some workers for a while, but the tradition of resistance persisted despite these murderous reprisals. Violent clashes became inevitable, whether or not they were preceded by legal formalities. In another case, in 1903, police violence was followed by legal formalities that clarified the nature of class law and power in this brutal colonial society. A gang of indentured workers at Plantation Friends in Berbice, which had been working on the rows for the replanting of cane tops, struck work on 6 May 1903 and marched to New Amsterdam to seek justice at the magistrate's court. They had been earning $1 per opening and asked for $1.44. Management had offered them $1.20 and then refused the compromise of $1.28, which the workers were willing to accept. Some workers were then charged with threatening the manager, on the word of a driver, and were arrested. The Riot Act was read outside the court, and six workers were promptly shot dead and seven seriously wounded. Four leaders were subsequently convicted of threatening the overseer and sentenced to 6-12 months' imprisonment each. One of the workers' leaders in this dispute was a veteran indentured woman, Salamea, who was said to 'urge the coolies who had assembled to fight' (Rodney 1981: 157). In this case, again, 'indentured resistance was met with preemptive force by the state apparatus acting on behalf of the plantation capitalists' (Rodney 1981: 159). Police violence and prison sentences were intended to intimidate the workers, but each such incident must have increased class consciousness and hardened class lines as it contributed to the history and tradition of militant resistance to oppression.

The widespread strikes and disturbances in Guyana in 1905 were the most serious in the British Caribbean in the period before the First World War.[17] The central issue of the 1905 labour disturbances was the persistently low rate of wages, which resulted in depressed living standards for the working people. Two decades of depression resulted in low wages, high unemployment and poverty on the sugar estates, in the villages and in Georgetown. Social and environmental factors, including poor and overcrowded housing, swampy conditions and lack of sanitation, resulted in high mortality rates, especially among infants, in Georgetown and the countryside. Families were crowded into single rooms, roofs leaked, cesspits overflowed and yards flooded. The infant mortality rate was over 200 per 1,000 live births, that is, mothers had a 20 per cent chance of losing a new baby before it was a year old.[18] A mortality commission held public hearings in Georgetown through November 1905, and this publicised the problems of which many people were all too well aware from their personal experience. The commissioners stated what was obvious: 'We are of the opinion that the excessive mortality in the colony occurs chiefly among the poorer classes of the community ... and the high rate among the poorer classes is in part due to the absence of adequate measures of sanitation; overcrowding in rooms, in ranges of tenement rooms and in tenement houses .... It is also due to poverty'.[19]

Although the sugar industry was beginning to emerge from its slump in the two years preceding the 1905 disturbances, wages were generally the same as they had been for 30 years, the cost of living was higher and work more scarce. Rent for the inadequate tenement rooms could consume at least one-quarter of the $3 or $4 a labourer might earn in a week, and one of the chief problems was that many workers were casually employed and might get only one or two days of work per week. Changes in the organisation of labour and technological innovations were making labour more productive and restoring the employers' profits, but many workers suffered de facto wage reductions and intensified exploitation. On the docks, for example, stevedores were loading ships with sugar in one and a half or two days in 1905 that they had previously loaded in four or five days. They got the same rate of pay, yet less work was available. Large numbers of unemployed workers gathered around the Georgetown docks hoping for some work, even if only for a day or two in the week, and this enabled employers to keep wages down. The stevedores felt that the shipping companies owed them back pay because they had been so underpaid for years.

It was on the Georgetown wharves, among stevedores who were poor and resentful, and who were in touch through sailors with the outside world, that the disturbances in 1905 began. There had been strikes among them in 1890, a year after the great London dock strike, and in 1905 they were the centre of militancy in Guyana. The stevedores had several complaints about their wages: first, that they had been too low for far too long; second, that they should be paid at a higher rate than the prevailing pro rata of 6 cents per hour for part of a day when work ran out; and third, that adults were often classed as boys and paid at a rate of 48 cents per day rather than the general rate of 64 cents for casual labourers. When the New Colonial Company offered a special rate of 16 cents per hour to complete the loading of a steamer, other workers went on strike on 28 November to back their demands that wages be raised to that level. The next day, the number of strikers increased and about 300 of them marched under a banner, saying '16 cents an hour or no work'. Some strikers intimidated workers on the wharves who had not joined them and others met in groups of 50 or 60 in parts of the business district.

Meanwhile, porters at Plantation Ruimveldt, the nearest estate just south of Georgetown, went on strike at midday. There was clearly contact between the strikers in Georgetown and workers on several sugar estates on the east and west banks of the Demerara and up the river, and strikes started among porters, sugar boilers, stokers and other workers near the sugar factories, as well as some Creole cane-cutters. These estate workers often were friends, relatives or former neighbours of some of the urban workers, many of whom had only recently moved to town in search of work. Although these occupations and places of residence are distinguishable, the mobility that was provoked by the depression emphasised the fluid nature of a casual workforce, and this fluidity encouraged the working people to make links and develop a broader class consciousness.

On 30 November large numbers of people demonstrated in the streets of Georgetown. Many of the strikers were then joined by domestic workers and unemployed people. Some workers, like those in the Railway Goods Wharf, were intimidated, but there was little violence and no arson. By evening the bakers had joined the strike because of a wage dispute and they marched down Carmichael Street. Around 6 pm the Riot Act was read at four points in the town and the crowds dispersed into smaller groups and outlying areas. The colonial state was overreacting, as if this was already a general labour rebellion, whereas it was still only a series of quite spontaneous and unorganised strikes and demonstrations, chiefly in Georgetown. As strikes spread in the next few days, however, there seems to have been more communication and perhaps even coordination among some groups of workers.

At about 5 am on 1 December, work ceased at the Ruimveldt Plantation factory. The manager rejected the strikers' wage demands and sent for the police, alleging that the workers were rioting. By 7.55 am the police and a detachment of artillery were in position by the Ruimveldt bridge. The Riot Act was read and the police opened fire, seriously wounding four workers, including a militant known as Long Walk and a porter named Haynes, both of them factory workers who were in the forefront of the demonstration. Police deliberately singled out those whom they considered ringleaders as targets. De Rinzy, who had been promoted to major since he fired on Indian workers at Non Pareil in 1896, ordered his men to shoot Robert Chapman, another leader. When one policeman missed, another was ordered to shoot him and Chapman died of his wounds.

News of the shooting and the sight of the wounded being brought to hospital inflamed people in Georgetown and, despite the reading of the Riot Act, thousands of people converged on the public buildings, seeking the inspector-general of police. Stones were thrown at magistrates, three of whom were injured, and some white people were beaten. Other people were shot by the police, who regained control of the western part of the town. People continued to resist by throwing stones and other missiles, and the police fired back. By the end of the day, which was dubbed Black Friday, seven or eight people had been killed and 30 wounded, 17 of them seriously.

On 2 December the strikers and demonstrators were more cautious, and moved in smaller groups. Women, in particular, engaged in stone throwing and a band of women attacked the police station in Hadfield Street at midday, scattering the meal that was being brought to the men besieged inside. Several women were arrested and the demonstrators split into smaller groups of four or five persons, thereby making the task of the police to control them harder. While Georgetown became quieter, however, the sugar estates of the east bank, Demerara, became more affected. At Houston, adjacent to Ruimveldt, the deputy manager was stoned, and at Plantation Diamond, further up the river, factory porters demanded an increase in wages from 36 cents to 48 cents per day, and sugar curers asked for 56 cents instead of the current rate of 40 cents per day. A force of 27 police and special constables was sent to Plantation Diamond to quell these demands.

On 3 December, a Sunday, while most workers were at rest, the tram conductors struck for more pay. Conductors received 5 or 6 cents an hour, depending on whether they had been employed for less or more than one year. By 5 December Georgetown was quieter but the wharves were still practically at a standstill. On 6 December, however, most of the strikes were over and the governor said that Georgetown was back to normal. Some sugar factory workers were still on strike in west bank estates and workers at Peter's Hall on the east bank struck for higher wages. On the west bank, Phillip Washington of Toevlugt became a recognised strike leader. He mobilised in Bagotstown and brought out the workers at Plantations Nismes, Schoonord and Wales. Workers at Plantation Versailles were also involved and some managers were now prepared to negotiate. On 12 December about 225 workers employed at an American-owned quartz mine in the Purumi River district went on strike, demanding $1.50 per day for men working underground, instead of their current wages of between 64 cents and $1.20 per day. By that time, however, the colonial state, strengthened by almost 600 men from HMS Diamond and HMS Sappho, had reacted with such repression that the labour disturbances subsided. So-called ringleaders were arrested and others were intimidated. Another problem was the strikers' 'sheer want, since the workers had no means of surviving without employment' (Rodney 1981: 194), and they lacked organisation and strike relief funds.

The colonial state's coercive apparatus was effectively brought to bear on the working people of Guyana in 1905. Without plans, organisation or support systems, this spontaneous workers' rebellion quickly ebbed. 'At best, ad hoc committees of workers sought audience with employers and with the colonial authorities. Alternatively, middle-class spokesmen presented themselves as negotiators.' (Rodney 1981: 198-9) The state's forces, acting on behalf of the employers to intimidate strikers, killed several people and jailed others, while reinforcing the authoritarian response to the workers' reasonable demands for wage increases, demands that were interpreted as criminal acts. As Rodney (1981: 199) states, 'There was certainly no plan to stage a violent rebellion. The corollary to this was that state agencies were largely responsible for forcing the wage protests in the direction of mass violence.' This pattern was repeated all too frequently in later years. Hardliners among the employers, who were unwilling to negotiate with their workers, were effectively supported by the state, and managers who were willing to compromise were undermined by the general show of force. Governor Hodgson, accompanied by troops from the naval ships, visited several west bank plantations and forced the managers to renege on new wage rates they had promised their workers, on the grounds that such concessions would encourage further wage demands. 'The governor told them plainly that they should follow his advice or he would withdraw the armed forces from their estates and leave them to the mercy of the "rioters"' (Rodney 1981: 200).

The colonial government did not try anyone by a jury because it was convinced that no jury would convict. Instead, using the Summary Convictions Ordinance of 1893, which was effective as soon as Georgetown was 'proclaimed' on 30 November, dozens of people were charged with disorderly conduct, possession of dangerous weapons, throwing stones and assaulting police. Many people were fined and imprisoned; some men were flogged and women had their heads shaved as additional punishments. These archaic and brutal penalties were possible under an amendment to the Summary Criminal Offences Ordinance in 1904, which had been passed with the intention of dealing with street people, who were known as centipedes. In this way, the working people who struggled for better wages were defined and treated as common criminals and social refuse by the authoritarian colonial state. The agents of the state, meanwhile, were not punished for their excesses. Patrick Dargan, a lawyer whose newspaper, the Creole, criticised the colonial administration for its handling of the disturbances, brought charges against Inspector-General Lushington and Major de Rinzy, alleging that they were criminally liable for the deaths of people at the hands of the police. These cases were dismissed.

The colonial administration could not be too complacent about these events, however, as there was evidence of quite widespread disaffection among the middle classes. A military tribunal dealt with some of the many militiamen who deserted or failed to answer the call to arms. Several were sentenced to imprisonment but were released after a month, and other pending cases, including one against Sergeant William Dathorne, a schoolteacher who had urged his fellow militiamen not to turn out, were dismissed. Over 100 men of this middle-class militia had failed to answer the call, and these defections suggest that many middle-class Guyanese sympathised with the strikers and could no longer be counted on as subalterns by the colonial authorities. Several middle-class people showed they could be active as allies in the workers' cause. Some educated people were alienated from the colonial regime because they were excluded from participation in the political process and discriminated against within the colonial establishment. A.A. Thorne, an educator from Barbados who became one of Guyana's trade union leaders in the 1930s, publicised the workers' grievances, but he was careful to disassociate himself from the centipedes who were alleged to have committed the violence. Thorne and some other members of the People's Association, which had been formed in 1903, including Dargan and Dr J.M. Rohlehr, won the respect and support of many working people. However, the People's Association, which had unsuccessfully called for the formation of a trade union, failed to organise the workers.

The actual leaders of this labour rebellion were themselves workers, who seem to have emerged at the local level in the course of the disturbances, and 'did not reappear subsequently as national trade unionists' (Rodney 1981: 208). Washington, Long Walk and Robert Chapman have already been mentioned. Another local leader was George Henry or George Beckles, a cane-cutter who led his mates out of the fields when he heard the factory workers had struck. Police stopped them and told them to give up their cutlasses. This they did, until the police tried to gather them up, when they objected. There was a scuffle and Henry, who had previously been identified as a ringleader, was arrested. He was subsequently sentenced to six months in prison with a flogging. Women, too, were active. Of the 105 people convicted in the magistrates' courts as a consequence of these disturbances, 41 were women, many of whom were probably domestic workers, washerwomen, street vendors and seamstresses in Georgetown. Though there were fewer Afro-Guyanese women working on the sugar estates, one of them, Dorothy Rice, was part of a workers' delegation from Ruimveldt. She explained that, though she worked cutting cane up to 7 pm each day and to midday on Saturdays, and had two daughters assist her with fetching the canes, she earned no more than 6 or 7 shillings per week (Rodney 1981: 207). These workers were evidently militant and courageous, but without organisation they could not win in a struggle that was not only against their employers but also the power of the colonial state.

One major problem that the workers faced in Guyana in 1905 was the racial split in their ranks. Though they succeeded to some extent in bringing together urban and rural workers, employed and unemployed, women and men, and they obtained some sympathetic support from members of the middle classes, the 1905 disturbances seem to have been limited to Guyanese workers of African descent. The workers who went on strike in the sugar estates were factory workers and cane-cutters who, according to the prevailing ethnic segmentation of the labour force, were largely Africans. Though management at Plantation Versailles promised wage increases to Indian as well as African workers, 'Indians were absent from the demonstrations' (Rodney 1981: 212). Some employers tried the old tactic of making Indians fill the places of Africans who were on strike, thereby fostering tensions between them. At Ruimveldt striking Africans kept Indians away from the job site, but no major conflict was provoked between them.

It was clearly official policy, as well as the employers' goal, to confine the disturbances to the African Guyanese and to 'prevent the spread of strike action and combination across racial lines' (Rodney 1981: 213), and in this they were largely successful. However, the need for a massive show of force, including two imperial warships, and the defection of so many members of the militia and middle classes in this critical time, indicate that, though the working class was not united, the colonial state was not entirely secure. The response of the state was to increase and reorganise its local armed forces, the chief function of which was to suppress the expression of discontent by working people. In place of the unreliable militia, a mounted police branch, comprising initially 40 mounted policemen, was created for riot control, and the government sought to start 'a volunteer force from among locally resident whites and senior employees of the large merchant firms' (Rodney 1981: 215). The resort to such means of force, however, was tantamount to an admission of failure by the colonial regime to establish its authority as legitimate. Moreover, the class and racial basis of this force was quite transparent to all concerned, which further undermined the regime's legitimacy in the minds of the majority.

Although the Guyanese labour rebellion of 1905 was not successful, it should not be seen as a complete failure. The divisions within the working people of Guyana, and particularly the great racial split which coincided with the division of labour, could not be easily overcome, so this rebellion did not come close to becoming a general strike or uprising as long as Indians did not participate. However, in the context of 1905, and viewed in comparison with other parts of the British Caribbean at the time, it contributed to the development of an especially militant class consciousness and the early formation of organised working–class institutions in Guyana.

The grievances of men and women from the sugar estates and Georgetown were articulated and fought for in 1905 and, though their leaders were victimised, the experience surely provided a basis for future action for many people. In 1906 the governor was still concerned that so many people in Georgetown showed disrespect to him, the representative of the king and the empire. Groups of people openly discussed the court cases of the militia and of Lushington and de Rinzy. In these ways, what had started as a specifically labour issue concerning wages was becoming a more generally political affair. Moreover, the grievances that had caused the disturbances of 1905 remained unresolved so they continued to ferment, and in 1906 there was another strike among Georgetown's stevedores.

Dock workers at Booker Brothers, McConnell & Co and at Sandbach Parker & Co went on strike at 1 pm on 25 September 1906. This time, it seemed that 'a secret underground movement was being built up' (Chase n.d.: 36) as the workers acted without warning, but also in a controlled way, without violence. This was a quiet, determined and organised strike, timed to coincide with the arrival of several ships in the port. On the second day the strike spread but, with mounted police patrolling the streets, there was no public disturbance. Some workers at Plantation Providence stopped work and came to Georgetown to make a complaint, but this was only a temporary stoppage and no other sugar workers joined them. The employers on the docks used strike-breakers and after three days the strike collapsed. Many strikers who returned to work were 'told with frigid politeness that their services were not required' (Chase n.d.: 37). During the strike a 22-year-old dock worker named Hubert Nathaniel Critchlow was charged with assault on 27 September. The magistrate dismissed the case and 'Critchlow left the Court a hero' (Chase n.d.: 37).[20] Critchlow was born in Georgetown on 18 December 1884, the son of a dock worker who had immigrated from Barbados. Although he left primary school at the age of 14, he became the greatest of the early leaders of organised labour in the British Caribbean.

There were several other strikes in Guyana in the following years, but it was during the First World War, when shortages provoked more demonstrations and disturbances, that Critchlow became more prominent. In 1916 he led a demonstration and delegation to the governor, Sir Wilfred Collet. As a result the dock workers gained a 10 per cent increase in wages and a reduction of their working day from ten and a half to nine and a half hours. Critchlow continued to agitate for reduced working hours, seeking an eight-hour day. A strike in 1917 obtained a nine-hour day, with a lunch break and rest period, and overtime pay for work after 5 pm and on Sundays and holidays. Many other strikes followed, at sawmills, on the railway, in the ice, match and soda factories, and among sea defence and road workers. These early efforts at collective bargaining led others, including post office workers, to petition for higher wages. Later, Critchlow negotiated a further wage increase with the Chamber of Commerce, but he lost his job in 1918 and was unable to find other work at the wharves because he was victimised by the Chamber of Commerce.

Critchlow was the recognised leader of Guyanese workers at this time. He led a massive demonstration in 1918, held talks with Governor Collet and on 11 January 1919 announced the formation of the British Guiana Labour Union (BGLU). Critchlow was the union's secretary, treasurer and organiser. By the end of the year the BGLU had about 7,000 members, including porters and labourers, tradesmen, sea defence and road workers, railway employees, factory workers, government employees, sugar estate workers and interior workers such as balata bleeders and miners, as well as dock workers, with branches in villages on the east and west Demerara coasts, on the Essequibo coast and in Berbice (Chase n.d.: 50). Critchlow's BGLU hosted the first regional labour conference in 1926 and was still active in the 1930s and 1940s. There are thus clear and direct connections between the waterfront strikes in Georgetown in 1905 and 1906 and the emergence of the first major trade union and the regional labour movement in the British Caribbean. The labour rebellion of 1905, far from being a failure, therefore, played an important part in the formation of a working class in Guyana and of organised labour in the Caribbean.

During this early phase of working-class activity, several small unions of skilled artisans were formed in Jamaica. Among them was the Carpenters, Bricklayers and Painters Union, organized in 1898, which became known as the Artisans' Union, officers of which helped form the Tailors and Shoemakers' Union in 1901. Short-lived unions of printers, in which Garvey was involved, and cigar makers were formed in 1907. A carpenter, W.G. Hinchcliffe, who had been the secretary of the Artisans' Union, started a Jamaica Trades and Labour Union in 1907, but two years later it ceased to function because its most zealous members had emigrated to Haiti and Central America. None of these early Jamaican unions survived into the second decade of the century (Hart 1988: 43-4).

One of the earliest and longest-lasting organisations of working people in the British Caribbean was the Trinidad Workingmen's Association (TWA), formed in 1897. Its core, like that of the early Jamaican unions, consisted of skilled workers, but the TWA also sought to include unskilled workers employed on the railway and waterfront, and to engage in reformist politics as well as trade union activities. Its first president, Walter Mills, was a druggist. He opposed Indian immigration but advocated free grants of 5 acres of land to labourers from Barbados, Tobago and Grenada. 'Labour by compulsion', he told the royal commission in 1897, 'can be nothing else but a state of half-slavery' (quoted in Ramdin 1982: 43).

The TWA was quite inactive until 1906, when Alfred Richards, an Afro-Chinese pharmacist, became president. The other members of the 1906 executive committee were a tailor, a mason, a carpenter, a planter and a commission agent. The chief activities of this largely petty bourgeois and skilled artisan group were in political reform rather than trade union affairs. The TWA worked in close association with the Ratepayers' Association and sought affiliation with the British Labour Party in 1906. It remained an urban-based organisation and its failure to recruit Indians was 'a major shortcoming, reflecting prejudice or neglect, or both' (Ramdin 1982: 46). Attempts were made in 1910 to form the Trinidad Bakers' Association and the Progressive Crafts Union of artisans, but both soon disappeared. Despite these efforts, by the First World War there was 'no combination of workers or body genuinely concerned with building a close-knit rank-and-file workers' organisation in Trinidad' (Ramdin 1982: 49). In 1914 there was a split in the TWA when one faction, led by John Sidney de Bourg, sought to end Richards' leadership, and by 1916 there were two branches of the TWA, neither of which 'could honestly claim to represent any important section of the people' (Ramdin 1982: 48).

The first wave of working-class unrest in the British Caribbean which had begun in the depression years of the nineteenth century had ebbed away by about 1907 and little was left to show for it by the time the First World War began. The most militant activity was in Guyana, but the most serious attempts at organisation before the war were in Jamaica and Trinidad. Though there were many self-help organisations, such as friendly societies and fraternal lodges, there were no trade unions in the smaller colonies. In some respects, the friendly societies served as proto-unions, providing some security in the form of sick and death benefits, and opportunities for working people to develop organisational skills and a sense of self-reliance. In some cases the friendly societies handled considerable sums of money, including contributions from overseas like Panama money.

More labour agitation occurred during the war. In addition to the working-class demonstrations and strikes in Guyana in 1916 and 1917, there were disturbances and strikes in Trinidad, St Lucia, St Kitts and Antigua in 1917 and 1918, but the wartime atmosphere and official restrictions were not conducive to the growth of organised labour or radical ideas, and political mobilisation did not progress until after the war had ended. The chief cause of discontent was 'the rapid increase in the prices of imported items of popular consumption during the course of the war, against a background of little or no increase in the level of wages' (Hart 1988: 50). According to Peter Fraser (1981), the price of flour, salted fish, salted beef and cotton manufactures rose in Guyana from a base of 100 in 1914 to 227, 228, 229 and 400, respectively, in 1918, and imports of flour, salted beef and cotton manufactures fell over this period to about two-thirds of the 1914 level and of salted fish by over 39 per cent. The governor of Guyana wrote to the Colonial Office on 31 January 1917, 'In view of the undoubted increase of prices due to the war, I fear the labour unrest in the Colony cannot yet be regarded as at an end'.[21]

This situation, which was common more or less throughout the British Caribbean during the war, caused considerable hardship and increasing discontent. In St Lucia there were several strikes both in the rural areas and in Castries in 1917. Stevedores obtained average wage increases of 25 per cent and the coal carriers 15 per cent. In St Kitts-Nevis workers tried to form a trade union in 1917. A small shopkeeper, J.A. Nathan, who had experienced trade unionism when he lived in the United States, was one of the organisers of the St Kitts-Nevis Universal Benevolent Association, which was registered under the Friendly Societies Act, and J. Matthew Sebastian, its president, began a labour-oriented newspaper, The Union Messenger, in 1921. Unions were illegal, however, and when some St Kitts workers went on strike in 1918 they were arrested and imprisoned for breach of contract, which was still a criminal offence. There was also a strike in Antigua in March 1918, provoked by an attempt to reduce the wages of cane-cutters. Canefields were burned and some planters were attacked. When protests spread to the town of St John, the police fired into a crowd, killing two people. An administrator alleged that one man, Arlington Newton, was behind the efforts to form a trade union in St Kitts in 1917 and the strike in Antigua in 1918 (Fraser 1981: 6). This may have been true, or it may reflect the administrator's paranoia about labour agitators.

In Trinidad, wartime restrictions checked the workers' protests, but in March 1917 workers in the oil and asphalt industries were involved in serious disturbances. Despite the fact that they were better paid than most labourers, they suffered as the others did from rising prices. Workers at the Point Fortin oilfields and the Asphalt Company refinery at Brighton went on strike between 19 and 26 March. Armed police went to other oilfields at Tabaguite and Fyzabad and the management dismissed and evicted some strikers at Fyzabad. George Richardson, the strikers' leader, rejected the oilfield company's effort to get them to resume work at the current rate of pay, but the strikers were at a great disadvantage because they had no strike funds or union organisation and they lived on company property. The leaders were ejected from the area and 50 soldiers were drafted to replace the strikers. In five days the Point Fortin strike collapsed. At Brighton, where the asphalt workers went on strike on 21 March, buildings and refined asphalt were destroyed by fire, but most of the 540 strikers returned to work by the sixth day. Three strikers and several other people, including a Seventh Day Adventist preacher who allegedly urged the men to strike, were arrested and some received prison sentences. The strikes had failed (Ramdin 1982: 49-51).

The TWA, meanwhile, was still divided into two factions. On the one hand, Richards tried to keep the TWA as a strictly political organisation involved chiefly in municipal politics, and, on the other hand, the rebel branch, whose leaders included David Headley, James Braithwaite, William Howard Bishop and de Bourg, behaved more as if it were a trade union. Several of these leaders were immigrants and hence vulnerable to threats of deportation. De Bourg, for example, who was from Grenada, and had been active in radical Trinidad politics from the 1880s, was deported in 1920. Braithwaite, a Barbadian dock worker, who became secretary of the TWA in 1918, and Bishop, a Guyanese journalist and teacher, were also vulnerable. These rebel leaders took over the TWA in 1918.

Though it was neither large nor well organised, the TWA 'became the main agency through which worker grievances were articulated, and it taught Trinidadians the methods of collective political and industrial action' (Brereton 1981: 160). In the first months of 1919 there were strikes by dockers, railwaymen, city council employees and workers at the electric and telephone companies, and the TWA leaders played an active role in the agitation for higher wages. When asphalt workers at La Brea asked TWA leaders to negotiate for them, the team achieved a 33 per cent wage increase, a reduction of working hours by 1 hour, and an increase in overtime rates of 150 per cent. This victory was important because it 'boosted TWA's status among workers, leading to an increase in its membership, and the establishment of two branches at La Brea and San Fernando' (Brereton 1981: 161). Though trade unions remained illegal, organised labour in Trinidad was clearly progressing by 1919.

In Jamaica, workers at the Kingston ice factory went on strike in 1917 and several were imprisoned (Hart 1988: 52). Cigar makers, led by J. A. Bain-Alves, who had been a member of their short-lived union in 1908, went on strike and formed a new union. In 1918 Bain-Alves organised unions among dock workers and tram workers in Kingston, and A.J. McGlashan[22] organised waiters. Several strikes erupted in Kingston, among employees of the fire brigade and then among the longshoremen and coal heavers on the wharves, and the sanitation workers. A strike among sugar workers at Amity Hall plantation at Vere in Clarendon, resulted in violent police action: three workers were shot and killed and a dozen wounded in 1918 (Eaton 1975: 20). Other strikes occurred at estates in Golden Grove in St Thomas and Annotto Bay in St Mary, but no attempt was made to organise agricultural workers at this time. In 1919 Hinchcliffe, a veteran of the early Artisans' Union and the Jamaica Trades and Labour Union, was again trying to organise workers in the building trades. Workers employed on the railway went on strike and formed a 'union under cover', called the Workingmen's Co-operative Association, in 1919 (Hart 1988: 52).

Bain-Alves, the president of the Longshoremen's Union, with the help of Alfred Mendes, who had been vice-president and secretary of the Artisans' Union in 1908, formed the Jamaican Federation of Labour (JFL), a group of embryonic unions under his presidency (Hart 1988: 52; Post 1978: 212). The JFL petitioned Governor Sir Leslie Probyn to give legal and official recognition to trade unions. As a result, the Trade Union Law, introduced into the Legislative Council in March 1919, became law on 25 October 1919. This law conferred legal status on registered trade unions and protected them from prosecution for conspiracy or unlawful combinations, but it neither conferred immunity for unions and workers from liability for tort or breach of contract, nor legalised peaceful picketing (Eaton 1975: 20; Hart 1988: 74). Similar legislation was passed in Guyana in June 1921, but not in Trinidad and other parts of the British Caribbean until the 1930s and 1940s.

The strikes and organisation of workers in Jamaica in 1917 and 1918 provided the necessary pressure that resulted in the significant, though still limited, legalisation of trade unions in 1919. There was important continuity, albeit interrupted, between the first, second and third waves of labour unrest in Jamaica, between the 1880s and 1908, 1917 and 1919, and the 1930s. Some people, including Bain-Alves, Mendes, Hinchcliffe, McGlashan and Garvey, like Critchlow in Guyana, were active as organisers in more than one of these periods, and some of them in all three.

Demobilised soldiers from the British West Indies Regiment

A new factor after the First World War, which was manifested in several parts of the British Caribbean, was the role of demobilised soldiers returning home from service with the British West Indies Regiment (BWIR). Bitterly disillusioned with the racial discrimination they had encountered during their wartime service for the mother country, and coming home to face un-employment and poverty, these men 'swelled the ranks of the discontented' (Hart 1988: 50) and as ex-soldiers they were not easily intimidated by the standard show of force.

Thousands of West Indians volunteered for service in the First World War, most of whom - 397 officers and 15,204 other ranks - served in the BWIR, which was created in 1915. The largest contingent by far, consisting of 303 officers and 9,977 other ranks, came from Jamaica. Another 40 officers and 1,438 other ranks came from Trinidad and Tobago, and 20 officers and 811 other ranks from Barbados. Even the small colonies contributed men, with 441 men from the Bahamas, 533 from Belize, 445 from Grenada, 700 from Guyana, 229 from the Leeward Islands, 359 from St Lucia and 305 from St Vincent. By 1917 Belize had sent 12.8 men per 1,000 of its population, well above the regional average of 4.9 per 1,000, so recruiting was suspended in that colony in order not to further affect the local labour supply (Joseph 1971: 110-11). Of the total of 15,601 men, 1,256 were killed or died of wounds or sickness, and 697 were wounded (Joseph 1971: 124).

Two battalions of the BWIR were involved in fighting in Palestine and Jordan against the Turkish army, but the War Office was determined that black colonial troops would not fight against Europeans. Consequently, most members of the BWIR functioned as if they were labour battalions, employed in handling ammunition and digging cable trenches and gun emplacements in France, often under heavy shell fire, and working on the quays in Taranto in southern Italy. Many West Indian soldiers served garrison duties in Egypt, and small parties were sent to East Africa and Mesopotamia, also in non-combatant roles. The racist policy of using West Indian soldiers primarily as labour battalions was compounded by the policy that the officers of these black troops must be white (Joseph 1971: 103). Further, towards the end of the war, when British soldiers received pay increases of 50 per cent, the War Office ruled that West Indians were not eligible because they were considered to be 'natives' (Elkins 1970: 100).

The pattern of discrimination continued after hostilities ceased, when the battalions of the BWIR from France and Egypt joined those already in Taranto. There the West Indians were not treated like British troops, but were 'humiliated and badly treated', and some of them had to wash dirty linen and clean latrines for other troops (Joseph 1971: 119). On 6 December 1918, members of the 9th Battalion of the BWIR attacked their officers, and 180 sergeants petitioned the secretary of state for the colonies, protesting against the discrimination they suffered. After several days of insubordination, during which the men refused to work, the 9th Battalion was disbanded and a machine-gun unit of the Worcestershire Regiment was sent to Taranto (Elkins 1970: 101). There were several other incidents of insubordination, as some West Indians refused to carry out the duties they were assigned, and on 17 December some 50 or 60 sergeants of the BWIR secretly formed a Caribbean League at Cimino camp. At several meetings through early January 1919, they discussed their grievances, including the replacement of black by white non-commissioned officers. They demanded that 'the black man should have freedom to govern himself' and declared that they were prepared to use force to that end, and to strike for higher wages after demobilisation. The Caribbean League was betrayed to the officers and it came to an end (Joseph 1971: 120). Some soldiers were convicted of mutiny, and received sentences of three or five years in prison. One was sentenced to 20 years in prison and another was executed by firing squad (Elkins 1970: 102). The decision was made to disarm the West Indian soldiers and to repatriate them as soon as possible (Joseph 1971: 118).

The Colonial Office was concerned that these men would promote disorder when repatriated and warned the West Indian governors. In February 1919 the Colonial Office secured the pay increases previously denied to the BWIR and applied them retroactively in order to allay their resentment, but also asked the Admiralty to make a warship available near Jamaica at the time of demobilisation. In March there was discussion about issuing machine-guns to West Indian police forces, provided they were supervised by white officers, to meet any disorders that might arise on the return of men from the BWIR. C.L. Joseph states: 'The disturbances expected in the early post-war period did not materialize, despite the fact that many ex-soldiers experienced difficulty in obtaining their pay and pensions' (1971: 121). In fact, however, there were some serious disturbances, in which demobilised soldiers of the BWIR played a major role, first in Belize in July 1919 and then in Trinidad in November and December 1919. These disturbances in their turn contributed to the development of racial and class consciousness and incipient nationalism in those colonies in the interwar period (Elkins 1970: 103).

In Belize, where 339 demobilised soldiers from the BWIR returned on 8 July 1919, the tensions of race and class that had erupted in 1894 continued to disturb the colony. During the administration of Governor Sir Wilfred Collett, between 1913 and 1918, there were several racial incidents, such as the exclusion of H.H. Vernon, a prominent middle-class Creole, from the governor's reception before the departure of the first Belizean volunteers to the BWIR in 1915. When the public buildings in Belize Town caught fire in August 1918, the colonial officials felt that the Creole public was indifferent (Ashdown 1981: 44). Copies of Garvey's paper, the Negro World, had been entering Belize in large numbers since 1918, and in January 1919 Acting-Governor Walter proscribed its circulation. This ban, which was ineffective as copies continued to be smuggled in, 'created much local resentment' (Ashdown 1981: 45). A deputation, led by a black radical, Herbert Hill Cain, demanded a revocation of the ban as the paper was allowed to circulate elsewhere in the West Indies.[23] Walter's dismissal of the deputation and maintenance of the ban was subsequently held to be one of the grievances that provoked the disturbances in July.[24] Cain published a newspaper, the Belize Independent, that emphasised black achievements and included a column called 'Garvey Eye', written by L.D. Kemp. On 16 July Cain published an editorial, under the heading 'Race Riots in the UK', about the recent anti-black riots in Liverpool and Cardiff, an article that the subsequent commission of inquiry into the riots concluded had 'a considerable effect in precipitating action'.[25] Samuel Haynes, who had been a corporal in the BWIR, wrote to the Belize Independent in 1919, complaining of their treatment by British soldiers in Egypt in 1916. Arriving hungry and tired, the Belizean soldiers were singing Rule Britannia when British soldiers demanded, 'Who gave you niggers authority to sing that? Clear out of this building - only British troops admitted here' (quoted in Foster 1987: 57).

The demobilised soldiers were reviewed and addressed by the new governor, Sir Eyre Hutson, and given a meal and $10 to keep them going, but some resented their exclusion from a social event at the golf club. On the night of 22 July resentment erupted in violence when ex-soldiers, led by

Sergeant Hubert Vernon, raged through the town smashing windows in the principal stores and assaulting some officials and employers. Joined by other working people of the town, a crowd of perhaps 3,000 people rioted through the night. The government remained helpless to stop them because it could not trust the local police and only some members of the volunteer territorial force responded to the authorities. Then some of the former soldiers, led by Haynes, helped to stop the looting and violence. Order was restored by the next morning, and the arrival of HMS Constance on 24 July brought the disturbances to an end. Haynes, as secretary of the British Honduras Contingent Committee, subsequently sought the release of several soldiers who had been imprisoned but, as an associate of Cain, he was seen by the governor as 'a troublesome agitator' (quoted in Ashdown 1981: 47).

The chief consequence of these disturbances was the heightening of racial and anti-colonial feeling in general, and of support for Garvey's philosophy in particular. In April 1920 a group of Belizean Creoles created a local branch of the UNIA. Haynes was the general secretary, and he subsequently became one of the principal leaders of the UNIA.[26] Others involved in the UNIA were Cain and Kemp of the Belize Independent, and Calvert Staine, who later became a city councillor and a nominated member of the Legislative Council from 1942 to 1947. This local UNIA branch received a visit from Garvey himself in 1921, when he held several public meetings, exhorting his supporters to purchase shares in the BSL. Though Garvey's visit encouraged interest in the UNIA, when Haynes left for the United States the Belize branch lost its most able member. A successful branch of the Black Cross Nurses was created in Belize by Vivian Seay in 1920 (Herrmann 1985: 39–46), but a split developed in the local UNIA in 1927 between Kemp, the executive secretary, and Benjamin Pitts, the president.

When Garvey again visited Belize, in 1929, his organisation was in decline internationally as well as locally. Nevertheless, his ideas influenced racial consciousness in Belize and several Garveyites, including Cain, Kemp and Staine continued to be politically active, and some of the leaders of the labour movement that began in 1934 were also followers of Garvey. In fact, the development of racial and class consciousness was so closely interrelated in the interwar years in Belize that it is somewhat artificial to try to distinguish between them. The emergence of racial and class consciousness, together, was a resistant response to the prevailing colonial political economy and began to shape a new anti-colonial and nationalist ideology in Belize.

There were demonstrations also in Jamaica in July and August 1919. F.E.M. Hercules, a Trinidadian resident in London who was the secretary of the Society of Peoples of African Origin, arrived in Jamaica in June and addressed several public meetings, advising workers to press for a minimum wage law.

During his visit, railway workers went on strike for a higher wage, white sailors were attacked and there were demonstrations in Kingston.

In Trinidad, as in Belize, the return of soldiers from the BWIR played a major part in the development of racial feeling and of serious unrest in 1919 and 1920. In July 1919 there was already evidence of anti-white feeling when British sailors were attacked in the streets of Port of Spain. The local press, particularly the Argos, had reported racial incidents in the UK, including the anti-black riots in Liverpool and Cardiff in which hundreds of black people were attacked and a Trinidadian sailor who had served in the navy during the war, Charles Wotten, was murdered (Brereton 1981: 161). Hercules, who was well-known for his defence of blacks in the UK, visited Trinidad in September 1919, where he 'contributed to the development of black nationalism' (Brereton 1981: 161). The unrest escalated and the governor refused to allow Hercules to return to Trinidad at the end of the year.

The Argos and the Negro World promoted race-conscious views in Trinidad and many sailors brought in Garveyite and socialist ideas. Members of the white community urged the colonial secretary to suppress the Argos, arm the white people and station British troops in the colony because of what they saw as the hostility of the black population. Returned soldiers who found it hard to obtain jobs and were annoyed at the delays in settling their claims for pay, allowances and pensions, formed the Returned Soldiers and Sailors Council, and contributed 'to the already deteriorating and explosive situation' (Basdeo 1983: 15).

The dock workers of Port of Spain, supported by the TWA, took the initiative in November 1919 and started what was to become more or less a general strike. These dock workers, as elsewhere, were a radical element in the emerging working class. Concentrated on the waterfront, they were in regular contact with international news and ideas, including radical ideas about trade unionism, socialism and Garveyism, disseminated through the sailors who brought in literature and engaged them in discussions. Many of the dock workers, like Braithwaite of the TWA, were immigrants from other colonies who brought with them broader experience and a wider perspective on local issues. They suffered in their work from irregular employment and great insecurity, as well as low wages and high inflation like other workers. In 1919 they demanded a wage increase, overtime pay and an 8-hour day, and were probably encouraged in this by the efforts of Critchlow and his BGLU in Guyana. The TWA, whose president and secretary were stevedores, sought to negotiate on the dock workers' behalf but the shipping agents refused, saying this was 'a piece of impudence on the part of those who had no authority from the men to make such representations' (quoted in Hart 1988: 53). On 15 November the dock workers went on strike. It was 'a well-planned strike, with a high level of collective organization and action among the workers on the waterfront. Scab labour was used to keep the docks functioning, and on 1 December dockers attacked warehouses, ran the scabs off the waterfront, and marched through the city forcing businesses to close. City council employees and coal carriers joined the strike.' (Brereton 1981: 162) The employers' attempt to use strike-breakers from rural Trinidad and Venezuela and to fire strikers backfired. Instead of intimidating the workers, it angered them and made them more determined, thus escalating the confrontation.

The strikers achieved extensive public support. Even the governor acknowledged that workers had been hard hit by uncontrolled inflation and price-gouging: 'the scandalous prices charged by the dry goods merchants have added to the difficulties of the poorer classes in maintaining themselves. As an illustration of the profits they are making, I may mention that one John Smith, owner of a business called Bonanza, who was supposed to be on the brink of bankruptcy when the war broke out in 1914, died six months ago leaving £250,000'.[27] On 1 December thousands of supporters joined the strikers in a march through Port of Spain that brought the city to a standstill. The police, volunteers and mounted infantry were mobilised and a warship and white troops were requested, and Dr Stephen Laurence, a popular coloured member of the Executive Council, urged Governor Sir John Robert Chancellor to compromise.

The TWA provided a structure within which the strikers and protesters could operate, encouraged collective action and became an agency through which grievances were articulated. A conciliation board was created, consisting of two shipping company representatives, two TWA leaders representing the strikers and two government appointees. The evident strength of the strike and support for the TWA had forced the employers and government to accept the TWA as the collective bargaining agency, effectively a union, of the workers. After a single meeting of the board, on 3 December, the shipping companies granted a 25 per cent wage increase to the waterfront workers.[28] This victory encouraged other workers to strike throughout Trinidad and Tobago. HMS Calcutta was sent to Tobago where estate workers struck and marched through Scarborough. The Riot Act was read and the police fired, killing one striker, Nathaniel Williams, and wounding seven others. Order was restored only after the marines landed. In Port of Spain, city council employees struck for higher wages and chose the TWA to represent them. Meanwhile, Indian estate workers went on strike at Montserrat, Couva, Cunupia, Esperanza, Sangre Grande, D'Abadie and Chaguanas. In a strike at Woodford Lodge an Indian worker was killed by a white plantation official.[29] Workers took to the streets in San Fernando, and at Central Oilfields in southern Trinidad fitters and labourers went on strike, demanding a 25 per cent wage increase. On 5 January oil workers on strike at Point Fortin returned to work only after the secretary of the TWA persuaded them to do so, but two weeks later the Asphalt Company workers at La Brea struck.

The governor and the Chamber of Commerce felt that black police and militia were unreliable in the circumstances as they could not be counted on to protect strike-breakers or to suppress riots. A white volunteer force of businessmen and their friends, called the Colonial Vigilantes, was formed and 350 soldiers of the Royal Sussex Regiment were despatched from the UK to ensure the maintenance of law and order in the colony. It became increasingly apparent that this was class law and a racist order, as the colonial government, feeling more secure with these white reinforcements, cracked down on the strikers and their leaders.

In the period of repression that followed the strikes and demonstrations of late 1919 and early 1920, 99 people were arrested and 82 of them were subsequently convicted and fined or imprisoned, among them Braithwaite and James Phillips, the secretary and assistant secretary of the TWA, respectively. Four leading members of the TWA who were not natives of Trinidad were deported for committing seditious activities: Brutus Ironman (from Guyana), Bruce McConney (Barbados), de Bourg (Grenada) and E. Sellier Salmon (Jamaica). The colonial government's action showed that as yet it saw 'little difference between industrial agitation and sedition' (Basdeo 1983: 29). The Trinidad Guardian in March 1920 published alarmist reports, lacking any factual foundation, that there was a conspiracy to massacre whites, overthrow the government and establish a black republic.[30] These were primal fears of the whites, as old as Caribbean colonialism itself.

In this atmosphere, the colonial government passed the Seditious Publications Ordinance in April 1920, banning the Negro World, The Monitor, The Crusader and The Recorder. One Colonial Office adviser saw this as an attack on 'fundamental liberties' but it received approval anyway (Basdeo 1983: 29). The strikes and lockout ordinance, passed in January 1920, prohibited strikes by workers and provided for compulsory arbitration in wage disputes. The head of the West India Department in the Colonial Office opposed this repressive legislation, on the grounds that something should be done to improve the economic situation and thereby reduce people's 'legitimate grievances'. He concluded,

> while the cost of living is more than doubled, wages have increased in general decidedly less than one half. The existing standard of living for the labourers is much below the standard prevailing in Cuba and San Domingo. No doubt racial feeling has played a considerable part in the troubles.... But experience in St Kitts, Sir Frederick Maxwell's report from British Honduras and the Admiral's

telegram ... just received from Trinidad all go to show that the predominant cause was economic. The labourer is badly paid and short of clothes and cash, and he sees the planters, with sugar trebled in price, making more money than they know how to spend. Evidently this position tends to exaggeration of the racial factor in the business.[31]

He followed these comments a year later with a more specific criticism of the steamship agents, who

in spite of the great increase in the cost of living ... asked for trouble by leaving the stevedores on pre-war wages, and even this they aggravated by refusing to receive the men's representatives when the strike broke out, and by importing Venezuelans and other foreigners in order to crush it. The result has been to provoke disorder, to stir up racial feeling and to inflict upon the whole colony the expense of maintaining white troops for a long period .... I cannot suppose that mob rule would have gone to such lengths if it had not been for the existence of genuine and serious grievances.[32]

While it is certainly true that there were serious economic grievances that needed to be addressed, the racial factor should not be underestimated. Racism, contrary to the denials of colonial officials and other whites, did constitute a genuine and serious grievance throughout the Caribbean colonies. Racial feelings had indeed been stirred up by the way the business community responded to the strikes in Trinidad and Tobago, but these feelings were already present and had a long history. Although racial feelings were certainly heightened just before these strikes by the return of angry soldiers of the BWIR, by the circulation of the Negro World and similar literature and by the agitation of men like Hercules, they were endemic in the colonial situation itself.

Labour organisations in the 1920s

There is no doubt that racial and class consciousness were increasing in many parts of the British Caribbean in the years immediately after the First World War as a result of great economic hardship, the influence of Garveyism and the returning soldiers from the BWIR. What was lacking in most colonies was an organised structure that could effectively channel this heightened consciousness into social action. Paradoxically, however, two of the colonies with the most racially divided working class, namely Guyana and Trinidad, were in 1919 and 1920 the most advanced in terms of organised labour. The BGLU was the only union created at this time in the British Caribbean that continued to function in the 1930s and 1940s, and the TWA pioneered the way for future political and labour organisations in Trinidad and Tobago. Together, these early labour organisations began to conceive and coordinate a regional labour movement in 1926, when the first British Guiana and West Indies Labour Conference was held in Georgetown. Yet both the BGLU and the TWA suffered from the fact that their members and support were drawn largely from the African segments of their respective societies and they neglected to organise the Indians; both had become less effective organisations by the late 1920s.

Despite the repression in 1920, the TWA emerged with greater prestige and membership. By early 1920 the TWA had about 6,000 members and by 1921 it was 'the sole representative organization of the Trinidad workers, recognized as such by the British Government and, reluctantly, by the local officials' (Brereton 1981: 164). However, just at this time the TWA became less of a trade union and more of a reformist political party. This change was reflected and reinforced by a change in the organisation's leadership. Bishop, the new secretary, began to publish a paper, the Labour Leader, in 1922 and to forge an alliance with middle-class liberals. The key figure became Cipriani, a hero of the BWIR soldiers, who had defended them against racism, joined the TWA in 1919 and was elected its president in 1923. The shift from black working-class leaders like Headley and Braithwaite to this white middle-class officer influenced the organisational transformation of the TWA, but it was also affected by the fact that in Trinidad, unlike Jamaica and Guyana, trade unions remained illegal in the 1920s. 'Cipriani's bias was towards reformist politics rather than working class struggles . . . . [As the TWA's president] he discouraged the trade union side of its activities and concentrated its attention on the achievement of political reforms' (Hart 1988: 57).

Cipriani had great faith in the British Labour Party and believed that constitutional reforms would enable the people of Trinidad and Tobago to achieve improvements. Of course, this may be seen as merely self-serving, at least in part, because Cipriani based his own political career on reformist politics. He entered the Legislative Council in 1925 when the TWA won three of the five elected seats under the new constitution. Although the TWA expanded and consolidated as an organisation in the 1920s, with at least 13 branches outside Port of Spain, its activities as a trade union declined under Cipriani's leadership. Even after legislation legalised trade unions in Trinidad and Tobago in 1934, Cipriani would not allow the TWA to register as a trade union, but instead changed its name to the Trinidad Labour Party (TLP). This 'merely confirmed a change of function that had long since been achieved in practice' (Hart 1988: 57). The constitutional reform of 1925 thus opened the way for middle-class political activity and confirmed the transformation of the TWA, leaving the majority of working people unenfranchised and without an organisation that was really their own. This pattern occurred in similar fashion in other parts of the British Caribbean in subsequent decades, as middle-class politicians used a working-class base from which to climb to power.

In Grenada an organisation modelled on the TWA, called the Grenada Workingmen's Association (GWA), was created in 1931, but it functioned more as a pressure group for political reforms than as a trade union. The Representative Government Association had been established in Grenada on 10 November 1918 and two years later a petition was sent to the Colonial Office demanding the abolition of Crown colony government and the introduction of popularly elected members to the Legislative Council. One of the leaders of this agitation was T. Albert Marryshow, a journalist who owned and edited The West Indian, who agitated for racial equality, political reforms and a West Indian Dominion within the British empire. However, like Cipriani, with whom he attended the Commonwealth Labour Conferences in London in 1928 and 1930, he had too much faith in the effectiveness and reliability of support from the British Labour Party.

After the Wood Commission's visit to the West Indies in 1922 the number of elected unofficials in Grenada's Legislative Council was increased from four to five, as Marryshow had urged, and he was elected unopposed as the representative of St George's in 1925. In response to the economic depression, which reduced the standard of living and the public revenue, the elected members established an economy committee in June 1931 and recommended a cut in officials' salaries. On 16 October the Legislative Council rejected this proposal and introduced a customs amendment ordinance to increase duties on several imported commodities. Marryshow and other unofficial members withdrew in protest and two days later the GWA, which was led by Marryshow, decided to protest against the new bill. According to The West Indian, some 10,000 Grenadians marched in silence to Government House on 28 October, carrying banners with such slogans as 'We cannot stand any more taxation' and 'Cut the salaries of the Officials'. George B. Otway, who was later the founder of the Seamen and Waterfront Workers' Union, presented a petition to the governor but the proposals were not accepted. All the elected members of the Legislative Council resigned, and meetings were held all over the island in February 1932 at which support was expressed for the elected members' stand, but this agitation did not develop into a labour movement. Marryshow devoted most of his efforts to the issues of constitutional reform and regionalism, the GWA was not much of a force and there was no labour rebellion in Grenada in the 1930s.[33] Marryshow organised a peaceful demonstration in 1938 'in order to show solidarity with the brothers in other islands' (Sheppard 1987: 37) and he may have actually helped prevent any violence (Singham 1968: 151). He was certainly a great admirer of the royal family and was rewarded for his repeated protestations of loyalty when he was made a Commander of the Order of the British Empire in 1943 and appointed to Grenada's Executive Council in 1944 (Sheppard 1987: 40). Though he was never much of a labour leader, Marryshow had considerable status among the rising West Indian nationalists in the 1940s and was elected the first president of the Caribbean Labour Congress (CLC) at the founding conference in Barbados in 1945.

Barbados in the 1920s lacked an organisation or pressure group as significant as the TWA or BGLU, but similar social and political forces were at work. The Barbados Labour Union was formed in 1919, and a branch of Garvey's UNIA in 1920. The two major figures in the 1920s were Clennell W. Wickham and Dr Charles Duncan O'Neale. Wickham's experience in the services in the First World War contributed to his anti-colonial consciousness, just as it did for others. He became the editor of the Barbados Herald, a weekly newspaper started in 1919 by Clemment Innis. Wickham 'developed a socialist agenda for action, and came close to being the country's first Marxist theoretician and activist' (Beckles 1990: 156). It was O'Neale, however, who launched the Democratic League (BDL), Barbados' first political party, in October 1924. Although O'Neale and other league leaders emphasised the moderate and Christian character of their goals, they were branded 'racists' and 'bolsheviks' by their conservative opponents (Beckles 1990: 157). In December 1924, C.A. (Chrissie) Brathwaite won a seat in the Assembly in a by-election for the league, and several others were won in the next decade.

O'Neale also started the Barbados Workingmen's Association (BWA), modelled on the TWA and acting as the 'industrial and business arm' of the league, in 1926. Working closely with the UNIA, led by John Beckles, the BWA spawned two working-class organisations, the Barbados Workers' Union Cooperative Company and the Workingmen's Loan and Friendly Investment Society. Trade unions were still illegal in Barbados, but during a dock workers' strike in April 1927, the BWA and O'Neale supported the strikers. Others, including a young lawyer named Grantley Adams, attacked O'Neale and other league leaders for supporting the strike. Representing a Bridgetown merchant, Adams won a libel suit in 1930 against Wickham for his editorials in the Herald. The judgement ruined Wickham financially and was 'a major blow for the Democratic League and the workers' movement' (Beckles 1990: 159). The BWA, which was created at a time when trade unionism was in decline elsewhere in the region, 'did not succeed in mobilising the workers for sustained trade union activity' (Hart 1988: 58). Adams, who was elected to the House in 1934, took up some liberal causes, but the reformist efforts of the league were frustrated in the Assembly and the Legislative Council remained dominated by the island's conservative merchant-planter elite. The BDL and its associated organisations did not survive after O'Neale's death in

1936, though friendly societies, lodges and UNIA branches maintained some political activity at the local level (Beckles 1990: 161).

In Guyana Critchlow's BGLU, which was formed in 1919, became the first legally recognised trade union in the British colonies. However, the union barely survived a crisis in the early 1920s. A group of middle-class people tried to take over the union in 1920 and in the struggle for leadership the workers' confidence and membership declined. In an economic crisis in 1921 the labour force was reduced by about 40 per cent and wages reduced by about 20 per cent. The BGLU, too weak to resist, gave in without a strike. The trades union ordinance was enacted in June 1921 and the BGLU was formally registered on 21 July 1922. By March 1923, however, the union had lost its headquarters because it was unable to make the mortgage payments, and it had only 205 members. By 1924, membership had recovered to 1,129, though only 418 of these were financial. The BGLU was open to all workers but its strongest support was on the docks, where the workers were the most militant (Chase n.d.: 56, 62-3, 69).

On 31 March 1924 the stevedores demanded an increase from $1.60 to $2 per day, truckers from 84 cents to $1.20, and packers from $1.12 to $1.44. The BGLU also demanded double time for night work, Saturday afternoons, holidays, and for work done between 4 pm and 6 pm. Another problem was the shortage of work, as most people got only 1 and a half days work per week on the waterfront, and the price of food had again been raised. The union called out the workers and, though the law still did not permit picketing, organised a picket line to help dissuade strike-breakers and to keep the strikers orderly. On the second day of the strike, 1 April, there was a huge demonstration of support in Georgetown, joined by several hundred women. The saw mill, tram cars and sewage works were closed down, and water supplies were interrupted. When they heard that strike-breakers were unloading a Canadian vessel, the crowd rushed to the wharf and drove them off. Other demonstrators closed the electric power company, the sewerage works and the railway, stopped the barges of the Demerara Bauxite Company; middle-class homes were invaded and servants told to quit work. The conservative Daily Argosy reported that some women attacked employers who had dismissed them from domestic work and said that 'what occurred yesterday was by no means a strike, but a war against the community' (Spackman 1973: 321).

Governor Sir Graeme Thompson, facing widespread unrest, issued a proclamation that invoked the provisions of the Summary Convictions Offences Ordinance of 1898, called out the active and reserve military forces, and banned all open air meetings and demonstrations, though there was little evidence of any violence or property damage. The Executive Council, led by the governor, 'issued instructions to the local forces to use all necessary force, including shooting, to control the situation' (Spackman 1973: 321). A conspicuous show of military strength and the arrest of many men and women were intended to intimidate the demonstrators. Critchlow, meanwhile, was pressured to urge the strikers to return to work before any wage increases had been conceded. Placing their trust in Critchlow, they resumed work and calm returned to Georgetown, but on 4 April the shipping agents and employers rejected the workers' demands. Critchlow appealed to the governor for arbitration, but this, too, was promptly rejected (Chase n.d.: 66-70).

Sugar workers went on strike on 2 April at Plantations Houston, Farm, La Penitence and Providence on the east bank of the Demerara. Creole and Indian workers marched to Diamond Estate and stopped the factory and field workers. A procession of Indian and Creole men, women and children, met by armed soldiers and police with machine guns, chanted, 'We ain't want to see soldier with gun and revolver, we want see money' (Chase n.d.: 71). On the next day, when about 4,000 people from several estates on the east bank headed to Georgetown, where the dock workers were still on strike and the proclamation was in effect, their way was barred by armed police at Ruimveldt. The Riot Act was read, the unarmed crowd tried to push through the guard, and mounted police charged them. The crowd then stoned the police, and the police fired. Within a few minutes 13 people were killed and 24 injured, 15 of them seriously. Captain Ramsay, who ordered his men to fire, later deposed that some of the dead and wounded, including a man and a child who were killed, were 'peaceful citizens who were in the line of fire' (Spackman 1973: 323), but an official enquiry approved his action. Several witnesses, including some English special constables, had testified that the 'crowd was peaceable' and that 'they were not attempting any violence at the time' they were fired on. However, C.R. Darnley of the Colonial Office minuted: 'We may congratulate ourselves on the restraint and firmness with which the police dealt with a most dangerous mob, on the point of sacking Georgetown'.[34] Once again, 'the state machinery was firm and merciless in dealing with the workers' (Chase n.d.: 72). The crowd dispersed and by the next day the east bank was quiet.

No evidence was found of collusion between the dock workers and the sugar workers. However, although most of the estate workers were not organised, the BGLU had distributed some pamphlets and called meetings on the east bank in March 1924 (Spackman 1973: 320), and at least one Barbadian worker from Diamond, a member of the BGLU, was reported to be a ringleader of the crowd at Ruimveldt. When work resumed no workers in the city or on the estates had made any immediate gains. The failure of the BGLU in 1924 'led to a slowing down in the recovery of the union' (Hart 1988: 59), as feelings of frustration and powerlessness rose. Nevertheless, the BGLU survived and it was the only union in Guyana in the 1920s. In fact, it was the only 'functioning trade union of manual workers' in the British Caribbean at the time the Great Depression hit the region (Hart 1988: 61).

Critchlow was a regionalist and internationalist. In 1925, he attended the British Commonwealth Labour Conference in London and was inspired to organise the first regional conference in the British Caribbean. From 12 to 14 January 1926, the BGLU hosted the first British Guiana and West Indies Labour Conference in Georgetown. Critchlow was joined by Cipriani and Bishop from Trinidad's TWA and two representatives from Suriname, W.J. Lesperan and W.H. Bastick of the Waterfront Workers' Union in Paramaribo. The participation of F.O. Roberts MP, representing the British Labour Party and International Trades Union Congress, initiated a long-term relationship between the British labour movement and West Indian trade unions. Roberts' reports to the British Labour Party and TUC were 'a glaring indictment of labour conditions' in the British Caribbean, including workers' wages and welfare, and the lack of labour legislation and of protection for working women and children (Basdeo 1983: 6). A.K. Amin and W.D. Dinally represented the British Guiana (BG) East Indian Association at the conference, and a message was received from the Indian Congress urging Guyanese Indians to 'organise in alliance with workers of other nationalities to build up a Socialist State' (Chase n.d.: 73).

On Critchlow's initiative, the conference approved a resolution to form a labour federation to be called the Guianese and West Indian Federation of Trades Unions and Labour Parties, and a committee was formed to draw up a constitution and rules. They passed many other resolutions, specific to both labour and political reform issues.[35] Critchlow represented the BGLU at another Commonwealth conference in London in 1930 and at an international trade union conference in Germany in 1931, and visited the Soviet Union in 1932. On his return to Guyana, the papers branded him a Communist and the governor referred to him as a 'Bolshie agitator'.[36] The regional Labour Federation remained an embryonic aspiration until 1938, when similar conferences were held in Trinidad and Guyana, and again in Guyana in 1944. When it developed into the Caribbean Labour Congress (CLC) in 1945, Hubert Critchlow was elected the first vice-president.[37] This pioneering labour organiser thus linked the militant strikes in Guyana at the turn of the century to the emergence of the first regional Caribbean labour organization.

Conclusion

The period from 1880 to 1930 was marked by great, if erratic, activity on the part of working people. It was during this half century that developing class and racial consciousness prepared the way for the formation of an active working class with its own labour organisations. However, as we have seen, the process was very uneven in different colonies, and there were many setbacks and tragic events, many frustrations and casualties. Though the aspiration for trade unions and political parties representing labour was emerging throughout the Caribbean – and was even expressed in 1926 as an aspiration for a regional labour federation and some form of self-government – the only two organisations with any real staying power, the TWA and the BGLU, were less effective in the late 1920s than they had been in the early 1920s.

The experience gained in this half century proved to be important, however, when economic distress and social disruption devastated the entire region in the 1930s and ushered in the third and greatest wave of working-class activity. The modern trade unions, political parties and the Caribbean Labour Congress, that were created during and soon after the wave of labour rebellions between 1934 and 1939, grew out of the efforts and organisations that had preceded them.

Notes

[1] Marcus Garvey, a Jamaican, founded and led the Universal Negro Improvement Association (UNIA), the largest international Pan-Africanist organisation of the twentieth century, until his death in 1940.

[2] Garvey had started branches of his UNIA in the United States in 1918 and in many parts of the Caribbean and Central America in the 1920s, and women started branches of the related Black Cross Nurses.

[3] Howard Johnson informed me (pers. comm. Aug. 1999) that reading and political clubs were decentralised in Jamaica, with 'vibrant groups … concerned with the issues of the day' in many parts of the country.

[4] *Our Own*, 1 Jul. 1911, quoted in Lewis 1987: 44.

[5] Cox 'was effectively driven out of the island by the sustained harassment of the colonial authorities' (James 1998: 74).

[6] This biographical outline depends on the chronology in Hill 1987: lxiii–lxviii.

[7] Munroe acknowledges that several activists and analysts, from Richard Hart to Horace Campbell, have long recognised the transformative political role of racial consciousness in the Caribbean.

[8] My thanks to Howard Johnson for this point. W. Arthur Lewis wrote in 1939 that the form of discrimination the small West Indian middle class resented the most was 'the reservation of certain appointments, both by the state and by private concerns, for white men …. The effect is as we should expect; some rebel, while others seek to conform' (1977: 13).

[9] 'Wharf Labourers' Strike in Kingston', *Jamaica Advocate*, 1 Jun. 1895, quoted in Bryan 1991: 268.

[10] *Ibid.*, quoted in Bryan 1991: 269.

[11] *Jamaica Advocate*, 12 Apr. 1902, quoted in Bryan 1991: 275.

[12] Herbert Thomas *Story of a West Indian Policeman* (Kingston, 1927), p. 122, quoted in Bryan 1991: 276.

[13] Cited by Ashdown 1979b.

[14] This account is based largely on Richards 1993.

[15] 'Act 20 of 1886-87, To Enable Sugar Plantations to be Cultivated and Managed for a

Limited Period', 9 Aug. 1886, CO 28/220, quoted in Richardson 1997: 64.

[16] Gov. Hemming to Joseph Chamberlain, 4 Mar. 1897, CO 111/493.

[17] This account is based largely on Chase n.d.: 20-7, and Rodney 1981: 190-216.

[18] Infant mortality rates fell to about 190 per 1,000 live births between 1911 and 1920, and then declined steadily to about 175 per 1,000 in 1921-5, to 146 per 1,000 in 1931-5, to 110 per 1,000 in 1941-5 and 64 per 1,000 in 1956-60 (Mandle 1973: 88).

[19] MCC Special Session, 1906, 'Report on General Mortality and Infant Mortality', quoted in Rodney 1981: 195.

[20] It has also been said that Critchlow was arrested for disorderly behaviour and assault, and later released, during the 1905 disturbances (Harry 1977: 14).

[21] Cited in Fraser 1981.

[22] McGlashan, a seaman himself, was a champion of Jamaican seamen in the mid-1930s, and a member of the committee of a labour union created by the Permanent Jamaica Development Convention in June 1935 (Post 1978: 241).

[23] Later, the Negro World was banned in 1919 and 1920 in Guyana, St Vincent and Trinidad, but after 1920 'the British rulers in the Caribbean generally did not consider the Negro World to be a serious threat to the colonial system' (Elkins 1971: 346).

[24] 'Report of the Commission appointed by the Governor to enquire into the origin of the riot in the Town of Belize which began on the night of 22nd July 1919', 10 Oct. 1919, CO 123/296.

[25] Ibid., deposition of Sir Eyre Hutson; Cain's editorial is Exhibit No. 4, CO 123/296.

[26] Haynes became one of the principal UNIA leaders in the United States, as a contributor to the Negro World and convenor of the large Pittsburgh branch. He became one of the four-member committee of presidents of the UNIA when Garvey was jailed in 1925 and by 1934 he had become the de facto leader of the UNIA in the United States. In 1936, however, Haynes broke with Garvey after failing to get him to change his policy regarding the Italian invasion of Ethiopia (James 1998: 67). He wrote the words of 'Land of the Gods', which has become Belize's national anthem.

[27] Gov. Sir John Robert Chancellor to Grindle, 20 Dec. 1919, CO 295/523. 'John Smith' and 'Bonanza' were presumably pseudonyms.

[28] Chancellor to Milner, 7 Dec. 1919, CO 295/523.

[29] Chancellor to Milner, 27 Jan. 1920, CO 295/526.

[30] Trinidad Guardian, 21 and 28 Mar. 1920; Basdeo 1983: 29-30.

[31] Minute by C.R. Darnley, 13 Dec. 1919, CO 318/352.

[32] Minute by Darnley, 23 Dec. 1920, CO 295/530.

[33] Richard Hart, in his introduction to my book, On the March, asked whether the fact that a labour rebellion did not occur in Grenada was due to 'a higher than average peasant component' in the population, or to the 'greater politicisation of Grenada under the popular leadership of T. Albert Marryshow and the workers' resultant belief that problems could be solved by means of political representations rather than strikes' (1995: viii). I do not think that Grenada was more politicised than most other British Caribbean colonies in the 1930s, and there is no evidence that the working people believed that their problems could be solved by political representations until the early 1950s. As we will see in chapter 8, the relatively large proportion of peasant farmers and the way that agricultural workers were tied to their employer-landlords made it harder to mobilise and organise rural workers in Grenada than elsewhere.

[34] Minute by Darnley, on deposition of R.C. Clegg, 17 Jul. 1924, CO 111/38708.

[35] Report of the First British Guiana and West Indies Labour Conference (Georgetown, BGLU, 1926).

[36] Gov. Denham to Sir Cosmo Parkinson, 25 Sept. 1933, CO 111/712/15140.

[37] Caribbean Labour Congress: Official Report of the Conference held at Barbados, 17-27 Sept. 1945, Barbados Department of Archives.

Chapter 5

The labour rebellions, 1934-9

A series of strikes, riots and other labour disturbances swept through the British Caribbean in the 1930s, beginning in Belize (then British Honduras), Trinidad and Guyana (British Guiana) in 1934, and culminating in Jamaica in 1938, and Antigua and Guyana in 1939. During these years there were disturbances also in St Kitts, St Vincent, St Lucia, Barbados and the Bahamas. As W. Arthur Lewis noted in 1939, it was not until then that there was 'anything that could be called a movement' among the working people of the British West Indies (Lewis 1977: 18). There had been many ostensibly similar events before 1934-9, disturbances which began in the late nineteenth century and contributed to the development of a greater consciousness of class and race among the working people of the British colonies in the Caribbean, but although they produced some labour organisations, they did not give rise to a lasting labour movement, as such. The BGLU was the only important organisation of manual workers in existence in the British Caribbean in the early 1930s, but by the end of the 1930s there were trade unions throughout. The rise of organised labour became the basis for subsequent political developments in the 1940s and 1950s, giving the labour rebellions of the 1930s their importance and distinctive sociohistorical meaning.

The labour movement in the British Caribbean was a regional movement, profoundly affected by common economic factors as changes in metropolitan capital penetrated these dependent colonial economies. British policies, such as the system of sugar preferences, affected the colonies throughout the region, and specific firms had branches in more than one colony. Tate and Lyle, the giant British sugar company, for example, acquired major plantations in Jamaica and Trinidad in the 1930s. The modernising orientation of this firm, along with the impact of oil companies and the UFC in Trinidad and

Jamaica, respectively, shaped the labour process in new ways. In particular, the economic and social pressures engendered by the Great Depression after 1929 had common and explosive consequences throughout the region, as sugar prices collapsed, unemployment and poverty increased, and emigrants returned home from overseas. To a large extent, the labour rebellions were in response to the economic distress of these depression years.[1]

There were other regional connections. Some labour leaders and activists were involved in more than one colony. For example, Clement Payne, who was the major figure in the Barbados labour rebellion in 1937, was active also in Trinidad in the National Unemployment Movement and the Negro Welfare Cultural and Social Association; subsequently he was a founder and leader of the Federated Workers' Trade Union in Trinidad. A large number of the labour activists were people who had worked as migrants in other countries and colonies, and several leaders were immigrants. For example, Elma Francois and Uriah Butler in Trinidad were from St Vincent and Grenada, respectively, and A.A. Thorne, leader of the British Guiana Workers' League, was from Barbados. Many working people in the Caribbean, then as now, were Pan-Africanist and knew about and responded to events elsewhere in the region and also further afield. The influences of Garvey's movement and of the Italian invasion of Ethiopia in 1935 are seen throughout the region in the developing racial and anti-colonial consciousness. At the other end of the social spectrum, some colonial officials were transferred from one Caribbean colony to another, most notably Sir Edward Denham who was governor of British Guiana before his last post as governor of Jamaica from 1934 to 1938. The experiences and responses of these officials to the labour rebellions were not confined to single colonies. The Colonial Office increasingly treated the Caribbean colonies as a region in terms of developing responses and policies to economic, political and social problems, not least with the appointment of the royal commission, known as the Moyne Commission, which travelled throughout the region in 1938 and 1939. Sir Walter Citrine, secretary of the British Trades Union Congress and a prominent member of this commission, was one of several British trade unionists and Labour MPs who sought to influence the development of trade unions in the British Caribbean, by sending information, giving advice and offering scholarships to selected personnel.

That the late 1930s constitute a kind of watershed in the modern history of the British Caribbean is generally accepted and not in dispute. However, my claim that this period began in Belize, Trinidad and Guyana in 1934 is not so widely accepted. The assertion that these upheavals began in St Kitts early in 1935, which was first made apparently in W.M. Macmillan's Warning from the West Indies in 1936[2] and repeated in Lewis's booklet for the Fabian Society in 1939, continues to be made. Meanwhile, some scholarly studies (Waddell

1961; Dobson 1973) of Belize either omit any mention of the 1930s events or fail to link them to the later labour and nationalist movements (Grant 1976: 61, 67; Ashdown 1978). However, the labour movement that began in Belize in 1934 is crucial in the political history of that country, as well as being one of the earliest manifestations of the labour rebellions that swept through the British Caribbean (Bolland 1986a: 33, 105-6, 1988a, 1991). Moreover, it is clear that the unrest that began in Trinidad and Guyana in 1934 and 1935 was linked to subsequent developments in those colonies.

My case for considering Belize to be one of the first examples of the West Indian labour rebellions is based on two points. First, Belize, though often viewed apart from the sugar colonies, should be considered as part of the British Caribbean with which it shares several sociohistorical, cultural, economic and even political links. Certainly, during the 1930s and 1940s, the UK considered its Central American colony as part of the West Indian region. Belize was included in Orde Browne's official Report of Labour Conditions in the West Indies (1939) and in the West India Royal Commission Report (1945) chaired by Lord Moyne. Belize was also included within the West Indies by the organisation established under the Colonial Development and Welfare Act of 1940 and in the discussions concerning the formation of the West Indies Federation. Moreover, in the 1940s there were links between Belizean labour organisations and those in the other British colonies, including participation in the regional Caribbean Labour Congress from 1947. Second, in Belize, as elsewhere in the British Caribbean, there were direct links, in terms of personnel and organisation, between the labour disturbances of the 1930s and the subsequent development of trade unions and political parties that formed the basis of the decolonisation movement. The Belizean developments of the 1930s and 1940s were not only a similar socio-historical phenomenon to those occurring elsewhere but were also a part of the regional labour movement that grew from those more discrete riots, strikes, and disturbances that had preceded them.

Belize

The early labour rebellion in Belize had three phases. The first, between February and October 1934, constituted the rise of the movement, and the second, from November 1934 to 1936, its decline. In the third phase, between 1938 and 1939, there was a revival of activity. In these five years, between 1934 and 1939, the basis for the formation of the first trade union and the emergence of anti-colonial and nationalist sentiments in the 1940s and 1950s was established.

The Great Depression and a devastating hurricane that destroyed Belize Town on 10 September 1931 (Bolland 1993) shattered the already fragile colonial economy and aggravated the chronically poor living conditions of the majority of people. The economy of Belize had been based on the export of forest products since its colonisation in the seventeenth and eighteenth centuries (Bolland 1973, 1977). First logwood and then mahogany predominated, and as they declined the export of chicle propped up a flagging economy after the 1880s. The timber trade revived briefly in the 1920s when tractors, bulldozers and mechanical saws were introduced, but the mechanisation of felling and hauling stripped forest resources and required less labour. Forest products accounted for over 80 per cent of exports by value and the 'forestocracy', led by the BEC, which owned over 1 million acres, suppressed agriculture and dominated the colony.

In 1931 most woodcutters and chicle gatherers were out of work and exports were half what they had been in 1930. The hurricane, which killed more than 1,000 of the 16,000 inhabitants and destroyed at least three-quarters of the housing in Belize Town, came on top of the economic disaster caused by the Great Depression. As the economy continued to decline after the hurricane, living conditions worsened and people became increasingly desperate. By 1932 the volume of exports was less than half of those in 1931, and the Colonial Report stated, 'Mahogany cutting was entirely stopped' and there was 'no market for the Colony's staple products, mahogany and chicle, and unemployment was more severe than in 1931'.[3] After the hurricane, the government opened soup kitchens, established a temporary camp and opened public buildings to shelter the homeless, but many people had to make their own shelters from the wreckage, pathetic shacks that they called 'dog-sit-downs'. Labour conditions and living standards in the 1930s were similar to what they had been in the nineteenth century. Yet such conditions in themselves could lead to despair rather than social action, so what accounts for the politicisation of the people in Belize in the 1930s?

Many people in the 1930s remembered the two previous popular protests in Belize Town, in 1894 and 1919, when the colonial system of government had been openly criticised. Judging by the nature of the protests and demands in the 1930s, the people held the colonial administration increasingly responsible for their situation. The British government delayed approving a reconstruction loan until the unofficial members of the Legislative Council agreed to the conditions, which were the imposition of treasury control and the restoration of reserve powers to the governor. The British government's treatment of the disaster as an opportunity to tighten its control over the colony must have seemed to Belizeans like kicking a man when he was down. Resentment against the administration's apparent callousness in delaying and imposing conditions over the hurricane loan increased when relief measures for the hungry and homeless proved woefully inadequate and insulting. The measures taken to quell the protests and restore order, which were initially quite successful, included relief work. On the one hand, this increased people's dependency and hence the government's ability to control them, but on the other hand the working people's demands escalated beyond the ability or willingness of the government to meet them. The resulting resentment smouldered throughout the 1930s and 1940s, providing the basis of the first protests, petitions and organisations, and eventually exploded when the governor used his reserve powers to impose devaluation in 1949.[4]

In the early 1930s there was little agitation in Belize. The branch of Garvey's UNIA that had been formed in 1920 was not very active, though Garveyites still ran the newspaper, The Belize Independent, owned by Herbert Hill Cain. The Black Cross Nurses (BCN) were engaged in community health and welfare activities, and after the hurricane the nurses helped in the hospital and in homes and staffed the hurricane refugee camp for four months (Herrmann 1985: 43). Their leader, Vivian Seay, as a member of the Belize Town Board in 1933, tried to establish a women's employment bureau where women could register as cooks, maids, washerwomen or nannies, and so avoid the degrading experience of begging for work door to door. Though the BCN 'focussed on acute social problems and provided the poor and un-employed with decades of service' (Macpherson 1993) and an opportunity for women to be active in the community, their social welfare approach was soon eclipsed by a new radical critique and more militant politics initiated by unemployed workers. When a group calling itself the Unemployed Brigade marched through Belize Town on 14 February 1934 it started a broad move-ment that had a lasting effect on Belizean politics.

Still in the depths of the depression, and two and a half years after the hurricane had destroyed the town, unemployment and poverty remained widespread and housing was deplorable. Although the people were desper-ate, this demonstration was orderly. The superintendent of police reported: 'Leaders were appointed and a march round the town arranged. After the march the leaders met the Governor by appointment. The leaders were men of the artisan and labouring classes . . . . The deputation represented to the Governor that their families were starving because the men could not get work'.[5] In answer to their appeal, Governor Sir Harold Kittermaster promised immediate outdoor relief for the hungry, told the unemployed to register at the Belize Town Board offices, and said that the Hurricane Loan Board would not foreclose on debtors. The police superintendent reported that the deputation 'was not too pleased with the result of the interview' as they wanted a cash dole of $1 a day. Moreover, the artisans were discontented with the unskilled nature of the relief work offered. A daily ration of 1 lb of cooked rice and 3 oz of local sugar, issued at the prison gate, was started on

21 February when 85 persons took the supplies. Within a week nearly 300 persons had accepted the ration but there were complaints that the food was not cooked properly and the number receiving rations soon declined to 35. On 10 March the ration was discontinued. At this time people were allowed to break rocks in the Public Works Department yard for 5-10 cents each day, or 20 cents for married people, to 'keep them from starving'. These inadequate measures, redolent of the nineteenth century, provoked further bad feeling against the government. Even the usually pro-government Clarion called the proffered relief 'degrading and humiliating'.[6]

The inadequacy of the governor's response can be gauged by the fact that 1,100 men and 300 women registered as unemployed as soon as the list was opened, and this was recognised by the governor to be a 'large Proportion' in a town of 16,000 people.[7] 'By this time', according to the police superintendent, 'the masses of the unemployed had become restless' and, thinking that the government was not doing all it should for them, 'commenced to be dissatisfied with their leaders. The leaders were not extreme enough for them and violence began to be talked about'.[8] A new leader emerged at a meeting held in front of the court house, in an open square called the Battlefield, on 16 March 1934.

Antonio Soberanis Gomez, a barber by trade, denounced the Unemployed Brigade's leaders and took over the movement. Soberanis' father, Canuto Soberanis, had come to Belize from Yucatán in 1894 and lived in San Antonio, Orange Walk, and his mother, Dominga Gomez, was born in Corozal, northern Belize. Antonio, the eldest of seven children, was born on 17 January 1897. He attended Roman Catholic primary school in Belize Town until 1912, was a member of the Volunteers Guard in the First World War and served in the Cayo expedition in 1914. He had travelled in all the Central American countries and the United States.[9] Soberanis, who died in 1975, has only recently been identified as a patriot and unofficial national hero.[10]

Soberanis held frequent meetings in the Battlefield, two or three times a week, when between 600 and 800 people attended. He was joined by a group of self-styled colleagues who constituted the co-leaders: Benjamin Reneau, John Lahoodie, James Barnett, Chano Lovell, James Middleton, Fred Allen and Alfred Hall.[11] The meetings in the Battlefield began at 8 pm and sometimes lasted until 1 am. According to the police superintendent, 'the more violent the language used from the rostrum the more the crowd enjoyed it. Soberanis was called the Moses of British Honduras who had been sent by God to lead the people to better things'. He noted that at least half of his followers were women and 'they were always more truculent than the men'.[12]

Though the governor first thought of him as a man of no importance, the organisation that Soberanis created and led, called the Labourers and

Unemployed Association (LUA), soon became a significant political force in Belize and was the prototype of future trade unions and political parties. It was reported that he 'always said that he was forming a labour Union',[13] though trade unions could not be legally registered at that time. His association, though not quite a union, was nevertheless far more political than the numerous friendly societies that existed to provide mutual aid and support for their members. The LUA organised food and medical care from time to time but its chief orientation from its inception was political in so far as it used such techniques as petitions, demonstrations, pickets, strikes and boycotts to pressure the employers, merchants and colonial officials into making concessions in favour of working people. Soberanis' attacks on the governor and various colonial officials, which were said 'to please the people immensely',[14] increasingly became an attack on the colonial government itself.

In April 1934 Soberanis was convicted of making a threatening remark about the police superintendent and was cautioned. Undeterred by the police, who were present at all the meetings, he organised a petition signed by several hundred people, demanding that the government find work for the unemployed at a minimum wage of $1.50 per day. He led a procession of about 500 people around the town and the crowd waited outside the court house while their leader presented the petition to the governor. The language of the petition gives some idea of the tone as well as the content of Soberanis' demands. He called for 'British Honduras for British Honduraneans.... We are a new People ... we are only asking for our rights. Justice to all men ... . British Honduras has been sleeping for over a century, not dead only sleeping .... Today British Honduras is walking around'.[15] Although the specific demands were for relief work and a minimum wage, they were couched in broad moral and political terms that began to define and develop a new nationalistic and democratic political culture hitherto unknown in Belize.

Kittermaster replied that wages were governed by the world market price. A minimum wage of $1.50 a day, he said, would force enterprises to close for lack of profit, so 'It is better to get work steadily at 50 or 75 cents a day all the year'. This was an astonishingly provocative recommendation when hundreds of Belizeans could obtain no work at all and where most labourers had never had contracts that lasted all year. The governor said he could do no more about the unemployed: 'It is only by asking for charity from England that there will be enough money this year to pay for services such as schools and hospitals. England herself has 4,000,000 unemployed and yet she is generously helping us here in our difficulties'.[16]

Soberanis rejected Kittermaster's argument and pointed out that many colonial officials drew large salaries but 50 cents per day was considered 'sufficient for the poor man and his family'. He also rejected the notion of

English charity: 'What we are receiving from England is only what belongs to us .... We will not throw up the sponge, but continue to agitate for our rights'.[17] At his next public meeting, when describing his interview to the crowd, Soberanis referred to the governor as a damn fool. At about this time he produced a flag in green and red, the colours of Garvey's movement, and said that 'he had no King, and no Queen, nor no Prince, but only his green and red flag, for which he was prepared to die'.[18] Soberanis and the LUA continued to agitate and developed new and successful tactics in the next few months.

In July Reneau was prosecuted for resisting arrest and was fined $25. The police superintendent reported that 'Soberanis and his colleagues considered they were their own law', and they publicly criticised the district commissioner, Denbigh Phillips, who had fined Reneau.[19] Meanwhile, Kittermaster obtained only $2,000 to provide relief work building the Northern Highway. Eighteen men were sent up every week on a rotation basis, each being given ten days' work; for each eight-hour day they received 60 cents, mostly in the form of credit for provisions at local stores. About 1,500 men were registered for work, so this was a hopelessly inadequate response.

On 1 August 1934 a march was held to celebrate the centenary of Emancipation. Led by the UNIA and the BCN, the marchers were joined by friendly societies and a 'Workers' Union', which was probably the LUA.[20] It was reported later in August that 'unemployment will get worse shortly. The Belize Estate and Produce Company are practically closing down'. The chairman of the Belize Town Board observed that there was 'considerable want and even distress', especially hungry children, among the unemployed.[21] Soberanis and the LUA responded to their urgent need by pressuring local merchants and tradesmen to donate to the poor. When some merchants refused (among the largest were Harley, Brodie and Melhado), the LUA organised a boycott. People bearing placards saying 'Don't buy from this store' paraded around the stores but were careful not to loiter or break the law in any way. According to the police superintendent, 'it was very evident that Soberanis was receiving legal advice as to how far he could go in various matters'.[22] A boycott procession, in which 50 banners were paraded around the town, showed who had and who had not contributed to the poor fund. During the celebrations on 10 September, commemorating the Battle of St George's Caye in 1798, the town was full of unemployed people and their families. Soberanis, on a horse, led a march of about 3,000 people, with many LUA members dressed in red and green, that culminated in a huge picnic for the poor. Even his opponents acknowledged that 'This procession and feed added greatly to the prestige of Soberanis and he was referred to as a "Moses" more than ever'.[23]

Encouraged by his success and widespread support, Soberanis broadened his attack and became increasingly militant. He demanded that Phillips, a notoriously severe magistrate, should be removed from the bench, and that C.S. Brown, the manager of the BEC and a member of the Legislative Council, should not be allowed to live in Government House. The acting governor refused to comply with these demands. Soberanis frequently held meetings in Stann Creek (now Dangriga), which was then the second largest town with a population of about 3,000, chiefly Garifuna. On 27 September, he organised a strike there among the stevedores who loaded grapefruit and achieved another encouraging victory when their pay was raised from 8 cents to 25 cents per hour.

Returning to Belize Town on 29 September, he was reported to have threatened to drag Phillips off his bench and to organise a strike at the BEC sawmill.[24] The police arrived at the sawmill at 6.15 am on 1 October, before Soberanis and 200 of his followers, so the mill started as usual at 7 am. When all seemed quiet the police dispersed, but by 8.45 am some 500 people 'armed with sticks' succeeded in closing the mill. When the police returned, the crowd split and went to different parts of the town. One group broke down the gates of the Public Works Department and told the director he should pay his labourers more; another group closed the office of Mr Esquivel, a coconut exporter; another stopped the dredger working at Fort George; and another closed Harley's lumber yard. According to the police superintendent, 'it was not a case of workmen striking for more pay but a case of unemployed men forcing employed men to strike for more pay'.[25] Elfreda Reyes, who was a 34-year-old domestic servant at the time, recalled that many women participated because 'men were so coward . . . they were afraid to lose their jobs' (Macpherson 1993: 11).

At 10.40 am about 300 men and women, armed with sticks, were at the Belize Town Board. When Superintendent Matthews tried to arrest a man for threatening the deputy chairman of the board, a struggle ensued. Eight men and one woman were arrested and when the crowd increased to about 1,500 the police, in two ranks, pushed it back down Queen Street. Several constables were assaulted, shots were heard and one of the crowd, Absolom Pollard, was wounded.[26] When the situation threatened to get out of control, the acting governor ordered the police to halt and return to their station while he talked to six of the crowd's leaders. It is not clear who these leaders were, or if, indeed, there were any at this point. None of the LUA leaders was named, nor were any of them among those arrested during the riot. At noon, Soberanis arrived at the police station, enquired who had been arrested, told the crowd to behave, and went away. At 2 pm he returned in a 'very truculent' mood and demanded bail for all those arrested. At 5 pm he bailed out 16 of the 17 persons who had been jailed, but he was promptly arrested himself and charged with threatening Phillips on 29 September. As news of this spread, the crowd increased to about 2,000. Several efforts to release Soberanis on bail were refused, and he remained in custody. One Christopher Velasquez brought two large snakes and told them to 'go and get Tony', but the police beat them off. Heavy rain dispersed the crowd, a planned meeting at the Battlefield was abandoned and the night passed peacefully.

The next day, in a court 'guarded by every available man', Soberanis was charged and refused bail.[27] About 500 people abused the magistrates and 1,000 gathered in the market square. Some, it was said, 'were inclined to be disorderly', and 'it was the women who were the most virulent', but no one was armed.[28] At 8 am on 3 October, about 150 men who had been assigned jobs refused to work for 60 cents a day and, demanding $1, they dispersed. On the following day a 'large gang of men' failed to stop others from working for 60 cents a day. The crisis was over and the British cruiser that the acting governor had inquired about turned out not to be needed. The sawmill remained closed until 18 October and the people obtained a promise of $3,000 for immediate outdoor relief. Meanwhile, 26 of the 32 persons who were prosecuted for participating in the riot were convicted, receiving sentences of between three days and one year of hard labour. The jurors having failed to agree, Soberanis was released on bail on 6 November and his freedom was celebrated by a big rally at Liberty Hall. In January 1935 Soberanis was acquitted of the charge of threatening Phillips who, it transpired, had threatened to horsewhip him. Soberanis continued to lead the LUA, but the movement was weakened by a split that had occurred while he was in jail, and the movement declined.

Shortly after the peak of the disturbances in October 1934, a new governor, Alan Burns, arrived. He viewed Soberanis as a professional agitator who should be locked up, and refused his request to meet to discuss the franchise. In February 1935 the LUA, which then included a Women's League, held meetings to discuss the restricted franchise and a petition was sent to Burns requesting 'that the women be given womanhood suffrage in voting for the coming election of the Legislative Council, and the age limit be 21 years' (Macpherson 1993: 14) but no change was made. Nevertheless, Burns was shocked by the people's condition and he made an effort during his six years in Belize to bring relief. In March 1935 the senior medical officer reported that the people, especially the children, were dangerously undernourished and hence susceptible to disease. Burns commented that the unemployment situation was still acute, that those who were employed were receiving reduced wages, and that when their contracts ended in June these wages would not tide them over the season. He considered 'the situation is most serious and that it will shortly become desperate .... The people have behaved, in the circumstances, with admirable restraint, but their temper is rising and matters must come to a head within a few months unless something is done'.[29] Soberanis continued to hold mass meetings and his speeches became increasingly 'offensive and inflammatory',[30] so Burns prepared legislation to facilitate control, namely bills to prohibit processions without police permission and to give the governor emergency powers to maintain order, as well as a seditious conspiracy bill so that 'Soberanis could be successfully prosecuted for sedition'.[31]

In May 1935 Soberanis helped to organise a strike among railway workers in Stann Creek, whose wage of 65 cents per day was below the rate for government workers elsewhere, which ranged between 75 cents and $1. Soberanis had made several visits to the Stann Creek and Toledo Districts in southern Belize, 'holding meetings and preaching discontent'.[32] On 20 May, following a meeting in Stann Creek Town, a crowd of about 300 unemployed men and women stopped the railway workers at Havana Bridge and told them to strike for $1 per day. The workers went home and made no attempt to go to work the next morning. That afternoon four railway employees who tried to pass the bridge were beaten by pickets and the police could not make arrests because of 'the very threatening attitude' of a crowd of about 400 people. Later, the crowd dispersed peacefully and the district commissioner spoke with two local leaders, Abraham Dolmo and Zacharias Flores, as Soberanis had already left by boat. That night, police reinforcements arrived from Belize Town 'to crush the disorders without bloodshed'. One woman and five men were convicted of impeding passage and disorderly conduct and were fined. None of the strikers was re-employed and those workers who were hired received the usual 65 cents per day. Police force had crushed the strike effort and Burns felt that 'in consequence Soberanis has suffered in repute as a leader'.[33] Burns claimed that Soberanis' support and influence in general was waning as a result of the colonial development grants that employed people in road work and thus changed people's attitude to the government, but he still kept the police 'constantly on the alert in case of a possible sudden outbreak'.[34] By July, Soberanis himself acknowledged that the LUA was declining. He blamed Lahoodie and Reneau for splitting the movement by creating the British Honduras Unemployed Association (BHUA), and suggested 'that they must have been paid to do so'.[35]

When Burns refused to allow Soberanis or any member of the LUA to Government House on the anniversary of Emancipation or on the anniversary of the Battle of St George's Caye, Soberanis responded in a rather quieter manner than usual. The LUA, he stated, was 'organised to agitate for a living wage and justice for the workers of British Honduras. The average personel [sic] of the General Membership earns between 1/50 to 1/200 part of Your Excellency's salary. We of the L. & U.A. do not believe God intended this to be so'. He insisted that they had the right to try to better their situation. He pointed out that by organising a band of 22 nurses they helped and cheered up the workers and unemployed and that the LUA's community work had benefited hundreds of people.[36] This suggests that Soberanis, like the UNIA and BCN, was emphasising a charitable social welfare role and a more reformist political stance, but he still expressed the workers' demands in terms of justice.

Shortly after the seditious conspiracy ordinance was passed on 24 October 1935, Soberanis was charged for using 'abusive and seditious language' at a public meeting in Corozal, though this meeting was held on 1 October, the first anniversary of the riot, before the bill was passed.[37] Burns was determined to put Soberanis behind bars, and to do so without provoking further disturbances. He instructed E.A. Grant, the magistrate of Orange Walk, to try Soberanis at Corozal because the Corozal magistrate was 'suffering from cold feet'. He added: 'One of my reasons for sending Grant to try "Tony" was that he was a black man. I did not want the trial to be a black v. white affair'.[38] He wanted Soberanis 'put away for a good long sentence'.

The trial was, as anticipated, a tense affair. Because there was 'a state of civil commotion which threatens the public safety', meetings were prohibited in the district, but people in Corozal and nearby Maya villages contributed over $200 to Soberanis's assistance. Soberanis was fined $85 (or four and a half months' hard labour), plus $30 costs, for using insulting words concerning various people. In January 1936 Soberanis was acquitted by the Supreme Court on the charge of attempting to 'bring His Majesty into hatred, ridicule or contempt', but the Corozal conviction, along with the prior split in his organisation, the muzzling effects of the new laws, the governor's efforts to expand relief work[39] and a temporary improvement in the economy in 1936, combined to spell the decline of his influence and the LUA. Although the LUA continued to hold meetings and processions in 1936, much of Soberanis' efforts consisted of attacking the BHUA.

The LUA disappeared but Soberanis did not, and when the economy slumped again in 1938 and 1939 he and several associates continued to agitate and organise until they had created a trade union. At a Battlefield meeting attended by about 500 people on 20 June 1938, Soberanis, along with James Barnett alias Bangula (who had helped in the Stann Creek strike in 1935), John Neal and Thomas Sabal, a Garifuna from Stann Creek, complained about wages and rations and demanded that Burns must go. Neal said that in Jamaica when Alexander Bustamante had demanded that Governor Denham must go, 'Denham go flying and Bustamante got what he wanted'. This refers to the fact that Bustamante started a 'Denham must go' campaign in 1937, and the governor's death after an abdominal operation during the labour rebellion was widely seen as a fulfilment of the labour leader's charge (Eaton 1975: 223). Soberanis addressed the crowd as 'Citizens of B.H. Comrades'. Speaking in Spanish and English, he said he had collected $40 from people in Stann Creek to register a union - 'we want a union and we must get it' - but when he asked for donations people began to leave. He chastised them and said they needed more loyalty, like the Jamaicans who had demanded Bustamante's release, if they were to get what they wanted.[40] As the Jamaican labour rebellion had begun scarcely a month earlier, and Bustamante was released from jail on 30 May and Denham died on 2 June, Neal's and Soberanis' comments on this occasion show that they knew what was happening in the labour movement in some other parts of the Caribbean.

Later that year Burns reported that unemployment was much worse and that he needed to provide work for more men so as to prevent disorder. On 19 November over 600 men gathered to apply for work at the Public Works Department where only 200 could be hired. One man was arrested for assaulting the clerk but danger of serious trouble was 'averted by a promise to the men that more would be taken on in a few days'.[41] Burns organised a series of roadworks, reclamation and drainage projects, as relief schemes for the unemployed. Under the quicena system, gangs of labourers were hired for two-week periods so that, by rotation, all the unemployed were given a chance of intermittent work. At one time there were about 600 men so employed, but Burns, concerned that about 1,000 fewer men would be hired in the mahogany industry in 1939, proposed opening a quarry at Gracy Rock to provide work for 300 men and stone for the Belize–Cayo road. The development of better communications in Belize through road construction was clearly of secondary importance to Burns, whose primary concern was to avoid trouble in the streets. He reported to the secretary of state, 'This year there appears to be very little money and crowds of unemployed men are in the streets. The local agitators have not missed the opportunity to stir up trouble'.[42] While the governor's strategy seems to have been largely successful, as further widespread disorders were avoided, it was not because Soberanis and his colleagues had retired. On the contrary, their continued agitation was clearly a factor in pushing Burns and the Colonial Office to expand the relief schemes.

The economy deteriorated further in 1939 and Burns had to lay off half of the men working on the Northern Highway, leaving 847 men in Belize Town seeking work.[43] In March, a telegram was sent from a public meeting to the secretary of state for the colonies: 'Suffering and uneasiness acute Belize. Due to unemployment. Developing into dangerous situation. Cannot continue without disastrous results. Government approached and admits situation grave but unable to help. Wholesale laying off by Government on public works not understood by the masses. Population pray for immediate intervention'.[44] Burns attempted to belittle this by saying that the chairman of the meeting, L.D. Kemp, was 'trying to make capital out of the situation'.[45] Kemp, an associate of Soberanis and cousin of Lahoodie, was a journalist who, under the nom de plume of 'Prince Dee', had for years attacked the colonial administration and supported Soberanis in his column, called 'Garvey Eye', in the Belize Independent. Kemp continued to be politically active and influential in the 1940s.

Soon after this meeting a crowd which became disorderly when only 75 men were engaged for road work out of 591 applicants, was ejected from the Public Works Department by the police.[46] Burns' letter to the secretary of state in April makes it clear that he viewed relief work as a way to avert further disturbances, but that the rate of wages paid for such work could itself become a cause of unrest:

> [T]he steps taken with your approval to relieve unemployment have averted what might have been serious disturbances, and have had an immediate effect on the people .... I considered it possible that the Belize labourers might refuse to work for 50 cents a day, and that rioting might result if Government should insist on paying no higher wage for relief work .... Your decision that the normal rate of wages should be paid for relief work relieves me of any anxiety regarding possible disturbances.[47]

The number of unemployed men registered in Belize Town alone rose from 1,200 in April to 1,953 in August.[48] Once again, public anxiety and the prospect of unrest were relieved by announcements of continuing relief work, though everyone knew this was only a palliative in a sick economy. It was in this context, early in 1939, that Soberanis and R.T. Meighan, a former member of the Belize Town Board, founded the British Honduras Workers and Tradesmen Union (BHWTU), the first organisation to be called a union in Belize, though it could not be legally registered as such. So some five years after the labour movement had started in Belize, it began to become institutionalised.

Throughout these years the increasing involvement of the colonial administration in relief work, made necessary by the deterioration of the economy and widespread hardship, had resulted in popular attention becoming focused on its responsibilities and shortcomings. Soberanis and his colleagues succeeded in channelling this attention into a labour movement and the first stirring of Belizean nationalism. Soberanis linked the pressing concerns of his followers, which were chiefly with wages, prices, employment, food, health and housing, to an attack on the colonial administration and the merchant elite, whom he characterised as incompetent and overpaid, ruthless and callous in their relations with workers and the poor, and as the cause of much of the poverty and injustice experienced by most Belizeans. Soberanis organised the working people who were not represented in the Legislative Council, and developed a variety of techniques to help the voiceless be heard, namely petitions, processions, boycotts, strikes and mass meetings, as well as mutual aid efforts. Though the core of these activities was in Belize Town, where a third of the colony's population was concentrated, Soberanis was active in the districts from north to south, among the Maya Indians around Corozal and the Garifuna in Stann Creek.

Never having been allowed to represent itself, the working class of Belize was used to looking to members of the elite to represent it. The 1936 constitution, which readmitted the electoral principle for the first time since 1871, though with high property and income qualifications and reserve powers for the governor, encouraged this, with the result that much of the political activity of the working people and the LUA in 1936 was focused on supporting the people's men in the elections. Endorsed by the LUA and a middle-class Citizens' Political Party, these men became the chief parliamentary opposition after 1936. With support from working people, who had neither votes nor candidates of their own, some of these early nationalists, like Arthur Balderamos, a black lawyer, Robert S. Turton, a chicle millionaire, and L.P. Ayuso, a local businessman, developed a 'Natives First' orientation because they resented the control of land, commerce and government by a coterie of expatriates. As working-class agitation continued, all six seats on the Belize Town Board, which was elected with a broader franchise, went to middle-class Creoles who appeared sympathetic to labour in 1939. Five years previously, in 1934, it was Soberanis who had initiated this growing working-class consciousness and proto-national movement, in which labour issues and interests were in the forefront of a critique of colonial government, thereby presaging the labour and national movements developing elsewhere in the British Caribbean.

St Kitts

The labour rebellion that exploded in St Kitts in January 1935 had been preceded by some efforts to raise the consciousness of the working class. As the law did not permit the formation of trade unions as such, the first popular organisation was the St Kitts-Nevis Universal Benevolent Association (SKNUBA), formed and registered under the Leeward Islands Friendly Societies Act in 1917. Two of its sponsors had clear ambitions to organise labour. J. Matthew Sebastian, the president, started a newspaper (of which he was the editor) called The Union Messenger in 1921 which was printed by the SKNUBA, and J.A. Nathan, the secretary, a small shopkeeper, had acquired some familiarity with unionism when he lived in the United States. The paper aired workers' grievances and problems and frequently reported news of labour discontent in Jamaica and Trinidad throughout the 1920s. Letters and articles often shared experiences, notably of migration for work and the restrictions that were imposed on such migration after 1929 (Richardson 1983: 129-31). In 1932 two federalist leaders and reformers, Marryshow of Grenada and Cipriani of Trinidad, visited St Kitts, met groups of workers and encouraged them to organise. The St Kitts Workers' League was formed that year, 'as an advocate of political and social reform in general and to promote the welfare of the working class in particular' (Richardson 1983: 166), but, like the Grenada Workingmen's Association and the Trinidad Workingmen's Association on which it was modelled, it could not legally act as a trade union.

In October 1934 the administrator of St Kitts received a letter from Rev. Newnham Davis of St Anne's in the west of the island, saying that the biggest employer of labour in the district, Bourke's Estate of Sandy Point, had dismissed all labourers except those required to care for the stock, because the owner had died intestate. 'As a result of so many people being thrown out of employment a very great deal of distress is bound to occur', he wrote, and raised the question of whether this situation 'will not result in much unrest amongst the labouring people'.[49] The administrator passed this news on to the governor of the Leeward Islands, adding that thousands of other field labourers might be thrown out of work if the planters, who were in an impasse over the cane prices with the St Kitts (Basseterre) Sugar Factory, ceased to grow more cane. 'There is already evidence of some disquiet which may possibly develop', he reported, and he attributed the main cause of this to agitation over the 'Elective Principle'. Since 13 December, when the Legislative Council voted down proposals for constitutional change, several cane fires had been lit, 'indicative possibly of a growing antipathy by labourers towards planters, and this is not unlikely being encouraged by the St Kitts Workers League, Ltd., and its thoroughly pernicious organ, the "Union Messenger".' Further, the fact that some planters had shared a bonus from the factory with their labourers while others had not, 'in itself led to dissatisfaction, with, of course, the inevitable suspicion in the minds of some that labourers have been exploited'. If these factors were not settled, he predicted, they 'will precipitate a difficult and serious condition involving civil commotion probably of an unprecedented kind'.[50] According to the chief colonial official on the spot, therefore, growing distress caused by unemployment and dissatisfaction with wages and the constitutional issue were provoking unrest for several weeks before the actual rebellion occurred. Yet nothing appears to have been done about it. As trade unions were illegal and Sebastian and his associates were labelled pernicious, there were no labour representatives with whom the colonial officials were prepared to discuss the problems.

By 1935 sugar production had been increasing for several years. Yet while the production of sugar per acre increased, the average gross receipts for sugar per acre declined, putting pressure on wages at the same time that fewer workers were employed by the industry. The wages of field workers employed by the planters as well as the employees of the St Kitts Sugar Factory at Basseterre, the only factory which purchased all the cane grown on the island, had been reduced in preceding seasons. The rate for cutting cane, having risen to 1 shilling per ton when sugar prices were high, was reduced to 8 pence per ton, the same rate as in 1881 before the first Great Depression (Richards 1987b: 1). This put even more pressure than usual on the workers to obtain decent rates at the start of the crop season.

Before the start of grinding at the factory, Nathan sent a circular to the principal labourers on the various estates, such as head cutters and head cartmen, inviting them to a meeting on 20 January 1935 at Union Hall, Basseterre, 'to discuss what wages should be demanded for reaping the present crop' and to be sure that 'no labourer should start to work until he or she knows what wages they are to obtain'.[51] The editorial in The St Kitts-Nevis Daily Bulletin, a conservative newspaper, suggested that the low price for sugar made it an inopportune time for labour to make demands. Nathan replied that, as 'the Planter has been recently granted a minimum price for their product (sugar cane), why should we not seek to get a minimum wage for the labourer?',[52] the factory having agreed to a minimum price of 14 shillings per ton for cane delivered. To this, the president of the Agricultural Society and an ex-member of the Legislative Council, E.J. Shelford, responded that it was indeed 'an inopportune time for any organisation to attempt to agitate the labouring classes to expect any higher rates for wages', given the low market price of sugar and dependency on British and Canadian government preferences. 'In fact, as sugar stands today - for agitators to endeavour to incite the labouring classes I take it as a mere manifestation of the rabidity of their rather Bolshivistic [sic] tendencies - agitators - some of whom in the near future perhaps - hope to become our local Legislators'.[53] To this provocative letter, Nathan replied that the St Kitts Workers' League was a political organisation, but the SKNUBA is 'strictly concerned with Labour and labour conditions in this Island ... [where] the labourer (not being organised) gets the worst end of it'. He stated that they are 'organising Agricultural Labourers' and that the meeting on 20 January will be 'the first Labour Convention ever held in this Island'.[54]

At the meeting, delegates decided that the SKNUBA 'should assume the responsibility of representing the Agricultural labourers interest throughout the Island, as far as wages and general working conditions are concerned ... and the Secretary promised to see what could be done to improve the wages paid'. Over 100 members were said to have registered by the meeting's close, and registration continued at the association's office.[55] On the eve of the crop season, 27 January, Nathan wrote in The Union Messenger that there was 'a little friction at Pond Estate' where labourers were threatened by management and told to remove their animals if they did not work as before. 'No definite news has reached us as to what price per ton the Planters intend paying for reaping the present crop. It is hoped that they will increase the labourers' pay at least 12 1/2% We have heard that quite a few Planters are willing to do this much, but there are some die-hards who are not willing to move one inch in this direction'. Nathan added that it was up to the planters 'to relieve the community from the terrible hardship suffered last year'.[56] In the light of all these activities and demands, it seems that the strike that began on 28 January 1935, a week after the meeting and on the opening day of the crop season, was not quite as 'spontaneous and unorganised' as has been claimed (Hart 1988: 66).

Governor Sir Reginald St-Johnston, certainly, believed that some 'agitators', including Nathan, had stirred up trouble. Before 28 January, he acknowledged, 'there had been a considerable amount of discussion among so-called labour organizations as to the prices that should be demanded by the labourers for their different varieties of work'. He thought that Nathan's comment about the labourers' pay being increased by at least 12.5 per cent would lead 'ignorant labourers' to 'jump to the conclusion that the pay had been so increased, and become enraged when the planters did not do this'.[57] Whatever Nathan's precise role may have been, there is no doubt that sparks touched some very responsive tinder on 28 January.

The strike began at Buckley's Estate, just northwest of Basseterre, when the workers, probably joined by some unemployed persons from the town, demanded that their wages be restored to the rate they had been in 1932, when the planters had reduced them from 11 pence to 8 pence per ton of cane. The manager, E.D.B. Dobridge, ordered them to work but they downed tools and walked off to begin spreading the word at other estates around the island. They went north, to the neighbouring estates of Shadwell and Monkey Hill, and convinced others to join them. At Monkey Hill, the police inspector, Major Duke, and the magistrate, Mr Bell, urged the crowd to disperse but the strikers went on to Douglas Estate where they collected the cane- cutters' cutlasses and threw them on the manager's veranda 'with various threats'.[58] Small groups of strikers went north to St Peters and Stapleton, but the chief crowd continued to Needs Must Estate and followed the main road around the northeastern bend, stopping at various estates. By noon the crowd, numbering between 300 and 400 and armed with sticks, had reached Brighton Estate. There the manager, Mr Yearwood, ordered them off the property. No violence was done to him, but the strikers took the mules and cattle out of the carts and cut the driving gear so they could not be used to haul cane.

Half a century after the event, a black schoolteacher who was teaching at the Cayun Village school, recalled the day of the riot and the mood of the crowd and the villagers.

> The Osbornes at the Telephone Exchange nearby had received a message that a band of rioters was coming our way, and the news spread through Cayon quickly. In a short time the main road was crowded with people, excitedly awaiting the arrival of the rioters, some curious to see them, others anxious to join them. The teachers tried to carry on school as usual, but there was little, if any, concentration on lessons. Every bit of news about the riot increased the excitement of the pupils. At about two o'clock in the afternoon, we heard the noise of pans knocking, shells blowing, and people shouting, coming up the Cayon Hill. Someone in the school shouted, "De Riot a come!"
>
> The children immediately made a mad rush for the door, and in a minute the school was empty. Teachers and pupils alike could not miss this once-in-a-lifetime event. There were the rioters - hundreds of them, all in their working clothes, barefooted, with sticks, bills, and other weapons in their hands, shouting: "We strike for higher wages! Everybody mus' stap wok today!" Some gave an occasional blow on a conch shell, between their shouts. But they all seemed fairly orderly as they followed their ring-leaders across Dunn's Cottage, heading for Brighton's Estate ...
>
> That same [more likely, the next] afternoon, Mr. Clarke, our headteacher and a member of the St Kitts Defence Force, was ordered to get into uniform and report immediately for service. The children, regarding what they were seeing as nothing but fun and excitement, cheered their headteacher as they saw him, dressed in khaki shirt and shorts with bayonet at his side, rush off to town on his motor-cycle (Sutton 1987: 148-9).

Not all was fun and excitement, however. One of the villagers who joined the crowd, named Ralston, was arrested and sent to prison; others remained in hiding while the police tried to pick up rioters (Sutton 1987: 150).

The crowd, still increasing in numbers, reached Lodge Estate at about 2.20 pm. The owner, Philip Todd, who like Dobridge and Yearwood was of European descent, ordered them off. Feeling threatened, he got a shotgun, but he was knocked down and beaten. His gun was broken and a few stones were thrown at his house servants. The crowd proceeded to other estates, 'unharnessing all cattle carts and damaging the working gear. From here onwards the leadership would appear to have been left to the labourers who constitute the working class on estates on the Northern portion of the Island'.[59] At Estridge's Estate, Major Duke and eight police, by now armed with rifles, intercepted the crowd and arrested five 'ringleaders'. Other strikers went on around the northern point at Dieppe Bay to Willet's Estate where the manager and overseer, who were of African descent, were threatened and carts were unharnessed, but no violence was done.

According to the chief justice, the police had not followed the crowd further because they were '12 to 13 miles from Headquarters and with hostile villages in their rear'.[60] This remark, and his comment about local leadership, contradicts an assertion made by the governor that the trouble was caused by agitators and loafers from Basseterre who ordered peaceful labourers to strike. It suggests, rather, that there was widespread sympathy with the strikers among villagers around the island. Some people, however, were intimidated and even wounded. A labourer who refused to join the crowd at Saddler's Village was struck down with a piece of iron pipe. A jury subsequently acquitted the man charged with wounding him, though the chief justice thought he had been convincingly identified.[61] This suggests that the members of the jury, too, may have been sympathetic with the strikers, or 'partisan' as the chief justice expressed it.

The next day, 29 January, a smaller gang of striking workers set off in the opposite direction to reach the west of the island, where they had not spread the news before, again visiting estates to urge others to join them. Quite evidently, they were aiming to achieve a general, islandwide strike on all the estates. The governor himself started a tour that morning, in the wake of the previous day's crowd, and he 'found very little work going on'.[62] As he reached Estridge's and Belleview Estates in the north, he received an urgent message asking him to return to Basseterre because there were further disturbances at Buckley's and West Farm Estates, just west of the town. At the latter, Magistrate Bell had read the Riot Act and the police fired three shots. 'Stone-throwing had been continuous on the part of the mob'.[63] As the violence escalated, the governor, on the advice of the Executive Council meeting in emergency session, sent telegrams asking Colonel Bell to bring police reinforcements from Antigua and the admiral at Bermuda to have a warship ready, if needed.

The main group of strikers, meanwhile, had marched to Sandy Point, the western point of the island, where they heard that Dobridge had employed strike-breakers to start cutting cane at Buckley's Estate. Many of them turned back and by 3 pm a crowd, estimated at 200-300 persons, armed with sticks, entered the estate yard and began to haul out a cart. Dobridge, accompanied by his overseer, both of whom had shotguns, ordered the crowd out. Stones were thrown at them and Dobridge fired, hitting several people with pellets and wounding two in the face and one in the shoulder. This enraged the strikers, but they retreated as Dobridge and his overseer had two revolvers and a rifle as well as the shotguns. An armed contingent of 11 police, led by

Major Duke and accompanied by Magistrate Bell, arrived at about 3.45 pm and lined up in the estate yard, facing the crowd at 10 yards' distance. Some of the strikers approached Duke and Bell and demanded that they arrest Dobridge. When Duke told them to come to the police station along with the injured parties to make statements, the crowd shouted angrily, 'We want Dobridge'. People taunted the police, shouting, 'Oh, you can't shoot because you have no ammunition', 'You only have blank cartridges', and 'See me here, shoot me if you have anything in your gun'.[64]

Major Duke arranged for reinforcements, asking the governor to sign the necessary proclamations to call out the Defence Force and Defence Reserve Force, which he did about 5 pm. Conveniently, the governor happened to be having a garden party at Government House, and he commented that 'a good many of the gentlemen of these forces were present',[65] as they were predominantly white planters and their associates, under the command of Geoffrey P. Boon, a leading planter and merchant. The Defence Force consisted of largely black and coloured men, commanded by white officers, and the Defence Reserve was formed in 1919 when whites objected to serving in the Defence Force because of its growing numbers of coloured men. At 6 pm the governor telegraphed for the warship and for the extra police from Antigua because, he averred, 'the affair was assuming some seriousness'.[66] And, a clear sign that he thought this was an emergency, he even concluded his garden party early so his guests could return home in daylight.

Though the striking workers appear to have been quite restrained, the governor reported that soon after 6 pm the combined forces, under the command of Major Duke, 'found it impossible to control the very large mob',[67] by then numbering 400-500 men, women and children.[68] The magistrate read the Riot Act and urged the strikers to disperse, but they continued to shout and to threaten Dobridge. When the Riot Act was read a second time, the crowd responded by throwing stones, some of which struck the police, none of whom was seriously injured. Major Duke ordered the police to press the crowd backwards towards St Johnston's Village. Orders were then given to fire on the crowd, though there 'were women and children in the main body of the rioters'.[69] In all, 55 shots were fired, resulting in three men being killed, J. Samuel, John Allen and James Archibald, and eight or nine were wounded.[70] Many of the shots were fired at people who threw stones from behind fences in the village as well as at persons in the crowd, and the men killed were on the street in the village, some 200 yards away from the estate buildings. The chief justice concluded that the shooting was justified because the angry crowd had refused to disperse, and that it was 'a serious civil disturbance which threatened the lives and property of law-abiding citizens of the Crown as well as the peace and good order of the Colony'.[71]

Major Duke reported that all was quiet by about 9.30 pm. At 2.30 am on 30 January the Lady Nelson arrived from Antigua with Colonel Bell and six men and the governor was informed that HMS Leander was on its way. He received messages from different parts of the island that morning, on the third day of the strike, that 'large bodies of men are parading about and still trying to intimidate the peaceably inclined labourers. They had also driven off the cattle and cut the harness on a number of estates'.[72] In the circumstances, he decided not to 'scatter and dissipate' his small forces into these different localities, but to wait until Leander came with reinforcements. The governor commented that, contrary to his usual experience, he 'was met everywhere by sullen and sulky looks' as he drove around town. 'Small knots of people had gathered at street corners and I could see but little was needed to start off further trouble at any moment'.[73] That night several cane fires were started, six of them near the town, and one a few yards from Government House. Colonel Bell, who seems to have been easily impressed, heard a rumour that Basseterre was to be burned down and all the white people exterminated, so he kept his forces on constant patrol. At about 1.30 am on 31 January HMS Leander arrived. Its searchlights were directed on the town and a party of 40 marines landed to intimidate the people. Subsequently, the marines were used to keep Basseterre secure while parties of police roamed the island searching for rioters and making arrests.

Looking at the pattern of these three days as a whole, it is apparent how little and how limited was the violence used by the strikers, despite considerable provocation, and how disproportionate was the violence employed against them. Though the workers were equipped with and accustomed to using long, razor-sharp cutlasses, no report suggests that they ever used them, even to threaten people. At one estate they threw cutlasses on to the manager's verandah and made threatening remarks, but the only arms they were reported having or using were sticks and stones, and on one occasion an iron pipe. There were few instances of physical harm committed on people by these hundreds of strikers over a 3-day period. Philip Todd was knocked down and beaten, in all, five or six blows;[74] Jonathan Moore, a labourer, was struck in Saddler's Village and the left of his face partially paralysed; and some of the police, including Major Duke, were struck by stones, 'but not seriously injured'.[75] The only other violence the strikers used was demonstrative and tactical, like cutting driving gear to immobilise carts and setting fire to canefields, but it was not against persons.

The reports by colonial officials often suggest how restrained the strikers were. They state, for example, that 'no personal violence was done' and that strikers 'used threats of violence but did not take any further action'.[76] Colonel Bell described, on the morning of 30 January, near two incendiary fires, 'a rather impudent demonstration by lawbreakers. A crowd, not a disorderly one, assembled in the public street near one of these fires … composed largely of persons of the field labouring class, men and women …. Someone in the crowd shouted out that the sugar factory was making big money and that the factory should share with planters and labourers'.[77] He heard of crowds armed with sticks 'inducing labourers willing to work to join them', yet when he received calls for protection from planters he did not feel justified to disperse the crowd because it was not violent. The commander-in-chief of the America and West Indies Station expressed doubt that the situation was ever sufficiently critical to justify landing a naval detachment. He pointed out that after 29 January 'the strikers appear to have confined themselves to normal strike picketing varied by occasional forcible persuasion of strike breakers to stop work and to scattered cases of cane burning, i.e. to activities which the police and local forces should be able to control and which are not appropriate to naval intervention'.[78] What these reports underscore is that this was a predominantly non-violent strike, a determined and militant labour action to stop the cane harvest until better wage rates could be obtained, not a violent riot. Yet the strikers were threatened with guns on several occasions, by the police and also by white managers and their overseers, were twice fired on and some people wounded, even before the 'riot' of 29 January.

Of course, the strikers were vocally threatening, often angry and sometimes disorderly, but they were desperate and frustrated because they had no legal or institutional means to make their case. To understand the escalation of the violence and the tragedy of 29 January we have to consider the racial factor. The chief justice identifies in his report various protagonists as of 'European descent', 'African descent', or 'coloured'[79] but, ironically, in his covering letter he urges that such references should be omitted when the report is published because he makes them only 'to distinguish the particular types of persons' and he would not want to 'create any ignorant misapprehension that I make distinctions between races as a Judge, which I do not in Court'.[80] What his original report reveals and the published version conceals is what one would expect, namely that the 'particular types of persons' involved in this confrontation reflected the history and social structure of St Kitts over 300 years. Repeatedly, the strikers, who were overwhelmingly of African descent, encountered managers of European descent, men who were accustomed to ordering them around and were quick to threaten them with guns when they were slow to obey. And these managers and their overseers had the confidence that they would be supported by the police and, if necessary, the navy. Even after Dobridge fired on and injured some of the strikers the police protected him, rather than arresting him as the crowd justifiably demanded. Not least, the 'gentlemen' whom the governor summoned from his garden party to support the police were the white planters with whom the strikers were in dispute. The purpose of these defence forces was not to defend the island against outside powers but to maintain public order and to control labour, in short, to maintain the social order, the old social hierarchy of whites over blacks, in which they were the beneficiaries. As Glen Richards writes (1987a: 7), 'The strikers at Buckley's Estate on 29 January were directly confronted with the physical embodiment of the source of their discontent. Drawn up before them, in the ranks of the Defence Reserve, were the visible representatives of the local planter class. But, in this undisguised class confrontation, the planters were armed with rifles and the plantation workers with sticks and stones'.

What the police and defence forces saw, from their viewpoint, was that they were greatly outnumbered by hundreds of angry black people who, far from being intimidated by this show of force, refused to do what they were told and were jeering and throwing stones. If Major Duke and Magistrate Bell had been willing to take Dobridge into custody the crowd might have dispersed, but, given their traditional roles, it was inconceivable that they would do that, nor did Chief Justice Rae seem to have considered that this was an option. Instead, he concluded that, to maintain law and order, 'the only course open to them was to maintain it by the only means open to them – that of firing on the rioters'.[81] Richards (1993: 19) points out: '[E]xisting labour legislation in the presidency made the preservation of public order indistinguishable from the maintenance of labour discipline. The armed forces at the disposal of the St Kitts administration, both local and imperial, found themselves enlisted in the task of guaranteeing the planters' control over labour on the sugar estates of the island .... Policing in St Kitts, therefore, became essentially the management of industrial relations in the interest of the employing classes'.

The strikers persisted, even after the marines landed to protect Basseterre and to enable police to go into the outer districts. When police made a road block, the marchers dispersed into the canefields and regrouped on the other side of the police. Each time the police tried to intercept a crowd, it had dispersed before they arrived, being warned on at least one occasion by a man on a motorcycle. On 1 February Colonel Bell patrolled the island to reassure planters and arrange 'armed pickets on each affected estate' to keep off the strikers. This arrangement worked, 'and the labourers gradually went back to work and molestation ceased. By Monday the 4th February all estates and the factory were working' and the marines re-embarked.[82] Though not all the 'ringleaders' were found, more people were arrested. The strike was effectively broken, but it was evidence of the strikers' determination that the harvest had to be commenced under armed guards. By 17 February some 63 persons were in custody. Of the 24 people who were charged with rioting at Buckley's Estate, only two were convicted. In all, only four were convicted of riot and two of wounding with intent, although others were punished for disorderly conduct.[83] Among those convicted, sentences ranged from two to five years' imprisonment with hard labour.

Although the governor and others claimed that Nathan and Sebastian, along with a mob of 'loafers' from the town who had picked up 'bad habits' while working on the Spanish sugar islands,[84] were responsible for instigating the disturbances, they produced no evidence of this. The extent to which the SKNUBA tried to act as a trade union at the beginning of January probably encouraged the workers to make demands and to press them militantly, so Nathan's efforts should not be underestimated. But they should not be exaggerated. From the moment the strike began it seems that only local leaders among the strikers themselves shaped the tactics and form of their action. The conservative newspaper, which had earlier criticised Nathan, reported, 'When the trouble started on Tuesday members of the St Kitts Workers' League and the "Union" did their best to pacify the people but to no avail'.[85]

Richards shows that the form of the protest, with labourers marching round the island, armed with sticks, calling on fellow workers to join the strike and demonstration, was the same as in the 1896 labour protest, which also lasted several days. As an editorial in The Union Messenger pointed out, it had long been the custom around Christmas for bands of masqueraders to parade through the villages armed with sticks, so 'the form of industrial protest adopted by the striking labourers was instinctively derived from their working–class cultural traditions' (Richards 1987a: 9). Nevertheless, Richards' conclusion that both the 1896 and 1935 protests 'were undeniably the result of the spontaneous action of the plantation workers', though largely true, underestimates the encouragement and preparation that Nathan and Sebastian appear to have provided, whether entirely intentionally or not, in 1935.

The chief reason for the St Kitts labour rebellion, unquestionably, remains the poverty and insecurity experienced by the sugar workers and their families, along with their growing sense of injustice about their obvious exploitation. Nobody had to point this out to them. They were also clearly aware that the sugar factory was making a lot of money and that the planters had been guaranteed a minimum price for their cane, while their own wages were less than they had been in 1932. The reduction of wages and the threat to their employment, in addition to the return of many workers from Cuba and the Dominican Republic, made these poor people increasingly desperate and angry. Whether they had an expectation or only a hope of an imminent wage increase in January 1935, we cannot doubt that they believed they deserved one. And although the labour rebellion began essentially as a strike over wages, the violent overreaction by the authorities made this an historic event in the shaping of Kittitian, and indeed West Indian, political consciousness.

On 4 February, while the workers were returning to the estates, Sebastian published an open letter to Mark Moody Stuart, the director of the St Kitts (Basseterre) Sugar Factory. He challenged the board of directors to share their profits with the planters, thus enabling them to pay more to their workers, for the good of 'the whole community':

> It is no secret that the shareholders of the company have received handsome dividends for many years. It is also no secret that during those years the planters have, more often than not, failed to make any money, or made very little, and the position of Labour during nearly all that period, has been, to say the most of it, worse than hand to mouth .... If the shareholders of your company would be satisfied with smaller profits ... would it not be possible to benefit the planter and through him the labourer? Every one concedes that the Sugar Factory is very efficiently operated. For this you and your co–Directors are mainly responsible. It should, therefore, be possible for you and them to make such re-adjustments in the distribution of profits as will result in disseminating contentment and happiness in place of the present conditions of discontent and poverty ...
>
> The key to the situation lies in your hands. Will you open the door to happiness and prosperity among planters and labourers alike, or will you keep the door firmly locked and thereby help to foster class and race hatred?[86]

At a meeting between Moody and Boon, representing the planters, no concessions were made. The governor's view was that 'the Factory Company is unreasonable in refusing to meet at least some of the requests of the Planters', who threatened to cease planting cane. According to the governor, the company's shareholders made big profits at the expense of the planters. Between 1930 and 1933, in 'good crop years', shareholders received £80,178 but the planters lost £57,642 .[87] Three months later the planters offered to buy the factory. The governor reported, 'Directors decline £200,000 offer for factory but am glad to report planters have agreed to continue operations for 1937 crop'.[88]

The workers of St Kitts gained nothing, not even recognised spokesmen, in the immediate aftermath of the 1935 labour rebellion. In March Nathan asked that the governor should appoint a 'special man' to represent the labourers' interest to the Legislative Council. 'Had the Labourers whom our Organisation represents been allowed a special Representative on the Legislative Council of the Presidency, the matter of wages which caused the recent disturbance would have been settled, and the whole trouble avoided'.[89]

Meanwhile, the situation in the sugar industry persisted. In the governor's words, 'though crops are more abundant and more is produced per acre more labour is not employed'.[90] Not surprisingly, there were reports of further restlessness among the workers, and planters expressed 'definite uneasiness'. Despite high property and income qualifications that limited the franchise to less than 5 per cent of the population, an election in 1937 resulted for the first time in victory for some popular candidates supported by the Workers' League, and the governor believed 'this will have steadying influence'.[91] Nevertheless, local police feared 'the possibility of disturbances at St Kitts',[92] perhaps as a repercussion of the dramatic events in Trinidad and Barbados.

In 1938 the Masters and Servants Ordinance (1922), with its penal provisions, was repealed.[93] The governor reported that in St Kitts there were about 9,000 wage earners, of whom probably 98 per cent were 'wholly dependent on wages'. Of these, some 7,400 worked in agriculture, chiefly in sugar and cotton, and fewer than 600 in sugar manufacture; most of the remainder produced salt or worked for the government.[94] A few hundred workers still migrated to the Dominican Republic and a handful to Curaçao and Aruba, the total number of whom had increased from 418 in 1936 to 706 in 1938. Although the migrants were sometimes ill-treated, 'the general attitude is maintained that it is advantageous to go to these islands to work', often in order to send or bring back money to build houses.[95] On the one hand, such labour migration served as a limited safety-valve to the unemployment problem at home, but on the other hand, the returning migrants may well have contributed to the unrest in St Kitts, both because they were out of work and because they may have had some politicising experiences abroad. Richardson argues that the periodic migration of young labourers from St Kitts afflicted the incipient labour movement with 'an inherent weakness' through 'inhibiting the local, long-term coalescence of a critical mass of laborers for a truly unified political organization' (Richardson 1983: 143). At any event, it was not until 1940, when the law prohibiting trade unions was rescinded, that the St Kitts-Nevis Trades and Labour Union was established, with Sebastian as president, five years after the historic strike. This union provided the base for the political rise of Robert L. Bradshaw, a labour leader who became the first premier of St Kitts-Nevis.

St Vincent

If the labour rebellion in St Kitts was more of a strike than a riot, then that in St Vincent was more of a riot than a strike. The occasion that sparked the St Vincent riot was a consideration of increased customs duties by the local legislature, but it was not limited to 'a protest against rising retail prices' (Hart 1988: 67). The facts that workers struck on two estates near Georgetown, on the other side of the island, before the riot occurred in Kingstown, and that demonstrators in the capital complained of unemployment and low wages, suggest that labour issues were also central to the disturbances. However, unlike St Kitts, retail stores were targets of the rioters and those Europeans who were subject to animosity were chiefly shopkeepers and merchants rather than planters and estate managers.

The governor of the Windward Islands, Sir Selwyn Grier, was convinced that agitators, particularly those who fomented hatred against Europeans, had organised the rebellion, but although they may have contributed, this was surely not the underlying cause he believed it to be.[96] Marryshow of the Grenada Workingmen's Association and Legislative Council had passed through St Vincent and given a 'provocative speech' in Kingstown on 16 October 1935.[97] Grier claimed also that the bishop of the Windward Islands had made an 'imprudent ... farewell speech' on leaving St Vincent, in which he 'advised the St Vincentians that they must fight for what they wanted',[98] but this would hardly have provoked a riot. The problem, rather than poor people listening to such supposed agitators, was Grier's reluctance to recognise or listen to representatives of poor people about their problems until it was too late, with the result that social tension built up, particularly in the capital.

On 18 October 1935 a bill was given its first reading at a meeting of the Legislative Council of St Vincent. It proposed to reduce the scale of import duties on motor vehicles and to raise them on other items, including matches, in order to produce more revenue. Among those present were members of the St Vincent Representative Government Association, an essentially middle-class organization, among whose leaders were Ebenezer Duncan, a teacher, and George McIntosh, a pharmacist. During the following days, before the second reading of the bill which was scheduled for 21 October, there were rumours, which may or may not have had a factual basis, that 'retail shopkeepers had increased the charges made for a variety of commodities',[99] including matches and also items that were not to be affected by the proposed taxation. The governor believed there was a 'deliberate campaign of misrepresentation' before the riot, 'undertaken for the purpose of causing discontent and ill-feeling'. According to him, 'The people were told and believed that the Government was largely increasing taxes on the necessities of life, was doubling the land tax, and was introducing increased licences on such animals as donkeys, dogs, etc. These statements though untrue were believed.' The governor acknowledged in retrospect that 'he should have taken steps' to explain the proposals better to the public in order to forestall 'the campaign of misrepresentation'.[100]

Whatever the real extent of such a campaign, the disturbances began on the morning of 21 October, when the bill was to receive its second reading in

Kingstown. That morning workers struck on two estates near Georgetown and the owner of one estate was slightly injured by a stone later in the day, but elsewhere 'people remained at work throughout the disturbance', so there was no attempt to produce a general strike as in St Kitts. At about 11.30 am, while the taxes were being discussed in the council chamber above the court house, a noisy crowd gathered outside. Seated among the public observers in the chamber was McIntosh of the Representative Government Association, who was then a popular member of the Kingstown Town Board. McIntosh, who was born on 8 March 1886 and died on 1 November 1963, was an important figure in the early struggle by the working people of St Vincent (Ryan and Williams n.d.: 6). The crowd was said to have gathered at his shop before moving to the court house. He delivered a letter to the governor, asking for an interview 'as he wished to represent the views of some of the people'. The governor sent a verbal reply that he would be willing to meet him at 5 pm, after the council's business had been concluded. The crowd, about 300 strong, feeling that he was putting them off, became angry and the police, who were then unarmed, could not control it. According to the governor, who went to the steps of the court house to tell the people to disperse, they were 'in a very excited condition', many carried heavy sticks and some were drunk. 'They were shouting "We want work", "We want money", "We want food"'. By ringing a bell, McIntosh quieted the crowd enough for the governor to make himself heard, but when he said he would speak to some representatives in the court house there was such a rush of people that the hall was immediately filled and the noise continued. 'The main cry of the crowd was unemployment and that they wanted work and that they wanted money; also that the wages paid were too low'. When the governor told them: 'If there was genuine unemployment among them road work would be found for the unemployed on the windward road within the next fortnight ... some raised the cry of taxation and that prices had gone up'.[101] The governor said that he could not speak to them when 100 people were talking at the same time, and told them to go outside and to send their representatives to meet him at the library at 5 pm.

Perhaps the governor underestimated the crowd's anger at this time, or maybe he simply did not know what to do, but it seems to have been the turning point when a noisy confrontation in which there was still opportunity for some dialogue became increasingly violent. Some of those who left the court house, presumably frustrated by the lack of results in their encounter with the governor, met a gang of prisoners with a stone cart on which there was a sledgehammer and a load of stones. The warder was driven off, the hammer was used to smash the doors of the prison behind the court house, and the prisoners were released. Two warders were injured in the attack. Another section of the crowd advanced on the court house and used the stones to smash doors and windows and to damage cars parked in front of the building. Others streamed across the market square to the dry goods store of F.A. Corea, a leading merchant and estate-owner, who was a member of the Legislative Council, and ransacked his place.

The police, meanwhile, sought reinforcements and arms from their barracks on the opposite side of the square, near the sea. Armed with rifles, a group of six police joined the governor and other officials at the court house and at about 1.50 pm the chief justice read the Riot Act. Across the square some people were breaking into a rum shop and a constable had been wounded and his rifle broken. However, the 'considerable body of people in front of the Court House ... were in a state of growing excitement but taking no actual part in the rioting'. As the crowd did not disperse, warning shots were fired in the air and then a volley was fired into Corea's store. Further firing took place and the rioters, who had suffered several casualties, streamed out of the square. One of the two women who were seriously wounded by this shooting, who subsequently died, was 'not in any way taking part in the rioting'.[102] The police were joined by some armed members of the local Volunteer Force. One of them, described as 'a prominent merchant in Kingstown who is a Lieutenant' in the force, when attacked by a man with a knife, shot him.[103]

When the governor's ADC tried to send a cable to Grenada to ask for naval assistance he found that the office had been broken into and the wires cut. He proceeded to the cable hut near the beach and used emergency equipment to send a telegram. When their car was attacked on the way back by 'a gang of men armed with cutlasses' they wounded one man with a revolver. Further damage was done to downtown properties on Hillsboro Street, Upper Bay Street and Bedford Street, where shops were damaged or looted. It was estimated that the total number of actual rioters was about 200, and that 'a great deal of damage was done by small boys and women'.[104] The captain of the Volunteer Force arrived with more men to secure the government offices and other buildings around the square, and the governor with his ADC joined the administrator and chief of police in the police barracks. While they were organising the volunteers and swearing in special constables whom they could trust, some houses on the outskirts of the town were attacked and looted. After they had got a sufficient force and mobilised vehicles, patrols of armed men were sent out to get the situation under control. During the afternoon telephone wires were cut near Kingstown.

At 5 pm the governor went with McIntosh to the library and met about 100 people. 'They were in an excited condition and their one and only cry was that they wanted work and money and that wages were low'. The governor 'gave them a very severe warning regarding their future conduct' and repeated that if there was 'genuine unemployment amongst them and they were anxious to obtain work', some additional road work would be created. 'No reference to any other grievance was made by this crowd than that of lack of employment and low wages'.[105]

Kingstown and its suburbs were reported quiet by 10 pm but there was a disturbance at Georgetown where police fired shots over a crowd that was breaking windows and doors. At midnight, HMS Challenger arrived in St Vincent and a party of 24 men and four officers, armed with rifles, landed in Kingstown, making it possible for armed patrols to be despatched towards Georgetown. Some of the Georgetown crowd went south to Byera where they began cutting telephone poles and wires until stopped by an armed patrol. Several were taken prisoner, including one who was wounded in the attack.

Early in the morning of 22 October a state of emergency was proclaimed and censorship was imposed on the local press and on news cables. Before 8 am rioting broke out at Camden Park, some 3.5 miles from Kingstown, and a house and store owned by a Portuguese shopkeeper were looted. An armed patrol of volunteers sent out to stop this was ambushed by rioters at a point where they could hurl stones on the truck from a steep hill alongside the road which they had 'blocked with fallen trees and telegraph posts'.[106] Two volunteers were injured and they opened fire, killing one man and wounding four others. More demonstrations, without rioting, took place in Lownams and Chauncey Villages, northwest of Kingstown, in Stubbs Village, about 5 miles east of Kingstown, and Park Hill and Grand Sable Estates near Georgetown on the east coast. Some other noisy demonstrations by young men armed with cutlasses and sticks were reported.

On 23 October the police began rounding up those who had taken part in the riots. The landing party returned to HMS Challenger on 24 October but the governor asked for the ship to remain at Kingstown until 29 October, after the Legislative Council had resumed the sitting which had been adjourned earlier. Ten Grenada police who had come on the Challenger remained as reinforcements until 5 November. On 12 November Grier admitted he did not intend to 'relax precautions ... for it is known that small gangs of men, wanted as ringleaders in the Kingstown riot, are in the hills and some of them are reported to be armed'. He said they had threatened to retaliate by attacking 'members of the community who assisted in restoring law and order',[104] but no such attacks were reported. The officially listed casualties of the whole event consisted of six people killed, 19 detained in hospital and 18 treated as outpatients. Of those wounded, 12 were police, warders, volunteers or special constables.[105]

The troubles continued as late as January. The administrator of St Vincent justified continuing the state of emergency on the grounds of the continuing trials, the volatility of about 200 persons in Kingstown's slums, and the need to censor newspapers and news telegrams which could 'increase tension at a time of unrest'.[106] A local planter, Claude Hadley, was killed by his chauffeur, Williams, who had been dismissed after being charged with an offence connected with the riots. In Kingstown itself there were 'still signs of sullen hostility'. Don Morgan, who was said to be 'one of the most notorious of the ringleaders', was shot and killed while resisting arrest, and two of his associates, Sutherland and McDowall, were arrested. Morgan had worked in Cuba and the governor believed that 'some of the worst characters' were labour migrants who had returned from the Spanish republics.[107] Morgan had led the uprising in the Camden Park district. They found it hard to arrest him because 'the hostility of many of the local inhabitants made it impossible for any enquiries to be made without warning being given to Don Morgan'. He came to be regarded among the people as 'something of a hero' and each time a police raid failed 'his prestige increased'.[108]

On 1 February 1936, as the situation at last appeared to be satisfactory, the state of emergency was ended. Of the most serious cases, 33 had already been tried and of these 29 were convicted and sentenced and the others acquitted.[109] Altogether, of the 114 persons (91 men and 23 women) who were tried only 14 were acquitted; 45 men and 5 women were sentenced to terms in prison.[110]

Governor Grier insisted that 'the Kingstown riot was organised',[111] but this is unlikely or at least exaggerated, in spite of the evidence of more or less simultaneous disturbances in Kingstown and Georgetown, and the fact that more than one group cut telephone and cable wires in different places. The governor sought to place most of the blame for what he believed to be 'a deliberate campaign of misrepresentation' on McIntosh, whom he said was 'mainly responsible for staging the whole business'.[112] McIntosh was arrested and charged with treason felony as the leader of an armed mob on 23 November. However, the charge was so ridiculous that the magistrate who heard the case dismissed it without even calling on the defence.[113] McIntosh, along with Duncan, was certainly critical of Crown colony rule and their opposition to the Italian invasion of Ethiopia, which began in 1935, probably encouraged racial consciousness and anticolonialism. Duncan published reports of the war in his newspaper, The Investigator, and McIntosh posted news and photographs about it on a bulletin board outside his Kingstown shop (Young 1993: 66-7). Others who participated in the demonstrations were also associated with advocating Ethiopia's cause. Sheriff Lewis, a working man who was said to have served as a volunteer in Ethiopia, was nicknamed Selassie, and Bertha Mutt, a labourer for the Agriculture Department, was known as Mother Selassie. These people have been characterised as working–class leaders of the rebellion (Hart 1988: 69). Lewis served 5 years of a 21-year prison sentence, the longest given to a convicted rioter (Young 1993: 68). However, there is no evidence that any of these people plotted or planned an uprising, or that it was organised at all. Though the government sought to portray McIntosh as the instigator of the riots, both he and Duncan soon condemned them. Duncan's editorial in The Investigator on 26 October described the riots as 'a blot on the history of the colony' and on 29 October McIntosh moved a resolution at a meeting of the Kingstown Town Board conveying its 'deep regret' about the riots and congratulating the government for 'the stand taken in suppressing the disorder' (quoted in Gonsalves n.d.: 13-14).

As for the underlying causes, Grier argued that 'the bitter and growing feeling of resentment against the white races . . . continually fomented by public speakers at pro-Abyssinia meetings' had been responsible.[114] Although in his own report he stated that the demonstrators complained only about unemployment, low wages and lack of money, he also asserted that 'the main driving force of those who rioted was a bitter hatred of the whites'.[115] His evidence for this is quite limited, however. Among threats made in the Market Square, the administrator heard, 'we lick all you white men up tonight,' and arrested rioters abused the police who had 'sided with the whites.' One 'ringleader' was said to have secured two black and two white fowls from a local merchant of Portuguese descent, and to have 'publicly decapitated the 2 white fowls with appropriate remarks.'[116] But such comments and demonstrations, particularly in such a heated moment, are better understood as the normal idiom of social tensions in a society rooted in slavery and colonialism than as evidence that racial hatred, as such, was the underlying cause of the riot. Perhaps more important is the evidence that shops and houses belonging to residents of European descent were singled out for attack, but even here it is impossible to distinguish the class from the race factor. Corea's store was probably a special target because he was a rich member of the Legislative Council, which was about to vote taxation measures that, it was believed, favoured people like him while making the poor pay more. Perhaps, too, the cars were attacked in market square because the council was proposing to reduce import duties on motor vehicles, used only by officials and the rich, but this was not simply 'bitter racial animosity'. On the other hand, if St Vincentians had known that Grier went so far as to say that 'if the Abyssinians achieved a similar success to that of 1896 [when Emperor Menelik II defeated an Italian army at the battle of Aduwa], the repercussions might be more dangerous than they will be if Italy succeeds in annexing Abyssinia',[117] they may have been provoked justifiably to such animosity.

Finally, Governor Grier blamed criminal gangs, including one called 'The Ranch Boys', named presumably after 'some American "gangster" film . . . The connection between this gang and another directing organisation which remained in the background is the subject of investigation'.[118] However, nothing more is heard about this sinister plot, the gangs or the unnamed 'directing organisation'. In fact, Grier seems to get the underlying causes and the symptoms or contributory causes mixed up. He could not admit that unemployment and low wages, combined with high prices and unfair taxation, could cause such a riot in his colony, though this is clearly what the demonstrators were repeatedly telling him. Instead, he had to look for agitators and criminal gangs, sinister designs and plots, which misled the normally peaceful and loyal working people of St Vincent in order to leave his paternalistic colonial vision intact. He admitted that wages for estate labourers were low, seldom exceeding 1 shilling a day for men and 10 pence for women, and that much of what was available for workers in town was 'casual employment as stevedores and porters and boatmen'. He also acknowledged that the 'position of estate owner is reminiscent of feudal times', yet he claimed that labour relations on the estates were 'most cordial' even when many estate-owners were in 'financial difficulties'.[119]

If the underlying cause was clearly economic, as the demonstrators repeatedly said, a contributory cause was that there was inadequate communication between the poor people and the colonial administration. Because the colonial officials contemptuously dismissed such men as McIntosh as agitators they cut themselves off from any popular representation of grievances, with the predictable result that poor people became increasingly frustrated and angry. Equally predictably, the governor, who was unable to acknowledge such a serious defect in the colonial system, argued for more police as he did not have 'the men available to keep in touch with the activities of local agitators who are well known to be exercising a subversive influence', though his volunteer force, numbering between 50 and 60 loyal men, 'proved of great value' during the crisis.[120]

One outcome of this labour rebellion, and more particularly of the subsequent prosecution, was that McIntosh 'emerged as unchallengeably the most popular leader of the working class' (Hart 1988: 69). Although it is true, as Cleve Scott states, that his 'entrance into local politics began with his election to the Kingstown Board in 1923' (Scott 1998: 1-2), and that the board provided him with political experience and a reputation as a man who represented working-class interests, it was the 1935 riot that expanded the arena of national politics to include working-class people and that raised McIntosh's status as a leader. In 1936 he organised the St Vincent Workingmen's Cooperative Association, the first organisation explicitly for working people in the island. It was registered as a limited liability company on 2 July, as it could not legally be registered as a trade union. Another outcome of the rebellion was that more attention was paid to the unemployment problem. An unemployment bureau, dealing with unemployment in an area up to 10 miles from Kingstown, was established on 7 August 1936. In the absence of accurate statistical information it was estimated that of some 11,500 workers and peasants 1,000 were 'more or less regularly employed' on sugar estates, another 1,000 had regular employment in Kingstown in various capacities, about 300 worked for government departments 'more or less regularly', and of the 3,000 who were partially employed on the windward coast and 1,500 who had partial employment on the leeward coast about half had access to small plots of land on which they grew food. Others made a living, or made do, by fishing or by obtaining casual employment but 'there are one thousand persons unemployable who exist by begging or by relying on their relations and friends' and 400 persons received poor relief. Of the 189 people registered at the bureau as in search of work, 32 were skilled, 137 unskilled and 20 were domestic workers. The number of persons for whom employment was found was said to be 'disappointing'. Seven of the skilled labourers found work in the Public Works Department, and two of the domestics and 24 of the unskilled laborers found work. Outdoor relief during the last three months of 1936 provided an average of 21 persons weekly with such employment as weeding and clearing the churchyard and cemetery.[121] This report reveals the extent of underemployment as well as unemployment, and shows that most St Vincentians had to mix casual work with their own food production. It also shows that the response of the bureau and of relief efforts was pitifully inadequate.

At the end of July 1936, McIntosh, in his capacity as president of the new St Vincent Workingmen's Cooperative Association (SVWCA), invited Marryshow to visit. The administrator of the island, Alban Wright, agreed to address a labour rally on 3 August provided they sang 'God save the King' instead of 'Toilers' and 'The Red Flag', and that he could speak after Marryshow. He was told this 'would be regarded as betraying the Labour Cause, if they were omitted, and that they had been sung at every Labour gathering in the West Indies', but he got his way. Some 3,000–4,000 women and men were in the procession, carrying banners proclaiming the villages whence they came and with such slogans as 'God Save the People', 'No sticks must be carried', 'Preserve perfect quiet and order', 'We demand employment' and 'The people must have land'. The procession 'moved quietly and in perfect order' to the Anglican cathedral and the rally in the park was also 'perfectly orderly and good-humoured throughout'. Wright thought Marryshow 'completely reasonable and in every respect moderate in his speeches and actions', and felt that the rally would help re-establish 'friendlier and more sympathetic relations' between white people and people of colour on the island.[122] These cooperative efforts, better communications and friendlier relations were achieved less than a year after the riots. In an election on 25 March 1937, under a still limited but somewhat more liberal franchise, McIntosh was elected to the Legislative Council, representing Kingstown, winning 364 votes to 178 for the Planters' and Peasants' Association candidacy (Scott 1998: 27). The SVWCA and the associated St Vincent Labour Party (SVLP), on a single ticket, won four of the five elected seats to the Legislative Council. At the end of that year the 1839 Masters and Servants Act, containing penal sanctions, was repealed.[123] The SVWCA/SVLP, led by McIntosh and Duncan, 'laid the groundwork for the growth of political unionism' in the period before adult suffrage in 1951 (Gonsalves n.d.: 19).

In spite of these gains and achievements in the two years after the labour rebellion, the endemic problems of St Vincent persisted. In 1938 Wright belatedly pointed out the obvious when he reported, 'One of the main difficulties in St Vincent is that there is no alternative employment for labourers other than agriculture which must be subject to seasonal inactivity'.[124] The SVWCA still could not register as a trade union, though it achieved some promising legislation on a minimum wage, work hours and a token land settlement scheme (Young 1993: 69). In 1939 W. Arthur Lewis wrote: 'In three short years the Association has become the focus of radical opinion in St Vincent, and a body of great political influence. It is not registered as a trade union, but it represents the workers in all negotiations. It has also attracted wide middle class support, and its candidates were enthusiastically returned at the last General Election. It is one of the new organisations which is changing the orientation of West Indian politics.' (Lewis 1977:21)

This organisation and McIntosh's leadership emerged directly out of the fiery crucible of October 1935. Had the colonial administration been willing to take McIntosh and his followers seriously in the first place, to listen to their grievances rather than dismiss them as criminals and agitators, the violence and tragic deaths in that month could have been avoided. However, it may be argued also that it was precisely those events that led to a modest re-evaluation of the situation. Colonial officials began to see that it was better to recognise and talk to moderate leaders of working people's organisations than to risk another outright rebellion.

St Lucia

On St Lucia, St Vincent's northern neighbour, most wage labour was on plantations, but there was also an important business supplying ships with coal at the port and capital, Castries. Although there was a history of strikes and militant workers in this trade, no working-class organisations had been formed. By the 1930s, as ships increasingly used oil, this business was providing less employment and it was the workers in this trade who started the labour unrest in St Lucia. These workers were most likely in fairly close touch with events on other islands, and even international labour issues, through the sailors with whom they would have come into contact.

On 4 November 1935, about 350-400 workers employed in unloading a collier went on strike at 1 pm. 'The strikers dispersed quite quietly', but it was said that some members 'of the hooligan class became increasingly offensive to any of the white community who were abroad in the town'.[125] For this reason, presumably, as there had been no public disturbance and the strikers had yet to make their demands, a detachment of 28 marines was landed from HMS Challenger to guard the police barracks during the night. At 11 am the next morning, a deputation from the strikers visited the governor. 'The men demanded double wages; they also complained about the overloading of baskets'.[126] Governor Grier argued that, in the present state of the trade, the coaling companies could not increase the wages. In 1934 one company had shown a loss of £900, and another was in liquidation.[127] Nothing was agreed, and the strike persisted.

The governor, who had proceeded directly from St Vincent to St Lucia on 1 November, was predisposed for trouble and quickly overreacted. He commented that the principal speaker of the deputation was 'a man who had at one time been in Cuba, and who speaks at times in a manner which is reminiscent of a communist orator in England'. He reported that anonymous letters, signed 'Hail [sic] Selassie our King', had been sent to a St Lucia police sergeant threatening 'all those who sided with the "whites" as well as against the "whites" themselves'.[128] Grier decided promptly that the situation on St Lucia 'had become threatening',[129] so he declared a state of emergency. The volunteers were mustered and special constables enrolled to support the 61 regular policemen and the marines, even though 'no trouble or rioting was reported from the town'.[130] The volunteers were led by a white man, Captain Wade, the inspector of schools.

At 1 pm on 6 November, about 50 persons, chiefly women and boys, were organised to carry on unloading the coal. 'These workers were threatened and intimidated, but suitable police protection was available. At 1800, attempts were made to molest them on their way home from the dumps. One arrest was quickly made and no further trouble was experienced throughout the night'.[131] The next day a gang of about 80 workers, 30 of whom were said to be regular coal workers, recommenced unloading the coal and no attempt was made to interfere with them. By the morning of 8 November, 'about 40% of the coaling gangs had returned to work ... without any interference or disturbance'.[132] By 11 November, the strike was said to be over and the situation remained quiet.

This was such a minor event that it could be argued there was no rebellion in St Lucia. The strike was a quite normal and orderly labour dispute. The only people threatened by the strikers were some strike-breakers who worked under police protection. But Governor Grier, with the St Vincent experience so fresh in his mind, reacted to this minor and reasonable labour dispute with an unnecessary show of force. Searchlights from HMS Challenger played over the town at night while marines patrolled the streets with the intention of disturbing and intimidating the inhabitants (Lewis 1977: 21). The police and the special forces were used by the colonial administration on behalf of the coaling companies to put down the strike. Despite this show of force, or perhaps in sympathetic reaction to it, a strike occurred among agricultural workers on Lime Estate, about 8 miles from Castries, on 12 November, but it was 'neutralised by borrowing labour from a neighbouring plantation'.[133] A committee set up by the governor subsequently reported that no wage increase for the coal haulers was possible.

Detectives were brought from Barbados to investigate 'sedition mongers'. One of them reported that the principal speaker at a meeting of the local branch of the UNIA, 'who had the reputation of a trouble maker urged the necessity of avoiding any trouble in view of what had taken place in Kingstown'[134] in neighbouring St Vincent. In February 1936 Grier wrote that 'the trouble makers were sufficiently frightened to remain quiet for the time being ... and interest in the Abyssinian War seems to have disappeared'.[135] Although Grier's efforts to intimidate people and to silence dissent appear to have succeeded, even he seems to have been aware that the underlying problems were unchanged, as he commented that the economic situation in St Lucia 'is pretty bad' and the minimum wage committee 'has a difficult task in front of it'.[136]

In spite of prolonged investigations into the activities of those believed to be responsible 'for the dissemination of subversive propaganda', no evidence was produced which would have justified legal proceedings against anybody. Nevertheless, the governor claimed that the enquiries themselves 'had the desired effect of discouraging for the time being subversive propaganda' and several people continued to be 'closely watched'.[137] In this way, any criticism of the administration or the society came to be defined as subversive activity and subjected to official intimidation. In the same process, the absence of any public dissent was construed as proving the effectiveness of such measures against agitators. Thus was a dangerously authoritarian pattern, subversive of democratic process, established within the colonial regime.

At the end of 1936 a minimum wage for agricultural workers was set in St Lucia that was the same as the normal current rate, namely 1 shilling for men and 10 pence for women for a day of not more than nine working hours.[138]

Nine months later, on 5 August 1937, a strike occurred on Cul-de-Sac Estate, one of the two largest plantations in St Lucia, about 10 miles from Castries. Some 1,500 workers were involved and the administrator called out the volunteer force as a 'purely precautionary measure'.[139] The strike spread to Roseau Estate, where the manager said he had heard threats that the radio station would be destroyed and all the Europeans slaughtered. More believably, it was said that higher wages were demanded because the workers had heard that the governor of Trinidad had recommended them there. To counter this, the administrator impressed on the manager of Cul-de-Sac Estate 'the necessity for a strict observance of the Minimum Wage Order .... It has been alleged that evasion is practiced by fixing task rates at such prices that it is impossible for the labourer to earn the daily minimum wage, also by the employment of juveniles at less than the full rates, and so on'.[140] The administrator expressed concern lest the owners of the two largest estates increase wages beyond the rates that small employers could afford, thereby resulting in 'a greater increase of unrest and discontent', so he kept the volunteer force mobilised.[141] However, if the large employers were paying below the minimum wage by cheating their workers, as he had previously suggested, then the smaller employers were surely not paying more. In effect, the so-called minimum wage was really a maximum, but one that many workers did not receive.

Governor H.B. Popham commented that several communities in the Windward Islands had been 'keyed up' in 1937 by the recent events in Trinidad and Barbados, and that the administrator of St Lucia had to 'allay the fears of the law-abiding elements and restore confidence'.[142] But there was no rioting in St Lucia where, once again, special forces were called out as soon as a strike occurred, in anticipation of disorder. Lewis commented that even the government's own nominees in the Legislative Council criticised 'the waste of public funds entailed by unnecessary mobilisation' (Lewis 1977: 22). It seems that the real function of these auxiliary police forces was to intimidate strikers and keep the labour situation favourable to employers.

On 6 December 1938 an ordinance repealing the penal sanctions in the old masters and servants law was passed in the St Lucia Legislative Council and it received the governor's assent on 14 December.[143] Early the next year, 1939, the first St Lucian trade union was formed, organising urban and agricultural workers (Lewis 1977: 22).

Trinidad

The working people of Trinidad were agitating and mobilising long before their great labour rebellion in 1937. As in Belize, returning soldiers from the West India Regiment in 1919 participated in a rash of strikes that began on the Port of Spain waterfront and spread round the island and to Tobago.

'The situation in December 1919 was the nearest thing to a general strike the colony had yet seen' (Basdeo 1983: 28). There followed a period of repression. Some of the earliest organisations oriented toward the needs of working people in the British Caribbean were created in Trinidad but, as elsewhere, legal restrictions on trade unionism blunted and frustrated these efforts. By the mid-1930s a more radical new leadership had developed, reflecting the degree of proletarianisation and urbanisation of the working people of Trinidad and their desperation in the depression years. Politically motivated militant groups began to agitate and organise workers and the unemployed in 1934 and 1935, but the rapid expansion of trade unionism started after the labour rebellion in June 1937. By the end of 1939 13 trade unions had been registered in Trinidad and Tobago,[144] and the labour movement was well on the way to becoming institutionalised.

Trinidad, along with Belize and Guyana, is one of the most racially diverse parts of the British Caribbean. This diversity has been evident in a segmented labour force that corresponds to a large degree to a sharply bifurcated economy. The salience of race and class, and their relationship to the structure and fluctuating fortunes of the economy, were central to the emergence of the labour movement in Trinidad. Three primary groups of trade unions emerged, among workers in the sugar industry and the oil industry, and the urban workers such as those on the docks and in public works. The oil industry, begun in the early twentieth century, had come to dominate Trinidad's exports by the 1930s, but it was a capital-intensive industry and far more people were employed in agriculture. Crude oil and its by-products accounted for about 60 per cent of the value of exports and sugar and rum, molasses and cocoa for about 33 per cent; however, the sugar and cocoa industries employed over 68,000 people compared with only about 8,000 employees in the oil industry. From the point of view of labour, therefore, plantation agriculture remained the dominant sector, but from the point of view of colonial officials the oil industry was critical, especially in terms of imperial defence policy. The fact that Trinidad had become the British empire's largest producer of oil 'was an important determinant of imperial policy towards the labour disturbances' (Johnson 1975: 29).

By the early 1930s the Trinidad Workingmen's Association (TWA), which was founded in 1897 and had been revived after the war, had become 'a less effective and united organization than it had been in the 1920s' (Brereton 1981: 170). Between 1919 and 1934 the TWA was a pioneering and progressive political force, but Cipriani's reformist leadership, which was committed exclusively to legal and constitutional methods, became challenged by younger and more militant leaders. As early as 1929 a rival organisation, the Trinidad and Tobago Trade Union Centre, was formed, claiming some 2,000 members, mostly in transport in 1930 (Lewis 1977: 27). However, trade unions were illegal until the Trade Union Ordinance of 1932 empowered the colonial government to register them, thereby making them legal - or not. But the law did not legalise peaceful picketing, nor protect unions from legal actions for damages arising out of strike actions, as was the case in the UK. In these circumstances, after seeking advice from the British TUC, Cipriani decided not to register his organisation as a union. Instead, he decided in 1934 to rename it the Trinidad Labour Party (TLP).

Cipriani's intolerance of criticism within his party and his refusal to challenge the limitations of the Trade Union Ordinance made his organisation increasingly marginal during the labour struggles of the next few years. 'It may be that Cipriani believed that the political strategy was more important than the development of trade unionism, or that he viewed the emergence of new leaders and new labour unions as a threat to his leadership of the workers, or simply that he had faith in the TUC's advice. In any case, there was increasing dissatisfaction within the TWA/TLP over Cipriani's authoritarian leadership.' (Brereton 1981: 170-1) As other, younger labour leaders developed new tactics and expressed the working people's demands more militantly, Cipriani and his TLP were overtaken and became an obstacle to the further development of the labour movement.

In the early 1930s a group of intellectuals developed a radical critique that helped shape a new political culture in Trinidad. C.L.R. James and Alfred Mendes started a literary journal called Trinidad, which appeared at Christmas 1929 and Easter 1930. Its portrayal of slum life was considered scandalous by middle-class society. This was the precursor of The Beacon, 28 issues of which appeared between 1931 and 1933, and which was financed and edited by Albert Gomes, who had recently returned from the United States. This magazine challenged conventions about culture and politics in exploring issues of West Indian identity, racial consciousness, socialism and communism. James's biographer writes that James 'insists that the magazine and the milieu around it dominated literary life, not only in Trinidad, where it had no competition, but in the English-speaking Caribbean, where it had next to none. And not only literary life, but also the maturing sensibility of the Caribbean's historical place within the century and the world.' (Buhle 1988: 27) Whatever influence this journal may have had upon the younger labour activists and cultural nationalists, James left before the real action started. In 1932 he migrated to the UK, carrying his manuscript of Minty Alley, a social realist novel written in the 1920s but not published until 1936, and his study of Cipriani and the movement towards self-government, The Life of Captain Cipriani: An Account of British Government in the West Indies (1932), revised as The Case for West Indian Self Government (1933). These intellectuals were imagining a new West Indian world that was soon to be actually initiated by the working people's movement. By the time James returned to Trinidad in 1958 the colony's political scene had been transformed.

A series of hunger marches and demonstrations, beginning in 1933 and accelerating in the next two years, moved beyond reformist politics and intellectual critique to a mass politics of the street. Several new organisations emerged, chief among them the Trinidad Citizens League (TCL) and the National Unemployed Movement (NUM), which became the Negro Welfare Cultural and Social Association (NWCSA). They attacked Cipriani's leadership of the labour movement, mobilised workers, and initiated a new, radical labour politics. Several of the leaders of these organisations had formerly participated in the TWA/TLP and had broken with Cipriani. A hunger march on the governor in the Red House, the seat of colonial government in Port of Spain, on 19 June 1933, took place against Cipriani's advice. The demonstrators demanded the reintroduction of rent control and relief work for the unemployed. The next year, a core of working people, Elma Francois, Jim Barrette and Jim Headley, formed the NUM. Francois was born in St Vincent in 1897 and migrated to Trinidad in 1919, where she worked as a domestic servant, became a member of the TWA and started to speak at public meetings. Barrette was her companion. Headley, as a ship's cook, had been active in the National Maritime Union and the Young Communist League in the United States, where he had been in touch with George Padmore, the Trinidadian revolutionary who was then a leading member of the International Trade Union Committee of Negro Workers of the Comintern. Headley, like Francois, had been a member of the TWA. They were joined by Dudley Mahon, a cook at the Port of Spain Colonial Hospital. The NUM organised demonstrations in 1934, the 'idea spread like wildfire throughout the country and "Hunger Marches" were organised by other groups' (Reddock 1988: 12-4).

As economic conditions worsened and increased mechanisation threatened employment, strikes and demonstrations occurred on the sugar estates, chiefly in central Trinidad (Basdeo 1983: 109-23). The NUM contacted the sugar workers, who were predominantly Indian. A militant Indian sugar worker, Poolbasie, informed the NUM members of living and working conditions on the estates. She said that a severe drought was making the earth particularly hard to work and that exploitative drivers were not only checking more frequently on the completion of tasks but were also taking young girls to their houses on pretexts. In addition to the inherent abuses of this situation, the sugar companies passed on the problems caused by the depression to their workers. "High unemployment and high rents for barrack accommodation were combined with unilateral increases in the size of tasks" (Reddock 1988: 14), but the workers still had no legally recognised representatives, organisations or negotiating processes.

The demonstrations began on 6 July 1934 among some 800 workers at the Brechin Castle and Esperanza Estates. When violence erupted and the police were attacked, 12 persons were arrested. Mass demonstrations were staged in Couva, Chaguanas, Tunapuna and San Fernando, involving some 15,000 estate workers in the sugar belt. 'Overseers, managers and policemen were attacked, company buildings set on fire, shops looted; it was the spontaneous violence of desperate men close to starvation. The disturbances were not organized, and no leaders were publicly identified.' (Brereton 1981: 171)

Although no people were killed by the police, many were arrested and fined or imprisoned. Basdeo concludes that the repressive activities of the police, including firing into the air and random arrests, 'helped to infuriate demonstrators' (Basdeo 1983: 114). A commission of inquiry stated that the sugar workers had legitimate grievances, but its recommendations were 'commonplace, simplistic and conservative, lacking in any fundamental provisions to remedy the situation' (Basdeo 1983: 119). The governor pointed out that 'callous retrenchment and overtasking by the sugar companies were the major causes of the riots, yet the only positive steps he could recommend were the distribution of the princely sum of £150 in relief for destitute workers and the irrigation of rice lands to enable them to plant rice' (Brereton 1981: 171). On 20 July 1934 a march from the Caroni area to Port of Spain was planned, to unite the Indian sugar workers with the predominantly African hunger marchers of the NUM, but a cordon of police stopped it. The important participation of Indians in these marches and the growing unity between rural Indian and urban African workers are remarkable features of these demonstrations, which were among the earliest in the growing labour rebellions of the 1930s in the British Caribbean.

The NUM organised a register of unemployed and collected 1,200 names within two weeks in 1934 in Port of Spain. In addition to organising the marches, they held public meetings at which they spoke about economic and labour issues. By the end of 1934 Headley had returned to his job as a seaman but the others, though harassed by the police, persisted. One of the leaders of the NUM, who were progressive in their attitude to gender equality, was Francois. Speaking at a meeting in Woodford Square early in 1935, she impressed Bertie Percival, an oilfield worker from Fyzabad, who subsequently joined the group. Other leaders included Clement Payne, who became a major figure in the Barbados labour rebellion in 1937, Christina King, who worked as a writer and undercover agent in the NUM and Rupert Gittens, who had been deported back to Trinidad for his activities with the French Communist Party in Marseilles. Gittens had previously worked for several years in the United States, where he was influenced by communist ideas and by radical black nationalism. Under his influence, 'the NUM was exposed much more to socialist thinking at an international level and became convinced of the limitations of "unemployment" as a political issue' (Reddock 1988: 16). By 1935 the NUM had transformed itself into an organisation with more broadly defined goals but a narrower social base, the NWCSA.

In March 1935 the workers at Apex Oilfields, which was the largest of the oil companies, producing 29 per cent of the total oil output of Trinidad in 1936 (Thomas 1987: 196), went on strike. Apex refused to redress the workers' grievances, which included 'low wages, long hours, wage deductions for late-coming and poor conditions' (Brereton 1981: 172), so the Fyzabad branch of the TLP asked Cipriani for help. When Cipriani refused to sanction strike action, the workers went ahead anyway and two members of the Fyzabad TLP executive, Tubal Uriah 'Buzz' Butler and John Rojas, organised a hunger march to Port of Spain, openly challenging Cipriani's leadership in the oil belt. Cipriani responded by joining the police to stop the march. He promised the demonstrators that he would arrange for a delegation to meet the governor to discuss their grievances, but 'no redress was forthcoming' (Ryan 1972: 40). Though the strike petered out and the workers settled for a meagre 2 per cent increase in wages, this event marked the start of Butler's rise as a labour leader in the oilfields of southern Trinidad.

Butler, born on 21 January 1897 in Grenada, had enlisted in the West Indies Regiment at the age of 17 in the First World War. An immigrant to Trinidad in 1921, he had worked as a pipe fitter until forced to retire as an oil worker in 1929 because of an industrial accident that left him with a permanent limp. From 1931 he was the chief pastor of the Butlerite Moravian Baptist church, and he joined the TWA about the same time (Jacobs 1982: 32-5). Working as a preacher around Fyzabad, where there were many other Grenadian immigrants, Butler became increasingly politicised as he witnessed the problems of his flock. Always flamboyant, he succeeded in dramatising the grievances of the oil workers and made them a national issue. 'Combining rhetoric culled from socialist vocabulary, with biblical phrases and images, and appeals to African race consciousness, Butler by early June, 1937, had become the catalyst that was needed for industrial action in the oil districts' (Singh 1982: 61-2).

Links were established between Butler and the NWCSA. Percival worked with Butler during the 1935 strike at Apex and lost his job in the oilfields as a result. Butler stayed at the home of Percival and King when he visited Port of Spain. They were all increasingly critical of Cipriani who, as mayor of Port of Spain, sought to prevent the NWCSA from using Woodford Square for their meetings. At a May Day meeting in 1935, Francois criticised Cipriani, calling him 'Britain's best policeman in the colonies' (cited in Reddock 1988: 22), and the NWCSA won over many former members of the TWA/TLP with its more radical ideology and militant activities.

The NWCSA played a major role in agitation against the Italian invasion of Ethiopia and this became, in Trinidad as elsewhere, a key aspect of raising racial and political consciousness. Dockers refused to unload Italian ships and the owner of a Port of Spain store was forced to take down the sign for an Italian shipping line of which he was the agent (Brereton 1981: 174). The NWCSA organised protest meetings, and contributed articles, leaflets and letters to newspapers on the issue. They handed in a petition to the Italian consul after a large demonstration. The climax of these activities was a meeting on 10 October 1935, at which speakers denounced the UK for refusing to sell arms to Ethiopia, condemned 'Italian Fascist Imperialism', and 'criticised the prohibition of meetings and marches as a direct attack upon the political rights of the working class by a government incompetent to solve the unemployment crisis' (Reddock 1988: 19–20). In these ways the NWCSA linked local and international political issues, and the connection between human rights and oppressive systems at home and abroad. The NWCSA continued its agitation through 1936, with a Friends of Ethiopia meeting on 9 May and a mass meeting in Woodford Square on 29 May, at which Francois was the chief speaker (Reddock 1988: 21).

By this time the NWCSA had extended its activities all over northern Trinidad and it cooperated with Butler and his southern-based movement. In 1936 the NWCSA took up the question of the cost of living and created the Condensed Milk Association to criticise the price of this commodity and the importers' advertising, which encouraged women to buy expensive brands for their babies. They did research on the cost of living, nutrition, health services, pensions and school meals and discussed the issues with other labour activists, including the Clerks' Union, which was founded by the TLP in 1933 but not registered as a union, and the Amalgamated Building and Woodworkers' Union, which was the first organisation to register as a trade union, on 30 March 1936. They went together with Butler to speak to the governor, Sir Murchison Fletcher, on 8 November 1936, but before the NWCSA members, many of whom were women, could deliver their memorandum, Butler fell to his knees, kissed Fletcher's hand and begged for his assistance. Francois, like others, was angered by Butler's behaviour as she was the designated leader of the delegation and Barrette had stepped aside in favour of Butler in order to promote unity and broader representativeness (Reddock 1988: 24–5). Francois disagreed with Butler on the questions of loyalty to the British monarchy and empire, and the relation of religion to the political struggle. Despite such disagreements, however, the NWCSA continued to work with Butler.

Another issue espoused by the NWCSA that showed their concern for the everyday problems of working people was the Shop Hours (Closing and

Opening) Bill, introduced in June 1936. This bill was promoted by the larger merchants, represented by the Chamber of Commerce, to stop the small shop-keepers from opening for longer hours. The 1921 Shop Hours Ordinance gave a 45-hour week to many clerks and shop assistants by limiting opening hours to between 8 am and 4 pm on five days and 8 am and 1 pm on the sixth, but in 1929 small stores, defined as those in which one proprietor and not more than two other persons worked, were allowed to stay open from 7 am to 7 pm on weekdays and up to 8 pm on Saturdays. The NWCSA opposed the new bill on behalf of the small shopkeepers and their predominantly working–class customers. On 25 June 1936 some 600 people passed a resolution against the new bill at a meeting in Woodford Square, but in July Cipriani refused to al-low the NWCSA to hold another meeting there (Reddock 1988: 26-7).

The NWCSA's influence peaked in 1936. Though Governor Fletcher later testified that it was the NWCSA that first drew his attention to the poor people's condition, and the colonial secretary, Howard Nankivell, is said to have 'maintained clandestine relations' with them (Reddock 1988: 24), they were frequently harassed by the police. The leaders, like the people they were organising, were all 'miserably poor', according to Gomes, who said he served his 'political apprenticeship' with the NWCSA (Gomes 1974:161). They faced great hardship and even hunger, as well as insecurity and imprisonment. Though these dedicated working–class intellectuals of the NWCSA 'never had the mass appeal that Butler developed' (Reddock 1988: 27), their persistent work 'did much to prepare the way for the 1937 riots' (Brereton 1981: 174).

Another organisation that helped prepare the way was the TCL, founded in 1935 by Adrian Cola Rienzi, another former TWA/TLP activist who had become disillusioned with Cipriani. Rienzi, born in San Fernando in 1905, changed his name from Krishna Deonarine in 1929. He had been involved with the TWA since 1925 and, as president of the San Fernando branch, developed it into an active base for local organisation. Always to the left of Cipriani, Rienzi had gradually withdrawn from TWA activities as he became increasingly enthusiastic about Indian nationalism and world socialism. He was elected general secretary of the Indian National Party in Trinidad in 1928 and campaigned for a shelter for destitute and homeless Indians. At this time, even as such a young man, the governor considered him notoriously seditious and refused to acknowledge his petitions or receive any deputation from his party. He left to study law in Dublin in 1930. When in the UK between 1931 and 1934 he associated with socialist, anti-imperialist and Indian nationalist groups, and he remained under British surveillance. He returned to Trinidad in 1934 as a qualified lawyer but the attorney-general refused to allow him to practise at the bar because of his political views. Only after Sir Stafford Cripps, the eminent Labour Party politician, intervened with the Colonial

Office on his behalf was his petition to practise granted (Singh 1982: 11-16).

Rienzi started the TCL in December 1935 with Butler and Rojas. The TCL, several of whose core members were of working-class status, 'immediately addressed itself to the more pressing problems of oppressive working-class conditions, maladministration and financial corruption' and petitioned for an inquiry into 'the general state of the colony' (Singh 1982: 17). The TCL soon became a serious rival to the TLP in the south, but on 27 July 1936 Butler seized the initiative by launching his own political organisation, the British Empire Workers and Citizens Home Rule Party (BEWCHRP), declaring himself the 'Chief Servant'. Rienzi was temporarily outmanoeuvred by Butler, but his professional skills were important and Kelvin Singh argues that his 'role in the labour movement, especially in the crucial years 1937-40, was not only critical but perhaps indispensable for the establishment and survival of trade unionism in Trinidad' (Singh 1982: 11). Whereas Butler's loyalty to the UK, and his desire to see the rights of British citizens extended to the colonies, is reflected in the name of his party, Rienzi's TCL, though it did not last long, helped politicise people in terms of nationalism and self-government. The explosion of June 1937 cast Butler and Rienzi into new roles and a difficult relationship in the labour movement.

Francois, Butler, Rienzi and others played a part in politicising and organising working people in Trinidad for several years before the labour rebellion exploded, but the fundamental cause of the 1937 riots was not their agitation so much as the continuing deterioration of the conditions of the majority of people through the economic crisis. Masses of evidence, including that given to the Forster Commission in 1937 and the Moyne Commission in 1938-9, shows that, 'for the labouring population, mere subsistence was increasingly problematic' (Brereton 1981: 177). However, it was not the absolute misery of the working people alone that provoked the rebellion. There was also 'the presence of an oil industry whose advanced structure and profitability brought into high relief the contradictions between capital and labour' (Cross 1988: 287). The labour leaders succeeded in politicising these class contradictions in connection with frustration about racial oppression so as to heighten dissatisfaction and produce the 'peculiar vibrancy of Trinidad's experience in the 1930s' (Cross 1988: 287). It was the combination of all these factors that produced the great labour rebellion.

As the price of sugar collapsed in the depression, the small cane farmers in Trinidad could not get a profitable price for their cane at the factories, so pressure on wages and employment was felt by all the sugar workers, whether they worked for the small farmers or the larger estates. The lowest rates of daily wages in the sugar industry fell from 1 shilling and 8 pence in 1930 to 10 pence in 1933 and rose to only 1 shilling and 5   pence in 1936, with women receiving less. This was for a nine hour day, from 7 am to 5 pm with an hour for lunch, six days a week. Skilled estate workers at the top end of the scale earned around 3 shillings per day and worked a 54-hour week.[145] These wage rates would result in annual incomes of £23-47 only if the workers were employed through the year, but of course most were not. Consequently, most workers received an annual income of £20-30, and some considerably less. Ten workers, selected randomly at Orange Grove Estate, earned between them only £113 for a total of 1,218 man-days in the 1936-7 season, an average of 9 pence per day. The two who worked the longest, for 237 and 202 days, received annual incomes of less than £22 and £19, respectively, in a context where an annual income of £158 was estimated to be required for the minimum needs of a family of five.[146]

Workers in the oil industry fared somewhat better if only because this capital-intensive and highly profitable industry with a low wage bill could easily afford to pay its workers more. Although many sugar workers received only 35 cents per day and worked up to 54 hours a week, oil industry workers received 72 cents per day for a 48-hour week.[147] Nevertheless, prices were high in the oil belt and they rose by at least 11 per cent, and perhaps as much as 17 per cent, between 1935 and 1937 (Basdeo 1983: 149). Even discounting inflation, 'wages were never restored to pre-Depression levels' (Cross 1988: 289), when the companies had reduced their labour costs. Moreover, the rate of profit had risen rapidly for the oil companies in the 1930s, resulting in total dividends of 25-35 per cent to the British shareholders (Singh 1987: 58) and smugness among the company directors. The chairman of Apex Oilfields, the largest oil company, reported a total dividend for 1937 of 45 per cent (52.25 per cent of gross), after some £2 million had been written off in depreciation and amortisation. He said just six months after the labour riots, 'I have no doubt you will agree that there is good reason to be satisfied with the position disclosed in our balance sheet'.[148] An assessment of the profits being made in the oil industry in the 1930s concludes that five of the six leading companies, together accounting for some 90 per cent of output, enjoyed great prosperity, particularly after 1933, a conclusion that concurs substantially with that reached at the time by the trade union leaders and W. Arthur Lewis (Thomas 1987: 211). The workers' awareness of the high profits that coincided with their low wages, at a time when prices were rising but the taxes and royalties paid by the oil companies remained low, was a cause of intense resentment. As Brereton writes (1981: 179), 'The rising cost of living while wages were not adjusted, in an industry known to be prosperous, was the major grievance of the oil workers, who had no recognized machinery of collective bargaining to articulate their demands or discuss conditions.'

The oil workers, concentrated together in the oilfields, were more easily mobilised than agricultural workers, though the pay and conditions of the latter were even worse.

One of the most intensely felt grievances of the oil workers, that was especially conducive to their politicisation, was the result of racial discrimination and victimisation. The black workers were well aware of the visible inequalities in standards of living between the white managers and employees and themselves. They objected particularly to their treatment by some white South Africans employed by Trinidad Leaseholds. The black workers objected to the use of racial epithets and insulting modes of address, such as 'boy', and the companies' practice of giving preference in the forms of higher wages and promotions to whites who were no more and sometimes less qualified or experienced. They objected, too, to the notorious 'red books', the records of service that companies shared with each other, the problem of job insecurity, the arbitrary fines imposed by companies and the absence of compensation for injuries sustained at work. Workers were fined for being late or misplacing tools, and could be dismissed without any compensation after years of service and then blackballed by other companies. They received little or no compensation for overtime or work on Sundays or public holidays and no pensions or gratuities on retirement. They suffered from chronic insecurity and low status but white employees were favoured.[149] In the wake of the publicity and agitation over the Italian war in Ethiopia, the oil workers' growing racial consciousness coincided with class issues in a most compelling fashion.

The experience of the Apex Oilfields strike and march in 1935 was still fresh in many people's minds early in 1937 and Butler made sure it was not forgotten in the southern oilfields where he held public meetings, appealing to the workers' racial feelings as well as their labour grievances. From 1935 he was the oil workers' leader and his messianic style and biblical rhetoric caught fire in the oil belt, where many Grenadian and other small-island immigrants like himself were concentrated. In many ways, however, Butler was a traditional rather than revolutionary leader. Far from espousing the socialist and anti-imperialist ideas of Rienzi and the NWCSA, Butler said he was conducting 'a heroic struggle for British justice for British Blacks in a British country' (quoted in Brereton 1981: 180). Although his radical tactics may be seen as pushing the apparent promises of imperial ideology beyond the limits the imperialists were prepared to permit, he displayed a loyalty to the empire and its symbols of authority that inhibited any long-term goal or strategy of national liberation. Partly for this reason, he seems to have been unprepared in terms of how to respond to the labour rebellion and the massive use of force with which it was crushed, though he himself had done more than any other individual to provoke it. Singh writes, 'Butler

suffered the fatal weakness of popular agitators: he had no strategy for dealing with the crisis that would inevitably develop in the event of a popular
confrontation with the establishment' (Singh 1982: 18). In the crisis after 19
June Butler gained popular status as a martyred leader while he was in hiding and in jail, but it was Elbert Redvers Blades, Rienzi and the members of
the NWCSA who provided leadership, direction and organisation for the
emergence of trade unions.

In June 1937 it was the police, not Butler, who triggered the widespread
rioting and violence. Butler struggled to deal with the oil companies at a
time when there was no trade union and the government viewed him as an
irresponsible if not actually crazy agitator. When he turned to strike action,
however, 'he envisaged a peaceful sit-down strike; he cautioned against demonstrations, looting or violence' (Brereton 1981: 180) and against encouraging
strikes in other industries. The strike was planned to begin on 22 June but
when the oil workers learned that the companies and the police intended
to frustrate them they brought the date forward to 18 June. At midnight oil
workers sat down on their jobs at Trinidad Leaseholds, in Forest Reserve and
Fyzabad. This tactic of a peaceful sit-in or sit-down was quite new; it had
been used effectively by rubber workers in Akron, Ohio, and in the creation
of the United Automobile Workers' Union in Detroit in 1935 and 1936.[150] The
employers and government in Trinidad, like those in the United States, were
prepared to use force against this peaceful tactic.

The oil companies pressed for Butler's arrest and police were deployed in
the oilfields and reinforcements sent to San Fernando. A warrant was issued
in the afternoon of 19 June to arrest him on charges of using violent language
and inciting breaches of the peace. While he was addressing a meeting of
400-500 workers in Fyzabad at about 6 pm, the police tried to arrest him but
'the crowd exploded in anger, rushed the police and hustled Butler out of
their grasp' (Singh 1987: 62-3). In the confusion and violence that followed,
Corporal Charlie King was beaten, soaked with paraffin and burned to death.[151]
Even though the telephone lines between Fyzabad and San Fernando had
been cut, police reinforcements arrived. They were stoned and fired on, and
Sub-Inspector Bradburn was killed. The police were forced to retreat without
having captured Butler or having recovered King's body. By 8.55 pm, when
the governor was informed of the situation, it was decided to mobilise the
Trinidad Light Horse, a mechanised volunteer unit, and to send for naval
forces. The determination of the government and oil companies to crush
the strike and arrest Butler triggered further violence, which soon escalated
into an islandwide rebellion. Before long, as Brereton writes, 'The unrest cut
across race lines, and affected every sector of the economy' (Brereton 1981: 181).

An armed police platoon and a detachment of the Trinidad Light Horse entered Fyzabad on the morning of 20 June and recovered King's body. In making a house-to-house search for suspects and arms, they 'encountered no opposition' (Singh 1987: 63). Nevertheless, HMS Ajax was ordered to Trinidad and press censorship was introduced. Governor Fletcher and the inspector-general of constabulary visited the troubled areas to quiet the unrest. But Timothy Roodal, a local businessman and prominent politician, member of the TLP and a friend of Butler, addressed a crowd and unintentionally inflamed them. Though the disturbances had occurred so far only in the south, more detachments were deployed in an increasing show of force in the oilfields and also on sugar estates. On 21 June the strikes spread, with action in Fyzabad, Point Fortin, San Fernando, Penal and Ste Madeleine, and a second cruiser was requested. At Point Fortin workers blocked the road to prevent access to the refinery and in San Fernando a crowd roamed the business section, closing shops and holding up traffic. Meanwhile, a group set off for the sugar factory at Ste Madeleine where they stopped the cane trains, called the workers out of the fields and the factory, assaulted company managers and closed down the water supply and lighting plant. In response, the first and second battalions of the Trinidad Light Infantry Volunteers, an almost exclusively white force armed with machine guns, was mobilised. Some were sent to San Fernando, where rioters armed with axes, cutlasses, sticks and stones had cut telephone lines to the power station and driven out its staff. When they attacked the telephone exchange, the first battalion of the volunteers fired on them, killing two and wounding eight. Later, a police patrol was fired on in Penal and a volunteer was wounded.[152]

On 22 June the resistance spread to Port of Spain and to more sugar estates. Several hundred people, armed with sticks and agricultural implements, invaded the Waterloo Estate and closed it down. They moved on to Wyaby Estate, which was also stopped, and then Woodford Lodge Estate, where they tried to break through a police cordon to close the factory. The police opened fire, killing one man and wounding two. More trouble broke out that morning at Tabaquite and Rio Claro. At the latter, the strikers stopped work on adjacent estates and took over the railway station but the police repulsed them, killing five men and wounding 20 more.[153] In Port of Spain members of the NWCSA, who had planned but then postponed a mass meeting on 18 June, had been taken by surprise. Francois spent 20 June in Fyzabad, 'investigating everything', before returning to Port of Spain to urge her comrades into action (Reddock 1988: 29). A strike among workers on the new Treasury Building was supported by a group from the NWCSA. A crowd demonstrated in the city, closing down stores and calling out workers at the Trinidad Trading Company and Harbour Scheme Works. By 22 June, according to the Trinidad Guardian, 'All Stores [were] closed in Port of Spain', but a raid on a train sending arms to San Fernando was repulsed when the police opened fire on the demonstrators. The strikes spread to Belmont, St James and Woodbrook, and schools and shops were closed. The Port of Spain Gazette noted that Trinidad was experiencing a general strike the proportions of which were 'previously unknown in the history of labour agitation' in the colony.[154]

The general strike continued to gain momentum round the island, as workers went on strike on the Caroni sugar estate on 23 June, and on several estates near Arima (O'Meara, Carapo, Esperanza, La Reunion, San Raphael and Golden Grove). Workers at the government farm and experimental station at St Augustine went on strike, as well as workers on the Port of Spain waterfront. Strikes spread among the employees of the Port of Spain City Council and the Public Works Department, then at the Bamboo Paper Pulp factory in Champs Fleurs, at Trinidad Clay Products, at Aranguez Estates, San Juan, and Black Estate in Flanagin Town. Under the headline, 'Strike Moves Fast', the Guardian reported, 'Men, young and old, women and children brandishing sticks, cutlasses and other weapons walked from factory to factory in the district, inflicting workers with the strike fever'.[155] Bus drivers went on strike, and schools and post offices were closed. By 26 June the strikes had reached Mayaro on the east coast, affecting the Beaumont, St Anns and Lagoon Doux Estates. On 27 June bus drivers struck at Arima and Tunapuna, as well as workers at Caigual and Fishing Pond, and on the Non Pareil and St Lawrence Estates. Though there was no coordinating revolutionary leadership, this spontaneous series of actions had evolved into a prolonged general strike, combining mass demonstrations with a few sporadic armed confrontations.

Butler remained in hiding and the workers, without any effective co-ordination, lacked a clear sense of direction. On 20 June and 22 June Butler smuggled brief notes to Rienzi, asking him to defend him and his followers against the legal charges brought by the police (Singh 1982: 18). Rienzi soon found himself thrust into a more active role as the workers perceived him to be a sympathetic lawyer. A 'strike action committee' of oil workers wrote to him on 24 June asking him to visit Fyzabad, preferably with other independent observers, to witness the military occupation and intimidation occurring there. Cipriani still opposed the formation of unions and Butler was not in a situation to organise them, but Rienzi became drawn into a leadership role. 'It was in these circumstances that Rienzi now re-emerged to make his most decisive contribution to the labour movement ... when Cipriani and the TLP were expressing undisguised hostility. Rienzi moved to salvage the gains that could still be made for the workers out of a situation in which the sheer military superiority of the ruling class could easily lead to the restoration of the status quo ante.' (Singh 1982: 18-9) On 26 June Rienzi sought a meeting with the governor, but it was not until 30 June that the

Executive Council's mediation committee met him in San Fernando.

In the meantime, the arrival of HMS Ajax and HMS Exeter on 22 and 23 June, respectively, changed the balance of force in the government's favour. Altogether, some 2,200 officers and men were mobilised. Most of the officers were white and many were expatriates. Of the 21 police officers, 13 were from England and two from Ireland and the 933 constables were predominantly black (Basdeo 1983: 150). The marines and sailors not only bolstered the tiring local forces but they also helped restore the confidence of the ruling class and intimidated many workers. The governor, who had a double policy of conciliation and repression (Brereton 1981: 183), announced on 24 June that he would seek a settlement 'which will be fair to employers and employees alike', while he deployed more troops and persistently sought to arrest Butler. A state of emergency was declared on 26 June,[156] and a committee of the Executive Council, including the colonial secretary, Howard Nankivell, was appointed to hear the workers' grievances and seek reconciliation between them and their employers. Given the importance of the oil industry to the empire and the danger of an expanding general strike, it was important 'for both the state and the capitalists ... to get the workers to return to work as quickly as possible' (Craig 1988: 28). Fletcher knew that it would be hard to arrest Butler, who was believed to have an armed escort of between 80 and 100 men with him at all times, so he sought to regain the initiative from the strikers by making offers to government workers and encouraging the oil companies to make similar offers to their workers. On 28 June when several NWCSA leaders, including Francois, Barrette and Percival, were arrested and held in jail, Fletcher complained, 'The Government's efforts to negotiate a settlement are seriously impeded by the lack of trade union or recognized leader of the oil workers and by the fact that the oil company managements are in London, out of touch with the local situation, with the result that prompt decisions which are so imperative cannot be taken.' (quoted in Craig 1988: 29)

The problem, of course, was partly of Fletcher's own making, as he refused to recognise or deal with the workers' leaders and preferred to jail them. He proposed to offer new wage rates to government workers, since he believed that the wages of unskilled labour were too low throughout the colony. Government workers' wages were to be increased to 72 cents per day for men and 60 cents for women in Port of Spain, and 60 cents for men and 36 cents for women outside the city, with the working week reduced from 54 to 45 hours. Fletcher's double policy was a way to enhance the paternalistic role of the state, by granting limited wage concessions while jailing the workers' leaders, but in so doing it unavoidably made the colonial administration more clearly political.

Butler, who was still in hiding, wrote to Rienzi on 1 July, saying he found himself in the position of not being able to call off the strike which had caused so much hurt to the colony and its inhabitants as a whole. 'The workers, I am told, are in the main prepared to put up a "last-ditch" fight to secure at least a general all-round increase in their wages as a prerequisite to going back to work . . . . I respectfully beg that you communicate this information to His Excellency the Governor.' (quoted in Craig 1988: 31) Governor Fletcher, who may have seen this as a confession of weakness, pressed his two-pronged policy. On the one hand, he reported on 2 July, 'With the cordial agreement of the Legislative Council, I have taken the opportunity of this unrest to fix a minimum wage only a fraction higher than that of pre-depression', while refusing to agree to a claim for a 25 per cent increase by the dock workers or to bargain with 'known agitators.' On the other hand, and on the very same day, three platoons were deployed throughout Fyzabad, the centre of the militancy, to 'comb out' the troublemakers, as they put it. Beginning at 6 am, the troops and police searched houses, seized arms and arrested 22 people, three of whom had been on the list of ten men Butler had nominated as workers' negotiators. Three more communities were combed out in dawn operations on 4 July and, though a few rigmen remained on strike at Forest Reserve and Fyzabad until 8 July, the strike was essentially broken. The Trinidad Guardian, 'organ of capitalist interests in the colony' (Singh 1982: 19), triumphantly exclaimed on 6 July, 'The strikes are now dead; only their ghosts remain to be buried'. The use of the press and press censorship had contributed to breaking the strike and rebellion, often by deliberately spreading lies and confusion. In an effort by the press to turn other poor people against them, the dock workers, one of the most militant sections, were accused of trying to raise food prices and starve the colony (Craig 1988: 32). In an attempt to counter this kind of propaganda, the NWCSA created a Workers' Defence Organisation consisting of three groups, the Defence Fund Committee, the Propaganda Committee and the Public Communication Committee. The last organised small groups of activists who travelled at night through the island, speaking unannounced in towns and villages in order to avoid the police (Rennie 1973: 96-100). Despite their efforts, most workers were prevented from having accurate information about the strikes and the actions of the armed forces.

The strike may have been broken, but when HMS Exeter left on 5 July, only government workers and dock workers had actually negotiated terms of work and all others were left with only offers and promises. That 'the situation remained explosive' (Craig 1988: 33) is suggested by the fact that the senior police officers wanted a warship stationed in the Gulf of Paria, to be available if required. Many people remained active. The NWCSA members, Percival,

Barrette, Caesar Ashby, and Francois, were eventually acquitted and they continued to organise meetings to collect defence funds and protest against the prosecution of strikers. Along with members of Butler's BEWCHRP they formed a Workers' Defence Committee and held meetings in Fyzabad, Point Fortin, Siparia and elsewhere. Butler himself, meanwhile, was not caught, which is a reflection of the loyalty of his supporters. He was arrested on 27 September 1937, when he came out of hiding to give evidence to the Labour Disturbances Commission.

On 9 July Fletcher and Nankivell spoke to the Legislative Council, castigating the oil and sugar companies for paying starvation wages, oppressing labour and repatriating profits. On the one hand, Craig suggests this was a tactic to 'play for popular support', mere rhetoric aiming 'to appease with words while repressing with deeds' (Craig 1988: 34), but there is reason to believe that they were sincere, as they wrote in similar fashion in confidential despatches to the Colonial Office. Their speeches were not merely a public posture but arose from their conviction that the low wages and general poverty were largely to blame for the widespread unrest. On the other hand, this did not make them 'champions of the working class', as Brereton, Ryan and Sahadeo Basdeo claim,[157] although the infuriated business community saw them that way. Fletcher cabled the secretary of state for the colonies, William Ormsby-Gore on 28 June, saying he was 'satisfied that the oilfield workers have legitimate grievances' and that 'the wages of unskilled labour throughout the Colony are admittedly too low'.[158] He reported on 5 July 1937: 'The roots of this colony-wide unrest go very deep. Labour has lived in conditions of extreme poverty and squalor, and the colour line has kept employer and employed at a long arm's length apart'.[159]

Fletcher acknowledged to the Legislative Council that the government shared the blame for not implementing a minimum wage and pressed the employers to make concessions in the interests of peace. He warned, 'I am certain that the white employer class in Trinidad will find in tact and sympathy a shield far more sure than any forest of bayonets to be planted here'.[160] At the same time, of course, he showed that he was willing to use bayonets and he dismissed Butler as a misguided agitator.

Nankivell, the Jamaican-born colonial secretary who was working on the council's mediation committee, was even more outspoken. Recalling that the Wages Advisory Board had received data the previous year about the workers' conditions and grievances, he pointed out that the cost of living had continued to rise and government revenues had increased while industry prospered and the workers' situation had clearly deteriorated. 'In the past' reproached Nankivell, 'we have had to salve our consciences with humbug and we have had to satisfy labour with platitudes. Those days have gone by'. He accused employers of treating 'the human element' worse than their machinery, of keeping people employed 'in conditions of economic slavery', and of branding workers as communist agitators as soon as they expressed their grievances. He went so far as to say that 'an industry has no right to pay dividends at all until it pays a fair wage to labour and gives the labourer decent conditions'. He concluded that it would be 'entirely in the interests of the colony' if the profits of the oil industry were transferred from the pockets of British shareholders to those of the workers, thereby stimulating consumption in Trinidad among 'our own people'.[161]

Rather than characterising these colonial officials as either champions of the working class or deceitful hypocrites, they are best understood as genuine liberals, exemplifying the contradictions of liberalism in a polarising situation. As the two senior representatives of British colonialism in Trinidad, they did take their 'trusteeship role seriously' (Ryan 1972: 55), but that meant that they would ruthlessly suppress disorder at the same time as seeking to reform the situation that they understood to have given rise to it. The difference between the views of the capitalists and the colonial officials is that, whereas the former were selfishly interested in their own particular profits, the latter had to be concerned about maintaining the general industrial peace and the social order as a whole. The rage of the capitalists, in Trinidad and the UK, over what they perceived to be the intemperate speeches of these officials, does not support the view that Fletcher and Nankivell set out to appease the workers for their benefit. These capitalists obstructed the mediation efforts, refused to make any substantial concessions to the workers and petitioned the Colonial Office to suspend the mediation committee. The Duke of Montrose, chairman of a Trinidad oil company, opined in the House of Lords that 'the trouble had nothing to do with wages and living costs, but was purely the result of communistic propaganda - the work of Communists who had been touring the islands stirring up racial conflict and urging the natives to grab all the wealth'. This was absurd. The chairman of Caroni Ltd was equally intemperate, claiming that the disturbances were 'an attempt at revolution by a minority of extremists. There was no question of unemployment, underpay, or undernourishment' (quoted in Brereton 1981: 182). These men, who sounded rather like slave-owners who claimed that their contented slaves were only led to rebellion by outsiders, wanted an overwhelming show of force and protection for their colonial properties without any diminution of their profits. Singh correctly concludes that 'both Fletcher and Nankivell, while not wishing for any fundamental re-ordering of worker-management relations, nevertheless took a far more humane view of the plight of workers in Trinidad than did the representatives of corporate management' (Singh 1987: 67). Whether or not their view was more humane, however, as the chief colonial officials on the spot they were responsible for suppressing the labour rebellion, and they did just that. By the time the combined armed forces had crushed the resistance, 14 people had been killed (two of them policemen), 59 wounded and hundreds arrested.

A commission of inquiry into the disturbances, chaired by John Forster, began its work on 6 September. Although the representatives of capital, who maintained an unrelenting lobby on the commissioners,[162] welcomed the report for supporting their contention that government had failed to promptly suppress the disorders at the outset, the commission was outspoken about the appalling conditions that working people suffered in Trinidad. The report stated that the condition of most agricultural workers 'justifies the view that many managements display a surprising indifference to the welfare of their labour', and that housing was very poor also in the oil belt and in Port of Spain. Fyzabad, they wrote, was 'a village which has grown up on the edge of the oilfields without any apparent regulation or control or observance of elementary rules as to structure, space, or sanitation', and they saw barracks in the capital that were 'indescribable in their lack of elementary needs of decency', yet charged rents at 12-15 shillings per month (Brereton 1981: 177-8). Although the commission agreed with Fletcher that low wages and poor working conditions had been the basic cause of unrest, it made no recommendations about these issues.

The commission did recommend the creation of a labour department and the appointment of a labour officer to act as a mediator and arbitrator between employees and employers, the establishment of an industrial court, and that the workers' compensation law should henceforth include agricultural labourers. To encourage industrial peace, the commission supported the development of trade unions, while saying that government should have the power to refuse recognition to unions whenever they viewed their leaders as unsatisfactory. The report rejected Cipriani's suggestion that a large measure of self-government was desirable. Most shockingly, the commissioners criticised the police for hesitating to fire on the crowd in Fyzabad on the evening of 19 June. The representatives of capital welcomed these conclusions when the Forster Report was published in February 1938, calling it a 'Law and Order Report'.[163]

Fletcher was forced to resign even before the Forster Report was published. As the winds began to turn, Fletcher had abandoned Nankivell, informing Ormsby-Gore that he 'has shown a bias towards labour',[164] and he called for more troops and riot control equipment in October. Imperial troops arrived in Trinidad in mid-November, but the business community remained opposed to him. Fletcher had strengthened the sedition laws and sought to restrain public meetings and public speakers. The Summary Jurisdiction Ordinance

(1937) made it illegal for more than ten persons to assemble in public. Fletcher's liberalism had crumbled under pressure, and he felt 'impelled to the conclusion that a small permanent garrison is inevitable', as the balance between capital and labour was fraught with difficulty and risk.[165] On 10 November, the day after Forster had returned to England and reported to Ormsby-Gore, Fletcher was recalled to London. He was forced to resign, supposedly on the grounds of ill health, in December 1937. The Colonial Office had concluded that he lacked 'independent capacity of decision, stability of character and constancy of purpose',[166] and that the 'possibility of achieving the desired industrial peace in Trinidad was endangered by Fletcher's erratic behaviour' (Johnson 1975: 44). Basdeo concludes that Fletcher's recall 'was a warning to labour in Trinidad that capital had still not lost its traditional allies in Downing Street. The dismissal of Fletcher was the work of the Colonial Office at its worst' (Basdeo 1983: 168). Fletcher was replaced by Sir Hubert Young, a choice that was believed to have been influenced by the absentee interests in London because he had crushed a strike in the copper mines in Northern Rhodesia in 1935 (Ryan 1972: 60).[167]

Malcolm Cross, referring to the manoeuvring by the capitalists against the colonial officials, concludes that 'the rift within the ruling elite of Trinidad galvanised support for class-based movements' (Cross 1988: 293). This support had been building for some time before the rift appeared, as we have shown, but it is probable that the awareness of these divisions encouraged the labour organisers. Certainly, the speed and effectiveness with which trade unions were organised in the months after the labour rebellion is astonishing.

The Oilfield Workers' Trade Union (OWTU), in particular, was formed extraordinarily quickly in July 1937, in the immediate wake of the labour rebellion. According to the union's official history, some informal and even clandestine meetings took place in Fyzabad in mid-July, before the more formal conference, at which representatives from most of the oilfields attended, that launched the union on 25 July.[168] The speed with which the OWTU was formed was possible because it was based on an extant organisation of workers that had been started two years earlier. According to a memorandum by Redvers Blades, the first general secretary of the OWTU, a small group of workers got together at Forest Reserve, Fyzabad, around the middle of 1935, to form a 'sort of cooperative movement whereby they could buy and sell to and from themselves'.[169] Their efforts were prompted by the fact that the cost of living was rising while their wages remained the same. The cost of food in the oil districts was exceptionally high, so some people even found it more economical to shop every two weeks or so in Port of Spain, over 50 miles away. Some workers approached the manager of Trinidad Leaseholds and asked him to use his influence to get the company to open a commissary for the workers, similar to one that supplied the staff with goods more cheaply than the workers could purchase them outside, but he replied that it was not the company's policy to make such a provision. In 1936, after this rebuff, a committee of the workers organised meetings in several oil districts and organised local subcommittees, each with a chairman and secretary, in order to start a business of their own. The organisation was called the United Workers Trading Association (UWTA). Blades, who was elected secretary of the main committee at Fyzabad, travelled frequently to different districts, 'making new contacts and setting up new groups'. This association was about to be registered in 1937, but 'the strike broke out and all activities ceased'.

When the mediation committee was formed during the strike, Blades, who was employed as a mechanic by Trinidad Leaseholds, was elected by his co-workers to represent the garage and transport departments, and to state their grievances. Later he spoke with Governor Fletcher, who urged him to 'tell the workers to form a Trade Union, and make it strong and powerfull [sic]'. Blades promptly addressed the workers and called for a meeting two days later. At that meeting he was elected provisional secretary and given the task of organising a meeting with representatives from other oilfields. The next day, he had some handbills printed which he circulated around the district committees of the UWTA, inviting its members to attend 'a monster meeting' in San Fernando on 25 July in order to formally create the OWTU. The UWTA members 'devoted all of their time to the formation of the Union', so the meeting was well attended and 'a great success'. Blades wrote in his memorandum that he asked Rienzi for some legal advice and also invited him to the meeting. 'He said if I gave him a written invitation he would attend. I wrote one in his office and handed it to him . . . . Mr. Rienzi attended and after giving a brilliant speech was elected President while I was confirmed in the post of Provisional Secretary'.

Blades' memorandum not only suggests that the invitation to Rienzi was an afterthought, and that Rienzi's speech was the immediate cause of his election as the first OWTU president, but also that the union was created and grew so rapidly because of the work of the district groups of the UWTA. Many leaders of the UWTA groups 'became union organisers and some became officers'. In addition to Blades himself, Alexander McNish, chairman of the UWTA and Frederick White, secretary of the Guapo branch of the UWTA, became president and secretary of the Cochrane Branch of the OWTU; Bertie Aberdeen, chairman of the Parrylands group of the UWTA became president of the Parrylands Branch of the union; and James Hall (or Halls), who represented a Fyzabad group of the UWTA, became a treasurer and trustee of the union.

When the UWTA was registered as a limited liability company in November 1938, with 48,000 shares selling at $1 each, about 97 per cent of its shareholders were members of the OWTU. A year later, when the company had sold about 16,000 shares, it opened a grocery, called the United Workers' Grocery, which 'was well patronised by the workers'. It is not clear whether the formation of the UWTA had anything to do with the hunger marches and demonstrations of 1934-5, but it was responding to the same issues. It is clear, however, that the OWTU sprang into being so swiftly in July 1937 because it was based on this already extant workers' organisation, and that Blades was the central organiser of both. The UWTA folded in 1940 and Blades was forced to resign his position in the OWTU in 1941, but they had played an important role in the early formation of Trinidad's greatest union.[170]

By the end of 1937 six unions had been registered: the Amalgamated Building and Woodworkers' Union (ABWU), already established in 1936; the Federated Workers' Trade Union (FWTU), registered on 27 August 1937; the OWTU, formed in July and registered on 15 September; the Seamen and Waterfront Workers' Trade Union (SWWTU), registered on 19 November; the All Trinidad Sugar Estates and Factory Workers' Trade Union (ATSEFWTU), registered on 24 November; and the Public Works and Public Service Workers' Union (PWPSWU), registered on 26 November (Ramdin 1982: 143). Three of these unions, the ABWU, SWWTU and PWPSWU, were based in Port of Spain and oriented towards the urban workers there, but the other three, which were led by Rienzi, were chiefly in the south.

While Butler was still in hiding, Rienzi, acting as his agent, met with Nankivell and the mediation committee and insisted that they recognise and meet the OWTU executive. The employers' union, the Petroleum Association, was determined to prevent the workers' unionisation, however, and manoeuvred to get the mediation committee suspended. Rienzi and a group of labour leaders, including Rojas, MacDonald Moses, Blades and Ralph Mentor, persisted in their unionisation drive and held meetings with oil and sugar workers. Rienzi became the president-general of both the OWTU and the ATSEFWTU in the south. The FWTU, which he served in an advisory capacity, organised railway and construction workers. Payne of the NWCSA, who had played a prominent role in the Barbados labour rebellion between his arrival there on 26 March 1937 and his deportation on 26 July, was a founding member and organiser of the FWTU. During the last months of 1937, Sir Arthur Pugh, a member of the Forster Commission and general secretary of the Iron and Steel Trades Confederation, addressed several union meetings, advising the organisers of unions to register under the 1932 Trade Union Ordinance (Basdeo 1983: 163). Undoubtedly, the rapid rise of trade unionism was the most important result of the labour rebellion and Rienzi played a leading role in the process, creating and consolidating organisations in the vanguard sectors of oil and sugar.

Although Butler was the more charismatic labour leader and was widely seen as a heroic figure, Rienzi was the more competent builder of lasting organisations. The problem of their compatibility arose in 1939. Rienzi had to work carefully because he was categorised as a communist by the authorities. On 20 July 1937 his home was raided, ostensibly in a search for arms but clearly in order to intimidate him, and he was under continual police surveillance (Singh 1982: 20). Despite the limitations of the 1932 ordinance, Rienzi thought that the registration of unions would 'strengthen the hands of a sympathetic government'.[171] and, in turn, recognition by that government would help the workers in their struggles with the oil and sugar companies. Registration and official recognition of the new unions did not lead the employers to recognise them at once, however. Rienzi and other union leaders gave evidence before the Forster Commission on behalf of the workers and this reinforced their standing. Rienzi's prestige among the oil and sugar workers rose and he won the support of The People, an influential labour-oriented paper edited by L.F. Walcott, who called Rienzi the 'idol of the South' and urged unity between Africans and Indians (Singh 1982: 22-3). The paper reported that Rienzi had told workers in San Fernando in September 1937 that Indian and African Trinidadians should unite as theirs was a class struggle in which the standard of living of each could best be promoted by mutual support. In January 1938 there was a joint demonstration of oil and sugar workers in San Fernando, and the line of marchers, many in uniform, extended for over a mile and a half.[172] Cipriani's support was on the wane, but Rienzi attracted sufficient middle-class support to be elected to the San Fernando Borough Council in late 1937 and then to the Legislative Council in early 1938, becoming representative of Victoria by 2,003 votes to 547. According to The People, the workers saw Rienzi as giving trade unionism a voice in the Legislative Council, as a 'tribune of the people', replacing Cipriani in this role.[173]

The governor and the Colonial Office recognised that if the trade unions developed under what they considered to be responsible leadership, it could help prevent further disorders, but the employers still opposed unionisation. The conviction that properly guided trade unions, avoiding extremists and extremism, would contribute to the industrial peace became part of a general shift in policy throughout the British West Indies in order to protect British property from further labour rebellions, but it was seen as particularly important in Trinidad because of the strategic role of the oil industry in the empire. In November 1937, as the possibility of war loomed larger, the British oil board produced a memorandum at Ormsby-Gore's request, stating that the maintenance of supplies from Trinidad, which was responsible for almost 40 per cent of the empire's production, was of 'paramount importance'. Consequently, it was deemed 'essential that all possible defence precautions should be taken to safeguard the refineries and oil shipping facilities' (Johnson 1975: 44), including maintaining peaceful labour relations. The oil companies still seemed to prefer to rely on force and intimidation, however, even though such an approach might have risked retaliatory sabotage. The employers considered Rienzi to be a dangerous communist, 'resisted the unions in every way possible, and the early organizers faced relentless victimization and persecution' (Brereton 1981: 186). Even local government officials and the police do not seem to have got the message from the Colonial Office, as they still treated trade unionism as seditious, scrutinised and harassed union organisers and often prohibited labour demonstrations. A British writer who visited Trinidad in 1938 described how the OWTU leaders were constantly shadowed by police spies and pointed out how absurd this was when the government's policy was to encourage trade unionism: 'Government can't expect to get it both ways. If they want to see trade unions established and their Industrial Advisor accepted without suspicion, they must stop shadowing the worker's leaders with a vigilance that they show towards no common criminal.' (Calder-Marshall 1939: 236)

In early March 1938, Rienzi, faced with this continuing police harassment and the employers' intransigence, urged both the oil and sugar workers to organise strike committees in case they should be needed. He made it clear that he preferred to reach a negotiated settlement through peaceful collective bargaining and advised against any violence or confrontation with police that might provoke further repression and endanger the young trade union movement, but he wanted to be ready for a strike.[174] Faced with this organised militancy, the Petroleum Association of Trinidad at last agreed to engage in direct negotiations with the OWTU, so the union won effective recognition. However, in the negotiations, chaired by the new labour officer, A.G.V. Lindon, a British official from the Ministry of Labour, the oil workers gained very little. Since June 1937 they had been demanding a general wage increase of 6 cents per hour, time and a half for overtime beyond a standard 8-hour day and double pay for work on Sundays and public holidays, as well as 2 weeks of annual vacation with pay and other minor concessions in their working conditions. But the employers conceded only an upgrading of the hourly rate to the minimum of 9 cents per hour, the rate that Public Works Department employees received from the government in Port of Spain, which would have benefited few oil workers, and time and a half for all overtime work, including that on Sundays and public holidays (Singh 1982: 24).

The OWTU executive, faced with a deadlock, agreed to accept Lindon's proposal to refer the dispute to an arbitration tribunal, under the terms of the recently enacted Trade Disputes (Arbitration and Inquiry) Ordinance of

1938, a law which Rienzi had helped to draft. Strategically, 'the acceptance of arbitration by the Petroleum Association represented a further gain in the struggle to legitimise the union' (Singh 1982: 25). Given the fact that the OWTU was still organising and had few resources, resorting to a strike at that stage might well have provoked further exercise of the state's armed forces and endangered the still weak trade union movement as a whole. When the award was finally made, on 21 January 1939, it provided for a wage increase of only 1 cent per hour retrospective from 1 February 1938 and an additional 1 cent an hour from 1 February 1939, along with one week's annual vacation with full pay for workers who had completed a year of continuous service.[175] The oil workers reacted to this with 'considerable dissatisfaction' but Rienzi pointed out that this, the first instance in which arbitration procedure had given an award to labour in the West Indies, further established the legitimacy of trade unions. He urged the OWTU to continue its membership drive so they would be able 'to exert the right degree of pressure at the right moment'.[176]

The sugar workers, meanwhile, faced with a similarly intransigent attitude by their employers in the Sugar Manufacturers' Association (SMA), had tried to use the strike weapon, but without success. In February 1938 the acting governor reported that there was an 'undercurrent of unrest among labour on sugar estates'. Some 'sporadic strikes of a minor character' had been settled without difficulty, with the Usine Ste Madeleine experiencing more strikes than other estates. The union asked for an all-round increase of 50 per cent in wage rates, but the SMA would not negotiate. 'The leaders of the Union appear to favour the calling of strikes in specified areas only rather than a general strike', because of lack of funds and, presumably, because they were better organised in some places than others. However, 'the demand for a general strike by a substantial number of the members of the Union remains insistent' and the union leaders, though opposed to such action, would give their support 'in the event of their hands being forced by the members . . . . While there has been some improvement in relations between labourers and employers in recent months, distrust still prevails'.[177]

The sugar workers, led by those at Ste Madeleine, tried to force the situation by going on strike. They demanded an all-round increase of 10 cents per day for field workers and 15-20 cents for factory workers. In early April 1938 Rienzi had been ready to seek arbitration but when the workers struck, the ATSEFWTU executive felt obliged to concur with the action in order to retain its legitimacy among its militant members. The union could not financially support the strike, however, and it collapsed in 16 days, leaving the SMA in the position of being able to refuse any renewed effort to have the dispute settled by arbitration. The fact that the SMA did not agree to a negotiated settlement with the union until 1945 suggests that Rienzi's tactic with the OWTU and the Petroleum Association had been the right one in the circumstances (Brereton 1981: 187).

The Colonial Office and the British TUC, and especially Sir Walter Citrine, encouraged Trinidadian unionists 'to model their unions on "sound", constitutional, British lines . . . to avoid politics or extremism and to work closely with the industrial advisor and the local government' (Brereton 1981: 188). Lindon, who had arrived in Trinidad in March 1938, helped arbitrate disputes and encouraged peaceful collective bargaining. Major G. St J. Orde Brown, labour adviser to the Colonial Office, credited him with the fact that trade unionism was more advanced along British lines in Trinidad in 1939 than in any other colony. However, Calder-Marshall, who interviewed Lindon, wrote that he 'tried to represent himself as the instructor of the ignorant trade unionists, too young in trade union experience to know what they wanted or how to get it', and that the union leaders did not trust him because the kind of trade unionism he wanted to see in Trinidad was based on 'the co-operation of Labour with Capital in the interests of Capital' (Calder-Marshall 1939: 202, 204). Clearly, credit for the rapid development of trade unionism in Trinidad should lie, not with Lindon or any other colonial official, but with the militant workers and their skilful and determined leaders, even when they decided tactically to work with Lindon in order to deal with recalcitrant employers.

While Rienzi was preoccupied with union developments in the south, in the oil and sugar sectors, the trade union movement was also emerging in the north where his role was minimal. Many labour organisers were persecuted. In October 1937 several NWCSA leaders were again arrested and tried, this time for distributing allegedly seditious literature in the oil belt in September, specifically pamphlets that called for Butler's release and an end to plans to deport militant workers. Percival, who had earlier been convicted for disorderly behaviour and using violent language, was convicted again in October and put on $100 bond for good behaviour for a year. Barrette was convicted and given a four-month suspended sentence, although he later won an appeal. The NWCSA people were linking local labour and human rights issues with British colonialism and international imperialism, so the government gave them its special attention. In February Percival and Francois, along with Darlington Marshall, who was not a member of the NWCSA, were tried for 'uttering words having a seditious intention'. Francois and Percival had spoken at a public meeting of about 150 persons on 13 October, the purpose of which was to get Butler released. According to the police informant, Francois had said that Barrette and Percival had been tried on 'framed up charges of Colonial Imperialism to strike terrorism into the hearts of the Negro and East Indian workers. The more prosecutions, the more jail sentences, the more ill-treatment of the workers by the police is the more hatred the workers will have for a British Colonial Imperialism. In the West Indies, the moment you say strike you get jail sentences because you are Negro and East Indian workers.... In Trinidad when the workers ask for bread they get bullets and jail-sentences'.[178]

Francois defended herself aggressively, saying that the subject of her speech that night was 'World Imperialism and the Colonial Toilers' and her intent was to link up world and local conditions, referring to Kenya, Nigeria, Germany and Russia, as well as the homeless, poverty-stricken workers of Trinidad. When asked by the court to define 'world imperialism', she 'described the relationship between the ruling classes of the world and the exploited workers of the colonies'. Asked why she persisted in 'causing disaffection', she boldly replied, 'I don't know that my speeches create disaffection, I know that my speeches create a fire in the minds of the people so as to change the conditions which now exist'.(quoted in Rennie 173: 112) The jury found her not guilty and she was discharged, but Barrette was convicted and imprisoned for nine months. Francois, far from being intimidated, continued to organise the struggle against the Shop Hours Bill, along with Payne, Percival and other NWCSA members, at the same time seeking defence funds for Barrette's appeal.

The northern trade unions were formed in the tense atmosphere created by harassment and the sedition trials. Although the main focus of the NWCSA was not on unionisation, several members, including Payne, Mahon, Gaskynd Granger and Christopher Harper, did work with the unions and as workers themselves they shared the unionists' struggles. Barrette was the first president of the SWWTU in 1937, and Payne and other NWCSA members were active in the formation of the FWTU. Gittens, along with Quintin O'Connor and Gomes, were leaders of the Trinidad and Tobago Union of Shop Assistants and Clerks (TTUSAC), registered on 30 August 1938. Granger was an organiser and acting treasurer of the PWPSWTU. When the May Day United Front Committee was formed in 1938, therefore, it included members of the NWCSA, the PWPSWU, FWTU and SWWTU. A resolution by the Workers' Defence Committee on May Day 1938 stated, 'We realise the burning need for the 8-hour day, 44-hour week in every Industry and undertaking in the Colony', with an increase in pay, first-aid kits in all working places, and seats for women.[179] At a meeting in the SWWTU Hall in Port of Spain to celebrate Butler's Day, the first anniversary of 19 June 1937, representatives of these unions were joined by NWCSA speakers Francois, Payne and Percival, among others. Francois was reported to have 'delivered a most interesting address, giving a thrilling experience of her activities in South Trinidad during the strike and the disturbances that followed'.[180] On 9 October 1938 the NWCSA joined members of the Chinese community of Trinidad in a demonstration in solidarity with the people of China in their struggle against the Japanese invasion and when a boat of refugees from the Spanish civil war landed in Trinidad the NWCSA mobilised to welcome them as fellow socialists with food and clothes (Rennie 1973: 124-6). We can see how, in the course of trade union formation, a new and radical political culture was shaping the labour movement, in northern as well as central and southern Trinidad.[181]

By the end of 1938 ten unions had been registered in Trinidad and Tobago. In addition to those already mentioned, there were: the All Trinidad Transport and General Workers' Trade Union (ATTGWTU), organised by Rojas with Rienzi's assistance and registered on 8 June 1938; the Railway Workers' Trade Union (RWTU), registered on 25 July; and the Printers' Industrial Trade Union (PITU), registered on 11 October. Three more were registered the next year: the Civil Service Association (CSA) on 23 March 1939; the Tobago Industrial Trade Union (TITU), on 3 September; and the Tailors' Industrial Union (TIU) on 10 October. There was more strike activity by workers seeking better wages and working conditions.

In July 1939 Payne, writing as the secretary of the Workers' United Front Committee to Arthur Creech-Jones, referred to a strike by women in the garment industry who demanded 'living wages' and 'better working conditions'.[182] This strike began at the Renown shirt factory on 20 June 1939 after negotiations between the owner and the TTUSAC broke down. There were at this date four small garment factories, each employing 50-100 workers, predominantly women (Reddock 1993: 253). After a week, workers in the other factories came out in a sympathy strike and the union declared they were 'determined to hold out to the bitter end'.[183] The industrial adviser's efforts at conciliation failed and by 8 July other trade unions pledged assistance and supported a boycott of all stores displaying Renown-made garments. Despite the employers' attempts to break the strike, by using strike-breakers protected by the police, the women won. They gained a 12 per cent wage increase, an eight hour day, two weeks' annual holiday after one year, protective clothing for pressers and a system of shop-floor representation. O'Connor, who lost his job as a hardware clerk for having been on the picket line, merged the TTUSAC with the FWTU, which subsequently represented the majority of garment workers. As Rhoda Reddock points out (1993: 255), the reports of this strike name several of the men who supported it, but none of the women who were at the heart of the struggle.

The rapid proliferation of union organisations in Trinidad between 1937 and 1939 was unique in the British Caribbean. In order to develop some coordination in the labour movement, Rienzi established a Committee of Industrial Organisation (CIO) in March 1938, and the ATTGWTU was intended to be a general union that would help link the northern and southern workers in different industries (Ramdin 1982: 144). The CIO was precursor to the Trinidad and Tobago Trades Union Council (TTTUC) which was formed in March 1939 on Citrine's advice and modelled on the British TUC (Nicholson 1986: 234). Rienzi, who had presided over the public meeting at which Citrine urged the establishment of the TTTUC, became its first elected president (Singh 1982: 28). In July 1938 Rienzi and Mentor represented the OWTU at the Second Guianese and West Indian Labour Conference in British Guiana where they supported the efforts towards regional labour organisation and the improvement of conditions of the West Indian working class in general (Basdeo 1983: 183-5). In 1939 Gittens, who had been corresponding with the British TUC, received one of the two scholarships it awarded to enable West Indian trade unionists to study at Ruskin College, Oxford (Ramdin 1982: 145). At the same time that some labour leaders were being harassed and imprisoned, therefore, others were achieving new prestige or were being chosen by the British TUC, working in close association with the Colonial Office, for training in responsibility.

On 6 May 1939 Butler was released from prison and greeted with spontaneous mass demonstrations. That Butler saw himself as the messianic leader of Trinidad is illustrated by the manifesto he issued on 8 May: 'To win out in the struggle, we must maintain the June [1937] leadership at all cost. The Holy Spirit of our Infallible Leadership so clearly and definitely manifested in June must be obeyed and maintained. That is easily done by following the example of your servant, Butler'.(quoted in Singh 1982: 28)

Although Butler acknowledged the contributions made by Rienzi in forming the OWTU, he did so in such a way as to leave no doubt that he saw himself, and expected to be seen, as the supreme moral leader of the labour movement: 'You praise and honour me for what I have done, but I assure you you owe more praise to Bonnie Prince, the Honourable Adrian Cola Rienzi, your president and leader, who risked his profession, his life, in building a solid structure on the foundation which I so humbly laid'. While calling for support for the OWTU executive, he declared himself the 'Servant of the Living God' and, on asking for a show of hands from those who were 'on the Lord's side', he was acclaimed by hundreds of raised hands.[184] The problem for the OWTU was 'how to integrate the charismatic leadership of Butler with the organizational leadership of Rienzi' (Singh 1982: 29). Both styles could be valuable and were not in conflict when they appeared in sequence, but there was a potential for conflict when they appeared simultaneously. With this in mind, a meeting of the OWTU executive with Butler and representatives of his BECWHRP decided to name him 'General Organiser' of the union, with a monthly salary.

Within months the accommodation broke down. Singh has suggested (1982: 29) that 'Butler deliberately provoked the conflict'. However, Blades, who was general secretary of the OWTU at the time, wrote in 1943 that the vice-presidents, Moses and Rojas, were anxious about their own positions after Butler was released, and so incited Rienzi

> to give Mr. Butler plenty of latitude and Mr. Butler, like a fool grasped at a shadow, possessed the idea that he should be the leader of the Union and worked in opposition to the officials.
>
> I am not saying that Mr. Butler was right, he was totally wrong in his calculations, but men with the brains of Messrs Rianzi [sic], Mentor, Moses and Rojas could have curbed him if they wanted, but instead they infuriated him by suddenly throwing him out.[185]

Certainly, the circumstances illustrate the nature of the difference between these kinds of authority and leadership.[186]

When a dispute arose on 26 July 1939 between the workers and management of the Lake Asphalt Company over the dismissal of an employee, the OWTU executive felt it could not support the strike. Some of the workers were OWTU members and others, including the dismissed employee, belonged to the FWTU. The OWTU had an agreement with the company which specified procedures that should be followed in such disputes and the executive thought it would be discredited if it did not follow these procedures. Both the OWTU and the FWTU advised the workers to return to work pending negotiations between the FWTU and the company. Butler, however, addressed workers at the La Brea branch of the OWTU and urged them to strike. Ignoring the executive's request for a meeting, he continued to associate with an unofficial strike committee. The OWTU executive, faced with this open defiance of its authority and fearing that its leadership would be dubbed irresponsible, decided to expel Butler on 4 August. The People, 'hitherto an ardent supporter of Butler' (Singh 1982: 30), argued that the movement was more important than any individual; most branches supported the executive's decision. The La Brea workers campaigned for Butler, however, and even threatened Rienzi and others with violence. Butler then formed a rival union. According to Blades, the executive's 'blunder' of expelling Butler, which was made against his advice, cost the OWTU a lot of support in the oilfields and some $7,000 in contributions that were withheld by disaffected workers.[187]

By November, when Butler was gaining considerable support, the governor felt that he could not risk further unrest in the oil industry during the war. Butler was arrested on 28 November and he remained imprisoned until 1945. Singh (1982: 30-1) concludes: 'Rienzi and the OWTU executive almost certainly viewed Butler's removal from the labour scene once more with considerable relief. For apart from the threat he posed to their control over the oil workers, Butler represented not a revolutionary force ... but an egotistical and apocalyptic force that was bound to alienate all those committed to secular organisation, sobriety and responsibility'.

It could also be argued, of course, that Rienzi's was the kind of trade unionism with which the British preferred to deal. While Rienzi continued to mobilise the oil and sugar workers, and others worked to organise many other unions, it was clear by 1939, even before the outbreak of war and Butler's imprisonment, that the next phase of the labour movement in Trinidad would include the institutionalisation of trade unions. Indeed, Trinidad and Tobago was already further along this path before the war than any other West Indian colony. In just five years, the unorganised 'barefooted men' whom Cipriani had sought to lead had become a class-conscious and organised proletariat, led by Trinidadians of African and Indian descent.

Barbados

Barbados has a reputation for being orderly and conservative, but in July 1937 a massive riot and several strikes broke out in Bridgetown. The disorders spread islandwide and persisted for three days. The situation on the island was explosive. Unemployment and poverty were widespread, frustration was increasing and workers at the Central Foundry had come out on strike three weeks before the disturbances. The spark that set off the riot was the deportation of Clement Osbourne Payne, who had been speaking to and trying to organise Barbadian workers since March. The governor's actions against Payne provoked his supporters and sympathisers into instigating the labor rebellion that became a turning point in Barbados history. Richardson writes:

> the 1937 flashpoint had been reached by a conflict between old and new. The white plantocracy of Barbados had attempted to maintain control over their black laborers in the 1930s as they had during the nineteenth century by keeping them tied to particular estates and by doling out tiny wages. But times had changed. A quasi-feudal system of labor control and the impersonal, monetized economy that the Barbadian emigrants had brought home from Panama were incompatible. And it had taken the desperation of the depression decade, combined with rising black expectations that had been awakened with Panama money, to bring the inherent conflicts between old and new to a head. (Richardson 1985: 242-3)

Some progress in modernising labour relations was being made in Barbados in 1937, but at a snail's pace. A bill to abolish the penal sanctions in the masters and servants law was introduced in 1936, but the governor feared that 'its effect on the relations between estate owners and agricultural labourers

who are their tenants may be detrimental to the labourers' interest',[188] so a
new bill was introduced in 1937. This bill, which was passed on 5 June 1937, removed the penal sanctions 'against servants other than domestic servants for
(a) neglect to perform stipulated work, (b) improper or negligent performance
of work, and (c) injury to employer's property entrusted to their care, by
negligence or improper conduct . . . [and] against employers for breach of
duty under the contract, or for injury to the person or property of the servant'.[189] Although this ordinance brought some aspects of Barbados' labour
relations into the twentieth century, labour conditions and unemployment
remained a severe problem.

Governor Mark Young's memorandum on unemployment, sent shortly
before the riots, acknowledged that the problem 'is likely to assume grave
proportions at any time when production is either curtailed by unfavourable
weather or rendered uneconomical by low market prices'. He drew attention
to the absence of opportunities abroad, in such places as Panama, Cuba, the
United States and other West Indian islands, where many Barbadian migrants
had found work previously, and that the 'closing of these avenues of emigration . . . had reduced the employment of Barbadian seamen' on various
shipping lines. Assistance for the unemployed was inadequate. Small grants
had been made in two parishes to provide relief work on road repairs and an
employment agency had helped find work for less than one-quarter of the
4,109 persons who had registered as seeking employment. According to official figures, most of the young people leaving school went into agriculture,
trades or domestic service, but more than one-quarter were unemployed.[190]
Evidence that some people had been desperate for several years came out at
the hearings of the commission of inquiry into the disturbances. An unemployed ex-policeman, Alphonso Ishmael, testified: 'Somewhere in 1935 or
thereabouts potato fields were raided at Crab Hill in St Lucy [the impoverished
northern parish]. I think that if Government had seen fit to investigate the
cause of those raids then they would have realised how bad things are in this
island, and things would not have gone so far as to develop into riots. Those
Crab Hill raids went to show that people were starving since that time'.[191]

The price paid for Barbadian sugar in the London market fell from 26
shillings per hundredweight in 1923 to 9 shillings in 1929, then plunged to less
than 5 shillings in 1934, staying at that level for three years (Deerr 1949: 531).
Together with emigration restrictions in the 1920s and 1930s, this produced
great pressure on wages and employment in Barbados. Wage rates were about
average for the West Indies, but the 'daily wage of most labourers remained
below the 1s. mark, hardly an improvement since the mid-nineteenth century' (Beckles 1990: 163).

The Barbados Democratic League and the Barbados Workingmen's Association, founded in 1924 and 1926 respectively, and led by Charles Duncan O'Neale, a Fabian socialist doctor, had laid a basis for a labour movement, but he died in November 1936 and the league disintegrated. About four months before the disturbances, between 100 and 120 bakers, most of whom were employed by the larger firms, tried to form a union in order to increase their wages and shorten their working hours,[192] but trade unions were still illegal. Branches of the UNIA remained active and a variety of friendly societies and lodges also provided some 'community politicisation' (Beckles 1990: 161) before Payne's arrival in Barbados, but his activities and the government's response to him accelerated the process.

Payne was born in Trinidad of Barbadian parents[193] and had first come to Barbados when he was four years old. He had later migrated to Trinidad, where he lived for ten years and associated with Butler and other radical former members of the TWA in the NUM and the NWCSA (Ramdin 1982: 86; Reddock 1988: 31-2). When he arrived back in Barbados on 26 March 1937, aged 33, he began holding public meetings with the intention of organising a trade union. He was joined by Fitzgerald Chase, Ulric McDonald Grant, Mortimer Skeete, Darnley Alleyne and Israel Lovell, who was a Garveyite. A series of about 17 public meetings at Golden Square, in a poor area of Bridgetown, attracted between 400 and 1,500 persons. A member of the Barbados Political Association testified, 'Payne's methods were different from ours .... We have been placing our ills in the hands of our representatives. Payne wanted to place them in the hands of the people directly'.[194] According to Hilary Beckles, 'He did not confine his speeches to the labour question, but spoke of race relations, black cultural suppression, the pan-American nature of Garveyism, and Italian aggression towards Ethiopia'. Payne drew attention to the agitation and strikes taking place in other parts of the West Indies 'as evidence of the rising consciousness of black West Indians' (Beckles 1990: 164-5).

Police accounts of some of Grant's speeches, even if unreliable, give some idea of the content and tone of these meetings. Grant, and presumably Payne as well, combined an analysis of social oppression and economic exploitation in terms of race and class with a militant tone, and urged people to organise. A strike at Central Foundry failed, Grant said on 15 July, 'because the masses failed to organise against the capitalistic element. We must start a form of organisation that will capsize the capitalistic element who is oppressing us . . . . Poor masses, we are mistreated. Let us seek our rights'.[195]

As Payne's support grew, so did the colonial government's anxiety. In July Payne was prosecuted for having wilfully made a false statement to the immigration authorities that he was born in Barbados, though he may well have believed that he was. His father testified that he might not have known where he was born, and Payne said he had always thought himself to be Barbadian. It was clear to all concerned that this was simply a pretence to get rid of him. On 22 July he was convicted and sentenced to a fine of £10 or three months' imprisonment. He appealed and while out on bail led a protest march to Government House. He carefully 'advised his followers that the procession should be conducted in an orderly manner and that no one should take offensive weapons'.[196] On this occasion Grant is reported to have said:

> The white man has no feelings for the poor negroes and if unrest starts in Barbados the capitalistic element will be responsible for it. We have to fight for what we want, not with sticks, except we are forced to. If we don't fight we will get nowhere, for it is a shame and disgrace to know that slavery still exists in Barbados. Organisation is essential to any people, so let us combine and get in mass formation. The capitalistic element is doing its best to get Payne out of Barbados. Payne and I will die for you. The sooner we get organised the better for the community. One of these days the capitalists will wake up and find things in a drastic way. The decision of Payne's case had me inflamed. I would rather die by the sword than by the famine. We must fight back at these people. Things in Barbados are going to be very serious. We are being educated and in the near future will demand our rights. Let us tell the powers that be that their time will come sooner or later. Let us assist Mr. Payne to pay the fine. We will pay now but when the time comes for the others to pay they may have to jump in the sea.
>
> The administration of justice today was done in a fraudish highhanded way. Before Payne entered the Court he was convicted. He had only tried to educate his people politically and the capitalistic element has started war against him. They have everything for themselves and are yet trying to exploit the poor masses.[197]

Grant referred to Garvey as 'a wonderful man', and urged people to 'remember your mother country which is Africa'.

The protesters were not allowed to see the governor and when the crowd refused to disperse, Payne and several others were arrested. For three nights, from 23 to 25 July, large protesting crowds gathered in Golden Square, Carrington's Village and the Lower Green, and threatened that they would release Payne from the police. With Payne in jail, Grant, Chase, Skeete, Lovell and others, unintimidated, addressed another crowd on 23 July in Golden Square. Grant criticised the police specifically:

> Tonight is a serious night and we are here fighting a just cause. The Constabulary has acted outrageously. Today Payne has been handled like a criminal. The capitalistic element has been trying long ago to get him out of the way. The white men are all for themselves and depriving us of bread and butter.

> Payne has made history in Barbados today . . . . The Police of this Island are only practising the capitalistic element and they have no sympathy for the masses. How long are we going to stand this? Don't let us be fools all the time but let us fight the good fight in spite of all their oppositions. I am saying that the Constabulary acted outrageously; however, they will not be able to get off as cheaply as they think. This is just the smoke, the fire is at hand . . . . We are going to make officers and organise them so that we can strike back and heavy too. Some of the Policemen are good but some of them are very brutal.[198]

While Payne was in custody, the Court of Appeal reversed his conviction, as it could not be proved that he knew he had not been born in Barbados or that he had intended to deceive. Payne's supporters, who had collected enough money to pay the fee requested for the appeal by the lawyer, Grantley Adams, gathered outside the court, but Payne was not released. On 26 July the police smuggled him on to a ship and deported him to Trinidad, where he was promptly arrested for possessing forbidden literature (Hart 1988: 71). At about 8 pm that night, the crowd, not realising that Payne had already been deported, gathered at the wharf to prevent his embarkation. When they discovered that they had been tricked, they responded in fury, spreading through the town, smashing cars and street lights. The police who tried to stop them were attacked with 'showers of stones and bottles'[199] and several were injured. Armed only with batons, the police were unable to make a single arrest.

The next morning large crowds again gathered in Golden Square. Incensed by a rumour that a child of one of Payne's followers had been killed by the police, people poured along Probyn and Bay streets, armed with sticks and stones. They smashed cars and garage show windows, and pushed some cars into the sea. Proceeding by Chamberlain Bridge and Trafalgar Square to Broad Street and the commercial district, they damaged more cars and shops and attacked the police, forcing them back to the central police station. One section of the crowd prepared to burn down the building of the Barbados Mutual Life Assurance Society, into which the occupants had barricaded themselves, until they were driven off by armed police. The commercial district, home to the profiteering merchants, was obviously a prime target for poor people who were hurt by rising prices, and the Mutual building 'symbolized economic and social apartheid in Barbados during the 1930s' (Beckles 1989: 42). The police were by then armed with rifles and fixed bayonets, and, 'as the town was now dominated by the mob, the Riot Act was read and steps taken to restore order'.[200] In other words, they fired on the crowd.

Several groups of workers went on strike. According to the evidence and the opinions of the commissioners who enquired into the event,[201] these

were serious strikes and they contributed to the disturbances. It is important to emphasise this, as the Barbados labour rebellion is often portrayed
merely as a riot. To the workers at Central Foundry, who were already on
strike, were added the waterfront workers and bus drivers and conductors,
who went on strike on 28 July.[202] The foundry workers had made written
demands on 6 July for a wage increase of 2 cents per hour, for overtime payment after an eight-hour day and for guaranteed employment throughout
the year. On 7 July 30 workers walked out. They were dismissed the next
morning when the manager refused to recognise their action as a strike.
Six more walked out on 9 July. They were still out on 26 July when they
wrote to the manager, asking that 'the dismissals be made null and void
without division'. These workers were still on strike, fighting for wage increases, recognition and reinstatement, the day that Payne was deported.
The commissioners blamed the manager for treating the walk-out as a
'breach of shop regulations' instead of a strike, and for deferring consideration of their grievances. The requests for wage increases and overtime pay
'demanded attention' and the commissioners expressed the opinion that it
was such 'unsympathetic action' by employers that drove the workers to
'extremes'.

The commissioners also treated the waterfront workers' strike seriously.
'One of the principal centres of unrest during the disturbances was among the
workers on the waterfront', who struck for higher wages on 28 July. The commissioners believed that 'the men had genuine grievances against which they
were justified in making a strong protest'.[203] As Barbados lacked a deepwater
pier, all cargo had to be loaded and discharged by longshoremen who worked
aboard the ships and lightermen who handled the cargo between the ships
and shore. The longshoremen were hired by and worked under stevedores,
labour contractors who worked for the steamship agents and employed the
labourers directly. The agents paid the stevedores at agreed rates, which they
had to recover from the ship-owners, and the stevedores generally paid the
gross amount for the labourers' wages to their foremen. The men were paid
as daily workers at the rate of $1.50 per day, and $2.25 for Sundays or public
holidays, with overtime at 18-20 cents per hour. The ordinary working day
began at 7 am and overtime began after 6 pm. The longshoremen complained
that the stevedores' profits were excessive, that they should receive a greater
share of the payment, and that the method of indirect payment led to many
abuses. The commissioners agreed, calling the stevedores' profits 'abnormal
and excessive' and pointing out that men often had to pay the foremen part
of their own wages in order to secure work. They also blamed the steamship
agents, 'who are not ignorant of the conditions', and who benefited by trans-
ferring all responsibility for damage to cargo or injury to employees to the

stevedores. They recommended that the system of independent stevedores be eliminated, that an adequate scale of wages should be adhered to, paid directly from the steamship agents to the workers, and that overtime rates should begin after 5 pm. In other words, the commissioners' recommendations went even further than the longshoremen's demands. The lightermen demanded an increase in wages of $1 per trip and a working day fixed from 6 am to 5 pm. As the captains of lighters often deducted sums from the lightermen's wages, the commissioners recommended that all lightermen, also, should be paid directly.

The bus drivers and conductors had been paid $5-7 per week before 1931 but the scale was subsequently reduced to $4-6, and they were paid as daily employees rather than weekly as before. They worked an average of 11 hours per day with no fixed time off for meals.[204] When a bus broke down the drivers and conductors had to stand by without remuneration. The commissioners recommended that 'drivers and conductors should not be in charge of a motor bus for a period exceeding nine consecutive hours', one of which should be for unrestricted rest and nourishment. It is quite likely that some of these bus drivers and conductors spread news of the Bridgetown protests in the country parishes before they went on strike.

The rebellion quickly spread through the island as some protesters and strikers commandeered buses and cars to spread the news, though 'there is no evidence to show that there was any concerted plan to have simultaneous outbreaks in the parishes .... Gangs were quickly organized for shopbreaking and raiding of potato fields and for the stoning of motor cars along the public highways'.[205] The commissioners concluded that hunger rather than racial hatred was responsible for these actions, as 'the number of persons who suffered injury at the hands of the lawless was insignificant and that the attacks were made against the property of persons of every colour without discrimination'.[206]

The commissioners, unlike the governor of the Windward Islands in 1935, were convinced that 'the real cause of the disturbances was in fact economic', that the 'Payne incident' was merely a 'detonator', and, further, that the explosive conditions 'which rendered this culmination possible still exist and demand immediate treatment'.[207] At the commission hearings, beginning on 13 August 1937, considerable convincing evidence was given about the high levels of poverty and dissatisfaction throughout Barbados. The commissioners were certainly convinced that this was the underlying cause of the disturbances and their criticisms were explicit. Although they believed the 'root cause of many, if not all, of the economic ills' was overpopulation and its 'inevitable concomitant', namely unemployment, they drew attention to many aspects of the economic situation and of traditional labour relations that were unjustifiable in so far as they resulted from the greed of the employers.

They recognised that the crisis in the sugar trade, along with the modernisation of sugar factories and the mechanisation of transport, had increased unemployment in agriculture and also in several subsidiary occupations. They heard 'abundant evidence that a considerable part of the population is permanently without employment, while an even larger proportion suffers from periods of unemployment of varying duration'. They attributed 'the growth of the class of idle and lawless vagrants who were chiefly responsible for the damage to property in Bridgetown' to this unemployment and to 'the effect of prolonged unemployment on the minds and characters of those who are forced to be idle', especially on those young adults who 'leave school to find themselves without occupation and without any prospect of steady and remunerative employment for years'.

Although the commissioners recognised the tendency in this situation for wages to decline, 'when for every place a man is eagerly waiting to supplant its holder', they believed the wages to be so shockingly and unnecessarily low that they resulted in discontent and feelings of injustice as well as material hardship. Wages paid to unskilled manual workers, clerks and shop assistants were 'definitely inadequate to provide the bare necessities of existence', and agricultural labourers who received no more than 30 cents per day, or a weekly wage of $1.78, were 'living from hand to mouth without reserves for times of scarcity and illness'. The commissioners expressed the opinion that 'in many cases the wages paid are inadequate and cannot be justified having regard to the prosperity of the businesses which employ these workers'. They pointed to 'the striking disparity' between wages paid to manual and clerical workers, on the one hand, and managerial staff, on the other. In one firm, eight employees received salaries totalling $1,243 per month and the 73 clerical workers received a total of $1,750, the average being $155 and $24 per employee, respectively.

Impressed by the high dividends and comfortable salaries and bonuses earned by some and the low wages paid to many, the commissioners urged 'a reconsideration of the fundamental conditions and organization of industry.... A fundamental change in the division of earnings between the employer and his employees is essential if hatred and bitterness are to be removed from the minds of the majority of employees .... It is clearly no less the duty of a Government to maintain a fair balance between capital and labour than to provide for the security of life and property'. The commissioners, commenting that 'the improvement of the condition of the agricultural labourer ... brooks no delay', recommended wages should be immediately increased by 20 per cent, to a minimum of 24 cents per 9-hour day for women and 36 cents for adult men, even though this 'is still below what we regard as a reasonable subsistence level', having calculated a working man's weekly budget at $1.97, not counting any recreations or margins for illness or misfortune. 'If the labourer has to provide for a partner in life and a family of three children .. . expenditure will be a minimum of forty six and a half cents per day'. (We should note that if a husband and wife both worked and received the recommended wages, they would together earn only 60 cents per day, while a single mother working to support two or three children would be hopelessly poor.) Moreover, the commissioners acknowledged that their calculation of the cost of living did not take into account the recent 'sudden and abnormal rise in the price of the basic foodstuffs in use by peasants, artisans and labourers', such as the 50–60 per cent rise in the cost of flour. This rise in the price of imported foodstuffs, which had effectively reduced the labourers' pay by around 25 per cent, 'coincided with a scarcity of locally grown provisions, and the resultant hardship quite naturally helped to swell the volume of dissatisfaction', much of it attributed to local merchants and shopkeepers.

The commissioners also drew attention to the poor housing and absence of recreational facilities for working people. They recommended that the government should provide playing fields, initiate slum clearance and build houses for working people in Bridgetown. They visited slum areas and commented that they were 'a standing reproach to local apathy and inertia'. Coincidentally, the commissioner of police complained of the difficulty of patrolling areas such as Golden Square where the police could be attacked in narrow and unlit alleys. As house rents were often 'exorbitant' and a major factor in poor people's budgets, the commissioners urged the government to 'plan boldly and on generous lines' in building houses and relieving the congestion. In addition to initiating public works schemes, the government 'should foster the development of new industries', such as dairy farming and soap manufacture, as well as supporting the local production of vegetables.

The commissioners commented that 'Barbados is singularly backward in the organization of labour' and they recommended the appointment of a labour officer 'before whom workers with a grievance may lay their demands', and who would act as 'a liaison officer between employers and workers'. Finally, they drew attention to the need for the police to be given 'adequate power for the control of public meetings'. This should include the authority to prohibit meetings, wider powers to search premises for 'suspected seditious literature', and widening the law on sedition, 'making it an indictable offence punishable by fine and/or imprisonment to make use in public speech or writing of language of such a nature as is likely to provoke public disorder or influence others to acts of violence by provoking class or racial antagonism or in any other way'. They even recommended that police should be able to enter 'any private premises on which a meeting of more than ten persons is being held', at which they suspected such 'inflammatory or seditious language' was being used. In other words, in spite of acknowledging that the causes of the rebellion were essentially economic and recommending some reforms to address these problems, the commissioners also supported strengthening the police powers of the colonial state to make it 'almost impossible for a campaign of inflammatory propaganda to be carried out'.[208]

The class factor in this rebellion is quite clear. On the one hand, many working people went on strike, and poor people sought food or attacked the property of the rich, particularly cars and stores in the business district, and on the other hand, planters enlisted armed special constables and other volunteers to restrain workers and assist the police in protecting their properties (Beckles 1990: 167). By the morning of 30 July these various armed forces had put down the rebellion. The police and volunteers fired 811 rounds of ammunition in quelling the protests, killing 14 people and wounding 47.[209] Some 666 persons were charged with over 700 offences, including shop-breaking, larceny, robbery, malicious damage, wounding, riotous assembly and sedition. Hundreds were convicted and imprisoned.[210] Alleyne and Lovell were each sentenced to five years and Skeete to ten years in prison. Grant, found guilty of sedition on four counts, was sentenced to five years' imprisonment on each count, two to run concurrently with the other two, making a total term of ten years.[211] Payne was not allowed back to Barbados to testify to the commission. He stayed in Trinidad where he became chairman of the NWCSA, a founding member and organiser of the FWTU, and a member of the radical Workers United Front Committee in 1938. He collapsed while speaking at a meeting on 7 April 1947, and died soon after (Hart 1988: 72).

Grantley Adams, who had been Payne's lawyer at the Court of Appeal, was the first witness to give evidence to the commission on 13 August 1937, and this began his rapid rise to power. At these hearings Adams was careful to situate himself as a spokesman for the poor and disenfranchised, while sharply distinguishing himself from radicals like Payne, Grant and Lovell. Payne, Adams claimed, was 'not sincere' and was 'willing to take money from either side', but he offered no evidence to support either accusation. It was during this period, in the months following the labour rebellion, that Adams' position was established in 'the reformist leadership which dominated the labour movement for the next two decades or so' (Beckles 1990: 168). Adams, as a member of the black middle class who, embracing the dominant system, sought a place within it, used his leadership of the working class to achieve political power. In November 1936 he had roundly criticised the power of Barbados' plutocracy and advocated a political solution to the island's economic problems. He wrote in the Barbados Observer, 'Power in this colony rests in the hands of a narrow, bigoted, selfish, grasping plutocracy. To financial pressure is added political overlordship and the powerful alliance of a state Church and various brands of religion whose ministrations help to delude the multitude. The remedy is, like the evil, primarily political. When the political fight is won, economic evils will disappear'.[212]

However, after the labour rebellion Adams spoke to the commissioners in a less radical and more conciliatory manner. He said that the key problems were unemployment, low wages and rising prices: 'When we get down to bed rock we find it is a question of food prices, poverty, starvation'.[213] People's dissatisfaction was aggravated by news of the Abyssinian war, which 'has accentuated the colour question', and of the riots and strikes in Trinidad and St Vincent, but not by 'Communist agitators', charges of which were 'sheer moonshine as far as Barbados is concerned'.[214]

Adams' message to the commissioners was essentially that people need representatives in labour organisations and in the House of Assembly to whom they can express their grievances. 'There are no labour organizations in Barbados, no Trade Unions, by means of which our people can air their grievances .... Many ... people - clerks, shop assistants and others - are afraid to come before this Commission and express their grievances with regard to wages. They are afraid that if they do so they will be fired by their employers who will have no difficulty in getting others to take their places. That is why grievances are bottled up'.[215] Voters can complain to their representatives, Adams pointed out, the average labourer 'knows practically nothing about making representations to members of the House, first of all, because, not being a voter, he does not come into contact with the members of the House. And so their grievances, whatever they may be, can find no means of expression, and become bottled up'.[216] He implied that, without representatives to whom dissatisfied people can express their grievances, the eventual result will be riots. Of course, the kind of constitutional reforms Adams had in mind would provide people like himself with a broader base of support in the House of Assembly for their struggle with the plutocracy, and this became Adams' strategy.

Adams' concern about Payne was likewise legalistic and constitutional. Distrusting Payne's aims and methods, Adams would have nothing to do with him until he was hired in his legal capacity to appeal his conviction. On 27 July Adams tried, apparently, 'to pacify the irate mob', but, as he told the crowd that the solicitor-general who prosecuted Payne had only been doing his duty, he was unlikely to succeed. It was, according to Adams' biographer, the 'legality of the whole proceedings' that continued to worry him and he suggested to the governor that Payne should be brought back in custody. He believed that the people 'would be pacified if they were informed that Payne was to return and that the question of his domicile would be determined in a court of law in Barbados' (Hoyos 1974: 62-4).[217] If Adams really thought that this would pacify people, he was out of touch with their mood. Despite his carefully legalistic stance, however, there were people who believed Adams was more closely connected with Payne and even involved in the disturbances. Some Barbadians were so opposed to any changes that they viewed even Adams as a threat. Adams and his family felt insecure and he mounted an armed guard at his house and fitted the grounds with lights so that the place could be floodlit at any sign of danger. 'Above all, there was the fear, ever present in the minds of his followers, that Adams would be arrested and tried for sedition along with the hundreds who were already in prison' (Hoyos 1974: 65), although there was never any real danger of that. Adams' friends collected money to enable him to go to the UK for a while, ostensibly to present a petition to the secretary of state. He left Barbados at the beginning of September and stayed away until the end of the year.

While in England, Adams became acquainted with Arthur Creech Jones and other members of the Fabian wing of the Labour Party and he won the favour of Ormsby-Gore, the colonial secretary. His reputation as a reliable reformer became 'of critical importance in understanding the remaining years of Adams' career .... He was considered the kind of man the Colonial Office wanted to lead the ethos of reform .... Adams enjoyed the status of a Colonial Office favourite from then until the 1950s.' (Beckles 1990: 168-9)

The crucial political outcome of the labour rebellion in Barbados, therefore, was the elimination through deportation and imprisonment of the radical nationalists and the strengthening of the reformist progressives, with Adams soon to become their chief. The Barbados Labour Party was started in March 1938 by Hope R. Stevens, a native of Tortola and resident of New York City, who had organised the St Kitts Workers Defence Committee to support those who had been arrested there in 1935. While Adams was off the island, Stevens met C.A. Brathwaite, J.A. Martineau, Dr H.G. Cummins, Dr Philip Payne, Wynter A. Crawford and C.E. Talma (Hoyos 1974: 81-2). The party's name was soon changed to the Barbados Progressive League (BPL) and it was officially launched in October 1938. Brathwaite, a black business-man who had formerly been in the Democratic League, became president and Adams vice-president. Herbert Seale, a radical Garveyite, soon became general secretary. Within a few months Adams came to dominate the BPL, and in the next decade he also dominated the labour movement in Barbados and became a leader of the West Indian federal movement.

The labour situation and the plight of the working people in Barbados did not improve immediately after the rebellion. Despite the recommendations of the commission, which were surprisingly far-reaching, the government was slow to respond. A Colonial Office meeting was convened on 13 May 1938 to consider the question of the provision of labour officers to Barbados and other West Indian colonies[218] and an act providing for a labour officer was passed in Barbados on 3 August 1938. His duties would include receiving and investigating all representations, whether of employers or workers, in order to settle disputes and grievances, 'especially regarding hours and conditions of work and regulation of wages'.[219] He would also prepare cost of living indices, statistics of earnings, employment and unemployment, and would advise on arbitration machinery and the establishment of industrial courts. He would register trade boards and trade unions, though the latter were not yet legal.

When a memorandum was sent to the secretary of state on 29 March 1939, reporting on the progress made on the commission's recommendations, no labour officer had yet been appointed. In fact, though some bills, studies and committees were being considered, no progress had been made in any area. No land had been acquired for providing playing fields, the question of wages for manual workers in Bridgetown was still being investigated, a bill to create machinery for establishing a minimum price for peasants' canes was being drafted, no steps had been taken to make the government responsible for social work and welfare, and proposals for the centralisation of health services were still being considered. No action had been taken on minimum wages, and the possibility of a building programme was still being examined. The tone of bureaucratic procrastination is conveyed in the comment on housing, the provision of which the commissioners described in 1937 as the 'most urgent need': 'Consideration is being given to the possibility of making a large scale survey of Bridgetown with the object of providing data for the drawing up of a plan for slum clearance'.[220]

In light of the colonial government's continuing inactivity, it is not surprising that there was widespread labour unrest, including another round of major strikes, in 1939. On 10 February Governor E. Waddington reported numerous strikes for higher wages on sugar estates, many of them accompanied by cane fires. Workers who swept the Bridgetown streets and labourers employed by a shipping firm went on strike briefly and obtained a promise of an increase in wages.[221] On 16 February the staff of the largest hotel went on strike, their wages were promptly doubled and they returned to work, but the next day workers at other hotels went on strike and some were still out a week later. Strikes among the dock workers were settled when they received 'considerable increases' but 'these concessions will be followed by further demands by labourers'. Waddington concluded: 'the position is far from satisfactory. Labour has become much more organised and I think that the leaders are anxious to avoid disturbances but I am doubtful of their ability to control their followers in an emergency'.[222] A week later he reported: 'Strikes and cane fires continue on many estates'.[223] As this was in the middle of the crop season, it was an urgent matter to settle the disputes and complete the harvest. On 21 February dock workers went on strike against 'the expressed advice' of Adams who, Waddington feared, 'may be losing control'. The next day many of the dock workers resumed work but Waddington was worried about 'an attempt to organise a general strike'.[224]

Waddington, in a secret report sent on 23 February 1939, commented that the West India Royal Commission, which was in Barbados between 14 January and 3 February, had inadvertently stirred up the unrest. He was careful to deny that 'the present state of unrest would not have occurred but for that visit', though many workers apparently believed that the commissioners had promised and brought benefits which the government was denying them. He thought that:

> the combination of unemployment, low rate of wages for agricultural labourers and the probability of a record sugar crop made discontent and strikes inevitable at this time, and that the Commission's visit created an atmosphere wherein the workers began to see the possibilities for them that lay in organised demands. This realisation has caused many workers to get the impression that they can dictate the terms of their employment and may lead to serious unrest unless they are controlled by leaders who can relate their aspirations to the economic facts.[225]

In the absence of legally constituted trade unions, 'a number of associations of workers at various trades' were forming related to the BPL, which Waddington thought 'expedient to recognise' in order 'to guide its activities along constitutional lines'. He believed Adams to be 'a Liberal and opposed to any form of communistic or other subversive activity'. After several discussions with the colonial secretary, Adams had undertaken 'to use all his powers to restrain his followers', and particularly to see that no members of the BPL would use expressions 'calculated to cause racial animosity'.[226] Nevertheless, 'cane fires and strikes of cane cutters increased daily' and Adams was warned about the 'inflammatory' speeches of Seale and John Hinds at BPL meetings in private rooms and houses, as reported by police spies. Waddington, believing that some increase in wages was 'reasonable in view of the heavy crop', urged the planters to deal promptly with the incipient labour organisation, lest it become controlled by 'extremists'. At the same time he warned Adams that 'any outbreak of disorder would necessitate prompt intervention by Government'.[227]

Waddington thought that some strikers had been 'fomented by the independent and unauthorised activities of the less responsible and less reputable members of the League', such as Seale, the secretary, and Sidney Skinner, who had been sentenced to nine months' imprisonment in 1937. He believed Adams 'took a firm line with his associates' against a general strike but he was not confident that he could continue to control the radical members of the BPL if discontent increased. Waddington concluded, 'I am not apprehensive that a general strike, if it is organised, would be protracted, for there would be many ready, provided that they were assured of protection, to take the places of the strikers, and the funds of the Barbados Progressive League are limited'. He felt there was a danger of clashes between those who wanted to work and strikers who sought to prevent them, but he was prepared to use 'forcible measures' to prevent disorder.[228]

On 28 February some bus drivers and conductors went on strike but, repudiated by leaders of the BPL, they applied for reinstatement on 1 March. Most cane-cutters and dock workers were by then back at work and a goodwill committee, which included Adams, was reviewing the wages of manual workers. The House of Assembly heard the Trade Union Bill for the first time on 28 February and the next day Adams and other members of the BPL addressed a large meeting in Bridgetown to explain the working of trade unions, pay tribute to the government and appeal for 'patience and good behaviour'.[229] The colonial secretary made it clear to Adams and Brathwaite, the 'responsible' league leaders, that Waddington saw the BPL as 'an instrument and symbol of unity' that the government would work with, 'so long as the leaders continued to fulfil their undertakings, and to advocate settlement of all labour disputes by constitutional methods of negotiation'.[230]

It was in this heated context of labour unrest and pressure from the colonial administration that Adams purged the BPL of its radical members and followed up by taking almost sole control of it. Former members of the defunct Barbados Democratic League shared the view of the Deane Commission and the colonial government that Payne's followers in the labour movement had to be isolated and kept from power. During the visit of the Moyne Commission, Morgan Jones and Citrine, the two Labour members, 'gave the organisers of the League invaluable advice as to how they should build up the political and industrial sections of the working-class movement in Barbados' (Hoyos 1974: 89), in the British fashion, by keeping them distinct. The BPL 'was essentially a middle-class-led organisation vying for a mass base in order to confront and eventually reduce the oligarchical political power of the consolidated merchant-planter elite' (Beckles 1990: 170), and in order to play with the colonial government it had to agree to abide by its rules. Within a few months the leadership was in conflict, with Adams leading the right and Seale on the left. Although Seale had support among Garveyites and some of the more radical urban workers, such as those on the docks, Adams had the backing of the colonial officials. In Barbados in the late 1930s there could be little doubt that the radical would lose to the reformer.

Adams, pushed by the colonial officials, criticised Seale's radicalism, though the latter was one of the BPL's most effective organisers during the five months he was secretary. In his key speech on 1 March 1939 Adams claimed, 'we have the government willing to assist us, we have an influential body of merchants willing to go thoroughly into the facts and figures connected with workers in Bridgetown. We give them the assurance that we as your officers of the Progressive League will keep the workers in check, and will tell them how stupid apart from being criminal it is to strike when negotiations are the correct way to improve conditions'. (quoted in Beckles 1990: 173).

Adams condemned the strikes that were taking place in the city and dissociated the BPL from such actions, thereby isolating Seale. He reminded people of the advice Citrine had offered, namely that a strike was a weapon of last resort, and claimed that without a trade union act strikes were probably illegal in Barbados. He pointed out that the last time a procession had gone to Government House it had resulted in a riot, so 'instead of forming a procession to Government House ... let the procession be that of the Progressive League to a seat at a conference table' (quoted in Hoyos 1974: 91). In short, Adams told the crowd to quit their militant leaders and militant actions and to rely henceforth on his advocacy. The Barbados Advocate approved, lending 'its wholehearted support to all those who are resolved to give labour such responsible guidance' (quoted in Beckles 1990: 173).

In a few days Hinds and Seale were expelled from the executive committee of the BPL and Adams' supporter, Talma, replaced Seale as secretary. In April, when members of the BPL committee of management voted to give Seale a $50 honorarium for his services to the organisation, Adams absented himself from the meeting and tendered his resignation as vice-president. This was a calculated power play, as Talma promptly suggested that Adams should be made president. F.A. Hoyos says (1974: 91-2), 'It seems clear that he chose to make the Seale issue the occasion to impose his will on the Committee of Management and to make a bid for the summit of power in the workers' movement.' Adams went secretly to the acting governor, behind Brathwaite's back, and explained why there was a power struggle in the BPL.[231] Adams then sought public support and Brathwaite and other members of the committee were heckled and harassed. They answered Adams in the press, charging that he was filled with 'an overmastering lust for power and overweening sense of his own importance' (quoted in Hoyos 1974: 92). On 1 July Brathwaite and Martineau, in a desperate effort, asked the acting governor to take control of the BPL's funds to keep them from Adams, but he refused.[232] Soon after, the executive committee resigned and Adams acquired the free hand he wanted. He was nominated by Talma for president-general and proposed a slate of his supporters for the executive committee. The election gave 12,332 votes for Adams and his committee and seven against (Hoyos 1974: 93). Adams' bid for power was complete.

In the two years following the labour rebellion, little advantage had accrued to the working people of Barbados and Adams' control of the labour movement was achieved at great price. Some workers had obtained wage increases and the Deane Commission had made a reasonable assessment of some of the problems and needs of the island, but it was not until August 1939 that the first labour officer was appointed and the Trade Union Act did not come into force until 1 August 1940. Of those who were imprisoned in 1937, Israel Lovell, aged almost 60, was pardoned and released on 19 August 1939, but others remained in jail. Several individuals and organisations petitioned for their release, including the National Council for Civil Liberties,[233] the League of Coloured Peoples,[234] Creech Jones, who called Grant's case 'an outrageous travesty of justice . . . a case of prejudiced victimization for trade union activity',[235] and Citrine, who thought the sentences passed on Grant and Lovell 'quite excessive' and 'altogether unjust'.[236] Alleyne was released in July 1940 and Grant, the last prisoner of the 1937 labour rebellion, was freed on 20 December 1941.[237]

If little concrete was achieved in the years immediately following the rebellion, Barbados was nevertheless transformed. George Lamming, whose first novel, *In the Castle of My Skin* (1953), reflects the emerging cultural nationalism of the period, has commented on how he perceived the shattering of illusions about his colonial society.

> I remember as a boy, a very young boy, Barbados being thought of as a very ordered, very conventional, very conservative society. But in July 1937 nobody on the island could have had those illusions when those barefooted men marched on Government House with the demand to see the Governor. And in the town, whites fleeing, cars overturned into the harbour, stores being smashed . . .
>
> There were very very violent moments, but more important than the violence was the creation of a confidence in very ordinary people that they could and should be heard by those who were called authority (Drayton and Andaiye 1992: 266).

The growing confidence among ordinary people that they could and should be heard by the authorities constituted a significant change in the political culture. However, the struggle with the old ways was far from over while the authoritarian tradition persisted.

The Bahamas

The Bahamas, like the rest of the British West Indies, suffered from the depression and from the closure of immigration possibilities to the United States and elsewhere. Many Bahamians who had migrated earlier returned home in the 1930s to face unemployment and poverty. 'Protest and change were generally slow in coming to the Bahamas' (Saunders 1990: 25), but some of the same factors that produced labour rebellions throughout the British Caribbean were present. Relatively isolated from the rest of the West Indies and with its small population dispersed throughout an extensive archipelago, communications within the Bahamas and between the Bahamas and other British colonies was difficult. Nevertheless, shortly after the Trinidad and Barbados labour rebellions a disturbance occurred at Matthew Town in Great Inagua, a remote island in the southern Bahamas, 65 miles north of Cuba, which has become known as the Inagua riot of 1937.[238]

The Bahamian economy, threatened by the decline in sponge and sisal prices, had benefited from proximity to the United States when the US Congress passed the Volstead Act in 1919 prohibiting intoxicating liquors in the United States. This led to large scale bootlegging in the Bahamas and, until the repeal of the Eighteenth Amendment in 1933, provided a windfall in profits not only for the bootleggers but also for the Bahamian government which, far from cooperating with the US Excise Service, obtained a fantastic increase in revenues from imported liquor. Craton says that 'to a limited extent, the whole of the Bahamas profited from the Prohibition goldrush', as construction and dock work increased and wages rose. However, 'one of the least happy aspects of the Prohibition boom was that it produced an even deeper separation between the "haves" and the "have-nots"' (Craton 1986: 253). The result was that when Prohibition was repealed there was a 'savage depression' as 'wages fell to starvation levels even where work was available' (Craton 1986: 255), and racial tensions increased between the poor black majority and the affluent white merchants, known as the Bay Street Boys, who dominated the colony politically, socially and economically. These were the social tensions, derived from the predominant class and race relations, that lay in the background. However, the Inagua riot was not a labour rebellion like those that occurred elsewhere.

Inagua had a successful salt industry in the nineteenth century which collapsed in the early 1900s. By the 1930s the population had declined as the islanders went to Nassau or the United States in a desperate search for work. In the early 1930s Inagua was dominated by Arthur L. Symonette, a coloured merchant who, as an agent for the Royal Netherlands Steamship Company, employed stevedores and kept them indebted by making their families purchase supplies at his store (Johnson 1986). 'There was a great deal of dissatisfaction among the stevedores as to the method whereby such stevedores were selected, the manner of making payments to them and ... the exorbitant rates charged for foodstuffs that they were compelled to purchase for the truck system was rampant'.[239] Symonette also engaged in a small way in the salt industry, paying his workers 1 shilling per day and compelling them to buy goods at his store. In 1934 there was a strike over wages by workers in the salt pans. A fledgling labour union was organised by Theodore Farquharson, who had spent 15 years in the United States before returning to the island to take over his father's general store. This union was said to be 'one of the sources of trouble in Inagua'.[240]

In 1935 some Crown lands were sold 'at a very low price'[241] to an American family, the brothers Josiah, Douglas and Wentworth Erickson. In January 1936 the Ericksons established the West Indian Chemical Company, employing about 50 men and a few women, to revive the salt industry in Inagua. They offered employment at wages of 2 shillings per day for men and 1 shilling and 6 pence for women, and so were seen by Symonette and some other local families as a threat to their traditional monopoly as employers. Consequently, when several strikes for higher wages occurred in December 1936 and early 1937 they were said to be 'instigated by several of the leaders in the town' (Saunders 1990: 55).

When the Ericksons imported strike-breakers from other islands, particularly Acklins Island, and took over the steamship agency from Symonette, 'an atmosphere of considerable hostility towards the Americans and these intruders rapidly developed'.[242] There was also an element of racial tension involved, as some Inaguans who had experienced discrimination in the United States resented white Americans taking superior positions in their own country. The Ericksons even threatened the acting colonial secretary that they would 'import a number of ex-Marines to the Island and run it as it ought to be run',[243] and they used an armour-plated car on the island. On 19 December 1936 a fight broke out between Charles Kaddy, a white American truck driver for the Ericksons, and George and Willis Duvalier, Bahamian brothers who had lived in the United States and were supporters of Symonette. Kaddy drove his truck into the side of Symonette's store, whereupon a brawl developed between the Duvaliers and their supporters, known as the 'Band of Inagua Terrors', and the white staff of the West Indian Chemical Company. Commissioner Fields, a coloured Trinidadian doctor, subsequently fined the combatants £2 each side for disturbing the peace, but it appears that the Duvaliers 'continued to harbour a grudge against the Ericksons' (Saunders 1990: 57).

In July 1937 Fields ordered two other members of the Band of Inagua Terrors to stand trial in Nassau for burning down a house. On 19 August George Duvalier was arrested for assaulting a witness in the arson case but he escaped from the courtroom. The policeman who pursued him was wounded by Willis Duvalier, who also threatened Fields with his knife. George obtained a gun and confronted Fields at the wireless station where he had gone to telegraph for help. George shot and wounded Fields, then ran to the Ericksons' and attacked Josiah Erickson. Josiah escaped with his brother Douglas. Arming themselves and accompanied by two of their American employees, including Kaddy, they went to the wireless station. They brought Fields out but were attacked, and three of them wounded, by Willis Duvalier. They all spent the night in fear at the Ericksons' house while the Duvaliers went on a rampage. They shot and killed John Munroe, a black employee of the West Indian Chemical Company whom they considered to be the Ericksons' informer, and then set fire to the commissioner's residence, the wireless station, the Ericksons' store and the company's salt house.

The next morning, the Ericksons, along with three of their employees, Fields and the wounded policeman, fled from Inagua in their motorboat. The Duvaliers, left in control of Matthew Town, 'terrorized the inhabitants'[244] for two days, 'though causing little further harm' (Saunders 1990: 60), and left in a sailing-boat on 22 August. They were later arrested in Haiti, brought to Nassau for trial, found guilty of murder and executed. According to Gail Saunders, this incident was 'blown out of proportion by the press within and outside the Bahamas' (Saunders 1990: 61), because of the recent labour rebellions in Trinidad and Barbados. Certainly, there was no actual riot, and this was not a labour rebellion as such. Yet to dismiss it as merely a 'local brawl', as did a report of the West Indian Department of the Colonial Office,[245] misses its significance.

There is little doubt that conditions similar to those that caused the labour rebellions in the rest of the British Caribbean gave rise to this incident, as there was 'a state of unrest' in Inagua, according to the commissioner, that was provoked both by labour and racial issues. The persistent use of the truck system to get employees indebted, and the Ericksons' use of strike-breakers, created resentment among Inagua's workers. Fields stated, 'While the rest of the inhabitants exhibited no willingness to help the Duvaliers, they equally made no effort and signified no willingness to stop them'.[246] This suggests that the majority of people may have sympathised with the Duvaliers, and not simply have been terrorised by them, and that there may have been mixed feelings about the Ericksons and Fields being chased off the island. The industry the Ericksons had brought offered some employment, but it also disturbed the established paternalistic relations of this little community. A Colonial Office minute commented: 'The impact of modern business methods on a community used to, and set in, old fashioned ways (however inefficient and corrupt) is liable to produce an explosion'.[247]

Perhaps this incident is best understood, then, not merely as a clash of personalities, but as a microcosm of social change and social tensions, and that the conflict broke out between these particular people because they embodied those tensions. The conflict did not spread, however, because of Inagua's isolation and also because the feelings of resentment against the Ericksons for employing strike-breakers, bringing in white American employees and taking over the stevedoring trade, were not universal, even on Inagua. So, as Saunders points out, the Inagua disturbance 'occurred in a potentially explosive atmosphere but failed to develop into a political or labour riot' (Saunders 1990: 68). A labour union led by a white Bahamian, Percy Christie, had about 800 members, but labour organisation and labour reform in the Bahamas lagged behind the rest of the British Caribbean. Orde Browne reported that although penal sanctions had been abolished by 1939, there was no measure for workmen's compensation and trade union organisation was still 'in an embryo form, being registered under friendly society regulations'.[248]

The Bahamian labour rebellion did not occur in Inagua in 1937, but a riot in Nassau in 1942 may be considered 'the last in the series of riots and strikes that had occurred throughout the British West Indies after 1934 ... [and] the beginning of a political movement when the black labourers made real demands for social and political change' (Saunders 1985-6: 117).

Jamaica

During the first 30 years of the twentieth century there was a good deal of labour organising in Jamaica, but no actual lasting organisations resulted. The law legalising trade unions in Jamaica, which was passed on 25 October 1919, did not confer immunity from liability for tort or breach of contract or legalise peaceful picketing (Hart 1988: 52). The most persistent of the early unions, the Jamaica Trades and Labour Union (JTLU), had an erratic existence. Founded in 1907, it ceased to function in 1909 but was revived in 1918, sponsored meetings in 1929 at which Otto Huiswood, the communist from Suriname, spoke, and was said to have about 600 members in 1930. Garvey cooperated briefly with the Jamaica Workers and Labourers Association, in which S.M. DeLeon played a major role, but he would not work with Huiswood (Post 1978: 4). None of the early unions survived into the mid-1930s.

In Jamaica, as elsewhere in the British Caribbean, the labour unrest in the 1930s was provoked by widespread poverty and unemployment, the return of migrant workers from overseas, frustration over the lack of labour reform and absence of political rights, and rage over the invasion of Ethiopia. Amongst other, more particular social, economic and ideological preconditions of the Jamaican labour rebellion were the crisis in banana production and changes in the sugar industry, the rapid urbanisation and immiseration of Kingston, the radicalisation of waterfront workers and the influence of Garvey. These factors and their mutual influences from the early to mid-1930s created an explosive mixture of racial and class feeling in a colony that has had a long tradition of often violent resistance to slavery and colonialism.[249]

Beginning in 1935, the Jamaican labour rebellion peaked in 1938 with widespread strikes, riots, demonstrations and other disturbances throughout the island. In the period between 1936 and 1939 organising resulted in lasting trade unions, the most important of which was the Bustamante Industrial Trade Union (BITU), which grew directly out of the rebellion. In this key period the early organisers played a role in the great labour rebellion of 1938 which in its turn mobilised the foundations of the first mass organisation of labour throughout the island. By 1939 the labour and political organisations and leaders that were critically important in shaping postwar Jamaica had already been established. The events of 1938 were the climax of the series of labour rebellions that spread through the British Caribbean after 1934.

In 1935 the population of Jamaica was 1,121,823. Although accurate employment statistics were not available, it was estimated in 1938 that of some 404,000 wage-earners, 231,000 were wholly dependent on wages. These were located in various sectors: 100,000 in bananas (43 per cent), 41,000 in sugar (18 per cent), 29,000 in road and construction work (13 per cent) and 6,000 on the waterfront (3 per cent). The remaining 55,000 were miscellaneous labourers and unemployed (23 per cent).[250] In many cases wage rates had remained the same since the First World War, and sometimes since the nineteenth century, but the problem of low wages was made more acute by the erratic nature of employment. As Orde Browne perceived, 'Manifestly a daily wage may be satisfactory in itself but quite inadequate if the possibility of earning it is restricted to two or three days a week'.[251] It was the combination of low wages and casual employment that created such dire poverty and insecurity. Thus, if a man earned 1 shilling and 6 pence per day for six days a week he would be poor, but if he could only get work for two days his weekly income would be a pitiful 3 shillings. There was much variation in actual wages received, as distinct from wage rates, therefore, from week to week, as well as from season to season, and between different industries, as a few examples illustrate.

On sugar estates during the crop season in 1935-6, some 22,200 men and 8,800 women were employed, but out of crop this fell to 13,600 men and 6,000 women, a reduction of 12,400.[252] Thus, not only was there greater hardship during the six months of the cropover season but there was also much movement of people migrating in the annual search for temporary jobs. Even among those who were 'permanently' employed during the crop season there was great variation in wages received. One man who was fortunate enough to work regularly during the harvest at Caymanas Estate earned an average of 21 shillings and 4 pence per week for 17 weeks, whereas a woman on the same estate earned an average of 6 shillings and 1 penny per week over ten weeks. Many people could not find work as regular as this so, even if paid at the same wage rate, they received less income. One young woman at Caymanas, for example, earned a total of 7 shillings and 9 pence for working over a period of three weeks (Post 1978: 123).

Though many sugar workers had access to a bit of land, it was often on the estate where they were employed, and hence a means of keeping them in the casual labour system, rather than an independent source of income. Not surprisingly, therefore, in these conditions, many workers desired more access to land, and this became one of their major demands, along with higher wages and more secure employment. A rural survey by Jamaica Welfare Ltd reported, 'The wish for land or more land, or more productive land, is almost universal .... Almost everyone thinks of a money crop in this connection.'[253] Such were the problems of small farming in Jamaica, however, that the conditions of peasant growers were no better than those of rural wage-earners (Post 1978: 124).

One of the chief problems was that Panama disease was destroying bananas, the main money crop of small farmers. The United Fruit Company (UFC) was abandoning some of its own estates in the 1930s, and many small farmers, unable to take advantage of market opportunities, were themselves being driven into failure and then wage labour. Some peasants joined local associations, but the Jamaica Agricultural Society and the Jamaica Banana Producers' Association represented and were controlled by the richer growers and 'never mobilised the peasants into an active, self-conscious and assertive force' (Post 1978: 131).

One consequence of the plight of the peasantry and rural wage-earners (two overlapping categories) was the increase of migration and urbanisation. As the opportunities overseas were curtailed, migration to the towns, particularly the capital, increased. In the 1920s and 1930s Kingston and the partially urbanised parish of St Andrew which surrounds it, grew rapidly, receiving a net inflow of almost 70,000 people between 1921 and 1943 (Roberts 1957: 153). In the mid-1930s, when thousands of Jamaican emigrants were repatriated, often bringing with them children who had been born abroad, the urban population of Jamaica swelled. Thousands of peasants who were being forced off the land, because rural employment opportunities were inadequate, joined some 30,000 emigrants who were repatriated between 1930 and 1934. This swelled the urban pool of unemployed and intermittently employed and the expanding shanty towns of the Kingston-St Andrew area. Between 1921 and 1943 the combined population of Kingston and St Andrew increased by 102 per cent, from 117,000 to 237,000 people (Clarke 1975: 30). Wages in Kingston, though higher than rural wages, were low in relation to the urban cost of living, at 3 shillings per day for men and 1 shilling and 6 pence for women, compared with an average rate of 1 shilling and 9 pence and 11 pence, respectively, in private employment in the rural parishes (Hart 1988: 63). The wage differential added to the attractions of the urban area, but the massive influx of workers kept the wages low. The Kingston metropolitan area grew most rapidly, but the population of smaller towns also increased as thousands of Jamaicans sought relief from rural poverty.

This concentration of poor people, many of whom had experience of work and politics abroad, had a major impact on the development of class and racial consciousness. The growth of Garveyism, the influence of Marxism and the emergence of Rastafarianism in the 1930s all contributed to the process in which the urban working class, and the waterfront workers in particular, pioneered powerful and lasting labour organisations.

Garvey, who had been an officer in the short-lived printers' union in 1907, was deported from the USA to Jamaica in December 1927, and was given a hero's welcome in Kingston. He quickly established UNIA branches throughout the island, held mass meetings and organised membership drives. The UNIA's Sixth International Convention, held in Kingston in 1929, drew thousands of people. Garvey and his organisation were an inspiration and provided a rare opportunity for many working people to develop skills as speakers and organisers. Although the restrictive franchise limited Garvey's participation in the formal political processes, 'the UNIA played a vital role in politicizing the masses, especially between 1928 and 1935' (Eaton 1975: 23). In 1929 Garvey was elected a councillor of the Kingston and St Andrew Corporation but his attempt to win a seat on the Legislative Council the next year failed and his efforts to launch a political party and a workers' association were abortive. Nevertheless, through Garvey's powerful message and inspirational leadership, 'black Jamaicans had not only been made aware of themselves as a race and the place they occupied in the Jamaican scheme of things, but had been given an institutionalized forum for talking about their problems, hopes, and aspirations' (Eaton 1975: 24).

When Garvey left Jamaica for the last time in 1935, Ethiopianism was becoming a significant force in the island. Garvey had encouraged a general reorientation towards Africa, but it was the coronation of Ras Tafari as the Emperor Haile Selassie in November 1930 and the Italian invasion of Ethiopia in 1935 that sparked the specific religion of Rastafarianism. Leonard Howell, amongst others, had preached the divinity of Haile Selassie in the early 1930s and by the time of Howell's arrest and trial for sedition in 1934 he had established a considerable following. When the wave of sympathy for Ethiopia swept Jamaica in 1935, Rastafarianism was only one part of a 'much broader front' of a pro-Ethiopia and anti-colonial movement (Post 1970: 195), similar to that in Trinidad. A Garveyite weekly newspaper, Plain Talk, edited by Alfred Mendes, 'succeeded in giving its readers a feeling of participation in defending Africa against this latest example of oppression by the white man' (Hart 1989: 21). By the mid-1930s, then, more and more Jamaicans were 'coming to see themselves as part of a scattered and exploited but nevertheless "chosen" people ... [and] to see white people increasingly clearly as their oppressors and the white (or near-white) establishment as "Babylon"' (Post 1970: 202). Garvey himself denounced Haile Selassie and his policies in 1936 from his exile in London, but a mix of Garveyism, Ethiopianism and Rastafarianism had become by then an important part of the political culture of resistance in Jamaica (Nettleford 1970; Campbell 1985).

In this turbulent context of economic deprivation, social volatility and heightened politicisation, labour protests took place in 1935 on the north coast. These were early warnings of the great labour rebellion three years later, especially since they involved banana workers and dock workers, who became the most militant rebels in 1938. The first issue of Plain Talk, on 18 May 1935, reported that banana workers in Oracabessa in the parish of St Mary had rioted five days before. A big grower had imported labourers from neighbouring Port Maria in order to increase competition and reduce wages. When the workers blocked roads and cut power lines, armed police were sent from Kingston to quell the disturbance (Post 1978: 240). A few days later, on 20 May, a more serious incident started at Falmouth in Trelawny, where the threat of using strike-breakers during a strike by dock workers provoked violence. At about 8 am on 20 May, Clinton Delgado of Delgado Bros reported to the Falmouth police inspector that the dock workers whom he wanted to load sugar on a ship had gone on strike, demanding 4 shillings for a 9-hour day instead of the usual 2 shillings and 6 pence. The inspector visited the wharf and found about 30 workers, who were 'quiet, peaceful and were laughing and joking among themselves',[254] but were determined not to work for less than 4 shillings per day.

During the course of the day the strikers' numbers increased and at about 1.30 pm they heard that workers were being brought to Falmouth from outside to load the ship. When they threatened 'to beat the persons so brought in and run them out of town', the inspector told them he would give the strike-breakers 'every protection and see that the ship was loaded'. The inspector accompanied three strikers to discuss the matter with the Delgados, but 'after some argument, no agreement could be reached and the conference broke up'. Although the crowd 'marched down the streets singing and waving sticks' there was no disorder. Nevertheless, the inspector obtained reinforcements from Montego Bay, as he must have anticipated that his actions would provoke the strikers. When the police advised the men 'to behave' and warned of 'the consequences of any disorder', there was still 'no antagonism towards the Police who were treated with respect', but the strikers remained determined that no outside labour would be brought in. As darkness fell the crowd had increased to about 500 or 600, many of them with sticks and iron bars, and some piled up stones at the side of the road. The strikers were stopping vehicles entering the town and searching them for strike-breakers. One car bringing police was damaged, but no arrests were made. More police reinforcements arrived from St Ann at 10 pm, and by about 2.30 am most of the crowd had peacefully dispersed to their homes.

At 4.45 am on 21 May, 40 armed police were posted to secure Delgados' wharf and to block all approaches from strikers. Two hours later Donat Delgado tried to hire labourers at 2 shillings and 6 pence per day and the few who accepted were escorted to the wharf by police. The strikers then became angry and shouted at Delgado. One man, Percival Brown, armed with an iron pipe, was said to shout, 'Lick him to rass, kill him to rass,' and the crowd surged toward the wharf. When the police arrested Brown, who 'put up a tremendous fight . . . several hundred men and women spread out facing the Police and commenced to throw stones, bricks, bottles, and conch shells', pressing forward and injuring several policemen. The police shouted warnings and fired some revolver shots over the crowd but this had no effect. The crowd jeered at the police and continued stoning them. The police then fired into the crowd, killing Sidney Black, a 37-year-old man who was shot in the face, and wounding another with a bullet in the thigh. The police took Brown to their lock-up, reformed with reinforcements outside the court house, and then charged with fixed bayonets through the streets of the town 'until the crowd was entirely dispersed', whereupon they 'scoured the town' to arrest those whom they considered to be ringleaders. Forty more police arrived in the afternoon and by 3 pm the next day 33 people had been arrested. The boat was subsequently loaded under police protection and left on 22 May.

According to the custos' report, the strike had been prepared. A meeting had been held on 15 May to discuss what should be done and on 19 May two or three young men 'of the radical element' were seen riding bicycles around town, 'stopping and speaking to people', and messengers went to neighbouring villages, such as Perth Town, Granville and Martha Brae, from which labourers were often recruited. The custos claimed that they referred to the Rev. J.W. Maxwell, a Baptist member of the Permanent Jamaica Development Convention, created at the UNIA convention in September 1934, who, when a candidate in the Legislative Council election in January 1935, had urged that: 'no man should work for less than a dollar [4 shillings] a day; that the estate owner and upper classes generally are grinding the population down and that he would enable the employer of labour to pay the dollar a day minimum wage by increasing the price of their produce; that the economic depression was entirely due to the upper classes etc. etc.'[255] Maxwell was a supporter of J.A.G. Smith, a black barrister and member of the Legislative Council from 1917 until his death in 1942, who advocated labour reform and had founded the Jamaica Representative Government Association in 1921.

The custos concluded that 'this disturbance is due to the economic conditions of this neighbourhood being exploited by the radical political element', conditions that he admitted were 'deplorable'. He commented that the area had not shared in the banana prosperity, that this 'portion of the parish is gradually going back to bush', and those people who had not already left 'have become poorer .... Their suffering and poverty is not a sudden thing of today, they have endured it for a generation with patience which entitles them to a degree of appreciation'.[256]

The claim that the Falmouth strike was prepared to some extent is supported by evidence of other 'agitation for increased pay on the part of loaders and stevedores' in Port Antonio and Kingston, which led to some shots and injuries in the latter. Governor Sir Edward Denham met with representatives of the leading shipping firms on 29 May and was 'satisfied that the agitation is largely fomented by a rowdy and disorderly element'.[257] On 18 July he reported there had been 'no recurrence of the disturbance at Falmouth or elsewhere' and that most of the 32 people convicted, out of 38 defendants, at Falmouth were imprisoned for between 3-12 months.[258] The Colonial Office commented ominously that the police were justified in shooting at Falmouth, but that 'armed forces should never fire over the heads of a crowd. If it becomes necessary to fire, the officer in command should, when it is possible, point out one or two ringleaders and have them shot. Aim should be taken at the lower part of the body'.[259]

No specific organisation resulted from these disturbances in 1935, but the next year the most important trade union to date, the Jamaica Workers and Tradesmen Union (JWTU), was founded and peasant unrest developed in the countryside. The JWTU, formed in 1936 and registered in 1937, was led by two men, Allan George St Claver Coombs and Hugh Clifford Buchanan, who played a pioneering role in organising labour in Jamaica over the next few years. Coombs, born of poor peasant parents in St Ann parish in 1901, served in the Jamaican police force from 1919 until 1922 and then in the West India Regiment until 1926. Working as a contractor for the Public Works Department, he started the union among his own labourers in May 1936 (Post 1978: 242).[260] A couple of weeks later, on 4 June, a series of hunger marches by the unemployed took place in Kingston, followed by several in Spanish Town, on 9 September, 9 October and 14 November, led by L.W. Rose, a shoemaker and UNIA organiser, and L.E. Barnett, who had returned from Costa Rica where he had been vice-president of the Limón Federation Union. One of the marchers, when offered lunch by the chairman of the St Catherine Parochial Board, responded, 'We are Naked . . . our children are naked, we are turned out of shelter, our families are turned out of shelter because we cannot pay the landlords their rent. What we do need is not the little lunch suggested but that the Parochial Board does find work, begin its work of magnitude and employ us now'.[261]

On 23 November Coombs met with members of the Ex-British West Indies Regiment Association and the Masons Cooperative Union[262] at Liberty Hall, the UNIA meeting place in Kingston. They created a council of action to organise more hunger marches to put pressure on the government. Coombs led a march of the unemployed in Kingston on 30 December, but the deputy mayor, Dr Oswald Anderson, advised them to turn back. When they hesitated, the police charged them and injured two men before they dispersed. Coombs later described the event to the Moyne Commission: 'The people all unarmed were only carrying flags and banners bearing the words "Starvation, Nakedness, Shelterless". The Union Jack was torn in pieces. The batons and clubs of the police were brought in play mercilessly on the people, while extra armed men kept the people covered with rifles, bayonets and pistols, while the poor and unfortunate people recieved [sic] their floggings which necessitated many going to hospital for treatment'.(quoted in Post 1978: 244)

Coombs responded by placing an advertisement in Plain Talk on 2 January 1937, calling for people from all over the island to come forward and join the JWTU because the key was in organised labour: 'the workers should organize solidly, because it is only through organization that any group of people can achieve success'. (quoted in Post 1978: 244) Six months later, Coombs described the dock workers whom he was organising:

> Women and children are among the banana carriers, pregnant women included. I stood up for about half an hour watching, the carriers running and trotting all along. The loaders receive the bananas with 'lightning' speed and accuracy, their clothing soaked with perspiration. The big bosses and managers paced lordly up and down the piers with their hands in their pockets, laughing and chattering with each other, while tourists take photographs of the workers, clad in tattered garments.[263]

By this time, Coombs had been joined in his efforts by Buchanan, 'Jamaica's first active Marxist' (Hart 1989: 18). Buchanan was born on 29 January 1907 and left his home at May Pen at the age of 12 to live with an aunt in Hanover. At age 16 he migrated with her to Cuba and there he learned the trade of brick mason and came to understand the Cuban sense of self-respect that was a source of powerful nationalism there. In December 1937, just a few months before the labour rebellion, he wrote to the new progressive paper, Public Opinion, comparing Cuban nationalism with the lack of such feeling in Jamaica:

> The illiterate Cuban guajiro beats his breast with pride and declares: "I am a Cuban".... This pride of even the most illiterate Cuban is due to the fact that at a certain time in the past they rose and did something monumental. The deeds of a Maceo, a Marti and a thousand patriots who distinguished themselves in the struggle are written in prose, and poetry, and in the text books of their schools. It is the source of a never-ending folklore, the vital chord to which every Cuban responds. "La Independencia" even though reduced to a solemn farce by the strangle-hold of Wall Street, is nevertheless the motive force, the ideal of a nation of progressive people less than one hundred miles from us.[264]

Buchanan may have had contact with Cuban communists but it is more likely that he was active there in the UNIA. According to Richard Hart, Buchanan was introduced to communism in Jamaica by Cleveland Antonio King, another Jamaican who had lived in Cuba and had been a member of the Communist Party there before returning home. Buchanan borrowed Marxist literature, including Lenin's The State and Revolution, from Audley Thomas, a senior civil servant in the Department of Education (Hart 1989: 18). In 1937 Buchanan met Hart, then a young law student, and before the end of that year they were meeting in Jamaica's first Marxist group with Wellesley A. McBean, Frank Hill, Albreath A. Morris, T.G. Christian, Cecil Nelson, and Lionel Lynch. Morris and Christian were tally clerks on the wharves and Lynch was a longshoreman and stevedore who had been introduced to communism while resident in the USA. They were soon joined by others, including Arthur Henry, who had been a railway fitter and an engine-room oiler on Canadian boats (Hart 1989: 19-20).

Hart writes that the group was 'loosely centred around Buchanan', but it was Hart himself who became the most important Jamaican Marxist. His father was Ansell Hart, a solicitor. Richard, born in 1917, was privileged enough to attend Munroe College and then spend three years at a minor English public school before entering the University of London in 1935. He returned to Jamaica in 1936, and became articled as a clerk in his father's firm. He had taken little interest in politics when in the UK but by 1937 was convinced he was a Marxist (Post 1978: 225) and, as part of the growing agitation of local intellectuals, started writing letters and articles for newspapers. Hill was a journalist who was one of the founders of a progressive weekly, Public Opinion, in February 1937, along with O.T. Fairclough, a Jamaican who had worked in Haiti, and H.P. Jacobs, a teacher from the UK who was Thomas' brother-in-law. Another focus of middle-class reform was the National Reform Association

(NRA), which held its inaugural meeting in March 1937. Noel N. Nethersole, a solicitor, became its president and its secretary was Ken Hill, Frank's older brother. In 1937 Ken Hill started the Jamaica Chauffeurs' Union for taxi and lorry drivers and the Motor Omnibus Drivers' Association. F.A. Glasspole, an accountant, organised shop assistants and clerks in Kingston and became secretary of the Jamaica United Clerks Association.[265] Thus by 1937 these people had formed a radical, socially active network.

These middle-class Jamaicans were trying to find a role in and provide leadership for the growing discontent in the colony, but they were not always trusted. At an early meeting of the NRA, on 28 April 1937, a popular Garveyite street orator, St William Grant, appeared and pointed an accusing finger at the dignitaries on the platform, demanding 'Are you leaders of this movement prepared, if need be, to die for the masses?'[266] Buchanan, who had joined the NRA immediately and was elected to its executive council, was certainly more radical than most of its members. A columnist asked in Plain Talk in August 1937, 'Must it be understood that this lofty association intends to reform the already poverty stricken inhabitants of this island through the opinion and sentiments of a few aristocrats thrown on them?'[267]

An attempt to launch a Jamaicans' Labour Party was made in April 1937, but when Norman Washington Manley, the colony's leading barrister and founder of Jamaica Welfare, was asked to stand as its candidate at the forth-coming Kingston and St Andrew Corporation election, he refused. Earlier he had turned down Fairclough's invitation to become president of the NRA, saying, 'The problems of Jamaica, my dear Fairclough, are social and eco-nomic, not political' (quoted in Post 1978: 220). Manley had won the trust of the colonial officials and was careful to keep it. Governor Denham described Manley in July 1937 as 'the ablest Jamaican of today ... very helpful, sane and conservative ... not a controversialist nor a politician, though a man of strong - but I believe loyal - views'.[268] So, although some people were trying to create a more openly political movement in 1937, others, including Manley, continued to drag their feet. Between December 1937 and April 1938 there was a lively debate about the need to form a political party, and what kind of party it should be, in Public Opinion. Participants included Fairclough, Buchanan and Hart, and three leading members of the Jamaica Progressive League (JPL), based in New York, that was formed in 1936: W. Adolphe Roberts, Wilfred A. Domingo and Jaime O'Meally, the last two former Garveyites. These people expressed strong nationalist and sometimes Marxist sentiments in debating issues of socialism and self-government for Jamaica. By the middle of 1938, however, this debate was overtaken by events. The situation changed dramatically - and so did Manley's attitude to political activity.

The two most serious attempts to organise working people before 1938 were by the JWTU and the Poor Man's Improvement Land Settlement and Labour Association (PMILSLA). The peasants' economic distress was evidenced in their inability to pay an annual land tax of 1 shilling for every £10 in value. By the end of March 1937 the total of arrears was £125,043 and the number of peasants imprisoned for non-payment increased from 57 in 1934-5, to 116 in 1935-6 and 153 in 1936-37 (Post 1978: 119). In 1935 a group of peasants in Golden Grove, St Thomas, a centre of Howell's Rastafarians, formed the Tax and Rate Payers Association. They called on the government for help, demanding a land settlement scheme, better roads and water supplies, and books for schoolchildren, but by 1936 they had faded from sight (Post 1978: 246-8). More serious was the PMILSLA, founded early in 1938 in Clarendon and led by Robert E. Rumble. A poor peasant who had worked in Cuban canefields in the 1920s, Rumble returned to Jamaica in 1932 and by 1937 was writing about 'the oppression of these iron-handed landowners in these parts of Clarendon'. He declared, 'We want no more landlords'.[269] Some land-hungry peasants who occupied land at Trout Hall and Cocoa Walk were arrested and tried. The PMILSLA, claiming a membership of 800, petitioned the governor on 23 April 1938: 'We are the Sons of slaves who have been paying rent to Landlords for fully many decades we want better wages, we have been exploited for years and we are looking to you to help us. We want a Minimum Wage Law. We want freedom in this the Hundredth year of our Emancipation. We are still economic Slaves, burdened in paying rent to Landlords who are sucking out our vitalities'.[270] Though Rumble appealed to the colonial authority as if it were a benevolent power above the local landlords, his tone was radical, and the demand for a minimum wage reflected the imminent proletarianisation of the peasantry and the discourse of modern labour reform. Many peasants believed, moreover, that 99-year leases had been given to landlords at the time of Emancipation and that the land was due to pass to its rightful owners, the descendants of the former slaves. This radical interpretation expressed the peasants' class grievances and a historical desire for compensation as well as further politicising them, but Rumble's organisation did not expand beyond the parish of Clarendon and it was 'swallowed up' by the general rebellion in 1938 (Post 1978: 249).

The JWTU, meanwhile, was trying to organise all kinds of workers on an islandwide basis. Coombs and Buchanan, financially pressed, accepted the assistance of a money-lender, William Alexander Bustamante, who became treasurer of the union in 1936. Born with his father's surname of Clarke on 24 February 1884, Bustamante subsequently created shadowy legends about his past. His father was the half-brother of Norman Manley's mother, so these two leaders of modern Jamaica, sharing a grandmother, were cousins (Eaton 1975: 1). Bustamante went to Cuba in 1905, moved to Panama two or three years later, returned to Cuba in 1919 or 1920, and tried a dairy business back in Jamaica in 1928. By 1932 he was in New York, calling himself Alejandro Bustamanti, but he finally returned to Jamaica, not notably prosperous, in 1934 (Eaton 1975: 14-15). He became a prolific writer of letters to the press (Hill 1976), and by May 1936 was speaking at meetings of the middle-class citizens' associations, which had grouped themselves into a federation the previous month and were intended to promote civic improvements.

During 1937 Coombs and Buchanan were trying to organise dock workers, railwaymen and banana workers in Kingston, Spanish Town, Port Maria and Oracabessa, and Bustamante was making several trips to the rural areas. When news came of the labour rebellion in Trinidad, Bustamante wrote to Plain Talk:

> We too in Jamaica must organize, unite, stick together, stay united to obtain a living wage and better treatment both from government, from the so-called Captain of Industries and other employers, and until then we will never [be] worth being called a people .... Labour of every class in this Island, white collars etc., I exhort you to organize. I will go [to] any part of this Island as I have been doing paying my own expenses to speak to you, to tell you the necessity and the beauty of Labour Organizations.[271]

In 1937 Bustamante began to establish his reputation, which may be characterised either as that of an inflammatory demagogue or as the workers' fearless champion. The workers grew increasingly militant and Bustamante got more publicity and rapidly became known as a labour leader. There was a one-day strike in the railway locomotive workshops on 12 July, several strikes among workers on banana estates in St James parish in September, and the banana loaders went on strike in Oracabessa in October.

Ken Post (1978: 225) has summarised succinctly the importance of the relations between the JWTU and Bustamante at this time, both for the individual and for the organisation of Jamaican labour:

> To the Union he brought his financial backing, his energy, and his capacities as a crowd-puller, with his commanding presence - tall, with a shock of hair - distinctive voice and rhetorical flair. For his part, he seems to have found in the Union two things, a chance to give the most effective expression to his pity for the poor and exploited and an organisation which he could dominate .... As for Jamaican labour, it found in Bustamante "the Chief", "Busta", "Labour Leader No.1", the man who was to lead it to apparent triumph and ultimate tragedy.

Bustamante's great ego and ambition created a crisis in the JWTU and friction developed because he wanted to become president. Coombs acknowledged he was losing authority to his treasurer and on 12 October he resigned as president and handed the position to his rival. However, Coombs 'never fully relinquished his claim to the leadership' (Hart 1989: 30) and in November Bustamante, facing opposition from Coombs' supporters, quit the union altogether. Bustamante had his own supporters, however, and the JWTU was badly divided. Buchanan attacked Coombs and resigned as general secretary in November and Rose, the vice-president from Spanish Town, also resigned. This was a serious split in the labour movement because at this time the JWTU claimed 88 per cent of the 1,080 members of the registered trade unions in the colony (Bakan 1990: 101). In late January 1938 a compromise was reached when Percy A. Aikan, a railway electrician who had been a leader of the railwaymen's strike at the end of the First World War, was made acting president, but the rivalry between Coombs and Bustamante re-emerged a year later in the struggle to control organised labour after the rebellion.

In September 1937, Governor Denham noted 'increased activity on the part of the various labour unions'.[272] The JWTU won a victory in St James in October when the banana growers agreed to pay carriers 2 pence a stem in place of the former penny, but the banana loaders' strike in Oracabessa later in the month petered out when the union could not persuade workers in Port Antonio and Port Maria to refuse to handle the diverted fruit. A union meeting at Port Antonio on 22 October was broken up by hired thugs and the police failed to intervene. This happened again on 28 January 1938. When unorganised workers on Serge Island sugar estate in St Thomas went on strike at the end of 1937, the JWTU was not involved. The strikers demanded 2 shillings for harvesting a ton of cane instead of 10 pence as paid by the estate. On 5 January some 1,400 strikers armed with sticks and cutlasses virtually shut down the parish of St Thomas. Bustamante, no longer a trade union official, offered to be a mediator but when the workers were told the employer was willing to pay only 1 shilling per ton they rejected the offer and Bustamante and the owner had to retreat with a police escort. A reinforcement of 50 police was brought from Kingston to quell the ensuing unrest in which 34 strikers were injured and 60 arrested (Phelps 1960: 422). This pattern of escalating violence was repeated on a greater scale within three months at Frome in Westmoreland parish, at the other end of the island.

It is now clear that the strike that erupted at Frome at the end of April 1938 was a continuation of the labour unrest and trade union politics that had been emerging for some months, but at the time many people were surprised by the event and amazed at the scale of the violence. Governor Denham's long message to the Legislative Council in March made only a brief comment about unemployment and no mention of labour relations. On 17 April 1938 Denham sent a telegram in response to what he called 'incorrect and misleading' statements by 'one Bustamante a local publicity seeker' concerning thousands of hungry schoolchildren. He assured the Colonial Office that 'Government is fully alive to present situation which does not appear to give any cause for alarm'.[273] Denham was not ignorant of the situation, nor was he as complacent as this telegram sounds. He was an active and liberal governor, as far as colonial governors in the 1930s could be, and had been involved in many relief efforts since his arrival in Jamaica in 1934. Legislation had been passed on workmen's compensation and slum clearance, and he had raised a loan of £2 million for land settlement schemes and irrigation projects, as well as building houses, schools, roads and hospitals. An effort had been made to create more jobs through public works and in the first months of 1938 several projects were started, including road improvement, building the new Palisadoes Airport and clearing slums in west Kingston. Nevertheless, Denham's claim that his 'Public Works Extraordinary programme amounting in coming year to over £170,000 will afford considerable relief to unemployment situation'[274] suggests that he was trying to reassure the Colonial Office that because he was doing his job they would get no trouble in Jamaica similar to what had occurred in Trinidad and Barbados in 1937.

On 20 April Bustamante, speaking to an estimated 2,000 people on North Parade in Kingston, described the governor as a 'misfit as an administrator', but he was careful to aver that he was 'not advocating a revolt'.[275] The next week Bustamante, who had won the trust of many poor people, spoke to an even larger crowd. A few days later, however, when the working people of Jamaica started their great rebellion in Frome, they did so without his leadership.

Though the various aspects of the Jamaican labour rebellion were actually closely interrelated, for purposes of clarity we may distinguish between three chief locations and phases: first, the riot and strike at Frome Estate in Westmoreland between 29 April and 2 May; second, the protests, strikes and uprising in Kingston between 2 and 28 May; and third, the many demonstrations, riots and rolling strikes throughout the island between 23 May and 11 June. Some of these events were organised and involved people we have already identified as labour leaders, but most were spontaneous responses with only local and anonymous leadership. Before the second week in June this rebellion had wrung several concessions from the colonial government and had promoted Bustamante and Manley to the status of leaders of the labour and nationalist movement.

The Frome affair, which started with a riot and developed into a strike, began because of anger about 'the dilatory payment of wages earned' (Phelps 1960: 424). On the afternoon of Friday 29 April the estate workers were paid more slowly than usual and, in the opinion of the commissioners who enquired into the disturbances, 'it was not unnatural that those who were waiting to be paid became impatient and discontented. The discontent resulted in the throwing of stones and in an attack by some of the labourers on the pay office. The discharge of several shots from a revolver to scare those who were committing these acts and to protect the clerks in charge of the cash did not improve the situation'.[276]

Although order was temporarily restored, some workers were angry and many were still unpaid when the office was closed at 10.30 pm. The next morning the estate manager failed to satisfy the workers and tension increased. In part, the immediate cause of the problem was bad management, and specifically 'the ingrained habit of estate operators of disregarding the convenience or point of view of labourers under their supervision' (Phelps 1960: 423), but there was more to it than that, and the incident at the pay office was simply the spark that ignited some very dry tinder.

The small riot at the Frome Estate pay office became a strike and then a large-scale violent confrontation because the hopes and expectations of hundreds of poor workers had been raised and then frustrated. The British sugar company, Tate & Lyle, having bought several properties in Jamaica, was scrapping some smaller factories and consolidating its facilities by establishing a large new central factory at Frome. The West Indies Sugar Company, a subsidiary of Tate & Lyle incorporated on 22 May 1937, controlled Frome, Bluecastle, Friendship, Shrewsbury, Masemure and Mint estates in Westmoreland, Prospect in Hanover and Monymusk in Clarendon, a total of 61,500 acres.[277] As part of its modernisation plans the company announced it would also be building housing for its employees and schools, churches and a hospital, all to be free to the workers and their dependents, as part of a £500,000 investment. An announcement in The Daily Gleaner to this effect on 26 March, and rumours of higher wages of up to 4 shillings or 5 shillings per day, encouraged the migration of hundreds of desperate workers, but the wages actually paid were less than half what was expected. Moreover, more workers came than would be hired, which was perhaps intended by the management, and even those who were hired did not have secure tenure.

Construction workers and general labourers were hired out of the great pool of available workers according to the company's needs of the moment, so the labour force was expanded one week and reduced the next, with a good deal of turnover and uncertainty among workers. Thus, at the end of March the labour force was 632, and this went up to 780 on 13 April and 911 on 20 April, but fell to 758 on 27 April, just before the riot began, and again to 380 on 11 May.[278] Accommodation for the permanent workers was poor and those people who were casually employed or still looking for work had to live in temporary shelters outside the estate. As Post writes, 'The Frome project reproduced in a microcosmic and intensified form, therefore, the situation of the Jamaican working class - poor living conditions, exploitation, those who were fortunate enough to have jobs feeling the hot breath of the reserve-army of labour always on their necks' (Post 1978: 277).

The mobility and the concentration of these workers facilitated their politicisation, even though it was hard to organise such a casually employed and mobile group of workers. The JWTU had not campaigned at Frome Estate, but some of the workers there had surely 'been exposed to its message' (Post 1978: 277). The construction work had been over-advertised to ensure a large pool of labour but the belief that pay rates would be higher may have resulted from rumours spread by unionists as much as by management. When the workers went on strike they demanded 4 shillings per day, just as the dock workers had in Falmouth three years earlier. When the company offered a revised scale of pay and hours of work, amounting to 2 shillings for a 10-hour day with an extra 4 pence per hour for overtime for general labourers, the workers asserted 'it did not substantially differ from the existing one, refused to accept it and the dissatisfaction was intensified'.[279] Not only were these rates less than the workers had expected, but they also objected to the arbitrary cutting of their pay, by sums ranging from 3 pence to 6 pence per day, so they did not always receive what they believed to have been agreed and earned. The confrontation intensified as cane fires were started[280] and police reinforcements rushed in. 'The representatives of Tate & Lyle were determined to stand firm against the strikers' demands and the colonial state was there to back them up to the full. But the strikers too were in a determined mood' (Hart 1989: 38). What began as an industrial dispute quickly became a violent confrontation. Perhaps, in this highly volatile situation and in the absence of any institutions or processes of mediation, the violence that transpired was inevitable.

Armed black policemen, commanded by white expatriate officers, faced about a thousand strikers who were armed only with bits of wood, iron pipes, and stones. A Daily Gleaner reporter witnessed the scene on 2 May. He heard glass at the old factory being broken and moved out of what he anticipated would be the line of fire. 'Behind me, I hear rifle firing, followed by shrieks and cries . . . . I can see men on the ground. Some are motionless, others are staggering to and fro or crawling away on their hands and knees. The strike has culminated in stark tragedy. A few minutes later I hear that three are dead, eleven wounded and that the police are making arrests'.[281]

By the end of the day four people were dead, three of them shot and one bayoneted by the police. Two of these were women, one of them old and the other pregnant. Somewhere between 14 and 25 people were reported wounded (including five policemen) but, as it was believed that people seeking medical attention for injuries would be arrested, the wounded were probably more numerous. According to the newspaper, 96 people were arrested up to noon on 3 May.[282]

People in Kingston responded to the news from Frome promptly. A protest meeting at North Parade on the evening of 2 May attracted 3,000 people and St William Grant led a march to the office of the Jamaica Standard to draw its British editor's attention to the conditions of Jamaica's working poor.[283] Bustamante left Kingston that night and, arriving at Frome on the morning of 3 May, conferred with the manager and endeavoured to play a mediating role. The Gleaner reported that he was satisfied by the medical facilities and promises of housing offered by the company but told the manager that the 2 shillings per day offered to workers was not adequate, and that there would not be 'peace at the factory so long as that scale of pay existed'.[284] As Hart points out, Bustamante was at Frome in 'the role not of a trade union leader representing workers but of a mediator between capital and labour' (Hart 1989: 41).

Grant, meanwhile, led another protest march in Kingston, and some people from the horrific area known as the Dungle (a dunghill of refuse in western Kingston) insisted on taking reporters from the Gleaner to see where they had to live. On 4 May Bustamante, who had returned from Frome where the workers had accepted the company's offer, spoke at a meeting in Kingston sponsored by the Social Reconstruction League, led by a former policeman called Barrington Williams. Although Denham considered Bustamante's speeches at meetings attended by as many as 3,000 persons to be 'distinctly inflammatory' and probably seditious, he decided to continue to watch him closely but not to arrest him. Denham believed that such a 'premature action might only result in creating a still greater amount of unrest and suspicion amongst the ignorant classes' while enhancing Bustamante's reputation.[285] Denham appears to have been trying to learn from what had happened in Trinidad and Barbados the previous year.

There was a relative lull in the rebellion for almost three weeks, though there were public meetings and sporadic strikes among dock workers in Kingston. There were marches of the unemployed on 9 and 13 May and the crowds became less orderly as tensions rose (Phelps 1960: 425). Buchanan, who was trying to organise the Jamaica Artisans' Federated Association after he left the JWTU, was active in Trench Pen, a slum area of Kingston where there was dissatisfaction with the hiring practices of labour contractors (Post 1978: 277). A crowd of 2,000 made some labourers on a public project quit work, but Bustamante 'helped quiet things down' (Phelps 1960: 425). On 14 May Buchanan and Stennett Kerr Coombs (not related to A.G.S. Coombs) brought out the first issue of the Jamaica Labour Weekly, the masthead of which displays a map of the island and two clasped hands, one black and one white, and the slogan, 'Workers of Jamaica Unite!' Though they never printed more than 2,000 copies this paper was, according to Hart, 'widely distributed throughout the island' and became 'a very popular voice of the workers' (Hart 1989: 123). Calling for unity but not for action, the paper advised the 'fellow workers' only to 'wait and watch'. But on 21 May the Kingston dock workers struck again and the rebellion intensified.

Dock workers on Lascelles Wharf had protested against the use of stevedores from Curaçao on 10 May and others struck at Grace's Wharf, demanding increased lunch hour rates (St Pierre 1978: 185). Workers on the UFC's wharf then demanded 1 shilling per hour instead of 9 pence and, as the strike spread, ships were diverted to Port Antonio in Portland. Meanwhile, people in Kingston followed the news from Frome where, on 19 May, the first lot of workers charged with riotous assembly had been convicted and sentenced, with prison terms ranging from 30 days to a year (Hart 1989: 43). On 22 May Bustamante and Grant encouraged the dock workers to hold out for higher wages. American seamen were offered 5 shillings per hour, five times what the Jamaican workers were demanding, to unload the Veragua but they refused when they received a telegram from the National Maritime Union (NMU) urging them to support the strike. The vice-president of the NMU since 1937 was a Jamaican communist, Ferdinand Smith.[286] Grant, speaking to a large crowd of strikers, with the police in attendance, was reported to have said, 'We want better living conditions ... we want our police to be better paid, we want the store clerks to be better paid, we want the ordinary Jamaican to get the wages of Englishmen'.[287] It has been suggested that Grant might have influenced the police not to interfere in the early stages of this strike (St Pierre 1978: 186), but it is equally likely that Denham hoped to avoid a repetition of the violence in Trinidad and Barbados in the previous year. Be that as it may, the situation on the waterfront became more disorderly the next morning and the police then reacted with force.

By 8 a.m. on 23 May, according to the report of the official enquiry,

> Disorder ... became general and the Police were insufficient in numbers to control the situation. Persons of all classes going to business were set upon, public property was destroyed, streets blocked and tramcars attacked. A hostile mob entered the Sewage Pumping Station and drove out the staff and another took possession of the Gold Street Power Station of the Jamaica Public Service Company. Several thousand persons collected in Harbour Street where Bustamante and Grant were endeavouring to hold a public meeting and refused to disperse at the request of the Police. They were eventually dislodged by a baton charge undertaken by 60 officers and men of the Police who were subjected to a rain of stones and brickbats.[288]

Bustamante, having been rebuffed as a mediator by the employers, was 'firmly committed to siding with the striking waterfront workers' by 23 May (Hart 1989: 48). That morning, he threatened 'to tie up every port in the Island' and the strike quickly spread among other workers. The street cleaners, who demanded a pay increase to a minimum of 30 shillings per week, with overtime for work on Sundays and public holidays, had stopped work on the previous day, and by 11 am all the bus and tram services in the city had ceased. Strikers moved through the city, closing down businesses, calling out other workers, stoning the police and erecting barricades.

Hart walked through the streets of Kingston that day and recorded what he saw in his diary the next day:

> Bands of workers closed all shops throughout the city. Was standing at door of Scotland's when small body of about twelve young men came up from Harbour Street and ordered his assistants to close the shutters. One shutter was closed and then about nine or ten police charged. The band scattered, and one man got hit over the head with a truncheon ....
>
> Outside Jamaica Fruit Bustamante and Grant were holding a meeting. There was a large crowd completely blocking the street. There was a detachment of police east of the meeting .... Bustamante finished his address and he and Grant moved east along Harbour Street. Some of the crowd started to follow. Then the police executed an absolutely unprovacated [sic] charge with batons, laying into men, old men and women indiscriminately ....
>
> [After 11.30 am] Proceeded up King Street to South Parade where Bustamante, Grant and others were holding a meeting from the statue. Bustamante told everyone to go home. On the statue there was a man who was offering to assist the strikers with food .... Bustamante then tried to get the people to sing "God Save the King", but very few obliged, and the meeting ended. The crowd however did not disperse ....
>
> It was now about [noon] ....There was a body of police, at a rough guess about 60 to 80 formed up at the junction of Temple Lane and the Parade ... .They spread across the road and advanced in a solid line mercilessly wielding their batons. They went right across clearing the Parade. I saw a ragged, bare-footed woman beaten till she fell to the ground, and the policeman stood over her and struck her across the back of the neck and shoulders as she lay there .... Another man was beaten badly and I saw him being escorted to safety between Bustamante and Grant (the Police did not touch them) ... he was in a pretty bad way when Grant was helping him along.
>
> In the wake of the police came four (or five) little army trucks manned by soldiers in tin helmets. The trucks lined up opposite and south of the statue, facing the Orange Street side of the parade.
>
> The police then formed up and systematically cleared the park working from south to north. As I with the rest was driven towards the north of the

park, I saw stationed there some of the little army trucks manned by soldiers. Most of the soldiers in the trucks had rifles ....

Bustamante and Grant were ... walking side by side ... down the side of the park on East Parade .... A crowd began to follow but a body of police drove them back with batons. My companion and I were ... turned back by the police ....

We ... went west along North Street to the Hospital as far as we could go. There was a guard of soldiers and police. The Laboratory was in a sorry state. Every window was broken .... [When the government epidemiologist drove his car through the demonstrators and knocked down three women], the strikers had cut up rough and he had drawn a gun and shot someone. He had escaped into the laboratory and the mob had besieged the place .... The police and soldiers had arrived and driven the people off.[289]

A crowd of 500 marched up from west Kingston, playing drums and singing "Onward Christian Soldiers". Others marched into the west 'to stop the country buses before they pulled out at three o'clock'.[290] The police were reinforced by six platoons of British troops from the Sherwood Foresters who were stationed in Jamaica. These drove the strikers from the power house, the railway station, the telephone company and the sewage works. By the end of the day the 400 police and 235 troops had been joined by some 400 special constables (Phelps 1960: 426). More barricades were erected across the roads to stop the movement of police and soldiers, and even when there was no barricade the amount of rubbish in the roads slowed traffic. Hart noted 'a mass of debris of all sorts, stones, rocks, an old motor car chassis, the body, an old engine, garbage cans, and God knows what else'.[291] The striking sanitary workers had left rubbish bins in the streets and these were overturned. People frequently fought back, stoning the police and smashing street lamps to hamper the patrols at night. The city was convulsed in a more or less total insurrection. The official report records:

> There were minor clashes between the Police and the populace throughout the day .... In Kingston from 6 pm on the Monday to 6 am on the Tuesday morning the city was patrolled by units of Police, Local Forces and Special Constables. They were frequently attacked by mobs concealed in dark lanes and alleys, which occasionally fired shots but in the main relied on stones . ... During the night three Chinese grocery shops were set on fire .... By 2.30 am the city was quiet.[292]

Meanwhile, unrest and strikes spread in other places, such as Spanish Town and Montego Bay, and Llandovery and Drax Hall Estates in St Ann parish.[293] To contain the unrest, the government recruited many 'light complexioned members of the upper and middle classes' as special constables because these people, with 'guns in their hands', could be relied on to subdue 'the rebellious black masses with enthusiasm' (Hart 1989: 52). These specials, who were responsible for many of the casualties, were undoubtedly hated by ordinary Jamaicans. As the violence escalated the social lines hardened, and as those lines hardened the violence escalated. When the number of special constables enrolled reached almost 5,000, however, it included many 'black men with a more mercenary motivation' (Hart 1989: 52).

On 24 May, which was ironically the old Empire Day, the unrest continued and so did the violence. 'Crowds began to gather in the capital early in the morning and police and military were engaged throughout the day in breaking them up .... Military trucks patrolled the streets at frequent intervals'.[294] At about 9.15 am a police patrol was stoned when it tried to disperse a crowd at the corner of Princess and Heywood Streets. The police fired into the crowd and also into the upstairs window of a nearby house, fatally wounding a woman who was looking on (Hart 1989: 53). At about 10 am a woman and her nine-year-old son were shot dead, and her six-year-old child seriously wounded, when police and special constables opened fire in Matthews Lane. A Gleaner reporter called it 'a scene of indescribable confusion. The remaining members of the unfortunate family were screaming hysterically while police clubbed men and women who assembled in the lane'.[295]

Bustamante and Grant, who had been prevented from addressing a crowd on the Spanish Town Road west of Kingston, went to the fire brigade headquarters where the firemen were demanding higher pay and threatening to strike. The governor decided to have them arrested, although Bustamante was offering to represent the firemen and they did not actually decide to strike 'until after their attempt to enlist Bustamante's support had been frustrated' (Hart 1989: 54). Bustamante and Grant were charged with sedition, inciting people to assemble unlawfully and refusing to move on when ordered to, and were taken to jail. With Bustamante and Grant in jail, Manley took a more prominent role, but, like Bustamante at the beginning, as a mediator rather than as a labour leader.

Manley was at Frome on 23 May, representing the West Indies Sugar Company at the commission of enquiry. Recalled to Kingston by a telegram, Manley 'perambulated' in the city on 24 March and in 1969 he recalled seeing 'knots of silent sullen people waiting in ugly frame of mind. I did not at all like what I saw'.[296] He spoke to the governor, who refused to release Bustamante but convinced Manley to intervene in the waterfront dispute. A special court was assembled at the central police station at 10 pm and Bustamante's lawyer, J.A.G. Smith, applied for bail, but it was refused. By the time that Manley's interview with a Gleaner reporter was carried in the paper on 25 May, announcing that he had 'placed his services at the disposal of the working classes to present their cases to the employers and the authorities',[297] the jailing of Bustamante had itself become a grievance. Manley said he was 'convinced that Government is anxious that the people should have an opportunity of making representations ... and that one of the greatest difficulties in the way of any desire on the part of Government to assist in these troubles is the difficulty of finding persons who are willing to assist the labouring classes and putting forward their grievances'.[298] Bustamante was willing, of course, but the government would not yet let him out of jail. Manley recorded in his diary that he thought this was a mistake because 'a martyr was being made' (Nettleford 1971: 26). The unrest persisted, meanwhile, as strikes were reported on 24 May among bus operators and road workers. A patrol of police and special constables was stoned in Spanish Town and four more people were injured, one by a bayonet and three by gun shots, by military patrols in Kingston (Hart 1989: 60).

On 25 May there were further signs of the strike spreading. Dock workers at Bowden and Port Morant in St Thomas refused to load bananas, and strikers demonstrated at Highgate in St Mary and Bog Walk in St Catherine. The sugar factory at Monymusk Estate, Clarendon, was closed by a strike and there was a hunger march in Montego Bay (Phelps 1960: 427). Special constables, commanded by the estate manager at Caymanas, shot and wounded six workers, three of them seriously. The manager said that 'a gang of hooligans' had taken 'control of the whole estate', so he 'read the Riot Act and then ordered my Special Constables to clear them out'.[299] The class nature of this confrontation is quite transparent.

In Kingston shop assistants and the subordinate staff at two hospitals came out on strike and the tram and bus operators of the Jamaica Public Service Company decided to continue their strike (Hart 1989: 61). Bustamante and Grant were again refused bail after a crowd was dispersed by armed force from the central police station. The governor declared a state of emergency, and Manley met representatives of several groups of workers as well as employers. It was clear that the Kingston waterfront strike was key to the whole situation and Manley arranged to meet the dock workers at No. 1 Railway Pier on the following morning. Before the meeting, Hart and Buchanan tried to persuade Manley that he should not advise the dock workers to give up their strike until Bustamante and Grant were released, but Manley recorded in his diary that he spoke bluntly with them. He had negotiated an offer of an increase from the employers and he and E.E.A. Campbell, a lawyer of the citizens' associations, intended to convey this to the strikers' meeting. Buchanan quickly printed up a leaflet and distributed hundreds of copies on the waterfront (Hart 1989: 66):

MANLEY AND CAMPBELL CANNOT BE TRUSTED
TOOLS OF THE CAPITALISTS
AWAY WITH THEM
SUPPORT BUSTAMANTE AND GRANT

At the mass meeting on 26 May the strikers, led by W.A. Williams, who had emerged during the strike as the longshoremen's leader, refused to resume work as long as Bustamante and Grant remained in jail. Manley's advice that they should accept a wage increase of 2 pence per hour and return to work was firmly rejected. According to the Gleaner, the workers chanted, 'No work, no work', and 'We don't want 1/- an hour. We want Bustamante'.[300] Bustamante was becoming a martyr and the hero of the workers' cause, as Manley had feared, and Manley had put himself in the role that, ironically, Bustamante had first sought, namely as a mediator between capital and labour.

When Ken Hill, the secretary of the NRA, suggested to Williams and other waterfront strikers that they should form a trade union, Bustamante indicated through his solicitor, Ross Livingston, that he was willing to be their president. 'In this way', Livingston announced, 'there will be a legal and organized body ready to hand to negotiate with wharf owners and shipping companies and Government'.[301] At the height of the rebellion, therefore, Manley's offer to be a mediator had been accepted by the government and employers but was rejected by the waterfront workers, who propelled Bustamante into the role of labour leader. This laid the foundation for the BITU.

HMS Ajax arrived from Bermuda on 26 May, and street cleaners and bus drivers, under police guard, returned to work in Kingston. There were large demonstrations in Spanish Town and on nearby estates in St Catherine, requiring the despatch of soldiers and special constables. Several people were wounded in confrontations as 'every inch of ground' was contested by the demonstrators and some of the armed forces were injured by 'heavy missiles'.[302] There were new strikes at Richmond in St Mary, May Pen in Clarendon and Bog Walk in St Catherine, as well as Montego Bay and Kingston. Some working-class women who had started cooking free meals for the waterfront strikers in Kingston were assisted by middle-class contributors, including Edna Manley, Norman's wife. Truck loads of bananas and coconuts were donated and sent from rural areas and by 27 May some 1,500 midday meals were being provided for strikers in Kingston (Hart 1989: 69). The rebellion was not only spreading and remaining militant, it was also becoming more organised.

Denham, like Fletcher in Trinidad the previous year, seemed to think that a combination of conciliation and intimidation would end the rebellion. So, while the presence of the warship added to the show of force and the government again opposed bail for Bustamante and Grant, Denham announced the appointment of a board of conciliation whose task would include bringing about settlements of labour disputes 'so as to secure continuation of work' and making recommendations 'to relieve unemployment'.[303] As no institution for the settlement of labour disputes existed before 1938, O.W. Phelps is correct in concluding that the appointment of this board was 'the first indication of official acceptance of negotiation between employers and employees as a basis for industrial peace, instead of reliance solely upon force' (Phelps 1960: 428).

The Royal Navy was preparing to protect the wharves and 'to relieve police and troops for duty outside Kingston if the situation became worse in the country'.[304] Meanwhile, the conservative Gleaner portrayed Manley as 'every working man's friend', in preference to Bustamante. Manley announced the creation of a labour committee 'to represent the different groups of workers before the Conciliation Board and to negotiate on their behalf', to help organise trade unions, to draw up recommendations for labour reforms and 'to try and lay a foundation for a genuine Labour Party in Jamaica'.[305] Hart, who was a member of that committee, concludes that at this point 'Manley saw his role to be merely that of an advisor, albeit a most influential advisor, and an advocate serving the workers, and the functions of his Labour Committee as temporary' (Hart 1989: 76), but it seems clear that Manley had by then become committed to a more overtly political strategy. Hart and Buchanan's Marxist group decided to cooperate with the labour committee which met in Manley's chambers on 27 May; this marked the beginning of an important coalition. At the meeting of waterfront workers that morning Manley defended himself against the accusation that he was a tool of the capitalists, saying 'I do not represent more companies than I represent poor people in our law courts' (Hart 1989: 78). However, the workers remained determined to make no deals until Bustamante and Grant were released. That night, Manley visited Bustamante in prison and got 'satisfactory assurances' that he would not make trouble if released. He then went to King's House and reassured the governor, noting, 'We agree Bustamante to come out next day' (Nettleford 1971: 27).

On 28 May bail was granted at a specially arranged court session, described by Manley as a farce and by Hart as a 'ridiculous charade' (Hart 1989: 79). It must have become clear to the governor that there was more chance of the unrest continuing if Bustamante and Grant remained in jail than if they were released. All charges against them were subsequently dropped.[306] Shortly after 4 pm Bustamante arrived with his lawyers, Manley and the mayor at No. 1 Railway Pier, to be greeted by a crowd of 15,000. Bustamante claimed credit for getting an increase in their overtime rates above what Manley had negotiated, though he was in jail when this concession was made the previous day

at a meeting of the conciliation board. Having impressed the workers that he
was able to get them a bit more than Manley, he urged them back to work.
The strike was promptly called off. Manley recorded in his diary, 'Smith and
Bustamante rush off in enthusiastic crowd. I go home sadly. The first round
is over' (Nettleford 1971: 27). Manley and Bustamante then worked with the
conciliation board to settle more claims for wage increases and negotiate an
end to other strikes, including that of the daily labourers of the Public Works
Department. Meanwhile, A.G.S. Coombs led a JWTU team in Montego Bay,
where they won a round of pay increases for banana carriers, wharf workers,
stevedores and waterworks labourers (Hart 1989: 82–3).

Although Kingston became quieter after 28 May, other parts of the island
remained in turmoil for two more weeks. Important as the events in the
capital were, clearly shaping the future of Jamaican politics, Post is right to
emphasise that what happened in the rest of the island, particularly among
banana workers and small peasants, was equally important for understanding the nature of the labour rebellion. This was recognised at the time by the
English journalist, William Makin, who wrote on 31 May: 'The disturbances
which have been going on for some days in the country have astonished those
who imagined that once the strikes in Kingston were settled, the whole island
would be quiet and peaceful. But it must be remembered that the real unrest
and discontent began in the country, and it is likely that it will be some days
before it ends in the country'. (quoted in Post 1978: 282)

The country around Mandeville in Manchester was full of demonstrators
on 30 May, and roads were blocked and fires started as they moved towards
the centre of town. Roads were blocked and telephone wires cut in the area of
Santa Cruz and Black River in St Elizabeth, and banana workers and carriers
went on strike in several places in St Mary, St Catherine and Portland. By the
first week of June, there was evidence of rebellion in every parish.

Just as in St Kitts in 1935, workers marched from estate to estate, singing
songs and waving sticks, calling out their fellows in a series of rolling strikes
through the countryside. Sometimes they stopped cars and demanded
money, and sometimes they looted groceries and fired canefields, but there
is little evidence that they committed serious violence to persons. A strike
at Prospect Estate in Hanover on 2 June seems to typify the spontaneity of
this unrest. About 1,000 workers gathered at the factory where the manager
addressed the strikers and offered a 25 per cent increase in wages and better working conditions. The offer was refused and when the crowd raided
the kitchens for food, five constables were unable to prevent them. Only
when reinforcements arrived in the afternoon was the crowd dispersed.[307]
Several clashes were more violent, however, especially when Sherwood Foresters and special constables supported local police in clearing road blocks

and dispersing marchers. At Balaclava in St Elizabeth, a man was wounded when police opened fire at a road block, and two strikers were badly wounded at Richmond in St Mary. That parish was described as being 'like an armed camp' and a serious incident occurred in Islington on 3 June. A crowd of about 100 strikers from nearby estates had cut telephone wires and gathered in the town. When police arrived and tried to disarm them, one man, Edgar Daley, refused to give up his stick, saying, 'No, not a rass. You have you gun. I have my stick'. He wrestled the policeman to the ground, was bayoneted and had his back broken by rifle butts.[308] The crowd surrounded the police and stoned them. The police fired, killing four people, Caleb Barrett, Archibald Franklin, Felix McLaglen and Thadeus Smith, and wounding others.[309] Near St Ann's Bay a crowd of about 40 people armed with sticks and cutlasses invaded the Greenwich Park property and demanded land. An armed party was sent to drive them out.

More roads were blocked, wires cut and clashes occurred in the next few days. Makin wrote on 4 June that 'the country districts of Jamaica are blazing with discontent and outbreaks are occurring with disconcerting frequency'. Even though Bustamante and Manley travelled around the island trying to get the strikers to accept the offers made by planters and the conciliation board, many refused to accept such settlements. According to Makin, 'The men argue that it is not a question of the day's wages being insufficient, but that the amount of work available is insufficient'.[310]

Since Denham had died after an operation on 2 June, the colonial government was in the hands of C.C. Woolley as acting governor. He continued the combination of intimidation and conciliation, but with important new initiatives. On 5 June HMS Ajax moved to Montego Bay, leaving two platoons of marines in Kingston, and Woolley made a dramatic announcement that £500,000 was to be spent on a land settlement scheme in a 'New Deal' for Jamaica. Although, as Post writes, 'this announcement was the decisive factor in bringing the rural rebellion to an end' (Post 1978: 284), the unrest and suppression continued for several days, and the official report described 6 June as 'the worst day in the parishes when the disorders reached their climax'. The Sherwood Foresters deployed patrols through the parishes of Clarendon, Manchester, St Ann, St Mary and Portland on 6 June and two platoons arrived in Savanna-la-Mar at dawn on 7 June to deal with widespread unrest in Westmoreland. Determined strikers at Worthy Park Estate in Lluidas Vale were fired on and several wounded, another striker manning a road block at Jericho was wounded, and a woman was killed and at least one person wounded at Tryall in St James where strikers had occupied the estate yard. An armed party that went to rescue an estate-owner and his staff in Trelawny was ambushed by a crowd that rolled boulders down a hill on to a road.

When the crowd was fired on, one person was killed and others wounded (Hart 1989: 94). Similar incidents occurred, with more shootings, in Hanover and St James over the next few days, but by 11 June the labour rebellion had petered out. In response to the acting governor's request, however, another company of British troops arrived in Jamaica on 20 June.

According to the commissioners' report, eight civilians had been killed (in addition to the four killed at Frome), 32 wounded by gunshots and 139 'otherwise injured', while 109 of the government's forces were injured and none killed.[311] In Jamaica, as in the other labour rebellions, it is clear that most violence against people was committed by the forces of law and order. Of some 745 persons who were prosecuted, 480 were convicted and given punishments ranging from 'admonished and discharged' to 9 months' imprisonment with hard labour.[312]

The price of the labour rebellion was high in another way, too, because of the latent rivalry between the two cousins, Bustamante and Manley. Their temporary coalition barely hid deeper divisions that were to emerge in the following year and that subsequently split the labour and nationalist movement in Jamaica. This was already apparent at the meeting on 28 May, when Bustamante had just been released from jail and claimed credit for obtaining a better deal for the waterfront workers than Manley had been able to. He told the crowd that he was glad Manley 'came down to enter the breach' during his enforced absence, but also made it clear that he himself was their only real leader: 'I was glad that he tried to do something to help you, but I was more glad that you all refused to work. When you did this, you gave definite proof that you respect your leader and that you accept but one leadership'.[313] This autocratic style defined Bustamante's leadership of the labour movement from the beginning. The martyred hero became the dictatorial leader soon after the labour rebellion. Even those, like Hart and Buchanan, who were concerned about Bustamante's authoritarianism, decided to support him. Hart writes that they were concerned that the workers, inexperienced as they were, did not as yet 'have a clear understanding of their strength as a class, and still saw their struggle in terms of response to a messiah. Bustamante was the personification of their will to resist oppression and fight for their rights' (Hart 1989: 105). Hart wrote to O'Meally in New York on 1 June 1938,

> The comet-like rise of Alexander Bustamante, Usurer, discredited officer of the Jamaica Workers and Tradesmen's Union, to the rank of deity among the masses, is nothing short of a miracle .... But ... it would be definitely foolish to oppose him now. He has taught the people the strength of unity, and that unity exists in loyalty to him alone. He has the power to organise the people into unions now, and must be assisted to that end. Therefore, most of us, from

the extreme left to the centre, are prepared to back him.[314]

Moreover, the left acknowledged that, such was Bustamante's popularity at the time, it would have cut itself off from the masses if it opposed him. Consequently, Buchanan accepted the post of general secretary, Ken Hill became a vice-president, merging his small unions with the BITU, and Lynch became an organiser in Portland, in Bustamante's growing union.

An advertisement, drawn up by Bustamante's solicitor, Livingston, appeared on 9 July: 'Look Out for the Name "Bustamante" on All His Unions'.[315] When Bustamante announced he would organise five trade unions, beginning with the Bustamante Maritime Union, they were conceived as his unions in a proprietorial sense and he expected to receive loyalty and obedience from the members. Hart writes that 'Bustamante did not regard a trade union as belonging to its members . . . . He conceived of a union as something more in the nature of a business and saw himself as its proprietor' (Hart 1989: 102). This was true from the start of his unions and it remained true. When his union was registered on 23 January 1939, under the Trade Union (Amendment) Law 1938, it was as the Bustamante Industrial Trade Union (BITU). The rules constituted him as its president for life, and gave him power to control its funds and to appoint the committee of management (Hart 1989: 104).

The distinctive forms of the labour rebellion in the country parts and the urban areas of Jamaica, particularly Kingston and Montego Bay, reflect the variations in the relations between capital and labour and the consequent differences in consciousness and organisation of the working people. These differences, in turn, correspond with the various ways in which the rebellion ended in these areas. Whereas the urban areas, in which waterfront workers were the militant vanguard, reached a temporary resolution of their demands around 28 May with concessions made to organised labour and the consequent strengthening of trade union organisation, the rural areas remained in turmoil, led by the strikes and demonstrations of banana workers and small peasants, until news spread about the acting governor's land settlement scheme after 6 June. The aspiration of most of Jamaica's rural population to an independent way of life based on small farming was apparent before legal Emancipation in 1838 with the persistence of Maroon communities and of a 'proto-peasantry' (Mintz 1974: 151) that grew provisions for their own consumption and for marketing even while they were still enslaved. The promise of emancipation and the high expectations created by the former slaves' pioneering of banana production were increasingly frustrated by the development of large-scale capitalist marketing and plantation agriculture, backed by the colonial state. This frustration lay behind Rumble's protests and the intense rebellion in rural areas of Jamaica in 1938, particularly around the banana estates in St Ann, St Mary, Portland and St Thomas.

Acting Governor Woolley, shaken by the intensity of this rural rebellion, had grasped at the idea of land settlement, an idea that had been around in official circles since the Norman Commission recommended in 1897 'the settlement of the labouring population on the land as small peasant proprietors' (Lobdell 1988: 200). Land settlement schemes had been discussed extensively and even tried on a small scale during Governor Denham's tenure. A few weeks before the rebellion a memorandum about unemployment in Jamaica assured that 'the additional land settlement schemes undertaken are proving of assistance to the agricultural population'.[316] Nevertheless, Post's description of Woolley's promised 'New Deal' as 'a desperate expedient' (Post 1978: 293) is appropriate in the sense that this was a hasty response, made without consulting his superiors in London, rather than a well-planned policy. Captain C.H.L. Woodhouse of HMS Ajax reported: 'By Saturday, 4th June, 1938, it was clear that Monday, 6th June, 1938, was likely to be a critical day in the country districts. There was apprehension that murderous attacks might be attempted on the white population in isolated positions and extensive blocking of roads, cutting of telephone wires and blowing up of bridges was anticipated'. (quoted in Post 1978: 293) Although there is no evidence of the attacks on people or 'racial animosity' that the colonial officials feared,[317] many roads were blocked, telephone wires cut and bridges damaged as the rebels tried to stop the movements of police and troops.

The intolerable pressure on the peasants and their experience of proletarianisation under conditions of casual and impoverished employment intensified their desire for land and made them listen to the acting governor's offer. As Post writes, 'When the banana workers struck and demonstrated they did so for land, even if their immediate demands were for higher wages' (Post 1978: 296). Woolley offered land, and also promised tools, seed, livestock, advice and a new government department to provide them. Special editions of the Sunday papers and meetings organised by local authorities publicised the scheme. A Gleaner headline on 6 June proclaimed just what people wanted to hear, that the scheme would 'Make people independent landowners'. (quoted in Hart 1989: 97) Bustamante and Manley supported it, saying, 'This new hope for Jamaica must not be dashed by acts of violence',[318] and Woolley was able to report on 7 June that his announcement had been well received and the disturbances were diminishing.[319]

The banana workers, unlike the waterfront workers, still hoped to avoid proletarianisation, so the promise of a land settlement scheme appealed to them, and the administration calculated that access to a bit of land would not only keep the rural poor from starvation but would also deter further unrest. So, while the urban workers and sugar workers, who were more remote from the possibility of tilling their own land, moved toward unionisation in the struggle for better wages and working conditions, the banana workers, in contrast, aspired to revert to their peasant status. We may conclude, therefore, that the outcome of the rebellion produced not only divisions within the movement towards organised labour but also reinforced the divisions between those workers who were more and those who were less proletarianised.

Though the crisis had passed by 10 June, when the newspapers reported that a royal commission would investigate conditions throughout the West Indies, the colonial government and capitalists were shaken by the great rebellion and were afraid of new disturbances. Specifically, they were concerned about the coming 100th anniversary of Emancipation, on 1 August, and anticipated land invasions by people who believed rights in land should now revert to them. The Jamaica Standard reported on 25 May that tenants in upper Clarendon, encouraged by Rumble's PMILSA, were refusing to pay rent to their landlords and that, in anticipation of acquiring formal ownership on 1 August, they were putting up fences and were even offering to pay taxes on their land in advance.[320] In June and July the acting governor and the Colonial Office were taking this matter seriously: 'In the Clarendon district there had been a no-rent campaign since the beginning of the year, and labourers have already staked out their plots and endeavoured to induce Government tax-collectors to accept land-tax on these plots in order to establish a claim to them at zero hour. It is said that owners who will not hand over are to be massacred . . . . If this is true it would explain the anxiety of the Officer administering the Government to have a warship available on 1st August'.[321]

There is no evidence that any widespread plot existed, however, and Woolley reported: 'August 1st passed off very quietly, much to my relief. I think the people understand now that we are not going to tolerate any further disturbances. We took every precaution of course and the Police, Military and some 2,000 Special Constables took up "battle" positions. There were no attempts at seizure of land as had been anticipated . . . . I think the worst is over, although there is a tremendous amount of mopping up to be done'.[322] Part of the mopping up involved Rumble. The government, fearing that Rumble's message might spread, arrested him on charges of committing an act of public mischief by inciting people to abstain from paying rents that were legally due. He was tried in December 1938 and sentenced to six months of hard labour (Hart 1989: 96).

While Bustamante was busy creating a trade union in his name and style, Manley founded the People's National Party (PNP), initially an organisation related and complementary to his cousin's union. Manley acknowledged that Bustamante had become 'Jamaica's Labour Leader by the only test which matters and that is the support and confidence of labour'.[323] In the tradition of

British Fabian socialism, Manley created a reform-oriented party that would appeal to elements in the middle class as well as cultivating a working-class base through Bustamante's union. When the PNP was launched in Kingston on 18 September 1938, the principal speakers were Manley and Sir Stafford Cripps, the prominent British Labour MP who happened to be on holiday in Jamaica. Bustamante, who was on the platform, was not invited to speak and 'he never played an active part in the affairs of the PNP' (Hart 1989: 118).

Whereas Bustamante's initial political orientation was entirely labouristic and limited to trade union activity, Manley's was more nationalistic in the sense that he 'saw the trade union organisation as a bridge between the middle class movement for self-government and the working class movement which implied social and economic reconstruction. He saw these as two sides of the same coin' (Nettleford 1971: 28). Manley's social background, education and professional experience all made him more cautious than Bustamante and he was careful to maintain his acceptability to the employers and government. Even after having launched the PNP, 'his nationalistic ideas were still undergoing a process of hesitant formation and development' (Hart 1989: 114). In his oral presentation to the West Indies Royal Commission, given on 14 November 1938, Manley stated he was against immediate self-government and that he was prepared to see suffrage limited by a literacy test. He eventually agreed that adult suffrage without such a test would be preferable only after being prodded to do so by the commissioners (Hart 1989: 115-16). Although it was common for educated middle-class Jamaicans like Manley to have such reservations about the qualifications of the masses to choose their government, his response was hardly what one would expect of a socialist and nationalist leader. When universal suffrage was proposed by J.A.G. Smith in the Legislative Council, it was approved by 12 votes to 1 on 13 December 1938, and even the nominated conservatives supported the motion. At the PNP's first annual conference, held in Kingston between 12 and 14 April 1939, Manley supported the goal of achieving 'a parliamentary democracy on the lines which obtain in other self-governing units of the British Commonwealth', but when the UK declared war on Germany in September he persuaded the PNP's executive committee to suspend agitation for self-government.[324]

In spite of Manley's evident caution, the Marxist group had already decided to cooperate with his nationalist party while preserving their own separate identity as leaders of a socialist movement within the broad anti-imperialist front. As early as 1 June 1938, Hart wrote to O'Meally informing him of this decision: 'Mr Manley and Mr Fairclough are engaged in the formation of a Labour Party .... It will be the duty of all earnest members of the movement to keep it really alive from within, and that is the line we of the left have decided to take'.[325] This decision to work for unity, taken during the labour rebellion, was crucial in the subsequent shaping of the labour and nationalist movement in Jamaica.[326]

Meanwhile, repression continued. The Marxist group's newspaper, the Jamaica Labour Weekly, attracted the government's wrath over an article in the issue of 18 June, headlined 'Police Terror in St. James. Innocent People Beaten and Shot. Jails Crowded'. The article made accusations about brutal activity by the special constables. 'Government is determined to kill every working man or woman... who raise their voices in defence of labour' (Eaton 1975: 60). Buchanan and Stennett Coombs, the editor and printer, respectively, were prosecuted for seditious libel. They were convicted in October and sentenced to imprisonment for six months. The paper was temporarily silenced, but Hart, with the help of Frank Hill and others, revived it on 17 December. Buchanan and Coombs were released on 3 April 1939 but they had quarrelled and the paper soon died.[327]

The chief problem of disunity at this time occurred within the trade union movement itself, in the continuing rivalry between Bustamante and A.G.S. Coombs, who was again president of the JWTU. On 30 November 1938 Citrine met with Bustamante, Glasspole, Campbell and others and urged them to form a Trade Union Advisory Council to coordinate their activities, but Bustamante declined (Post 1978: 395). Bustamante's union expanded rapidly in the second half of 1938. In November he claimed he had 50,000 supporters, half of them active members, but government figures suggested there were about 8,000 regular members, including 2,000 dockers and 4,000 agricultural, mostly sugar, workers (Eaton 1975: 69). Many local JWTU leaders had transferred their allegiance to Bustamante. Rose, who led the St Catherine branch of the JWTU, for example, was persuaded to switch unions and bring the membership with him, and he was rewarded by being appointed a vice-president in Bustamante's union (Eaton 1975: 61). The BITU was rapidly becoming the only major union, as Bustamante co-opted or eliminated his rivals.

Coombs remained entrenched among the banana and dock workers in St James, however, so Bustamante sent Grant to Montego Bay in February 1939 to start organising a challenge. Grant was told by a member of the JWTU, an employee of the UFC, that Bustamante's union was not wanted there. An altercation developed and Grant sent for Bustamante who promptly demanded that the company dismiss the man. Coombs insisted that he be allowed to continue working and the company agreed, so Bustamante called a strike on the Montego Bay wharves. The Standard Fruit Company and Jamaica Banana Producers' Association wharves were closed, and these companies diverted their fruit to Kingston, but the UFC wharf remained open under police protection. Bustamante impulsively and autocratically called for an islandwide general strike, 'without any proper preparation or consultation with the workers' (Hart 1989: 127).

Dock workers in Kingston and Port Antonio and sugar workers in St Thomas responded to Bustamante's call, and so did Governor Sir Arthur Richards who, just as impulsively, declared a state of emergency on 14 February and mobilised the local forces and special constables. Protection was given to strike-breakers on the wharves, where members of H.M. Reid's Jamaican Ex-Servicemen's Union (JESU), sometimes known as the Ex-Servicemen's Trades and Labour Union No. 1, provided scab labour. Thus, a local dispute between unions, which had started as an altercation between two individuals, exploded within two days into a political struggle between the infant labour movement and the colonial government as a result of Bustamante's precipitate action.

The strike was a complete failure and some workers who had responded to Bustamante's call suffered victimisation. The weakness of the labour organisation and the inexperience of its leader were revealed, as Bustamante's 'ill-considered move ... jeopardized the whole future of the new trade union movement' (Hart 1989: 128). On 16 February Richards assured the Colonial Office that 'while the strike is maintained in places it is generally losing ground and public opinion is against it'.[328] Manley tried to salvage the movement by proposing what Citrine had suggested earlier, namely the formation of a Trade Union Advisory Council. Bustamante and Coombs agreed and Richards accepted the idea. On 20 February the strike notices were withdrawn, Richards ended the state of emergency at midnight, and the next day the advisory council's formation was publicly announced, with Nethersole as its chairman. At a public meeting at the Kingston Race Course on 25 February 1939, the chief speakers were Bustamante, Coombs and Manley. According to the Jamaica Standard, 'A historic scene was witnessed ... when before thousands of labourers, shouting themselves hoarse, the union of Jamaica's two rival labour chiefs, Alexander Bustamante and A.G.S. Coombs was at long last accomplished as they shook hands, embraced warmly, and pledged themselves to fight together and as never before in the cause of labour'. (quoted in Hart 1989: 131)

Hart, who was the provisional secretary of the advisory council, describes this public reconciliation as one-sided because Bustamante was less generous to Coombs[329] than the latter was in his praise for Bustamante. 'The truce between Bustamante and Coombs had not solved all the problems of a divided labour movement, but it was a step in the right direction', according to Hart. However, Bustamante regarded the truce 'as a temporary expedient' to save him from the trouble caused by the failure of the strike he had so impulsively called (Hart 1989: 133). Glasspole became the secretary of the advisory council in March and it was renamed the Jamaica Trade Union Council (JTUC) in April. The affiliated unions were the BITU, the JWTU, the Montego Bay Clerks Association, the Northern Longshoremen Union, the Northern Fruit Clerks Association, the Builders and Allied Trades Union and the Jamaica United Clerks Association.[330]

In March a group of union members, including Lynch, challenged Bustamante to democratise his union, as he had agreed during the negotiations in February, calling for the election of officers and for proper records of union decisions and activities. Bustamante's response at a meeting in Edelweiss Park was to call them 'tools of the capitalists'. The truce soon fell apart, as Bustamante broke with the advisory council and 'reverted to his own way of achieving unification under his personal control - the destruction of all other organisations'.[331] When Buchanan was released from prison on 3 April he was not reinstated as general secretary of the BITU, and the post went instead to J.A.G. Edwards, a former Garveyite who had been appointed to act in his absence.[332] The public passenger transport workers split with Bustamante and formed their own union, the Tramway Transport and General Workers Union, on 23 May. Their president was Ken Hill, who had originally led the bus drivers and had brought them into the BITU but had resigned as vice-president of the BITU on 17 April. The BITU was supreme, however, and on 24 May, in order to demonstrate its continuing support, a mass demonstration was staged, honouring Bustamante and Grant as the heroes of the previous year's labour rebellion.

At about this time the Marxists, who were then quite isolated, started the Jamaica Unemployed League (JUL), with Buchanan as secretary. During its brief existence, several leaflets were issued, demanding that relief workers should be paid at the rate of 3 shillings and 9 pence per day, as recommended the previous year by the conciliation board, and charging that the government was undermining the general level of wages by paying them only 1 shilling and 6 pence for an 8-hour day, up to four days a week for a maximum of 6 shillings. From 10 May demonstrations prevented the implementation of this scheme as so few workers signed on that the project could not be started. By 9 June the new labour advisor, F.A. Norman, had persuaded the government to announce a reduction of the daily hours to six and a free meal to supplement the 1 shilling and 6 pence daily rate, but the weekly maximum remained 6 shillings. Bustamante then encouraged his unemployed followers to accept these terms and begin to register (Post 1978: 423).

This issue became linked with the attempt by the principal shipping companies to employ members of the JESU as strike-breakers. On 16 June a crowd attacked the JESU headquarters and threw stones at the police who opened fire on the crowd. The next day, the government mobilised 400 special constables and a battle ensued in Kingston between people protesting against the government's terms of relief work and the armed forces. On 18 June police escorting members of the JESU to work at No. 2 Pier at 7.30 am were attacked by a crowd of 600. When the police opened fire, one man, who the London Times said 'was not one of the rioters',[333] was mortally wounded. The governor proclaimed a state of emergency on 19 June, rushed through legislation to control public meetings and demonstrations, and ordered intensive patrols of the streets. The disturbances ended.

This violence, the worst since the 1938 rebellion, occurred at the confluence of two of the chief sources of conflict, the unemployed and the dock workers. Several hundred dock workers who had been victimised since February's strikes were looking for work on the Kingston wharves. They refused to accept the terms the government offered for relief work and objected to their places being taken by members of the JESU, whom they saw as scab workers. Their bitterness and the subsequent violence reflected not only the divisions that characterized the working class but also the determination of the shipping companies and the government to keep wages low.

However, this also exposed one of the fundamental contradictions in the functions of the colonial state and contributed to the further politicisation of the working class. On the one hand, the colonial government was forced into expanding relief work for the unemployed. In January 1939 some 12,000–14,000 people were registered as unemployed in Kingston alone, out of perhaps 50,000 in the island as a whole (Post 1978: 420). After the experience of the labour rebellion in 1938, the colonial government took the advice of the Colonial Office to expand relief work as an 'insurance against disorder'. (quoted in Post 1978: 348). However, on the other hand, the government retained its role of helping to maintain a suitable supply of cheap labour for the employers, so it was essential that the rate offered for relief work should not compete with and drive up wages in the private sector. As the wages paid for casual employment in this sector were reduced to a minimum by competition, the relief worker had to be paid at less than minimal rates. Orde Browne had concluded that a rate of 12 shillings per week was just above the minimum subsistence level for a man without dependents, so the rate allowed for relief workers was to be no more than half that, namely a maximum of 6 shillings per week.

The unemployed resented not only these pitifully inadequate wages, but also the fact that the government gave armed protection to the strike-breakers who undermined their efforts to raise wages in the private sector. The contradictions of the economy were therefore forcing the colonial government into becoming a cut-rate employer at the same time that it maintained its role as the policeman of labour for private capitalists. It was therefore not just the economic conditions of a casual labour market, characterised by poverty and insecurity, but also the expanding and highly visible role of the colonial government that politicised the working class. The fact that the government could not meet the people's demands led to this synergy between the labour and nationalist movements, as it was widely believed that economic needs and reconstruction could not be achieved without self-government. However, by the middle of 1939, these two aspects, which should have come together, remained badly divided in practice. The JTUC, which was led by PNP people, could not seriously rival the BITU on the labour front, and the nationalist movement, as represented by the PNP, had lost its roots in labour. These divisions remained a serious and persistent problem in Jamaica.

Antigua

Labour unrest, but not a labour rebellion as such, occurred in Antigua, which was 'one of the more quiet areas of the region' between 1934 and 1938 (Henry 1985: 84). As elsewhere, earlier unrest had petered out without resulting in any lasting organisations. Workers used friendly societies and lodges for political and economic purposes in the early twentieth century. At one of these, the Antigua Progressive Union, there was in 1917 a discussion of wages and the Contract Act, the means by which the planters recruited and secured their labour. At the end of the First World War, a central factory was able to pay its workers slightly higher wages than the planters who owned small estates, so many workers felt the estate-owners were not paying them enough. A retired estate worker, Samuel Smith, recalled bitterly, 'After the nega reap the cane, the estate owner use to collect the money for it from the factory and pay the croppers what the owner decide was enough. Crop after crop them robbed us' (Smith and Smith 1989: 129). In 1918 some sugar workers went on strike and battled against the police. As Smith recalled, the reinforcement of the police by the militia and the defence force made it, in Antigua as elsewhere, more of a racial confrontation: 'The massas call out the militia and when they come the riot really spread. No longer was it riot between the Point people and the police, now it was between nega and white. The militia and the defence force - except for a few high-coloured police - was all white.' (Smith and Smith 1989: 131-2)

After reading the Riot Act, the armed forces fired on the demonstrators and several people were wounded. According to Smith, people were intimidated by this violence: 'I think it was after the riot that the people of Antigua gòt to be afraid of guns. Everything went still. Small farmers decided to make out, no more public grumbling from them. Them just grunt and bear it. No more refusal to work from anybody - at least that I know of - for quite a while.' (Smith and Smith 1989: 133) One of the workers' leaders in 1918 was George Weston, who subsequently became a vice-president of Garvey's UNIA in New York. On return visits to Antigua he spoke of Garvey and Pan-Africanism at the local UNIA branch, trying to keep alive a degree of community politicisation.

An effort to create an organisation oriented towards the working class was made by Harold Wilson when he formed the Antigua Workingmen's Association (AWA) in 1933, but it 'had only a small impact' (Henry 1985: 83). The labour rebellions elsewhere between 1934 and 1938 largely passed Antigua by, but people were certainly aware of them. Governor Lethem of the Leeward Islands reported that, before the rebellions in Trinidad and Barbados in 1937, a strike among Antiguan dock workers at the end of April 'collapsed after small increases of pay were given and alternative supplies of labour found', but that there was 'an indefinite restlessness' among Antiguan workers.[334] At the end of July, he reported anxiously that 'no immediate indications of trouble are evident but that possibility cannot be excluded'.[335] From the opposite end of the social spectrum, Samuel Smith recalled, 'news were reaching Antigua of disturbances in the other islands, something that the Antigua planters take very seriously. A whole lot of them gather at the great house at Collin's to talk about the riots in the other islands. At that meeting the bakkra pledge to do everything to keep that kind of thing from reaching Antigua.' (Smith and Smith 1989: 142)

The Contract Act was repealed in 1937 and the colonial government announced the Antigua Recovery Programme that included a small land settlement scheme for peasants and an expansion in public works activities, such as road construction (Henry 1985: 85).

The visit of the royal commission to Antigua stimulated labour activities and the formation of the first trade union. In the early months of 1939 labour unrest was reported to be common, 'with sporadic strikes in numerous sections of the labouring community'.[336] On 27 March a dispute at the Antigua Sugar Factory started a wider disturbance. The strikers wanted to form a union to represent them in their demand for higher wages but, according to Governor Lethem, 'it does not appear that this embryo trade union had in any way engineered the strike'.[337] On the evening of 28 March a pay rise of 20-25 per cent was conceded and work resumed but the next day workers at a smaller factory, known as Bendals, went on strike to claim a similar raise. Workers from the factory joined field workers from various estates and waterfront workers, and some travelled in bands armed with sticks and cutlasses from one estate to another to promote a general strike. Some cane fires were set and work stopped for two days. The police and defence force were mobilised, reinforced by an officer and ten men from St Kitts, and despatched to the estates. Eleven arrests were made, but there were no violent confrontations.

Two weeks elapsed before these factory workers received a small raise and returned to work, but other workers got no increase. Lethem admitted that the wages of agricultural workers were 'definitely low' but thought the estates could not afford to pay more. Bendals, which was already in difficulties, soon sold out to the Antigua Sugar Factory. On 9 April the dock workers and porters went on strike, demanding a substantial raise. After a committee of enquiry was appointed they returned to work on 12 April. An increase was granted, though not so much as was demanded. On 3 May the Antigua Sugar Factory workers struck again, but the government insisted this was 'utterly irresponsible' and they returned to work immediately.[338]

The labour officer, who had been appointed in November 1938, failed to win the confidence of either the employers or those who were emerging as labour leaders, and in May the members of the Legislative Council who had been elected in 1936 voted against him. One of these men was Reginald Stevens, a middle-class politician, described by Smith as a 'brown-skinned man' and 'a big man in the Odd Fellows Lodge' (Smith and Smith 1989: 144). Soon after the commission's visit, during which Citrine spoke of the value of trade unionism, Norris Allen, who had experience of unions in the United States, brought together several men to create the Antigua Trades and Labour Union (ATLU). These men included Stevens, who became the first president, Berkeley Richards, the general secretary, Wilson of the AWA and Vere Bird, who later replaced Stevens and soon became the chief figure in Antigua's politics. The Trade Union Act, No. 16 of 1939, was modelled on British legislation and contained 'provisions for the immunity of trade union funds in relation to actions for tort and for permitting peaceful picketing'.[339] The ATLU held its first annual conference in February 1940 and was officially registered on 3 March 1940. The creation of the ATLU, which 'marked a very important turning point in the political organization of Antigua workers' (Henry 1985: 86), was thus relatively peaceful, but these developments in Antigua were largely the result of the impact of the labour movement in the British Caribbean as a whole.

Guyana

While Guyana[340] did not experience a massive labour rebellion such as occurred in Trinidad, Barbados, or Jamaica, it certainly shared the characteristics and consequences of similar rebelliousness in the 1930s. Indeed, the history of persistent labour militancy and labour organisations is longer in Guyana than elsewhere in the British Caribbean.

Rodney wrote critically of the tendency among those who trace the origins of trade unionism in Guyana 'to skim over the last decades of the nineteenth century' (Rodney 1981: 219) and to commence with the years after the First World War or, sometimes, to start with the riots of 1905. Certainly, 'it was in the late nineteenth century that the modern political economy of Guyana took shape', and this constitutes the context within which the Guyanese working people began to shape itself into a class, as Rodney eloquently described, through extensive political struggles. However, as he himself wrote, in the 1905 riots 'spontaneity was much more evident than organization' (Rodney 1981: 221), so the history of organised labour may be said to have commenced in 1919 with the formation of the British Guiana Labour Union (BGLU).

The strikes, demonstrations and riots of 1905 did indeed 'set the stage for advance toward trade union organization' (Rodney 1981: 219), but this organisation emerged on a lasting basis only in 1919. Subsequently, a series of sporadic but persistent strikes and demonstrations by the Guyanese working people gave rise to the formation of 12 more trade unions in the 1930s. Guyana has the longest history of continuous organised labour and a record of great labour militancy, but by 1939 the labour movement was not as strong there as it was in Jamaica or Trinidad. Among the reasons for this are the facts that Guyanese labour organisations came to reflect the racial or ethnic segmentation of the population and they were not linked to any broader nationalist movement in the colony at that time. There were, however, growing links between some labour organisations in Guyana and those in other West Indian colonies, which were largely inspired and promoted by Guyana's labour leaders. It was in Guyana, in this period, that the foundations were laid for the Caribbean Labour Congress.

Guyana is an unusual part of the British Caribbean, less because of its continental location than because of its population distribution. Apart from the indigenous people of the interior, most of the colony's population became concentrated in the coastal belt that was drained and cultivated to produce coffee, cotton and sugar. The overall population density remained low, therefore, but the pattern of colonisation concentrated about 90 per cent of the people into the 4 per cent of the total land area that constitutes this coastal belt. As we have seen, the planters maintained political hegemony after the termination of apprenticeship in 1838 and used a combination of legal sanctions and massive immigration to keep their control over labour. Protracted strikes on the sugar estates by former slaves in the 1840s were defeated and planters reduced wages and turned to indentured immigration from Madeira, Africa, China and India. Portuguese immigration peaked in 1846 and African and Chinese immigration virtually ceased in the 1860s, but Indian immigration continued until 1917. The several thousand indentured immigrants who were brought to Guyana in the 1840s were so successful for the planters that annual shipments occurred without interruption between 1851 and 1917. The introduction of a further 228,743 Indians in this period dramatically changed the racial and cultural composition of the colony's population. By the 1890s the newer immigrants amounted to 43.6 per cent of the total population and the fact that they were brought to Guyana in order to supplant the former slaves and to reduce their wages 'created an atmosphere of suspicion and animosity between these ethnic sections' (Moore 1987: 178).

Although all these working people were being exploited, they were pitted against each other in ways that tended to increase competition and communalism. Serious communal conflict between Guyanese of Indian and African origin was minimal in these early decades, but Moore argues that this 'did not mean an absence of serious conflict ... at a localized and individual level'. Moreover, 'the incidence of communal conflict was kept to a minimum by the high degree of physical separatism which characterized the coexistence of these two large differentiated ethnic groups, but which at the same time accentuated and perpetuated their social and cultural differences' (Moore 1987: 184). Tragically, one of the ideas that these people came to share, which was derived from the dominant colonial culture, was that racial differences and identities were primordial and paramount. To the extent that this idea was shared, then, it promoted ethnic divisions in the colonial society, including divisions in labour organisations. Despite the fact that the working people of Guyana were in the same leaky colonial boat, or perhaps because they were put in the situation of competing with each other for their places in that boat, their labour organisations came to reflect the ethnic segmentation of the wider society, and the more divided the labour movement, the weaker it was.

The discovery of bauxite about 70 miles up the Demerara River from Georgetown led to the establishment of the Demerara Bauxite Company, a subsidiary of Alcan/Alcoa, and the company town of Mackenzie, now Linden, during the First World War. In the 1920s and 1930s, however, the Guyanese economy remained largely agricultural, producing chiefly sugar and rice. In 1931, only 2,867 labourers, or less than 3 per cent of all wage-earners, worked in mines and quarries, compared with 46 per cent in agriculture.[341] The vast majority of sugar and rice workers was Indian, some of them immigrants who still spoke only Indian languages. Though unindentured Indian adults resident on the estates already outnumbered indentured immigrants by 1880, the last indentures were cancelled on 15 April 1920 (Rodney 1981: 34). The interests of the Indian indentured workers were supposed to be looked after by an official protector of immigrants until the post was abolished in 1932. The presence of such indentured labour had a depressing effect on wage rates not only because they were the lowest paid workers but also because these bound labourers reduced the ability of other workers to bargain for wage increases.

The combination of low wages and a sharp rise in the cost of living during the First World War led to many labour disturbances and the creation of Critchlow's BGLU, but no other union was registered in the 1920s. The dramatic effect of falling sugar prices in the depression after 1929 provoked demonstrations in Georgetown in February 1930, and on 28 January 1931 a second trade union, the British Guiana Workers' League (BGWL), was registered. Led by A.A. Thorne, a Barbadian, this union lasted until 1951, but its membership was less than 500 until the 1940s. Most members were sugar factory workers, or municipal, hospital and other government employees in Georgetown, and were predominantly of African descent.

As the depression worsened, hundreds of Guyanese migrated to Georgetown to look for work, thereby increasing job competition in the capital. The government started some road work to relieve unemployment in 1930 but paid only 50 cents for a nine-hour day. In 1931 the BGLU pressed for a dole for the unemployed, and when the colonial government rejected this demand the union continued to agitate. A march was held on 11 May 1933, and a rally was planned in Georgetown for 1 August, the anniversary of Emancipation, 'to celebrate National and International Day of Solidarity'. The BGLU's publicity called for workers to prepare themselves for the coming struggle: 'Emancipate yourself from Imperialist and Capitalist economic slavery'.[342] Governor Denham dictated that 'no demonstrations would be allowed' and 'everything passed off quite quietly'. Nevertheless, Denham was concerned about the situation and felt that without 'the assistance given from home for works to relieve the situation ... there would undoubtedly have been disturbances to be quelled by force'.[343] On 14 August the BGLU organised a token 'Down Tools Day' as part of their struggle for an 8-hour day and a 44-hour week, without a reduction in pay. The 'Down Tools Day' did not have the intended impact on the Legislative Council, which met on the next day, and a strike among sugar workers at Diamond Estate, demanding the removal of the manager and large wage increases, continued until early in October.[344] Members of the East Indian Association, a largely middle-class group, provided food for the strikers and asked the government to support arbitration. The strike ended without violence, but 17 employees were convicted of intimidating non-strikers in the fields. According to the governor, 'The influence of Mr Critchlow and his supporters has undoubtedly been considerably weakened by the failure of the demonstration and strike', but he continued to be concerned that the thousands of unemployed in Georgetown 'form ready material on which agitators can work'.[345] A Workmen's Compensation Ordinance was passed in 1934, but its value was limited as about 75 per cent of the workers, including all agricultural and domestic workers, were excluded.

The depression persisted through the mid-1930s. In 1935 the yield of sugar per acre reached 3.02 tons, a record, and the total output was another record, namely 178,041 tons, compared with the previous record of 148,634 tons in 1932. However, although the total yield and the yield per acre increased substantially in the 1920s and 1930s, the falling price of sugar meant that the gross receipts for sugar, and even for sugar per acre, were falling. Thus, the average annual gross receipts for sugar per acre between 1921 and 1928 were $166.70, whereas between 1929 and 1935 they were $117.70, though the average yield per acre in those periods had increased from 1.96 tons of sugar to 2.55 tons.[346] The sugar workers were producing more sugar, and producing it more efficiently, but they continued to receive the same low wages. The result, in terms of housing, diet and nutrition was appalling. Many sugar workers continued to live in run-down and overcrowded barracks left over from the indenture period, surrounded by stagnant water and without adequate sanitation or water supplies. A visitor to Guyana in 1936 reported that 'The diet is mainly starch foods .... Milk foods are lamentably lacking ... generally speaking, a child once weaned never tastes milk again'. And, as someone in the Colonial Office noted on this report, 'milk is beyond the reach of the labouring classes, even where available'.[347] As the economic crisis continued, serious disturbances broke out on several sugar estates in 1934 and 1935.

In the 1930s Indians, who constituted 42.3 per cent of the Guyanese population, were 44 per cent of all wage-earners. However, they were over-represented in sugar and rice production and underrepresented in most other occupations: 75 per cent of all agricultural wage-earners were Indian, whereas they were only 19 per-cent of wage-earners in the public services, clerks and shop assistants, and transport workers, 14 per cent of mechanics, artisans and engine drivers, 8 per cent of domestic servants, and 2 per cent of wage-earners in mining, quarrying and forest work.[348]

Not only was there a great deal of ethnic segmentation of wage-earners between economic sectors, but there were also substantial differences in the occupations and wages paid within these sectors. Resident estate labourers were almost entirely Indian but many non-residents who lived in villages worked in the factories or cutting the cane, and a higher proportion of these were of African descent. Whereas the average annual wage for all workers in the sugar industry in 1935 was said to be $112, that for Indians was less than $98, so the minority of sugar workers who were of African descent were better paid. Moreover, although the average earnings of all workers increased slightly between 1931 and 1935, those of Indians declined. The average weekly earnings of Indian resident labourers between 1925 and 1928 was $2.03, corresponding to annual average earnings of $105.69. This fell to $1.92 and $99.84, respectively, in 1929, and fell further to an average of $1.74 weekly and $90.27 annually between 1930 and 1934. After the agitation and strikes in 1934 and 1935 these rates rose slightly in 1935, to $1.88 and $99.76, respectively, but this was still less than the workers had received ten years before. There were also significant wage differentials between occupations on the sugar estates. For example, the best paid African male cane-cutters in 1935 could earn $1.39 per day, but Indian male cane-cutters received no more than $1.05 per day. All other African male field workers (including punt loaders, cane transporters, fork and shovel workers, trench cleaners and weeders) received 62–81cents per day and Indian male field workers were paid 52–77 cents per day for the same jobs. Women field workers' pay ranged from a maximum of 90 cents for Indian cane cutters to a minimum of 24 cents for those who worked at grass banking. In the factory, average daily earnings (not distinguished by the workers' ethnicity) varied from $1.05 for fitters to 50 cents for unskilled labourers, with engine drivers, blacksmiths and carpenters receiving 73, 89 and 90 cents, respectively.[349]

The distinctions and competitions between workers made it extremely hard to organise labour across ethnic lines, even in the general economic crisis of the 1930s when the vast majority of the working people, whether employed or unemployed, and whatever their skill, ethnicity or gender, suffered so badly. The fact that Guyanese sugar factory workers and cane-cutters of African descent did join Indian sugar workers on several occasions and that there were no reported cases of conflict between these communities, is eloquent testimony to the growth of class consciousness in Guyana in these years.

Surprisingly little has been written about the labour rebellion in Guyana in the mid-1930s. Some Colonial Office files were destroyed[350] but much material remains on industrial unrest and labour disturbances in these years. According to a report by J. Nicole, a county inspector and district commissioner, 'there was a noticeable undercurrent of unrest' on several sugar estates in September 1934.[351] The trouble began at Plantation Leonora on the west coast of Demerara, one of several estates owned by the Demerara Company and managed by the local agents, Sandbach, Parker & Co, whose relations with Leonora dated from the nineteenth century. On 7 September about 600 shovelmen quit work and complained to Mr Lywood, the manager, about the price being paid, which would not enable them to earn more than 20–24 cents per day. They also complained that the work was not priced when it was allocated, that the overseers and deputy manager cursed workers unnecessarily, and that the head driver, Hassanalli, 'was overbearing and did as he pleased'. Nicole added that he thought the removal on the same day of the three senior staff members, to whom the workers felt 'they could carry their troubles', and the refusal of the new manager to participate in a system by which labourers contributed from their wages to a local Hindu temple, contributed to the trouble. This is a fairly typical mixture of grievances, including as it did concerns over pay rates and relations with management.

It is clear that the workers felt abused in several ways. On 10 September, a 'noisy and excited crowd of over 1,500' demanded Hassanalli's immediate dismissal and saying they did not want the manager or his deputy on the estate either, roughed them up and drove them off. Nicole sent for 12 police to keep order but the strikers refused to return to work until 12 September, after Hassanalli had been dismissed and the deputy manager had left the firm. But that same day 200 people left work when a driver assaulted a labourer. They returned only after Nicole told them the driver had been charged with assault and locked up. These workers, in the absence of any formal procedures for expressing their grievances, were finding an effective way of dealing with abuses by management.

On 21 September between 250 and 300 workers, shovelmen, punt-loaders and weeders, from Plantation Uitvlugt, owned by Booker Brothers, McConnell & Co (Bookers), which owned and managed most of Guyana's plantations, came to Nicole. They, too, 'complained about the low prices paid for work and the fact that work was not being priced when allocated'. The next day the whole estate was on strike and when the manager tried to restart grinding more than 2,000 strikers 'made an ugly rush towards the factory'. Nicole called for 'every available man to come armed with ammunition' and the factory was started under 'a strong armed guard'. The workers, like those at Leonora, 'complained against several drivers and the punt-loaders asked for adjustments to their pay, hours of work and the amount of load per punt'. Some of these demands reflect the distinctive nature of the organisation and tasks of sugar production in Guyana, but the general problems were essentially the same as elsewhere, namely too little pay for too much work and resentment about the abusive behaviour of supervisors.

No sooner had the workers at Uitvlugt returned to work on 24 September than, the next day, those at two other estates, De Kinderen and Tuschen, also belonging to Bookers, went on strike. Then the manager at Uitvlugt claimed his workers had 'gone absolutely mad' and had tried to beat him. By 26 September all three estates were on strike and pickets turned back the few who turned up to work. At De Kinderen, Nicole found a large and threatening crowd and when he urged them to return to work 'about a dozen men, blacks and East Indians, shouted that they must not believe me and that no one must work'. The next day some strikers assaulted a driver and two workers whom they 'suspected of carrying news to the Manager'. Three people were arrested that night and after 'several displays of force' and three more arrests, the people 'were subdued and frightened'. What Nicole's report shows is that, though the workers could still be forced into submission, there was in 1934 a mood of anger and a willingness to engage in militant action on the estates.

The acting governor, Sir Crawford Douglas-Jones, commented early in

1935 that although these disturbances had never got 'out of hand', they, like other disputes on other estates in the colony, showed there was 'a growing spirit of unrest amongst the labourers'. He attributed this in part to the new generation of Indian workers, Guyanese Indians who could read and write English and who 'are beginning to realise the benefits which can be obtained by collective bargaining'.[352] Resentment about the arrogant style of supervision, along with the fact that workers were not informed about the rate of pay at the time tasks were assigned, were major sources of dissatisfaction, and a contributing factor was that the workers knew many managers had been paid considerable bonuses in the previous two or three years and felt 'it should be also possible to increase slightly the wages paid to them'.[353] Finally, Douglas-Jones thought that managers on the sugar estates should deal with most 'ordinary labour troubles' without invoking the aid of government and should seek police protection only as a last resort if life and property were threatened. 'It is well known that serious trouble, which might otherwise have been avoided, may be created by the premature interference by Police Forces.... The premature invoking of outside assistance must have the effect of reducing the authority of the management over its employees .... It is quite evident that the troubles which recently occurred on the West Coast, Demerara, were the result of tactless handling by those in authority'.[354] These remarks proved prophetic of the tragedy at Leonora in 1939. However, while such tactless handling surely contributed, the fact that the troubles were more deeply rooted became evident as they spread in 1935.

Heavy floods on the east coast of Demerara in January 1934 had destroyed some of the small farms and livestock of workers in that area, making them even more dependent on wage labour. Several hundred villagers, mostly of African descent, obtained government work repairing sea defences until March 1935, but then joined all the others who sought employment in that year's sugar harvest. The workers anticipated it would be a bumper year because they could see 'the unprecedented heavy stands of cane'[355] resulting from the enrichment of the land by the floods, and they expected a share in this apparent prosperity. Agents of the BGLU had been active in the area and Critchlow was said to have encouraged the sugar workers to hold out for better wages at harvest time. The demand for higher wages was a major factor in these disturbances, as most people's wages had been declining since 1929, but at least as important was the workers' resentment about the way they were treated by the drivers and managers. Many of the disputes were triggered by anger about the way they were paid, or wages they thought were due were withheld, added to which was the abuse they suffered. What lay behind this growing unrest was generally a combination of demands for better pay and working conditions along with demands for rights as workers and dignity as human beings.

In no case did the BGLU call a strike, nor were these workers organised; on the contrary, their actions seem to have been almost entirely spontaneous and local, though there was a certain amount of imitation by the workers of adjacent estates and villages. We can also see that various categories of workers were joining together and increasingly forging a common purpose and united strategy, between field and factory workers, estate residents and villagers, women and men, and Guyanese of African and Indian origin. Though some workers did intimidate others to join them in strike action from time to time, the only recorded violence was that directed against their supervisory personnel, often Europeans, who were sometimes beaten and humiliated. However much the plantation system had divided these workers in the past, their actions in this period indicate a growing class consciousness as they united against managers, employers and police. The lines that were hardening in the course of these confrontations in the 1930s were class not ethnic lines.

The labour unrest in September and October 1935 was described as 'continuous though sporadic'.[356] Strikes occurred on the west coast of Demerara and in Berbice but the most militant were on the east coast of Demerara. On 30 August workers at Plantation Leonora, where there had been trouble the previous year, complained that their head overseer, Mr Rigden, was 'too pressing' and demanded his removal. They said he habitually cursed and abused them and was cruel to them. They also complained that they were not told the price to be paid for task work until it was almost completed, and objected to the long hours in the factory, and that mule boys who got home at 1 am and had to be out again by 3 am were getting only 2 hours sleep in 24. 'Most stress however was laid upon abuse by Mr Rigden whom they wanted dismissed'.[357] On 2 September the workers, armed with sticks, said that 'if Mr Rigden was not off the estate by 11 am they would make a row',[358] and everyone went on strike. The next day a deputation of 300–400 strikers met the estate's attorney at the district commissioner's office. There they raised more complaints, including some about the treatment of women, saying in particular that old women should not have to walk long distances to get to their assigned work places and that pregnant women should be allocated lighter work. The main complaint was still about Rigden's abusive behaviour, but the attorney refused to dismiss him. Later that day some canefields were fired and over 1,000 tons of cane burnt. Work did not resume in full at Leonora until 10 September.

The commissioners concluded that another contributing cause of the strike at Leonora was the system called 'Jeribandan' by which workers were defrauded of part of their earnings by drivers who assigned their cronies to complete other workers' tasks at the end of the week and then took a portion of the pay. This was a widespread abuse on sugar estates where the workers were assigned tasks that would take several days to complete instead of daily tasks. All the workers involved in this strike were Indian, and it is clear that men spoke up for women and village people spoke up for estate residents. The latter is particularly significant as estate residents, who were the tenants as well as the employees of the estate, felt so vulnerable to victimisation that not a single one came forward to give evidence to the commission about any of the disturbances. The commissioners bluntly stated that the obvious reason was their fear, 'the fear of retaliatory action and possible eviction from house and subsistence plot with but three days notice ... and the knowledge that no alternative means of earning a livelihood is readily available'.[359] (In this connection it is worth noting that three lawyers of the British Guiana Sugar Producers' Association were present at all the commission's meetings, which would have intimidated many workers, particularly the estate residents.) A few villagers did come forward, however, presumably because they felt a little more independent. One of these was a man named Basdeo who, with his brother Arjun, had 'taken prominent parts' in the strike at Leonora in 1934. After being refused employment at Leonora he had sought work on an estate in Berbice, some 60 miles away, under an assumed name, and had succeeded in this for seven weeks. When a suspicious manager had his photograph taken to verify his identity, Basdeo returned to his village near Leonora, but found it hard to earn a livelihood. He and three other villagers, Assick, Sookdeo, and Manna Singh, 'expressed the hope after giving their evidence they would not suffer through having come forward'.[360] The commissioners heard complaints of Rigden's 'harsh, exacting, autocratic and unsympathetic treatment' of the workers. A woman, for example, complained that he had caught her fishing and destroyed her seine, then fined her husband 2 shillings and told him that if he did not like it he could leave the estate. The commissioners concluded that such acts would 'account for the animosity directed against the perpe-trator culminating with a unanimous wish for his removal'.[361]

These examples are included at some length because it is through such details that we learn more of what the workers had to contend with and why they responded as they did. There is often a sense of accumulated frustra-tion, of a whole series of overlapping complaints that spill over from work situations to community and social life, any one of which may not seem major but that together eventually tip the balance and provoke the work-ers to risk strike action. It is also clear, in Guyana as elsewhere in the 1930s, that the workers had no other recourse so long as there were no established procedures or institutions to enable them to express their grievances without fear of victimisation. This left strike action as virtually the only way they could get something done about their problems.

Several other strikes occurred in the next few weeks, on Plantations Vry-heids Lust and La Bonne Intention between 11 September and 20 October, at Plantation Enmore between 18 and 24 September, at Lusignan between 7 and 17 October, at Plantation Ogle between 8 and 15 October, at Plantation Farm between 15 and 22 October, and also at seven plantations in Berbice between 11 and 14 October.

At Vryheids Lust the shovel gang, comprised entirely of Indians, stopped work when told the price offered, and a few days after threatened to beat Ramsingh, a driver who was cheating them. Others demanded increases in the rates for loading a punt, for half-banking and planting. The manager made some small concessions and suspended Ramsingh on half pay, pending investigations into his conduct. On 30 September a gang of cane-cutters refused the rate offered and demanded to know the price before they commenced work. One of the problems, the commissioners thought, was that 'the growth of cane is often very unevenly distributed in fields and that a flat rate might operate very unfairly to workers'.[362] These cane-cutters, who were all villagers and mostly Creole, made sure estate workers would not be brought to cut the canes, saying that 'they had planted the canes and were not going to permit others to reap them'.[363] On 2 October, 22 policemen were brought in to escort 80 estate workers to cut cane but some of the villagers chased them off. The next day the manager agreed to a higher rate as the canes were deteriorating and there was then 'a scramble for the work'. News then came that some gangs intended to stop the factory, so more policemen were brought to the estate. A crowd of about 400 strikers, armed with sticks and cutlasses, waving flags and beating drums, got into the factory and stopped the mills, but when the manager pleaded with them that the estate could not afford to pay any more the factory was restarted and the demonstrators quietened down. When ten mounted and 40 armed police arrived, however, the strikers got angry and accused the manager of being responsible for this, which he denied. At La Bonne Intention, as at Vryheid Lust, workers complained about a driver and wanted him dismissed, but the manager informed them that he kept fines in his own hands and the driver was not in any way responsible.

At Plantation Enmore grinding started at the end of August. On 18 September some punt loaders demanded an increase from 9 cents to 10 cents for loading each ton of canes. The 15 punt loaders on the estate earned an average of 94.6 cents per day, so each person was loading over 10 tons of cane per day. They also complained about the long hours they had to work to earn these wages. The manager declined to make any increase, so that afternoon the punt loaders went to the cane hoist at the factory and stopped all the work. Two of them attacked a driver and broke his arm. At the district commissioner's request, 24 policemen arrived on the estate and the trouble escalated. The punt loaders were joined during the night 'by Blacks and other East Indians from adjacent villages'.[364] They picketed the entrance to the estate, cut the telephone wires and set fire to several acres of cane. When the manager tried to restart the factory the next morning the strikers objected, shouted down the manager and the district commissioner, who was on the scene, and 'all work on the estate was paralysed'. At 9.30 pm the electric wires were cut, plunging the factory and managerial staff residences into darkness, and more canefields were set on fire. The strikers were using their own methods of counter-intimidation. At the strikers' request, the member of the Legislative Council for the East Coast Demerara District and an Indian doctor, Dr Jung Bahadur Singh, who was the member for Western Demerara, visited the estate to investigate the complaints. In addition to demanding a general increase in wages, the strikers now asked for the dismissal of the deputy manager who was said to use 'bad language to their wives'. The next day they were told their complaints were not justified. An attempt by the strikers to involve the workers at the neighbouring estate, Non Pareil, failed because they had just got a wage increase. On 23 September a large force of police arrived early in the morning to ensure the restart of grinding, 'the crowd melted away', and people returned to work.

At Lusignan a group of cane–cutters, described as half black and half East Indian, demanded an increase in pay and the manager promptly raised their rate from 36 cents to 40 cents per opening. These men agreed to this, but soon the manager encountered about 120 other workers, beating drums and waving red flags, who demanded $1.08 an opening and a flat rate of 24 cents for cutting all canes. When the manager said he could not agree to such a rate, they said they would not go to work and nor would anyone else. Soon after, the place was deserted and at 9 am about 100 strikers 'forced their way into the factory, drums beating, flags flying and waving cutlasses'.[365] They kept up the demonstration for about 15 minutes, with no violence, and then 'danced themselves out of the factory'. When they returned, five police had arrived and they were kept out. They then went behind the factory, stopped a string of loaded punts and released the mules. It was not until 17 October, ten days later, that the factory could work again. On 16 October a crowd of strikers beat an overseer and forced him to march in front of them, naked to the waist and carrying a red flag. These strikers, who were Creoles from nearby villages, armed with sticks and cutlasses, were shouting: 'Bad Abyssinia - all you white bitches got no business here - our country - you go back where you come from'.[366] One man, named Murray, ordered the overseer to dance to a drum and when he said he did not know how, they 'gave an African exhibition dance' round him, but let him go when armed police arrived. After several arrests had been made, work resumed the next day under an armed guard of 12 police.

On Plantation Ogle on 8 October, the punt loaders obtained an increase from the manager, simplifying the payment system by eliminating extras and bonuses, and receiving instead a flat rate of 48 cents per punt, as they demanded. The next morning some shovelmen took an overseer's saddle off his horse and threw it into a trench. A 'gang of East Indians and Blacks' beat the deputy manager and forced him to carry a red flag at the head of their procession. Between 200 and 300 strikers, 'waving cutlasses and sticks and carrying red flags', said they wanted more money and the deputy manager and a driver named Manoo dismissed, as these people ill-treated them. They complained also about not being told the price before they started work, that the wages for field labour were insufficient, that they had to pay rental for their rice lands although these were free on other estates, that there was favouritism in allocating work, that reductions were made from men's wages when their wives did not work regularly, and that women were required to do unsuitable work in the water. The manager found that Manoo had indeed been 'showing favouritism' so he was transferred, but he declined to dismiss his deputy. The strikers were not satisfied, so carrying a banner that said 'War Declared' they barricaded the bridge to the estate to try to prevent mounted police from entering and prepared to 'rush the factory'. They quieted down when the police arrived, however, and a few days later, after they were told the deputy manager 'was going away on leave' and that some wages were to be increased, work was resumed.[367]

On Plantation Farm on 15 October, a crowd of workers, led by a former policeman named Joseph Barlow, shouted at the manager, 'We want more money'. When he said their demands were unreasonable, they shouted 'Slavery done long time' and became 'threatening in their demeanour'.[368] The next day two overseers were assaulted and by 18 October police were stationed on the estate and the overseers were sworn in as special constables. By 22 October work was returning to normal. One of the workers, a shovelman named Soobrian Singh, later gave evidence that workers felt they could not ask for more money because if they did the overseer and driver 'would tell such a man "no work for you"', so they could only make demands when they were emboldened as a group: 'when the strike come on they get a little pluck otherwise the game would have continued so always'.[369] Barlow himself testified that they had actually planned to strike, having decided on 12 October that if they were not told the price of work for new tasks on 15 October they would strike. He also objected that the manager had implied that if they did not like the price they should take their wives to the bars in Georgetown where they could earn money as prostitutes. 'I turned to him and said "Oh, you take us then to make slaves", and he said yes if we does not know that we are still slaves. I said if we are slaves then nobody goes to work and I will see that no man work'.[370] Barlow, who was described by the commissioners as 'a capable and industrious worker', said he went about persuading people to stop working because of these insults.

These examples show that much of the labour unrest on these Guyanese estates was about how the workers felt they were treated. Workers demanded wage increases and better working terms and conditions, of course, but they were often provoked into strike action by the attitudes and abuse of the drivers, overseers and managers who carried on in a manner reminiscent of the days of slavery and indentured labour. The workers were sensitive to this and in 1935 a good deal of their militancy and some of the symbolic acts of resistance they displayed were focused on the issue of authority and their struggle for rights at the workplace, including the right to be treated with respect as human beings.

Governor Sir Geoffrey Northcote reported that Guyanese people of African origin were 'most powerfully affected by [the] Italian Abyssinian conflict which presents itself to them as [a] colour question',[371] and attributed the assaults on European estate officials to this. Although there is some evidence that anger about this colonial war was a contributing factor, it would be an error to deny that the behaviour of these managers was itself a reason, as Northcote implied. Opinion about the Abyssinian invasion reinforced the workers' anger about the racism that was deeply rooted within the culture of the British colony itself and that was manifested so frequently in labour relations on the plantations. The BGLU's publicity that 'employers are making too big profits and labourers are getting too little pay'[372] and that the start of the harvest was the best time to strike, was certainly another reason for the timing of these strikes. Having started on the west coast of Demerara the action spread to the east coast and then to Berbice in October, 'actuated no doubt by rumours that substantial increases in remuneration had been wrested from employers in this way'.[373] The governor acknowledged that the practice of not fixing the price of a task before the worker had 'gone aback' to start 'prejudiced the labourer', but his response to the prolonged unrest was to issue a proclamation on 17 October, make many arrests, enlist 100 extra police and put the militia on standby, after which, he said, 'the situation rapidly improved'.[374]

The strikers' tactics suggest a growing militancy, beginning with a verbal expression of demands backed up by strike action, and then often continuing by invading factories and firing canefields. Telephone lines were cut on five estates and roads were blocked with felled trees and barbed wire, and some bridges were destroyed. The inspector general of police commented on the similarity of the strikers' tactics to those used during the 1924 strikes, in which 'East Indians and persons of African descent banded together for a common purpose ... waving red flags, beating drums', and creating a common tradition of resistance and rebellion. He added that with armed and truculent crowds of between 200 and 700 people, 'a mere demonstration of force was not sufficient to set down the steadily rising tide of unrest'.[375] Given the scale of the unrest and the intensity of feelings involved, there seems to have been very little actual violence, by either strikers or police, in 1935 but the governor and his police chief were clearly prepared to use more force to suppress the growing disturbances if they felt it necessary.

The persistence of low wages, long hours of work, irregular employment and ill-treatment by supervisors caused continuing discontent and strikes on the sugar estates, but the BGLU and BGWL remained small and their activities were chiefly in Georgetown.[376] On 7 October 1936 Critchlow sent a letter to several firms, asking for higher wages for dock workers and stevedores. He argued that a reasonable living is 'made difficult owing to the limited number of days per month during which these labourers are employed'.[377] The speeding up of their work and the smallness of the gangs resulted in 'excessive physical strain on the workers ... [and] fewer days' work being available to them', as three days' work was compressed into two. Critchlow asked for an increase in the size of the gangs from three to four men, an increase of stevedores' wages from $1.60 to $1.80 per day, with double time for night and holiday work, and of dock workers' wages from $1.12 to $1.28 per day for men and from 84 cents to 96 cents for boys. The employers admitted that wage rates had remained stationary since 1922, but said it was 'impossible to contemplate any increase in the wages paid on the wharves'.[378] The strike called among the wharf workers of Georgetown lasted from 26 October to 10 November but was unsuccessful because 'many unemployed took advantage of the strike situation to obtain work' and the police ensured that the situation remained orderly.[379] The number of unemployed workers in Georgetown continued to rise in 1936 and 1937: on 31 December 1937 there were 5,047 people registered at the government labour bureau, of which 3,403 were described simply as labourers.[380] The absence of a strong union and the police protection provided for strike-breakers meant that the competition provided by the unemployed people in the town, many of them migrants from depressed rural areas, undermined the efforts to raise wages and improve working conditions on the wharves.

In September 1936 a Colonial Office minute on the commission's report into the 1935 disturbances commented that 'present conditions in the sugar industry preclude a cash rise in wages, but ... some shortening of hours without reduction of wages seems to me unavoidable'.[381] The official noted that the hours worked by field labourers, mule boys and factory workers were far too long, particularly in relation to their income, and that such conditions 'cannot be allowed to continue . . . . In the absence of a powerful trade union movement which could bring pressure to bear on the employers, some authority must be set up to watch over the interests of the labourers'. The official was concerned not only about the workers' low wages and long hours but also by their obvious 'fear of retribution' from management if they complained about their conditions. He commented that all the managers of the estates who gave evidence and said that the disturbances had surprised them, were either 'liars, or . . . extraordinarily ignorant of the feeling among their employees'. These comments, which were made before there was a strong union movement anywhere in the British Caribbean and even before the major labour rebellions in Trinidad, Barbados and Jamaica, indicate that some people in the Colonial Office were thinking that something had to be done about the exploitation and oppression of Caribbean workers. Another minute, written four months later, when it was anticipated that the price of sugar would rise, argued that the Colonial Office should press for 'action to improve the working conditions throughout the sugar producing Colonies', as the industry was dependent on government policy by way of preferences: 'Every endeavour should be made to ensure that a full share of the benefits of those improved conditions [in sugar prices] is passed on to the labourers, partly in increased wages, and, perhaps more important, in better conditions, shorter hours, etc., throughout the Colonial sugar industry. Present conditions vary no doubt, and perhaps they are not everywhere as bad as in British Guiana, but I am sure that they are everywhere capable of improvement'.[382]

While this sense of paternalistic responsibility was being expressed in the Colonial Office, a new union was emerging in Guyana, the most important to be formed in the 1930s. This was the Manpower Citizens' Association (MPCA), formed in 1936 and registered on 5 November 1937. The MPCA focussed on organising the sugar workers, especially the field workers, and it grew rapidly. Founded and led by Ayube M. Edun, the president, with the assistance of Harri Barron, general secretary, and C.R. Jacob, treasurer, the MPCA claimed about 10,000 members in 1939 and 20,000 by 1943 (Chase n.d.: 85). Edun and Jacob were already well known as advocates of the political rights of Indians. Jacob, a merchant and elected member of the Legislative Council, was president of the East Indian Association and wrote articles for the Guiana Review calling for Indian communal representation. W. Arthur Lewis wrote in 1939 that the Indian workers were easier to organise than the Creoles because they have 'a greater sense of national solidarity, being bound together by their own languages, religions and social customs' (Lewis 1977: 25). Though these languages, religions and customs actually divided the

Indians in many ways, a communal feeling of being not-Creole may have contributed to the MPCA's success in organising them. Although there were some people of African descent in the MPCA, this union was seen from its inception as a largely Indian organisation.

Meanwhile, some other trade union leaders were active in voluntary associations that were largely composed of and oriented towards people of African descent. Critchlow of the BGLU, for example, was involved in the Negro Progress Convention, founded in 1922. Six other trade unions, registered in 1938, organised primarily African Guyanese workers in Georgetown: the British Guiana Seamen's Union, the Transport Workers' Union, the Post Office Workers' Union, the Subordinate Medical Employees Union, the British Guiana Congress of General Workers and the Subordinate Government Employees Association, registered respectively on 16 February, 23 March, 30 June, 28 September, and 3 and 6 October.[383] The most important of the four small unions registered in 1939 was the British Guiana Clerks Association (Chase n.d.: 92). What was emerging in the late 1930s, then, was a trade union movement that was largely divided along ethnic lines, and some of the leaders of the trade unions were also leaders or active members of ethnic associations.

In a confidential section of his report on labour conditions, Orde Browne noted that in his first general meeting with all the unions the MPCA, which he described as 'overwhelmingly Indian', was 'conspicuous by its absence'. He commented, 'While the various trade unions all stoutly maintain their disregard of racialism, there is a very perceptible mistrust between brown and black', and a rivalry that could all too easily be aggravated if employers took advantage of it 'for purposes of strike-breaking, a quite possible development which would … produce most mischievous results'.[384] The ever present danger was that racial divisiveness would permeate down the society from the top and that the resulting disunity of labour would negate efforts to achieve progress for all Guyanese working people.

The number of labour disputes, which had declined in 1936 to two and 1937 to four, rose sharply in 1938. Between January and September 1938 there were 30 disputes involving over 12,000 workers. None of these strikes was called by the MPCA, but the union became involved in negotiations. When strikes happened in June, the MPCA advised the workers to return to work while it secured wage increases for them by negotiation (Lewis 1977: 26). Most of the strikes involved demands for wage increases, but seven of them included calls for the dismissal of unpopular heads of gangs. The Sugar Producers Association (SPA) complained that the activity of the MPCA was affecting the white staff on the estates and that some were quitting as the workers became 'more and more truculent'.[385] The racist attitudes of the planter class and their managers was made shockingly explicit in an exchange with

Citrine during the royal commission's visit to Guyana between 27 January and 20 February 1939. The SPA's memorandum to the commission referred to the workers' requirements as 'food, shelter, bright and attractive clothing, a little spare money for rum and gambling, and the opportunity for easy love making' (quoted in Chase n.d.: 85). A mass meeting was held in Georgetown on 12 February to protest against these remarks and Citrine attacked the president of the SPA, Frederick Seaford, about the planters' profiteering and exploitation of labour. Seaford tried to defend himself by saying his remarks were directed only at Guyanese of African descent, not at Indians, and accused Citrine of threatening the 'well being of the colony' by setting up 'labour against capital'. The terms of this debate, which had 'all the ingredients for a powerful class reaction against entrenched, external capital' (Cross 1988: 300), could have clarified the real bases of exploitation in Guyana. However, the commission hearings were overtaken by a major strike and rebellion at Plantation Leonora, which had been the scene of strikes in 1934 and 1935.

A strike by a shovel gang on 14 February was preceded by a complaint by the 15 firemen at the Leonora factory on 13 February that they worked an hour longer than other factory workers. They worked for 11 hours per day, in two shifts. While their request for an hour's extra pay was being considered they returned to work. The next day, the 80 or 90 workers on shovel gang no. 2 complained to Lywood (the same manager as in 1934) that their rate of pay was so low that they could not earn an adequate sum in the course of a week. They spoke to the district commissioner who advised them to accept the rate offered. Dissatisfied, the men said they wanted to speak to Edun, president of the MPCA, and that they would go to Georgetown to see the royal commission.

On 15 February no field workers turned out to work and entrances to the estate were picketed. At 7.40 am, while a small deputation went to see Edun and the commissioner of labour in Georgetown, the police prevented a large crowd from boarding the train, so they left on foot, shouting that they would go to Georgetown. Before 11 am they had reached Vreed-en-Hoop where a party of police stopped them. At noon Jacob, the MPCA's treasurer, arrived and heard the workers' complaints about rates of pay, hours of work and the method of marking punts. Jacob said he would make representations on their behalf and advised them to go home and await results. When he returned to Georgetown, 'the crowd became more disorderly' and tried to board the ferry to cross the river, but the police prevented them.[386] The crowd was reinforced by a party of women who arrived at Vreed-en-Hoop at about 1.30 pm. Later in the afternoon the crowd 'tried to push through the police cordon' to cross to Georgetown, 'but at no time used any form of violence'.[387] Arrangements were eventually made to take them back to Leonora by train, which left at

5.33 pm. Over 30 police were present and, apart from one isolated incident, it was said that no violence was used on either side. Meanwhile, Edun and Jacob told the SPA that they wanted to be able to carry on negotiations on the estates whenever disputes arose, because Lywood had said they could meet the workers only on the public road. The problem was that the SPA had not yet recognised the MPCA as a legitimate union, so the MPCA's officers, rather than pressing the specific demands of Leonora's workers, were using the dispute to struggle for recognition and their right to organise on the estates.

On 16 February about 200 factory workers turned up and were work-ing at about 8 am when a crowd of 70-100 strikers entered the factory and, without violence, got them to leave. This action was so orderly that some of the strikers even assisted a pan-boiler to remove sugar before he left the building. At 8.20 am, after the strikers, now joined by the factory workers, had left the building, 19 police arrived, armed with rifles and greenheart batons. Their bus was pelted with missiles and a large crowd gathered on the road by a bridge at the entrance to the factory. When District Superintendent Weber arrested five men the crowd attacked the police and demanded their release. People complained that PC Bijadder had injured a man and some strikers threatened him. At about 10.30 am another 12 police, also armed with rifles, arrived. The prisoners were released on bail at about 11 am and the crowd moved away from the factory.

Some strikers then approached the manager's house and the police who were sent to guard it were stoned and their bus's windshield was broken. Some workers said they had come because the manager had agreed to inspect the site where they were working, others demanded more pay, and some asked to be allowed to see Edun and Jacob. The MPCA officials had communicated that 'they were unable to attend on the estate without full recognition by the management'.[388] When the manager spoke to the strikers they threw things at him and the police escorted him back to his house. The district commis-sioner arrived at about 2 pm. His explanation that Edun and Jacob could not come because 'the estate authorities would not permit them to enter on the estate'[389] was unpopular and the police drove the crowd back with fixed bayonets. A police car drove up at 2.30 pm was attacked and damaged and the occupants injured. When the police threatened to fire on the crowd some people shouted, 'You are not allowed to shoot' and 'don't be frightened, they cannot shoot', 'the riot act has not been read and they cannot shoot'.[390] But when the police raised their loaded rifles to the 'present', a large part of the crowd moved away, towards the factory.

The situation at the factory was quiet until after 3 pm. Among the eight police then guarding the factory was PC Bijadder. As the crowd approached the factory, he was separated from the other police and fled across the road to a shed. Some strikers followed him and others pelted the remaining police on the bridge. The police fired some shots in the air but with no apparent effect. Fearing for the safety of Bijadder, Weber ordered his men to 'fire on the ringleaders'. Several shots were fired, both by the police on the bridge and those who had followed Bijadder. Four people were killed, one of them a woman named Sumintra, four more were admitted to hospital with bullet wounds, and at least six others were injured. Of the 32 police who were on duty, 23 were said to have been injured to some degree. No more shots were fired and the crowd 'almost immediately' dispersed. Edun arrived at about 5.30 pm, met a large number of people whom he said were very quiet, and spoke to them at the Hindu temple before they went to their homes.[391] Work resumed at Leonora the following day.

The commission appointed by Governor Sir Wilfred Jackson to enquire into the Leonora disturbances met for 12 days of hearings. The commissioners concluded that the firemen had acted reasonably on 13 February, and that their action 'appears to have been symptomatic of a more general discontent with conditions rather than a contributory cause of the strike'.[392] They thought that the members of the shovel gang who were dissatisfied with their rate of pay and went on strike on 14 February 'felt that they had legitimate cause for complaint' and that they were 'not altogether unreasonable' in assuming the manager had prejudged the matter and was trying to trick them back to work without any better rate when he agreed to inspect the field. They found no evidence of 'any deliberately concerted or organised determination' either among the workers or by people from off the estate to develop a more general strike. The march towards Georgetown and the more general strike resulted rather from 'an infection of immediate discontent which spread through the estate' after the shovel gang failed to get satisfaction. The commissioners concluded that the strike was caused by 'a general feeling of discontent with wage rates, earnings, hours of labour and conditions of living' throughout the colony, by an awakening and intensification of that discontent through the formation of trade unions, the unrest in neighbouring colonies, and the proceedings of the royal commission, by the immediate grievance, 'genuinely felt', by a section of the estate workers, by the failure of the manager 'to meet this grievance in a sufficiently conciliatory manner', and, finally, by: 'The absence of any effective means whereby the trade union would have been enabled to make representations directly to the management on behalf of these labourers at the time when the grievance first arose and to secure at that time adequate investigation of the matter in dispute'.[393]

Although the commissioners believed that the police had used 'proper and necessary' force against the strikers, it is clear from their report that the intervention of the police so early in the dispute contributed to the rebellion by provoking the strikers. The commission's report states clearly that there was no violence, nor was any intended, even when the field workers persuaded factory workers to cease work and join them, until after the police arrived. 'The determination of the crowd which had now gathered to effect a complete stoppage of work but not at that time, it would appear, to commit acts of violence led them to resent the arrival of the police upon whom assault was immediately made by the throwing of missiles at the bus which conveyed them'.[394]

The efforts of the police to clear the factory and make arrests 'further incensed the crowd who then resumed their attack on the police with greater violence'. The police were within the law in repelling these attacks, but their methods of dealing with the strikers created still more resentment and anger against particular policemen, like Bijadder, who took part in the arrests and used their large greenheart batons too vigorously. When the escalating violence resulted in threats to Bijadder and perhaps to burn the factory, the police were prepared to fire on the crowd. Though the commissioners supported the order to fire at the so-called ringleaders in these circumstances, they concluded, 'There is no sufficient evidence from which we can conclude that any of the persons who were killed or injured by rifle fire were actually engaged at that moment in acts of violence'.[395]

One must conclude, as the commissioners did not, that the presence of armed police at an early stage of a labour dispute in which there had been no violence to persons or damage to property was perceived by the strikers as inappropriate and an attempt to intimidate them. The fact that the manager could bring the police on to the estate so promptly, at the same time denying access to their chosen representatives in the MPCA, who could have helped to negotiate a peaceful resolution of the dispute, incensed the strikers, quite understandably. The readiness of the police to intervene in a labour dispute on behalf of management further identified the interests of capital and the colonial state in the strikers' consciousness.

In this way, the evolution of a labour rebellion out of a small labour dispute, and of a national incident out of a local problem, such as occurred at Plantation Leonora, itself became a factor shaping the emerging character of the labour movement and the anticolonial movement, though this did not really begin in Guyana until the 1940s. The death of several strikers, who were not themselves involved in acts of violence, at the hands of the police further strengthened this character of the movement in the consciousness of the working people, as the martyrs of the Leonora rebellion became part of Guyana's nationalist history.

Soon after the Leonora rebellion, on 2 March 1939, the SPA agreed to recognise the MPCA 'for purposes of collective bargaining, giving it the right to negotiate in any case of dispute, and to hold meetings on the plantations' (Lewis 1977: 26). The commissioners expressed the hope that 'more orderly negotiation and settlement' of disputes would result and that the MPCA would use its influence to control and limit work stoppages, of which there had been 37 in 1938, involving a loss of 147,461 aggregate working days.[396] The SPA was also concerned about the security of its factories. The recognition of the MPCA as representing the largely Indian field workers, while the BGWL represented the largely Creole factory workers, encouraged a division among estate workers as a whole, a division that actions such as the Leonora rebellion seem to have transcended, if only temporarily. The joining together of field and factory workers in a more general strike at Leonora indicates the development of a class consciousness that, by bridging ethnic divisions, created unity among labour vis-a-vis management. This was exactly what the president of the SPA told the royal commission would be 'most disturbing to the well being of the colony', meaning the well-being of the SPA and their shareholders.

One positive consequence of the strike and the subsequent recognition of the MPCA, which was surely not intended by the SPA, was the facility and encouragement it gave the union to organise and unite field workers throughout the colony. 'Union recognition throughout the industry made possible communication between sugar workers throughout the country. A unity of purpose, and at times of action, thus developed among the plantation labour force that had never been possible in Guyana before.' (Walker-Kilkenny 1992: 8)

However, the rapid growth of the MPCA after 1939 came at the expense of a broader, more inclusive labour unity precisely to the extent to which it was seen as a union of Indian workers under Indian leadership. Labour organisation in Guyana, because it 'started from the assumption of ethnic separation ... became a vehicle for ethnic interest' (Cross 1988: 304-5). The early trade unions of Guyana, instead of overcoming the ethnic divisions of the colonial society, reflected and ultimately reinforced them, to the long-term detriment of the society.

Comparisons and Conclusions

Despite considerable diversity in the British Caribbean, there is a degree of unity that enables us to conceive of these various colonies as parts of a regional whole. Important as the individual rebellions are in the social and political history of each country in which they took place, the impact of the rebellions as a whole was greater than merely the sum of the parts. This summary of the major causes, characteristics and consequences of the labour rebellions indicates the need to understand the relationships between local and global, and between economic, political and ideological factors, as well as the need to see the interconnections of these colonies in the region.

In this section we will see that these rebellions constitute a kind of watershed in the region in much the same way that legal Emancipation did one century earlier. I mean a watershed not in the extreme sense of everything changing, because there were important continuities after 1939 just as there were after 1838, but in the more limited sense that after these events, and largely because of them, the political culture and institutions of the British Caribbean were irrevocably changed in several crucial ways.

Caribbean intellectuals as different as James and W. Arthur Lewis recognised the epoch-making nature of these events at the time they occurred, but it is now possible, over a half century later, to understand the period in a different fashion. James and Lewis hoped that the birth of this workers' movement would not only give rise to labour and political reforms but would also form the basis of a new nation. They differed in their political responses to this project, but they shared the goal of a free West Indies. Though we must now concede that this project was aborted, it was nevertheless a real project at the time.

In The Black Jacobins, published in 1938, James wrote his analysis of the Saint Domingue revolution that produced the first independent Caribbean nation in 1804 because he believed there was a parallel, and a lesson to be learned, in the way the Haitian people had transformed themselves while breaking out of the old colonial system. James believed that this had to be a revolutionary struggle. Lewis, whose Labour in the West Indies had first been published by the Fabian Society in 1939, was a reformer who believed that the liberalisation of the political system, along with economic growth and social welfare, would promote the development of the West Indian people. Like James, Lewis understood the transformative political influence of the labour movement in the 1930s and hoped it would provide the basis for the aspiration to West Indian nationhood. He concluded his pamphlet: 'The Labour Movement is on the march. It has already behind it a history of great achievement in a short space of time. It will make of the West Indies of the future a country where the common man may lead a cultured life in freedom and prosperity.' (Lewis 1977: 52)

More than half a century later, when each of the former colonies has gone its separate way to nationhood, it is hard to comprehend the strength of this West Indian aspiration. But if we fail to comprehend it we will also fail to comprehend the regional dimension that was part of the movement at the time it took place. The embryonic aspiration to West Indian nationhood that was encouraged by the labour movement in the 1930s and 1940s subsequently became fragmented and frustrated in the 1950s and 1960s. A comparative regional analysis of the labour rebellions between 1934 and 1939 is therefore essential for the further understanding of this whole historical process.

First, the common causes of the labour rebellions include the impact of the economic crisis in the capitalist world, known as the Great Depression, and the related reduction of opportunities for labour migration and the return of many migrants to their countries of origin. Further, colonial policies were changing, particularly with regard to labour reforms and the return of the elective principle on a limited suffrage, that encouraged people in the British Caribbean to demand further reforms. Although British legal and political institutions were slow to change in the colonies, and generally lagged behind the liberalisation of the metropole, some British companies were modernising more rapidly in terms of technology than in their labour relations. Finally, the deeply rooted colonial political culture, based upon racism and rigid social hierarchies, was being challenged in the 1930s by the influence of various ideologies, including Garveyism and Ethiopianism, on the one hand, and Fabian socialism and Marxism, on the other. These factors had varying impacts in different places, but they were present more or less throughout the British Caribbean in the 1930s.

The Great Depression, which was an international catastrophe, shattered the dependent monocrop economies of the Caribbean. About half of the 2.5 million people in the British Caribbean were then engaged in agriculture, many of them dependent still, as they had been for a century, upon seasonal wage labour on the sugar plantations. Endemic unemployment and underemployment, resulting in widespread and persistent poverty, became suddenly worse in the 1930s. Sugar workers and their families throughout the Caribbean suffered, as did those who depended on forest products in Belize or bananas in Jamaica. Everywhere employment was intermittent and insecure, wages were low and hours long, and working and living conditions were severe. Poor housing, malnutrition and ill-health conspired to produce declining living standards and social conditions, particularly for the children of the poor. The royal commissioners' account of the terrible conditions they saw in 1938 and 1939 was suppressed by the War Cabinet for fear that it could provide useful material for 'enemy propaganda'. Lord Moyne agreed to 'moderate the tone' of the report and to cut particularly dangerous sections, such as those on housing and the position of women, from the published report.[397]

The closing of work opportunities in Central America, Cuba, the Dominican Republic and the United States, and the return of many West Indians who had migrated to those places in the more prosperous 1920s, swelled the ranks of the unemployed in the 1930s. Many of these returning migrants, who may have had some experience of unionism and politics, often associated with the Garvey movement, became active in the labour rebellions in the British Caribbean, for example, in Belize, St Kitts, Jamaica and Trinidad. The impact of the depression was not only direct, therefore, in terms of the deteriorating conditions affecting the working class, but also indirect in so far as it caused many people, who had been influenced by ideas that were then new and radical in the British Caribbean, to return home. Buchanan in Jamaica was one of the most prominent of these, but hundreds of others who have remained anonymous contributed to the labour rebellions through this period.

Changing colonial policies between the wars, particularly in labour reform and legislative systems, had an effect throughout the British Caribbean, often provoking further demands rather than satisfying them. Differences existed in the legislative systems in these colonies, from Barbados which had never been a Crown colony to Trinidad which had always been one. Most colonies had a semi-representative system in which part of the legislature was elected, and the rest were either officials or were unofficials nominated by the governor. Generally, the officials could prevail by means of the governor's veto and the Colonial Office was unwilling to give up this power. After Major Wood's Report (Wood 1922), however, some concessions were made to increase the popularly elected element, though still maintaining tiny, restrictive electorates. Even in Jamaica, 'politically the most advanced of all the units, only one-twelfth of the population qualified for the taxpayers' franchise, while in all the colonies high property and income qualifications restricted candidacies for election to the legislative councils to the small groups of the well-to-do classes' (Lewis 1968: 102). Not surprisingly, 'all self-respecting West Indians despised' (Lewis 1968: 100) this half-baked system and agitation for further reforms persisted throughout the 1930s.

The British labour movement's involvement in influencing its Caribbean counterpart began in 1925 when Critchlow of the BGLU participated in the British Commonwealth Labour Conference in London and in 1926 when F.O. Roberts attended the British Guiana and West Indies Labour Conference hosted by the BGLU. Lord Passfield, the Fabian socialist who became secretary of state for the colonies in the second Labour government in 1929, and his talented subordinate Shiels, showed a commitment to reforming the archaic labour laws in the West Indies. Prompted by the conventions proposed by the International Labour Organization, Passfield indicated to all the colonial governments that henceforth they would have to pay attention to the organisation and conditions of 'native labour'.[398] A Colonial Office conference, held in June and July 1930, discussed a variety of topics, the most important of which was colonial labour reform. Passfield urged the colonial governments 'to deal ... with Trade Unionism, and to provide for its organization"[399] and

Shiels pressed them to repeal the obsolete master and servant ordinances that still defined a breach of contract by a labourer as a criminal offence.[400] West Indians who participated in this conference included Cipriani, Critchlow and Marryshow. There is no doubt that they felt encouraged by what they heard and returned home with renewed enthusiasm for their workingmen's associations and infant unions, but perhaps they had too much faith in what they thought the British Labour Party would achieve on behalf of the Caribbean working people.

The workingmen's associations of Trinidad and Grenada and the BGLU began to look to the British labour movement for guidance and assistance at this time. Even after the fall of the Labour government, the appointment of the young Malcolm MacDonald as secretary of state for the colonies in June 1935 ensured that the concern with labour issues would not die. When, in response to the disturbances, Orde Browne was appointed labour advisor to the secretary of state in March 1938, the Labour Party, which had originally proposed this position in 1936, welcomed the move. MacDonald advised Orde Browne to cooperate with Citrine and the TUC on colonial labour problems (Basdeo 1983: 174-5). In December 1937 the general council of the TUC had established a new colonial advisory committee, the 13 members of which included Professor W.M. Macmillan, author of *Warning from the West Indies* (1936), Shiels, former under secretary at the Colonial Office, C.R. Buxton, vice-chairman of the Anti-Slavery and Aborigines Protection Society, and Creech Jones. This group not only began to shape the Labour Party's colonial policies but also sought to influence the new labour movement in the British Caribbean. On 31 March 1938, for example, a booklet for the guidance of colonial organizations, called Model Trade Union Rules, Agendas, and Standing Orders, was sent to 'all the known colonial unions'[401] and in February 1939 Creech Jones sent his account of the British trade union movement to several Trinidadian labour leaders: C.P. Alexander of the SWWTU, Rienzi of the OWTU, Francois of the NWCSA and Sylvestre Patrick of the FWTU.[402] The paternalistic attitude of the British labour movement to its Caribbean counterpart took on an urgency after the labour rebellions when the British Fabian socialists became anxious that the Caribbean trade unions should be led by people who, in their view, were responsible. Consequently, their advice and assistance were intended to guide and support those leaders whom they identified as responsible, at the expense of others.

This issue was especially salient in the late 1930s because of the revolutionary potential and radical ideological currents sweeping the entire Caribbean. Although in the British Caribbean Marxism appears to have had an influence only in Trinidad and Jamaica in this period, which was quite circumscribed, Garveyism was both more widespread and more deeply rooted in the political culture of the region. Many labour leaders of the 1930s were followers or former followers of Garvey, some with experience in UNIA branches in Cuba, Costa Rica or the United States. So it was not only the ideas of Garvey that were important but also the experience of public speaking and organising, and of recognising the need for unity, self-reliance and solidarity. After the Italian invasion of Ethiopia, in particular, the Pan-African and anticolonial aspects of Garvey's philosophy became a major force in the labour rebellions. Members of the British labour movement, as well as colonial officials, were antagonised by what they saw as an anti-white racial hostility in this reaction because they were unwilling to acknowledge how deeply rooted and interrelated with the class struggle the phenomenon of race and racism is in Caribbean societies. The British government's failure to satisfy the people's growing political aspirations, the increasing unemployment and poverty in the Great Depression, the spread of new radical ideas that challenged the colonial political culture, and a host of local grievances specific to each place, gave rise to the labour rebellions that swept across the region like a cane fire between 1934 and 1939.

Because many of the causes were common, there were also many characteristics common to these rebellions, in terms of issues and concerns, situations, tactics and responses. As is to be expected in a situation of such widespread economic deprivation, two of the key issues that recurred repeatedly across the region were the demands for jobs and higher wages. Several disturbances began with demonstrations of the unemployed who demanded work or relief, and others were by people who demanded more regular and secure work. The extent to which the unemployed and employed united in these actions is impressive because it shows that working people understood the relation between their low wages and casual employment, as well as the threat to the efforts to raise wages that was posed by the reserve army of unemployed. Though some unemployed were recruited as strike-breakers, we see the working people struggling simultaneously for jobs, more security, shorter hours and higher wages.

These economic issues were not their only nor always their first concern. We see also, repeatedly, demands for the end to racial discrimination and abuse at the workplace and for the rights to organise and negotiate. These workers' rights became increasingly linked to demands for rights as citizens. These human rights issues were less often expressed as demands for specifically political rights, however, than for decent and respectful treatment as human beings. Over and over again, the working people of the British Caribbean, most of them the descendants of slaves and indentured workers, made it clear that they resented being treated as if they were still in bondage. Their view of themselves as free people, a century after the end of legal slavery, was inseparable from their sense of dignity and the respect that they, like all other people, deserved. For them, as for anyone else, self-respect depends largely upon the respect one receives from others, and the entire colonial system, economically, politically, socially, culturally and psychologically, conspired to deprive the majority of people of such respect. A century after formal Emancipation, several factors conjoined, including the working people's economic deprivation, frustrated political aspirations, ideas about human rights and racial pride, and often their experiences overseas, to encourage so many people to struggle for these rights and this respect.

An important example of how the working people perceived and responded to this struggle has to do with their relations with the police and other armed forces. The police forces, and especially the various volunteer groups, were not only the frontline of protection for colonial property arrangements and social institutions, they were also the visible embodiment of racial privileges and hierarchy, which were maintained through violence. The officers and volunteers were largely white or 'near white', from the privileged social sectors of the colony or from outside the society, while the rank-and-file were brown and black. To many working people the police constables, who were in other respects like themselves, may have appeared as traitors or mercenaries, paid and ordered to oppress their own people. But the greatest anger was directed against the volunteers, the militia and special constables, who were often the strikers' employers, managers and overseers, now given licence by the state to use violence against the workers. In these situations, time and again, the colonial power structure was dramatised and clarified. The employers and managers, who were often racially distinct from their workers, armed themselves and called for armed police as soon as a labour dispute began, and this was frequently enough to enrage workers who had until then been peaceful. The ready use of armed force to intimidate workers in a labour dispute itself became an issue as the workers struggled for the right to express and negotiate their grievances. If the strikers defended themselves or were provoked into attacking the police, this often led to bloodshed and escalating violence, and in many cases to the introduction of more armed force, including the British army and navy. Even before it reached such extremes, however, the escalation of the struggle made the role of the colonial state in relation to labour disputes quite transparent. As the conditions provoked the workers into disputes and rebellion, so the labour rebellions provoked the state to defend with violence the economic and social order.

We see a frequent pattern in these rebellions. A local and quite specific labour dispute, having to do with rates of pay or methods of payment, or an abusive overseer, or not enough work to go round, became a source of confrontation with management who promptly sought the backing of the police. The workers' tactics, which were generally peaceful, often included mass meetings, processions and demonstrations, sometimes with a petition to someone in authority, and strikes that frequently developed as rolling strikes with occupations or sit-ins, as more militant workers encouraged others to join them in a more general strike to bring broader pressure to bear on the employers and the colonial administration. The workers, who began without legal or recognised representation or grievance procedures, often directed their frustration and anger at the police and special constables who were sent to intimidate them, and violence, once started, quickly escalated. The forces of law and order, therefore, often provoked violence and disorder and then suppressed it by arresting and shooting people. If the governor felt it necessary, he declared a state of emergency, enlisted volunteers and called in the army and navy to restore order. The courts subsequently convicted and sentenced many of the arrested people to make an example of them, while a commission of inquiry showed concern about the causes of the riots but expressed satisfaction that the police and volunteers had acted appropriately in difficult circumstances.

The common consequences of the labour rebellions were the responses of the imperial system, the institutionalisation of the labour movement and the development of its links with modern politics and nationalism. The responses of the various colonial governments were similar in part because some administrators, like Denham, went from one colony to another, and in part because all were following broadly defined Colonial Office policies for the region (and even for the entire empire). But they were also alike because they followed the logic of a colonial system in which similar structurally and culturally defined conditions limited the options. One of the chief functions of the colonial state was to maintain the security of capitalist property, which was particularly important in the case of Trinidad's oilfields, and, in relation to that function, to ensure the supply of a cheap and manageable labour force. By the 1920s this could no longer be provided by enslaved or indentured labour, and the system of coercion codified by the masters and servants acts that made workers' breach of labour contracts a criminal offence was under attack, even within the imperial government itself, by 1930. But it was the challenge to this system by the working people themselves, between 1934 and 1939, that provoked a crisis and exposed the contradictions within it.

The colonial governments throughout the British Caribbean responded to this challenge essentially in three ways: by police action, by making limited concessions and then by trying to institutionalise and control the labour movement. First, police action, as we have seen, involved surveillance, intimidation, armed force and legal action through the courts. When existing laws were inadequate new ones were quickly passed in order to detain, punish and isolate the more radical elements and divide the movement. Such laws, which included new definitions of sedition and the prohibition of meetings and demonstrations, generally inhibited democratic discourse and procedures, as well as workers' rights.

Second, colonial governments made concessions to some demands, particularly for relief, by providing (or sometimes only promising) help in the form of relief work and land settlement to assuage a proportion of the working people and so to divert them away from the growing labour movement. This part of the strategy was begun early in Belize and became a widespread response as an insurance against disorder in Jamaica and elsewhere. As social welfare it became the central part of the Colonial Development and Welfare programme throughout the British Caribbean after 1940. The launching of urgent relief schemes became a standard tactic for heading off disturbances and a key component of public welfare programmes for controlling the political responses of the poor.[403]

Third, the colonial governments appointed labour advisors and created labour departments, ostensibly 'to assist and guide the labouring classes in the formation of trade unions along the right lines'.[404] Where trade unions were still weak, however, the labour departments tended to dominate and control industrial relations and actually retard the development of autonomous trade unions by usurping their functions (Hamill 1978). The paternalistic approach taken by the Colonial Office, in conjunction with the British TUC, sought to establish what they defined as sound trade unions under responsible leadership. In 1938 MacDonald circulated copies of the TUC's booklet, Model Trade Union Rules, to all the colonies.[405] Several prominent British trade unionists and Labour Party leaders, including John Jagger, Cripps and, above all, Citrine, played a direct role in shaping labour organisations during their visits to the Caribbean. In early 1939 Arthur Creech Jones, a Labour Party and trade union leader who was a member of the new Colonial Advisory Committee of the TUC, sent copies of his book, Trade Unionism Today, to Ken Hill in Jamaica, C.R. Jacob and Hubert Critchlow in Guyana, and Adrian Rienzi and Sylvestre Patrick in Trinidad.[406] The TUC, working in support of the Colonial Office, was engaged in a programme of activities that included the distribution of guides to trade unionism and the offer of scholarships to selected labour leaders to attend Ruskin College, Oxford. Working in conjunction with the new local labour departments, this programme was aimed at shaping the development of the Caribbean unions, to propagate what they defined as responsible trade unionism by emphasising 'the separation between industrial disputes and militant political action' (Lewis 1977: 79). The articulation of this goal and the creation of labour departments to implement it were in response to the labour rebellions which had shown the possibility of a more radical labour movement, developing under leaders who linked it to a broad anti-imperialist project that could be both nationalist in orientation and regional in scope.

The logic of the colonial system meant that the Colonial Office and its local administrators had to retain their role of maintaining a suitable supply of cheap labour even when their more urgent task was to quash the rebellions and restore order. It was here that the colonial governments became entangled in blatant contradictions. At the same time that they offered relief work, promised minimum wages and intervened in labour disputes in order to circumvent further rebellions, they could not do so in such a way that would antagonise the capitalist class. When Governor Fletcher and his colonial secretary chastised and offended the employers and shareholders of Trinidad in 1937 they were removed. Yet when the colonial governments intervened to keep wages low and workers disciplined, and paid miserable pittances for relief work so as not to compete with local employers, the workers quite reasonably resented them. Facing the crisis in the capitalist economy and an increasingly militant response from the working people, the colonial governments became more directly engaged in labour affairs, in some cases even becoming one of the largest employers in the colony[407] and not simply the means of ensuring a supply of labour to private capital.

The colonial state was pressured, by the bankruptcy of the capitalist economy it was there to serve, to set up an economy based on long-term relief work and public welfare while becoming more openly involved in disciplining the labour force that rebelled against being exploited. As working people's demands rose, the role of the colonial government expanded and became more transparent, which only served to broaden the demands made of it. The structural conditions of the colonial economy, based as it was on the perpetuation of a cheap and casual labour market in which seasonal low-paid work and frequent unemployment were the norm, denied the colonial government the possibility of meeting the people's economic demands, with the result that criticism was increasingly focused on the inadequacies of this government and the imperial system it represented. Thus, the increasingly obvious inability of the colonial governments to satisfy the people's demands fed the seeds of nationalism within the labour movement in the 1930s and the anticolonial and independence movements that followed. Despite the efforts of these colonial governments to divert or suppress such movements, through land settlement schemes or imprisoning the leaders, as we have seen, and despite the diversion of the war years when many colonised people rallied round the Union Jack, the momentum that was established in the labour rebellions between 1934 and 1939 developed into modern political parties, the evolution of self-government and constitutional decolonisation in the next 30-40 years throughout the British Caribbean.

As is well known, some of the leaders of these political parties and movements had already emerged by 1939, including Bird in Antigua, Adams in Barbados and Bustamante and Manley in Jamaica. In many cases, such as Barbados, Belize and Jamaica, middle-class politicians used the trade unions as vehicles for their own advancement and the labour movement in these places lost autonomy. In some cases, such as Belize, Grenada and Guyana, the intimate connections between trade unions and nationalist parties did not emerge until the late 1940s and early 1950s. By 1939 there were already some crucial differences between the colonies. Although trade unions were forming in most of the British Caribbean by that date, they remained weak in most places, such as Belize, St Kitts, Antigua and Barbados and in Guyana where they were sharply divided by ethnicity. Unions were strongest in Jamaica and Trinidad, but whereas in the former one man had already come to dominate organised labour while his rival had formed a political party, in the latter there was a proliferation of trade unions without any political unity. These differences shaped the subsequent genesis of politics and the relations of political parties to trade unions in those colonies.

These brief conclusions have only identified some of the chief consequences of the labour rebellions, along with their similarities and differences, but something more needs to be said about the regional nature of the movement at that time. The institutionalisation of trade unions and their relations with political parties took an increasingly insular form but the aspiration towards some kind of regional movement was quite strong in 1939.[408] The first British Guiana and West Indies labour conference, organised and hosted by Critchlow and his BGLU in Georgetown in 1926, included representatives from Trinidad and Suriname. This embryonic regional labour organisation advocated broad social and political reforms within a federal concept of nationhood. Resolutions were passed recommending the introduction of compulsory education throughout the West Indies, along with workmen's compensation, an 8-hour working day, minimum wages, non-contributory old-age pensions, national health insurance and prison reform. The conference called for a federation of the West Indies and British Guiana, with some form of parliamentary self-government and dominion status. A committee was charged with drafting the rules for a Guianese and West Indian Federation of Trade Unions and Labour Parties.

The second and third conferences were held in 1938, in Guyana in July and Trinidad in November, with Critchlow of the BGLU, Thorne of the BGWL, Cipriani of the TLP, and Rienzi and Mentor of the OWTU. Messages were received from workers in Barbados, St Kitts and St Vincent, and delegates from Barbados attended the Trinidad conference. The executive members of the British Guianese and West Indies Labour Congress were

Cipriani as president, Thorne and J.H. Helstone, vice-presidents, Rienzi as general secretary, Critchlow, assistant secretary, A.N. Gooding, treasurer, and Jacob, Edun, Mentor, J. Van Eer and Theophilus Lee as committee members (Basdeo 1983: 257). The delegates reaffirmed their primary goal, namely 'To strengthen intercolonial solidarity of the workers in the various trade unions' (Chase n.d.: 75). The conferences aspired to embrace both trade union and broader political and cultural aspects of the workers' struggle. It was hoped to establish regular communication between this organisation and the British TUC, whose general council agreed to send a representative to the West Indies. However, this regional labour congress remained at that time more of an aspiration than an institution and its work, interrupted by the war, was not resumed until 1944.

Another aspiration toward regional unity manifested itself in 1938. Though it does not seem to have had a serious or organised basis, it shows that even some of the West Indians resident in Cuba shared in a federal ideal. In 1938 David S. Nathan, a Trinidadian resident in Guantanamo, Cuba, sent a resolution from the British West Indies Labour Party (BWILP), of which he was said to be the vice-president and Cipriani the president, to the Colonial Office. Nathan worked among West Indians in Oriente and Camaguey provinces. He claimed that the BWILP had received 'the endorsement and support of workers' in Belize, Guyana, the Bahamas, the British Virgin Islands and West Indies, as well as West Indians 'temporarily residing in foreign countries', to create a British West Indian government, with Cipriani as prime minister.[409] He wrote that the BWILP, 'situated in and around the Caribbean Sea', strongly protested against 'the abuses of the capitalist class upon the workers' that were responsible for 'the revolution in the colonies during these several months'.[410] The British government took this seriously enough to make enquiries about Nathan in Cuba and Trinidad. Cipriani had apparently accepted Nathan's invitation to lead the BWILP but had not heard from him since.[411] When Nathan sent a declaration of independence on behalf of the BWILP to Washington in 1940, Cipriani repudiated the action.[412]

The aspirations of the labour movement towards closer regional cooperation and a federal ideal were institutionalised within a few years of the labour rebellions when the Caribbean Labour Congress (CLC) was created in Barbados in 1945. Many of the participants in the events between 1934 and 1939, including Adams, Bird, Critchlow, Hart and Manley, along with Robert Bradshaw, Gomes, Marryshow and Hugh Springer, played leading roles in the development of trade unions and the CLC. Most of them, in the 1940s, saw the need for labour unity and West Indian unity as connected and interdependent. In these early years the labour leaders, who had not yet become insular nationalist politicians, still dreamed of a strong federal state, including Belize and Guyana, with full self-government and dominion status, that would be capable of planning regional economic development on behalf of the entire West Indian working class.[413] Gordon Lewis (1968: 343) wrote, 'The recognition of the seminal truth that only a unified Caribbean, politically and economically, can save the region from its fatal particularism is at least a century old'. Although proposals about a federation had started in the nineteenth century, it was not until organised labour emerged out of the labour rebellions in the 1930s that the idea had a base in popular organisations. When the newly formed regional labour movement became divided in the late 1940s the federal ideal lost its labour voice, so the compromise federation that was worked out by middle-class politicians and British officials, without popular support, was doomed to failure. Nevertheless, the extent to which the movement that emerged from the labour rebellions of the 1930s included a regional impetus is an important part of the history of the Caribbean.

What were the chief achievements of the labour rebellions? They must include, of course, the formation of trade unions and the passage of a variety of labour reforms in the colonial legislatures. They must include also the new attention that the British government focused on its Caribbean colonies, marked by the royal commission of 1938-9, and resulting in the Colonial Development and Welfare organisation and then, beginning in Jamaica in 1944, universal adult suffrage. Above all, however, the rebellions achieved a shift in the political culture, as the working people of the British Caribbean made it clear that they would no longer be defined as merely the cheap labour of sugar kings and oil lords. In Lamming's words, which were written with reference to Barbados but could apply throughout the region, there was after the labour rebellions a new 'confidence in very ordinary people that they could and should be heard by those who were called authority'. These people placed their demands for improved conditions at the centre of the Caribbean agenda, and their struggle for respect and a better life became the basis of modern Caribbean politics.

Notes

[1] There were also major strikes and rebellions in other parts of the Caribbean, such as Cuba in 1933 and Puerto Rico in 1934.

[2] Macmillan 1936 does not mention Belize.

[3] Colonial Report for 1932, No. 1 1647 (London, 1933): 12, 31.

[4] It is to this explosion that the beginning of modern politics is generally attributed (Waddell 1961: 109). However, as I have shown, the birth of the nationalist movement cannot be understood without consideration of its long period of gestation.

[5] P.E. Matthews' report to governor, 27 Nov. 1934, CO 123/346/35524.

[6] Clarion, 22 Feb. 1934: 165.

7   Gov. Sir Harold Kittermaster to Secretary of State (SS), 7 Mar. 1934, CO 123/346/35524.
8   Matthews' report, op. cit.
9   See the autobiographical letter, A. Soberanis to Vernon Leslie, 10 Jul. 1973, BA, SP 27;
    also 'Oral History: The L. and U.A.', National Studies 2:3 (1974): 3-10.
10 A government-sponsored school textbook lists him as a national hero; A History of
    Belize: Nation in the Making (Belize City, 1983): 53.
11 Matthews' report. op. cit.
12 Ibid.
13 Ibid.
14 Ibid.
15 'Memorial in regard to conditions in the Colony', Soberanis to Kittermaster, 17 May
    1934, BA, MP 700-34.
16 Kittermaster to Soberanis, 18 May 1934, BA, MP 700-34.
17 Soberanis to Kittermaster, 21 May 1934, BA, MP 700-34.
18 Matthews' report, op. cit.
19 Matthews' report, op. cit.
20 Belize Independent, 1 Aug. 1934.
21 See reports enclosed in Acting Gov. Hunter to SS, 14 Aug. 1934, CO 123/346/35524.
22 Matthews' report, op. cit.
23 Ibid.
24 Ibid.
25 Ibid.
26 He recovered from the wound and it was never discovered who shot him. The police
    contended that it was a member of the crowd but it was widely believed that Corporal
    Building was responsible.
27 Matthews' report, op. cit.
28 Ibid.
29 Gov. A.C. Burns to SS, 31 Mar. 1935, CO 123/352/66554.
30 Burns to SS, 26 Jul. 1935, CO 123/353/66571.
31 Att.-Gen. S.A. McKinistry to Burns, 22 Jul. 1935, CO 123/353/66571.
32 Matthews' report, 12 Jun. 1935, included in Burns to SS, 13 Jun. 1935, CO 123/253/66568.
33 Burns to SS, 13 Jun. 1935, CO 123/253/66568.
34 Burns to SS, 23 May 1935, CO 123/353/66571.
35 Serg. A.B. Clarke's report, 20 Jul. 1935, CO 123/353/66571.
36 Soberanis to Burns, 23 Sept. 1935, CO 123/353/66571.
37 Burns to SS, 30 Oct. 1935, CO 123/353/66571.
38 Burns to Beckett, 15 Nov. 1935, CO 123/354/66648. A Colonial Office official approved
    of Burns' action: 'The Governor took the right line in putting Mr. Grant on to try
    Tony, so as to avoid any suspicion of colour clash', Rootham's minute, 13 Dec. 1935,
    CO 123/354/66648.
39 The amount spent on outdoor relief, distributed largely in Belize Town, had increased
    rapidly from $2,600 in 1931 to about $10,000 in 1935 and 1936; see Cheverton and Smart
    1937: 47.
40 Corp. Cornelius A. Building to Supt. of Police, 21 Jun. 1938, CO 123/367/66648.
41 Burns to SS, 22 Nov. 1938, CO 123/366/66553.
42 Ibid.
43 Burns to SS, 5 Jan. 1939, CO 123/366/66553.
44 Encl. in Burns to SS, 13 Mar. 1939, CO 123/373/66553.
45 Ibid.
46 Burns to SS, 24 Mar. 1939, CO 123/373/66553.
47 Burns to SS, 3 Apr. 1939, CO 123/373/66553. The same issue arose in Jamaica at this time;
    see below.
48 Act. Gov. Sir Reginald St-Johnston to SS, Aug. 1939, CO 123/373/66553.
49 Rev. N.W. Newnham Davis to D.R. Stewart, 23 Oct. 1934, encl. in Stewart to Gov. Johnston,

2 Jan. 1935, CO 152/454/15.

50 Stewart to Johnston, 2 Jan. 1935, CO 152/454/15.

51 St Kitts-Nevis Daily Bulletin, 12 Jan. 1935, in CO 152/454/15.

52 Ibid., 14 Jan. 1935.

53 Letter from E.J. Shelford, St Kitts-Nevis Daily Bulletin, 18 Jan. 1935, in CO 152/454/15.

54 Letter from Nathan, St Kitts-Nevis Daily Bulletin, 19 Jan. 1935, in CO 152/454/15.

55 Letter from Nathan, The Union Messenger, encl. in Johnston to SS Sir Philip Cunliffe-Lister, 30 Jan. 1935, CO 152/454/12.

56 Ibid.

57 Johnston to SS, 30 Jan. 1935, CO 152/454/12.

58 Ibid.

59 Chief Justice James S. Rae's report, 8 May 1935, encl. in Johnston to SS, 13 May 1935, CO 152/454/12.

60 Ibid.

61 Ibid.

62 Johnston to SS, 30 Jan. 1935, CO 152/454/12.

63 Ibid.

64 Rae's report, op. cit. They may have been taunting the police by suggesting that they were impotent in more ways than one.

65 Johnston to SS, 30 Jan, 1935, CO 152/454/12.

66 Ibid.

67 Ibid.

68 Rae's report, op. cit.

69 Ibid.

70 Rae's report says eight and Johnston's letter nine.

71 Ibid.

72 Johnston to SS, 30 Jan. 1935, CO 152/454/12.

73 Johnston to SS, 31 Jan. 1935, CO 152/454/12.

74 Rae's report, op. cit.

75 Ibid.

76 Ibid.

77 Lt. Col. Edward Bell's report, 17 Feb. 1935, encl. in Johnston to SS, 16 Mar. 1935, CO 152/454/12.

78 J.S. Barnes (Admiralty) to under SS (CO), 17 Apr. 1935, CO 152/454/12.

79 Rae's report, op. cit.

80 Rae to Johnston, 11 May 1935, CO 152/454/12.

81 Rae's report, op. cit.

82 Bell's report, op. cit.

83 Rae's report, op. cit.

84 Johnston to SS, 12 Apr. 1935, CO 152/454/12.

85 St Kitts-Nevis Daily Bulletin, 2 Feb. 1935, in CO 152/454/15.

86 The Union Messenger, 4 Feb. 1935, in CO 152/454/15.

87 Johnston to SS, 15 Feb. 1935, CO 152/454/15.

88 Johnston to SS, 31 May 1935, CO 152/454/15.

89 Nathan to Cunliffe-Lister, 8 Mar. 1935, CO 152/454/12.

90 Gov. G.J. Lethem to SS, 8 Jun. 1937, CO 318/427/3.

91 Lethem to SS, 29 Jul. 1937, CO 318/427/11.

92 Lethem to SS, 30 Jul. 1937, CO 318/427/11.

93 Official gazette, St Kitts-Nevis, 27 Jan. 1938, CO 318/431/1.

94 Lethem to SS, 28 Oct. 1938, CO 318/434/8.

95 Lethem to SS, 15 Sept. 1939, CO 318/440/14.

96 Gov. Sir Selwyn M. Grier to SS Malcolm MacDonald, 12 Nov. 1935, CO 321/363/64320. He claimed to know that 'a Russian Jew, an accomplished linguist who professed a philanthropic interest in the slums of Kingstown and Castries [St Lucia], where he spent

much of his time, was present in these islands in 1934 and early 1935. He is also known to have visited St Kitts'. A marginal minute identified him as Nathan Leipziger and refers to 'No.10 in 7057/35 General'. That file appears in CO 378/106 (Colonies General: Register of Correspondence) as 'General suspects', but was 'destroyed under statute'.

[97] Ibid.

[98] Grier to Sir Cosmo Parkinson, 17 Nov. 1935, CO 321/363/64320.

[99] Grier to MacDonald, 12 Nov. 1935, CO 321/363/64320.

[100] Ibid.

[101] Ibid.

[102] Ibid.

[103] Ibid.

[104] Commander A. Jones, HMS Challenger to C-in-C, 29 Oct. 1935, CO 321/369/64320.

[105] Grier to MacDonald, 12 Nov. 1935, CO 321/363/64320.

[106] Jones to C-in-C, 29 Oct. 1935, CO 321/369/64320.

[107] Grier to MacDonald, 12 Nov. 1935, CO 321/363/64320.

[108] Ibid.

[109] A. Grimble to Grier, 24 Jan. 1936, CO 321/369/64320.

[110] Grier to Parkinson, 20 Jan. 1936, CO 321/369/64320.

[111] Lt. Comdr. C.D. Milbourne to A. Grimble, encl. in Grimble to Grier, 22 Jan. 1936, CO 321/369/64320.

[112] Grier to SS, 31 Jan. 1936, CO 321/369/64320.

[113] Grier to J.H. Thomas, 28 Mar. 1936, CO 321/369/64320.

[114] Grier to MacDonald, 12 Nov. 1935, CO 321/363/64320.

[115] Grier to Parkinson, 17 Nov. 1935, CO 321/363/64320.

[116] Grier to Parkinson, 18 Dec. 1935, CO 321/369/64320.

[117] Grier to MacDonald, 12 Nov. 1935, CO 321/363/64320.

[118] Ibid.

[119] Ibid.

[120] Ibid.

[121] Ibid.

[122] Ibid.

[123] Ibid.

[124] Report by Administrator Alban Wright, in Gov. H.B. Popham to Ormsby-Gore (SS), 2 Jun. 1937, CO 318/427/3.

[125] Wright to Popham, 2 Sept. 1936, encl. in Acting Gov. Edward Baynes to Ormsby-Gore, 8 Sept. 1936, CO 321/369/64354.

[126] Popham to Ormsby-Gore, 29 Dec. 1937, CO 318/431/1.

[127] Acting Gov. Alban Wright to MacDonald, 27 Sept. 1938, CO 318/434/8.

[128] Jones to C-in-C, 9 Nov. 1935, CO 321/369/64320.

[129] Ibid.

[130] Ibid.

[131] Grier to MacDonald, 12 Nov. 1935, CO 321/363/64320.

[132] Ibid.

[133] Jones to C-in-C, 9 Nov. 1935, CO 321/369/64320.

[134] Ibid.

[135] Ibid.

[136] Letter of proceedings of HMS Dundee, 25 Nov. 1935, CO 321/369/64320.

[137] Grier to Parkinson, 20 Jan. 1936, CO 321/367/63796.

[138] Grier to Parkinson, 27 Feb. 1936, CO 321/367/63796.

[139] Grier to Parkinson, 15 Mar. 1936, CO 321/367/63796.

[140] Grier to J.H. Thomas, 6 May 1936, CO 321/367/63796.

[141] St Lucia Rules and Orders, No. 55, 26 Nov. 1936, encl. in Grier to Ormsby-Gore (SS), 5 Jan. 1937, CO 321/368/63834.

[142] St Lucia Gazette, 6 Aug. 1937.

[143] Administrator Edward Baynes, to Popham, 6 Aug. 1937, encl. in Popham to Ormsby-Gore (SS), 12 Aug. 1937, CO 318/427/11.

[144] Baynes to Popham, 7 Aug. 1937, encl. in Popham to Ormsby-Gore (SS), 12 Aug. 1937, CO 318/427/11.

[145] Popham to Ormsby-Gore (SS), 12 Aug. 1937, CO 318/427/11.

[146] Popham to MacDonald, 24 Dec. 1938, CO 318/437/13.

[147] Of these unions, only the Public Works and Public Service Workers' Union, registered on 26 November 1937, and the Tobago Industrial Trade Union, registered on 3 September 1939, were organising in Tobago, where the Public Works Department was the chief employer of wage labour outside agriculture. A more self-sufficient peasantry and less dependence on wage labour in Tobago made that island less fertile ground for trade unions. As no strike occurred there in 1937, this account deals solely with Trinidad (Craig 1988: 8-12).

[148] Memoranda on labour conditions, 23 Feb. 1938, CO 318/432/6.

[149] Evidence to the Moyne Commission, cited by Cross 1988: 287.

[150] Memoranda on labour conditions, 23 Feb. 1938, CO 318/432/6. Singh's figures of 40 cents and 91.5 cents per day in 1936, though slightly higher, show a similar 1:2 ratio (Singh 1987: 59).

[151] Financial News, 13 Jan. 1938, cited in Cross 1988: 288-9.

[152] Gov. Sir M. Fletcher to W. Ormsby-Gore, 5 July 1937, CO 295/599/70297.

[153] There were 170 sit-downs in General Motors plants between March and June 1937; see Brecher 1972: 251.

[154] King probably had a bad reputation among working people. He tried to stop a NWCSA demonstration on behalf of the poor in 1936 (Rennie 1973: 75).

[155] 'Trinidad and Tobago Disturbances, 1937: Report of the Commission', Cmd. 5641, 1938 (hereafter Forster Report), and Singh 1987: 64-5.

[156] Forster Report.

[157] Port of Spain Gazette, editorial, 22 Jun. 1937.

[158] Trinidad Guardian, 25 Jun. 1937, quoted in Reddock 1988: 30.

[159] Fletcher to Ormsby-Gore (SS), 26 Jun. 1937, CO 295/599.

[160] Brereton 1981: 182. Ryan calls Fletcher 'the champion of the interests of the worker' (1972: 55), and Basdeo writes that they 'took their trusteeship role seriously and emerged, if only for a short while, as the champion [sic] of the interests of the working class' (1983: 153).

[161] CO 295/599/70297.

[162] CO 295/599/70297.

[163] Legislative Council debates, 9 Jul. 1937.

[164] Ibid.

[165] Sir Alexander Roger, managing director of Trinidad Leasehold's parent company, travelled to Trinidad with the three British commissioners in August and on his return to England dined with the secretary of state for the colonies on 16 December. He convinced Ormsby-Gore that Fletcher was a 'vacillating' person and that he 'must go'. A few days after, Fletcher was forced to resign (Johnson 1975: 46).

[166] West India Committee Circular, 10 Feb. 1938, cited in Singh 1987: 71.

[167] 22 Oct. 1937, CO 295/600/70307.

[168] Fletcher to Ormsby-Gore (SS), 31 Oct. 1937, CO 295/600/70307, quoted in Craig 1988: 40.

[169] Notes, 28 Feb. 1938, CO 295/606/70307, quoted in Craig 1988: 45.

[170] Nankivell, removed from office a few months after Fletcher, died in peculiar circumstances in France in late 1938.

[171] Oilfield Workers' Trade Union 50 Years of Progress, 1937-1987 (San Fernando, Vanguard Publications, 1988): 11.

[172] Elbert Redvers Blades to Sir Walter Citrine, 21 Apr. 1943, OWTUL. Subsequent quotations are from this document.

[173] Singh's study of the struggle in Trinidad from 1917 to 1945 does not mention the UWTA

and mentions the origins of the OWTU only briefly: 'the oilworkers announced that they had formed a trade union with Adrian Cola Rienzi as their president' (1994: 175). He refers to Earl [sic] Blades only with regard to his later contributions, along with John Rojas, Ralph Mentor, and MacDonald Moses, to organising oil and sugar workers (p. 203).

[174] Report of his address to oil workers, The People, 4 Sept. 1937, quoted in Singh 1982: 20.
[175] The People, 4 Sept. 1937 and 22 Jan. 1938, cited in Singh 1982: 23.
[176] The People, 15 and 29 Jan. 1938, cited in Singh 1982: 23.
[177] The People, 5 Mar. 1938, cited in Singh 1982: 24.
[178] Council Paper No. 25 of 1941: Industrial Adviser's Report for the Years 1938-40, p. 8, cited in Singh 1982: 26.
[179] The People, 4 Feb. 1939, quoted in Singh 1982: 26.
[180] Acting Gov. Mark Young to Ormsby-Gore (SS), 22 Feb. 1938, CO 318/430/5.
[181] Trinidad Guardian, 15 Feb. 1938, quoted in Reddock 1988: 35.
[182] Signed by D. Isaac, Printers Industrial Workers Union, Gaskynd Granger, Public Works Workers Union, Sylvestre L. Patrick, Federation of Workers of Trinidad Union, and John Broomes, Workers' Defence Committee; Arthur Creech-Jones papers, MSS Brit. Emp. S332, Box 25, file 4, RHL.
[183] The People, 2 Jul. 1938, quoted in Reddock 1988: 48.
[184] Many calypsos commented on the events of the 1930s and contributed to shaping this new political culture, for example the CD 'Calypsos from Trinidad: Politics, Intrigue and Violence in the 1930s' (El Cerrito, Arhoolie Productions, 1991).
[185] Payne to Creech-Jones, 10 Jul. 1939, MSS Brit. Emp. S332, 25/4, RHL.
[186] The People, 1 Jul. 1939, quoted in Reddock 1993: 254.
[187] The People, 13 May 1939, in Singh 1982: 28-9.
[188] Blades to Citrine, 21 Apr. 1943, OWTUL.
[189] See Braithwaite 1987: 15, on the use of Weber's discussion of types of authority for analysing trade union leadership in Trinidad and Tobago.
[190] Blades to Citrine, 21 Apr. 1943, OWTUL.
[191] Gov. Mark Young to Ormsby-Gore (SS), 5 Apr. 1937, CO 318/426/10.
[192] Young to Ormsby-Gore, 5 Apr. and 21 Jun. 1937, CO 318/426/10.
[193] Young to Ormsby-Gore, 5 Jul. 1937, CO 318/427/3.
[194] Deane Commission hearings, 16 Aug. 1937, CO 28/319/9.
[195] Report of the Commission appointed to enquire into the Disturbances, 2 Nov. 1937 (hereafter Deane Report), CO 28/319/8.
[196] Reddock says he had a Barbadian father and a Trinidadian mother (1988: 32).
[197] Deane Report, CO 28/319/8.
[198] Account of Grant's trial, 12 Nov. 1937, encl. in Acting Gov. W.H. Flinn to Ormsby-Gore, 14 Mar. 1938, CO 28/321/12.
[199] Deane Report, CO 28/319/8.
[200] In Flinn to Ormsby-Gore, 14 Mar. 1938, CO 28/321/12.
[201] Ibid.
[202] Deane Report, CO 28/319/8.
[203] Deane Report, CO 28/319/8.
[204] The Commission of Inquiry consisted of Sir George C. Deane (chairman), Matthew A. Murphy and Erskine R.L. Ward.
[205] Hilton Augustus Vaughan's evidence, 16 Aug. 1937, CO 28/319/9; Deane Report, CO 28/319/8.
[206] Dean Report, CO 28/319/8.
[207] Orde Browne later remarked, 'Major Flinn [the acting governor] has obviously never had the unnerving experience of passing buses driven by a Barbadian chauffeur fatigued to the verge of sleep at the wheel. Whether from the point of view of the menace to the public, or from consideration for the drivers, the hours ought to be reduced'. Minute by Orde Browne, 7 June 1939, CO 28/324/11.
[208] Deane Report, CO 28/319/8.

[209] Ibid.

[210] Ibid.

[211] Ibid.

[212] Ibid.

[213] Young to Ormsby-Gore, 2 Oct. 1937 and 1 Dec. 1937, CO 28/319/8.

[214] Flinn to Ormsby-Gore, 14 Mar. 1938, CO 28/321/12.

[215] Barbados Observer, 14 Nov. 1936.

[216] Adams' evidence to commission, 13 Aug. 1937, CO 28/319/9.

[217] Ibid.

[218] Ibid.

[219] Ibid.

[220] The fact that Hoyos was Adams' brother-in-law, which may have provided him with some inside knowledge, should be borne in mind when considering his perspective. My thanks to Howard Johnson for this point.

[221] Note of meeting convened by Lord Dufferin, 13 May 1938, CO 28/322/3.

[222] Gov. E. Waddington to MacDonald, 26 Aug. 1938, CO 28/322/3.

[223] Flinn to MacDonald, 29 Mar. 1939, CO 28/324/11.

[224] Waddington to MacDonald, 23 Feb. 1939, CO 28/324/11.

[225] Waddington to SS, 10 Feb. 1939, CO 28/324/11.

[226] Waddington to SS, 18 Feb. 1939, CO 28/324/11.

[227] Waddington to SS, 22 Feb. 1939, CO 28/324/11.

[228] Waddington to MacDonald, 23 Feb. 1939, CO 28/324/11.

[229] Ibid.

[230] Ibid.

[231] Ibid.

[232] Waddington to MacDonald, 14 Mar. 1939, CO 28/324/11.

[233] Ibid.

[234] Flinn to MacDonald, 3 Jul. 1939, CO 28/324/11.

[235] Ibid.

[236] Resolution passed at a meeting on 4 Mar. 1938, encl. in Flinn to Ormsby-Gore (SS), 3 May 1938, CO 28/321/12.

[237] Harold A. Moody to MacDonald, 16 Jun. 1938, CO 28/321/12.

[238] Creech Jones to George H. Hall, 24 Apr. 1941, CO 28/328/2.

[239] Citrine to Lord Moyne, 29 Sept. 1941, CO 28/328/2.

[240] Waddington to Sir Alan Burns, 27 Jun. 1941; Gov. Sir G. Bushe to SS, 18 Dec. 1941, CO 28/328/2.

[241] See Saunders 1988, reprinted in Saunders 1990: 49-75. This section draws largely on this article.

[242] Report by Commissioner J.A. Hughes, 'Inagua disturbance and present conditions', 23 Feb. 1938, encl. in Gov. Charles Dundas to Ormsby-Gore (SS), 19 Mar. 1938, CO 23/638.

[243] Report by Att.-Gen. G.W. McL. Henderson, 7 Feb. 1936, encl. in Dundas to Ormsby-Gore (SS), 21 Feb. 1938, CO 23/638.

[244] Report by K.E. Robinson, 'The disturbances in Inagua', n.d., CO 23/618.

[245] Ibid.

[246] Report of Acting Col. Sec. Charles P. Bethel re Inagua disturbance, 6 Sept. 1937, encl. in Administrator J.H. Jarrett to Ormsby-Gore (SS), 17 Sept. 1937, CO 23/618.

[247] Robinson's report, op. cit., CO 23/618.

[248] 20 May 1938, CO 318/433/1.

[249] Votes of Legislative Council, 1937-8: pp. 42-3, quoted in Saunders 1990: 65.

[250] Minute by H. Beckett, 4 Jun. 1938, CO 23/638.

[251] Orde Browne's report, 4 Apr. 1939, CO 23/682.

[252] Bakan (1990) and Holt (1992) provide useful analyses of many of the key issues in the century before the labour rebellion.

[253] Gov. A.F. Richards to MacDonald, 21 Oct. 1938, CO 318/434/8.

[254] Orde Browne's provisional report, 25 Jan. 1939, CO 137/837/68989.

255 From Gov. to SS, 18 May 1938, CO 137/825/68729, quoted in Post 1978: 122.

256 In CO 950/110, quoted in Post 1978: 125.

257 The quotes in this account are from Inspector George O'Toole to Inspector General Owen F. Wright, 22 May 1935, encl. in Gov. E. Denham to Cunliffe-Lister, 30 May 1935, and The Daily Gleaner, 30 May 1935, CO 137/806/68557.

258 Guy S. Ewen to Denham, 25 May 1935, encl. in Denham to Cunliffe-Lister, 30 May 1935, CO 137/806/68557.

259 Ibid.

260 Denham to Cunliffe-Lister, 30 May 1935, CO 137/806/68557.

261 Denham to MacDonald, 18 Jul. 1935, CO 137/806/ 68557.

262 Minute by F.J. Howard to Parkinson, 10 Jul. 1935, CO 137/806/68557.

263 Coombs died in 1969, without public acknowledgement of his pioneering role.

264 Plain Talk, 17 Oct. 1936, quoted in Post 1978: 243.

265 The latter may have been started by Buchanan, who was a master mason.

266 Letter in Plain Talk, 19 Jun. 1937, quoted in Post 1978: 137.

267 Letter in Public Opinion, 18 Dec. 1937, quoted in Post 1978: 5-6.

268 Report of the Trades Union Congress of Jamaica, 30 Jun. 1946, for report to conference on 21 Sept.1946, HP. However, Post cites the Jamaica Standard, 13 May 1938, that Hill started these unions in early May 1938 (Post 1978: 350).

269 Plain Talk, 8 May 1937, quoted in Post 1978: 219.

270 Plain Talk, 28 Aug. 1937, quoted in Post 1978: 219.

271 Denham to Parkinson, 30 Jul. 1937, CO 318/427/13.

272 Letter in Plain Talk, 20 Feb. 1937, quoted in Post 1978: 248.

273 Petition published in Plain Talk, 30 Apr. 1938, quoted in Post 1978: 249.

274 Plain Talk, 3 Jul. 1937, quoted in Post 1978: 256.

275 Denham to SS, 20 Sept. 1937, CO 137/820/68868.

276 Copy of telegram, 17 Apr., in Denham to MacDonald, 21 May 1938, CO 318/430/5.

277 Ibid.

278 Jamaica Standard, 21 Apr. 1938, quoted in Post 1978: 276.

279 Report of the Commission appointed to enquire into the Disturbances which occurred on Frome Estate in Westmoreland on 2nd May, 1938 (hereafter Frome Report) Kingston, 1938: 1.

280 Notes on Tate and Lyle's interests in the West Indies, 8 Feb. 1938, encl. in Charles Watney to Ormsby-Gore, 15 Feb. 1938, CO 318/432/5.

281 Frome Report, p.8.

282 Frome Report.

283 As burnt cane can be salvaged if harvested quickly, the firing of canefields should not necessarily be understood as sabotage but may be a way for workers to try to hasten a settlement.

284 The Daily Gleaner, 3 May 1938, quoted in Hart 1989: 39.

285 Daily Gleaner, 4 May 1938.

286 The editor, William Makin, wrote a book, Caribbean Nights (1939), about his Jamaican experience.

287 Daily Gleaner, 4 May 1938, quoted in Hart 1989: 41.

288 Denham to MacDonald, 21 May 1938, CO 318/430/5.

289 Smith, born in 1893, worked for five years in the Canal Zone and 33 years in the United States, where he became vice-president of the NMU in 1937 and national executive secretary in 1939. Deported to the UK in 1951, he returned to Jamaica in 1952 and continued to be involved in trade union organising; see Hart 1953.

290 Daily Gleaner, 23 May 1938.

291 Report of the Commission appointed to enquire into the Disturbances which occurred in Jamaica between the 23rd May, and the 8th June, 1938 (hereafter Jamaica Disturbances Report) Kingston, 1938: 4-5.

292 Hart's diary, typed copy, HP.

293 Ibid.
294 Ibid.
295 Jamaica Disturbances Report: 5.
296 Ibid.: 6.
297 Ibid.: 6.
298 Daily Gleaner, 25 May 1938.
299 Quoted in Hart 1989: 55.
300 Ibid.: 57.
301 Ibid.
302 Daily Gleaner, 26 May 1938, quoted in Hart 1989: 60.
303 Daily Gleaner, 27 May 1938, quoted in Hart 1989: 67.
304 Daily Gleaner, 27 May 1938, quoted in Hart 1989: 70.
305 Daily Gleaner, 27 May 1938, quoted in Hart 1989: 68-9.
306 Daily Gleaner, 27 May 1938, quoted in Hart 1989: 73.
307 Jamaica Disturbances Report: 7.
308 Daily Gleaner, 27 May 1938, quoted in Hart 1989: 74-5.
309 Makin had earlier realized that Bustamante had actually discouraged rioting and attempted negotiations. 'Bustamante may not be the leader that all men want', he wrote, 'but he is the only leader available to them', Jamaica Standard, 25 May 1938, quoted in Post 1978: 288.
310 Jamaica Disturbances Report: 10.
311 He was never able to work again and died a pauper; Hart 1989: 91.
312 Jamaica Disturbances Report: 10-14.
313 Jamaica Standard, 4 Jun. 1938, quoted in Post 1978: 283.
314 Jamaica Disturbances Report: 1.
315 Ibid.
316 Jamaica Standard and Daily Gleaner, 30 May 1938, quoted in Post 1978: 291.
317 Richard Hart to Jaime O'Meally, 1 Jun. 1938, HP.
318 Jamaica Labour Weekly, 9 Jul. 1938, quoted in Hart 1989: 100.
319 Undated memo prepared for answer to Parliamentary question by Mr Day on 30 Mar. 1938, CO 318/427/3.
320 Woolley to SS, 5 Jun. 1938, CO 137/826/68868.
321 Jamaica Standard, 6 Jun. 1938, quoted in Post 1978: 294.
322 Woolley to SS, 7 Jun. 1938, CO 137/826/68868.
323 Jamaica Standard, 25 May 1938, cited in Post 1978: 249.
324 Minute by J.H. Emmens, 23 Jun. 1938, CO 137/827/68868.
325 Woolley to Sir Henry Moore, 3 Aug. 1938, CO 137/826/68868.
326 Daily Gleaner, 27 Aug. 1938.
327 'This decision, though largely ignored in practice, was not formally reversed until the party's Second Annual Conference on August 28, 1940', Hart 1989: 143.
328 Hart to O'Meally, 1 Jun. 1938, HP.
329 Domingo and O'Meally's JPL in New York joined Manley's new PNP in September.
330 An attempt to create a similar paper, called The Worker, edited first by Arthur Henry and then Frank Hill, lasted only a few weeks, between Nov. 1939 and early 1940 (Hart 1989: 123-5).
331 Gov. Sir Arthur Richards to SS, 16 Feb. 1939, CO 137/836/68868.
332 Bustamante is reported to have said, 'The reason why Mr Coombs is here is not because I personally need him, but because it was necessary for all branches of labour to unite for the good of Jamaica', quoted in Eaton 1975: 76.
333 Report of the JTUC, 30 Jun. 1946, HP.
334 Ibid.
335 Ibid.
336 The Times, 20 Jun. 1939, quoted in Hart 1989: 135.
337 Gov. Lethem to SS, 29 Jul. 1937, CO 318/427/11.

[338] Lethem to SS, 30 Jul. 1937, CO 318/427/11.

[339] Lethem to SS, 19 Mar. 1940, CO 318/439/12.

[340] Lethem to SS, 8 Nov. 1939, CO 152/485/61760.

[341] Ibid.

[342] Lethem to SS, 19 Mar. 1940, CO 318/439/12.

[343] Now formally called the Cooperative Republic of Guyana, and known as British Guiana between 1831, when Berbice was united with Essequibo and Demerara, and independence in 1966.

[344] Figures from the 1931 census.

[345] BGLU fliers, 14 Jul. and 1 Aug. 1933, CO 111/712/15140.

[346] Denham to Parkinson, 25 Sept. 1933, CO 111/712/15140.

[347] Denham to Cunliffe-Lister, 17 Oct. 1933, CO 111/712/15140.

[348] Ibid.

[349] Calculated from figures in 'Report on Sugar Industry in British Guiana' by J. Sydney Dash, 24 Feb. 1936, encl. in Gov. Northcote to J.H. Thomas, 5 Mar. 1936, CO 318/421/3.

[350] Notes on a recent visit to British Guiana and the West Indies by Sir Edward Davson, 29 May 1936, CO 318/423/4.

[351] Data from 1931 census and 1936 Economic Survey, encl. in Orde Browne's provisional report to SS, 18 Oct. 1938, CO 111/756/60338.

[352] Figures from Report of the Commission of Enquiry into the 1935 Disturbances, 24 Aug. 1936 (hereafter Report of 1935 disturbances): 7, 30, CO 111/732/60036.

[353] For example, CO 345/28 refers to 1934 'industrial unrest,' file 35156 as destroyed, and CO 345/29 refers to two files for 1936, 'Lucius O'Brien, activities of. Suspected of Communistic activities & requests that enquiries be made into his past activities', file 60148, and 'Political situation', file 60206, which were also destroyed.

[354] Report by J. Nicole, 3 Oct. 1934, encl. in Acting Gov. Sir Crawford Douglas-Jones to Cunliffe-Lister, 24 Jan. 1935, CO 111/726/60036.

[355] Douglas-Jones to Cunliffe-Lister, 24 Jan. 1935, CO 111/726/60036.

[356] Ibid.

[357] Ibid.

[358] Report of 1935 disturbances: 4.

[359] Gov. Sir Geoffrey Northcote to SS, 17 Oct. 1935, CO 111/726/60036.

[360] Report of 1935 disturbances: 18.

[361] Ibid.: 19.

[362] Ibid.: 16.

[363] Ibid.: 21. The commissioners, by publishing their names, would scarcely have helped them.

[364] Ibid. 21.

[368] Ibid. 21.

[366] Ibid. 22.

[367] Ibid. 23.

[368] Ibid. 24.

[369] Ibid. 25.

[370] Ibid. 26.

[371] Ibid. 27.

[372] Ibid. 27.

[373] Ibid. 28.

[374] Northcote to SS, 17 Oct. 1935, CO 111/726/60036.

[375] Northcote to H. Beckett, 18 Oct. 1935, CO 111/726/60036.

[376] Report of 1935 disturbances: 29.

[377] Northcote to Thomas, 7 Dec. 1935, CO 111/726/60036.

[378] Report of W.E.H. Bradburn, 15 Nov. 1935, encl. in Northcote to Thomas, 7 Dec. 1935, CO 111/726/60036.

[379] Northcote to SS, 17 Feb. 1936, CO 111/732/60036.

[380] Letter from Hubert Critchlow, 7 Oct. 1936, encl. in Northcote to Ormsby-Gore, 4 Dec. 1936, CO 111/732/60036.

[381] Report of meeting, 19 Oct. 1936, encl. in Northcote to Ormsby-Gore, 4 Dec. 1936, CO 111/732/60036.

[382] Northcote to Ormsby-Gore, 4 Dec. 1936, CO 111/732/60036.

[383] Report of government labour bureau, encl. in Gov. to SS, 12 Feb. 1938, CO 318/427/3.

[384] Minute by J. St J. Rootham, 29 Sept. 1936, CO 111/732/60036.

[385] Minute by S. Caine, 22 Jan. 1937, CO 111/732/60036.

[386] Orde Browne's provisional report, 16 Oct. 1938, encl. in Orde Browne to SS, 18 Oct. 1938, CO 111/756/60338, and Chase n.d.: 90.

[387] Orde Browne's provisional report, 16 Oct. 1938, encl. in Orde Browne to SS, 18 Oct. 1938, CO 111/756/60338.

[388] Memorandum encl. in Edward J. King, secretary of WI Committee, to private secretary of SS, 7 Jun. 1939, CO 111/758/60036/1.

[389] Report of Leonora Enquiry Commission, 23 Mar. 1939 (Georgetown, 1939), CO 111/762/60270 (hereafter Report of Leonora Commission): 5.

[390] Ibid. 6.

[391] Ibid. 8.

[392] Ibid. 8.

[393] Ibid. 9.

[394] Ibid. 13.

[395] Ibid. 15.

[396] Ibid. 16.

[397] Ibid. 18.

[398] Ibid. 22.

[399] Ibid. 23.

[400] Correspondence and memoranda between Lord Moyne and the War Cabinet, 30 and 31 Jan. 1940, CO 318/443/6.

[401] Circulars, Lord Passfield to all colonies, protectorates, etc, 19 Aug. 1929, CO 854/73, 12 Mar. 1930, CO 854/173, and 29 Apr. 1930, CO 854/76.

[402] Minutes of CO conference, 23 Jun. 1930, CO 854/173.

[403] Ibid., 10 Jul. 1930, CO 854/173.

[404] Creech Jones Papers (CJP), Mss Brit. Emp. S332, box 14/1, RHL.

[405] Ibid., box 14/4.

[406] The general case about welfare as a means of social control is made in Piven and Cloward 1971.

[407] Labour Department Annual Report, 1939, Belize.

[408] Circular, MacDonald to governors, 12 Jul. 1938, CO 854/110.

[409] Creech Jones to K. Hill, 12 Feb. 1939; A. Rienzi to Creech Jones, 1 Mar. 1939; S. Patrick to Creech Jones, 16 Mar. 1939, CJP Mss Brit. Emp. S332, box 25/5; Creech Jones to C.R. Jacob, 11 Feb. 1939; H. Critchlow to Creech Jones, 17 Mar. 1939, Fabian Colonial Bureau Papers (FCBP) Mss Brit. Emp. S365, box 137/1, RHL.

[410] In Belize, for example, by 1950 the Public Works Department alone employed 1,284 workers, exclusive of relief work, compared with 1,091 employed by the BEC, the largest firm in the colony; Gov. R.H. Garvey's report on Economic Development and Employment, 30 Sept. 1950, CO 123/406/66985.

[411] This topic was explored in a preliminary fashion in my paper, 'The Caribbean Labour Congress and the Federal Ideal', presented at the 20th annual conference of the Association of Caribbean Historians in St Thomas, 27 Mar. - 2 Apr. 1988.

[412] David S. Nathan to SS, 15 Jun. 1938, CO 318/428/1.

[413] Nathan to Ormsby-Gore, 12 May 1938, CO 318/428/1.

[414] Acting Gov. John Higgins to MacDonald, 20 Dec. 1938, CO 318/436/1.

[415] Gov. Sir Hubert Young to Lord Lloyd, 27 Jul. 1940, CO 318/442/1.

[416] The Federation of the West Indies that was created by an act of the British Parliament in 1956, initiated in 1958, and disintegrated in 1962, lacked these features.

Part 2

The Institutionalisation of Labour Politics

Chapter 6

The colonies at war, 1939-45

The UK fought the Second World War 'to defend the empire as well as to defeat fascism' (Cain and Hopkins 1993: 234). The debate about colonial policies continued during the war. The Caribbean colonies played a part in that debate that was out of all proportion to their relative scale or importance in the empire as a whole because of the political pressures resulting from the labour rebellions of the 1930s and the proximity of the United States. In June 1940, when France fell to the Axis powers, the UK and its empire stood alone. The war 'revealed Britain's inability to defend a two-hemisphere empire, plunged the country deeper into debt, encouraged nationalist resistance and subjected Britain to American anti-imperialism' (Porter and Stockwell 1987: vol. 1, 25). The UK became increasingly dependent on the United States, even before the latter entered the war in December 1941, and by February 1942, when Singapore fell, the empire was in jeopardy. The United States took advantage of the UK's wartime difficulties and, despite its anti-imperialist rhetoric, strengthened its own position and became the principal power in the Caribbean. Of course, this was simply a regional manifestation of the global expansion of the US economy relative to that of the UK and other European powers. This shift was accelerated by the Spanish–American war and also both world wars. The UK waged these wars far beyond its means but they were, uniquely, good for the US economy because the United States was remote from the fighting and was the chief arsenal of its allies (Hobsbawm 1994: 46-8).

Several of the shifts in the global distribution of power were specific to the ways the world powers preceived the strategic significance of the Caribbean. The destroyers-for-bases deal that was made between the UK and the United States in 1940 was, in this light, simply another link in a chain of events that

384 The Politics of Labour in the British Caribbean

included the US invasion of Cuba and Puerto Rico in 1898, the occupation of Haiti and the Dominican Republic in 1915 and 1916, respectively, and the purchase of the Danish Virgin Islands in 1917. Until the Second World War, the influence of the United States was felt more in these territories than in the colonies of the UK, France and the Netherlands, but by 1940 the German threat had become a critical factor in the US expansion in the Caribbean. The military, political, economic and cultural penetration of the Caribbean by the United States not only reflected this changing global balance of power, but it also affected the tendencies towards fragmentation and nationalism within the Caribbean. In the British Caribbean, the impact of the destroyers-for-bases deal was greatest in Trinidad, but the war and growing US influences affected all the colonies.

The relative decline in the UK's power and the rise of the United States coincided with a change in the approach of British officials to the development of the colonies. The consecutive impact of the Great Depression and the Second World War, combined with burgeoning movements of resistance to colonialism, resulted in a crisis in the British imperial system. Consequently, when the UK sought to reform its social welfare and development policies in its colonies it did so in a time of diminishing resources. There was a tense relationship between the UK and the United States, as the former increasingly came to rely on the latter, while resenting its growing power. The destroyers-for-bases deal and the Anglo-American Commission (Johnson 1984a, 1984b) [both] represented and produced further US influence in the British Caribbean, specifically, at the time that these colonies were beginning a process of constitutional decolonisation. The impetus towards democratisation that had started in the labour rebellions of the 1930s was slowed by the pressures of wartime, when authoritarian controls and repression were reinforced, but it revived again towards the end of the war as the general imperial crisis meant that decolonisation was again on the agenda. Between 1944 and 1946 elections in Jamaica, Trinidad and Tobago, and Barbados moved these colonies towards democratic self-government. Several of the labour leaders who had emerged before the Second World War, including Norman Manley and Alexander Bustamante in Jamaica, Grantley Adams in Barbados, and Adrian Cola Rienzi and Albert Gomes in Trinidad and Tobago, became political leaders in the decolonisation movement. Other labour leaders, such as Vere Bird of Antigua and Robert L. Bradshaw of St Kitts-Nevis, who became prominent political leaders, emerged during the war.

The Colonial Development and Welfare Act

The labour rebellions in the British Caribbean colonies in the 1930s demonstrated all too publicly that all was not well in the old empire. The great Jamaican rebellion provoked several reports in The Times[1] and a lively debate in the House of Commons on 14 June 1938.[2] The government's response was to appoint the royal commission of inquiry into West Indian social and economic conditions, under the chairmanship of Lord Moyne, 'as one method of restoring Britain's credibility as a benevolent colonial power' (Johnson 1977:70). The commission's personnel and terms of reference were announced by the secretary of state for the colonies, Malcolm MacDonald, on 28 July 1938[3] and the commissioners toured the Caribbean in late 1938 and early 1939. Before the commission completed its report war broke out, and when its findings were presented to the government in February 1940 they were suppressed for fear of providing information that could be used by enemy propaganda against British colonial policies[4]. The recommendations of the Moyne Commission were published immediately but the report itself was not released until July 1945. In the meantime, the report of Major G. Orde Browne, Labour Conditions in the West Indies, was published in July 1939. The chief result of these reports and recommendations, along with Professor W. M. Macmillan's Warning from the West Indies (1936), was to reinforce the conviction that was emerging among some British officials that long-term reconstruction was needed. The first practical consequence was the passage of the Colonial Development and Welfare Act, which established a budget and an organisation to allocate it in 1940.

Members of the British official classes had been gradually reassessing colonial development policies before the labour rebellions of the 1930s but, as Howard Johnson argues, the 'more precise formulation of new approaches to colonial development was a consequence of the West Indian disturbances of 1937-38' (1977: 55). Earlier commissions had been appointed to enquire into the problems of the sugar industry, chaired by Lord Olivier,[5] and into the disturbances in Trinidad and Barbados,[6] but it was the Jamaican rebellion that convinced the British government to think of the disturbances as a more general West Indian problem that warranted a broader study and an imperial response.

The Colonial Office was also pressured to reconsider its policies by the parliamentary questions posed by a group of Labour Party MPs, including Arthur Creech Jones, T.W. Sorensen, Ben Riley and Wilfred Paling, who had developed a particular interest in colonial problems. The Labour Party's imperial advisory committee developed an interest in labour issues in the Caribbean colonies and Creech Jones, in particular, established links with many individuals and organisations concerned with West Indian affairs (Gupta 1975: 225-31). After Orde Browne was appointed labour adviser to the Colonial Office in March 1938, two successive Conservative secretaries of state for the colonies, Ormsby-Gore and MacDonald, encouraged him to communicate with these Labour MPs and with Sir Walter Citrine, the general secretary of the TUC.[7] Calls for a commission to investigate West Indian social and economic conditions were rejected, however, until late May 1938.

Until the Jamaican labour rebellion, the West Indian Department of the Colonial Office felt that gradual reforms, financed by the individual colonies, could ameliorate the problems and that a strong enough case could not be made to the Treasury for large-scale financial assistance from the UK. However, the West Indian Department report of 20 May 1938 noted that there had been eight disturbances in six Caribbean colonies since 1935, resulting in 44 people being killed and 183 wounded.[8] Though we now know that this actually understated the scope and cost of the rebellions, the report shows that some officials were considering that there was almost an emergency in the Caribbean colonies. Two advisers to the department, Sir Frank Stockdale and Sir John Campbell, who were convinced of the need for a long-term policy to address economic issues, favoured the appointment of an appropriate royal commission. Campbell, the financial advisor, commented on 23 May 1938 that the West Indies were 'the British show-window for the U.S.A. - I am afraid it is not a very striking exhibit'.[9] He argued that financial assistance from the UK was required and that recommendations for such assistance would carry great weight if they came from a royal commission. The department as a whole changed its opinion about the need for such a commission at a meeting on 31 May 1938, when news was received that the rebellion in Jamaica had become islandwide (Johnson 1977: 67).

The Colonial Office, having reached the conclusion that a long-term policy for reconstruction was needed for the rehabilitation of the Caribbean colonies, sought the appointment of a royal commission as a necessary preliminary. The need for the commission was not so much to collect information, though it could fill some gaps with its overview of social and economic conditions, as to assure people in the colonies that something was being done to address their problems and to lend greater prestige to the shift in policy. With the approval of the prime minister, Neville Chamberlain, and the chancellor of the exchequer, Sir John Simon, MacDonald announced in Parliament on 14 June that a royal commission would be appointed. The government, in appointing the commission, was already agreeing that considerable financial expenditure would be required. At the cabinet meeting the next day, the prime minister noted,

> there was no short cut to the rehabilitation of the Islands. There were only a limited number of industries in the West Indies, and all were of an agricultural nature. The market for their products was limited, and, so far as sugar was concerned, was decreasing. It might be possible to make the sugar industry more efficient, but the probable consequence would be to increase unemployment, for example, by the adoption of labour-saving machinery. It might be necessary to take steps to enable the natives to obtain subsistence from the land without exporting the product of their labour. For that, more finance would be necessary, and he did not think that further expenditure could be avoided.[10]

Cognisant of the shortcomings of the Colonial Development Act of 1929, the Colonial Office's committee on colonial development used the term 'development' quite broadly, to cover medical, educational and social welfare schemes as well as material and economic development, and in December 1938 senior officials agreed to establish a Social Services Department to deal with labour as well as social services (Johnson 1977: 72-3).

The Colonial Office's proposals for a new approach to colonial development, requiring substantial financial assistance from the Treasury and close cooperation between the Colonial Office and the individual colonial governments, was complete months before the submission from the Moyne Commission, whose report was signed on 2 December 1939. MacDonald wanted to wait for the report before submitting his proposals, but he felt that the outbreak of war made the reforms even more urgent. He met his advisers on 4 September 1939, the day after the UK declared war, and they drafted a memorandum to take to Cabinet. MacDonald thought it was 'very important too that we should keep the colonies content during the war, and he felt that a big scheme of colonial development, announced quite soon, would impress people here and abroad'.[11] The chief reason for MacDonald's urgency was clearly political, in terms of both impressing the UK's domestic and foreign critics that it was a benevolent empire and also restoring loyalty among the colonised peoples themselves and so avoiding the possibility of further disruptive strikes and disturbances.

The draft memorandum proposed the creation of a Colonial Development and Welfare Fund with £10 million per year for ten years, and a Colonial Research Fund of £1 million per year for ten years. Though these funds were to be available for colonies in Africa, Asia and elsewhere, the Caribbean colonies were a priority because of the crisis there and because the United States was already initiating New Deal programmes in its own Caribbean colonies.[12] Meetings between Colonial Office and Treasury officials took place in early 1940. The Treasury remained unconvinced, and Sir Henry Moore of the Colonial Office felt that they had not understood what was to be gained politically by welfare expenditure: 'Politically the whole point is that we should be able to make a big thing out of the "welfare" side. If it is just going to be "development" on the old lines it will look merely as if we are going to exploit the Colonies in order to get money to pay for the war!'[13]

The Moyne Commission's report was critical of British colonial policies and it came at a critical moment in the debate. Though MacDonald had been assured that the report would be more moderate in tone than it would have been had it been drafted in peacetime, it was still too strong for the Cabinet which decided on 30 January 1940 not to publish it. MacDonald felt that the effect of delaying its publication, along with the rise in the cost of living caused already by the war, could result in more disturbances. His draft Cabinet memorandum made this view clear:

> The comparative quiescence of the West Indies in the last 18 months, after 2 years of disturbances, is largely attributable to the knowledge that an authoritative Commission was looking into their affairs, and the note for many months has been one of keen expectancy. I am not confident that this position can be held for much longer; a rise in the cost of living inevitable as a consequence of the war has already set in ... and all the causes of general unrest are near the surface .... From a purely propaganda point of view, then, we must consider whether riots are preferable to the publication of the Report. Also, the renewal of disturbances might well occasion demands for the diversion of His Majesty's forces which could be very ill spared at this time.[14]

Extracts from chapters 9 and 11, on housing and other social needs and services, respectively,[15] apparently convinced the Cabinet that they could be used by the enemy for propaganda and, though Lord Moyne offered to cut the dangerous sections in the hope of publishing the rest,[16] the report was not published until 1945.

The recommendations were published, however, and MacDonald argued that 'there is serious danger of trouble in the West Indies if no action is taken to implement the recommendations of the Royal Commission'.[17] This is a clear and documented example of the way that civil disturbances, and the threat of more, have brought some rewards, however limited, to the poor people of the Caribbean. Perhaps reading the extracts that had provoked the Cabinet to delay publishing the report, that described seriously overcrowded and unhealthy housing, overcrowded schools, widespread poverty and ill-health, convinced Cabinet members that the British government should be seen to be doing something for its colonies. At any rate, in February 1940, a compromise was reached, to create the Colonial Development and Welfare Fund with £5 million per year and the Colonial Research Fund with £500,000 per year, half what the Colonial Office had requested, with £1.4 million committed to fund the recommendations of the Moyne Commission. By pushing the political point, namely to encourage the loyalty of the colonised and to deny propaganda opportunities to the enemy, 'The Colonial Office achieved in wartime what was probably beyond its reach in peace time, that is, a greatly enlarged measure for colonial development and social services' (Havinden and Meredith 1993: 204). Although the Moyne Commission did not provide any startling new information, it did contribute, in the way that was intended, to marshalling 'support for a line of action which the Colonial Office had already decided on' (Johnson 1977: 76). This line of action, involving an unprecedented degree of financial assistance from the UK for colonial development and welfare, was chiefly the result of the labour rebellions of the 1930s and the implied threat of more disturbances in the 1940s. In time of war, the UK could ill afford such financial assistance, but also it could not afford to risk the political consequences of not providing it.

Although a fund of £5 million per year had been approved, colonial governments were told in September 1940 that, unless their proposed scheme was 'of such urgency and importance as to justify the expenditure of United Kingdom funds in present circumstances',[18] the UK could not afford it. Between the inception of the act in July 1940 and October 1942, approval was given for the expenditure of about £2 million, an average of only £833,000 per year, 'which was about the same as the level of expenditure on colonial development in the 1930s' (Havinden and Meredith 1993: 218). The rate increased, with £1.6 million approved between 1 November 1942 and 31 March 1943, but the total funds allocated up to March 1943 were only 26 per cent of what was permitted under the act, and a mere 5 per cent of the possible £1,375,000 of research funds was spent. In the next financial year, £4.1 million was allocated, but two-thirds of this sum accounted for just 15 expensive projects. Between 1 April 1944 and 31 March 1945, when a total of £15.9 million was allocated to development and welfare projects, 44 per cent of these funds were for Nigeria alone. Allocations were reduced in the financial year 1945/6 to £5.5 million and, as in the previous year, the ten most expensive schemes absorbed about half of all the allocations (Havinden and Meredith 1993: 219-23).

It is striking, nevertheless, how much of these colonial development and welfare funds were allocated to the Caribbean colonies, particularly in the first years. Between 1940 and 1944, the Caribbean colonies were allocated 60 per cent of all the funds under the act, and although this declined to 30 per cent in the period 1944-6, it remained very high on a per head basis compared with other colonies. Altogether, between 1940 and 1946, the Caribbean colonies were allocated 38 per cent of the funds.

Among the more expensive schemes in the Caribbean during the first two years were those for agricultural development in Dominica, yaws and malaria control in Jamaica, yaws control in Dominica, housing and land reclamation and construction of a reservoir in Jamaica, road developments in Belize, Dominica and Montserrat, water supply, drainage and irrigation projects in Guyana, and airfields in Belize and other places. In 1943 and 1944, projects funded were for agricultural development in Jamaica and Barbados, more water supply, drainage and irrigation schemes in Guyana, and land settlement and housing projects in Jamaica and Antigua. Together, between 1940 and 1946, schemes for agriculture and veterinary care, communications and transport, educational, housing, health and sanitation, social services, and water supply and irrigation projects accounted for about 91 per cent of all the funds allocated under the act. Schemes for industrial development and public utilities, fisheries and forestry, and labour, received very small shares of the funds. 'Overall, "Welfare" received more attention than "Development": water supply, housing, medical, public health and education took 58 per cent of funds allocated' (Havinden and Meredith 1993: 223).

This emphasis on welfare projects and, particularly in the early years, on schemes in the Caribbean colonies, reflects the concerns about social conditions and the potential for more disturbances, as publicised by the Moyne Commission's report. It also reflected the view that the activities of the commission itself had raised expectations in the Caribbean colonies, expectations that, if not addressed promptly, could become frustrated and lead to renewed rebellions. Anxiety about further protests in the Caribbean increased because of fears that the economic impact of the war would aggravate the already poor material and social conditions.

The economic impact of the Second World War

Correspondence from several governors in the Caribbean colonies to the Colonial Office early in 1940 emphasised the dangers of grave and general unrest, and the need for prompt relief work in order to avoid such trouble. The essential problem was that colonial trade, already depressed in the 1930s, suffered a further decline as a result of the war, reaching a low point in the Caribbean between 1940 and 1942. Although special efforts were made to increase the supply of oil and other essential resources for the war effort, the export of most Caribbean products declined as a result of the diversion of shipping to routes that the British government decided were more important. Meanwhile, the prices of most imports, including such essentials as flour, increased, with the result that the colonies' terms of trade and the people's standard of living deteriorated.

The export of sugar from Guyana, Jamaica and Trinidad fell from a total of 8.2 million cwt in 1938 to 6 million cwt in 1940, and the export of bananas from Jamaica fell from 23.8 million stems in 1938 to less than 300,000 stems in 1943. The export of sugar from Guyana and of sugar and bananas from Jamaica recovered somewhat by the end of the war, but Trinidad's sugar exports remained quite low and Trinidad's cocoa exports in 1946 were less than one-sixth of what they had been in 1938. The export of bauxite from Guyana, in contrast, increased from 376,000 tons in 1938 to 1,901,000 tons in 1943 because it was a strategic resource. Overall, the value of exports from Barbados, Belize, Guyana, Jamaica and Trinidad declined from £15.2 million before the war to the low point of £11.3 million in 1942, recovered to £16.2 million in 1945 and rose to £27.5 million in 1946 (see Table 6.1).

Meanwhile, the cost of living rose sharply in most places in the early years of the war. Consumer prices in the Caribbean colonies had risen generally by about 65 per cent in 1943 from their prewar levels, but inflation abated in some places where price and wage controls were instituted in 1944 and 1945 (see Table

TABLE 6.1 EXPORTS FROM CARIBBEAN COLONIES, 1938-46

	1938	1939	1940	1941	1942	1943	1944	1945	1946
Sugar, '000 cwt, from Guyana, Jamaica, Trinidad	6,174	7,248	6,029	6,000	6,000	6,528	7,291	6,208	7,662
Cocoa, '000 cwt, from Trinidad	57.9	159	232	166	90	72	95	88	59
Bananas, m. stems from Jamaica	23.6	18.6	6.6	5.6	1.3	0.3	1.1	1.6	5.6
Bauxite, '000 tons from Guyana	374	478	634	1073	1116	1301	694	739	1120
Total exports, £m, from Barbados, Belize, Guyana, Jamaica, Trinidad	15.2	15.2	12.6	12.6	11.3	13.3	14.3	16.2	27.5

Source: Havinden and Meredith 1993: 207-9.

6.2). Some imported consumer items became much more expensive. In Jamaica, for example, between 1939 and 1945 the price of flour rose by 119 per cent and of footwear by 373 per cent (Havinden and Meredith 1993: 207-9). The spread of hardship and malnutrition was apparent.

TABLE 6.2 COST OF LIVING INDICES IN SELECTED COLONIES, 1940-6, 1939-100

	1940	1941	1942	1943	1944	1945	1946
Barbados	120	130	151	165	179	187	207
Jamaica	125	145	157	158	160	159	175
Trinidad	113	123	148	164	163	170	183
St Lucia	111	127	150	176	182	170	185

Source: Havinden and Meredith 1993: 214.

As conditions deteriorated and the threat of unrest grew, several governors sought an increase in financial aid, not only for more schools, better medical facilities and the infrastructure for economic development, but also for immediate relief work. MacDonald was anxious lest the royal commission's long-term recommendations would disappoint West Indians who hoped for provisions for 'immediate betterment of their conditions and ... this may lead to violent reactions'.[19] The governor of Guyana replied that there was indeed such a danger and was especially concerned by the rise of unemployment 'which has been inevitably aggravated by restriction of works in the effort to balance the budget[,] by the rise in living costs and by severe drought'.[20] He requested $250,000 in additional funds for relief works. Two weeks later, he reported the spread of general unrest and considered the extension of relief works to be 'most urgent' to alleviate the situation.[21] Governor Richards of Jamaica, meanwhile, advised that the Colonial Office should announce 'immediate interim help' along with publication of the commission's recommendations in order to improve public opinion. He sought £200,000 for relief work, as 'conditions are getting worse'. 'Robbery and burglary and such crimes are increasing and after several unsuccessful attempts train has recently been derailed by sabotage. Unemployment is increasing and will only certainly be relieved by Panama scheme and sugar subsidy'.[22] A month later, Richards referred to 'grave unemployment distress' in areas that lacked relief work on roads or land reclamation projects. He expressed the view that 'the necessarily slow initiation of long-range policies would be valueless without the temporary expedients which prevent a complete present collapse'.[23] In May Richards said there was 'an astonishing amount of fundamental disloyalty in the urban areas'.[24]

A senior official at the Colonial Office, commenting that conditions were bad and deteriorating in most of the Caribbean colonies, sought about £320,000 from the Treasury for immediate expenditure, 'to give work for the many in the W.I. who are at present urgently in need of it'.[25] He increased the request on 7 February 1940 to £350,000, of which £200,000 was for Jamaica, £52,000 for Guyana, £45,000 for Belize, £38,000 for the Windward Islands and £15,000 for the Leewards. Barbados and Trinidad and Tobago, however, were allocated nothing.[26]

The problems persisted in Jamaica and Guyana. Richards reported that, despite proposals for Panama Canal work and on a local US base, unemployment in Jamaica was a persistent problem, and 'Alternative to relief works is serious privation and grave unrest'.[27] The governor of Guyana commented, 'At least 1/5 of the population of this colony depends upon relief grants for bare subsistence and serious political trouble will ensue if this is abolished or reduced'.[28] Early in 1941, a Colonial Office official requested a further £300,000 for more relief work, as 'prudent insurance' against disturbances:

> Throughout the West Indies there is a rising tide of unemployment and under employment with all its concomitants of destitution, malnutrition and the danger of political unrest .... The year 1940 cannot be described as a very favourable one for the West Indies, and we feel strongly that the comparative absence of unrest may be attributed in large part to the provision of employment by the £350,000 grant.
>
> There is little likelihood that the year 1941 will be any better ....
>
> We should like to emphasise our view that provision such as we desire is no more than a prudent insurance which may not only save a great deal of money in dealing with disturbances, but prevent the considerable harm which would be done to our prestige abroad by disturbances requiring to be put down by force.[29]

It is clear that the expenditure of British funds on relief work in the Caribbean colonies, which had been initiated in response to the labour rebellions in the 1930s, was still necessary in wartime conditions, though the exigencies of war ensured that less was actually spent than the government had approved. Despite some colonials' protestations of loyalty to the empire, the Colonial Office itself remained clear about the continuing need to purchase 'further insurance against disorder'.[30] While it may be argued that the UK was largely successful in containing further unrest by buying such insurance, it should also be acknowledged that the labour rebellions of the 1930s and the persistent threat of further unrest in the war brought the poor and unemployed of the colonies a small degree of actual, though limited and short-term, material relief. Such relief work was not intended to create permanent jobs, of course, but it did establish the expectation that government had a continuing responsibility to meet people's basic needs when a crisis resulted in unusually hard times. At the same time, however, the British government sought to control labour conflicts by other means, including the appointment of labour officers and the creation of labour departments in the colonies.

In addition to the endemic problems of organising a largely casual or seasonal labour force in conditions of widespread unemployment, the political conditions of wartime raised further problems. As the labour officer of Barbados indicated in 1940, the employers as well as the colonial officials were willing to permit the development of trade unions only if their leaders were deemed by them to be 'responsible', but many labour leaders, because of their origins, were judged to be too political. 'I have not met objection on the part of employers to the formation of trade unions properly led. They have told me that they would welcome a responsible body with whom they could treat. There is however, considerable opposition to politically actuated organisations led by the "agitator" type of person.... For the time being I am afraid that use must be made of such political organisations as already exist'.[31] In Jamaica, the labour adviser, who had been appointed in 1939, established four district offices during his first year, at Montego Bay, St Anne's Bay, Port Antonio and Mandeville, explicitly in order to 'watch for signs of friction with a view of pouring oil on the troubled waters'.[32]

Although the trade unions and the practice of collective bargaining were still in their embryonic stage in the early 1940s, the impact of the colonial labour officers and departments, and of the many advisory committees, boards and arbitration tribunals, eroded the functional autonomy of the unions. The Colonial Office, whose primary functions remained keeping order and ensuring a supply of cheap labour to the capitalist class, was not interested in helping powerful trade unions to develop. On the contrary, trade unions were valued as a way to help maintain order and predictability in labour relations and so they had to be tractable. Consequently, when the colonial governments passed a variety of labour regulations and ordinances in these years, it was generally only 'as a sop for unity and support for the allied war effort' (Chase n.d.: 106).

The political conditions of wartime and the efforts of colonial government officials made it hard to develop autonomous trade unions, but the economic conditions reinforced the need for a strong labour movement. The combination of rising prices and high unemployment, after years of severe depression, resulted in widespread and persistent poverty, often manifest in appalling housing and malnutrition. Such problems, in turn, led to, and were often heightened by, migration and urbanisation. The labour adviser in Jamaica reported in April 1940 that serious unemployment was particularly evident in the towns because of the 'drift of population from the country areas' and the return of Jamaicans who had been working in Cuba and Panama. He estimated that the 2,500 persons then employed on relief work were only half of the total unemployed in the Kingston area alone. He commented that relief work, 'by way of useful public works', helped 'to cope with the destitution', but that 'Public Works cannot . . . go forward on a large scale indefinitely, and the hope of the situation is that accelerated and developed land settlement may draw off people from relief works'. However, he recognized that 'the unemployed man without resources does not profit as adequate Government aid is not forthcoming to enable him to take up a holding, purchase necessary tools and seeds, prepare the soil and plant it and wait until the produce is ready for sale'.[33] The Olivier Commission of 1930 and the Moyne Commission of 1938-9, like the Norman Commission of 1897, recommended land settlement schemes and the development of the class of peasant proprietors as a solution to the problems of unemployment (Momsen 1987: 53), and in wartime intensive cultivation was also seen as a way to increase the domestic supply of food. Land settlement schemes, however, continued to run into the problem of competition with the entrenched power of the plantocracy, so these schemes often only made use of land that was too poor or remote for estates or on which estate agriculture had failed.

Land settlement schemes, which have generally been initiated only in response to crises, but have responded to the symptoms rather than the causes of such crises, have been a dismal failure in the British Caribbean colonies (Braithwaite 1968: 273). Although more than 16,000 persons were settled in the Jamaican land settlement scheme by 1941, the average holding was only just over 4 acres and there was little money available for loans for the farmers. The Food Production Board, launched in July 1940, offered loans at 6 per cent interest to the settlers and other peasants, but by late 1941 defaulters on the unpaid loans were being prosecuted. About 5,000 tenants on Crown land who held less than an acre each on average were said, not surprisingly, to be producing scarcely enough for their own subsistence and were living in poor conditions. By the middle of 1942, when about three-quarters of Jamaica's population lived in peasant households, the colony was in another crisis and the government instituted agricultural centres. 'The proposal is that properties be purchased in areas where there is unemployment and the need for land and that unemployed persons in such areas be put to work on the land as relief workers and trained in agriculture, the aim being to settle them ultimately on the land. At the end of a reasonable period selected persons would be settled on the property'.[34] Sir Frank Stockdale, the comptroller for colonial development and welfare in the West Indies, found it hard to ascertain what part of these centres was 'purely relief for unemployment' and what was 'definitely developmental'.[35] Although the Jamaican government sought to ameliorate the crisis by turning some unemployed workers into peasants, it was ultimately unwilling 'to face up to the structural incompatibility of peasant and capitalist agrarian sectors which had lain at the heart of Jamaica's economy since the late nineteenth century' (Post 1981: Vol. 1, 253).

Other colonies faced similar problems, but sometimes in different circumstances and so sought different solutions. In Belize, for example, where forest workers and chicle gatherers were still viciously exploited, the Moyne Commission had recommended stamping out the truck system and 'its attendant evils of chronic indebtedness and fraud'.[36] Governor J.A. Hunter sought to control the truck system by reducing the limit of advances to one month's wages.[37] However, a Mr Norris of the Colonial Office pointed out that though the 'system of advances is the cause of a good deal of the poverty especially among the women and children', it was hard to estimate the forest workers' wages in advance as they were so often paid by the task.[38]

The governor of the Windward Islands blamed intermittent employment rather than low wages for the widespread poverty: 'It is a chronic condition in towns, and is aggravated by casual labour from rural districts, lacking employment through the economies brought about by low prices and minimum wage legislation, and attracted by higher rates of pay for town labour, however short the period of employment offered'.[39] He recommended the encouragement of peasant agriculture and industry, but a Colonial Office man noted that it was 'useless to build hopes on a development of peasant industries' which rarely survive 'when they have met the competition of factory produced articles'.[40]

For Trinidad, where Rienzi's OWTU was judged to be orderly and responsible, it was recommended by C.Y. Carstairs of the Colonial Office that the larger firms should employ personnel managers to iron out small difficulties before they became grievances that would poison the whole climate of labour relations. Orde Browne supported the introduction of such 'welfare officials' as a useful step to reduce the causes of tension and disorder, but argued that this measure did not address the underlying causes of unrest:

> At the same time, my observations led me to believe that one of the most potent causes of well-founded discontent is the under-employment (not complete unemployment) that exists in almost all West Indian towns. This suits the employers, as it gives them a large and elastic supply of labour, and also tends to keep down wages; so the evil system of rotational engagement flourishes, especially on the waterfronts. This cannot be remedied by the raising of wages, although the workers' leaders always advocate this; it proved to make the position worse rather than better, in the case of the Jamaica riots, since it acted as a magnet to draw still more workers to Kingston. Action by government to eliminate part of the superfluous labour in the towns is essential, in the form of assisted land settlement or other such schemes. I suggest that any move to press the employers to adopt modern methods should be accompanied by the stressing of the need for government action on lines calculated to reduce the urban population.[41]

It is clear that in these cases the war was not itself the cause of the problems; rather the cause lay in the nature of the conditions of production and employment under capitalism, and none of these proposed solutions addressed seriously the fundamental structural conditions of the system that gave rise to these chronic problems. The lesson of wartime for the Colonial Office was limited to welfare measures to ameliorate the problems in order to avoid social unrest, but not to undertake the serious re-evaluation of development policies. Indeed, this could not be done within the shackles of colonialism and capitalism which limited the officials' thinking. The wartime crisis, like the crisis of the labour rebellions in the 1930s, drew the attention of the Colonial Office to conditions in the Caribbean colonies that even they admitted were intolerable, but their proposed solutions were limited to reforming the system in order to keep it functioning. Meanwhile, the logic of the imperial system required them to take repressive measures to keep the lid on, lest these colonies boil over again.

Emergency powers, repression and resistance

Although the people of the British Caribbean colonies were overwhelmingly opposed to fascism, their expressions of loyalty towards the UK were sometimes joined to demands for an extension of democratic rights to themselves. For some of the new labour and political leaders the war occasioned a partial truce in their struggle as they agreed to suspend anticolonial agitation and not to strike for the duration of the war. The colonial governments, however, often used the war as an excuse to expand their powers, under the guise of emergency wartime regulations, and to tighten their control of political and trade union activities by detaining leaders and censoring communications and publications. Such official actions, though they were resisted, reinforced the pattern of authoritarian responses to the labour and anti-colonial movements. Hence, the war, far from suspending the struggle between the authoritarian and democratic tendencies in the political culture, revealed it in some new ways. It was in Jamaica and Trinidad, where the labour rebellions of the 1930s had given rise to the most militant and organised labour movements, that government repression and resistance to such oppression was most marked during the war.

Jamaica

In Jamaica the governor reported positively on 6 September 1939 on the people's general reactions to the war and, in particular, the political and labour leaders' expressions of cooperation:

> The reaction in Jamaica has been unanimously loyal. The way in which all classes have publicly expressed their loyalty and their desire to help is most gratifying and has completely belied the prophecies of unrest. For example Manley and his followers of the national party have called off all meetings and

> political agitation and have publicly said that this is no time for domestic strife.
> Bustamente [sic] in private correspondence and in published letter has placed
> the services of himself and the labour unions unreservedly at my disposal.
>   A wave of patriotism is passing over the country.[42]

Governor Richards was aware, however, that economic hardships could
produce more negative reactions and that the previous war had 'left many
bitter memories' about discrimination in the services. Certainly, such patriotic
fervour as was aroused by the war did not ensure the complete absence of class
conflict, as prices rose and the number of people on relief increased to about
18,000 in 1940-1 (Post 1981: Vol. 1, 34).

The great labour rebellion of 1938 did not change the fundamental dimensions of the class struggle in Jamaica, but it did provide experience in labour
politics that changed irreversibly the colony's political culture. The political
scene was generally quiescent during the first months of the war, but Richards
had to acknowledge that conditions were worsening and unemployment and
crime were increasing. By early 1940, there were signs of renewed militancy. The
leaders might be affirming their loyalty and postponing agitation for constitutional change, but the effects of price inflation and wage cuts provoked sugar
workers in St Thomas to strike in January 1940. Frank Hill, a journalist and member of the PNP's left wing, wrote in The Worker that 'the spirit of May 1938 still
lived and flowered' among the 2,000 strikers at Serge Island Estate.[43] Bustamante
wrote to assure the secretary of state of his 'unflinching loyalty and allegiance
to the throne', but added that he felt his 'responsibility as Leader of the great
masses of this island'.[44] A leader in The Worker reacted strongly to the news that
the Moyne Commission's report would not be published and, while thousands
of workers were still on strike, threatened to end the truce in the class struggle:

> This may suit the Chamberlain clique who are more concerned about the
> profits from their Colonial possessions, which Hitler covets, than about the
> living conditions of semi-civilised natives who dare to question the English-
> man's divine right to rule over their bodies as well as their souls.
>   But we, the semi-civilised natives, will not be content with things as they
> are. We cannot be satisfied with postponing the solution until Chamberlain
> has got through with Hitler....
>   We demand publication of the Commission's report. We demand it in the
> name of the entire working class of Jamaica.[45]

The strike, which may have involved almost 10,000 workers at its peak,
spread briefly to two estates in Clarendon, but by 8 February it was over and
the workers got no pay increase. Within a few days, however, relief workers and
dock workers in Kingston struck. When the former were allowed back to work

on 21 February, each of them had to sign an undertaking of good behaviour (Post 1981: Vol. 1, 77). Although these strikes had failed, they pushed Bustamante back into a more radical posture and he declared that he would join with Manley's PNP to 'change this government'.[46]

Meanwhile, Leonard P. Howell's Rastafarian Ethiopian Salvation Society held mass meetings at which it was said that the white man's time was over, that all European powers would be overthrown in 1940, that black people would be liberated, and there would be a distribution of land and money (Post 1981: Vol. 1, 95). The chairman of the Negro Workers' Educational League (NWEL), an organisation of the PNP's left wing that worked in the slums of West Kingston, wrote to The Worker indicating a desire for unity between movements based on racial and class consciousness:

> We do not know Mr Leonard Howell and we hold no brief for the Ras Tafari Society, but we do know that they represent a united Negro Movement with a membership drawn exclusively from the working class; so naturally we sympathise with them and regard them as comrades. Their methods are different from ours but we feel that ultimately they will join us in the class struggle to achieve the emancipation of the entire working class of the world.
>
> The more we unite the stronger we become; and by the strength of our unity we are confident that in spite of any curtailment of our civil liberties we will secure the liberation of the Ethiopians and all other oppressed peoples from the unmerciful exploitation of the capitalists.[47]

In May 1940, when German armies had overrun Denmark, Norway, the Netherlands, Belgium and Luxemburg, and the Chamberlain government had quit in favour of Winston Churchill's national government, Richards felt obliged to report that there was 'an astonishing amount of fundamental disloyalty in the urban areas of Kingston, St Andrew and Spanish Town' and a 'growth of racial feeling'.[48] The temporary truce in Jamaica was unravelling under the pressure of wartime conditions. Racial and class consciousness, though not well integrated, played significant roles in the struggle at this time and contributed to the continuing growth of the anticolonial and nationalist movement.

At a meeting in the Majestic Theatre, Kingston, on 24 May 1940, to celebrate Labour Day, representatives of several distinct political tendencies came together: Bustamante, Manley, Noel Nethersole, Frank Hill, and Amy Ashwood Garvey (Marcus Garvey's first wife). Bustamante announced: 'For some months I have made up my mind not to allow anything whatever to separate me and the Bustmante Industrial Union from the People's National Party .... I now join hand and heart with Mr Norman Washington Manley ... and with the other officers of the PNP'.[49]

In the months after this coalition began to form two important events occurred: the Allied armies retreated from Dunkirk and France fell (22 June), and the Colonial Development and Welfare Act became law (17 July). These events tested the unity of the coalition. Under the pressures of the war crisis, some PNP leaders, like Manley and Nethersole, still sought to cooperate loyally with the government, and others, such as Richard Hart, took the opportunity to press for 'a democratic Government of our own' (Post 1981: Vol. 1, 107-8). Moreover, when the United States responded to the German threat to the Dutch, French and British Caribbean colonies with the Act of Havana in July 1940, members of the Jamaica Progressive League (JPL),[50] based in New York, pressed for democratic self-determination, declaring, 'The status of an independent nation is the only status that could automatically follow the demise of British imperial authority' (quoted in Post 1981: Vol. 1, 115). Although the United States was expanding its involvement in the Caribbean in mid-1940, the Jamaican left 'put in a strong bid to be the spearhead of resistance to that involvement, a position it and its successors were to retain until the early 1950s' (Post 1981: Vol. 1, 117).

By August 1940, with the Battle of Britain under way, the PNP declared 'its faith in the Socialist cause', the goals of which were indispensably linked to that of self-government. In presenting his party's policy statement, Manley linked these goals to the class politics of Jamaica and the UK and to the dangers of the international situation. The problem was that if the UK fell, then its Caribbean colonies would be taken over by the United States, and most of the people would be treated like the people of African descent in the southern states. This was a realistic fear in 1940. The report of the PNP's second annual conference, held in August, stated:

> If owing to the difficulties of the situation it became necessary for England to concentrate all her efforts in the European sphere and if the large sections of opinion in America which are now in favour of taking over West Indian territories were in consequence to have their way we cannot be found without any strong national movement. The result would be that the merchants and capitalistic classes in Jamaica represented by the Chamber of Commerce and the Imperial Association and similar bodies would be regarded as representing public opinion in this Country and it would suit their interests to have America impose on West Indian Colonies a form of Government which ought to be unacceptable to the people of this Country and would be harmful to our political progress . . . . [A]ny real programme for the development of the Country is dependent upon our being responsible for our own Government and able to introduce measures which could never obtain the approval of the Colonial Office dominated as the British Government is by the financial interests in England.[51]

Manley continued to affirm his loyalty and support in the struggle against fascism and it is significant, as Post points out, that the PNP consistently referred to self-government for Jamaica within the British empire rather than to independence from it. Perhaps the possibility of US domination seemed even worse. At any rate, when the party's left, led by Hart, Arthur Henry and Frank Hill, sought a more political and militant analysis of Jamaica's situation in terms of class struggle and imperialism, and demanded immediate full independence and the election by all people over 18 of a constituent assembly, it was defeated. Nevertheless, at this conference the PNP formally reversed its decision to suspend agitation for self-government during the war (Hart 1989: 143).

The official commitment of the PNP to socialism and a renewed campaign for self-government came on the eve of a confrontation between Bustamante and Richards. The BITU, which was effectively the organised labour movement in Jamaica at this time, was highly centralised and Bustamante was its unchallenged leader (Post 1981: Vol. 1, 125). At the same time, Richards sought to tighten his control of the colony. On 26 August 1940, he issued a list of the items banned under the recently passed Undesirable Publications Act, including Irish and Indian nationalist literature and communist literature, such as London's Daily Worker and George Padmore's What is the International Trade Union Committee of Negro Workers? When Bustamante called for a strike in a dispute with the Shipping Association, Richards promptly had him and W.A. Williams, the vice-president of the maritime section of the BITU, detained under the defence regulations, 'on account of his increasingly inflammatory utterances and influence over workers'.[52] According to a police report, Bustamante said, 'We want our own government and it must be self-government too. The niggers of this country shall rise. We do not want to go to war like a timid dog. This will be war. We want revolution in this country and before whites destroy us we will destroy them. I am going to paralyse all industrial works of the country. There will be shedding of blood . . . . This time it is a race war. Down with the white man down with capitalists. We want self-government'.[53] Whether or not Bustamante actually said this, and it is as likely that the police agents exaggerated as it is that Bustamante got impulsively carried away in his speech, the report provoked Richards to detain him indefinitely.

Bustamante was interned under military guard, without a trial, from 8 September 1940 to 8 February 1942. During this period of 17 months the BITU, which had languished during the first year of the war, was revitalised by Manley and members of the PNP, particularly its left wing of Hart, Henry, Frank and Ken Hill. Bustamante, however, emerged as a martyr and hero, with his reputation dramatically enhanced among the rank and file.

Bustamante's detention did not stop the dock strike on Kingston's wharves and Hart and Henry led a protest demonstration on 9 September. They were arrested but Manley defended them in a magistrate's court and they were acquitted. Then, in a clash between banana workers and the police in St Thomas on 10 September, one striker was shot dead and 11 arrested. Some strike-breakers worked under police protection at United Fruit's wharves, and the sugar workers did not join the strike. By 19 September, with a promise of government arbitration, if needed, the strike ended (Post 1981: Vol. 1, 131).

The coalition between the BITU and the PNP was created, with Bustamante's approval, at a joint public meeting on 15 September 1940, and in October a contact committee to provide a permanent link between the organisations was created. Richards had demonstrated his power by locking up Bustamante, but the Colonial Office was concerned lest the detention of such a popular labour leader could provide material for anti-British propaganda. Consequently, the secretary of state urged Richards to expedite an inquiry into wages in the sugar industry, as 'it is my desire that workers in the sugar industry should receive a fair wage and should share in any increase in profit made by the industry and that they should be subject to reasonable hours of employment'.[54] In wartime conditions Bustamante could be detained indefinitely without trial, but the UK wanted a good press, supplies of sugar and industrial peace in its colonies. The opportunity for the sugar workers to make the most of this situation came early in 1941.

By October 1940 the cost of living was officially 25 per cent higher than in August 1939, and exports in the first nine months of 1940 were down almost 40 per cent in value from what they had been in the same period the previous year. Shipping was a major problem, of course, but also the imperial government decided that sugar was more important than bananas in the British diet. As a result, banana exports in 1940 were only 42.8 per cent in value of those for 1939, and sugar was being restored to its earlier position of predominance (Post 1981: Vol. 1, 141-2). Sugar workers, facing inflation, were increasingly dissatisfied and there were frequent stoppages at the start of the crop season in January 1941. The BITU, led by its vice-president, H.M. Shirley, who kept in close touch with Bustamante through Gladys Longbridge, the union's treasurer and its president's secretary and confidante, made demands for wage increases in the sugar industry. The union was now strongly supported by the PNP, as Ken Hill, a former BITU vice-president, made clear in a letter to Creech Jones: 'The Party is doing all it can sincerely and genuinely to help the Bustamante Union and Labour in general and I am happy to say that relations between the two are friendly and cordial. It is my belief that if this relationship continues to exist and more active and practical collaboration should develop between the Party and the Union, the Labour Movement will be much strengthened and the workers will benefit correspondingly'.[55] Hill's assessment was correct, in so far as a continuing collaboration between the PNP and the BITU would surely have strengthened the labour movement in Jamaica. However, the collaboration was brief, reaching its peak between February 1941 and February 1942, after which it disintegrated.

Talks at the Minimum Wages Board, appointed on 7 January 1941, between the Sugar Manufacturers Association (SMA) and the BITU, then being led by Shirley, Manley, Nethersole and Ken Hill, were deadlocked by the end of January. The union demanded an immediate 10 per cent wage increase but the SMA argued they could not afford this. The employers claimed that they needed more time before making an offer, so the BITU issued an ultimatum, demanding that they make an offer by 5 March or strike action would result. Unrest grew during February, while Ken Hill worked with local BITU organisers to prepare for a strike. A series of meetings and a pamphlet called 'Sugar Workers of the Bustamante Union,' distributed on 3 March, helped inform the workers. Hill reported later, 'The result confirmed and proved all the more what we, who have the honour and privilege to work among the masses of our people, have always known. With all his limitations of education and social training the Jamaican worker is as much amenable to discipline and training as any other worker. He is eager to be organised, is willing to follow honest, sincere and intelligent leadership, and is grateful for the opportunity, when he is convinced that it is a genuine one'.[56] What was 'probably the first really organized strike in Jamaica's history' (Eaton 1975: 79) ended in a victory for the workers and a terrific boost for the BITU.

The strike lasted for two weeks, from 5 March to 19 March. Richards got involved initially by appealing to the workers' loyalty to the 'Motherland', meaning the UK. In a speech to the Legislative Council on 10 March, he said it would be 'to the everlasting disgrace of this Island if labour troubles should add to our present difficulties, preventing the Island from giving the fullest measure of assistance in its power to the Motherland in her life and death struggle with her enemies'.[57] This appeal failed to break the strikers' resolve. Ten centres had been established in St Thomas and the organisers had sworn in many delegates to uphold the cause. When delegates in Clarendon were sworn in and the strike threatened to spread and paralyse the entire sugar industry, Richards brought pressure to bear on the SMA. As he put it, he made 'a personal appeal to them on purely sentimental and patriotic grounds', to make concessions as 'a patriotic gesture - as part of their contribution to the war effort'.[58] The governor's class bias was clear: the workers were accused of threatening the colony with 'everlasting disgrace', and their employers could make a 'patriotic gesture'. However, it is also clear that he needed the strike settled quickly and that he had to acknowledge the union's determination.

The outcome was a collective agreement, the first in Jamaica's history, which not only gave sugar workers an increase of 1 penny in 1 shilling and tied future wages to the cost of living with an escalator clause, but also gave the BITU the right to organise throughout the industry. There was to be no victimisation of strikers, and the agreement was to last through two crops, until July 1943. 'Over

35,000 field and 6,000 factory workers benefited directly' (Eaton 1975: 79). Another important sector of workers, the Kingston dock workers, won a 20 per cent wage increase, tied to the cost of living, in July 1941, when Nethersole negotiated on behalf of the union. As a result of these victories, membership in the BITU rose dramatically from 8,133 (5,200 of them paying members) in March 1941, to 20,612 (13,741 paying) in February 1942. The sugar strike had firmly placed the BITU 'at the centre of all future labour relations' (Post 1981: Vol. 1, 160) and, ironically, created a situation in which the PNP leaders who had contributed so much to the strike's success would find in future that the BITU was the greatest obstacle to their own attempts to organise workers. Manley and Nethersole, as presidents of the PNP and the Jamaica Trade Union Council (JTUC), respectively, campaigned and petitioned for Bustamante's release from detention.[59] As soon as Richards released Bustamante on 8 February 1942, however, the martyred labour leader attacked those people who had strengthened the union during his enforced absence. The unwavering personal loyalty of BITU members, which became legendary, provided him with an unassailable power base.

The result was a profound and permanent break between the PNP and the BITU, which were in 1942 the only significant political and trade union organisations in Jamaica. Although the governor had failed to weaken the union or to separate it from its leader, henceforth the powerful core of the labour movement was divorced from the political agitation for self–government, as the cousins, Manley and Bustamante, developed their lasting rivalry. The long–term consequence of these wartime events in 1941 and 1942, therefore, was the profound division in the politics of labour in Jamaica, up to independence and beyond.

In May 1941, Ken Hill, who had been directing the sugar workers' strike, published an astute assessment in an article entitled 'What Our Workers are Thinking'. According to him, the workers had little access to the media and little knowledge of the war. They were less fatalistic than previously but still intensely religious, were clearer about the 'struggle of race' than the class struggle, and sought heroic leaders to fight for them.

> So, they regard the Union and PNP, Manley, Bustamante, Garvey[60] and the rest as being raised up specially by God to right the wrongs that oppress them. To these workers, the cleavage of class is not as clear as what they consider the struggle of race. Garvey came before Bustamante, who came before Manley. This conditions their way of thinking. Garvey represents to them the ideal of a coloured nation. Hence they think of Jamaica first as a nation to whom the members of all other races are alien. Bustamante is the consummation of the dire necessity to organise as workers against employers.[61]

If this was indeed the prevailing consciousness among most workers, and there is no reason to believe otherwise, it was more or less inevitable that Bustamante would win back the leadership of his union after his release in 1942 and that he would soon challenge Manley's political leadership. The PNP and its labour adjunct, the JTUC, engaged in considerable organising to broaden its base outside Kingston in the second half of 1941. By the new year of 1942, however, the PNP 'had not yet fully established itself as a leading force in the labour movement, had not found any positive position with regard to the issue of Black Nationalism, and had not yet succeeded in taking over from the Colonial Office, or even the Elected Members, the dictation of the pace on constitutional reform' (Post 1981: Vol. 1, 208). Consequently, the PNP and TUC were unable to meet Bustamante's challenge.

When Bustamante was abruptly released on 8 February 1942, after 17 months in detention, he was forbidden to leave Kingston without notifying the police and could not speak in public or to more than 49 persons in a building without official permission. When invited by the BITU's executive committee to attend a reception to celebrate his release, Bustamante declined and published a letter in the Jamaica Worker, the union's newspaper, charging that 'certain officers' in the union had helped 'to hinder, obstruct and delay' his release. Moreover, he charged, 'there has been and still exists an unholy combination of certain persons with political ambition whose objective is that of destroying me and then to assume control of the Union as a political machine and to serve their own big friends' (quoted in Post 1981: Vol. 1, 219). Although Bustamante's most immediate target was Shirley, the acting president of the BITU, Manley promptly took up the challenge.

Although it was charged that Bustamante had made a deal with the governor to take the BITU out of politics in return for his release, no direct evidence has been found to support this (Munroe 1972: 23). The chief issue of the debate between the cousins, which became public and acrimonious, concerned accusations about the misuse of union funds. Bustamante alleged that Shirley had used the union's car and expense account without his authorisation. Manley responded by accusing Bustamante of squandering union funds when he controlled them[62] and that his charges against Shirley were just a cover-up. Further, Manley accused his cousin of ingratitude for all that he and the caretaker administration had done for the BITU and for Bustamante during his detention, and asked, 'Is it true that the Union constitution provides that Bustamante shall be a standing committee of one with power to hire and fire all officers, including every member of the Managing Committee with the exception of Shirley who holds a position which is elected by Annual Assembly and to control all funds of the Union?' (quoted in Eaton 1975: 81). This was a direct challenge to Bustamante's authoritarian control and the undemocratic nature of the union's constitution.

Bustamante responded by saying he had not even drawn the salary to which he was entitled, much less the £2,000 a year which he was accused of taking. 'But even ... if they paid me £5,000 per annum it could not repay me for the loss of my own financial business which I have had to close down, much more for my health, the effort and energy I have expended, the night and day work which I have had to do' (quoted in Eaton 1975: 81). Bustamante's ability as a 'trickster', like the admired Anansi of West Indian folk tales (Post 1978: 252), enabled him to turn this issue to his own advantage. Most Jamaican workers agreed that he had helped them more than he had helped himself, and his reputation with them proved to be largely impervious to allegations of financial improprieties. As Ken Hill had predicted, Bustamante appeared to many workers to be a saviour sent by God to help those who could not help themselves, to defend those who were themselves defenceless, and if he helped himself a bit in the process that was only to be expected. His popularity among the bulk of the workers was unassailable. Consequently, when Bustamante fired several senior BITU officials within a few weeks of his release, and reconstituted an executive committee that pledged unswerving loyalty to him personally, his victory 'was never in doubt' (Eaton 1975: 81).

The split between the BITU and the PNP left the latter with little organised grassroots support and Bustamante was 'reaffirmed as hero and saviour of the working classes' (Eaton 1975: 82). Whether or not Richards released Bustamante on condition that he split with the PNP,[63] Bustamante would have split with Manley anyway. There is no doubt that he saw himself as a 'labour boss' and desired to be supreme in that capacity, known as 'Labour Leader No 1'. Although he does not seem to have had explicitly political ambitions at the time of the rupture, his undoubted popularity and his purging of potential rivals from his union left the way open. Richards certainly appreciated the political consequences of the conflict between the cousins and in June 1942 he wrote a personal letter in which he made his preference clear:

> Bustamante is a damned nuisance, admittedly, and he too is stirring up trouble all over the Island. The difference is that he is first and last out for Bustamante and Bustamante's credit. He is not fundamentally anti-Government and subversive. On the other hand the Manley group is fundamentally anti-Government and subversive. It is out to discredit and if possible to break the present administration and it works, night and day, for that end under Manley's guidance. It aims - now openly - at conscription of all wealth and property, at complete self Government and at an entirely Communist set-up....
>
> Nuisance, though Bustamante is, there is no doubt that had he not been released or had he gone in with Manley the situation would be far more serious than it is.[64]

Bustamante publicly announced in July 1942 that he intended to launch a new political party, but he did not actually carry this through for a year (Post

1981: Vol. 1, 248).

As the war situation deteriorated, the PNP was increasingly involved in the class struggle and nationalist movement, though not aiming at the 'entirely Communist set-up' that the paranoid governor feared. The split between Manley and Bustamante resulted in part from the personal rivalry of ambitious men but also from their different styles of leadership that, as Post points out, 'exposed at a deeper level the continuing ideological differences between the social forces who represented the centre of gravity of the PNP and those which were being drawn into the labour movement' (Post 1981: Vol. 1, 223). Bustamante's assertion of personal authority as a labour boss, controlling his own organisation as if it were his property, and boldly challenging the powerful as if he himself was a poor sufferer, coincided with the limitations of the workers' consciousness at the time. As a former general secretary of the BITU who was dismissed by Bustamante put it in 1942, 'the political philosophy of the PNP . . . is not of the people's voluntary choice, as is the case of the BIT Union, which came about as the outburst of tied up feelings of the bulk of the people'.[65] Bustamante's authoritarianism was extreme. As he could be removed only by a two-thirds majority of all members gathered at a general meeting, which was practically impossible, he was effectively president for life. He had the power to appoint or dismiss all other officers or employees, except the vice-president who was elected, and he alone controlled the union's finances. Less than a month after his release, he announced a new union rule, that no agreement could last more than three months without the workers' ratification, thereby making void such agreements as Manley had achieved for the BITU the previous year (Post 1981: Vol. 1, 223).

The PNP leaders, who sought to relate the workers' struggle to the more middle-class concerns of the franchise, civil rights and self-government, took up Bustamante's challenge by trying to create their own, more democratic trade unions in 1942. In a letter to the newspaper, Manley challenged: 'I wager a day will come when a real labour movement will be led by real workers, by the Shirley's of Jamaica and men of that class, when persons like Bustamante and I, men of means, won't do more than give their help when it is wanted and our advice when it is sought - a time when fat jobs won't be set up for rich men out of the pennies of the poor'.[66]

A few days later, on 3 March 1942, Shirley, with S.T. Morais and other former BITU organisers, created the Jamaica United Workers Union (JUWU), aligned with the JTUC and supported by the PNP. However, although welcomed by Manley and the JTUC, it turned out to be a failure, and it was dissolved in November 1945. The BITU's base was among the sugar workers, dockers, and other largely unskilled labourers, and the JTUC unions were smaller, separate industrial unions of more skilled workers. The chief point, however, was not simply that these were different kinds of unions but that this 'division in the labour movement was also a division in the working class, and that was to remain central to the development of Jamaican politics' (Post 1981: Vol. 1, 224).

The left of the PNP led the party's efforts to create and support unions and to raise the consciousness of the working class. A provisional joint committee, chaired by Hart, was set up after a meeting by representatives in the Kingston-St Andrew area on 9 February 1942 to coordinate organising activities. In late March, a Workers Correspondence College was created. The director, B.B. Wilson, who had been sentenced to 18 months' imprisonment for sedition for organising street meetings of the native defenders committee in 1930 (Post 1978: 208-9), said it was 'a purely educational institution. It is not a union or a political party .... Rather, the knowledge we disseminate will help members of the unions and the PNP to improve their work in these organizations'.[67] Some of the material Wilson's group used, such as a pamphlet called 'Elementary Study Course, Six Lessons on Political Economy', were based on notes by Hart, Jamaica's chief Marxist.

The JTUC, led by Nethersole, a solicitor and close associate of Manley in the PNP, had tried, after Bustamante withdrew his union, to integrate and support the remaining small, chiefly craft-oriented unions, such as the Printers and Allied Workers Union (PAWU) and the Builders and Allied Workers Trade Union (BAWTU). In order to create a broader working-class base for the PNP and to bring increasing popular pressure on the colonial administration, the PNP left, led by Hart, Henry and the Hill brothers, started organising government workers and affiliating the new unions with the JTUC. Richards promptly issued, in April 1942, the Defence Projects and Essential Services (Trade Disputes) Order, imposing severe restrictions on strikes and requiring disputes to be referred to the labour adviser and, if conciliation failed, to compulsory arbitration. The emerging confrontation between the labour left and the colonial government therefore became framed in terms of democratic rights versus emergency war powers, but it was essentially the core of a broader political struggle.

That this broader struggle involved racial as well as class consciousness may be seen from the efforts made by two brown leaders of the PNP, Manley and Hart, to build bridges with the black nationalist leaders of the UNIA, such as S.V. Smith, president of the Harmony Division. The New Negro Voice, a UNIA paper that had supported the goal of self-government for Jamaica since November 1941 (Post 1981: Vol. 1, 206), reported on a UNIA meeting in April 1942, at which Manley and Hart spoke as well as Amy Jacques Garvey. Hart reminisced about hearing Garvey speak in London and said, 'Mr Garvey had done his duty and wiped out the "Yes massa and yes missis" idea out of at least 50 per cent of the people. It was therefore our duty to wipe [it] out of the other 50'. And Manley declared, 'The spirit of having a "superior" man with more money and a straighter nose as a leader is dying in Jamaica. We are learning that true leadership comes from the people'.[68] The emerging alliance between the PNP and UNIA grew with a series of meetings at the Harmony Division, beginning on 26 April, on the subject of social reconstruction at which Hart and Nethersole spoke, and a New Negro Voice editorial on 2 May that proclaimed self-government was an 'Outgrowth from Garveyism' (Post 1981: Vol. 1, 230). Simultaneously, then, the PNP leaders were developing their working–class, trade union base while creating a coalition with the largely middle-strata black nationalists of the Garvey movement. The PNP Executive was also meeting the Federation of Citizens' Associations (FCA) and some elected members of the Legislative Council to present a more united voice on constitutional reform (Post 1981: Vol. 1, 233). Dr Ivan Lloyd, a former government medical officer, was elected to the Legislative Council as a PNP representative, despite the still limited suffrage (Post 1981: Vol. 1, 238). The core of the broader political struggle in 1942, however, lay in several small trade unions affiliated to the JTUC.

On 5 February a strike sponsored by the PAWU at the Daily Gleaner plant resulted in a pay increase of 12.5 per cent. In April, Ken Hill's Tramway, Transport and General Workers' Union (TTGWU) won a 24 per cent raise, tied to the cost of living, free uniforms, a 48-hour week after a year's service and two weeks of paid leave per year, from Jamaica Public Services Ltd. The Government Railway Employees Union (GREU), with Hart as president and Henry as secretary, was formed in March and by late April was pressing the government on issues of long hours of work and safety (Post 1981: Vol. 1, 234). In April and May, Shirley's JUWU challenged the BITU, both in its new weekly paper, Democrat, in which its members were promised democratic leadership, and in direct confrontations at the Machado Tobacco Co. and the Jamaica Biscuit Co. in Kingston. After the JUWU called a strike at the former in April, Bustamante could not get workers back into his union, and BITU members assaulted JUWU organisers. In the latter case, in May, a JUWU supporter who had struck a BITU member was dismissed and then reinstated, and became the focus of rivalry about union representation. After a BITU demonstration, management told JUWU workers that reinstatement could take place only with the approval of the BITU, so the JUWU called a strike on 27 May. When Bustamante and his followers confronted the picket line the police had to keep the two sides apart. Although this incident was minor in itself, it suggests that Bustamante would work with some of Jamaica's leading capitalists to maintain his domination of the labour movement and intimates that 'inter-union - and later inter-party - violence was to become a very important part of Jamaica's political practice' (Post 1981: Vol. 1, 236).[69]

By mid-1942 Jamaica was in a serious crisis. As losses to Allied shipping peaked in June, Governor Richards decreed the end of all private motoring and the drastic reduction of public transport. Unemployment rose dramatically as hundreds of workers at a US base were laid off at the same time that the sugar harvest ended. Casual employment in the Kingston–St Andrew corporate area fell from 14,250 in March - April to 8,500 in June, and again to 7,350 in August.[70] There were shortages of food and other consumer items, even of staples such as rice, and the cost of living index climbed from 146.56 in March to 153.14 in June, and to 155.77 in July.[71] With the threat of imminent disaster at hand, various groups joined together on 16 May to form the Citizens Emergency Council (CEC), groups that included the JTUC, JUWU, UNIA, FCA and the Jamaica Union of Teachers, as well as the capitalist Imperial Association. The CEC, whose intention was to address the issues of food production and distribution, markets, transport, health and nutrition, started operations on 12 June (Post 1981: Vol. 1, 238-9). The PNP and JTUC leaders, Manley and Nethersole, were prominent in the CEC, but Bustamante chose this crisis to announce at a meeting at the Kingston race course that he would form a new political party to fight for a minimum wage, an 8-hour working day and old-age pensions.

Richards now began to see Manley as a 'self-less patriot' and potentially 'a great leader',[72] while Bustamante appeared more of a maverick. Manley chose not to exploit this critical situation by increasing pressure on the government, but the governor reinforced the state's repressive apparatus. In July 2,500 special constables were added to the Jamaica Constabulary and the Legislative Council passed 'A Law to make provision during the Present Emergency with respect to sentences of Corporal Punishment for certain Crimes of Violence' (Post 1981: Vol. 1, 250). At the same time, the prices of some essentials were controlled and some items were rationed, and the governor sought finance for public works projects lest even larger sums should be required for 'putting down large-scale disorder'.[73] In spite of these efforts, the crisis took a specifically political form by October, when the PNP executive publicly criticized the governor's efforts. In November Richards had the PNP left interned.

At the PNP's fourth annual conference, held on 19 and 20 September 1942, the left, led by Hart and the Hill brothers, criticised Manley for devoting too much time to the CEC, which meant that he was associating the party too much with middle-class and even capitalist elements in Jamaica. Manley survived the challenge, with the support of such men as Lloyd, William Seivright and Nethersole, but the left gained more representation on the executive committee and, according to an FBI memorandum, permission 'to go ahead with what they intend to do, if they think that they can gain anything by it'.[74] The immediate result, then, was not a breach in the party, which transpired several years later, and in Manley's favour, but a renewed breach between the PNP and the colonial government.

When Richards was interviewed for the Daily Gleaner at the end of September, he claimed that 'much is being done in the way of relief' for unemployment and that 'already the situation has greatly improved'. Moreover, he claimed that it was only a vocal minority that wanted self-government: 'The great majority

of the Jamaicans do not want self-government'.[75] The PNP executive committee replied by calling Richards' picture of Jamaica distorted, as the shortages
resulted from 'Government's negligence' and not solely from the war. Whereas
the war had 'created new avenues of employment' in other countries, the PNP
argued, the government in Jamaica was actually following the business community's policy of retrenching workers, specifically at the Railway and Public
Works Department. 'The middle class are facing just as serious a position as the
labourer. Old employment avenues are closing. No new ones are being opened
up .... But our people are waking up. Every day more and more realize that our
future security can only be achieved when we govern ourselves'.[76]

The PNP was publicly challenging Richards by linking the rising unemployment to the colonial government's negligence and to the need for
self-government. Party members were busy organising unemployed as well as
employed workers, in rural and urban areas. One of the organisers in Clarendon
was Robert Rumble, the militant peasant leader of the 1930s, who was elected to
the PNP's general council in September (Post 1981: Vol. 1, 261). Ken Hill and Cecil
Nelson, who were directing the party's labour and unemployment departments
respectively, drew up plans for organising activities, and Vernon Arnett, the party
secretary and head of the organization department, urged that they should plan
so as 'to lead decisively in any crisis that develops' (quoted in Post 1981: Vol. 1, 261).
Hart, who was president of the GREU and head of the department of internal
party finance, expressed great confidence in the growing strength of the party
and the labour movement: 'The present wave of Trade Union development and
organisation which is proceeding so rapidly is strengthening the position of
the Party as the political organisation of the working class. Party members are
obtaining positions of leadership in union after union and the labour movement
itself is increasing in strength' (quoted in Post 1981: Vol. 1, 262). Hart's optimism
was soon to be proved premature, however, because the badly divided labour
movement left him and other leaders of small unions without adequate support
when the governor moved against them.

October and November may have been the worst months, economically,
for many people in Jamaica. The number of people employed in casual labour
in the Kingston-St Andrew area continued to decline, reaching about 6,500 in
November (compared with 14,250 in April), and the cost of living rose again in
October to 159.77 (Post 1981: Vol. 1, 263). Richards reported that the number of
people employed on relief works had increased between 18 July and 5 December
from 3,577 to 10,611, but he admitted that between 150,000 and 200,000 persons
were seriously affected by unemployment and underemployment in the island
and that the situation was 'unstable'. Much of the problem could be attributed
to the restriction on fuel oils resulting from the extension of the U-boat war
into the Caribbean; construction had ceased at the US base and the banana

industry was in decline.[77] Restrictions on transport made it hard for higglers to get their produce to urban markets. Urban consumers felt the higglers were profiteering and called on the government to control the prices (Post 1981: Vol. 1, 264). The GREU confronted the government against this background of rising prices and unemployment.

The JTUC and PNP had made a special effort to organise government workers in 1942, first the railwaymen in March, then postal and telegraph workers in July, and Public Works Department employees in October. Henry, the GREU secretary, and several other union activists lost their jobs on the railway and on 26 September the union was told it would not be recognised. When the GREU asked the labour adviser to arbitrate, Richards ordered him not to because the PNP, he claimed, sought 'to undermine discipline in the Government service and to reach a position where they can paralyse [the] transport system'.[78] While there is no evidence of a plot to paralyse Jamaica's transport system, the PNP left was effectively organising government employees and becoming increasingly influential in the JTUC and PNP: Hart and Henry in the GREU, Ken Hill in the Postal and Telegraph Workers' Union (PTWU), and Frank Hill and Henry in the Public Works Employees Union (PWEU). Frank Hill was also editing the left's weekly paper, The Masses (Post 1981: Vol. 1, 265–6). The goals of the Four H's, as they came to be known, were to organise workers who were not in the BITU and to organise government employees, in particular, so they could both benefit the workers and 'embarrass the Colonial administration' (Eaton 1975: 86). The governor's intransigence was largely responsible for the rapid escalation of the confrontation.

In pursuit of recognition, the GREU cabled Citrine to put pressure on the Colonial Office and asked Manley to obtain a writ to the Supreme Court seeking an injunction on the governor to permit arbitration. Such procedures were not revolutionary. The Supreme Court fixed a hearing for 2 November. Meanwhile, on 19 October, the GREU executive decided to affiliate with the JTUC. Richards' response on 22 October was the Authorized Associations (Government Departments) (Defence) Regulations which forbade membership or leadership of such unions of people who were not government employees. This would not only have made it impossible for non-government employees to lead the unions, but would also make the unions vulnerable to victimisation because leaders who were employees could be fired by the government and then could no longer be members.

All three of the new unions of government employees were soon declared illegal, and on 25 October the police raided the GREU office and the printery where The Masses was produced. That same day, the GREU executive, consisting of Hart, Nethersole and Henry, asked their comrades to support them: 'We are fighting a great battle for the right of free trade unions to elect freely their own officers'.[79] On 2 November, the Supreme Court reserved its judgment because, though the unions were now illegal under the new regulations, the case raised problems about the use of defense regulations. The next day, 3 November, Richards had Hart, Henry and the Hill brothers interned at Gibraltar Camp under the defense regulations, and six other PNP leaders and organisers were detained in the next few days.

Though it is clear that 'the Left had every intention of increasing its influence through the nationalist struggle and eventually of pressing much more strongly for socialism than the PNP centre was ever going to do', there is no 'evidence of revolutionary conspiracy or even intent to profit directly from the existing social crisis' (Post 1981: Vol. 1, 269). Moreover, the left was quite unprepared for the internment of its leaders and there was no call for protest action. On 20 November, Richards, on instructions from the British government, had to revoke his Authorized Associations Regulations and subordinate government employees were restored the right to select their own union officials. However, the Four H's remained in detention, and Nethersole of the PNP's centre replaced Hart as head of the GREU.

The impact of these events in October and November 1942 was far-reaching. On the one hand, Richards' authoritarian actions stimulated Jamaicans' demands for self-government. As George Eaton says,

> In his attempt to deny representational and bargaining rights to the T.U.C. affiliates under their professional leadership, Richards had shown that he was prepared not only to interfere with the internal structure and government of the unions, but also with the due processes of law. His high-handed action did much to foster a sense of Jamaican identity and nationalism. Middle-class Jamaicans and professionals of diverse social and political outlook joined in denouncing Richards' escalating encroachment on civil liberties (1975: 87-8).

On the other hand, the effective decapitation of the left on 3 November meant that the PNP's centre, which lacked a strong enough base in the labour movement, could not compete successfully, in terms of political mobilisation, with Bustamante's organisation. Consequently, although Manley's PNP contributed to the constitutional change towards self-government in 1943, Bustamante and his new Jamaica Labour Party won the resulting electoral competition in 1944. The wartime crisis of 1942 provided the particular context that established the conditions in which this broader political struggle was played.

The inability of the PNP left to establish an adequate popular base in 1942, much less to take control of the labour movement, left the PNP centre-right to struggle with Bustamante for political power within a slowly evolving process of constitutional change, defined by the British in terms of the liberal democratic model of the Whitehall-Westminster system. By the end of 1942, the demand for

constitutional change was so broadly based that even the new Jamaica Democratic Party, an organ of capitalist and upper middle-class interests, was calling
for universal suffrage and a bicameral legislature in Jamaica (Post 1981: Vol. 1,
279). These constitutional developments gave the Jamaican middle classes some
local political power but left the basic economic structure unchanged, so the
vast majority of Jamaican peasants and workers remained poor and powerless.

Trinidad and Tobago

The great growth of trade unions in Trinidad and Tobago that followed the
labour rebellion of 1937 strengthened the voice of organised labour but resulted
also in a fragmented labour movement that was often characterised by bitter
rivalries. Not only were there persistent divisions between unions that failed to
unite in an effective TUC, but there continued to be competition between rival
leaders for support from workers in particular industries, as, for example, the
split among oilfield workers between the supporters of Butler and Rienzi. During
the war, the actions of the colonial government, in dealing with some labour
leaders and repressing others, deepened these divisions, and the constitutional
changes towards universal suffrage and self-government gave rise to a parallel
proliferation of small political parties, most of which appealed to trade unionists
and labour sympathisers. The outcome, in the first election held with universal
adult suffrage in 1946, was that, while most of the successful candidates had
the support of labour, no particular group emerged as a clear political winner.

The British government was particularly concerned about maintaining industrial peace and security in Trinidad's oilfields during the war. The contrasting
treatment by the colonial authorities of the two chief labour leaders of the oilfield
workers, Butler and Rienzi, reflected these concerns at the same time as deepening the rift between the rival leaders and their supporters. While Rienzi built up
the OWTU in 1937 and 1938, Butler was in hiding and then in prison. Released
from prison on 6 May 1939, Butler was initially welcomed by the OWTU leaders
but, as we have seen, continuing disagreements and rivalries led to his expulsion
from the union on 8 August. In order to avoid the risk that Butler would incite
further unrest in the oilfields, the colonial government interned him under the
emergency defence regulations for the duration of the war. Efforts were made
by people in Trinidad and the UK to obtain his release, but in vain. When he
eventually emerged in 1945 from his incarceration his reputation as a martyred
hero was considerably enhanced, but he had no organisation and constitutional
changes were moving the colony's politics towards a system in which his style
would be less effective than it had been in 1937.

Meanwhile, Rienzi had enhanced his own reputation with the colonial
authorities as a responsible labour leader, the head of the OWTU and the
Trades Union Congress (TUC). Rienzi sought to organise labour in a legal and

bureaucratic way in order to extend benefits and rights to Trinidadian workers, and this also provided his solid base for entry into electoral politics and a post in government in 1944. While Butler was being excluded from participation, therefore, Rienzi was becoming co-opted into the colonial power structure.

On 2 June 1940, the Trinidad and Tobago TUC (TTTUC), led by Rienzi, passed a resolution condemning fascism:

> The Council feels that while the workers in Trinidad do not enjoy the same democratic rights which the workers in Great Britain and other self-governing dominions enjoy, they still enjoy greater rights and privileges than the workers under Nazi Germany or any other Fascist State.
>
> The Council desires to point out that if the rights and privileges thus far won are to be maintained and if the workers are to move forward to the attainment of greater rights, it is essential that Hitlerism and Fascism must be defeated.
>
> The Council regards it as a historic mission to mobilize the moral and material resources of the workers for the defeat of Hitlerism and Fascism.[80]

Rienzi was attacked by Bertie Percival and Elma Francois of the NWCSA, who despite their differences with Butler expressed their solidarity with the interned labour leader, and by E.M. Mitchell of the FWTU and Albert Gomes and Quintin O'Connor of the Shop Clerks and Shop Assistants Union (SCSAU). These people got together at a memorial day for Butler on 23 June 1940 at La Brea. Mitchell declared Butler to be 'the only true and original working class leader', while Percival critically referred to other 'leaders who felt that they could ride to power on the backs of those who really struggled',[81] which was surely aimed at Rienzi. C.Y. Carstairs, an official in the Colonial Office, evaluated Rienzi quite differently when he minuted that the TTTUC resolution was a 'most significant document. It shows a judiciousness and balance which is uncommon in the West Indies, and which is probably a product of the present stage of the war. Mr Rienzi is plainly adding to his stature'.[82]

While Butler was incarcerated and Rienzi was adding to his stature by adopting a more conciliatory mode of operating, Arthur Cipriani, who was still the leader of the TLP, took an anti-union position and became regarded 'by those committed to the working-class movement as an undisguised supporter of ruling class interests and British imperialism' (Singh 1994: 212). Cipriani, once the champion of West Indian soldiers and the 'barefooted man', had become an obstacle to the labour movement after 1937. During the war, as the mayor of Port of Spain, he denied unions the use of Woodford Square for public meetings, sought to have strikes outlawed and supported press censorship. His nomination to the Executive Council in May 1941 was criticised by labour leaders who had come to see him as authoritarian (Singh 1994: 212). By the time Cipriani died in 1945, his TLP was 'a spent force' (Brereton 1981: 194).

The chief labour agreements in which Rienzi was involved occurred early in 1940, following some unofficial but orderly strikes in the sugar and oil industries. A stoppage occurred at Point Fortin on 22 January and mass demonstrations were held the next day. Even after the Oilfields Employers' Association of Trinidad (OEAT) agreed to pay a 1 cent per hour war bonus, stoppages continued at Apex Oilfields and the Point-a-Pierre refinery.[83] The governor was pleased to report on 27 January that, following talks he had held with employers and unions in both the oil and sugar industries, settlements had been reached. Stoppages continued for a while at some places, supported by some local union officials. At Barrackpore, where men had suffered reduced earnings when they were transferred from work on drilling crews to poorer paid jobs as pipe fitters, a 'field caught fire in circumstances which suggested sabotage'.[84] The OEAT insisted that the OWTU honour their joint agreement and that they 'had a positive duty to see that their members did so'. By 18 February they reported that 'the undercurrent of unrest ... subsided'.[85]

Field and factory workers in the sugar industry received a wage increase of 3 cents per day or task, and members of the Joint Sugar Board would enquire into wages to be paid for the 1940 crop season. In the oil industry the standard wage rate was increased by 2 cents per hour, with a war bonus to be calculated on a sliding scale of   cent per hour for every complete rise of 5 points in the government index of the cost of living. Effective from 24 January, this war bonus would add another cent per hour to the wage. Most significant was the fact that the OWTU 'undertook not to request any further increase in the standard wage during the war and 6 months thereafter or for 2 years, whichever period is longer', and Rienzi agreed that his unions would not strike for the duration of the war.[86]

Nearly four months after this declaration of an industrial truce, the governor reported that 'industrial relations in the Oil Industry have not only improved considerably but are on a sounder basis than ever before', and that though the situation in the sugar industry was not so satisfactory he expected it to improve.

> In general it may be said that the attitude of the majority of work people and of organised labour is entirely peaceful. The policy of the Trade Unions especially those operating in major industries is to avoid disorder, and although spasmodic strikes may periodically occur I have no reason to apprehend that they will be conducted in an irresponsible manner. Trade Unions in the south on their own initiative decided not to organise any May Day Demonstration this year, and one demonstration that took place in the north was conducted in an orderly manner. Owing to cooperation of all concerned and excellent work of Industrial Advisor labour difficulties in Trinidad have been reduced to a minimum.[87]

A report by the industrial adviser, who chaired a meeting of the Joint

Conciliation Board for the oil industry on 30 April 1940, claimed that Rienzi had 'frequently poured oil on the waters as they became troubled during the conference', with both sides deploring the stoppages of work at Point Fortin, which had occurred 'without using the successive stages of procedure for settlement of grievances' that had been agreed to in February. The result was that 'the Union officials had expeditiously assumed control of the stoppages and secured early resumption of work'. Although Ralph Mentor was said to have been unwilling 'to accept a complete condemnation of the men without an equal condemnation of the Machine Shop Superintendent whom he considered was as much responsible for the stoppage on the 1st April as the men themselves .. .. Mr Rienzi was extremely helpful in ... placating his colleagues'. Rienzi again 'jumped into the breach' and 'placated his colleagues', Mentor and MacDonald Moses, when they became angry about the use of Red Books and discharge tickets to victimise workers.[88] Orde Browne subsequently commented on what he and the secretary of state viewed as a satisfactory meeting, saying that there was a die-hard element among the employers but that Rienzi had been 'more conciliatory than I should have expected'.[89] In spite of the fact that Rienzi had become so conciliatory, and that the governor had come to view him and his unions in a positive light, some representatives of the sugar and oil companies remained strongly anti-union. Governor Young commented that 'while ostensibly accepting Trade Unionism and collective bargaining they feel strongly that any step in this direction is a mistake and are full of suspicion and fear'.[90] At about this time, in June 1940, the OWTU was said to have 3,817 contributing members,[91] but this was in a workforce of over 13,000, so much organising still needed to be done in the oilfields.

Despite the efforts of Young and his industrial adviser and the cooperation of Rienzi, the industrial truce merely papered over the cracks in labour relations in Trinidad and Tobago. The cost of living continued to rise sharply and many workers were not covered by the war bonus agreements. Many people were angered by 'the government's repression of political and union activity under the pretext of the war' (Brereton 1981: 192) and were disillusioned about the slow progress being made towards democratic rights and constitutional change. West Indians were expected to make their contributions and sacrifices towards the war effort on behalf of democracy, but they themselves lacked the most basic rights of citizenship.

In 1941 some minor constitutional changes were initiated. In the Legislative Council the number of officials was reduced and the number of electives was raised. The new council consisted of three ex officio members, six nominated unofficials and nine electives, so the governor's casting vote still gave the non-elected element a majority (Brereton 1981: 192-3). In the Executive Council the number of elected members was increased to two, but there were still three nominated unofficials and the governor, who was not obliged to take the council's advice, remained very much in charge. A large committee was created in 1941 to study the question of broadening the franchise. On a committee of 33 persons, three men, Rienzi, Mentor and Gomes, represented trade unions, but the conservative wing, led by the chairman, Sir Lennox O'Reilly, dominated the committee (Brereton 1981: 193). Despite increasing political activity, this franchise committee did not report until 1944, and universal suffrage was delayed until the elections of 1946.

Although a general election based on universal adult suffrage was postponed, several elections for seats on the Legislative Council and for borough councils encouraged political activity and the formation and growth of political parties during the war. The new parties, like the established but declining TLP, appealed to the cause of labour, and were connected to organised labour, even though most labourers were disqualified from voting. The chief new parties were the Socialist Party of Trinidad and Tobago (SPTT), launched by Rienzi and the OWTU in 1941, and the West Indian National Party (WINP), formed by Dr David Pitt and Roy Joseph in 1942. Rienzi had won the Victoria seat on the Legislative Council in 1938 when he was supported by The People as the champion of 'the two great races, the African and the Indian, who constitute Trinidad's working classes'.[92] Rienzi and his largely African associates in the OWTU continued to press for working-class solidarity across racial lines, as did Dr Tito P. Achong, the Chinese mayor of Port of Spain's council.

Rienzi, Mentor and Joseph were all elected to the San Fernando Borough Council with OWTU support. Some trade unionists began to feel that the involvement of their colleagues in politics conflicted with the 'purely trade union work', and E. Redvers Blades, the OWTU's general secretary, objected to a proposal to increase the salaries of his colleagues Moses and John F. Rojas so that they could qualify for election. Blades wrote in 1943, 'I am not against politics, but when leaders are bent on politics and not planning future moves, and not aiming at a rich and financial movement, and not partaking in real trade union work as they should that movement is doomed'. Of Rienzi, Blades wrote,

> He has a great love for politics, even more than real trade union work, and has a tendency to mix the two issues.
>
> He did much valuable work ... but the higher he goes the less the workers see of him.
>
> For the last three years or at least since he has reached the top of the ladder he is a changed man, and neglects his trade union work.[93]

Soon after Blades objected to his colleagues' voting to raise their own salaries in February 1941, they forced him to resign his position as general secretary. Mentor replaced Blades and charged him with embezzling union funds, but the magistrate dismissed the case for lack of evidence.[94]

The chief officers of the OWTU, Rienzi, Mentor, F.J. Morgan, Rojas and Moses, were also the principal officers of the TTTUC. In May 1943, the TTTUC advocated Rienzi's nomination to the Executive Council in order that he could counteract Cipriani's influence. This was the high point, but also 'the beginning of the end of Rienzi's career as a labour representative' (Singh 1994: 213). Predictably, members of the capitalist class were outraged when Governor Sir Bede Clifford included Rienzi in the Executive Council, and when Gomes, the president of the FWTU, and Pitt and Joseph, of the San Fernando Borough Council, turned against Rienzi it was apparent that his popular base was eroding. Anti-Rienzi candidates defeated the SPTT's nominees in the San Fernando borough elections in November 1943, soon after Pitt and Joseph had formed the rival WINP. This second southern-based party, which supported Butler's release, further divided the labour cause. Rienzi became increasingly preoccupied with the franchise committee, the majority of whose members advocated a language test that would disadvantage many of the Indian population. Even Gomes, Mentor and O'Connor supported the proposal that only persons who understood English should be allowed to vote, so Rienzi was becoming isolated from his colleagues. On this issue, Singh writes, Rienzi began 'to abandon his class position and rally to the cause of his race' (1994: 217), but it may also be said that the other trade unionists should have supported him on this issue. Rienzi correctly contended that the language qualification would 'deprive a large proportion of the Indian community of the right to vote'.[95]

Governor Clifford supported Rienzi's minority position when the committee's report was submitted in December 1943,[96] and in February 1944 he offered him the position of acting Second Crown Counsel in the Colonial Service. Acceptance of this appointment, which was conditional on Rienzi disengaging from political activity, marked the end of his involvement in the labour movement. Rojas, who had been first vice-president of the OWTU since 1937, succeeded Rienzi as president and held the post until 1962. Rienzi, who became the president of the India Club, behaved increasingly like the middle-class Indian professional that he was. His departure from the labour movement weakened efforts to make it a truly multiracial movement as Trinidad and Tobago moved further towards biracial party politics in the decade after the achievement of adult franchise (Singh 1994: 226).

Meanwhile, the WINP gained the support of Gomes and O'Connor of the FWTU and adopted quite a radical programme. The programme's vision extended beyond Trinidad and Tobago in aiming to develop 'a West Indian national consciousness based not on racial origins but on the community of interests of all West Indians'.[97] The party sought to work through trade unions, study groups and local party branches to develop the people's confidence and consciousness in preparation for an active role in postwar reconstruction. Its programme stated in 1942: 'The time is ripe for the West Indian peoples themselves to make a constructive contribution towards the solution of the economic, social and political problems of these islands instead of waiting for action by the Colonial Governments. There is need for an organised body to express the West Indies' viewpoint and to assist in the re-organization of the economic and political structure of these islands which will come at the end of the war'.[98]

More specifically, the WINP called for 'redistribution of the land, so that the landless may, by means of planned land settlement schemes, acquire holdings adequate to the maintenance of the settler and his family'.[99] The party proposed an ambitious programme of nationalisation, including the oil and asphalt industries, while sugar estates and factories would become state-sponsored cooperatives; the country's wealth would be used to finance a social welfare system. It called also for industrial and agricultural diversification, state control of public utilities and communications, the West Indianisation of the managerial strata and of the education curriculum, free primary and secondary education, free health services, protective insurance and improved work conditions - in short, a programme similar to that of the British Labour Party (Ryan 1972: 73). The time was not as ripe as the WINP leaders anticipated, however, and they failed to involve many Trinidadian Indians, much less to make this a party of wider West Indian peoples. Attempts were made to unite some of these labour-oriented parties, but the labour vote, though strong, was so fragmented in the first election with universal adult suffrage that 'middle-class politics would dominate the scene in the years after 1946' (Brereton 1981: 195).

Barbados

On the eve of the Second World War, in July 1939, Grantley Adams packed the executive committee of the Barbados Progressive League (BPL) with his loyal followers. Adams was the new president, after C.A. Braithwaite's removal, Edwy Talma the treasurer, Hugh Springer the vice-president and C.A. Nurse the general secretary. 'The Progressive League was ... essentially a middle-class-led organisation vying for a mass base in order to confront and eventually reduce the oligarchical power of the consolidated merchant-planter elite' (Beckles 1990: 170). In order to create this mass base and to consolidate Adams' power within the BPL, the Barbados Workers' Union (BWU) was formed in 1941. Though some opposition to Adams' leadership and policies persisted, his dominance of the Barbados labour movement became firmly established during the war and provided the basis for his rise to political power.

While purging the BPL of its radical Garveyite, Herbert Seale, and assuring the governor and others that he was not a communist, Adams did argue, in an exchange with Lord Moyne during the royal commission's hearings in 1939, for a partial nationalisation of the sugar industry, that is, 'government ownership of sugar factories, cooperative production, and marketing' (quoted in Beckles 1990: 176). Lacking a mass base at that time, however, the BPL backed away from talk of nationalisation in 1940, and Adams sought to promote more limited reforms through legislation by staying 'close to executive power' (Beckles 1990: 177).

The BPL organised three sections under the slogan, 'Three units, one aim; raising the living standards for the working classes' (Hoyos 1974: 97). The Peasants' Association, formed by A.G. Gittens early in 1940, sought to organise peasant farmers and to raise their income by means of cooperative production and marketing. The BPL also organised a friendly society, and its political council organised the campaign for the 1940 general election. Adams and his colleagues called for a broad programme of social and political reform, including a redistribution of land to the peasants, more progressive taxation, universal adult suffrage and the abolition of property qualifications for membership in the House of Assembly (Hoyos 1974: 96). In spite of the fact that the franchise was restricted to about 3.5 per cent of the population, five of the BPL candidates were elected in 1940: Adams, Springer, Gittens, V.B. Vaughan and Dr H.G. Cummins. Wynter A. Crawford, a radical anti-colonialist who had just left the BPL, won as an independent. For the first time there was a substantial reformist element in the House, though it was unlikely to increase without a broadening of the franchise.

The Trade Union Act of 1940, which had been recommended by the Moyne Commission, provided the legal basis for the trade union that would become the BPL's mass base. Several people had advocated the creation of a trade union for some time. Among them were three journalists, Crawford and Clement Sobers, the editor and a leading writer, respectively, of the Barbados Observer, and Clennell Wickham, a columnist in the Barbados Advocate Weekly. They drew attention to the fact that trade unions already had become part of the life of Trinidad, Jamaica and Guyana. The acting attorney-general spoke in favour of the Trade Union Bill at its second reading on 2 August 1938, referring to the fact that the report of the Disturbances Commission in 1937 had stressed Barbados' backwardness with regard to organised labour. However, the bill was delayed in select committee and was not assented to until 27 December 1939, to come into force on 1 August 1940.

The BWU's rules were drafted and adopted in May 1941, and it was registered on 4 October. It was created as a single union, organised with divisions to represent the various trades and occupations, with each division responsible for electing its own officers and collecting fees from members for transmission to the central office. Matters concerning wages, conditions and grievances could be raised at the division level and voted on before being sent to the central Executive Council, whose first officers were Adams, president general, Springer, general secretary, and Hilton Coulston, treasurer (Dixon 1991: 17). The structure of the BWU appeared to be decentralised and democratic, and the annual delegates conference was nominally the supreme authority, but actually the union was dominated by Adams and it provided the mass base for his rise to power.

During the remaining years of the war there was sporadic working-class discontent and protest in Barbados, while Adams and his organisations gained strength, as evidenced in a strike and general election in 1944. This meant that by 1946, when a general election was held in order to create a semi-ministerial government on the way to internal self-government, Adams' BPL, reconstituted as the Barbados Labour Party (BLP), was poised for victory. Adams became the first premier in 1954 and the BLP dominated politics in Barbados until 1961. In Barbados, therefore, where Adams was the head of both the BWU and the BLP, there was much greater unity between the chief political party and the dominant trade union in the early years than in either Jamaica or Trinidad and Tobago.

In early 1941, in spite of a rapid rise in the cost of living since the beginning of the war, the head of the Colonial Development and Welfare organisation commented that there was 'a general air of prosperity [in Barbados]…but there is also much poverty in places, brought about mainly by under-employment'.[100] The poverty was eased to a degree by remittances from relatives in Trinidad and elsewhere, and by the fact that almost 57,000 people were members of the various friendly societies that provided a measure of security and paid out Christmas bonuses. More serious problems were expected at the end of the sugar crop, but a planting programme to produce food was instituted by the government under the defence regulations and 1,792 workers left to work on the US bases in Trinidad. When most of them returned in 1942 they went to various parts of Barbados, so Governor Bushe did not perceive an 'immediate necessity for the provision of relief measures'.[101] Three months later, however, he complained that news of thousands of Bahamians and Jamaicans being recruited to work in the United States had embarrassed him, and he requested that Barbados should be included in this scheme in order 'to relieve local unemployment'.[102]

On 29 June 1943 a mass meeting of some 6,000 persons was organised by Crawford, who urged a quota of Barbadian workers for the United States.[103] Since 1942 Adams had been a member of the Executive Committee, appointed by Bushe, and he seems to have stayed closer to the seat of power while Crawford agitated in the streets. A petition signed on 19 July, encouraged by Crawford, stated that there were 25,000 unemployed in Barbados and sought the recruitment of workers for the United States. The British Foreign Office then instructed its Washington embassy to ask the US authorities if, 'in the event of recruiting being continued, [the] claims of Barbados, where [the] unemployment situation is worst of all in the West Indies', could be considered.[104] By July, Bushe had to admit, 'Unemployment and under-employment constitute a serious social and economic problem in Barbados', relieved only partly and temporarily by the departure of some workers for employment elsewhere and the enlargement of local armed forces.[105] In November Bushe stated that about 5,000 men and as many women 'could be supplied from Barbados without risk of dislocation of local labour supply', and that this would both diminish unemployment and raise national income through remittances; it would create a problem only if all the persons so recruited were to be repatriated at the same time.[106]

Most of the labour required for essential industries in the United States was poorly paid work picking crops and most people were repatriated as winter came on.[107] About 4,700 Bahamians and 9,000 Jamaicans were recruited to work in the United States in 1943, and the reason for not recruiting Barbadians was political and, according to the Anglo-American Caribbean Commission (AACC), could not be publicly revealed. The problem for the US government was that if they took workers from Puerto Rico, who were US citizens, 'they could not be sent back against their will. This cannot, of course, be stated, and [the] reason given is lack of shipping facilities. If workers were brought from Barbados, [the] falsity of the reason given would be apparent'.[108]

The advantage of recruiting migrant workers from the Bahamas and Jamaica to pick crops in the United States clearly was that they could be sent home against their will when they were no longer needed. The governor of Barbados was still hoping for a 'favourable decision to employ [a] Barbadian quota' in 1944, as the 'widespread disappointment' about the lack of recruitment could be exploited by Crawford and others to promote unrest and disturbances.[109] By that time it could no longer be denied that large-scale unemployment had become 'a chronic problem' in Barbados.[110]

When Bushe eventually succeeded in obtaining a quota for almost 5,000 Barbadian workers in the United States,[111] the planters objected 'because it is likely to increase the difficulty of obtaining cheap plantation labour', though almost 10,000 persons had registered in the hope of gaining work in the United States,[112] which suggests that there would still be a substantial surplus of labour on the island. On 11 June 1944, the first 2,060 agricultural workers sailed to the United States and by the end of the year there were 3,659 Barbadians working there. By August 1945 there were 5,655 Barbadians among the 38,152 West Indians working in the United States,[113] but most were soon repatriated and in early 1946 there were only 327 Barbadians among the remaining 7,238 West Indians working there.[114] Some 3,000 Barbadians were recruited for the 1946 season but by the end of that year only 1,211 remained, among a total of under 10,000 West Indians.[115]

The limited opportunity afforded a few thousand Barbadians as temporary agricultural workers in the United States towards the end of the war constituted something of a safety valve as unemployment and poverty increased on the island. Nevertheless, some protests occurred about the recruitment of migrant labour and the planters themselves were unhappy about the reduction of what they saw as their labour supply. Although some employers had been persuaded to deal with representatives of workers on conciliation committees, others were still unwilling to accept that the BWU had become part of the labour relations of the colony. Since the disastrous strike of 1939, which provided Adams with the opportunity to purge and take complete control of the BPL, he had generally proved a conciliatory labour leader, which was one reason why he and Crawford soon parted company.

Adams worked with the labour officer, Guy Perrin, who organised a system of voluntary conciliation boards and a Central Labour Advisory Board 'to provide for the regulation of wage-rates and of working conditions in various occupations and industries' (Mark 1966: 70). The Labour Department report of 1944 stated that the BWU had established agencies in the parishes but its financial membership, which had grown to 3,680, was 'drawn for the most part from the urban area where workers are quicker to appreciate the advantage of collective action. The assistance and cooperation given by this organisation was much appreciated, and its selection of suitable workers' representatives to sit on Conciliation Boards which have during the year dealt with the affairs of seven different trades, has been particularly helpful' (quoted in Dixon 1991: 17-18). Adams' willingness to work with the labour officer and to use his BWU, which was still the only registered trade union in the colony, to help resolve the workers' disputes and grievances, earned him the continuing favour of the governor.

Adams and Crawford demanded but failed to get universal adult suffrage in 1943 when the House debated the Representation of the People Bill. Instead, a reduction of the income qualification to £25 and the extension of the franchise to women, for the first time, broadened the electorate somewhat before the 1944 election. Contesting the election were the conservative Barbados Electors' Association (BEA) of the planters, Adams' reformist BPL, and Crawford's new West Indian National Congress Party (WINCP), which was 'rooted within radical elements of the working class' (Beckles 1990: 180). Crawford, who was born in 1910, had been associated with Adams and Seale in 1937 and 1938, and had been elected to a seat in the House for St Philip in 1940 and 1942. The WINCP, formed early in 1944, seriously challenged Adams' BPL from the left, thus dividing the labour movement politically between 1944 and 1951, when the BLP won overwhelmingly in the first general election with universal adult suffrage.

Towards the end of the war, Adams was in a difficult position. He had been appointed a member of the Executive Council in 1942, but could not push the government to more liberal policies any faster than Bushe would permit. As he had failed to obtain a much broader franchise he was still dependent on the support of the middle strata and he could not afford to alienate the powerful planter-merchant elite without first developing a firmer base. At the same time, he was in danger of losing some of his popular support to Crawford, who was not tainted by association with the colonial government and who took a more militant stance on such issues as the recruitment of labour for the United States. It was not until the middle of 1945 that the BWU executive began to discuss the sugar workers and to hold meetings in several parishes 'to encourage the workers to come together and join the Union so as to enhance the bargaining power of the workers' representatives in a Conciliation Board'.[116]

The most active division of the BWU was that of the engineers who were foundry workers. Central Foundry workers, who had struck on 6 July 1937, probably played an important role in the labour rebellion that year. In early 1942, the Vaucleuse Factory engineers had obtained a wage increase and improvement in their working hours and conditions through negotiations by the BWU. Six ship's carpenters stopped work at the Central Foundry on 21 February when they found that some house carpenters were being employed, and the BWU negotiated a settlement after instructing the men to return to work.[117] Another strike began at the Central Foundry on 16 January 1943 and the governor rebuked the employer for refusing to have the matter, which concerned a dismissed employee, investigated by the Conciliation Board.[118] Another dispute arose at the end of the year when an engineer at the Barbados Foundry was dismissed.[119]

Much of the BWU Executive Council's business in these early years concerned complaints about dismissals, including some where workers thought they were being victimised because they were seen to be 'leaning toward Trade Unionism'.[120] This was a central issue in 1944 when 121 engineers walked out of the foundries because McDonald Brathwaite, a turner with 25 years of service at the Barbados Foundry[121] and the secretary of the BWU Engineers' Division, had been dismissed. The union received support in this struggle from the Trinidad and Tobago TUC and a contribution of $90.60 from Barbadian workers in Curaçao.[122] The strike lasted for eight weeks, with pickets organised and pay from the union for the strikers, and 'the Union came triumphantly through the ordeal .... Not only did the strike achieve its principal objectives, but after the battle the agricultural labourers joined the Union in force and all the divisions were invigorated by a new sense of vitality.' (Hoyos 1974: 99-100)

Despite the growing strength of the BWU, however, the WINCP laid claim to be the radical vanguard of the labour movement in the 1944 election. Using his position as editor of the Barbados Observer, Crawford criticised the planters' party and urged people to 'Bring Socialism to Barbados': 'Barbados is in revolt against the status quo. Throughout the country thousands of middle and working class men and women are voicing the most determined protests against poverty and unemployment. These thousands are resolved to put more of the wealth in the colony at the service of the people; these thousands are in deadly earnest, this spirit may well be called NEW DEMOCRACY' (quoted in

Beckles 1990: 181).

In spite of the narrow franchise, which left thousands without a vote, and the split of the labour movement's vote between two parties, the planters' BEA won only eight seats, to eight for the WINCP and seven for the BPL (Beckles 1990: 181).

At the start of the crop season in 1945 Crawford and other WINCP members were trying to organise a cane-cutters' union.[123] In February Bushe reported that 'workers are refusing to cut, and in the last ten days some 1,000 acres have been burnt. Threats and intimidation are increasing'. Although acknowledging that the parties had failed to agree on wages or the method of calculating them, he thought the reason for the problem was more political than economic, and that it was 'fostered by Crawford's new party in a bid to win the votes of the agricultural labourers'.[124] Bushe disapproved of Crawford and his radically socialist and anti-colonial party and preferred the more moderate and loyal BPL. Consequently, instead of appointing Crawford and Adams to the Executive Council, where they could have worked together on behalf of labour, Bushe ignored Crawford and appointed Springer of the BPL-BWU along with Adams. This deepened the rivalry between these leaders of the labour movement, while the relationship between Adams and the colonial governor grew still closer.

Bushe rewarded Adams for his moderation and was grooming him for semi-ministerial office in the next, reformed constitution, but excluded Crawford and thus drove a wedge into this division in the labour movement. Bushe's strategy helped to ensure that even while democracy and responsible government was allowed, in gradual stages, to transform Barbados' political system, they would not lead to a serious threat to the continuing economic predominance of the planter-merchant elite, who could no longer control the colony's politics. Ironically, Adams, who in the 1930s had argued that Barbados' essential problem was economic, dominated the new political system through his control of the monolithic BLP-BWU, but failed to transform the economy.

Antigua, St Kitts, Guyana, the Bahamas, Belize and St Lucia

Most of the other colonies in the British Caribbean where there had been labour disturbances and rebellions in the 1930s experienced unrest during the war, but not to the same extent as in Jamaica, Trinidad and Barbados. As in Jamaica and Trinidad, early reports of workers' loyalty and support for the UK were some-times followed by other reports of discontent, labour disputes and strikes. The pressure of unemployment and rising prices and the widespread growth of trade unionism gave rise to both organised and spontaneous action. The colonial governments often urged strikers to return to work on patriotic grounds, while protecting strike-breakers in the name of the war effort.

The Antigua Trades and Labour Union (ATLU), at its first general conference in February 1940, pledged its 'unwavering loyalty' and 'whole-hearted support' to the UK during the war.[125] ATLU representatives met Acting Governor J.D. Harford before the start of the sugar crop, and discussed wages in field and factory, the after-crop bonus and the shift system in the factory. Negotiations started between the ATLU and the management of the Antigua Sugar Factory[126] on 28 February and between the ATLU and representatives of estate owners on 1 March, with Harford acting as chairman. Factory workers wanted an eight-hour day and a 25 per cent increase in wages, but the management said it could not introduce a three-shift system and offered only a 5 per cent war bonus on wages in recognition of the increased cost of living. Field workers sought an end to cutting sugar by the ton, and pay of 4 pence per line for cutting plant cane and 3 pence for ratoons, not including tying. Estate owners replied that they were faced with substantial losses and that the proposal to abolish cutting by the ton was unacceptable. They offered to pay 1 shilling per ton, without tying, compared with 10 pence the previous year. Harford met the ATLU executive committee on 3 March and told them it was a bad year for sugar, with production down even if the price was up, that the estate owners could not pay workers more, that the union had 'a grave responsibility' at this time when 'Empire unity' was essential, and urged them to pursue long-range aims rather than bringing the island to a standstill. The union officers responded on 4 March with new proposals: an eight-hour day plus 10 per cent increase in wages for the factory workers, and for the field workers 3 pence per line for plant canes and 2 pence for ratoons, not including tying. They also demanded that the system of a voluntary after-crop bonus should be discontinued, and that if the total price per ton of cane exceeded 17 shillings then half of the excess over the price of 16 shillings and 10 pence the previous year should be distributed among the workers.

Negotiations continued and resulted in an agreement of a 5 per cent bonus, payable weekly to factory workers, with an additional bonus on a sliding scale if production exceeded 14,000 tons, and 'an understanding on the subject of the three shift system for the future'. Field workers received the same rates as before, except that first and second ratoons were to be paid at equal rates instead of 2 pence and 1 pence, respectively. Harford praised the union's officers, who 'fought hard for their aims' and 'were not browbeaten', and the 'rank and file who loyally accepted the decisions arrived at and entered on the labours of the crop in conditions of order and good temper'. He told the Legislative Council on 27 March 1940 that 'Trades Unions in Antigua are going to play a valuable and indeed an indispensable part in promoting better understanding and relations between employers and employed, to the benefit of the community as a whole'.[127]

A few weeks later the ATLU president, Reginald St Clair Stevens, negotiated on behalf of striking dock workers in St John's harbour. They refused to load a ship with 3,000 tons of sugar on 1 May while negotiations were under way. When lightermen were offered 25 cents per ton as a temporary measure, above the regular rate of 21.5 cents per ton, they rejected it. Harford, when Stevens declined to meet him, expressed 'grave disappointment' to the Legislative Council. Although Harford claimed that his was not a 'strike-breaking Government', he nevertheless arranged 'for the loading of the ship by such labour as might be available'.[128] He asserted that it was 'not considered to be the proper role of the Government as such formally to intervene',[129] but labour disputes increasingly involved the government, whether in informal or more formal ways.

During the war, using such slogans as 'Empire unity', the colonial governments advocated a kind of partnership between workers and capitalists, while accepting a growing responsibility for people's welfare, if not for economic development. Harford indicated this in his speech to the Legislative Council on 27 March 1940:

> If in fact it was the case that on the one hand the labourer could not receive during this short crop a sufficiency of earnings to serve him in the way he relied upon, and if on the other hand the estate owner was literally not in a position to pay him more, then I would say that the situation came back on the Government, and that the Government had not shirked it and would not shirk it. It was not in a position at this time directly to subsidise the industry, but as a result of unemployment the Government had during the past six months expended very considerable sums of money on relief work and also had done all it could by careful examination of ways and means to relieve actual destitution. The Government was prepared to continue to accept and fulfil as far as practicable that responsibility.[130]

The problem for the colonial government was simply that it could not meet the people's growing demands, particularly during such a period of extended crisis and war. The inevitable result was that people became more critical of the government, began to seek more control over their own resources and developed an increasingly anti-colonial and nationalist agenda. The labour leaders, like the colonial administrators, were caught up in this situation: damned by the colonial government and employers if they did not control their union members, they would be damned by the latter if they were perceived as not tough enough. Although Harford had praised the labour leaders for their cooperation in March, Governor Lethem soon criticised Stevens for failing to cooperate with government and the ATLU's executive committee for failing 'to control their ignorant followers'.[131] Lethem claimed that the government's act in securing strike-breakers to load the ship on 4 May and 'in effect breaking the incipient strike, was thoroughly justified; it was prompt, effective, and has been most salutary'.[132] While Lethem acknowledged that a long history of 'deep-seated distrust' existed between labourers and employers, and that the latter were far from blameless, he felt that the government had 'to intervene in the public interest' on the side of the employers.

The dock workers had actually made representations as early as 28 March and 'negotiations were still dragging on' when the first sugar boat arrived to load on 22 April. The shipping agents tried to handle the dispute without government intervention and had put an elderly solicitor who was strongly opposed to trade unionism in charge of the negotiations. When the second boat arrived on 1 May, almost five weeks after negotiations had started, 'the men had become very restive and exasperated'. Consequently, in the governor's opinion, 'The Union Executive were pushed along the line of an active demonstration' on behalf of the dock workers.[133] Although Stevens had spoken to the superintendent of public works, who was speaking for the acting governor on 2 May, Governor Lethem found his failure to meet with him that day 'inexcusable', and the ATLU president subsequently 'apologised profusely by letter'.[134] Lethem described Stevens as weak, but added 'he is responding to responsibilities'.[135]

Other members of the ATLU must have thought that Stevens was becoming too responsive to the colonial government and not responsible enough to the members. The lightermen of St John's received a minimal raise, from a rate of 23 cents per ton to 25 cents per ton of sugar carried.[136] When Stevens agreed to a ban on strikes until the end of the war, a more radical faction within the union's leadership opposed him and forced him out. Samuel Smith, an old Antiguan worker, described Stevens as a 'brown-skinned man' who was 'accustom to deal with planters'. He credited Stevens with giving the ATLU 'a flying start and a solid foundation in the early days' and did not understand exactly why he 'was remove from office .... That change sure cause stir for awhile. I was wondering if the planters' hope that the union was going to destroy itself was coming to pass' (Smith and Smith 1989: 144-6). In 1943 Vere Bird became the ATLU president and proposed major plans for nationalisation (Henry 1985: 88, 153). Bird rose to power on the base of the ATLU, and he and his sons have dominated Antiguan politics ever since.

In St Kitts there was an important strike in 1940 when workers at the Basseterre sugar factory sought higher wages. According to Governor Lethem, the factory workers struck on 1 April against the advice of the St Kitts-Nevis Trades and Labour Union (SKNTLU), whose executive 'showed vacillation and inability to control', and never 'officially countenanced the strike'.[137] Lethem characterised the manager's actions, particularly his posting up an ultimatum and addressing a letter to 11 workers that was deemed threatening, as 'ill-advised'. The union's head, told that the government would protect the factory when it employed strike-breakers, began on 18 May 'to urge patriotic motives on the men to return to work', which they did soon after. Lethem argued that the situation of reciprocal distrust on the part of workers and employers was 'affected by the growing awareness on the part of the population at large of the financial strength and annual profits of the factory', which had even been selling sugar locally at a higher price than was obtained for sugar exported. 'The recent strike, I fear, was bringing out a marked anti-capital and anti-employer feeling'.[138]

According to the provisional head of the union, Edgar O. Challenger, however, the union officials were caught unawares as the union was 'still in the process of formation'. He wrote that the men had been 'the butt of broken promises' by the factory manager for over two years, while the gap increased between their fixed wages and the rising cost of living. He thought also that the men were deeply offended by the way the manager treated them and that they walked out as a result of the offensive notice he posted up around the factory.

The workers had tried to negotiate for a considerable time, at least since January when the crop season began, and struck because they felt the manager was stalling and breaking his promises. Challenger said that the workers, though rejecting his appeal to return to work, had been for over a month 'loyal and peaceful in an amazing degree', despite what they saw as the manager's attempts at victimisation.[139] Both sides agreed to submit to arbitration but the manager refused to discuss any wage increases until the men resumed work, which they refused to do without a guarantee of a minimum increase of 15 per cent on basic rates of pay, subject to any adjustment as a result of an arbitration award. In the ensuing deadlock the factory took on more outside labour and gradually resumed work, but feelings were hardening on both sides. The government sent around notices appealing to the workers to return to work on patriotic grounds, as part of the 'struggle for freedom - our freedom!'.[140] Eventually, the war bonus of 15 per cent was increased to 20 per cent, and pay adjustments 'varying greatly in extent but averaging at about 15 per cent' were made throughout the factory.[141] The factory workers of Basseterre appear to have won these increases through their own disciplined militancy and determination, rather than through the union leaders who tried from the beginning to get them back to work.

Although the secretary of state was concerned about the 'responsibilities as well as rights' of organised labour in the Leeward Islands,[142] C.Y. Carstairs of the Colonial Office commented on the 'ineptitude on the part of all concerned', including some local government officials, but added, 'The only redeeming feature appears to be the action of the workers in buckling to after the dispute was settled. They have shown a most praiseworthy and patriotic attitude, which constitutes both an opportunity and a danger: if something is not done to make them feel that their loyalty is not misplaced, their eventual reaction may have serious and lasting consequences'.[143] Although this suggests that the Colonial Office was at last taking the working people seriously, it is apparent that it was chiefly concerned with how they could be controlled.

The wartime situation strengthened the resolve of the Colonial Office to continue to try to work with the new trade unions rather than against them, in order to foster what they defined as responsible trade unionism.[144] On 19 January 1941 the executive committee of the SKNTLU, led by Challenger and J.N. France, the general secretary, voted to banish strikes for the duration of the war.[145] This prompted a comment from the Colonial Office: 'The spirit shown is excellent: I only hope that they can keep it up and maintain control over the rank and file'.[146] The central question was the role of the trade union officials, namely, whether they would encourage their rank and file to engage in militant action or, as the colonial governments and employers hoped, use their influence to control them. In these circumstances union officials could become important power brokers in their societies. One of the workers who was involved in the 1940 strike was Robert L. Bradshaw. Born in 1916, he was apprenticed in the factory's machine shop in 1932 and became active in the Workers' League that was organised in the same year. He became prominent in subsequent strikes and was elected to the Legislative Council in 1946. As the president of the SKNTLU, he dominated politics in St Kitts-Nevis until his death in 1978 (Richardson 1983: 167-8).

In Guyana, where a labour ordinance came into force in 1942, creating the posts of commissioner and inspectors of labour, a strike occurred among waterfront workers in January 1942. When Hubert Critchlow called off the strike as a result of negotiations between the BGLU and the government officers, the workers 'raised a hue and cry of "he sell we"' (Chase n.d.: 101). There is no evidence that Critchlow actually sold out the workers, but the fact that he was so accused suggests that the strikers were suspicious of the new conciliatory mechanisms in which he was required to participate. An advisory committee, appointed under Section 6 of the ordinance, submitted an interim report on 2 February in order that work would be resumed, and after the final report was made in April the government approved wage increases, to $2.08 per day for winchmen, $1.84 per day for stevedores, $1.04 for truckers and 84 cents for women (Chase n.d.: 102).

The first commissioner, Colin Fraser, arrived in August 1942 and the new Labour Department had a tremendous influence on the development of trade unions and labour relations, particularly through helping settle disputes by facilitating collective negotiations and, when these failed, by conciliation (Chase n.d.: 103). This was an example of the British government's new colonial labour policy at work, promoting industrial peace through a tripartite system of labour administration consisting of trade unions, employers and government officials.

Critchlow had problems also with the bauxite workers whom he had been trying to draw into the BGLU since 1942. During the war strict security measures were in force around MacKenzie because of the strategic importance of bauxite so, with the employers opposed to trade unionism, it was hard for union organisers to work in the area. Union officials could not obtain the necessary passes to visit, so a shoemaker at Wismar became one of the chief organisers. The workers suffered from long hours - a 60-hour working week in 1943 - when bauxite was in high demand, but a fall in demand after 1943 resulted in a massive retrenchment and reduction of working hours, with corresponding loss of pay. In 1942 there were 3,600 employees in the bauxite industry. This declined to 2,950 in 1943, to 1,100 in 1944 and 1,030 in 1945 (Chase n.d.: 126). In 1944 the ten-hour working day was reduced to eight hours and workers earned less money.

The low wages, threat of unemployment, bad working conditions and poor relations with management led many workers to join the BGLU, despite the obstacles put in their way, but when they went on strike for higher wages and better conditions in 1944 the union's officials were taken by surprise. When Critchlow hurried to MacKenzie and met the management in the Demerara Bauxite Company's offices, no workers were present. Critchlow was overawed, gave instructions for work to be resumed, and 'left hastily for Georgetown' (Chase n.d.: 127). The strike 'petered out in failure' and the waterfront workers' call, 'he sell we', echoed through MacKenzie. Few bauxite workers subsequently retained union membership after this 'brief but unhappy excursion into trade unionism' (Chase n.d.: 128). This case illustrates some of the difficulties that union leaders faced, when even a respected veteran leader such as Critchlow had to deal not only with the wiles and pressure of the employers and government but also with the suspicions of the workers. And the workers themselves were in such a weak position that it was hard for them to organise to improve their situation.

There was also unrest during the war in the Bahamas. In 1942 a protest about wages turned into a riot in Nassau.[147] There was little in the way of organised labour in the Bahamas, although a Federation of Labour was established in May 1942. The powerful Bay Street merchants still had firm control of the reactionary House of Assembly, and the small coloured and black middle class was largely conservative and politically weak. All but five of the 29 members of the House were members of the white oligarchy and few Bahamians attained the property qualifications to be able to vote. As social divisions by colour were so clearly correlated with class, power and privilege in Bahamian society, particularly in Nassau, the rising racial consciousness and increasing unemployment characteristic of the 1930s had created a tense and volatile situation. The impact of changes resulting from the war set a spark to this and produced what may be considered as the Bahamas' delayed labour rebellion.

In addition to the endemic problems of the Bahamas, which included unemployment, poverty, high land prices, poor housing, and inadequate health and educational services, the war resulted in higher prices and the collapse of the tourist industry. When the United States and the UK selected New Providence as the site for two landing fields, known together as the Project, expectations were high among Bahamian workers, many of whom had come to Nassau in the preceding years in search of work. Over 2,000 men were employed on the

Project, where work began on 20 May 1942. The workers promptly protested to Charles Rhodriquez, a coloured merchant who was head of the Labour Union and Federation of Labour, about two interrelated grievances: they expected a higher wage than the local rate, which was 4 shillings for an eight-hour day for unskilled construction workers, and they objected to white American employees earning much more for doing the same work.

Class and race issues were coming together in an explosive mixture, but the explosion might not have occurred if the government had acted more promptly in response to the demands. On 22 May Rhodriquez met skilled and unskilled workers and they adopted a new scale of wages, beginning with 8 shillings per day for unskilled workers, and this was delivered to the labour officer. The governor, the Duke of Windsor, had left for Washington on 28 May, so the acting governor promised Rhodriquez that an advisory board would be appointed to consider the demands. However, at about 4 pm on 31 May a crowd of some 400 workers, perhaps feeling that the government was engaged in delaying tactics, gathered outside the construction company's offices, shouting 'We want more money'. In addition to demanding higher wages, they complained they had not been paid when rain prevented them from working. The police dispersed the crowd but the next morning, 1 June, most of them refused to work. Although there had been some talk of a strike their action seems to have been essentially spontaneous. At about 8 am a crowd of them, armed with sticks and tools, marched to the town and assembled outside the colonial secretary's office. The attorney-general failed to pacify them and a group of angry young men, who believed that they would be replaced by Americans if they did not return to work, attacked the commercial centre of Nassau, breaking windows and looting stores. When the police and British troops pushed the rioters over to Grant's Town, the poor black section, they were stoned and hit by bottles. Although the anger was directed against property rather than persons, the Riot Act was read at 12.15 pm and the police and troops opened fire. One man, Roy Johnson, was killed and another, David Smith, died of his wounds later. Forty other civilians were treated for injuries. Later that day a crowd attacked the Grant's Town police station, library and post office, and damaged an ambulance and fire engine. A curfew was instituted at 8 pm and the night passed quietly, but the next day other shops and the house of a police corporal were attacked and the military again intervened. A shopkeeper's son killed one rioter, Donald Johnson.

Altogether, five people were killed and considerable damage was done to property. Of the 80 persons who appeared in court, 67 were convicted, the longest sentences being given to Leonard Storr Green and Harold Thurston, who were considered to be ringleaders and were sentenced to eight years in prison. The governor lifted the curfew on 8 June and, to avoid further trouble, negotiated a free midday meal and 1 shilling per day wage increase for the Project workers; he also censored the press and forbad public meetings except with police permission.

On 31 March 1943 a Trade Union Act was passed providing for the registration of trade unions, but strikes were still deemed illegal if they intended to coerce the government, or inflicted hardship on the community, or had any object other than the dispute within the trade or industry in which they occurred. Moreover, hotel, domestic and agricultural workers, and civil servants were barred from joining unions. On 21 June 1943 a Workmen's Compensation Act provided for the payment of compensation to workmen for injuries they received in the course of their employment. The Duke of Windsor, in his closing speech to the House on 14 September 1943, admitted that these acts fell short of modern standards, but the reactionary House resisted further changes.

Social and constitutional reforms were even slower in coming to the Bahamas than to other parts of the British Caribbean, in part because black and coloured leaders were slow to take up the challenge. Milo Butler, a coloured member of the House who had been elected in the Western District in 1939, and who later became a leader of the Progressive Liberal Party and a government minister in 1967, was deemed a troublemaker by the Americans, even though he had tried to pacify the strikers. According to Saunders (1990: 27), for the black middle class at this time, 'who worked to safeguard their increasingly comfortable lifestyles, it would have been economic suicide to attempt to overthrow the system, and the absence of political parties or effective trade unions gave them little clout'. The strike and riot in Nassau in 1942 were a harbinger of developments which were to parallel the changes occurring elsewhere in the British Caribbean, but the Bahamas still lagged behind other colonies in terms of organised labour, political parties and constitutional changes.

In Belize, Antonio Soberanis Gomez had pioneered organised labour in the 1930s and, together with R.T. Meighan, he founded the first trade union, the British Honduras Workers and Tradesmen Union (BHWTU), in 1939. In July 1939, when Meighan was its president, the BHWTU supported a strike of about 170 Garifuna road workers near Stann Creek Town, now Dangriga. These road workers demanded a wage increase from 75 cents to $1 per day and 'guaranteed minimum earnings of $10 for each fortnight's work irrespective of loss of time through bad weather'.[148] They also complained about their leaky camps and that two foremen abused them, making derogatory remarks about Caribs. Six representatives travelled to Belize Town to speak to the acting governor who said their claims would not be considered until they returned to work because the road needed to be completed in order to export grapefruit in August. At first they refused to return to work, but work was recommenced on 11 July without reprisals against the strikers. There was said to be 'no disorder at any time, and no need for police action'.[149]

The colonial administrators were concerned about the strike for two reasons.

First, relief work had expanded in order to quell the demands of hundreds of unemployed mahogany workers, and even while the economic outlook remained poor the government was spending some $3,900 per week on relief projects. In April Governor Alan C. Burns had made it clear that this expenditure was not only to build roads but was also, and more urgently, in order to avoid a repetition of the labour disturbances that had occurred before:

> [T]he steps taken with your approval to relieve unemployment have averted what might have been serious labour disturbances, and have had an immediate effect on the people .... I considered it possible that the Belize labourers might refuse to work for 50 cents a day, and that rioting might result if Government should insist on paying no higher wage for relief work .... Your decision that the normal rate of wages should be paid for relief work relieves me of any anxiety regarding possible disturbances and I welcome it on that account ... . About 500 men can be employed on the Cayo road (including the quarry).. .. Some 1,000 men resident in Belize [Town] have registered their names ... as unemployed. About 200 men more now employed on the Belize–Orange Walk road will presumably register when they return to Belize, bringing the total number of registered unemployed in Belize alone to 1,200. Of these about 100 will continue to be employed on the Belize–Orange Walk road and on feeder roads already approved, and about 500 will be employed on the works referred to ... [various canal and road maintenance projects around Belize Town] and on the Cayo road (including the quarry). The remaining 600 will have to await their turn, as I propose to continue the existing system of changing the gangs every fortnight. It is a bad arrangement but there is no alternative at present. It must also be remembered that towards the end of May some 500 mahogany labourers will be returning to Belize [Town] to swell the ranks of the (temporarily) unemployed.[150]

As anticipated, the unemployment situation became worse between June and August when hundreds of workers returned to Belize Town from the mahogany camps.

> They had a certain amount of money in their possession as a result of work during the past mahogany season and none was allowed to register as unemployed unless more than one month had elapsed since his last employment. ... During July the unemployment position became more acute, the number of registered unemployed men in Belize [Town] alone having risen gradually from 1612 on the 3rd of June to 1953 on the 5th of August ...
> I authorized an increase of 50 men in the number employed from the 10th of July and a further 50 from the 24th of July and it seems unlikely that the total number of men employed in fortnightly periods of relief work can be

reduced below the present figure of 500 for at least two months. In practice a man gets a fortnight's work every six to eight weeks.[151]

A few days later it was reported that although over 500 men had been signed on by chicle contractors there was still 'a considerable amount of unemployment ... [and] considerable distress' in Cayo District where people who sold bananas and corn were suffering from the effects of a long drought.[152] The governor stated in November that there was 'no prospect of any material improvement in the unemployment situation in the New Year' and urged an early announcement of continuing relief work 'to relieve growing public anxiety'.[153] One problem the colonial government faced, therefore, was the growing number of people who had to be provided with relief work in order to avoid disturbances, and this involved increasing costs at a time when revenues were especially low.

The other problem was that government had become a major employer of labour in the colony and this was having an effect on the private employers, as Acting Governor Johnston indicated in August 1939: 'In the Stann Creek district the labourers employed by companies or private individuals are generally engaged by the task. The cleaning of farm lands enables a man to earn from 70 cents to 90 cents per day and the earnings from fruit picking which is only seasonal work vary from 40 cents to 90 cents per day. Any increase in the rate of wages paid by Government would of course create difficulties for other employers of labour in the locality'.[154] Workers employed by the government had been paid only 65 cents a day until 1937, and then 75 cents, while workers on the Belize-Cayo road received $1 a day. The governor rejected the Stann Creek workers' demand for $1 a day, not just because it would increase the wage bill but also because it would tend to drive up wages in the vicinity, thereby making it harder and more expensive for local employers to obtain workers.

Further slumps in the mahogany industry and chicle trade and the failure of the banana industry in the south led to further increases in unemployment. The labour officer reported 1,964 people registered on the unemployment roll in January 1940, of whom 304 were on relief work, and by July there were 2,315 people unemployed.[155] Governor J.A. Hunter stated bluntly, 'Our immediate problem is unemployment with attendant starvation and social unrest. Things here are bad, very bad. Trade is stagnant, money is not coming into the Colony, revenues are falling ... '[156] The number of people registered as unemployed rose to 2,596 in August and of these 1,662 were in Belize District. The number of unemployed on other districts' rolls remained stable, probably 'due to sloth on the part of the Labour Department',[157] but those on the Belize District roll increased to 1,869 in October 1940.[158] In this context Hunter reported that 'there is no possibility of my being able to reduce the numbers on relief work in the near future without grave risk of creating a serious and possible dangerous situation',[159] though he also recognised that the intermittent nature of the relief afforded under the present system was itself a source of discontent. Soberanis, L.D. Kemp and others organised a march to Government House to protest about the widespread distress, dissatisfaction and even starvation. Hunter observed, 'While allegations of widespread starvation seem to be exaggerated there is no doubt that serious distress is increasing and present method of relief is neither economical nor effective. It is however essential to continue it until trade improves or practicable alternative has been devised'. He requested authority to increase the numbers on relief work by 30 per cent for three months at an extra cost of up to $5,000 a month.[160] However, it was not until 1941 when hundreds of Belizean workers migrated to work in Panama and Scotland that critical unemployment temporarily eased.

During the war there was continuing labour agitation and a growing sense of nationalism in Belize. Demands for democracy and improvements in the economic situation developed into a radical but still quite inchoate nationalism in which there were strong elements of Garveyism. In a confidential report after the visit of the Moyne Commission in 1938, Governor Burns attributed most agitation and discontent to what he called 'colour feeling . . . fomented by a small group, of whom the principal is R.S. Turton'. He named four professional agitators (Soberanis, Kemp, Gabriel Adderley and Arthur Balderamos, a black lawyer), but devoted most of his report to Robert Turton, a chicle millionaire.[161] Turton's business connections were with the US rivals of the BEC in the chicle and mahogany industries, namely Wrigley's of Chicago and I.T. Williams Company, respectively. In 1936, after Turton had defeated the BEC's local manager in the first elections to the Legislative Council, the governor nominated the defeated representative of the British firm. Burns accused Turton in 1938 of financing the agitators 'in order to discredit and embarrass the administration and its officers. The agitation appears to be on behalf of the working class: actually it is in the interests of the worst type of capitalist', meaning Turton. Whatever may be the truth of Burns' assertion, it cannot apply to Soberanis who was always desperately poor and whose efforts over eight years to create a union were independent of Turton and were certainly inspired by working-class interests. Perhaps the organisations formed by John Lahoodie and Benjamin Reneau (British Honduras Unemployed Association) and by Kemp (British Honduras Federation of Workers Protection Association), neither of which functioned as trade unions, were supported by Turton.[162]

A radical nationalist group, first called the British Honduras Independent Labour Party, then the People's Republican Party and finally the People's Nationalist Committee, was formed in 1940. It may have been supported by Turton because its anti-British and pro-American stance (which became confused after the United States joined the UK in the war) reflected his business interests. The leaders of this group included Lahoodie and Adderley, who had been with Soberanis in the LUA, but the chief figure was Joseph Campbell, known as the 'Lion of Judah'. Born in 1901 of a Belizean mother and a Jamaican father, Campbell had worked for many years for the United Fruit Company in Honduras. In 1941 he was said to attack the British every day, and predicted their defeat in the war as a just punishment for all the 'dirt the English had done'.[163] The radical nationalists demanded the expulsion of all white people, the creation of a local republic in union with the United States and the replacement of the Union Jack with a national flag of Belize Honduras. They were often attacked at their meetings by loyalists who called themselves the Unconquerables. The name Lion of Judah suggests that Garveyism was a link between the early social movements of the 1920s and 1930s and this more explicitly nationalist group in 1940 and racial consciousness was a prominent aspect of their ideology. Campbell was imprisoned repeatedly and the governor tried to deport him in July 1941.

Mass meetings were held in several parts of Belize in 1941 to demand adult suffrage and the right to elect the government. A broad spectrum of Belizean politicians took part in these meetings, including middle-class elected members of the Legislative Council and Belize Town Board, like Balderamos and E.S. Usher, as well as Garveyites, trade unionists and other radicals, such as Kemp and Meighan.[164] On 5 September, with Campbell already in jail, Lahoodie and Adderley were detained in a special camp in Corozal. Governor Hunter indicated that he was avoiding a trial and was holding the prisoners far from Belize Town in order to keep trouble from spreading. The 72-year-old Lahoodie stubbornly refused to appeal and was reported to have 'asserted his desire to be rid of the British administration of this colony and would have no truck with it'.[165] By 14 February 1942 Hunter felt confident enough to release Lahoodie and Adderley, subject to certain restrictions, and they went to live in Guatemala.[166]

Governor Hunter, while repressing these radical critics, thought that the council over which he presided was 'undemocratic if not oligarchic',[167] but the Colonial Office decided that Belize, unlike Jamaica, was too backward for democracy and so made only minor constitutional changes in 1945. The new Legislative Council consisted of 13 members, six of them elected, three official and four nominated, and the governor retained his reserve powers. The franchise remained extremely narrow. In a population of about 64,000 there were only 822 registered voters in 1945 and 1,772 in 1948 (Shoman 1987: 18). The constitutional issues did not go away, however, and they became a prime part of the platform of the People's United Party (PUP) in the early 1950s.

Garvey's influence was strong in Belize in the 1930s and 1940s. He had visited Belize between 1910 and 1912, when he travelled widely in Central America, and again in 1921 and 1929. Several leading members of Soberanis's LUA were members of the Belize branch of the UNIA that was founded in 1920 and the flag and colours of the LUA were the red and green of the UNIA. Kemp was a Garveyite, as was Calvert Staine, who was a vice-president of the Belize UNIA and later the chairman of the Belize Town Board. When the parent UNIA split in 1929 over the disposal of the estate of Isaiah Morter, a wealthy Belizean benefactor who had died in 1924, there was a split in the local branch but Staine, along with Cain and Kemp of the Belize Independent, remained loyal to Garvey (Ashdown 1981: 50-2). In February 1941 Lionel Antonio Francis, a Trinidadian physician who was president of the rival New York-based UNIA Inc., came to administer the Morter estate and settled in Belize. Contending, 'if we can solve our economic problem, then to hell with the white man' (Cronon 1969: 165), Francis started an Economic Society and became a respectable spokesman of labour. In 1942 he won a seat on the Belize Town Board, displacing Staine, and he and his People's Group, which was based on his UNIA supporters, controlled the Belize City Council (as it became in 1943) until 1947 (Ashdown 1981: 53). As president of the British Honduras Trades and Labour Union he attended the CLC meeting in Jamaica in August 1947.

In the meantime, the struggle to legalise and organise trade unions continued in Belize. Soberanis, as president of the BHWTU from 6 March 1941, said: 'Trade Unionism is … the only medium by which the working class can get a square deal'.[168] The BHWTU had branches in Stann Creek, Corozal and San Ignacio, that is, in the south, north and west of Belize. Trade unions were legalised in 1941 but breach of contract was not removed from the criminal code and several wartime emergency laws were in force that made it difficult to protest and organise. Hunter amalgamated a Masters and Servants Bill and a Truck Bill in order to 'control the issue of advances and the grant of credit in the forest commissaries'[169] in accord with the Moyne Commission's recommendations, but the bill was defeated by the employers among the unofficial members of the Legislative Council. Hunter blamed Turton and his 'former henchman', Balderamos, for the defeat. This became an election issue in 1942 when Balderamos's opponents 'attacked him strongly for scuttling the Masters and Servants Bill'[170] and he was defeated. Unemployment declined temporarily when hundreds of workers went to Panama and Scotland,[171] but the infant trade union movement found it hard to pursue the struggle to improve conditions. In 1942 Soberanis, discouraged by trying to organise people under wartime conditions when they 'could not give vent to their feelings',[172] went to Panama himself, where he stayed for six years.

Staine was nominated to the council by Governor Hunter in 1942. With Meighan, the former president of the BHWTU, he was a member of a middle-class creole group called the Progressive Party. These men made the crucial difference in the council when the Employers and Workers Bill was passed on 27 April 1943. Breach of labour contract was removed from the criminal code and so trade unions were more free to pursue the struggle for improving conditions. The next month, in May 1943, the BHWTU was formally registered.

The BHWTU changed its name to the General Workers' Union (GWU) and quickly expanded into a nationwide organisation, the only one at this time to unite people of various classes and ethnic groups in different parts of the colony.[173] Beginning with only 350 members in the forest industry and on the waterfront, the GWU engaged in a militant struggle to improve workers' wages and living conditions, even though strikes in the mahogany industry were forbidden by a wartime essential services law that was not amended until 1953 and the monopolistic BEC refused to allow union officials to visit the lumber camps. The chronic unemployment problem of Belize was temporarily in remission in the middle of the war, partly because of a revived demand for mahogany but largely because about 900 men were recruited into a forestry unit to work in Scotland (Ford 1985) and even more went to work in the Panama Canal Zone. By early 1944, however, 420 of the men who had gone to Scotland and about 1,000 of the workers from Panama returned to Belize.[174]

A petition to the secretary of state for the colonies, signed by 367 Belizeans in the forestry unit, drew attention to their problems and sought assistance in the form of agricultural development and land settlement schemes for Belize:

> Termination of our contract nearly a year before it would other-wise have ended has been a shock to us .... Those of us who will be repatriated will face greater difficulty. We will return to a country in which unemployment has been the greatest evil for many years and we are appealing to you to initiate some industry in the Colony which would give us lasting employment .... We appeal to you, Sir, to initiate a scheme of agricultural development in our country which will assure employment permanently not only to the 700 odd of us who will be returning there in search of work, but to the even larger number there are who are unable to find work and the means of satisfying the needs of themselves and their families.[175]

In response to this petition the secretary of state recommended to Governor Hunter only limited road work and forest regeneration.[176] People demonstrated in Belize in 1944, hoping for some war work in the United States, and recruiters arrived on 1 June.[177] Although some people were recruited to work in the United States (919 Belizeans were working there in August 1945),[178] the unemployment problem in Belize was again acute.

In this context, a successful strike of unionised stevedores in July 1944 and the election of a radical president, Clifford E. Betson, were responsible for the rapid growth of the GWU, which became the principal popular national organisation. Betson was a former boat builder who had been a member of the Belize Town Board and a leader of the Progressive Party in the 1930s. He had advocated lowering the franchise during debates about the constitution at that time (Shoman 1994: 193). As the GWU's president he conducted organisational and educational work all over the country. Based in Belize City, with branches in the districts and even in remote chicle and mahogany camps, this union, more than any other organisation, raised the political and class consciousness of the working people of Belize in the 1940s and thus established the necessary base for the rapid rise of the PUP after 1950. C.H. Grant claims that the 'political calm remained generally unruffled throughout the first fifty years of the twentieth century and in particular during the 1930s' and that it was not until devaluation on 31 December 1949 that 'Belize was rudely awakened from its apparent slumber' (Grant 1976: 61). Far from slumbering, however, from as far back as 1934 and periodically throughout the war there was frequent and widespread political agitation in Belize and the organised labour movement, led by Soberanis and Betson, provided the essential basis for the later nationalist movement.

Agitation about unemployment and the recruitment of workers for war work in the United States also occurred in St Lucia. There were two demonstrations in Castries in 1945.[179] The administrator of St Lucia wrote to the governor of the Windward Islands that the rejection of St Lucians on the grounds of their patois 'will not be found convincing as the majority of St Lucians are bi-lingual, thousands worked for Americans on the Bases without any language difficulty'.[180] The recruitment of 65 men for work in Curaçao and 190 for Aruba created a little relief in the unemployment situation in St Lucia, and work on Colonial Development and Welfare schemes promised more jobs, but the administrator remained anxious about continuing discontent.

British West Indians in Cuba also expressed discontent during the war but they appear to have been split between Jamaicans, who predominated in the British West Indian Cultural Association, founded in 1932 and led by a Jamaican building contractor, G.E. Lord, and the more radical British West Indies Labour Party, led by the Trinidadian David S. Nathan. When Nathan and others sent a 'Declaration of Independence' on behalf of the British West Indies to Washington, Cipriani, who was said to be the president of this party, repudiated their action.[181] The head of the British delegation in Havana reported that Nathan's party failed because Jamaicans, who were the majority of West Indians in Oriente Province, were against it, 'partly from loyalty and also because of their condescension for the ... so-called "Little Islanders"'.[182] Five years later, however, Nathan, then the president of the Inter-Caribbean Labour Party, based in Cuba, was enquiring about the ill-treatment of Caribbean workers in the United States.[183] The Cuban Communist Party focused its organisational activities among black workers in Oriente and fought for the rights of foreign workers to remain (Petras 1988: 249, 257), but more work needs to be done on the political influence of this party on West Indian workers. Some repatriated Jamaican labour leaders of the 1930s and 1940s, like H.C. Buchanan and Robert Rumble, were influenced by their experiences when working in Cuba, but we know little about those West Indians who, like Nathan, remained in Cuba throughout the war.

The influence of the United States

US influence in the Caribbean did not begin in the Second World War. Its economic, political and military involvement in the Caribbean expanded in the nineteenth century, particularly with the taking of Cuba and Puerto Rico in the Spanish-American war, and again in the early twentieth century with the opening of the Panama Canal in 1914, the occupation of Haiti in 1915 and the Dominican Republic in 1916, and the purchase of the Danish Virgin Islands in 1917. Rationalised by the unilateral Monroe Doctrine and Theodore Roosevelt's corollary to that doctrine in 1904, US interventions had demonstrated its expansionist geopolitical ambitions in the region long before the Russian revolution and any communist threat. Even after Franklin D. Roosevelt announced a shift from a 'Big Stick' to a 'Good Neighbor' policy in 1933, the United States continued to intervene in Cuban politics. What was new during the Second World War was the growing influence of the United States in the British colonies in the Caribbean. Although this stemmed initially from concern about German power in the Caribbean, by late 1943 the United States was preoccupied with the shape of the postwar peace, and particularly with anti-communism in the region. Even before the end of the war, therefore, and certainly well before Winston Churchill's speech in Fulton, Missouri, declared the opening of the cold war in 1946, the influence of the United States was felt in labour and political affairs in the British Caribbean colonies.[184]

The United States had for many years considered the strategic control of the Caribbean as essential for the security of the Panama Canal, which was crucial to its global ambitions. Hence, the War Department designated the Caribbean as an 'area of main resistance' (Leighton and Coakley 1955) because of the need to control access to the canal, but it was not until late 1939 that the fortification of Puerto Rico, the chief US colony in the Caribbean, was expanded. The chief danger was perceived to be from submarines: although the many narrow straits of the Caribbean made protection from surface vessels easier, they provided many opportunities for underwater predators. The success of German U-boats in 1917 and the vulnerability of crucial oil supplies from the Caribbean gave rise to great concern in the UK and the United States, and prompted secret Anglo-American negotiations on naval bases in Bermuda, St Lucia and Trinidad in 1938-9. Anglo-French talks on naval cooperation in 1939 assumed that the United States would become involved in Caribbean defences, and that bases at Bermuda, Jamaica, Trinidad and Martinique would be vital to regional security. In August 1939, just before the UK declared war, the United States made leasehold arrangements for aviation facilities in several British colonies (Baptiste 1988: 12). Although the

United States remained officially neutral, by March 1940 there was increasing collaboration between it and the Allies, especially concerning naval activities.

The crisis came with the defeat of the Netherlands in May 1940. Aruba, Curaçao and Venezuela had been the source of 44 per cent of Germany's oil imports in 1938 and for over one-third of the UK's oil imports. The protection of oil supplies from the southern and eastern Caribbean became 'a matter of the highest priority for the Allies' (Baptiste 1988: 32), so British and French forces occupied Aruba and Curaçao on 11 May. In June France fell and the chief of French naval forces in the Atlantic and Caribbean ordered the French out of Aruba and declared loyalty to the Vichy government of Marshal Pétain. The United States was forced not only to consider what to do about the colonies of European powers conquered by Germany, but also to contemplate the possible defeat of the UK and the need to defend itself from a potential Axis advance in the Americas.

The outcome of this crisis was the destroyers-for-bases agreement, made on 2 September 1940, which was 'the culmination of the United States' quest for a lodgement in the British possessions in the Western Hemisphere, a quest that dated back to World War I' (Baptiste 1988: 60). This agreement, out of which the UK got 50 First World War destroyers and the United States received 99-year leases on land for air and naval bases in the Bahamas, Jamaica, Antigua, St Lucia, Trinidad and Guyana, was important not only in relation to the Allies' defence strategy but also in the Caribbean colonies where US bases were built, particularly Trinidad.

By late 1940 British and US planners were devising a global strategy against the Axis powers in which 'Defense of the inner Caribbean perimeter figured prominently' (Baptiste 1988: 74). The Caribbean base area was to consist of three sectors: first, Puerto Rico, with Antigua and the US Virgin Islands; second, Guantánamo, Cuba, with Jamaica and the Bahamas; and third, Trinidad, with St Lucia and Guyana. These bases were to protect oil supplies and other shipping, together with the Caribbean coastal frontier of the United States, by connecting with the Middle and North Atlantic base areas and those of the Gulf of Mexico, located in Florida, and the Panama Canal (Baptiste 1988: 80). The new base to be constructed in Trinidad was intended to play a principal role in this plan, along with those in Guantánamo and Puerto Rico. However, when a US team in October 1940 proposed Chaguaramas as a site, Governor Sir Hubert Young objected on the grounds that it would interfere with the normal life of the island and he offered Caroni Swamp instead (Baptiste 1988: 87).

A serious problem arose about sovereignty and the governor's role in local defence. Young was concerned about his constitutional position and British sovereignty over the colony because the United States claimed 'an overriding right to regulate and to control all internal and external communications of whatever nature from, to, and within the areas leased' (Baptiste 1988: 91). Lord Moyne, who succeeded Lord Lloyd in the Colonial Office, also objected to the extent of US 'rights, power and authority' within and outside the bases and to its demand to control military operations. The United States 'rejected any suggestion that the British governors could have a controlling role in local defense, even under normal conditions prior to the United States entry into the war' (Baptiste 1988: 95). The Colonial Office was also concerned about the reactions of labour and political organisations, such as the Trinidad and Tobago TUC and West Indian groups in New York, to the reproduction of the 'patterns of racial segregation and discrimination' on the bases which existed in the United States and the Panama Canal Zone (Baptiste 1988: 96). In spite of these concerns, Churchill essentially accepted the US version, capitulating to superior power in order to get the agreement, in March 1940. Actual construction work began in Jamaica in January 1941 and in Trinidad in May 1941. A US presence was established already in Trinidad, Antigua and St Lucia by March 1941 and in Guyana by June 1941, several months before the attack on Pearl Harbor that brought the United States into the war. Even before it formally entered the war, therefore, it was clear that it would dominate military arrangements, with the British governors having only a nominal role in matters of local defence, as 'fitted the power reality by 1941' (Baptiste 1988: 114).

The construction of the bases had a great impact in Trinidad, in particular. The projects not only employed thousands of people and brought a massive infusion of Yankee Dollars into the economy, but they also had an impact on labour relations and trade union development and effected long-term changes in the culture of the colony. Construction expanded in Trinidad in 1942, when piers and roads were built, new channels dredged for anchorages, airfields enlarged and storage and repair facilities built. By July 1942 the projects employed some 26,000 persons in Trinidad. The naval base alone employed about 9,000 local civilians, as well as about 3,000 American civilians (Baptiste 1988: 163). Most people were only temporarily employed, however, so unemployment increased again as soon as the major construction phase ended.

In Jamaica Governor Sir Arthur Richards reported that by July 1942 'the employment situation was deteriorating rapidly' due in part to the cessation of construction on the US base there.[185] In Guyana Governor Lethem reported in October 1942 that 2,718 workers had been laid off from the bases by 18 August and 'another 1,150 workers will be discharged very shortly'.[186] Meanwhile, 1,638 of the 1,792 Barbadian workers who had been recruited to work on the bases in Trinidad had returned to their island.[187] In Trinidad the number of workers employed on the bases was reduced by November 1942 to 7,239, though the governor reported there was still difficulty finding certain kinds of labourer, particularly for 'the main agricultural industries of the Colony'.[188] In St Lucia, too, the number of workers at the base of Vieux-Fort peaked around the middle of 1942 at 4,496 and by October 1943 was only 600. The governor commented that unemployment was worsening, that in 1943 it was reaching proportions similar to those in 1939 when there were about 3,000 people unemployed, and that 'some now unemployed are disinclined to work at rates of pay lower than those which they received on the American Bases'.[189]

The governors' despatches suggest that the recruitment of workers for the US bases, which temporarily alleviated the unemployment problem in several colonies, actually contributed to endemic labour problems. First, the employment of so many people on the bases in Trinidad had drawn workers away from other sectors where employers could not pay so well, and second, when they were laid off the bases many of these workers had higher expectations about what they should be paid. The sugar industry and most other agricultural enterprises in the Caribbean still could not offer acceptable wages or employment throughout the year, so poverty and underemployment, particularly between harvest seasons, remained a persistent problem. In addition, the curtailment of tourism and shipping that resulted from the intensified U-boat offensive in 1942, when about 130 ships were sunk off Trinidad alone, reduced employment among waterfront workers, and the coaling industry in St Lucia virtually ceased. Moreover, there were shortages of imports, including basic food items. Trinidad and other colonies introduced rationing and Dominica and Guyana ran out of flour for two weeks in 1942.

The temporary boost in wages from the bases, combined with the shortages, resulted in rising prices, although exports were declining. Many people in the Caribbean resorted to growing food to provide for themselves, and many migrated to find work in the armed forces, in the oilfields and as domestic servants in Aruba and Curacao, and as agricultural and factory workers in the United States and the UK. Wages from the bases and remittances from abroad helped many people, but the chronic unemployment and underemployment meant there was persistent and widespread poverty and insecurity. Not surprisingly, therefore, despite the appeals made to loyalty during the Battle of the Caribbean in 1942 and 1943, there was some labour unrest, such as in the Bahamas and Jamaica. Although the construction of US bases had an impact, therefore, most particularly in Trinidad in 1942, it was beneficial only in quite limited ways and did not solve any of the endemic problems.

Local responses to the increasing US presence reflected ambivalent attitudes. 'At first the Americans were enthusiastically welcomed, but gradually resentment against them grew' (Braithwaite 1975: 128). On the one hand, access to thousands of jobs, higher wages, and the circulation of dollars and supplies in the poor colonial economies were welcomed for obvious reasons. And for so long as the jobs lasted, workers felt they could leave one job and obtain another, so they lost 'the servile fear of the boss, the clinging to the job at all costs' (Braithwaite

1975: 128). On the other hand, there were 'the usual complaints which accompany any concentration of troops: increased prostitution, venereal disease, fighting, in short, affronts to morality' (Maingot 1994: 64). US labour practices specifically exhibited clear contradictions between egalitarian principles of workers' rights and the persistence of racial segregation and discrimination, even within the armed forces fighting for freedom and democracy. The influence of the American occupation, as it was popularly called in Trinidad, was similar to that of migration, in so far as it exposed large numbers of workers to new arrangements and practices of labour relations, new ways that often led them to question the old. This period undoubtedly 'brought about a tremendous acceleration in the exposure of Trinidadians to the outside world' (Oxaal 1968: 81), but the influences and reactions were mixed.

There were situations in which the established customs and values of Caribbean workers were affronted by the ways of the Yankees, as the Americans were generally known. A Barbadian worker said, over 50 years after the event, that he had been fired by the Americans for whom he had been working, building a road to Maracas Bay in northern Trinidad. As soon as we protested, he said, we were fired and put on the next plane home. What seemed most important to him in retrospect was not the original grievance, but rather the arbitrary and authoritarian way in which the workers were treated by their new bosses. This man subsequently became active in the Barbados Workers' Union.[190] If US personnel practices 'influenced the aspirations of Trinidadian workers for more dignified treatment and better working conditions' (Brereton 1981: 189), it was as often in reaction against them as it was by positive example. 'The Americans were admired for their competence, their modern personnel practices and their aura of easy money, but their racial attitudes were cruder and more obvious than the subtler racism of the British' (Brereton 1981: 192). Trinidadians reacted against the Jim Crow racial behaviour and to the vice associated with the influx of easy money. A popular calypso expressed local reactions:

> Rum and Coca-Cola; go down Point Cumana,
> Both mother and daughter working for the Yankee Dollar.[191]

The amount of finance and work devoted to the construction of the military bases, roads and other facilities was in sharp contrast to the achievements of the colonial state with regard to people's welfare. In Trinidad, in spite of the potential promise of the Moyne Commission's recommendations and the establishment of the Colonial Development and Welfare fund, and the booming oil industry, the colonial government increased its revenues largely by imposing greater fiscal burdens on the working people, while postponing plans for renovating and extending hospitals, health centres and schools, or the supply of piped water and electricity, for the duration of the war. Moreover, the movement of people that resulted from the construction of the bases, as people were displaced from the Chaguaramas area and migrated from rural areas and other islands in search of work, aggravated the already notorious housing situation, especially in Port of Spain and San Fernando. Rising demand for cheap housing benefited landlords, of course, and an increasing proportion of working people, not to say the unemployed and underemployed, had to live in barracks and single-room tenements (Singh 1994: 193-5). On the reverse side of the new jobs and higher wages provided by the bases, therefore, were the higher rents and prices, along with social disruption and abominable housing that heightened social tensions. The American occupation, far from being a panacea, was at best a mixed blessing.

In Trinidad, where the US bases had the greatest impact, oil exports had become increasingly important and a 'grow more food' campaign had been quite successful by 1943. However, this was not a permanent restructuring of the agricultural economy in favour of small farmers and the traditional plantation interests moved quickly to reassert their domination over the labour supply. The Agricultural Society, the Trinidad Chamber of Commerce and the Trinidad Guardian supported the immigration of West Indians to work on the bases in order to limit the opportunities of the rural workers, who were largely Indian. According to the Benham committee, before the war only about 25,000 of the 34,000 rural workers normally available to the sugar industry were employed at any one time and the considerable labour surplus helped keep plantation wages low (Singh 1994: 197, 258). Although the government announced a war bonus to sugar workers of 10 cents in 1942, in addition to a 5 cent bonus they had begun to receive in 1940, the increased cost of living and expansion of what was required in task work, and hence a lengthening of the working day, caused many workers to be worse off.

An agricultural policy committee, chaired by A.J. Wakefield, was appointed in mid-1943. Its report, in January 1944, reasserted the priority of large-scale agricultural enterprises in Trinidad and the need for a regular supply of labour on the plantations. Like the Benham committee, the Wakefield committee's 'principal concern was the retention of the plantation economy' (Singh 1994: 200). The colonial government, having already relieved most estates of the obligation to grow food crops by August 1943, withdrew state guarantees on prices for locally grown food 'to ensure that Indian labour flowed back to the sugar plantation sector' (Singh 1994: 202). The resurgence of the plantation economy in Trinidad was further ensured by divisions, defections and weakness in the ranks of organised labour. Butler remained in prison and Rienzi, who was appointed to the Executive Council in May 1943 and then to the post of Second Crown Counsel in February 1944, left the labour movement. The bases had brought many changes to Trinidad, but much remained the same.

Another new source of US influence in the British Caribbean, in addition to the military bases, was through the Anglo-American Caribbean Commission (AACC). In April 1941, while the Stars and Stripes was being raised over bases in several British Caribbean colonies, the US government was suggesting the creation of a joint British-US advisory committee, to cooperate in such fields as agricultural research, land tenure issues, labour problems, and health and education services in the Caribbean area (Post 1981: Vol. 1, 168). The AACC was formally constituted on 9 March 1942 and its leading figure was Charles W. Taussig, chief stockholder in American Molasses and a confidant of President Roosevelt. During the war the chief concern of the United States in the Caribbean was strategic, but Taussig also pressed for political changes that 'would open the British colonies to American enterprise' (Johnson 1984b: 192). Beginning in March 1945 the AACC held a series of conferences, attended chiefly by expatriate officials and advisers, and issued reports on such topics as public works, fishing and agriculture, tourism and health, but the emphasis was quite different from that of the Caribbean Labour Congress (CLC) in September 1945. The AACC assumed that whatever limited developments occurred would be coordinated by its industries section, making it a coordinating agency for further external – largely US – investment in and economic control of the region. The CLC, in contrast, warned against an extension of such external control and urged a bold policy of regional development that would be premised on the organisation of strong local political institutions that were 'democratically accountable to the peoples of the individual territories' (Lewis 1968: 350). This conflict between Caribbean and imperial aspirations that was already taking a characteristic shape before the end of the war became intensified during the Cold War.

By the time of the AACC's first West Indian conference, which was convened in Barbados between 21 and 30 March 1945, Taussig had come to understand that West Indian labour and political leaders sought a self-governing federation that would be more democratic than the systems that then operated in Puerto Rico and the US Virgin Islands. Important constitutional reforms were being introduced in Jamaica, Trinidad and Tobago, and Barbados to democratise their political systems. President Roosevelt, who as early as 1942 had a vision of a Caribbean federation under some kind of international supervisory authority (Baptiste 1988: 216), pressed the UK to decolonise. Churchill accepted that British and US interests in the Caribbean were becoming increasingly mingled, but would not be pushed on the pace of democratisation and decolonisation, particularly because colonies like the Bahamas and Barbados had influential white minorities that felt threatened by these processes. Although Roosevelt, by the time of his death on 12 April 1945, had resolved to let the UK work out its own timetable on decolonisation, the period of the Second World War had 'marked a decisive phase in the United States' strategic penetration of the British, French, and Dutch Caribbean possessions ... [which] came to constitute part of a hemispheric security system as defined by the United States' (Baptiste 1988: 217), a system that lasted for at least half a century after the end of the war. The new warfare, with its use of planes and submarines, along with the increased importance of oil and bauxite supplies, reinforced the much earlier concept of the so-called American lake. The UK had to adjust to the preponderance of US power in the Caribbean, and the destroyers-for-bases agreement was both the product and the means of further implementation of this strategic reality, whose shape was simply accelerated by the events of the war.

Dr Eric Williams, the Trinidadian Island Scholar and Oxford graduate, who had taught social and political science at Howard University in Washington, became a consultant and then a full-time official of the AACC between 1943 and 1955. His pan-Caribbean orientation was undoubtedly strengthened by the opportunities he had in the AACC, though his contribution was expected to be technical, not political. His frustration with and eventual dismissal from the AACC precipitated his entry into nationalist politics (Sutton 1992: 101-2). Thus the imperialist AACC, rather like the US bases, provoked reactions that stimulated the growth of nationalist and democratic politics. The two stories of the bases and the AACC came together in 1957 when Williams and his People's National Movement (PNM) sought to have the base at Chaguaramas returned to the West Indies in order to become the site of the federation's capital. The issue, which was symbolically important, came to a head in 1960 when Williams led a march to demand the return of Chaguaramas. This was 'the militant high point of Trinidadian nationalism' (Oxaal 1968: 133) and the base was finally abandoned in 1967.

Moving towards self–government: Jamaica, Trinidad and Tobago, and Barbados

In spite of the frequent repression of many political and trade union activities under emergency wartime regulations, the British government initiated some important constitutional reforms in Jamaica, Trinidad and Tobago, and Barbados. These reforms, which included the granting of universal adult suffrage in Jamaica in 1944 and Trinidad and Tobago in 1945, moved these colonies decisively towards democracy and self-government. Most of the smaller colonies followed a similar pattern of democratisation shortly thereafter and all had entered the period of mass politics by the 1950s. In this evolutionary process of constitutional decolonisation, many of the men who had started as labour leaders became the chief politicians who controlled local affairs through the 1950s and into the period of independence that began in 1962 in Jamaica and Trinidad and Tobago.

What was happening in the bigger colonies, such as India, Ceylon, Kenya and Nigeria, had more impact on the imperial system, and hence on the smaller colonies such as those in the Caribbean, than vice versa. Soon after the Colonial

Development and Welfare Act (1940), and certainly with the fall of Singapore on 15 February 1942, there was a 'stocktaking and review' of colonial affairs.[192] The Japanese success, in particular, provoked this reassessment because it destroyed most lingering assumptions about British superiority and revealed internal weaknesses in the colonial system. Those colonies that were ethnically plural societies, in which there were marked social divisions and rivalries based on differences in race, language and religion, were seen as especially vulnerable because they were held together only by the colonial power and administration. This became a greater issue in constitutional reform in Trinidad and Tobago than in Jamaica or Barbados.

Jamaica

The changes made in the Jamaican constitution in 1944 were in part the consequence of the labour rebellion of 1938 and the agitation and debates over the Moyne Commission's report. Thus the working people of Jamaica precipitated the development of democracy and their own decolonisation. But the constitutional reforms also reflected a general reassessment of colonial policy that resulted from the long-term and irreversible decline of British imperialism.

Advocates of colonial reform sought to move beyond the old paternalistic formula of trusteeship towards the notion of partnership (Macmillan 1967: 177). While falling far short of an unequivocal abandonment of the empire, this shift in imperial ideology acknowledged that native peoples, but more precisely the Westernised colonial elites, had a legitimate political role to play in the colonies. The deeply rooted racial attitudes and economic assumptions that lay at the heart of imperialism were essentially unchanged, however, as the point of reforms was to make such limited changes as would enable the threatened system to survive. Lord Hailey's influential notion of a colonial charter (1942), for example, embodied the pragmatic traditions of British imperialism in so far as it called for a new vision of the empire, while warning that such ideals as self-government were not appropriate everywhere. Hailey's advocacy of partnership influenced Harold Macmillan who, as the new under-secretary of state for the colonies, introduced the concept in a House of Commons debate on 24 June 1942. He was challenged by Dr Leslie Haden Guest, a Labour MP, who asked whether he meant an 'equal partnership or just another form of words to delude people'. Macmillan's rhetoric about 'a spirit of partnership' was defined only in terms of 'understanding and friendship', not in terms of the equal control of economic resources and political power.[193] Arthur Creech Jones and others in the Fabian Colonial Bureau also criticised the limitations of partnership for failing to address such fundamental issues as the control of land and other resources, or racial discrimination in civil and political rights. In short, the shift to reform policies in 1942 made some concessions to pressure from the colonised, while trying to keep control - in fact, so as to be able to keep control - of the colonies

(Louis 1978: 134–46).

In Jamaica the development of colonial policy during the war meant that 'the struggle for a parliamentary democratic constitution... began effectively in 1938 and ended by and large in 1944' (Munroe 1972: 26). In other words, the struggle between the nationalist and democratic movement, as represented by Norman Manley and the PNP, and the imperial government was largely resolved in the form of the 1944 constitution and the recognition that this was a transitional moment in the transformation of the state framework into more democratic self-government. The adoption of British-style political procedures and institutions, known as the Westminster model, was acceptable to both the colonial elite and the Colonial Office. The Moyne Commission, which did not go to the Caribbean to consider constitutional reform, strictly speaking, recommended nonetheless that 'the representatives of popular opinion... be converted from criticism to cooperation'[194] and the 1944 constitution was intended to do just that, to deflect radical agitation by co-opting the local elite into government while retaining British control. Henceforth, the chief struggles were to be contained within this new legal framework, namely the struggle between sections of the elite and administration, on the one hand, and the Jamaican left, on the other. The expulsion of the chief members of the left from the PNP in 1952 meant that politics became focused on the rivalry between Manley and Bustamante. The PNP's success in rapidly building the National Workers Union (NWU) in 1952-3, which filled the vacuum left in trade unions by the expelled left wing, was largely responsible for its success in the 1955 elections. The rivalry between the JLP-BITU and the PNP-NWU further institutionalised the division within the working class, however, and the predominant issue remaining in Jamaican politics during the decade before independence was the question of federation, with Manley in favour and Bustamante opposed. But this model decolonisation, in which sections of the elite used organised labour in their competition to succeed the coloniser, fell short of a real decolonisation, to the extent that the status and condition of the majority of Jamaicans 'remained fundamentally unchanged' by independence in 1962 (Munroe 1972: 179).

The constitutional framework and party structure of this formal competition was worked out during the war. A memorandum, drafted on 6 May 1942 by Manley and supported by representatives of the PNP, the Federation of Citizens' Associations and the Elected Members' Association, was forwarded by Governor Richards to the secretary of state for the colonies.[195] The memorandum demanded a bicameral legislature, an Executive Council that would be the 'principal instrument of policy' and would contain a majority of elected members who would have ministerial responsibility, the abolition of the governor's veto power and a federation of the British colonies as 'a logical West Indian development'. Lord Cranborne, in his final days as secretary of state, accepted the advice to proceed without delay to a new constitution along the lines demanded in order to avoid 'a smouldering agitation, which may at any time burst into flame, with most unfortunate results on our relations with the United States'.[196] The Colonial Office hoped that the new constitution would 'split apart' those whom they defined as 'reformers' and the 'subversive elements' in the PNP, and that Bustamante would stand aside from 'overt opposition to the Government because of the conditions on which he was released from internment'.[197] In other words, the new constitution was promulgated in the hope that it would prevent further political trouble in Jamaica.

The PNP continued to campaign for constitutional change towards self-gov-ernment at the end of 1942, and Bustamante reasserted 'his dominance in the labour movement . . . [and] held it outside the constitutional campaign' (Post 1981: Vol 1, 295). When the Jamaican administration used its wartime powers to fix a minimum daily wage in the sugar industry on the eve of the harvest (2 shillings and 6 pence for men and 1 shilling and 6 pence for women), Bustamante responded by demanding a wage higher than 18 shillings per week. The chief problem, he insisted, was that of sporadic earnings, which a higher daily rate did not really resolve. Most significantly, in the political situation, Bustamante had appealed directly to the secretary of state, over the head of the governor, insisting that only he and his union represented labour in Jamaica.[198] Two weeks after restrictions on his appearances at public meetings were lifted, Bustamante ordered striking sugar workers at Serge Island in St Thomas back to work, saying that he would renegotiate their wage rates in July.[199] Strike action spread in late January, however, as dock workers refused to handle produce of strike-breakers on the coconut estates. On 16 February Bustamante was reported to have said, 'I would rather see those 15,000 [sugar] workers die of starvation than have them return to work at low rates of pay. I shall let the employers know that Labour loves me; I control Labour; Labour will follow me'.[200] While not campaigning for constitutional reform, therefore, Bustamante was positioning himself so as to be able to take advantage of it whenever it came.

Constitutional reform was already on its way. On 2 February 1943 the new secretary of state for the colonies, Colonel Oliver Stanley, presented his pro-posal for constitutional changes in Jamaica to the War Cabinet. 'The political uncertainties of the last three years', he argued, 'have created in Jamaica a most unhappy spirit, and I am afraid that, unless in some way we can bring this con-troversy to an end and establish an atmosphere of co-operation and goodwill, we shall be faced at the end of the war, if not before, with serious trouble'.[201] The Cabinet approved the proposal on 8 February, and on 23 February the new constitution, which yielded to most of the Jamaican demands, was presented to the Legislative Council. Within a few weeks, Governor Richards was able to report optimistically that all sections of the public, including the PNP, had greeted the reforms and seemed likely to make a 'genuine constructive effort to work within the new constitution'. The only reservations were those expressed privately by 'the propertied classes' who 'wonder whether the offer is not too generous for the present stage of development and education of the people'.[202]

The new constitution, promulgated on 20 November 1944, replaced the single-chamber Legislative Council with a bicameral legislature, consisting of an elected House of Representatives and a Legislative Council. The former consisted of 32 representatives chosen by universal adult suffrage in single-member constituencies and the latter, which could delay bills that had been passed in the House for up to a year, consisted of three officials and ten nominated unofficials. The governor was to be advised by a Privy Council, consisting of four officials and two nominated unofficials. The Executive Council, which was the instrument of policy, was to include five members elected from and removable by the House of Representatives in addition to three officials and two nominated unofficials. The five elected quasi-ministers, who were empowered to represent certain departments of government, introduced the first element of responsibility in a cabinet system, but the governor retained the 'paramount power' with respect to the veto, reservation and certification of bills, without the consent of the legislature, as 'the single and supreme authority responsible to, and representative of, His Majesty' (Hurwitz and Hurwitz 1971: 204). As in the UK, a plurality was required for election and the maximum life of the House of Representatives was five years. The general election which would create this semi-responsible government was set for 14 December 1944.

With the achievement of universal adult suffrage the electorate increased tenfold, from about 63,000 in 1937 to 663,069 in 1944. However, instead of the Jamaican people becoming united by participating in their first real general election, the organisation and appeal of the different parties reflected and reinforced the divisions of class and colour in the social structure. Hence, 'the initial impact of the PNP, the Jamaica Labour Party and the Jamaica Democratic Party was divisive rather than integrative ... [which] meant that the new Constitution which was presented as the first stage in nation-building threatened to open further the traditional divisions between existing groups.' (Munroe 1972: 36)

At the same time that traditional social divisions were reinforced, however, some important political realignments developed as a result of the election, the most important of which was that the old propertied elite, which was the biggest loser in the election, moved towards support of Bustamante's JLP, which it saw as less threatening to its interests than the avowedly socialist PNP. The shifts in the class struggle, therefore, were not the result of changes in the social structure or in class relations but were caused 'by the new political form given to it by constitutional change which remained under Colonial Office control' (Post 1981: Vol 2, 369). The emergence of new political parties and their appeal to the electorate, between February 1943 and December 1944, needs to be examined in this light.

The various political groups established and positioned themselves in readiness for an election. The Jamaica Democratic Party (JDP), which was formed in 1942, had attracted some capitalist backers but revealed no clear programme at its second all-island conference in March 1943. It was described accurately in September 1943 as 'a weak conglomeration of conservative elements'[203] and was too obviously backed by the wealthy to achieve popular support. In its declaration of principles in March 1944 the JDP presented the view that 'Labour and Capital are the inevitable help mates of Civilization' that should work together to produce 'a prosperous Jamaica', and that 'the island's resources can best be developed by the enterprise and initiative of the individual as opposed to State-ownership'.[204] The JDP sought to be the class organ of the capitalists, but it was dominated by the commercial element of importers and exporters rather than the planters. Though essentially conservative, the JDP accepted the goal of 'self-government within the democratic framework of the British Commonwealth of Nations' and sought working-class support from the JUWU, but this union had little influence. H.C. Buchanan, the veteran Marxist trade unionist, had tried to create a United Negro Party in April 1943, but it failed to get off the ground and by 1944 he was a JDP organiser in Clarendon (Post 1981: Vol. 2, 426). Buchanan's former comrades derided him as a 'political Humpty-Dumpty' and accused the JUWU journal, The Democrat, of accepting a weekly subsidy from the JDP in return for supporting the party.[205] The JDP attacked the PNP as not merely socialist, but as communist and irreligious: 'Communism is anti-God. Vote for the JDP' (Post 1981: Vol. 2, 487). In spite of the widespread respect for religion and private property in Jamaica, the JDP failed to benefit from this slogan, won few votes and disappeared soon after the election.

Although some PNP leaders advocated using the BITU to win mass support, as during Bustamante's internment, by early May 1943 Manley decided it was impossible to work with his cousin's union. 'The PNP has taken what, I trust, will prove a final decision not to co-operate with Bustamante himself. It puts us in an extremely difficult position but his tactics are such that we have no choice in the matter'.[206] Manley defended sugar workers who had participated in a strike in defiance of the defence regulations, but 44 of them were convicted. The Masses publicly accused Bustamante of 'displays of personal glamour which merely obscure the realities of the position' and attacked his union's undemocratic structure.[207] This confirmation of the split in the labour movement was the paramount factor in the coming elections.

The left of the PNP, consisting of Richard Hart, Arthur Henry, and the brothers Ken and Frank Hill (who became famous as the Four Hs), released from internment on 18 March 1943 (Hart 1999:218), was creating and leading several new unions, including the Municipal and Parochial Workers Union and the Garment Workers Union, and expanding the Postal and Telegraph Workers Union, the Railway Employees Union and the Public Works Department Workers Union. Nevertheless, the combined strength of all the JTUC affiliated unions was only about one-sixth of the BITU, which reported 28,700 members in July (Post 1981: Vol 2, 321-2). The JTUC unions were generally composed of more skilled and educated workers, and were quite disciplined and democratically organised. Bustamante's blanket union, however, was the more formidable political force. On 8 July 1943 Bustamante reacted to the new political situation by launching his Jamaica Labour Party (JLP) in Kingston.

Bustamante declared, according to a report of his inaugural speech, that he would 'pack Labour Members' into the new legislature and 'fight for a New Deal for Labour in this country',[208] but he cunningly left a door open for the capitalists. The JLP programme advocated a conservative reformist policy:

> The aims and objects of the Jamaica Labour Party are to work for the improvement of the social, economic, educational and political improvement and development of the condition of the small taxpayers, the workers, and the masses on the whole. At the same time, the Party is pledged to keep within a certain moderate conservative policy in order not to reduce beyond reason, or destroy the wealth of Capitalists to any extreme that will eventually hurt their economical [sic] inferiors, but to advocate for the introduction of such measures and Laws that will shorten the terrible wide economic and social gulf that exists today, that almost inhuman disparity between the haves and the have-nots - the rich and the poor, and which indeed is a reflection on the sense of honour, justice and democracy of a civilised country.
>
> Summed up, the whole object of the Party boils down to a few things, a few positive points, points not based upon extreme political philosophies incapable of attainments, but practical points which involve in the main a better Jamaica, stronger and healthier population, more intelligence, a balanced relationship between Employers and Employees, Government and people, moderate and timely evolutionary progress in the march with other countries in the world, less poverty and distress, less abuse of the weak and defenceless, more unity and comradeship amongst all, and the dispensation of some equality which does not today exist.[209]

Soon after the JLP was launched, Bustamante won a concession from the powerful Sugar Manufacturers' Association (SMA). The concession was not over rates of pay, which would have hurt the capitalists who were then experiencing a decline in their average rates of profit, but was the recognition by the SMA that the BITU was henceforth to be the sugar workers' sole bargaining agent.[210] This concession cost the capitalists nothing, while boosting Bustamante's prestige and power. It was a sign of a new deal in labour politics, of an emerging tacit alliance between the leading labour chief and the leading capitalists, which succeeded in keeping the PNP out of power for many years. Bustamante's shrewd populist programme thus appealed to peasants and workers by responding to some of the immediate problems of their existence without challenging the dominant power structure of the ruling class and the colonial elite. Henceforth, the primary confrontation in Jamaican politics, which was between the followers of the BITU-JLP and the JTUC-PNP, detracted from the primary contradictions of society, namely the class struggles between capitalists on the one hand, and workers and peasants on the other.

When the PNP challenged Bustamante's supremacy among dock workers and held a big rally after its fifth annual conference, BITU militants tried to intimidate them. On 13 August 1943 the new Port Workers' League, led by Wills Isaacs, Ken Hill and St William Grant, a former BITU militant, held a mass meeting. At a second meeting a week later there were clashes between the rivals and on 29 August BITU supporters who tried to disrupt a big PNP rally at the Kingston Race Course had to be beaten off. The police, apparently, did not intervene to stop the BITU assaults (Post 1981: Vol. 2, 364, 410). The emergence of these violent street battles between rival trade unionists in 1943 was an ominous development in Jamaican politics.

At the PNP conference several members of the left were elected to the executive, including Hart and Frank Hill, and Ken Hill was third vice-president. Whatever the role of the left, the party's policy statement, which was analytically clearer than the JLP's programme, offered little in concrete terms on the issues of work and wages. Under 'Trade Union Relationship', the PNP pledged to encourage and cooperate with trade unions, to seek 'social legislation' and to 'secure political power for the workers, small settlers, and those who supply services to the community'.[211] If this was meant to be a rallying cry in response to Bustamante's powerful labour organisation and militant tactics, it was too weak to work. The PNP was compromised: trying to unite all classes of Jamaicans with a policy that was formally socialist but that obscured class contradictions, it could not win against the JLP's programme which was 'an almost brilliant stroke of populism' (Post 1981: Vol. 2, 356). Bustamante succeeded in uniting conservative labour politics with moderate nationalism, and in attacking the 'extreme political philosophies' of the PNP while seeming to promise something for everyone else.

Even more important than the fact that the JLP was set to win the competition for votes, however, is the fundamental fact that the division of the labour and nationalist movement along political party lines in 1943 sabotaged the class struggle. Jamaica was thus the first example in the British Caribbean of the way in which parliamentary elections and the evolution of self-government, that is, the

British model of representative democracy and constitutional decolonisation, actually weakened the ability of organised labour to decisively influence the class structure and class relations. Political reforms created formal competitions which precluded more fundamental and substantial social change.

Trinidad and Tobago

Gordon Lewis described the period from 1938 to 1956 in Trinidad and Tobago as one in which 'the local political scene was a wild circus of electoral independents and trade union "czars" having nothing to unite them in a national front' (Lewis 1968: 208). This characterisation of the period draws attention to the key weakness of the politics of labour in Trinidad and Tobago but does not explain its origins. The disunity of labour was to a great extent a result of divisions in the social and economic structure. There was, on the one hand, a division in the economy between the sugar and oil sectors that were dominated by imperial capital and the cocoa, coconut and food-crop sector that was in the hands of local capitalists and small farmers. There was, on the other hand, the racial division of the working class that stemmed from the indenture period when Indian workers competed with and replaced many African or Creole Trinidadians in agricultural labour. By the 1930s and 1940s the new trade unions faced the virtually impossible task of trying to bring together the mostly Creole workers of the urban and oilfield areas with the mostly Indian workers in the rural areas.

Although most labour leaders and political parties in the 1940s espoused some form of socialism, they did not unite in their political struggle against the colonial regime. On the contrary, many of them spent most of their efforts competing with each other for popular support and for the favour of the colonial officials. This was why there were so many political independents and trade union 'czars' in Trinidad and Tobago. The pattern was established in the elections in 1946 and was overcome, but not destroyed, by the rise of Eric Williams' PNM in 1956. The strong trade unions in Trinidad and Tobago did not provide the basis for successful political parties, as in Jamaica and Barbados, and later in Antigua, Belize, Grenada and St Kitts-Nevis, but they contributed to the fragmentation of the politics of labour.

The governor's announcement in 1941 that constitutional changes were imminent was preceded by a serious bifurcation in the labour movement, and the growing split was then exacerbated by political competition for the elected positions on the Legislative Council. In late 1939, soon after Butler was reincarcerated, the labour organisations led by Rienzi launched their own paper, The Vanguard, to give more attention than The People to the struggle of Indians. By mid-1940 Rienzi's largely southern movement, focused as it was on the struggle of oil and sugar workers, was challenged by a loose northern coalition that included Gomes, a Portuguese creole, Mitchell of the FWTU, O'Connor of the Shop Clerks and Shop Assistants' Union (SCSAU) and FWTU, and Francois and

Percival of the NWSCA. They joined with Butler's British Empire Workers and Citizens Home Rule Party (BEWCHRP) in a Memorial Day at La Brea, Butler's base, to celebrate him, in Mitchell's pointed words, as 'the only true and original working class leader' (Singh 1994: 211). Percival criticised 'leaders who felt that they could ride to power on the backs of those who really struggled'[212] and the rift with Rienzi widened. Cipriani's authoritarian leadership of the TLP, meanwhile, had reduced the influence of that organisation, and his nomination to the Executive Council in May 1941 was protested against by his labour critics. Rienzi and his OWTU launched the Socialist Party of Trinidad and Tobago (SPTT) in March 1941 and they campaigned for adult suffrage and self-government, but they failed to integrate the northern unions into an islandwide organisation.

Constitutional change and the debate over the franchise proceeded at a slow pace. The number of electives on the Legislative Council was raised from seven to nine in 1941, so it consisted of the governor, three ex officio members, six nominated unofficials and nine elected members. The governor retained his reserve power as well as the casting vote. On the Executive Council, which advised the governor, the number of nominated unofficials was reduced to three and the number of elected members was increased to two. In 1944 the elected members were increased to four and the nominated unofficials reduced to one, but as the governor did not have to take the Exective Council's advice it is clear that 'the ultimate responsibility for government still rested with the governor' (Brereton 1981: 193).

The committee of 33 local notables that was appointed in May 1941 to make recommendations about extending the franchise did not report until 1944. By a majority of one it recommended the adoption of universal suffrage of all adults over 21 but, against the objections of three union representatives on the committee (Rienzi, Gomes and Mentor), candidates for election had to be literate in English, with an income of not less than $960 per year or property worth at least $5,000. Mentor wrote in the minority report: 'The idea of income at certain levels and the possession of property being criteria of fitness and suitability of persons to take part in the business of government is a relic of an age that is long past and is not in keeping with democratic ideals'.[213] O'Connor, general secretary of the TTSAC and FWTU, argued that it was the right time to introduce democracy: 'The people of this country have been encouraged to believe in democracy and no better time could be chosen to introduce them to the democratic way of life than when they are being asked to and they are making sacrifices to ensure the continued existence of democracy'.[214] Rienzi objected to the use of a language qualification for voters on the grounds that it would disenfranchise many older Indians and the secretary of state agreed with him, contrary to the recommendation of the committee. The protracted debate about the language test mobilised the Indian population into 'a state of unprecedented communal consciousness'

(Singh 1994: 222), thus weakening the chance of achieving working-class solidarity between Creoles and Indians. An order in council subsequently extended the vote to all adults over 21, without any language qualification, and the number of electoral districts was increased to nine.

By the time of the elections, on 1 July 1946, Cipriani had died and Rienzi had withdrawn from politics. But far from leaving an opportunity for a new, unifying political organisation, this merely created more opportunities for other ambitious politicians and new parties to come forward. The WINP, another southern-based party, formed in November 1942 by Joseph and Pitt, became more active in 1944 and gained the support of Gomes and O'Connor of the FWTU. The WINP advocated a self-governing, federal West Indies, immediate responsible government for Trinidad and Tobago, and the eventual nationalisation of the oil and asphalt industries. Their agitation for Butler's release embarrassed the OWTU executive, whose leading members, Rojas, Mentor and Moses, were the leaders of the rival TTTUC and Socialist Party of Trinidad and Tobago (SPTT). Rojas, after he returned from the Pan-African conference in Manchester in 1945, argued that British policy was 'directed towards building a sectional coalition of reactionary Western imperialism', but he opposed the nationalisation of the oil and sugar industries.[215]

Meanwhile, the TLP split again. Several TLP leaders, including Gerald Wight who had replaced Cipriani in 1945, left the old organisation to form a business-oriented Progressive Democratic Party (PDP), but neither the TLP nor the PDP had any success in 1946. Butler, released from detention in 1945, continued to lead his BEWCHRP, a loose but important grouping of his supporters. Shortly before the elections, a Marxist lawyer who had served in the Canadian Air Force, Jack Kelshall, joined some of the labour-oriented groups, including the WINP, into a United Front (UF). The movement remained divided against itself, however, with the chief groups, the UF, the BEWCHRP and the SPTT, all appealing to working-class voters. Despite all their talk of socialism, this was not close to being a revolutionary situation in 1946, as has been claimed (La Guerre 1972: 189), because these groups were fighting each other.

Five political parties and 42 candidates contested the election to fill the nine seats. Although working people were the majority of the 46 per cent of the total population who registered as voters for the 1946 elections, and most of them voted for the parties advocating some kind of labour or socialist programme, no single party emerged as a winner. The UF and BEWCHRP each won three seats and the SPTT won two, but the leaders of the most sucessful parties, namely Kelshall and Pitt of the UF, Butler of the BEWCHRP, and Rojas and Mentor of the SPTT, failed to get elected.

For the UF, Gomes beat Butler in North Port of Spain by taking about 70 per cent of the votes, Dr Patrick Solomon beat C.B. Mathura of the TLP in South Port of Spain, and Joseph beat Mentor in San Fernando. For the BEWCHRP, Timothy Roodal, the outgoing member, beat both Kelshall and Rojas in St Patrick with the biggest majority of the election, and Chanka Maharaj and Alfonso James won St George and Tobago, respectively. For the SPTT, Victor Bryan won Eastern Counties and C.C. Abidh won Caroni. The sole independent who was elected was Ranjit Kumar, a businessman who was born in India in 1912, had moved to Trinidad in 1935, and had been associated with Butler. Kumar, with 51.2 per cent of the vote, beat Pitt, Moses and George Fitzpatrick, the outgoing member, in Victoria, where the racial factor seems to have played a larger role than elsewhere (La Guerre 1972: 195).

The trade unions were a major influence in the election but no group won a majority among the electives in the Legislative Council. Moreover, Trinidad and Tobago had only got adult suffrage, not self-government, and members of three parties, Gomes, Roodal, Joseph and Abidh, were absorbed into the Executive Council as advisers to the governor. In November 1946 when Gomes called the Executive Council an anachronism,[216] Joseph tabled a motion on further constitutional reform. The politicians continued to fight with each other, and the UF soon split.

In order to understand why the labour movement in Trinidad and Tobago did not emerge in the 1940s as a unified political movement, despite its potential in the late 1930s to transcend ethnic and regional divisions, we must examine both the nature of the political aspirants and the social and cultural heterogeneity of the society. Certainly, a society as plural as Trinidad and Tobago in 1946 was prone to sectoral politics. In a total population of less than half a million people, a slender majority of 54.6 per cent was of African descent, the remainder being Indian (41 per cent), European (3.2 per cent), Chinese (1.2 per cent), or other, according to the census. These racial-ethnic groups were further divided and cross-cut by class, place of residence (85 per cent of the Indians were distributed in the largely rural areas of the four western counties, St George, Caroni, Victoria and St Patrick), and religion (34.5 per cent were Catholic, 24.2 per cent Anglican, 22.7 per cent Hindu, 5.8 per cent Muslim and 3.6 per cent Presbyterian). With this degree of pluralism it is perhaps surprising that politics was not even more sectarian than it was in 1946.

The strength of class consciousness and the emerging politics of labour, along with a kind of national consciousness fostered by the problems and sacrifices of wartime, and the general demand for democratic reforms, overlaid some of these other divisions, at least in much of the political rhetoric. What could not be overcome, and was to be fomented by the electoral competition for nine seats in a government that still had no responsibility, was the aspiration for personal power of most political leaders, at the expense of the long-term development of a powerful labour movement. Each of the chief political aspirants of this period, namely Cipriani, Butler, Rienzi and Gomes, who were members of all the chief ethnic groups in the society, desired to be the maximum leader and sought to bring their rivals down. Consequently, while each deserves some credit for the development of modern politics in Trinidad and Tobago in the 1930s, each must also share some of the blame for the disunity of the 1940s. But the new political system must also be blamed for creating the situation that encouraged these men to compete in ways that divided the labour movement.

Singh (1994: 224) has pointed out that Rienzi was a central figure between 1937 and 1944 in the forging of a 'trans-ethnic alliance between the African and Indian working masses.' Rienzi, a middle-class Indian professional, became the leader, like the white Creole Cipriani before him, of a largely Creole labour movement, and his withdrawal from politics 'virtually destroyed whatever chances of success that movement retained in the period' (Singh 1994: 225). But perhaps Singh exaggerates Rienzi's importance, as it is hard to imagine any fundamentally different outcome to the 1946 election if Rienzi had remained in politics. Even if he had been re-elected in 1946, the labour movement and the Legislative Council would still have been divided along similar lines. It was hard for any of these men to consistently transcend the parochial expectations that were endemic in their plural society, and none of them, not even Rienzi, really seemed likely to do so.

The problem seems to have been not simply that they were all too personally ambitious and unwilling to share the limelight, though this was largely true, but that too many people expected them to be leaders only of their own social sections and, despite occasional heroic efforts to overcome this, such constraints limited their national effectiveness. Thus, as Singh says of Rienzi (1994: 225), the 'conclusive factor' in his decision to opt out of working-class politics 'was his unwillingness to sacrifice the interests of his race on the question of the franchise.' When push came to shove, Rienzi withdrew from the emerging politics of labour on parochial, though undoubtedly important and principled, grounds. The tragedy of Trinidad and Tobago, therefore, is that despite the potentially powerful trans-ethnic labour movement of the late 1930s and early 1940s, by the election of 1946 politics had become characterised by individual opportunism, parochial allegiances and middle-class control, all of which were encouraged by the modified Westminster model. Gomes, who became 'the virtual chief minister ... [and] then ... essentially a collaborator of the ruling class' (Singh 1994: 226) between 1946 and 1956, epitomised this development.

Barbados

In Barbados the fratricidal struggle of rival trade unions and political parties that characterised Jamaica and Trinidad and Tobago was largely avoided with the successful development of the BWU after 1941. This was a general union that was organised in industrial sections under a united leadership. The monolithic quality of this organisation, which was a branch of the chief political party, and the growing personal power of Adams, were confirmed after the elections of 1946 when he and his BLP (formerly the BPL), drawing its support from the BWU, led the first quasi-democratic Barbadian government. However, this monolithism, which reflected the simpler nature of Barbadian society and politics, gave rise to its own particular problems for the labour movement. The BLP-BWU, constrained by Adams' liberal constitutionalism as well as the entrenched power of the largely white plantocracy and commercial elite, imagined nothing more radical than a Fabian colonial socialism, and so failed to challenge the dominant structures of this classic plantation society. The outcome of these developments in the 1940s was that 'a conciliatory arrangement between white corporate power and black political administrations emerged as the dominant political thrust of the post-independence period' (Beckles 1990: 203).

In 1940 it appeared that Adams' BPL might seriously challenge the colony's entrenched power structure. Despite a still restricted franchise, the BPL campaigned in the election that year on the basis of a living wage for all workers, the abolition of the plantation system and distribution of land to small farmers, and for adult suffrage and the abolition of property qualifications for membership of the House of Assembly. Needless to say, if these goals had been achieved at that time, Barbados would have changed unrecognisably. The BPL won five of the 24 seats in the house in 1940, but it was clear that little further progress could be made without a broader franchise and an organised popular base. The first meeting of the Executive Council of the BWU, with Adams as general president and Springer as general secretary, was held on 26 February 1942. The minutes were kept on the letterhead of the BPL, the 'Parent Body of Unions', which shows the relationship of the political and union wings of Adams' organisation.[217] Following Citrine's advice, the BWU was formed as a general union 'with as many divisions as was necessary to cover the Island's various trades and occupations' (Hoyos 1974: 97). By mid-1942 there were several divisions, including ships' carpenters, engineers, seamen and bakers, but the BWU did not start organising sugar workers until July 1945. During the war many employers were 'diehards, who saw no reason to negotiate wages and conditions' (Mark 1966: 75) and voluntary arbitration was employed only three times between 1941 and 1946.

The BWU was slow to organise working people and the BPL won only four seats in the House of Assembly in 1942 but Governor Bushe encouraged Adams by appointing him to the executive committee that year. Adams was in a difficult situation, however. On the one hand, according to his biographer, he 'was not prepared to evade any responsibility that came his way as the people's tribune and he regarded his appointment as an opportunity to advocate the case for the workers in quarters where he could, if successful, produce fruitful results'

(Hoyos 1974: 98). On the other hand, he ran the risk of becoming increasingly associated with the government while having little influence upon its policies. In this context, a former member of the BPL, Wynter Crawford, took up a position to the left of Adams. When the Representation of the People Bill was debated in April and May 1943, Adams and Crawford both demanded adult suffrage, but it was Crawford 'who carried the debate for the workers by illustrating the rigid conservatism of the governing merchant-planter elite' (Beckles 1990: 178). Adult suffrage was not achieved, but the income qualification was reduced and women were able to vote for the first time.

Under this newly extended franchise, which increased the electorate by over 500 per cent, there was a more serious and aggressively contested election than ever before. In 1944 the BPL faced a challenge from both right and left, respectively the planters' Electors' Association (EA) and Crawford's newly formed West Indian National Congress Party (WINCP). While the latter promised to break the planter-merchant political leadership, as represented by the EA, and to move rapidly towards socialism, Adams's BPL, 'critical of both these right and left parties, pledged itself to labour reforms, social welfare policies, and a gradualist approach in the search for liberal political democracy' (Beckles 1990: 180). The result was an even split, the WINCP and EA each winning eight seats and the BPL seven. Although those representing the elite in the House of Assembly were now a minority, those who claimed to represent labour were badly divided.

Governor Bushe decided that, although the WINCP had won more seats than the BPL, Crawford was too radical, so he appointed Adams and Springer to the executive committee. This obvious favouritism, which deepened the rift between the labour parties, was rewarded when Adams and Springer voted to increase the governor's salary; Crawford voted against it (Beckles 1990: 182). In 1946, Bushe initiated a further moderate constitutional reform, known as his experiment, whereby membership of the executive committee would actually reflect the distribution of seats held by the different political parties within the House of Assembly. This timid move towards Cabinet government, known as semi-ministerial government, was nevertheless a partial victory for the advocates of democracy in the labour movement.

In the 1946 election Adams's party, renamed the Barbados Labour Party (BLP), was favoured by Bushe as the moderate party. Crawford, whose attempt to lead the sugar workers' struggle for wage increases in 1945 had been stifled by an alliance between the BLP and the EA, with the governor's support, 'accused Bushe of fostering the development of an accomodationist labour movement with the assistance of Adams and the Electors' Association, as part of a stategy to suppress worker radicalism, slow down the pace of decolonisation, and derail the movement toward socialism' (Beckles 1990: 183). After a bitter campaign, the BLP won nine seats, the EA eight and the WINCP seven, with one independent elected. Adams was called upon to lead the House, but he had to cooperate with Crawford in order to achieve a working majority. According to Bushe's rules, Adams and Springer of the BLP and Crawford and Blackman of the WINCP were nominated to the executive committee. This was 'an uncomfortable coalition from the beginning' (Beckles 1990: 184), as Adams wanted to move reforms more slowly than Crawford. In October 1947, Crawford resigned from the executive committee and Adams enticed three members of the WINCP to join the BLP, thereby obtaining 12 seats out of the 24 in the House.[218]

Crawford's challenge had lasted only a couple of years and Adams, whose consolidation of power was supported by the governor, achieved a virtually authoritarian control over the parliamentary representation of the labour movement, even while further constitutional changes led to adult suffrage and self-government. This was the context within which there emerged the 'conciliatory arrangement between white corporate power and black political administrations' (Beckles 1990: 203) that has subsequently characterised Barbados.

The imperial crisis, the war and the decolonisation process

When the constitutional evolution from colony to independent state is examined in each Caribbean nation, the historical narrative usually emphasises a relatively orderly progress from stage to stage, marked particularly by the formation of political parties, the achievement of adult suffrage, and the development of ministerial responsibility and self-government. From this perspective, we can identify the variations among the three examples we have analysed: Jamaica was the first to achieve adult suffrage, and exhibited a severe split in its labour movement that gave rise to a bitter struggle between rival political parties; Trinidad and Tobago developed a proliferation of trade unions and several competing labour parties in its first general election with adult suffrage; and Barbados, several years before suffrage was achieved, witnessed the growing dominance of one party and its associated trade union, both led by the same man. These variations may be explained largely in terms of the different characteristics of these societies in the 1930s and 1940s, but they led in turn to variations in the nature of the democratic process, and in the relations between leaders and their organisations, and between the trade unions and political parties. By 1946, in all three of these colonies, and in most of the rest of the British Caribbean within a few years, the different patterns in the politics of labour were established. From this perspective, then, the internal variations are highlighted and, from a comparative point of view, this is important.

There is a more pan-Caribbean and global perspective, however, that complements the focus on the internal histories of each Caribbean nation. This perspective emphasises what all the parts of the British Caribbean experienced in common, as a result of the interrelated factors of the imperial crisis and changing policies of the UK, the increasing and pervasive influence of the United States in the region and the impact of the Second World War. What happened in each country was shaped not only by the particular structure and culture of that society, and by its particular labour leaders and their political organisations, but also by these broader forces that to a great extent underlaid what was common in the overall pattern of decolonisation during this period.

An excessive focus on the global perspective overlooks the important variations as well as the crucial role of individuals, organisations and local social movements in shaping the political processes and cultures of their societies, but such a focus on the biographies of particular leaders, or on the history of each nation in isolation, underestimates the importance of the global forces that shaped the history of the region. Both perspectives are necessary in order to achieve a fuller understanding of the changes that took place in the British Caribbean in these crucial years during and immediately after the Second World War.

The war had a huge and complex impact on the political culture of the British Caribbean, especially as it followed so soon after the Great Depression and the labour rebellions of the 1930s. One way that the relationship between these internal and external aspects may be seen is in terms of how the war affected some of the new labour leaders and organisations in the colonies, some of them becoming more anti-colonial and others less so, as they attacked or gathered around the flag of the motherland in its crisis. Of course, this polarisation oversimplifies what was actually happening, as many people adopted coherent middle positions of critical support in the struggle against fascism, and others vacillated between more extreme positions or held contradictory positions simultaneously. With this qualification in mind, I will illustrate the general point with the example of Ebenezer Duncan of St Vincent.

Duncan was a schoolteacher and prominent citizen who had achieved some influence in the 1930s and 1940s, though he is not mentioned in a local popular history of the anticolonial struggles (Ryan and Williams n.d.). He was a leader of the St Vincent Representative Government Association in the 1930s and published critical accounts of the Italian invasion of Ethiopia in his newspaper, *The Investigator*, in 1935. Duncan, along with George McIntosh, helped associate racial consciousness with a rising anticolonialism at this time, but whatever part they played in the disorders in Kingstown in 1935 they soon tried to disassociate themselves from the rioters. Duncan's editorial on 26 October referred to the disorder as 'a blot on the history of the colony'. McIntosh subsequently formed the St Vincent Workingmen's Cooperative Association, and he and Duncan led the associated St Vincent Labour Party that established the basis for political unionism in the 1950s.

In 1941, ten years before the achievement of universal adult suffrage in St Vincent, Duncan wrote a school textbook, A Brief History of St Vincent with Studies in Citizenship. This text, which was reprinted five times, was read by most secondary-school students until the early 1970s and presumably affected an entire generation's thoughts about the history and political culture of their nation.

Young shows how Duncan's book was 'a manual for Commonwealth citizenship as well as a history of St Vincent' (1993: 19). The book reveals and promotes an implicit but distinct view of political culture. Duncan interprets two dramatic aspects of St Vincent's history, namely slavery and the Black Carib war, so as to encourage Vincentians to feel pride in their English-derived system of government, although this system was far from being achieved there when he wrote the book in 1941. St Vincent's population grew from the roots of slavery, but Duncan praises all the things associated with their enslavers, the British. Thus, the English language, Magna Carta and Queen Victoria are all symbols of the unity, identity and rights that Vincentians are supposed to enjoy as a result of their colonisation by the British. The Caribs, who loved their beautiful island and were valiant warriors, were portrayed from the dominant British viewpoint as savages. Duncan thus accepted and fostered a dualism that contrasted the savage Caribs with the civilised English, and he clearly preferred the latter, with all their values, symbols of authority and social hierarchies.

What is critical, of course, is that the slaves did not ally themselves with the Caribs in the 30-year struggle that threatened the existence of the British colony in the eighteenth century. Duncan, by depicting the Caribs as savages, albeit as worthy enemies of the British, implies that the slave forbears of modern Vincentians chose to stand with their masters in defending civilised life. The reward for the slaves' loyalty, though a long time coming, was the act of Parliament that gave them their freedom. Duncan portrays the parliamentary process and the abolition of slavery at length in order to instruct his students, and concludes, 'This glorious triumph in a fight for freedom is an example of what can be accomplished by trust in God and the employment of constitutional methods' (Duncan 1941: 33). Duncan's Anglophilia is an expression of admiration for a system of colonial government, a set of values and a hierarchical social order that continued to exclude the vast majority of Vincentians until 1951.

The point is that Duncan's school text, written in the middle of another fight for freedom in the Second World War, taught a generation of Vincentians to play by the rules that the British imposed and to have faith that their loyalty, like that of their slave ancestors, would eventually be rewarded. Duncan had rejected the idea of people taking the law into their own hands in 1935, and the crisis of the empire at war, which he saw as rather like the Carib Wars in St Vincent's history, prompted him to promote a political culture that he associated with the struggle for civilisation itself. In this way, then, and to the unmeasurable extent that Vincentians were influenced by Duncan's ideas, the values of democracy and independence, which were seen as part of the British heritage, became part of the social identity of Vincentians. Like the end of slavery, the achievement of democracy and independence was portrayed as a reward given to loyal Vincentians, rather than something to which they themselves contributed, and least of all as something that they achieved in the course of a protracted struggle for freedom.

The coloniser's political culture, mediated by people like Duncan in the course of the global crises of the 1930s and 1940s, became part of the political culture of the colonised. The dialectics of colonial history, and the interrelations between the internal and external factors, which are really two aspects of the same process, are thus revealed in a deeply rooted process of power, resistance and accommodation. In the Second World War, as in other critical periods of Caribbean history, people responded to the crisis in many complex ways, but within broad parameters that they had largely inherited from the past and that were shaped by wider forces and structures that were beyond their control.

Notes

1   The Times, 25, 26 and 27 May 1938.
2   Hansard (Commons Debates) 5th series, v. 338, 110, 14 Jun. 1938.
3   Hansard (Commons Debates) 5th series, v. 338, 3299, 28 July 1938. In addition to Lord Moyne, the members of the commission were Sir Edward Stubbs (a former governor of Jamaica), Hubert D. Henderson (research fellow of All Souls College, Oxford), Professor Frank Engledow (Professor of Agriculture at Cambridge University), Ralph Assheton (a Conservative MP), Dr Mary Blacklock (Curator of the Museum of the Liverpool School of Tropical Medicine), Sir Walter Citrine (joint secretary of the Trades Union Congress), Morgan Jones (a Labour MP), Sir Percy MacKinnon (a former chairman of Lloyds Bank) and Dame Rachel Crowdy (former head of the League of Nations Social Questions and Opium Traffic Section).
4   Memos on Cabinet decision, Jan. 1940, CO 318/443/6.
5   Report of the West Indian Sugar Commission, Cmd. 3517, 1930.
6   Report of the Commission on Trinidad and Tobago Disturbances, 1937, Cmd. 5641, 1938; Report of the Commission appointed to enquire into the disturbances which took place in Barbados on the 27th July 1937 and subsequent days (Barbados, 1937).
7   Ormsby-Gore to Orde Browne, 8 Apr. 1938, Orde Browne papers box 2/5, f. 83; MacDonald to Creech Jones, 14 June 1938, ACJ papers box 14/1, f. 101, RHL.
8   Report of West Indian Deprtment, 20 May 1938, CO 318/433/1.
9   Minute by Sir John Campbell, 23 May 1938, CO 318/433/71168.
10   Cabinet minutes, 15 Jun. 1938, CO 318/433/1.
11   Quoted in Havinden and Meredith 1993: 201.
12   Orde Browne commented that the US enterprises 'afford a somewhat humiliating contrast in certain ways to the British West Indies'; memorandum, 23 Jul. 1939, CO 852/250/15606.
13   Quoted in Havinden and Meredith 1993: 203.
14   Draft Cabinet memo by MacDonald, n.d. [Jan. 1940], CO 318/443/6.

15   Extracts from the Report of the Royal West India Commission, CO 318/443/6.
16   Moyne to MacDonald, 31 Jan. 1940, CO 318/443/6.
17   Quoted in Havinden and Meredith 1993: 204.
18   Colonial Development and Welfare, Report on the Operation of the Act to 31 October 1942, PP 1942-3, IX (Cmd. 6422), 601, p.4.
19   SS to WI governors, 16 Jan. 1940, CO 318/443/7.
20   Gov. of British Guiana to SS, 18 Jan. 1940, CO 318/443/7.
21   Gov. of British Guiana to SS, 3 Feb. 1940, CO 318/443/7.
22   A.F. Richards to MacDonald, 18 Jan. 1940, CO 318/443/7.
23   Richards to MacDonald, 19 Feb. 1940, CO 318/444/22.
24   Richards to Lloyd, 27 May 1940, CO 318/443/8.
25   H. Beckett to E. Hale, 26 Jan. 1940, CO 318/443/7.
26   Beckett to G.L. Syers, 7 Feb. 1940, CO 318/443/7.
27   Richards to MacDonald, 14 Nov. 1940, CO 318/443/7.
28   Gov. of British Guiana to SS, 29 Nov. 1940, CO 318/443/7.
29   C.Y. Carstairs to Davidge, 24 Jan. 1941, CO 318/443/7.
30   C.G. Stevens memo, 22 Dec. 1938, CO 137/830/689/89.
31   Guy Perrin, memo, 3 Apr. 1940, encl. in Gov. Waddington to MacDonald, 13 Apr. 1940, CO 318/443/8.
32   F.A. Norman, memo, 25 Apr. 1940, CO 318/444/22.
33   Norman, memo, 25 Apr. 1940, CO 318/445/13.
34   Gov. of Jamaica to SS, 28 Oct. 1942, CO 137/854/69205.
35   Stockdale to Beckett, 13 May 1943, CO 318/455/17.
36   Moyne Commission Report, paras 27-9.
37   Gov. J.A. Hunter to Lloyd, 16 Sept. 1940, CO 318/444/30.
38   Minute by Norris, 7 May 1940, CO 318/444/30.
39   Gov. Sir H. Popham to MacDonald, 26 Apr. 1940, CO 318/445/13.
40   Minute by S. Caine, 29 Jun. 1940, CO 318/445/13.
41   Orde Browne's comments on Carstair's memo, 8 Aug. 1940, CO 318/445/48.
42   Richards to SS, 6 Sept. 1939, CO 318/441/4.
43   'Labour and the War', The Worker, 2 Feb. 1940, quoted in Post 1981: Vol. 1, 74.
44   Bustamante to SS, 29 Jan. 1940, CO 137/840/68511/229.
45   The Worker, 30 Jan. 1940, encl. in Richards to MacDonald, 3 Feb. 1940, CO 318/445/42.
46   The Worker, 13 Feb. 1940, quoted in Post 1981: Vol. 1, 79.
47   Cecil Nelson, letter, The Worker, 10 Feb. 1940, quoted in Post 1981: Vol. 1, 95-6.
48   Richards to Lloyd, 27 May 1940, CO 318/443/8.
49   Daily Gleaner, 25 May 1940, emphasises in the original, quoted in Post 1981: Vol. 1, 104.
50   The JPL, led by W.A. Domingo, was in close touch with Richard Hart of the PNP left and with George Padmore, the Trinidadian socialist then living in London. On 17 June 1941, Domingo was arrested on returning to Jamaica, on the grounds of fostering anti-British and racial animosity. Manley, who had invited Domingo to return and work for the PNP, severed all personal contact with the governor, and a broadly based Council for the Protection of Civil Liberties was formed. After 20 months of detention, Domingo was released on 19 Feb 1943 (Post 1981: Vol. 1, 177-9, 299).
51   Quoted in Post 1981: Vol. 1, 115.
52   The People's National Party Report of the 2nd Annual Conference (Kingston, PNP, n.d.), p.16, quoted in Post 1981: Vol. 1, 118-19.
52   Richards to SS, 8 Sept. 1940, CO 137/840/68511/229.
53   Quotations encl. in Richards to SS, 13 Sept. 1940, CO 137/840/68511/229, quoted in Post 1981: Vol. 1, 129-30.
54   SS to Richards, 24 Oct. 1940, CO 137/846/69120.

55 K. Hill to A. Creech Jones, 7 Jan. 1941, FCBP 142/1A.
56 'The Romance of the Strike', Public Opinion, 19 Apr. 1941, quoted in Post 1981: Vol. 1, 159-60.
57 Daily Gleaner, 11 Mar. 1941, quoted in Post 1981: Vol. 1, 160.
58 Daily Gleaner, 25 Mar. 1941, quoted in Post 1981: Vol. 1, 160.
59 The sugar workers' union in Guyana, the MPCA, also petitioned in 1941 for his release (Post 1981: Vol. 1, 166).
60 Garvey had died in London on 10 June 1940.
61 'What Our Workers are Thinking', Public Opinion, 3 May 1941, quoted in Post 1981: Vol. 1, 165.
62 The union's treasurer, Gladys Longbridge, was Bustamante's 'devoted companion' (Eaton 1975: 27), who became his wife in 1962.
63 In 1968, Richards, then Lord Milverton, admitted he had had a long private talk with Bustamante before he was released, but denied that a deal had been struck (Munroe 1972: 23).
64 Richards to H.F. Downie, 1 Jun. 1942, CO 137/852/69120.
65 J.A.G. Edwards' letter, Daily Gleaner, 27 Feb. 1942, quoted in Post 1981: Vol. 1, 223.
66 Daily Gleaner, 26 Feb. 1942, quoted in Post 1981: Vol. 1, 224. Of course, this sentiment did not stop Norman Manley's son, Michael, from becoming the head of the National Workers Union (NWU), the chief rival to the BITU, that was linked to the PNP (Manley 1975).
67 B.B. Wilson circular, 20 Mar. 1942, quoted in Post 1981: Vol. 1, 225.
68 New Negro Voice, 11 Apr. 1942, quoted in Post 1981: Vol. 1, 229.
69 More violence between workers occurred in August when Bustamante intervened in a dispute at the Jamaica Shirt Factory in Kingston. Bustamante was fined £10 with costs for incitement (Post 1981: Vol. 1, 263).
70 'Agricultural Policy and the Labour Situation', CO 318/455/71335.
71 F.A. Norman, 'Survey of the Labour Position in the British West Indies', May 1943, CO 318/452/71265.
72 Richards to Downie, 1 Jun. 1942, CO 137/850/68714/6.
73 Richards to Downie, 1 Jun. 1942, CO 137/854/69202.
74 FBI memorandum, 16 Nov. 1942, quoted in Post 1981: Vol. 1, 258.
75 Richards, interviewed by Reynolds Packard, Daily Gleaner, 30 Sept. 1942, in CO 318/447/2.
76 Daily Gleaner, 15 Oct. 1942, in CO 318/447/2.
77 Richards to Col. Oliver Stanley, 29 Dec. 1942, CO 318/447/20.
78 Richards to SS, 12 Oct. 1942, CO 137/851/69016.
79 25 Oct. 1942, HP 1/63.
80 Resolution of the TTTUC, 2 Jun. 1940, encl. in Gov. Hubert Young to Lloyd, 2 Jul. 1940, CO 318/446/8.
81 The People, 29 Jun. 1940, quoted in Singh 1994: 211.
82 C.Y. Carstairs' minute on the TTTUC resolution, 6 Aug. 1940, CO 318/446/8.
83 R. Gavin, report to OEAT, 'Survey of Industrial Relations in Trinidad Oil Industry 1937-41', OWTUL.
84 ———Ibid.
85 ———Ibid.
86 Gov. Hubert Young to Lloyd, 27 Jan. 1940, CO 295/619/70392.
87 Young to Lloyd, 10 May 1940, CO 295/619/70392.
88 A.G.V. Lindon, report of the first meeting of the Joint Conciliation Board for the oil industry, 1 May 1940, encl. in Young to Lloyd, 31 May 1940, CO 295/619/70392.
89 Orde Browne's minute, 19 Jul. 1940, CO 295/619/70392.
90 Young to Lloyd, 20 May 1940, CO 318/445/48.
91 OWTU files, OWTUL.
92 The People, 8 Jan. 1938, quoted in Singh 1994: 208.
93 Blades to Citrine, 21 Apr. 1943, OWTUL.

94   Port of Spain Gazette, 15 Mar. 1942.

95   Report of the Franchise Committee (Port of Spain, 1944: 10).

96   Clifford to Stanley, 9 Dec. 1943, CO 295/630/70097/44.

97   Statement of Policy, Programme and Constitution of the West Indian National Party (Port of Spain, 1942).

98   ———Ibid.

99   ———Ibid.

100   Sir F. Stockdale to Mr Beckett, 15 Jan. 1941, CO 318/448/3.

101   Gov. Sir G. Bushe to Lord Cranborne, 24 Oct. 1942, CO 318/447/20.

102   Bushe to SS, 3 Apr. 1943, CO 318/448/10.

103   Bushe to SS, 3 Jul. 1943, CO 318/448/10.

104   FO to Washington Embassy, 20 Jul. 1943, CO 318/448/10.

105   Bushe to Stanley, 30 Jul. 1943, CO 318/448/10.

106   Bushe to SS, 16 Nov. 1943, CO 318/448/10.

107   Anglo-American Caribbean Commission to SS, 20 Oct. 1943, CO 318/448/10.

108   Anglo-American Caribbean Commission to SS, 11 Mar. 1944, CO 318/460/1.

109   Bushe to SS, 14 Apr. 1944, CO 318/460/1.

110   R.H. Whitehorn, note, 20 Apr. 1944, CO 318/460/1.

111   Bushe to SS, 31 May 1944, CO 318/460/1.

112   Bushe to SS, 12 Jun. 1944, CO 318/460/1.

113   Herbert G. Macdonald, report, 8 Sept. 1945, CO 318/460/2.

114   Macdonald, report, 2 Apr. 1946, CO 318/460/3.

115   Macdonald, reports, 3 Jun. and 2 Dec. 1946, CO 318/460/3.

116   Minute 59, 17 Jul. 1945, BWU Executive Council minute book, hereafter BWUMB.

117   Minutes 1, 26 Feb. 1942; 2, 27 Feb. 1942; 3, 4 Mar. 1942, BWUMB.

118   Minute 15, 3 Feb. 1943, BWUMB.

119   Minute 24, 28 Dec. 1943, BWUMB.

120   Minute 37, 21 Aug. 1944, BWUMB.

121   TTTUC circular, 4 Dec. 1944, OWTUL.

122   Minute 40, 14 Feb. 1945, BWUMB.

123   T. Walker Paton, reports, encl. in Bushe to Stanley, 28 Feb. 1945, CO 537/1682.

124   Bushe to SS, 21 Feb. 1945, CO 537/1682.

125   J.D. Harford, letter with copy of ATLU resolutions, 26 Feb. 1940, encl. in Gov. Lethem to SS, 10 Mar. 1940, CO 318/445/42.

126   The smaller factory, Bendals, was sold to the Antigua Sugar Factory after the 1939 strike; Lethem to SS, 8 Nov. 1939, CO 152/485/1760.

127   Supplement to the Leeward Islands Gazette, 4 Apr. 1940, p. 7, CO 152/493/61760.

128   Supplement to the Leeward Islands Gazette, 9 May 1940, CO 152/494/61783.

129   Harford to SS, 8 Apr. 1940, CO 152/493/61760.

130   Supplement to the Leeward Islands Gazette, 4 Apr. 1940, pp. 4–5, CO 152/493/61760.

131   Lethem to SS, 28 Jun. 1940, CO 152/494/61783.

132   Ibid.

133   Ibid.

134   Ibid.

135   Lethem to SS, 29 Jun. 1940, CO 152/494/61783.

136   Lethem to SS, 30 Jun. 1940, CO 152/494/61783.

137   Lethem to SS, 28 Jun. 1940, CO 152/494/61783.

138   Ibid.

139   Edgar O. Challenger to Peter Blackman, 3 May 1940, CO 152/494/62245.

140   Government Notices, 30 Apr. 1940, CO 152/494/62245.

141   Lethem to SS, 30 Jun. 1940, CO 152/494/61783.

142   SS to Lethem, 20 Jun. 1940, CO 152/494/62245.

143   Minute by C.Y. Carstairs, 7 Aug. 1940, CO 152/494/61783.

144   Minute by H. Beckett, 19 Jun. 1940, CO 152/494/61783.

145 St Kitts-Nevis Daily Bulletin, 21 Jan. 1941, CO 152/494/62245.
146 Beckett to Lethem, 28 Feb. 1941, CO 152/494/62245.
147 This account is based on Saunders 1985-6, reprinted in Saunders 1990.
148 Act. Gov. Johnston to SS, 22 Aug. 1939, CO 123/377/66853.
149 Johnston to SS, 13 Jul. 1939, CO 123/377/66853.
150 Gov. A.C. Burns to SS, 3 Apr. 1939, CO 123/373/66553.
151 Johnston to SS, 10 Aug. 1939, CO 123/373/66553.
152 Johnston to SS, 15 Aug. 1939, CO 123/373/66553.
153 Gov. to SS, 6 Nov. 1939, CO 123/373/66553.
154 Johnston to SS, 22 Aug. 1939, CO 123/377/66853.
155 E.P. Bradley's labour reports, 29 Jan. 1940 and 6 Jul. 1940, CO 123/378/66553.
156 Gov. J.A. Hunter to Beckett, 15 Jul. 1940, CO 123/378/66553.
157 Minute, P. Rogers to Beckett, 9 Feb. 1941, CO 123/378/66553.
158 Bradley's labour reports, 13 Aug. 1940 and 21 Oct. 1940, CO 123/378/66553.
159 Hunter to SS, 26 Apr. 1940, CO 123/379/66871.
160 Hunter to SS, 7 Apr. 1940.
161 Burns to SS, 28 Dec. 1938, CO 123/376/66824.
162 Kemp was said to live rent-free in one of Turton's houses; Burns to SS, 28 Dec. 1938, CO 123/376/66824.
163 Hunter to Lord Moyne, 24 Oct. 1941, BA 174.
164 Belize Independent, 27 Aug. 1941.
165 Hunter to Cranborne, 5 Mar. 1942, BA 174.
166 Adderley, having taken Guatemalan nationality, was deported from Belize when he tried to return in 1950 (Gov. Garvey to SS, 6 Nov. 1950, CO 537/6132).
167 Hunter to Stanley, 8 Feb. 1943, CO 123/380.
168 Belize Independent, 26 Mar. 1941.
169 Hunter to Moyne, 27 Mar. 1941, CO 318/447/16.
170 Hunter to Downie, 26 Apr. 1942, CO 318/447/16.
171 Hunter to SS, 5 Dec. 1942, CO 318/447/20.
172 A. Soberanis to Vernon Leslie, 10 Jul. 1973, BA, SP 25.
173 Annual report of the Labour Department, 1943.
174 Greenidge to Lloyd, 23 Dec. 1943; Lloyd to Greenidge, 4 Jan. 1944, CO 123/384/66897/1.
175 Petition signed by 367 Belizeans to SS, 11 Feb. 1944, CO 123/388/66925.
176 SS to Hunter, 9 Mar. 1944, CO 123/388/66925.
177 Hunter to SS, 1 Jun. 1944, CO 123/388/66925.
178 Macdonald, report, 8 Sept. 1945, CO 318/460/2.
179 Gov. Sir A. Grimble to SS, 10 Mar. 1945, CO 318/460/2.
180 Admin. to Grimble, 4 Apr. 1945, CO 318/460/2.
181 Gov. Sir Hubert Young to Lloyd, 27 Jul. 1940, CO 318/442/1.
182 George Ogilvie-Forbes to Young, 7 Nov. 1940, CO 318/442/1.
183 David S. Nathan to Attlee, 8 Sept. 1945, CO 318/460/2.
184 British and US interests coincided, but they did remain distinct. While the UK was chiefly concerned with maintaining its empire, the United States defined its imperial ambitions in terms of an anti-communist crusade that was less meaningful to the British.
185 Richards to Col. Oliver Stanley, 29 Dec. 1942, CO 318/447/20.
186 Lethem to Cranborne, 19 Oct. 1942, CO 318/447/20.
187 Gov. Sir G. Bushe to Cranborne, 24 Oct. 1942, CO 318/447/20.
188 Gov. Sir Bede Clifford to Cranborne, 5 Nov. 1942, CO 318/447/20.
189 Gov. Sir Arthur Francis Grimble to Stanley, 23 Oct. 1943, CO 318/447/20.
190 Interview in Barbados, Jan. 1994.
191 Lord Invader, 1941.
192 'The Need for Stocktaking and Review', The Times, 13 Mar. 1942, in Perham 1967: 225-8.

193   Parliamentary Debates (Commons), 24 Jun. 1942, cols. 2014-15.

194   Moyne Commission Report, p. 374.

195   Richards to SS, 5 Nov. 1942, CO 137/849/68714/42.

196   Lord Cranborne, minute, and Sir William Battershill, memorandum, 16 Nov. 1942, CO 137/849/68714/42.

197   Battershill, quoted in Post 1981: Vo. 1, 288.

198   Bustamante to SS, 14 Dec. 1942, CO 137/852/69130.

199   Daily Gleaner, 9 Jan. 1943, 1.

200   Daily Gleaner, 16 Feb. 1943, 4.

201   Stanley, memo, 'Constitutional Changes in Jamaica', 2 Feb. 1943, CO 137/850/68714/7.

202   Richards to Stanley, 12 Mar. 1943, CO 137/849/68714/1943.

203   Paul Blanshard, 'The Political Situation in Jamaica', 20 Sept. 1943, quoted in Post 1981: Vol. 2, 352.

204   Daily Gleaner, 4 Mar. 1944.

205   The Masses, 4 Mar. and 8 Apr. 1944, cited in Post 1981: Vol. 2, 426, 441.

206   Norman Manley to Rita Hinden, 7 May 1943, FCBP Box 142/1B, f.88, RHL.

207   The Masses, 8 May 1943, cited in Post 1981: Vol 2, 321.

208   Daily Gleaner, 10 Jul. 1943.

209   'Aims and Objects of the Jamaica Labour Party', Daily Gleaner, 12 Aug. 1943.

210   Daily Gleaner, 16 Jul. 1943.

211   'Statement of Policy', fifth annual conference of the PNP, 21-22 Aug. 1943, quoted in Post 1981: Vol. 2, 364.

212   The People, 29 Jun. 1940.

213   Report of the Franchise Committee of Trinidad and Tobago; Council Paper No. 35 of 1944 (Government Printer, 1944).

214   ___Ibid.

215   The Vanguard, 16 Mar. 1946.

216   Legislative Council Debates, 22 Nov. 1946.

217   BWU minute book, BWU Archives, Bridgetown.

218   This was reduced to 11 when Springer resigned to become the registrar of the University of the West Indies, established in Jamaica in 1948, and the BLP candidate was defeated in the subsequent by-election.

Chapter 7

The Caribbean Labour Congress
and the Cold War, 1945-52

In 1945, the year that the Caribbean Labour Congress (CLC) was established, several world events encouraged Caribbean people to continue to aspire towards democracy and national liberation. In south and southeast Asia the process of decolonisation and national liberation was already in an advanced stage. The San Francisco conference, convened in April 1945 to establish the United Nations, encouraged nationalist aspirations in the colonies. The Sixth Pan-African Congress, held in Manchester in October 1945, brought together about 100 delegates, 33 of whom came from the Caribbean (Turner and Turner 1988: 192). In a short time, however, the beginning of the Cold War changed this context of decolonisation. The United States, in particular, formulated its policy with regard to the colonial question in the Caribbean and elsewhere in terms of its own self-interest, narrowly defined. Henceforth, issues of democracy and self-determination in colonies were to be evaluated against such priorities as the security of the so-called free world and the value of the colonies to the Western powers in their struggle against international communism. The end of the Second World War marked the end of the old European imperialisms of the UK, France and the Netherlands, and the expansion of the United States' empire that had been firmly established since 1898 (LaFeber 1963).

The Second World War had barely ended when relations between the erstwhile Allies deteriorated rapidly and the Cold War started. The break-up of the economic and political power of Germany and Japan after 1945 appeared to have created power vacuums in eastern Europe and east Asia and this provoked the capitalist world's containment strategy (Van der Wee 1986: 351-2). Winston Churchill's speech at Fulton, Missouri, in March 1946 announced the Cold War and on 12 March 1947 President Truman declared his crusade against communism, known as the Truman Doctrine or the containment policy. On 5 June 1947 the Marshall Plan to reconstruct western Europe was announced and in September 1947 the Soviet Union established Cominform, a new version of the Communist International. Though there were certainly crises and local hot wars, such as occurred in Berlin in 1948 and Korea in 1950, the tensions of the Cold War were manifest primarily in an arms race and a global political polarisation that were quite unprecedented in their scope and nature. The division of the world into two hostile camps, led respectively by the two superpowers, seemed to leave little room for neutrality or for alternative third paths. The Cold War took on the characteristics of a religious war, one of the chief casualties of which is tolerance for the views and values of others.

The impact of the Cold War was pervasive in the Caribbean, both in the nominally independent states and in the colonies, where political and ideological pressures sharply divided many labour movements and political parties supported by labour organisations. Most catastrophic, from the perspective of the growing labour movement and the struggle for democracy and independence in the British Caribbean, was its effect on the CLC, the new regional organisation which seemed to offer the possibility of a popular basis for a federation of socialist-oriented nations. Within a few years the CLC was eviscerated by internal rivalries fed by the Cold War. The demise of this regional organisation and the growth of 'fragmented nationalism' (Knight 1990) in the 1950s contributed to the failure of the Federation of the West Indies, which lasted only from 1958 to 1962.[1] The emergence of independent nations in the British Caribbean after 1962, along with the variety of relations between labour organisations and political parties and the polarisation of political culture in these societies, cannot be explained solely with reference to so-called internal factors, important as they are. Rather, the accelerating crisis in the British empire and the growing influence of the United States, and the political polarisation that was exacerbated by the Cold War, were major factors in shaping the labour movement and the emergence of modern politics in the British Caribbean in the decade after the Second World War.

The origins of the CLC, 1926–45

A Caribbean labour leader and historian has written: 'Most attempts at bringing together Caribbean people into some form of regional political entity, have been impositions from the metropolitan area. This has not been so in relation to the regional labour movement.' (Morris 1985: 1). The origins of the organisation of the CLC lay in the first British Guiana (BG) and West Indies (WI) labour conference, hosted by Hubert Critchlow and his BGLU in Georgetown between 12 and 14 January 1926. Arthur Cipriani and William Howard-Bishop of the TWA, and W.J. Lesperan and W.H. Bastick from the Surinam Porters' Union, participated, along with F.O. Roberts, representing the British Labour Party and TUC, and A.K. Amin and W.D. Dinally of the BG East Indian Association. The conference passed many resolutions on labour reforms and political issues, called for a federation of the West Indies with self-government and dominion status, and appointed a committee to draw up a constitution and rules for a labour federation to be called the Guianese and West Indian Federation of Trade Unions and Labour Parties (GWIFTULP).[2]

The GWIFTULP was little more than an aspiration, as it was virtually inactive between conferences, failed to develop communication between its affiliates and lacked 'even the most rudimentary function of a regional organization' (Harrod 1972: 237), but the ideas expressed in 1926 persisted into the 1940s and were incorporated in the creation of the CLC. The most important ideas were that improvements in the lives of working people depended on legislation and self-government as well as on their own trade unions, and that there should be a federal government as well as a federal labour organisation. The chief purpose of the CLC, when it was created in 1945, was to develop a strong regional labour movement by linking existing trade unions and labour parties, in order to provide a powerful popular base for a strong federal government that would enable Caribbean people to improve their living and working conditions not only through labour and welfare reforms but also by promoting economic development.

Three other labour conferences were held before 1945. The second Guianese and West Indian labour conference, held in Guyana in June 1938, was attended by Cipriani, A. Gooding and L. Thomas of the TLP, Adrian Cola Rienzi and Ralph Mentor of the OWTU, as well as delegates from Guyana and Suriname. Rienzi, who had more influence at this conference than Cipriani, argued that the British Guiana and West Indies Labour Congress (BGWILC), which was formed to replace the GWIFTULP, should aim to transfer 'political and economic power' from the small class of capitalists to the West Indian working class, and coined the slogan, 'Organise, Centralise and Revolutionise' (Basdeo 1983: 183). Rienzi advocated the nationalisation of key industries, particularly oil and sugar, because if 'we desire real freedom and the right to live and to pursue our happiness in the Guianas and West Indies then we must carry out a militant struggle to revolutionise the relationship between man and man – between capital and labour' (Basdeo 1983: 183-4).

The third conference convened in Trinidad between 22 and 30 November 1938, with Grantley Adams from Barbados as well as delegates from Guyana, Trinidad and Suriname. The executive of the BGWILC reflected the fact that support was essentially from the last three of these colonies: Cipriani (Trinidad) president, A.A. Thorne (Guyana) and J.H. Helstone[3] (Suriname) vice-presidents,

Rienzi (Trinidad) general secretary, Critchlow (Guyana) assistant secretary, and C.R. Jacob, A. Edun, Theophilus Lee (Guyana), Mentor (Trinidad), and J. Van Eer (Suriname) committee members. The chief purpose of this conference was to define a regional position that could be presented to the Moyne Commission, whose visit was imminent. The BGWILC pledged to secure the rights of workers to form trade unions and to help organise them, to promote the principle of collective bargaining and the improvement of the conditions of the working class, and to strengthen the intercolonial solidarity of the workers by maintaining contact with trade unions and labour movements in the Caribbean and other parts of the world (Basdeo 1983: 184–5). In addition to this ambitious labour agenda, this conference demanded constitutional reforms, including adult suffrage, purely elected legislatures, executive councils to be elected by and responsible to the legislatures, and the creation of a federated West Indies (Lewis 1977: 53), in short, democracy in a regional nation. Hoyos, who wrote (1974: 84) that Adams drafted a bill embodying a federal constitution, says, 'From this it may be fairly assumed that West Indian federation was regarded as part and parcel of the radical programme that was designed to secure the salvation of the people of the British Caribbean as a whole.'

The fourth BG and WI labour conference, held in Guyana from 28 February to 1 March 1944, followed a 25th anniversary celebration of the BGLU on 27 February. T.A. Marryshow, the veteran West Indian leader from Grenada, and Albert Gomes, the president of the FWU and deputy mayor of Port of Spain, participated. A significant difference of opinion emerged between Gomes and Colin Fraser, the commissioner of labour in Guyana. When Fraser commented that it was 'nothing short of a disgrace' that the BGLU had only 500 members (it claimed to have 1,489 members, of whom 437 were financial), Gomes retorted that 'this sententious and patronizing manner must cease once and for all'. He added that he recognised the limitations of trade unions, and said that 'ultimately the salvation of these Colonies will not come through Trade Unionism' but 'only by establishing political organizations on very broad lines'. The next day, when Fraser's deputy argued that it was a trade union conference and he was concerned only with trade union issues, Vivian Henry of the TLP responded that it was a conference of both trade unions and political parties, dealing with industrial, social, and political issues. H.J.M. Hubbard, general secretary of the British Guiana TUC, urged the closer cooperation of trade unions because 'any political development that is to benefit the working people must be based on a strong Trade Union movement.'[4]

This exchange revealed two sources of tension: first, between the colonial officials and the labour delegates, and second, between delegates whose interests emphasised working–class or more general political goals. On the first, it was clearly the colonial administration's goal, following the policy of the Colonial Office and the practice of the British TUC,[5] to keep trade union issues apart from political ones, whereas the new labour leaders in the British Caribbean saw the two as intimately interrelated in the broad labour movement. On the second, however, it appears that tensions were emerging between those like Gomes and Henry, who saw the trade unions essentially as vehicles for their middle-class political ambitions, and those like Hubbard for whom the growth of a powerful political movement, that would be based on and also controlled by the organised working class, was essential for the establishment of a socialist society, the chief beneficiaries of which would be the working people themselves. These tensions and distinctions became sharper in the next decade when middle-class politicians, like Gomes and Adams, became dominant with the support of British policy. The labour movement that had emerged, at considerable cost, from the rebellions of the 1930s became captured by these aspiring and largely middle-class politicians, and most trade unions became essentially subservient to the political parties, whether or not they were called labour parties. Hence, the working class lost its autonomous voice and organisations almost as soon as they had appeared. But in 1944 this outcome was far from clear and was yet to be contested in most of the colonies.

Among the other issues discussed in the 1944 conference, two seem to have been novel, suggesting important future developments. First, a resolution was passed calling for the free and unimpeded movement of labour leaders between the colonies, an issue that arose again in the 1950s as a result of Cold War hysteria. Second, Henry introduced a motion deploring the 99-year leases the UK had given to the United States for its Caribbean bases, and Gomes added that 'the Americans have come here and have simply become a party to the whole existing feudal set up'.[6] The resentment about this deal between the imperial powers, made over the heads of West Indians, continued to provoke nationalist feelings. The protracted struggle over the Chaguaramas base in Trinidad re-emerged in 1957, when Eric Williams tried to have the base returned to the West Indies as the site for the federal capital. The issue took on symbolic significance and the march that Williams led to the US consulate in 1960, demanding the return of the base, has been called 'the militant high point of Trinidad nationalism' (Oxaal 1968: 133). The West Indian nationalists insisted that it was their right to be able to negotiate this matter. It is important to note that the issue of American power being allowed into the British Caribbean through the back door, before West Indians themselves had any say in the matter, was already being discussed at this regional labour conference in 1944.

Marryshow, who had led the Grenada Workingmen's Association (GWA), attended the regional conference in 1944 as the president of the Grenada Labour

Party (GLP). He had organised a peaceful demonstration in Grenada in 1938, in solidarity with the workers' struggles in other colonies, but at that time the GWA was 'virtually extinct and in the process of being replaced by the Grenada Labour Party - General Workers' Union' (Sheppard 1987: 37). His presence not only marked the first participation of a Grenadian, thereby broadening the regional representation at the conference, though it was still from the south-eastern Caribbean, but also emphasised its West Indian orientation. In 1944 the BGWILC moved from a British-influenced labour movement in 1926 to a more middle-class nationalist movement, with a strong federal and socialist component (Braithwaite 1957), reflecting the influence of men like Cipriani, Marryshow, Adams and Gomes. Its officers in 1944 were Cipriani, president; Marryshow and Thorne, vice-presidents; Henry, general secretary; Critchlow, assistant secretary; Gooding, treasurer; and Jacob, Lee, Edun, Adams, Gomes and T.O. Jean (of the OWTU) were committee members.[7] The labour delegates in Guyana agreed to meet in 1945 in Barbados, to develop a stronger regional labour congress.

The founding conference of the CLC was held in Barbados between 17 and 27 September 1945, convened by the Barbados Workers' Union (BWU). Twenty-six delegates and five observers came from many parts of the British Caribbean and from Suriname. For the first time there were delegates from Antigua (Vere Bird, Harold T. Wilson and J. Oliver Davis), Bermuda (Dr E.F. Gordon), Jamaica (Richard Hart, representing the PNP and JTUC), St Lucia and St Vincent (St Clair Bonadie and George McIntosh). Notably, this was the first time there was direct contact between labour organisations in Jamaica and those of the eastern Caribbean and Guyana, though the largest Jamaican union, the BITU, eschewed participation. Among the other delegates were Adams, Springer and Frank Walcott of Barbados, G.A. Glean and Marryshow of Grenada, Critchlow, Lee and Thorne of Guyana, G. Van den Stoom and Lesperan of Suriname,[8] and Gomes, Henry, Dudley Mahon, C.B. Mathura, Mentor, McDonald Moses and T.E. Simpson from Trinidad and Tobago. Among this virtual 'Who's Who' of Caribbean labour leaders there were several veterans, including Critchlow and Lesperan, who had been at the first regional conference in 1926.

The most obvious omission at the conference was Alexander Bustamante. Apparently, he had been sent an invitation but did not reply (Hart 1982: 84). Nor was there any representation from the Man-Power Citizens' Association (MPCA), which was the chief union of the mostly Indian field workers in the Guyanese sugar industry, though its leaders, Jacob and Edun, had been committee members of the CLC's precursor in 1944. Thorne's BG Sugar Estates and Factory Workers' Union had declining support among the mostly African factory workers and none among the field workers. Nor was Uriah Butler's organisation in Trinidad or Wynter Crawford's in Barbados represented, apparently because of the influence of their rivals (Hart 1982: 85). In spite of these omissions, however, the number of delegates, together with the number and range of organisations and colonies they represented, indicates that this was the first broadly Caribbean labour conference.[9] Even St Kitts, which was unable to send a delegate, participated by briefing Hart with proposals. On 20 September the conference received a cable from three other prominent labour leaders, Rupert Gittens, Ken Hill and John Rojas, who were on their way to the World Trade Union Conference in Paris and asked if they could be authorised to represent the West Indies collectively. The delegates in Barbados agreed to this unanimously.[10]

The conference began with the delegates standing in silence to honour the late Captain Cipriani. Adams, as the host, made the opening address in which he opined that 'there is no hope for the West Indies unless they become a Socialist Commonwealth. On any other condition, with mingled races, with insular prejudices and with the age-old habit of suspecting everybody else - and at sometimes even ourselves - we will get nowhere'.[11] There was outspoken criticism of US influence and ambitions in the Caribbean. Marryshow was cheered when he said they were all loyalists who wanted to stay in the British Commonwealth because there were 'certain American Senators who desire to take over the West Indies as though we were so many chattels'.[12] Several delegates spoke against the US bases continuing, some of them specifically referring to the obnoxious social influences of US personnel in their societies. Wilson said that the bad behaviour of US troops in Antigua had accentuated racial feeling and demoralised the people, and McIntosh said that in St Vincent, where there was not a base, women were still debased by visiting US troops.[13]

Hart made an important speech in which he urged that theirs should be one congress for both democratic trade unions and pro-labour political organisations, presumably intending thereby to exclude or put pressure on Bustamante's union for its undemocratic structure and procedures. Hart developed a strong economic argument for a political federation, as the dependent economies could develop only as a whole. This whole was to include the mainland territories of Belize and Guyana where, as in Jamaica, there were many acres of unused but cultivable land. Hart argued that the people of the region should import less and produce more food for local consumption. He continued, 'Economics could not of course be divorced from politics. Only by achieving power to control their own affairs would the West Indies be able to protect their new or developing industries from the dumping of European or American or other foreign goods'.[14]

Mentor said that 'it would be a waste of time to have merely a loose federation .... What was wanted was the transfer to the West Indies of the political power at present exercised at Downing Street'.[15] Springer urged the conference to establish an organisation through which they could work together, for as long as necessary, until 'the ultimate goal was reached of federation with real autonomy for the whole region'.[16] The delegates agreed to recommend the establishment of a West Indian university. (Two years later, when the University College of the West Indies was established in Jamaica, Springer left the BWU to become its registrar).

Adams addressed a vitally important economic issue when he urged the delegates to declare a policy on land tenure, advocating the nationalisation of the sugar industry and the abolition of the private ownership of large units of land.[17] He also supported the idea that the different constitutional statuses of the various colonies should not impede progress towards federation. He proposed that a federal constitution similar to Australia's should be a model, but that 'federation should not await the establishment of representative government in every colony. Each colony must work out its own pattern of development'.[18] In accordance with Adams' suggestion, the conference, while advocating that all the colonies of the British Caribbean should be granted entirely elected legislatures, based on universal adult suffrage and with executive councils responsible to them, agreed to keep this issue distinct from the establishment of a West Indian federation. The secretary of state for the colonies, Oliver Stanley, had stated on 14 March 1945 that a self-governing West Indian federation was the ultimate goal of the British government, so Adams and the other delegates were supporting and trying to advance this accepted policy more rapidly. However, the delegates, following those to the other regional labour conferences since 1926, viewed the federal ideal as a crucial goal and a means to their pursuit of democracy, socialism and national liberation, which was not how the British government saw it.

Marryshow was elected the president of the CLC and the other officers were Critchlow, Adams and Gomes, as first, second and third vice-presidents, respectively, Springer as treasurer, and Henry and Hart as the secretary and assistant secretary, respectively. The membership of the provisional council, which consisted of Hart, Bird, Grant, Walcott, Mentor, Mahon, Thorne, Lee and Lesperan, shows that the intention was to maintain broad representation and involvement from all the participating parts of the region. Henry, who was a solicitor and member of the TLP, had been the secretary of the previous conference in 1944. According to Hart, he 'did not conceive of his office as requiring any activity between conferences' and 'dissatisfaction at the Secretary's inactivity increased' (Hart 1982: 85). Consequently, at a meeting of the CLC council in Antigua in January 1947, Hart was appointed in his place. He became the most energetic member of the CLC in its most active period.

The growth of the CLC and
the conference in Jamaica, 1947

The broad coalition of labour leaders and politicians that constituted the CLC in its first years represented a socialist spectrum from social democrats of Fabian complexion to Marxists who wanted working–class control and regional economic planning. Whatever brand of socialism they espoused, however, the CLC Council members adhered to a strong federal ideal. Unlike the Colonial Office, which saw federation as a convenient administrative device, for the CLC members 'federation meant self–government and dominion status, those concepts in turn being conceived as essential instruments for the overall planning and development of the Caribbean area as an integral part of the larger world economy' (Lewis 1968: 345). For just three years the CLC, with a strong voice, articulated the need for unity in the regional labour movement and connected this with the aspiration towards democracy, independence and a socialist Caribbean federation.

The CLC council met in Antigua in January 1947 in order to discuss federation proposals. The council consisted of the president, Marryshow (Grenada); the vice-presidents, Critchlow (Guyana), Adams (Barbados) and Gomes (Trinidad and Tobago); the treasurer, Springer (Barbados); the secretary, Hart (Jamaica); the assistant secretary, Robert L. Bradshaw (St Kitts); and the members, Bird (Antigua) and Manley (Jamaica). The membership shows that, while there was broader participation from the British Caribbean colonies than before, Suriname, which had been active for 20 years in the CLC and its predecessors, seems no longer to have been involved. The council circulated a statement concerning federation proposals to all CLC affiliates before the CLC conference, which was to be held in Kingston, Jamaica, in September 1947, just a few days before the Montego Bay conference organised by the Colonial Office to discuss closer union of the British colonies. Although delegates from trade unions and political parties from other states and colonies were invited, the chief focus of the agenda and the concern of most delegates was the political and constitutional development of the Commonwealth Caribbean.

Thirty-four delegates from 15 colonies, representing 27 trade unions and labour parties, participated in the CLC conference in Kingston. This was the high point for the CLC. No delegates came from Suriname but the Aruba Labour Union was represented. The vice-president of the Socialist Party of Panama, José Brouwer, attended as an observer and was applauded when he warned the delegates of the dangers of 'American Imperialism'.[19] There was a popular struggle in Panama at that time against the continuing US occupation of military bases obtained during the war (Priestley 1986: 15), an issue that echoed around the Caribbean. Trade unions and political organisations in Puerto Rico and the French and Dutch colonies were invited to send delegates. The Communist Party in Martinique declined and there was no reply from Guadeloupe, Curaçao or Puerto Rico.[20] A delegate, Henry Middleton, came from the General Workers' Union (GWU) of Belize, and representatives of the MPCA of Guyana and the Congress Party of Barbados also participated. The participation of delegates, like the membership of the CLC Council, shows that the organisation was expanding within but not really beyond the British Caribbean colonies, and the concerns of the conference reflected this.

On the eve of the CLC conference in Kingston, Bird, the president of the Antigua Trades and Labour Union, said that he wanted to see 'one big socialist labour union throughout the Caribbean .... We want a West Indian nation'.[21] When referring to the Caribbean, however, he, like so many people from the English-speaking West Indies, meant only the Anglophone Caribbean. Manley, in a speech at the conference on 2 September, likewise focused on the future of the British Caribbean colonies: 'I reject totally any sort of mis-marriage between colonial rule and federation and I would predict for such a marriage such an abortion as politics has never seen, and I say that a federated West Indies cannot aim at any smaller immediate objective than dominion status (applause). I cannot imagine what we should be federating about if it is not to achieve the beginning of nationhood'.[22]

Richard B. Moore, the Barbadian secretary of the New York-based American Committee for West Indian Federation, submitted his 'Memorandum on Federation and Self-Government of the West Indies', in which he advocated a democratic and independent federation (Turner and Turner 1988: 279-83). The delegates agreed 'that the West Indies must unite with the mainland colonies of British Honduras and British Guiana, under one flag, for one Caribbean Commonwealth'.[23] It was resolved that each territory should be granted a similar constitution, providing universal adult suffrage and internal self-government, simultaneously with the creation of the federation, which would have a prime minister and Cabinet responsible to the federal Parliament and having power over 'regional planning and economic development'.[24]

Those delegates from the CLC who were going to the Montego Bay conference were expected to press for the policy decided upon at the CLC conference in Kingston. However, Arthur Creech Jones, the secretary of state for the colonies who chaired the Montego Bay conference, undermined the CLC's position by stating that the subject of a self-governing federation 'was rather outside the immediate terms of reference of this Conference' (quoted in Mordechai 1968: 36). Whereas the concept of federation for the Colonial Office 'meant merely a loose confederal association', for the CLC 'it meant a strong federal state ... a vehicle for democratic social growth' (Lewis 1968: 348). Hart, the CLC's secretary, subsequently wrote that the principal differences between the Colonial Office plan and the CLC's proposals were:

(a) The constitution would not provide for Independence simultaneously with the inauguration of the Federation, but instead would provide for a federal government enjoying less self-governing powers than the constitution already obtained by Jamaica.

(b) The federal constitution was to be a loose structure and the federal government was not to enjoy strong centralized powers such as would have enabled it to plan industrialization of the whole area according to a unified plan and control customs duties in a manner which would have facilitated implementation of a common trading policy.[25]

The fundamental difference between these conceptions of the federation was less political and constitutional than economic. After the Second World War, as in the 1930s, the UK's colonial development policies were driven chiefly by its own economic crisis. Consequently, the Colonial Office sought to increase the productivity of the colonies to meet the UK's urgent needs, not to develop the colonial economies in order that they should become more self-sustaining and meet the needs of their own people, as the CLC desired. The most striking example of the distortions and failures of this policy was the Tanganyika groundnut scheme, a project that demonstrated how 'colonialism and development were largely contradictory' (Havinden and Meredith 1993: 317). Some labour leaders of the CLC, like Hart, understood this point in 1947, which is one reason why they wanted to achieve an independent federation at an early date.

The federal concept held by the CLC was a progressive ideal in this period after the Second World War, and with a well-run and unified campaign the CLC could have obtained broad support for its proposals. However, divisions began to appear among some of the CLC's leaders, in part because some of them were poised to benefit from proposed constitutional reforms in their own colonies and were consequently unwilling to offend the Colonial Office by promoting public agitation for a more radical programme. Hence, when the Colonial Office rejected the CLC's proposal for federation as 'precipitate and unfeasible' (Mordecai 1968: 38), some of the political leaders in the CLC, including Adams, Gomes and Manley, accepted the fateful compromise of the gradual, reductive approach in which each territorial unit was left to secure what constitutional advance it could. Above all, however, the CLC's preoccupation with the issue of constitutional reforms in the British Caribbean colonies, a preoccupation that reflected and favoured the parochial inclinations of the middle-class politicians, led the labour organisation to neglect the broader development of a strong regional labour confederation and its local components. The result was an increasing focus on local campaigns for constitutional reform, and when the CLC was threatened by the splits in the international trade union movement caused by the Cold War it was too weak and divided to survive.

Divisions in the CLC, 1948

Cracks were beginning to appear in the CLC in 1948, between Hart on the left wing and Gomes and Adams on the right, but it was the great split in the international labour movement in 1949, when the superpowers' Cold War rivalry divided the World Federation of Trade Unions (WFTU), that led to the division and destruction of the CLC in the early 1950s.

Hart organised a meeting of trade unions and political organisations in Trinidad on 4 July 1948, to agitate against the majority report of a constitutional reform committee that had been created in 1947 to recommend changes. Gomes, a former vice-president of the CLC who had called for responsible government in 1946, had reversed his position and, as a member of the Executive Council of Trinidad and Tobago, he claimed that abandoning the nominated system would be a threat to stable government. Progressive members of the committee, like Mentor and Dr Patrick Solomon, resigned from the committee, but Gomes signed the majority report which called for a majority of elected members in the legislature and an equal balance between elected and nominated elements in the Executive Council. After the meeting organised by Hart, which unanimously supported the recommendations of the minority report calling for a fully elected single chamber legislature of 25 members elected on the basis of adult suffrage, Quintin O'Connor, secretary of the FWTU, who had originally agreed with the majority report, agreed to withdraw his signature and support the demand for an elected majority on the Executive Council.

The secretary of state for the colonies decided against the majority report and in favour of an elected majority on the council (which would consist of five elected members, three ex officio and one nominated), which was a 'marginal improvement on what had been asked for in the majority report' (Hart 1998: 148) and a cautious step towards a quasi-ministerial constitution. When it became law in April 1950 the constitution was attacked by nationalist groups and the labour movement for not going far enough, but Gomes continued to oppose unequivocal self-government (Brereton 1981: 196-7). What emerged in mid-1948, therefore, was a public division between the CLC's secretary and Gomes over the development of fully responsible government in Trinidad and Tobago.

Hart went on to Guyana where he organised a public meeting of labour and political organizations in favour of self-government, at which Critchlow and Cheddi Jagan were said to be the most popular speakers.[26] In 1946, Cheddi and Janet Jagan, with the trade unionists Hubbard and Ashton Chase, had formed the Political Affairs Committee (PAC), a group that crossed ethnic divisions to assist the progressive labour movement and achieve self-government.

For the elections in late 1947, the first held in Guyana since 1935, qualifications for voters were reduced to an income of $10 per month, so the number of employed voters increased. A hastily formed Labour Party[27] contested three seats and, because of the broader franchise, Cheddi Jagan won in Central Demerara, with the support of an Afro-Guyanese schoolteacher, Sydney King. Jagan entered the Legislature on 18 December 1947 at the age of 29 (Spinner 1984: 24-5). Critchlow won in South Georgetown, but the Supreme Court declared his election null and void and barred him from contesting a seat for five years (Chase n.d.: 125). Although elected members were in the majority for the first time since 1928, and the Executive Council had an unofficial majority, the latter could only advise the governor, who retained considerable power.

On 16 June 1948, after five sugar workers were shot and killed by police at a strike on the Enmore Estates, the Jagans led a funeral march 16 miles from Enmore to Georgetown. It was in this politically charged context that Hart visited Guyana in July, when he conferred with leaders of the BGLU, MPCA, BGTUC, PAC, the League of Coloured People and the East Indian Association, who co-sponsored the public meeting at which Hart, Cheddi Jagan and Critchlow spoke for the campaign for self-government. It was agreed that the campaign should be coordinated by the BGTUC, and on 1 August a demonstration marched through Georgetown demanding self-government (Hart 1982: 87-8).

In July 1948, therefore, in Trinidad and Guyana, Hart was promoting the goals of the CLC as they had been articulated at the 1945 and 1947 conferences, specifically to encourage the campaign for self-government in the several units of the proposed federation, none of them at that time having progressed as far as the Jamaican constitution of 1944. In so doing, however, Hart, who was one of the leading figures of the Jamaican left and an outspoken anti-imperialist, was involved with some of the more radical people in Trinidad and Guyana, a fact that was not lost on Adams, who had become the CLC president. It was Adams' speech at the United Nations in Paris on 13 October 1948 that widened the rift between him and Hart and seriously damaged the unity of the CLC.

Adams was invited to join the British delegation at the United Nations General Assembly meeting in Paris to debate the issue of decolonisation. He had ostensibly espoused the cause of socialism for many years, had taken an interest in colonial territories beyond the Caribbean and had been influenced by the Fabian Society and Creech Jones, with whom he had been in contact since the time of the Barbados labour rebellion in 1937 (Hoyos 1974: 133). Creech Jones, who was the colonial secretary in 1948, trusted Adams to defend the empire in this debate. Adams did not let him down, but in so doing he aroused the feelings of African and Asian nationalists as well as the anti-imperialist forces in the Caribbean.

The issue being debated in Paris was whether the United Nations should exercise any control or supervision over colonial affairs, comparable with the mandates system of the former League of Nations. Adams accepted the colonial policy of the British government, so the Fabian Society in its journal welcomed his appointment to the delegation:

> Mr Grantley Adams, leader of the Barbados House of Assembly and an out-standing figure in the Caribbean Labour Congress, regards his inclusion in the delegation as an indication of Britain's willingness to give colonials more say in their own affairs, and he believes that the Labour Government is prepared to grant complete responsibility as soon as the colonies are in a position to take it. He is all the more anxious, therefore, to avoid increased intervention from outside and is implacably opposed to all attempts to place the colonies under the supervision of the United Nations.[28]

Adams had stated, in an interview with George Padmore, the Trinidadian Pan-Africanist: 'The future political status of the West Indies is an issue between the peoples of these colonies and the British Government and any attempt to divert this struggle and turn the colonies into political footballs in the game of international power politics will be strongly resented and resisted by respon-sible leaders of all shades of opinion'.[29] Perhaps Adams, like Cipriani before him, placed too much trust in the British Labour Party to promote the process of decolonisation, and perhaps he hoped the trusteeship council of the United Nations would not become a mere platform for political propaganda struggles between the superpowers in their Cold War. He may also have thought that his rising position in Barbados and in a potential West Indian federation depended on his continuing good relations with the British government. Whatever his motives, Adams' speech to the UN actually provoked the kind of clash that he said he aimed to avoid.

In response to a Russian proposal calling upon the colonial powers to provide the trusteeship council with information concerning the political and constitu-tional status of non-self-governing territories, Adams declared, as Creech Jones wanted him to, that the British government made such changes public but did not feel required to provide changes in such a way that they could become the subject for debate at the United Nations. He added, provocatively:

> The colonial peoples, as the months pass and as we read the accounts of what goes on in the various organs of the United Nations are inclined to become disillusioned, even somewhat cynical, as to the practical contributions the United Nations seem to be making to the advancement and welfare of the Trust Territory peoples. It seems that their affairs are being discussed within

the context of power politics – and more particularly rival ideologies – and that in the clash of their extraneous interests the real interest of the colonial peoples tends to be overlooked.[30]

Colonial affairs have always been a matter of 'power politics', of course, but Adams opposed the Russian proposal on the grounds that its subject was simply a domestic affair between the British government and its colonial territories. In response to the criticism that he was merely the mouthpiece of a metropolitan power and a traitor to his own people, Adams claimed that he spoke as the elected representative not only of the Barbados House of Assembly but also of the CLC: 'I shall be so immodest as to say that I have been elected President of a Congress of all the democratic labour organisations and trade unions in the British Caribbean area – a socialist Congress which includes even some organisations in the Netherlands Antilles. These people know whether I am merely the mouthpiece of an oppressing, exploiting Government or not'.[31]

Whether Adams was or was not anyone's mouthpiece, the British authorities were undoubtedly delighted when he staunchly defended their colonial policy, as this was what Creech Jones had chosen him for. The governor of Barbados reported that Adams' speech made a 'profound impression' when it was broadcast there, 'First, that it fell to a coloured son of Barbados to defend British Colonial Policy and, second, that it was "de leader" who was that man'.[32] Whatever feelings people in Barbados may have had, Adams' support of British colonial policy provoked widespread criticism elsewhere, from Africa, from the Pan African Federation[33] in London, from the American Committee for West Indian Federation and from the secretary of the CLC, Hart. Stating that Adams had not consulted other leaders of the CLC and so should not have claimed to have spoken on this topic on their behalf, Hart denounced Adams in the CLC Monthly Bulletin:

> We of the Caribbean area hoped for a clear enunciation of our demand for a self-governing Dominion . . . . We were disappointed. But our disappointment cannot be compared to the sense of betrayal which must have been felt by the workers' movements in other parts of the colonial empire where the hand of imperialism is today falling more heavily and viciously than anything we can conceive from our experience . . . . The President of the Caribbean Labour Congress has, on one of the most important issues of all time, thrown away the golden opportunity to be the champion of the cause of colonial peoples everywhere struggling for freedom.[34]

Adams responded by saying, 'The most charitable construction I can put on Mr Hart's indifference to the truth is that an attack on his beloved Russia has temporarily unbalanced the state of his mind'.[35]

Hoyos, Adams' biographer, avers that Hart naively ignored the realities of the international situation, but this may be said more accurately of Adams. Adams' charge that Hart was motivated solely by his love of Russia was accompanied by a complaint that the issue of decolonisation should not become part of a Cold War struggle, which was surely a naive position to take in 1948. It is true that Cold War propaganda, from both sides, would affect the terms of the debate about decolonisation, but the 'cause of colonial peoples' was not invalidated simply because it received support from the USSR. In fact, Adams had been used by the British government in a propaganda counter-offensive to defend its colonial policy, as the governor of Barbados said, and this sorely divided the CLC. Walcott, general secretary of the BWU, sprang to Adams' defence and denounced Hart's charges as 'highly irresponsible' and unauthorised by the CLC executive,[36] and Wills Isaacs, vice-president of the PNP, made a similar criticism of Hart in Jamaica.[37]

Divisions were deepening in the CLC, along lines shaped by the Cold War, even before the crucial split in the WFTU in 1949. Even if there had not been a climate of Cold War propaganda, the division between Adams and Hart would probably have occurred because they perceived the nature and urgency of the anti-imperial struggle quite differently. Adams was in the middle of a campaign for the Barbados general election of December 1948 and his return from the United Nations trip was the occasion of a massive rally by his supporters, organised in part by Walcott. Adams' speech at the United Nations in Paris had made him appear an international spokesman and helped increase his stature in relation to Crawford of the Congress Party. The BLP's campaign 'reflected more the increasing political conservatism of Adams' leadership than an interest in socialism which had been the vision of the party's rank and file' (Beckles 1990: 188). The result confirmed the trend of 1946, with the BLP increasing its share of the popular vote to 60 per cent and winning 16 seats, to four for the Electors' Association and only two for the Congress Party. Adams, whose 'vision of political change and development in the island was in line with imperial policy' (Beckles 1990: 188), was the chief beneficiary of these changes and policies in Barbados, as Bustamante and Gomes were in Jamaica and Trinidad, respectively, at this time. These three men, who began their political careers as labour leaders and critics of colonialism, and even as self-professed socialists, became the leaders of conservatism under the Cold War guise of anti-communism.

The split in the WFTU in 1949 and the decline of the CLC

From the inception of the WFTU in 1945, there were differences among its members, including ideological differences expressed in terms of whether trade union work should or should not be closely linked with broader political action, such as the anticolonial struggle. With the development of the Cold War these differences became irreconcilable and the WFTU split in 1949 along Cold War lines, with drastic consequences for many colonial trade unions including the CLC. British and US trade unions, as well as the British and US governments, played a key role in these developments.

The Colonial Office encouraged the participation of the British TUC in its policy of attempting to duplicate the British pattern of trade unions and indus- trial relations in its colonies. The assumption was that the new colonial unions needed supervision, control and guidance (Harrod 1972: 371). As we have seen, some members of the British labour movement had shown an interest in the emerging Caribbean labour movement for several years before the Second World War. Sir Walter Citrine, the general secretary of the British TUC from 1926 to 1946, went to the Caribbean as a member of the Moyne Commission 'equipped with rule books and union publications in readiness for discussions with existing and potential union leaders' (Nicholson 1986: 228). Citrine gave advice, whether solicited or not, to labour organisations in Trinidad, Jamaica, Barbados, St Vincent, St Lucia and Antigua. Gomes later referred to the British TUC's involvement as 'an instance of colonial paternalism at its best' (Gomes 1974: 42), but not all the British involvement was as innocent as it was made to seem. After Fred Dalley, a British TUC adviser, visited Trinidad and Tobago in 1947 he sent his 'Notes on some of the personalities in the Trade Union and Labour World of Trinidad' to the Colonial Office.[38] He was, to put it bluntly, a spy.

British trade union leaders assumed that their movement and organisations, their goals and procedures, provided the model for the nascent unions of the colonies. One consequence of this assumption was that the TUC's definition of responsible trade unionism, which 'stressed the separation between indus- trial disputes and militant political action' (Craig 1977: 79), coincided with the Colonial Office's labour policy. This paternalistic policy of the British TUC, which encouraged colonial trade unions and tried to develop a trade union international organisation which would not be engaged in the anti-imperialist struggle, helps to explain what happened to the CLC between 1945 and 1952.

The British TUC hosted the world conference of trade unions in London in February 1945 that established the basis for the Paris conference that became the first congress of the WFTU in October of that year. The London conference emphasised the need to end economic exploitation and to work for protective labour legislation and trade union rights in the colonies, issues that were still highly political in the colonies themselves, where they were generally linked to the issues of democratic rights and self-government. Nevertheless, Citrine pointedly told delegates at the Paris conference:

> Our job here is to build a trade union international, an International to carry

on practical day-to-day trade union work, to guide the activities of our different trade union centres and to receive practical results for the individual members of our unions . . . . I heard one speaker say yesterday that his organization was going to join the International because his country wanted their national independence and he wished to establish socialism. However laudable these desires may be, the World Federation of Trade Unions is not the medium whereby that is to be done . . . . If once we get into the maze of politics, as surely as I am standing at this rostrum, the International will perish. It will split, because the different conceptions of political aspiration, desire, method and policy are so wide that they would divide us. (Quoted in Nicholson 1986: 249)

The British TUC actively cooperated with the WFTU which, at the executive level, was controlled administratively by British and French unions which insisted on their prerogatives in areas for which they claimed responsibility. Thus, when Russian and US delegates attempted in 1947 to set up a fund to help colonial trade unions, this was vetoed by Arthur Deakin, the British president of the WFTU (Davies 1966: 190). The problem for liberal unionists like Citrine and Deakin was that, in the colonies at least, trade unionism was irrevocably inside 'the maze of politics'. When the metropolitan trade unionists, who had their own conception of the politics of labour, found they could no longer control the activities and agenda of the WFTU, they withdrew and set up a rival international organisation that would play by their rules.

Labour leaders in the British Caribbean were optimistic that the WFTU would prove helpful in their struggle and some participated in the international organisation from its beginning. Ken Hill, of the Jamaica TUC, was a participant at both the London and Paris conferences in 1945 and he was also at the WFTU meeting in Rome in 1948. As we have seen, he, Rojas and Gittens of Trinidad and Tobago were authorised by the founding conference of the CLC in Barbados to represent the West Indian labour movement collectively at the Paris conference. As the British TUC did not permit the affiliation of colonial unions, these Caribbean labour leaders saw the WFTU as providing an opportunity for international affiliation and perhaps also for financial support. However, from the beginning, the political goals of these men contradicted Citrine's more limited conception of the role of the international organisation. When the split occurred in the WFTU in 1949 it created a massive and irreversible division within the labour movement in the British Caribbean, some of whose leaders adhered to the rump of the WFTU while others joined the new rival International Confederation of Free Trade Unions (ICFTU).

After the British, Dutch and US unions withdrew from the WFTU in 1949 the British government quickly brought pressure to bear on the unions in the colonies to follow suit. In August the secretary of state for the colonies wrote to the Caribbean governors about the world labour congress that was being planned for November, at which the new international organisation would be created:

> In view of the special attention which is now being given to the Colonies by the Communist dominated World Federation of Trade Unions, it is of the highest importance that Colonial trade union bodies should be affiliated where possible to the new non-Communist Organisation. I hope therefore that it will be possible for the representatives selected by the local unions to take advantage of the invitation and I should be grateful if all possible assistance including if necessary financial assistance could be given to this end.[39]

The Colonial Office was not suddenly converted to help the colonial unions in their struggle, but was trying to recruit support for an anti-communist crusade in the intensifying Cold War.

Although some Caribbean labour leaders, such as Hart and Rojas, held a view of imperialism that led them to adhere to the rump of the WFTU, others, such as Adams and Manley, had become 'wedded to the parliamentary system in which they had already begun to share ... [and they] shared to an exceptional degree the British Labour view of politics and of trade unionism' (Nicholson 1986: 258). The split in the WFTU and the creation of the ICFTU, which reflected the deepening rift of the Cold War, not only divided the emerging Caribbean labour movement but also led to the disintegration of its regional organisation, the CLC, which Adams and Manley dismantled when their unions became affiliated with the ICFTU.

Several Caribbean labour leaders promptly accepted the invitation to participate in the inaugural meeting of the ICFTU, including Bradshaw, president of the St Kitts-Nevis Trades and Labour Union (SKNTLU) and the assistant secretary of the CLC, and Adams, who was president of both the BWU and the CLC. Some problems were created in Guyana, where separate invitations were sent to the BGTUC, the BGLU and the MPCA. When Critchlow, who was said by the secretary of the BGTUC to represent only the 'negligible minority' of trade unionists who were in the BGLU, was offered a grant to attend the conference, this created friction between the BGTUC and its affiliates.[40] The BGTUC, which had joined the WFTU in 1945, left it but did not try to affiliate with the ICFTU until 1952, by which time Guyana was becoming drawn into a Cold War crisis.

The situations in Trinidad and Jamaica in 1949 were far more complicated than that in Guyana. In both places serious divisions in the labour movement, caused by the international split resulting from the Cold War, were already apparent in that year. By the end of 1948, the TTTUC represented some 27 registered trade unions, including nine of the major unions, claiming a combined membership of 20,000 workers who were concentrated in key industrial areas including the sugar and oil industries, the waterfront and public works. Unions began to work more closely together at this time. According to Ron Ramdin, 'This consolidation of labour meant that the TUC, largely composed of all the active and influential Unions, came to be regarded as being fully representative of all organised labour' (1982: 163), but this unity was brief. Up to 1949, all the unions affiliated with the TTTUC regarded the WFTU as their international labour organisation, but the invitation to participate in the new ICFTU led to a split in the TTTUC.

In 1949 the TTTUC was led by Rojas and Mentor, who were also the president and secretary, respectively, of the OWTU. In January, in an article in Vanguard, Rojas condemned the effort to split the world labour movement, saying that, while the British TUC had never granted affiliation to colonial trade unions, the WFTU had 'proven to be a useful instrument in fighting the workers' battles. Colonial workers are shamelessly exploited and . . . have very strong reason to frown upon the move calculated to destroy the effectiveness of the Federation'.[41] In May some 5,000 workers in San Fernando heard Rojas pledge the TTTUC's support for the CLC and WFTU.[42] In July Rojas followed this with an article in the CLC Monthly Bulletin in which he criticised the British TUC for having done or said nothing when the British government denied Trinidad and Tobago the right to self-determination. He urged all trade union organisations to pledge loyalty to the WFTU.[43]

Trinidad's commissioner of labour, Solomon Hochoy, met several trade union leaders, separately, early in October in order to ascertain their positions vis-a-vis the WFTU and the invitation to the rival conference in London. The TTTUC met on 5 October and divided, with the majority of delegates voting to reject the invitation.[44] On the one hand, Rojas and Mentor of the OWTU, and Mahon, O'Connor and Simeon Alexander of the FWTU, declined the invitation on the grounds that participation in the proposed conference would be inconsistent with their affiliation with the WFTU. On the other hand, leaders of the Seamen and Waterfront Workers' Trade Union (SWWTU) and the Railway Workers' Trade Union (RWTU) opposed this decision and promptly withdrew from the TTTUC. C.P. Alexander, the president of the SWWTU, agreed to represent his union and the RWTU at the London conference.[45] The acting governor of Trinidad and Tobago indicated that Hochoy had tried, on his instructions, to get the TTTUC to associate with the new international organisation by offering them financial assistance. He commented that Rojas, Mentor and O'Connor 'have no particular liking for Moscow doctrines, but that they are ready to embrace any cause which will embarrass the Government'. He appeared pleased that:

Mr Hochoy's efforts, at any rate, ensured that the invitation was known and the importance of the decision was fully appreciated. The result has been a split in the Colony's trade unionism .... But the main body of trade union-ism in the country ... will remain affiliated to the WFTU so long as Messrs. Rojas, Mentor and Quintin O'Connor retain their dominant positions.... The Caribbean Labour Congress is a body of some influence in the area to which the Trinidad and Tobago Trades Union Council has long affirmed its loyalty and support, and whether it finally decides to support the Free World Trade Union Organisation or the WFTU will have a considerable effect on the final decision in Trinidad.[46]

The colonial administration had not sought deliberately to divide the TT-TUC, and the acting governor advised that they should take no further action at that time concerning 'their domestic argument about the rival merits' of the two international federations, but the effect of these events was a split that weakened organised labour and its political influence in Trinidad and Tobago for many years. The OWTU and FWTU remained in the TTTUC, affiliated to the WFTU, but a new Federation of Trade Unions (FTU), headed by Alexander of the SWWTU and including five other unions, was formed in 1951 and affiliated with the ICFTU. This split remained so long as the TTTUC and its unions were in the WFTU, and it was not until 1957 that the trade unions reunited when the TTTUC and FTU were dissolved and the National Trade Union Congress was formed, with most leading trade unions taking part.[47] Although the work-ing class was relatively well organised in Trinidad and Tobago, this split in the labour movement weakened its political influence.

In Jamaica the labour movement, which was already deeply divided between the BITU and the JTUC, became further fragmented as the pressures of the Cold War were felt within the JTUC. The BITU was always a parochial union and it never affiliated with the WFTU or the CLC, but the JTUC was associated with both these international organisations. Indeed, two of the most prominent men in the JTUC, Hart and Ken Hill, were active in the WFTU and CLC from 1945. In 1949, mindful of the forthcoming general election and the increasing anti-communist climate of the Cold War, Manley and other centre-right members of the PNP sought to distance themselves from the left, which was prominent in the JTUC. The PNP, which was also affiliated to the CLC, asked the JTUC to withdraw from the WFTU for political reasons. The US consul-general, Nelson Park, reported to the State Department that there was 'considerable skepticism ... in various quarters as to the sincerity of the PNP's attitude in bringing pressure on its affiliate Trade Union Congress to sever its association with WFTU' and that these (unspecified) sectors had concluded this pressure was 'a manoeuvre of political expediency, carried out ingeniously'.[48] Park's appraisal was mistaken as there is no doubt that the JTUC General Executive Council took the pressure seriously and its impact was real and far-reaching. The issue proved divisive even before it was put before the delegates to the JTUC congress in September 1949. The JTUC general secretary, Florizel Glasspole, resigned over it, declaring that there was a fundamental difference between himself and other JTUC leaders.[49]

A special committee of the JTUC, appointed on 11 September and consisting of Henry and Ken and Frank Hill, faced with a unilateral decision by the PNP executive to terminate the party's special relationship with the JTUC, recommended that they should disaffiliate from the WFTU in order to restore their relationship with the PNP. The committee referred to the 'alarming situation which developed between the PNP and the TUC as well as the dissension which took place inside the TUC' and recommended that the PNP Executive Council should be told that 'we regret deeply their action in abruptly terminating the working agreement between their organisation and ours, without previous notice or warning'.[50] The minutes of the JTUC General Executive Council meeting of 19 September 1949, which were not for public consumption, reveal the members' anger and frustration about being forced into this disaffiliation by what they called the 'extreme pressure' and 'precipitate and ruthless' action of the PNP executive. T.A. Kelly stated that he felt the JTUC had been 'treated as an appendage rather than as a sovereign body'. Grant said it was:

> necessary for a Trade Union being a working class organisation to lean to the left. But it was clear that the TUC did not have sufficient numerical strength otherwise the party would have come to us and not we have to go to them. If the TUC were numerically stronger then neither would we have to worry about money from our international affiliations nor would the PNP have to worry about votes. But as things are now we have to accept things which as a Trade Union movement we do not like to.[51]

With these regrets and reservations the JTUC General Executive Council, including Hart, voted unanimously to disaffiliate from the WFTU, but they also expressed their confidence in those officers of the JTUC who had been requested to resign from the PNP. Nevertheless, the next day Hart, the first vice-president of the JTUC, tendered his resignation as a member of the executive committee of the PNP, as the latter had requested:

> In doing so I wish to make it clear that I do not consider that I have conducted myself in any way improperly or done or said anything which could be construed as a breach of party discipline. I feel that I and my comrades have been very unfairly treated by the Executive.
> My resignation is therefore tended solely with a view to assisting in heal-

ing the breach which has arisen within our ranks with a view to ensuring the maximum unity possible within the party for the purposes of the forthcoming general elections and the future of the national movement, and to preserving the trade union movement which would be greatly damaged by further disunity.[52]

Although the differences were publicly papered over, a wedge had been driven by the PNP executive between the PNP left, who were the leaders of the JTUC, and the rest of the party, and also between the JTUC and the CLC because the latter, for which Hart was still the secretary, remained affiliated to the WFTU.

The importance of these events should be understood. The events of September 1949, clearly brought about by political pressure following the British withdrawal from the WFTU and the worsening Cold War, foreshadowed the disintegration of the CLC and the purge of the left wing of the PNP in 1952. They are important evidence of the way that external political pressures, initiated as early as 1949, acted upon the personnel and relations within the labour movement, fostering disunity and weakness. Grant's statement to the JTUC Executive Council meeting, quoted above, shows that some participants realised and resented that their labour organisations were becoming dominated by the political parties, whose leaders were being influenced by considerations that were extraneous to the labour issues of the Caribbean. Cold War pressures, which were created by the superpowers' rivalry and imposed upon the politics of labour in the Caribbean, contributed to a divided and weakened labour movement, the disintegration of the first regional labour organisation and the dominance of middle-class controlled political parties over the workers' trade unions. These pressures began in 1949 and worsened in the following years.[53]

When the CLC council met in Kingston on 19 October 1949, just a month after this crisis between the PNP and the JTUC, Adams tried to persuade a Jamaican representative (possibly Ken Hill) to attend the forthcoming London conference, but he refused on the grounds that there was racial discrimination in US unions but not in those in the USSR. At this council meeting Gomes 'denounced socialism and resigned'.[54] Gomes, whose earlier radicalism faded after he became a member of Trinidad's Executive Council in 1946, was 'almost certainly the single most influential politician in Trinidad' (Brereton 1981: 197) at this time and he remained so until the rise of Williams in 1956. After Gomes defected from the CLC he led the Political Progress Group (PPG), a middle-class party backed largely by white planters and businessmen, in the 1950 elections. As the quasi-minister for labour, commerce and industry, he played a leading role in the red-baiting and purging of the trade unions in Trinidad and Tobago in the early 1950s. These problems in the CLC, like those in the JTUC, had nothing to do with local labour issues and policies but were the result of pressure and posturing associated with the international politics of the Cold War.

The British government and TUC heated up their campaign against the WFTU as the London conference approached. On 8 November 1949 the Central Office of Information issued a 900-word article for general distribution, called 'New World Trades Union Organisation', written by Denis Healey, the secretary of the Labour Party's International Department. Just two years earlier, Healey, on behalf of the Labour Party, and Vincent Tewson, general secretary of the TUC, turned down the CLC's request for observers and funds for the important conference in Kingston,[55] but by 1949 the commitment of resources to a global propaganda war with the WFTU had become a high priority. The British Labour Party and TUC were unwilling to support the CLC, which they did not control, but were willing to be used by the British government as adjuncts in an anti-communist crusade.

The Foreign Office instructed His Majesty's representatives worldwide to give prudent help in publicising the forthcoming London conference: 'This operation is in the front line of the world struggle against Communism, and its effectiveness depends largely upon the publicity which it receives. I realise that in many countries any suggestion of government sponsorship may do more harm than good in the trade union and left-wing circles at which the operation is aimed; but even in those countries discreet ways can no doubt be found to ensure that the facts are prominently reported'.[56] In addition to the usual news channels and press services, it was said that arrangements were being made 'for special articles to be written' to influence public opinion.

In a revealing statement, Creech Jones, the secretary of state for the colonies, told the general secretary of the British TUC that the governor of Sierra Leone had suggested that:

> the popularity in West Africa of the WFTU is due not to its communist associations, but rather to the fact that it takes a real and live interest in the Colonial labour organisations, and goes to a lot of trouble to keep them informed of what is going on elsewhere in the world. He points out that if the new organisation is to win and retain the allegiance of local unions it will have to do so in competition with the WFTU. It will have to show that it is at least equally if not more interested in local trade unions . . . . There is no point in pressing local unions to switch their affections from the WFTU to the new organisation simply on the grounds that the former is communist and the latter is not . . . .
>
> A great deal will depend on the extent to which the subtle influences of the WFTU can be countered by the Secretariat of the new Organisation and by a closer linking of the Colonial unions with the TUC. In any case I am sure you will agree that much will need to be done in the way of good propaganda to break the hold that the WFTU has on the trade union councils of many of the

Colonial territories.[57]

Creech Jones was here acknowledging that they were involved in a propaganda war with the WFTU, a struggle, as it has come to be expressed, for the hearts and minds of trade unionists in the colonies. Moreover, in saying that the new international organisation would have to compete with the WFTU for the allegiance of these trade unionists, he admitted that the WFTU had taken a real interest in the colonial unions and had kept them informed about what was going on in the world. He urged Tewson to link the colonial unions more closely with the British TUC in order to be able to influence them more effectively. The colonial unions had sought in vain to obtain affiliation with and support from the British TUC, which to date had offered only paternalistic advice about how they should run their affairs. It was only the exigencies of Cold War politics in 1949 that made the assistance and control of colonial trade unions a British priority. The relationship, instead of being determined by the needs and goals of the colonial unions, was to be dictated by the imperialist countries' need to break the colonial unions away from the WFTU and secure their allegiance to the new anti-communist international organisation.

The examples of Trinidad and Jamaica show that what determined the allegiance of the colonial unions was not a local competition over labour and union issues, but a power struggle influenced by external forces. In Trinidad the TTTUC suffered a split but remained loyal to the WFTU, and Gomes resigned from the CLC, while in Jamaica the dependency of the JTUC on a political party that was anxious to disassociate itself from any links with communist organisations led to intense pressure that resulted in the disaffiliation of the JTUC from the WFTU. It was the pressure of the international politics associated with the Cold War, sometimes channeled through local parties, that reoriented the allegiances of colonial politicians and trade unions. Ironically, this was contrary to the publicly expressed dictum of the British TUC and Labour Party which claimed that they wanted to keep these unions and international labour organisations out of the 'maze of politics'. In fact, however, their pressure, exerted on behalf of the British government, was politicising the colonial trade unions according to the terms of the Cold War, and the political and propaganda struggle polarised, divided and weakened the Caribbean labour movement.

The founding of the ICFTU and CADORIT, 1949-52

Eight delegates went from the British Caribbean colonies to the London conference in December 1949 at which the ICFTU was founded: Adams of the BWU, Middleton, secretary of the GWU of Belize, Chase of the BGLU, Bradshaw of the SKNTLU, E.A. Mitchell of the Grenada Workers' Union (GWU), Christopher Loblack, President of the Dominican Trades Union (DTU), G.F.L. Charles of the St Lucia Workers' Union (SLWU), and Alexander of the SWWTU. Together they represented only about 23,000 trade union members[58] and the largest and most powerful unions in the British Caribbean, including the BITU, JTUC, OWTU and TTTUC, were unrepresented. However, these West Indian delegates outnumbered those from the seven other British colonies represented (Sierra Leone, Mauritius, Malta, Malaya, the Gambia, Hong Kong and Cyprus) and played an important symbolic part in lending an apparent legitimacy to the new international labour federation. This was especially true of the two CLC council members, Adams and Bradshaw, although the CLC remained officially affiliated with the WFTU. Adams was made a vice-chairman of the conference and Bradshaw, representing the West Indies, was elected one of the 19 members of the executive board and a member of the standing orders committee of the ICFTU. Mitchell and Charles became members of the constitution committee, and Alexander and Middleton were members of the committee on economic and social demands.[59]

The appearance of participation by colonial trade unions in the ICFTU, which was a prime part of the propaganda struggle with the WFTU, was thus assured and perhaps, in return, the participation of these men in the ICFTU committees enhanced their reputations when they returned home.[60] The real effect of Cold War politics on the labour movement of the British Caribbean was deeply divisive, however, as may be seen by the continuing decline and eventual destruction of the CLC and its replacement by the Caribbean Area Division of the Inter-American Regional Organization of Workers (CADORIT), affiliated to the ICFTU, in 1952.

While the CLC struggled for survival after 1949, tentative steps towards a West Indian federation continued. At the CLC council meeting in October 1949, the secretary of state's proposed constitutional reform of the Leeward and Windward Islands was discussed in relation to the question of the federation. Several members of the Standing Closer Association Committee (SCAC), which had been appointed at the Montego Bay conference in 1947 to present a report on the implications of federation, were members of the CLC, including Adams, Gomes, Bird, McIntosh, Maurice Davis of St Kitts and Austin Winston of Dominica, and Adams urged that the SCAC should accept the draft constitution prepared by the CLC. However, the final report, named after the committee's chairman, Sir Hubert Rance, accepted the recommendation of full adult suffrage but fell short of proposing complete independence.

Manley thought the Rance Committee's proposal was completely unsatisfactory, and Adams, though he had signed the report, described the proposed West Indian Federation as 'not much more than a glorified Crown Colony' (quoted in Mordechai 1968: 41). Progressive West Indians rejected the proposal that the governor-general would retain reserve powers and demanded nothing less than fully responsible government and independence. The secretary of the London branch of the CLC, Billy Strachan, sent a resolution to the secretary of state demanding immediate and full independence for the West Indies, with autonomy for each individual territory.[61] Adams himself wrote that 'federation is the only hope for our stability and our progress and that any federal structure that is to be of use to the people of this area must rest on the sure foundation of ultimate power resting unequivocally in the hands of the adult population. The actual exercise of this power must lie with their elected representatives and with them alone'.[62]

The ideal of a democratic, independent West Indian Federation, which had been developing in the British Caribbean since the 1920s and which had been a major goal of the CLC since its founding in 1945, was one of the last of the hopes and aspirations about which organised labour in the region could agree in 1949. After lengthy debates in the several colonial legislatures, however, the Rance Committee's proposals were endorsed by all except Guyana, Belize and the Virgin Islands. Even the Jamaican Legislature, in August 1951, unanimously endorsed the report and reaffirmed its acceptance of the proposed West Indian Federation.

The proposed federal constitution was a far cry from what the CLC had been proposing since 1945. Far from aiming at a rapid transition to full self-government with a strong federal centre, as the CLC advocated, the ideology of the Rance Report (British Caribbean Report, 1949) was of gradualism in the process of constitutional decolonisation, with each unit of the federation retaining its powers except in so far as it specifically surrendered them. Instead of a single-chamber parliament, as the CLC recommended, the West Indian Parliament was to be bicameral, with an elected Lower House and a Senate appointed by the governor-general, who would continue to possess reserve powers. Moreover, no period was specified for graduation to dominion status. In Lewis's opinion, 'on every crucial issue the Rance Report was uncannily wrong' (1968: 355), yet two of the most prominent federalists, Adams and Manley, who had shaped the CLC's original ideal, split from the CLC and left it impotent at this crucial time instead of encouraging a bold drive for the independence of a strong federal state of the West Indies.

While negotiations concerning the West Indian Federation were continuing at the London conferences in 1953 and 1956, the CLC struggled and died. A CLC conference was scheduled for April 1950 in Trinidad but supporters in New York who sought to raise $10,000 to fund it experienced the political pressure of the McCarthy era. According to Richard B. Moore, some former supporters withdrew 'because of the association of the United Caribbean American Council with progressive leaders and organizations militantly fighting against reaction in the country and for that reason branded by the current hysteria' (Turner and Turner 1988: 84). Hart's urgent appeals for funds were in vain and the Trinidad conference was cancelled. The critical year was 1952 when, at the height of the McCarthy witch-hunts in the United States, the left labour leaders in the British Caribbean came under great pressure not only from the colonial governments but also from their centre-right colleagues in the trade unions and political parties. Details of the relations between the unions and the parties, and of the purges that occurred, will follow in the next chapters, but the outline must be told here in order to make sense of the sequence of events that left the CLC in total disarray and supplanted in most colonies by the US-dominated CADORIT.

Two developments occurred in the first half of 1952 that undermined the effectiveness of the left labour leaders to support the CLC. First, colonial governments made it harder for some of them to travel between Caribbean territories, on the grounds that they were dangerous subversives. In 1948 the Colonial Office had agreed with the governor of Guyana that Butler should not be allowed to land in Guyana, but the ban was not used as he did not try to go there.[63] Early in 1949 the Jagans had been humiliated by the immigration authorities in St Vincent when Cheddi Jagan's passport was seized and Janet Jagan was declared a prohibited immigrant. There were protests from several Caribbean unions and parties, including the GWU of Belize which made a 'strong protest' at this 'unwarranted act' of interference with the freedom of movement of Caribbean leaders,[64] the BGTUC and GIWU, the St Lucia Seamen and Waterfront Workers' Trade Union, the CLC, with Adams and Hart joining in protest,[65] and from Manley on behalf of the PNP.[66] Cheddi Jagan sought to discover the reasons on his return to Guyana but the governor arranged a cover-up of the fact that he had told the St Vincent administration that Janet Jagan was a communist.[67]

In February 1952 the Jagans received letters from the governments of Trinidad and Tobago and Grenada informing them they were prohibited immigrants, which caused a stir throughout the British Caribbean as these were the first of such formal bans (Jagan 1972: 103). This was followed by the passage of the Undesirable Publications Act in Guyana, and in June 1952 the government of Trinidad and Tobago banned 'red' publications, making it an offence even to possess a copy of Soviet Weekly.[68] These bans were clearly contrary to the Universal Declaration of Human Rights of the United Nations, agreeing to the freedom 'to seek, receive and impart information and ideas through any media regardless of frontiers'. The movement of several other labour and political leaders was restricted in parts of the British Caribbean. Victims included Strachan, Hart, Critchlow, Eric Gairy of Grenada, John La Rose, president of the West Indian Independence Party (WIIP), Rojas, O'Connor and Ferdinand Smith, the Jamaican secretary of the US National Maritime Union who was deported from the United States in 1951, put in charge of the Colonial and Dependent Territories Departments of the WFTU in London, and returned to Jamaica in 1952. In early 1952, therefore, the governments of the self-declared free world nations and their colonies were becoming increasingly restrictive of the movement of people, literature and ideas of which they disapproved, in an hysterical atmosphere of anti-communism.

The second development was the purge of the left wing of the PNP, known as the Four H's: Hart, Henry, Frank Hill and Ken Hill. In this Cold War climate it was not only the colonial governments and conservative politicians, like Bustamante and Gomes, who attacked the left-wingers, but also those, like Manley, who considered themselves to be socialists and friends of the left. In the current climate of witch-hunting, they were anxious not to be labelled as fellow travellers of the communists. This climate encouraged some Caribbean politicians and labour leaders to behave in authoritarian ways such as purging their ranks, whether or not they could actually find any communists among them. Some even went so far as to label their opponents as communists in order to get rid of them and to make it appear they were serious anti-communists. Although many labour leaders on the left sought to defend the rights of those who were deemed to be subversives, the labour right split the labour movement and destroyed the CLC, its only home-grown regional organisation.

The Four H's, who had been interned in the war and who were instrumental in developing the base in organised labour for the PNP in the form of the JTUC and its unions, were investigated and then expelled from the PNP. The signs of this purge, as we have shown, were revealed in 1949 over the question of the JTUC's affiliation with the WFTU. In 1952 the question was the survival of the CLC, of which Hart was still the secretary, and which remained affiliated with the WFTU, to the obvious embarrassment of politicians like Adams, Bradshaw and Manley. Unlike Gomes, who simply left the CLC, these others sought to get the organisation, which still had legitimacy as the regional labour federation, to transfer its allegiance to the ICFTU, while Hart and others fought a rearguard action. Soon after the Four H's were investigated by a PNP committee, where they were denounced by former associates who had started a rival union, they were expelled from the party by a vote of 128 to 75.[69]

On 3 April 1952 Hart, Henry and Frank Hill resigned from the executive of the JTUC in order to counter the rumour that they were somehow controlling Ken Hill.[70] Within a few months Hart was complaining that he was being excluded from speaking on platforms at public meetings, although he had been elected a vice-president of the JTUC by a substantial majority of the delegates at the last congress.[71] By 14 September, Ken Hill had become anxious to disassociate himself from Hart, when he launched the National Labour Party (NLP). On 19

January 1953, as president of the NLP, he repudiated Hart, saying he could not retain membership in the NLP, hold NLP meetings or organise NLP centres.[72] Within a few months of their being expelled from the PNP, therefore, the four H's were themselves at odds, with Hart becoming increasingly isolated.

While Hart was becoming separated from his base of popular support in Jamaica, steps were being taken to replace the CLC with a new organisation. It is clear that the initiative, and perhaps even pressure, for this new labour organisation came from outside the region, and that one of the chief actors was Serafino Romualdi, an Italian immigrant to the United States who had worked on Nelson Rockefeller's staff in the Office of Inter-American Affairs during the war. The American Federation of Labor (AFL), unlike the Congress of Industrial Organizations (CIO), had never joined the WFTU because it objected to the membership of unions from communist countries in the international. From 1946, Romualdi, as the AFL's representative in Latin America, assisted in splitting the WFTU's regional organisation, the Confederation of Latin American Workers (CTAL) and some of its national affiliates. In January 1948 he launched the Inter-American Confederation of Workers (CIT) and on 5 April 1950 met with representatives of the AFL and CIO in New York to create 'a regional organization comprising North, Central, and South America, including British, Dutch, and French possessions', which would exclude 'organizations under direct or indirect control of the Communist Party' (Romualdi 1967: 110). This agreement by US labour leaders 'was subsequently approved informally by the Canadian, Cuban, and Chilean ICFTU-affiliated organizations' and accepted by the ICFTU executive board (Romualdi 1967: 111). The Inter-American Regional Organization of Workers (ORIT) was formally launched at a conference in Mexico City in January 1951[73] and it became an affiliate of the ICFTU (Radosh 1969: 359-71). The origins of ORIT and its continuing relationship with the AFL, which was its major financial sponsor, meant that it was quite independent of the ICFTU. Romualdi, who continued to play a key role in ORIT and its offshoot CADORIT, claimed that 'until 1954 the ICFTU Secretariat in Brussels left ORIT pretty much alone' (Romualdi 1967: 128). So CADORIT, which was created in June 1952 at the height of McCarthyism in the United States, was the child of the conservative AFL and was known to be 'an anti-communist organisation, specifically designed to combat the CLC' (Harrod 1972: 285).

In April 1952 Francisco Aguirre, general secretary of ORIT, presided over a meeting in Trinidad with Walcott of the BWU, who was Adams' right-hand man, Alexander of the SWWTU, F.J. Carasco from St Lucia and L.F. Eliazar from Suriname. They agreed to hold a conference in Barbados of regional unions that were already affiliated to the ICFTU, thereby creating a federation to rival the CLC.[74] On 30 April Walcott announced to the BWU that a committee of the

ICFTU would hold a conference of affiliates in the area in Barbados and it was at that conference in June that CADORIT was created. Barbados[75] was chosen as the site to launch CADORIT in order to strengthen Adams' hand, and plans may have been laid for this when Adams attended the ICFTU meeting in Milan in July 1951, when he was appointed a member of the international's executive board (Hoyos 1974: 170). At the opening of the Barbados conference, Adams made an 'eloquent plea on behalf of the ICFTU' and urged every Caribbean trade unionist to support it (Hoyos 1974: 171) though he was still president of the CLC.

At the same time that this meeting was being planned and the four H's were expelled from the PNP in Jamaica, the leaders of the TTTUC, Rojas and O'Connor, who were among the CLC's staunchest supporters, were attacked in the Trinidad press. An editorial in March 1952 praised Manley for expelling the 'Left Wing extremists' who were accused of taking over the CLC 'to infect the BWI with Communist ideas'.[76] In May Gomes, the minister of labour, industry and commerce, stated there was 'unmistakable evidence' of subversion and 'Communist infiltration' in the trade unions,[77] and this was followed by dozens of articles, letters and editorials in the press about 'local Reds' and 'Red agents.' On 1 June an editorial attacked the TTTUC for being affiliated to the WFTU, 'from which the Western unions withdrew in disgust in 1949',[78] and on 8 June, the day after the creation of CADORIT was announced, the Sunday Guardian editorial urged Rojas and O'Connor to 'break the Moscow affiliation'.[79] In Trinidad and Tobago, unlike Jamaica, the TUC leaders could not be directly pressured and expelled by a political party, but the media were involved in what looks suspiciously like an orchestrated campaign to put pressure on the leading trade unionists to withdraw their support from the CLC and WFTU just at the time that the rival CADORIT was created. This pressure was resisted for a while, and Rojas and O'Connor joined Hart and other prominent labour leaders in a last-minute effort to save the CLC. Between June, when CADORIT was created, and November, when this last effort was made to save the CLC, there was some crucial manoeuvring by both sides.

By 1952 the campaign against the CLC's association with the WFTU had become a united front of colonial governments, newspapers, churches and all the major political parties (with the exception of Jagan's People's Progressive Party, PPP, in Guyana), as well as several trade unions. Adams could count on Manley's support. Manley had expelled Hart and the others from the PNP but he did not have the authority to expel them from the JTUC, the president of which was the popular mayor of Kingston, Ken Hill. Instead, Manley authorized the creation of a rival union, the National Workers' Union (NWU), to be associated with the PNP, and it grew very quickly. When Ken Hill sought to have the JTUC affiliated with the ICFTU the application was held up pending an investigation. In June 1952 CADORIT decided that the Jamaican situation should be investigated before it was decided which of the Jamaican unions should be admitted to affiliation. Then, at the meeting of the executive board of the ICFTU in Berlin in July, 'Grantley Adams came out unequivocally on the side of the National Workers' Union. He convinced the Board that the NWU, which was to be affiliated to the PNP, was a free and democratic union and urged that it should be recognized as such without any investigation. As a result of his stand, the Executive Board made a decision that was of timely assistance to Manley.' (Hoyos 1974: 177)

Manley expressed his appreciation to Adams at a BWU conference when he visited Barbados in July. The NWU was accepted by the ICFTU, became affiliated in October 1952 and remained the only Jamaican union recognised by the ICFTU-ORIT for 15 years (Harrod 1972: 284). From June 1953 the NWU became the basis of Michael Manley's rise to power (Manley 1975: 81-2), as his father's successor.

There was clearly an understanding between Adams and Norman Manley, who were still the president and vice-president of the CLC, respectively, to do away with the CLC if they could not control it. This decision was reached, at the latest, in July 1952, several months before Hart's delegation met Adams in Barbados. Adams had stated in June, when CADORIT was created, that it would become the 'medium of regional thinking and consciousness among West Indian workers',[80] so if he could not incorporate the CLC into CADORIT then the CLC would have to be smashed. Adams's biographer writes that the question of the CLC 'had long been uppermost in Adams's mind and that there can be no doubt that, when Manley came to Barbados, the two socialist comrades discussed the grave situation facing the trade union movement in the Caribbean. In due course, Adams came to a firm and irrevocable decision. The Caribbean Labour Congress must be dissolved'. (Hoyos 1974: 178)

Adams presumably felt confident that, with the support he had from ORIT and from Manley, he could oust Hart and defeat the WFTU supporters in the CLC. Hart concluded some years later, 'It was Adams who, with Manley's approval, played the leading part in smashing the CLC when he was unable to incorporate it into the ICFTU'.[81]

The Daily Gleaner of Jamaica reported in September that the CLC factions were 'lining up for battle' and that Adams and Manley had decided the time was 'ripe to remove Mr Richard Hart as Secretary of the CLC'.[82] The CLC council had the power to suspend the secretary, as had been done in Antigua in 1947 when Henry was replaced by Hart; so Adams and Manley wanted a CLC council meeting, while Hart sought to convene a full congress in order to have a broader debate. There is little doubt that Adams and Manley discussed their tactics about this struggle when they met in Barbados between 25 and 29 July because on 2 August Adams sent a circular to the remaining affiliated organisations proposing a split in the CLC on the basis of the unions' international affiliations. He urged that a council meeting should be held in Jamaica to sanction this. The Hill brothers supported this call for a council meeting but, despite this, the JTUC executive voted to support Hart's counter-proposal for a congress. So the BWU and BLP, the PNP and Bradshaw's SKNTLU supported Adams's proposal for a council meeting, and the TUCs of Jamaica, Guyana, and Trinidad and Tobago supported Hart's proposal for a full congress. However, Hart had no effective office or sufficient funds to organise such a congress, particularly in the face of the opposition of the CLC's president and vice-president. Hence there was a stalemate, which Hart tried to break with a new initiative in November.

According to Hart, it was the CLC's policy that the international affiliations of each Caribbean trade union were their own concern and that it would not interfere with them. However, with the escalation of the Cold War and the creation of CADORIT, which opened its office in Barbados in October 1952, with Walcott of the BWU as its head, this policy was no longer being practised. What Hart proposed, therefore, was a new Caribbean federation of trade unions to which all unions would affiliate, irrespective of their international connections with the WFTU or ICFTU. Hart organised a delegation consisting of himself, Rojas, O'Connor, Cheddi Jagan, La Rose, Ebeneezer T. Joshua (president of the Agricultural and Industrial Workers' Union of St Vincent) and Smith, the Jamaican head of the Colonial and Dependent Territories Department of the WFTU. Most of these delegates were supporters of the WFTU, but Joshua said that he knew very little about the two internationals and was simply supporting an effort to preserve unity among Caribbean unions.[83]

Hart's effort was obstructed. The Trinidad government refused to allow Hart or Smith to pass through the island, or even to remain on a plane while it refuelled there, and then the Barbados government banned Smith from entry. When the other delegates arrived in Barbados, Adams initially declined to meet them. He said he was in favour of West Indian self-government and West Indian trade unionism, but had no intention 'of allowing the CLC to be used as a pawn in the game of Cold War power politics'.[84] This was ironic, of course, as Adams and Walcott were allowing the BWU to be used as a pawn in the creation of CADORIT, which was the Cold Warriors' answer to the CLC. On 3 November Adams and Walcott met the delegation and heard their case. The delegates asked Adams to approach the ICFTU while Rojas would approach the WFTU, to inform them that it would be in the best interests of the Caribbean workers to establish a new Caribbean federation of trade unions which would embrace all unions in the region regardless of their international affiliations and would control its own affairs. They said also that they should 'tell both organisations that if they are really concerned with the welfare of the Caribbean workers, they should be prepared to assist us in equal proportions without attaching any strings to their assistance and leaving it to us to use the assistance to develop a united organisation under our own control'.[85]

Adams rejected these suggestions and, according to Hart, admitted that the ICFTU would not agree because it was their policy to divide the workers on ideological grounds. In Hart's words, 'he turned us down flat. He said he had made up his mind to have a federation of unions exclusively under ICFTU and if the CLC wouldn't play that role, they would organise a federation anyway'.[86] This was disingenuous as CADORIT's office had already been opened in Barbados on 20 October. Adams would not even agree with the delegates on a date at which to hold a third congress of the CLC. Hart suggested mid-January, but presumably Adams did not want to provide him with the opportunity that he wanted to rouse opposition to what Adams and Manley were doing. Consequently, Hart had to circulate the members of the CLC to ask if they agreed with the proposal for a Caribbean federation of trade unions as proposed by the delegation, and whether this organisation would be represented at a third congress if it were held either in Barbados or Antigua in the second week of January 1953.[87] But such a conference was never held. On 26 February 1953 the SKNTLU revoked its affiliation with the CLC and Bradshaw resigned as the CLC's assistant secretary.[88] Hart tried for a couple more years to carry on some activities for the CLC, 'mainly of a publicity nature'.[89] Hart and Rojas, together with delegates of the Post Office Workers' Union and the Sawmill Workers' Union of Guyana, attended the WFTU conference in Vienna in October 1953, but the CLC lacked funds to organise a third congress.

The continuing Cold War pressures that led Rojas and O'Connor to pull their unions and the TTTUC out of the WFTU, and to the overthrow of Jagan's first government and the suspension of the constitution in Guyana in 1953, meant the defeat of the last left labour leaders who had supported Hart in the CLC. The CLC became defunct without having been formally dissolved, although the London branch carried on some activities. In August 1955 Hart tried to revive the CLC and to transfer its secretariat to London in order to respond to the 'advanced stage that the federation proposals have now reached',[90] but this effort failed. On 1 July 1956, the London branch of the CLC, at its ninth annual general meeting, agreed to dissolve itself and to form a new organisation, the Caribbean National Congress,[91] but the CLC had really been dead already for several years.

Conclusion

One of the chief problems that faced the CLC, of course, was a lack of funds.

The 1947 conference in Jamaica was partially funded by the American Committee for West Indian Federation, whose chairman donated $10,000, but the CLC received no significant funds from the WFTU or any other international trade union organisation. Harrod concludes (1972: 243), 'During its short history there is no evidence that it was heavily dependent on politically donated funds nor is there any indication that the leaders uniformly pursued policies or followed models promoted by international or national trade union organisations.' Whereas CADORIT and its parent ORIT were financially dependent on the AFL, and were 'an important instrument of North American trade union organisations rather than an entity pursuing its independent policies' (Harrod 1972: 296), the CLC was a remarkably independent and regionally oriented trade union federation. Indeed, because the United States sought to create and control labour organisations that would serve its own superpower purposes, it was the CLC's independence and regional orientation that made it a target and victim of Cold War politics.

In addition to the obvious lack of funds, there are three other reasons why, despite the great enthusiasm with which it had begun in 1945, the CLC failed after so few years. These factors, though analytically distinguishable, actually interacted in ways that proved fatal. First, the federal ideal, which had been an element in the aspirations of Caribbean labour leaders from as early as 1926 and which was a major topic in the CLC Conferences in 1945 and 1947, distracted their attention and activity from trade union issues and from the necessity of building their own permanent labour organisation. This is not to say, as British and other metropolitan trade unionists argued, that Caribbean labour leaders should keep trade union matters separate from politics - far from it. The problem was that the largely middle-class lawyers who quickly dominated the CLC subordinated the labour issues and the CLC itself to their own political agendas. So long as federation was their priority, as it clearly was between 1945 and 1947 for men like Marryshow, Gomes, Adams and Manley, they became caught up in the agenda that was still controlled by the British government. Questions concerning the nature of the federal constitution, the timing of gradual decolonisation, the disparities between political reforms in the several territories and the degree of responsibility held by the quasi-ministers in the executive councils, predominated over labour issues. Although some labour leaders of the 1940s had risen through the ranks of the trade unions, including Bird, Bradshaw, Betson and Rojas, most of the CLC leaders, including Adams, Gomes, Hart, Manley and Marryshow, were middle-class leaders of trade unions or political parties associated with trade unions. Some of them were elected by their members, but the rank and file of these infant labour organisations rarely shaped their leaders' policies and priorities directly. These

CLC leaders generally neglected the development of organised labour in the region, a development which could have provided a popular base – the only popular base possible – to support a genuinely West Indian conception of a strong and independent federal government.

Second, and closely related, is the question of nationalism. There was a distinct contrast between a unifying regional West Indian nationalism and the fragmentary insular nationalisms in each colony. In retrospect, it is easy to see that the latter was stronger, but it is necessary to explain why several of the labour leaders who initially espoused a strong federal ideal reverted so quickly toward insular nationalisms. One reason is the effect of the British responses to federation, which left each colony to go at its own pace toward democracy and decolonisation. This certainly encouraged multiple bilateral negotiations and fostered disparities that undermined regional unity among the constituent parts. Another reason is the impact of the Puerto Rican model of economic development that, along with Lewis's theory of economic growth (Lewis 1950), became the focal point of development strategy in the early 1950s. In this view, 'foreign business investment was the sine qua non of West Indian industrial development' (Mandle 1989: 243), and West Indian politicians were seduced into competing with each other to attract such investment. In Hart's words,

> Mr. Manley's whole conception of how to industrialize had changed. He now saw industrialization, not as a process to take place under local ownership and against the interests of imperialism, but as a process actually to be performed by foreign investors to whom incentives were to be offered to develop our resources under foreign ownership. He therefore no longer wanted a strong federal government with power to control investment in the entire area. Instead he wanted a weak central government, so that he would have the right to pursue an independent policy of attracting foreign investment by tax and other incentives in Jamaica (1982: 89).

The logic of this development strategy, consequently, led to each independent national government competing with the others, rather than a strong federal government that would coordinate their cooperation in development for a common good.

An important feature of this changed conception of development was that trade unions would have to be subordinated in order to ensure an attractive climate for the potential foreign investors. In short, the new strategy for economic development promoted competition between the several parts of the Caribbean, that simultaneously fragmented nationalism and relegated trade unions to a subservient role that foreign investors would perceive as responsible. In this new conception, therefore, there was simply no place for an independent CLC that aimed at a strong federal government and placed the

Caribbean workers' needs above those of foreign investors.

Third, the CLC was the victim of Cold War politics. As so often in the past, international superpower rivalries affected the Caribbean in ways that interfered with the goals and realities of the people of the region. Although the UK did not enter the Cold War with the same crusading zeal with which the United States led it, the British colonies in the Caribbean were deeply affected because the UK acknowledged that the United States increasingly treated the Caribbean as its backyard. It has been said that in terms of domestic politics communism was as insignificant in the United States as Buddhism in Ireland (Hobsbawm 1994: 237), and the same could be said of the British Caribbean. Yet the apocalyptic tone of US politics, and absurdly exaggerated claims about Red agents and Communist conspiracies, permeated domestic politics in the British Caribbean colonies just as they did in the United States in the early 1950s. One effect was the emergence of similar patterns of paranoia, red-baiting and witch-hunts, that encouraged labour and political leaders in the Caribbean to purge their organisations of rivals in the guise of defending democracy. In short, the Cold War provided a pretext and an ideological rationale for authoritarian actions on the part of these leaders as they consolidated their power bases in the course of the process of constitutional decolonisation.

The CLC was one among many victims of these developments. There were left members of the CLC and of its affiliated unions, of course, as was to be expected in any broad and democratic labour movement. Many of them called themselves socialists, and some called themselves Marxists, but very few were actually communists. Their problem was that in the ideological climate of the Cold War, distinctions between various positions on the left were eroded, since guilt was determined by innuendo and association. Thus, Hart felt compelled to make a press statement: 'I am a Marxian socialist .... I am not a member of a Communist Party or organisation. But I am not afraid to associate with Communists.'[92] Most labour leaders did become afraid of such associations, however, or even became afraid of being accused of having such associations. This fear, which was deliberately fomented by the Cold Warriors and their associates in the media, churches and other organisations, severely split many of the young trade unions and political parties in the British Caribbean. And this fear, and the pressures and purges that it induced, provoked the fatal blow to the CLC, which was the only home-grown, genuinely independent federation of labour organisations in the British Caribbean.

Notes

1 A history of the English-speaking Caribbean 'from occupation to independence' by Richard Hart, the former secretary of the CLC, makes surprisingly few references to the CLC and even less to the Cold War's effects on Caribbean decolonisation. Hart says in his Preface that to 'do justice' to the CLC's contribution 'would require a separate study' (Hart 1998).

2 Report of the First British Guiana and West Indies Labour Conference, Georgetown, BGLU, 1926.

3 Ashton Chase says S.F. Helstone.

4 Official Report of the BGLU Silver Jubilee Celebration, 27 Feb. 1944, and Third BG and WI Labour Conference, 28 Feb.-1 Mar. 1944, Georgetown, BGLU, n.d., Archives of Barbados. It was actually the fourth conference.

5 Despite the TUC's close relationship with the British Labour Party, a model that was being adopted to some extent in Trinidad and Tobago.

6 Ibid.

7 Ibid.

8 They represented the Harbour and Transport Workers' Union of Paramaribo.

9 The Official Report reveals that very little was said about Suriname, however, and the delegates were entirely concerned with the British Caribbean colonies.

10 Official Report of the CLC Conference held at Barbados, 17-27 Sept. 1945, Archives of Barbados.

11 Ibid., p. 2.

12 Ibid., p. 7.

13 Ibid., p. 13.

14 Ibid., pp. 22-3.

15 Ibid., p. 24.

16 Ibid., pp. 27-8.

17 Ibid., p. 30.

18 Ibid., pp. 20-1.

19 Daily Gleaner, 8 Sept. 1947.

20 Hart suspected that his letters were intercepted by the colonial authorities in some cases (Hart 1982: 86, and pers. comm. 31 Dec. 1994).

21 Daily Gleaner, 30 Aug. 1947.

22 Daily Gleaner, 3 Sept. 1947.

23 Spotlight, Sept. 1947, HP, R1/151.

24 Daily Gleaner, 9 Sept. 1947.

25 Hart, 'The History of the Caribbean Labour Congress', Dec. 1966, HP, R4/35.

26 See HP, R4/35.

27 Chase, its assistant secretary, said it was 'nothing but a collection of individuals primarily seeking political honours and working together for mutual aid and assistance. It had no mass appeal whatever ... and the Party disintegrated shortly after the elections' (n.d.: 126).

28 Empire, Nov. 1948, quoted in Hoyos 1974: 133-4.

29 Barbados Beacon, 25 Sept. 1948, quoted in Hoyos 1974: 134.

30 Barbados Beacon, 30 Oct. 1948, quoted in Hoyos 1974: 138.

31 Ibid.

32 Gov. of Barbados to Secretary of State, 3 Nov. 1948, CO 537/3824.

33 Richard B. Moore, the secretary of the ACWIF, who was born in Barbados, wrote, 'Every intelligent native of the Caribbean and every thinking, liberty-loving person, devoted to the freeing of millions of colonial and semi-colonial peoples from the yoke of imperialist oppression, must repudiate and condemn the statement of Grantley H. Adams'; statement from the Pan-African Federation, in Barbados Observer, 13 Nov. 1948, quoted in Hoyos 1974: 141.

[34] CLC Monthly Bulletin, Sept. - Oct. 1948, HP, R2/20.

[35] Barbados Beacon, 11 Dec. 1948, quoted in Hoyos 1974: 143.

[36] Walcott to Hart, letter published in Barbados Beacon, 6 Nov. 1948, quoted in Hoyos 1974: 143.

[37] Isaacs' letter to Daily Gleaner, reprinted in Barbados Beacon, 13 Nov. 1948, quoted in Hoyos 1974: 145.

[38] 'Notes . . . ' by F.W. Dalley, Nov. 1947, Mss Brit. Emp. S365, Box 145, RHL.

[39] 24 Aug. 1949, CO 537/4282.

[40] SS to Gov. Sir Charles Woolley, 18 Nov. 1949; Woolley to SS, 21 Nov. 1949, CO 537/4282. Curiously, though Chase (n.d.: 118) wrote that Critchlow attended the London conference in 1949 and does not mention his own participation, the record of the election of the General Council states that Chase was himself the BGLU delegate (8 Dec. 1949, CO 537/4283).

[41] Vanguard, 29 Jan. 1949, quoted in Gov. Sir John Shaw to Creech Jones, 6 Aug. 1949, CO 537/4282.

[42] Trinidad Guardian, 3 May 1949, in CO 537/4902.

[43] CLC Monthly Bulletin, Jul. 1949, HP, R2/49.

[44] S. Hochoy, minute of 11 Oct. 1949, encl. in Acting Gov. to Creech Jones, 22 Oct. 1949, CO 537/4282.

[45] Gov. to SS, 24 Nov. 1949, CO 537/4282.

[46] Acting Gov. to SS, 22 Oct. 1949, CO 537/4282.

[47] Discussion papers for OWTU 46th annual conference, 22 Feb. 1986, OWTUL.

[48] 30 Sept. 1949, quoted in Munroe 1992: 88.

[49] Daily Gleaner, 23 Sept. 1949.

[50] Interim report of JTUC special committee, 19 Sept. 1949, HP, R2/37.

[51] Minutes of TUC General Executive Council meeting, 19 Sept. 1949, HP, R2/39.

[52] Hart to V.L. Arnett, 20 Sept. 1949, HP, R2/41.

[53] This not to deny that there were internal rivalries in Jamaica and elsewhere. Rather, the point is that the intensity and focus of the external pressures shaped the form of these rivalries and resulted in irreconcilable differences and destructive conflicts. There was a comparable crisis in Grenada in 1983, when internal rivalries within the PRG imploded as a result of intolerable external pressures.

[54] CLC Monthly Bulletin, Dec. 1949, HP, R2/51. The council members present were Adams (president), Manley (vice-president), Bird, Gomes, Hart (secretary), McIntosh, Lee, Lloyd, Ken Hill and A. Winston, representing Barbados, Jamaica, Antigua, Trinidad and Tobago, St Vincent, Guyana and Dominica. Marryshow and Critchlow were unable to attend.

[55] Denis Healey to Hart, 25 Feb. 1947, HP, R8/113; Vincent Tewson to Hart, 6 Mar. 1947, HP, R8/120.

[56] Foreign Office to HM representatives worldwide, 20 Nov. 1949, CO 537/4282.

[57] Arthur Creech Jones to Tewson, 15 Nov. 1949, CO 537/4282.

[58] Election of General Council, 8 Dec. 1949, CO 537/4283.

[59] Annex on ICFTU, 1949, CO 537/4283.

[60] Bradshaw had already shown the inclination to enjoy and make a political asset of such connections when he returned from England to 'a great reception' and 'now flies a Union Jack from the Bonnet of his car of which he is proud' (Gov. Leeward Islands to Creech Jones, 23 Jul. 1949, CO 537/48837).

[61] Barbados Beacon, 25 Mar. 1950, quoted in Hoyos 1974: 158.

[62] Barbados Beacon, 15 Jul. 1950, quoted in Hoyos 1974: 159.

[63] Woolley to SS, 2 Sept. 1948, CO 537/3785.

[64] Gov. R.H. Garvey to SS, 8 Feb. 1949, CO 537/4905.

[35] Barbados Beacon, 29 Jan. 1949, cited in Hoyos 1974: 156.

[66] Manley to SS, 7 Feb. 1949, CO 537/4905.

[67] Woolley to SS, 9 Mar. 1949, CO 537/4905.

[68] Trinidad Guardian, 24 Jun. 1952.

69 Hart, the lone surviving member of the Four H's, was restored as a party member in 1998 (pers. comm. July 2000).

70 Hart, F. Hill and Henry to K. Hill, 3 Apr. 1952, HP, R2/127.

71 Hart to F. Hill, 5 Sept. 1952, HP, R2/153.

72 Circular from K. Hill, 19 Jan. 1953, HP, R2/142.

73 Henry Middleton of Belize's GWU was present at this conference (Romualdi 1967: 113).

74 Trinidad Guardian, 29 Apr. 1952, OWTUL.

75 BWU minute book, 30 April 1952, BWU, Bridgetown.

76 Sunday Guardian, 9 Mar. 1952.

77 Port of Spain Gazette, 20 May 1952; Sunday Guardian, 25 May 1952.

78 Port of Spain Gazette, 1 Jun. 1952.

79 Sunday Guardian, 8 Jun. 1952.

80 Barbados Beacon, 7 Jun. 1952, quoted in Hoyos 1974: 178.

81 Hart to Hoyos, 17 Feb. 1963, quoted in Hoyos 1974: 178.

82 Daily Gleaner, 25 Sept. 1952.

83 Hart's circular to CLC members, 14 Nov. 1952, HP, R2/134.

84 Barbados Recorder, 3 Nov. 1952, quoted in Hoyos 1974: 173.

85 Hart's circular to CLC members, 14 Nov. 1952, HP, R2/134.

86 Hart to Hoyos, 17 Feb. 1963, quoted in Hoyos 1974: 173.

87 Hart's circular to CLC members, 14 Nov. 1952, HP, R2/134.

88 Joseph Bance to Hart, 26 Feb. 1953, HP, R8/157; Bradshaw to Hart, 26 Feb. 1953, HP, R8/158.

89 Hart, 'The History of the Caribbean Labour Congress', Dec. 1966, HP, R4/35.

90 Hart's circular letter, 24 Aug. 1955, HP, R8/159.

91 G. Bowrin to Hart, 13 Nov. 1956, HP, R6/227.

92 Hart's press statement, n.d. (c. 1952), HP, R2/125.

Chapter 8

Authoritarianism in the institutionalisation of the labour movement

Since the nineteenth century European popular movements of the left have tended towards either the democratic or the authoritarian political tradition. The latter, drawing on the Jacobin phase of the French Revolution and culminating in the Bolsheviks, emphasised a political vanguard whose 'centralized action-oriented revolutionary efforts' (Hobsbawm 1994: 385) were intended to create the conditions that would benefit the masses. The former consisted of trade unions, labour parties, cooperatives and combinations of all of these that emerged as mass movements whose political aspirations were expressed internally in democratic procedures and organisational structures and externally in the demand for a broader franchise. In other words, the democratic tradition sought reforms, some of them far-reaching and profound, within the existing society, rather than a revolutionary break with that society.

The democratic tradition prevailed in the labour movement in the British Caribbean colonies in the 1930s and 1940s, including the Marxist left, but there were also frequently signs of more authoritarian tendencies within the movement. These, however, far from being oriented towards revolutionary goals, were generally associated with the more conservative side of the labour movement. Authoritarianism was often associated not only with charismatic leaders, like Alexander Bustamante and Eric Gairy, but also with the bureaucratisation of labour organisations, and it was generally strengthened by imperialism. Thus, despite the pro-democratic rhetoric from the UK and the United States, which became particularly strident from the latter during the Cold War, imperialism hindered democratic developments and reinforced authoritarianism in the Caribbean colonies. By the early 1950s, when most of these colonies were participating in democratic political systems and were coming closer to self-government and independence, authoritarian tendencies were becoming more pronounced in many trade unions and political parties.

Several factors coincided during the 1940s and early 1950s to promote this authoritarianism in the new trade unions of the British Caribbean. Among these were the extraordinarily powerful influences of a few popular labour leaders, the bureaucratisation of the unions that institutionalised a hierarchy of power, and the influence of the new colonial labour departments and the British TUC that reinforced the control of the leaders at the expense of the rank and file. Regardless of whether authoritarianism took a more populist or more bureaucratic form, however, it was inimical to the democratic aspirations and tendencies of the labour movement in the British Caribbean. Moreover, the development of authoritarianism in the labour movement had wider political implications because of the close connections between the trade unions and emerging political parties during this period of decolonisation and evolving self-government.

In this chapter the relations between democratic and authoritarian tendencies will be examined in the context of the institutionalisation of trade unions and the emergent political parties associated with the labour movement. During the final phase of British colonialism in the Caribbean, when mass politics emerged out of anticolonial agitation in the global context of the Cold War, the conditions under which ostensibly democratic procedures and institutions developed were conducive to the persistence of authoritarianism even within these organisations. Moreover, as Clive Thomas argues, the constitutional struggles for independence at that time were linked to 'struggles against the colonial division of labor and its emphasis on primary commodity production, export specialization, and minimal industrial development; against forced trade and financial links with the metropole, designed to reproduce the world market internally' (1984: 44). To the extent these struggles were unresolved they further promoted authoritarianism in the post-colonial states, so, despite the prevalence of democratic forms, working people, the majority, remained effectively excluded from real power in both the economy and the state.

The institutionalisation of trade unions and their close relations with emerging political parties in this phase of decolonisation established a pattern of labour politics that has generally persisted in the post–colonial states. By the late twentieth century, in the period after the Cold War, characterised by economic depression, the debt crisis and structural adjustment, the associated problems of powerlessness and poverty were persisting throughout the Caribbean. The only real solution to regional development for the benefit of the 'poor and the powerless' lies in overcoming the longstanding and deep-rooted authoritarian traditions and 'the democratisation of all the decision-making structures in the society, from the level of the workplace and community right through to central government' (Thomas 1988: 358).

A framework for analysing trade unionism

Lloyd Braithwaite advocated a Weberian framework for the analysis of trade unionism in the Caribbean. In both Jamaica and Trinidad, he pointed out, there was 'the emergence of "a charismatic personality", who in each case came into conflict with a legally-trained person more suited perhaps for bureaucratic organization-building' (1987:14). Braithwaite saw the relevance of Max Weber's classic discussion of authority 'in the specifically West Indian context of the end of colonial rule and the emergence of a popular political and labour leadership' (1987: 15). For example, a leader like Uriah Butler was undoubtedly charismatic in the sense of being a powerful individual whose exceptional powers and willingness to break the rules endowed him with a particular kind of authority among his followers, while a leader like Adrian Cola Rienzi depended more on bureaucratic authority based on a system of rules and regulations. Braithwaite concluded: 'The trade union has developed from this phase dominated by personal leadership to the period of democratic organization. This tension between charismatic personality and bureaucratic order remained (and some would say persisted) as a constant theme in the trade union movement in Trinidad and Tobago.' (1987: 15)

This is largely true, but Braithwaite's proposed framework is one-dimensional. The tension between charismatic and bureaucratic constitutes one dimension of analysis, but each varies in the degree to which it may be authoritarian. I propose, therefore, a two-dimensional framework of analysis for the study of trade unionism, one dimension being that of charismatic versus bureaucratic authority, in the Weberian sense, and the other being the distinction between democratic and authoritarian procedures and structures within the institutions.

Figure 8.1

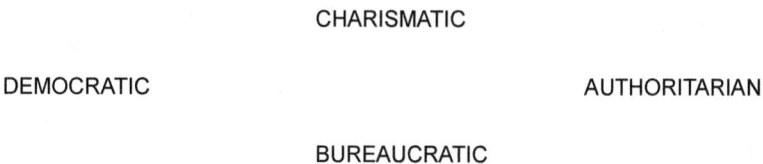

CHARISMATIC

DEMOCRATIC   AUTHORITARIAN

BUREAUCRATIC

The notion of charismatic authoritarian leaders, or 'populist auth-oritar-ianism', is quite familiar, and the history of the Caribbean offers numerous examples, but the notion of 'bureaucratic authoritarianism' requires some explanation. The concept was developed by the Argentinian political scientist Guillermo O'Donnell (1973, 1979) to account for the emergence of a distinctive form of politics associated with the military regimes that followed the crisis of populism in Argentina under Juan Perón and in Brazil under Getúlio Vargas. According to O'Donnell, the new form of politics emerged in part because a growing sector of technocrats sought a coalition with middle- and upper-class elements in order to deactivate popular sectors by instituting a repressive kind of state authoritarianism. Bureaucratic authoritarianism, then, became a way to deactivate a popular sector, which may include elements of the middle class as well as the working class and peasants, that is already active by effectively excluding it from political participation. This limitation of democracy could take place both at the societal level of national politics and at the institutional level in labour and political organisations. The political exclusion and deacti-vation of the popular elements is typically achieved in this bureaucratic form by an emphasis on order, rules, hierarchy, technical qualifications and so on, with a high degree of coercion that may be obscured by the ostensible use of democratic forms and procedures.

It has been argued that the term 'bureaucratic authoritarianism' should be restricted 'to situations in which military intervention occurred in reaction against leftist movements' (Cardoso 1979: 38), but this is too restrictive a use of the term which is more useful as an ideal type than a specific and narrow label. Using the notion as an ideal type, we may look for elements of bureaucratic authoritarianism in a variety of situations that may in other respects be quite different. Hence, any regime that exhibits bureaucratic and authoritarian fea-tures, such as the civilian rule of the PRI in Mexico, may be analysed in terms of bureaucratic authoritarianism. Many Latin American nations have a history of militarism and caudillismo, so what is distinctive about the more recent political role of the military is that it has taken a less personal and more insti-tutionalised and bureaucratic form. However, bureaucratic authoritarianism appears in many institutions, including trade unions and political parties, and occurs frequently in societies undertaking decolonisation when the organised popular forces pressing for extended civil rights and independence come into conflict with the state's need to create an attractive climate for foreign inves-tors. Restrictions on trade unions, economic austerity programmes and wage controls may be opposed by popular organisations, but trade unions and labour-based political parties themselves become vehicles of social control when their middle-class leaders, often in collusion with the retiring colonial regime that they will replace, seek to develop the economy in the context of dependent capitalism. The emergence of varieties of bureaucratic authoritarianism, including but not limited to its military form, is related, therefore, to many political and economic contingencies. What they have in common is that they seek to deactivate leftist movements by bureaucratic methods.

Analysis in terms of bureaucratic authoritarianism should help us to understand how the growth of trade unions, and the increasing ties between them and political parties, may have debilitating effects on a democratic labour movement. My suggestion, therefore, is that the history of the labour movement, and of the changes in the social relations of domination during the period of decolonisation, may be analysed in terms of tensions between charismatic and bureaucratic authority, on the one hand, and democracy and authoritarianism, on the other. In short, we may observe in the institutionalisation of trade unions, and in the changes in the wider political culture, forms of charismatic and bureaucratic authority and organisation that are more or less democratic or authoritarian. This additional dimension provides a better framework for, and hence a more complete understanding of, trade unionism and the labour movement in the British Caribbean. The next two sections of this chapter examine, first, Bustamante, Butler and Gairy as charismatic authoritarian labour leaders, and, second, the Barbados Workers' Union and the Oilfield Workers' Trade Union of Trinidad in terms of bureaucratic authoritarianism.

Charismatic authoritarian labour leaders

Alexander Bustamante is almost an archetypal charismatic authoritarian labour leader, but he is not the only figure of this kind in the British Caribbean. Among the many early labour leaders there were several others, including Butler, Robert Bradshaw, Vere Bird and Gairy. Butler was a truly charismatic leader[1] in the sense that his authority among his followers was based on the belief that he was a man possessed of special, and perhaps even supernatural, powers and that he could break the rules by which others were governed. Butler was a messianic figure, whose influence over his followers relied on a distinctly religious appeal and his ability to use words in a highly charged manner. The traditions of eloquence in the Caribbean and the performance aspect of the man of words are well known (Abrahams 1983). Several leaders used this cultural tradition - using words to influence people - in order to achieve and maintain a powerful sway over their followers. Here we will focus on Bustamante, Butler and Gairy. All three were royalist-loyalists whose faith in God was associated with their faith in king and queen. Their radical rhetoric was aimed at their local opponents, not at the central symbols of the British empire. They sought home rule within the empire, and all desired acceptance by their social superiors. Bustamante and Gairy eventually and gratefully accepted knighthoods.

Jamaica

Bustamante was a man of words, renowned for his fiery rhetoric, and he resorted to histrionics in ways that bonded his audiences to him. Eaton recalls, as a teenager, 'seeing Alexander Bustamante demonstrate to an enthralled audience in Kingston how Manley and the P.N.P. candidates would writhe from his political whiplash, as if beaten with cow-itch (a vine which produces severe itching and irritation on contact with the human body) and then proceed, with mock contortions, to take off his shirt, all the while 'scratching' the supposedly affected areas. The performances kept his supporters in 'stitches' of laughter.' (1975: 172)

This was not merely a manner of speaking or a performance. Rather, the effective use of a rhetorical style established and maintained a particular kind of relationship between the leader and his followers, and it is this relationship rather than the style itself that concerns us because it promoted a profoundly undemocratic spirit and structure within the Bustamante Industrial Trade Union (BITU) and its associated political party, the Jamaica Labour Party (JLP). Bustamante succeeded in being both popular, in the sense of a man of the people, and aloof, a leader apart from the crowd. People who were not his followers often viewed him as a buffoon and contrasted him with his intellectually brilliant and more reserved rival, Norman Manley. My point, however, is not simply to contrast these two personalities or their political styles but to examine the nature of the relationship the leader had with his followers. Bustamante's followers could laugh with Bustamante but they did not see him as a buffoon.

Bustamante's platform and speaking style has been described by people who knew him:

> As he strode through the streets of Kingston and major rural towns, tall, gaunt, with high cheek-bones, flashing eyes and unruly hair, he was the warrior knight, the St. George, breathing denunciations and threatening to slay the offending dragon. On public platforms, he displayed even greater flamboyance and melodrama, gesticulating, baring his encased dagger, occasionally brandishing his revolver, especially when reporting alleged plots against his life because of his identification with the cause of the common man. He spoke in short, clipped phrases, repeating his points as if to hammer them home into the consciousness of his listeners (Eaton 1975: 54).

Bustamante manipulated the mythology about his mysterious background, his youthful travels and foreign experience, and his martyrdom after his arrest and imprisonment. He also made use of his economic and racial status, which was considerably higher than that of his followers. In a society in which many black people still doubted their own abilities, even if they did not believe in the supposedly superior nature of the white man, Bustamante throve on the notion that he was 'every bit as good as the bosses were' (Eaton 1975: 55) and that they could not outwit him or intimidate him. Sometime in the 1940s, Vernon Arnett, the secretary of the People's National Party (PNP), invoked the folk character of Anansi, the trickster spider, to describe the relations between Bustamante and his followers:

> He has been put at the head of an organisation by the people in the belief that he will serve them, and they cannot believe that he is merely serving his own interests. His cunning appeals to them that he is doing it to trick the employers and gain more power. The 'nancy' complex of his is strong within us. For in the days of slavery when the slaves gathered together in the evenings, it was these tales of how the little anancy with his cunning could outwit the strong and powerful that they loved to hear. We must remember that in thinking of conditions today.[2]

Post, too, refers to Bustamante as 'the trickster leader, who…invoked status. Coming to the workers 'from above', he was able to convince them that he understood the system and could manipulate it for their benefit' (1978: 252). Bustamante was known as 'Labour Leader No. 1', or simply 'the Chief', and his followers pledged, as their song says, 'to follow Busta 'til we die'.

Bustamante created and exploited a reputation for brinkmanship, while confident that he could lead the masses into situations where, by virtue of his own social status, he would be less susceptible to police harassment or brutality than his followers (Eaton 1975: 26). This is not to deny that Bustamante possessed great personal courage, but rather to point out that his display of courage, often in confrontations that seem to have been created to provide the opportunity for such display, became a basis for hero-worship. Bustamante's carefully staged performances when negotiating with employers, cajoling or threatening them, and storming out of meetings, impressed the worker delegates because they 'imparted a sense of power and gave deep psychological satisfaction' (Eaton 1975: 215). These performances were also crafted in such a way that the workers remained dependent on their chief.

Bustamante was a man of rural background, of considerable charm and generosity, who succeeded in creating a relationship with 'the illiterate peasants and workers who not only believed in him, and revered him, but who were prepared to die for him' (Eaton 1975: 55). His rhetoric and histrionics helped create this reverence but so, too, did his actions as a labour leader and negotiator. His reputation as a fearless and cunning leader, earned through countless confrontations, not only inspired loyalty among his followers but also enabled him to claim that he was indispensable. Expectations of loyalty and support then became demands for total commitment and absolute obedience to the boss. Though Bustamante could easily fraternise with the rank and file, he was never one of them, and his relationship with them was paternalistic, if not despotic. He accepted the familiar shortening of his name to Busta as a token of the affection in which the masses held him, but he tolerated no opposition or rivals and ruled the union that he named after himself as if it were his personal business.

'As a labour leader, Alexander Bustamante exercised a truly remarkable authority over the B.I.T.U.'s rank and file' (Eaton 1975: 214), for whom he was the hero and champion. He also exercised absolute control over the senior officers in the union. This control over the union hierarchy, and subsequently the JLP hierarchy also, was evident in his intolerance of rivals and opposition. He also deflected criticism when something went wrong by claiming that it was because somebody had given him less than full support. His 'habit of publicly denouncing alleged challenges to, or usurpations of, his authority' (Eaton 1975: 218), both within the BITU and the JLP, obtained for him a degree of immunity from criticism and, by appearing to stand above petty matters, this further enhanced his heroic stature. In the event of a crisis he would demand a vote of confidence in the chief, which was a way to avoid debating the merits of a particular issue while reinforcing his personal authority. 'At no time, therefore, during his active career as labour leader and politician was there ever the slightest possibility of Bustamante being persuaded to function as "the first among equals" ... the "Chief" exacted absolute loyalty and obedience' (Eaton 1975: 218).

The absolute authority that Bustamante demanded and exercised was based on his personal qualities, but it became embedded in the constitution of his union and reinforced by a system of patronage. Bustamante was installed as the leader of the union for life, unless two-thirds of the union's members, who had to be gathered at a general meeting, voted to remove him, which was practically impossible (Post 1981:Vol. 1, 241). Bustamante took the extraordinary step of naming the unions that were being organised in 1938 after himself, soon after his release from prison. The draft constitution that Hart and others wrote for the fledgling unions provided for the election of officers and an executive committee, but Bustamante instructed his solicitor to amend the constitution so as to make him president for life and to give him the power to appoint its managing committee. 'Bustamante did not regard a trade union as belonging to its members. Nor did he see himself in the role of a servant or employee of the workers. He conceived of a union as something more in the nature of a business and saw himself as its proprietor. The union would offer a service to the workers in return for their money and support. In Bustamante's book unionism was a straight commercial transaction.' (Hart 1989: 102) When Bustamante's proprietary approach to trade unionism was challenged in 1939 he responded by expelling or demoting experienced leaders like Hugh Buchanan,

St William Grant and Ken Hill. He wrote to The Daily Gleaner in response to criticism on 31 August 1938: 'It has been stated that I want to be a dictator. Yes, I do want to dictate the policy of the Unions, in the interests of the people I represent and the only ones who are giving results today are the dictators ... . The voice of labour must be heard and it shall be heard through me.'³ Other trade unionists were concerned about Bustamante's contempt for democracy. The president of the Chauffeurs' Union, which held out against merging with the BITU, warned that 'when you name a union after any one man, it is a sure sign that somebody is going to be a dictator' (quoted in Eaton 1975: 62-3).

When Bustamante was released from internment in 1942 he reasserted control over the BITU by firing several senior officers. He refused to attend a reception organised by the union's managing executive committee in his honour, saying, 'There are certain officers right in the office, whom my blood has almost been depleted in order to provide them legitimate employment, whose conduct has helped materially to hinder, obstruct and delay my release from detention .... To aggravate matters there has been and still exists an unholy combination of certain persons with political ambition whose objective is that of destroying me and then to assume control of the Union as a political machine and to serve their own big friends.'⁴

Bustamante's targets were H.M. Shirley, the BITU's vice-president, who had taken the chair in the leader's absence, and Manley, the chief of the 'big friends'. Although Bustamante could constitutionally appoint or dismiss all the other officers, the vice-president was elected. It is unclear whether Shirley was dismissed or resigned (Post 1981: Vol. 1, 223), but it is clear that Bustamante used a pretence to remove possible rivals and to re-establish his absolute control of the union. His biographer says, 'Alexander Bustamante's victory over Manley and Shirley was never in doubt,' and at a meeting on 31 March 1942 he 'was reaffirmed as hero and saviour of the working classes" (Eaton 1975: 81-2). However, his personal victory came at the expense of the widening split between the BITU and the PNP and of Bustamante's increasingly dictatorial control of Jamaica's greatest trade union. Even the control of union finances was in the hands of a standing committee consisting of one person, President Bustamante. His private secretary, Gladys Longbridge, whom he had met when she was a cashier at a restaurant and who became his wife after 30 years of attachment, was the BITU's treasurer (Eaton 1975: 27,78).

The patronage system came later when Bustamante, as minister of communications, had funds, jobs and contracts to dispense. Part of his role as messiah consisted of dispensing and protecting jobs and contracts for his supporters. Eaton points out that some of the old pattern of patronage and allegiance that existed under the traditional estate system, which was dispensed and exacted by the planters and managers, was transferred to Bustamante as chief of his BITU, and then to Bustamante as minister in the JLP government:

> One immediate consequence of Bustamante's political unionism, therefore, was that political and trade union affiliation became the main criterion govern-ing the employment of labour on governmental work projects as well as the recruitment of employees at the subordinate levels in the public services. This held true for both levels of government, central and municipal or parochial.
> To the victor, then, went the spoils. (Eaton 1975: 115)

Bustamante's enhanced ability, as minister of communications as well as president general of the BITU, to determine the levels and allocation of public funds and contracts for public works became a source of further power not only through patronage but also through denying opportunities to his union and political rivals. During 1945 there was a record of 145 labour disputes, 97 of which resulted in strikes involving some 11,600 workers, and 53 per cent of which occurred in agriculture. The BITU was expanding its power through closed-shop agreements that excluded the rival JTUC. Bustamante clearly stated his view in a debate in the House of Representatives concerning claims by the Railway Employees' Union, an affiliate of the JTUC, for higher wages and shorter hours: 'I am the only leader in this country and the only leader of a union that can protect the people' (quoted in Eaton 1975: 116). Bustamante, having used his union base to rise to political prominence, then openly used his ministerial position to promote his union. In April 1946 he stated to the House of Representatives, 'The Sugar Manufacturers have an obligation to see that unionists are first employed by them in the field and factory, because workers in the field and factory are members of the Bustamante Industrial Trade Union, skilled workers and unskilled' (quoted in Eaton 1975: 115-16). The BITU benefited at the expense of the JTUC, as membership of the former rose from 30,000 to 46,000 while that of the latter declined from 14,000 to less than 10,000. This success occurred at the expense of labour solidarity.

One of the issues causing rivalry between the unions was the recruitment of workers to go to the United States. In March 1945 it was confirmed that the local agents who were to recruit the workers would be appointed by the members of the House of Representatives. Even if this did not involve direct corruption and kickbacks, leaders of the BITU-JLP were provided with an opportunity to influence the job opportunities of thousands of workers. In March 1945 there were 15,423 Jamaicans (along with 957 Belizeans and 1,736 Barbadians) working in the United States, and by August this had risen to 31,578 Jamaicans (and 919 Belizeans and 5,655 Barbadians).[5] A pattern of rivalry, animosity and even violence arose as workers competed with each other for access to the limited employment opportunities that were dispensed or withheld on the basis of trade-union and political-party affiliations.[6] This pattern became well established in Jamaica where it was both a cause and an effect of the party machine, and where it reinforced the relations between the leader and that machine, which Bustamante developed and kept tight control of in order to extend his personal power. His charismatic authority remained predominant over the bureaucratic elements, and the entire BITU-JLP system became more authoritarian.

This was evident in a series of events in 1946 and 1947, during which the increasingly violent union rivalries and political partisanship pushed Bustamante into a law-and-order stance. On 15 February 1946 a crisis began when about 280 nurses and attendants at the Kingston Mental Hospital, most of whom were members of Florizel Glasspole's JTUC-affiliated Government Hospital and Prison Employees' Union, went on strike. They sought the dismissal of the senior medical officer, whom a review committee in 1943 had found responsible for employee problems and which had recommended his retirement. Bustamante's government demanded that they return to work unconditionally, but the JTUC retorted that the government had not adopted this position when Bustamante had led strikes on the waterfront and sugar estates during the war. Mental patients escaped and the police, who were reported to be sympathetic to the strikers, were slow to recapture them. Bustamante claimed that the strike was aimed at his government and advised the governor 'to take an iron hand in this matter. No sympathy whatsoever must be shown'.[7]

The government brought in military personnel to run the hospital and Bustamante assembled thousands of dockers who were BITU members, ostensibly to round up the inmates but really as a show of force. On 16 February they marched to the hospital, some singing, 'We will follow Bustamante till we die'. One BITU member, Clifford Reid, did die. J. Nicholas, a PNP supporter who was not connected with the dispute, when threatened by a BITU gang, shot and killed Reid before he was himself trampled to death by the enraged mob. The JTUC called out prison guards, firemen and railroad workers, and pitched battles ensued in the streets of Kingston, during which three more men were killed and scores wounded. An inmate of the hospital, inadequately supervised, started a fire that burned 15 patients to death. Nethersole, president of the JTUC, sought intervention from Britain. He wrote to Creech Jones, 'Since Bustamante's rise to power as Head of the elected section of Government in Jamaica, he has adopted a deliberate strategy of coercion through his trade union organisation and to establish a political power machine . . . . Bustamante, shortly after his election, declared his intention to destroy the subordinate government employees union … [and] to compel workers to join his union as a condition of obtaining work'.[8]

The government of Jamaica, meanwhile, declared a state of emergency. Thirty-seven JTUC pickets were arrested and charged with unlawful assembly. A settlement was reached in March, strikers returned to work and the state of emergency was relaxed. In April Bustamante and Frank Pixley, the minister for social welfare, were charged with manslaughter in the death of a bystander at the hands of the BITU gang. Although they were acquitted in June, the violence, charges and trial had further polarised the two sides.

PNP supporters and the unemployed joined in marches to protest against discrimination and victimization in employment on government projects, so Bustamante's government passed a bill in May 1947 to prohibit marches within a specified distance of several government offices. As the opposition became more determined, with the PNP creating its own strong-arm groups to protect their meetings and members, political violence continued. On 20 October 1947 a clash between rival political groups in Trench Pen left several BITU-JLP supporters dead and wounded. As a result, 'Bustamante became more and more preoccupied with the maintenance of law and order and with the containment of political protest' (Eaton 1975: 121). The chief rabble-rouser himself became a law-and-order authoritarian, and this development, while certainly not unique to the Jamaican situation, was enhanced by the 'ambiguity of the roles being played concurrently by Bustamante as head of the B.I.T.U. and elected head of the B.I.T.U-based Government' (Eaton 1975: 121). Bustamante's charismatic leadership of his union was based on his reputation as a tough man who was willing to break the rules for his followers, but as head of the JLP government he could use the rules, and create new ones, to shackle his opponents when they played the same game.

In this way, tragically, the intense rivalry and political violence between the two union-based political parties of Jamaica became institutionalised and in this political culture authoritarianism flourished at the expense of democracy. Popular participation was largely a matter of mass protests and shows of strength, and rewards for support were handed out in the form of patronage when leaders acquired power. The spoils of patronage, in turn, reinforced inequalities in the party machines and also fuelled the intense competition and partisanship that led to greater political intolerance and violence. Over the years this violence escalated from the use of stones and clubs to automatic weapons.

Bustamante's 'paternalistic concern for labour's welfare' (Eaton 1975: 126) became increasingly evident, and it became clear that the JLP was not a labour party in the British sense but really a party with a strong commitment to private enterprise. Bustamante led a conservative party based on a proprietary union. Although officially Bustamante did not become chief minister until May 1953, when the ministerial system was inaugurated, he was always the Chief, who demanded absolute personal loyalty and obedience, whether as president of his union, leader of his party or chief minister of his government. Bustamante epitomised the charismatic - authoritarian form of leadership in the Caribbean, but he was not the only example.

Trinidad

Butler, the self-styled 'Chief Servant of the Lord', who relied even more than Bustamante on charismatic qualities, failed to create an organised movement to compare with the BITU-JLP, and never achieved power in Trinidad and Tobago in spite of having a larger and more faithful following than any other labour leader. We have seen in chapter 5 how Butler sparked the labour rebellion in Trinidad in 1937 and how, on his release from prison in 1939, he was soon expelled from the Oilfield Workers' Trade Union (OWTU). Rearrested in November 1939, Butler remained in prison until 1945, leaving the way for Rienzi, Mentor, Rojas and Moses to institutionalise the OWTU. By 1945, after Rojas had succeeded Rienzi as president general, and a historical agreement had been signed with the oil companies containing a cost-of-living allowance clause, the OWTU appeared impregnable. Rojas, in fact, held the leading position for 19 years, until 1962. Butler, however, was not finished. Soon after his release from internment he roused his followers and started another period of agitation in the oilfields. Unlike Bustamante and Gairy, Butler really was a worker among workers, and his support was quite widespread and very committed. However, Butler never achieved the kind of power that Bustamante and Gairy came to enjoy, and within a decade of his release 'Butlerism was a spent force' (Ryan 1972: 138).

After Butler's release on 9 April 1945 he was prevented from entering the oilfield area by a restriction order.[9] Nevertheless, he revived his British Empire Workers' Peasants' and Ratepayers' Union and the British Empire Workers' and Citizens' Home Rule Party (BEWCHRP) to contest the general elections in 1946. The BEWCHRP won three of the nine seats but Butler himself lost to Albert Gomes, the United Front candidate, in Port of Spain. Butler's strength was in the oilfields where he remained very popular, and where he turned again to direct action. Workers were dissatisfied because of high inflation and the decline in the number of jobs after the war. 'Butler's issues were the cost of living, unemployment, racial discrimination in industry, neglect by the government and the apparent inactivity of the recognized trade unions' (Brereton 1981: 190). The central question was who would represent the workers, and union rivalry among the oil, asphalt and sugar workers continued to divide the labour movement in Trinidad.

On 11 November 1946 Butler's union issued a demand to the Oilfields Employers' Association (OEA) for a general increase of 10 cents per hour for all hourly-paid workers and 80 cents per day for all other categories of workers.

Later that month, during a well-organised waterfront strike in Port of Spain, led by the Seamen and Waterfront Workers' Trade Union (SWWU), Butler distributed a handbill demanding more pay for all workers and urging them to join his union. But, the handbill said, 'they must wait for the order to strike which can only come from Butler and Butler alone' (Dalley 1947: 46). When Butler called on oil workers to strike on 19 December 1946, the OWTU countermanded his instructions. As the OWTU had a contractual agreement with the OEA, effective from 13 December 1945, they could hardly do otherwise, even though the 2 cents per hour wage increase they had negotiated was lost through inflation. The official cost of living index had risen from 100 in 1935 to 109 in 1939, and then to 216 in 1946 and 221 in 1947, but because of 'excessive commercial profits' the actual cost of living was 'far above that indicated by the official index' (Dalley 1947: 4). When a large number of workers responded to Butler's call, the OWTU joined the OEA and the colonial government in trying to crush Butler. Tensions rose and Butler's supporters became frustrated when people whom Rojas and other OWTU officials had recruited to break the strike were driven under police guard to the oilfields.[10] Two oil wells were set on fire on 17 January and the government introduced an emergency powers ordinance, ordering Butler and five of his cohorts to leave the county of St Patrick, and controlling the movement of people in the oil district. The Public Works Union (PWU), meanwhile, called a strike in Port of Spain on 8 January, and some 1,200 of Butler's supporters staged a protest march in the capital. When the crowd occupied the Red House, the government building housing the legislature and the secretariat, the police cleared it and the adjacent square. Butler's headquarters was raided and his printing machine damaged. Sugar workers on the Caroni Estates, led by Ranjit Kumar who opposed the Sugar Workers' Union,[11] went on strike on 5 May 1947, but they did not unite with the oilfield and urban workers, and Butler's efforts to create a broader strike failed.

Butler was squeezed out by the 'responsible' labour leaders and the government and employers who regarded him 'as a threat to orderly trade unionism' (Brereton 1981: 190). F.W. Dalley, a British trade unionist who arrived in Trinidad on 3 April 1947 to make a report on the labour situation, concluded, 'Responsible Trade Unionism and "Butlerism" cannot exist side by side; they are incompatibles, and the workers of Trinidad should be helped to realise this by all the responsible elements in the Colony' (1947: 35). When the TTTUC endorsed Dalley's report, the rift between Butler and the other unions widened. The OWTU later described its role in the strike of 1946-7 as 'unforgivable', but says that the influx of many Butlerites strengthened the union in 1948-50 by increasing its size and militancy. In the early 1950s, consequently, the OWTU 'recaptured some of the fire for which it was first known. Marches and demonstrations were held regularly - and with tremendous support from oilworkers and their families'.[12] Although the OWTU, in particular, benefited from Butler's eclipse, he again attempted to win political power in the 1950 elections.

On 28 April 1949, while Butler was in the UK where he petitioned the colonial secretary, several of his supporters held a meeting in the dock area of Port of Spain. They protested against the new constitution which provided for a legislature in which eight of the 26 seats would not be elected. On May Day, when the TTTUC held a demonstration with some 1,100 people in San Fernando, Butler's party held a demonstration in Port of Spain with about 3,000 people, many of whom came from the south by special trains. Timothy Roodal, Chanka Maharaj, C.B. Mathura, Benjamin Alves and Pope McLean, members of Butler's BEWCHRP, spoke against the new constitution.[13] Eighteen seats were contested in the elections on 18 September 1950 by several labour-oriented groups and parties, including the Caribbean Socialist Party (CSP), led by Patrick Solomon, the old Trinidad Labour Party (TLP), led by Raymond Hamel-Smith, the TTTUC, which although not officially a political party did contest the election, and Butler's party, which formed an alliance with some key Indian leaders including Mitra and Ashford Sinanan (brothers) and Ranjit Kumar. Finally, there was the Political Progress Group (PPG), led by Gomes and backed by mostly white planters and businessmen. Efforts to create a labour coalition failed and Butler's party was the only one to contest all 18 seats.

The Butler party candidates won 41,644, or 23 per cent, of a total of 180,386 votes, which was enough to win six seats: Butler in St Patrick West, Chanka Maharaj in St Joseph, Mitra Sinanan in Caroni South, McLean in Victoria North, Ashford Sinanan in Victoria South, and S. Maharaj in Ortoire/Mayaro. The PPG and TLP each won two seats and the CSP one; the other seven were won by independents. Butler's victory was achieved despite the fact that he and his candidates had spent less money on their campaigns than their rivals.[14] Solomon and Hamel-Smith were both defeated, so Gomes was the only party leader other than Butler to win his seat. When two independents attached themselves to Butler's group this bloc expanded to eight, by far the largest group in the Legislative Council but still a small minority of the total of 26, consisting of 18 elected, five nominated unofficials and three ex officio members. Governor Sir Hubert Rance, who was convinced that Butler lacked the ability to fill a role on the Executive Council, manoeuvred among the members of the Legislative Council to exclude him. Not only was Butler himself denied the ministerial office that he was justified in claiming but, astonishingly, no member of his party was chosen for the Executive Council. Of the five elected members given seats on the Executive Council, three were independents, one a member of the CSP and one, Gomes, was the leader of the PPG, but Butler's party was shut out completely.

Butler and his colleagues had protested against the shortcomings of the constitution with good reason. After winning the election, he lost to the conservative and official members of the Legislative Council who made a mockery of democracy. Understandably, Butler characterised his exclusion from the Executive Council as a 'political blasphemy' and 'a spectacle … never surpassed even in the most distasteful era of British Crown colony government in the West Indies' (quoted in Ryan 1972: 91). The chief beneficiary of the quasi-ministerial system that emerged in Trinidad and Tobago between 1950 and 1956 was Gomes, who dominated the political stage in those years although he lacked the popular support of Butler.

It has been generally accepted, not least by Eric Williams, that Butler had great leadership ability in the sense of being able to inspire support among thousands of people, but that his failure as an organiser explains why he never achieved power. He 'proved inadequate to the task either of forming a political party or of organizing the oilfield workers; and whilst his popularity was undoubted and was fully deserved, and whilst he never swerved in his demand for self-government for Trinidad and Tobago, he proved as inadequate as Cipriani had proved before him in the sense of mobilizing the mass movement that he had helped to develop and guiding it along the inevitable organizational channels for the capture of political power and for the use of that power when it had been captured'. (Williams 1964: 235) Similarly, Ryan (1972: 92) argues, 'Butler's weaknesses as a leader go a long way towards explaining the failure of the nationalist movement to develop more fully and powerfully in the early fifties …. He was a mesmerizer par excellence, but his leadership abilities ended there.'

There is a good deal of truth in these views, but it probably only amounts to half the truth when it comes to explaining Butler's failure. There is no doubt that his union and party lacked adequate organisation and that his personal vanity and jealousy of rival leaders inhibited the kind of cooperation that could have built a broader and more powerful movement. Dalley reported in 1947 that 'there was a constant succession of appointments and dismissals' in Butler's union because the 'Chief Servant' removed officers who opposed him or appeared too co-operative with employers (Dalley 1947:15). Financial contributions, often obtained by passing a hat around at meetings, were also kept in Butler's personal control, and the union's books were said to be 'inexpertly kept' (Dalley 1947: 16). Much the same may be said of many of Butler's contemporaries in Trinidad and elsewhere, yet some of them succeeded when Butler did not. Bustamante, too, was vain and his organisations were built to an extraordinary degree around his person in order to fulfil his ambitions. Gomes was also a colourful egoist who is said to have boasted, 'I am the Government of Trinidad and Tobago' (Ryan 1972: 94), but he achieved higher status with even less organisation than Butler. One crucial difference between these men is that Butler was unwilling to compromise with the employers and colonial administrators, as both Bustamante and Gomes did, in such a way as to negotiate a position for himself in the emerging system of self-government. Bustamante and Gomes became acceptable in the eyes of the economic and political elite, but because Butler remained an outsider in their eyes he remained one in fact, excluded from an office that he reasonably claimed to have won. The fact that Butler, unlike Gomes and Bustamante, was black probably contributed to the elite's view of him as an outsider.[15]

Whatever the shortcomings of Butler and his organisations, and they are clear and important, we should acknowledge that he succeeded in organising well enough in the five years between his release from internment in 1945 and the elections in 1950, and against the opposition of better established trade unions and better backed political parties, as well as the implacable opposition of the employers and colonial government, to win more than any other labour or political leader in those elections. Perhaps the weakness of the labour movement and the nationalist movement in the early 1950s in Trinidad and Tobago should be attributed, not only to Butler himself, but also to those other, lesser leaders who failed to rally around him and chose instead to pursue their own selfish ambitions. Certainly, their eagerness to squeeze him out and then to share the major spoils among themselves was quite shameful, even if realistic politically in the light of the UK's refusal to deal with Butler. And the willingness with which the governor, and the Labour government which he represented, manoeuvred a transitional constitution in order to deny office to those who had succeeded in a democratic contest is also shameful.

Whatever judgement is made about Butler's failure or the culpability of his opponents, it is clear that Butler, unlike Gomes and Bustamante, had no power or patronage because he was denied office, and without the opportunity to dispense patronage his weak organisation soon fell apart. Butler, more than anyone, succeeded in bringing together Creole and Indian Trinidadians, workers from the canefields and the oilfields, the rural and the urban poor, but, denied the rewards of jobs, contracts or resources, many of his supporters simply sought coalitions elsewhere with people who could offer them something. Denied office, Butler could only threaten more agitation and disruption, but to what end when others were stepping in to share the spoils of the emerging system of self-government? Butler's threats to form the greatest opposition bloc and to agitate inside the Legislative Council made people anxious, but a new wave of unrest did not materialise. Butler spent much of the next few years in the UK, ostensibly petitioning the Colonial Office for home rule. He returned to contest the 1956 elections, but Butlerism was a spent force and Williams succeeded in defining himself as Butler's logical and historical successor (Ryan 1972: 137). Butler won his seat in the oilbelt in 1956, but in 1961 he polled only 517 votes in his old stronghold, which was a 'humiliating defeat' (Brereton 1981: 246). Although jailed for squatting in 1966, Butler was awarded a national medal in 1971, and 19 June 1972, the anniversary of the labour rebellion in 1937, was declared Butler Day, a national holiday (Kambon 1988: 278). Butler was brought back into the OWTU and awarded its labour star, the union's highest award, in 1969. He died on 20 February 1977.[16]

Butler, like Bustamante, was capable of working a crowd and inspiring support, and both men suffered in jail for being associated with the labour rebellions in the 1930s and for leading the labour movements that emerged from them. Both men had huge egos and were unwilling to share their leadership with others who might become rivals, or even to permit a more democratic, rational legal trade union to represent their people. Their messianic style and proprietorial approach to labour organisation led them to define the trade unions, and subsequently also their political parties, as if they were their personal property, with a consequent authoritarian disregard for accountability or democratic procedures. They and their organisations had much in common. Where they differed was partly in their social background and status, but also in their circumstances and success. Bustamante, whose social status was higher than Butler's, managed to outmanoeuvre his rivals, first in the trade unions and then in politics, so he was the first to benefit from the quasi-ministerial system in Jamaica, and used his new office, power and resources to reward his followers and to build his BITU-JLP into a successful patronage machine. Butler, who was an unemployed oil worker, was himself outmanoeuvred, first by his trade union rivals within the OWTU, then by other labour and political leaders, and finally, after he had won more seats than his rivals in the 1950 elections, by the colonial officials. 'Deprived of patronage and the fruits of power, the party fell apart' (Brereton 1981: 227) and Butler could not recover. His messianic skills and ambitions retained considerable support in the oilfields for a few more years, but his role as a labour and political leader finished in the early 1950s, while Bustamante's power rose to new heights.

Grenada

Another West Indian leader who used his personal charisma to develop an authoritarian trade union and labour party was Eric Matthew Gairy of Grenada. Grenada was one of the few British Caribbean colonies where there was no labour rebellion in the 1930s and this fact has generally been attributed to the 'higher than average peasant component' in the population (Hart 1995: viii).[17] This is not to say that most Grenadians were really better off, or even that they were more comfortable or economically secure than other people in the region. Rather, Grenadians who worked the land were embedded in social relationships that, although they were unsatisfactory, made it harder for them to combine in actions, such as strikes and demonstrations, to improve their situation. Grenada exhibited many features of the plantation economy, but the prevailing social relations of its economy established strong links of personal dependency between the workers and land-owners. These links were weakened in the 1930s and 1940s but were not challenged until the early 1950s.

The basis of Grenada's economy was still export crops, but the predominant crops changed between the period of slavery and the 1950s. Low sugar prices in the 1840s led the planters in Grenada as elsewhere to try to reduce wages and to import indentured workers from Madeira and India. Workers who demonstrated against wage reductions in the northern parish of St Patrick were suppressed by troops, and about 2,500 Indians were brought in before 1863. By 1856 47 sugar estates had been abandoned and the export of sugar declined from over 9 million lb in 1846 to about 2 million lb in 1881. However, cocoa production trebled between 1846 and 1855, and continued to rise until in 1881 almost 6 million lb of cocoa was exported (Smith 1965: 268). Nutmeg production, which was established in the second half of the nineteenth century, also expanded rapidly and nutmeg exports increased fourfold between 1900 and 1925, while cocoa production declined. By the early 1950s the cultivation and export of cocoa, nutmeg and mace (dried nutmeg husks, also used as a spice) constituted the basis of the Grenadian economy. From 1950 to 1954 these three products together accounted for 88 per cent of the value of all exports (Smith 1965: 264).

Most production of cocoa and nutmeg was undertaken by worker-tenants who cultivated subsistence crops such as bluggoes, plantains and ground foods while tending the cocoa and nutmeg trees. The land-owners granted the workers what they perceived to be privileges: to live on the estate rent-free, to work small gardens near their homes or to rent additional plots at nominal rates, to tether livestock on the estate, to have a first claim to paid estate labour, and so on. The workers, naturally, perceived these traditional privileges as their rights which they received in return for supplying cheap and reliable labour on demand. So long as the export crops remained profitable and adequate land was available this traditional system of planter-peasant relations, though embedded in unequal patronage, cushioned the workers' poverty and provided a measure of economic security. The system relied, above all, on persisting social bonds between those whose ancestors had been slave-owners and those whose ancestors were predominantly slaves, sometimes linking successive generations of planters and their people on the estates. These social bonds, in Grenada as elsewhere, were rationalised in terms of ideologies of cultural and racial inequalities. The privileged social status of the land-owners, who were often linked by kinship and marriage with each other, and who, along with a handful of colonial administrators, merchants and professional people, comprised the island's tiny elite, was not seriously challenged until the 1950s, although it was certainly resented by some people who sought to be upwardly mobile.

The inequalities of the colony were grounded in the unequal distribution of land ownership. The governor of the Windward Islands sent evidence to the royal commission in 1938, including data on the distribution of land in Grenada. There was just one estate of 1,202 acres, and 130 estates of 101 - 1,000 acres. These 131 estates, together constituting only 0.7 per cent of the farms, held 51.6 per cent of the farm land. Middle-sized farms, of 11 - 100 acres, comprised 2.2 per cent of all farms and occupied 15.2 per cent of the farm land. The vast majority of farms, 97.1 per cent of the total, were less than 10 acres. These 18,004 farms occupied 24,977 acres, or just 33.2 per cent of the farm land, an average of less than 1.4 acres per farm.[18]

Twenty years later there were fewer farms, down from 18,545 to 12,673, and less acreage was being farmed, down from 75,199 to 62,767 acres. The number of farms of less than 10 acres had declined from 18,004 to 12,067, those of 100 acres or more from 131 to 95, and those of 50 - 100 acres from 58 to 53. Only farms of 10 - 50 acres had increased, from 352 to 458. The distribution of land remained similar, however: 0.7 per cent of farms, those with 100 acres or more, accounted for 49 per cent of the acres in farms; 95.3 per cent of the farms were less than 10 acres and together occupied only 31.9 per cent of farm acreage; and middle-sized farms of 10 - 100 acres were 4 per cent of farms and occupied 19.1 per cent of farm acreage (Singham 1968: 45). These figures, strikingly unequal though they are, do not indicate the whole structure of inequality, however, as the larger estates tended to have better-quality land and many of the smaller farms were actually fragmented into parcels, making them harder to work. In 1957, for example, farms of 5 - 10 acres averaged 3 parcels per farm (Singham 1968: 47).

In 1938 most estates were occupied and managed by their owners, but some of the most important ones were owned by absentee landlords and managed by paid managers. The majority of agricultural workers had provision plots on these estates and this subsidised their low wages. Nevertheless, according to the governor, there was widespread and endemic poverty.

> The standard of living of the agricultural labourer is low and that of the peasant proprietor little better. The plantation owner on account of low prices is at present living under frugal conditions ....
>
> Up to five or more years ago labour employed on the plantations was permanent, that is at least 5 days per week work was always given. At the pres-

ent time on the majority of estates labourers are lucky if 3 days a week work can be obtained. Labour is employed by the day. According to law ablebodied adult men must be paid 1/3 for an 8 hour day and ablebodied adult women 1/- for an eight hour day. Work is also done by task which is usually assessed at a days work but very often the task is completed in 3 or 4 hours in which case the labourer can either go to his own garden or obtain work at overtime rates. In a majority of cases labourers live in huts in close proximity to the estates on which they are employed. In a few cases barracks are provided on estates. This system is dying out. The general practice is for estate owners to allow labourers to erect their huts on estate owned land. The security is that approximating to a yearly tenant ....

There is little total unemployment but considerable under employment.[19]

Although there was an independent peasantry in Grenada, there was also a continuum between, at one end, the peasant proprietor working on his own account on a few acres, and, at the other, the dependent worker-tenants who combined wage labour on the estates with their own subsistence farming. Few, if any, of these peasant workers had any opportunity for mobility or improvement through working the land in Grenada. In the face of this ingrained poverty, what inhibited the emergence of radical class action, such as occurred in the other colonies, was the highly paternalistic system of 'contracting-out', along with heavy migration to neighbouring Trinidad, Aruba and Venezuela, where many Grenadians worked in the oilfields.

M.G. Smith summarised the social differentiation and social ties in Grenada:

A handful of planters ran the estates, each with its own resident laborers. Casual workers were recruited as required from the "peasantry" on the estate margins. Many "peasants" depended on wage labor on or off the estates. Others occasionally hired help. Laborers living on estates were expected to take wage-work when it was offered. Wage rates were low, but the "privileges" of resident workers and the ill-defined obligations of their planter patrons prevented the situation from becoming intolerable. (1965: 279)

This situation explains why there was no labour rebellion among these workers in the 1930s. In 1938, Marryshow, the founder of the Grenada Working-men's Association, led a peaceful demonstration in Grenada to show solidarity with West Indians struggling elsewhere (Sheppard 1987: 37). The franchise was restricted then to a small propertied elite: only 4,005 people, less than 15 per cent of the adults of the colony, were entitled to vote in the general election of 1944. Marryshow's Grenada Labour Party (GLP) and General Workers' Union (GWU) consisted chiefly of people who lived and worked in St George's, Gouyave and Grenville, the largest towns, rather than the rural workers. The ways in which agricultural workers were linked with their employer-landlords, along with the large proportion of more independent small farmers, made it even harder to organise rural workers in Grenada than elsewhere. The paternalism of the contracting-out system and 'the almost total feeling of dependency leaves the Grenadian with little sense of being able to exercise control over his economic life, which places severe constraints on political development' (Singham 1968: 61). Nevertheless, there was a labour rebellion in Grenada in 1951, when thousands of rural workers joined a new trade union, and their leader, Gairy, and his political party, the Grenada United Labour Party (GULP), swept the first general elections held on the basis of universal adult suffrage on 10 October 1951. So Grenada did follow a similar pattern as other colonies in the British Caribbean, though somewhat later.

The characteristics of this belated labour rebellion reflected the prevailing social and economic relations in the predominant system of agricultural production. The workers' aspirations were more for a restoration of what they conceived as their traditional rights on the estates than for a transformation of the system, and they turned to Gairy as someone who offered to represent them when they felt unable to represent themselves. So long as Gairy articulated their aspirations and achieved some of their goals they gave him overwhelming support, but when he used the trade union and political party that he had based on their support for other goals the support dwindled. To the extent that Gairy's appeal to his followers was built on confrontations with the rich landowners and colonial administrators he could demand the workers' support, but when these land-owners and administrators made concessions independent of Gairy's intervention his support was undermined. Gairy's leadership was intensely personal and charismatic, and his failure to create more firmly based bureaucratic organisations resulted in considerable volatility in Grenadian politics. However, though Gairy's personality was somewhat unstable, the volatility of Grenadian politics resulted chiefly from the structural and cultural conditions of the society.

Small-island politics tends to be strongly personalist and, as Gordon Lewis (1968: 155) pointed out, 'What Governors liked to call "irresponsible" politicians were, after all, only local expressions of an irresponsible system,' the Crown colony system. The imposition of this authoritarian system on a plantation society, which itself promoted authoritarianism, produced 'the class struggle out of which Gairyism emerged' (Lewis 1968: 157). Neither M.G. Smith nor A.W. Singham adequately analysed this class struggle. Smith erroneously sought to separate the economic sphere from the structure of social relations of Grenada (1965: 294) and then claimed that it was the social and not the economic factors that created the crisis in the 1950s. He rejected what he saw as economic determinism by defining Grenadian labour relations as simply social rather than economic. Many of the workers' grievances clearly were social but their social problems were inseparable from the economic system. Singham understated the importance of the class struggle by overemphasising the conflict between Gairy's charismatic leadership and the government as the embodiment of rational bureaucracy. Although this distinction is useful, I agree with Lewis that 'charisma is not a self-generating first cause; it grows out of deep social crisis' (1968: 157). Hence, in order to understand how Gairyism became such an important political phenomenon, we must analyse the crisis in terms of the social relations that prevailed in the economic system, as well as the limits on political expression imposed by the colonial constitution. The politics of labour, in Grenada as elsewhere, grew out of the changing economic and social structure.

Before the outbreak of strikes and violence in 1951 there had been little intimation of serious labour or political unrest in Grenada. The monthly political reports that went to the Colonial Office in the late 1940s confirmed that there were 'no known Communist organisations', though it was believed that a sailor who was a member of the Canadian Seamen's Union, and who had contacts in Barbados, may have distributed 'Communist literature' to the small labour union, the Grenada Workers' Union, that was led by E.A. Mitchell.[20] In 1948 Marryshow was known for 'his efforts towards political advancement and the policy of "West Indies for the West Indians" .... His oratory can still sway crowds though he is not taken as seriously now as he might have been some years ago'.[21] Grenada was said to be 'particularly free from labour disputes except of a minor character, largely because of its widespread peasant proprietorship'. There was concern, however, about influences from Trinidad which had returned 'a large batch of Grenadians, followers of Butler, who were giving trouble' there, and the rising cost of living and knowledge about the higher world prices for cocoa and nutmeg were causing some unrest and 'agitation for higher wages all round'.[22] Towards the end of 1948 the Grenada Workers' Union, with about 1,614 members, and the General Workers' Union, with only 425 members, united in the Trades Union Council (GTUC).[23] These unions, like Marryshow's support, however, were largely in the urban area of St George's, and the more numerous rural workers remained unorganised.

The prevailing situation became a social crisis in 1950-1 when rural workers began to feel that their traditional rights were threatened. Although Smith states that 'the workers' resentment and insecurity reflected social rather than economic factors' (1965: 296), this imposes an arbitrary distinction. The workers' rights and security were social and economic. Threats of unemployment and wage reductions, together with loss of access to land, are social and economic issues because they undermine the economic position of individual workers and their dependants and weaken the ties between workers and their employers. When the workers took collective action about these issues through protests, strikes and acts of violence, the social crisis developed rapidly into a political crisis that the government defined primarily in terms of law and order. This was the situation that Gairy took advantage of, and he used it to establish a basis of rural support for his trade union and political party.

The spark to the crisis occurred on a large estate that was sold early in 1950 by a leading local family, who had owned it for decades, to a British buyer. Favourable prices for cocoa and nutmeg on the world market enabled many planters to pay off their debts; the land values rose and estates, as valuable investments, began to change hands. The transfer of estates was often complicated by the presence of tenants who claimed customary rights, but no trade union or other organisation represented the rights of these worker-tenants. The purchaser of this large estate understood by the contract that it was free of encumbrances, but on arrival in Grenada he found people living there. When he tried to evict them, as he thought the contract of sale legally entitled him to, the people asserted their customary rights and sought someone to help them. Gairy, a young black schoolteacher, offered to help.

Gairy, who was born in 1922, had left Grenada to work on the American base in Trinidad in the war and had gone on to Aruba where he worked as a clerk in the oil refineries. There he became active in trade unions and 'received his first political training, for, as he recalls, the Dutch authorities were not kindly disposed toward labor organizers' (Singham 1968: 153).[24] He met Marryshow in Aruba and became interested in Grenadian affairs, so when he was deported from the Dutch colony and returned home in December 1949 he was ready to get involved. Gairy claimed full cash compensation for the evicted worker-tenants under the tenants' compensation ordinance. The purchaser denied liability but compensation, said to be worth about £3,000, was obtained from the former owner. Gairy's intervention was seen as a complete success and, as the people's spokesman, he 'became the Galahad of the workers and peasants in this part of the island' (Smith 1965: 283).

In March 1950 Gairy was said to have been 'implicated in the strike amongst the workers of the Grenville branch of the Nutmeg Association', and in June he was holding meetings throughout the colony, having created a new union and political party, naming himself the president-general of both.[25] Gairy was not the only person involved in labour agitation in the first half of 1950. The Grenada Workers' Union was negotiating wage increases for clerks and shop assistants in St George's, stevedores were negotiating increases with the shipping agents and the GTUC was negotiating increases based on cocoa prices for farm workers. However, it was Gairy who moved most decisively and quickly when he registered his new trade union, the Grenada Manual and Mental Workers' Union (GMMWU) in July 1950.

On 31 July Gairy demanded a 50 per cent increase in wages for all workers employed by the Grenada Sugar Company, whose estates lay near the scene of his first triumph. The company, claiming to have an agreement with the Grenada Workers' Union, asked the advice of the labour officer about recognising Gairy's union. The labour officer met the sugar workers on 9 August, ascertained that they wanted to be represented by the GMMWU and advised the company to recognise that union 'as the body possessed with authority to negotiate on behalf of the workers'.[26] He offered to convene a meeting of the company and union but the company delayed replying. On the morning of 24 August Gairy called the company's 496 workers out on strike and at noon asked the labour officer to convene a meeting between his union and the company. The chairman and secretary of the company agreed to the meeting on 26 August. On 25 August 430 workers on 11 other estates in the parish struck in a forceful show of sympathy. The directors of the company did not attend the meeting, as they had agreed, but the chairman, S.A. Francis, intimated that he would participate in his capacity as the owner of the Grand Anse Estates. He agreed to some of the union's demands, including the payment of time-and-a-half for hours of work in excess of eight hours or on Sundays and public holidays, but he said he would wait for the company's decision on the demands for 50 per cent wage increases and a paid yearly vacation. Gairy, probably feeling that this was not a serious negotiation on the part of the company, indicated 'the workers would not be required to return to work'.[27]

Soon after the start of the strike there were several acts of sabotage and violence, including road blocks, cutting telephone wires and cables, and stoning motor cars; and one of Francis's cattle was killed and its hind legs stolen. On 29 August a party of armed police was sent to the area and the governor asked for extra police to be sent from St Lucia. By the end of August a storehouse had been burned down on a sugar estate and the violence was spreading beyond the sugar belt. Gairy met the governor on 1 September and discussed unemployment and the strike situation.

> His case was that he had been asked by the strikers to look after their interests; he did not call the strikes but had told the workers what their rights were; the Sugar Factory strike had followed only after his attempt to get the Directors to meet the workers had been unsuccessful; other strikes have occurred in sympathy; others will take place shortly as the result of decisions already reached; he is a friend of the underdog and his heart bleeds for them; he has no personal ambition save to help his fellowmen; evernone [sic] has reviled him but those who have met him have been surprised to find him a "very decent

chap." Gairy protested again that he was not responsible for any violence. On the contrary he had told his people that they must do nothing bad - nothing to let him down - and that they must report to him and the police any of their members who did bad things - such people would be expelled from the Union forthwith.[28]

Gairy indicated that if the sugar company could not afford even a 20 per cent increase or less the union would accept this, but 'they would not call off the strike while the Directors refused to meet them'. This suggests that Gairy was less focused on the actual wage increase at this time and more on being treated with respect by the company directors. When the governor said that his concern was law and order, and that Gairy should 'do everything possible to prevent the strike from spreading', Gairy 'gave his personal undertaking to co-operate whole-heartedly ... in the maintenance of law and order' but said he could not stop strikes that were already arranged or 'stop any workers who wanted to strike against his advice'.[29]

On 2 September the directors of the sugar company told the governor they would negotiate with the union as soon as the workers returned to work, but they insisted that 'Gairy was directly responsible for the acts of violence and intimidation which were taking place'.[30] The next day, Gairy went with Marryshow and the labour officer to impress upon the strikers their responsibility for keeping law and order, and he wrote to the Agricultural Employers' Association (AEA) asking for an all-round increase of 20 per cent for agricultural workers. It was widely known, apparently, that nutmeg prices and sales continued to be good and that the price of cocoa had again risen, so the workers wanted a share. By 5 September all the strikers were back at work. Meetings were held between the sugar company and the GMMWU on 7 September and 12 September, and they agreed to arbitration proceedings. Meanwhile, negotiations between the AEA and the GTUC, which was asking for a 25 per cent wage increase for agricultural workers, resulted in an agreement in the form of a bonus of 3.75 per cent on the existing statutory minimum wage for each 10 cent rise in the price of cocoa over 20 cents per lb, amounting at that time to a 15 per cent increase, or 12 cents for men and 10 cents for women.[31] Gairy was said, in the meantime, to be 'expanding his activities generally' in other parts of Grenada 'to foster his political aims', and choosing candidates for the various districts for the forthcoming elections for the Legislative Council.[32]

The arbitration tribunal released its report on 31 October, awarding an increase of 25 per cent to the statutory minimum wage to sugar workers, with retrospective effect to 27 July, a week's holiday with full pay to those who worked for not less than 200 days in a calendar year, and the payment of double wages to workers who were required to work on public holidays.[33] This award was higher than the more numerous cocoa and nutmeg workers received, and was clearly a victory for Gairy and his new union. He called on the workers to contribute to a special fund for honoraria to the union's representatives and planned a public celebration on Armistice Day, 11 November. Gairy, dressed in a 'tail coat, bowler hat, white gloves and a cane, and carrying a bible', addressed a crowd of 3,000 people, 'the majority of whom were women', in Market Square, St George's. He eulogised himself and claimed victories on all fronts. Having issued a handbill to the crowd, he read from it and called on them to shout his name in response:

> Who has got 25% (the biggest in history) increase for workers in Grenada? UNCLE GAIRY.
> Who is responsible for workers getting 'double pay' when they work on Bank Holidays? UNCLE GAIRY.
> Who has seen to it that labourers get '7 days vacation with full pay' at the end of every year? UNCLE GAIRY.[34]

Within three months of being registered the GMMWU had a membership of over 2,000.

When cocoa prices began to fall the bonuses negotiated by the GTUC also diminished and the daily wages fell from 94 cents to 91 cents for men and from 78 cents to 76 cents for women. The GTUC requested that the AEA let the current wages stand, arguing that 'any fall in the wages of the workers might lead to other disturbances', but the employers replied that the terms of the agreement should stand.[35] Gairy asked the AEA to grant a 46 per cent increase on the minimum estate wage, but he received no reply. In January 1951 he intensified his new campaign. On 29 January he visited the estate for whose evicted members he had obtained compensation the previous year; when the owner interrupted him work ceased. Workers on an adjoining estate joined this spontaneous strike the next day and others joined within the next two weeks. The employers insisted that they had an agreement with the GTUC, and the labour officer delivered three broadcast talks on responsible trade unionism. On 18 February, in response to Gairy's plans for a general strike, the heads of the four leading religious denominations together issued an appeal to their congregations to stop the strike. Despite this united opposition from the employers, colonial officials and churches, 19 February was the start of the first islandwide general strike in Grenada's history. It lasted a month and ended in complete victory for Gairy and his GMMWU.

Gairy appeared to deliberately provoke the government by staging a mass demonstration outside the Legislative Council all day on 21 February, and meanwhile he kept demanding a meeting with the acting governor. The economic issues immediately became social and political issues as Gairy's rural supporters packed St George's. Gairy 'was determined to show the employers that if they would not deal with him as the spokesman for the workers and as a social equal he would force them to deal with him through the government' (Singham 1968: 159). In the middle of the morning he spoke dramatically and provocatively to the crowd:

> I am leaving you now, don't follow me, to return at 12 o'clock. It is ten past ten now, if I don't return at twelve, find me!
>
> Things have come to a stage when I may be arrested at any time [murmurs of protest from the crowd], but you shall not sleep a night or do a stroke of work until I am released.[36]

Gairy kept leaving and returning, and reported to the crowd that the acting governor was frightened. The crowd responded by chanting, 'Don't study him [the acting governor], Gairy is Governor now'. The acting governor probably was afraid to provoke the crowd by arresting Gairy, but he would not accord him legitimacy by meeting him. Instead, Gairy and his associate, Blaize, were smuggled on to a British gunboat that night, whisked off to Carriacou and held there.

The colonial authorities, as well as the business people and middle classes of St George's, dealt with Gairy as if he was a dangerous threat to the social and political peace. Marines were landed from HMS Devonshire on 22 February to take over guard duties at vital points in order to free police for the task of restoring order. Some arrests were made for unlawful assembly and violence broke out in several areas on 23 February. There were fires on some estates and a school in Grenville was burned to the ground on 27 February. Meanwhile, a crowd gathered in Woodford Square in Trinidad to condemn the actions of the British government and Bustamante sent a telegram from Jamaica, protesting against the victimisation of the trade union movement (Singham 1968: 162).

Gairy's enforced absence, far from ending the protests, appeared to provoke more. According to a Labour Department report,

> for one month, commencing 19th February 1951, Grenada experienced a strike of agricultural and road workers which caused an upheaval such as has not been known within living memory. Workers who showed a disinclination to go on strike were intimidated and beaten by their co-workers, by the un-employed and by the unemployables; estates were looted in broad daylight, while Management stood by unable to interfere; valuable produce trees were deliberately damaged; estate buildings, medical health centres, schools, and privately owned residences were burnt; rioting and bloodshed occurred; the small police force appeared totally inadequate to deal with the situation.[37]

Road blocks isolated the capital; some workers divided an estate among themselves, and others disposed of the products of cocoa and nutmeg trees that they claimed their ancestors had planted. Angry planters armed themselves and at least one fired on people approaching his house (Smith 1965: 286). Police reinforcements came from St Lucia and Trinidad, the British navy was summoned and a garrison of British troops remained in Grenada for some months. Although the protesters did not kill anybody, the police killed four people and wounded five in quelling the disturbances. Of the 98 people who were arrested during the period of the strike, 81 were convicted for various breaches of the law (Singham 1968: 163).

When Gairy was released on 6 March he returned to Grenada. It was clear that he had won. Although the employers did not want to deal with him or to accept trade unionism, the governor and his labour advisor began negotiating with him. The official government newsletter described these negotiations on 13 March:

> Mr. E.W. Barltrop, Labour Advisor to the Secretary of State, yesterday met Mr. Gairy and members of the Executive of the Manual and Mental Workers' Union when the idea of forming Wage Councils was discussed and favourably received. After seeing Mr. Gairy, Mr. Barltrop saw employers and understood that they would cooperate in any wage councils created. The Government have therefore agreed to introduce a law which will enable employers and workers to meet on Councils created by the Government. The representatives on both sides will be chosen by the Government after consultation with the organisations appearing to represent employers and workers in any industry for which Councils are created. A Council will also have independent members, that is persons who do not represent employers or workers, and there independently will have the power to decide disagreements between the parties. The decisions of the Councils will have the force of law.[38]

It was clear that trade unionism had arrived in Grenada and that the colonial government was seeking to control it. Under pressure from Gairy's GMMWU, the colonial government found a way to institutionalize negotiations with the wages councils.

Gairy and his followers had virtually coerced the government into these extraordinary measures by their threat of violence, and part of the deal he made with the authorities was to help restore law and order. Gairy made an appeal on 8 March for the violence to end, but since it continued he made an islandwide broadcast on 15 March for people to cooperate with the police and stop the arson, theft and intimidation. Gairy agreed to use his personal influence to help restore social peace in return for getting the employers to deal with his union. This broadcast displays something of his style and relationship with his followers.

Yes folks, this is your Leader, 'Uncle Gairy' speaking to you.

My dear Fellow Grenadians, you know that I am deeply concerned over the present state of affairs in this our dear little Island. You too - every one of you - are concerned one way or the other. As head of Grenada's two largest Organisations - the Grenada People's Party [which became GULP] and the Grenada Manual and Mental Workers' Union (the one now involved in the wage dispute), I feel obligated morally and spiritually to do something to alleviate, to stop, and when I say stop I mean stop, the burning of buildings and fields; interfering with people who are breaking your strikes (leave them alone); stop taking away things from the estates that are not belonging to you, particularly cocoa and nutmegs; I want you to stop now every act of violence and intimidation. I am aware of the fact that it is greatly felt that most of the wrongs are committed by people outside our Organisation and are connected in no way with the strike. Nevertheless, I say this: Union members and non-Union members, strikers and non-strikers - everyone has that love for 'Uncle Gairy', everyone was disturbed when Blaize and myself were arrested and detained, and as a result lots of bad things happened - things that brought bad name for us all - bad name for Government, bad name for employers, bad name for workers, bad name for the Union members and bad name for everyone of us that lives in Grenada. Gairy and Blaize are out again with you; therefore now is high time to stop. I told his Excellency the Governor that I have gained your respect and your implicit confidence and you will obey me without fail. Now don't let me down. I ERIC MATTHEW GAIRY, am now making this serious appeal to you to start living your normal peaceful life, take my example and be a respectful decent citizen, as I say starting now. Let me make this point, however, everyone knows that I am a serious young man and when I say 'No,' I mean 'No;' and when I say 'Yes' I mean 'Yes.' Now listen to this: I am now in the search for gangsters and hooligans, I ask every one of my people to help me, and if anyone is found setting fire to any place, breaking open or robbing in any way, interfering with people who are working, there will be nothing to save you, because the law will deal with you most severely, and 'Uncle Gairy' will turn you down completely. So join me now in saying no more violence. Come on now those of you listening, let's say no more violence three times together, 'No more violence,' 'No more violence,' 'No more violence'.

And now we take another matter - the going back to work - when I lifted my little finger on the 19th of February and said 'strike' several thousands went on strike, that is because you have the confidence in me and you know very well that 'Uncle Gairy' knows his whereabouts. Well, you're correct, I know my onions. Listen carefully. Are you ready? This is an instruction coming from your Leader and I expect it to be carried out without failure. All workers who were on strike report to work on Monday coming, Monday, the nineteenth of March. I am going to speak to you about it at length at a series of meetings starting from tonight. Listen … [he listed the times and places for six meetings].

Thank you very much for listening, thank you.[39]

In addition to Gairy's tone, which was like a Victorian schoolmaster, there is an extraordinary arrogance about this talk and his instructions. From being essentially unknown a year before, Gairy had proclaimed himself the island's leader, whose little finger could instruct thousands to strike or to work, and who must be obeyed. The government had recognised that Gairy was capable of bringing the island to a standstill, or of restoring law and order, and by calling on him to make this unprecedented broadcast they reinforced his popular standing. Within one year Gairy had become Grenada's most powerful popular leader and then, 'Almost overnight, Gairy had changed his status from a small-island trade union leader to a West Indian political leader' (Singham 1968: 167). His meteoric rise was acknowledged and approved by leaders of the earlier generation. On 22 March Bradshaw of St Kitts addressed meetings in Grenada, saying, 'I welcome Gairy to the ranks of leading Labour Leaders in the British West Indies', and Butler and Bustamante sent Gairy messages of support (Singham 1968: 168).

Under the agreement signed by the GMMWU and the Grenada Agricultural Employers' Society (which replaced the AEA) after this strike, wages were raised to $1.20 per day for men and $1 for women, and those who worked 200 days or more in a year were entitled to seven days' paid leave, as Gairy had demanded in October. Gairy promptly proceeded to translate the popularity he had achieved as a trade union leader into political power by taking advantage of the constitutional changes that granted universal adult suffrage in 1951. However, this power was circumscribed, not only by the limits of the colonial constitution but also by his own inability or unwillingness to create a well-organised political party.

The 1951 constitution was contradictory: 'While the constitution recognized the potential strength of mass organizations (like Gairy's trade union), it made no provision for involving such organizations in a meaningful way in the exercise of power. It had the effect of deluding the participants into believing that they had actual power, when in effect they had only titular power.' (Singham 1968: 120) This constitutional limitation was exacerbated by Gairy's sense of himself as an absolute and indispensable leader, his distrust of potential rivals and intolerance of differences of opinion, and his unwillingness to delegate authority, the result of which was a weak union and party organisation, despite the strength of his personal following. 'Gairy saw himself as an uncompromising charismatic leader to whom all workers owed devotion and unswerving obedience. But he did not succeed in winning the workers' loyalty fully. Intimidation was constantly necessary to ensure a solid front' (Smith 1965: 301). Gairy's exaggerated sense of his own status and control led to a decline in support from the working people who were his chief followers. Membership in the GMMWU declined from about 6,000 paid and 10,000 unpaid members in 1951-2 to about 4,500 and 6,000, respectively, in 1958, and to 3,600 and 4,100 in 1959 (Singham 1968: 185). The decline of support for Gairy's party through the 1950s was not reversed until the elections of 1961, when there was a very low voter turnout (see Table 8.1).

TABLE 8.1 GRENADA ELECTION RESULTS, 1951-62

	% voting	% voting for GULP	Seats won by GULP
1951	69	63	6 (out of 8)
1954	67	46	6 (out of 8)
1957	68	44	2 (out of 8)
1961	55	53	8 (out of 10)
1962	73	46	4 (out of 10)

Source: Singham 1968: 173-9, 286, 289.

Gairy was helped by the fact that his was the only political party in 1951, and the high voter turnout suggests enthusiasm in Grenada for the new experience of the democratic process. Gairy's support was strongest in the rural areas, where the GULP obtained 71 per cent of the votes cast, but even in the towns and St George's GULP received 52 per cent of the votes. The seats the GULP lost in 1951 were in St George's, which was won by Marryshow whose following was strongest among the middle class, and in the island of Carriacou where Gairy never had much support. Though the GULP retained six seats in 1954 it is evident that there was a decline in support for Gairy himself. Whereas 71 per cent of the eligible voters voted in Gairy's constituency in 1951, compared with 69 per cent overall, this fell to 58 per cent, the lowest proportion voting in any constituency, compared with 67 per cent overall, in 1954.

Gairy's strength in 1951 lay in his personal support and his disruptive potential. Many workers made significant gains for the first time in 1951 and the Grenadian elite was certainly anxious about Gairy's rise to political power. However, his failure to create a really new pattern of labour relations, relying as he did on the workers' personal loyalty and obedience rather than on democratic organisation, left him vulnerable to a conflict in terms of competition for their loyalty. When Gairy called another general strike of agricultural workers in November 1953, he miscalculated and lost this struggle to the planters. At the height of his power in 1952 Gairy acted arrogantly and recklessly, as if he was above the law. He refused to register his union's accounts, as required by law, called impromptu strikes on individual estates, threatened another islandwide strike and even drove without a valid driver's licence. By 1953 more planters were willing to treat their workers' demands seriously and Gairy's weaknesses were revealed. When Gairy called the strike on 26 November he was ill-prepared.

> No demands were made on the employers, nor was a request received for consideration by the Reference Board of any issues in dispute. About one-third of the estimated 6,000 agricultural workers stopped work - many of them because of the fear of arson, violence or intimidation - but the week preceding Christmas, the vast majority were back at work or had been replaced by the unemployed, except in the parishes of St. John's and St. Mark's where the majority of workers remained on strike. There was the usual crop of incidents - arson, stone-throwing at night, intimidation - but this was on a vastly reduced scale .... Larceny of licensable produce - cocoa, nutmegs, coconuts ... was effectively checked by the prompt introduction of legislation prohibiting the sale or transfer of such produce without a permit.[40]

Gairy made an effort to revive the strike in January 1954 by calling out the sugar workers who were due to start the harvest.

> At the same time the Union renewed its efforts to obtain the support of those agricultural workers who had previously shown an unwillingness to associate themselves with strike action. The response was a little better than previously, as about 50 per cent of the labour force did not turn out to work. By the end of January 1954 there was however a gradual ... return to work which became complete by the end of February .... On 26th April 1954 ... at a time when relations between the employers and the workers' Unions were strained, the Employers' Union [Grenada Agriculturalists' Union, GAU] announced a voluntary increase of 24 cents to men and 20 cents to women on the basic daily rate ... to $1.44 and $1.20 for men and women respectively. In addition ... the Employers' Union announced that the customary perquisites enjoyed by their workers would be continued so as to augment the daily wage rates.[41]

The GAU, by volunteering these increases, outflanked Gairy. Although he tried to claim that the increases were concessions resulting from the pressure of his union - and there was some truth in this - the planters had 'restored the traditional pattern of relations with its old privileges, obligations, and loyalties, and which also granted wage increases freely ..... Whereas the first strike followed a specific demand to which there had been no reply, the reverse was the case with the second' (Smith 1965: 293).

Gairy's first strike, in 1951, caught the planters by surprise and threatened to disrupt the traditional pattern of labour relations. But Gairy did not follow it up with organisational efforts to empower the workers, relying instead on his personal support and the workers' loyalty and obedience. The planters could play this game in traditional terms and, because Gairy was not yet in a position to manipulate political patronage, the planters won over the second strike.

> By first defeating Gairy's second strike, and then trying to meet the grievances of their workers, the planters simultaneously achieved several objectives, reestablishing direct relations with their people while denying Gairy and his union coordinate status. These objectives were political rather than economic; but the crisis was also political in nature, though economic in form. In Grenada during these years the issue at stake was nothing less than the continuity or modification of the social structure of which the planters were the guardians, leaders, and chief beneficiaries. In essence the conflict became a struggle between Gairy and the planters for the workers' loyalty, the government being primarily concerned with the preservation of law and order. The planters' decisions of April 26, 1954, marked the end of the Grenadian crisis, and Gairy lost his disruptive potential. (Smith 1965: 293)

Although it is true that Gairy lost his disruptive potential, at least for a while, and this first phase of modern Grenadian politics ended with a victory for the traditional elite, Gairy had succeeded in introducing a new element in the political culture. He was himself a symbol of this change: a black man of humble origins had brought the poor rural people of Grenada on to the political stage in St George's. For the first time, in 1951, they had challenged the establishment, and they won. The planters won in 1954, and Gairy lost a great deal of support in the elections in September, but the planters had been forced to acknowledge that the workers had potential power and they had to respond to the workers' grievances. What Gairy had failed to do was to take advantage of the momentum achieved in 1951 to build democratically-based organisations that would consolidate the workers' new power in the society. The growth of rival trade unions and the emigration of many workers to Trinidad and the UK further eroded Gairy's support between 1954 and 1957, and the GMMWU called no further strike in the decade. In the general election of September 1957, the GULP won 44 percent of the votes but only two seats. However, Gairy, unlike Butler at this time, was far from being a spent force.

Gairy dominated Grenadian politics between 1967 and 1979. He developed a virtual dictatorship through extensive and corrupt distribution of patronage, known as squandermania, intimidation and violence, epitomized by his paramilitary thugs, the Mongoose Gang. 'The middle classes became, in effect, dependent upon him, their political loyalty (and financial kickbacks) purchased through import licenses and monopolies, tax concessions and many legal and illegal incentives .... Anti-labour legislation was passed and his erstwhile base, the Grenada Workers' Union, became just another source of patronage and revenue .... Victimization of those who opposed him - employer, landowner, worker and peasant alike - became widespread'. (Thorndike 1985: 38-9) Gairy's charismatic appeal and authoritarian leadership remained a central political feature of Grenada until the overthrow of his government on 13 March 1979 by the New Jewel Movement.

Singham argues that the 'hero', like Eric Gairy, 'does not have a genuine mass party, he has supporters who are personally committed to following him but who are not controlled by him .... For the most part, members of the mass do not find the party an institution that provides sustained psychological support for their values, beliefs, and attitudes. When they participate in politics they participate as members of a crowd rather than a movement'. (1968: 190) Although this is true, it does not appear to be a sufficient explanation of the political situation and events in Grenada. Gairy's followers may not have found 'sustained psychological support', though it would be hard for anyone to measure that. However, this underestimates their need for sustained material support, as it was for such help that the workers and peasants of Grenada first turned to Gairy, and his initial successes here established his reputation. His failure to produce a comparable success in the strike of 1954 was a blow to his followers whose loyalty was tested when the traditional elite restored its system of patronage. Gairy, like Butler in Trinidad, did not achieve the political position in the 1950s that would have enabled him to develop his own system of patronage, or even to use his still limited political power to obtain further concessions from the employers and landlords for his supporters. The quasi-ministerial system, which Bustamante utilised in building his political patronage machine in Jamaica, was not introduced into Grenada until 1956, when Gairy was at one of the lowest points of his career and a year before the GULP lost the elections. The psychological support that the hero gives the crowd, to use Singham's terms, depended on a personal charisma that was sustained only so long as the hero won his battles. Without more consistent material rewards this was a fragile support, so the hero's following was volatile. In turn, the apparent unreliability of his supporters tended to reinforce Gairy's authoritarianism, so the self-styled uncle of the masses castigated his followers for what he saw as their disloyalty and he often resorted to threats and intimidation to keep them in line. This problem resulted not merely from a flaw in Gairy's personality, nor simply from a weakness in the colonial constitution, though these were factors that contributed to the situation. The fundamental cause of the problem lay rather in the structure of social relations and the political culture of Grenada, which invested so much in the personal abilities of the people's leader that his downfall, which was almost inevitable in the circumstances, was almost catastrophic.

The chief differences between Bustamante, Butler and Gairy were not in their kinds of leadership or political philosophy, which were quite similar in many respects, but in their circumstances. What needs to be understood, therefore, is not the variations in their personality, interesting as these may be, but the variations in their relations with their followers as these were shaped by social, economic and political circumstances. First, the prevailing structure of social relations in each society provided different opportunities and limits to the kinds of aspirations, support and organisation that were possible for the working people at any given time. Second, what may be described as the uneven development of the constitutions of these colonies offered different political opportunities to these pioneering labour leaders. Between 1950 and 1954, the constitutions of Jamaica, Trinidad and Tobago, and Grenada varied in the degree to which they provided opportunities for these men to organise systems of political patronage. Butler never got as far politically as Gairy, so his decline was less dramatic, whereas Bustamante got further than either of the others because he operated in a political system that enabled him to sustain his supporters through patronage. What was common to all three of these pioneering labour leaders was a highly charismatic form of leadership, and each defined his personal will as pre-eminent and his goals as equivalent to the goals of the labour movement itself. This kind of leadership depended upon a certain kind of relationship with the followers. In each case, though in different ways and with different results, this dynamic reinforced authoritarian rather than democratic tendencies in the labour organisations and the associated political parties over which they presided.

Bureaucratic authoritarian trade unions

The Barbados Workers Union (BWU) and the OWTU of Trinidad were two of the most important trade unions in the British Caribbean in the 1940s and 1950s, as they still are, and the most powerful unions in their respective countries. Although their membership and structure differed, the BWU aiming to include various trades and occupations while the OWTU concentrated initially on workers in the oilfields, both unions tried to influence progressive legislation through political involvement while continuing to work for improved wages and working conditions for their members. As the legislatures of Barbados and Trinidad and Tobago became increasingly democratic, therefore, several of the chief officials of these unions contested elections and sought to participate in government. In many respects, also, these unions in their branch meetings and annual conferences, their internal election of officers and decision-making procedures, were democratic institutions. However, both unions exhibited persistent authoritarian tendencies, not only in the sense that their leaders sought to maintain their power by stifling opposition, but also in the ways that dissent was suppressed, sometimes in the name of freedom during the early years of the Cold War. These two unions were not extreme examples of bureaucratic authoritarianism, but they illustrate the conflicting tendencies of democracy and authoritarianism within trade unions as they became increasingly bureaucratised.

Barbados

The BWU was registered on 4 October 1941, taking advantage of the Trade Union Act that was passed in 1939 and came into effect on 1 August 1940. It was created out of the economic units of Grantley Adams' Barbados Progressive League (BPL). The minutes of the first meeting of the BWU Executive Council, with Adams as president-general and Hugh Springer as general secretary, held on 26 February 1942, were kept on the letterhead of the BPL, the 'Parent Body of Unions'.[42] The BWU started with divisions of ships' carpenters, bakers and foundry mechanics, then started growing as a more general trade union in late 1944 when the port workers in Bridgetown became organised. The next big step forward came in 1945 and 1946 when the sugar workers were organised.[43] The BWU continued to be a general union, organised by divisions according to industry, including bakers, engineers, seamen, dockers, stevedores, postmen, workers in waterworks, light and power, cable and wireless, telephone, hotels, sugar workers and so on. The success with which the BWU included all categories of workers within its organisation meant that there were few other unions and little union rivalry.[44] Adams, by presiding over 'the two offsprings of the Progressive League' (Hoyos 1974: 106), the Barbados Labour Party (BLP) and the BWU, was the predominant leader and he remained so until February 1954.

In October 1946, when Adams had become the leader of a semi-ministerial and semi-responsible government, he addressed a large demonstration from the BWU headquarters in quite radical, even socialist terms.

> I want every one of you to look upon this day as a milestone on the road to democracy in industry .... The people of this country make the wealth of the country, and it is for the organised might of this country to say how that wealth is to be distributed. For centuries it has been the practice of the capitalist class to amass wealth out of the toil and sweat of the labourers. If it has been the unfortunate lot of the labourers not to have a vote in this government, it is our duty to change that .... If we stand solidly together, we can, and should, be masters of this country.[45]

This was a time when the BLP, like the Labour Party in the UK, sang the Red Flag at its meetings, but Adams did not want to push reforms as fast as Wynter Crawford and his socialist Congress Party. The BLP lacked a majority in the House, however, so Adams and Crawford formed a temporary coalition in order

to pass reform legislation. When Crawford resigned from the Executive Committee in October 1947, Adams enticed three of the Congress Party's leaders to
defect to the BLP, and in the general election in 1948 the BLP won 12 of the 24
seats (Beckles 1990: 184). When Springer left Barbados to become registrar of the
new University College of the West Indies, which was established in Jamaica
in 1948, he was replaced by Frank Walcott as general secretary of the BWU.
By 1948 Adams had outmanoeuvred the Congress Party and consolidated his
dominance of labour politics in Barbados.

In 1950 Adams introduced a bill to remove the remaining property or
income qualifications for both voting and membership in the House. In the
1951 general election, the first with universal adult suffrage, the BLP won 60 per
cent of the popular vote and 16 seats, to four seats for the conservative Electors'
Association and only two for the Congress Party. On 1 February 1954, when a
new ministerial system of government was introduced, Adams became the
first premier of Barbados and he resigned as president-general of the BWU. But,
with Walcott in firm control of the union, continuity and cohesion seemed
assured. However, the apparent unity of the labour movement was achieved
by 'the almost authoritarian power' that Adams exercised, as he 'found himself having to perform the role of critic and suppressor of political radicalism'
within the BWU and BLP (Beckles 1990: 189).The rift that occurred in 1954
and 1955 was presaged in 1952, when Adams purged some of his critics from
the BWU on the spurious grounds that they were communist sympathisers.
Adams' authoritarian actions were parallel to Manley's purge of the Four-H's in
Jamaica and with their joint campaign to take over or, failing that, to destroy
the Caribbean Labour Congress in 1952.

Adams' expulsion of the two men whom he denounced as communist
sympathisers reflected the intensified paranoia of the Cold War, though there
is no evidence that these men, or any others in Barbados, were actively involved
in the communist movement. Rather, the Cold War climate provided a political
culture that enabled, and perhaps even encouraged, Adams to consolidate his
power by purging the BWU's executive of embarrassing critics on the pretext
that they were communist sympathisers. Minutes of the BWU Executive Council show that one of the two men, D. Farrell, was an active member of the union
from 1948, as an employee of the Barbados Electric Supply Corporation (BESC),
and the other, N. Layne, who worked for Radio Distribution (Rediffusion), was
first mentioned in 1949. They were elected grassroots leaders of their industrial
divisions in the union and, as such, were often demanding action from the
BWU leaders on behalf of the rank-and-file members. The evidence suggests
that they became increasingly frustrated with Adams' reluctance to act on the
members' behalf and so became more critical of the BWU leaders. That these

men became known as members of a so-called Iron Curtain group gave them a certain notoriety, but there is no evidence that any such communist faction ever existed in the BWU. One of the expelled men told me in 1994 that there was no such group, and the first that he had heard of it was when he read about it in the papers. He said the name was conjured up by the BWU leadership in order to smear him, and he was still bitter about it.[46]

On 4 August 1948 a delegation of BWU members who worked for the BESC met the Executive Council to notify them of the company's attitude towards Farrell, who had been 'removed from his post and placed on one of the main gangs. After a long discussion, the Council informed Comrade Farrell to continue on the job given to him and note any inconsistencies'.[47] Like many of the other cases referred to in the Executive Council's minutes in these early years, this one was concerned with the employer's attitude towards employees, and possibly also with the victimisation of a union activist. Several material issues were being raised at the time, including wage rates, hours of work and the designation of a pay day. On 12 January 1949 several members of the division who worked for the BESC collected in the street facing the BWU headquarters after a council meeting and created a 'rather disorderly scene'. Presumably frustrated by their leaders' lack of support, they 'subjected the members present at the Executive Meeting held that evening to insult and abuse'. Farrell reported that 'the men had been annoyed' because they were summoned to the council meeting scheduled for that evening but 'had not got a call to the Council'. Adams' response was to point out the 'seriousness of such misconduct' and to threaten those who could be identified by council members that they would be summoned to answer charges.[48] Meanwhile, Adams's position as the predominant labour leader was strengthened when the 600-strong Clerks Union, said to be 'predominantly white', voted unanimously to amalgamate with the BWU.[49] This came after the BLP had organised two days of demonstrations in support of A.E.S. Lewis, who had been dismissed after 28 years of employment by a commercial firm. Though the amalgamation did not take place because the necessary five-sixths of the members were not present to ratify the decision by a written ballot, many members did join the BWU.[50]

The issues still remained alive in May when Walcott reported that he had not met the electrical division workers on account of having other business but that he had taken up their concerns with the labour commissioner.[51] Later in the month, Walcott informed Adams about the situation and, after a long discussion, the council 'decided to ask for arbitration if a settlement is not reached'.[52] In June the Executive Council accepted the offer of an increase of 5 cents on the existing rates up to 29 cents per hour and 3 cents on rates of 30 cents per hour, with retrospective payment from 1 August 1948.[53] The question of hours and the pay day remained, and the council decided on 45 hours per week and a Friday pay day.[54] The workers were not satisfied, however. When a committee of BESC workers met the council, Walcott said, 'he is not hearing Layne in any matters concerning these workers', read them the rules about the duties of a division secretary, and after 'a lengthy discussion' the committee withdrew.[55] This suggests that there was already bad feeling between Layne and Walcott, and that BWU leaders were responding bureaucratically to their members.

Although the BWU leaders may not have been as active and decisive as the rank and file wanted, the acting governor of Barbados laid much of the blame for this prolonged dispute on the employers. 'The Barbados Electric Supply Corporation ... not content with spinning out a labour dispute for a whole year, issued a provocative notice on the 1st of July that they had been forced to advance their rates by 7 % because of the terms of the award in the dispute. This stupid announcement has had the effect of re-opening the whole controversy again in the newspaper press, with the Company and the Union slanging each other like lower school boys'.[56]

Another workers' delegation met the council in August and 'Farrell said that he cannot understand why when they interview the manager [of the BESC] he always vary'. The manager had argued that not all workers could be paid by 4 pm on Fridays, when the office closed, because they worked on distant jobs. He also complained that nine workers had left work to go to the races, and asked the union to help stop such 'gross insubordination'.[57] Then, when a committee of the electric division workers made a donation to Layne, presumably to thank him for his efforts on their behalf, Adams said they were wrong.[58] These minutes demonstrate that the chief officers of the BWU were dealing with the minutiae of union affairs and were unwilling to delegate them to the grassroots leaders. Moreover, the officers frequently distrusted and even resented these leaders when they took the initiative or pressed for concrete results. Such behaviour on the part of the union's officials, and the problems associated with it, may have stemmed in part from inexperience during these early years of the union's life, and in part from the politically motivated desire of the BWU leaders to control affairs, but nothing suggests that Farrell or Layne were communists.

In 1950 the workers at Radio Distribution (later called Rediffusion Service) were engaged in negotiations. Layne, the secretary of this union division, said, 'the manager was discourteous to the delegates during discussions', so they withdrew from the meeting.[59] Walcott had two meetings with the labour commissioner about this situation and, after being told that Layne had misinformed the workers about wage rates, he headed a committee to investigate.[60] This matter was said to be settled in May, and a wage of $15 per week was accepted. But the workers at the BESC were active again. Apparently, the manager of the company said he 'did not want Farrell to represent the workers at the Conciliation Board Meeting' and Farrell reported he had been threatened with dismissal if he was seen at the Labour Department meeting.[61] The manager refused to meet Farrell at the Labour Department, but Walcott did the right thing and told the labour commissioner he 'would not negotiate if Farrell was not allowed to be present'.[62] The following month, however, Walcott told a delegation of the electric workers who came to the Executive Council that they had not submitted a letter about the subject matter, as had been requested. Adams imperiously told them the council would not hear them, and they withdrew.[63]

In 1950, Ulric Grant, one of the major figures in the 1937 labour rebellion, was dismissed as an area organiser of the BWU, ostensibly for inefficiency, but it was believed that Adams and Walcott thought 'that he was being disloyal by giving confidential information to the Opposition'.[64] Adams did not tolerate disloyalty and he used the union's rules to emphasise his own status and power. He also seemed willing to make agreements over the heads of the workers and their grassroots leaders, and even to use his prestige and the influence of the union to discipline workers on behalf of management. In October 1950, for example, a maintenance worker named Thornhill at Radio Distribution was dismissed, allegedly for refusing to go to a job during his breakfast time. When Thornhill and Layne met the BWU Executive Council, they were told 'that they should carry out the instructions given by their employers and avoid being rude to the manager'. Council minutes record that the company was to be informed 'that the men were spoken to'.[65] Later, the manager of Radio Distribution informed Walcott that 'Layne had refused to do certain duties in connection with the maintenance staff and he would be glad if the Council investigate the matter'. The council agreed to call in Layne and Thornhill.[66] Meanwhile, Farrell complained about the manager of the BESC who, he said, 'had requested linesmen to do work ... [they] considered was not in keeping with their obligations to the company'. He enquired 'what attitude should the men adopt in these circumstances', and the council agreed to send the assistant secretary, K.N.R. Husbands, to interview the manager.[67] Perhaps in connection with this, Husbands complained at a council meeting in February about 'certain members' of the union who 'had made reference to his position', presumably critically. Adams and Walcott then informed the council of unspecified reports reaching them 'about subversive activities of a certain group within the Union and mentioned that this sort of a resistance movement appeared to be working against the best interests of the Union and especially against the Secretaries'. Adams formally moved that Farrell and Layne 'be summoned before the Executive

Council at its next meeting to defend their position as to why they should not be expelled from the Union since they were accused of being associated with a movement designed to work against the best interests of the organisation'. The motion was passed by five to four, though there were 14 members present.[68] This was the first mention of 'subversive activities' or a 'resistance movement', and nothing about these members' activities as previously reported could be so characterised. Moreover, Adams, as a lawyer, knew the difference between demanding that these men should say why they should not be expelled for having been accused, and their being presumed innocent until found guilty of what they had been accused. He also knew that in his Executive Council the rules of a legal court did not apply and all he had to do was to persuade enough council members to vote for their expulsion.[69]

On 21 February 1951, at an Executive Council meeting, Adams charged Farrell and Layne with being 'ring-leaders who by design intended to get rid of certain officers of the Union and supplant them by others and that this was conducting subversive activities against the interest of the Barbados Workers' Union'.[70] It was not clear how they would 'get rid of certain officers', as they lacked the power to do such a thing. Adams himself had said in 1950 that the general secretary did not need to be elected, but he holds office 'during the pleasure of the Union ... until he is dismissed for some action contrary to the rules of the Union',[71] but how he could be dismissed, whether by the president or a majority of the council, was not specified. The two accused men were tried separately. First, Farrell told how he had got a job at the electric company, had enquired of the men if they belonged to a union, and how, after many setbacks, he had got the majority of the men organised and had formed a division of the BWU. After he became the head of that division he met Layne, whom he had known since their schooldays, and he 'got to know more of the other divisional Officers and the members of the Union'. Williams of the Licensed Carters asked him to an interdivisional meeting and he 'thought he would gain knowledge at such a meeting'. Farrell said that he and D. Clarke intended to form the BWU Combined Committee, and to ask Adams and Walcott to speak to them.

> They were to go around and get people to support the B.W.U. and the Barbados Progressive League. They had no ulterior motive. Layne suggested to him that in his traveling around the country as a worker at the Electric Co., he might spread ideas about the movement. He got to know more of the Comrades.[72] He attended meetings of other divisions. He declared that if any member of any division might be summoned to the Council and asked if he [Farrell] had said anything against the Union. He had never taken part in any discussion in connection with the dismissal of any Officer of the Union. He had never told any division to go out on strike.[73]

Farrell added that he thought the utilities workers ought to be organised in one division. Walcott asked Farrell 'if he had received the utmost support of the Officers in presenting a case for his division'. Farrell replied that 'matters could have been settled quicker', but

> the workers had appreciated how much had been done for them. He knew nothing of any subversive activities of any movement within the Union. He knew nothing of any organisation called "The Iron Curtain."
>
> The Committee of the B.W.U.C.C. was dissolved when the Council refused to allow of its formation. They had met at the homes of Comrades R. Clarke, and G. Hepburn. He had never heard Layne say that he was starting any organization.

Farrell withdrew, and by a vote of two to none the council decided to expel him, though he was told he would have a rehearing at the next annual conference.

Then Layne appeared. He was asked 'why he should not be expelled from the B.W.U. since he was alleged to be head of a revolutionary organisation within the Union and which was charged with working towards the dismissal of certain Officers of the Union'. Layne denied any knowledge of the Iron Curtain group and 'said that he heard of the Iron Curtain over the radio and the newspapers'. V. Lynch asked 'if he had never remarked that neither the President, the General Secretary, nor the Assistant Secretary could represent him but that he preferred two members of the Executive Council to do so'. Layne denied having said so, but Husbands said he had heard Layne make 'such a remark in the hearing of many others'. T. Ishmael asked Layne if he had said 'that the Officers were not working in the interest of the workers'. Layne denied this also and said that 'he could not remember having abused the Council in public'. After Layne withdrew, Hepburn said he 'had associated himself with the movement', and said there had been 'some misunderstanding as to the election of the General Secretary' at the last annual conference. He had attended three meetings of the so-called Iron Curtain group, he said, but 'had heard nothing against the Union at any of them. He simply did not like Layne's way of putting up things'. Two members then voted for Layne to be expelled, and none against, and he, like Farrell, was told he had a right to appeal at the next annual conference.

Judging by these minutes, no evidence was offered of any subversive activities or organisation. There may have been some sort of faction of younger and more radical union men, focused on those who organised the utilities workers, and they may have expressed criticism of the BWU leaders at times. Farrell had certainly raised questions in at least two council meetings about the regular presentation of the financial statement of the BWU,[74] and this may have embarrassed the leaders. Walcott had earlier asked about this himself, remarking that he was unwilling to continue as general secretary 'with the existing state of affairs, and that there must be a change by the time the

Annual Conference takes place',[75] so it is possible that others were asking about the accounting of the union's finances. Certainly, no evidence was presented that there was a communist political faction within the BWU. Moreover, it is not clear why only two members of the Executive Council voted on these expulsions, or who they were, though we may surmise that one was Adams, as he had pressed the charges. The whole 'trial', despite the semblance of legal and democratic proceedings, seems to have been a modern version of the Inquisition, with the leader using his power over his followers to crush people whom he deemed to be heretical. In so doing, of course, he further impressed those who remained in his organisation with his power, which was probably one of the chief reasons for the trial.

These problems in the BWU persisted and came to head in 1952, the same year that Adams and Manley worked to break the CLC and helped inaugurate CADORIT. Farrell remained the head of the BESC workers' division and in October 1951 he pressed for the 'various Public Utility Groups in the Union getting together and submitting similar proposals for the respective workers'. The council, with both Adams and Walcott present, agreed to his proposals.[76] Both Farrell and Layne remained active and may have made themselves felt as thorns in the leaders' sides. Early in 1952, for example, both men were agitating for more action on the labour front. Farrell led a delegation of his BESC workers to complain that 'the Council had not been giving this division sufficient attention in the matter of having the recent disputes between the workers and the management settled', and that the grievance committee had not gathered a quorum in order to consider their report. Layne, meanwhile, led a delegation of Rediffusion Service workers, saying that the management could improve their offer of 4 cents per hour to 5 cents, but the council decided to refer this matter to the Labour Department.[77] Two weeks later, the grievance committee told a delegation of BESC workers that it was still unable to report on their problems,[78] and a week after that the council referred the matter to the Labour Department.[79]

The minutes of these affairs suggest not only that the BWU Executive Council was slow to respond to the problems expressed by its rank and file, but also that it was excessively eager to refer matters that should have been negotiated directly between the union and the employers to the Labour Department. Both these responses, of delay and referring matters to a third party, reduced the participation of the rank and file and their grassroots leaders, and so would increase their frustration with the union's chief officers. In April 1952 this situation got worse as Adams and other BWU officers appeared to side with the employers against the workers and their grassroots delegates. When letters from the Rediffusion Service management were read to the Executive Council, in Layne's presence, saying Layne was 'a poor worker and a disturber', Walcott described Layne's manner as 'incompatible as far as the Secretaries of the B.W.U. was [sic] concerned'.[80] On 30 April Farrell and Fields of the electric workers met the council, but Walcott said he was dealing with their matter 'and it was nothing for the attention of the Council'. Layne and workers from the Rediffusion Service then met the council, and Walcott said the BWU supported the labour commissioner 'in saying that overtime should be performed'. Layne asked about the right of a worker to refuse overtime, and Adams 'informed him that overtime should be performed at all times provided adequate notice was given'. The council, after 'a brief discussion', accepted their president's ruling.[81] In spite of a semblance of discussion and democratic procedure, the BWU's president and general secretary were imposing their rulings on what matters the council would discuss, and what the outcomes would be, in an authoritarian manner.

In May a worker named Phillips said he wanted a decision from the council about compensation due to his wife who worked at a laundry, but he was told it would not make a decision at that stage. Walcott told the council of 'Comrade Phillips' disloyalty to the Union and stated that he was informed that Phillips said that the Union was not interested in his case'. Phillips then said that the union had not done anything for him. Walcott announced that there would be a May Day demonstration, but Layne told him that if Phillips was not reinstated there would be no such demonstration. Walcott read a letter from Rediffusion Service stating that 'three of the workers has [sic] used remarks against the Union and that the management had refused to pay the 5c increase to all of the workers at the Company'.[82] These workers were summoned to the council, but a week later Layne told the council that they would not attend and that he had heard them say 'that the Union did not employ them and that they did not care anything about the Union'. The council agreed there was not enough evidence to find these men guilty but asked them to 'pull their weight and work together in the interest of the Union'.[83] In the next two months, three other men complained about BWU officers and trustees. Charles Shepherd of the Knitting Mills wrote a letter in June complaining that Walcott had 'accused him for association with some underground association'.[84] In July J. Cabral criticised the trustees for not 'carrying out their duties'. He was informed that they were not elected annually, and Hepburn asked that they 'present themselves before the Council' for interrogation, but his motion was not seconded.[85]

These criticisms came at an especially sensitive time for Adams and Walcott. On the one hand, Adams was having to defend his party's policies in the House of Assembly, not only against Crawford of the Congress Party but also against Errol Barrow and other young backbenchers in his own Labour Party. They were unhappy about the Revenue Equalisation Fund Bill, which they criticised as an old-fashioned and conservative financial measure, and in their view the government should be spending more on social services and economic development. Adams attacked Barrow for making 'dogmatic and pontifical utterances', and Barrow responded by saying that he did not think it was right for Adams 'to get up and unwarrantably attack other members'. Barrow argued that he had simply pointed to some mistakes. 'For members to be attacked when they have not criticised the Government is irrelevant and unnecessary',[86] he said. The debate about this bill was 'at times bitter and acrimonious' (Hoyos 1974: 191) and it demonstrated Adams' impatience with criticism and his anger against Barrow. He bluntly challenged his critics: 'If members feel that they cannot agree with the Government, that they cannot even trust the Government, let them form their own party, the Government will still get on'.[87] Adams' actions, both in his party and his union, were authoritarian and his response to criticism was to expel dissidents rather than to seek a basis for compromise.

Adams was surely sensitive to the ideological dimensions of the Cold War as they were affecting the Caribbean labour movement and politics of labour in parties such as his own and Manley's PNP in Jamaica. The ICFTU's choice of Barbados for its first Caribbean conference in June 1952 added to the pressure Adams must have felt to clarify his credentials as an outspoken anti-communist labour leader. Serafino Romualdi, the assistant secretary of ORIT, Latin American representative of the AFL and a renowned communist-fighter, assisted Adams in the chair at this conference.[88] Adams and Manley were certainly comparing notes at this time and developing their strategy to deal with Hart and the CLC, the continuing affiliation of which with the WFTU was embarrassing to them.

It is not too fanciful to say that, following Manley's lead in the expulsion of the Four-H's, Adams did not want to be perceived as any less forceful in his own anti-communism, and if he did not have any real communists to purge then Farrell and Layne would suffice as substitutes. On 24 July 1952, at a public meeting in Bridgetown at which Manley and Marryshow were guest speakers, Adams 'warned that as he had purged the Progressive League of such radicals over a decade ago, it was his intention to do likewise' with the BWU and BLP (Beckles 1990: 190). He was upset that Farrell and Layne had been elected by their divisions to the BWU Executive Council and made members of its standing committee for 1952-3.[89] Neither Farrell nor Layne backed down, and they were joined by several others in protesting against the BWU leaders' actions, so matters came to a head between July and November 1952.

On 13 August Farrell asked in the Executive Council about the union's accounts and Walcott responded that he could not answer for Adams 'as he was not informed'.[90] A week later, Hepburn moved, and Layne seconded, that H.D. Blackman, the BWU's treasurer, should be asked at the next council meeting 'to explain why the financial statements had ceased to appear regularly'. The motion was carried. At this meeting, also, a discussion arose about another dispute at the BESC. Walcott wanted to leave the matter to the labour commissioner, but Hepburn argued that in the absence of an agreement at the coming meeting, 'the General Secretary as head of the Union delegation should be authorised to give the employers a seven days' notice of strike action'. He then moved, and Layne seconded, that if at the proposed meeting agreement was not reached to reinstate five workers, 'the employers be immediately given seven days' notice of the Union's intention to declare a strike'. This motion, too, was carried. The council also approved a letter to Hart about his proposal for a meeting of CLC representatives in Jamaica in November.[91]

The radicals in the union were pushing forward a more active agenda. In Adams' absence they succeeded in passing their motions, which suggests not only that Adams had a big influence when he was present at the council but also that the more radical division delegates could get support, at least on some issues. Adams counterattacked a few days later. The representatives of the BESC did not attend the meeting arranged under the chairmanship of the labour commissioner and Walcott did not serve them the notice of strike action as decided by the council. Adams, feeling his responsibilities as a quasi-minister of government, reminded the council that the Better Security Act (1920) restricted strike action in essential services and 'stressed the wisdom of the Union taking the right constitutional course of action under these circumstances'. Hepburn and Layne condemned the act and provocatively moved that the BESC workers 'be summoned to the Council and told that the existence of this act rendered it impossible for the Union to do these workers any good in their present dispute with the Company'. The chairman disallowed their motion, so Hepburn and Layne 'withdrew in protest'. The council then agreed the matter should be sent to arbitration.[92] Once again Adams had prevailed by invoking procedural rules and avoiding a showdown, but the disagreements persisted within the BWU. A conflict between Adams' roles as president of the BWU and leader of the BLP was suggested a few days later when two members of the council, Cabral and Clarke, complained about the expense to the union of Manley and Marryshow's visit to the island. There was 'a strong feeling of the Council' that the BLP did not pay a fair share.[93]

There was nothing politically subversive about these issues, though Adams may have felt that the questions and motions were deliberately provocative and were embarrassing him just at the time he was seeking the maximum support for his efforts in the House and for the establishment of CADORIT's office in Barbados. What the questions do suggest, certainly, is that several members, and perhaps a majority, of the BWU's Executive Council were not pleased about the inactivity of their leaders on labour issues and about the financial affairs of the union. Some of them may have thought that Adams was not only neglecting them but was even using them as the base for his own rising political career. The concern of these union members coincided with Adams' embarrassment in the House of Assembly as divisions within his own party appeared in an important vote. C.E. Talma moved a resolution to nationalise a central sugar factory and F.E. Miller called for the nationalisation of Rediffusion Service. Though the first motion was withdrawn and the second was defeated, the 'criticism of the Government by its back-benchers was clearly becoming more and more bitter' (Hoyos 1974: 191). In August some workers broke with the BLP-BWU and formed a new party, the Barbados United Party, led by Grafton Clarke, which 'in its own words was dedicated to the protection of workers' interests' (Beckles 1990: 190).

On Labour Day, 6 October, Adams warned workers at the BWU headquarters that 'it was not all roses in the garden' and they should be prepared to pluck out 'undesirable weeds', a clear threat to those members of the union whom he called rebels (Beckles 1990:191). The crisis in the BLP was addressed but not resolved at a special meeting of the party executive, held on 18 October. According to his biographer, Adams 'intended to use a heavy hand against the back-benchers and would not replace the "old Brigade" with the young back-benchers. He regarded the attitude of the "Young Turks" as a challenge and as a "parting of the ways".' (Hoyos 1974: 192). The conflicts and divisions were publicly revealed again during the House debates about the Five Year Plan of Development and Taxation at the beginning of November (Hoyos 1974: 192-5). A.E.S. Lewis, V.B. Vaughan and Barrow of the BLP, as well as Crawford and J.E.T. Brancker of the Congress Party, attacked the plan's provisions and omissions, and Cameron Tudor resigned from the BLP over the government's financial policy. While this was happening, on 3 November Adams met the CLC delegation led by Hart, rejected their proposal for a new Caribbean federation of trade unions, and would not agree on a date for a third congress of the CLC.

These events constituted the background for the last act in the expulsion of Farrell and Layne from the BWU. On 14 November, at a public meeting in Queen's Park, Adams attacked the critics of his five year plan, Hart and Jagan. He said that he was running out of tolerance for such radicals and that he would not 'allow the labour movement in Barbados to be weakened by people who were in their diapers when it started' (Beckles 1990: 192). By lumping these unconnected critics together Adams implied that there was some sort of rebel or communist conspiracy directed against the legitimate labour movement. The fact was rather that Adams was intolerant of his critics and made a variety of enemies through his authoritarian political style and his increasingly conservative agenda. Farrell and Layne were the victims of the former.

At the meeting of the BWU Executive Council on 17 November 1952 Adams declared that Farrell and Layne 'had been guilty of conduct prejudicial to the interest of the Barbados Workers' Union and that they by devious and unconstitutional devices had been trying to influence groups within the Union to work against the interest of the organisation as a whole'. They had even used the union's premises to hold their meetings, he asserted, and he 'further declared the existence of the so-called Utilities Workers Division as a piece of evidence that could be brought against these comrades. Such tactics ... were calculated to split the Union into two hostile camps and these comrades had recently re-doubled their efforts openly with the express object of having nothing to do with those who were not on their side'. Adams also referred to 'the insults and abuses to which the officers of the Union had been regularly subjected by these Comrades'. R. Clarke then told the council that he had attended a meeting of the electric company's workers at Farrell's invitation and 'had heard the President-General accused for calling the Council a Communist body'. Further, he understood that 'Farrell had advised his division not to pay their Union contributions because of the existence of the Better Security Act and that the Union could do nothing for them since the President would do nothing about this act'.

Farrell responded that 'he would not reply to these charges until he was able to call members of his division before the Council'. Clarke went on to say that Farrell and Layne had been 'very active under the trees amongst waterfront workers in such a manner as was detrimental to the welfare of the Union', and he mentioned Layne's 'activities in Fairchild Street and on the lower wharf'. Layne then said he would not defend himself until witnesses were brought against him. Adams, who was effectively the prosecutor and chief judge in this trial, ruled that 'such statements as had been made were evidence against these Comrades', thereby making the council members both witnesses and jurors. Walcott said the two men had abused officers of the union. Farrell began an explanation, saying his remarks 'had been twisted and used against him', and Layne walked out of the meeting. Some members defended the accused men. One said that Farrell had told members to pay their dues, and another said that he had been present and had not heard Farrell make the remarks attributed to him. He asked that a vote be postponed until the council heard from workers of the electric division. He was overruled, however, and the vote was taken. It resulted in a tie, 3 against 3, so Adams cast his deciding vote to expel both men from the union.[94]

A careful reading of the minute book of the Executive Council of the BWU, which is the official record kept by the union's leaders, shows little real evidence against either Farrell or Layne, and they were not allowed to bring in witnesses in their defence. What the book reveals, however, is the way that bureaucratic procedures, covered by a veneer of legal and democratic proceedings, were used by the people in power to suppress dissent and expel their critics. Repeatedly, the union's leaders appealed to rules and regulations, as, for example, when a workers' delegation would not be heard by the council because they had not submitted a letter in advance, or deflected problems to the Labour Department when they should have taken responsibility. Above all, the two trials, on 21 February 1951 and 17 November 1952, were conducted with a semblance of legal procedures, and the outcomes were decided by votes, as if this was a process of democratic decision-making in a context of law. In both cases, however, the president-general of the union was really the accuser, prosecutor and judge, in a case in which he was extremely partial. Adams' mind was evidently made up before any evidence was heard and he controlled the meetings in such a way as to control the outcome. The accused were not permitted to call witnesses on their behalf, so the 'jurors' heard only one side of the case. Under the guise of a legal and democratic process, therefore, this was really a bureaucratic authoritarian process which was used to deactivate a popular sector and to expel critics through the use of procedures that emphasised order, rules and hierarchy. In short, the process used the semblance of democratic forms to achieve an undemocratic and authoritarian result.

At the end of 1952 Adams seemed to be in complete control of the situation. He had expelled his most vocal critics from the BWU, outmanoeuvred his backbenchers in the BLP, and deflected Hart's last efforts to keep the CLC alive. But many of the issues remained alive, and fresh critics emerged. When D. Holder commented on the minutes of the 17 November council meeting, wanting to amend them to the effect that Adams had said 'he wanted the Council to vote for the expulsion of Comrades Farrell and Layne', Adams objected and refused to accept the insertion.[95] This suggests that Adams tried to cover up the extent of his role in their expulsion in order to make the proceedings appear more democratic and less authoritarian than they really were. Later, in January 1953, Walcott reported that he had spoken with the labour commissioner about workers who had been fired by the BESC, and advised that 'the Union should await the future employment policy of the Company before any action is taken'. Cabral responded, saying that 'whenever there was a case of laying off workmen the Union was useless'. Walcott challenged Cabral, saying 'it was a very serious statement for a member of the Council to make', but Cabral reiterated his view and the 'meeting became noisy'. The chairman, failing to restore order, adjourned the meeting.[96] When a delegation of members from Rediffusion Service met the council in February and protested about the way it had dealt with one of their members, presumably Layne, the chairman ruled them out of order.[97]

In March the issue of the union's accounts reappeared. Holder said he had seen the auditor general and the registrar, who had told him that the BWU had sent in no returns for three years. Walcott asked that the minutes record 'that Comrade Holder was acting inimically to the interests of the Union'.[98] Two weeks later, when Cabral asked about auditing the union's accounts, the acting general secretary, Husbands, said 'he had no information on this matter'.[99] At the annual delegates' conference in August 1953 the expulsion of Farrell and Layne was briefly mentioned. Ironically, it was also stated that the public services divisions, such as telephone, electric and rediffusion, 'have continued to be well organised sections of the Union'. The comment on the waterfront workers, however, suggests that the BWU preferred inactive members: 'the absence of a major strike on the waterfront is a credit to the Union which has maintained discipline and settled the many issues in a constitutional manner'.[100] The Executive Council's 12th report stated that Romualdi, the assistant secretary of ORIT, had paid his second visit to Barbados and gave a 'brilliant address'. The council also reported, not coincidentally, that the BWU had agreed to disaffiliate from the CLC, which 'has become the chief instrument of the communist front organisation in the area'.[101]

Adams, as president-general of the BWU, leader of the BLP and Barbados government, and former president of the CLC, and Walcott, as the general secretary of the BWU, a member of Barbados' quasi-cabinet and chairman of CADORIT, had played important parts in destroying the CLC and promoting its rival, CADORIT. Within a few years, however, Barrow and other members of the BLP resigned to form the new Democratic Labour Party (DLP), and Walcott withdrew the BWU's support from Adams' BLP. Though these events lie beyond the period examined in this study, the seeds of these splits had been sown in 1951 and 1952. In 1954, when Adams became the first premier of Barbados and resigned his presidency of the BWU, he confidently left the union in charge of Walcott. In April 1955 Barrow and other former members of the BLP formally created the DLP to challenge 'Adams' growing conservatism and softness on the colonial question' (Beckles 1990: 193). In the 1956 general election, when Walcott ran and won his seat as an independent, the BLP still won 15 of the 24 seats, but with an ominous reduction of its share of the popular vote, to only 49 per cent (Beckles 1990: 194). The young Turks were defeated and Adams received a knighthood early in the following year for his public services, but the grand old man was resoundingly beaten in the 1961 elections, when the BLP won only five seats to the DLP's 14. The DLP won again in 1966 and Barrow became the first prime minister of independent Barbados on 30 November 1966.

The shift in Barbados' political spectrum that had started in the early 1950s became entrenched by the 1960s when the BLP drifted further to the right and the BWU, under Walcott's leadership, gave firm support to the DLP. Nominally, two labour parties contested for power but, as Beckles points out, there was a broad consensus regarding the real division between economic and political power. 'Both parties had cultivated traditions of criticism of the oligarchical political attitudes and practices of the planter-merchant elite, but both had also sought to court its economic power and managerial expertise within their developmental strategies. These positions were not considered contradictory; a conciliatory arrangement between white corporate power and black political administrations emerged as the dominant political thrust of the post-independence period'. (Beckles 1990: 203) The only possible alternative to this political development would have lain with a radical and democratic labour movement, based in a united trade union with strong regional links, but this possibility became derailed in the early 1950s.

Trinidad

Unlike the BWU, which aimed to organise all Barbadian workers in a series of divisions, the OWTU focused chiefly on the workers in Trinidad's oilfields. Though oil had come to dominate exports, few workers were employed in this capital-intensive industry. After the Second World War, when oil accounted for 80 per cent of the exports of Trinidad and Tobago, about 14,000 people were employed in this sector, compared with 16,000 - 18,000 people in the sugar industry (Dalley 1947: 3). This meant that a well-organised union of oilfield workers ought to be able to exercise an influence out of proportion to its numbers, and this has generally been the case.[102] However, the OWTU's political influence has never been as direct as that of most other major trade unions in the British Caribbean, such as the BITU or the BWU, because it was not linked to a successful political party as they were. During the late 1940s and early 1950s, the OWTU maintained a radically socialist and anti-imperialist stance in national and regional politics, but in its own organisation the union became increasingly bureaucratic and authoritarian. Thus its socialist ideology provoked repression from the colonial state, and its authoritarianism resulted in the emergence of a radical democratic reform movement within the union, known as the 'Rebels'. It is easy to personalise these conflicting tendencies by focusing on Rojas, who was the OWTU president from 1943 until 1962, and his opponent and successor, George Weekes, president from 1962 till 1987. But however responsible Rojas was for his union's affairs, the causes of these tendencies were both deeper and more widespread than the OWTU itself, so reference must be made to some of the other developments among Trinidadian trade unions in this period.

We have seen already how Rojas succeeded Rienzi as president of the OWTU in 1943, and that the union signed a historic agreement with the OEA in 1945. This agreement contained the first cost-of-living allowance negotiated in the country, a half-cent increase for every 5-point rise in the cost-of-living index. The colonial government and the OEA were especially concerned with maintaining industrial peace in the oilfields. Good profits were made during the depression and war years in this strategic industry and by 1946 Trinidad was providing 65 per cent of the oil produced in the British empire. The number of people employed in the oil industry was small, so the employers could afford to pay the workers more, but they found it hard to buy them off. The colonial government and the oil companies had come to agree that responsible trade unionism, as they defined it, was preferable to spontaneous protests and strikes or to the radical and unpredictable leadership of a man like Butler. So, when Butler started to revive his movement in the oil belt after his release from prison in 1945, the OWTU joined with the government and the oil companies to suppress him.

The strike that Butler started on 19 December 1946 was most effective in the deep south, especially around Point Fortin where the refinery and most producing fields were closed down. The OWTU's position was that it had a contract and was not in dispute with the oil companies, so it would not join Butler's strike,[103] but the union went further and actively intervened. The efforts it made to help break the strike were aimed at destroying a rival labour leader. The OWTU executive not only issued instructions that members should not strike, it even went so far as to recruit strike-breakers, workers who were bussed to the oilfields under armed police guard. A waterfront workers' strike, that had begun on 8 November 1946 and lasted a month, led to the government using troops to offload supplies and to the passage of the emergency powers ordinance in January 1947. Among the extensive powers this gave the governor was 'the power to restrict the movement of people with respect to their employment or business, their places of residence, and their associations or communications with other persons' (Thomas 1989: 32), and this new power was promptly exercised by ordering Butler out of the oilfields area (Dalley 1947: 16). Butler, as we have seen, was effectively squeezed out by the responsible labour leaders, the government and the oil companies, and the OWTU was the chief beneficiary of his 1946-7 strike.

The OWTU celebrated its tenth anniversary on 27 July 1947 at the Palm's Club, San Fernando, in the presence of the governor, the colonial secretary, Adrian Cola Rienzi and other dignitaries. Rojas referred in his speech to wage increases that had been achieved, but warned that there was a 'falling off in the purchasing power of working class populations'. He linked future gains to economic development and full employment through industrialisation, and emphasized the union's willingness to cooperate. 'The O.W.T.U. during its ten years of existence has always maintained its industrial agreements and obligations to the community.... It is known to cooperate with Government .... We are as equally anxious as the employers to see the industry prosper and expand'.[104]

Mentor, the general secretary, similarly emphasised that 'this union has, in a spirit of goodwill and compromise always resolved its differences across the conference table and, therefore, has never had cause to order a cessation of work.[105] He drew attention to the frequency with which OWTU officers served on government boards and committees, and were elected to public offices.[106] The governor responded by saying, 'I believe that the machinery exists for discussion and surmounting trouble without recourse to stoppage of work and all the disastrous consequences which flow therefrom'. He emphasised that every element in the community was cooperating.[107] This spirit of compromise and cooperation was clearly seen by all those present at these celebrations as contrasting with Butler's approach.

As the OWTU became institutionalised in its first decade, it became more responsible and respectable in the view of the government and the oil companies, particularly when contrasted with the alternative of the mass, militant agitation that was threatened by Butler and his movement. In 1948 the oil companies, a decade after recognising the OWTU, conceded the check-off and the closed shop, thereby completing its official status in the oilfields. The legal rational bureaucratisation of the union was more or less inevitable in these circumstances, as the officers' credibility during negotiations depended, in part, on their ability to keep their agreements, and therefore on their ability to control their members. However, their credibility with their rank and file could be compromised if the latter were more militant and demanding than their leaders. The companies could afford to make financial concessions and preferred to make them in order to preserve the industrial peace, but it is noteworthy that the union did not call an official strike until 1960.

Rojas and the other OWTU officers faced a problem after 1947 that was in part the consequence of their success in quelling Butler's challenge. Many of Butler's supporters in the oilfields, realizing that they had no real alternative, joined the OWTU. Although this influx of new members between 1947 and 1950 increased the size of the union substantially, it also brought a Butlerite militancy that pushed the executive into a more radical stance than it might have otherwise adopted. Workers recognised that, as individuals, they could not deal with the powerful oil companies and that they needed a strong union. The OWTU's blue-shirted army, as it was called, was famous for its marches and demonstrations, including a well-organised women's auxiliary. According to the

OWTU's official history, 'Every May Day, in particular, the OWTU would show their solidarity with the workers of the world in their struggle to free themselves from the shackles of capitalism. An interesting feature of this period was the tremendous strength and activity of the Union's Women's Auxiliary who were always in the forefront of all the demonstrations. Often too, they would take the initiative and organise their own marches and protests'.

Rojas encouraged these demonstrations as they gave him an air of militancy.[108] However, his growing reputation as a militant socialist got him into increasing trouble with the colonial authorities as the Cold War intensified in the early 1950s. Rojas, like many of the other early labour leaders in the British Caribbean, espoused a socialist and anti-imperialist position, advocated West Indian independence and supported the CLC in the mid-1940s. Unlike most of the other leaders, however, he kept to these positions in the late 1940s and early 1950s, and resisted the considerable pressure that was brought to bear on him by the colonial authorities and other trade unionists to renounce his commitment and his union's affiliation with the CLC and WFTU. In March 1938, just before the oil companies recognized the OWTU, Rojas, then the union's vice-president, celebrated Rienzi's election to the colony's legislature in terms of the class struggle.

> The struggle against capitalist exploitation is necessarily a political struggle. The working class cannot develop its economic organization and wage its economic battles without political rights, and without first coming into political power. In securing a seat in the Legislative Council, we have secured a strategic position in our class struggle. But we need to reinforce this by action to convince employers of our willingness to fight. No weeping, beseeching, or kneeling at the feet of capitalists or any commission of inquiry can bring about our salvation.[109]

Rojas was one of the founders of the Socialist Party of Trinidad and Tobago (SPTT) in 1941, and one of the principal officers of the TTTUC. The SPTT won two seats in the 1946 election, but Rojas himself was beaten by Roodal of Butler's party in St Patrick, the oilfield area of southwest Trinidad.

Rojas attended the first WFTU conference, held in Paris in September 1945, and the Pan African Congress Conference in Manchester in October 1945. The delegates of the inaugural meeting of the CLC in Barbados authorised Rojas, with Rupert Gittens and Ken Hill, to represent the West Indies collectively at the WFTU conference. Rojas was outspoken in Paris. As president of the OWTU and the TTTUC, and a delegate of the new CLC, he chastised British imperialists and capitalists for the suffering of working people in the West Indies, and looked with fresh hope to the WFTU. 'These British West India islands are still an oppressed group suffering from the exploitation of British imperialism and

British capitalism. The history of the workers in the West Indies is a history of murder, suicide, malnutrition, bad housing conditions and poor wages . . . workers in that part of the world are looking forward to this World Trade Union Congress for assistance, for salvation, and for guidance'.[110]

In 1949, when the commissioner of labour, Solomon Hochoy, pressured the chief labour leaders to associate with the emerging Free World Trade Union Organisation that became the ICFTU, Rojas and Mentor of the OWTU, along with Quintin O'Connor, Dudley Mahon and Simeon Alexander of the Federated Workers' Trade Union (FWTU), declined the invitation to participate and remained loyal to the WFTU. The acting governor reported that Rojas, Mentor and O'Connor, 'whether from conviction or for political purposes are strongly anti-Government and anti-British. My own judgement would be that they have no particular liking for Moscow doctrines, but that they are ready to embrace any cause which will embarrass the Government and show His Majesty's Government and the United Kingdom Trades Union Congress that they are able to get on without them'.[111]

By 1950 the colonial officials were more concerned about Butler's political resurgence in the elections than the ideological orientation of Rojas and other leaders of the OWTU and the TTTUC. The signing of an agreement between the OEA and OWTU in May, according to Governor Sir Hubert Rance, put 'wages in the oil industry very much above those in Government employment and other industries . . . [and] incensed the Butlerite officials who have long sought to discredit the Oilfield Workers' Union'.[112] The OWTU membership was said to have increased since the agreement was signed, but Mentor, the general secretary, 'who tried to hold an electioneering meeting at Point Fortin where Butlerite influence is at its strongest, was forced to abandon the attempt owing to heckling by Butlerite supporters'.[113] In the general election on 18 September, when his party won more votes and seats than any other, Butler won that constituency.[114]

A political development that proved to be significant was the activities of several Marxist study groups in 1950, including the Point Fortin Study Group, the West Indian Proletariat Group in Curepe and the Workers' Freedom Movement (WFM) which was formed in 1948 in Port of Spain. These groups held a conference on 15 October in Port of Spain and a week later, 22 October, the WFM held a meeting of some 45 people at the public library in Port of Spain.[115] Among the leaders of this group were John La Rose (secretary), Llewellyn Cross, Jim Barrette and Christina King, some of whom had been leaders of the NWCSA since the 1930s (Reddock 1988: 55-6). In November, the governor reported that members of the WFM had 'intensified their activities' and

were considering plans for obtaining the sympathies of the Butler Party, who, in the opinion of some of the members of the Movement, have a considerable influence over the masses ....

Possibly with a view to infiltrating into other political bodies and Trade Unions in the colony, the Movement has succeeded in getting Vincent Bowles, an active member of Point Fortin Study group, elected to serve on educational committee of the Oilfield Workers' Trade Union (Point Fortin branch) and Bowles has proposed to conduct a course of lectures on Socialism to members of the Oilfield Workers' Trade Union.

It is reported that the Movement in conjunction with the other two groups, one at Point Fortin and the other at Curepe, intend to publish a magazine under the caption "Freedom." Both the Point Fortin Study Group and the West Indian Proletarian Party at Curepe are already well known for their communistic tendencies. A suggestion was made that Butler should be exposed in the "Freedom," with the hope that his party would lose faith in him and become an easy prey to the principles of the Movement, but this suggestion was turned down by other members who probably felt that it would be a better plan to befriend Butler.[116]

The WFM made a mark on politics in Trinidad and Tobago, not by infiltrating the Butler movement or the trade unions, as these official reports suggest, but by joining the leaders of the most powerful trade unions, the OWTU and FWTU, to create a new political party, the West Indian Independence Party (WIIP) in 1952. The WFM was joined by Lennox Pierre, a Marxist solicitor who led the youth council and who, along with La Rose, was a member of the Civil Rights Action Committee which was formed to protest against the actions taken by several British Caribbean governments to prohibit the movement of Caribbean people and to ban what they defined as subversive literature. The WIIP, formed on 30 July, held its inaugural meeting on 21 October 1952. Defining itself as a nationalist party with a socialist outlook, the WIIP declared its basic policy was 'to struggle for the abolition, once and for all, of British imperialist rule, for the establishment of an independent Trinidad and Tobago in a federated independent West Indies'.[117] This was essentially the goal declared by all the labour leaders at the founding conference of the CLC in 1945, but by 1952 most of these people had turned against the CLC and some of those who were nominally still its leaders were even trying to destroy it. The central executive committee of the WIIP consisted of Pierre, chairman; Rojas, first vice chairman; Oli Mohammed, second vice chairman; La Rose, general secretary; O'Connor, treasurer; and Osmund Fletcher, Cyril Gonzales, Barrette, Mahon, Simeon Alexander, Rita Scott and John Poon. On paper, at least, this was a powerful coalition. Rojas, O'Connor and Mohammed were the leaders of the OWTU, FWTU, TTTUC and the All Trinidad Sugar Estates and Factory Workers' Trade Union (ATSEFWTU). The WIIP never really got off the ground, however. Within two years the alliance with the labour leaders was broken and Williams and the PNM swept the new party aside in 1956. The WIIP failed to develop in part because of internal problems in the labour movement, but also because of heavy pressure from the colonial government and the conservative media in the paranoid anti-communist atmosphere of the Cold War.

Brereton says that 'organized labour had its own divisions and weaknesses, which forced it to play a secondary role on the political stage in the 1950s. Inter-union rivalries and disputes were intense in this period, aggravated by politicians who used the unions as bases for their own careers' (1981: 228). This is true, but, as we have seen with the case of Butler after the 1950 elections, the failure of the labour movement was as much the consequence of external pressures which forced divisions, exploited weaknesses and refused to allow radical labour leaders to take advantage of democratic opportunities, as it was the consequence of weaknesses or opportunism on the part of the labour organisations and leaders themselves.

We may see the dynamics of the politics of labour exemplified within the sugar industry in Trinidad. The ATSEFWTU, founded in 1937, was the oldest trade union of sugar workers, led initially by Rienzi, but the Sugar Manufacturers' Association (SMA) did not agree to a negotiated settlement with the union until 1945. This first agreement, signed in January 1945, was followed by two more 12-month agreements, signed in April 1946 and March 1947. They provided for increases in wages, though sugar workers remained 'among the lowest paid in Trinidad' (Dalley 1947: 19), seven days' holiday with pay per year, an eight-hour day for all daily-rated time workers, with extra rates for overtime, Sundays and public holidays, and the establishment of a joint consultative committee for settling disputes and other matters arising concerning the employment of field and factory workers in the sugar industry. There remained many variations in how tasks and payments were defined from one estate to another, however, and the union was 'faced with complicated methods of work and remuneration which would tax a well-equipped British Trade Union to deal with'. Nonetheless, Dalley believed, 'The Union has done well and should be encouraged' (1947: 37).

A strike began among the sugar workers on the Perseverance Estate of Caroni Ltd on 5 May 1947, involving some 1,400 workers. It was fomented, and possibly started by Butler and his followers, not by the ATSEFWTU. Kumar, an independent member of the Legislative Council, Indian nationalist and supporter of Butler, characterised the ATSEFWTU as incompetent, and Butler threatened that 'if prompt action is not taken the strike may extend even outside the sugar industry to encompass other industries as well' (Dalley 1947: 20). Kumar pressed for an inquiry and Chanka Maharaj, another of Butler's Indian supporters, seconded his motion, saying that the cause of the strike was the payment of starvation wages. The president of the ATSEFWTU, C.C. Abidh, who was also a member of the Legislative Council, repudiated the attack on his union and drew attention to the improvements that it had secured. He denied that the strike was spontaneous and condemned the actions of certain members of the council who, instead of urging the workers to put their grievances through their union, had belittled the union and its officers, thereby encouraging an unauthorised strike and fostering unrest. Gomes suggested that it was Butler and Kumar who had engineered the strike. Kumar's motion was defeated by ten votes to five on 16 May. The strike declined over the next two weeks and gradually came to an end. In a report on labour leaders marked strictly private and confidential, Dalley stated that he had been told that Kumar had tried to create a rival union of sugar workers, and that Abidh said he had appealed to Kumar to assist him in rebuilding the ATSEFWTU, but had got no response because Kumar 'does not believe in trade unionism'.[118] Undoubtedly, Butler was trying to extend his influence into the sugar industry, and Indian politicians like Kumar and Chanka Maharaj thought this could be a useful coalition to expand their own influence. While they were largely unsuccessful, their efforts did weaken the existing trade union.

The situation recurred the following year when a three-month strike began in February, chiefly on the Usine Ste Madeleine estate, near San Fernando. According to Governor Shaw, over 20,000 tons of cane were burned in acts of sabotage, but the strike did not become more general. 'From first to last no "demands" for increased wages or anything else were made by the workers on the employers . . . . Butler's motives must be presumed to be . . . general chaos and disturbance . . . and to smash his hated rivals, the orthodox, but as yet not wholly stable and representative trade unions in both the sugar and the oil industries'.[119]

Police repression was also effective: a police sergeant fired on and wounded three leaders of a demonstration in Point Fortin and, under the emergency powers ordinance, Butler and his principal colleagues were prevented from entering the counties of Caroni, Victoria and St Patrick, that is, the oil and sugar regions of central and southwestern Trinidad.

Even in this context, Governor Sir John Shaw reported there was no tangible evidence of any organised communist activity in Trinidad and Tobago.[120] In November 1948, however, Shaw reported a Marxist study group, led by Jack Kelshall, a solicitor, meeting weekly at his home in San Fernando,[121] and Darlington Marshall, speaking at a meeting of Butler's in Port of Spain on 10 November, was alleged to have said 'that the only way the black man would attain equal rights with the white man was in a communist state'.[122]

By 1948 two tendencies were developing in Trinidad. First, Butler's agitation, while not resulting in any major organisation of his own, affected the existing trade unions in the oil and sugar industries, but in different ways. The

OWTU, which was well established, benefited from the absorption of Butlerites into the organisation, not only in the sense that they swelled numbers
but also because they revived the union's militancy. The ATSEFWTU was a
weaker organization, however, and the combined attacks it sustained from
Butler and his Indian colleagues in the Legislative Council encouraged other
would-be politicians of Indian descent to try to use this same social base as a
springboard for their own power. The next few years, consequently, saw the
creation of other rival unions, thereby further diluting the latent strength
of the sugar workers by severely dividing them. By the early 1950s, as the
earlier Indian leaders, like Abidh, Roodal and Sarran Teelucksingh, were losing their political strength, new ones sought their bases among Trinidad's
sugar workers, either by leading existing unions or by starting their own in
competition. Thus, Mitra Sinanan started the Sugar Industry Labour Union
(SILU) and Lionel Frank Seukeran started the Sugar Workers' Union (SWU).
In 1952 Seukeran suggested dividing the sugar belt between three unions,
with the ATSEFWTU in the north, the SILU in the centre and his own SWU,
based in San Fernando, in the south.[123] Then Ashford Sinanan started a new,
subscription-free union, the Cane Farmers and Sugar Workers' Association, said
to be funded by prominent citizens, in competition with the ATSEFWTU and
the SWU.[124] These labour leaders did not emerge from the ranks of the workers,
'but rather imposed themselves on the Hindu community' which they used
'as a political base of support'.[125]

In 1953 there were between four and six unions claiming to represent sugar
workers and the SMA refused to recognise any of them. The weakness of the sugar workers, and the rivalry between the unions that sought to represent them, is
reflected in the fact that four boards of inquiry were established between 1948
and 1960 to investigate aspects of the sugar industry such as wages and conditions of work, rival unionism and arrangements on collective bargaining. The
strategy of 'industrial relations by board of inquiry' (Thomas 1989: 36), and the
determination of remuneration and holidays by wages councils, provided for
by the wages councils ordinance of 1949, reflected the weakness of trade unions
and negotiating machinery, but they also contributed to it. The governor, by
referring matters concerning wages, conditions or representation to a wages
council or a board of inquiry, moved the resolution of serious disputes another
step away from the unions themselves. Moreover, many routine disputes were
resolved in the Department of Labour, where the official strategy of building
up 'a strong conciliation unit' (Thomas 1989: 36) further reduced the role of
the trade unions in industrial relations, and hence also the faith workers might
have in their organisations.

In this context, it was a major achievement when Bhadase Sagan Maraj federated two of the unions, the ATSEFWTU, of which he had become president in 1953, and Mitra Sinanan's SILU. Maraj had come to prominence in 1952 when he merged the two leading Hindu organizations into the Sanatan Dharma Maha Sabha (Singh 1996: 244). He soon became the 'strong man in the sugar belt' (Brereton 1981: 228) and his union achieved recognition by the SMA. The chaotic years of the late 1940s and early 1950s were resolved, therefore, in a way that defined the chief sugar workers' union as the base for the man who became the most powerful Indian politician in Trinidad. Fear of Maraj's growing political strength among Indo-Trinidadians, following the creation of the People's Democratic Party (PDP) in 1955, helped to push the middle-class Creoles into creating the rival People's National Movement (PNM) in 1956, so the organizational strength of the sugar workers, when it finally came, was channelled into ethnic politics at the expense of a multi-ethnic labour party. The persistent politicisation of ethnicity in Trinidad and Tobago stemmed directly from these developments in the early 1950s.

The second tendency was the development of a new litmus test for responsible, that is non-political and non-militant, trade unionism, inspired by the global ideological struggle of the Cold War. The fanatical and ruthless application of this test to some of the leading trade unions and labour leaders created further divisions that weakened the political effectiveness not only of the left wing but also of the entire labour movement. We have seen how the split in the WFTU and pressure from the British TUC and Colonial Office led to a split within the TTTUC in 1949. Rojas and Mentor of the OWTU, with Mahon, O'Connor and Simeon Alexander of the FWTU, remained with the WFTU, and C.P. Alexander, president of the Seamen and Waterfront Workers' Trade Union (SWWTU), along with the Railway Workers' Trade Union (RWTU), affiliated with the new ICFTU and withdrew from the TTTUC and the CLC. This split persisted, so when Rojas, O'Connor, Mahon and Simeon Alexander helped to create the WIIP in 1952, they were not speaking for a united labour movement. The rivalries and divisions within the labour movement, exacerbated by the ideological frenzy of anti-communism at this stage in the Cold War, spelled the doom of the WIIP which never became the trade union-based political force in Trinidad and Tobago that it was intended to be.

Rojas and O'Connor, in particular, became the targets of an intense witch-hunting campaign in the Trinidad press. On 9 March 1952, an editorial in the Sunday Guardian praised Manley for expelling the 'Left Wing extremists', known as the Four H's, who were accused of using the CLC 'to infect the BWI with Communist ideas'.[126] The Four Hs were reported to have been excluded from Trinidad and Tobago.[127] Dozens of articles, letters, editorials and cartoons followed through May and June, about 'local Reds' and 'Red agents', while

Gomes, the minister of labour, industry and commerce, warned of 'unmistakable evidence' of subversion and 'Communist infiltration' in the trade unions.[128] Butler, Rojas and O'Connor would not comment on Gomes' accusations, but C.P. Alexander said they were 'most timely'. An editorial in the Sunday Guardian commented on 'the extraordinary laxity of the Government in allowing the free flow into Trinidad of the most rabid and subversive Communist literature . . . . All this hate-mongering Communist literature must be banned from the Colony, and the sooner this is done the better'. The article reported that Bertram Jack, the general secretary of the Public Works and Public Services Workers' Union (PWPSWU), agreed there was an 'insidious' communist-inspired attempt, backed by the WFTU, to agitate among the trade unions, and C.P. Alexander agreed, calling them 'subversive elements'.[129] A week later, the Port of Spain Gazette attacked the TTTUC for being affiliated to the WFTU, 'from which the Western unions withdrew in disgust in 1949',[130] and a week after that the Sunday Guardian editorial urged Rojas and O'Connor to 'break the Moscow affiliation'. There were op-ed 'letters' in this issue, by people identified only as 'Telescope' and 'Common Sense', with the headlines, 'Reds Use Forced Labour on Enormous Scale' and 'Soviet Worker of Today Only a Robot'.[131] The Port of Spain Gazette kept up its end of this public campaign by criticising 'the two responsible officials' of the TTTUC for retaining its affiliation to the WFTU. It went on to say that the WIIP's advocacy of 'freedom for Trinidad in a Federated West Indies' would open the country to '"influences" we could not escape', and implied that people would not 'risk investing all they possess in industry unless they are absolutely certain that things will be properly conducted and the unions themselves are prepared to put a stop to any subversive propaganda'. It urged the government to take action.[132] On 10 June a letter from 'Common Sense' claimed that 'a certain labour union leader' went 'behind the Iron Curtain' and returned to spread communism in Trinidad.[133] This press campaign occurred just at the time that the ICFTU was holding its first Caribbean conference in Barbados.

Rojas responded to the Guardian with a forceful letter. 'Your editorial . . . prompts me to ask since when has this journal, the champion of capitalist interest in the Colony, become so solicitous of the interests of the workers? The workers are rightly suspicious when the Capitalist Press offer [sic] them gratuitous advice'. He argued that the WFTU is 'supported by all class conscious workers of the world' and 'continues to work for the achievement of its original aims', while the Anglo-Americans 'impair the solidarity of the workers, and thus make it easier for them to continue the ruthless and heartless exploitation of the workers . . . . We refuse to preach to the workers that they should hate their comrades'.[134] The Trinidad Guardian kept up the attack, urging a ban on subversive literature and 'foreign propaganda', and Seukeran joined the bandwagon with a letter, claiming that 'the T.U.C. is as democratic only as the Kremlin is . . . . Rojas is the dictator of the T.U.C. . . . . As a trade unionist and leader of sugar workers I affirm my pledge to fight Communism to the bitter end, and I will see to it that Moscow's agents have little success in the sugar zone . . . . Communism has infiltrated into our midst to a larger extent than either the Government or we ourselves realise'.[135] He had discovered the political potential of denouncing the enemy within, and of declaring himself a real champion of the workers' freedoms in contrast to those who were alleged to be Moscow's agents.

The scope of the attack was broadened when an editorial and an article by Alderman E.J. Lange of San Fernando referred to local red agents attacking all religions and churches of all denominations, but without giving any particulars.[136] On the same day the Sunday Guardian editorialised, 'Pro-Communists Belittle the Church', and carried an article by Canon M.E. Farquhar called 'Workers of West Menaced by Attitude of W.F.T.U.', and a reprint of another of his articles, 'Communism in Trinidad', from the Catholic News.[137] Before the end of June the government had banned 'red' publications and made it an offence to possess copies of Soviet Weekly or World Trade Union Movement, the WFTU publication. In the name of freedom, the government was preventing the free flow of literature into the colony, as the papers had advocated the previous month. There appears to have been a more or less concerted campaign to rouse the public's support for such restrictions and to turn the trade unions' rank-and-file members against their leaders.

Not all voices contributed to the campaign, however. An article by Charles H. Archibald, contrary to this red scare and the government's panic measures, headlined 'Jamaica Dealt with Communism Without Help from Government', concluded that 'Gomes has greatly overstressed the danger' of communist tendencies. 'The marvel is that Communism has not taken wide and deep root in the Caribbean', he observed, as the 'extreme poverty' provides such a suitable breeding-ground. He pointed out the absurdity that Ken Hill, after being expelled from the PNP for communist activity, had just been admitted to the ICFTU conference in Barbados as the principal figure of the JTUC. He added that 'corruption in public places' was a more serious threat than communism in Trinidad.[138] Three weeks later, Archibald, writing again from London, opined that if 'Rojas and his colleagues persist with their relationship with the W.F.T.U., they cannot be expected to be treated quite like other unions'. But he urged government restraint: 'How valuable is political freedom to Trinidadians? The Communist menace will be doing its dirty work if it leads to curtailment of freedom'.[139] The simple comparison he made between Jamaica and Trinidad misses some crucial differences, however. First, at the time the Four H's were expelled the Jamaican premier, Bustamante, was content to see his rival wrestling with his left wingers because it helped reinforce his own credentials as someone further removed from communism than the tainted PNP. It seemed to be in the Jamaican government's interest, as seen by Bustamante, not to intervene in the case but to continue to snipe at the PNP socialists as untrustworthy supporters of the free world. Second, in Trinidad and Tobago, unlike Jamaica, the leaders of the TUC could not be directly pressured and expelled by a political party. Rojas and O'Connor, on the contrary, had just helped to create a new party which was clearly dependent on their support if it was to expand its base in the labour movement. This is why the government in Trinidad and Tobago had to resort to the public opinion campaign, with the media joining in an inflated red scare, in order to pressure the labour leaders to change their minds, or to get their followers to push them to do so. The problem for the government in Trinidad and Tobago, therefore, was precisely that Rojas and O'Connor were independent labour leaders, whereas in Jamaica the Four H's were not independent of the PNP leadership.

Rojas and O'Connor did not capitulate after the first round of pressure in 1952. They kept the TTTUC affiliated to the WFTU and their unions, the OWTU and the FWTU, remained affiliated with the CLC, which was itself still officially connected to the WFTU. In November 1952, as we saw in the previous chapter, Rojas and O'Connor, along with La Rose of the WIIP, Cheddi Jagan from Guyana and Joshua from St Vincent, joined Hart in Barbados to try to convince Adams to support a new Caribbean federation of trade unions to which all regional unions would affiliate, irrespective of whether their international connections were with the WFTU or the ICFTU. When Adams turned down this proposal in favour of a federation that would be affiliated exclusively with the ICFTU, namely CADORIT, it was another blow to those labour leaders, like Rojas and O'Connor, who wanted to retain their affiliations with the WFTU.

The CLC lacked the funds to organise a third congress, but CADORIT and its affiliates were relatively rich in resources. In addition to providing material assistance, unionists from the region attended the second congress of ORIT in Rio de Janeiro in December 1952, where Walcott of the BWU was elected to represent the English-speaking territories. In March 1953 several area unionists, including Walcott, Lionel Luckhoo of the MPCA in Guyana, Florizel Glasspole of the Jamaican NWU and Osman Mohammed of the SILU, attended the Sugar Workers' and Plantation Workers' conference in Havana under ICFTU auspices. In June Violet Lynch of the BWU represented the area at the ICFTU International Summer School for women in France, and at the third congress of the ICFTU in Stockholm Walcott replaced Adams as the Caribbean area representative on the ICFTU executive board.[140] CADORIT's monthly Information Bulletin first appeared in February 1953 as a medium for disseminating selected trade union news and ideas, and the Trinidad and Tobago Federation of Trade Unions, the rival to the TTTUC, organised a course for its members. The chairman and secretary of CADORIT paid visits to various territories 'with a view to binding the forces of the democratic trade union movement closer together'.[141] While CADORIT flourished the CLC declined, just as the leaders and backers of the ICFTU and ORIT intended. Hart and Rojas attended the WFTU conference in Vienna in October 1953 but they could not revive the CLC and continuing Cold War pressures led Rojas and O'Connor to pull their unions and the TTTUC out of the WFTU in 1953.

On his way to the WFTU conference in Vienna Rojas sent a defiant message to OWTU members, saying he was going to 'a mass congress of unity . . . a movement, of remarkable scope and strength, of the working people in the capitalist, colonial and semi-colonial countries'.[142] Rojas, Hart, La Rose and others were encouraged by the fact that the People's Progressive Party (PPP), led by Cheddi Jagan, having won the first election with universal adult suffrage in British Guiana, had formed a government in May 1953. However, as will be seen in the next chapter, the UK suspended the constitution on 9 October 1953 and brought down Jagan's government. Hart, in his speech to the Vienna congress, warned about 'the penetration of the working class ranks by opportunism', and of labour movements being 'too readily open for bourgeois nationalist politicians to use the trade unions simply as vote-catching machines for their own purposes', but the danger in Guyana was both more direct and violent. Even as Hart was saying that British imperialism was employing 'more subtle methods of attack' by using the ICFTU, combining rewards and flattery to entice some labour leaders and destroy unity, the British government was actually deploying troops in Georgetown.[143] The CLC and WIIP had links with Jagan, so the British action in Guyana increased the pressure on Rojas and O'Connor to withdraw their unions from the WFTU and to leave the WIIP.

The Trinidad press escalated the scale of red scare headlines in order to justify the overthrow of British Guiana's constitution and to increase pressure on the leaders of the WIIP. On 6 November it was reported that the Venezuelan government would soon celebrate the fifth anniversary of 'the ousting of the Communist-influenced Acción Democrática Government in 1948'. They were said to have posted guards on the border to stop reds coming from British Guiana: 'Reds will not be tolerated', the Venezuelan consul was reported as saying.[144] The next day, under the headline 'Link between B.G., Guatemala and Br. Honduras Reds', the British colonial secretary was reported to have said there was a 'definite link' between opposition elements in Belize, presumably George Price and other members of the People's United Party (PUP), and communists in

Guatemala and Guyana.[145] Gomes and Hochoy, meanwhile, undertook a secret mission to London, where they discussed the recent events in Guyana and the situation in Trinidad and Tobago with the colonial secretary and leaders of the British TUC. On their return, it was announced that Dalley would pay another visit to Trinidad, to report 'on a West Indian trade union movement which it is feared may have become affected by Communist infiltration'.[146]

The day after Dalley's mission was announced, and just a week after Rojas returned from Vienna, the TTTUC held an emergency meeting at which it was decided to end its affiliation to the WFTU. The TTTUC resolution stated, 'in view of the misconceptions of the role of the T.U.C. as an affiliated unit of the W.F.T.U., and in the interest of the continuance of industrial relations with Government and employers and to avoid any future misunderstanding of the aims of the unions affiliated, the Council decides to withdraw its affiliation to the W.F.T.U.' Rojas added that 'The resolution embodies fully the position of the T.U.C. in respect to the W.F.T.U.', and pointed out that, originally, 'it was under Government's encouragement and assistance that the T.U.C. had affiliated to the W.F.T.U.' and that 'the T.U.C. had not been convinced that there was good reason for disaffiliating'.[147] O'Connor was reported as saying that 'the T.U.C. was socialist in outlook' and remained sympathetic to the WFTU which, unlike the ICFTU, supported the liberation of colonial territories. He said that the decision had been under consideration for about six months and was 'in the air' when Rojas went to Vienna. The Guardian's response was, 'Who's Fooling Whom?'[148] Undoubtedly, given the pressure they were under, the TTTUC leaders must have been considering this option for some time but, just as surely, the actual decision was made precipitately after the dramatic events in Guyana and the announcement of Dalley's mission. It is also quite likely that Rojas realised, after his visit to Vienna, that he would get little real support from the WFTU other than rhetoric and that the CLC was defunct. Therefore, although they would have nothing to gain from stubbornly maintaining the affiliation with the WFTU, they nevertheless felt, for ideological reasons, that they should not denounce the federation or affiliate with its rival. At a labour rally, where the TTTUC, FWTU, OWTU, and WIIP were represented by O'Connor, Mahon, Simeon Alexander, Pierre, Barrette and La Rose, Rojas explained why the TTTUC had joined the WFTU and why it now withdrew. The WIIP paper, Freedom, edited by La Rose, stated: 'He went on further to point out that if the oil bosses believed that they could get away from recognizing the union [OWTU] by raising the Communist bogey they were in for a big surprise'. It also warned that, under 'the pretext of fighting communism', the big interests of Tate & Lyle, the World Bank and the bauxite companies would seek to smash every labour party and trade union, and that every West Indian government was 'charged with these designs'.[149]

This tone of militant defiance did not last much longer, however. Dalley dutifully reported that the WIIP was 'communist inspired and directed' and that the trade union leaders were acting irresponsibly by participating in it (Dalley 1954). Rojas and O'Connor withdrew from the WIIP in 1954 and the party, lacking any mass base in the union organisations, soon withered away. La Rose was the only party member to contest a seat in the national elections in 1956 and he got little support. In 1958 he left Trinidad to live in Venezuela and subsequently moved to the UK. Rojas, frustrated in his political ambitions and in the failure of the labour movement to become a major political force, moved politically to the right and became increasingly authoritarian within the OWTU. After forces outside the labour movement had broken up the attempt to create a strong left-wing party, Rojas moved to break the militants within his own union. The Butlerites within the OWTU included supporters of the WIIP, such as Walter Annamunthodo and Weekes, who were participating in a struggle for internal democracy within the union. According to the OWTU's official history, 'Workers were becoming more and more suspicious of the representation they were getting and there were many who felt that "sellouts" were taking place'.[150] A group of workers who called themselves the Reformists held regular caucuses to discuss union affairs, but the newspapers dubbed them the Rebels and the name stuck. Weekes, an admirer of Pierre and La Rose and a member of the WIIP, was elected a branch committee member for Point-a-Pierre, the biggest branch of the union, in 1955.

At the 1956 annual conference of the OWTU the Point-a-Pierre branch delegation raised questions about the union's finances, concerning irregularities in accounting procedures and waste of resources, and about the constitution and rules of the union, in order to bring more democratic procedures into the organisation. The annual conference usually began with a series of speeches by the chairman, government officers and officials from other unions, and continued with the general secretary's report and other speeches by members of the executive, until many delegates had left. Then the election of executive officers was rushed through and at the end of the day a motion was passed to leave any other matters to be dealt with by the council. The semblance of democratic procedures obscured the fact that a small group, with Rojas in charge, really ran the union without participation from the rank and file. The Rebel's motions in 1956 succeeded in prolonging the conference for an unprecedented three days, during which there was a great deal of debate, but the Rojas loyalists retained their control. The Rebels' motions were defeated but, according to the OWTU history, 'The eyes of many workers were opened. They now began to understand the importance of democracy, and members recognised that all was not well with the existing policy of the OWTU'.[151] The executive's response was not to open up the union, but to crack down on the Rebels: three members of the Point-a-Pierre Branch - Annamunthodo, Cecil Mitchell and Hugh Norton - were expelled from the union in 1957 for plotting. Annamunthodo appealed against the union's action, fought his case all the way to the Privy Council, and won. The action against the Rebels and Annamunthodo's legal victory further clarified the authoritarian nature of the union's executive and 'workers were more than ever convinced of the need for a change to be made'.[152]

In 1958, the Rebels gained control of the Point-a-Pierre branch, with Israel Yearwood and Weekes elected as president and vice-president, respectively. In 1959 Weekes was elected president of the branch, and this democratic example spread elsewhere in the union. A year after a strike, the first official strike in the OWTU's history, shut down Texaco, Shell, British Petroleum, Apex and other oil-fields, Weekes became the first vice-president of the OWTU. In 1962 the annual conference of OWTU delegates instructed the General Council to take action, and strike action if necessary, on behalf of 38 workers dismissed by BP, but Rojas agreed with the company that 22 of the workers would be given employment with a contractor. This did not placate the union, however, as these workers lost their job security. A motion of no-confidence in the president and general secretary was passed by the General Council on 27 March 1962, Rojas resigned and Weekes took over as acting president general. On 25 June 1962 Weekes was confirmed as president general by 'the first popular democratic vote for the Executive of the union .... The victory was total as the entire Reformist team was voted into office' (Kambon 1988: 65). According to the OWTU history, this election 'was the first time in the Union's history that every member was entitled to vote for the leadership of his choice ... the Rebels had restored democracy to the OWTU'.[153]

As an endnote to this story of the democratisation of the OWTU, it may be pointed out that Rojas turned full circle and accused the trade unions of harbouring Marxists and communist elements. Appointed to the Senate in 1962, Rojas launched a campaign against alleged communist infiltration in the trade unions, and identified Weekes as one of the chief agents of this 'alien ideology'. When Williams established a commission of inquiry into subversive activities in 1963, with a Nigerian chief justice, L. Mbanefo, in the chair, Rojas was one of the principal witnesses. He claimed that there was a plot by com-munist trade union leaders to take over the country. The commission was not convinced by Rojas's claims, however, and pointed out that the 'fact that the strikes [of 1962 and 1963] were spread over all the major unions negatives the suggestion of subversion' (Mbanefo Report 1965: 45). The Mbanefo Commis-sion's report was presented in January 1964, but it was not until March 1965, when sugar workers were on strike, that the government laid the report before the House of Representatives and declared a state of emergency, as a prelude to opportunistically rushing through the Industrial Stabilisation Act.

The events of the 1950s, then, provide the necessary background for understanding the political and labour struggles that continued in the 1960s in Trinidad and Tobago. Indeed, the roots of the black power rebellion of 1970, in which the working class of the urban north and the oilfields played a major role, of the United Labour Front, an alliance of progressive trade unions formed in 1975, and of MOTION, the Movement for Social Transformation formed in 1989, all lay in the struggles of democratic and socialist trade unionists in the 1940s and 1950s. What this analysis shows is that the admitted weakness of the labour movement and of the politics of labour in Trinidad and Tobago by the mid-1950s was not simply the result of internal factors, such as the failure of key labour leaders or the ethnic divisions among the workers, though these factors certainly played a role. Rather, these failures and divisions were exacerbated by the conflicts and problems created within the labour movement by 'external' factors, including the slow pace of democratisation of the political system and the pressures of Cold War ideology. These factors coincided in the late 1940s and early 1950s in such a way that they divided and weakened the political voice of organised labour.

> The repercussions of the split in the WFTU were felt in the Trinidad and Tobago labour movement in several important ways. First, the split was connected with the beginnings of rival federations of trade unions of different ideological orientations; this feature has persisted to the present day. Second, the developments that followed from the split facilitated a strategy on the part of the political authorities of isolating the left wing of the trade union movement and putting it on the defensive. Third, the persisting division in the ranks of the labour movement became a formidable obstacle to the formation of a trade union-based political force. (Thomas 1989: 36)

In the early 1950s the politics of labour became a free-for-all for independent political aspirants who sought to use working-class support, to the exclusion of the ideological left. This left the way open from 1955 for the ethnically-based and middle-class dominated parties, the People's Democratic Party (PDP) and its successor the Democratic Labour Party (DLP), and the PNM.

The WIIP, an avowedly Marxist party, attempted to unify the socialist elements of the labour movement with a militantly anti-imperialist nationalism, defined in a broadly West Indian fashion that expressed similar goals and aspirations to those of the CLC in the mid-1940s. But the hysterical and paranoid climate of the early 1950s, and particularly the impact of events in Guyana in 1953 and Guatemala in 1954, doomed the WIIP to isolation, division and destruction. The leaders were frequently and publicly chastised as the subversive agents of an alien ideology, but there is no evidence that the WIIP, or any of the left labour leaders, received instructions or financial assistance from foreign organisations or governments, whereas this could not be said of those who affiliated with the ICFTU and CADORIT. Selwyn Ryan said that 'Trinidadians have never looked beyond Britain for their political ideology' (1972: 136). Although this is not true of those ideological elements that originated in Pan-Africanism and Garveyism, it is true of the democratic socialism that characterises the political left wing of the labour movement. Rojas, O'Connor, Pierre and La Rose used the methods and values of the democratic socialist tradition to criticise the capitalist imperialist system as they saw it work in Trinidad and Tobago. However, they were trying to create their Marxist, trade-union based party for national liberation at the worst time, when the political climate of the US-led Cold War, at its hysterical peak, allowed them no opportunity to develop.

Conclusion

The early 1950s were a critical period in many parts of the British Caribbean for the institutionalisation of the labour movement. This was a period of transition between the militancy of the 1930s, when the series of labour rebellions resulted in dozens of inchoate trade unions, and the eve of independence in the late 1950s and 1960s, when many of these trade unions constituted the organised bases for political parties that competed for votes and political power. The next chapter will focus more on the relations between the labour movement and nationalist political parties, in particular those in two multi-ethnic societies, Guyana and Belize. In this chapter we have seen that, along with substantial variations, there were certain clear tendencies in the development of trade unions in the British Caribbean.

One such tendency was the dominance of a trade union by a charismatic figure who treated the labour organisation as if it was his personal vehicle rather than the organised expression of working-class aspirations. Bustamante, Butler and Gairy all exemplify this tendency, but with interesting variations. In large part, their success or failure may be attributed, not to their different personal qualities, but to the different social and political circumstances in which they became leaders of their trade unions. Butler was the first of these three to achieve national prominence, but he was the most hampered and harassed, first by being jailed and expelled from the chief trade union and then by being excluded from participating in trade union and political developments by a conspiracy of employers, colonial officials and other labour and political leaders. The zenith of his career was in 1950, when his party won more seats than any other in the general elections, and yet he was excluded from the Executive Council.

Bustamante, the next of these three on the scene of labour politics, was also jailed and, like Butler, was soon involved in rivalry with other labour and political leaders. His timing was more fortunate, however, as the Jamaican constitution was liberalised in 1944, enabling his JLP, with just 41.4 per cent of the vote, to capture such power as was then permitted. He was therefore able to use his powerful trade union base to achieve a political position that provided him with the patronage to consolidate his power. He also became more acceptable to the employers and colonial officials than Butler was in Trinidad and Tobago. The JLP's share of the vote increased to 42.7 per cent in 1949, which, though slightly below the 43.5 per cent won by the PNP, was enough for it to retain office, as the number of independents declined from five to two. Bustamante's power increased in the early 1950s but his party's popularity declined and the PNP won overwhelmingly in 1955 with 50.5 per cent of the vote to the JLP's 39.3 per cent (Kuper 1976: 112).

Grenada was not involved in the labour rebellions of the 1930s and Gairy was a newcomer in labour politics. The different social and economic circumstances in Grenada delayed the demands of working people and universal suffrage did not come until 1951. Gairy was the first labour leader to take advantage of this new situation, stirring up and leading Grenada's belated labour rebellion, and leapfrogging over Marryshow in the process by creating a new trade union and political party. However, Grenada's constitution was not as developed as Jamaica's, so Gairy did not gain such early access to the sources of patronage and power as did Bustamante. Gairy failed to consolidate his early gains, as Bustamante did, and he lost a lot of support in Grenada's second and third general elections, in 1954 and 1957. However, Gairy, unlike Butler, was not a spent force in the mid-1950s. Like Bustamante, he returned to power in the early 1960s. His subsequent abuse of that power led to his removal by force in 1979.

The second marked tendency was for a trade union to develop along bureaucratic lines, unlike the more personal followings that supported Butler, Bustamante and Gairy. Both of the examples examined, the BWU and the OWTU, had, in Adams and Rojas, respectively, strong and long-lasting leaders, and these men ran their unions along more legal and bureaucratic lines than did Butler, Bustamante and Gairy. Adams and Rojas consolidated their power within these trade unions and had little tolerance for rivals or even for people who questioned how they ran the union's affairs. I have characterised their kind of leadership as bureaucratic authoritarianism to distinguish it from the more charismatic or populist authoritarianism of Butler, Bustamante and Gairy. However, Adams and Rojas were strikingly different from each other in terms of their political success, in large part because of the difference in their relations with the colonial authorities. Both men had serious political rivals as well as strong trade union bases, but Adams' chief rivals were to his political left and he was early on accepted by the colonial authorities as the most responsible labour leader. Rojas, on the contrary, though initially favoured over Butler, became at odds with the colonial administration when he refused to take his union and the TTTUC out of the CLC and WFTU, as he was pressed to do. The politics of the Cold War interceded in local labour politics, therefore, with different consequences for Adams and Rojas. Adams renounced the initially socialist position of the CLC and became a staunch anti-communist in the paranoid years of the early 1950s. He was rewarded with a knighthood and he became the first, and only, prime minister of the short-lived West Indies Federation between 1958 and 1962. Rojas failed in several efforts to achieve political power on his labour base, with the Socialist Party of Trinidad and Tobago in 1946, the WIIP in 1952 and the Caribbean National Labour Party in 1956. In 1962 he was appointed a senator by the governor, but this was a position without political power.

Both Adams and Rojas tried to suppress their rivals and critics within their unions by ostensibly legal and bureaucratic means, thereby obscuring essentially authoritarian actions under a thin guise of democratic procedures. The regular conferences and meetings, procedural rules and elections of officers, the keeping of minutes, the motions and votes, all suggest democratic forms and processes, but a small group of officials led by a powerful individual actually dominated trade union affairs in both cases. Although the style of trade union leadership, management and decision-making was more legal and bureaucratic than in the organisations led by Butler, Bustamante and Gairy, these trade unions were also very authoritarian. In none of these cases was there any real control, and scarcely any real input, into trade union affairs by the rank and file. On the contrary, decision-making was concentrated at the top, and communications were largely from the unions' officers down to the members. Those members who objected or called their officers to account were dealt with severely, even by expulsion, and it was not until 1962 that the reforming Rebels succeeded in taking the OWTU away from Rojas' control.

Ironically, the leaders of the BWU and OWTU used the ostensibly democratic forms and procedures to ensure their authoritarian control, and Adams even went as far as to use anti-communist rhetoric about freedom to suppress the more democratic tendencies in his union. The politics of the Cold War, and specifically anti-communist rhetoric and resources from outside the region, was used by Bustamante and Gairy, Adams and Manley, and later even Rojas, to reinforce authoritarian tendencies against the democratic aspects within the labour movement.

Notes

[1] The concept is often used loosely, but I am using it in the more specific Weberian sense.
[2] V.L. Arnett, 'Lecture on the History of the People's National Party', n.d., quoted in Post 1978: 252.
[3] Quoted in Eaton 1975: 65. Presumably, Bustamante refers here to Hitler, Franco and Mussolini as the dictators who are giving results.
[4] Daily Gleaner, 21 Feb. 1942, quoted in Post 1981: Vol. 1, 219.
[5] Reports of Herbert G. Macdonald, BWI Central Labour Organisation, 3 Apr. 1945 and 8 Sept. 1945, CO 318/460/2.
[6] Some Jamaicans were aware at this time that the limited employment opportunities coincided with a rapid growth in the population from 858,118 in 1921 to 1,321,054 in 1946.
[7] Quoted in Eaton 1975: 118.
[8] N.N. Nethersole to Arthur Creech Jones, 18 Mar. 1946, FCB Papers, Mss Brit. Emp. S365, Box 142/2 Rhodes House Library.
[9] W.I. Department Report, Jul. 1948, CO 537/3812.
[10] OWTU, 50 Years of Progress (San Fernando, 1988), p. 14.
[11] Kumar, the Indian-born president of the East Indian National Congress, was elected to the House as an independent by a mostly Hindu vote in 1946 and was a rival of C.C. Abidh, the president of the Sugar Workers' Union, who was elected in 1946 as a TUC/Socialist Party candidate. Kumar cooperated with Butler for a while but he depended on Indian communal support, and proposed separate seats for Indians in the House, and even a voting system that would permit Hindus and Moslems to vote only for members of their own religion (Clarion, 17 Apr. 1948).
[12] OWTU, 50 Years of Progress, p. 15.
[13] Gov. Sir H. Rance to Creech Jones, 4 May 1949, CO 537/4902.
[14] Rance to James Griffiths, 25 Nov. 1950, CO 537/6149. Butler was said to have obtained a personal loan from a bank for $150 for his campaign.
[15] My thanks to Howard Johnson for this observation.
[16] OWTU, 50 Years of Progress, pp. 27, 37.
[17] The same was observed about Dominica.
[18] Gov. H.B. Popham to Macdonald, 31 Oct. 1938, CO 318/434/1.
[19] Ibid.
[20] F. Kennedy, West Indies Report, 27 Aug. 1948, CO 537/3824.
[21] Gov. R.D.H. Arundell to G.F. Seel, 1 Aug. 1948, CO 537/3824.
[22] Ibid.
[23] Arundell to Seel, 3 Dec. 1948, CO 537/3824.
[24] Gairy probably exaggerated the extent of his involvement with Aruba trade unions, as part of his 'reinvention of himself' (Howard Johnson, pers. comm. Aug. 1999).
[25] Arundell to SS, 6 Jun. 1950, CO 537/6124.
[26] Administrator of Grenada, Political Report, 3 Sept. 1950, CO 537/6124.
[27] Ibid.
[28] Ibid.
[29] Ibid.
[30] Ibid.
[31] Gov. to Griffiths, 9 Oct. 1950, CO 537/6124.
[32] Ibid.
[33] Gov. to Griffiths, 9 Nov. 1950, CO 537/6124.
[34] Gov. to Griffiths, 5 Dec. 1950, CO 537/6124.
[35] Report on the Labour Department, 1951, p. 3, Council Papers, Grenada, 1954.
[36] The West Indian, 22 Feb. 1951, quoted in Singham 1968: 159-60.
[37] Report on the Labour Department, 1951, p. 4, Council Papers, Grenada, 1954.
[38] Grenada Government Official Newsletter, 13 Mar. 1951.
[39] Ibid., 16 Mar. 1951.

[40] Report on the Labour Department, 1953, Council Papers, Grenada, 1956, quoted in Smith 1965: 292.

[41] Report on the Labour Department, 1954, Council Papers, Grenada, 1956, quoted in Smith 1965: 292.

[42] BWU Executive Council and Annual Conference Minute Books (henceforth BWUMB) 26 Feb. 1942.

[43] CADORIT pamphlet, Mar./Apr. 1959.

[44] The Caribbean Workers' Union, formed in 1950, was founded by a conservative businessman, Ernest Mottley, to organise working-class support for the Electors' Association (Beckles 1990: 186-8).

[45] Barbados Advocate, 3 Oct. 1946, quoted in Hoyos 1974: 106.

[46] Interview with Napoleon Layne, 19 Jan. 1994, Solidarity House, Bridgetown.

[47] BWUMB, 4 Aug. 1948.

[48] BWUMB, 19 Jan. 1949.

[49] Governor to SS, 3 Feb. 1949, CO 537/4907.

[50] Gov. to SS, 4 Mar. 1949, CO 537/4907.

[51] BWUMB, 18 May 1949.

[52] BWUMB, 25 May 1949.

[53] BWUMB, 1 Jun. 1949.

[54] BWUMB, 22 Jun. 1949.

[55] BWUMB, 29 Jun. 1949.

[56] Acting Gov. to SS, 31 Jul. 1949, CO 537/4890.

[57] BWUMB, 10 Aug. 1949.

[58] BWUMB, 17 Aug. 1949.

[59] BWUMB, 1 Mar. 1950.

[60] BWUMB, 22 Mar. 1950.

[61] BWUMB, 31 May 1950.

[62] BWUMB, 7 Jun. 1950.

[63] BWUMB, 19 Jul. 1950.

[64] Gov. to SS, 8 Sept. 1950, CO 537/6127.

[65] BWUMB, 25 Oct. 1950.

[66] BWUMB, 1 Nov. 1950.

[67] BWUMB, 10 Jan. 1951.

[68] BWUMB, 18 Feb. 1951.

[69] It is not clear when Farrell and Layne became members of the BWU Executive Council, but Farrell certainly was by October or November 1950.

[70] BWUMB, 21 Feb. 1951.

[71] BWUMB, 26 Jul. 1950.

[72] All the unionists, including Adams and Walcott, called each other comrades at this time. However, at the conference of the ICFTU held in Barbados in June 1952, in deference to the ideological and semantic distinctions made in the free world, the word brother was used instead (BWUMB, 25 Jun. 1952).

[73] BWUMB, 21 Feb. 1951.

[74] BWUMB, 29 Dec. 1950 and 21 Feb. 1951.

[75] BWUMB, 31 Oct. 1949.

[76] BWUMB, 10 Oct. 1951.

[77] BWUMB, 1 Feb. 1952.

[78] BWUMB, 14 Feb. 1952.

[79] BWUMB, 21 Feb. 1952.

[80] BWUMB, 3 Apr. 1952.

[81] BWUMB, 30 Apr. 1952.

[82] BWUMB, 7 May 1952.

[83] BWUMB, 14 May 1952.

[84] BWUMB, 18 Jun. 1952.

85 BWUMB, 16 Jul. 1952.
86 Barbados House of Assembly Debates, Official Gazette, 12 Jun. 1952, p. 156.
87 Ibid.
88 CADORIT pamphlet, Barbados 1954, Mss. Brit. Emp. S365, Box 140/2, RHL.
89 BWUMB, 30 Jul. 1952.
90 BWUMB, 13 Aug. 1952.
91 BWUMB, 20 Aug. 1952.
92 BWUMB, 24 Aug. 1952.
93 BWUMB, 27 Aug. 1952.
94 BWUMB, 17 Nov. 1952.
95 BWUMB, 7 Jan. 1953.
96 BWUMB, 28 Jan. 1953.
97 BWUMB, 27 Feb. 1953.
98 BWUMB, 4 Mar. 1953.
99 BWUMB, 18 Mar. 1953.
100 BWUMB, 2 Aug. 1953.
101 BWUMB, 2 Aug. 1953.
102 The OWTU has subsequently expanded and represents workers in a wide variety of industries, including chemicals, manufacturing, construction, transport, hotels and catering, and agriculture.
103 See statement issued by the OWTU on the strike in the oilfields, Dec. 1946, in Dalley 1947: 41-3.
104 Vanguard, 2 Aug. 1947, p. 2.
105 Ibid., p. 7.
106 Rojas had served on the Public Works Advisory Committee, the Transport Board and the Full Employment Committee; Mentor on the Trinidad and Tobago Joint Sugar Board, the Unemployment Committee, Franchise Committee, Demobilisation Committee, Resettlement Committee, Social Welfare Committee, Trade Unions Ordinance Amendment Committee, and chaired the Full Employment Committee; Moses on the Price Control Committee, the Labour Recruitment Committee, the Poor Relief Board and the Unemployment and Health Insurance Committee. Mentor was elected to the San Fernando Borough Council in 1940, 1942 and 1945, and was the deputy mayor and then mayor of that town, and John E. Commissiong, the OWTU treasurer, was on the Victoria County Council and was an elected representative of Naparima Ward.
107 Vanguard, 2 Aug. 1947, p. 11.
108 OWTU, 50 Years of Progress, p. 15.
109 People, 5 Mar. 1938.
110 WFTU, Report of the Congress, Paris, 25 Sept.-8 Oct. 1945, pp.65-7, quoted in Thomas 1989: 34.
111 Act. Gov. P.M. Renison to Creech Jones, 22 Oct. 1949, CO 537/4282.
112 Rance to Griffiths, 12 Jun. 1950, CO 537/6149.
113 Ibid.
114 Rance to Griffiths, 25 Nov. 1950, CO 537/6149.
115 Ibid.
116 Ibid.
117 Document in OWTU Library.
118 F.W. Dalley, 'Notes on some of the personalities in the Trade Union and Labour World of Trinidad', Nov. 1947, CO 537/3814.
119 Gov. Sir John Shaw to Creech Jones, 16 Aug. 1948, CO 537/3816.
120 Shaw to Creech Jones, 16 Aug. 1948, CO 537/3816.
121 Shaw to Creech Jones, 25 Nov. 1948, CO 537/3816.
122 Shaw to Creech Jones, 25 Dec. 1948, CO 537/3816.
123 Port of Spain Gazette, 20 May 1952.
124 Trinidad Guardian, 31 July. 1952.

125 Davenand Rajbansee, 'The East Indian Impact on Trade Unionism and Politics in Trinidad and Tobago, 1946-56', unpublished paper, West Indiana Collection, UWI Library, St Augustine, Trinidad, p. 52.
126 Sunday Guardian, 9 Mar. 1952.
127 Trinidad Guardian, 14 May 1952.
128 Port of Spain Gazette, 20 May 1952; Sunday Guardian, 25 May 1952.
129 Sunday Guardian, 25 May 1952.
130 Port of Spain Gazette, 1 Jun. 1952.
131 Sunday Guardian, 8 Jun. 1952.
132 Port of Spain Gazette, 8 Jun. 1952.
133 Port of Spain Gazette, 10 Jun. 1952.
134 Trinidad Guardian, 15 Jun. 1952.
135 Trinidad Guardian, 19 Jun. 1952.
136 Port of Spain Gazette, 22 Jun. 1952.
137 Sunday Guardian, 22 Jun. 1952.
138 Trinidad Guardian, 3 Jul. 1952.
139 Evening News, 25 Jul. 1952, p. 11.
140 CADORIT pamphlet, 1954, Mss. Brit. Emp. S365 Box 140/2, RHL.
141 CADORIT, Report of the Second Conference, Port of Spain, 6-8 Apr. 1955.
142 'President General's Message to Members', 1 Oct. 1953, OWTUL.
143 Hart's speech to the WFTU congress, Vienna, Oct. 1953, HP, 2/202.
144 Port of Spain Gazette, 6 Nov. 1953.
145 Port of Spain Gazette, 7 Nov. 1953. An attempt was made in Belize to associate Price's People's United Party with communism and Guatemala in the months before the first election with adult suffrage in April 1954 (see chapter 9).
146 Port of Spain Gazette, 4 Dec. 1953.
147 Trinidad Guardian, 4 Dec. 1953.
148 Trinidad Guardian, 1 Dec. 1953.
149 Freedom, Feb. 1954.
150 Ibid.
151 OWTU, 50 Years of Progress, p. 17.
152 Ibid., p. 18.
153 Ibid., p. 18.
154 Ibid., p. 20.

Class and ethnicity in the politics of decolonisation

Whether or not the outcome of the struggle for national liberation results in a democratic or an authoritarian post-colonial state (or, more realistically, whether the post-colonial state is more or less democratic or authoritarian) depends on the specific interrelations in each particular society between its internal social structure and politics, on the one hand, and its relations with the global capitalist system of which it is a peripheral part, on the other. This chapter examines the relations between democratic and authoritarian tendencies in the political cultures of three nations in terms of their particular structures of class and ethnic differentiation in the period of decolonisation.

Decolonisation in the British Caribbean in the 1940s and 1950s gave rise to a set of democratic authoritarian states, as distinct from the clearly undemocratic authoritarian states that had been created by the colonial power. The timing of this process showed how the dialectical interrelations of the internal and external aspects produced certain social and political changes while maintaining important continuities. On the one hand, the economic crisis of the 1930s and the political crisis of the Second World War provoked increasing demands within these colonies for democracy and decolonisation. These demands, so forcefully expressed, resulted in the legalisation of trade unions, the expansion of the franchise, and the emergence of modern political parties: in short, they resulted in significant democratisation in the sense of the first legal and institutionalised popular participation in the political process. On the other hand, changes were occurring in this same period in the global capitalist system in two respects: first, the centre-periphery relations had developed to the extent that direct colonialism was no longer the necessary, or even the most effective, framework for the exploitation of the periphery; and second, the centre of the system moved from western Europe to the United States. This imperial succession, which was everywhere quite transparent by the end of the twentieth century, was not so clear in the middle of the century when the new political leaders in the colonies were establishing themselves, though it was already affecting the situation.

The legitimacy of these political leaders at the time, and their subsequent heroisation, depended to a large extent on the perception that they had won both democracy and national liberation. To some extent, of course, this perception was correct, but the mythology surrounding the birth of the new nations has obscured the contradictory tendencies of the complex processes of democratisation and decolonisation. Two factors have generally been important in perpetuating the authoritarian tendencies inherent in colonial societies. As the newly emerging labour and political leaders struggled against refractory and powerful employers and colonial officials, and with each other, they were inclined to use authoritarian methods. This is not to say that authoritarianism was embodied in dictators, but, on the contrary, that the structure and culture of these societies promoted authoritarian behaviour. The second factor was the expanding role of the state, particularly in the economics of development, which was widely accepted even in capitalist societies in the period of reconstruction after the Great Depression and the Second World War. In response to this experience of profound crisis, the ideology of laissez-faire was temporarily abandoned, and in the New Deal era in the United States and the Labour government in the UK, along with the reconstruction of postwar western Europe and Japan, a newly expanded role for governments was accepted in economic as well as social affairs. This new role was soon applied to the decolonising societies.

Governments were expected to lead in the development of housing, health care, education, the infrastructure for transport and communications, and even in economic investment and the expansion of employment opportunities. The popular demand for improvements in the standard and quality of life were, indeed, central to democratisation, and governments were evaluated increasingly on the basis of their perceived ability to deliver, so they had to implement development strategies, such as industrialisation, which appeared to promise economic improvements. In the peripheral, decolonising societies, however, there was a contradiction. At the same time that the majority of people were achieving for the first time the right to negotiate through trade unions and to vote for political parties of their choice, the centre of the global capitalist system was intent on maintaining its exploitation of the periphery. Consequently, there was continuing pressure to increase productivity while decreasing real wages in these societies. At the same time the popular demand was for greater economic security and an improved standard of living. Hence, a rising tide of popular expectations, promoted by the new labour and political leaders, confronted global capitalism. It was crucial for the global centre, therefore, that the process of decolonisation should be controlled in such a way as to ensure that the popular demands would be kept in check, and this required handing over the administration of the state, while not really handing over power per se, to a class that would be legitimate in the eyes of the people even while it acted to maintain the interests of the global centre. The best way this could be achieved was if the new political leaders were labour leaders who could use or manipulate, but certainly control, the trade unions, and whose political prestige would be enhanced by the formal trappings of constitutional decolonisation and, eventually, national independence. It was important, therefore, that one of the expanding roles of the state was to control, and if necessary actually suppress, the demands of the newly organised labour movement. At the same time the political leaders generally derived their legitimacy from this movement with its central political role in the process of decolonisation.

In order to run the post-colonial state in these circumstances, this new class of political leaders and administrators, who replaced the colonial officials, had to disguise their authoritarianism under a veil of democratic forms, procedures and ideology. This is why we can speak of the emergence of the democratic authoritarian state in these post-colonial societies. The decolonisation process had two successive stages. First, beginning in the labour rebellions in the 1930s, the new labour leaders engaged in the politics of confrontation, using protests and strikes as their chief weapons, in order to win concessions from employers and to press for constitutional reforms in the direction of democracy and self-government. Second, as constitutional decolonisation occurred and these labour leaders became political leaders with increasing responsibility in government, their methods and priorities shifted. Increasingly, they tried to control the trade unions and political parties that they led and so to demonstrate that they were now capable of being responsible ministers of governments that were on the eve of independence.

The shift between these two phases, which was sometimes quite dramatic, often coincided with two other, related changes: the turn from the respectability of socialism associated with the UK's postwar Labour government to the red-baiting of the early Cold War years, and the change from a commitment to the local control of economic resources via nationalisation to the effort to attract more foreign investment as the stimulus for economic development. To a large extent, these changes reflected the expanding influence of the United States, not only because its government was at the centre of the crusade against international communism and anything that remotely resembled it, but also because it was the US economic empire that was capable of providing new investment, whether in oil or bauxite, bananas or tourism. The US economic and political ideology became the only permissible game just at the time that the new labour and political leaders of the British Caribbean colonies began to inherit the apparatus of the state. Rising to prominence in a more radical phase of labour and nationalist politics, they had to consolidate their power in a situation where such politics was no longer tolerable to the UK or the United States. These leaders had to become more conservative and even authoritarian in controlling the own supporters, or risk being denied the governmental offices they sought.

In this chapter we will examine and compare three cases, Antigua and Barbuda, British Guiana and British Honduras (or Antigua, Guyana and Belize, respectively). They are similar in certain respects and differ in others. In Antigua class and race largely coincided, with the upper class being exclusively white while most Antiguans are of African descent, so labour issues have often been seen, in Samuel Smith's words, as 'between nega and white' (Smith and Smith 1989: 131). Both Guyana and Belize, however, are ethnically diverse as well as class–stratified societies, in which the varying concepts and relations of class and ethnicity were central in the decolonisation process and subsequent internal political struggles (Bolland 1997a: 259–313). In Antigua the leader of the trade union became the dominant political leader; in Belize the rising political leader took over and made use of an already existing trade union, ousting the original labour leaders in the process; and in Guyana the first political leader did not succeed in becoming acceptable to the British government, as did his peers in Antigua and Belize, so he remained for years in the political wilderness, while the leaders of Antigua and Belize led their countries into independence. In all three societies a democratic authoritarian state developed, though it was much more authoritarian in Antigua and Guyana than Belize, and in all three societies ethnicity as well as class was politically significant, though much more so in Guyana than in Antigua or Belize. Further, in all three societies the roots of the political developments of the 1960s and subsequent decades were established in the late 1940s and early 1950s when the first modern political parties were created in these colonies.

Labourism and authoritarianism in Antigua

The Antigua Trades and Labour Union (ATLU) emerged during a strike among sugar workers in 1939, held its first annual conference in February 1940 and was officially registered on 3 March 1940. The beginning of organised labour in Antigua was also the beginning of political organisation, because the ATLU soon became the basis of the Antigua Labour Party (ALP), which won every general election until 1971. The ALP pressed for and benefited from the democratisation of the political system in the 1940s and early 1950s, but 'the party system, quite paradoxically, has become both the center of democracy and the biggest threat to it' (Henry 1985: 150). The authoritarian tendencies within the ATLU and ALP were personified in the dominance of Vere Bird, but they cannot be explained simply by his dictatorial nature. Rather, we must also understand the limitations of the ATLU-ALP's labourist ideology, the nature of the relations between the union and the party, and the constraints and influences in the structure of the society and its connections with the wider world that shaped this ideology and these relations.

The first president of the ATLU was Reginald Stevens, described as a 'brown-skinned man' who 'give the union a flying start and a solid foundation in the early days' (Smith and Smith 1989: 144-6). Stevens, who had been elected a member of the Legislative Council in 1936 but was forced out on the grounds that he had not met the property qualifications for candidates, was a middle-class politician who was associated with the working people's cause (Henry 1985: 84). Stevens was elected to the council in 1943 but when he agreed to a ban on strikes for the duration of the war there ensued a power struggle within the union. He was replaced as president of the ATLU by Bird in 1943, and when he died in 1945 Bird was elected without opposition to complete his term on the council. Bird, who had been a member of the ATLU's executive committee from its beginning, consolidated his control of the union through what has been called a 'centralized democracy' (Henry 1985: 152). What this meant was that there was a formal democratic structure, consisting of the executive committee (president, general secretary, treasurer and eight members) which was elected at the annual convention, and a series of section leaders who were responsible for conveying demands and grievances to the executive. However, important decisions were centralised and opposition was not tolerated. 'Although within these structures it was possible to tolerate differences of opinion, they provided no space for a legitimate opposition. Consequently institutional support for the resolution of factional differences has been very weak. Because of this inability to resolve factional conflicts, they have systematically led to purges.' (Henry 1985: 152)

When the ATLU created a political arm of the union to contest the 1946 elections, which were still severely limited by literacy and property-owning requirements, this centralised democracy was reproduced in the political process. Indeed, the leadership of the party that emerged from this process was essentially the same as that of the union, with Bird the president of both, and the party did not really have an existence independent of the union (Henry 1985: 152). All five of the ATLU-ALP candidates, led by Bird, were successful in 1946 when the election was held on the basis of a single islandwide constituency. The ATLU-ALP continued to dominate elections, and Bird himself was returned unopposed in 1951, 1956 and 1960. For years the ALP was the only political party, receiving token opposition from independents and weak quasi-parties. From 1951, when universal adult suffrage was achieved, it won every general election with large voting majorities (87.4 per cent in 1951, 86.7 per cent in 1956, 85 per cent in 1960 and 78.9 per cent in 1965), and won every seat in the legislature, until 1971, when the Progressive Labour Movement (PLM), which was created by a schism in the ATLU-ALP in 1968, won 57.7 per cent of the vote and 13 of the 17 seats to the ALP's 37.9 per cent and four seats. A subsequent split in the PLM led to its decline and demise, however, and the dominance of Bird's ALP was re-established (Emmanuel 1992: 19-23). With the rise of Bird's sons, Vere Jr, Lester and Ivor, this became a politically dominant dynasty, leading Antigua to independence in November 1981. Bird retired in 1994, making way for his sons. When he died in 1999 Lester said, 'He raised us and produced us to continue in his footsteps.'[1]

There is no doubt that Bird and his ATLU-ALP had a widespread and popular base in Antigua's working people. This popularity was achieved by continuing the politics of confrontation and challenge that had started in the 1930s, and in the 1940s, with more organised confrontations and strikes, the 'workers were successful in winning concessions from both the economic and political elites' (Henry 1985: 90). Bird received much of the credit for these successes. Influenced by the British Labour Party and by other West Indian leaders, like Adams and Manley, he sometimes used socialist rhetoric in the 1940s. On the eve of the CLC conference in Jamaica in 1947, for example, he said he wanted to see 'one big socialist labour union throughout the Caribbean . . . . We want a West Indian nation'.[2] Essentially, however, the ATLU-ALP ideology is better described as labourism than socialism. 'No socialist reorganization was envisaged, but strong anti-planter and anti-upper class sentiments were expressed, especially during strikes' (Thorndike 1987: 103). The ALP, as the political arm of the ATLU, placed the interests of labour at the top of its agenda and, in the circumstances of the 1940s, this also meant pushing for universal adult suffrage. In order that labour's interests could be achieved by political means it was necessary to democratise the political system by including the votes of the masses of working people. The first elections held under universal adult suffrage were on 20 December 1951, when 70 per cent of the registered voters voted and 87.4 per cent of them gave their votes to the eight ALP candidates (Emmanuel 1992: 8, 22).

As well as standing as the champions in the struggle for democratisation in the 1940s, the ATLU-ALP took a radical position over the control of economic resources. Modelling its demands on the process of nationalisation in the UK after the Second World War, the ATLU-ALP wanted local public ownership of the Antigua Sugar Factory and the creation of a lands authority that could redistribute plantation land. In 1946 the ATLU-ALP put a resolution before the Legislative Council: 'Be it resolved that this Council strongly recommends that the Government take all steps necessary and calculate to obtain the consent of, and secure permission from, the proper responsible authorities in the United

Kingdom, to use part of the Colonial Development Welfare ten year grant for the colony (Antigua) for the acquisition of the Antigua Sugar Factory, and its operation as a public concern, under the direction of a statutory factory management board, constituted on the lines of the coal mines [in the U.K.]'.(quoted in Henry 1985: 89)

Similarly, the ATLU-ALP called for the establishment of a statutory lands authority which could acquire lands from the planters and distribute it, according to the best interests of the economy and society, between large-scale and peasant production. As Henry (1985: 89) says, 'Together, these positions on resource ownership amounted to radical programs of nationalization that would have transferred the control of economic resources into local hands'. However, as may be gathered from the tone of the resolution quoted above, this was not a revolutionary programme so much as an attempt to achieve a kind of state capitalism, which would concentrate economic as well as political control in the same, few local hands.

This concept of state capitalism reflected, on the one hand, the influence of the British Labour government after 1945 and, on the other hand, the popular response to the prevailing social and economic structure of Antigua, which had been completely dominated by plantations since the late seventeenth century (Dunn 1973: 141). In an economy that was traditionally so dominated by sugar production, most people wanted either to improve their remuneration and working conditions on the plantations or to gain access to land in order to become independent small farmers. A Land Settlement and Development Board, which was formed in 1943, had settled some 1,220 persons on 6,219 acres by the end of the war, but little of the land was arable, so not many of these people became independent farmers (Henry 1985: 105). By 1948 the board had almost 12,000 acres under its control but only 913 acres were arable, so it is clear that the 'planters were making available to the board only the worst lands' (Henry 1985: 106). The ATLU-ALP was therefore articulating the aspirations of the majority of Antiguans in the traditional conflict between the planters and those who, like the Nevisians Richard Frucht described, were neither peasant nor proletarian but who were moving toward 'a curious mixture of dependence upon proletarian-like relationships, peasant-like holdings, and bourgeois aspirations and consumer behavior' (Frucht 1967: 299). The class conflict in Antigua was reinforced by sharp distinctions of race and nationalism, as the big planters, like the Moody Stuart family, were white and British, and the vast majority of Antiguans are of African descent. In 1949 the governor, Lord Baldwin, reported there was a 'growing feeling that the African population, being the majority, should rule themselves. This is merely the result of the constant meetings held by the Trades Union agitating against the New Constitution not giving them a majority of elected members over all others .... The Planters paper continues to attack the Labour Party and vice versa'.[3]

During a serious strike that began on the waterfront on 3 April 1950 and then spread to the sugar factories and estates, this racial consciousness provided an element of solidarity among Antiguan workers. The governor observed, 'The tendency of the Union is towards "Antigua for the Africans" while real Trades Unionism is not understood, and Socialism never mentioned'.[4] The ATLU wanted a closed shop on the waterfront but when a compromise solution 'established a Port Labour Committee for the selection and rotation of workers on the waterfront',[5] the strike ended, on 5 May. Nevertheless, Bird continued to draw parallels between the South African and Antiguan situations at public meetings. The acting governor reported in November 1950 that the ATLU was not 'subject to communist influence', contrary to the allegations of some residents with 'extremely right-wing views', but when the union demonstrated against the government's proposals to increase taxation Bird spoke of the policies of the South African government and of white rule in colonies like Rhodesia and Kenya.[6] In 1950, while universal suffrage was not yet achieved, Bird could use these analogies to rouse the majority of Antiguans against the colonial government.

Samuel Smith (1877 - 1982), who was a sugar worker at this time, gives us a sense of the workers' consciousness as he describes the changes that resulted from the ATLU's activities. During the war, he said, 'There was some improvements in the land, but the laws that treat nega people like the beasts of the fields was still going strong and the planters never miss any opportunity to punish nega people'. But in 1946, when the ATLU 'got into politics . . . the people was ready to do anything and everything to make life come better'. The planters, however, 'determine to fight against anything and everything that look like it is in the favour of the people'. Following a successful nine-week strike over the method of paying cane–cutters, Smith felt:

> Things was starting to look up. Workers was demanding and getting respect from the planters. Gov. Baldwin was giving some backing to the demands of the union . . . . A lot of people was still living on the estates at the time. The planters wanted them off because they said the people didn't have to pay house rent or have to meet bank. The times was already changed and the planters couldn't handle the workers like they use to in the old days . . . .
>
> In 1951, it was strike from the word go. Like I tell you, force make water go up hill. The president of the AT & LU declared that not a blade of cane would get cut till the price got settled. The strike went on for several weeks. After it was over the workers decide for the first time to celebrate May Day. When the people went back to work on the next day the planters drove them off the estates and closed down the reaping. The planter boss, Alexander Moody

Stuart, decide not to recognize the unions anymore. That was the first time that happen since 1939 .... That wasn't all. Then he made it known all around that nobody was going to be allowed on any land belonging to the syndicate. He was going to be the one to say where the people should walk.

At the same time, the union wanted them lands to be taken away from the syndicate. The union was of the belief that the government should own the land so that the small farmers couldn't be driven off at any time. The union hit back by calling a general strike .... Antigua was hot like fire. The people was behind the union. Moody Stuart said he was going to starve out the people. The fight was on. There was violence here and there. Some buildings in St. John's was set ablaze. Gov. Blackburn got afraid the thing would get out of hand and he called in the British fleet from Jamaica ...

The workers didn't let Moody Stuart starve them out. The end was victory for the union, but quite a few of the strong members suffer the consequences of Magistrate Athill. Men from Bethesda, All Saints, Sea View Farm and Parham all did time in jail.

In my mind, 1951 got to be the best year since the end of slavery. What happen that year set the stage for what was going to come. The union was also doing other serious business. It was advancing in politics .... When the Council hold the elections in 1951 and the union got all the elected seats, the two sides really start to square up.

Negas was scoring great gains. The union winning on all sides in 1951 gave a very clear sign that it was just a matter of time before massa have to go back home to England.

Smith also described problems within the union, including the purge of several of its founders.

My good friend Ashley Kirwan was out, so too was Leonard Benjamin - former Vice-president of the AT & LU and member of Council. Hugh Pratt - he was once the AT & LU Treasurer and also a member of Council - was gone. I am of the belief that Pratt got forced out because he didn't vote the way the president wanted him to in some Council matter .... Samuel James - he was the union's third General Secretary - was out and so was Ken Roberts - one of the most militant men I ever knew .... Roberts was the first Vice-president and was the union officer that organize the powerful waterfront workers. He was a forceful speaker for the union and doing everything to defend the workers....

There was a strong rumour going around that Roberts could get to be the president of the union and so the president make sure that never happen. Maybe the ousting of Luther George, another founding father of the union, was the most painful thing to see....

While all this going on, any new ideas or programmes that come from anybody or any group of persons that wasn't a union big shot was looked down on. If it wasn't the president's idea, it wasn't any good. (Smith and Smith 1989: 146-51)

Smith's account of Bird's intolerance of rivals within the union is followed by his criticism of Bird and his associates becoming 'planters and union leaders at the same time' because this led to a conflict of interest. By 1957 'the union leaders was in the planters' place and at the same time they was running the union'. The union leaders were also in government by then and their conflicting roles led to more disillionment among union supporters. Smith says, however, that he was not against the union, as such, just against the way it was being run by the people in power.

> Disgruntlement were in the union and amongst the workers generally. It appear like the union was losing its drive. The leaders was in an embarrassing position. Myself, too, was in conflict with some of my family. I was of the view that the leaders of the union shouldn't be planters and union leaders at the same time, that the union should get somebody else to keep up the fight for the workers. Some of my people didn't think so. They got to feel that I was against the union, but that wasn't the case at all. (Smith and Smith 1989: 154)

When Bird got to be chief planter as well as the union's president, Smith said,

> The first thing he went to do as chief planter was to cut into the wages of the workers. The money that he fight Moody Stuart to pay them he went and slice in two. The rates under him in 1967 was lower than what the white planters have to pay in 1963. What a thing! The rest of the union officers couldn't say a thing. There wasn't even a squeak from the AT & LU. The premier was still the boss of the union .... The new sugar boss then start to punish a lot of people that wasn't in agreement with him. (Smith and Smith 1989: 158-9)

In the absence of organised political opposition the ATLU-ALP had a clear labourist ideology, popular appeal and widespread support, but its centralised democracy moved rapidly towards authoritarianism. In 1949, the governor reported that Bird had got his yes-men to remove the general secretary and two other officers from the union. 'Mr Bird is suffering from a lust for power and it looks as if he may well smash the Union .... Mr Bird wishes to be sole big boss after the U.S. Labour Pattern'.[7] Three months later he reported a further purge in the union.[8] Apparently, Bird had accused the men he purged 'of being disloyal to him'.[9] What began as a debate about policies, concerning the appropriate response to make to planters' complaints about the dilatory manner in which workers reaped the sugar crop, became a factional struggle between one group led by Bird and another by the general secretary, Samuel James.

Unable to reach a compromise, the resulting deadlock degenerated into a power struggle. At the end of this struggle some of the executive's most active members were forced out. These included Douglas (Kem) Roberts, Samuel James, Joe Stevens, Rolston Williams, Musgrave Edwards, and William Jeffrey. Starting a pattern that would develop more fully later, many of these ousted individuals formed the nucleus of an opposition; they were not so much opposed to the ideals of the movement but to the Bird faction. (Henry 1985: 153)

By 23 March 1950, the year before the first elections with universal adult suffrage, as the governor claimed, 'Mr Bird's egomania is on the increase, and he is developing into a local Hitler. No man must be against him, and what he says must be obeyed'.[10] Although Bird's psychological disposition towards authoritarianism is not in doubt, it is too simple to attribute Antigua's descent towards authoritarianism solely to his personality. Rather, in a context in which social and political gains could be most effectively sought through confrontation and challenge, and in which the class - race conflict between a small elite and the vast majority was so clearcut, there were no structural or institutional constraints on the leader's will to power. The result was factional infighting, followed by purges.

The identity of trade union and political party organisation gave Bird extraordinary popular authority by the early 1950s while he still had no responsibility in government. When he achieved some responsibility in the 1960s, the concentration of power in his leadership of the sole trade union and political party led to further conflicts and schisms because he would not tolerate opposition. Whereas, in the early years, the ALP had been merely an arm of the ATLU, the growing power of politicians that resulted from constitutional decolonisation reversed the situation, and the ATLU became dependent on the political party. What had started as the dominant faction in the union, therefore, became the dominant faction in the party and, hence, in the government. 'By staying on top of this type of factional politics, the Bird faction was able to maintain its control over the union and the party. It is this strong tendency towards political self-perpetuation, both within parties and at the state level, that has constituted the major source of authoritarian tendencies in the postcolonial period'. (Henry 1985: 153)

In 1956 a quasi-ministerial system was introduced and Bird became minister of trade, and in 1961, when the number of elected seats in the legislature was increased from eight to ten, Bird became chief minister in a largely self-governing associated state. In this halfway stage between colony and nation, local leaders who controlled the state could acquire economic advantage which reinforced their political power through clientelism and patronage. In 1966, as the sugar industry entered a deepening crisis, the government assumed control of the industry, with the result that Bird was the premier of the government that employed the sugar workers while he was still the president of the trade union that represented them. Many old union supporters, like Smith, became disillusioned with the turn of labour politics when Bird became authoritarian, but they were not disillusioned with trade unionism as such.

In 1967 matters came to a crisis when the ATLU's general secretary, George Walter, called a strike to back up wage demands for workers in the nationalised sugar industry. Bird dismissed Walter and two other officers of the union, Donald Halstead and Keithlyn Smith, who promptly formed a rival union, the Antigua Workers Union (AWU) and took about 70 per cent of the ATLU's rank and file members. A period of intense industrial strife ensued and Walter called a general strike in 1968. Protests and demonstrations, and a petition demanding Bird's resignation, resulted in a state of emergency and riots. A compromise was worked out that permitted Bird and his government to continue in office, on condition there was a lifting of the state of emergency, an end to the strikes, recognition of the AWU and agreement on a mechanism to allow for workers' choice of union representation, and the creation of four new seats in the legislature, to be filled by a special by-election. Walter, like Bird before him, created a political arm of his union, the PLM. The PLM won all four seats, with 71 per cent of the vote, in the by-election in August 1968, shattering the dominance of the ALP, and it went on to win the general elections on 11 February 1971, with 57.7 per cent of the vote to 37.9 per cent for the ALP (Midgett n.d.: 21-7). In 1976, after a period of inflation, the abandonment of the sugar industry, and 'repressive legislation, reminiscent of the previous ALP regime, aimed at curbing expression of opposition' (Midgett n.d.: 25-8), Bird and the ALP resumed power, winning just 49 per cent of the vote and 11 seats, to 49.9 per cent and five seats for the PLM. By 1980, with the PLM in terminal decline, the ALP won 58 per cent of the vote and 13 of the 17 seats, and in the first election after independence, in 1984, the ALP won an impressive victory, with 67.9 per cent of the votes and 16 out of 17 seats (Emmanuel 1992: 22). The foundation of this pattern of one-party dominance, conflict and schism, and the restoration of one-party dominance, was laid in the 1940s and early 1950s when the ATLU-ALP, under Bird's leadership, achieved its hegemony. Control of the state during the period of constitutional decolonisation enabled Bird's ATLU-ALP, through a combination of popular support, patronage and repression, to virtually monopolise political power in a democratic authoritarian system.

Democracy against authoritarianism in Guyana

The story of British Guiana (which became Guyana) in the 1940s and 1950s is one of paradox and tragedy; paradox because the colony that produced the most class-conscious political party nevertheless devolved into the most racialised party politics, and tragedy because the racialisation of politics led to many deaths and to the decline of democracy and development for many years after independence in 1966. The People's Progressive Party (PPP), which was officially launched in 1950 with ethnically diverse leadership, won the first general election with universal adult suffrage in April 1953. However, on 9 October 1953, the British government suspended the new constitution, threw out the PPP ministers and fomented a split within the PPP. By 1955 the PPP was divided and race quickly emerged as the central political issue between Cheddi Jagan's PPP and Forbes Burnham's People's National Congress (PNC). Although the PPP won the elections in 1957 and 1961, Jagan was not allowed to lead his country into independence. His government was destabilised between 1962 and 1964, when a new constitution enabled Burnham to create a coalition government consisting of two minority parties. The 1964 election was the last free and fair election until 1992, when the PPP, still led by Jagan, was once again returned to power.[11] The origins of this situation, which was catastrophic for the people, lay in the political developments of the early 1950s (Bolland 1997a: 284-305).

Several new trade unions were formed in Guyana in the years after the strike at Plantation Leonora in 1939 but progress was slow on the political front. In part, this may be because the unions mostly organised either African or Indian workers but rarely both, so the labour movement was divided along ethnic lines. Thus, the largest union, the Man–Power Citizens' Association (MPCA), which was registered in 1937 and claimed 20,000 members by 1943, organised the predominantly Indian field workers in the sugar industry, and the British Guiana Workers' League (BGWL), registered in 1931, was a much smaller union whose membership, hardly exceeding 1,000 members, consisted chiefly of African factory workers. Hubert Critchlow's British Guiana Labour Union (BGLU), which was the oldest union, and seven small unions registered in 1938 and 1939 (the British Guiana Seamen's Union, the Transport Workers' Union (TWU), the Post Office Workers' Union, the Subordinate Medical Employees' Union, the British Guiana Congress of General Workers, the Subordinate Government Employees' Association and the British Guiana Clerks Association) consisted largely of African Guyanese workers (Chase n.d.: 90-2). By 1947 there were some 20 trade unions, the MPCA being the largest, but there were no political parties and all the members of the Legislative Council elected in 1935 served as individuals. Although the constitution was liberalised in 1943, elections were delayed until 1947. A Labour Party was hastily created by some Georgetown trade unionists but it was, according to its assistant secretary, Ashton Chase, "nothing but a collection of individuals" (Chase n.d.: 126) and no real political party existed. Nevertheless, the political movement out of which the PPP emerged was initiated and deliberately developed along multi-ethnic lines.

In 1946 the Political Affairs Committee (PAC) was formed by Jagan, the grandson of indentured workers from Uttar Pradesh who had qualified as a dentist in the United States, Janet Jagan, his American wife, Chase, an Afro-Guyanese trade unionist, and H. Jocelyn M. Hubbard, a white Marxist who was the general secretary of the Clerks Association and the British Guiana TUC. 'The appeal of the PAC crossed ethnic lines by basing itself upon a class analysis aimed at unifying the largest body of people in British Guiana, the working class of urban blacks and rural East Indians' (Spinner 1984: 24). The PAC embarked on a programme 'to provide information and to present scientific political analyses on current affairs both local and international', through the publication of the PAC Bulletin, other printed matter and discussion groups, in order 'to assist the growth and development of Labour and Progressive Movements of British Guiana to the end of establishing a strong, disciplined and enlightened Party, equipped with the theory of Scientific Socialism'.[12] The PAC, distinguishing itself from earlier political parties which 'were invariably ephemeral groups organized at election time to promote a limited number of specific issues' (Premdas 1974: 7), explicitly aimed to provide the ideological and organisational basis for a permanent political party, based on the working class and oriented towards replacing the authoritarian, colonial and capitalist society with one that would be democratic, independent and socialist. The PAC, unlike previous organisations, had a comprehensive national goal. Whereas the League of Coloured Peoples (LCP) and the East Indian Association (EIA) made sectoral ethnic appeals, the PAC sought to create a classless society free from racialism, and unlike the BGLU and MPCA, which aimed for limited goals within the capitalist system, the PAC advocated the abolition of the existing economic system and the 'establishment of a well-planned collective industrial economy'.[13] Political and economic development were to be encouraged by educating and mobilising the working people: 'Between 1946 and 1952, over half a million publications were distributed in Guyana by the PAC and its successor the PPP' (Premdas 1974: 10).

Members of the PAC became involved in assisting bauxite workers and presenting their case during a strike at MacKenzie in April 1947. Between 1942 and 1944 the BGLU had tried to organise the bauxite workers, but with little success. Bauxite was defined as a strategic resource during the war and strict security measures, along with a restrictive company policy, made it almost impossible for union officials to visit MacKenzie, where most bauxite workers lived. The BGLU was not recognised by the Demerara Bauxite Company (Demba) and a brief strike in 1944 resulted in failure. After this 'unhappy excursion into trade unionism' (Chase n.d.: 128), the workers asked the MPCA if it would organise them. A group of machine shop workers struck on 12 December 1946, ostensibly because a worker had been suspended but also because they sought recognition for the MPCA. A few days after the Labour Department intervened an agreement was reached between the MPCA and Demba, but when other workers were dismissed in January, apparently because they had been pickets and advocates for the union, tensions increased. In March the MPCA sent an eight-point package of demands concerning wages and working conditions to the company, but officials refused to discuss them, although advised by the labour commissioner to do so. The workers, without referring to the union's executive, decided on 13 April to go on strike.

In addition to the questions of wages and leave policy the bauxite workers were frustrated about the issue of union recognition, as well as the racial segregation and discrimination that were rife in MacKenzie. Moreover, most of the workers had to sign contracts giving the company the right to evict them from their homes without notice. 'Constables frequently entered the workers [sic] homes without search warrants to ascertain if persons other than authorised tenants were in the rooms' (Chase n.d.: 130). The strikers were supported by donations and subscriptions from sympathisers in other parts of the country and Hubbard, as general secretary of the BGTUC, played a leading role in their assistance. The result of the strike, which lasted until 16 June, and a committee of inquiry's report, completed in July, was an agreement signed on 16 December 1947. This victory 'secured the complete establishment of trade unionism at MacKenzie and full recognition of trade unionism by the Demerara Bauxite Company' (Chase n.d.: 132), as well as a general increase in wages of 3 cents per hour and some improvements in working conditions. One of the workers who had been dismissed, Charles A. Carter, became a full-time trade union official and a principal founder of the BG Mineworkers' Union (BGMU), which was established in 1950 and took over from the MPCA (Chase n.d.: 133). Carter was elected to the House of Assembly in 1953.

In November 1947 Cheddi Jagan was elected to the Legislative Council to represent the villages and sugar estates of the lower east coast of Demerara. Jagan won with 1,592, or 45 per cent, of the 3,572 votes cast, the remainder being divided between his three opponents.[14] He was able to win because of the liberalisation of the franchise, but he and several others were elected because of their appeal to the working people of Guyana and their pressure for further constitutional reforms. The number of eligible voters had increased negligibly from 9,513 in 1937 to about 11,000 in 1944, and then expanded to over 59,000 in 1947, and many of the new voters were wage-earners. In addition to the PAC, there were two labour-oriented parties, one based on the MPCA and the other based on the other trade unions, and 31 independents, contesting 14 seats. The Labour Party won five seats and the MPCA Party won one, and most of the eight victorious independent candidates, including Jagan, 'appealed mainly to workers in their campaigns' (Premdas 1974: 11).

The question of adult suffrage was complicated by the fact that in Guyana, as in Trinidad, many members, or about 44 per cent, of the Indian community were illiterate, compared with only 3 per cent among Guyanese of African descent. When motions requesting the immediate introduction of adult suffrage were introduced into the Legislative Council, the governor reported that debates

> indicated very clearly the racial feeling between Africans and East Indians. While universal adult suffrage is generally assured of staunch support from individuals and groups of either race identified with labour movements, yet when the Motion came up in the Legislative Council amendments were moved to provide for a literacy test and in one case for a literacy test in English; eventually the Motion for the immediate introduction of universal adult suffrage was defeated with the help of the votes of the African members who were elected on a labour ticket.[15]

Indians opposed any literacy test, of course, and pressed strongly for universal adult suffrage, 'by which means only can this community get fair and proportional representation in the Legislature'.[16] The issue of constitutional reform was further complicated by different attitudes towards the proposed federation of the West Indies. According to Governor Sir Charles Woolley, the underlying cause of the tension between the two chief ethnic communities 'is the fear of domination of one by the other and it is this fear which colours the attitude of the Guianese East Indian towards federation. He feels that if federation comes about the African will certainly predominate and that his community will suffer in consequence. It is this reason also which accounts for an increasing Indian nationalist attitude in the Colony.'[17]

In these ways, therefore, many vital political, constitutional and labour issues became immediately racialised in the discourse of the colony. It is to the credit of Jagan and his group that they sought to transcend such racial mobilisation by creating a labour-based multi-ethnic national movement in the late 1940s (Premdas 1974).

Labour unrest increased in 1948, including struggles between a union and the colonial administration and between two unions, as well as between organised workers and their employers. The events of that year provided a basis for the great struggles of 1953, so they need to be examined in some detail. The unrest began among the largely Afro-Guyanese members of the TWU and continued with a strike by cane-cutters, chiefly of Indian descent, on sugar estates on the east coast of Demerara. The TWU went on strike on 17 April because Colonel Robert V. Teare, the general manager of the Transport and Harbours Department, had reassigned five workers, three of whom were TWU executive members, from Georgetown to Bartica and Issano in the interior. They were given less than 24 hours' notice of their new assignments, but when the union objected the colonial secretary confirmed the general manager's right to make these transfers. The strike, which effectively paralyzed rail and steamer transport, became a 'Teare must go' strike (Chase n.d.: 135), and thus a confrontation with the colonial authorities. The strike lasted four days and ended when Governor Woolley appointed a commission of inquiry into the strained relations between the management and workers. A report on the possible need for naval assistance stated: 'The Union clearly feel [sic] strongly that Colonel Teare should go. If it is decided that he should remain, there may be a danger that it might spread to other workers. An effective strike of transport workers would seriously disrupt the life of the Colony'.[18] The strike resumed when Teare appeared at the head office so he had to stay away pending the commission's report.

The commission held 12 public sittings at which 33 witnesses, on behalf of the TWU, spoke of Teare's arrogant manner, insulting language, refusal to negotiate cases of dismissal, and his way of imposing a system of retrenchment and reorganisation which was not in line with normal industrial practice. There was no doubt that Teare was using the transfers to try to destroy the union and that this was done with the connivance of the colonial secretary. The commission reported in May. It deprecated the strike, which it said contravened the Trades Disputes (Essential Services) Ordinance of 1942, but recommended that the transfer of the union executive members be stayed as they had received inadequate notice. Although the commission recommended the retention of Teare's services, Governor Woolley had him removed and transferred to Bermuda, and the workers were not transferred. The TWU interpreted the outcome as a complete victory, and it was followed soon after by a revision of salary grades and rates of pay, awarding higher wages and substantial back pay (Chase n.d.: 138). Just over a year after this strike, the TWU negotiated a check-off agreement, the first union in Guyana to achieve this, and it resulted in an improvement in the union's membership and finances. According to Chase (n.d.: 140), the 1948 strike by the TWU 'marked the turning point in the tide of trade union affairs'.

The strike of sugar workers was longer, and more dramatic and tragic in its outcome. In addition to the sugar workers' dissatisfaction with general conditions and rates of pay, two major issues were involved in this strike, namely the basis on which cane-cutters were paid and the desire 'to secure recognition of the Guiana Industrial Workers' Union (GIWU) as the bargaining agent on behalf of field and factory workers in the sugar industry' (Chase n.d.: 141). Workers were dissatisfied with their wages because basic wage rates had remained fixed since 1939 and a war bonus of 10 per cent in 1940, increased to 15 per cent in 1944, had not kept pace with the rising cost of living. In February 1948, when pushed by the workers' demands, the MPCA began negotiations with the Sugar Producers' Association (SPA). The workers wanted an increase in the rate of pay and were also concerned about the introduction of a new method of calculating pay, changed from the old cut-and-drop system to the new cut-and-load system.

In the old system the cane-cutters cut the canes and dropped them on the bank of the trench, from where they were taken by loaders who put them in punts. The cane-cutter was paid for cutting the canes in what was known as an opening, consisting of two rows of canes, on the overseer's estimate of what tonnage an acre would yield at a rate of 45 cents per ton. This system gave rise to conflicts when cutters disagreed with the overseer's estimate, and appeals could be made to the deputy manager who arbitrated when he saw fit to do so. The loaders in this system were paid 15 cents per ton. The dissatisfaction with this system, as well as with the wage rates, led to the introduction of the cut-and-load system, under which the cutter completed the task by loading his cut canes into the punt, for a payment of 60 cents per ton, that is, the sum of the 45 cents for cutting and the 15 cents for loading under the old system. It was believed that this new system, by eliminating the estimates (because it relied on the canes being weighed in the punt, or after being unloaded from the punt) would reduce the bickering and conflicts endemic in the old system. But there were problems with the new system also, though it seemed more straightforward. First, loading the punts took time away from cutting and often kept the cutter in the fields after dark in order to complete his task. Second, delays in supplying punts disrupted and retarded the cutters' work, often leaving them waiting to complete their task, even until the following day. Third, workers did not trust the weighing of the canes and felt they were sometimes cheated. Fourth, fetching and loading the canes was strenuous, taking energy as well as time away from the more lucrative work of cutting the cane, and was often dangerous when punts became slippery. Fifth, the problem of favouritism, which existed in the old system, was not eliminated as some assignments were further away from the dam bed, and some punts were higher than the parapets, which meant that some workers had a harder time loading the punts than others. And sixth, by combining two jobs into one, some jobs were eliminated, older workers found the work too strenuous, and the workers who remained felt they deserved an increase in pay for the extra time, strain and difficulties involved in their extra tasks. Although they were receiving 15 cents more per ton, they were doing a lot more work to earn a little more money, and in some cases the wage packet contracted (Rose 1994: 8).

When the MPCA signed an agreement with the SPA in mid-April, agreeing to new rates that amounted to an overall increase of only 7 cents per ton, when the workers had sought an increase of 40 cents to make a rate of $1 per ton for cutting and loading cane, there was widespread dissatisfaction. The general secretary of the MPCA responded by claiming that this was only an interim and not a final agreement, but there was nothing in the agreement he had signed to support this claim. Workers felt betrayed and frustrated, so when the GIWU castigated the MPCA for signing the agreement the workers turned to this new union for help.

The GIWU, which was formed in 1946 and registered on 5 April 1948, was led by Dr Joseph Prayal Lachhmansingh and Amos A. Rangela, who were also the leaders of the EIA. Though the MPCA had fewer than 600 members on the sugar estates in 1948, the SPA refused to deal with the GIWU because it said the MPCA was the recognised trade union for field workers throughout the colony.

> The Labour Department also refused to consider representations on behalf of particular sugar workers or group of workers where those representations were made by the GIWU. There was clearly no legal authority for this refusal by the Labour Department. To refuse to listen to representations by the GIWU was a demonstration of profound misunderstanding of the Department's functions, or at worse showed partiality on the part of the Labour Department. The GIWU was a registered trade union and in the eyes of the law it had a legal standing which the Government was bound to recognise, however much the sugar producers cared to ignore its existence. (Chase n.d.: 148-9)

On 22 April some 1,200 field workers, principally on Plantations Enmore, Non Pariel, Lusignan, Mon Repos, La Bonne Intention, Vryheid's Lust and Ogle, on the east coast of Demerara, went on strike. This strike, by bringing together several related issues, heightened the workers' consciousness of their role in the wider political struggle. Their basic economic concerns were linked to the question of their right to choose which trade union would represent them, and this, in turn, was linked to the role of the Labour Department and the labour commissioner, W.I.L. Bissell, who seemed to work hand in hand with the SPA and MPCA. The GIWU counselled the workers not to 'be fooled by the MPCA officers' and 'impeached the bona fides of Mr. Bissell ... declared that the sugar estates were making huge profits ... [and] urged Government to take over the estates and transfer the land in sections to the workers who would profitably cultivate it' (Chase n.d.: 149). On 5 June the strikers passed a resolution asking the governor to terminate Bissell's services (Rose 1994: 11). The strike action was encouraging a broader critique of the colonial administration and the capitalist economy.

On 16 June, five workers – Rambarran, Lall (known as Pooran), Lallabagee Kisson, Surujballi and Harri – were killed and 14 wounded by the police at Enmore. Seven police, armed with rifles, had reported to the management at Enmore at 4 am to protect the property. They claimed that a crowd of 400 people, armed with sticks and similar weapons, intended to enter the estate factory. A commission of inquiry, chaired by Frederick M. Boland, a judge of the Supreme Court, found that, although no policeman had received serious injury at the time of the shooting, they were nevertheless justified in opening fire. However, the commission also concluded that, as several people were shot in the back while trying to escape, the firing after the first few shots 'went beyond the requirements of the situation'. Lachhmansingh and the Jagans declined to testify before the commission as they felt it would be a waste of time and would serve no useful purpose (Chase n.d.: 150). The funeral march for the Enmore Martyrs, as they became known, stretched 16 miles from Enmore to Georgetown, and was led by the Jagans, Lachhmansingh, Rangela and Jane Phillips-Gay, the general secretary of the GIWU. Some 5,000 people participated[19] and they were barred from entering Georgetown by steel-helmeted police.[20] 'Dr. and Mrs. Jagan addressed several meetings of strikers and inspired them to keep united in the struggle for their rights. At all the meetings, policemen took copious notes. Dr. and Mrs. Jagan also paid considerable attention to the day to day organisation of the strike and to many details. They helped in raising funds for the strikers, in organising "soup kitchens" and in the general propaganda work. The ... PAC agitational bulletins were widely circulated at the GIWU meetings'. (Chase n.d.: 141) Janet Jagan is alleged to have told a journalist that 'Enmore made us', and certainly the Jagans 'were idolized by the sugar workers' after this strike (Premdas 1974: 12, 19). The Jagans' involvement in this strike helped achieve a broader base and greater national prominence for the PAC.

The strike continued throughout July but remained limited to the same estates. Governor Woolley noted on 23 July, 'No sign of general return to work .... Meetings, which have been orderly, are being held by strike leaders almost nightly in Georgetown for purpose of collecting funds and enlisting sympathy'.[21] The strike ended without the SPA recognising the GIWU but, as Chase (n.d.: 152) says, 'The Enmore Martyrs did not die in vain.' One result of the strike was that the secretary of state for the colonies appointed a commission, that became known after its chairman, J. A. Venn of Queen's College, Cambridge, to enquire into and report on the sugar industry in Guyana, with particular reference to the system of production, wages and working conditions, and the experience of women, who constituted 28 per cent of the labour force employed on the sugar estates. The Venn Commission made many recommendations, including the provision of plots of land for regular workers to cultivate their own rice and ground provisions, the clearance of all the old housing and the rehousing of sugar workers within five years, and the title of 'drivers', redolent of the days of slavery and indenture, should be changed to 'headmen'. It recommended that creches should be provided on each estate and tasks arranged so as to enable women to care for their children. Women and girls should not have to work in water, and female gangs should be under the charge of women. Fresh water should be supplied in the fields 'aback', and shelters built to protect workers from rain and to provide places where they could eat their meals during the working day. It was recommended that further measures, beyond the Education Ordinance of 1946, needed to be taken to prevent the employment of children. All these recommendations indicate that the labour conditions and relations of the sugar industry of Guyana in 1948 resembled those of the nineteenth century. Finally, the commission favoured the cut-and-load system in general, but suggested that the cut-and-drop system should be used when not enough punts were supplied.

On the recommendation of the commission the SPA recognised the three small unions that represented particular groups of workers and that had been trying to get recognised for years: the Sugar Estates Clerks' Association, registered in 1946, the BG and WI Sugar Boilers Union, registered in 1944, and the BG Drivers Association, registered in 1945, which became the BG Headmen's Union in 1950 (Chase n.d.: 154-5). The commission also noted that there were in all 27 trade unions in a colony with 400,000 people,[22] of which nine represented workers in the sugar industry, so it proposed that five of them should form a council to coordinate all trade union activity in the sugar industry. Strikingly, the commission found the GIWU's claim for recognition to be unwarranted as it was duplicating the work of other unions, and noted that it was opposed to the Labour Department, adding: 'when the strength and financial membership of the GIWU have been maintained over a period of, say, three to five years, there will be some ground for considering whether its influence justifies its being given the recognition that the steady work of past years has brought to the established unions' (quoted in Chase n.d.: 156). In fact, this issue came to the fore just five years later, in 1953. In the meantime, the leaders of the PAC learned important lessons from the 1947 elections and the 1948 strikes that led to their establishing the PPP in January 1950. The party's name was influenced by Henry Wallace's Progressive Party in the United States, and its constitution and organisation was based on Jamaica's People's National Party (PNP) (Jagan 1972: 98).

The PAC-PPP strengthened its trade union base and ensured that its leadership was ethnically diverse. Cheddi Jagan became president of the Sawmill Workers' Union in 1949, and Chase, another PAC founder, became secretary general of the BGLU. But Chase stepped aside to let Forbes Burnham, a middle-class Afro-Guyanese lawyer who had just returned from London in 1949, become the new party's chairman. Burnham had won the Guiana Scholarship and had studied and worked in the UK since 1945. He won a speaker's award in the law faculty at London University, and was politically active as president of the West Indies Student Union in 1947 and vice-president of the London branch of the CLC. He also helped organise demonstrations by the League of Coloured Peoples (LCP)[23] in London (Spinner 1984: 29). Burnham was a dynamic speaker and he became president of the BGLU, a union composed chiefly of black waterfront workers in Georgetown, which he used as his own political base. Lachhmansingh, the president of the GIWU, became senior vice-president of the PPP. Cheddi Jagan, though designated a second vice-chairman, was the real party leader, and Janet Jagan was the general secretary. Sydney King and Rory Westmaas, both Afro-Guyanese, became assistant secretary and junior vice-chairman, respectively. Clinton Wong was senior vice-chairman, and Ram Karran the treasurer. Jai Narine Singh, another prominent East Indian leader, was a member of the executive committee. The party executive had great power, although local cells and constituency committees sent delegates to the party congress, the first of which was held in April 1951.

The PAC Bulletin, renamed Thunder, became the official PPP organ and it aimed 'to help counter the propaganda of government and big business' (Jagan 1972: 99). Thunder also declared, unequivocally, the new party's goals and purpose:

> The People's Progressive Party, recognizing that the final abolition of exploita-
> tion and oppression, of economic crises and unemployment and war will be
> achieved only by the Socialist reorganization of society, pledges itself to the
> task of winning a free and independent Guiana, of building a just socialist
> society, in which the industries of the country shall be socially and democrati-
> cally owned and managed for the common good, a society in which security,
> plenty, peace, and freedom shall be the heritage of all.[24]

Despite the socialist goals and a class-based analysis, the party's programme called for a populist strategy, to unite all the various sectors and segments of the society: 'The PPP will strive for unity of workers, farmers, cooperatives, friendly societies, progressive businessmen, professional civil servants, and cooperation of all racial groups'.[25] The party had a central office in Georgetown and two auxiliary arms, the Women's Political and Economic Organization and the Progressive Youth Movement, to help mobilise women and young people (Premdas 1974: 14). Independent Indian candidates and LCP candidates made racial appeals for votes, but PAC and PPP candidates tried 'to make inroads upon the sectional voting patterns because of their ideological programmes' (Premdas 1974: 13) and to forge and promote a multiracial image. Though Janet Jagan and Hubbard, both of European descent, lost in predominantly African constituencies in the Legislative Council elections in 1947, the former won another predominantly African constituency in Georgetown in municipal elections in 1950, when Cheddi Jagan and Burnham were defeated in other wards. It became clear that they not only needed to garner support from all the major groups of the society, but also that the country should have a more liberal franchise and constitution, such as were already being established in other British Caribbean colonies.

A constitutional commission[26] had been promised since 1948, and when the Waddington Commission arrived in December 1950, Burnham and Cheddi

Jagan were among the principal witnesses to petition for universal adult suffrage and self-government. The commission was encouraged by 'the development of a genuine Guianese outlook', and by the ambition of younger East Indians to seek 'their permanent place in Guianese life' and by their equal participation in the society. It rejected the advice given by some witnesses to retain literacy or property restrictions and endorsed universal adult suffrage for men and women. The commission was divided over whether there should be a unicameral or a bicameral legislature, but recommended that the governor should retain specified reserve powers for emergencies.[27] After discussing the report with Governor Woolley, the Colonial Office announced in October 1951 that there would be universal adult suffrage, though elected members should be literate in English, and there would be a bicameral legislature. The House of Assembly would consist of 24 elected members from single-member constituencies and three ex-officio members (the colonial secretary, financial secretary and attorney-general). The State Council, an upper house, would consist of nine members, six selected by the governor, two by the majority group in the Assembly and one by the minority group. The Executive Council would consist of the governor, the three ex-officio members of the House of Assembly, six ministers from the House and one from the State Council. The ministers were to be individually responsible to the governor, who retained the authority to veto legislation and also maintained great influence through his official appointees. Although this was an advanced constitution compared to most others in the British Caribbean at the time, the PPP argued that the people should elect a constituent assembly which would be empowered to write a constitution, providing the country with internal self-government immediately (Spinner 1984: 34). Nevertheless, the PPP prepared for the elections which were scheduled for April 1953. By the time a new governor, Sir Alfred Savage, arrived early in 1953 the election campaign was in full swing.

Of 130 candidates who contested the 24 seats, some 78 or 80 were independents.[28] The PPP ran 22 candidates, ignoring the two seats in remote Amerindian areas, and the hastily formed National Democratic Party (NDP) was the only other serious organized party that attempted to appeal to more than one ethnic group. The United Farmers and Workers Party (UFWP) was an all-Indian group, the United Guianese Party (UGP) was backed by whites and the People's National Party (PNP) was an 'overtly racialist' splinter of the NDP (Premdas 1974: 16). The NDP, formed in 1952, was led by Lionel Luckhoo, a wealthy East Indian merchant, and John Carter, a lawyer of African descent who was general secretary of the LCP. The NDP 'thundered, ad infinitum: the PPP is dominated by Soviet-line communists' (Spinner 1984: 35). Jagan had made contact with members of the Communist Party of Great Britain during his first trip to the UK in 1951, and he went on to the World Youth Festival in the German Democratic Republic, where he 'saw at first hand how workers were building socialism' (Jagan 1972: 106). However, the PPP campaign was pragmatic and strongly nationalistic in its appeal, rather than communist. In addition to opposing British imperialism and advocating self-government, the PPP advocated the mass construction of cheap housing, the reduction of indirect taxes and an increase in direct taxation, the development of a free health service, a workers' compensation scheme, more nursery schools and secondary-school scholarships and the removal of denominational control of schools, and the support of new industries. The PPP also urged the strengthening of trade unions and wanted to take away unused land from the sugar estates so that more independent farmers could have secure access to land. 'The PPP advocated a comprehensive drainage and irrigation system for the uncultivated land hoarded by the great sugar companies' (Spinner 1984: 36). This was not a communist programme, but it was certainly progressive in the backward context of colonial British Guiana and it provoked opposition from various vested interests.

The Anglican and Roman Catholic churches and the organised Hindu and Muslim groups all attacked the PPP because of the policy about the control of schools; and the MPCA and big business interests, particularly the sugar industry, used the press to attack the PPP. Instead of debating the party's programme, however, these accused the PPP of receiving 'red gold' and being entirely subservient to the Soviet Union. Sugar-industry money financed the MPCA to produce a free four-page supplement in all three newspapers on the Sunday eight days before the election. Among other irrelevant diversions, the supplement emphasised that Janet Jagan, née Rosenberg, was Jewish. The PPP was, according to Cheddi Jagan, caught in a 'cross fire of racism' (1972: 114). While the NDP and LCP people argued that the PPP was Indian-dominated and that Burnham was being used, Daniel P. Debidin's UFWP and the Hindu Maha Sabha argued that Indian interests would be lost in an African-dominated West Indies federation, a federation which the PPP supported even while calling for a referendum on whether or not Guyana should join it. However, the PPP won a major victory in these elections, and the fact that there was a significant amount of intersectoral voting showed how many people were persuaded more by the PPP's broad radical programme than by narrow racialist appeals.

With a turnout of about 75 per cent of the registered voters, the PPP won 51 per cent of the vote and 18 seats, to the NDP's 13 per cent of the vote and two seats. Independents won the remaining four seats, as the other parties failed to win any. As the vote was often split between many candidates,[29] and the PPP did not contest two seats, it was a clear and outstanding victory for the PPP to win an absolute majority of the total votes cast, and far more than the NDP. Moreover, the racial cooperation and cross-voting in several constituencies indicated that the PPP was getting its multi-ethnic message across. For example, in the largely East Indian constituency of Demerara/Essequibo, the PPP's African candidate, Fred Bowman, beat Dr J.B. Singh, who was endorsed by the EIA. True, the Indian vote was divided between three East Indian opponents, but Bowman nevertheless won 42.3 per cent of the votes, including many from Indians who were prepared to elect an Afro-Guyanese candidate. The PPP, though characterised by the NDP and LCP as an Indian-dominated party, won all five seats in Georgetown, as well as winning all eight in the sugar belt. For the PPP, Janet Jagan won in Western Essequibo, Wong in Georgetown South central and King in Central Demerara, all constituencies where most voters were ethnically different from the successful candidate. And, in a struggle between rival trade unions' leaders, Ajodha Singh, vice-president of the GIWU, defeated Sheik M. Shakoor, general secretary of the MPCA, in Berbice. Although race was clearly a factor in these elections, it was subsumed by other issues. Africans and Indians who were interviewed some 20 years later said they believed that this period, when Burnham and Jagan were allies, was a 'Golden Age of Racial Harmony' (Premdas 1974: 17). This does not mean, of course, that this single election, or even the four years of intersectoral cooperation that followed the formation of the PPP in 1950, had disposed of the tensions between Africans and Indians in Guyana, but the cooperation of Burnham and Jagan, however superficial, certainly made this historic victory possible.

> Both Jagan and Burnham were dynamic sectoral leaders whose private political futures would have suffered immeasurably had each contended the elections as individual candidates. The social structure with its inherent sectoral predilections inevitably would have given only sectoral support to each leader. But the unity of the two leaders evidently overcame the strong sectoral voting pattern embodied in the social structure and consequently resulted in intersectoral political cooperation among Africans and Indians. (Premdas 1974: 37)

Trouble developed within the PPP, however, as soon as the leaders of the party began to select names of people to submit to the governor for appointment as ministers. Signs of such trouble had surfaced at the third party congress held in Georgetown in March 1953. Burnham had urged that this congress should be held in the capital because he thought his supporters there could dominate proceedings. One of his lieutenants introduced a motion that the leader of the party should be chosen by the general council after the general election, in anticipation of Burnham capturing a majority of members beforehand. Countering this plan, King made an impassioned plea to reject the motion, which was tantamount to one of 'no confidence in our leader' (Jagan 1972: 117), and the majority agreed. Consequently, the executive members were confirmed in their party offices: Jagan as leader and Burnham as chairman, Janet

Jagan and King as general secretary and assistant general secretary, respectively, and Ram Karran as treasurer. Jagan retained the support of most of the black leaders, including King, Chase, Martin Carter and Westmaas. Jagan attributed this success to 'the good common sense of the working people who attended the congress', most of whom were from Georgetown, and who 'were very conscious of my leadership in the political and trade union fields long before Burnham's return in late 1949' (Jagan 1972: 117).

In the week after the election Burnham again sought to become the principal leader, by refusing to discuss the selection of ministers until the leadership question was settled and by organising an impromptu mass meeting in Georgetown to rouse the rank and file in his support. Once again it was clear that Burnham was not challenging Jagan on any issue but that he simply sought to usurp him. The meeting broke up and Burnham dropped his ultimatum and agreed to discuss the selection of ministers. The original plan was to nominate Cheddi and Janet Jagan, Burnham, Chase, King and Lachhmansingh as the ministers, and George Robertson and W.H. Thomas to the State Council. Under Burnham's pressure a compromise was reached, with Janet Jagan named deputy speaker and replaced as a minister by Jai Narine Singh, and Thomas was replaced by Ulric Fingal.[30] These people marched proudly from the party headquarters to the Public Building to take their places at the opening of the new legislature on May 30. What started as a new democratic era, however, ended abruptly when the UK suspended the constitution after the PPP ministers had held office for only 133 days.

With the wisdom of hindsight, it may be judged that the PPP ministers made some unnecessarily provocative gestures. For example, they refused to appropriate funds to send representatives to greet the Queen when she visited Jamaica, ostensibly on the grounds that too much had been spent already on sending a Guyanese representative to her coronation in London. Moreover, the PPP members who took their seats in the new House, though proud of their achievement, told their supporters that they were still the opposition to Her Majesty's government in order to emphasise the persisting constitutional limitations that left the elected representatives of the people of Guyana subordinate to the metropolitan power. As symbolic gestures, of course, these seemed to be important, but they surely raised a red flag to the conservative forces in Guyana and the UK. However, even if the PPP had not waived these particular red flags, the reforms and changes they introduced would still have resulted in the British intervention, which was not provoked by perceived insults to the Queen.

The People's Opposition, as they called themselves, was led by Cheddi Jagan as the minister of agriculture, Burnham as minister of education, Chase as minister of labour, King as minister of communications and works, Lachhmansingh as minister of health, and Narine Singh as minister of local government. Unlike the JLP and BLP governments in, respectively, Jamaica and Barbados, which were labour parties only in the sense that they were based on trade unions, the PPP seriously 'declared open war upon the colonial economic-political alliance that dominated the territory' (Lewis 1968: 272). The JLP and BLP governments had accepted the colonial rules, 'in which the native political class enters into a "partnership" with a benign officialdom which means, in effect, partnership on imperial, not local terms, that is, terms envisaging not the socialist elimination of the colonial "enclave economy" but its continuing existence with minor modifications' (Lewis 1968: 273). The PPP did not accept these rules in 1953, hence their self-designation as the People's Opposition rather than the government. As Jagan wrote several years later,

> The changes we began to introduce now seem quite modest - to bring all schools under the supervision of government and local education committees; to reform local government so that on this level, too, there would be universal adult suffrage without property qualifications; to appoint working people to government boards and committees; to revise the fees of government medical officers in order to make medical care possible for the poor; to curtail unnecessary expenditure of public funds; to provide more scholarships; to bring about social security and workmen's compensation; to improve drainage and irrigation; to make available and usable large tracts of land then uncultivated; and to review and act on the recommendations of the Central Housing and Planning Authority. We wanted improvements in the areas of domestic service; holidays with pay; reductions in the cost of living; removal of restrictions on trade, with Japan for example; rent adjustments; setting up of an agricultural machinery pool; encouragement of diversified farming and the application of scientific methods to agriculture; tax reform; encouragement of local industry; development of the fishing industry and aid to fishermen.
>
> We succeeded in prescribing increased rates for certain categories of workers, primarily the sawmill workers, employees in cinemas and hire-car chauffeurs; an eight-hour day for factory watchmen; a \$13 weekly minimum wage for employees at drug, hardware, grocery and dry goods stores. (Jagan 1972: 119)

This list of reforms does not appear controversial, much less revolutionary, but some items, such as the control of schools, 95 per cent of which were run by Christian denominations, were very controversial in the local context. Moreover, the whole programme was more than the simple sum of its parts because it claimed an active role for government in promoting people's rights and welfare, which amounted to a frontal challenge to the entire colonial capitalist system. Some changes were direct reversals of colonial policy, such as the lifting of the ban on the entry of 'subversive' West Indian labour leaders and the repeal of the Undesirable Publications Ordinance, both of which had been imposed to restrict the freedom of Jagan and his associates, among others. The PPP government received support for some of its measures even from establishment figures. During the debate on the Undesirable Publications Ordinance in the State Council, for example, the archbishop of the West Indies called the law 'ineffective, ill-timed, undesirable and entirely mischievous.... With all my heart I have revolted against this Ordinance ever since it was first put out in the form of a Bill, and I am only thankful for this opportunity to say something to support its repeal. This is an infringement of the liberty of the individual. This is not just restraint ... this is tyranny'. (Quoted in Jagan 1972: 121)

Although the archbishop joined the PPP in considering that this law's repeal was necessary for the restoration of democratic freedoms, the British government portrayed it as enabling the PPP to flood the colony with dangerous communist literature, and the official view of what was dangerous was absurdly broad. When Janet Jagan was being tried in 1954 for addressing an illegal meeting, the prosecuting officer described Nehru's autobiography, Towards Freedom, which was found in her possession, as communist (Jagan 1972: 121). Undoubtedly, the PPP's actions were viewed by the British government as provocative, particularly as they occurred while the United States was in a peak of anti-communist hysteria and anxieties about communist influences in Guatemala. The chief problems, however, were caused by an amendment to the Rice Farmers (Security of Tenure) Ordinance and the Labour Relations Bill, because these were seen, correctly, as part of a broader and long-term plan to reform land utilisation throughout Guyana and to confront the power of King Sugar.

The original Rice Farmers (Security of Tenure) Ordinance of 1945, while ostensibly providing penalties for landlords and tenants who failed to practise good estate management, was actually one-sided. Whereas the tenants could be evicted for deficiencies, there were no effective penalties for the landlords. If, for example, the landlord failed to provide proper drainage facilities, there was little the tenant could do. In effect, landlords could allow drains and trenches to become choked with weeds or dams to fall into disrepair, as a way of putting pressure on tenants to quit, with no danger to themselves. The PPP rushed an amendment through the House, on the grounds that a drought had created an urgent situation, empowering district commissioners to give the landlord a specified period to complete the work he was required by law to do, and if he failed to complete it the government officer could have the work done and then charge it to the landlord. If the landlord refused to pay the costs, the land could be sold. The State Council rejected this amendment by six to two, with only the PPP nominees supporting the measure. Luckhoo, the defeated NDP leader who had been appointed to the council, and who had introduced the

Undesirable Publications Ordinance in 1952, denounced the amendment as an 'invasion and infringement of the personal rights of the subject'.[31] The PPP intended this amendment to be the start of a broader plan of action, including the establishment of a land authority. They refused to grant automatic leases of more Crown lands to landlords who already had large holdings, as many Crown lands were held idle by both expatriate sugar companies and big local land-owners. 'In various parts of the country, particularly in the county of Essequibo', Jagan wrote, 'landlords held their tenants in almost feudal bond-age', with Crown lands that were leased at nominal rates of 5 - 20 cents per acre being sublet to farmers at very high rentals ranging between $10 and $12 per acre, or about 25 - 30 per cent of the rice produced (Jagan 1972: 122). With the PPP threatening the possibility of the expropriation and redistribution of unused lands, this clearly indicated the emergence of a fundamental conflict concerning property, profits and power in the colony.

The growing crisis intensified over the politics of labour and the introduc-tion of the Labour Relations Bill. The long-term rivalry between the MPCA and the GIWU was a focus of this struggle. The BGTUC, which had left the WFTU, was trying to affiliate with the ICFTU in late 1952, but after Serafino Romualdi, the head of ORIT, had met Luckhoo, then the president of the MPCA, he be-came convinced that the BGTUC was dominated by PPP communists and its application was rejected (Romualdi 1967: 345-8).[32] ORIT, beginning a long period of support for the PPP's opponents, supplied equipment to the MPCA (Chase n.d.: 206). Lachhmansingh, president of the GIWU and minister of health in 1953, knew that the sugar workers preferred the GIWU and tried, as in 1948, to replace the MPCA. Unauthorised strikes had taken place on some sugar estates in 1951 and 1952 and in November 1952 the GIWU called a strike for recognition on the east coast estates. The GIWU, at its fifth annual conference in March 1953, approved resolutions calling for minimum wages for field and factory workers, a plebiscite to determine which union was the workers' choice in the sugar industry, and the suspension of trespass notices to enable candidates for the general election to visit workers on the sugar estates. 'None of these demands was conceded' prior to the general elections (Chase n.d.: 207).

A strike at Leonora Estate from 5 May to 18 May was followed by strikes in most of the sugar estates from 31 August into September. The strikers demanded higher wages and better working conditions but, as in 1948, the key issue was about representation, 'a battle to the death between GIWU, supported by the PPP, and the company union, the MPCA. The conflict lasted for twenty-five days and eventually brought out sympathetic strikers from other unions' (Spinner 1984: 41), including the Public Works, Pure Water Supply and Sea De-fense Union, the Subordinate Government Employees Union and the Sawmill Workers' Union, but the SPA would not budge (Chase n.d.: 208). The PPP leaders, sure of winning a representation vote, introduced a Labour Relations Bill in September to provide for the compulsory recognition of trade unions based on the workers' choice in a secret ballot. A union would need 51 per cent of the vote to claim recognition as the workers' bargaining agent when no other union was recognised, but the PPP was so confident of the GIWU's popularity that the bill stated a new union could replace an old one only if it received 65 per cent of the vote (Spinner 1984: 43). The enemies of the PPP still called this another communist measure, however, and they spread rumours about a collapse of the economy and the imminent suspension of the constitution. Conservatives expressed outrage that Lachhmansingh remained the head of the union even while he was a minister in the Executive Council, though there did not seem to be a problem with Bustamante being Jamaica's premier while he was president for life of the BITU. The reason why this situation became a crisis in Guyana, however, was not because of who led the GIWU, but because it was thought that if the GIWU-PPP won this round it would then seriously challenge the sugar industry.

On 24 September Lachhmansingh announced that the strike was over but Chase, the minister of labour, explained that the workers returned to work only because the government had promised them the opportunity to choose their union. Chase introduced the Labour Relations Bill and asked for a suspension of standing orders so that this urgent measure could pass the Assembly in one day. The Speaker rejected this motion on the grounds that this was an 'important piece of domestic legislation' that required lengthy discussion. The PPP members then marched out of the House, whereupon the NDP member for New Amsterdam, W.O.R. Kendall, shouted, 'I say now on behalf of all right-thinking responsible persons in this country, that the quicker this Constitution is taken away from us the better it will be'.[33]

On 29 September, when the House met in session again, debate began on the Labour Relations Bill. The urgent need for the bill was connected with the sugar workers' strike and their persistent demand, five years after the Enmore Martyrs' strike, for the democratic right to be able to choose by secret ballot which union would represent them. Important as this was, however, both the advocates and opponents of the bill recognised that its implications went beyond this immediate occasion and issue. Employers had been initiating joint consultative committees, which included ad hoc representatives of workers who were unconnected with trade unions, in order to take the place of trade unions. The bill provided for the compulsory recognition of trade unions, the workers' preference being ascertained by means of a secret ballot, and for a penalty of $500 for any employer who refused to recognise a union that had obtained a certificate of recognition from the commissioner of labour, with a further penalty of $100 for each day the employer remained in default. The bill also provided penalties for employers who victimised workers, including the use of such methods as eviction notices, trespass notices and unreasonable transfers, and gave courts the authority to order an employer to pay compensation to a worker who was dismissed, demoted or unreasonably transferred in what amounted to victimisation. 'In other words', wrote the author of the bill, 'the Bill aimed not only at guaranteeing to workers the right to join trade unions and to have trade unions of their choice recognised by their employers, but it also attempted to prohibit unfair labour practices by employers which made their recognition of trade unions a hollow sham' (Chase n.d.: 210). An American historian contended, 'While slightly more advanced than the Wagner Act [in the United States], it was certainly not as radical as its enemies contended .... [T]he primary purpose of the bill was to establish machinery for fair collective bargaining elections' (Spinner 1984: 43). This is true, but the bill, if implemented as its authors intended, would have transformed the entire pattern of labour relations in Guyana. Not surprisingly, therefore, the SPA and the MPCA opposed it, and the GIWU and the BGTUC supported it.

On 4 October the colonial secretary, Oliver Lyttelton, with the home secretary and the senior legal assistant to the Colonial Office, obtained the Queen's signature to an order-in-council to suspend the constitution of British Guiana, and the necessary arrangements were made to send troops to enforce the order. Lyttelton was 'very much a hardliner in coping with colonial disturbances' (Goldsworthy 1990: 86) and Winston Churchill's government was determined to demonstrate that it maintained control in Guyana, as also in Kenya and Malaya. The frigates Bigbury Bay and Burghead Bay steamed from Bermuda towards Guyana, the cruiser Superb left Jamaica with 500 troops and the cruiser Sheffield and aircraft carrier Implacable were prepared to support them. Incredibly, an Admiralty spokesmen claimed that these events had nothing to do with what was happening in Guyana but were simply normal moves that had been planned months before. Guyana was full of rumours, despite the secrecy, but the Assembly went ahead with the second reading of the Labour Relations Bill on 5 October, passing it by a vote of 16 to six. The next day, the BBC confirmed that the UK was sending ships and troops, though British newspapers said there was no evidence of any disturbances in Guyana. The Daily Mail reported on 7 October that a reporter had spoken by phone with the deputy police commissioner in Georgetown and he 'sounded calm and unperturbed'. He said, 'There are no demonstrations, there is no general strike, there is nothing abnormal happening here whatsoever' (quoted in Jagan 1972: 126) The Daily Mirror's reporter, Ralph Champion, wrote from Georgetown on 7 October, 'I was the first British newspaperman to arrive in this "crisis" colony and when I flew in yesterday, I was greeted with amazement. There seemed to be little idea that there was a crisis over alleged moves by the government's People's Progressive

Party to convert the colony into a Red Republic' (quoted in Jagan 1972: 126).

In the House, on 7 October, Jagan tried to discuss the troop movements, saying that, while the PPP was acting constitutionally and not violently, the presence of British troops might provoke trouble. On the grounds that insufficient notice had been given, the Speaker refused to entertain Jagan's motion and added that there was no proof of Jagan's assertions about the British troops and ships. When Jagan asked on the next day, the day the troops landed, that the rules be suspended so that his motion against British intervention could be debated, the Speaker acknowledged the existence of the intervention but said he was confident the governor would soon inform them why troops had been sent. Jagan's motion could be debated the next day, he ruled.[34] But the Assembly was not allowed to meet again.

The House passed the Labour Relations Bill again on 8 October with only four elected representatives voting against it. Charles Carter, the representative for the Upper Demerara, who was a member of the opposition and who had played a prominent role in the bauxite workers' strike in 1948, voted with the PPP in support of the Bill (Chase n.d.: 210). On the same day British troops landed and overthrew the PPP government. This Assembly did not meet again, the constitution was suspended, and the bill lapsed. On procedural grounds, under a thin smokescreen of legality, the democratically elected representatives of the colony were denied the opportunity to debate the constitutional crisis before the constitution was suspended. The reason is obvious, and unconscionable: the British government had already taken the decision to suspend the constitution and would not allow the Guianese House of Assembly to debate its decision. The chief secretary, John Gutch, read an official statement over the radio on 9 October:

> Her Majesty's Government has decided that the Constitution of British Guiana must be suspended to prevent Communist subversion of the Government and a dangerous crisis both in public order and in economic affairs…. The faction in power have shown by their acts and their speeches that they are prepared to go to any lengths, including violence, to turn British Guiana into a Communist state. The Governor has therefore been given emergency powers and has removed the portfolios of the Party Ministers. Armed forces have landed to support the police and to prevent any public disorder which might be fomented by Communist supporters.[35]

This announcement may be characterised by George Orwell's word 'double-think'. What is referred to as the 'faction in power' and the 'party ministers' was a government elected according to the constitution, by universal adult suffrage and by a majority of the people who voted (which is quite uncommon in British elections). The government was called a faction in order to make it appear illegitimate and so to legitimise its removal by force. Moreover, there was no violence, or even the threat of violence, on the part of the PPP or its supporters. The strike was over before the troops were sent and there was no disorder. The suspension of the constitution and overthrow of the elected government was the real act of subversion and it was that violent act, rather than anything the PPP was doing, that threatened to provoke public disorder. Gutch and other officials tried to obscure the fact that the troops had been landed in order to prevent popular reactions to the illegitimate overthrow of the democratically elected government. The worst charge brought against the PPP was that there was a Red plot to burn down the city of Georgetown, though why this would bring any advantage to ministers who were pursuing their goals by constitutional means was not explained. In any case, Lyttelton said that this plot was disclosed by the police agents to the governor on 7 October, but this was three days after he had already received the Queen's signature on a decree to suspend Guyana's constitution, so this supposed evidence seems to be no more than a trumped-up excuse made after the deed was done.

The British government, responding to criticism that it had overreacted in Guyana, published a White Paper, but it contained no new evidence of communist subversion. It contended that the PPP ministers had fomented strikes for political ends and that they planned to secularise the schools and to rewrite the textbooks, that they undermined the loyalty of the police and sought to gain control of the civil service, but failed to prove that 'their objective is to impose a totalitarian control on the PPP, the Trade Unions, the police force, the youth organizations and the State itself'.[36] If there was evidence of a plot to burn Georgetown, as was claimed, then criminal charges could be brought and people brought to trial, but no charges were made, so the evidence was never examined. In a debate in the House of Commons on 22 October Harold Macmillan defended the government against charges that it did not have to suspend the constitution, saying that under the constitution the governor could not remove the PPP ministers from the Executive Council and that if he had simply dissolved the Assembly a new electoral campaign would have focused on that act rather than on the policies of the PPP. 'The Governor would in fact have announced in advance that he was unwilling and unable to co-operate with the leaders of one of the parties, and that the larger party. That would be the most complete interference with the whole spirit of the Constitution'.[37]

This effectively admitted that the British government chose to suspend the constitution because it recognised that the PPP would win another election if the governor's interference became a central campaign issue. In other words, the PPP ministers had to be dismissed in this way precisely because they had such broad popular support and were not merely a faction, and the troops were needed because dismissing them by suspending the constitution and reverting to the old autocratic ways was going to be very unpopular with the people. Rather than pit the governor against the most popular party, which would have been interference with the democratic constitution, the British government decided to suspend that constitution altogether, under the pretence that they were saving the colony from a communist plot. The Conservatives won the debate in the Commons, as was expected, by a vote of 294 to 256.[38]

As the governor had the power of veto, which he could have used to check the PPP ministers, the extraordinary measures taken by the British government were 'unquestionably excessive' (C. Singh 1988: 25), so how may they be explained? In the first place, at the local level, Governor Savage did not simply overreact. On the contrary, the constitution made it quite difficult for him to exercise his power over an issue that had broad popular support. In late July, before the sugar strike and the Labour Relations Bill, concern was raised about the governor needing 'to boost his popularity in the colony in the event of a crisis' (Fraser 1994: 128), as the colonial administration felt it was losing control to the PPP leaders more quickly than it wanted. The Labour Relations Bill did not create this crisis in the local power struggle, but it was the event that precipitated it. The State Council could delay the passage of the Labour Relations Bill for up to a year, but the governor was empowered by the constitution to summon a joint meeting of the House of Assembly and the State Council to act without delay if a bill was deemed to be of vital importance. The governor would not choose do this in this case, of course, but the PPP, having calculated that they could win a vote in such a meeting by 20 to 16, had indicated that they would ask him to convene such a joint meeting if the State Council voted down the bill, as they were expected to. So the governor, knowing that the PPP would use this issue to expose the limits of the current constitution, was in a difficult situation. As Jagan put it, 'if we had remained in office more than a few months the position of the Governor and the whole constitutional machinery would have been thoroughly exposed in the eyes of the people' (quoted in Spinner 1984: 52). Rather than risk a political crisis on terms that suited the PPP, therefore, reasons had to be found and evidence fabricated to justify the suspension of the constitution, simultaneously putting the PPP ministers in a bad light and removing them from office.

Second, at the international level, the political climate made Guyana, 'in effect, the victim of the Cold War' (Lewis 1968: 273). As anti-communist hysteria grew in the United States, the unexpected victory of the PPP in the 1953 election attracted more attention. Jagan did not have access to United States files but he was convinced that 'the main cause ... for the suspension of our constitution was pressure from the government of the United States' (1972: 138). Certainly, the US government was concerned about the PPP's victory and its ideology, so it closely monitored events in the colony in 1953. In June, the US consul-general visited Guyana from Trinidad, but after speaking to PPP leaders he reported that the British government would probably offer further constitutional devolution. He 'did not appear to anticipate the crisis that exploded within the next three months' (Fraser 1994: 128). As late as 7 September, the consul was expressing concern but not urgency when he reported on the PPP's education policy: 'Although the development of state-operated schools is not in itself objectionable, the apparent intention to give them a monopoly in the field of education savors of totalitarian policy'.[39] The struggle over trade union representation in the sugar industry may have tipped the balance so far as US attitudes were concerned. Precisely because the MPCA was identified as 'a nucleus of anti-Communist and anti-Jagan leadership' (Fraser 1994: 130), the threat of its displacement by the GIWU was seen as critical. Romualdi advised that the GIWU's effort to displace the MPCA was a 'Communist takeover' (quoted in Fraser 1994: 161); once that button was pushed US policy became predictable. The consul cabled on 1 October: 'With PPP leaders pressing hard to establish complete control colony, consolidated Communist bridgehead this area distinctly possible unless menace firmly met'.[40]

Though the US government was kept informed of British plans, the evidence suggests that it gave general support for British policy rather than pressure to shape that policy over Guyana. On 6 October the secretary of state, John Foster Dulles, sent a telegram to all US diplomatic posts in Latin America and the Caribbean, stating: 'Although we not officially consulted re. Situation in British Guiana or action contemplated, we have been generally informed of developments. Our view if that establishment Commie bridgehead there would be matter deep concern all republics hemisphere which value their sovereign independence .... FYI only, we have expressed deep concern to British re. developments and opinion situation should be met with great firmness'.[41] The United States, concerned that the PPP's success may have encouraged other left-wing nationalists in the hemisphere, promptly instructed its missions in Latin America to take the position that 'forthright British action has apparently thwarted' the communist threat posed by developments in Guyana.[42]

Contrary to what Jagan believed, therefore, it is unlikely that United States pressure was crucial in shaping British policy. The United States' concern about the spread of communism in the hemisphere, and even particular concerns about access to the high-grade bauxite from Guyana, were certainly behind the United States' support of British action in Guyana, but Churchill did not need American pressure to prompt him to send gunboats to the colonies. Though the UK was a second-order power after the Second World War, Churchill's Cabinet in the early 1950s was dominated by old-style imperialists, including Churchill himself, Sir Anthony Eden, Oliver Lyttelton and Lord Salisbury.[43] The

United States' hysteria about communism in the early 1950s coincided with the Churchill government's desire to slow the process of decolonisation started by its predecessor (Goldsworthy 1990). The Waddington Commission conducted its investigation when Clement Attlee's Labour government was in office and the constitution it recommended presupposed that the British and Guyanese governments would agree on the sharing of powers and the pace of further constitutional decolonisation. The chief problem was that they did not agree.

The PPP interpreted its unexpected victory in the 1953 elections as a mandate to pursue its radical nationalist agenda and its campaign, though conducted within constitutional bounds, resulted in a collision with the co-lonial policies of the Conservative government in the UK. During the debate in the Commons on 22 October Lyttelton made use of the fact that certain prominent West Indian leaders, including Adams, Manley and Bustamante, had supported the British government's action in suspending Guyana's constitu-tion. This support showed how far these leaders had come to accept that the UK would control the pace of constitutional devolution. 'The concurrence of other nationalist movements with the British campaign to portray the PPP as Communist reflected both the consensus among the nationalists that Fabian socialism should represent the leftward limits of ideology in the Caribbean, and a tactical unwillingness to pursue the path followed by the PPP in forcing the pace of constitutional devolution' (Fraser 1994: 131). Jagan, unlike Adams and Bustamante, 'meant what he said when, with his colleagues, he declared open war upon the colonial economic–political alliance that dominated the territory' (Lewis 1968: 272). The PPP sought fundamental political, economic and social changes, and they collided with a constitution 'in which they held the shadow of power while British officialdom held the substance' (Lewis 1968: 272-3). The UK was intent on 'keeping change within bounds', and this meant 'that Britain must remain always in full "control" of colonial events, and demonstrably so' (Goldsworthy 1990: 84). The UK had long since come to accept that leaders like Adams and Bustamante posed no real threat to continuing imperial control because they were content and even willing to keep change within bounds. But Jagan was not so content and it was because he threatened British control over decolonisation in Guyana that he was forcibly removed.

The consequences of the suspension of Guyana's constitution and subse-quent British actions were devastating for the development of politics in the colony.[44] The British government fomented a split within the PPP by referring to one group as a communist clique and another as moderates and by treating each group differently. Burnham and other moderates were restricted in their movements for a short period, but the Jagans were imprisoned for six months for minor infractions of the emergency regulations. King, Westmaas, Martin Carter, Bowman and Karran, as Jagan's supporters, were regarded as communists and were imprisoned without trial. This provoked distrust and resentment within the party and encouraged Burnham, whom the British openly preferred to Jagan, to bid for control of the PPP in February 1955. Burnham drew two of the prominent Indians, Lachhmansingh and Narine Singh, to his support but he failed to win control because several prominent blacks, including King, Martin Carter, Chase, Westmaas and Brindley Benn, supported Jagan. Effectively, there were then two PPPs, one led by Jagan and the other by Burnham, and the potential for a racial rift, which had always existed, now developed further. 'There was a clear potential for economic competition between the Indians and Africans becoming transmuted into racial conflict. The emergence of the PPP as a multiracial organization contributed immensely to the promotion of racial amity between the Africans and the Indians. However, Burnham's departure from the PPP in 1955 created a situation in which racial appeals could be used to some advantage'. (C. Singh 1988: 26)

Race emerged as a central issue in 1956, when Martin Carter and Westmaas, and later King, broke with Jagan. The potential for racial politics became clearer in the 1957 elections and it became increasingly hard for the PPP to present itself as a multiracial nationalist organisation. Though Chase and Benn stayed in Jagan's PPP, the party was increasingly perceived as the party of the Indians, and the term apan jhaat, meaning vote for your own race, was current in Indian communities. King ran as an independent candidate in 1957 but he was assisted by Burnham. He joined Burnham's faction, which was now named the People's National Congress (PNC), in 1958 and became the party's general secretary and editor of the party newspaper, The New Nation. Burnham and King were developing a more explicitly racial politics based on the Afro–Guyanese electorate (C. Singh 1988: 27).

Jagan's PPP won the 1957 elections convincingly and his second government lasted until new elections in 1961. During this period, Jagan's veto of Guyana's participation in the West Indies Federation further eroded his support among the African Guyanese who feared that they would become dominated by the increasingly numerous Indians in an independent Guyana. Burnham, meanwhile, moved to the right in order to attract the middle classes who opposed Jagan's socialism. He courted the United Force (UF), a conservative group launched in 1960, representing business and supported by Amerindian, Chinese and Portuguese voters, led by Peter D'Aguiar. Burnham demanded proportional representation in order to increase his chances of winning a parliamentary majority, but the constitutional conference held in March 1960 rejected this proposal and opted for an expanded Legislative Assembly of 35 members to be elected on the basis of single-member constituencies. The leader of the party winning a majority in the lower house would be designated premier and would nominate eight of the 13 senators in the upper house, with three of the others nominated by the opposition and two by the governor, who would retain control of defence and foreign affairs. These changes were within the usual process of constitutional decolonisation through an evolving pattern of self-government based on the Westminster model. After a bitter contest and growing racial tension, the PPP won 20 seats with 43 per cent of the vote, to the PNC's 11 seats and the UF's four. Racial politics was clearly becoming predominant. During the campaign King even suggested a partition of Guyana into three zones, one for Africans, one for Indians and one for people who wanted to live together. Burnham dissociated himself from this proposal by expelling King from the PNC, but violence increased at meetings where some candidates were stoned (C. Singh 1988: 28-9).

It was generally understood that Guyana would achieve independence some time during the four years following the 1961 elections, a goal that both Jagan and Burnham sought, but the UK and US governments became increasingly concerned about Jagan's socialism, especially in the light of the changes taking place in Cuba in the early 1960s. After Jagan visited Washington in October 1961, President J.F. Kennedy was convinced that 'an independent British Guiana under Burnham (if Burnham will commit himself to a multi-racial policy) would cause us fewer problems than an independent British Guiana under Jagan' (Schlesinger 1965: 778-9). Between 1962 and 1964 the United States, through its Central Intelligence Agency (CIA), supported Burnham's efforts to destabilise the PPP government by fomenting strikes, riots and demonstrations. Burnham and D'Aguiar opposed an austerity budget, drafted by Nicholas Kaldor, a distinguished Cambridge economist, that aimed to reform the tax system and increase national savings by taxing capital gains and luxury items. The government agreed to postpone consideration of the budget until after talks with the BGTUC on 15 February 1963, but on 13 February a general strike was organised by opposition forces. Large sections of Georgetown were burned down in the riots that followed, five people were killed and many injured, and looting was widespread.

Burnham and D'Aguiar exploited this situation and insisted that new elections under proportional representation should be held before independence was granted. Jagan opposed this change but invited Burnham to form a coalition government. However, by this time it was clear that 'Burnham would settle for nothing except a complete capitulation by Jagan' (C. Singh 1988: 31). Once again, a crisis emerged in the sugar industry because the Guyana Agricultural Workers' Union (GAWU), supported by the PPP, sought to replace the discredited MPCA. The head of the MPCA, Richard Ishmael, was also the president of the BGTUC and stood to lose both positions if the GAWU won the struggle for representation. The PPP government introduced a Labour Relations Bill on 25 March 1963, similar to the one it had proposed ten years before, calling for a poll in any industry in which there was a jurisdictional dispute between two or more unions. The BGTUC called for a general strike to oppose this bill on 20 May. Although only about 2,000 of the 20,000 sugar workers that the MPCA claimed as supporters responded, the others were locked out by the sugar companies which also opposed the bill. Burnham, who had supported the 1953 bill, and D'Aguiar rallied their Georgetown supporters, including members of the Civil Service Association and the postal and transport workers' unions. This became 'the occasion for massive US intervention against the PPP government' (C. Singh 1988: 32), including direct support from the AFL–CIO, the American Institute for Free Labor Development (AIFLD), which was formed in 1961 and funded by the US government, and the ICFTU, which supported Ishmael. The CIA spent more than $1 million to keep the strike going and Romualdi admitted that the opposition to the government was 'ably coordinated by Andrew C. McLelland, my successor as AFL–CIO Inter-American Representative' (Romualdi 1967: 351). The strike brought the economy to a standstill and social tensions to a head. After 80 days of demonstrations and violence in and around Georgetown, during which nine people were killed and many wounded, the PPP government capitulated.

The US government then persuaded the UK to introduce proportional representation into Guyana, a system that neither the UK nor US governments accept at home, in order to remove the PPP from office. In 1961 the PNC had gained 41 per cent of the vote and the UF 16 per cent, so it was calculated that they could win more seats than the PPP under the new system and then form a coalition government. When a constitutional conference in London in 1963 resulted in a stalemate, Jagan agreed to abide by whatever solution was determined by the colonial secretary, Duncan Sandys. Sandys' solution was not a compromise between the contending parties, however. Instead, conceding everything that Burnham and D'Aguiar had demanded, he imposed proportional representation, with the voting age remaining at 21 years, with new elections to be held in 1964, after which a date would be fixed for independence. 'This decision sealed the fate of the PPP and set the stage for Burnham's elevation to power' (C. Singh 1988: 33), as it was intended to do. It also confirmed the predominance and institutionalisation of racial politics in Guyana.

Following Sandys' decision, there was a politically motivated strike in the sugar industry from February to August 1964, ostensibly to win recognition for the GAWU but also to bring pressure against Sandys' plan. When African Guyanese from Georgetown were transported to the plantations as strike breakers, racial violence erupted. Even after the strike ended the violence continued, including arson and bombings. About 176 people lost their lives and almost a thousand were injured. Over 1,400 homes were destroyed by fire and some 15,000 persons resettled in communities where their own ethnic group predominated.

Governor Sir Richard Luyt, a rabidly anti-communist South African, used his emergency powers to detain 32 persons, most of them PPP officials, including Benn, the deputy premier, and four other Assembly members, so the government lost its majority in the legislature. When Patrick Gordon Walker, the foreign secretary in the UK's new Labour government, visited Washington in October 1963, the New York Times reported that 'Mr Rusk [Kennedy's secretary of state] had left Mr Gordon Walker in no doubt that the United States would resist a rise of British Guiana as an independent Castro-type state' (Spinner 1984: 110). Jagan still hoped that Harold Wilson, who had recently ridiculed the 'fiddled constitutional arrangement' when he was in opposition, would reverse Sandys' plan now that he was Britain's prime minister, but he was disappointed. When elections were held on 7 December 1964 the voting largely followed racial lines. The PPP received 45.8 per cent of the vote and was awarded 24 of the 53 seats, the PNC received 40.5 per cent of the vote and 22 seats, and the UF 12.4 per cent of the vote and 7 seats. Although the PPP had increased its share of the vote and would have won under the old system, it was outmanoevred under the new rules. Burnham rejected Jagan's invitation to form a coalition and formed one with the UF. His PNC-UF government took office on 15 December. Guyana became independent under this government, as the UK and the United States had planned, on 26 May 1966.

What had started in the late 1940s as a multi-ethnic struggle for independence 'became transformed into an internal struggle for power, one that resulted in the racial polarization of Guyanese society' (C. Singh 1988: 36). The efforts of the PAC and PPP to overcome ethnic tensions in Guyana and to create a united class-based nationalist movement between 1946 and 1956 were reversed in the next decade. Although the potential for racial polarisation had existed ever since the indentured Indians were brought in to compete with the ex-slaves of African descent, this potential was realised only after the split in the PPP in 1955. The UK and US governments promoted racial polarisation through violence in order to stop Jagan from leading Guyana to independence. For the next quarter century, as the PNC manipulated and rigged the electoral system to remain in power, racial politics predominated in Guyana (Bolland 1997a: 300–304). The 1964 election was the last fair and free election until 1992, when Jagan was re-elected. He remained in office until his death in March 1997, and in December of that year Janet Jagan was elected president.

The elections in 1968, 1973, 1980 and 1985 were not only fraudulent but also deepened racial tensions and provoked racial hostilities. Moreover, to the extent that 'race remains the dominant factor in the formation and manifestation of political attitudes of the Guyanese electorate' (Greene 1974: vi), the promotion of racial politics was at the expense of progressive labour politics, democracy and civil society.

Undoubtedly, the structure of Guyanese society and its colonial traditions of racial ideology made the nationalist movement in the early 1950s susceptible to segmental division, and also undoubtedly the faults of the leaders, including Jagan's 'inflexibility' and Burnham's 'opportunism' (Lewis 1968: 275), contributed to the political division of the mid-1950s. But the politics of plural societies are not determined by cultural pluralism (Bolland 1997a: 259-313). Rather, as may be seen quite clearly in the case of Guyana, more profound social forces, including those of imperial intervention, may shape the political culture and possibilities. The politics of labour in Guyana between 1946 and 1953 gave rise to a remarkably unified and militant movement of national liberation, but when this movement collided with imperial policies and Cold War priorities it provoked an imperial backlash in 1953 that it did not have the resources to resist. The UK, supported by the United States, restored its control, ensured that the more radical leader would not lead his nation into independence, and helped to create a monstrous authoritarian state based on racial mobilisation. The irony in this story is that Jagan, who was branded a totalitarian communist, continued to act within the constitutional framework, whereas Burnham, who was supported by the imperial powers because he was identified as more moderate, perverted the constitution in order to ensure his increasingly authoritarian rule. The priorities of the imperial powers led them to prefer Burnham's authoritarianism to the unacceptable idea that a Marxist party would come to power by free elections. The ordeal of independent Guyana, characterised by political assassinations, racialised politics and deepening poverty, was largely determined by the outcome of the crisis of 1953.

The origins of authoritarian democracy in Belize

In Belize, as in Guyana, there were elements of a Red scare in the early 1950s when nationalist leaders were accused of being communists, but the UK and the United States treated Guyana more seriously than Belize, remaining adamantly opposed to Cheddi Jagan in the 1960s. George Price, the leader of Belize's nationalist movement, was defined as a dangerous radical in the early 1950s but, unlike Jagan, he was accepted by the early 1960s. Under the self-government constitution, he became Belize's first premier in 1964 and as prime minister he led his country to independence in 1981. Price's People's United Party (PUP), like Jagan's PPP in the early 1950s, was a populist, multi-ethnic party, the first modern political party in the country. Unlike the PPP, however, the PUP has remained a multi-ethnic party and, apart from two periods when the United Democratic Party (UDP) won the general elections and formed the government (1984-9 and 1993-8), the PUP has dominated the political scene. And from 1951, just one year after the PUP was founded, until 1996 when he resigned, Price was the dominant leader of the PUP.

Price's personal influence extended beyond the terms of the formal constitutions of both party and government. According to one of his former Cabinet ministers, 'Price was the undisputed chief' (Shoman 1987: 63). In the 1970s several younger party leaders sought to democratise the PUP and a new party constitution was approved in 1975, but Price retained his centralised grip on party and government affairs because 'the new constitution provided a model for the renewal of democracy within the Party, but it was never allowed to work' (Shoman 1987: 65). A pressure group within the PUP, called the Democratic Direction, was defeated in the national convention in 1983 and the autocratic control of Price and his ageing loyalists was reasserted. Politics in Belize has never been so violent or so racialised as in Guyana, but Assad Shoman, who was a minister in Price's government between 1974 and 1984, characterizes Belize as an 'authoritarian democratic state' that reproduces the politics of the colonial era (Shoman 1995: 189-219). The origins of this authoritarian democratic state lay in the early 1950s, when the PUP leapfrogged into prominence on the back of the General Workers' Union (GWU) and won the first election based on universal adult suffrage in 1954.[45]

Antonio Soberanis and R.T. Meighan founded the British Honduras Workers and Tradesmen Union (BHWTU) in 1939 and soon after it was registered in 1943 it became the GWU. Before the end of the Second World War it had become the most important popular national organisation in Belize, raising political and class consciousness in all its branches throughout the country. After the war the GWU's president, Clifford E. Betson, continued to conduct organisational and educational work all over the country, and wrote articles for a weekly newspaper, the Belize Billboard, founded by a Cuban national, Narciso Valdes, in 1946. This newspaper 'quickly developed an interest in the working class . . . championed the cause of the GWU and in the process made the union a household name in various parts of the country. In so far as the ordinary people could grasp the essential features of colonial rule, the newspaper served another useful function by placing the social and political malaise in Belize in its wider colonial context' (Grant 1976: 113-14). The GWU successfully managed several strikes that won concessions from employers, including strikes among citrus workers in Stann Creek in 1946, sugar workers in Corozal and sawmill workers in Belize City in 1947 and dock workers in Punta Gorda in 1948.

An example of the GWU's growing power and influence in this period is the strike against the Belize Estate and Produce Company (BEC) at the sawmill in Belize City in 1947. The sawmill workers had been negotiating for a raise since 3 January when Betson urged them to unite: 'The inertia of B.H. workmen in respect of their rights must disappear and there must be an end to the exploitation of workers'.[46] By early February some 300 men were on strike and Betson told them, 'we are dealing with a company who are in a position to pay what we ask of them .... It is only right that we should share some of the profits of our land'. This nationalist note was echoed by the GWU treasurer, who said, 'a meeting of this kind stretches into the life and economy of British Honduras. You men are here to decide whether you shall live as slaves or as freemen in your homeland'.[47] For 20 days the employer ignored the GWU's demand for a raise from $1.25 to $2 and when he eventually offered a 10 per cent increase the men refused it. Farmers from Santana, Salt Creek and other villages on the northern highway, many of whom were formerly unemployed people from Belize Town who were settled there in the mid-1930s, offered free food for the strikers. In early March an arbitration board awarded the sawmill workers $1.90 a day, which was a major victory for them and their union.[48]

The success of this strike in early 1947 led to others at the Corozal sugar factory and on the Belize City waterfront where 45 longshoremen walked off the job in a wildcat strike. The GWU's achievements and national visibility enabled it to expand quite rapidly. Embracing all kinds of workers, including domestic servants, the GWU reported 1,943 financial members by 1948 and it soon claimed over 3,000 members. More than any other organisation, the GWU, which was based in Belize City but had branches in the districts and even in remote chicle and mahogany camps, raised the political consciousness of the working people in the 1940s. The wretched conditions in which most of these people lived and worked were translated, through protracted and organised struggle with employers and the colonial government, into a protest against colonialism itself. In municipal elections in 1947 GWU candidates won all five seats in Stann Creek Town (now Dangriga), 'presaging the greater role the GWU was to play in the first universal suffrage national elections seven years later' (Shoman 1994: 194). The GWU was planning to create a Labour Party, led by Betson and Henry Middleton, the GWU secretary, at the end of 1947, but the next year it was said that 'plans for the formation of a Labour Party have not been pursued'.[49] GWU leaders also began playing an international role at this time and this must have enhanced their status at home. The GWU had been affiliated with the CLC since 1947[50] and when Middleton attended the first ICFTU conference in London in December 1949, he was elected a member of the Committee on Economic and Social Demands.[51] The part played by the BHTWU-GWU, in the 11 years of its existence before 1950, in establishing a basis in people's consciousness and of an organisation for the nationalist movement and the PUP, can hardly be exaggerated.

It was in the context of this growing labour movement that Price and some other middle-class alumni of St John's College, who were members of the Christian Social Action Group (CSAG), got their feet on the bottom of the political ladder. The CSAG was connected with the Jesuit-led Credit Union Movement, which from 1945 promoted Catholic ideas of social justice inspired by the papal encyclical, Rerum Novarum (Bolland 1998: 31). Price, who was middle-class by family background and education, had studied for the priesthood in the United States, but on returning to Belize in 1942 he became secretary to Robert S. Turton, the chicle millionaire. He failed to get elected to the Belize City Council in 1943 but in November 1947, when he opposed immigration schemes and import controls and rode a wave of feeling against participation in the proposed federation of British Caribbean colonies, he topped the polls. Price, along with John Smith, Herbert Fuller and Karl Wade, and the editors of the Billboard, Philip Goldson and Leigh Richardson, belonged to the Natives First Independent Group. These middle-class Creole Catholic nationalists succeeded in ending the domination of the Belize City Council by Lionel Francis's People's Group, by linking Belize's social and economic troubles to the wider colonial context. However, when Betson, in his New Year message to the GWU in 1948, called for a 'united front, the election of representatives of labour' and the introduction of socialism in Belize, the Billboard editors, although they published his message, dissociated themselves from what they called its 'dangerous tendency'.[52] Goldson and Richardson, a former teacher and a former civil servant, respectively, proclaimed that socialism was the enemy of 'individual progress and national unity'. These members of the CSAG were anti-socialist as well as anti-colonial, and in favour of free-enterprise capitalism as well as being pro-American.

Soberanis returned to Belize in 1948 and joined Ethelbert "Kid" Broaster and L.D. Kemp in an 'Open Forum' at the Battlefield, a popular square in Belize City, to challenge British colonialism.[53] Their meetings were characterised by pro-Americanism, complete with renditions of the 'Stars and Stripes' and 'God Bless America', and a rather equivocal attitude towards the Guatemalan territorial claim to Belize. Although their goal was political independence, they argued that 'The Guatemalan stand opens the gateway for natives to have legal rights to self-determination' (Soberanis and Kemp 1949: 10). By September 1948 the acting governor was concerned enough about this group to consider taking action against them.

> A group of orators known as the "Open Forum" held meetings throughout the month on the Battlefield.... The principal speakers were Broaster... and Antonio Soberanis.... The speakers complained against import control restrictions, attacked the Police, and urged their listeners to boycott the September 10th celebrations. Unemployment and poverty in the Colony were described as deliberately encouraged by the Government, and particularly the British, "a lot of bloodsuckers." All these ills would vanish, according to these orators, if "the British" would get out and leave the people of British Honduras to manage their own affairs. Incorporation with Guatemala was not however suggested as

an alternative .... They are ... endeavouring to recruit a following among the unemployed, particularly ex-servicemen. It may therefore become necessary to take action against them before long.[54]

This Open Forum group sharply distinguished itself from those Legislative Council members who expressed loyalty to the British Crown and who, like the establishment lawyer W. Harrison Courtenay, favoured the proposed West Indies federation. Soberanis and Kemp saw advantages for Belize, especially in labour opportunities, in a closer association with the Central American republics, and particularly with Guatemala which, between the revolution of 1944 and the counter-revolution of 1954, had a popular and progressive democratic government.

Belize was in a political ferment. Among the chief issues that caused agitation, including universal suffrage and constitutional reform, West Indian federation, import controls and immigration, was the widespread economic distress and unemployment that followed the return of almost 2,000 workers from abroad after the war and the renewed depression in the chicle and ma-hogany industries. Of the many groups and organisations involved in politics after the war, including the People's Group, the Natives First Independent Group, the CSAG and the Open Forum, the only mass organisation involved in political issues was the GWU. The intense labour and political activity of this union throughout the country prepared the ground for the middle-class politicians of the CSAG who seized the opportunity provided by devaluation at the end of 1949. The independence movement in general, and the PUP in particular, grew out of this labour movement, which had been developing for 16 years before devaluation.

In Belize, as elsewhere in the British Caribbean colonies, the working people began to act as a class in the 1930s and 1940s, yet they unwittingly served as the vehicle for the weak but manipulative middle classes who rose to political power during the process of decolonisation. The working people's immediate concerns about jobs, food, wages and housing, quickly grew into demands for rights, respect and social justice, and then into nationalist demands for self-government and independence. The reaction of the colonial administration in Belize was similar to that of colonial administrations elsewhere, in part because they all followed broadly defined Colonial Office policies but also because similar structurally defined conditions limited their options. One of the chief functions of the colonial state was to maintain the property of capitalists (whose leading local representatives were invariably nominated to the Legislative Councils) and, as part of this function, to ensure the supply of a cheap and manageable labour force. When this could no longer be provided by the immigration and coercion of slaves or indentured workers, the colonial judicial and police system enforced labour laws that made breaches of labour contract by the workers a criminal offence. It was this system which was challenged by the working people in the 1930s and which was modified by the legalisation of trade unions and the decriminalisation of breaches of the labour contract that were passed by the Legislative Council in 1941-3. This was part of the colonial administration's response to the determined labour action by the working people, who meanwhile were becoming increasingly class-conscious. Without universal suffrage or any political parties to articulate and further the particular interests of this class, however, the working people remained in subjection to the coercive state.

In addition to the usual police action, surveillance, intimidation, force and legal action, the colonial administration made concessions, largely in the form of providing limited relief work for some of the unemployed. This policy was still prevalent in 1949, when Governor R.H. Garvey wrote, 'Very early launching of relief schemes is necessary owing to the serious position in the Belize and Cayo districts particularly, where I am advised riots might break out if quick action is not taken'.[55] Relief work had become less of a temporary palliative during a downturn in the economy and more of a permanent necessity. More and more people looked to the colonial government rather than private employers to provide employment and the government became the largest single employer in the colony, even not including those who were on relief work. In 1950 it was reported that the 'Public Works Department employs the largest labour force in the Colony ... (exclusive of relief work)', namely 1,284 workers compared with 1,091 employed by the BEC.[56] Since the colonial state was forced, by the bankruptcy of the very capitalist economy it was there to serve, to substitute a long-term relief work economy, this welfare became a permanent means of social control.

Working-class action had certainly won concessions from the colonial government, and as demands on the government increased, criticism of its economic role, which was increasingly transparent, expanded into a more general criticism of the colonial system. On the one hand, the expanding economic role of the government and its inability to meet the people's demands sowed the seeds of nationalism within the labour movement in the 1930s and 1940s, and this fuelled the anticolonial and independence movement that followed. On the other hand, within the context of this colonial capitalist state, the working people became increasingly dependent upon a state which they did not control. Before the constitutional changes that allowed universal suffrage and self-government, and before the creation of modern political parties, mechanisms were in place that limited the scope and effectiveness of the labour movement. The establishment of the Labour Department in 1939, for example, 'was the institutionalisation of the colonial approach to trade unionism' (Hamill

1978: 12), namely to paternalistically encourage responsible labour leaders and to take over some of the functions of trade unions in order to control the labour movement. Moreover, the 1947 strike was resolved in the end by arbitration under the trade disputes ordinance of 1939, with the GWU being represented by Courtenay, who, as a member of the Legislative Council, became 'a pillar of the anti-nationalist crusade in the 1950s' (Shoman 1994: 195). However important the GWU was by 1949, and however much it had achieved on behalf of the working people, it remained fundamentally dependent and hence vulnerable to being taken over by the aspiring new middle-class politicians who, claiming to represent the interests of the new nation, seized the opportunity provided by working-class agitation to negotiate the process of decolonisation, which was still controlled by the UK, to their own benefit. It was middle-class leaders like Price, not working-class leaders like Soberanis and Betson, who inherited the colonial state, including the relations that state had with the working class and its organisations. While the working people's actions achieved a great deal, therefore, they did not achieve political autonomy at this crucial moment in the emergence of the new nation state.

By 1949 'all the principal actors in the nationalist drama that was about to unfold were in place' (Shoman 1987: 21) and the devaluation of the British Honduras dollar on 31 December precipitated the beginning of modern Belizean politics. Social and economic conditions deteriorated towards the end of 1949, with a severe drought in the northern and western regions, 'seriously aggravated by the virtual cessation of activity in the mahogany and chicle industries'.[57] It was estimated that in the mahogany and chicle industries some 1,200 and 1,600 workers, respectively, had been thrown out of work and many were not even registering as unemployed because 'it is generally known that the Labour Officer has no employment to offer'. The economically active population was growing rapidly in this period from about 20,000 people in 1946 to about 27,000 in 1960, but at least 15 per cent of them were unemployed at the end of 1949 and many other people were adversely affected by the drought and economic crisis. Without the prompt offer of relief work, the governor noted, there was a danger of riots.[58] An orderly demonstration and a mass meeting in the Battlefield took place in Belize City on 29 August 1949. The governor was aware that, in the light of the recommendation of the Evans Commission[59] that unemployed people from the Caribbean islands should be settled in Belize and Guyana, there would be 'political turmoil' if Belize's unemployment problem was not solved first.[60] With starvation threatening, he announced more rotational relief work 'in order to avert widespread destitution and the concomitant possibility of demonstrations against the Government and rioting'.[61] In October 1949 there were 1,166 people registered as unemployed in Belize City alone.[62] Relief work was distributed throughout the districts, chiefly on road-building, in order to deter the unemployed from flowing into the urban areas.

Some people explicitly linked their criticism of the economic situation to the shortcomings of the political system. A pamphlet called 'A Downright Shame', said to be written by Lloyd Griffith and produced in Guatemala in 1948, was distributed in Belize in 1949. It complained that Belizeans who had contributed to the British war effort, 'today can be seen tramping the streets of Belize looking for jobs and finding none, because the government is not concerned about their welfare .... We have been called the most law-abiding part of the Empire; what we really are is the most dumb, subservient, spineless, cold, cowish part of the Empire .... Democracy as practiced in British Honduras is a complete failure because it has fallen short of the marks it professes to attain'.[63]

A political intelligence report in October 1949 stated that there had been further demonstrations by the unemployed in Belize City and San Ignacio, that they had formed an Unemployed Association and that some had made plans to 'obtain control of the arms and ammunition of the Volunteer Guard with the object of staging a labour rebellion'.[64] Meanwhile, the BEC was criticised in October 'in a press campaign for refusing to grant access to their lands by officials of the General Workers' Union and for having disgraceful labour conditions'.[65] Clearly, feelings were strong in 1949 and among people's many concerns labour issues were very important but until the devaluation the various strands of protest remained inchoate and uncoordinated.

The several strands of Belizean politics came together in 1950 because the devaluation provided a clear rallying point for the various labour and nationalist forces. First, devaluation was effected by the governor using his reserve powers, in defiance of the Legislative Council and after repeated assurances by the British government since the devaluation of sterling the previous September that the BH dollar would not be devalued. This action, then, exposed the limits of the existing representative system and the extent of the colonial government's power over all Belizeans, even including the more privileged members of the council. Their inferior colonial status was an aggravating insult to the educated middle classes who wanted a more representative and responsible form of government. Second, the devaluation led to an immediate and easily calculable fall in the purchasing power of the people while at the same time it protected the interests of big transnationals like the BEC, whose trade with the sterling area would be at a disadvantage without devaluation. The working people, subjected already to widespread unemployment and poverty, were the chief sufferers when devaluation resulted in a rise in the price of imported US goods, including food. Thus devaluation provided a clear issue to unite the working and middle classes in nationalist opposition to the governor and the colonial administration. The creation of the People's Committee (PC) was provoked by the devaluation, and this group was to form the core from which

Belizean party politics developed in the 1950s.

The night that Governor Garvey used his reserve power to override the unofficial members of the Legislative Assembly and devalue the BH dollar, the Open Forum held a protest meeting at which Smith and Price were speakers. The PC was formed a few days later with Smith as chairman and Price as secretary, and Betson was one of the members. The PC immediately linked the devaluation to the issue of colonial exploitation, as the root cause of the crisis, and began to advocate self-government. Before the end of January 1950 the Open Forum, the PC and the GWU had 'started a vigorous campaign by means of public meetings, processions through Belize [City], and petitions',[66] discussing issues ranging from devaluation to labour legislation, federation and constitutional reform. On 6 January, for example, a 'large torchlight demonstration' was held; the police estimated that 6,000 persons attended and the PC claimed there were 16,000.[67] Among the chief supporters were those who were most dramatically affected by the rise in prices, namely, women and the unemployed, and the GWU threw its organizational weight and national reputation behind the agitation. On 23 January Betson and Middleton, the GWU president and secretary, respectively, demanded wage increases from the colonial government, and Middleton wrote to the colonial secretary, accusing him of subterfuge and speaking of colonial exploitation: 'We hold that the poor and destitute, the unemployed and under paid workers, are citizens (unfortunate and neglected though they may be); and as citizens they should be especially protected, and their state of life made more tolerable by the Government. To defend economic enslavement of the under paid workers by artificial and vague phrases violates all social justice'. Middleton demanded 'a minimum wage of 25 cents an hour for an eight hour day, plus cost of living allowance sufficient to offset adequately the rise in living expenses brought on by an unpopular and unjust devaluation of our currency'.[68]

The Executive Council condemned this letter and the colonial secretary demanded its withdrawal and a written apology. Governor Garvey commented, 'It has become clear that Middleton is now working hand in glove with the People's Committee who are, in effect, conducting the present campaign on his behalf'.[69] On 13 February 1950, after some stone-throwing incidents, the governor prohibited public gatherings in Belize City without a written permit from the police and the next day police used tear gas to disperse a crowd (Shoman 1973: 12). This prohibition remained in force until 1 July but the PC was able to hold some meetings under the auspices of the GWU outside Belize City. At one meeting, which was broken up by the police, stones were thrown at Broaster and Soberanis, who subsequently decided not to appear on any platform with the PC.[70] When Broaster organised an Open Forum meeting in June some 500 people attended but he was heckled and eventually retired 'in high dudgeon'.[71] By this time the new political leaders from the CSAG clearly had replaced those who had predominated in the 1940s.

Without the support of the GWU, the only extant mass organisation of the working people, the early success of the PC and subsequently that of the PUP would have been impossible. On 28 April 1950, however, the middle-class members of the CSAG took over the leadership of the union. Nicholas Pollard, who was already president of the small and weak Mercantile Clerk Union (MCU), became president, Smith vice-president, and Price and Goldson members of the Executive Council. Middleton remained the secretary because that post did not come up for election. Betson preferred the idea of a confederation of trade unions and he fought this takeover but 'the PC leaders were not content with either the GWU's voluntary support or its idea of a loose association. They sought complete control of the union's organizational machinery' (Grant 1976: 127). So, after seven years as a militant, pioneering union chief, Betson was replaced, condescendingly given the dubious honorific title of Patriarch of the Union and allowed to sit on the Executive Council. The governor commented, 'from now on we shall not be dealing with a trades union proper, but with an anti-Government political organisation. None of the new officers ... has any labour background or experience'.[72] According to Grant (1976: 27), who studied these developments in Belize in the 1960s,

> The political leaders had assumed control of the GWU not only for its organizational value in the districts but perhaps more important because they believed that industrial objectives could be more effectively pursued by political means. As the union gained in strength it was increasingly dominated by politicians. These leaders extended their personal patronage to the GWU to such an extent that the fortunes of the union depended upon those of the individual politicians. Indeed this dependency, which the politicians seldom admitted, was the dominant feature of the trade union movement during the 1950s.

However, even if the political leaders believed initially that they would pursue labour issues by political means, it soon became clear that political and constitutional issues took precedence over the labour issues, with the result that working people no longer had an independent organisation that would make their concerns its priority. The PUP leaders, unlike Betson, never espoused any form of socialism, nor even labourism, in the sense of making the interests of working people the focus of their political agenda.

On 21 July, a meeting of some 3,000 people was held on the return of Price from the United States. He claimed to have contacted the United Nations, and presented Belize's case to the Trusteeship Council and the Commission on Human Rights, and the Pan-American Union Secretariat in Washington. Governor Garvey reported that all Price's movements were being checked by the police and that 'fairly large crowds' were now attending weekly Battlefield meetings where the speakers urged people 'to stage counter demonstrations and to dis-organize the programme being arranged by the Loyal and Patriotic Order of the Baymen .... Price, in particular, has suggested that this year's celebrations should take the form of anti-British demonstrations'.[73] Meanwhile, Pollard, using the GWU's organisation, was 'holding meetings both in Belize and the country districts ... making no effort to keep any division between the legiti-mate business of the Union and politics'.[74] The governor judged that the 'People's Committee grip on the G.W.U. is of considerable value to them in their general subversive and anti-government campaign'.[75] The traditional celebration of St George's Caye Day, held on 10 September, was 'an occasion for addresses of loyalty to the King and ... a parade through the streets under the Union Jack' (Shoman 1973: 13). In 1950 the PC made this a test of strength. Thousands of supporters under the PC's blue-and-white flag sang 'God Bless America' and drowned out the British anthem, while 'boos and shouts greeted the loyalty address given by Herbert Fuller as well as the governor's reply' (Shoman 1973: 13). The governor attacked those who incited disloyalty and tried to scare people by saying that the agitators were creating an atmosphere in which anarchy and communism would flourish. The extent of the anti-British feeling at this time was extraordinary in a country where, apart from the small groups of radical colonial critics in the 1930s and 1940s, 'the Union Jack had been revered, the King adored, all things British treated with awe and respect' (Shoman 1973: 12). In 1950 for the first time, thousands of people, incited by the PC, were publicly demonstrating against the symbols of imperial domination. But it had also become clear that the PC needed to be reorganised as a political party in order that this popular feeling could lead to further progress. Richardson, who had been studying in London, was one of the first to advocate this change in an article in the Billboard on 17 August:

> To free ourselves from colonial status we must have national unity against mental enslavement and to achieve that national unity we need a national party dedicated to the preservation of our inalienable human rights, not the preservation of rights and privileges conferred upon us by Britain and subject to interpretation by persons resident thousands of miles from us and having no desire to set us free.
>
> Now that we know what must be done I am eager to begin the task of ob-taining constitutional advancement. But [this task] demands a united national front, a national political party supported in ideology and with finance by the citizens of the country.
>
> The People's Committee, it is happy to note, is forming such a party and formulating a policy that will enable that party to work successfully in the dank political climate provided by Britain.

On 29 September 1950 the PC dissolved itself, to be replaced by the PUP, the first modern political party to be organized on a countrywide basis in Belize. The provisional leaders were Smith as party leader, Richardson as chairman, Price as secretary and Goldson as assistant secretary. Richardson and Goldson, the editors of the Billboard, were charged with sedition on 4 November, when the colonial government counter-attacked and the PUP responded by holding a series of large public meetings to win support in the coming Belize City Council elections. The editors apologised for calling the governor dishonest and the charges were dropped, but they insisted on their right to criticise the government. The PUP candidates used the municipal election, which enjoyed a more liberal franchise than elections for the Legislative Council, to demand better living and working conditions, economic development, universal adult suffrage and self-government (Shoman 1973: 15). On 20 November the PUP fielded six candidates and won five of the nine seats on the Council with 48.7 per cent of the votes cast, despite the restricted franchise 'that was more advantageous to the middle-class Creole professional and business groups that had dominated the Council for decades' (Grant 1976: 147). Smith, Price, Cameron Gabb, Richardson and Goldson won, and Middleton lost. Meighan and Soberanis, who ran as independents, also lost. According to a police report, Price was the only one of the PUP candidates to attack colonialism: 'He said that now that the forces of the people are on the march ... their success in the City Council is only the beginning of the new British Honduras that will end the rule of British Colonial slavery'.[76] Within a year of the devaluation, therefore, the new party had proved its viability at the polls and was confidently announcing a general assault on British colonialism. Early in 1951, however, there were reported to be differences of opinion among the PUP leaders and even open hostility between Smith and Price over seeking assistance from Guatemala. Price was said to have declared at a GWU meeting 'that whilst British colonialism remains, unions cannot prosper, that the laws are only made to protect the capitalist and that conditions in Guatemala are far more favourable for the working classes than in British Honduras'.[77]

On 28 April 1951, at the GWU's annual convention, the PUP leaders who had come from the CSAG completed their takeover of the union and the two organisations became more or less identical. Pollard was re-elected president, Price became vice-president, and Goldson and Richardson became assistant secretary and corresponding secretary, respectively. Two days later, the first PUP convention confirmed Smith as the party's leader, Richardson as chairman, Price as secretary, and Goldson as assistant secretary. Pollard, meanwhile, had become an International Organizer for the newly created Organizacion Regional Interamericana de Trabajadores (ORIT) of the ICFTU. While Pollard was on ORIT business in Cuba, El Salvador, Guatemala and Mexico between 11 May and 4 June, Price was said to be 'taking every advantage of Pollard's absence to win the members of the Union over to his cause'.[78] Middleton, who had been elected to the Executive Committee of ORIT in Mexico City in January 1951 (Romualdi 1967: 119), was dismissed from the GWU in July by its newly elected officials. They 'alleged that he had organized a petition to protest against the last elections in which the P.U.P leaders took over power .... The majority of the union workers appear to have sided with the new committee against Middleton'.[79] Kemp was then expelled from the GWU by the new committee for 'allegedly publishing defamatory articles against the union' in the Daily Clarion, and at a Battlefield meeting on 5 July Price, Pollard, Goldson and Richardson explained why Middleton and his followers had been dismissed from the union.[80] It was later reported that Betson, who had been appointed a life-member of the GWU's Executive Council at the 1950 conference, 'failed to attend any Council meetings since June, 1951'.[81] The takeover was complete.

At least one of the earlier nationalists welcomed these developments, however. According to a police report of a PUP meeting at the Battlefield in August 1951, Joseph Campbell, one of the radical nationalist leaders during the war, said, 'the P.U.P have some educated young men to lead them, and he is very glad that at last some young fellows have come along to form this movement, for it was never done before'.[82] All the speeches at that meeting, however, were about the governor's dissolution of the city council after the PUP members refused to have the King's picture in the chamber, and nothing was said about the union or continuing problems of unemployment. The struggle between the governor and the PUP at that point focused on symbolic and constitutional issues, not labour issues. These middle-class political leaders had taken control of the GWU to use its strength, but the labour movement declined in the 1950s as it became increasingly dependent on the politicians. Rivalries and splits between these politicians resulted in a badly divided and weakened labour movement, with the result that constitutional rather than labour issues continued to predominate.

Between 1950 and 1954 the PUP established its popular base, articulated its chief demands and consolidated its organisation. It concentrated on agitating for constitutional reforms, including universal adult suffrage without a literacy test, an all-elected Legislative Council, an Executive Council chosen by the leader of the majority party in the legislature, the introduction of a ministerial system and the abolition of the governor's reserve powers. In short, the demand was for the Westminster-style of representative and responsible self-government that was being introduced elsewhere in the West Indies. On 30 April 1951 the commission of inquiry on constitutional reform made its report.[83] The chairman of the commission, Courtenay, was a prominent Creole lawyer and member of the Legislative Council who had demanded constitutional reform, including universal adult suffrage without a literacy qualification, in 1947, although by 1951, with the rise of the new nationalist politicians, his position had become more conservative. Other members of the Courtenay Commission were Herbert Fuller, C.M. Staine, Karl Wade, all members of the Legislative Council, and James Waight, a government surveyor. The keyword of their report was caution and their chief goal was to slow the pace of political change in order to ensure the advantage of the old Creole elite in the process of decolonisation. The report drew particular attention to what the commission considered to be the problems of introducing democracy in this multi-ethnic society.

> It is our view that there is far less risk in giving more power to and placing greater responsibility in the hands of the people in a homogeneous society than in a society of a cosmopolitan character, where the process of integration is still in a state of flux, and where there is the subtle ferment of racial cleavage arising from differences of language, culture and outlook, and inequality in educational progress....
>
> It should be clear that the advance in general and political education has not been uniform among all the races which comprise the Colony's population, and that the lack of balance arising from the long lead which the largest group enjoys over the minorities calls for the establishment of a system which, while meeting the legitimate aspirations of the one does no violence to the interests of the other[84].

The fact is that all the ethnic groups, including the Creoles who were the most numerous, were minorities. While the PUP was boldly promoting national unity in the cause of independence, and urging everyone to join its cause on an equal basis, the Courtenay Commission advocated enshrining differences in the constitution in such a way that Creoles would be privileged over others.

The Courtenay Commission recommended a new Legislative Council, consisting of 15 unofficial members, 11 of whom would be elected and four nominated, three official members and a non-voting president. They recommended adult suffrage, though retaining the literacy qualification that would exclude many people, especially in the rural areas among those for whom English was not their first language, and a complicated system of voting. The Belize District, centre of the Creoles, would elect three members directly, two from urban constituencies and one rural, but each of the other five districts (Corozal, Orange Walk, Cayo, Stann Creek and Toledo) would elect one indirectly by means of an electoral college comprised of members of the district town board and village councils. These five districts would then combine as a single constituency to elect three more members at large. Grant (1976: 150-2) evaluated this proposal succinctly:

> Designed to perpetuate the old structure of political influence... the real aim of the proposal was not to raise local horizons beyond the village or the town

or even to lay the foundation for a nationally integrated local government system that would be a training ground for national leaders .... Rather the election of the district representatives in two stages was an attempt to minimize the impact of the PUP leaders on the rural population .... Altogether, the constitutional provisions constituted a stand-still policy which imputed a second-class status to the outdistricts and the unlettered population.

Because of the residence pattern of the various ethnic groups and the concentration of educational opportunities in Belize District, this second-class status of the 'outdistricts and the unlettered population' would have also meant second-class status for those who were not Creole. While the Colonial Office and a select committee of the Legislative Council were considering the commission's proposals, the PUP increased the pressure for more unequivocal democratic reforms. Smith took the PUP's proposals for a straightforward self-government constitution, similar to those being instituted in other British Caribbean colonies, to London, and other PUP leaders, in articles in the Billboard, in the Belize City Council and at frequent public meetings, kept up the agitation at home.

The colonial government, alarmed by the growing support for the PUP and its militant anticolonial rhetoric, retaliated by attacking two of the party's chief public platforms. The governor dissolved the Belize City Council on 7 August 1951,[85] on the pretext that it had shown disloyalty by refusing to hang a picture of the King,[86] and in October the publishers and owners of the Billboard, including Goldson and Richardson, were charged with sedition. They were convicted and sentenced to 12 months' imprisonment with hard labour and two more years on good behaviour, which they began to serve on 7 November. A few days later, on 19 November, Smith resigned from the PUP when he failed to get the party to agree to fly the British flag at its public meetings in order to counter the accusations that it was anti-British and was receiving aid from Guatemala. Guatemala had revived its territorial claim to Belize in 1938 and in 1945 wrote into its constitution that 'Belice' was part of its national territory. Guatemala's irredentist claim was an explosive issue and the charge that Price was pro-Guatemalan haunted him for years. It has been suggested, however, that Smith wanted to leave the PUP at this time because he was uncomfortable with its strongly anti-British tone and that he might have been intimidated by the imprisonment of Richardson and Goldson (Shoman 1973: 18). At any rate, although the removal of three of the party's four chief leaders in 1951 was a temporary blow to the PUP, it left Price in a powerful position. A pragmatic and skilled politician, he took the opportunity of the absence of any possible rivals to consolidate his position. He remained the PUP's undisputed leader from 1951 until 1996.

Meanwhile, in late August 1951, the anti-PUP middle-class Creoles created the National Party (NP). Its leaders included two people who were members of the Legislative Council and former members of the Courtenay Commission, and other prominent members of the older generation of Creole politicians and social leaders. Courtenay himself was the first NP president and Fuller a vice-president. The other vice-presidents were H.W. Beaumont, a retired colonial postmaster who had urged the governor to dissolve the Belize City Council in July, and Vivian Seay, who led the Black Cross Nurses from their inception in 1920 until her death in 1971. The Black Cross Nurses, though formed with the inspiration of the Universal Negro Improvement Association (UNIA) and a pioneering women's organisation in Belize, had accommodated themselves to the colonial establishment and represented a model of respectability. Francis and E.O.B. Barrow were the chairman and secretary, respectively, and M.S. Metzgen, a captain in the volunteer force and president of the Loyal and Patriotic Order of the Baymen, was the treasurer (Grant 1976: 148). This 'collection of old empire loyalists' (Shoman 1987: 22), supported by the colonial government, won four seats in the Belize City Council in early 1952, to three for the PUP, with the remaining two independent. The PUP had nominated Goldson and Richardson but they were not allowed to stand on the basis of a law stating that a person could not be elected if they had been sentenced to a term of imprisonment exceeding 12 months. As their original sentence had been 18 months, which had been reduced to 12 upon their entering into a recognisance of good behaviour, the election officials interpreted that they were ineligible, but waited until nomination day to announce their ruling (Shoman 1973: 19). This left some inexperienced and quite unknown PUP candidates running against NP veterans like Francis, Fuller, Barrow and Middleton, the former GWU secretary who had switched parties. The PUP did quite well, in the circumstances, as three (Price, William Coffin and Joe Rivero) of their five candidates won. Price again topped the polls, gaining almost twice as many votes as Smith, who stood as an independent. Though Belize City was the home of the old Creole elite and almost the sole source of the NP's support, Price could still win there and he was a national force with which the colonial government had to reckon seriously.

In July 1952 the Legislative Council approved a version of the Courtenay Commission's proposals modified by a select committee consisting of the unofficial members. The committee recommended eliminating the literacy test in general elections but retaining the income and property franchise for municipal elections.[87] Courtenay responded to this by arguing that it was unreasonable to deny universal suffrage in municipal elections when it was granted at the level of national government.[88] The PUP protested against both the original commission's proposals and the committee's modifications. In any event, the British government rejected the idea of different voting systems and insisted on a simpler and more consistent suffrage, rejecting the proposal that district representatives should be selected by electoral colleges and ending existing income and property qualifications for membership of the Legislative Council. Although the Colonial Office made sure that the governor's powers remained extant and stated that the proposal to make the Executive Council responsible to the Legislative Council was premature, the changes it announced in January 1953 were closer to the reforms demanded by the PUP than to the Courtenay Commission's proposals.[89] The Legislative Council was to consist of nine members to be elected by universal adult suffrage, three nominated and three official members, and the Executive Council was to consist of four official, two nominated and four elected members. This proposed Legislative Council was called the Legislative Assembly when it was inaugurated in 1954, exactly a century after the first Legislative Assembly had been established in Belize. The period between this announcement and April 1954, when the general elections were held, has been described as a 'prolonged election campaign' in which 'the colonial government openly took sides in favour of the "responsible" leaders of the so-called National Party against the PUP' (Shoman 1973: 22).

The prelude to this campaign began on 20 October 1952 when the GWU commenced what it called a national strike. The union had pressed for months for the wages of manual workers to be increased but while prices continued to rise, the government and other employers maintained a freeze on wages. The GWU called for a two-day strike of all workers in the Public Works Department, the Colonial Development Corporation, the United Fruit Company's port and the BEC's sawmill in Belize City. The strikers then decided to stay out indefinitely, until their demands were met, and support came from other people and parts of the country in the form of money and goods. After a week the governor appealed on the radio for them to return to work and government workers were threatened with dismissal. On 28 October the government agreed to negotiate with the GWU and two days later the union agreed to suspend the strike of all but the sawmill workers while negotiations were in progress. On 16 November the GWU obtained a general increase of 22 cents a day which, though less than their original demand of $1, was still a victory. The BEC, however, refused to agree. The 268 men employed there were all dismissed and the company appealed for strike-breakers over the government-controlled radio. Only three showed up and when a large crowd tried to stop them the police arrested 28 people. By 4 December there were still only 31 workers at the mill but by 8 December, when 47 workers showed up, the strikers decided they could not hold out any longer. The company re-employed only about 70 of the men who had gone on strike. Though this appeared to be a defeat it proved to be a rallying point for the PUP-GWU and attracted widespread support.

Workers had showed great determination and prolonged a strike originally

> planned for two days to one lasting forty-nine days.... If nothing else, the strike had attracted additional support for the union - in late November it reported that it had 8200 members over the entire country, more than a thousand of whom had joined since 1st October. And the People's United Party, which had virtually the same leaders as the General Workers' Union was firmly established in the public mind as the champion of [the] workers' cause. (Shoman 1973: 21)

Grant characterised this strike as 'the high point of the PUP counter-pressure on the colonial government' (1976: 154). Certainly, it showed that the PUP leaders who had taken over the GWU could successfully use a labour issue to make political gains on the eve of the constitutional reform. And the PUP-GWU was the only countrywide organisation capable of taking advantage of those reforms.

The PUP contested all nine constituencies in 1954 whereas the NP ran in only seven, and unlike the NP, issued a manifesto stating its goals and plans. The NP candidates issued some individual programmes but the only elements they really shared were a fanatical loyalty to the British monarchy and the symbols of empire, and opposition to the PUP, which they said was trying to sell out Belize to Guatemala. Governor P.M. Renison, who had replaced Garvey in 1952, played an active part in the anti-PUP campaign by attacking the PUP-GWU connection and by accusing the PUP leaders of disloyalty and of having had contacts with Guatemala. Both these attempts failed. On 5 June 1953 the colonial government informed the GWU, which for some time had sought to get an agreement concerning the wages and conditions of manual workers in the Public Works Department, that it 'would find very great difficulty in entering into any collective bargaining agreement with a Union closely linked with a political party which is openly disloyal and subversive' (quoted in Shoman 1973: 22). The government declared that the GWU should hold a poll among its members on whether it should adopt political goals and maintain a political fund. In general, of course, this was in line with the British policy that trade union matters should be kept separate from political affairs in the colonies (even though trade unions in the UK were related to the Labour Party), but the timing of this particular initiative was clearly intended to embarrass the PUP and split the party from its union support during its campaign for the first elections based on universal adult suffrage. It may also have been a response, so far as the British government was concerned, to the recent victory of the PPP in Guyana. However, when the poll was conducted on 17 September, 1,357 of the 1,361 union members who voted were in favour of adopting political goals and maintaining a political fund, two voted against and two ballots were spoiled (Shoman 1973: 22), so it was clear that the GWU members did not share the governor's view of the relationship between labour and political affairs.

The charge that the PUP leaders were selling out the country to Guatemala was linked to two other charges, that they were communist and that they were racially and religiously prejudiced. The charge that the PUP-GWU leaders were communist had no basis whatever, but it did make them defensive. PUP leaders found it necessary to condemn communism as well as colonialism, even though the former had no discernible influence in their country. The Cold War climate, nevertheless, had entered the political discourse in Belize. Romualdi, the communist-hunting assistant secretary of ORIT, visited Belize twice in 1953, in April and again in November. He wrote (1967: 238) later, 'I arrived in British Honduras with open eyes, having been tipped off to be on the lookout for possible Communist influence. I found that nothing could have been further from the truth. The officers and members of the GWU, who also constituted the bulk of the PUP, were convinced anti-Communists, mostly of the Catholic faith'.   Nevertheless, soon after the Guyana crisis, the London Daily Telegraph carried accusations that the GWU and PUP were under communist influence,[90] and Governor Renison reported in November 1953 that the Billboard had made no comment on the crisis in Guyana, as it 'would hardly be in its interests overtly to associate itself with the P.P.P. cause, in view of the Party's necessity to disassociate itself from Communism'. Romualdi, at a meeting on 4 November, praised the PUP leaders as 'good people, religious people, morally sound, and in no danger of imitating the People's Progressive Party in British Guiana', but Price, Pollard and Richardson still felt it necessary at a meeting on 26 November to repudiate 'the charge of Communist influence in the movement'.[91] In a letter to the Billboard Price wrote,

> The PUP's statement of policy contains a resolution condemning Communism, Colonialism, Fascism, and all other undemocratic systems of government .... The colonial conditions which would ordinarily cause Communism do exist in this country, but the threat of Communism does not exist here because the Christian leaders of the PUP came to rally the masses and give them a practical solution to their economic, social, and political problems before any Communists could appear and win the people's misguided confidence.[92]

The chief PUP-GWU leaders were Catholics, graduates of St John's College, the prestigious Jesuit school, and former members of the CSAG, who were inspired by the papal encyclical, Rerum Novarum, but 'were unmistakably opposed to "leftist" ideologies' (Grant 1976: 134). The NP leaders, however, like the colonial administration, were chiefly Anglicans and Methodists who were traditionally anti-Catholic. The Anglophile Creole elite charged the PUP with promoting Catholic, Latin or Spanish and more specifically Guatemalan interests. The Protestant Creoles saw a sinister Jesuit plot, believing that 'if the Jesuits did not foster the [PUP's] anti-British campaign and Price's Latin aspirations they at least welcomed them' (Grant 1976: 141). The charge that the PUP was pro-Spanish and pro-Catholic became an accusation that they were also anti-Creole, because most Creoles are Protestant and most Belizeans who are not Creole are Catholic. When, in March 1953, the Billboard protested against the appointment of a Jamaican to a civil service post over the heads of locals, the NP accused the PUP-GWU of racial prejudice against people of African origin and of trying to lead Belize into Guatemala. The PUP's response to these specific charges was consistent with its general position, that it was against the West Indies Federation because it would displace local workers and tend to reduce wages, and that Belize, though geographically part of Central America, 'belongs neither to Britain ... nor to Guatemala ... but to us who for a couple of centuries have inhabited it and are now as much a nation as any other'.[93] The fact that the PUP-GWU leaders were themselves Creoles, albeit Catholic Creoles, was not lost on most people and the charge of racial prejudice, like that of communism, did not achieve much credibility. However, the charge that they had Catholic or Latin aspirations stuck with more people, probably because of the combination of the inherited anti-Catholic and anti-Spanish prejudices of the British tradition and continuing fears provoked by Guatemala's irredentist claims to Belize. These fears were heightened at this particular time by the attacks made by the United States on the Guatemalan government which, it was claimed, was pro-communist or at least communist-inspired. These attacks, coming hard on the heals of the UK ousting Jagan's government in Guyana, culminated in the US secretary of state denouncing Guatemala's government as an agency of the international communist movement and a threat to the hemisphere at the Organisation of American States meeting in Caracas in March 1954, on the eve of the Belize elections. The United States provided arms, training and finance for Colonel Carlos Castillo Armas who in June invaded Guatemala from Honduras and provoked the overthrow of the government. It is in this context, not only of general anti-Catholic and anti-Spanish prejudices but also of a particular international anti-communist campaign directed against the Guatemalan government, that we need to understand the seriousness of the charges brought against the PUP on the eve of the 1954 elections.

In March 1954, the month before the elections, the British government announced that, in view of allegations of contacts between the PUP and Guatemala, a commission of inquiry would soon be held. Though this was expected to intimidate and confuse the PUP and its supporters, the PUP responded that it had nothing to fear from such an inquiry and sent a scathing telegram to the secretary of state for the colonies: 'Consider your investigation of People's United Party on eve of elections political trick stop protest appointment any British Commissioner as impossible be impartial stop issue international therefore suggest you request United States Senator McCarthy greatest Communist hunter conduct inquiry'.[94]

The commissioner, Sir Reginald Sharpe QC, arrived on 23 March and made his report on 29 March, a month before the elections. Smith, the principal witness against the PUP, alleged that the party had received BH$500 from the Guatemalan consul in 1951 and the colonial government produced two unsigned documents as evidence there had been contacts between PUP leaders and the Guatemalan government. Price, Richardson and Goldson denied receiving the money and disclaimed knowledge of the documents. In his report, Sharpe was satisfied that Price had received this money to help with the cost of Richardson and Goldson's legal defence but he could not say from what source in Guatemala it came, that Goldson and Richardson had had interviews with government officials in Guatemala in 1951 and 1953, respectively, and that a PUP policy document had been sent to Guatemala.[95] However, the PUP's opponents were disappointed that Sharpe had found so little and that the report 'did not amount to a total and unqualified condemnation of the PUP leaders' (Grant 1976: 160). Most people considered the allegations and the inquiry to be a politically motivated red herring and the election slogan was coined: 'Contact or No Contact, Vote PUP All the Way' (Shoman 1973: 25). Moreover, an unintended result of the inquiry was that it revealed to the public the extent to which the government's director of information and telecommunications, Commander John Proud, 'was involved in the political process' (Grant 1976: 160), including tampering with documents and encouraging Smith to form a new political party.[96]

Governor Renison would not drop the allegations but tried again to discredit the PUP in a radio address on nomination day, 6 April. Explaining that it was the UK's policy to guide its colonies towards self-government, Renison warned of the problems of trusting leaders who started as trade union agitators.

> You can use all the usual stepping stones of trade unions and other associations which provide a good audience .... Once you start off as an agitator you need a very strong character not to be corrupted by it .... If like the Irish you're agin' the Government you will find on your doorstep all sorts of cranks and perverts and criminals who for obvious reasons are agin' the Government too .... You've got to be on your guard all this time against International Communism ... there are foreign states who do not wish us well who are eager to embarrass us by assisting agitators. (quoted in Shoman 1973: 26)

Renison referred to the PUP–GWU leaders as 'disloyal and subversive' and concluded by urging the voters 'to decide by the use of their vote whether those concerned have gone too far or not for there ever to be a chance of their becoming leaders who will be valuable to the country' (quoted in Shoman

1973: 26). Though the government tried to shift the agenda of the election by making it a referendum on the loyalty of the PUP leaders, the latter largely ignored these attacks and kept the election focused on the central issue, namely the rejection of colonialism.

The need for national unity in the process of decolonisation led the PUP–GWU to campaign throughout the country, in rural as well as urban areas and among all classes and ethnic groups, in a way that was unprecedented. The PUP leaders were all based in Belize City, so they relied on the organisation of the union in the districts to register voters and campaign for the party. By the end of November 1953 there were 20,784 registered voters and Renison acknowledged that GWU representatives had 'conducted an extensive registration campaign' on behalf of the PUP in the districts. In Corozal, for example, they used a mobile public address system and registered people in the various villages as well as at a meeting at the town hall. He mentioned also meetings in Maskall, Punta Gorda and Orange Walk. In contrast, he reported that the NP, with the exception of Fuller, who had succeeded Courtenay as leader in September 1953, had 'done no campaigning'.[97] Perhaps, as Shoman suggests, the NP felt that given the government's anti-PUP efforts, 'it need not campaign too actively, and it did not' (1973: 26). The NP candidates, who came from an older generation of politicians than the PUP,[98] may also have been stuck in the more limited politics of 1948 when there were only 1,772 registered voters, 70 per cent of whom were in the Belize District. The PUP and its GWU campaigners were actively broadening the distribution and national representativeness of the electorate, however, and in 1954 the three constituencies in Belize City accounted for only 43 per cent of the voters. Nevertheless, this was not an election of a rural PUP versus an urban NP, since the PUP's grassroots campaign was successful throughout the country, except for the far south.

On 28 April 1954 over 68.6 per cent of the registered voters (14,274 of 20,801) voted for 19 candidates contesting the nine seats. Just under 66.3 per cent (9,461) voted for the PUP candidates, 23 per cent for the NP and 10 per cent for independents. The result was that the PUP won eight seats and the NP just one. In Belize City the PUP won all three seats with an average of 70 per cent of the votes, higher than their national average.[99] Price, with 75 per cent of the votes, easily beat Smith who ran as an independent. Goldson beat Fuller, who ran the best NP campaign, by 53 to 47 per cent, and Richardson, winning 78 per cent, overwhelmed Francis. In Belize Rural, Herman Jex, who had succeeded Pollard as the GWU president in April 1953, won with 52 per cent in a three-way contest with NP and independent candidates. In Cayo District the PUP candidate, Enrique De Paz, won hugely with 86 per cent, while in Corozal, Orange Walk and Stann Creek the PUP candidates won with 63 per cent, 65 per cent and 61 per cent, respectively. The sole NP winner was in the small southern district of

Toledo, where the PUP candidate received 46 per cent of the vote. In short, in the first elections held under universal adult suffrage the PUP won an overwhelming victory and the NP suffered a shattering defeat. The governor reluctantly conceded that 'it cannot be said that the results do not show the will of the people' while the PUP said it would cooperate with the colonial government only in so far as that 'will not retard the campaign against the colonial system' (quoted in Shoman 1973: 28). Though there were subsequently splits within the PUP and several new opposition parties arose, the PUP under Price's leadership went on to win every national election until 1984.

In Belize as in other British Caribbean colonies, the working people, who began to act as a class in the 1930s and 1940s, unwittingly served as the vehicle for the weak but manipulative middle classes in their rise to political power. Trade unions always found it exceptionally hard to organise workers in Belize because most labour was seasonal, unskilled and insecure, and workers were often in isolated camps, dominated by companies that were able to determine wage rates, working conditions and even living conditions. Moreover, the biggest private employer, the BEC, would not allow GWU officials to visit the workers at their camps.[100] In the 1940s and early 1950s the GWU was struggling to overcome these disadvantages and was making rapid progress. By 1952 the GWU had 6,171 members, of whom 3,921 were in Belize City and 1,050 in Stann Creek.[101] However, when the GWU threw its support behind the PC it was taken over by the middle-class politicians, Betson and Middleton were ousted, and the union lost its autonomy. Two years after the 1954 election, at the PUP convention in September 1956, there was a split in the party. Goldson, Richardson and ten other officials resigned from the PUP, leaving Price as the sole and unchallenged leader. Pollard, a supporter of Price, was expelled from the GWU for allegedly mishandling funds and he created the Christian Democratic Union (CDU) with many of the GWU rank and file. The CDU, in turn, was dominated by the PUP. It helped the party in the 1957 elections but it 'became a tool of the PUP rather than its partner' (Shoman 1987: 25) and the labour movement remained divided and weak. Price, meanwhile, 'established a personalistic and paternalistic style of leadership, relying on his charismatic appeal with the rank and file and his considerable talent at manipulating the divisions and personality differences among other leaders of the party' (Shoman 1987: 25-6).

The various parties that opposed the PUP in the 1950s and 1960s were poorly organised and quite ineffectual (Shoman 1987; Bolland 1991). They drew too exclusively on Protestant Creole support in and around Belize City, whereas the PUP succeeded in maintaining a broader national appeal across ethnic groups. Several opposition leaders, including Goldson who formed the Honduran Independence Party and then merged it with the NP to form the National Independence Party (NIP) in 1958, were former members of the PUP.

Guatemala's irredentist claim continued to be a major issue and threatened to reduce politics to pro-Price or anti-Guatemala reactions, but as long as the NIP appeared to be a Creole party it could not win against the PUP. In 1958, after the governor had accused Price of preparing to sell Belize to Guatemala and removed him from the Executive Council, the PUP won 29 of the 33 seats in seven municipal elections around the country and Price became the mayor of Belize City, the centre of the Creole community. In the early 1960s Price came to accept the British process of constitutional decolonisation and the British government accepted him as the authentic national leader. The PUP consolidated its dominant position and Price became the premier in a ministerial system of government in 1964. As Price learned to cooperate with the UK in the process of decolonisation his leadership became unassailable and he and the party he dominated eventually led Belize to independence on 21 September 1981.

Conclusion

The UK was withdrawing from its colonies everywhere by the 1950s in a process that has been called 'constitutional decolonization' (Munroe 1972), but variations in particular local situations affected the timing and character of the transition from colonial to national governments. Bird, Burnham and Price became dominant political leaders in Antigua, Guyana and Belize, respectively, during the decolonisation process but the political culture was different in each case. In Antigua the racial division between blacks and whites largely coincided with class differences, whereas in Guyana and Belize there were ethnic divisions among the working people. Although racial consciousness was a factor in the early struggles between the ATLU-ALP and the planters it was not a factor in subsequent splits within the trade union and political party. In Guyana and Belize, however, after an early period of national unity, organised in each case within a single political party, ethnic differences became more politically salient, particularly in Guyana. Bird, Burnham and Price came to power on a rising tide of anticolonialism but the social basis of their legitimacy was quite different. In all three cases, moreover, their legitimacy coexisted with authoritarianism, although this, too, was manifested in quite different ways.

In the examples of Guyana and Belize we can identify several common features, but also distinguish some striking differences. Among the common features are the facts that these were the most culturally heterogeneous of the UK's Caribbean colonies and that ethnicity has played a part in politics in both societies. Further, in each country the emergence of a popular mass-based nationalist party occurred later than in many of the other colonies, these parties were dominated almost from the outset and until recently by a single man, and in both cases the intense nationalist campaigns led by these men and their parties were met with opposition from the British colonial governments.

Both parties relied on support from trade unions, but the initial development of working–class consciousness and of strong labour organisations quickly declined and trade unions have not played the major role in either country that it appeared they would in the late 1940s and early 1950s. Both the PPP in Guyana, beginning in 1953, and the PUP in Belize, beginning in 1954, won elections based on universal adult suffrage. Until Price resigned as the PUP leader in 1996 and Jagan died in 1997, these men remained among the dominant political figures of their countries.

One of the chief differences, however, was that the Jagans and several other leaders of the PPP were openly Marxist while, contrary to some wild accusations, this was not true of any of the PUP leaders. Although the PUP relied on the GWU to win the first national elections, it eschewed class politics as well as ethnic politics, developing instead a typical populist party of national unity. The PUP was initially opposed by the British government, largely on grounds of its supposed disloyalty and suspicions that it would sell out to Guatemala, but the Colonial Office eventually came round to accept the idea that Price and his party were legitimate and could safely inherit the state without threat to British (or other capitalist) interests. The acceptance of Price by the 1960s was also a function of the failure of his local opponents to create a political party that could beat the PUP in national elections, a failure that was in large part the consequence of the anti-PUP forces being too narrowly based in the Anglophile Protestant Creoles of Belize City, while the PUP's broader ethnic coalition was repeatedly successful in its nationwide appeal. In Guyana, by way of contrast, the British government, supported by the United States' crusade against international communism, took extreme measures, including overthrowing the elected government, and suspending and then rewriting the constitution, to ensure that Jagan, unlike Price, would not lead his country to independence. The split that occurred in the PPP resulted in a more viciously racialised politics in Guyana, spurred on by continuing British and US interference, than ever existed in Belize and the change to proportional representation enabled Burnham's minority PNC to become the dominant political force in Guyana, as the UK and the United States intended.

The outcome of the national struggle for decolonisation was therefore different in Belize and Guyana. Whereas in Guyana the first popular national leader was excluded from power by the UK, first in 1953 and again in 1964, in Belize Price remained the dominant politician and he led his country to its delayed independence in 1981 (Bolland 1997a: 259-313). Since independence, governments have changed in Belize by peaceful democratic means, with the UDP winning in 1984 and 1993, and the PUP winning in 1989 and 1998. However, despite the apparent success of the democratic system and the absence of ethnic sectarianism, both political parties espouse a conservative social and economic policy that precludes the involvement of the working class as organised labour. Since the PUP took over the GWU there have been several attempts to develop strong and independent trade unions but they have not lasted long and some were repressed (Shoman 1995: 152–89). Politics remains an essentially middle-class business and the parties, though ostensibly democratic, are quite authoritarian in their procedures and structures. This pattern and culture of democratic authoritarianism was established in the 1950s when the aspiring middle-class politicians of the PUP ousted the pioneering labour leaders of the GWU and used the union for their own political purposes. In Guyana, by contrast, there was initially a stronger class consciousness and a pervasive Marxist or Socialist rhetoric, but from the mid-1950s party politics became racialised to a degree unknown elsewhere in the former British Caribbean. Burnham's PNC, as the party of an ethnic minority that felt it should inherit the state and was afraid that it would be excluded, was intent on retaining power by any and every means, however fraudulent and violent, whereas Price's PUP, without any effective opposition until the late 1970s, continued to appeal to all groups throughout society. The states that followed the colonial system in Guyana and Belize are both authoritarian, but in quite different ways. In short, we may say that the PUP developed a paternalistic style of politics, personified by Price's leadership, that was democratic in form but authoritarian in substance, while Guyana descended to a more brutal kind of authoritarianism with scarcely any pretence at democratic processes.

Notes

1. New York Times, 30 June 1999, p. B9.
2. Daily Gleaner, 30 Aug. 1947.
3. Gov. Leewards (Baldwin) to Creech Jones, 23 Sept. 1949, CO 537/4883.
4. Baldwin to SS, 24 May 1950, CO 537/6118.
5. Act. Gov. P.D. Macdonald to SS, 26 Jun. 1950, CO 537/6118.
6. Macdonald to SS, 5 Dec. 1950, CO 537/6118.
7. Baldwin to Creech Jones, 24 Aug. 1949, CO 537/4883.
8. Baldwin to SS, n.d., but about 28 Nov. 1949, CO 537/4883.
9. West Indies Political Report, Summary No. I 1, IO Sept. 1949, CO 537/4907.
10. Baldwin to SS, 23 Mar. 1950, CO 537/6118.
11. Jagan remained the president of Guyana until his death in 1997.
12. PAC Bulletin, 6 Nov. 1946, p. 1.
13. Ibid., p. 2.
14. Gov. Sir Charles Woolley to SS, 13 Sept. 1948, CO 537/3782.
15. Ibid.
16. Ibid.
17. Ibid.
18. W.D. Sweeney to Major Digby Bell, Naval Intelligence, 25 May 1948, CO 537/3783.
19. Woolley to SS, 17 Jun. 1948, CO 537/3784.
20. Times, 18 Jun. 1948.
21. Woolley to SS, 23 Jul. 1948, CO 537/3784.

22. Of the 55 unions that had been registered by 1948, 13 had ceased to exist, five were employers' associations and six were really trade protection societies (Chase n.d.: 156).
23. The LCP, a Pan-African Organisation, was founded in London in 1931 by a Jamaican doctor, Harold Moody.
24. 'Aims and Programme of the People's Progressive Party', Thunder, 1:4 (Apr. 1950), pp. 6-7.
25. Ibid.
26. The members were Sir E.J. Waddington, a former colonial official, Professor V.T. Harlow and Dr Rita Hinden, an active member of the Fabian Society's colonial bureau.
27. Report of the British Guiana Constitution Commission (London: HMSO Colonial No. 28, 1950-1).
28. Premdas (1974: 15) and Jagan (1972: 107) say 78, and Spinner (1984: 36) says 80.
29. One independent candidate, Theo Lee, won his seat with only 26.8 per cent of the votes (Premdas 1974: 16).
30. Singh and Fingal were supporters of Burnham, along with Lachhmansingh, when the split occurred in 1955.
31. Debates of the British Guiana State Council, 23 Sept. 1953.
32. Romualdi (1967: 346) did not deny Jagan's charges that he and the AIFLD conspired to overthrow the PPP government: 'I publicly acknowledged the fact that, having become convinced of Dr. Jagan's subservience to the Communist movement since my first visit to British Guiana in 1951, I did everything in my power to strengthen the democratic trade union forces opposed to him and to expose Jagan's pro-Communist activities from the day he was elected Prime Minister, following the general election of April 27, 1953' and this was despite the fact that the PPP had won a majority of the votes.
33. Debates of the British Guiana House of Assembly, 24 Sept. 1953.
34. Debates of the British Guiana House of Assembly, 7 Oct. and 8 Oct. 1953.
35. See the Colonial Report, British Guiana, 1953 (London 1955).
36. Suspension of the Constitution in British Guiana, Colonial Office, Cmd. 8980, 1953, p. 11
37. Hansard's Parliamentary Debates, 518, 22 Oct. 1953.
38. Not everyone was convinced by the evidence presented in the white paper and the Commons debate. Several British newspapers and journals, including the Times, the Economist and the New Statesman, expressed skepticism, and the Spectator reported, What Mr. Lyttelton has failed, or declined, to establish is the precise nature of the threat and the precise reason for the remedy employed. Though Dr. Jagan emerges as beyond all doubt a potential Guy Fawkes, his gun powder and his plot are still missing. It is one thing to encourage a strike and incite a riot; but it may be still another to plan a Communist coup .... The removal of democratic rights is not a matter which can, or should, be left to the imagination and the Colonial Office should be the last to overrate this particular faculty. (23 Oct. 1953, quoted in Fraser 1994: 130).
39. Consul Maddox to Department of State, 7 Sept. 1953, quoted in Fraser 1994: 128.
40. Maddox to D. of S., 1 Oct. 1953, quoted in Fraser 1994: 129.
41. Dulles circular, 6 Oct. 1953, quoted in Fraser 1994: 129.
42. Dulles to US embassy, Rio de Janeiro, 20 Oct. 1953, quoted in Fraser 1994: 129.
43. In early 1953, Salisbury, a former colonial secretary, commented as lord president of the council on a memorandum concerning colonial territories, 'These small countries inhabited by primitive peoples ... are in fact not adult nations'. DO 35/5056/6, quoted in Goldsworthy 1990: 85.
44. The following section draws on Bolland 1997a: 295-301.
45. The following section draws on Bolland 1988, 1991; Shoman 1973, 1987.
46. Belize Billboard, 12 Jan. 1947.
47. Belize Billboard, 2 Feb. 1947.
48. Belize Billboard, 9 Mar. 1947.
49. CLC Monthly Bulletin, May 1948, HP, 11155.

50. The GWU did not send delegates to the CLC conference in Jamaica; the Belizean delegates to that meeting were Lionel Francis and E.E.A. Grant (Spotlight, Sept. 1947, HP, 1/1 5 1).
51. Annex on ICFTU, election of General Council, 8 Dec. 1949, CO 537/4283.
52. Belize Billboard, 3 Jan. 1948.
53. Broaster had been deported from the United States after being imprisoned for advocating the non-participation of African-Americans in the war. Joseph Campbell was probably one of this group, as it was later reported that he had 'preached anti-British propaganda' in 1948 (Gov. R.H. Garvey to SS, 5 Sept. 195 1, CO 537/7375).
54. Act. Gov. Hone to George F. Seel, 7 Sept. 1948, CO 537/3824.
55. Garvey to SS, 26 Aug. 1949, CO 123/394/66620/5.
56. Garvey's Report on Economic Development and Employment, 30 Sept. 1950, CO 123/406/66985.
57. Garvey to SS, 12 Aug. 1949, CO 123/394/66620/5.
58. Garvey to SS, 26 Aug. 1949, CO 123/394/66620/5.
59. The settlement commission, chaired by Godfrey Evans and generally named after him, investigated the possibilities of the settlement of people from the islands in Belize and Guyana; see Report of the British Guiana and British Honduras Settlement Commission, Cmd. 7533 (London, HMSO, 1948).
60. Garvey to J.E. Marnham, 3 Aug. 1949, CO 123/401/66985.
61. Garvey to SS, 31 Oct. 1949, CO 123/394/66620/5.
62. E.P. Bradley, labour officer, Report on Unemployment in Belize, 31 Oct. 1949, CO 123/401/66985.
63. Enclosed in Act. Gov. to SS, 24 Jan. 1949, CO 123/401/66985.
64. West Indies Department A, WI Political Report, Summary No. 12, 12 Oct. 1949, CO 537/4907.
65. West Indies Department A, WI Political Report, Summary No. 14, 22 Dec. 1949, CO 537/4907.
66. Garvey to SS, 26 Feb. 1950, CO 537/6132.
67. Garvey to SS, 12 Jan. 1950, CO 537/6131.
68. Henry Middleton to colonial secretary, 3 Mar. 1950, encl. in Garvey to SS, 31 Mar. 1950, CO 123/408/67034.
69. Garvey to SS, 31 Mar. 1950, CO 123/408/67034.
70. Garvey to SS, 29 Mar. 1950, CO 537/6132.
71. Garvey to SS, 3 Jul. 1950, CO 537/6132.
72. Garvey to SS, 2 May 1950, CO 123/408/67034.
73. Garvey to SS, 6 Sept. 1950, CO 537/6132.
74. Ibid.
75. Garvey to SS, 4 Oct. 1950, CO 537/6132.
76. Police superintendent's Report, encl. in Garvey to SS, 25 Nov. 1950, CO 123/403/66512/2.
77. Garvey to SS, 3 May 1951, CO 537/7375.
78. Garvey to SS, 4 Jun. 1951, CO 537/7375.
79. Garvey to SS, 3 Jul. 1951, CO 537/7375.
80. Garvey to SS, 4 Aug. 1951, CO 537/7375.
81. GWU newsletter, 25 Apr. 1952, CO 1031/784.
82. Police report by C.M. Flores, 14 Aug. 1951, CO 123/403/66512/6.
83. Report of the Commission of Inquiry on Constitutional Reform 1951 (Belize City, Government Printer, 1951).
84. Ibid., paragraphs 40 and 49.
85. Garvey to SS, 5 Sept. 1951, CO 537/7375.
86. For 46 years the council had managed without a portrait of the monarch, so the opposition Councillors (E.O.B. Barrow, Fuller, Francis, and L. Bracket) who moved a resolution to introduce the King's portrait did so in order to embarrass and trap the PUP councillors (Grant 1976: 147). When a non-PUP member moved that a portrait of the King

should be prominently placed in the chamber, Price countered with an amendment that a decision on that motion should be deferred until after such time as the people's grievances were justly dealt with. The Legislative Council then passed a resolution demanding that the Belize City Council should be dissolved for showing disloyalty. Despite a petition with over 1,000 signatures that the PUP obtained in a few hours asking the governor not to dissolve the council, he did so, replacing the elected body with an entirely nominated one. This was a 'blatant abuse of power' (Shoman 1973: 17) that reinforced the lines of the struggle between the authoritarian and undemocratic nature of the colonial regime and the democratic and anticolonial stand of the PUP.

[87] Report of a Select Committee of All the Unofficial Members of the Legislative Council, Sessional Paper no.40 of 1952.

[88] Legislative Council Debate, 28 Jul. 1952, pp. 6–12.

[89] Colonial Office, Constitutional Reform in British Honduras. SS to Garvey, No. 3, 17 Jan. 1953. Cited in Grant 1976: 153.

[90] Reports by T.S. Steele, 2/3 Nov. 1953 (cited in Romualdi 1967: 240).

[91] Gov. Renison to SS, 4 Dec. 1953, CO 1031/137.

[92] Belize Billboard, 16 Nov. 1953, quoted in Romualdi 1967: 267.

[93] Belize Billboard, 10 Mar. 1953.

[94] Belize Billboard, 12 Mar. 1954.

[95] Colonial Office, 'British Honduras. Report of an Inquiry held by Sir Reginald Sharpe, Q.C., into Allegations of Contacts between the People's United Party and Guatemala', London, HMSO, Cmd. 9139, 1954.

[96] Belize Billboard, 24 Mar. 1954.

[97] Renison to SS, 6 Nov. 1953 and 4 Dec. 1953, CO 1031/137.

[98] Fuller, at age 42, was the youngest of the NP candidates; almost all the PUP candidates were in their twenties and thirties (Grant 1976: 163).

[99] Grant states incorrectly that 'the four successful GWU candidates in the outdistricts won by larger margins than their PUP colleagues in Belize City' (1976: 164). In fact, only one of them won with a larger margin than Price and Richardson, or larger even than the average of the three Belize City candidates. The average for all six of the PUP-GWU candidates outside Belize City was 62.5 per cent, and the average for the five of them who won was 64.6 per cent, compared with an average of 70 percent for the three winning PUP candidates in Belize City. Grant is correct in attributing the PUP victory in the districts to the efforts of the GWU, but wrong in stating that the PUP was stronger in the districts than in Belize City. The fact is that, thanks largely to the GWU, it was strong everywhere except in the least populated and most remote district of Toledo.

[100] Middleton to Albert Gliksten, 15 Mar. 1950, CO 123/409/67034/1.

[101] GWU newsletter, 25 Apr. 1952, CO 1031/784.

Chapter 10

Conclusion

The history of the politics of labour in the British Caribbean reflects the fact that Caribbean society is complex and often contradictory. Caribbean political culture, also, contains contradictions that may be understood dialectically. C.L.R. James argued that in the continuing dialectic of Caribbean societies freedom is imminent within the structures of domination, but domination reappears 'at the very moment when freedom was won' (1980: 184). Thus, the persistent and pervasive authoritarian influences of centuries of colonialism and coerced labour regimes provoked struggles for freedom, but within the transition to more democratic structures and procedures aspects of the despotic tradition continued. The working people of the Caribbean, even as they participated in the labour movement that created trade unions and political parties, and led to an extension of civil rights and eventually national independence, were often tempted to support leaders, either of their own or of middle-class origins, who were more authoritarian than democratic. Further, many of the new organisations, though ostensibly democratic in formal structure and procedures, became increasingly authoritarian in practice. Consequently, the transition from the colonial to the independent state was all too often a transition from one kind of authoritarian state to another.

Throughout this book I have shown how external forces, that is forces outside the Caribbean that are a constituent of the world system, have affected the labour movement in these societies. The growth of racial and class consciousness in the 1920s, the impact of the Great Depression and the Second World War, the decline of the British empire and the rise of the United States, and the effects of the Cold War all interacted with internal factors and influenced the politics of labour in the British Caribbean colonies. In the middle of the twentieth century, at the height of the Cold War, when the colonies were moving towards self-government, the Puerto Rican model of dependent capitalist development became widely accepted by the nationalist leaders, such as Grantley Adams, Norman Manley and Eric Williams. As a result, just as their countries became independent they were competing with each other, and with many other countries round the world, to attract foreign, largely US, investment. At the same time that they sought to create jobs, therefore, they had to offer tax concessions to foreign corporations, thereby losing potential revenue, and keep wages low and trade unions under control. These countries became constitutionally democratic and independent, but the development strategy imposed by the world capitalist system reinforced their economic dependency and their new rulers became more authoritarian.

Since the middle of the twentieth century most Caribbean societies have experienced considerable political and cultural change, but there has been little change, generally, in terms of the structures of social inequality and the distribution of resources. In most countries a truce developed between the local political regimes, that are mostly brown or black, and the holders of economic power, still largely white, foreign and corporate. The establishment of democratic, Westminster-style, politics and government during the process of 'constitutional decolonization' (Munroe 1972) ensured not only a smooth transition from colonial to independent status (except in Guyana), but also the entrenchment of the middle classes that controlled the political parties, including those with bases in organised labour. In 1966 C.L.R. James drew attention to 'the savage ferocity of some of the West Indian rulers today to the populations who have put them in power' (1980: 184). The achievement of formal democracy and independence, therefore, disguised the fact that organised labour, which had provided the basis for this achievement, was suppressed or controlled and excluded from political power. This is the reason why radical political ideologies, such as Black Power, developed in several of these countries in the late 1960s and 1970s.[1]

Although colonial rule could not obscure conditions of economic exploitation and racial oppression, the appearance and ideology of democracy and independence in the latter half of the twentieth century often did obscure the persistence of widespread authoritarianism and inequality in the political system. The culture of resistance that developed during the centuries of colonialism and slavery necessarily involved the 'weapons of the weak' (J. Scott 1985), some of which were drawn from the culture of the powerful. Among the weapons of resistance in the past were 'appeals to God and Crown' (Bakan 1990: 17), and these weapons only substituted a kind of authoritarianism that seemed more benevolent and remote for that which was more obviously oppressive and imminent. Many powerful leaders exploited the religious idiom in the struggle for freedom, claiming special charismatic qualities and demanding unquestioning loyalty. As would be expected, the British government and local colonial authorities tried to intimidate and suppress these early labour leaders, many of whom, like Alexander Bustamante and Uriah Butler, were interned in the Second World War. The UK preferred to deal with those leaders it defined as responsible rather than those who were more political and militant, and the leaders who were favoured by the authorities tended to have an advantage over others when the political system became more democratised. During the Cold War the anti-communist crusade invaded the Caribbean and provided a pretext for purges of the left in trade unions and political parties, ironically strengthening authoritarian tendencies in the name of defending freedom and democracy. This process, which occurred during the earliest years of political parties and universal suffrage, and on the eve of self-government, gave rise to institutions that were less than democratic, so the struggle for real democracy continues.

The roots of the political culture are deep. During slavery and indenture most working people were engaged in plantation production, often under close supervision and the threat of violence, but in many parts of the Caribbean these same people also worked on provision grounds as a proto-peasantry, when they had a greater sense of control over their labour and their lives. After slavery and indenture these contradictory labour processes continued and were the locus of prolonged struggle between those who needed labour and those who provided it. Many workers alternated between the desire to work more independently on their own land, or at least on land that they controlled, and the need to work for wages on the estates; they were neither peasant nor proletarian, but something of both (Frucht 1967). Their ability to bargain with employers was enhanced if they could withdraw their labour from the estates by falling back on subsistence plots. As independent producers their bargaining power, as well as their economic and social security, increased, so the planters who sought to control their labour either denied them access to land or made such access conditional upon their supplying labour. In places where a substantial peasantry developed the planters sought to replace them with immigrants who were coerced in a system of indentured labour.

The tension between peasant and plantation production persisted in the late nineteenth and early twentieth centuries, but conditions were changing. The population grew after Emancipation, especially in those colonies where it was augmented by large-scale immigration, and the number of estates generally declined. Thus, a period of labour shortage on the estates, or at least of a shortage of the dependent and controllable labour that the planters wanted, changed to one of labour surplus, with consequent unemployment, underemployment and downward pressure on wage rates. Dreams of peasant prosperity, meanwhile, evaporated under the pressure of a growing land crisis and this provoked massive migration, both internally to the towns and also overseas.

The struggle over the control of land was fundamental to this crisis. In Jamaica, for example, the amount of land under cultivation increased,[2] and so did the pressure on small farmers. The number of small and medium peasants, with farms of 50 acres and less, increased from 52,512 in 1882 to 184,444 in 1930, and then to 209,834 in 1943 (Stone 1974: 151). The smallest farms, those with less than 5 acres, increased more, from 74 per cent of all farms of 50 acres and less in 1882, to 83 per cent in 1930, and 86 per cent in 1943. People who could not find employment strove to make their living on small plots of land, and the small and medium farms were often subdivided between children each generation. It was hard for small peasants to expand their landholdings sufficiently to join the middle peasants, while most farm land remained concentrated in the big plantations which became both fewer and larger. In 1882 there were 895 plantations of 500 acres or more, with an average size of 1,338 acres, but in 1943 there were only 540 large plantations, with an average size of 1,976 acres (Stone 1974: 150). The large landholdings occupied most of the farm land. In 1943 landholdings of 200 acres or more, which were a mere 1.4 percent of the farming units in Jamaica, occupied 66 percent of the total farm acreage, but 92 percent of all the farms were less than 25 acres and together occupied only 21 percent of the acreage under cultivation. Moreover, the larger estates generally occupied better land and benefited from better roads, while the smaller farms were often remote and on poor-quality and more easily eroded land. The larger and more successful estates, of course, also had more access to capital and so were able to take advantage of technical innovations, often merging into even larger units in the process, while the peasants became poorer. The increase in the number of small peasants, those with less than 5 acres, stopped sometime in the 1940s and it declined thereafter, from 179,788 in 1943 to 138,761 in 1954, and 113,239 in 1961 (Marshall 1968: 258). This was also true in the Lesser Antilles, where the opportunities offered by small farms became exhausted in the 1940s as the unavailability of land for expansion, and the increasing pressure of population on the small amount of inferior land that was available, resulted in a flow of former peasants to the towns and overseas.

Throughout the Caribbean, though to different degrees in different places, in both rural and urban sectors, two simultaneous processes were shaping the structure and experience of the working people in the first half of the twentieth century. On the one hand, some members of the working class, predominantly men, were concentrated in relatively large and modern sectors of employment, such as the surviving sugar plantations and factories, the docks, the oilfields and the bauxite mines. Much estate work was only seasonal and dock work casual, but the experience of such concentrated centres of labour tended to increase class and racial consciousness and the opportunity for organisation. On the other, many working people, a high proportion of whom were women, experienced long periods of unemployment or underemployment, increasing poverty on tiny and uneconomic farms, insecure domestic service or self-employment as seamstresses, laundresses, vendors or peddlers. This section of the work force was more socially atomised and thus much harder to organise. The reason for these simultaneous changes in the labour force is simply that capital was becoming increasingly concentrated in fewer and larger enterprises, while the potential labour force continued to grow beyond the needs of capital. The results of these changes were increasing unemployment, pressure on wages and a more politically volatile labour force.

The economic crisis of the 1930s intensified these two contradictory processes, resulting in further social polarisation: the large estates with the best land, most capital and advanced technology became ever more concentrated, but did not provide work for all those who needed it, and the small plots became increasingly uneconomical, often unable to provide even a minimum of security for all those who sought it. This is why, for so many people who were part peasant and part proletarian, life was a continual hustle between casual, poorly paid labour in the harvest season on the estates and hard but unremunerative labour on unproductive little plots the rest of the year. And this is why so many of the same people in the 1930s sought jobs, higher wages and land. In these circumstances, access to a piece of land was for many people both an immediate fall-back measure and a long-term aspiration, but not enough land was available and displaced agricultural workers went to towns or overseas seeking employment. The existence of a greater variety of jobs and the hope of better opportunities attracted people to the towns, but there were never enough jobs and certainly not enough good ones, so urban unemployment and shanty towns rapidly developed. These circumstances explain why many small farmers as well as sugar plantation workers, bus drivers, dock workers and oilfield workers participated in the labour rebellions. They also help explain why women participated but played only secondary roles in the emerging labour organisations.

Most women in the Caribbean have always worked, of course, but they were generally limited to a small range of occupations in agricultural work and domestic service, and as seamstresses, laundresses, hawkers and peddlers. Limited educational opportunities and gender discrimination by employers, including the government, meant that few women entered the professions or even white-collar jobs, though some became teachers, nurses, clerks and shop assistants. Women, who were generally employed in the less-skilled, labour-intensive tasks in agriculture, were especially affected by mechanisation and were more likely to be laid off in the 1930s

	1921	1931	1946	1960	1970	1980
Barbados	61.4	-	45.5	41.0	39.3	42.6
Belize	15.9	14.4	18.6	17.9	19.0	19.9
Grenada	58.2	-	48.2	39.5	37.8	37.5
Guyana	43.1	33.5	27.8	22.7	19.0	22.7
Jamaica	49.5	-	33.8	37.1	32.5	39.2
Trinidad & Tobago	41.0	33.2	24.9	26.2	25.0	30.4

Source: Senior 1991: 124.

The proportion of women in the working population was highest in 1921 in most places, except in Belize where it was unusually and persistently low. The period of the emergence of trade unions, therefore, coincided with a general decline in the proportion of women in the working population, and many were domestic workers who were hard to organise. Nevertheless, it is striking how much the trade unions have been completely dominated by men and this fact cannot simply be explained by the decline in the proportion of women in the working population.

Lynn Bolles, in her study of women trade union leaders of the English-speaking Caribbean, draws attention to the 'invisibility of women in the region's labour history' (1996: 8). This is partly due to the historians' failure to seek or to recognise women's contributions to the labour movement, but it is also the result of sexism in the movement itself. Bolles, writing of the 1980s, states several 'indisputable facts: No woman could claim to be the

CEO of a trade union; rarely did a woman engage in collective bargaining or know even rudimentary negotiation procedures; and, although women performed a wide range of functions, most of these involved clerical, secretarial, and catering services' (1996: 4). The point is not so much that women leaders have been ignored as that, for about 50 years, women have not been able to engage in leading roles in the trade unions or, for that matter, in most political parties. Shocking as this is in mass organisations that are supposedly democratic in form and serving democratic functions, it is scarcely surprising, given the traditional sexism of the political culture and the wider social context.

Although it is true that women's real contributions have too often been overlooked and denied, it is also true that women are under-represented because they have been denied opportunities in a labour movement that reflected the patriarchal biases of the British model upon which it was largely based (Bolles 1996: 7). In general, also, women who are active in the labour movement have to balance this with their work and their commitment to families, which they often take more seriously than men. Many women, like men, still feel that men should be in charge, at least in public life, and are perhaps less willing than men to run for office in the dangerous, dirty and unfeminine business of labour and political struggles, which is still perceived as a man's world. While men seem more willing to engage in the expected abuse, slander and ridicule associated with public life, and expect their families' support, women are less likely to risk the effect on their families of attacks on their reputation and may be less able to count on their mates' support (Senior 1991: 159-61). 'Most importantly, women's responsibilities in the home leave them little time for participation in public life, while precisely this freedom from domestic labour and child-care duties is what "frees up" men to engage in activities outside the home' (Senior 1991: 165). Moreover, many women and men who are of middle-class background or who aspire to middle-class status probably accept the traditional Eurocentric ideal that a sign of a man's success is that his wife does not work outside the home, except in a voluntary capacity in religious or social and charitable organisations.

Whatever the precise combination of causes, 'the trade union movement reflected the stratification based on class, race, ethnicity, and gender that could be found throughout the West Indies' (Bolles 1996: 7), so very few women appeared in leading roles in the movement in its early years. It was not until the late 1970s and 1980s, with the stimulus of the United Nations Decade for Women (1976-85), that women came to more openly criticise the sexism they experienced not only from their employers and supervisors but also within the trade unions and political parties to which they belonged. Even today, and despite the pressure from a growing women's movement, women are largely involved in auxiliaries of organisations, and 'they are hardly represented at all in the highest reaches of political power'; such leadership roles as they occupy 'are usually the preserve of upper- and middle-class women' (Senior 1991: 153). Some 50 or more years after the emergence of trade unions and political parties dedicated to the achievement of civil rights and democracy this persistent and widespread discrimination against women constitutes one of the chief failures of the labour movement to democratise itself.

In spite of its shortcomings, the labour movement has achieved a great deal, both for its members and for society as a whole. The many thousands of active participants, including those who were eminent and anonymous alike, exhibited qualities of courage, determination, interpersonal skills, patience, honesty and reliability, in order to achieve their goals. Although some dropped out when they felt threatened or frustrated, others persisted and endured, establishing a tradition in the politics of labour of which they may be justifiably proud. Trade unions in the Caribbean, no less than those in the UK and the United States, have been under threat for some time, and in many places it is hard to discern a labour movement, as such. The politics of labour in the Caribbean enters the new millennium facing enormous challenges, but this great tradition and the depth of experience of so many trade unionists are grounds for optimism.

Notes

[1] For example, versions of Black Power emerged in Jamaica, Trinidad and Tobago, Guyana, Belize and Grenada.

[2] The amount of land under cultivation even increased per person, from 0.771 acres in 1871 to 1.393 acres in 1911 (Eisner 1961: 348).

Bibliography

Abrahams, Roger D. The Man-of-Words in the West Indies: Performance and the Emergence of Creole Culture (Baltimore, Johns Hopkins University Press, 1983).

Abrams, Philip 'History, Sociology, Historical Sociology,' Past and Present 87 (1980), 3-16.

Adamson, Alan H. Sugar Without Slaves: The Political Economy of British Guiana, 1838-1904 (New Haven, Yale University Press, 1972).

Alleyne, Mervyn Roots of Jamaican Culture (London, Pluto Press, 1988).

Ashdown, Peter 'Antonio Soberanis and the Disturbances in Belize 1934-1937', Caribbean Quarterly 24 (1978), 61-74.

- 'Control or Coercion: The Motive for Government's Nurture of Organised Labour,' Journal of Belizean Affairs 9 (1979a), 36-43.

- 'Race, Class and the Unofficial Majority in British Honduras 1890-1949', unpublished PhD thesis (University of Sussex, 1979b).

- 'Marcus Garvey, the U.N.I.A. and the Black Cause in British Honduras, 1914-1949', Journal of Caribbean History 15 (1981), 41-55.

Augier, Roy 'Before and After 1865', New World Quarterly 2:2 (1966), 21-40.

Austin, Diane J. Urban Life in Kingston, Jamaica: The Culture and Class Ideology of Two Neighborhoods (New York, Gordon and Breach Science Publishers, 1984).

Austin-Broos, Diane J. 'Class and Race in Jamaica', unpublished paper (conference on 'The Meaning of Freedom', University of Pittsburgh, 1988).

- 'Redefining the Moral Order: Interpretations of Christianity in Postemancipation Jamaica', in The Meaning of Freedom: Economics, Politics, and Culture after Slavery ed. by Frank McGlynn and Seymour Drescher (Pittsburgh, University of Pittsburgh Press, 1992), 221-43.

Bacchus, M.K. Utilization, Misuse, and Development of Human Resources in the Early West Indian Colonies from 1492 to 1845 (Waterloo, Ontario, Wilfred Laurier University Press, 1990).

Bakan, Abigail B. Ideology and Class Conflict in Jamaica: The Politics of Rebellion (Montreal and Kingston, McGill - Queen's University Press, 1990).

Baker, Patrick L. Centring the Periphery: Chaos, Order and the Ethnohistory of Dominica (Kingston, University of the West Indies Press, 1994).

Baptiste, F.A. War, Cooperation, and Conflict: The European Possessions in the Caribbean, 1939-1945 (Westport, CT, Greenwood Press, 1988).

Barraclough, Geoffrey An Introduction to Contemporary History (London, C.A. Watts, 1964).

Basdeo, Sahadeo Labour Organization and Labour Reform in Trinidad, 1919-1939 (St

Augustine, ISER, University of the West Indies, 1983).

Beckford, George L. Persistent Poverty: Underdevelopment in Plantation Economies of the Third World (New York, Oxford University Press, 1972).

- (ed) Caribbean Economy: Dependency and Backwardness (Mona, ISER, University of the West Indies, 1975).

Beckles, Hilary McD. Corporate Power in Barbados: The Mutual Affair (Bridgetown, Lighthouse Communications, 1989).

- A History of Barbados: From Amerindian Settlement to Nation-State (Cambridge, Cambridge University Press, 1990).

Beckles, Hilary McD., and Verene A. Shepherd (eds) Caribbean Freedom: Economy and Society from Emancipation to the Present (Kingston, Ian Randle, and London, James Currey, 1993).

Belle, George 'The Abortive Revolution of 1876 in Barbados', Journal of Caribbean History 18 (1984), 1-34.

- 'The Struggle for Political Democracy: The 1937 Riots', in Emancipation III: Aspects of the Post-Slavery Experience of Barbados ed. by Woodville Marshall (National Cultural Foundation and University of the West Indies, 1988), 56-91.

Bennett, Louise Jamaica Labrish (Kingston, Sangster's Book Stores, 1966).

Besson, Jean 'A Paradox in Caribbean Attitudes to Land', in Land and Development in the Caribbean ed. by Jean Besson and Janet Momsen (London, Macmillan Caribbean, 1987), 13-45.

- 'Freedom and Community: The British West Indies', in The Meaning of Freedom: Economics, Politics, and Culture after Slavery ed. by Frank McGlynn and Seymour Drescher (Pittsburgh, University of Pittsburgh Press, 1992), 183-219.

- 'Reputation and Respectability Reconsidered: A New Perspective on Afro-Caribbean Peasant Women', in Women and Change in the Caribbean ed. by Janet H. Momsen (Kingston, Ian Randle, 1993), 15-37.

Bolland, O. Nigel 'The Social Structure and Social Relations of the Settlement in the Bay of Honduras (Belize) in the 18th Century', Journal of Caribbean History 6 (1973) 1-42.

- The Formation of a Colonial Society: Belize, from Conquest to Crown Colony (Baltimore, Johns Hopkins University Press, 1977)

- 'Systems of Domination after Slavery: The Control of Land and Labor in the British West Indies after 1838', Comparative Studies in Society and History 23 (1981), 591-619.

- 'Reply to William A. Green's "The Perils of Comparative History",' Comparative Studies in Society and History 26 (1984), 120-5.

- Belize: A New Nation in Central America (Boulder, Westview Press, 1986a).

- 'Labour Control and Resistance in Belize in the Century after 1838', Slavery and Abolition 7 (1986b), 175-87.

- 'The Labour Movement and the Genesis of Modern Politics in Belize', in Labour in the Caribbean: From Emancipation to Independence ed. by Malcolm Cross and Gad Heuman (London, Macmillan, 1988a), 258-84.

- Colonialism and Resistance in Belize: Essays in Historical Sociology (Benque Viejo del Carmen, Cubola Productions, and Belize City, SPEAR, 1988b).
- 'Society and Politics in Belize', in Society and Politics in the Caribbean ed. by Colin Clarke (London, Macmillan, 1991), 78-109.
- 'The Politics of Freedom in the British Caribbean', in The Meaning of Freedom: Economics, Politics, and Culture after Slavery ed. by Frank McGlynn and Seymour Drescher (Pittsburgh, University of Pittsburgh Press, 1992a), 113-46.
- 'Creolization and Creole Societies: A Cultural Nationalist View of Caribbean Social History', in Intellectuals in the Twentieth-Century Caribbean, Vol. 1, Spectre of the New Class: The Commonwealth Caribbean ed. by Alistair Hennessy (London, Macmillan, 1992b), 50-79.
- 'The Social and Political Consequences of the 1931 Hurricane in Belize', unpublished paper (Association of Caribbean Historians conference, Mona, 1993).
- 'Colonization and Slavery in Central America', in Unfree Labour in the Development of the Atlantic World ed. by Paul E. Lovejoy and Nicholas Rogers (London, Frank Cass, 1994), 11-25.
- 'Proto-Proletarians? Slave Wages in the Americas: Between Slave Labour and Free Labour', in From Chattel Slaves to Wage Slaves: The Dynamics of Labour Bargaining in the Americas ed. by Mary Turner (Kingston, Ian Randle, Bloomington, Indiana University Press, and London, James Currey, 1995a), 123-47.
- On the March: Labour Rebellions in the British Caribbean, 1934-39 (Kingston, Ian Randle, and London, James Currey, 1995b).
- Struggles for Freedom: Essays on Slavery, Colonialism and Culture in the Caribbean and Central America (Belize City, Angelus Press, 1997a).
- 'Democracy and Authoritarianism in the Struggle for National Liberation: The Caribbean Labour Congress and the Cold War, 1945-52', Comparative Studies of South Asia, Africa and the Middle East 17:1 (1997b), 99-117.
- 'United States' Influences in Belize in the Twentieth Century', Journal of Social Sciences 4:1 (1997c), 23-46.
- 'Religious Influences on Education and Politics in Colonial Belize', in Before and After 1865: Education, Politics and Regionalism in the Caribbean ed. by Brian L. Moore and Swithin R. Wilmot (Kingston, Ian Randle, 1998), 23-35, 377-8.
Bolland, O. Nigel, and Assad Shoman Land in Belize, 1765-1871: The Origins of Land Tenure, Use, and Distribution in a Dependent Economy (Mona, ISER, University of the West Indies, 1977).
Bolles, A. Lynn We Paid Our Dues: Women Trade Union Leaders of the Caribbean (Washington, DC, Howard University Press, 1996).
Braithwaite, Lloyd Social Stratification in Trinidad [1953] (Mona, ISER, University of the West Indies, 1975).
- 'Federal Association in Institutions in the West Indies', Social and Economic Studies 6:2 (1957), 286-312.
- 'Social and Political Aspects of Rural Development in the West Indies', Selected

Papers from the Third West Indian Agricultural Economics Conference (St Augustine, University of the West Indies, 1968), 264-75.

- 'Introduction', The Trinidad Labour Riots of 1937: Perspectives 50 Years Later ed. by Roy Thomas (St Augustine, Extra-Mural Studies Unit, University of the West Indies, 1987), 1-20.

Brecher, Jeremy Strike! (Greenwich, CT, Fawcett Publications, 1972).

Brereton, Bridget Race Relations in Colonial Trinidad, 1870-1900 (Cambridge, Cambridge University Press, 1979).

- A History of Modern Trinidad, 1783-1962 (Kingston and London, Heinemann, 1981).

- 'Society and Culture in the Caribbean: The British and French West Indies, 1870-1980', in The Modern Caribbean ed. by Franklin W. Knight and Colin A. Palmer (Chapel Hill, University of North Carolina Press, 1989), 85-110.

- 'Family Strategies, Gender and the Shift to Wage Labour in the British Caribbean', in The Colonial Caribbean in Transition: Essays on Postemancipation Social and Cultural History ed. by Bridget Brereton and Kevin A. Yelvington (Kingston, University of the West Indies Press, and Gainesville, University Press of Florida, 1999), 77-107.

Bristowe, Lindsay W., and Philip B. Wright The Handbook of British Honduras for 1888-89 (London, Blackwood, 1888).

British Caribbean Standing Closer Association Committee (1948-9) Report (London, HMSO, Colonial No. 255, 1949).

British Guiana. Report of the Constitutional Commission. 1950-51 (London, HMSO, Colonial No. 280, 1951).

British Guiana. Suspension of the Constitution (London, HMSO, Cmd. 8980, 1953).

Bryan, Patrick The Jamaican People, 1880-1902: Race, Class and Social Control (London, Macmillan, 1991).

Buhle, Paul C.L.R. James: The Artist as Revolutionary (London, Verso, 1988).

Burdon, Sir John Alder Archives of British Honduras, 3 vols (London, Sifton Praed, 1931-5).

Burton, Richard D.E. Afro-Creole: Power, Opposition, and Play in the Caribbean (Ithaca, Cornell University Press, 1997).

Butler, Kathleen Mary '"Fair and Equitable Consideration": the Distribution of Slave Compensation in Jamaica and Barbados', Journal of Caribbean History 22:1&2 (1988), 138-52.

- The Economics of Emancipation: Jamaica and Barbados, 1823-1843 (Chapel Hill, University of North Carolina Press, 1995).

Cain, P.J., and A.G. Hopkins British Imperialism: Crisis and Deconstruction, 1914-1990 (London, Longman, 1993).

Calder-Marshall, Arthur Glory Dead (London, Michael Joseph, 1939).

Cambridge, Alrick 'C.L.R. James: Freedom Through History and Dialectics', in Intellectuals in the Twentieth-Century Caribbean, Vol. 1 Spectre of the New Class: The Commonwealth Caribbean ed. by Alistair Hennessy (London, Macmillan,

1992), 163-78.

Campbell, Carl Colony and Nation: A Short History of Education in Trinidad and Tobago (Kingston, Ian Randle, 1992).

Campbell, Horace Rasta and Resistance: From Marcus Garvey to Walter Rodney (London, Hansib, 1985).

Cardoso, Fernando Henrique 'On the Characterization of Authoritarian Regimes in Latin America', in The New Authoritarianism in Latin America ed. by David Collier (Princeton, Princeton University Press, 1979), 33-57.

Chace, Russell E. 'Protest in Post-emancipation Dominica: The "Guerre Negre" of 1844', Journal of Caribbean History 23:2 (1989), 118-41.

Charles, George F.L. The History of the Labour Movement in St Lucia 1945-1974: A Personal Memoir (St Lucia, Folk Research Centre, 1994).

Chase, Ashton A History of Trade Unionism in Guyana, 1900-1961 (Ruimveldt, New Guyana Company, n.d., [c. 1968]).

Cheverton, R.L., and H.P. Smart Report of the Committee on Nutrition in the Colony of British Honduras (Belize, Government Printer, 1937).

Clarke, Colin G. Kingston, Jamaica: Urban Development and Social Change, 1692-1962 (Berkeley, University of California Press, 1975).

Clegern, Wayne M. British Honduras: Colonial Dead End, 1859-1900 (Baton Rouge, Louisiana State University Press, 1967).

Craig, Susan 'The Germs of an Idea', in W. Arthur Lewis Labour in the West Indies: The Birth of a Workers' Movement (London, New Beacon Books, 1977).

- 'Sociological Theorizing in the English-speaking Caribbean: A Review', in Contemporary Caribbean: A Sociological Reader (Maracas, College Press, 1982), 143-80.

- Smiles and Blood: The Ruling Class Response to the Workers' Rebellion of 1937 in Trinidad and Tobago (London, New Beacon Books, 1988).

Craton, Michael Searching for the Invisible Man: Slaves and Plantation Life in Jamaica (Cambridge, MA, Harvard University Press, 1978).

- Testing the Chains: Resistance to Slavery in the British West Indies (Ithaca, Cornell University Press, 1982).

- A History of the Bahamas (Waterloo, Ontario, San Salvador Press, 1986).

- 'Continuity not Change: The Incidence of Unrest Among Ex-Slaves in the British West Indies, 1838-1876', Slavery and Abolition 7:1 (1988), 144-70.

- Empire, Enslavement and Freedom in the Caribbean (Kingston, Ian Randle, 1997).

Craton, Michael, and James Walvin A Jamaican Plantation: The History of Worthy Park, 1670-1970 (London, W.H. Allen, 1970).

Cronon, Edmund David Black Moses: The Story of Marcus Garvey and the Universal Negro Improvement Association (Madison, University of Wisconsin Press, 1969).

Cross, Malcolm Urbanization and Urban Growth in the Caribbean: An Essay on Social Change in Dependent Societies (Cambridge, Cambridge University Press, 1979).

- 'The Political Representation of Organised Labour in Trinidad and Guyana: A Comparative Puzzle', in Labour in the Caribbean: From Emancipation to Independence ed. by Malcolm Cross and Gad Heuman (London, Macmillan, 1988), 285-308.

Cross, Malcolm, and Gad Heuman (eds) Labour in the Caribbean: From Emancipation to Independence (London, Macmillan, 1988).

Cumper, George E. 'Labour Demand and Supply in the Jamaican Sugar Industry, 1830-1950', Social and Economic Studies 2:4 (1954), 37-86.

Curtin, Philip D. 'The British Sugar Duties and West Indian Prosperity', Journal of Economic History 14:2 (1954), 157-64.

- The Atlantic Slave Trade: A Census (Madison, University of Wisconsin Press, 1969).

- Two Jamaicas: The Role of Ideas in a Tropical Colony, 1830-1865 [1955] (New York, Atheneum, 1970).

Dalley, F.W. Trade Union Organization and Industrial Relations in Trinidad (London, HMSO, 1947).

- General Industrial Conditions and Labour Relations in Trinidad (Trinidad, Government Printing Office, 1954).

Davies, Ioan African Trade Unions (Harmondsworth, Penguin, 1966).

De Certeau, Michel The Practice of Everyday Life trans. by Steven F. Rendall (Berkeley, University of California Press, 1984).

Deerr, Noel The History of Sugar, 2 vols (London, Chapman & Hall, 1949).

Despres, Leo A. Cultural Pluralism and Nationalist Politics in British Guiana (Chicago, Rand McNally, 1967).

Dixon, William From Riots to Responsibility: History of the Barbados Workers' Union, 1941-91 (Bridgetown, 1991).

Dobson, Narda A History of Belize (London, Longman Caribbean, 1973).

Drayton, Richard, and Andaiye (eds) Conversations: George Lamming: Essays, Addresses and Interviews 1953-1990 (London, Karia Press, 1992).

Duncan, Ebeneezer A Brief History of St Vincent with Studies in Citizenship [1941] (Kingstown, 1970).

Dunn, Richard S. Sugar and Slaves: The Rise of the Planter Class in the English West Indies, 1624-1713 (New York, W.W. Norton, 1973).

Eaton, George E. 'Trade Union Development in Jamaica', Caribbean Quarterly 8:1/2 (1962), 45-53, 69-75.

- Alexander Bustamante and Modern Jamaica (Kingston, Kingston Publishers, 1975).

Edgell, Zee Beka Lamb (London, Heinemann, 1982).

Eisner, Gisela Jamaica, 1830-1930: A Study in Economic Growth (Manchester, Manchester University Press, 1961).

Elkins, W.F. 'Black Power in the British West Indies: The Trinidad Longshoremen's Strike of 1919', Science and Society 33:1 (1969), 71-5.

- 'A Source of Black Nationalism in the Caribbean: The Revolt of the British West Indies Regiment at Taranto, Italy', Science and Society 35:1 (1970), 99-103.
- 'Suppression of the Negro World in the British West Indies', Science and Society 35:3 (1971), 344-7.

Emmanuel, Patrick Elections and Party Systems in the Commonwealth Caribbean, 1944-1991 (Barbados, Caribbean Development Research Services, 1992).

Engerman, S.L. 'Economic Change and Contract Labour in the British Caribbean: The End of Slavery and the Adjustment to Emancipation', in Abolition and its Aftermath: The Historical Context, 1790-1916 ed. by David Richardson (London, Frank Cass, 1985), 225-44.

Fanon, Frantz The Wretched of the Earth, trans. by Constance Farrington (New York, Grove Press, 1968).

Finley, M.I. 'Between Slavery and Freedom', Comparative Studies in Society and History 6:3 (1964), 233-49.
- Ancient Slavery and Modern Ideology (New York, Viking, 1980).

Fogel, Robert William, and Stanley L. Engerman, 'Philanthropy at Bargain Prices: Notes on the Economics of Gradual Emancipation', Journal of Legal Studies 3 (1974), 377-401.

Foner, Eric Nothing but Freedom: Emancipation and its Legacy (Baton Rouge, Louisiana State University Press, 1983).
- Reconstruction: America's Unfinished Revolution, 1863-1877 (New York, Harper & Row, 1988).

Ford, Amos A. Telling the Truth: The Life and Times of the British Honduran Forestry Unit in Scotland (1914-44) (London, Karia Press, 1985).

Foster, Byron The Baymen's Legacy: A Portrait of Belize City (Benque Viejo del Carmen, Cubola Productions, 1987).

Foster, Cecil No Man in the House (New York, Ballantine, 1991).

Frank, Andre Gunder Capitalism and Underdevelopment in Latin America: Historical Studies of Chile and Brazil (Harmondsworth, Penguin, 1971).

Fraser, Cary Ambivalent Anti-Colonialism: The United States and the Genesis of West Indian Independence, 1940-1964 (Westport, CT, Greenwood Press, 1994).

Fraser, Peter D. 'The Immigration Issue in British Guiana, 1903-1913: The Economic and Constitutional Origins of Racist Politics in Guyana', Journal of Caribbean History 14 (1981), 18-45.

Frucht, Richard 'A Caribbean Social Type: Neither "Peasant" nor "Proletarian"', Social and Economic Studies 16:3 (1967), 295-300.

Gibbs, Archibald Robertson British Honduras: An Historical and Descriptive Account of the Colony from its Settlement, 1670 (London, Sampson Low, 1883).

Girvan, Norman P. 'The Political Economy of Race in the Americas: The Historical Context of Garveyism', in Garvey: His Work and Impact ed. by Rupert Lewis and Patrick Bryan (Mona, ISER and Department of Extra-Mural Studies, University of the West Indies, 1988), 11-21.

Goffman, Erving Asylums (Harmondsworth, Penguin, 1961).

Goldsworthy, David 'Keeping Change Within Bounds: Aspects of Colonial Policy During the Churchill and Eden Governments, 1951-57', Journal of Imperial and Commonwealth History 18:1 (1990), 81-108.

Gomes, Albert Through a Maze of Colour (Trinidad, Key Caribbean Publications, 1974).

Gonsalves, Ralph 'The 1935 Labour Riots in St Vincent and their Political Significance', unpublished paper (Institute of Commonwealth Studies Library, University of London, n.d.).

Gordon, Shirley C. Reports and Repercussions in West Indian Education, 1835-1933 (London, Ginn, 1968).

Grant, C.H. The Making of Modern Belize: Politics, Society and British Colonialism in Central America (Cambridge, Cambridge University Press, 1976).

Green, William A. British Slave Emancipation: The Sugar Colonies and the Great Experiment, 1830-1865 (Oxford, Clarendon Press, 1976).

- 'The Perils of Comparative History: Belize and the British Sugar Colonies after Slavery', Comparative Studies in Society and History 26:1 (1984), 112-19.

- 'The Creolization of Caribbean History: The Emancipation Era and a Critique of Dialectical Analysis', Journal of Imperial and Commonwealth History 14:3 (1986), 149-69.

Greene, J.E. Race vs Politics in Guyana: Political Cleavages and Political Mobilisation in the 1968 General Election (Mona, ISER, University of the West Indies, 1974).

Gupta, Partha Sarathi Imperialism and the British Labour Movement, 1914-1964 (New York, Holmes & Meier, 1975).

Gurney, Joseph John Familiar Letters to Henry Clay of Kentucky Describing a Winter in the West Indies [1840] (New York, Negro Universities Press, 1969).

Hall, Douglas Free Jamaica, 1838-1865: An Economic History (New Haven, Yale University Press, 1959).

- Five of the Leewards, 1834-1870. The Major Problems of the Post-Emancipation Period in Antigua, Barbuda, Montserrat, Nevis and St Kitts (Barbados, Caribbean Universities Press, 1971).

- 'The Flight from the Estates Reconsidered: The British West Indies, 1838-1842', Journal of Caribbean History 10/11 (1978), 7-24.

Hall, Stuart 'A Conversation with C.L.R.James', in Rethinking C.L.R. James ed. by Grant Farred (Cambridge, Blackwell, 1996), 15-44.

Hamill, Don 'Colonialism and the Emergence of Trade Unions in Belize', Journal of Belizean Affairs 7 (1978), 3-20.

Haraksingh, Kusha 'Control and Resistance Among Overseas Indian Workers: A Study of Labour on the Sugar Plantations of Trinidad, 1875-1917', Journal of Caribbean History 14 (1981), 1-17.

- 'The Worker and the Wage in a Plantation Economy: Trinidad in the Late Nineteenth Century', in From Chattel Slaves to Wage Slaves: The Dynamics of Labour Bargaining in the Americas ed. by Mary Turner (Kingston, Ian Randle, Bloomington, Indiana University Press, and London, James Currey, 1995), 224-38.

Harrod, Jeffrey Trade Union Foreign Policy: A Study of British and American Trade Union Activities in Jamaica (London, Macmillan, 1972).

Harry, Carlyle Hubert Nathaniel Critchlow: His Main Tasks and Achievements (Ruimveldt, Guyana National Service Publishing Centre, 1977).

Hart, Richard 'Trade Unionism in the English-speaking Caribbean: The Formative Years and the Caribbean Labour Congress', in Contemporary Caribbean: A Sociological Reader, Vol. 2, ed. by Susan Craig (Maracas, College Press, 1982), 59-96.

- 'Origin and Development of the Working Class in the English-speaking Caribbean Area: 1897-1937', in Labour in the Caribbean: From Emancipation to Independence ed. by Malcolm Cross and Gad Heuman (London, Macmillan, 1988), 43-79.

- Rise and Organise: The Birth of the Workers and National Movements in Jamaica, 1936-1939 (London, Karia Press, 1989).

- 'Introduction', in O. Nigel Bolland On the March: Labour Rebellions in the British Caribbean, 1934-39 (Kingston, Ian Randle, and London, James Currey, 1995), vii-viii.

- From Occupation to Independence: A Short History of the Peoples of the English-Speaking Caribbean Region (London, Pluto Press, 1998).

- Towards Decolonisation: Political, Labour and Economic Development in Jamaica 1938-1945 (Mona, University of the West Indies Canoe Press, 1999).

Havinden, Michael, and David Meredith Colonialism and Development: Britain and its Tropical Colonies, 1850-1960 (London, Routledge, 1993).

Henry, Paget Peripheral Capitalism and Underdevelopment in Antigua (New Brunswick, Transaction Books, 1985).

Herrmann, Eleanor Krohn Origins of Tomorrow: A History of Belizean Nursing Education (Belize, Ministry of Health, 1985).

Heuman, Gad Between Black and White: Race, Politics and the Free Coloreds in Jamaica, 1792-1865 (Westport, CT, Greenwood Press, 1981).

- The Killing Time: The Morant Bay Rebellion in Jamaica (London, Macmillan, 1994).

Higman, B.W. Slave Population and Economy in Jamaica, 1807-1834 (Cambridge, Cambridge University Press, 1976).

- Slave Populations in the British Caribbean, 1807-1834 (Baltimore, Johns Hopkins University Press, 1984).

- 'Theory, Method and Technique in Caribbean Social History', Journal of Caribbean History 20 (1985-6), 1-29.

- Writing West Indian Histories (London, Macmillan, 1999).

Hill, Frank Bustamante and his Letters (Kingston, Kingston Publishers, 1976).

Hill, Robert A. (ed.) Marcus Garvey: Life and Lessons (Berkeley, University of California Press, 1987).

A History of Belize: Nation in the Making (Belize, Sunshine Books, 1983).

Hobsbawm, E.J. The Age of Empire, 1875-1914 (New York, Pantheon Books, 1987).

- The Age of Extremes: A History of the World, 1914-1991 (New York, Pantheon Books, 1994).

Hodge, Merle Crick Crack, Monkey (London, André Deutsch, 1970).

- 'The Shadow of the Whip: A Comment on Male-Female Relations in the Caribbean', in Is Massa Day Dead? Black Moods in the Caribbean ed. by Orde Coombs (New York, Anchor Books, 1974), 111-19.

Hoefte, Rosemarijn 'Control and Resistance: Indentured Labor in Suriname', New West Indian Guide 61: 1 & 2 (1987), 1-22.

Holt, Thomas C. '"An Empire Over the Mind": Emancipation, Race, and Ideology in the British West Indies and the American South', in Region, Race, and Reconstruction ed. by J. Morgan Kousser and James M. McPherson (New York, Oxford University Press, 1982), 283-313.

- The Problem of Freedom: Race, Labor, and Politics in Jamaica and Britain, 1832-1938 (Baltimore, Johns Hopkins University Press, 1992).

Hoyos, F.A. Grantley Adams and the Social Revolution (London, Macmillan, 1974).

Hurwitz, Samuel J., and Edith F. Hurwitz Jamaica: A Historical Portrait (New York, Praeger Publishers, 1971).

Jacobs, Harriet A. Incidents in the Life of a Slave Girl, Written by Herself ed. by Jean Fagan Yellin (Cambridge, MA, Harvard University Press, 1987).

Jacobs, W. Richard 'Butler: A Life of Struggle', in In the Spirit of Butler: Trade Unionism in Free Grenada (St. George's, Fedon Publishers, 1982), 32-44.

Jagan, Cheddi The West on Trial: The Fight for Guyana's Freedom [1966] rev. edn., (Berlin, Seven Seas Publishers, 1972).

James, C.L.R. Minty Alley (London, Secker and Warburg, 1936).

- The Black Jacobins: Toussaint L'Ouverture and the San Domingo Revolution [1938] (New York, Vintage Books, 1963).

- Spheres of Existence: Selected Writings (London, Allison & Busby, 1980).

James, Winston Holding Aloft the Banner of Ethiopia: Caribbean Radicalism in Early Twentieth-Century America (London, Verso, 1998).

Johnson, Howard 'Oil, Imperial Policy and the Trinidad Disturbances, 1937', Journal of Imperial and Commonwealth History 4:1 (1975), 29-54.

- 'The West Indies and the Conversion of the British Official Classes to the Development Idea', Journal of Commonwealth and Comparative Politics 15:1 (1977), 55-83.

- 'The United States and the Establishment of the Anglo-American Caribbean Commission', Journal of Caribbean History 19:1 (1984a), 26-47.

- 'The Anglo-American Caribbean Commission and the Extension of American Influence in the British Caribbean, 1942-1945', Journal of Commonwealth and Comparative Politics 22:2 (1984b), 180-203.

- '"A Modified Form of Slavery": The Credit and Truck Systems in the Bahamas in the Nineteenth and Early Twentieth Centuries', Comparative Studies in Society and History 28:4 (1986), 729-53.

- 'Merchant Credit and the Dispossession of the Cocoa Peasantry in Trinidad in the Late Nineteenth Century', Peasant Studies 15:1 (1987), 27-38.

- The Bahamas in Slavery and Freedom (Kingston, Ian Randle, 1991).
- The Bahamas from Slavery to Servitude, 1783-1933 (Gainesville, University Press of Florida, 1996).

Jones, Jacqueline Labor of Love, Labor of Sorrow: Black Women, Work, and the Family from Slavery to the Present (New York, Vintage, 1995).

Joseph, Cedric L. 'The British West Indies Regiment, 1914-1918', Journal of Caribbean History (1971), 94-124.

Judd, Karen H. 'Elite Reproduction and Ethnic Identity in Belize', unpublished PhD thesis (City University of New York, 1992).

Kambon, Khafra For Bread Justice and Freedom: A Political Biography of George Weekes (London, New Beacon Books, 1988).

Kiely, Ray The Politics of Labour and Development in Trinidad (Kingston, University of the West Indies Press, 1996).

Knight, Franklin W. The Caribbean: The Genesis of a Fragmented Nationalism (New York, Oxford University Press, 1978, 2nd edn, 1990).

- 'Columbus and Slavery in the New World and Africa', Revista/Review Interamericana 22: 1 and 2 (1992), 18-35.

Knight, Franklin W., and Colin A. Palmer (eds) The Modern Caribbean (Chapel Hill, University of North Carolina Press, 1989).

Kuper, Adam Changing Jamaica (London, Routledge & Kegan Paul, 1976).

Knowles, William H. Trade Union Development and Industrial Relations in the British West Indies (Berkeley, University of California Press, 1959).

LaFeber, Walter The New Empire: An Interpretation of American Expansion, 1860-1898 (Ithaca, Cornell University Press, 1963).

- Inevitable Revolutions: The United States in Central America (New York, W.W. Norton, 2nd edn, 1993).

La Guerre, John Gaffar 'The General Elections of 1946 in Trinidad and Tobago', Social and Economic Studies 21:2 (1972), 184-204.

- 'The Moyne Commission and the Jamaican Left', Social and Economic Studies 31:3 (1982), 59-94.

Lamming, George In the Castle of My Skin (London, Michael Joseph, 1953).

Laurence, Keith 'The Development of Medical Services in British Guiana and Trinidad 1841-1873', Jamaica Historical Review 4 (1964), 59-67.

- 'The Evolution of Long-term Labour Contracts in Trinidad and British Guiana, 1834-1863', Jamaica Historical Review 5 (1965), 9-27.

- Immigration into the West Indies in the Nineteenth Century (Barbados, Caribbean Universities Press, 1971).

- 'Comments on Green, Marshall, Engerman and Emmer', in Abolition and its Aftermath: The Historical Context, 1790-1916 ed. by David Richardson (London, Frank Cass, 1985), 267-73.

- A Question of Labour: Indentured Immigration into Trinidad and British Guiana, 1875-1917 (Kingston, Ian Randle, and London, James Currey, 1994).

- 'A Note on the Suspension of the Constitution of British Guiana (1953)', Journal of Caribbean History 29:1 (1995), 59-76.

Leighton, Richard M., and Robert W. Coakley Global Logistics and Strategy (Washington, DC, Department of the Army, US Government, 1955).

Levitt, Kari, and Lloyd Best 'Character of the Caribbean Economy', [1975] in Caribbean Freedom: Economy and Society from Emancipation to the Present ed. by Hilary M.D. Beckles and Verene A.Shepherd (Kingston, Ian Randle, 1993), 405-20.

Levy, Claude Emancipation, Sugar, and Federalism: Barbados and the West Indies, 1833-1876 (Gainesville, University Presses of Florida, 1980).

Lewis, Gordon K. The Growth of the Modern West Indies (London, MacGibbon & Kee, 1968).

Lewis, Rupert Marcus Garvey: Anti-Colonial Champion (London, Karia Press, 1987).

Lewis, W. Arthur Labour in the West Indies: The Birth of a Workers' Movement [1939] (London, New Beacon Books, 1977).

-   'The Industrialization of the British West Indies', Caribbean Economic Review 2 (1950), 1-39.

Lobdell, Richard 'Patterns of Investment and Credit in the British West Indian Sugar Industry 1838-1897', Journal of Caribbean History 4 (1972), 31-53.

-   'British Officials and the West Indian Peasantry: 1842-1938', in Labour in the Caribbean: From Emancipation to Independence ed. by Malcolm Cross and Gad Heuman (London, Macmillan, 1988), 195-207.

Look Lai, Walton Indentured Labor, Caribbean Sugar: Chinese and Indian Migrants to the British West Indies, 1838-1918 (Baltimore, Johns Hopkins University Press, 1993).

Louis, W. Roger Imperialism at Bay, 1941-1945: The United States and the Decolonization of the British Empire, (New York, Oxford University Press, 1978).

Lowenthal, David West Indian Societies (New York, Oxford University Press, 1972).

Macmillan, Harold The Blast of War (London, Macmillan, 1967).

Macmillan, W.M. Warning from the West Indies (London, Faber and Faber, 1936).

Macpherson, Anne S. 'Gender and Nation: Belizean Women in the Process of Decolonization', unpublished paper (University of Wisconsin-Madison, 1993).

Magid, Alvin Urban Nationalism: A Study of Political Development in Trinidad (Gainesville, University of Florida Press, 1988).

Maingot, Anthony P. The United States and the Caribbean: Challenges of an Asymetrical Relationship (Boulder, Westview Press, 1994).

Makin, William J. Caribbean Nights (London, Robert Hale, 1939).

Mandle, Jay R. The Plantation Economy: Population and Economic Change in Guyana, 1838-1960 (Philadelphia, Temple University Press, 1973).

-   'British Caribbean Economic History', in The Modern Caribbean ed. by Franklin W. Knight and Colin A. Palmer (Chapel Hill, University of North Carolina Press, 1989), 229-58.

Manley, Michael A Voice at the Workplace: Reflections on Colonialism and the Jamaican Worker (London, André Deutsch, 1975).

Mark, Francis The History of the Barbados Workers' Union (Bridgetown, Barbados

Workers' Union, 1966).

Marshall, Woodville K. 'Peasant Development in the West Indies Since 1838', Social and Economic Studies 17 (1968), 252-63.

- 'Vox Populi: The St Vincent Riots and Disturbances of 1862', in Trade, Government and Society in Caribbean History, 1700-1920 ed. by B.W. Higman (Kingston, Heinemann Educational Books Caribbean, 1983), 84-115.

- 'Apprenticeship and Labour Relations in Four Windward Islands', in Abolition and its Aftermath: The Historical Context, 1790-1916 ed. by David Richardson (London, Frank Cass, 1985), 203-24.

- 'Provision Ground and Plantation Labour: Competition for Resources', unpublished paper (Association of Caribbean Historians conference, St Thomas, VI, 1988).

- The Post-Slavery Labour Problem Revisited (Mona, University of the West Indies, 1991).

- '"We be wise to many more tings": Blacks' Hopes and Expectations of Emancipation', in Caribbean Freedom: Economy and Society from Emancipation to the Present ed. by Hilary Mc D. Beckles and Verene A. Shepherd (Kingston, Ian Randle Publishers, 1993), 12-20.

McFeely, William S. Frederick Douglass (New York, W.W. Norton, 1991).

Midgett, Douglas Eastern Caribbean Elections, 1950-1982: Antigua, Dominica, Grenada, St Kitts-Nevis, St Lucia, and St Vincent (Iowa City, University of Iowa, n.d.).

Millette, James 'The Wage Problem in Trinidad and Tobago 1838-1938', in The Colonial Caribbean in Transition: Essays on Postemancipation Social and Cultural History ed. by Bridget Brereton and Kevin A. Yelvington (Kingston, University of the West Indies Press, and Gainesville, University Press of Florida, 1999), 55-76.

Mills, C. Wright The Sociological Imagination (New York, Grove Press, 1961).

Mintz, Sidney W. Worker in the Cane: A Puerto Rican Life History (New Haven, Yale University Press, 1960).

- 'The Question of Caribbean Peasantries: A Comment', Caribbean Studies 1 (1961), 31-4.

- 'The Caribbean as a Socio-cultural Area', in Peoples and Cultures of the Caribbean ed. by Michael M. Horowitz (Garden City, Natural History Press, 1971), 17-46.

- Caribbean Transformations (Chicago, Aldine Publishing Co., 1974).

- 'The So-called World System: Local Initiative and Local Response', Dialectical Anthropology 2:4 (1977), 253-70.

- 'Was the Plantation Slave a Proletarian?' Review 2:1 (1978), 81-98.

- 'Epilogue: The Divided Aftermaths of Freedom', in Between Slavery and Free Labor: The Spanish-Speaking Caribbean in the Nineteenth Century ed. by Manuel Moreno Fraginals, Frank Moya Pons and Stanley L. Engerman (Baltimore, Johns Hopkins University Press, 1985), 270-8.

- 'Panglosses and Pollyannas; or, Whose Reality are we Talking About?' in The Meaning of Freedom: Economics, Politics, and Culture after Slavery ed. by Frank

McGlynn and Seymour Drescher (Pittsburgh, University of Pittsburgh Press, 1992), 245-56.

- 'Introduction', in Indentured Labor, Caribbean Sugar: Chinese and Indian Migrants to the British West Indies, 1838-1918 by Walton Look Lai (Baltimore, Johns Hopkins University Press, 1993a), xxiii-xxviii.

- 'Goodbye, Columbus: Second Thoughts on the Caribbean Region at Mid-millennium', Walter Rodney Memorial Lecture (Coventry, University of Warwick, 1993b).

Moberg, Mark 'Crown Colony as Banana Republic: The United Fruit Company and British Honduras, 1900-1920', Journal of Latin American Studies 28:2 (1996), 357-81.

Momsen, Janet 'Land Settlement as an Imposed Solution', in Land and Development in the Caribbean ed. by Jean Besson and Janet Momsen (London, Macmillan, 1987), 46-69.

Moohr, Michael 'The Economic Impact of Slave Emancipation in British Guiana, 1832-52', Economic History Review 2nd series, 25 (1972), 588-607.

Moore, Brian L. Race, Power and Social Segmentation in Colonial Society: Guyana after Slavery, 1838-1891 (New York, Gordon and Breach Science Publishers, 1987).

- Cultural Power, Resistance, and Pluralism: Colonial Guyana, 1838-1900 (Montreal and Kingston, McGill-Queen's University Press, 1995).

Mordecai, Sir John The West Indies: The Federal Negotiations (London, George Allen and Unwin, 1968).

Morris, Robert L. 'Historical Outline of the Regional Labour Movement', (Bridgetown, BWU History Module Study Material, 1985).

- 'The Effects of the Great Depression', in Emancipation III: Aspects of the Post-Slavery Experience of Barbados ed. by Woodville Marshall (National Cultural Foundation and University of the West Indies, 1988), 39-55.

Munroe, Trevor The Politics of Constitutional Decolonization: Jamaica, 1944-62 (Mona, ISER, University of the West Indies, 1972).

- 'The Left and the Question of Race in Jamaica', in Garvey: His Work and Impact ed. by Rupert Lewis and Patrick Bryan (Mona, ISER and Department of Extra-Mural Studies, University of the West Indies, 1988), 283-98.

- The Cold War and the Jamaican Left, 1950-55: Re-opening the Files (Kingston, Kingston Publishers, 1992).

Nettleford, Rex Mirror Mirror: Identity, Race and Protest in Jamaica (Kingston, William Collins and Sangster, 1970).

- Manley and the Politics of Jamaica: Towards an Analysis of Political Change in Jamaica, 1938-1968 (Mona, ISER, University of the West Indies, 1971).

Newton, Velma The Silver Men: West Indian Labour Migration to Panama, 1850-1914 (Mona, ISER, University of the West Indies, 1984).

Nicholson, Marjorie The TUC Overseas: The Roots of Policy (London, Allen and Unwin, 1986).

O'Donnell, Guillermo A. Modernization and Bureaucratic-Authoritarianism: Studies in

South American Politics (Berkeley, Institute of International Studies, University of California, 1973).

- 'Tensions in the Bureaucratic-Authoritarian State and the Question of Democracy', in The New Authoritarianism in Latin America ed. by David Collier (Princeton, Princeton University Press, 1979), 285-318.

Orde Browne, Major G. St J. Labour Conditions in the British West Indies (London, HMSO, 1939).

Oxaal, Ivar Black Intellectuals Come to Power: The Rise of Creole Nationalism in Trinidad and Tobago (Cambridge, MA, Schenkman Publishing Company, 1968).

Parry, J.H. and P.M. Sherlock A Short History of the West Indies, 3rd edn (London, Macmillan, 1971).

Patterson, Orlando The Sociology of Slavery: An Analysis of the Origins, Development and Structure of Negro Slave Society in Jamaica (London, Macgibbon and Kee, 1967).

- Slavery and Social Death: A Comparative Study (Cambridge, MA, Harvard University Press, 1982).

- 'Slavery: The Underside of Freedom', in Out of Slavery: Abolition and After ed. by Jack Hayward (London, Frank Cass, 1985), 7-29.

- Freedom, Vol.1 Freedom in the Making of Western Culture (Basic Books, 1991).

Perham, Margery Colonial Sequence, 1930 to 1949, a Chronological Commentary upon British Policy Especially in Africa (London, Methuen, 1967).

Petras, Elizabeth McLean Jamaican Labor Migration: White Capital and Black Labor, 1850-1930 (Boulder, Westview Press, 1988).

Phelps, O.W. 'Rise of the Labour Movement in Jamaica', Social and Economic Studies 9:4 (1960), 417-68.

Piven, Frances Fox, and Richard A. Cloward Regulating the Poor: The Functions of Public Welfare (New York, Pantheon Books, 1971).

Porter, A.N., and A.J. Stockwell British Imperial Policy and Decolonization, 1938-64, Vol. 1 1938-51 (New York, St Martin's Press, 1987).

Post, Ken 'The Politics of Protest in Jamaica, 1938: Some Problems of Analysis and Conceptualization', Social and Economic Studies 18:4 (1969), 374-90.

- 'The Bible as Ideology: Ethiopianism in Jamaica, 1930-38', in African Perspectives ed. by C.H. Allen and R.W. Johnson (Cambridge, Cambridge University Press, 1970), 185-207.

- Arise Ye Starvelings: The Jamaican Labour Rebellion and its Aftermath (The Hague, Martinus Nijhoff, 1978).

- Strike the Iron: A Colony at War - Jamaica, 1939-45, 2 vols (Atlantic Highlands, NJ, Humanities Press, 1981).

Premdas, Ralph R. 'The Rise of the First Mass-based Multi-racial Party in Guyana', Caribbean Quarterly 20 (1974), 5-20.

Priestley, George Military Government and Popular Participation in Panama: The Torrijos Regime, 1968-1975 (Boulder, Westview Press, 1986).

Proctor, Jesse Harris, Jr. 'British West Indian Society and Government in Transition, 1920-60', Social and Economic Studies 2:4 (1962), 273-304.

Purcell, Trevor W. Banana Fallout: Class, Color, and Culture Among West Indians in Costa Rica (Los Angeles, Center for Afro-American Studies, University of California, 1993).

Quamina, Odida T. Mineworkers of Guyana: The Making of a Working Class (London, Zed Books, 1987).

Radosh, Ronald American Labor and United States Foreign Policy (New York, Random House, 1969).

Ramdin, Ron From Chattel Slave to Wage Earner: A History of Trade Unionism in Trinidad and Tobago (London, Martin Brian & O'Keefe, 1982).

Rance, Sir Hubert Development and Welfare in the West Indies (Barbados, Advocate, n.d.).

Reddock, Rhoda Elma Francois: The NWCSA and the Workers Struggle for Change in the Caribbean in the 1930s (London, New Beacon Books, 1988).

- 'Transformation in the Needle Trades: Women in Garment and Textile Production in Early Twentieth-Century Trinidad', in Women and Change in the Caribbean: A Pan-Caribbean Perspective ed. by Janet Momsen (Kingston, Ian Randle, and London, James Currey, 1993), 249-62.

- Women, Labour and Politics in Trinidad and Tobago: A History (London, Zed Books, 1994).

Rennie, Bukka The History of the Working-class in the 20th Century (1919-1956) – The Trinidad and Tobago Experience (Trinidad, New Beginning Movement, 1973).

Report of the British Guiana and British Honduras Settlement Commission, Cmd. 7533 (London, HMSO, 1948).

Report of the Commission of Enquiry into Subversive Activities in Trinidad and Tobago (Mbanefo Report) (Port of Spain, House Paper No. 2 of 1965).

Report of the First British Guiana and West Indies Labour Conference (Georgetown, British Guiana Labour Union, 1926).

Rich, Paul 'Sydney Olivier, Jamaica and the Debate on British Colonial Policy in the West Indies', in Labour in the Caribbean: From Emancipation to Independence ed. by Malcolm Cross and Gad Heuman (London, Macmillan, 1988), 208-33.

Richards, Glen 'Collective Violence in Plantation Societies: The Case of the St Kitts Labour Protests of 1896 and 1935', unpublished paper (Institute of Commonwealth Studies Library, University of London, 1987a).

- '"The Maddened Rabble:" Labour Protests in St Kitts, 1896 and 1935', unpublished paper (Society for Caribbean Studies conference, Hoddesdon, 1987b).

- 'Order and Disorder in Colonial St Kitts: The Role of the Armed Forces in Maintaining Labour Discipline, 1896-1935', unpublished paper (Association of Caribbean Historians conference, Mona, 1993).

Richards, Novelle H. The Struggle and Conquest: Twenty-five Years of Social Democracy in Antigua (St John's, Workers Voice Printery, 1964).

Richardson, Bonham C. Caribbean Migrants: Environment and Human Survival on St Kitts and Nevis (Knoxville, University of Tennessee Press, 1983).

- 'Slavery to Freedom in the British Caribbean: Ecological Considerations', Caribbean Geography 1 (1984), 164-75.
- Panama Money in Barbados, 1900-1920 (Knoxville, University of Tennessee Press, 1985).
- 'Caribbean Migrations, 1838-1985', in The Modern Caribbean ed. by Franklin W. Knight and Colin A. Palmer (Chapel Hill, University of North Carolina Press, 1989), 203-28.
- The Caribbean in the Wider World, 1492-1992: A Regional Geography (Cambridge, Cambridge University Press, 1992a).
- 'Depression Riots and the Calling of the 1897 West India Royal Commission', New West Indian Guide 66: 3 & 4 (1992b), 169-91.
- Economy and Environment in the Caribbean: Barbados and the Windwards in the Late 1800s (Gainesville, University Press of Florida, and Mona, University of the West Indies Press, 1997).

Riviere, W. Emanuel 'Labour Shortage in the British West Indies after Emancipation', Journal of Caribbean History 4 (1972), 1-30.

Roberts, G.W. The Population of Jamaica (Cambridge, Cambridge University Press, 1957).

Roberts, George, and Joycelyn Byrne 'Summary Statistics on Indenture and Associated Migration Affecting the West Indies, 1834-1918', Population Studies 20 (1966), 125-34.

Robotham, Don 'The Development of a Black Ethnicity in Jamaica', in Garvey: His Work and Impact ed. by Rupert Lewis and Patrick Bryan (Mona, ISER and Department of Extra-Mural Studies, University of the West Indies, 1988), 23-38.

Rodney, Walter A History of the Guyanese Working People, 1881-1905 (Baltimore, Johns Hopkins University Press, 1981).

Romualdi, Serafino Presidents and Peons: Recollections of a Labor Ambassador in Latin America (New York, Funk and Wagnalls, 1967).

Rose, James G. 'The Enmore Incident of 1948', History Gazette 69 (1994).

Rouse, Irving The Tainos: Rise and Decline of the People Who Greeted Columbus (New Haven, Yale University Press, 1992).

Russell, Horace O. 'The Emergence of the Christian Black: The Making of a Stereotype', Jamaica Journal 16 (1983), 51-8.

Ryan, Cecil, and Cecil A. Blazer Williams From Charles to Mitchell, Part 1 (St Vincent, Projects Promotion Limited, n.d.).

Ryan, Selwyn D. Race and Nationalism in Trinidad and Tobago: A Study of Decolonization in a Multiracial Society (Toronto, University of Toronto Press, 1972).

Samaroo, Brinsley 'The Trinidad Workingmen's Association and the Origins of Popular Protest in a Crown Colony', Social and Economic Studies 21:2 (1972), 205-22.

Sampson, H.C. Report on Development of Agriculture in British Guiana (London, HMSO, 1927).

Satchell, Veront M. From Plots to Plantations: Land Transactions in Jamaica, 1866-1900 (Mona, ISER, University of the West Indies, 1990).

Saunders, D. Gail 'The 1942 Riot in Nassau. A Demand for Change?' Journal of Caribbean History 20:2 (1985-6), 117-46.

- 'The 1937 Riot in Inagua, the Bahamas', New West Indian Guide 62: 3,4 (1988), 129-45.

- Bahamian Society after Emancipation: Essays in Nineteenth and Early Twentieth Century Bahamian History (Nassau, the author, 1990).

Scarano, Francisco A. 'Labor and Society in the Nineteenth Century', in The Modern Caribbean ed. by Franklin W. Knight and Colin A. Palmer (Chapel Hill, University of North Carolina Press, 1989), 51-84.

Schlesinger, Arthur Jr A Thousand Days: John F. Kennedy in the White House (Boston, Houghton Mifflin, 1965).

Schuler, Monica "Alas, Alas, Kongo": A Social History of Indentured African Immigration into Jamaica, 1841-1865 (Baltimore, Johns Hopkins University Press, 1980).

Scott, Cleve McD. 'The Politics of Local Government in St Vincent and the Grenadines: The Kingstown Town Board, 1897-1937', unpublished paper (conference on 'Caribbean Intellectual Traditions', University of the West Indies, Mona, 1998).

Scott, James C. Weapons of the Weak: Everyday Forms of Peasant Resistance (New Haven, Yale University Press, 1985).

Scott, Rebecca J. Slave Emancipation in Cuba: The Transition to Free Labor, 1860-1899 (Princeton, Princeton University Press, 1985).

- 'Comparing Emancipations: A Review Essay', Journal of Social History 20 (1987), 565-83.

- 'Labour Control in Cuba after Emancipation'" in Labour in the Caribbean: From Emancipation to Independence ed. by Malcolm Cross and Gad Heuman (London, Macmillan, 1988), 80-87.

Senior, Olive Working Miracles: Women's Lives in the English-Speaking Caribbean (Kingston, Ian Randle, London, James Currey, and Bloomington, Indiana University Press, 1991).

Sewell, W.G. The Ordeal of Free Labor in the British West Indies (London, Harper and Brothers, 1861).

Sheppard, Jill Marryshow of Grenada: An Introduction (Barbados, Letchworth Press, 1987).

Sheridan, Richard B. Doctors and Slaves: A Medical and Demographic History of Slavery in the British West Indies, 1680-1834 (Cambridge, Cambridge University Press, 1985).

- 'From Chattel to Wage Slavery in Jamaica, 1740-1860', Slavery and Abolition 14:1 (1993), 13-40.

- Sugar and Slavery: An Economic History of the British West Indies, 1623-1775 [1974] (Kingston, Canoe Press, 1994).

Shoman, Assad 'The Birth of the Nationalist Movement in Belize, 1950-1954', Journal of Belizean Affairs 2 (1973), 3-40.

- Party Politics in Belize, 1950-1986 (Benque Viejo del Carmen, Cubola Produc-

tions, 1987).
- Thirteen Chapters of a History of Belize (Belize City, Angelus Press, 1994).
- Backtalking Belize: Selected Writings, ed. by Anne S. Macpherson (Belize City, Angelus Press, 1995).

Singh, Chaitram Guyana: Politics in a Plantation Society (New York, Praeger, 1988).

Singh, Kelvin 'Adrian Cola Rienzi and the Labour Movement in Trinidad (1925-44)', Journal of Caribbean History 16 (1982), 10-35.
- 'The June 1937 Disturbances in Trinidad', in The Trinidad Labour Riots of 1937: Perspectives 50 Years Later ed. by Roy Thomas (St Augustine, Extra-Mural Studies Unit, University of the West Indies, 1987), 57-80.
- Bloodstained Tombs: The Mulharram Massacre 1884 (London, Macmillan Caribbean, 1988).
- Race and Class Struggles in a Colonial State: Trinidad 1917-1945 (Alberta, University of Calgary Press, and Kingston, University of the West Indies Press, 1994).
- 'Conflict and Collaboration: Tradition and Modernizing Indo-Trinidadian Elites (1917-56)', New West Indian Guide 70:3 and 4 (1996), 229-53.

Singham, A. W. The Hero and the Crowd in a Colonial Polity (New Haven, Yale University Press, 1968).

Sio, Arnold 'Commentary on "Slavery and Race"', in Roots and Branches: Current Directions in Slave Studies, ed. by Michael Craton, Historical Reflections 6 (1979), 269-74.

Smith, Keithlyn B., and Fernando C. Smith To Shoot Hard Labour: The Life and Times of Samuel Smith, an Antiguan Workingman, 1877-1982 (London, Karia Press, 1989).

Smith, M.G. The Plural Society in the British West Indies (Berkeley, University of California Press, 1965).
- Culture, Race and Class in the Commonwealth Caribbean (Mona, University of the West Indies, 1984).
- Pluralism, Politics and Ideology in the Creole Caribbean (New York, Research Institute for the Study of Man, 1991).

Smith, Raymond T. 'Social Stratification, Cultural Pluralism and Integration in West Indian Societies', in Caribbean Integration: Papers on Social, Political and Economic Integration, ed. by S. Lewis and T. Mathews (Rio Piedras, Institute of Caribbean Studies, 1967), 226-58.
- Kinship and Class in the West Indies: A Genealogical Study of Jamaica and Guyana (Cambridge, Cambridge University Press, 1988).
- 'Race, Class, and Gender in the Transition to Freedom', in The Meaning of Freedom: Economics, Politics, and Culture after Slavery ed. by Frank McGlynn and Seymour Drescher (Pittsburgh, University of Pittsburgh Press, 1992), 257-90.

Soberanis, Antonio, and L.D. Kemp The Third Side of the Anglo-Guatemala Dispute (Belize City, Commercial Press, 1949).

Spackman, Ann 'Official Attitudes and Official Violence: The Ruimveldt Massacre, Guyana, 1924', Social and Economic Studies 22:3 (1973), 315-34.

Spinner, Thomas J. A Political and Social History of Guyana, 1945-1983 (Boulder,

Westview Press, 1984).

Stein, Judith 'The Ideology and Practice of Garveyism', in Garvey: His Work and Impact ed. by Rupert Lewis and Patrick Bryan (Mona, ISER and Department of Extra-Mural Studies, University of the West Indies, 1988), 199-213.

Stewart, Robert Religion and Society in Post-Emancipation Jamaica (Knoxville, University of Tennessee Press, 1992).

Stone, Carl 'Political Aspects of Agricultural Policies in Jamaica (1945-1970)', Social and Economic Studies 23:2 (1974), 145-75.

St Pierre, Maurice 'The 1938 Jamaican Disturbances. A Portrait of Mass Reaction Against Colonialism', Social and Economic Studies 27:2 (1978), 171-96.

- Anatomy of Resistance: Anti-Colonialism in Guyana 1823-1966 (London, Macmillan Caribbean, 1999).

Sutton, Constance, and Susan Makiesky-Barrow 'Social Inequality and Sexual Status in Barbados', in Sexual Stratification: A Cross-Cultural View, ed. by Alice Schlegel (New York, Columbia University Press, 1977), 292-325.

Sutton, James W. A Testimony of Triumph: A Narrative of the Life of James Sutton and Family in Nevis and St Kitts, 1920-1940 (Scarborough, Ontario, Edan's Publishers, 1987).

Sutton, Paul 'The Historian as Politician: Eric Williams and Walter Rodney', in Intellectuals in the Twentieth-Century Caribbean, Vol.1 Spectre of the New Class: The Commonwealth Caribbean ed. by Alistair Hennessy (London, Macmillan, 1992), 98-114.

Taylor, Frank Fonda To Hell with Paradise: A History of the Jamaican Tourist Industry (Pittsburgh, University of Pittsburgh Press, 1993).

Thomas, Clive Y. The Rise of the Authoritarian State in Peripheral Societies (New York, Monthly Review Press, 1984).

- The Poor and the Powerless: Economic Policy and Change in the Caribbean (New York, Monthly Review Press, 1988).

Thomas, Roy D. (ed.) The Trinidad Labour Riots of 1937: Perspectives 50 Years Later (St Augustine, Extra-Mural Studies Unit, University of the West Indies, 1987).

- The Development of Labour Law in Trinidad and Tobago (Wellesley, MA, Calaloux Publications, 1989).

Thorndike, Tony Grenada: Politics, Economics and Society (London, Frances Pinter, 1985).

- 'Antigua and Barbuda,' in Politics, Security and Development in Small States ed. by Colin Clarke and Tony Payne (London, Allen and Unwin, 1987), 96-112.

Trotman, David Vincent Crime in Trinidad: Conflict and Control in a Plantation Society, 1838-1900 (Knoxville, University of Tennessee Press, 1986).

Trouillot, Michel-Rolph 'The Inconvenience of Freedom', in The Meaning of Freedom: Economics, Politics, and Culture after Slavery ed. by Frank McGlynn and Seymour Drescher (Pittsburgh, University of Pittsburgh Press, 1992), 147-82.

Tucker, Robert C. (ed.) The Marx-Engels Reader (New York, W.W. Norton, 1972).

Turner, Mary 'Chattel Slaves into Wage Slaves: A Jamaican Case Study', in Labour in the Caribbean: From Emancipation to Independence ed. by Malcolm Cross and Gad Heuman (London, Macmillan, 1988), 14-31.

Turner, W. Burghardt, and Joyce Moore Turner Richard B. Moore, Caribbean Militant in Harlem: Collected Writings, 1920-1972 (Indianapolis, Indiana University Press, 1988).

Van der Wee, Herman Prosperity and Upheaval: The World Economy, 1945-1980 trans. by Robin Hogg and Max R. Hall (Berkeley, University of California Press, 1986).

Waddell, D.A.G. British Honduras: A Historical and Contemporary Survey (London, Oxford University Press, 1961).

Wagley, Charles 'Plantation America: A Culture Sphere', in Caribbean Studies: A Symposium ed. by Vera Rubin (Seattle, University of Washington Press, 1957), 3-13.

Walker-Kilkenny, Roberta 'The Leonora Strike of 1939', History Gazette 46 (1992).

- 'Women in Social and Political Struggle in British Guiana, 1946-1953', History Gazette 49 (1992).

Ward, J.R. Poverty and Progress in the Caribbean, 1800-1960 (London, Macmillan, 1985).

West India Royal Commission Report (London, HMSO, 1945).

Williams, Eric The History of the People of Trinidad and Tobago (London, Andre Deutsch, 1964).

- From Columbus to Castro: The History of the Caribbean, 1492-1969 (London, Andre Deutsch, 1970).

Wilmot, Swithin 'Emancipation in Action: Workers and Wage Conflict in Jamaica 1838-1848', in Caribbean Freedom: Economy and Society from Emancipation to the Present ed. by Hilary Beckles and Verene Shepherd (Kingston, Ian Randle, 1993), 48-54.

- 'The Growth of Black Political Activity in Post-Emancipation Jamaica', in Garvey: His Work and Impact ed. by Rupert Lewis and Patrick Bryan (Mona, ISER and Department of Extra-Mural Studies, University of the West Indies, 1988), 39-46.

Wilson, Samuel M. 'Introduction to the Study of the Indigenous People of the Caribbean', and 'The Legacy of the Indigenous People of the Caribbean', in The Indigenous People of the Caribbean ed. by Samuel M. Wilson (Gainesville, University Press of Florida, 1997), 1-8, 206-13.

Wood, Bryce The Making of the Good Neighbor Policy (New York, Columbia University Press, 1961).

Wood, Donald Trinidad in Transition: The Years after Slavery (London, Oxford University Press, 1968).

Wood, E.F.L. West Indies and British Guiana (London, HMSO, 1922).

Worsley, Peter Marx and Marxism (Chichester, Ellis Horwood, 1982).

- The Three Worlds: Culture and World Development (London, Weidenfeld and Nicolson, 1984).

Young, Virginia Heyer Becoming West Indian: Culture, Self, and Nation in St Vincent (Washington, Smithsonian Institution Press, 1993).

Grenada Manual and Metal Workers' Union (GMMWU); and the labour movement, 536-543, 546-548
Grenada United Labour Party (GULP); 533
Grenada Workingmen's Association (GWA); formation of, 204, 533
Grey, Governor Charles (Jamaica); and resistance, 80
Grey, Earl; 33
Grier, Sir Selwyn (Governor St Vincent & St Lucia); and labour protests, 238, 240, 241, 243-244, 247-248
Guatemala; and territorial claim to Belize, 643-644
Guiana Industrial Workers Union (GIWU); and the sugar workers strike, 605-609
Guianese and West Indian Federation of Trade Unions and Labour Parties (GWIFTULP); 475-478
Guyana; administrative system in, 65-66, 135-137; bauxite mining in, 123, 337; class structure in, 181; constitution reform in, 615-619; suppression of the constitution in, 619-629; democratic movement in, 600-629; economic conditions, 184-185, 338-340, 343-344, 349-350; education system in, 75, 132; elections (1947), 485-485, 603, (1953), 610-613, (1957), 625; election fraud, 628-629; exports, 388-390; franchise in, 65-66, 136, 603; health issues in, 129, 131, 184; indentured immigrants in, 61-62, 80, 117, 129, 181, 182-183, 337-338; labour contracts in, 81; labour patterns in post-emancipation, 45-46; labour protests in, 51, 70-71, (1842-1848), 80-82; 181-191, 193, 206-208, (1930s) 336-356, (1940s), 604-609, 617-618; labour relations in post-emancipation, 50-53; land tenure in, 45, 111; growth of peasantry in, 117-118; political development in, 601-629; race issues in, 182, 189-190; rice production in, 118; consolidation of sugar estates in, 112, 114, 118; sugar production in, 117-120; trade union movement in, 191, 336-356, 350-353, 430-431; trade union rivalry in, 617-618, universal adult suffrage, 604; working class conflict in, 337-340; welfare projects in, 387

Haiti; independence of, 2; US occupation of, 5
Haitian revolution; 16, 80
Hailey, Lord; and constitutional reform in the colonies, 450
Harford, J.D. Acting Governor (Antigua); and the labour movement, 426-427
Hart, Richard (Jamaica); and the CLC, 367, 479-480, 482-483, 483-485, 504-506; criticism of Adams, 487-488; and the labour movement, 316-317, 321-322; and the Marxist movement, 307, 500-501, 577; WFTU affiliation, 493-494
Health care; in the British Caribbean, 129-131
Hennessey, Governor John Pope (Barbados); and constitution change, 87-88
Hill, Frank (Jamaica); and the Marxist movement, 307, 500-501
Hill, Ken (Jamaica); and the BITU, 401-403; and the Marxist movement, 307, 500-501, 575; WFTU affiliation, 493-494
Hodge, John, 109-110
Hosein riots (1884, Trinidad); 80, 88-90
Howell, Leonard (Jamaica); and the nationalist movement, 397; and Rastafarianism, 302
Hunter, Governor J.A.(Belize); and the labour movement, 436, 437-438
Hutson, D.M. (Guyana); and political reform, 135-136
Hyde, James, 109

Identity; of former slaves, 76
Immigration See also Migration; labour supply through, 58-62
Indentureship system; as a strategy for labour control, 2, 10-11, 35-37, 58-62, 114
Indian National Party (Trinidad); and the labour movement, 257
Indigenous peoples See also Amerindians, Tainos; 4-6, 8
International Conference of Free Trade Unions (ICFTU); impact on the Caribbean labour movement, 491, 493, 576; formation of the, 497
International Labour Organisation (ILO); and labour reform in the British Caribbean, 144-153

Jagan, Chedi and Janet (Guyana); and 1947 elections 484-485, 603; and the PAC, 602; and the PO government, 615-629; and PPP government, 577
Jamaica; administrative structure in, 64-65, 76-77, 141-142; constitution reform in, 450-456; economic conditions in, 82, 299-301, 304-305, 332-333; education system in, 132; exports, 388-390; franchise in (1859), 64-65; free villages in, 98-99; health care in, 129-131 labour patterns in post-emancipation, 44-45; labour protests in, 79-80, 82-86, 174-177, 194-195, (1930s) 223-224, 299-333, (1940s) 400-402, 410-412, 452; labour relations in post-emancipation, 48-49; land control in, 82, 110-111; land settlement schemes, 326-327; Marxism in, 307, 329, 331-332; rural-urban migration, 161-162; growth of peasantry in, 41, 44-45, 98-99, 110-111; political development in, 396-412; slave rebellions in, 9; 16 sugar production in, 112, 114; squatting in, 47; trade union movement in, 191-192, 194, 299-333, 399-412, trade union rivalry in, 522-524; universal adult suffrage in, 449; welfare projects in, 326-327, 387
Jamaica Agricultural Society, 301

www.ingramcontent.com/pod-product-compliance
Lightning Source LLC
Chambersburg PA
CBHW071129270326
41929CB00012B/1695